TOPOGRAPHICAL DESCRIPTION

OF THE DOMINIONS OF THE

UNITED STATES OF AMERICA

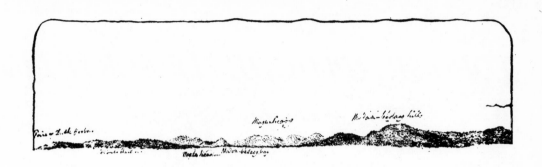

A topographic sketch by Thomas Pownall—among the large amount of manuscript material he tipped into his own copy of the first edition (published 1776), anticipating a second edition for 1779, an edition which is published only now—170 years later.

A
TOPOGRAPHICAL DESCRIPTION

OF THE DOMINIONS OF

THE UNITED STATES OF AMERICA

———

[BEING A REVISED and ENLARGED EDITION of]
A TOPOGRAPHICAL DESCRIPTION
of SUCH PARTS of NORTH AMERICA
as are CONTAINED in
THE (Annexed) MAP of the MIDDLE BRITISH COLONIES, &c.
in
NORTH AMERICA

———

By *T. POWNALL*, M.P.
Late GOVERNOR, CAPTAIN-GENERAL, VICE-ADMIRAL
and COMMANDER IN CHIEF of His Majesty's Provinces now States,
Massachusetts Bay and South Carolina,
and LIEUTENANT GOVERNOR of New Jersey.

EDITED BY *Lois Mulkearn*, LIBRARIAN
DARLINGTON MEMORIAL LIBRARY
UNIVERSITY OF PITTSBURGH

PITTSBURGH:
UNIVERSITY OF PITTSBURGH PRESS
1949

To Jim

FOREWORD

OF all the British administrators who served in America in the eighteenth century none showed a more sustained and lively interest in New World developments than did Thomas Pownall. The year after his arrival in New York we find him present at the Albany Congress of 1754 in an unofficial capacity and presenting to the consideration of the delegates a plan for the defense of the colonial frontiers, for which he received the thanks of the Congress. The following year he was at Alexandria, Virginia, also in an unofficial capacity, in attendance at the Governors' Conference called by General Braddock. Among the friendships he formed in America those with Benjamin Franklin and Lewis Evans were of more than usual significance. Through these various contacts he was introduced intimately to a host of problems connected with British colonial Indian relations, westward expansion, and Anglo-French rivalry in North America. In 1754 he drew up a plan for regulating Indian trade and land purchases and in 1755 he prepared his "Considerations on yᵉ Means, Method & Nature of Settling a Colony on yᵉ Lands South of Lake Erie" and a map with elaborate notations to accompany it—which are among the Loudoun Papers in the Huntington Library at San Marino, California. Both as Lieutenant Governor of New Jersey and as Governor of Massachusetts Bay he was actively and officially concerned in the war in North America that was waged from 1754 to 1763 and, especially in his latter capacity, wrote voluminous reports to his superiors in London on the progress of events in New England and also made various suggestions to both Loudoun and Abercromby—each in turn serving as commander-in-chief of the British forces in North America—for the successful prosecution of hostilities. Although he returned to England before the close of the war, his attention continued to be centered on the colonies and, among other publications credited to him, there appeared in 1764 *The Administration of the Colonies* that went through six editions; in 1776 the *Topographical Description of North America;* in 1780 *A Memorial to*

ix

*the Sovereigns of Europe on the present state of affairs between the old and
new world;* and, finally, in 1783, the year of the Peace of Paris, *A
Memorial addressed to the Sovereigns of America.*

Among Thomas Pownall's various works none has greater interest
for the present-day student in the field of either American colonial
history or American historical geography than the *Topographical Description.* The book, however, has been out of print and is therefore not
easily available. Moreover, Pownall thoroughly revised it in the year
1784, and also made many additions to it, with the expectation of its
being reissued from the press, but this was not done. Happily, Mrs.
Lois Mulkearn, librarian of the Darlington Library of the University
of Pittsburgh, was in a position to set herself the task of editing the revised work, which, after the lapse of so many years, is now presented
to the public by the University of Pittsburgh Press.

The lives and reputations of Thomas Pownall, the colonial adminis-
trator and political theorist, and Lewis Evans, the Pennsylvania cartog-
rapher and geographer, were closely linked from the year 1754. Pownall
spent some time in Philadelphia assisting Evans with the latter's
famous *General Map of the Middle British Colonies* and his equally
famous *Analysis* to accompany it, both of which appeared in 1755.
Although Evans passed away the following year Pownall continued his
interest in his friend's map and geographical guide to it and ultimately
used them as the basis for both the map and the *Topographical Description* that he himself issued. In view of the fact that both the Evans' *Map*
and *Analysis* were reissued in the writer's *Lewis Evans,* published in
1939 by the Historical Society of Pennsylvania, it is perhaps not in-
appropriate that he should write this Foreword to this revised edition
of the *Topographical Description.*

There are many ways of editing a document. No two people are apt
to approach the task in quite the same manner. In this instance Mrs.
Mulkearn was content to give her efforts largely to the important and
sometimes baffling work of identifying eighteenth-century incidents,
places, and persons—letting the reader arrive at his own opinion of the
soundness of Pownall's occasional excursions into the realm of scientific
hypothesis respecting the origins of the topography of North America.
In view of the fact that valid criticisms of such hypotheses call for very
different training than that possessed by most students of colonial
history, the writer is persuaded that the editor of this volume chose
wisely not to attempt to enter a field in which theories, as against
ascertainable facts, still so largely dominate discussion. Nevertheless,

for those interested in the history of science the *Topographical Description* is at least now readily available and it will be a matter of surprise if advantage is not taken of this fact to explore some of the scientific theories embodied in it. The book, however, will doubtless make its chief appeal to those who seek rather to recapture the American eighteenth-century scene. For such it is a mine of information.

LAWRENCE HENRY GIPSON

Lehigh University

EDITOR'S PREFACE

THOMAS POWNALL, in 1753, came to America to serve as Secretary to the newly appointed royal Governor of the Province of New York, Sir Danvers Osborne. The death of the Governor, only a few days after Pownall's arrival, relieved him of his official duties. Nevertheless, he remained in America and interested himself in colonial affairs. It is said that this early interest, especially in the French-English controversy, caused him to make a thorough study of the waterways which could be used in the transportation of troops in the open conflict that he recognized as inevitable.

When Pownall assumed his duties as royal Governor of the Massachusetts Bay Colony in 1757, the French had become a real threat to the very existence of the English colonies. His intimate knowledge of the topography of the country and his constant study of the "Scouts Journals" helped much in the planning of the strategy against the French.

Late in 1759, when the American part of the "Seven Years' War" had been won by the British, Governor Pownall was transferred from the governorship of Massachusetts Bay to that of South Carolina. Instead of going from New England to South Carolina, he returned to England, and although he did not resign his position in South Carolina for almost a year, he remained in Great Britain. In fact, he never returned to America.

After a brief withdrawal from activity in colonial affairs Pownall resumed his unofficial interest, in 1764, with the publication of *The Administration of the Colonies.* This book was designed to influence public opinion on the treatment of the American colonies. In it he set forth not only his plan to knit more tightly the interests of the Colonies with those of the mother country, but also his belief that the Americans were loyal Englishmen, who, if treated fairly, were a great asset to the mother country.

*   *   *   *

A Topographical Description of Such Parts of North America as are Contained in the (Annexed) Map of the Middle British Colonies, &c., in

North America by Thomas Pownall was published in 1776. The book was a detailed topographical description of New England and the Middle Colonies. The *Map* within the volume was a revised edition of Lewis Evans' *Map* of 1755, and the information about the Ohio Country was quoted from Lewis Evans' *Analysis* of his map of 1755. In 1779 Pownall began a revision of this work. By 1784 he had completed the revision and had written the preface to his self-styled third edition, which is this book, published now as Pownall's revised and enlarged edition.

Why this edition was not published in 1784 is unknown to the present editor. In 1854 the manuscript was sold.[1] It came later into the possession of William M. Darlington, the collector of the basic collection of books in the Darlington Memorial Library, University of Pittsburgh, Pittsburgh, Pennsylvania. The additions to the first, or 1776 edition, add about one-third in volume to the publication. Pownall made corrections and minor additions on almost every page, especially in the first part of the work. The large additions are descriptions of New York City, Boston, and the Connecticut Valley and "Extracts" from a Journal of his travels through New Jersey to Bethlehem and Philadelphia, Pennsylvania. Facsimiles of some of the holograph additions are used to illustrate this book.

* * * *

The 1949 publication has been projected to make available at reasonable cost to students of history Pownall's authentic, contemporary topographic description of the American colonies in an edition augmented by his own hitherto unpublished writings.

The editor's notes are intended to make Pownall's work more intelligible to the modern reader; they identify proper names, names of places, topographic features, and events, familiar to the reader in Pownall's time, but often unfamiliar or even unknown today. Since Pownall's work is chiefly topographical, the annotations, for the most part, are limited to identifying (according to present and past location) forts, Indian towns, early settlements, and theaters of activity during the French and Indian War. Explanations of historical matters are given only when they are judged necessary to explain Pownall more fully.

When the spelling of the names of persons, places, and topographic features is different from today's, the correct or modern spelling is placed

---

[1]"This interesting volume was sold by Messrs. Bangs, Bros., & Co., at New York, in 1854." Joseph Sabin, *A Dictionary of Books Relating to America, From its Discovery to the Present Time* (New York, J. Sabin, 1868-1936), No. 64835.

in small brackets ([]) within the body of the work; when names are completely different, the modern equivalent is given in a footnote. Since names of persons and places given in the marginal notes appear in the body of the book, no bracketed respellings appear in the marginal notes.

Source material has been used, whenever possible, for the location and identification of persons, places, and events mentioned by Pownall; secondary material has been used for the identification of modern equivalents or present sites of colonial settlements, forts, Indian towns, and trails. No citations are given for information obtained from general reference works. Identification of topographic features described by Pownall, but not named, has been made from modern maps. Names of places and topographic features that appear in the same form in any of the general reference works given in the bibliography receive no comment.

Pownall's corrected publication and holograph additions are faithfully copied. His errors in spelling, punctuation, and sentence structure are printed as they appear in the manuscript and printed composite.

It is, of course, difficult to indicate typographically the very great number of changes Pownall made in his edition of 1776; therefore, no attempt has been made to do this.

The footnotes in this edition include those made by Pownall, for both the published and unpublished editions; those made by Lewis Evans, which were copied by Pownall; and those contributed by the present editor. It is advisable, therefore, for the reader to examine carefully the *Guide to Footnotes* printed on page xvi.

*   *   *   *

For typing the manuscript the editor thanks Miss Ann Retterer and Mrs. Mildred Winner; for assistance in obtaining materials, members of the staff of the University of Pittsburgh Library, Carnegie Library of Pittsburgh, William L. Clements Library, Massachusetts Historical Society Library, New England Historical and Genealogical Society Library, Massachusetts Archives, New York Public Library, New York Historical Society Library, Lehigh University Library, Henry E. Huntington Library, Historical Society of Delaware Library, and the Library of the Historical Society of Pennsylvania. Special thanks go to the following individuals at the University of Pittsburgh: Dr. John W. Oliver, head of the history department; and Drs. Russell J. Ferguson, Leland D. Baldwin, and A. P. James of the same faculty; Dr. Arthur M. Young, head of the classics department; Dr. Putnam F. Jones, head of the English department; Dr. O. E. Jennings, director of the Carnegie Museum, Pittsburgh; and Mrs. Agnes L. Starrett, editor of the University of Pittsburgh Press. These special thanks go, too, to Dr. Douglas Adair, College of William and Mary; Dr. Julian P. Boyd, librarian of Princeton University; and Dr. Howard N. Eavenson of Pittsburgh, Pennsylvania. Particular gratitude goes to Dr. Lawrence H. Gipson, of Lehigh University, whose *Foreword* appears in this volume, and whose untiring interest and constructive criticism have been a chief source of inspiration; to Dr. A. L. Robinson, acting librarian, University of Pittsburgh, who made this publication a library project; and to my husband whose patience made the whole work possible.

LOIS MULKEARN

University of Pittsburgh,
Pittsburgh, Pennsylvania
July 17, 1948

GUIDE TO FOOTNOTES

Thomas Pownall's note Pownall's note	Footnotes copied from 1776 edition.
Pownall's note for revised and enlarged edition	Additions and corrected notes made by Pownall for revised edition.
Lewis Evans' note Evans' note	Lewis Evans' notes published in Pownall's 1776 edition.

THE
PREFACE
TO THE FIRST EDITION[1]

Philadelphia. Aug. 9, 1755.

T HE Map,[2] which these Sheets accompany, and which they are intended to explain, is presented to the Public, when a longer Time was indeed necessary to have given it the Degree of Correctness that was intended it. But the Conjuncture of Affairs in America,[3] and the generous Assistance of the Assembly of Pennsylvania,[4] have brought it to Light, when the Public will, it is hoped, receive Advantages from it, that will render an Apology for its premature Publication needless; and think it worthy the Encouragement of a Body who devote the Public Money to the Public Service.

It comprizes such an Extent, as is connected with that very valuable Country on the Ohio, which is now the Object of the British and French Policy, and the different Routs of both Nations thither. The Lake Ontario is equally open to both; to the One by the River St. Lawrence; to the other by the Rivers Hudson, Mohocks [Mohawk], and Seneca. But the French having, 30 Years ago, fixed themselves on the Streights of Niagara, by building Fortresses on Lands confessedly British, secured the Key on that Side to all the Country Westward. Those in Power see at last its Consequence, and are projecting the Recovery of it; and with great Judgement, for that Purpose, are establishing[5] a Naval Force on

---

[1]This preface is a copy of the preface to Lewis Evans' *Geographical, Historical, Political, Philosophical and Mechanical Essays. The First, Containing an Analysis of a General Map of the Middle British Colonies in America* . . . (Philadelphia, B. Franklin and D. Hall, 1755), pp. iii-iv. This essay is reprinted in Lawrence H. Gipson's *Lewis Evans* . . . (Philadelphia, Historical Society of Pennsylvania, 1939), preface, pp. 143-144. Thomas Pownall has made a few minor changes in words and phrases.

[2]*A General Map of the Middle British Colonies, in America* . . . By Lewis Evans, 1755. Engraved by Ja[s] Turner in Philadelphia. Published according to Act of Parliament, by Lewis Evans, June 23. 1755 and sold by R. Dodsley, in Pall-Mall, London, & by the Author in Philadelphia.

[3][Thomas Pownall's note for revised and enlarged edition] At the commencement of the last Warr in America, 1755.

"No doubt refers to the rapidly increasing encroachments of France on the back settlements." Henry N. Stevens, *Lewis Evans. His Map of the Middle British Colonies in America* (3d ed., London, H. Stevens, Son and Stiles, 1924), p. 9.

[4]The Province of Pennsylvania voted Lewis Evans £50 toward the expense of having this map engraved and printed. Pennsylvania (Colony) General Assembly. House of Representatives, *Votes and Proceedings of the House of Representatives of the Province of Pennsylvania . . . from 15th Day of October, 1744 to September 30, 1758* (Phila., Henry Miller, 1744), IV, 330, 334, 481.

[5][Pownall's note for revised and enlarged edition] Vida *Appendix* to the *Administration of the British*

I

Lake Ontario, as very necessary in the Recovery and securing of it. The Issue of this Enterprize will have great Influence on our Affairs, and of all Things it becomes the Colonies to push it on with Vigour. If they succeed here, the Remainder of the Work will be easy; and nothing so, without it. The English have several Ways to Ohio; but far the best is by Potomack[1] [Potomac].

By reason of the little Acquaintance the Public has with these remoter Parts, where the Country is yet a Wilderness, and the Necessity of knowing the Ways of travelling there, especially by Water, in the Map is pointed out the Nature of the several Streams; as where rapid, gentle, or obstructed with Falls, and consequently more or less fitted for Inland Navigation with Canoes, Boats, or larger Vessels; and where the Portages are made at the Falls, or from one River, Creek, or Lake to another. And for distinguishing the Extent of the Marine Navigation, the Places that the Tide reaches, in the several Rivers, are pointed out. And in these sheets, both the Marine and Inland Navigation are treated of at Length.

As the Nature of the Soil and Streams depend upon the Elevation and Depression of the Land, I have particularly explained here the different Stages that it is divided into. It were to be wished, that we had like Accounts of all Countries; as such would discover to us great Regularity, where an inattentive Observer would imagine there was nothing but Confusion; and at the same Time explain the Climates, the Healthiness, the Produce, and Conveniences for Habitations, Commerce, and Military Expeditions, to a judicious Reader in a few Pages, better than Volumes of Remarks on Places, drawn without these Distinctions.

To render this Map useful in Commerce, and in ascertaining the Boundaries of Lands, the Time of High Water at the Full and Change of the Moon, and the Variation of the Magnetical Needle, are laid down. But as these deserve particular Explanations, I have, for want of Room, concluded to treat of them at large in a separate Essay.[2]

Along the Western Margin of the Map is drawn a Line representing

Colonies where the Reader will see the Proposition of this measure as made to the Congress mett at Albany by Governor Pownall.

[1]For criticism and Evans' defense of this statement read Lewis Evans' *Geographical, Historical, Political, Philosophical and Mechanical Essays Number II containing a Letter Representing the Impropriety of sending Forces to Virginia ... Published*

in the New York Mercury, No. 178, January 5, 1756. With an Answer to so much thereof as concerns the Public (Philadelphia, Printed for the Author, 1756) and reprinted in Gipson's *Lewis Evans ... op. cit.,* pp. 177-219.

[2]This essay was never written, for Lewis Evans died on June 11, 1756, a few days after the publication of his Essay Number II. Gipson, *op. cit.,* p. 77.

the greatest Lengths of Days and Nights (without Allowance for the Refraction) which will assist Travellers in forming some Judgment of the Latitude of Places, by the Help of their Watches only.

Though many of these Articles are almost peculiar to the Author's map, they are of no less Importance than any Thing that has yet had a Place amongst Geographers. But want of Room in the Plate has obliged me to leave out what would have very much assisted my Explanation of the Face of the Country, I mean a Section of it in several Directions; such would have exhibited the Rising and Falling of the Ground, and how elevated above the Surface of the Sea; what Parts are level, what rugged; where the Mountains rise, and how far they spread. Nor is this all that a perpendicular Section might be made to represent; for, as on the superficial Line, the Elevations, Depressions, outer Appearances, and Names of Places may be laid down; so within the Area of the Section, the Nature of the Soil, Substrata, and particular Fossils may be exprest. It was with Regret I was obliged to omit it. But in some future Maps of separate Colonies, I hope to be furnished with more Room.[1]

The present, late and antient Seats of the original Inhabitants are expressed in the Map; and though it might be imagined that several Nation are omitted, which are mentioned by Authors, it may be remarked, that Authors, for want of Knowledge in Indian Affairs, have taken every little Society for a separate Nation; whereas they are not truly more in Number than I have laid down. I have been something particular in these Sheets in representing the Extent of the Confederates or Five Nations; because whatever is theirs, is expressly acceded to the English by Treaty with the French.[2]

[1][Pownall's note for revised and enlarged edition] The Materials, so far as taken from the Itinerary Observations of the present Editor, which were in Part to have composed those Sections, are now inserted in the following *Topographical Description.*

[2]By the Treaties of Breda (1667) and Westminster (1673) the English gained control over all the Dutch lands in North America. These possessions included the land of the Iroquois. The Iroquois reaffirmed their possession by the Dongan Treaty (1684) and the sale of their lands to the English in 1701. Again this English sovereignty was reaffirmed in particular at their Lancaster Treaty (1744). The terms of the Treaties of Utrecht (1713) and Aix-la-Chapelle (1748) returned the French and English territory in North America, which was gained by Wars between them, to the respective owners before their conquests.

PREFACE

TO THE

SECOND AND THIRD EDITIONS[1]

Albemarle Street 1775

THE Western Division of this present Map was composed and published at the Commencement of the late War in America.[2] It was found by the Officers and Servants of the Crown to have such a Degree of Precision, that it was used by them both in England and in America,[3] and served every practical Purpose during the Warrs. Those who have served and travelled in America, have had few Occasions of correcting it; on the contrary, its Exactness as far as a general Map means to go, has generally been confirmed by Experience on the Spot. In any Transactions since the War, where local Precision has been necessary, this Map has been referred to, not simply in private but public Transactions, such as the great Indian Purchase and Cession.[4] The Boundaries by which the Propositions for the Purchase of Lands on the Ohio were made to the Boards of Trade and Treasury, were marked and settled on this Map.[5] When the Servants of the Crown proposed in the House of Commons the Clause for the Limits of the Government of Quebec; and when the Line of those Limits were there opposed, both Sides, with this Map in their Hands, argued from it.[6]

[1]This preface is in two parts. The first part (Albemarle Street, 1775) published in Pownall's *Topographical Descriptions* . . . (1776), is here greatly revised and enlarged. The second part or preface to his self-styled third edition (Richmond Hill, 1784), is printed for the first time in this, a revised and enlarged edition.

[2]1755.

[3]Evans' *Maps* figured largely in Braddock's Campaign. The 1752 edition was used both in England and America. Prepublication copies of the 1755 edition were rushed to Braddock on his arrival in Virginia. Hazel Shields Garrison, "Cartography of Pennsylvania" in *Pennsylvania Magazine of History and Biography* (Philadelphia, Publication Fund of the Historical Society of Pennsylvania, 1877—), LIX (1935), 269.

[4]See "Map of the Frontiers of the Northern Colonies with the Boundary Line Established Between Them and the Indians at the Treaty Held by Sr. Will Johnson at Fort Stanwix in Nov'r 1768, Corrected and Improved from Evans Map. By Guy Johnson, Agt Indian Affairs." Sir William Johnson, *Papers of* . . . (Albany, University of the State of N.Y., 1921-39), VI, map opposite 450.

[5]See "Vandalia as Originally Plotted on Evans' Map." Thomas Perkins Abernethy, *Western Lands and the American Revolution* (N.Y., D. Appleton-Century Co., 1937), map opposite p. 39.

[6]Published debates on the Quebec Act are not in accord with this statement. See title page: Great Britain (1760-1820, George III) House of Commons, . . . *Debates of the House of Commons in the Year 1774, of the Bill for Making More Effectual Provision for the Government of the Province of Quebec. Drawn up from the notes of Sir Henry Cavendish. With a Map of Canada, copied from the Second Edition of Mitchell's Map of North America referred to in the Debates* (London, Ridgway, 1839).

In Mr. Evans's First Publication of this Map, the Parts within Virginia were copied from Fry and Jefferson's Map[1] of that Province, a Work of great Merit, composed from actual Surveys, and published by Jefferys in 1751. It has in this Edition been improved by later Informations. A Map engraved by Jefferys, and called, 'A new and accurate Map of Virginia,' by John Henry,[2] was published 1770. I was in Hopes to have derived Information from this, but upon Examination of it, it appears to me to be a very inaccurate Compilation; defective in Topography; and not very attentive even to Geography; The Draughtsman or the Engraver has totally omitted the South Branch of Potômack [Potomac] River: Nor is that curious and interesting Piece of Information, the Communication between the Waters of Virginia and the Waters of the Ohio, which were known when this was published, marked in it. This Map of Mr. Henry has indeed the Division Lines of the Counties of the Province drawn on it, and if they are rightly drawn, it is certainly an Improvement: But while I doubt the Accuracy of the Geography, I cannot be assured of these.

If there be any Map of Maryland published since this of Evans's, I have never seen such. There have been many new Settlements and many Improvements made in that Country since this Map was published: I have applied to Quarters whence, I did suppose, there might be derived Information in these Matters, but without Success.

Mr. Scull[3] in 1770, published a new Edition[4] of his Uncle Nic. Scull's[5] Map of Pennsylvania,[6] published in 1759. Mr. Evans in his First Edition of his Map was greatly assisted by Mr. N. Scull. The western Parts of

[1]*A Map of the most inhabited part of Virginia containing the whole province of Maryland with part of Pensilvania, New Jersey and North Carolina.* Drawn by Joshua Fry and Peter Jefferson in 1751. Printed for Robt. Sayer at No. 53 in Fleet Street & Thos. Jefferys at the Corner of St. Martins Lane, Charing Cross, London.

[2]*A New and Accurate Map of Virginia Wherein most of the Counties are laid down from Actual Surveys. With a Concise Account of the Number of Inhabitants, the Trade, the Soil, and Produce of that Province* by John Henry. Engraved by Thomas Jefferys, Geographer to the King. London, February 1770, Published according to act of Parliament for the author, by Thos. Jefferys at the corner of St. Martins Lane, in the Strand.

[3]William Scull. Birth and death dates are unknown. Evidently he was a native Pennsylvanian who was assistant to Robert Erskine, geographer and surveyor general for the Continental Army under Washington, and was, in 1755, sheriff in Northumberland County, Pennsylvania. Garrison, *op. cit.*, pp. 277-78.

[4]*To the honorable Thomas Penn and Richard Penn, esquires, true and absolute proprietors and Governors of the Province of Pennsylvania and the territories thereunto belonging and to the honorable John Penn, esquire, lieutenant governor of the same, this map of the province of Pennsylvania is humbly dedicated by their most obedient serv't W. Scull.* Philadelphia, James Nevil, for the author, April 1st, 1770.

[5]Nicholas Scull (1687-1762) surveyor general of Pennsylvania, was William Scull's grandfather not his uncle. *Pennsylvania Archives*, 1st series (Phila., Joseph Severns & Co., 1852-56), VIII, 94.

[6]*To the honourable Thomas Penn and Richard Penn, this map of the improved part of the province of Pennsylvania is humbly dedicated by Nicholas Scull.* Philadelphia, J. Davis for the author, 1759.

this Province were in Evans's Map done with a Degree of Accuracy, which I do not find this New Map can any where essentially correct or amend. The Names of new Counties, Settlements, and Townships, erected since the First Publication, are in this Edition added from the New Map of 1770.[1]

I do not know of any printed Map of New Jersey in particular. A Projection of that Province, done by Mr. Alexander,[2] Surveyor General, in which were laid down all the Stations that have been occasionally fixed by Astronomical Observation, and all the Lines which have been run by actual Survey, in the Course of the several Disputes in which that Province was involved between the East and Western, the Elizabeth Town, and other Proprietaries, as also with the Province New York, was very obligingly copied for and given to me by his Son Lord Sterling.[3] The Parts of Mr. Evans's Map within that Province have been corrected from these Papers. The Boundary Line betwixt this Province and New York was drawn on this Map by Capt. Holland,[4] who was employed to run it.

There has, (in 1778) since the time[5] of the publication of this work, been published by Mr. Faden A Map of New Jersey[6] which is said to be laid down in ye parts near the boundary Line betwixt that Province & New York from a survey made by Lieut. Ratzer[7] under ye Orders of the Commissioners appointed to settle it & in the Northern Parts in general from a Survey by Gerard Barker, in the possession of the Earl of Dunmore.[8] I have examined this and compared with Mr. Alexander's

[1]William Scull's *Map, op. cit.*

[2]James Alexander (1691-1756), surveyor general for the Province of New Jersey.

[3]William Alexander (1726-1783), son of James Alexander.

[4]Samuel Holland, British surveyor general of lands for the Northern district of America. In 1767 while serving in this capacity Captain Holland was one of the Commissioners appointed to settle the controversy concerning the boundary line between the provinces, New York and New Jersey. *Documents relating to the Colonial history of the state of New Jersey* (Newark, Daily Advertiser Printing House, *et al.*, 1880-1928), IX, 624. (Hereafter cited as *New Jersey Archives*). Holland's appointment to service in North America may have been made in 1765 for by 1772 he had spent seven years in surveying part of the coast of North America. In a letter to General Thomas Gage he estimates the survey will take five years longer. Thomas Gage, *The Correspondence of* . . . , edited by Clarence Edwin

Carter (New Haven, Yale University Press, 1933), II, 601.

[5]1776.

[6]First published in 1777. "The province of New Jersey, divided into east and west, commonly called the Jerseys. Drawn from the survey made in 1769 by order of the commissioners appointed to settle the partition line between the provinces of New York & New Jersey by Bernard Ratzer, and from another large survey of the northern parts by Gerard Barker, Engraved by Wm. Faden. London, W. Faden, Dec. 1, 1777." Wm. Faden, *The North American Atlas* (London, for W. Faden, 1777), no. 22.

[7]Bernard Ratzer, British Army engineer. Leland DeWitt Baldwin, *Pittsburgh, the Story of a City* (Pittsburgh, University of Pittsburgh Press, 1938), p. 57.

[8]John Murray, *4th Earl of Dunmore* (1730-1809). Lord Dunmore was governor of New York, 1770-71, governor of Virginia, 1771-76, and governor of the Bahamas, 1787-96.

Surveys of Lines & Patents and find nothing new or more detailed than what I had seen.[1]

A Map of New York and New Jersey,[2] published by T. Jefferys, to which Publication the Name of Capt. Holland is put,[3] without his Knowledge or Consent, is little more than a Copy of those Parts contained in Evans's Map, or, if not a Copy, a Compilation from the same Materials on a larger Scale, without any essential Amendment, without scarce a Difference, except in the County of Albany, corrected from a Map of that County which Capt. Holland copied for me in 1756, from Draughts of Mr. Bleecker,[4] Deputy Surveyor in that County. The only Parts contained in the Map, thus published by Jefferys, which were surveyed by Capt. Holland are, "the Passage of the Hudson's [Hudson] River through the Highlands, "and the Parts on the Banks from Viskill[5] to Croton's [Croton] River," a Distance of about 20 Miles; and even in these Parts the Compiler has omitted to notice that remarkable Pass Martlaer's Rock.[6] The Boundary Lines of the great Patents and Manors; of some of the Counties; and some of the new Townships are drawn over this Map in their Squares: But I am not able to collect any Improvement in it either as to Topography or Geography. The present Jefferys[7] is, as I understand, in Possession of an excellent Draught of the Province of New York,[8] done under the Direction of Governor Tryon:[9] I hope the Publication will be made in a Manner worthy of it. This Map[10] is now (1779) published by Mr. Faden, a very accurate, industrious

---

[1]This paragraph is a 1784 addition to the 1776 publication of Pownall's *Topographical Descriptions*.

[2]"The Provinces of New York and New Jersey with part of Pensilvania, and the Province of Quebec Drawn by Major Holland, Surveyor General of the Northern District in America, Corrected and Improved from the original materials by Governor Pownall, M.P. 1776. London, printed for Robert Sayer & John Bennett 17 Aug., 1776." Thomas Jefferys, *The American Atlas* . . . (London, R. Sayer and J. Bennett, 1776), no. 17.

[3][Pownall's note] Advertisement published by Capt. Holland, "Nor have I at any Time published or given my Consent to the publishing of any Plan, Map, or Survey now extant, that bears my Name. Sam. Holland."

[4]John Rutger Bleeker, (bap. 1713-1800), surveyor of Albany County and deputy surveyor for the Northern Department under Samuel Holland. The name is written both Bleeker and Bleecker.

[5]Fishkill Creek, New York.

[6]Now Constitution Island. This island projects halfway across the Hudson River and forms the left bank opposite West Point. Edward C. Boynton, *History of West Point* . . . (London, Sampson Low, Son, & Marston, 1864), pp. 20-21.

[7]Evidently William Jefferys to whom Library of Congress, Division of Maps attributes *The American Atlas. op. cit.*, for T. Jefferys died in 1771. U.S. Library of Congress. Division of Maps, *A List of Maps of America in the Library of Congress* (Washington, Government Printing Office, 1901), p. 505. Hereafter cited as Phillips, *List of Maps*.

[8]*A Chorographical map of the province of New York, divided into Counties, Manors, etc. Compiled from actual surveys deposited in the patent office at New York by order of Gen. William Tryon*, by Claude Joseph Sauthier. London, W. Faden, Jan. 1, 1779.

[9]William Tryon (1729-1788) lieutenant governor North Carolina, 1765-1771, and governor New York, 1771 to the Revolution. In 1777 Tryon obtained permission to command a force of Loyalists in America, a commission he carried until 1780 when he was forced by ill health to retire and return to England.

[10]See *note* 8, above.

young Man. I saw some of the Proofs of it & made some few corrections in it. Mr. Faden has done it Justice in his attention to accuracy & by his skill in the engraving. As the scale gives room for such, I wish the Soundings up ye Hudson's [Hudson] R^r & several noted points of land on Long Island & in the Sound had been marked on it. Perhaps before any future impression these things may be putt into the plate.

Of New England there has been no new Map[1] published since that by Dr. Douglas,[2] dedicated to the several Assemblies of Messachuset's [Massachusetts] Bay, New Hampshire, Connecticut, and Rhode Island. So far as that went it was composed from actual Surveys of the Boundary Lines of the several Provinces, Colonies, Grants, and Townships: The Courses of the Rivers and the remarkable Mountains were traced and fixed with great Care and Attention. What there was wanting to a compleat Map of New England, is now added from later Information, and from later Draughts and Surveys[3] deposited at the Board of Trade, which the Earl of Dartmouth[4] permitted me to have copied for the Benefit of the Public. These new Parts which I have added are plotted down in the Form in which I think every Map which can offer to give the Face of the Country, should be drawn, tracing the Features of it, and not in Default of that, filling up the Map with Writing. Instead of Writing I have put *Figures of Reference*, and the Writing is put in the Margin and in other blank Places. The Surveys which give this Map its Accuracy in the Maritime Parts of New England were chiefly made by Capt. Holland,[5] or by his Deputies under his Direction.

Many Tracks which the Geographer will see marked in the western Parts of the Map, as it was first published at Philadelphia in 1755, were mere Indian or Traders Paths through the Wilderness,

............per avia quâ Sola nunquam

Trita rotis............

but are now in the Course of a very few Years become great Waggon Roads, & are here mark'd as such.

Et modo quae fuerat Semita, facta via.

[1]Map of New England published by Dr. Douglass. *Plan of the British Dominions of New England in North America Composed from Actual Surveys.* By Dr. William Douglas. Engraved by R. W. Seale, London, 1753. "Published by the executors of dr. William Douglas from his original draft." Phillips, *List of Maps, op. cit.,* p. 469.

[2]William Douglass (1691-1752).

[3]See Great Britain. Board of Trade and Plantations, *List of Maps, Plans, &c belonging to the Right Honble the Lords Commissioners for Trade and Plantations under the care of Francis Aegidius Assiotti, Draughtsman,* 1780. P. R. O. CO 326/15.

[4]William Legge, *2nd Earl of Dartmouth* (1731-1801). Dartmouth was President of the Board of Trade and Plantations, 1765-66, Secretary of State for the Colonies and President of the Board of Trade and Plantations, 1772-1775, Lord privy seal, 1775-1782.

[5]See *note* 4, p. 7.

Many *Indian Settlements*, being then merely a *Collection of Wig-wams* or Cabins, must now in this Edition of 1755[1] marked as COUNTY TOWNS. Many other Particulars marked in the Map, and noticed in the original Analysis, which were, 20 Years ago, Matter of practical Information, and useful to the Service, ceasing, perhaps now to have that Use, may yet be amusing as *Matters of curious Antiquity*, become so at this early Period. It will be curious in a few Years, as the Face of the Country changes and is totally altered, to view in this Map, and to read in this Description, what it was in its natural State, and how the Settlements began to expand, and had extended themselves in 20 Years.

A pirated Copy of this Map, soon after it came to England, was in a most audacious Manner published by the late Thomas Jefferys,[2] under a false Pretence of Improvements, Lewis Evans's Name was put to it; and this Plagiarism was falsely sold as Evans's Map improved; by which that very laborious and ingenious, but poor Man, was deprived of the Benefit of his Work. The Engraver was so totally ignorant of the Principles on which the Original was formed, that although he traced the Lines of the Rivers and Roads in the usual Way, yet it can scarce be called a Copy. The Mountains in America, which give the real Features to the Face of it, run in Ridges of a specific Direction, do in Places here and there run up into Peaks; do in others end abruptly in Knobs and Bluff-points; do interlock and have Gaps; all which Particulars were in the Original with a scrupulous Attention plotted and set down; as also the Parts where these Ridges spread into hilly Land. The Officer or the Geographer will look in vain for this Precision in the pirated Copy. The blundering Copyist thought, that the filling the Places where he happened to meet with the Word, *Mountains*, with the Engraver's common Marks scratched in at random, was doing the Business, by which he has put Mountains where they are not; and has converted great Swamps into Mountains; and in other Parts has totally omitted the Marks of high Ground, because he did not understand those Marks which were used to express such high Ground, without presuming to give the Range and Form, where that was not yet known. So far as respects the Face of the Country, this Thing of Jefferys might as well be a Map of the Face of the Moon. Further, in the Original there was

---

[1] Since this is a correction made in 1784, Pownall may have intended the date, 1785.

[2] *A General Map of the Middle British Colonies in America: viz. Virginia, Maryland, Delaware, Pensilvania ... By Lewis Evans. Corrected and improved in the addition of the line of forts on the back settlements,* by Thomas Jefferys. London, R. Sayer & T. Jefferys, 1758.

Henry Stevens says that Pownall unjustly accused Jefferys, for he, Jefferys, merely reissued T. Kitchin's 1756 edition of Evans' *Map*. Stevens, *op. cit.*, p. 16.

observed a scrupulous Caution not to deceive; the Parts which were drawn from Report and Computation, and collected from Journals, are in the Original engraved in a slighter Manner, and very differently from those Parts which are laid down from actual Surveys; neither the Eye, the Ideas, nor the Spirit of the Copyist went to the Marking this; and all Parts stand equal in Authority in his false Copy.

The Plate of this blundering Copy has, in the Course of Trade, by Purchase, fallen into the Hands of Mr. Sayer[1] of Fleet-Street, a Man of Reputation in a very extensive Line of Business. He very honourably told me, that if the Plate[2] stood as a single Article in his Shop, he would destroy it directly; but that it made Part of an Atlas[3] already published by him; and was also Part of another very soon to be published[4] by him, which cost many thousand Pounds; and that he did not know how to take it out of these Collections. I can only say, it will disgrace any Collection in which it stands, and that I am sorry it is to disgrace any coming from a Shop in which there are so many valuable Maps and Charts.[5]

Richmond hill, 1784.

The very great Sale which the following Work has experienced hath intirely taken off the last impression; although it consisted of Double the number of Copies usually put into one Edition. It has been now three or four years out of Print. I have been applied to repeatedly from abroad as well as in England, to put out another Edition. In the year 1779 I undertook to revise it. I look'd out my own papers. I applied also to Lord George Germain[6] at that time the Secretary of State to whom his Majesty had assigned the American department, for leave of access to such geographical papers, & surveys of different parts in the Southern Colonies, were in his office. He granted this Favor with a degree of politeness & liberality which I beg here to make my acknowledgements to. I collated and . . . [The remainder of this preface is missing.]

[1]Robert Sayer.

[2]See *note* 2, page 10.

[3]Thomas Jefferys, engraver, *A General Topography of North America and the West Indies* (London, for R. Sayer & T. Jefferys, 1768). Lewis Evans' *Map* is number 32.

[4]T. Jefferys, engraver, *The American Atlas . . .* (London, R. Sayer & J. Bennett, 1775). It is interesting to note that the 1776 edition of this atlas, unlike the 1775 edition, does not include the Lewis Evans *Map*. See U.S. Library of Congress. Division of Maps, *A List of Geographical Atlases in the Library of Congress . . .* compiled under the direction of Philip Lee Phillips (Washington, Government Print-ing Office, 1909-20), I, nos. 1165-1166. Hereafter cited as Phillips, *List of Atlases.*

[5][Pownall's note for revised and enlarged edition] He has had it since corrected from my Map for the purpose of making part of a Collection in a Pocket Atlas of North America. R. Sayer and J. Bennet, *The American Military Pocket Atlas . . .* London, for R. Sayer & J. Bennet 1776. Known as the "Holster Atlas" since it was made for the use of mounted British officers. Phillips *List of Atlases, op. cit.,* I, no. 1206—Ed.

[6]George Sackville Germain (1716-1785). Known as Lord George Sackville, 1720-1770, and as Lord George Germain, 1770-1782.

A

TOPOGRAPHICAL DESCRIPTION

Of Such Parts Of

NORTH AMERICA

As Are Contained In

THE MAP

The Parts of this Work marked with inverted Commas[1] are reprinted from Mr. Lewis Evans's Analysis, *printed in Philadelphia 1755; the other Parts are by Governor Pownall.*

"AS different Parts of this Map are done with very different Proportion of Exactness, Justice to the Public, requires my distinguishing the Degree of Credit every Part deserves; and to make some Recompence for the Defects of those Places, where no actual Surveys have been yet made, by giving such a Description as the Nature of the Subject will admit; which may, at this Time, be of as much Consequence as the nicest Surveys destitute of this Advantage.

"The British Settlements are done, for the greater Part, from actual Surveys. The Latitudes of many Places taken with good Instruments, and the Longitudes of Philadelphia and Boston, observed by different Persons, and well agreeing, give a Foundation for the Projection of the Map. And as Philadelphia is a fine City, situate near the Center of the British Dominions on this Continent; and as, whether it is inferior to others in Wealth, or Number of Houses, or not, it far excels in the Progress of Letters, mechanic Arts, and the public Spirit of its Inhabitants; I thought this Reason sufficient for paying it the particular Distinction of making it the first Meridian of America. And a Meridian here I thought the more necessary, that we may determine the Difference of the Longitude of Places by Mensuration; a Method far excelling the best astronomical Observations; and as we may be led into several Errors by always reckoning from remote Meridians, those who have only seen the Plans and Maps of this City, must be cautioned not to give

Philadelphia made the first Meridian.

---

[1]In this present edition the inverted commas have been replaced by quotation marks.

any of them Credit, for it extends only on the West Side of Delaware,[1] about a Mile and a Half in Length, and about Half a Mile in its greatest Breadth. Near the Western Extremity is the Statehouse, the Spot proposed for my Meridian to be drawn through.[2]

"The Longitude at the Top is computed from Philadelphia; at Bottom from London, according to the late Mr. Thomas Godfrey's Observations[3] and my own at Philadelphia. And I was induced to give these the Preference to that made at New York by Mr. Burnet,[4] because of their Agreement with Mr. Th. Robie's Observations[5] at Boston. The Distance from Philadelphia to Conohasset [Cohasset], at the Mouth of Bound Brook, on Massachuset [Massachusetts] Bay, has, the far greater Part, been measured in long Lines, on public Occasions, and the Rest is supplied by Surveys[6] of particular Tracts of Land and Roads. And if Bound Brook is 19 or 20 Miles Eastward of the Meridian of Boston, as I imagine it is, there is no sensible Difference between the Observations, but what arises from the Difference of 4° between the Two Places, as laid down.

"The principal Observations of Latitude are these,

Boston, – – – – – – – 42 : 25

N. Boundary of Connecticut, – 42 : 2
New York, – – – – – – – 40 : 42 } By Governor Burnet[7]

N. Station Point, – – – – 41 : 40 } By the Jersey and N. York Commissioners 1719[8]

Philadelphia, – – – – – 39 : 57
Shamokin, – – – – – – 40 : 40
Owege, – – – – – – – 41 : 55 } By L. Evans[9]
Onondaga, – – – – – – 42 : 55
Oswego, – – – – – – – 43 : 17
Sandy Hook, – – – – – 40 : 28

[1][Pownall's note] This was written in 1755.

[2]Quoted from Evans' *Analysis, op. cit.*, p. 1; reprinted in Gipson's *Lewis Evans, op. cit.*, p. 145.

[3]Thomas Godfrey (1704-1749). Godfrey's observations are recorded by Lewis Evans. *A Map of Pensilvania, New Jersey, New York . . . By Lewis Evans*, 1749. Published by Lewis Evans March 25, 1749, According to Act of Parliament, Philadelphia, Benjamin Franklin? 1749.

[4]William Burnet (1688-1729), colonial governor of New York, New Jersey, and Massachusetts. "Observations" in Royal Society of London, *Philosophical Transactions . . .* (London, The Society, 1665-date), no. 385 (1724).

[5]Thomas Robie (died 1729). "Meteorological Observations," *ibid.*, nos. 270-272 (1701).

[6][Evans' note] We call nothing *Surveys* but actual Mensurations with a Chain, and the Course taken with a good surveying Instrument. Courses with a Pocket Compass and computed Distances we call *Computations*.

[7]See *note* 4, this page.

[8]Read "Tripartite Indenture settling the North Partition Point between New Jersey & New York," in New Jersey *Archives, op. cit.*, IV, 349-99.

[9]These observations may have been made in 1743 when Lewis Evans traveled with John Bartram to Onondaga. John Bartram, *Observations on the Inhabitants, Climate, Soil, Rivers, Productions, Animals and other matters worthy of Notice . . . In his Travels from Pensilvania to Onondaga, Oswego and the Lake Ontario* (London, J. Whiston and B. White, 1751).

Ray's Town,	– – – – –	39 : 59	} By Col. Fry[1]
Shanoppen's Town,	– – –	40 : 26	
S. Side of S. St. Louis	– – –	45 : 18	} By Champlain, in 1603[2]
Ville Marie –	– – – – –	45 : 27	

"Though there have been many other Observations made in several Places in the Settlements, I have always chosen to adjust their Situations by Actual Mensurations; because many of the Instruments yet used are not sufficiently accurate to determine the Latitude of Places with Nicety."[3]

Many very accurate Observations of the Latitude and Longitude of many Places have been since made, which chiefly confirm the Positions in this Present Map—where they differed materially it has been corrected by them.

"A Map I published of PENNSYLVANIA, NEW JERSEY, NEW YORK, and DELAWARE[4] in 1749,[5] is reduced to a smaller Scale in this,[6] and forms those Four Colonies. The Errors are rectified, the principal of which were, Albany placed too far North, Shamokin too far West, and all the Route thence to Oswego Five Miles altogether too much North; besides several Imperfections in Places which later Observations and Discoveries have given us Knowledge of. In the first Impression[7] of my former Map I committed some Mistakes in the Names of Places near the Entrance of Delaware Bay on the West Side[d8]

Capes of Delaware.

d H d

[1]Joshua Fry (1700?-1754). William West reported this observation by Col. Fry to be 40°27′. Pennsylvania (Colony). Provincial Council, *Minutes of . . . from its organization to the termination of the Proprietary Government* (Phila., Jo Severns & Co. [and others], 1852-53) V, 761. Hereafter cited as *Colonial Records of Pennsylvania.*

[2]Samuel de Champlain (1567-1635). The latitude for the vicinity of Ville Marie is given by Champlain in 1603 as "45° and some minutes." Samuel de Champlain. *The Works of . . .* translated . . . by H. P. Biggar (Toronto, Champlain Society, 1922), I, 153. The latitude for the south side or end of Lake St. Louis is given by Champlain in 1613 as 45°18′ *ibid.* (1925), II, 261.

[3]Quoted from Evans' *Analysis*, pp. 2-3; reprinted in Gipson's *Lewis Evans*, pp. 146-47.

[4][Evans' note] So the *Three Lower Counties of Newcastle, Kent, and Sussex, upon Delaware,* were called before they were annexed to Pennsylvania, when this Name was given in Contradistinction to the *Three Upper* Counties of Chester, Philadelphia, and Bucks. As this Name exceeds in Length and Barbarity all the Savage Ones in my Title put together,

I have restored the Colony its old Name of *Delaware.*

[5]*A Map of Pensilvania, New Jersey, New York and the Three Delaware Counties. By Lewis Evans, 1749, op. cit.*

[6]Refers to Evans' *Map* of 1755.

[7]*A Map of Pensilvania . . . , By Lewis Evans, 1749, op. cit.*

[8][Pownall's note] Upon this first Reference, by Letters in the Margin, it may be proper to acquaint the Reader, that the Reference is to the Letters H and d in the Margin of the Map. The Capitals are on the eastern Margin between the Parallels of Latitudes; the small Letters in the upper Margin between the Meridians of Longitude. They are meant to direct the Reader (without perpetually repeating Degrees and Minutes of Latitude and Longitude) to a ready Manner of finding any Place mentioned in these Sheets. For instance, in this first Case: Look for H in the eastern Margin, and for d in the Northern; and in the Square where the Parallels of Latitude between which H is, intersect with the Meridians of Longitude between which d is, the Reader will find the Place referred to.

and in my Attempt to rectify them, in the second Edition,[1] did but add to the Confusion. I have since had an Opportunity of making a thorough Enquiry into this Affair, and conclude, that the Names which the Places thereabouts are now called by, and are the same as laid down in my general Map, are the only Names they ever had,[2] and still retain amongst those acquainted with them; as Lewes, Whorekill Road, Cape Hinlopen, False Cape, and Fenwick's Island: Excepting, that Mr. William Penn called Cape Hinlopen by the Name of Cape *James;* and Whorekill *Lewes,* on his first Arrival in 1682; the former is scarce known at this Day, and the Name *Lewes* is confined to the Town, while the Creek still retains the Name of *The Whorekill.*

"All must admit that the present Names are rightly laid down; but what is related in regard to the ancient Names must be Understood as only my Opinion. There are others who think, on no less Opportunity of forming a Judgement, that Cape Hinlopen was formerly called Cape Cornelius; and that *Fenwick's Island* was the *False Cape,* or *Cape Hinlopen* of the Dutch, and others, till the Arrival of the English in those Parts under Mr. Penn.

"To complete what was left imperfect in my former Map, especially in *New York,* I have been in a particular Manner assisted by Mr. William Alexander,[3] whose numerous Observations and Collections add greatly to the Merit of this Part of the present One, as they will Authority with all who know him."[4]

The upper Part of the County of Albany, in New York, together with the Country on the Mohawks [Mohawk] River, is corrected and rendered more perfect in its Topography, from a Map[5] laid down by John Rulse Bleecker,[6] Deputy to the Surveyor of the Province, which Map is composed from actual Surveys as far up the River as Orhiscony [Oriskany], the rest is traced by the Journals of the Oswego Traders, and of this Deputy Surveyor himself.

[1]*A Map of Pensilvania, New Jersey, New York and the Three Delaware Counties: By Lewis Evans, 1749, The Second Edition, July 1752;* Reprinted in Gipson, *op. cit.*

[2]Read Gipson, *ibid.,* p. 47.

[3][Pownall's note for the revised and enlarged edition] This Gentleman afterward took the Title of Earl of Sterling and was a General Officer in the Service of the States.

[4]Quoted from Evans' *Analysis,* pp. 3-4; reprinted in Gipson's *Lewis Evans,* pp. 147-48.

[5]Probably a "Map of Albany County with the Country of the Five Nations," 1750-1770?, By Jno. R. Bleecker. Manuscript map in the New York Historical Society.

[6][Pownall's note for the revised and enlarged edition] This Man though a good practical surveyor being no Draughtsman, Capt. Holland drew the Map for me at Albany in 1756. It was the first Draught he made in America.

John Rutger Bleecker. Here Mr. Pownall has confused the middle name, Rutger, with the middle name of the Indian interpreter, John Rulse Bleecker—Ed.

The Parts about Lake George, Wood Creek, and the Drowned Lands are corrected from a Draught[1] of that Part given to me by my Friend the late Sir William Johnson;[2] the Figures on it are placed for Reference to the Names written in a vacant Part of the Map, as also to the Account that I shall give of it in this Description, as there was not room to write the long Indian Names by which the several Parts here were marked; this Draught was made for Practice while he commanded there, and has on it all the Indian Paths and Tracks of the Scouts; I have examined it by the Journals of the Scouts which I have by me,[c] Two or Three of which I shall annex, as giving the best Account [c Vide Appendix] of the Face of the Country in those Parts; I have also compared it with the Surveys, since made, which lie at the Board of Trade, but find nothing which exceeds this in its Topography. The River St. Francis, and the Communication by Land between that River and the River Connecticut, is corrected and laid down in the present Map from an actual Survey[3] given to me by Capt. Holland.[4] It was made by Mr. Grant[5] his Deputy.

When Mr. Evans rectified the northerly Projection of some Parts, in his Map published in 1749, and placed Albany lower (and right as now is confirmed by the Observations made by Order of the Governor of New York) in Lat. 42° 36'. He omitted to bring down the Parts of the Hudson River above Albany, by which Means the Distance betwixt Albany and Saratoga remained Five Miles too great, and the Distance [Cc] betwixt Saratoga and Fort Edward a Mile at least. I have in this Edition corrected the upper Parts of this River from Bleecker's Survey, which Corrections fortunately coincided with my Friend Sir William Johnson's Map; as also with a Sketch wherein the Courses and Distances between Fort Edward,[6] the Old Fort Ann,[7] and Lake George, are laid down by Mr. Grant who ran them. The relative Distances are thus rectified to great Exactness; but the Whole of this Map in these Parts (as also Lake

[1]"Johnson's Map of Lake George and Vicinity." William Johnson *Papers . . . op. cit.*, II, opp., 422.

[2]Sir William Johnson (1715-1774), superintendent of Indian Affairs in the Northern department.

[3]Probably "A Plan of a Survey made to explore the Country for a road between Connecticut River & St. Francis," attributed to Hugh Finlay. Manuscript map, in Library of Congress, Map Division. Phillips, *List of Maps, op. cit.*, p. 248.

[4][Pownall's note] Capt. Holland is surveyor general of Canada, and of the Northern District of America.

[5]James Grant, deputy surveyor under Samuel Holland, surveyor general for the Northern department.

[6]Built in 1755 at the Great Carrying Place on the Hudson River, about 45 miles north of Albany. On the present site of Fort Edward, New York.

[7]At the Wood Creek terminus of the Great Carrying Place between Hudson River and Lake Champlain. Built about 1709. On the present site of Fort Ann, New York.

Champlain and Montreal)[1] remaining still projected near Three Miles too much to the North, the South End of Lake George is about Three Miles more Northward than the New York Observations place it, being in North Latitude 43° 16′ 12″. It was proper I should mark this, but I believe it will not be thought of much Consequence.

The Observations were as follow, which I insert, that where there is any Difference the Reader may compare them, and decide for himself.

	o	′	″
Light-house at Sandy-hook – – – – – – – – –	40	27	40
New York Fort – – – – – – – – – –	40	41	50
Albany – – – – – – – – – – – –	42	36	0
South End of Lake George – – – – – –	43	16	12
Crown Point – – – – – – – – – – –	43	50	7
Windmill Point – – – – – – – – –	44	59	18
Point au Pines – – – – – – – – – –	44	58	48
Moor's Point – – – – – – – – – – –	45	0	0

"Besides a general Map of Connecticut, which the Rev. Mr. Clap[2] favoured me with, I have been assisted in drawing the EASTERN COLONIES now States by Memorials, preserved in Douglas's [Douglass'] Summary,[3] of the Colony Lines, as actually run round Three Sides of CONNECTICUT and RHODE ISLAND, and between NEW HAMPSHIRE and MASSACHUSET [TS]; and the Extension of these Lines in Two Places to Hudson's [Hudson] River. As for that said to be run from Deerfield to this River, there is certainly a Mistake of several Miles in the length of it. These, with several Surveys by Messieurs Helm, Kellog, and Chandler, amongst which is an entire one of Connecticut River from No. 4[e] to the North Side of Connecticut Colony,[f] given me by Mr. Pownall,[4] *together with his own itinerary Observations on the Face of the Country, the Ranges and Bearings of the Hills, and Distances of Places*, contribute to give these Parts a great Degree of Exactness. Nor am I obliged, in these Parts alone, to this Gentleman, but for the Corrections of many Articles, which had escaped me in the former Map, and for some other valuable Papers he procured me."[5]

eCb fDb

[1][Pownall's note] According to an Observation made by Monsieur Gillion, Montreal is in North Lat. 45 27. Variation 10 38 West.

[2]Rev. Thomas Clap (1703-67) president of Yale College, 1740-1764.

[3]William Douglass, *A Summary, Historical and Political of the First Planting, Progressive Improvements, and Present State of the British Settlements in* North America (Boston, New England, printed: London, reprinted for R. Baldwin, 1755), 2v. Dr. Douglass summarizes the surveys and settlements of boundary lines between several New England Colonies.

[4]Thomas Pownall.

[5]Reprinted from Evans' *Analysis*, p. 4; reprinted in Gipson's *Lewis Evans*, p. 148.

The Remainder of Connecticut River to its Spring Head is now first published and added to this Map: It is laid down from an actual Survey made of it by Mr. Grant, one of Capt. Holland's Deputies, which is deposited at the Board of Trade, a Work of great Labour and Merit.

The Provinces now States Massachuset's [Massachusetts] Bay and New Hampshire are now first added to this Map. The Parts contained within the Old Province, and within the Colony of Plymouth, are laid down from Dr. Douglas's [Douglass'] Map[1] corrected by myself from particular Surveys and other local Informations which came to my Knowledge during my residence therein. Capt. Holland's Surveys do not extend to these Parts. Dr. Douglas's [Douglass'] original Map is the *Fond* for the Interior Parts of New Hampshire. Capt. Holland's Surveys[2] of those Parts correct this, and give it its Accuracy. The Maritime Parts of New England from Rhode Island to Kenebaëg [Kennebec] River, and from Penobskaëg [Penobscot] River to Passam-aquâda [Passamaquoddy] are copied in Part from Surveys made by Order of Governor Bernard,[3] and in Part from Capt. Holland's Survey,[4] a Work of the very Highest Degree of Merit.

The Kenebaëg [Kennebec] and Penobskaëg [Penobscot] Rivers, with the Country contained between them, are plotted down from Journals of the Officers of the Scouting Parties, and from the Draughts of Surveyors sent out by me to examine and make a rough Survey of those Parts.

The Earl of Dartmouth, in a Manner most obliging, permitted me to have Captain Holland's Surveys, lying at the Board of Trade, copied, that the Public might Profit of the Knowledge which they give. Mr. Lewis, a Clerk at the Board of Trade, made the Copies; as he is an exceedingly neat and accurate Draughtsman they will be found to have, although on so small a Scale, a Degree of Precision and Accuracy which many larger Maps will not pretend to.

The following Observations of Latitudes were made by Capt. Holland in the Years 1773 and 1774, in the Course of this Work;

	°	′	″
The most southerly Part of Mount Desert Island	44	12	0
Fort Pownall on Penosbcot [Penobscot] River –	44	24	30

[1]*Plan of the British Dominions of New England . . .*, *op. cit.*

[2]*A Topographical Map of the Province of New Hampshire surveyed by Mr. Thomas Wright and others. Author S. Holland*, London, 1784. Printed for William Faden Mar. 1, 1784. Great Britain, Board of Trade and Plantations. *List of Maps . . .*, *op. cit.*, p. 27.

[3]Sir Frances Bernard (1712-1779), colonial governor of New Jersey and Massachusetts.

[4]See *note* 4, p. 7.

	°	′	″
Pemaquid Point – – – – – – – – –	43	48	15
Cape Elizabeth – – – – – – – – – –	43	33	0
Cape Porpoise – – – – – – – – – –	43	21	0
Cape Neddock – – – – – – – – – –	43	9	30
Thatcher's Island Lights – – – – – – –	42	38	0
Cape Ann Harbour East Point – – – – –	42	35	0
Cape Cod Most northerly Point – – – –	42	4	20

In Addition to the Topographical Notices which these Surveys give, I have been able, by my new method of putting Figures of Reference instead of writing the Names of Towns and Places, to fill up the interior Parts with a Delineation of the Face of the Country, such as will be sought for in vain in the great Maps of the largest Scale hitherto published, such perhaps for the Future will be inserted in other mapps.[1] The Ranges of the Mountains and the Bearings of the high Pikes in them are pretty accurately laid down from Observations begun long ago by Dr. Douglas [Douglass], and from others made by myself: The Returns made on the plan of Instructions I gave for that Purpose, by the Officers of the Scouting Parties, which I kept as a Guard ranging on the back Parts of the Province during the Whole of the late War; as also by Surveyors which I sent out to search and examine the Routs which the Country offered, and particularly that by Kenebëag [Kennebec] to Chaudiere; as also to examine the East Branches thereof, and the Interlocking of those with the West Branches of Penobscëag [Penobscot], are the Authorities for the rest. The Description given of the Face of the Country will be found in the following Treatise. Accurate and detailed as these Maps are they should always be accompanied by this Description in the Hands of those who wish to have a practical Knowledge of the Country.

"The greatest Part of VIRGINIA is composed with the Assistance of Messieurs Fry[2] and Jefferson's[3] Map[4] of it, and as this had the Assistance of actual Surveys of the Division Line with *Carolina*, and of the Rivers *Rapahannock* [Rappahannock] and *Potomack* [Potomac] from their Entrances to their Heads, joined to the Experience of Two skilful Persons, it would have been Affectation to have omitted the Advantage

Fry and Jefferson's Map of Virginia.

[1][Pownall's note] I should not have ventured to have inserted these in this Map, had I not found them to coincide with those Parts of Capt. Holland's Surveys, wherein any Notice is taken of the Mountains, these are indeed very few, but the Coincidence is a corroborating Authority which justifies me.

[2]Joshua Fry, (d. 1754) master in the College of William and Mary and member of the House of Burgesses of Virginia.

[3]Peter Jefferson (1708-1758), father of Thomas Jefferson.

[4]Fry and Jefferson *Map*, 1751. *op. cit.*

of it. But however, an actual Survey from Philadelphia to the Mountains, near the great Bent of Potomack [Potomac], by the Pennsylvania Surveyors in 1739,[1] enabled me to give the just Longitude of that Place from Philadelphia, which they mistook by 10 or 12 Miles; and this obliges me to give Potomack [Potomac], and the whole Country, a Position something different. As that Performance is very valuable, I contrived mine to interfere as little as possible with it; and omitted the Counties and numerous Gentlemens Seats that it contains, to give room for the Roads, Inspection-houses, Court-houses, and the Seats of some Half a Dozen Gentlemen noted in the literary Way.

"I am obliged to the Same Map and Capt. Hoxton's Chart of *Chesopeak* [Chesapeake], Bay for MARYLAND.[2] But this Colony is the worst done of all the Settlements in mine, yet the Bay from Annapolis to the Head I have lately had an Opportunity of adjusting; as well as to measure the Isthmus across from the Head of Elk to Delaware River, about Three Miles below Newcastle. There is a considerable Error in my General Map, which came Time enough to my Knowledge to be mentioned here, though not to be rectified; and that is, I make the Breadth of the Peninsula from Fenwick's Island to the South Side of Little Choptank 65 Miles, whereas Mr. Parsons,[3] One of the Surveyors, who ran the Line across, informs me, that it should have been 70."[4]

Maryland but imperfect.

Whoever shall trace the Country along which the Line, that divides the Provinces, now States, Maryland and Pennsylvania, runs, will find every River and Mountain, every Creek, Hill, and Road of any Consequence crossing it in their Courses exactly in the Point where the actual Survey made by Authority, and engraved by J. Smither,[5] places them: The western Parts of this Line where it should become the Boundary between Virginia and Pennsylvania remain yet unsettled and a disputed Point.

The Map[6] of the Southern Colonies is an exact Copy of a large

---

[1] *A Map of Part of the Province of Pennsylvania and of the Counties of New Castle, Kent, and Sussex on Delaware: Showing the Temporary Limits of the Jurisdiction of Pennsylvania and Maryland. Fixed According to an Order of His Majesty in Council Dated the 25th Day of May in the Year 1738. Surveyed in the Year 1739.* Phillips, *List of Maps, op. cit.,* p. 672.

[2] Walter Hoxton, *To the Merchants of London Trading to Virginia & Maryland This Mapp of the Bay of Chesepeack, with the Rivers Potomack, Potapsco North East, and Part of Chester,* London: W. Beitts and E. Baldwin, 1735.

[3] William Parsons (d. 1757), surveyor general for Pennsylvania and founder of Easton.

[4] Quoted from Evans' *Analysis,* pp. 4-5; reprinted in Gipson's *Lewis Evans,* pp. 148-49.

[5] *A Plan of the West Line or Parallel of Latitude which is the Boundary between the Provinces of Maryland and Pennsylvania engraved by J. Smither 1770.* Great Britain. Board of Trade and Plantations, *List of Maps . . . , op. cit.,* p. 33.

[6] *A General Map of the Southern British Colonies in America . . . By B. Romans, 1776.* London. Printed for R. Sayer and J. Bennett, 15th Oct[r] 1776. This map is reproduced in this book.

Map in Manuscript at the Office of the American Secretary composed from diverse works of Persons employed by Government.

Delaware Colony. "The DELAWARE Colony," now State, "is adjusted by Part of a Circle of 12 Miles Radius, run round Newcastle as a Center, and an actual Mensuration of the whole Length of the Colony, by the late Mr. Thomas Noxon.[1]

The Author's Acknowledgment of Assistance given him. "To recount all the Surveys of Roads, Tracts of Land, and general Lines that I have been favoured with in the Composition of my Map" of 1749, "which makes so considerable a Part of this, would be endless: But I must not omit here to repeat, with Gratitude, my Thanks, not only for the Favours many Gentlemen did me, but the Chearfulness they shewed in assisting in a Design intended for public Service. It would have been almost impossible to have succeeded in the Composition, notwithstanding all These Helps, without my personal Knowledge also of almost all the Country it contained. One of the greatest Mistakes in it arose from my going from Kinderhook to Albany by night, where the Skipper deceived me in the Distance."[2] The Passage of the River through the Highlands is in this Edition corrected by Capt. Holland's Draught; he surveyed these Parts from Croton River to Vish-kill [Fishkill]: The rest is corrected by the Courses which I noticed, and more than once revised, in my Passages up and down this River.

[1]Thomas Noxon, planter and gristmiller who, in 1740, built *Noxon House* near present Noxontown Pond and Silver Lake, Delaware. Federal Writers' project. Delaware, *Delaware, A Guide to the First State* (N.Y., Viking Press, 1938), p. 465.

[2]Quoted from Evans' *Analysis*, p. 5; reprinted in Gipson's *Lewis Evans*, p. 149.

SECT. I.

Of the Face of the Country

HAVING given an Account of the Authorities whereon the several Parts of this Map rest, the Editor[1] now proceeds to describe the Face of the Country in its natural State; its Mountains and Rivers, and its Vegetation, which is always the most natural and just Description of the Powers of its Soil.

This Globe, the Earth which we inhabit, is, in its natural State, in a continued Progress of Exsiccation, and is universally, wherever the Waters do not prevail, covered with Woods, so that viewing this great Continent America (as yet a new World to the Land-workers of Europe) we see it a Country of Woods and Lakes or Rivers. Except where the Land is worn to the Bone, and nothing remains on the Surface but bare Rocks, every Soil, even the poorest, hath its peculiar Cloathing of Trees and Shrubs. There are Spots here and there scattered over the Face of this Country, which, seen amongst the Woods from a Distance, seem as though they were Plains of clear'd Land, but these are covered with a Species of Dwarf of Shrub Oak which grows about the Height of a Man's Shoulder, and bears very good Acorns. There are also in many, I might say most, Places, between the Banks of the Rivers and the Hills or Mountains through which these Rivers run, Margins of rich Meadow Land clear of Trees; this peculiar State is owing to the annual Inundations that these Meadows are covered with, and to a constant Accretion of Soil which is left on the Surface after the Waters retire; these the Settlers call, by a very expressive Name, *Interval Lands*.[2] In some Parts, as on the Mohawk and Connecticut River, these Interval Lands are of a Soil so rich that they may be tilled, some have been tilled incessantly for a Century or more, and yet continue as rich as the Vale of Egypt itself. I know but of one Place which is totally without Trees, and that is a Tract of Land upon Long Island, in New York State called Jamaica or Hampstead Plain, on which a shrubby Kind of Heath only grows.

[1]Thomas Pownall.

[2]A New England colloquialism. "That extent of ground, which lay between the original bank of the river and the river itself. The New Englander relishes it (interval) more than flats or bottoms." Timothy Dwight, *Travels in New England and New York* (London, W. Baynes & Sons, 1823), II, 310.

23

The particular Kind of Tree which grows in each Tract is always determined by the peculiar Soil or Nidus which is suited to produce it in Preference to other Species. This does not exclude other Species also from growing at the same Time, but some one Species always predominates in each Tract; the Soil therefore is best known and always described by the European Settlers from its peculiar Vegetation, as Oak Land, Birch, Beech, or Chestnut Land; Pine-Barren, Maple Swamps, Caedar Swamps. Walnut or Hickory, Firs, White and Red Elm, Magnolias, Locusts, Sassafras, and various other Trees are mixed with all these.

The Fruits which grow wild, as far as my Observations went, I here set down from my Journals. The Wild Vine of different Sorts, in general produce a very small sour thick-skin'd Grape, but the Plants themselves are in their Growth luxuriant beyond the Conception of those who have not seen them. The Wild Cherry, a Tree of which I saw near Scenectady [Schenectady], appeared to me One of the largest Trees I ever saw. Mulberry Red and White, but these latter are scarce. Hickory or Walnuts of several Sorts, Hazel, Wild Prune or Plumb, Chestnuts of different Sorts, Wild Pear and Crab, a Sort of Cervice or Medlar, Bilberry, Gooseberry, and Strawberry. The individual Trees of those Woods grow up, have their Youth, their old Age, and a Period to their Life, and die as we Men do: You will see many a Sapling growing up, many an old Tree tottering to its Fall, and many fallen and rotting away, while they are succeeded by others of their Kind, just as the Race of Man is: By this Succession of Vegetation this Wilderness is kept cloathed with Woods just as the human Species keeps the Earth peopled by its continuing Succession of Generations. As it happens to Man in the Course of Fate that sometimes epidemic Distempers, Deluges, or Famine have swept whole Nations off at once, so here, by a like Fate, Epidemic Distempers, to which even the Forests are liable, have destroyed whole Tracts of Woods at once. Deluges in the Vallies, Fire & Hurricanes on the mountains have also in their course often done the same. Wherever this at any Time hath happened, one sees a new Generation bearing all the Appearance of an European new Plantation growing up. If the Soil has suffered no great Change, Woods of the same Genus arise; if it hath undergone any Change, either for the better or for the worse, then, as from a Nidus prepared for a new Brood, we see Woods of a different Species, which before appeared rarely, and as Aliens in the Place, now from a new power of Vegetation, springing up and possessing the Land as the predominant Wood.

If here I should attempt to describe the Colouring of these Woods, I should be at a Loss what Season of the Year to choose, whether the sober Harmony of Greens that the Woods in all their various Tints give in Summer; or whether the flaunting Blush of Spring, when the Woods glow with a thousand Tints that the flowering Trees[1] and Shrubs throw out. If I should persuade the Painter to attempt the giving a real and strict Portrait of these Woods in Autumn, he must mix in upon his Canvass all the Colours of the Rainbow, in order to copy the various and varied Dyes which the Leaves at the Fall assume: The Red, the Scarlet, the bright and the deep Yellow, the warm Brown, the White, which he must use, would give a prismatic motley Patch-work that the Eye would turn away from, and that the Judgement would not bear; and yet the Woods in this embroidered Garb have in real Nature a Richness of Appearance beyond Conception. But this is not the only Instance, there are many which I, who have used myself to draw from Nature, have observed, wherein Nature will not bear a Portrait, and wherein she is never less imitated than when she is attempted to be literally copied.

Some few Observations in these Matters, corrected on Enquiry, which I noted and set down, although they be those of a very unskilful Naturalist, may yet suggest some Hints to those who know how to derive Advantages from the meerest Trifles.

The Grapes of European Vines which are transplanted to America do not so well bear the sudden Changes of the Weather, nor the Extreams of the Dry and Wet which the Climate is liable to, as the native Grapes. If there be much Thunder, and that attended with heavy Showers, and followed by Gleams of excessive Heat, at the Time that the Exotic Grapes are growing to their Maturity, such Grapes are apt to burst; whereas the thick Skin of the native Grapes preserve them against this Mischief; When therefore I have seen with what abundant Luxuriancy these native Vines grow, and have been taught that the coarsest Fruits by Cultivation may be meliorated even into Sorts which are delicious; When I have read how Change of Soil and Cultivation have succeeded, I have always thought that the American Settlers would do more wisely in trying to cultivate and meliorate their native Vines,

[1][Pownall's note] I am no Botanist, but I will here transcribe from my Journal the Names of some of the flowering Trees and Shrubs which I find inserted there; the Red Flowering Maple, the Sassafras, the Locust, the Tulip Tree, Chestnut, the Wild Cherry, Prune, Crab, Sloe, Pear, Dogwood, Hawthorn, Elm, Leather Tree, a Sort of Gilder Rose, Swamp Laurel or Magnelia Honeysuckle; there were Multitudes of Flowers which I saw in the Pine-barrens and Swamps, but which I know not the Names of.

small and sour as their Grapes may appear at present, than by endeavouring to force the Nature of the foreign Vine. It takes always a great Time to accommodate an Exotic to a foreign Clime, and does not always succeed at last; the Native, whose Nature is already assimilated to its own Clime, might sooner, and with better Hopes of Success, be improved under the present State and Progress of American cultivation.[1]

Mr. Gist,[2] in his Journal (vide Appendix N° VI.)[3] says, that in some of the Plains of the Oïlinois [Illinois] Country, a Species of *Wild Rye*[4] grows spontaneously, that it shoots in Winter so as to appear Green through the Snow, though Two Feet deep; I have heard the same from others, but as neither they nor I were Botanists, I never was able to ascertain what this Plant so called was. The very first and most learned of Botanists in England never heard any Thing of it. I have oftentimes, on the same Principles as above, wished that Experiments were made as to the Cultivation and Melioration of it. The Wheat Plant, which now in its cultivated State gives Bread to great Part of the human Species, was most likely brought to this State by some such Cultivation, from some such humble wild Plant: It is singular, and a curious Fact, that no History gives us any Account of the native Place of this Plant as indigenous.

Since the Paragraph above was written I have received from Lieut. Governor Mercer,[5] a Native of Virginia, who has seen the Plant growing, and has eaten the Seed of it, the following Account: "The Wild Rye, which grows every where in the Ohio Country, is a Species of the Rye which is cultivated by the Europeans. It has the same bearded Ear, and produces a farinaceous Grain. The Ear and Grain, in the wild State of this Plant, are less, and the Beard of the Ear is longer than those of the cultivated Rye, which makes this wild Plant resemble more the Ryegrass in its Appearance; but it differs in no other Respect from the Rye, and it shoots in its spontaneous Vegetation about the Middle of November as the cultivated Rye doth." The Fact ascertained as above, that

[1][Pownall's note] Vide Mr. Anthill's Observations on the Culture of the Vine in the *Transactions* of the Philosophical Society at Philadelphia, Vol. I. See "An Essay on the Cultivation of the Vine, and the Making and Preserving of Wine, suited to the different Climates in North America, by Edward Anthill" American Philosophical Society, *Transactions* . . . (Phila., Wm. and Thomas Bradford, 1771), I, Section II, 117-197.

[2]Christopher Gist (*ca.* 1706-1759), surveyor and agent for the Ohio Company of Virginia.

[3]Read entry dated January 27, 1751, p. 181 this work.

[4]Wild rye was indigenous grass growing along the Atlantic Coast from Virginia northward. The grass beards resemble wheat or rye. Lyman Carrier, *The Beginnings of Agriculture in America* (New York, McGraw Hill, 1923), pp. 27-28.

[5]George Mercer (1733-1784), agent for the Ohio Company of Virginia, later lieutenant-governor of North Carolina.

there is in this Part of the World a Plant of spontaneous Growth which produces Bread-corn, lead me to inquire a little more into the History of the Plant called *Wheat*, hitherto, as I said above, unnoticed and unknown; and I found in Diodorus Siculus a *Traditionary* Piece of History which almost gives the Form of a Fact to what I had before put down merely as an Opinion; he says,[1] "That Isis was the Discoverer to Mankind of the Fruit of Wheat and Barley (growing perchance amongst the other wild Plants of the Earth unknown to Men) and that Osiris taught them the Manner of cultivating this to Use." But Polyhistor (as quoted by Eusebius) giving an Account, which he took from Berosus of the ancient natural State of Mesopotamia where Babylon was built, says, that in the earliest Times it abounded with *Wild Wheat* (Πυροὺς ἀγρίους) amongst the other indigenous Plants. There is a passage in Diodorus Siculus which asserts that wheat[2] *grows wild* in Sicily, & that it was so even in the Author's time. This very circumstance leads me to think, that Although such wheat might *grow wild*, yet that it was but the self sown remains of fields once cultivated. It is not at least to me a proof, of its being *indiginous* in those parts. These passages however in History respecting the original State of the Ancient World throw a kind of reflected light of Truth on the accounts which I have receiv'd & which I here give, of the New One.

From the Accounts I have had of the Indian wild Hemp, from the Specimens which have been sent to me; from the Judgment which some of our Ropemakers of the first Class here in England have given of it; I have persuaded myself that something more might be done in America by the Cultivation of the Native than by the transplanting of a foreign species.

The Bark of the Bass or Leather Tree, with a little more Attention than is at present given to it, might be applied to all the ordinary Purposes of Country Tackle with great Benefit.

There is a Sweet Maple, from the Juice of which, extracted from the Tree, the Indians and Back Settlers make a Sugar, and from which many of the German Settlers make a rich Liqueure. I have had a considerable Quantity of this Sugar, it is very sweet, and even in its first State of Granulation has, though a peculiar, yet no unpleasing Taste:

---

[1] Εὑρούσης μὲν Ἴσιδος τόν τε τοῦ πυροῦ καὶ τῆς κριθῆς καρπὸν (φυόμενον μέν, ὡς ἔτυχε, κατὰ τὴν χώραν μετὰ τῆς ἄλλης βοτάνης, ἀγνοούμενον δὲ ὑπὸ τῶν ἀνθρώπων) τοῦ δὲ Ὀσίριδος ἐπινοησαμένου τὴν τούτων κατεργα-σίαν τῶν καρπῶν.   Diodorus Sic. Lib. I, 14.

[2] Ἔν τε τῷ Λεοντίνῳ πεδίῳ καὶ κατὰ πολλοὺς ἄλλους τόπους τῆς Σικελίας, μέχρι τοῦ νῦν, φύεσθαι τοὺς ἀγρίους ὀνομαζομένους πυρούς.   *Ibid.*, Lib. 2, [?]

These Trees properly cultivated, and the Sugar carefully manufactured and refined, would supply that Article of Consumption, in some degree to the people inhabiting the interior parts of the Country.

My Friend Mr. Pratt,[1] than whom there was not a wiser or more knowing Man in the Country, was always of Opinion, that the Juice which can be drawn, by Incision, from the Poison Vine is that Material which the Chinese and Japonese make their Vernice with.

He also recommended it to his Countrymen, that instead of attempting to breed the Silkworm of Asia, they should make many Trials on various Species of Spinning worms, with which the Woods in America abound. His necessary Attention to his Business as a Lawyer, and his very disinterested meritorious Labours in the public Service as a Representative of ye Town of Boston & a leading Member of the House of Assembly did not permit him to follow his Biass to the Study of Nature; but he used to tell me, that from Trials he had made he was sure a native Silk-worm would some Day or other be found in America; such when found, he said, might turn to practical Account, whereas the Thunder, the boisterous and sudden Changes of Weather, under the present State of the Climate of America, disturbed the foreign Silk-worm, so as that it would never be cultivated to any Advantage equal to what the native Silk-worms might be. At the Time that these Things were with us in New England a Subject of Speculation, they were, by the Experiments made by Madam Hubert, a Provençal settled in Louisiana, become actual Facts; This lady made many comparative Experiments on the native and foreign Silk-worm, fed on different Leaves of different Mulberry Trees; the native Worm of America, though larger and stronger, yet being wild and not settled like the domiciliated Worm of Europe, did not produce an equal Quantity of Silk; but she imputed this wholly to its wild unsettled Nature; their Silk, although coarse, was strong and thick. Since the Remark above was set done, I have been informed that 10,000 Weight of Cocoons of the *native* Silk-worm of America was sold in 1771[3] at the public Filature in Philadelphia, and that the Silk produced from them was of a good Quality, and (a Sample being sent to England) was much approved of in London. I find also in the Transactions of the American Philosophical Society

Monsieur de Ptatz.
Hist. de Louisiana[2]
Liv. 2., Ch. 2.

[1]Benjamin Pratt (1710-1763), representative of Boston, in the Massachusetts Bay General Assembly, and later chief justice of the province of New York.
[2]Le Page du Pratz, *Histoire de la Louisiane* . . . (Paris, De Bure, 1768).

[3]"About 1770 the planting of mulberry trees to feed silk worms had quite a boom in Pennsylvania. A public filature for unwinding cocoons was established in Philadelphia. Prizes were given and £850 was raised for the enterprise." Carrier, *op. cit.*, pp. 178-79.

held at Philadelphia, printed in 1768, that Mr. Moses Bertram [Bartram] had made many curious Experiments on the native Silk-worm.[1]

The fine soft Hair which grows on the Bunch of the Buffalo is of that woolly or rather silken Texture, which from the Corruption of a Dutch Word we call *Mohaire*. Mrs. Wright,[2] a Woman of very uncommon Ingenuity, and possessing an uncommon Share of Science, one of a Quaker Family, that lived and had a fine Farm at the Ferry on Susquahanna [Susquehanna] River, which bears their Name, gave me, when I was at their House, a Pair of Muffeties, and shewed me a Pair of Stockings, which she had spun and knit of it. This Manufacture made of these Materials as much exceeded in Pliability, Softness, and Warmth any Woollen or Cotton, as the East Indian Fabrick called the *Shaul*[3] doth silk. The finest and most luxurious Fabricks might be made of this.

Asbestos is very common in America; and this same Gentlewoman had contrived a Method of spinning the Thread-like Fibres of this Stone into a continued consistent Thread, of which she made a Purse; she mingled and, in the Spinning, twisted it in with Flax, and of the Thread so spun knitted or netted her Work. The Whole, when finished, was thrown into the Fire, the Flax burnt away, the Fabrick remained firm and wholly of Asbestos. I mention this merely as a Curiosity, because it has been a Kind of Desideratum with the Antiquaries how the Cloth of Asbestos, which was used by the Ancients to wrap the Corps when burnt, so as to preserve the remains in the Ashes, was fabricated.

From the Nature of the Surface and interior Contexture of this American Part of our Earth, the Mountains, as we in our relative Language call them, do all run in Ridges, with almost even Tops in parallel Lines; those to the West of Hudson's [Hudson] River N.E. and S.W. those to the Eastward of it nearly N. and S. between which, in like parallel Lines, run the great Rivers.

As the general Surface of the Land slopes to the S.E. and as the Heights of the Tops of the Mountains decrease gradually on the Eastern Side, so the general Flow of the great Rivers have a Course which such a Face of Country naturally gives: While they continue to run in any one Vale their Course is S.W. whenever through the Gaps or Intersections of the Mountains they can force a Way Eastward they do, tumbling over Rocks, Rifts, and Precipices in continual Falls and Cataracts South Easterly, and so along each Stage, and so from one

[1] See American Philosophical Society, *op. cit.*, I, Section II, 224-230.

[2] Mrs. John Wright. John Wright was a justice of the peace in Lancaster County, Pennsylvania and owner of Wright's Ferry across the Susquehanna.

[3] Probably cashmere.

Stage to another, is their Course in great Zigzags S.W. and S.E. Such is the Course (speaking generally) of the Delaware, Susquehanna, and Potomack [Potomac] Rivers. The lesser Rivers, which run only from off the Eastern Slope of these Mountains (such as Rapahanoch [Rappahannock], James River, Roanoch [Roanoke] and the other Rivers of the Carolina's) urge their Course in all Ways and Windings to the Sea at S.E.

The Vales between the Ridges of these Mountains have all one and the same general Appearance, that of an Amphitheatre enclosing, as it were, an Ocean of Woods swelled and depressed with a waving Surface like that of the great Ocean itself: Though the Ridges of the Mountains run, as I have said, in nearly parallel Lines, yet at Times, by the Means of Branchings and Spurs of Mountains, they every here and there seem to close, and where they do so, the Land of the Vale also rises in irregular hilly Land, which is the Circumstance that gives this general Appearance of an Amphitheatre to these Vales, when from any of the Mountains above one looks down into them. If the Spectator hath gotten a Stand on some high Mountain so as to look across any Number of the Ridges which may be less high than that he stands on, he then sees a repeated Succession of Blue and Purple parallel waving Lines behind each other, with here and there a Breaking-off or Gap in them; here and there sudden Endings of them in perpendicular bluff Points and Knobs, as they are by the People called; and here and there high elevated Peaks; all which, together with the general Direction of the Ridges, are Points which mark the Geography of the Country to the Indians, and even in a very sufficient practical Way the general Bearings to the Geographical Surveyor. In like Manner the Courses and the Currents of the great Rivers, with their attendant Streams and Rivulets, by the Line of their Course, and by the Nature of the Current with which they flow, mark the Height of the Land, the Declination of its Sides, and its abrupt Descents or its level Plains. Those who have attentively studied this Subject, and who have accustomed themselves to apply the Knowledge, which it gives, to Cases in Fact, will soon derive from it such Information respecting a Country as will answer every Purpose of Practice; and very often such a Precision of Acquaintance with the Face of the Country, as will astonish even those who have resided in it: To give this Knowledge, as far as Information went at the Time[1] that the First Edition of this Map was published, to those whose Duty it was to know these Matters, the Ranges of the Mountains, the

[1] 1755.

Gaps in them, and the Knobs where they end, are laid down with great Attention, and, where it could be obtained, with great Precision by the Compass. The Point to which the Tide Flows, on the Rivers, the swift currents, the Rifts, the Falls, the still Water or the slowly flowing Course, are either marked in the Map or described in the following Sheets. As the general, and I had almost said, the only Way of travelling this Country in its natural State is by the Rivers and Lakes, the Portages or Carrying-places from one Water to another, or along the Shores where the Navigation is obstructed by Rifts or Falls in the same River, are particularly and pretty exactly marked and set down. The general Face of the Country, when one travels it along the Rivers through Parts not yet settled, exhibits the most picturesque Landscapes that Imagination can conceive, in a Variety of the noblest, richest Groupes of Wood, Water, and Mountains. As the Eye is lead on from Reach to Reach, at each Turning of the Courses, the Imagination is in a perpetual Alternative of curious Suspense and new Delight, not knowing at any Point, and not being able to discover where the Way is to open next, until it does open and captivates like Enchantment.

> Ignotas tentare Vias, atque inter opacum
>   Allabi nemus——
> Olli Remigio Noctemque Diemque fatigant,
>   Et longos superant Flexus, variisque teguntur,
> Arboribus, viridasque secant placido Æquore Sylvas.

But while the Eye is thus catching new Pleasures from the Landscape, with what an overflowing Joy does the Heart melt, while one views the Banks where rising Farms, new Fields, or flowering Orchards begin to illuminate this Face of Nature; nothing can be more delightful to the Eye, nothing go with more penetrating Sensation to the Heart. To any one that has the Habit of Drawing from Nature, the making Sketches of these picturesque Scenes would be ample Employment: Some are so astonishingly great, that none but those who have made the Trial know how difficult it is to bring up the Scale of the ordinary Objects to this, which is (as it were) beyond the Garb of Nature. I made many Draughts and Sketches; some few, which were characteristic, I let the Public have in Engravings: I have seen since many fine Drawings done by our Officers and Engineers, a Collection of Engravings from all which got together would surely be curious, and not unuseful. So much for the Coup d'Oeïl of the Païsage of this Country. But pursuing the Line which I laid down of a practical Knowledge of it, we must proceed in another Train of Ideas.

SECT. II.

Description of the Tract which divides this Continent into two distinct Parts

The Two
distinct
Tracts of this
Continent.

WHEN we proceed to a more exact Detail of this Country, so as to examine it in its Parts, we must observe, that as the Country in general is divided into different Stages, so the general Face of it contained in this Map is divided into Two distinct and very different Tracts of Country, viz. Into that Part which lies W. and S.W. of Hudson's [Hudson] River, and that which is E. and N.E. of Hudson's [Hudson] River and Lake Champlain. This specific Difference will be marked in the Descriptions which I shall give of each Part. It will be sufficient here to say, that the Mountains of the Western Division, beginning from an immense high Tract of Land lying in the Angle formed by the Mohawks [Mohawk] and Hudson's [Hudson] Rivers, go off from Hudson's [Hudson] River in one general Trending in parallel Lines and in uniform Ranges of Ridges South Westerly to West Florida and Louisiana. The Mountains of the other Division on the East Side of the River run in like uniform Ranges, but in a Direction almost due North and South parallel to the River, and end in steep Ridges and bluff Heads at or near the Coast on Long Island Sound: And in the Latitude 45 or thereabouts, turning Eastward run away to the Gulf of St. Lawrence. The Hudson's [Hudson] River, and the Lakes George and Champlain, and the River Sorel form the very peculiar Line of this Division of the Country. The Bed of the Hudson's [Hudson] River (as if it were a great deep Chasm formed in the Body of the Country by its being split down to the Level of the Sea) is a strait deep Channel running (to speak generally) North and South betwixt Two Tracts of very high Land, and admits, amidst and through high Mountains, the Flow of the Tide more than 180 Miles up it. Where it lies thus (180 Miles from the Ocean) on a Level with the Flow of the Tide, the Rivers which have their Sources in the high Lands on each Side of it, the Delaware and Susquehanna Rivers particularly, which are very great Rivers, run tumbling with a precipitate Course over Rifts and Falls for many hundred Miles S. and S.E. before they reach the same Level; even the

D c

The very
particular
Nature of
this Division.

32

Connecticut River on the east of it & parallel to it runs with many a Swift and over many Falls above 100 Miles South before it reaches the same Level.

The Northern Part of this peculiar Division of the main Continent is formed by a Succession of deep Lakes, the Lakes George and Champlain, which issue the Waste of their Waters through the little River Sorel into Canada[1] River; the Bed of these Lakes is likewise formed by a deep Chasm amidst Mountains, running North and South, as continuing the same Line of the Hudson's [Hudson] River.

This River is usually, & especially by the Dutch Inhabitants of this Country, called *North River*. As I do not recollect to have seen anywhere the reason for this name given, I will insert it in this Edition. The Tract of Country lyeing between This River & the Delaware River inclusive was possessed by the Dutch under the Name of New Netherlands. They gave the two relative names of North & South River to this & the Delaware River. Their Chief Post & Town was New-Amsterdam which the English afterwards called New-York.

The Hudson's [Hudson] River arises from Two main Sources derived by Two Branches which meet about Ten Miles above Albany, the one called the Mohawk's [Mohawk] River (rising in a flat level Tract of Country, at the very Top or Height of the Land to Westward) comes away E. and S.E. at the Foot, on the North Sides of the Mountains, which the Indians call by a Name signifying the Endless Mountains.[2] It runs in a Vale, which it seems to have worn itself, with Interval Lands on each Side, for about 100 miles.

Hudson's River Mohawk Branch.

The soil at the height of the Land & at the head of this River doth appear to be Low Land, that is, It is flatt, & a deep Rich Soil not yet worn away & full of bogs, ponds, & springs from whence not only this Mohawk River But the Onondaga[3] River which empties itself into Lake Ontario at Oswego derive. The River keeps on with a quiet still Stream to Burnet's field[4] having Lands of a deep & rich soil on both sides. At Burnet's field (a very fine settlement so called from Govr Burnet) The Vale & Interval Lands form a Space from ye west or upper end to ye Falls about 11 miles long & from 2½ to 3½ miles wide. This Settlement[5] in 1754 consisted of about 120 Houses. The Stream after this quickens

[1]St. Lawrence.
[2]Read description by Evans. Printed on his *Map*, 1749, *op. cit.*
[3]Oswego.
[4]Burnet's Field patent (1725) extended 24 miles

from Little Falls, New York, west along both sides of the Mohawk River. Nathaniel S. Benton, *A History of Herkimer County* . . . (Albany, J. Munsell, 1856), p. 42.
[5]*Ibid.*

in its motion & begins to Wear a Valley by washing away the soil of the Lands through which it runs, but has however rich *interval Lands* on both sides which Produce Wheat Peas & Hemp without Dunge or Manure. The lands were said in 1754 to be worth 45 £ p^r Acre. About six or seven miles below Burnet's field the River running across a Rocky Stratum tumbles in a Fall by which the Navigation is interrupted. There is a good road on the side of the River by means of which all Goods & Batteaus also are carried over Land for about a mile. At this Place the Vale is narrow & the river runs close under the Hills on ye southside. After this The Vale widens again to the breadth of a mile & half or two miles, as ye River passes the Indian Castles,[1] till it comes to Schyelers[2] & Zimmermans[3] where the River runs rapid, through a narrow between three Islands: After this the Vale widens to a Triangular space of about 5½ miles long & 3¼ broad a little above, or west of Stoney-Arabia [Stone Arabia], a fine settlement so called. From hence the River runs about 7½ miles till it comes round a high point of Land called Anthony's Nose in a narrower vale of about a mile over. From hence to the Settlements at Fort Hunter[4] the Vale widens again to two & four mile breadth. After this till it comes to the west or upper End of the Precinct of Schenectady Township. The Vale is again narrow but begins to Widen at Van Eps's Farm.[5] At the Scite of Schenectady. The Vale forms the most pleasing prospect one can Imagine. The Eye from ye Hills with which it is surrounded Views is one Landschape an amphitheatre of about 4 or 5 miles long & about 2 miles broad with level lands & inclosing a rich Vale of Corn & Meadow of ye most Luxurious vegetation watered by a Beautifull River running in two Streams through it; on ye Banks of which stands a Pretty & Regular built Little Town of about 150 Houses with a Fort, a Dutch Church, & Stadthouse, in three Streight Streets parrallel to ye River & 4 at right angles with these. I speak of it in 1754. The Hills which surround this Fertile delightfull opening of the Vale rise in two ridges. The first consists of Pine Land and the second of Oak Land rising behind it.

It appeared to me seen from the little Lake by Major Glen's[6] not

[1]Mohawk Castles.

[2]Colonel Peter Schuyler was one of the grantees for the Oriskany Patent lands along the Mohawk near the mouth of Oriskany Creek. George W. Schuyler, *Colonial New York*, (New York, Charles Scribner's Sons, 1885), II, 133. Near the present site of Utica, New York.

[3]Probably near the mouth of Zimmermans Creek.

[4]Fort Hunter (1710-1776?), a frontier military post situated at the junction of the Schoharie and Mohawk rivers. Present site of Fort Hunter, New York.

[5]John J. Van Eps, one of the first land owners in the vicinity of Schenectady. John F. Watson, *Annals and occurrences of New York City and State in the Olden Time* . . . (Phila., H. F. Anners, 1846), p. 32.

[6]Jacob Glen. Johnson, *Papers, op. cit.*, I, 122;

unlike in form to the Vale between Hartford & Ware, but infinitely more picturesque in its dress as not yet totally derobed of its Native Ornaments. This Vale is narrow'd below & again widened into a lesser but somewhat similar Spott. And the River being near Two Furlongs broad, falls over a Ledge of Rocks 75 Feet perpendicular in one Fall; these Falls the Indians call by the expressive Name *Cohoes:* This is so singular an Object, that I will here insert a Description as I take it from my Journal noted down, 1754, on the Spot.

Going from Albany one rides along the banks of the Hudson river for six miles through most delightfull meadows, that is what we should call meadows in England, but all in tillage form. The river is on the right hand: The bank on the opposite shore is high woodlands sloping gently down to the Waters edge; on the left are these meadows from half to three quarters of a mile in breadth, then hilly woodlands rising gently. For two miles further through the commencement of settlements but in part clear'd. Then through Woods, Oak, Chestnut Walnut, Chesnut-oak & Elm & so for the rest of the way about four or five miles more. Here one begins to hear the *Pouiflosboish* noise of the Tumultuous rushing & dashing of Waters which amidst the stillness of the Woods is like the roar of a Storm at Sea heard from the Land in the dead of night.

I went Twice to view this; the first Time there was but little Water in the River, and what came over the Fall ran in the Cliffs and Gullies D c of the Rocks in Three or Four different Channels. The View of them in Cohoes Falls this State given in Mr. Calm's [Kalm] Account of America[1] would have been pretty exact, had the Draughtsman in the Composition known how to have given a Scale to them; as it is, they appear to have a Magnitude not much more than that of a Mill-dam.

Upon a great Flood coming down the River on the 25th of June, I went a second Time to view these Falls; they were then a most tremendous Object. The Torrent, which came over, filled the whole Space from Side to Side; before it reached the Edge of the Fall it had acquired a Velocity which the Eye could scarce follow; and although at the Fall the Stream tumbled in one great Cataract: yet it did not appear like a Sheet of Water; it was a tumultuous Conglomeration of Waves foaming, and at Intervals bursting into Clouds of Vapour, which fly off in rolling Eddies like the Smoak of great Guns. In that Part of the Fall where

William Shirley, *Correspondence* . . . , ed. by Charles Henry Lincoln (New York, Macmillan Co., 1912), II, 177.

[1]Per Kalm, *Travels in North America* . . . , translated into English by John Reinhold Forster (London, the Editor, 1770-71), II, 275-77.

the large Rock shoots forward, the Torrent as it falls into the Angle formed by it seems to lose the Property of Water; if the Eye tries to pursue it in its Fall, the Head will turn giddy; the great and ponderous Mass with which it ingulfs itself makes the Weight of it (one may almost say) visible, however it makes itself felt by keeping the whole Body of the Earth on the Banks on each Side in a continued Tremulation; after having shot down as though it would pierce to the Center, it rebounds again with astonishing Recoil in large Jets and Columns of Water to the very Height from which it fell,

———Ter Gurgite vastos
Sorbet in abruptum Fluctus, rursusque sub auras,
Erigit alternos———

This is not Poetry but Fact, and a natural Operation. In other Parts, where it shoots over in a Sheet of Water, there is a peculiar Circumstance which struck me, and which I will endeavour to explain; there are every now and then violent Explosions of Air which burst through the Surface of the Torrent, and as I considered it attentively on the Spot, I explained it as follows to myself; the Air which is contained and pent in between the Rock and the Arch of the Torrent, which shoots over it must, by the violent Motion of this Torrent, be heated and rarefied, and if so, will of course break out in Explosions; however the Fact was as I state it, and better Philosophers than I pretend to be may give better Accounts of it.

The Vapours which fly off from this Fall disperse themselves and fall in heavy Showers for near Half a Mile round the Place. Whenever the Spectator can gain a Position in a proper Angle between the Falls and the Sun, he will always see it reflected in a Rainbow.

While we are contemplating this Object, there came on a most violent Thunder Storm: Any one who has been in America knows how exceeding loud the Sound of these Explosions of the Thunder are: Yet so stunned were we with the incessant hoarse Roar of this Cataract that we were totally insensible to it.

I made a Sketch of this Fall upon the Spot, I afterwards composed a Drawing from it, wherein I was happy enough, after several Trials and Devices, to succeed in giving it it's proper Scale. Mr. P. Sanby[1] made a coloured Drawing for me from this, and an Engraving[2] has been made after it and published.

The Mohawk River runs hence with a tumbling rapid Course till

[1]Paul Sandby was the first engraver to practice aquatint engraving in England (1775).

[2]"A view of the Great Cohoes Falls on the Mohawk River; the Fall about Seventy feet; the River near a

it falls into the main River called Hudson's [Hudson]. Many little Rivers and Streams fall into this Branch; those which come from the North rise in a Tract of Country called Couxsachrâgé,[1] the Principal of which is that called Canada Creek: Those which fall into it from the South C d rise in and tumble from the high Ranges of the Endless Mountains, and interlock with the Heads of the Delaware and Susquehanna Rivers: One of these high Ridges, in which the Canajohary [Canajoharie] Creek C d rises, is called Brimstone Hill.[2] It has not run farr before it falls from a Cliff 300 feet in height. Schohary [Schoharie], which falls into the Mohawk's [Mohawk] River a little below Canajohary [Canajoharie], rises in the western Parts of the highest of the Mountains call Kaat's-kill D c [Catskill] Mountains, and runs through a deep Vale for 50 or 60 Miles. But this River is so intirely obstructed from one end to the other (except a Tract of Land about Five Miles long, 14 Miles from the Mouth) with Rifts and Falls that the Inhabitants do not use even Canoes. As the Mountains which close in this Vale are very high, the Settlements are confined to the Interval Land: These Settlers had no Communication with Hudson's [Hudson] River but by Albany, and this was by Land over the *Helleberg*,[3] in Winter Time only, with Sledges. When I was there they had proposed to make a new Road from a Point about 40 Miles up the River to a Point on the South Line of Renslaer's Manor,[4] where that Line at 12 Miles Distance from Hudson's [Hudson] River strikes the River called Kaat's-kill [Catskill].

The other or northern main Branch of this River Hudson rises from Lakes in the Mountains of Couxsachrâgé to the West of Lake Champlain, and is called Sacondaga [Sacandaga] River; it comes from the Sacondaga North with a direct southern Course till it comes within 12 Miles of the Branch Mohawk Branch,[5] then turns short back to the North, till it comes with-

---

Quarter of a Mile broad, Sketched on the spot by Governor Pownall, painted by Paul Sandby and Engraved by William Elliott." In *Scenographia Americana; or, A Collection of Views in North America and the West Indies. Neatly Engraved by Messrs. Sandby, Grignion, Rooker, Canot, Elliot, and others; from Drawings on the Spot, by several Officers of the British Navy & Army* . . . , (London, Printed for John Bowles, Robert Sayer, Thomas Jefferys, Carington Bowles & Henry Parker, 1768).
There is, in the Map Division of Library of Congress, a manuscript pen and ink sketch, "A View of the Cohoes or Great Falls of the Mohawk River," which may be by Thomas Pownall. Phillips, *List of Maps, op. cit.,* p. 239.

[1]The early settlers around Albany knew this region as the "proper hunting grounds" for the Five Nations. Watson, *Annals of . . . New York, op. cit.,* p. 15.
[2][Pownall's note] Bituminous springs here.
[3]A ridge in the Catskill Mountains.
[4]Rensselaerwyck, a Dutch manor of about 700,000 acres on the Hudson, comprising most of the present New York counties of Albany and Rensselaer.
[5][Pownall's note] I find in my Journal of 1755 the following Observation, written down from Sir William Johnson's Information on the Spot. A convenient and advantageous Communication may be opened between the Mohawks [Mohawk] and

in Five or Six Miles of the South End of Lake George, and then winds round to the South till it meets the Western or Mohawk Branch. Where this River, about Four Miles above Fort Edward, descends from the Oak-land Tract to the Pine-land, there are Falls upon it which obstruct Navigation, above these Falls it is navigable not only for Canoes but for large Boats. There are also Two other Falls below Fort Edward. In this Bend is included the Tract of Country which the Indians call Kaiaderossoras.[1] From the Junction of these Branches, under the Name of Hudson's [Hudson] River, it runs nearly South, and passing what is called the Narrows, between Long Island and Staten Island, runs out to Sea by Sandy Hook; in its Course it passes by the City of Albany.

Albany

This City is a Corporation. It consisted in 1755 of 378 Houses, of 2972 Regular Inhabitants in Families. It has two Streets running parrallel to the bank of the River & one very broad noble Street at Right Angles with these. There is a Dutch Church & an English one; a Statehouse; & on the ground rising above it at the upper end of ye broad Street a Fort[2] which Commands the Town; but which is itself Commanded by the Ground that rises behind it, & is not tenable against a proper regular Force. The Whole Town except a Few New Houses, is intirely built after the Dutch mode. While ye Dutch had it it was called Orange. When the Duke of York had it granted to him, It took ye Name of Albany. It arose into a Town from being originally the most advanced Trading Post, in the Indian trade which the Dutch had, & which they, called by a name signifying, The Fore-sail. The River runs hence by Kinderhoëk [Kinderhook] and then under the eastern Foot of the Kaat's-kill [Catskill] Mountains and the Highlands of 'Sopos [Esopus]; but the extraordinary and very singular Passage which it has, is through a Range of very high and mountainous Lands, about 12 Miles across, called the Highlands, running directly athwart its Course; for as though a Chasm had been split in this Range of Mountains to make Way for it,

E c

it passes in a deep Channel near a Mile broad, with one Zigzag only,

Sacondaga [Sacandaga] Branch by cutting a Road of only Seven Miles from Johnson-hall to Sacondaga [Sacandaga] Creek; the Half of this Road next to Sacondaga [Sacandaga] is sandy Land, of White Poplars, and White and Black Pine, like the Sand betwixt Albany and Sckenectada [Schenectady]. The other Half is hilly, the Growth on the Ridges Beech and some Oak, in the Bottoms Maples. There is good Navigation from this Creek to the Falls of Sacondaga [Sacandaga].

[1]Kayaderosseras or Cayaderossoras. A large tract of Indian land beginning at the Half Moon (Waterford) to the third fall, then west to Canada Creek. *Documents relative to the Colonial History of the State of New York* . . . , ed. by E. B. O'Callaghan (Albany, Weed, Parsons & Co., 1853-87), VI, 866. Hereafter cited as *N.Y.C.D.* This tract was the most valuable part of the Mohawks' hunting ground. *Ibid.*, VII, 576-77.

[2]Fort Frederick (Albany).

through these Mountains piled up almost perpendicular to a most astonishing Height on each Side of it.

> Hinc atque hinc vastae Rupes, geminique minantur
> In Coelum Scopuli: quorum sub vertice latè
> Æquora tuta silent; tum Sylvis scena coruscis
> Desuper.—

Just after having entered into this Pass, a very peculiar Rock called E c
Martler's Rock[1] projects from the East Side into the River; and at the Foot of these immensely high Mountains, although it is as high as a Sloop's Mast, looks like a Wharf or Mole. The Eddy which this occasions in the Current, and the Wind which is always flittering here, makes this a puzzled Pass. This I find marked down in my Journal 1755, October 22, as a Spot on which a Fort placed would have great Command of this Pass; and I understand now, 1775, that the Americans have taken post and built a Fort[2] upon it. They however found afterward other positions for forts equally commanding & less commanded.[3]

After emerging out of this Pass, it spreads itself in the Form of a E c
great Lake 15 Miles in Length by one Way of reckoning,[4] and by another 20, and about Four Miles broad, and is called the Topang [Tappan] Sea: The western Banks are perpendicular rocky Cliffs of an immense Height, Covered with Woods at the Top, which from the great Height of the Cliff seem like Shrubs. The Eastern Coasts are formed by a gently rising Country, Hill behind a Hill, of fruitful Vegetation at the back of which lye the White-plains: It then again for 20 Miles more or thereabouts takes the Form of a River, but above a Mile and Half broad, and passes by New York.

The Reader may imagine that the Scenes on this River must exhibit some of the finest Landscapes in the World; I thought so, and made many Sketches of the different Scenes, particularly of Windy Gate, the Entrance of the Highlands,[5] with a View of Martler's Rock, and of others[6] which the Passage through the Highlands gives. The Islands which may be said to lie at the Mouth of this great River, are first New F C
York Island,[7] about 12 Miles long and scarce Two broad in the greatest New York Island

[1]See *note* 6, p. 8.

[2]Read *American Archives, Fourth Series, Containing a Documentary History of the English Colonies in North America . . . By Peter Force.* (Wash., M. St. Clair Clarke and Peter Force, Dec. 1840), III, 1657. The fortress was called Fort Constitution.

[3]*American Archives, op. cit.,* III, 1657.

[4][Pownall's note] This is reckoning Haverstraw Bay as Part.

[5]"A View of Hudson's River of the Entrance of What is Called the Topan Sea . . ." In *Scenographia Americana . . . , op. cit.*

[6]"A View of Hudson's River of the Pakepsey and the Catts-kill Mountains from Sopos Island in Hudson's River." In *Scenographia Americana . . . , op. cit.*

[7]Present Manhattan Island.

Breadth of it, lying in the Course of the River North and South; it is at the north end separated from the Continent which forms the eastern Banks of the River by a very narrow Channel, through which the Tides flow with great Rapidity; there is a Bridge built over it, a Toll-bridge,[1] of private Property: This Island is in general of a rocky stony Texture, with a light Soil, scarce enough to cover the Rocks, and yet from rich Bottoms which there are in it, and from a certain Moisture which Stones retain in the Soil amidst which they lie, it is of a very kindly Vegetation. There is remarkable fine Water in many Parts of this little Island. From its Scite and Position it rather may be described as forming the eastern Banks of this lower Part of the River, than that it can be said to lie in the Mouth of it. After passing by this Island and the southern Point of it, at which the City of New York stands, the River opens again into a wide Bay 10 or 12 Miles broad, with Two or Three little Islands in it, and then passing between Long Island and Staaten [Staten] Island, through a Straight called the Narrows; it then forms a second Bay, and thence issues out between Sandy Hook and Long Island to Sea.

New York

There is a certain affectation of prudent secrecy always observed by Writers of all Nations, that avoids the giving of too particular descriptions of the principal Ports & Harbours of their own Country. Although I believe that a knowledge of these parts of any Country may be had & are had by their Enemies: & that ignorance in these matters never remains but from indolence: Yet I restrained myself in the first editions[2] of this work from all descriptions of Ports or Harbours or Towns. Now that They cannot be any longer supposed to be unknown to other nations One may venture to give a description of them so farr as they come within the Geography and Topography of the Country. The account so farr as respects the navigation, of the Port & Harbour of New York I shall give as I received it from the regulated Pilots of that Port signed by them in the year 1755, which I brought over to England for the information of our own Government, which at that time would not be persuaded that large Shipps of Warr could with safety enter there. The General Descriptions of these as well as of the City I take from my own remarks & notes.

In approaching the Coast at about 20 leagues SW distant from the Hoëk,[3] The sounding are 35 fathoms a gritty mud with very small

[1][Pownall's note] A free Bridge has been built at the Public's Expense since I was there.

[2]Here Thomas Pownall appears to take full credit for Lewis Evans' *Analysis . . . , op. cit.*

[3]Sandy Hook, New Jersey. Hereafter in the text *Hook.*

a text reference at this mark ⎯⎯ in page 32.

There is a certain affectation of prudent secrecy always observed by writers of all Nations, that forbids the giving of too particular descriptions of the principal ports & Harbours of their own country. Although I believe that a knowledge of these ports of any country may be had & are had & that ignorance in these matters never recovers but from indolence; yet I restrained myself in the first editions of this work from all descriptions of Ports or Harbours or Towns. Now that They cannot be any longer supposed to be unknown to other nations One may venture to give a description of them so far as they come within the Geography and Topography of the Country. The account so far as respects the navigation of the Port & Harbour of New-York I shall give as I received it from the regulated Pilots of that Port signed by them in the year 1756. which I brought over to England for the information of our own Government which at that time would not be persuaded that large Ships of War could with safety enter there; The General Descriptions of these as well as of the City I take from my own remarks & notes.

In approaching the Coast at about 20 leagues SW distant from the Hœk. The sounding are 35 fathoms a gritty mud with very small shining particles: at 25 fathom gravel of very small round pebbles red & black: in 23 fathom the ground partakes more of white sand. The soundings shoal very regularly as you advance from 20 to 4 fathom which it is off the river.

The first Land you discover in coming from sea is the High-land of the Neve-sinks called by its Indian name, but vulgarly called neve-sink or reven sunk. These run in a rocky high manner

The new material added by Pownall, anticipating a second edition, is among the most interesting in the book.

shining particles: at 25 fathom gravel of very small round pebbles red & black: in 23 fathom the ground partakes more of white sand. The soundings shoal pretty regularly as you advance from 20 to 4 fathom, which it is off the barr.

The first Land you discover in coming from Sea is the high-land of the *Nave-sinks* so called by its Indian name, but vulgarly called *Neversink* or *never sunk*. These Lands are a rocky high Hummock covered with Woods. As you approach you begin to see on the right hand faintly the line of the land of Long island: also under the Nave-sinks stretching from their foot for about 4 miles to the right or northward of this high land a neck of low sandy hills coverd with Cedars & holly, ending in a low sandy point. Between this neck called the Cedars & the Navesink is a beach which the sea sometimes breaks through so as to seperate the Cedars from the Navesink.

This was the first land of America that I saw & here I first landed. My Eye was upon the watch, and everything struck it. My imagination was all suspense & every thing made a vivid impression on my mind. I made a scetch of these Highlands & Hoëk [Hook] & the approach: there is not much picturesque matter in the view but it would make a pretty back ground to a Sea-piece of shipping. There was a trifling circumstance scarce worth remark, but as it struck my senses & I putt it down in my notes, I will transcribe it. My senses, as I advanced up towards the City were struck with a high odorous smell of burning of cedar. The inhabitants I found light their fires with cedar chips. The boatmen who row'd me up when I noticed this were insensible to it being nothing uncommon to them. In like manner when an American first comes to England, His senses are struck with the suffocating smell of our Coal Fires to which we dwellers are insensible. Having at that time my School-books in my head I recollected that Homer had thought this peculiar though trifling circumstance worthy notice in his description of Calypso's Island τηλόθι δ' ὀδμὴ κέδρου τ' εὐκεάτοιο θύου τ' ἀνὰ νῆσον ὀδώδει δαιομένων and that Virgil thought fitt to copy this in his description of the Island of Circe.

Urit odoratam nocturna in Lumina Cedrum

Eneid. Lib. 7. line 13

The Cedar point which runs like a mole from the Navesinks was with the Navesinks called by the Dutch Sandy-Hoëk. It forms one side of the Entrance of Hudson's [Hudson] or North River & Long Island which is about 8 or 9 miles distant from this point the other. As a large Bank of Sand runs off from Long-island to within a mile & half of the

Hoëk [Hook] the entrance into the River is between this bank (called the east-bank) and a shoal which lyes E, off the Hoëk [Hook] & runs parrallel to it, called middle-ground, a thread of Sand about half a mile over, runs from the E bank to this middle ground, which forms a kind of barr at the entrance, over which the soundings were, in my time, one or two & twenty feet. I remember striking on this in passing over in a twenty-gun ship. There is another very narrow passage between the middle-ground & the Hoëk [Hook]. After a Ship is over the barr it soon finds 5, 6, or 7 fathom water. The course up to the Narrows (a narrow pass between two bluff points of Staten & Long Islands) in the way to ye City is round the East-bank & must be kept on, W Southerly, five or six miles. It then rounds Northward Easterly to go up to the Narrows, Between this E bank & the W bank (A long bank running off Staten Island 5 miles). The Narrows are about three quarters of a mile across from point to point. The pass not a furlong. The soundings in these narrows are 13 & 14 fathom. As some of these soundings & some of these courses here in before mentioned may have changed in a period of near 30 years, the nautical reader is desired to compare these with later observations.

After having passed the Barr & come from sea within the Hoëk [Hook], & under the pleasant feel of still Water, the Eye is delighted with the View of a most noble bay. On the left are the rocky & high woodlands of the Navesink wild & Picturesque, contrasted by the settlements & cultivated land of Long Island on the right. The Farms on Staten Island & the very Peculiar View of the Narrows meet your Eye upon the Ships bow, the bay & harbour of Amboy lyeing right before you. These pleasing & thus varied Objects form the sides of this Noble Bay. As you advance through the Narrows the Eye expands its view again into a still more pleasing second bay, a kind of Amphitheatre, to appearance Circular, of about 12 Miles Diameter. This being constantly Covered with Boats Sloops & every kind of Shipping passing & repassing through it & across it in all directions seems all alive with bustle & buisness. As you advance you see in the center of the Background on the Point of an Island the City of New York having the opening of Hudson or North River with the high lands of Bergen & New-Jersey on the right of it & the opening of the Harbour & Quays in the East River bounded by the bluff points of Red Hoëk [Hook] & Yellow Hoëk [Hook] & the Heights of Brook line[1] in Long Island on the left of it. This populous &

¹Present Brooklyn Heights.

well built Town with the Fort[1] in front with the many steeples of its Churches the Turret of the Stadthouse & [Ex] Change dispersed amidst its buildings & the multitude of Shipping with which it is thronged perpetually makes a very striking appearance & alltogether as fine & as pleasing a View as I ever saw. I made a Scetch of this View taken from the narrows as the Foreground, correcting the bearings of all the points by the Compass. I never look at it but with a revived feel of the many pleasing daies I spent at New-York; but a certain painful regrett has always at the same time so wrought upon my mind that I have never yet found myself in a disposition to finish a drawing from it. I also copied from a Dutch Picture, and keep by me as a matter of Curiosity & Antiquity, a View of this town as it was, when a Dutch Town called Nieu-Amsteldam. One sees in this old view rows of the Gabel-ends of Houses, built under the Fort also repeated rows of the like Gabel-ends rising on the rising ground behind it mixed with the high roofed Churches & Stadthouse. On the Parapets of the Fort one sees a Flag staff of the Beacon-kind, & a Windmill. All the Houses & Public buildings were of the Dutch taste. Since it came into the hands of the English New Churches & New Houses have been built in a more modern taste & many of the Gabel-ends of yᵉ old houses, just as is done in Holland, have been new fronted in the Italian stile. The City however still retains the general appearance of a Dutch-town with its row of Gabel-ends & the rows of Trees on the sides of the Streets. It is Cheifly in its publick as well private buildings built with brick & neatly paved.

There are four Principal Streets as nearly parallel to each other as the uneaveness of the ground will permitt, all the cross streets the lesser & secondary streets are at right angles with these & in general run from shore to shore across the narrow point whereon the town stands. The Principal Street is a noble broad Street 100 feet wide called Broad Way. It commences at the north gate of the Fort by a kind of Square or Place formerly a Parade[2] now (1755) a bowling green railed in, & runs directly in a strait line NE better than half a mile where it Terminates by another intended square. On the west side[3] of the Street are Several very

[1]Fort George 1726-1788. *N.Y.C.D.*, V, 782; John F. Watson, *Annals of Philadelphia* (Philadelphia, For sale by Uriah Hunt, 1830), Appendix, p. 29.
[2]Known as The Parade. *Valentine's Manual of Old New York, 1924*. Edited by Henry Collins Brown ... (N.Y., Gracie Mansion, c. 1923), p. 58.
[3][Pownall's note for revised and enlarged edition] This west side, The Churches & other buildings mentioned here have been burnt down since this was written. The great fire of 1776 burned up Broadway on the Western side from the wharf near White Hall slip to St. Paul's Church at the entrance to The Common. Watson, *Annals of Philadelphia, op. cit.*, Appendix, p. 57.—Ed.

handsome spacious Houses of the principal Inhabitants, the Lutheran Church & the English Church called Trinity Church a very large plain brick Building, but within as spacious commodious & handsome a Place of Worship as I ever saw belonging to a private Parish. In the S.E. part of the City there is another handsome modern built Church called St. George's Chapel.[1] I am told that a third English Church called St. Pauls[2] was built in broad Way: & that the intended Square above mentioned hath been built. How much of these have been burnt down I don't know.

The next principal Street called broad street being about 80 feet wide commences at the landing at west dock, where stand the [Ex]Change[3] & runs about a quarter of a mile up to the Stadthouse[4] or Townhouse, An old Dutch building very spacious & well adapted to all the Offices kept therein, In apartments within which the Council Assembly & Courts of Justice hold their Sessions.

The third principal Street is called Hanover Street[5] & runs from Hanover-square,[6] in the form of an S running in its course round the sides of a high piece of ground.

The fourth principal Street like Tower Street[7] in London runs along the Vlys Quays wharfs & docks on the eastern bank of the town. The numbers of Houses & Buildings in the year 1753 were as follows:

Publick Buildings	25
Dwelling Houses	1991
Store-houses	207
Stables	150
Distilling houses	10
Sugar Houses	2
Brew houses	4
Rope Walks	4
Total	2393

The Inhabitants of the City extending through out the Island were about 15,000. The average of the Rent of the Buildings were estimated

[1]At Beekman and Cliff Street. *Plan of the City of New York in North America. Surveyed in the years 1766 & 1767. To His Excellency Sir Henry Moore . . . is dedicated . . . this Plan of the City of New York and its Environs . . . B. Batzer . . . . Surveyed in the years 1766 & 1767.* London, Jefferys & Faden, 1776. Hereafter cited as Ratzer's *Map of New York.*

[2]On Broadway between Partition and Veasyes Streets, at the entrance to The Common, Ratzer's *Map of New York, op. cit.*

[3]Over Broad Street at Dock Street. *Ibid.*

[4]Corner Broad Street and Wall Street. *Ibid.*

[5]Hanover Street, or Queen Street. Queen Street is now Pearl Street. Watson, *Annals of Philadelphia, op. cit.*, Appendix, p. 36.

[6][Pownall's note for revised and enlarged edition] Those broad openings in a Town, which the French call Places, We call Squares. This Appellation becomes ridiculous as all these Squares are Triangles.

[7]Water Street. Ratzer's *Map of New York, op. cit.*

at 25£ p^r Ann. To give some idea of the manner in which their Houses were furnished I here insert from a speculative estimate made for me by the Vendue-master[1] extracts of the averages of the value of the Plate and furniture of the First, Middling and lower Class of Householders. He averaged the first at 700£, The second at 200£, The third he subdivided into two Classes & averaged the value of the furniture of the first of these at 40£ the second at 20£.

This pleasant City standing in a most charming situation, & enjoying the most delicious Climate in the world was inhabited by an hospitable cheerfull social people living by their extensive fortune Landed & Commercial & from the plenty & cheapness of every article of living better & more hospitably without parades than I ever saw any people in the old world live.

The North or Hudsons [Hudson] river, at opening which into the bay this City stands, is of the most perfect navigation; is seldom frozen up in Winter which the Delaware on which Philadelphia stands generally is, as also often the harbour of Boston. This North River carries from New-York to Kinder-hoëk [Kinderhook] which about 20 miles below Albany pretty uniformly 7 fathom water except where it passes through the Highlands there its depth is from 15 to 30 fathom. From Kinder-hoëk [Kinderhook] to the overslough (a barr of shallows) the depth is from 7 to 12 feet. After you are over the shallows of the overslough it deepens somewhat again up to Albany. The Navigation from New York to Albany was intirely carried on in a kind of Sloop of about 60 tons called a Yacht. The Dutch Schippers of Albany are the Cheif Navigators. They had in 1754 twenty three of these Vessels in constant employ. From the Commodiousness & Cleanliness of these Vessels one enjoys the most agreeable passage that can be wished. These Yachts brought down the Produce of Albany County Wheat Flour Pease. The Produce of the Indian Trade &c to New York & their Back carriage was all sorts of European Goods & Produce Rum Sugar Salt & every article of manufacture both for the use of the Inhabitants & for the Indian Trade.

Staaten [Staten] Island is included within the Province of New York, and is of itself one of the Counties of that Province called Richmond: This Island is about 12 Miles long, and about Six Miles broad, it is high, dry, and hilly, pleasant and fruitful; the County Town Richmond lies near the Center of it.

[1][Pownall's note for the revised and enlarged edition] A Public Auctioneer Commissioned by Government.

Long Island, formerly called by the Dutch Nassau Island, (separated from New York by the East River of Half a Mile Breadth, over which is a Ferry) is included within the Province of New York, and contains Three Counties,[1] viz. King's, Queen's, and Suffolk Counties: This Island lies nearly East and West, is more than 100 Miles long, and taking one Place with another at a Medium about 16 Miles broad. When Lewis Evans describes this Island as formed by and consisting of Sand only, he was not apprized that a Ridge of Hills beginning from the Ferry at the Narrows runs rounding across the West End of the Island to the North Side, and continues in a Range along that Side almost to the End: This Ridge forms the substantial Part of the Island; it is said that there is a Straum of Coal in this Island. The South Side of it is indeed a level Plain formed by the Accretion of Silt and Sand at the Foot of this more elevated Ridge; this Plain extends with a long slope to the Ocean, but has (as Land thus formed always has) a high Beach or Bar in the Front of it, a little below Low Water Mark.

"Hudson's [Hudson] River, at whose Entrance stands the City of New York,[g] has good Depth of Water for Sloops, and the Tide extended above Albany,[h] more than 180 Miles into the *Upland*. While all the Rivers, from thence South-westward, are navigable with Sea Vessels in the *Lower Flats* only, this opens Communications with the Inland Parts of the Continent, of the utmost Importance to the British Interest. The Communication between Albany and Montreal[i] is described below. A Route of no less Importance in the immediate Affairs of the English opens from Albany westward into the Heart of the Continent, and is performed commonly in the light flat-bottomed Boats.[2] To avoid a great Cataract of 75 Feet,[3] in the Mohocks [Mohawk] River,[k] they carry all the Goods, destined for the Inland Trade,[4] 16 Miles over Land to Skenèctady [Schenectady][l] in Waggons. There they embark on the Mohocks [Mohawk] River, which in general is pretty rapid and shallow, and proceed to the Long Fall,[m][5] where they are obliged to carry their

g F e
h D c
Hudson's river navigable with Sloops to Albany
i Page 19 Evans' *Analysis* inland Navigation from Albany to Oswego
k D c
l D c
m C d

[1]At present Four Counties: Kings, Queens, Nassau, and Suffolk.

[2]Small batteaux known as three handed and four handed boats. Jeptha R. Simms, *History of Schoharie County and Border Wars of New York* . . . (Albany, Munsell & Tanner, 1845), p. 139.

[3]Cohoes Falls.

[4][Pownall's note] The soil of the Land through which this Road goes is Sand for the first Seven Miles, the Timber nothing but Pitch Pine, the Underwood Fern in great Quantities, some Shumack and Dwarf Oak, Four Miles more the same; a wet Bottom crosses the Land here of about a Mile; the Wood Birch, Aspin, Chestnut, Oak; the remaining Five Miles much the same again as before. I observed in the Woods many Flowers, as the Heart's-ease, the Blue Lupin, the Convolvolies; and in the swampy Bottoms, the Orange Lilly, and the Iris.

[5]Known as the Little Falls in comparison with the great Cohoes Falls. This was the first carrying place on the Mohawk west of Schenectady. Simms, *op. cit.*, pp. 138-39. Present site of Little Falls, N.Y.

Boats and Goods a Mile over Land. The same River conducts them again to the Great Carrying-place,[n][1] where, according as the Season is wet or dry, they are obliged to carry over Land Four or Eight Miles to Wood Creek.[2] This Creek is very gentle and crooked, and together with Onoyda [Oneida] Lake and Onondaga River,[o][3] furnishes an easy passage to the Seneca River; which at 12 Miles above Oswego[p] has a Fall,[4] where they carry their Boats about 100 Feet, and Goods liable to damage by wet near a Mile and a Half; besides Three very bad Rifts, and several small ones in other Places. The Whole is performed in a Week.

n The Dragplat C d

o C e

p C e

"But if you intend to go to the Onondágas or Cayúgas Country,[5] you turn up the Seneca River, and in Half a Mile come to a little gentle Rippling, where the River may be forded on Horseback:[q] From hence upwards it is very deep, and so gentle as scarce to discover which Way it runs."[6]

The Passage up Seneca River q A Ford C e

The Tackonaëg [Taconic] Mountains, hereafter mentioned in the Description of the Eastern Division, run nearly parallel to Hudson's [Hudson] River at the Distance of 16 Miles one Place with another; the Land between these Mountains and the River is hilly, stony, and but indifferent Soil; the Timber White and Black Oak on the Hills, Hickory in the Valleys, with Swamps of Ash.

"Hudson's [Hudson] River has no Branches navigable with Ships or Shalops; for it is truly but a single Channel extended into the Land, where the Country East and West of it afford those Two Series already mentioned."[7]

The northern Part of this peculiar Division of the Country is formed by a Succession of Drowned Lands and Lakes,[8] lying in deep Chasms, that have the same Direction North and South.

Between the northern Part of the Hudson's [Hudson] River and the southern Parts of the Lakes and Drowned Land is the Height of the

[1]Site of Fort Stanwix, *N.Y.C.D.*, VII, 985. Present site of Rome, N.Y.

[2]Wood Creek in the vicinity of Rome, N.Y. Not to be confused with the Great Carrying Place (Fort Edward) and Wood Creek east of Lake George.

[3]Oneida River.

[4]Oswego Falls. On present maps that part of the Seneca River from Onondaga Lake to Oswego on Lake Ontario is called Oswego River.

[5]The Iroquois' lands extended from the Hudson River west along the Mohawk, and connecting waterways to Lake Erie. The five original tribes in the league were the Mohawks who lived in the east, the Oneidas and the Onondagas, who occupied the central portion, the Cayugas, in the Finger Lakes region, and the Senecas whose land bordered on Lake Erie. Lewis M. Morgan, *League of the Ho-Da'-no-Sau-nee, or Iroquois*. (Rochester, Sage & Brother, 1851), pp. 42-43. For location on map see: John Mitchell, *A Map of the British and French Dominions in North America . . .* London Published by the Author Feb[ry] 13th 1755, according to Act of Parliament.

[6]Quoted from Evans' *Analysis*, p. 20; reprinted in Gipson's *Lewis Evans*, p. 164.

[7]*Ibid.*

[8]Lake George and Lake Champlain region.

Land of about 12 or 14 Miles Breadth, whence the Waters run different Ways, Part to the South, Part to the North; over this Portage to Lake George is a Waggon Road about 13 Miles.[1]

Vide Appendix Van Schaik's Journal

The Country Between the Drowned Lands and Lake George, as the Journals of the European Scouts both French and English describe it, also according to the Information which the Indians give of it, is a very impracticable Country. The Mountains are high, steep, and abrupt; and the Vales filled with deep Lakes and Ponds. The deep narrow Vale through which the Wood Creek creeps, is a Mixture between Lake and Swamp. The great western Vale or rather Chasm is an intire Lake, the Lake George, deep, narrow, and bounded on both Sides to the Water's Edge with exceeding high Mountains. Kankusker Bay[2] indeed runs up into a swampy Cove between Two Ridges. The Navigation which this Lake affords is obstructed at its northern Embouchure by a Ridge or Ledge of Rocks over which the surplus Issue of its Waters falls. Here is a Portage, I mean the old Indian Hunters and Traders Portage, over a high Hill on the South East Side to Tiëonderôga [Ticonderoga]. The Course which our Troops took was generally to land on Sabbath-day Point, whence a Road, by a Mill which stood on a small Rivulet, leads

Ticonderoga

to Fort Carillon[3] at Chëonderôga [Ticonderoga] or Trois Rivieres. This word denotes the Fork of a River or the confluence of two branches which go off in one united Stream. This the French always translate *Trois-rivieres* The Dutch who first improved this rout, using the letters *tie* to express the sound, *che* as we do yᵉ letters *tion* to express *çhon* wrote the word Tiëonderôga, and the letter *e* in the correspondencies being mistaken for *c* this place gott the name of Ticonderoga. Custom has adopted this original mistake, And the using the real name in its true orthography looks so like affectation That I cannot but think this Explanation, by way of Apology at least has become necessary. The Situation on yᵉ Ohio, on which Fort de Quesne, afterwards called *Fort Pitt* was built, was by the Indians called Chëonderôga, & accordingly by the French called *Trois-rivieres*. It is recorded by that name in the famous *Leaden Plate*,[4] which was buried there as a Memorial of their

[1] See "A Map of the Site of the Battle of Lake George, September 8th, 1755." William Johnson, *Papers . . . , op. cit.,* II, map opposite 2.

[2] North Arm of Lake George. A high ridge of Tongue Mountain rises between this bay and Lake George proper.

[3] Fort Carillon (1756-1759). This fort was abandoned and burned by the French.

[4] According to the "Official Statement" of Celeron there was on the third of August, 1749 a leaden plate buried "upon the southern bank of the Ohio, at four leagues distance below the River aux Boeufs, directly opposite a naked mountain, and near an immense stone upon which certain figures are rudely enough carved." This plate was buried on the Allegheny 115 miles above Pittsburgh. Charles

Possession. Untill I had occasion to explain this it was always a matter of Puzzle to our Ministers what Place in those Quarters the French meant to design by Trois-rivieres. Here follows an exact copy of that plate.

L'an 1749 Du Regne de Louis XV Roy de France Nous Celeron Commandant d'un detachment Envoie par Monsieur Le Mis de la Gallisoniere Commandant General De la Nouvelle France pour retablir la tranquillite dans quelques Villages Sauvages de ces cantons avons enterré Cette Plaque A. [3[1] rivieres dessous la riviere au beouf ce 3 Aoust] pres de la Riviere Oyo autrement belle Riviere pour Monument de Renouvellement de la Possession que nous avons pris de la ditte Riviere Oyo & de toutes celles qui y tombnt[2] & toutes les Terres des deux Cotes jusque aux Sources des dittes Rivieres ainsi qu'en ont jovy ou du jovir les precedent Roy de France et qu'ils s'y sont maintenûs par les Armes & par les Traites speciallement par ceux de Reswick du Trecht & d'Aix la Chapelle.

on ye Back is

Paul Labrosse Fecit

[Endorsed on back of Manuscript] Copy of the Leaden Plate Buried at the Forks of Monongahela & Ohio by Monsr Celeron by way of taking Possession & as a memorial & Testimony thereof 1753 or 2.

The Navigation from hence[3] to Crown Point and Fort Frederick[4] is uninterrupted through a River; the Narrows between these Points, which form the Entrance into Lake Champlain, the Indians call Teck-ya-dough Nigarêgé.[5] The Point on which Fort Frederick stands is not, as has been vulgarly imagined, Crown Point; it is the opposite Point, so

---

B. Galbreath, ed., *Expedition of Celeron to the Ohio Country in 1749.* (Columbus, Ohio, The F. J. Heer Printing Co., 1921), pp. 26, 64. Mr. Pownall has interpreted *3 rivieres*, scratched on the plate, to be *Trois Rivieres*. Probably the inscription was intended to connote the third stream below Riviere au Beouf. The *Proces Verbal* and inscription on the plate was not, in every case, identical.

[1][Pownall's note for revised and enlarged edition] This is only scratch'd with ye point of a knife & scarce legible in a space which was left blank to be fill'd up when buried.

[2][Pownall's note for revised and enlarged edition] It is so written in the Plate.

[3]Ticonderoga.

[4]French fort (1731-1759). For routes from Albany see "Trails, Military Roads and Forts from Albany to Crown Point." Johnson, *Papers, op. cit.,* I, map opp. p. 896.

[5]Johnson, *Papers, op. cit.,* II, map opp. 422, *note* 22.

called, by the Dutch Crun [Crûm Pᵗ] Punt,[1] by the French, Pointe à la Chevelure,[2] from a remarkable Action of Scalping committed there: The Point on which the Fort stands, a long Point, and low in Comparison of the Mountains which surround it, runs into the Lake, having the River to the East and a narrow Bay, which runs up South, to the West of it; at the South Head of this Bay was a Carrying-place to the River, much used in order to avoid passing by the Fort, by the French Indians and Traders in their smuggling Intercourse with the People of Albany.

Lake Champlain, as the French call it; Corlaer, as the Dutch call it; but according to its Indian Name, Caniaderi Guarunté [Caniadere'-guaront'], signifying the Gate or Mouth of the Country,[3] lies in a deep narrow Chasm of the Land, bounded up to the Water's Edge with steep Mountains on the western Shore, which continue thus to bound it as far as Cumberland Bay; the Ranges of the Mountains then trend off North West, and the Shore is low and in many Parts swampy. Many Streams, some which at Times issue an Abundance of Waters, fall into this Lake on the West Side, but they cannot be called Rivers; they are mere Cataracts, and so barred with Rocks and Sand there is no Entrance to them.

b
Vide Capt. Hobbs' and Van Schaik's Journals Appendix B b

The eastern Shores are formed by a low swampy Tract of Land; the Mountains keep off at the Distance of about 12 Miles.[b] The Soundings of the Lake are very deep in general, in many Places 60, 70, and 80, and in some Parts 100 Fathom. There are Three or Four considerable Streams fall into the Lake on the East Side. Otter Creek is the most considerable; an Account of which you have in Captain Hobbs's Journal in the Appendix.

Although these Lakes, Swamps, and Drowned Lands consist of such a Multitude of Waters, yet the Issue of their Surplus by the Sorel River is very small, and bears no Proportion to the Mass which seems to require an abundant Torrent. This is no singular Phaenomenon, it would have been singular were it otherwise than it is. The Issue of no River bears any Proportion to the Mass of Water which seems to flow in all the Parts of it.

B c d

Before I proceed to the Description of the Two principal Divisions of the Country, I must just passing (rather to mark my Ignorance than

---

[1]Johnson, *Papers, op. cit.,* II, map opp. 422, *note* 22.   [2]Peter Palmer, *History of Lake Champlain . . .* (Albany, J. Munsell, 1866), p. 3.

[3]Johnson, *Papers, op. cit.,* II, map opp. 422, *note* 22.

presuming to give Information) observe, that the Country, lying to the West of these Lakes, bounded on the North West by Canada River,[1] and on the South by the Mohawks [Mohawk] River, called by the Indians Couxsachrâgé, which signifies the Dismal Wilderness or Habitation of Winter, is a triangular, high mountainous Tract, very little known to the Europeans; and although a hunting Ground of the Indians, yet either not much known to them, or, if known, very wisely by them kept from the Knowledge of the Europeans. It is said to be a broken unpracticable Tract; I own I could never learn any Thing about it.

[1]St. Lawrence River.

SECT. III.

Eastern Division

FROM a Review of this Division, collected from a thousand Particulars, we may here begin by saying, that the great Portion of this Country which lies East of Hudson's [Hudson] River and Lake Champlain, lies in the Form of a Lunet or the Quarter of a Circle. The range of the Land of this First Part, beginning at Long Island Sound, runs nearly North and South, and then in about North Lat. 45, curves away Eastward to the Gulf of St. Lawrence. It consists of a high, hilly, and in some Part mountainous, Tract of Land, running in Ranges which follow the general Course of the main Land, and in general keep nearly parallel to each other; it is from 180 to 200 Miles across: It is divided into several principal or main Ranges, each consisting of a Multitude of parallel Ridges, each also having many Spurs and Branches deviating from the Course of the general Range, which Branches are sometimes broken into irregular hilly Land.

The highest Part of this Tract of Mountains may be defined by a Line drawn North westerly from the White Hills (which will be hereafter described) to the 45th Parallel of North Lat.

A a 1

Beginning from this Point in Lat. 45, and tracing this Tract to Long Island Sound, it is found to be divided into Two Parts by a great Vale through which Connecticut, or Long River (as its Indian Name signifies) flows; this Vale is from 12 to 20 Miles, in some Parts, broad. One of the main Ranges runs between Hudson's [Hudson] River, Wood Creek, Lake Champlain, and Connecticut River: Between Wood Creek, Lake Champlain, and Connecticut River it trends North North East, and afterwards North East. It consists of One high Range[1] only with hilly Lands, and not Ridges on each Side, suited for very fine Settlements.ᵉ This is The Tract of Country now settled & called *Vermont.*

c
Vide Capt. Hobbs' Journal in the Appendix

Capt. Holland has since the War run a Line from Connecticut River to the Mouth of St. Francis River, 90 Miles. The Topography of his Survey gives the same Account. On each Side of this great long Vale, at the Distance of about 100 Miles from Long Island Sound, the Two main

[1]Green Mountains, Vermont.

52

Ranges which form its Boundaries are again sub-divided into Two Parts, each by a Vale of near 100 Miles long; that on the West by the Vale through which the Hoosatonick [Housatonic] or Westonhoek River runs, passing to Sea by Milford, bounded on the West by the Taconick [Taconic], and on the East by Hoosatonick [Housatonic] Mountains, which also make the western Bound on the Vale of Connecticut. The most eastern Ridge of this main Range ends in a Bluff-head at Meridon [Meriden]: A Second ends in like Manner at Walingford [Wallingford]: A Third at New Haven: Where these Ridges terminate, the Face of the Country breaks into irregular hilly Ground. The Range of hills on the eastern Side of this Vale is subdivided by the Vale, beginning near the South of the great Ouätchuset [Wachusett], through which the River that hath acquired the Name of the Thames runs, passing to Sea by New London. This Vale is bordered on the West by a Range of the Chicabé [Chicopee] Mountains,[1] these terminate a little below East Hadham [Haddam], and the Face of the Country spreads in like Manner into hilly Land (These form the East Boundary of the Vale of Connecticut) and on the East by One of the Ranges of the Ouätchuset [Wachusett] Mountain continuing South to Stonington. Going from the same Line in Lat. 45, of the greatest Height of these Range of Mountains, and following them to the East northerly: They all seem to range as united until again divided by the Bay of Chaleurs [Chaleur], an Arm of the Gulf of St. Lawrence.

All the Rivers which have their Sources amidst the northern Ridges of this great Range fall into Canada or St. Lawrence River, as the St. Francis, Chaudiere, and many others. All which have their Sources amidst the southern Ridges fall into the Bay of Fundé [Fundy] or into the main Ocean; their Rise are almost universally from Lakes and Ponds, great Part of their first Courses lie in the Valleys amidst the mountainous Ridges in the Forms of drowned swampy Lands, or a Succession of Ponds, and while they do so their Courses are generally, I might say universally, from West to East: Whenever through Gaps or Intersections they can get away Southward they do so, tumbling over almost continued Falls across the Ranges. If they happen to find a Course along the Side of any Spur or Branch which runs South, it is otherwise, and their Courses are free. But the other Circumstance being that which forms in general their characteristic Nature; these Rivers in general are very little capable of Marine Navigation to any Length of Course within the Country; St. John's River in Nova Scotia excepted.

[1]Only the river retains this name. See p. 60 this work.

CONNECTICUT RIVER. This River rises in North Lat. 45°10′, at the Height of the Land, in Long. 4, East of the Meridian of Philadelphia. It hath its Birth in a swampy Cove at the Height of the Land; after having slept for Eight or 10 Miles in this State of Infancy, it leaves the Place of its Birth by tumbling over Four separate Falls; it then turns to the West, and keeps close under the Hills which form the northern Boundary of the Vale in which it runs; and in 10 Miles further Course runs under the Little Monadnaëg [Monadnock] Mountains for about Four Miles, at the End it turns round a high sharp Point, and for about a Mile runs North West, till coming under a high Hill it turns again to the South West; at Two Miles and a Half Distance from hence a little River called Leack's [Leech's] Stream[1] falls into it, coming down a Valley from the North West. This Stream[2] interlocks with some of Heads of St. Francis's Waters, and has been formerly an Indian Road. From hence, running under the Hills of the western Boundary of the Vale, it comes in Six or Seven Miles Course to the Grand Monadnaëg [Monadnock] Mountains on the West; as it runs Eight or 10 Miles further Course, it approrches the Mountains on the East Side of the Vale, and runs under rocky Mountains on the East. Almost opposite to this, in a flat swampy Interval on the West Shore, there is a Mineral Spring.[3] About Eight Miles below this is the Beginning of a new Settlement,[4] the First in the Course of this River; about Four Miles lower, opposite to Amanuseag [Ammonoosuc][5] River, which falls into it from the East, are Two more Settlements. Three Miles lower there is a Fall in the River. Here, once for all, let me observe, that these Ledges of Rocks over which the Rivers fall, serve in Nature the same Purposes which our Locks, that Art erects across our Rivers, are meant to serve: They hold up the Waters, and aid also the Navigation by causing Still Water above them. Three Miles below this Fall there is a very con-

[1]Probably the small unnamed stream which flows into the Upper Connecticut River at Stewartstown. For location on contemporary plan see *A Plan of a Survey Made to explore the Country for a Road between Connecticut River & St. Francis, op. cit.*

[2][Pownall's note] Here the Rout by Land from St. Francis's River, not 30 Miles, comes into the Connecticut River according to the Survey given to me by Capt. Holland Jan. 1776, which confirms what I had above noted.

[3]Near North Stratford, N.H. *A Map of the Province of New York, Reduc'd from the large Drawings of that Province, compiled from Actual Surveys by order of His Excellency William Tryon Esq[r] . . . . By Claude Sauthier . . . Engraved by William Faden, 1776.* London, Wm. Faden, 1776. Reprinted by the United States Constitution Sesquicentennial Convention under the title, *New York at the time of the ratification of the Constitution from 1776 and 1787 originals in the Library of Congress at Washington.* Hereafter cited as Sauthier's *Map . . . 1776.*

[4][Pownall's note for revised and enlarged edition] This was transcribed in the year 1774.

[5]Upper Ammonoosuc River. Present Ammonoosuc River flows into the Connecticut south of Israel River.

siderable Settlement begun by ———— Burnside,[1] Esq; Five Miles below this Settlement Capt. Page's[2] Settlements lie on the Intervals amidst the Windings of the River, under a high Hill on the West; on the East Israel's [Israel] River comes in, and Two Miles lower are several Settlements on the Intervals called Cahass [Cohass], the Upper or Lesser Cahass [Cohass]: The River keeps its Course South westerly, and then quitting the Hills on the East, and the Vale in which it hath hitherto ran, crosses the western Range, and tumbles with a Course South West for 15 Miles together over Rifts and Ledges of Rocks[3] till it meets the high Lands on the West Side; and then, under the Foot of these, resumes its old Course South-westerly, in a Second Vale, or rather Second Stage of the same Vale. Here again on the Interval Lands are several new Settlements begun. In about Two Miles further Course the River gets again under the Hills on the eastern Side where comes in Hurd's River,[4] and running under them for about Two Miles falls Four Feet over a Ledge of Rocks which run across its Bed. Four Miles below this it passes a Strait betwixt Two Rocks. After this the New Settlements are found pretty thick upon the Meadows and Intervals of the Lower or Great Cohass. Townships are settling very fast on the Banks on both Sides. Running along the Township of Lebanon, under high steep Hills, on the West, called Cunney Mountain,[5] the River tumbles over several Falls. In Plainfield Township a Ledge of Rocks about Three Feet high crosses its Course: in Eight Miles further Course it runs close under the Ascutney Mountains which rise high on the West Side the Vale; it next runs under the Casowetchawêgê[6] Mountains on the same Side, close under the South Point of which a Road[7] goes off West to Crown Point. About Eight Miles further with a still deep Course the River passes by Charles Town [Charlestown], late a Garrison Number

Vide Capt. Hobbs' Journal Appendix

[1]Thomas Burnside, one of Roger's Rangers. Jeanette R. Thompson, *History of the Town of Stratford, New Hampshire, 1773-1925* (Concord, N.H., Rumford Pub. Co. 1925), p. 31.

[2]David Page. *Ibid.*, p. 31.

[3]Fifteen Miles Falls above Barnet, Vermont. Walter Hard, *The Connecticut* . . . (N.Y., Rinehart & Co., c. 1947), pp. 9, 168.

[4]Not located. Probably a stream flowing into the Connecticut in the vicinity of Hards Island Falls in Lyman township, New Hampshire.

[5]Probably Sawyers Mountains. See "A Map of the Most Inhabited part of New England Containing the Provinces of Massachusets Bay and New Hamp-shire with the Colonies of Conecticut and Rhode Island.". . . November 29th, 1774. Published according to Act by Tho[s] Jefferys. Jefferys, *American Atlas, op. cit.*, nos. 15 and 16.

[6]Near the junction of Williams and Connecticut Rivers. Sauthier's *Map . . . 1776, op. cit.*

[7]Crown Point Road, an old military road from Amherst, Mass. to Crown Point, N.Y. This road has been marked by a granite marker set up near Charlestown, N.H. Federal Writers' Project, New Hampshire, *New Hampshire, a guide to the Granite State* (Boston, Houghton, Mifflin, Co., 1938), pp. 366-367.

4,[1] a little above which comes in Black River from the North West. About Seven or Eight Miles below this the River runs under a very high Mountain,[2] rising on the East Shore opposite to Rockingham Township: Here are the great Falls,[3] in passing which the River shoots with great Rapidity between Two Rocks scarce 30 Feet asunder, and then extends itself into a wide Bason. The River continuing to run nearly the same Course in the same Kind of Vale amidst the like new Settlements for Two or Three Miles, then runs under the West River Mountains,[4] so called being opposite to a considerable River called West River, which runs from the North West; these Mountains are on the East Side the Vale. In these Mountains there is the Appearance of there having been some Eruption or Volcano. In 11 Miles more making a great Bend directly South West, and short back again North East. The River comes to the Boundary Line between the Provinces Massachuset's Bay [Massachusetts] and New York; a little to the North of which Line the Ashewelot [Ashuelot] River coming from the East falls into it; its Course then through Northfield Township is for Two-thirds of its South-Easterly, for the remaining Third South westerly; it continues winding in the same Course through Part of Deerfield, till it comes to where Miller's [Miller] River falls into it from the East; the River then turns short to the West, and in a sinuous Course comes to a Fall, which from a Battle fought with the Indians there, is called *The Fighting Falls*;[5] it hence turns South-westerly and tumbles over Deerfield Falls,[6] which Falls are impassable for Navigation. Above these Falls the River is wide and the Current slow. A little below these Falls Deerfield River coming from the West and making a Turn Northward falls into Connecticut from the South. Hence running in a broad and still Current between Deerfield and Sunderland Townships it passes just above Sunderland Meeting-house between Two Peaks of Mountains, Mount Toby on the East, and the Sugar Loaves[7] on the West: It then runs South through Hatfield and Hadley Townships, and just opposite to Hadley Meeting-house makes a great western Bend, returning to the East it then runs

[1]No. 4, as it was called, was a famous military post throughout the French and Indian War.

[2]Great Falls Mountain. Sauthier's *Map . . . 1776*, *op. cit.*

[3]At Bellows Falls, Vermont. Hard, *op. cit.*, pp. 21, 168-69.

[4]Not located on contemporary or modern maps. Probably the Northfield Mountains on "A Map of the Most Inhabited Part of New England Containing the Provinces of Massachusets Bay and New Hampshire with the Colonies of Conecticut and Rhode Island". . . November 29th, 1774. Published According to Act by Tho[s] Jefferys. Jefferys, *American Atlas, op. cit.*, nos. 15 and 16.

[5]Fighting Falls as mentioned by Pownall may be part of Deerfield Falls. The Fall fight, an Indian battle, took place at Deerfield Falls in May 1676. Samuel G. Drake, ed., *The Old Indian Chronicle* . . . (Boston, Samuel A. Drake, 1867), pp. 259-62.

[6]Now Turner's Falls. *Ibid.*, p. 260n.

[7]Mt. Sugarloaf.

South-westerly along under a high Ridge of Mountains called the Holy Oaks [Holyoke], which are on the East Side of the Vale, and making, just below Hampton Meeting-house, a great Bend to the West, returns again East directly against the Foot of these Mountains, and passes between that and a high Peak called Mount Tom, over a very bad Rift; hence it runs South, and then taking a South-eastern Course tumbles over Two Falls, the one called Hampton Upper Falls, the Lower one called the Fishing Falls, both these are passable. These Falls[1] are about a Mile and Half asunder, and the River between is broad and deep. Two or Three Miles below, the Chicabee [Chicopee] River, so called as coming from the Chicabee Ridge[2] of Mountains which form here the East Boundary of the Vale, a pretty large Stream runs into it on the East Side. There is another Rift[3] lower down the River just above Enfield Meeting-house, but passable. The River runs hence by Suffeild [Suffield], Simsbury, and Windsor in a strait South Course, with an easy though pretty quick Current, 12 Miles to Hertford [Hartford]. The Tide flows up very near, but not quite to Hertford [Hartford] Town. The River, where it is a Tide River, is said to be filled up from the Soil which is brought down by the Freshes mixing with the Silt which is rolled up by the Tide. But this I apprehend not to be the true Cause, because this Case being common to all Tide Rivers it must equally operate in all, which is not so. The River here ceases to run through a sloping decided Valley. The Land of the Bed of the Valley rises here in broken hilly Ground, and the River ceasing to have the same Slope as above, runs more upon a Level and more crooked: Wherever this happens, the Soil which was before kept suspended by the swifter Current always begins first to subside where the Current is first checked. Hence for 35 or 36 Miles running by Weathersfield [Wethersfield], Kensington, Middleton [Middletown], Haddam, and Durham on its West Banks; Glassenbury [Glastonbury] and Windham on its East Banks, it passes between Seabrook [Saybrook] and Lyme[4] to Sea that is, into Long Island Sound.

It will give some Idea of this delightfull Country & Vale, If one pursues the Account of yᵉ Road through it, as I find it in my Journal. Going From New York into New England one leaves the Dutch towns & the little French Settlement of New Rochell [Rochelle], & Comes to Towns assuming the appearance of English Market Towns. The Spired Churches & Square Townhouses & Porched Houses give yᵉ striking

---

[1]South Hadley Falls. Hard, *op. cit.*, p. 23.
[2]See p. 60 this work.
[3]Enfield Falls. Hard, *ibid.*, p. 23.
[4]Old Lyme, Connecticut.

Features of this likeness. The Road after Passing over a Bridge across Byram River which divides New York from New England & by Horsneck,[1] Coscal [Cos Cob], Stamford, Middleton [Middlesex],[2] Norwalk, Fairfeild [Fairfield], Stratfeild[3] & Pembroke,[4] rises up a very high hill called Stoney brook hill from whence The Traveller has a very fine View of the Country every way. On one side He views the Sound with all its Islands, bounded by the hilly shores of Long Island. In another Stratford Stratfeild[5] & ye sweet vales in which their Lands lye in every ye most pleasing Groupes of Habitancy Culture Woods & Water. The Road then runs through Stratford & over Stratford River[6] by a Ferry to Milford, hence 10 miles to Newhaven. Newhaven lyes at the NW end of the Harbour or Bay so Called in a Charming Vale, surrounded from the NW round to ye NE with high Cliffs of hills. The Vale is full of Culture in alternate Tillage & Meadows about two miles broad on each side the River. Just as the Road descends at about two miles from Newhaven, The Traveller has from the hills an enchanting view of the Vale & the Town; a Town of Trading, & ye Harbour full of Vessels. The Town is built on a regular designed Plan. Is a Square, has a Place or Square in the Middle, from the Angles of which go off in right lines eight Streets. The Houses are all built in the English Fashion. In the Center of the Square is a fine Meeting house with its Spire like our English Churches. On the East side is another like Meeting: at the South east corner of this Square is an English Church & on ye south side of this Square is a Third Meeting. The College, Called Yale College takes up the west side of the Square. It consists of Two buildings each of three Story besides the Garret. The Old one[7] has three Stair Cases like the sides of our Colleges. The New One[8] has two Staircases. The Old Building is a Framed Wooden Building. The New One is of Brick. From New-haven to Wallingford the road goes up north along ye same Vale[9] in which Newhaven stands. It is 8½ miles to North Haven & 6 to Wallingford. The Road continues in the same Vale four miles beyond

[1]Near the New York state line. Christopher Colles. *A Survey of the Roads of United States of America, 1789.* [New York, 1789] Sheet 4. Not indicated on present maps.

[2]Darien, Connecticut, post office. Connecticut (State) *Register and Manual, 1939,* (Hartford, the State, 1939), p. 374.

[3]Bridgeport, Connecticut. *Ibid.,* p. 390.

[4]Danbury, Connecticut post office. *Ibid.,* p. 392.

[5]Bridgeport.

[6]Housatonic.

[7]This building, erected in 1717, stood, in part, until 1782. All except the kitchen and dining room were razed in 1775. Yale University, *Historical Register . . . 1701-1937* (New Haven, Conn., Yale University, 1939), p. 9.

[8]Connecticut Hall (1750) later known as South Middle College. J. W. Barber, *History and Antiquities of New Haven, (Conn.)* . . . (New Haven, J. W. Barber, 1831), p. 21.

[9]Quinnipiac Valley.

Wallingford then crosses north east several ridges & comes into a second Vale called Great Swamp or Kensington. From Wallingford to Meridon [Meriden] 8 miles to Kensington 7. This is a rich well cultivated Vale thickly settled & swarming with People. From Kensington to Weatherfield [Wethersfield] 10 miles. At seven miles of this way, as it runns N East it crosses yᵉ ridges. From yᵉ last ridge three miles from Weathersfield [Wethersfield] The Traveller has a view of the Great Vale of Connecticut up the River, a Landschape picturesque in every assemblage of beautifull Objects that gives a View of a rich populous Inhabitancy of the Human Race enjoying in peace & Liberty every happiness that a *Heaven upon earth* can give. The Vale is from 12 to 8 miles broad, bounded on both sides with high blue hills in parts mountainous. The River runs through the middle of it & Go which you will on each side of it, It is as though you were still travelling along one continued town for 70 or 80 miles on end. At 6, 8, or 10 miles distance you come to yᵉ Body of a Large regular built town,[1] but yᵉ View of the Vale itself in the whole Like a most noble amphitheatre will at first possess the Eye & Mind. Strait, as Milton says, the Eye catches new pleasure when it fixes in detail on yᵉ Multitude of Towns the innumerable farms & settlements, The Groups of Woods & rivulets, amidst cleared & cultured lands teeming with abundance. How other People may be made I don't know and what the Reader may think of me I don't care, but I declare I could never view this scene of happiness nor do I now write yᵉ account of it without an overflowing of heart that putts a tear in My Eye, which Tear that was Sweet is now become a bitter one when I reflect that that Happiness has been destroyed; And most likely can never exist there again in the same degree.[2] From Weathersfeil [Wethersfield] the Road runs 8½ miles to Hertford [Hartford], To Windsor 10 miles coming down from hilly Land upon Windsor another Charming Prospect. To Southfeild[3] 10 miles: To Springfeild 10 miles.[4] Here the Road that goes to Boston goes away East. The Traveller crosses the River by a Ferry boat, and Leaves this charming Vale.

To describe now the Ranges of this Eastern Division, which lie between Connecticut Vale and the Ocean, one may in general state it as an Opinion formed from a Multitude of collected Facts, that this Tract, which is from 50 to 60 Miles broad consists of Three principal Ranges; the First is that which with its many subordinate Ridges forms the

[1]Hartford, Connecticut.

[2]Pownall here refers to the Revolutionary War crisis.

[3]Not indicated on present maps.

[4]Springfield, Massachusetts.

eastern Boundary of the Vale of Connecticut, running generally North and sometimes to the Eastward of North from East Hadham [East Haddam] in Connecticut Colony to the Head of the Vale: The Middle Range runs from Stonington in the same Colony along the great Ouätchuset [Wachusett] Mountains, and so away Northerly (as shall be particularly described) in a Direction nearly parallel to the former. The Third rising in the Townships of Hopkinton, Holliston, and Medford, in Massachuset's Province runs North in a like Direction by Watertown and Concord across the Merrimaeg [Merrimac] River and Pantookaëg [Pawtucket Falls][1] fall away to the White Hills [Mountains].

The First Ridge of the westernmost Range keeps in the Massachuset's Province about 10 or 12 Miles from Connecticut River; and the easternmost Ridge of the eastern Range runs in a Meridian about 11 Miles West of Boston, forming a Tract about 60 Miles across. These Ranges do not keep the same Height, but are in some Parts depressed and lowered greatly; in others again they run up into high Peaks of Mountains, or high mountainous Tracts. They are sometimes broken and discontinued, but take up again ranging in the same Direction. Within the Bounds of the Massachuset's Province the middle Range, by the high mountainous Tract called Great Watchusets [Wachusett], is the highest. In New Hampshire Province, about 20 Miles North of the Boundary Line, the western Range, by means of the high Peaks of Monadneag [Monadnock], is the highest. In Lat. 44, within the same Province, the eastern Range, by means of the *White Hills* [Mountains], is beyond all comparison the highest.

To give now some Description of each of these Ranges. The Western one, which as I said, begins in East Hadham [East Haddam], in the Colony of Connecticut, forms the East Boundary of Connecticut Vale; in this Colony, and in the Province of Massachuset[ts], it was called the Chicabee, though the River[2] which runs from and falls into Connecticut River at Springfield seems now to have appropriated that Name to itself alone; it is not very high while it ranges through these Provinces, but after it hath passed the Boundary Line between Massachuset[ts] and New Hampshire about 20 Miles, it runs up into a very high Peak called Monadneag,[3] the Ridge in which Monadneag [Monadnock] rises seems here to be discontinued, but the next West Ridge in the same Range keeps on, and in about Lat. 43° 20′ runs up into another

[1]At Lowell, Massachusetts.

[2]Chicopee River.
[3]Grand Monadnock.

high Peak called Sunapee Mountains, on the West of which is Sunapee Pond [Lake]; it continues on, and in Lat. 44 rises again into a high Tract called Mooscoog [Moose] Mountain; beyond this my Information does not go.

The Middle Range may be taken as rising about Stonington, in the Colony of Connecticut, on the Sound; it ranges hence North-easterly, and in Rutland District, in the Province Massachuset[ts], runs up into a very high Tract of Land called the Great Watchuset [Wachusett]; this is the highest Land in all this Tract of Country: From the South Side of it springs the River which finally acquires the Name of the Thames; from the West Side the Chicabee [Chicopee]; from the North East Side the Nashaweag [Nashua] River, which runs away North East to Merrimac River; from the South East Side, the principal Branch of the River, afterward called Naraganset[1] River, which runs into Naraganset [Narragansett] Bay by Rhode Island. Ranging still North it rises again just at the Boundary Line into another high Mountain called Wadadeag;[2] keeping the same Course it lowers its Crest, and alternately rises again in Peaks Three or Four Times,[3] and at length in about the Lat. 43° 25' runs up into a high Peak called Cowesawaskoog:[4] Here my Information stops.

The Eastern Range begins by an humble lowly Birth about Hopkington, Holliston, or Medford; the eastern Ridge of this keeps a Course North by Concord, and runs across the River Merrimac at Pantookaëg [Pawtucket] Falls;[5] it begins to grow more considerable in the Province New Hampshire, and runs up into a high Ridge called Tower Hill;[6] it is depressed again, and again rises into rather a higher Ridge called Saddle-back Mountain:[7] It subsides, but soon again rises in what is called Packer's Hill,[8] it then ranges along the East of Winipissiocket [Winnipesaukee Lake] Pond, and at the North East Bay of that runs up into very high Mountains called Ossipee Hills; it continues then the same northern Course, and in Lat. 44 rises into the highest Mountains of this whole eastern Division called the White Hills, the Peak or

[1]Blackstone, named Providence River where it empties into Narragansett Bay.

[2]Watatic Mountain.

[3]From the south summit [Ragged Mt.] is a view of Mts. Kearsarge, Sunapee, Cardigan, and other peaks. Federal Writers' Project. New Hampshire, *op. cit.*, p. 452.

[4]Ragged Mountain is approximately in this latitude.

[5]At Lowell, Massachusetts.

[6]Not located on modern maps. Near Chester, Rockingham County, New Hampshire.

[7]Not located on modern maps. Probably Leavitts Hill, New Hampshire.

[8]Not located on modern maps. Probably mountains in Gilford Township, Belknap County, New Hampshire.

The White Hills B a

Top of which being bare Rocks of a white Grit and Talk [Talc], and bleached by the eternal Beating of the Weather, has a very uncommon Appearance: These Hills; although more than 70 Miles within Land, are seen many Leagues off at Sea,[1] and always appear like an exceeding bright Cloud in the Horizon. A Ridge of the same Range, the next to the Westward, running on the West Side Winipissiocket [Winnipesaukee Lake] Pond, runs up at the North West Bay into a high Mountain of red shelly Land, and is called the Red Hill[2] or Mountain; this Range falls also in with the White Hills. A Range running hence crosses the East Boundary Line of New Hampshire in Lat. 44½, and trending North East forms the Height of the Land between Kenebaëg [Kennebec] and Chaudiere Rivers: Of the Nature and Course of this high Land in these Parts I am totally uninformed; and I have directed that the Map in these Parts should be so engraved as not to assume any great Authority.

All the Rivers in the Eastern Parts of New England, arising amidst the South and Southeastern Ridges of this high Range, generally spring from Lakes, great Ponds, or boggy Swamps in the Vales: While they run or rather creep along the Course of these Vales their Beds are broad and seem rather like a Succession of Ponds than the Channels of Rivers; but as the southern Ridges are much lower than the Northern ones, these Rivers get away South through the first Gap or Interlocking, or along the first Spur which sets off, and tumble across the several Strata in broken Currents over Rifts and Cataracts almost to their Mouths. They are from this Circumstance capable of admitting Marine Navigation but a very little Way within Land. It is generally stopt at about 20 or 30 Miles by Falls. The Projection of the Rivers in this Part of the Map may be depended upon, being laid down from actual Surveys. Of each of these Rivers and of the Coast I shall speak separately.

All the Rivers which arise amidst the northern Ridges fall into St. Lawrence River, the Heads of these Two Sets of Waters interlock with each other, and in the travelling this Country in its natural Wilderness State, which is conducted by means of and along these Waters, very short Portages over Land form the Communication.

B C D a

To speak of that Part of this high Tract in its northern Range through the Provinces Massachuset[ts] and New Hampshire, one finds

[1][Pownall's note] Nobody has been at the Summit of these Hills, the craggy Tops are perpendicular; some People impute this singular Appearance to their being always covered with Snow; but by what I learnt from Mr. Grant, who passed over Part of these Hills by a Passage through them, called THE NOTCH, I am induced to adopt the Opinion as above.

[2]East of Center Harbor, New Hampshire. Federal Writers' Project, New Hampshire, *op. cit.*, p. 416.

a numberless Multitude of Lakes and Ponds amidst the Ridges, whence spring a Multitude of Streams and Rivers, all interlocking in every Direction with each other; those of the western Side fall into the River Connecticut, those which run East into the Merrimac River.

Between this high mountainous Tract and the Ocean, both in its northern and in its eastern Range, there is a Piedmont of irregularly broken hilly Land. Of that in the eastern Parts of New England, especially East of Penobsceäg [Penobscot], I can say nothing with Accuracy, and will therefore say nothing at all. I have struck out of my Map most of the Hills which I found drawn in the Surveys whence I had the Rivers copied, as I suspected they were laid down too much *ad libitum*. I will not in these Parts vouch for even those which remain, except within the Line of my Scouting Parties from Penobscot to Kenebeäg [Kennebec], and on the Back of the Settlements of the Counties of York and Cumberland. Of the Piedmont which lies upon the western Division of the Massachuset[ts] Province I can speak with some Accuracy, from my own Knowledge, formed by collating the Observations of Dr. Douglas[1] and others on the Spot.

This Piedmont, which a Tartar[a] would call Mas-Tchudi, has been called by the Indians here Mais-Tchuseäg, which signifies the same Thing, namely, *The Country on this Side the Hills*. It doth not range in Ridges, but lies in irregular hilly, though not high Land. The Rivers within this Tract, which run in all Directions, mark this, if the Eye had not. First, Concord River,[3] which rises in One Branch from a Pond[4] in Framingham, and in Two others from amidst the eastern Ridges of the high Range about Marlborough [Marlboro], runs along the East Side at the Foot of the easternmost Ridge North to Merrimac River, a little below Pantucket [Pawtucket] Falls. Mystick and Medford[5] Rivers on the North of Boston Harbour run from the North to the South; across their Heads the Ipswich River, rising in Wilmington, in the County of Middlesex, runs East and then turns North East.

Charles River arises in Five or Six Sources[6] on the South East Side

Margin notes: Piedmont or Tract towards the Coast. — A B a 4 — a Vide Van Stralenberg's Account of Siberia,[2] &c — D a 1 Concord River — D E a 2 Ipswich River. — D E a 1 Charles River

---

[1]Wm. Douglass. A Summary, Historical and Political . . . *op. cit.*

[2]John Philip von Strahlenberg. *An Historico-geographical description of the North and Eastern Parts of Europe and Asia; but More Particularly of Russia, Siberia and Great Tartary . . .* now faithfully translated into English (London, printed for W. Innis and R. Mansby, 1738), p. 42.

[3][Pownall's note] Sudbury River, a Branch of Concord River, rises in Westborough.

[4]Lake Cochituate.

[5]A stream, fed by ponds, flowing into the Mystic River at Medford, Massachusetts.

[6]Beaver Pond, Hoppin, Chicken, Mine and Shephard's Brooks, Mill River, and Archer's Pond. Nathaniel Shurtleff, *A Topographical and Historical Description of Boston* (3d ed., Boston, By Order of the Common Council 1891), p. 154.

of Hopkington and Holliston Ridge, all running South; the main Stream runs North East, then North round this Ridge, then North-easterly, and then in Natick Township, runs away with a sinuous Course East-northerly till it meets Mother Brook, in Dedham. The other Branch called Mother Brook, hath Three Sources, Two on each Side Mooshill,[1] Naponset [Neponset], and Mashapoog [Massapoag],[2] which runs North East; a Third[3] which springs from the high elevated Tract South the Blue Hills; these all join in the Branch above-named, and meet the western Branch or real Charles River, in Dedham. Hence, running West in Needham, it tumbles in Falls[4] across the South West End of Brooklin [Brookline] Hills, till it comes near Framingham Pond; it then runs away North East to Cambridge, where, winding round in a South West Course, it falls into Boston Harbour. The Hills of Roxbury and Dorchester are not Ridges, and are confined to the Northward of Mother Brook; the Part of this Piedmont, on the West and South West of Boston Bay, is divided by an elevated Tract of Land, whose general Direction may be described by a Line drawn from Squantum [Squantum's] Neck[5] to Mount Hope[6] at the Head of Naraganset [Narragansett] Bay. At the Back of Milton and Braintree it runs up into high Peaks of Hills called, by Sailors, the Blue Mountains.[7] The main Drain of the District on the East Side of this high Tract is Taunton River, which runs nearly a straight Course South West under the East Foot of it to Tiverton on Naraganset [Narragansett] Bay; all the Streams which fall into the North West Side of this River, come down South East from the High Land; not more than Two or Three, and those very small ones, falling into it from the South East.

The natural Vegitation of this Country, which I have been describing, is Pine of many Sorts, The White Masting Pine, and the Pitch Pine; Firs, Cedar, and Spruce; Oaks of many Sorts, Red, Black, and White; Beech, Birch, Maple, and Bass; Ash and Elm, both Black and White; Walnut, Hickory, Hornbeam, and Acacia. As these different Species of Wood predominate in each Place, the Soil may be pronounced to be of Mould, loomy and moist, stony or sandy, light or stiff.

In Tillage it produces Maize, Rye, Barley, Buck-wheat, and Pulse well; there is something in the Soil (at least as the New England Farmers

[1]Mouse Hill. Jefferys, *The American Atlas, op. cit.*, Map no. 16. Probably present Sharon Heights.
[2]Brook with Massapoag Pond as its source.
[3]Ponkapog with Ponkapog Pond as its source.
[4]Newton Upper and Newton Lower Falls.

[5]In 1855 Squantum's Neck was annexed to Quincy, Massachusetts. Shurtleff, *op. cit.*, p. 505.
[6]Bristol, R.I. Federal Writers' Project, Rhode Island . . . *Rhode Island* . . . (Boston, Houghton, Mifflin Co., 1937), pp. 183-84.
[7]Blue Hill Range near Milton, Massachusetts.

husband it) which does not well for Wheat; it is chiefly a grazing Country, and feeds many Sheep and immense Numbers of Oxen, and many Horses. Apples thrive in it to a great Degree, Peaches also, but not equal to what they do more to the Southward. Connecticut grows a great Quantity of Flax for Seed, which causes a considerable Export from thence.

The Fisheries on the Coast: The lesser Fisheries in those Rivers, amongst which are Shad, Sturgeon, and Salmon in the Season: The Ship Timber, the Masting, the Lumber, the Naval Stores, and of late Pot Ash, are its peculiar and native Staples. The eastern Parts of Massachuset[ts] Province, and the interior Parts of New Hampshire Province, being towards the Coast, of a strong moist Soil, did contain a Source of this Naval Supply, which might have been inexhaustible; but Plunder and Waste profiting of bad Regulations, have well nigh exhausted this Store near the Rivers.[1]

I shall here as I did through Connecticut Transcribe my Journal of y[e] Road from Connecticut River to Boston as it appeared to me in 1754. From Springfield on Connecticut River to Day's[2] Tavern 10 miles sandy Land & Pine Woods: from Day's to Scott's[3] 5 miles; to Shaw's[4] 2 miles. At Scott's one crosses the Chicabee [Chicopee] River over a long Wooden bridge. Scotts' & Shaws both in a very pleasant Valley along which the Chicabee [Chicopee] runs winding from side to side. At the end ford the Chicabee [Chicopee] then over high & stoney mountains here & there pretty prospects of y[e] valleys which are settled particularly coming down to Cutlers:[5] to Cutlers 8 miles. To Brookfield 6 miles. To Leicester 11 miles. This stage over hilly Country but not mountainous. To Worcester 9 miles, a Beautiful Clear New & Young looking Town in a pleasant broad Vale. This has been so settled about 23 Years. To Shrewsbery [Shrewsbury] 8 miles, about 6 miles of this over hills, the soil a white sand mixt with Isinglass, talck [talc] like that at New York in the Jerseys & Pensylvania [Pennsylvania]. This Country does not lye in steep hills & narrow vallies but in easy slopes & spacious bottoms. The Prospects charm the Travellers with their woody hills & with the Farms,

[1][Pownall's note] There are some few Furs; I have met with some black Fox Skins from the Parts about Ponobskaeg [Penobscot].

[2]Not identified.

[3]John, William, and William Scott Jr. were proprietors in the "Elbow Tract" which lay along the Chicopee River east of Springfield, Massachusetts. J. H. Temple, *History of the Town of Palmer, Mass., early known as The Elbow Tract* . . . (Palmer, Mass., published by the Town, 1889), p. 131; "Orig-inal Elbow District, Mass., 1716 to 1752. Compiled by E. B. Gates." *Ibid.*, Map no. 1.

[4]Samuel, David, and Seth Shaw, names in "Petition of the Inhabitants of Elbow Tract," October, 1751. Massachusetts Archives, Manuscript Folio CXVI, 137. The Massachusetts Archives are housed in the Office of the Secretary of the Commonwealth, State House, Boston.

[5]Not identified.

Rivulets, little lakes, orchards & Feilds, in the bottoms. This cheifly a grazing Country. Of Sheep scarce any Flock above 40 or 50. But Multitudes of Oxen. To Marlborough [Marlboro] 7 miles; to Sudbury 11. The Vales here larger & wider rather swampy with extensive meadows. As the road advances from the interior & distant parts, The Farmers engage more in Tillage yet there is a great deal of Pine Land & Sandy Soil All the way intermixt. To Saltmarshe's[1] Tavern in Watertown 11 miles: The first six miles of this over ridges of Mountains; but the road is pretty easy & not steep, running through the Gaps; In this six miles little or no Tillage that I could observe. The other 5 miles across a spacious level plain of a mixt soil but good for tillage. Here Multitudes of Pretty Farms all with orchards round their Houses. To Boston 9½ miles. The Face of the Country in this Stage Hilly & rather Stony & of light soil: but better cultured than the rest.

Detailed and tedious as the Remarks above will seem and perhaps prove in the Reading, they always appeared to me necessary to be observed by any who wished, or whose Duty it was, to have a Knowledge of the Country. When I first went to America the Subject and the Object were both new to the Europeans; I thought the Situation in which I was employed required Attention to this Point; I never travelled without a Compass and a little Level, of my own Contrivance, for taking Elevations; besides that, from an Habit of Drawing from Nature, my Eye could mark an Angle with Exactness sufficient for Practice. I was very particular in observing and noting, not only from my own Observations but from Surveys, where such were projected with Care, the Ranges of the Hills and Mountains, I also marked the *Sections which their Out-lines formed*, also the Knobs or Bluff-endings, and the Peaks. I was particular in my Observations and Inquiries into the Courses and Nature of the Currents of the several Rivers, their Falls and Fords, wherever I had Opportunity. The Passes and Gaps in the Mountains, and especially the Places where Posts fixed might give a Command in the Country. The Reader may see a very early Use which I made of this Knowledge (such as it was) in the State of the Service,[2] which I drew up for the late Duke of Cumberland in the Year 1756; as also in the itinerary Observations[3] referred to by LEWIS EVANS, which gave some ad-

[1]Not identified.

[2]"A Memorial: Stating the Nature of the Service in North America, and proposing a General Plan of Operations, as founded thereon. Drawn up by Order of, and presented to, his Royal Highness the Duke of Cumberland, 1756." Thomas Pownall, *The Administration of the Colonies* (2d ed., London, Dodsley 1765), Appendix, pp. 2-49.

[3]See *note* 1, p. 3.

ditional Topographical Merit to the First Edition of this Map in 1755.

When I was afterwards in a Situation[1] to direct the Inquiries of others, I formed a Set of Instructions for directing the Observations and Remarks of such as were sent out to reconnoitre; and the Returns I received gave very sufficient Information as far as it could go. If the Plan, which I proposed and began, had been observed through the War, namely, that of obliging every Scout to keep a Journal with Topographical Remarks; and, upon the Returns of these, of copying into a Book (under a general Head, each within their respective District) all these Informations so returned; a very ample-Store of Topographical Knowledge of the Country might have been collected and classed, which is now dispersed and lost. I can speak from Experience of the Use of this; I experienced it in my own Province; such classed and posted Accounts would have proved a good Check on the Unfaithfulness of many an artificial Journal cooked up by the Scouting Parties; moreover the Habit of keeping such Journals, and making such Remarks, would have trained many a good Regimental Officer to become a real General. Without this Knowledge and practical Readiness in applying it, no Officer ought to be trusted with the Command of a Body of Men. It would be invidious, but it would be easy to show, how strongly this Truth was evinced in the Events of the last War in America. The Americans have been much used to this Habit. They will always have amongst their Officers good Partizans;[2] and I shall never be surprized to see Generals formed from these. I say this not to disparage but to excite the Emulation of the British Officers.

There are in many Parts of New England Mines of Iron Ore,[3] some of Copper; but I must suppose that either the Ore is not good, or that

---

[1]Governor of Massachusetts, 1757-60. Pownall's official title was "Captain-General and Commander-in-Chief of Massachusetts Bay in New England," Charles A. W. Pownall, *Thomas Pownall . . .* (London, Henry Stevens, son & Stiles, 1908), p. 71.

[2][Pownall's note] This remark was written in 1774.

[3][Pownall's note] Although what I have said above be the Fact as to New England in general, yet there are Iron Mines in some Parts of this main *Eastern Division;* I may instance those of Mr. Levington [Livingston] in particular: This famous Iron-work is

b D b   at ᵇAncram, in the Manor of Levington [Livingston]; there are Two Beds of Ore which supply this Furnace, the One in the Tachonic [Taconic] Mountains near

c E b   it, and the other by Salisbury Fallsᶜ in Connecticut, about 12 Miles off. The Tachonic [Taconic] Ore is

richer than that from the New England Bed. The Salisbury Ore costs 2s. 6d. per Ton raising, and 8s. per Ton carting to the Furnace: 2000 Tons of this Ore make 900 Tons of Pigs, and expend about 200 Tons of Limestone: 2700 Loads of Coals serve the Furnace to make 900 Tons of Pigs, and Three Fires in the Forge in the mean while. N.B. Small Coals that will not do for the Furnace serve the Forge. The Coals cost 12s. 6d. per Load, and 3s. Cartage from the River. A Load of Coals is 100 Bushels on the Bank. Mr. Levington [Livingston] pays 2s. per Cord for cutting the Wood, which is repaid to him by the Collier. The People employed, and their Wages are as followeth: The Founder has 5s. a Ton for his Pigs, and finds his Keeper, who is a second Hand to watch the Furnace while he sleeps. The

the Mines are not worth the Working, as most of the Iron which is forged in New England is brought from the southern Provinces in Pigs: And none of the Copper Mines are worked.

There is a great Quantity of Bog-Iron, which is used for Cast-metal, and is much esteemed.

I have been told, when I was in the Country, of a Mine or Bog in which Lumps of Native Steel were found; but I never saw Reason to remove the Doubt and Suspense of Opinion with which I always received the Account. There may be, for ought I know, a Species of Bog-Iron, which is peculiarly adapted to the Process by which Steel is formed from Iron, and which more readily receives that Temper. I always understood, however, that Steel is not Native but Artificial.

Having thus given a Description of the Interior of the Country, I shall now describe the Coasts and Rivers which run into the Ocean as far as falls within this Map.

B a 5 a 6
Pasama-
quady Bay
and Rivers
St. Croix, a
general
Adjunct

The River Pasam-Aquâda [Passamaquoddy],[1] or Possam-Accâda, which runs into a Bay so called, is the supposed eastern Boundary of New England; To the East of this begins Aquâda [Acadia] or Nova Scotia; an incertain River St. Croix in the nominal Boundary. But as the French, according to their Mode of taking Possession, always fixed a Cross in every River they came to, almost every River on this Coast of Sagadahoc has in its Turn been deemed by them La Riviere de St. Croix. Under Equivocation of this general Appellative they have amused our

---

Jobber, whose Business it is to clear the Casting-room, has 3£ per Month. Two Mine Pounders, One Limestone Pounder, each 3£ 10s. per Month. Two Fillers at 4£ per Month. One Banksman at 3£ per Month. Two Coal-stockers 6d. a Load. Clerk 45£ per Ann. Carpenter 60£ per Ann. Blacksmith 40£ per Ann. One Ore-burner 3£ per Month. Two Men, Two Waggons, and Four Horses for fetching Lime-stone and Wood, and splitting Ditto.

The Furnace when in good Order makes 22 Tons of Pigs a Week, but generally on an Average 20 Tons.

The Forge; making Bar iron from the Pigs 4£ per Ton, or 2£ 5s. per Ton for making from the Pigs into Anchories, and 1£ 15s. from Anchories to Bars. They find the most profitable Way of working in the Forge is to keep Two Fires, One for refining, and One for Drawing. When the Forge is in Order and full Work, they can make 500 Weight of Anchories in a Day at each refining Fire, and 1000 Weight for Bar-iron. To make a Ton of Bar-iron it requires 2700 Weight of Pigs, and expends Four Load and an Half of Coals. The Iron in Pigs sell in New York at 8£ Currency, and 6£ Sterling per Ton. Bar-Iron from 24£ to 26£ New York Currency per Ton.

N.B. These Observations were noted down in 1754, the Sums are in Currency, which was as 4 to 7 in its Proportion to Sterling.

Ancram Works. Philip Livingston erected Ancram Iron Works, consisting of a furnace and a forge. He used the rich ores from his newly discovered mines in Salisbury as well as New York ores. Ores were discovered on a tract of land granted by the Colony to Yale College. The tract was transferred in 1734 to Philip Livingston who built a blast furnace at Lime Rock. Arthur Cecil Bining, *British Regulations of the Colonial Iron Industry*. Ph. D. Thesis, University of Pennsylvania (Philadelphia, 1933), pp. 23-24.—Ed.

[1]Schoodic, named St. Croix River in the Treaties of 1783 and 1842. Read Israel Washburn's "The North Eastern Boundary," in the Maine Historical Society *Collections* (1st series, Portland, The Society, 1831-87), VIII, 3-106.

Negotiators on every Occasion. I am ashamed but surprised that I must here add to the foregoing remark that the adroitness of the Americans taking advantage of the ignorance of our Minister and Negotiators at the late treaty of peace,[1] was in a more special manner exemplified in the settling the boundary, in this part, between the British & the American Empires. By which The Massachusetts State has gained a large Tract of fine land bordering on Passam-aquaâda [Passamaquoddy] bay: as also the Bay, & the Island Grand Manan & several lesser Islands.[2]

The Source of Pasam-Aquâda [Passamaquoddy][3] River is formed by a Succession of Lakes[4] and Swamps running East 42 Miles; it then takes the Form of a River and runs East North East Eight Miles and an Half; then South and by East 12 Miles; then makes a Bend of about 10 Miles Course, running round by South, till it returns to the same Parallel at the Distance Five miles and an Half East; it turns then to the South, and here are the great Falls where Marine Navigation ends; hence it runs South East Six Miles, and then South and by East Six more to its Mouth.

In and off Pasam-Aquâda [Passamaquoddy] Bay are many fine Islands, as Grand Manán.

All the Land lying between Pasam-Aquâda [Passamaquoddy] and Penobskaëg [Penobscot] is White-Pine Land, a strong moist Soil, with some Mixture of Oaks, White Ash, Birch, and other Trees, and in the upper Inland Parts has almost generally Beech Ridges.

Mount Desert is a little Island of very high Land, which being B a 5 covered on the South with a String of little Islands forms a very fine and safe Harbour. The Entrance is from the Eastward; I went into it in my own Province 20 Gun Ship, the King George,[5] and found sufficient Depth; however there is a Middle Ground at the Entrance, of which the Navigator must take Cognizance.

[1]Definitive treaty of peace, signed at Paris, the third day of September, 1783.

[2]Massachusetts Second Charter, dated Oct. 7th, 1691 gave the colony "all islands and islets lying within 10 leagues directly opposite to the main land" within the boundaries set by the Charter. By the Treaty of Peace, Sept. 3rd, 1783 the United States gained all islands "within twenty leagues of any Part of the Shores of the United States." However the boundary line between British and American territory in North America was not set finally until the Webster-Ashburton Treaty, 1842. By the terms of this Treaty Great Britain gained over 571,570 acres of land in excess of the award by the Treaty of Ghent, 1814. For a full discussion on this subject read "The Webster-Ashburton Treaty," *U.S. Treaties, etc.* edited by Hunter Miller (Washington, U.S. Gov't. printing office, 1934), IV, Doc. 99.

[3]St. Croix River.

[4]North, Grand, and Chiputneticook Lakes.

[5]"The King George was a 20 Gun Ship fitted out at the Expense of my Province Massachusetts bay & Commissioned by me, Cap.t Benj Hollowell Commander under my Commission." [Thomas Pownall]. This is a holograph note written on verso of pen sketch of Penobscot Bay by Thomas Pownall in 1769. See reproduction, frontispiece.

Behind this Island, which lies near the Shore, is a very large Opening that forms the Mouth or Bay[1] of Mount Desert River.[2]

To the East of this the Land advances South in Form of a Promontory, on the Front of which are Four large Islands and a Multitude of little ones; the large ones are, Deer Island, the Two Foxes Islands,[3] and Holt Island;[4] these, with the Promontory, form the East Side of Penôbskeäg [Penobscot] Bay.

Monhagon [Monhegan] Island, which lies between Three and Four Leagues South South West from Duck Harbour,[5] may be said to form the West Point of Penôbskeäg [Penobscot] Bay; Duck Harbour forms the South Point of the West Side on the main Land; hence the Shore trends North East Five Miles to Terrant's [Tenants] Harbour; the Land a pretty high Ridge; hence North North East Four Miles, then rounding Four Miles more so as to make a North Course.

Here the Ridges of the Land rise higher and continue to range hence about Three Miles and a Half to Owl's Head, so called from a Bluff Point which the Sailors imagine to bear some Resemblance to an Owl's Head; round this Point is Madom-bédeäg [Medomak] Bay, about Two Miles and Half broad, lying at the Foot of Madom-bédeäg [Medomak] Hill,[6] a high Ridge which goes off North: Behind this is another Ridge running further North, called Magunticoog [Meduncook];[7] about here begins the South Point of an Island, which lies Length-ways in the Middle of the Bay, is about 12 Miles long, and is called Long Island: The North Point, from the Shape in which it makes from Sea exactly resembling a Turtle, we called Turtle Head.[8] If I had, as I once intended annexed any Drawings to this Description, I should here have given Sections of Out-lines of the Forms of all the Ranges and Heads as they present themselves to the Eye out at Sea. From the North East Point of Madombédeäg [Medomak] the Shore trends North East and by North, about 15 Miles to Pasaôumkeäg (or Pumpking) Point, which forms the West Point of the Mouth of Penôbskeäg [Penobscot] River, as Peguoit or Cape Razier [Rosier] does the Eastern. The River at this Entrance is about point blank Shot over.[9]

Passing between these Two Points, one finds the River opening on

---

[1]Present Union Bay.

[2]Present Union River.

[3]Present Vinalhaven. William D. Williamson. *The History of the State of Maine* ... (Hallowell, Maine, Glazier, Masters & Co., 1832), I, 72.

[4]Present Isle au Haut. *Ibid.*, I, 74.

[5]Probably present Port Clyde.

[6]Camden Mountains. Williamson, *op. cit.*, I, 95.

[7]Probably a ridge in the Camden Mountains.

[8]Not identified.

[9]Maine Historical Society, *op. cit.*, V, 380.

the West into a circular Bay; to the East is another Bay, called, by the French, Pentagoät or Pentooskeäg [Penobscot],[1] where I saw the Ruins of a French Settlement,[2] which from the Scite and Nature of the Houses, and the Remains of Fields and Orchards, had been once a pleasant Habitation; one's Heart felt Sorrow that it had ever been destroyed.

There is a large Island at the Entrance into the Channel of the River above this broad Part, called Bethune Island; the Land is pretty high on each Side the River. As one approaches to the Falls one sees on the North very high Hills, which, to distinguish from the Lesser ones, we call Mountains. At 35 Miles above the Mouth the River tumbles for near two Miles over Falls[3] which totally put a Stop to all Marine Navigation: About Two Miles North West above these are other Falls.

The Courses up the River from the Mouth to the Falls are as follow: From Peguoit N. 3 Miles, N. and by E. 2, N.W. and by N. 2, N.W. 8, N.N.E. 4½, N. 2, N.W. and by N. 1½, and N. by W. 12. Total 35.

In the Front of the Falls there runs across the River a Row of pointed Rocks,[4] which at Low Water appear like the Pickets across the River; I got over these at High Water in a large armed Sloop, the Massachuset[ts], and stuck upon a round smooth Rock in the Middle of the River while the Tide was running down Three Knots. Capt. HOLLOWELL,[5] who commanded the King George, and who went up the River with me, by running the Men from Side to Side of the Sloop, so as to give her a great Roll, rolled her off, and she tumbled off like a Seal into the Water. It was well that he was so quick in his Resource, and so ready in executing it, for soon after at Low Water this Rock stood more than a Fathom above the Water, the Tide running down Five Knots.

For Nine Miles above the Falls the River puts on the Appearance of a Lake Two Miles wide, lying North and South, and being full of Islands: The old Penôbsket Indian Town[6] stood at the Bottom of this, at the Head of the Falls. Here, and below on the western Banks of the River, were old worn-out clear Fields, extending Four or Five Miles.

[1]The French spelled Penobscot more than fifty different ways. Maine Historical Society, *ibid.*, VII, 3.

[2]The French settlement founded by Baron de St. Castine in 1677. Maine Historical Society, *ibid.*, p. 385 n. On the present site of Castine, Maine.

[3]Probably Treats Falls, Bangor, Maine. Federal Writers' Project. Maine, . . . *Maine, a Guide 'Down East'* (Boston, Houghton, Mifflin Co., 1937), p. 130.

[4]Champlain's rocks, off the foot of Newbury Street, Bangor, Maine. Maine Historical Society, *op. cit.*, VII, 6.

[5]Captain Benjamin Hallowell (1725-1799), a landed proprietor of the Kennebec Region. As a loyalist he was banished in 1778, and his entire estate was confiscated. Massachusetts Historical Society, *Proceedings* . . . (Boston, The Society, 1791-date), LXIII (October, 1929-June, 1932), 260.

[6]On the present site of Old Town, Maine.

Six Miles higher up North, where Passadâmkeäg [Passadumkeag] River comes in from the East, is Passadâmkeäg [Passadumkeag] Indian Town,[1] to which Site the Penôbskeägs [Penobscots] were removed. About Two Miles and Half above this One meets another Fork of Two Branches,[2] One comes South East about 11 Miles from Sebaëg [Sebec][3] Pond, the main One[4] from the North Two Miles. East North East Six Miles higher is Ma-âda-ôuamkeäg [Mattawamkeag] Indian Town, the River comes to this Place South East about 16 Miles from some Ponds whence it takes its Source.

This River and District of Penobskeäg [Penobscot] remained at the time of the last War in Possession of the Natives[5] who had put themselves and lived under the Patronage and Authority of the French, and were governed by a Jesuit as their Priest and Superintendant:[6] In the Year 1759 when we were in open War with the Indians as well as French, the Governor[7] of Massachuset[ts] took Possession of it by armed Force, which gives a title that the Indians distinctly understand & always acquiesce in: To maintain this Title & Possession He built a Fort, which the People of the Province were pleased to call FORT POWNALL,[8] and which, to all Purposes wanted, held command in it. This was the last River and District on the North American Coast unpossessed, and which thus taken completed the British Possession of that Coast.

St. George's River

At the Distance of about Two Leagues West-northerly is the Mouth of St. George's River, near a Mile wide at the Mouth; in going up to the Bason at the Forks, where stood Fort St. George,[9] it is a strait Course North East and by North about 16 Miles, the Land on each Side high; at Three Miles from the Mouth you pass the First Narrows, made so by

[1]On present site of Passadumkeag, Maine.

[2]At Howland, Maine, the Piscataquis River flows from the east into the Penobscot.

[3]The Sebec River, which has its source in Sebec Lake, flows into the Piscataquis.

[4]Pleasant River. Although the author states this is the main river of the forked branch of the Penobscot, modern maps show the Pleasant River is a small tributary of the Piscataquis.

[5]The Abnaki Indians were in sympathy with the French from early times to the end of French power in North America. This attachment was due chiefly to the influence of the French Missionaries. Frederick W. Hodge, ed., *Handbook of American Indians North of Mexico* (Washington, Government Printing Office, 1907), I, 2-5.

[6]Father Sebastian Ralé (Rasle) (1657-1724), massacred by the English at Norridgewock in 1724, was the missionary priest most hated by the English and best loved by the Abnaki Indians. Read Pierre F. X. de Charlevoix, *History and General Description of New France translated . . . by John Gilmary Shea* (New York, John Gilmary Shea, 1871), V, 272-282.

[7]Thomas Pownall, governor of Massachusetts, 1757-60.

[8]"In the present town of Prospect [Maine] at the mouth of Penobscot River." Maine Historical Society, *op. cit.*, V, 377n.

[9]Fort Georges, built in 1719-20 by the proprietors of the Waldo Patent and made a public garrison soon after this date. On the present site of Thomaston, Maine. Maine Historical Society, *op. cit.*, V, 367n.

the Points of the high Land running in; above this the River is wide again, and a Cove runs up on the Right Hand North East and by East Four Miles in Length, reckoned from the Narrows; from the Head of this Cove there is a Portage over the Neck to Terrant's [Tenants] Harbour; from the Lower Narrows to the Upper like Narrows is Seven Miles and an Half, from thence to the Bason Four Miles and an Half; from the Entrance of this up to the Fort One Mile. The Breadth of this Bason is nearly Two Miles, from hence there is an Indian Path and Portage of about a Mile to a little Creek which falls into Pen-ôb-skeäg [Penobscot] Bay. The Fort George[s] stands upon a Point of Land in the Forks between Two Branches of this River, the one coming from Two Ponds on Ma-adombedeäg [Medomak] Hill[1] about Six Miles, at a Mile and Three Quarters above the Fort is obstructed by the Falls; The other Branch at 10 Miles above the Fort hath Falls.

Five Miles West of [St.] George's River is Broad Bay; a Number of Islands lie in the Front of all this Coast, so that Sloops and small Vessels may sail within them as if in a covered Harbour. It would become tedious to give a List of all; the Principal beginning from the West Point of Pen-ôb-skeäg [Penobscot] Bay are, Metin-eäg [Metinic], Monhêgan, Duck Island, Planting Island, Crooked Sand, Leveret's Island; Ma-adom-côg off Point Pleasant, the West Point of [St.] George's River, Hatchet Island, Muscongus Island, Hog Island, and Oar Island; the Five last are in Broad Bay and in the Mouth of the Muscongus River.[2] — Broad Bay C a 4

Broad Bay runs up 10 Miles, and carries a Breadth from Two Miles to One Mile and a Half: Two Branches fall into it at the Head, the East one is stopped by a Fall at Two Miles and a Quarter, called Ma-adamëg[3] Falls: The other at Five Miles has Falls, called Cheôuanasäg.[4] — C a 4

There are Three little Rivers betwixt Broad Bay and Kenebaëg [Kennebec] River, Pemequid [Pemaquid], Damariscotta, and Sheepscut [Sheepcot], all having Falls on them.

As the River KENEBAEG [Kennebec] has been now rendered famous as a Pass, by a March[5] of some Spirit and Enterprize made by the Americans, following its Course, across the Land to St. Lawrence or Canada River, I shall here give a more particular and detailed Description of it than I should otherwise have entered into. — A B C a 3 Kenebaëg River

[1]Camden Mountains.
[2]Planting, Crooked Sand, Leveret's, Ma-adom-côg and Hatchet Islands are not indicated on modern maps or on *Topographic sheets* of the U.S. Geological Survey.
[3]Not identified.
[4]Not identified.
[5]Benedict Arnold's expedition against Quebec, 1775.

This River, in the Year 1754 and 1755, was talked of as a Rout by which an Army might pass, the best and shortest Way to attack Canada and Quebec. The Rout was supposed to be by an Indian Path and Carrying-place, which going off from Kenebaëg [Kennebec] about Eight or 10 Miles above Noridgewaëg [Norridgewock], in a North West Course of Six or Seven Miles, came to a Pond which issued into the River Chaudiere. Some such Information had been given to Government; it was of the utmost Importance that Government should not be misled. In the Year 1756, I had an Opportunity of inquiring into this Matter by scrutinizing a Journal[1] given to me, and signed by Capt. Hobbs[2] and Lieut. Kenedy,[3] and by examining the Journalists themselves as to the Authority of the Particulars. I found enough to be convinced that this supposed Pass was mere Conjecture, taken upon trust of BARTHOLEMON [Bartholemew][4] an Indian, who was found to be false and a Spy, and was in 1755 shot by our own People as he was attempting to desert. Government therefore was early cautioned against this Misinformation. When I was Governor of the Province of Massachuset's Bay, I had this Rout particularly investigated, by Ensign Howard[5] a Country Surveyor, under the Direction of Capt. Nicholls [Nickels][6] who commanded at Fort Frederick.[7] Instead of a short Pass of some Eight or 10 Miles of easy Portage, this Indian Path turned out to be a Rout, on a Line as the Bird flies, of near 50 Miles over Land, *impracticable to an Army that hath a Train of Artillery and heavy Baggage.* It appeared however that (although a difficult and very laborious Rout) it was practicable to any Body of Men who should go light armed, as a

[1] "Captain Hobbs and Lieut. Kennedy's Account of the River Kennebeck and Carrying Place to the River Chaudiere, Septemb[r] 17th 1756." Manuscript copy in Henry E. Huntington Library, LO 1824.

[2] Captain Humphrey Hobbs, the "Fighting Deacon" of Souhegan [Amherst], N.H., served in King George's War, in the Beauséjour campaign in Acadia in 1755, in John Winslow's expedition to the Kennebec River to build Fort Halifax in 1754; also as captain of a company of Rangers raised by Governor Shirley in 1756. Captain Hobbs died of smallpox early in 1757. Burt Garfield Loescher, *The History of Rogers Rangers* . . . , (San Francisco [the author] 1946), I, 101-03, 421.

[3] Lieutenant Samuel Kennedy, noted surveyor for Capt. John Winslow on the Kennebec in 1754 and lieutenant in Captain Thomas Speakman's regiment of Rangers. *Ibid.*, pp. 102-03. Lieutenant Kennedy was killed in the action near Ticonderoga January

21, 1757. Caleb Stark, *Memoir and Official Correspondence of General John Stark* . . . (Concord, G. Parker Lyon, 1860), p. 413.

[4] While acting as a guide to Governor Shirley on his trip to Oswego, this Indian, Bartholomew, attempted to desert and was shot. Capt. Hobbs and Lieut. Kennedy's Account . . . LO 1824, *op. cit.*

[5] Sergeant John Howard of Captain Humphrey Hobbs' Rangers was killed in the action near Ticonderoga January 21, 1757. Stark, *op. cit.*, p. 413.

[6] Capt. Alexander Nickels. A prominent man of New Castle and Pemaquid near Pemaquid Fort. Nickels was with Governor Pownall on his trip to Penobscot (1759) and afterwards commanded a company at Fort Pownall. William Otis Sawtelle, "Thomas Pownall," in Massachusetts Historical Society, *Proceedings, op. cit.*, LXIII, 254n, 268n, 274.

[7] On the east bank of the Pemaquid River. Also known as Fort William Henry and Fort George. Williamson, *op. cit.*, I, 57.

Scouting Party, either to reconnoitre or to break up Settlements. The Sort of March which Arnold[1] and his People experienced, has confirmed this Account given 17 or 18 Years ago. After taking Possession of the Penobskaëg [Penobscot] Country, I had all the eastern Branches of this River[2] traced to their Sources, and the Communications between them and the Waters of Penobskaëg [Penobscot] scrutinized by constant Scouting Parties. A general Map which I had plotted down from these Routs and Journals, together with Surveys of the Rivers, is the Authority to this Map in these Parts.

This River Kenebaëg [Kennebec], to begin from its principal Branch,[3] may be described as rising on the Height of the Land in North Lat. 45° 20′, and in East Longitude, from Philadelphia, 5° 10′ or there- A a 3 abouts; its Source is from a little Pond, and the first Courses of its Birth a Succession of Ponds or drowned Lands, Swamps, and Falls. Its first general Course is 30 Miles South East, it then makes a great Bow whose String (lying East and by South and West and by North) is 12 Miles. It then runs North-easterly Nine Miles and an Half, and then tumbling over Falls North East 10 Miles, joins the North Branch.[4] The North Branch is said (I speak not here from the same Degree of Authority) to arise in and issue from a little Pond[5] about 16 Miles North of this Crotch,[6] from whence (it is likewise said) there is a Carrying-place of 13 or 14 Miles to an eastern Branch of the Chaudiere River. This was represented to me as the shortest Rout to Canada, but I do not find in my Journals that I have set this down as confirmed or sufficiently authenticated. After these Two Branches join, they run South-easterly about Three Miles, when a small River tumbling over Falls, and running between high perpendicular rocky Banks for Seven Miles and an Half, and issuing from a great Pond full of Islands, called Sebaïm [Sebec],[7] or by some such Name, North East 12 Miles distant comes into the Kenebaëg [Kennebec]. This Stream is impracticable for any Navigation at these Falls, but there is a Carrying-place on the East Side from a Cove to the Head of the Falls. From the Junction of this Stream the River has its Course South-westerly 12 Miles, when one comes to the Place whence the Indian Path goes off to the North West, as shall be hereafter de-

---

[1]Benedict Arnold (1741-1801), see *note* 5, p. 73.
[2]The Chaudiere.
[3]Dead River. Williamson, *op. cit.*, I, 47.
[4]North Branch of the Kennebec. Williamson, *op. cit.*, I, 47.
[5]Moosehead Lake.
[6]Mouth of Dead River known as The Forks. Williamson, *op. cit.*, I, 13, 47.

[7][Pownall's note] From this Lake there is a Communication by a short Portage to the One of the Sources of Penobskaeg, and I have been told with an eastern Branch of Chaudiere also; but I do not give this last as from Authority.

scribed. Hence with many Windings the River keeps its southern Course to Noridgewaëg [Norridgewock], where it has the Appearance of a Lake full of Islands. On the Banks of this was the Indian Dwelling of the Tribe of that Name. A little below are the Falls.[1] The River then runs in a winding Course Five Miles East, and at the Point[2] where it turns again South the River Wesseronsaëg [Wesserunsett][3] comes in from the North East. Keeping on the same Course 12 or 14 Miles more it comes to Tachonaëg [Ticonic] Falls,[4] below which Sebastoocoog [Sebasticook] comes into it, from a Pond[5] bearing North East, and distant about 25 Miles: In the Fork between these Two Streams Mr. Shirley[6] built Fort Halifax.[7] From hence the River runs in a Course South-westerly 17 Miles to Cushnoog;[8] here is a little Blockhouse called Fort Western.[9] The Fall at Cushnoog is the Head of Tide Water; Sloops of 90 Tons Burthen come up hither from Sea, which, if the River is reckoned to Small Point, is about 30 Miles distant. This River is in general narrow, and continued between high Banks, it runs through a ridgy rather than hilly Country; about Five or Six Miles below Cushnoog[10] the Stream Cobessiconti [Cobbessecontee] comes in from the West, running out of a Pond of the same Name, full of Islands, lying Five Miles West of Kenebaëg [Kennebec]. The River in the same Course, Distance about Eight or Nine Miles lower, comes to Swan Island; just above which, on a Point on the West Side of the River, is a Blockhouse called Richmond Fort;[11] from this Point to the North Point of Merry-meeting Bay is Four Miles.

This Bay, so called from some Event interesting to the First Adventurers, is formed by the Junction of the River Sagadahoc[12] (Ammerescoggin or Pejepschaëg) with the River Kenebaëg [Kennebec].

To describe next the River Kenebaëg [Kennebec] as a Rout[13] to Quebeck [Quebec], in the first Place the Reader has been told that Sloops of 90 Tons Burthen can go up to Cushnoog Falls, about 30 Miles from

[1]Norridgewock Falls just above the mouth of Sandy River, Maine. Williamson, *op. cit.*, I, 49.

[2]Skowhegan, Maine.

[3]Wesserunsett River flows through Cornville from the north into the Kennebec at Skowhegan. Williamson, *op. cit.*, I, 49.

[4]Ticonic, also spelled *Taconic*. At Waterville, Maine.

[5]Sebasticook Lake.

[6]William Shirley (1693-1771), Governor of Massachusetts from 1741 to 1757.

[7]Built in 1754 on the eastern bank of the Kennebec. Present site of Winslow, Maine, which is opposite the city of Waterville.

[8]Present site, Augusta, Maine. Williamson, *op. cit.*, II, 301.

[9]Built by the Plymouth Company in 1754. *Ibid.*, I, 50.

[10]Augusta.

[11]A very old fortification on the western side of the Kennebec nearly opposite the upper end of Swan Island. Williamson, *op. cit.*, I, 51.

[12]Androscoggin River.

[13]Here the author follows closely Arnold's march to Quebec in 1775. For a full account read William Allen's "Account of Arnold's Expedition," in Maine Historical Society, *op. cit.*, I, 499-532.

Small Point. From thence to Fort Hallifax [Halifax], at Tackonic [Ticonic] Falls, 17 Miles, is a Waggon Road.[1] Thence a certain Degree of Navigation for Bateaux takes Place, which is interrupted by Falls[2] and Rapids below Noridgewaëg [Norridgewock], at which Places all Baggage must be again carried over Land, where a Waggon Road might be made between the Hills and the River. Half a Mile above Noridgewaëg [Norridgewock] there is a long sharp Fall,[3] but that a good Waggon Road might be made quite up to the *Great Carrying-place*.[4] Hence the Indian Path goes off West from the River over Land about Four Miles and an Half to a Pond about Three Quarters of a Mile long; a good Waggon Road might be made here: This First Pond has been found to issue its Waters into the Kenebaëg [Kennebec]. Hence the Path runs over the like Grounds West-northerly about a Mile, and comes to a Second Pond, this has been found to issue its Waters into Sagadahoc[5] River. Hence over the like Land, and in the same Course about a Mile more, it comes to a Third Pond,[6] which issuing its Waters to the North, and falling into a River which runs North-easterly, gave rise to the Misinformation that here went the Rout to Canada by Chaudiere; but the River which this Pond empties itself into is found to be the Kenebaëg [Kennebec], which in this Place runs North-easterly; from this Pond the Path runs West-northerly near Four Miles, and strikes the southermost Bend of this main Branch of Kenebaëg [Kennebec]; up this Stream there may be an imperfect Navigation for Indians, and Traders, or Hunters, somewhat better in the Time of Freshes, but both the Navigation is bad and the travelling between high Ranges of Mountains, and in swampy boggy Vales very troublesome to Individuals, very arduous, and almost impracticable to Bodies of Men. When you get higher towards the Source of the River, you come to a Chain of Ponds which makes the Navigation better, but this is interrupted with Falls. From the Head of the River to a little Stream which falls into Agamuntaëg Pond,[7] is a Carrying-place of about Four Miles. That is the Indian Carrying-place, but I apprehend that if a Body of Men would transport any Baggage which requires a Depth of

[1]In 1754 Governor Shirley ordered a wagon road to be made from Fort Western (Augusta) to Fort Halifax. Williamson, *op. cit.*, II, 301.

[2]Skowhegan Falls. *Ibid.*, I, 49.

[3]Norridgewock Falls. Maine Historical Society, *op. cit.*, I, 459.

[4]This is a twelve mile portage from the Kennebec River above Cariotunk Falls to the Dead River. This portage was made in preference to ascending the Kennebec twenty miles to the mouth of the Dead River and then up the Dead River through shallows and rapids, a total distance over fifty miles. Maine Historical Society, *op. cit.*, I, 505.

[5]Androscoggin.

[6][Pownall's note] The Pond, which was falsly said to be the Head of the River Chaudiere, and so set down in a Map published in 1754, has a Mark set upon it in this Map.

[7]Lake Megantic, the source of the Chaudiere River.

Water before it can be embarked, the Portage must be to, or near to, the Lake, about 10 Miles. This Lake[1] is the Head of Chaudiere River, and is about 40 Miles above the present Settlements of the Canadians.

The River *Sagadahock*,[2] Ammerescoggin, or Pejepschaëg, which properly speaking is but the main western Branch of Kenebaëg [Kennebec], rises in Lat. 44° 50′ North-easterly of the White Hills in New Hampshire, not far from the Head of Connecticut River; it has its Source in a Lake called Umbagoog [Umbagog]. Two or Three other lesser Streams[3] issuing from little Ponds to the East of this join it after it has run South about 26 Miles; it then turns East North East 60 Miles, and meets a Second main Source[4] rising from a Lake about 19 Miles West of Noridgewaëg [Norridgewock]. These Two Streams after the Western One has run about 86 Miles East South East, and the Eastern One about 34 Miles South join;[5] and hence the River runs South 40 Miles. In this Course it runs within Two Miles of the Sea Coast, but then turns short about North and runs over a Fall called Pejepskaëg [Pejepscot][6] into Merry-meeting Bay. In this Bay Kenebaëg [Kennebec] and this River unite, this loses its Name, and the River Kenebaëg [Kennebec] continues its South Course about Five or Six Miles to its Mouth, in which are two pretty large Islands, Arrôsaëg [Arrowsic] and Reskêgon.[7] If *Small-point* be reckoned to be the Mouth of the River, instead of Five or Six it is 16 or 17 Miles from Merry-meeting Bay to its Mouth. Round *Small-point* to the East is a deep Bay with a large Island in it called Sebasedâgon [Sebascodegan],[8] included between Long-reach and Merriconaëg Neck. This Neck is about 11 Miles long, and about Three Quarters of a Mile broad. It was in my Time incorporated into a District, and I named it *Harpswell*, from the Seat of my old Friend Mr. Wichcot of Lincolnshire, where I had spent many a happy Holiday when a School-boy. This became a very considerable Settlement last War; it had 84 taxable Polls in it, a Company of Militia, and paid besides Fifty Pounds per Ann. to the Province Tax.

Casco Bay: This Bay, if reckoned from Cape Elizabeth to Small Point, is 25 Miles wide, and about 14 deep; it is a most beautiful Bay, full of little Islands. Brunswick stands at the North East Cove of it,

[1]Lake Megantic.
[2]Androscoggin, Maine.
[3]Sunday, Bear, and Ellis Rivers, Maine.
[4]Swift River, Maine.
[5]At Rumford, Maine.
[6]Falls of the Androscoggin, Brunswick, Maine.

Federal Writers' Project. Maine, *op. cit.*, p. 144.
[7]Island of Georgetown formerly Parker's Island. Federal Writers' Project. Maine, *op. cit.*, p. 263. Parker's Island was originally Eraskohegan [Reskegon]. Williamson, *op. cit.*, I, 53.
[8]Great Island, known locally as East Harpswell. Federal Writers' Project. Maine, *op. cit.*, p. 257.

and Falmouth,[1] a sweet pretty Town, on a most delightful Scite, on a hilly Neck of Land at the South West End of it. As this is now no more, I will from my Journal describe what Falmouth was in 1759, when I was there: The Township consisted of 600 Families settled in Three Parishes, New Casco, Sapoodock, and Stroud Water: The Body of the Town sat elevated on a Neck of Land stretching out East from Stroud Water, and forming a kind of Mole to a little Cove within it. This Part consisted of a Church and Townhouse (this being a Country Town) and about 112 Houses. This Town was laid out in Lots forming Two Streets parallel to the Harbour, and Five at right Angles to them: Inhabitants were settling and building fast on these Lots. The Harbour is extremely fine, large, and commodious; Masts and Naval Stores were loaded here. There was much Trade carried from hence directly to the West Indies in Lumber, Boards, Staves, and Fish of the small Kind. Many Ships were also built here. Royal's [Royale's] River runs into the Bay at North Yarmouth, and the Presumskeag [Presumpscot] rising in Great Tobago [Sebago] Pond runs into it at New Casco. Stroud Water running East on the Back of the Scite of Falmouth, falls also into this Bay South of Falmouth. None of these Rivers are capable of marine Navigation to any Length, in most it is stopped by Falls.

Rounding Cape Elizabeth to the South West, and between that Point and the East Point of Winter Harbour,[2] is Scarborough Bay, into which Two or Three inconsiderable Streamlets run. C a 2

Rounding this last Point and Southak's Isles,[3] you come to Winter Harbour and Saco Bay, contained within this Point and Cape Porpoise.

The River Saco has Two principal Sources, one springs from the Ossipee Pond near Ossipee Hills, the other rises from the Notch amidst the White Hills; the one called Ossipee, the other Pigwaket River. These soon unite, and the River, keeping in general a South-eastern Course for about 60 or 70 Miles, runs between Scarborough and Biddiford Townships into Saco Bay by Winter Harbour: Marine Navigation is stopped in this River very near the Mouth of it by Saco Falls. Saco River

Rounding Cape Porpoise is Well's Bay, contained within this Cape and Cape Nedock [Neddick] or Bald-head [Cliffs]. Into this runs Kenebunk River, which has its Source in the Northernmost of Lovels [Lovewell's] Ponds in Lat. 43° 53'.

---

[1]Named Portland, July 4, 1786. Federal Writers' Project. Maine, *op. cit.*, p. 167.

[2]Biddiford Pool. Williamson, *op. cit.*, I, 26-27.

[3]Wood and Negro Islands. In 1808 a lighthouse was built on Wood Island. Williamson, *ibid.*, I, 27. *Wood Island Light* is in Biddiford Pool. Federal Writers' Project. Maine, *op. cit.*, p. 256.

Between Cape Nedock [Neddick] and Piscatua [Piscataqua] River is York Harbour.

Piscatua [Piscataqua] River being the Boundary between the eastern Division of the Massachuset[ts] and New Hampshire Province, I will here, before I proceed further, give such an Account as I am enabled to do with any Degree of Certainty, of the Ranges of the Hills in these Parts.

As I kept up, during the last War,[1] a constant Line of Scouting Parties on the Back of the Settlements in these Parts, and as I gave Instructions amongst other Points for their marking the Nature of the Land; and as these Scouts, after I took Possession of the Penobsceäg [Penobscot] Country, extended to that River, the Returns of the Officers did, in some small Degree, answer my Design as to this Point. I may state in general that the Parts towards the Coasts are White Pine Land. The upper or interior Parts Oak, with high Chesnut Ridges, having Birch in the Vales; these Vales are almost intirely occupied by Swamps, Ponds, and little Lakes. There is a Communication between Penobsceäg [Penobscot] and Kenebek [Kennebec] Rivers, with very short Portages from Fort Pownall[2] to Fort Hallifax [Halifax], by a Succession of Ponds and by Sebastoocoog [Sebasticook] River. There is a like Communication of a still shorter Course between the Branches of these Rivers at their Heads. There is likewise a very easy Communication between the East Branches of Penobsceäg [Penobscot] and the Sources of Passamaquada[3] [Passamaquoddy] Rivers.

At the Back of York Township is a very high Peak called Agamanticoos [Agamenticus], from hence the Ridges of the Hills of these Parts range North East under various local Names.

The Ranges in York and Cumberland Counties trend to the Northward of North East, those in the County of Lincoln East of Kenebaëg [Kennebec] next the Coast do so likewise, but within Land they trend more and more to the East of North East. All the Heads of Kenebaëg [Kennebec], Penobskaëg [Penobscot], and Passam-aquâda [Passamaquoddy] River are on the Height of the Land running East North East.

Piscatua [Piscataqua] River is the only Port of the Province of New Hampshire; the Embouchure of this River for 10 Miles on one Course (reckoning this Course upwards as you enter it) North West, and then

---

[1]French and Indian War.
[2]Fort Pownall (1759-1775), built by Governor Pownall. For details read "Governor Pownall's Voyage from Boston to Penobscot River [1759]" in Maine Historical Society, *op. cit.*, V, 365-387. On the present site of Bangor, Maine.
[3]St. Croix River, Maine. See *note* 1, p. 68.

Five or Six Miles South into Little Bay and Exeter Bay,[1] has more the
Appearance of a deep Bay than a River; there is in the Mouth of it the
Island Newcastle, about a Mile and Half long and a Mile and Quarter
broad. It is navigable up the First Course for Ships of any Burthen,
for Nine Miles more up the West Branch to Exeter it is navigable for
Sloops; and also up the East Branch or main River to the Falls. This
River springs from the southernmost of Lovels [Lovewell's] Ponds, and
tumbling over several Falls under the Name of Salmon [Falls] River,
and running South and South-easterly falls into the broad Bay-like Part
called Piscatua [Piscataqua]. A Line drawn North from the Head of this
River till it meets the Boundary of the Province of Quebec, is the
Boundary betwixt the Two Provinces of Massachuset[ts] and New
Hampshire. In the Description which I gave of the Country at large, the
Province of New Hampshire as well as the western Division of Massachuset[ts] was included. I therefore here pass on to Merrimaeg, com-
monly called Merrymack [Merrimac], River in Massachuset[t]'s Bay
Province.

Continuing along the Coast South about 20 Miles, one comes to the
Mouth of Merrimack [Merrimac] River, about a Quarter of a Mile
broad; this River has Two principal Sources, the Western one is Squam
Pond[2] in Lat. 43° 50′: The Branch which runs from this South bears the
Indian Name Oûïïnaoûasset.[3] The eastern Branch springs in Oûini-
pissiocket [Winnepesaukee] or Richmond Lake; the Dimensions and
Shape of this are accurately laid down in the Map, and need no further
Explanation. Between these Two Ponds or Lakes run the Red Hills, so
called from their apparent Soil being chiefly of the red shelly Land
taken Notice of in other Parts of this Work. This Eastern or Merrimaeg
[Merrimac] Branch runs out of the West or South-western Bay of this
Lake. After Four or Five Miles tumbling over Falls it meets the western
Branch which joins it. Its Course from hence to the Line which divides
the South of New Hampshire, and the North of Massachuset[ts] is
South according to the Course of the Ridges amidst which it runs. There
are numberless Multitudes of Streams which run into it from the West,
all which rise from little Ponds and Swamps in the Vales of the great
middle Range. The first principal Stream which runs into it is the
Conticoog [Contoocook] Branch from the West. Just below where this
Stream enters, the River takes a turn East, and crosses through Pene-

D a 2
Merrimack
R^r

[1]Great Bay, New Hampshire.   [3]Pemigewassett River, New Hampshire.
[2]Squam Lake, New Hampshire.

coog Ridge,[1] a little Stream called Sowcoog [Soucook] comes in from the North. About two Miles below this, coming also from the North, from a Pond[2] South of Oûinipissiocket [Winnepesaukee] Lake, comes in the Suncoog [Suncook]; below this the River runs through or across a Ridge of Hills, which range North East, called Amaiskaeg [Amoskeag], and here are the Amaiskaeg [Amoskeag] Falls.[3] Just above the Narrows where the Pitch of the Fall commences, the Waters of the River, pent up, spread to the Breadth of Half a Mile; at the Narrows the Channel is about 40 Rod across. The Stream after tumbling over Ledges of Rocks, at the Narrows shoots away in Three principal rocky Channels and over craggy Ledges, twisted round to the South West; the Fall is above 26 Feet in the Perpendicular. The Banks at the Narrows are steep Rocks, those on the East Side 10 Feet high. After this the River continues its Course uninterrupted to Pantucket [Pawtucket][4] or Pantoocoog great Falls.[5] About Three Miles before it crosses the Division Line, the Nashawaeg [Nashua] River, which I took Notice of before as arising on the Sides of the Watchuset [Wachusett] and Wadadeag [Watatic] Peaks, runs into it from the West. At these Falls the River turns East, and crosses a Ridge before noticed, ranging North; above the Falls the River is wide, at the Falls narrow; the rocky Ledge of the Falls is Slate; there are Two Pitches and the Stream shoots with an inconceivable Rapidity between the upper and lower Pitch or Falls. The upper Fall is 10 Feet perpendicular; the *Rapid*, between the Two Falls descends also 10 Feet in the Course of its Shot; the latter has 24 Feet Fall in 65 Rods Course. The Whole of these Falls is above 40 Feet.

A little below these Falls, the Concord River, running North along the East Foot of this Pentoocog Ridge,[6] comes into the Merrimaëg [Merrimac]. There are two lesser Falls[7] between this and Haverhill; that at Haverhill stops Marine Navigation.

C a   The Country in which this River takes its Rise, as well as that through which it and its many attendant Waters run, is the great living Magazine of Masts and Naval Timber. These are floated down this River; but as very many fine Masts, and much valuable Timber, have

[1]Pawtuckaway Range. Federal Writers' Project. New Hampshire, *op. cit.*, p. 486.

[2]Suncook Pond.

[3]At Manchester, New Hampshire. Federal Writers' Project. New Hampshire, *op. cit.*, p. 54.

[4]At Lowell, Massachusetts.

[5][Pownall's note] Two large and principal Branches which come into the Merrimaeg [Merrimac] from the West (viz. The Piscatagnage [Piscataquog] and Sowhaeg or Sowhaegon [Souhegan] Rivers) are by an Oversight neglected to be inserted into the Text, which is supplied by their being mentioned in this Note. They run between Conticoog [Contoocook] and Nashawaeg [Nashua].

[6]Pawtuckaway Range.

[7]Mitchell's Falls. Massachusetts Historical Society, *Collections* . . . (2d series, Boston, John Eliot, 1814-23), IV, 121.

Pownall shows himself an intelligent and accurate observer of the contemporary colonial environment.

been lost or at least spoiled in shooting the Falls, especially those of Amiskeag [Amoskeag][1] and Pentoocoog [Pawtucket],[2] I had, when I was Governor, several Projects and Proposals laid before me, for making Channels at those Falls, through which the Masts and Timber might be shot without Danger. Besides the Difficulty of the Measures proposed, and my Apprehension of the Damage which the River must sustain elsewhere by being drained off too low if the Measure did succeed, I had other Reasons for not entering into them. While I saw the almost invaluable Interest of this great Naval Magazine neglected and abandoned to every Waste and Rapine, for Want of common Attention to Regulations which had been repeatedly proposed to Ministers, and which would have cost nothing but Attention, I did not wish to propose a Jobb that would have expended Four or Five Thousand Pounds, and not have mended the Matter. From Haverhill the River runs winding along a pleasant rich Vale of Intervals, and passing between Newberry [port] and Salisbury runs to Sea.

Ipswich is the next River Southward on this Coast; that I have already taken Notice of.

Hence rounding Cape Ann to the West, one enters the Massachusett's Bay and so by the Harbours, Cape Ann, Salem, and Marblehead, between Nahant and Alderton [Allerton] Points, into Boston Harbour. It is sufficient here to say, that this Harbour is full of Islands, threading amidst which the Ship Channel runs.

The reason which induced me to repress the description of the Harbour & of the Town of Boston, in the last Edition, no longer subsisting, I shall here insert it in this. The Entrance into the Great Bay Massachusett[s] is Between Cape Cod & Cape Ann an opening of about 40 or 50 miles. And from a Line drawn across this opening to the Entrance of Boston harbour by yᵉ Light house is about 30 miles.

In advancing to the Harbour of Boston upon the Starboard or right bow of the Ship lyes Nahant Point, on the Larboard, or left, Point Alderton [Allerton], at the distance of about 7 or 8 miles from each other. These are Generally Reckoned the two points of the Entrance of the Harbour; & are so taken to be, in a very silly Act of Parlt[3] of yᵉ 14th of yᵉ Reign of George yᵉ 3d enacted to *Disport this Harbour* of Boston, that is to disallow the Lading or Landing of Goods or Merchandise at the Town or within the Harbour of Boston. As Nahant Bay is very little if at all, used as an Anchoring and Broad Sound on account of the

[1]At Manchester, New Hampshire.
[2]At Lowell, Massachusetts.
[3]Boston Port Bill, Mar. 25, 1774.

Danger from the Shoals & Sunken rocks very seldom Navigated but by small Vessels, I always Considered Shirley Point & Point Alderton [Allerton] as the points of the Entrance of the Harbour. These Points are nearly Five Miles Distance From Each other. In a Direct Line Between these Points beginning From Point Shirley lye Deer Island Lovels [Lovells] Island Gallops [Gallups] & George's Island. In the Front of Lovels [Lovells] & George's Islands advanced towards yᵉ Bay lye several Rocks & Rocky Small Islands called the Breakers[1] on one of which called Becon Island[2] is a Lighthouse. Deer Island is of high elevated Ground with a cliff towards Point Shirley & is about a mile long & somewhat better than a quarter of a Mile Broad. The other three are oval & from a Quarter to a half a mile Diameter. Between Deer Island & Shirley Point is an Entrance for small Craft, called the Gutt.[3] Between Deer Island & the other three is the Entrance by Broad Sound.[4] But Between George's Island Point Alderton [Allerton] & Hull Is the real Entrance & Ship Channel. Passing by Hull & Pettocks [Peddock] Island on the left & George's Island on the right through a Channel about a Mile broad, You advance into a kind of bay surrounded with Islands called Nantasket Road. Point Alderton [Allerton] is high land toward the Channel & slopes off from it to a Beach by which it is join'd to the Main Land. Nantasket (on which is Hull) in like Manner is high & Bluff toward yᵉ Channel but slopes off at yᵉ side to a beach by which joins Point Alderton [Allerton]. It slopes off also behind. Georges Island, is elevated but not so high as yᵉ last mentioned. Nantasket Road may be described as a Circular Bay enclosed by Long Island Gallop's [Gallups] George's Pettocks [Peddocks] & Sunken[5] behind which is Hangmans Island; with a very small Island in the Center called Rainsford Island. A Center being fixed on this Island a Radius of about a mile will sweep Long-Island Gallops [Gallups] George's Petticks [Peddocks] & yᵉ Sunken Island, with soundings from 3½ to 9 fathom all round. This road is out of & to the left of the Ships Channel which runs betwixt Georges & Gallops [Gallups] Island on one hand & Lovels [Lovells] on the other rounding to the left by an Island almost washed away to nothing & hence called Nix's Mate[6] through which passage called the narrows the Channel carries a Depth of 5, 6, & 7 fathom water. Hence

[1]"The Brewsters" named for William Brewster, elder of the first church of Plymouth, Shurtleff, *op. cit.*, pp. 435-36.

[2]Light House Island, sometimes called Little Brewster. *Ibid.*, p. 436.

[3]Shirley Gut. *Ibid.*, p. 437.

[4]Broad Channel. *Ibid.*

[5]Sunken ledge near Quarantine Rocks. Shurtleff, *op. cit.*, p. 519.

[6]Marked by a monument in the Ships' Channel called the Narrows. *Ibid.*, pp. 538-39.

between the S point of Deer Island & N point of Long Island about three quarters of a mile distant from each other it runs by the North point of Spectacle Island for about a large league to Castle Island in a Channel rather confined by shoals on each side. There is a shoal called yᵉ Middle group to yᵉ right as you advance to Castle Island which is dry at low water. I take notice of this because on Castle Island, as part of yᵉ works of Castle William,[1] was a well placed Battery of heavy Cannon called Shirley's Battery which raked this Channel the whole way. Hence Passing Close under Castle Island on yᵉ left also between a middle ground to the right & the Shoals of Dorchester[2] again on yᵉ left & Governor's Island, Bird Island[3] & its shoals, & Noddles Island[4] on the right; The Channel leads up to the Town at three miles Distance.

As to the Nautical & Sailing Directions I should wish to referr to the Atlantick [Atlantic] Neptune[5] published by Mʳ Des Barres under the Directions of the Lords of the Admiralty & from Surveys made at a great expence paid by the publick, If I could settle which of the three several ones given to that work I could depend upon. They differr from each other in some bearings & distances And from yᵉ Printed Nautical Remarks and Directions in many instances. The second of Holland[6] mistakes the name of Spectacle Island calling it Hospital Island a name given, on account of a Lazarett or Pest house, to Rainsford's Island.

This Harbour is about 9 miles from the Light House at the Entrance to the Town & is from 3 & 4 & 5 miles wide in different parts from Point to point. It is rounded with several Points of Elevated Land that have the Appearance of Islands & has besides sett within it like a Clustered Jewell, 22 Islands most of them of elevated land with Bluff Points at their Ends & sloping sides. Some of them are a Mile, a Mile & ¾ a Mile & ½ by half a Mile in size, others a little round or oval ones of ¾ to ¼ of a mile diameter. These are all Cultivated as farms & some have very pretty Farmers Dwellings on them so as that any one of them would form a pleasing Landscape. Lett now the Reader prepare his mind to conceive what a most strikeing & even enchanting Picture The

[1]This was a fortification on Dorchester Neck, now South Boston. The fort was built between 1701 and 1703, burned by the British in 1776, repaired and renamed Fort Independence in 1797, converted into a prison in 1785, ceded to United States government in 1798, rebuilt 1801, and abandoned in 1880. Shurtleff, *op. cit.*, pp. 484-97; Federal Writers' Project. Massachusetts, . . . *Massachusetts; A Guide to its Places and People* . . . (Boston, Houghton Mifflin Co., 1937), p. 168 (Castle Island).

[2]South Boston.

[3]Bird Island has disappeared, only Bird Island Shoals remain. Shurtleff, *op. cit.*, pp. 442-43.

[4]East Boston. *Ibid.*, p. 443.

[5]*The Atlantic Neptune*, published for the use of the Royal Navy of Great Britain, by Joseph F. W. Des Barres . . . [London, 1774-1781] 3v.

[6]Samuel Holland. See *note* 4, p. 7.

Voyager sees as he Enters this Harbour & sails threading in amidst these beautifull Objects presenting themselves in perpetually varying shapes & varying groups releived by a thickly Inhabited Country on ye Sides of the Harbour. As He advances first up to Castle Island a high rising knol with its Fortress[1] on the Top & all its works on ye Sides forming a most Picturesque Foreground to the Town which Sitts on three hills[2] & therefore originally called Tremontane in all its pride of Populous Buisy Wealthy Inhabitancy at three miles distance. This Particular Scite of the Town Placed on a Peninsula a Group of three Hills forms with all its Shipping by its side & at its wharfs with all its Houses, Publick Buildings & Spired Churches grouped in sweeping lines around this hilly spott; a most peculiar & most pleasing view. I made Drawing of This View & Mr Marlow[3] painted me a picture from it. It makes one of the most pleasing Landschapes I ever saw.

The Shape of the Town is somewhat like a Cross the triangular Space however between the stem & branches especially ye South end filled up with Buildings, the Head at ye North End rounded. The triangles between the head & branches are form'd to the East & SE by an indenture of ye Water into the Line of the Town & to the West & NW by the Common, a Cove of ye Harbour, & the Water called the Mill pond.[4] The Length is nearly from the South End to ye North Ferry one mile & three quarters. The breadth from Barton Point[5] to the south side of Fort Hill[6] one mile one furlong.

The Town was originally built as all our old English Towns were of Timber-framed Houses. And although one of the first Laws one meets with in their Law book directs that all Houses after the Passing of that Act in 1692[7] shall be built of Brick or Stone, Many of ye Houses under the pretext of repairing instead new building, are still of the same framed materials. The Principal Part & Body of the Town is of Brick as are most of the Public Places of Worship. The Church called the King's Chapel[8] is of Stone or at least cased with stone. There are 16 of these Places of Worship Ten Churches of the Congregationalist; Three of the Church of England, most of these are very spacious & Commodious:

---

[1]Castle William.

[2]North to east, namely: Copps, Beacon, and Fort Hill.

[3]Probably William Marlow (1740-1813), English landscape painter.

[4]Early in the 1800's Mill Pond, covering about 50 acres in the vicinity of present Haymarket Square, was filled in and made available for building sites. Shurtleff, *op. cit.*, pp. 108-10.

[5]At Barton Street near North Station. *Ibid.*, p. 107.

[6]Fort Hill Square, Oliver and High Streets.

[7]Massachusetts (Colony) Statutes. *Acts and laws, passed by the Great and General Court or Assembly of their Majesties Province of Massachusetts Bay . . .* (Boston, Benjamin Harris, 1692), p. 4.

[8]Present King's Chapel built in 1749 at School and Tremont Streets. Shurtleff, *op. cit.*, p. 195.

There are besides these an Anabaptist, a Friends or Quaker Meeting, & a Presbyterian Meeting. The Other Public Buildings are the State-House[1] in which are Council Chamber, Chamber of Representatives, Secretary's Office, And those of the Clerks of the Two Houses of Legislature & The Courts of ye Assises. Fanueil Hall[2] is the Town Hall, a Place build for the assembling of ye Town-meetings & other convocations of the People. There is a Public Granery[3] an Alms House[4] & Publick school.[5] The Province House[6] which is appropriated for the Governor's Residence is a very decent comfortable Dwelling. The House was that of a Private Merchant[7] & Bought for this purpose. It is a plain brick square building. There is a very neat elegant Building also called Concert hall at which the young People hold their Balls & Concerts. There is one Principal Street which runs direct from ye South Entrance at ye Neck to ye State-house somewhat more than a mile in length and continues by one or two detours to the North End & Ferry in all 2 miles. It is spacious well built especially towards the Body of the Town, & well paved & makes a handsome Appearance. A Second Street strikes off north from this at about a Quarter of a mile from ye South Entrance & then runs lateral to it for near three Quarters of a Mile whence it runs north to the Part called New Boston. The High Street[8] with the long wharf in one straight Line of half a mile in Length is a Spacious broad Street & really handsome as it approaches ye State House at the upper end of it. The rest of the Town consists of various Cross Streets built without any regular design, many of which are narrow like those of our old English Market Towns. I remember that People use to reckon the Number of Houses & Buildings in Boston at 4,000. I cannot find amongst my papers the account which states the Number of Houses in my Time but as well as I can recollect I do not think that they exceeded 3,000. The Number of Inhabitants of this Town including the average of those birds of passage the sailors was stated at 22 or 23,000. If I were to State the Plenty & Abundance of the Market Supply in all Articles of Provisions Fish Flesh & Poultry & Game & add to this the common rates & prices of my time

[1] Built in 1712 at the head of State Street. *Ibid.*, p. 592.

[2] Original Fanueil Hall, completed in 1742, was destroyed by fire in 1762. It was rebuilt after the original plan and enlarged in 1805. The building still stands in Dock Square. Federal Writers' Project. Massachusetts, *op. cit.*, p. 157.

[3] Built in 1737 on Park Street. Shurtleff, *op. cit.*, p. 21.

[4] The old Almshouse stood on the corner of Beacon Street near the present City Hall Annex. Shurtleff, *ibid.*, pp. 309-10.

[5] Not identified.

[6] Built in 1679 for a private residence and acquired by the Province in 1716. On Washington Street opposite Old South Church. For history and description of the building read Shurtleff, *op. cit.* pp. 596-604.

[7] Peter Sargeant. *Ibid.*

[8] King Street and Queen Street, now State Street.

as they stand in my house keeping books, People of these Times would Scarcely beleive me. Boston was originally the Principal almost the Sole Port & Mart of America, When Philadelphia had scarce any Trade & New York not above 7 or 8 Ships which came to Europe the major part of which too went to Holland, their fatherland, instead of coming to England. Since the amazing advance of Commerce in Rhode Island New York & Philadelphia, The Encrease of the prosperity Town of Boston has been checked. But another & Internal Reason has operated strongly in this event, but I deferr the discussion of that part where I shall speak of the Nature of the Inhabitancy of America.

Between the South Battery under Fort Hill & Hancock's Wharf[1] is the semicircular indenture of the Water into the Line of the town before mentioned the shores of this enclosed Water are lined with Quays, wharfs, & Docks of Private Property. The Long Wharf[2] a noble Publick Structure runs out across & nearly through the middle of this; into the main Harbour. It is projected for above a quarter of a Mile & runs into deep Water so that a Twenty Gun Ship of Warr can lye along side of it. It is so broad that there are Warehouses all on the north side of it the whole length with a road of sufficient breadth for Carts & Trucks to pass each other & not disturb ye business of lading & unlading on ye Quays as it going on at the same time. Hollowell's [Hallowell's] Ship & Dock Yard[3] with several other Quays of private property were to the South of this long Wharf & multitudes of others Along ye Shore to the north of it. This whole water thus inclosed between Hancock's Wharf & the South Battery is fronted with a line of Isolated or Island Wharfs. There are also several Wharfs & Quays of Private Property in the south end part of the town.

There are three elevated points of Ground within the Town which commands all the rest. Fort Hill, Becon [Beacon] Hill & Cops [Copp's]-Hill. The Peninsula on which the Town stands is joined to the Continent by a low beach called the Neck about half a mile in length along which a good road, thrown up & shaped like the English turnpike roads, is made. This Neck & all the South-end parts of the Town is Commanded by the high grounds of Dorchester-Neck on a point which called Forsters [Fox] hill a Center being placed & a Circle with a radius of 5 furlong struck will over reach the neck & sweep ye Southern Shores of ye town.

[1]Hancock's Wharf was formerly Clark's Wharf, located at the eastern end of present Fleet Street. Shurtleff, *op. cit.*, p. 115; *The Town of Boston in New England.* By Capt. John Bonner (1722). Known as the Bonner *Map.*

[2]Built by Governor Jonathan Belcher.
[3]Near the foot of Milk Street. Shurtleff, *op. cit.*, p. 134.

Before I return & quitt this Harbour I cannot but take notice of the Town of Cambridge which stands on the Charles River that runs into the Harbour & is about three miles to the NW of Boston. The River runs through a Salt Marsh or Meadow overflows with the tides about three Quarters of a mile broad opposite to the Town of Cambridge. There is a Bridge over the River; and an elevated Causeway made across yᵉ Marsh. On the Cambridge side at about a furlong & a half from yᵉ river, the Ground rises & on this rising ground upon a level spott is the Town of Cambridge situated. Its Platform is laied down on a regular Plan of a Parallelogram with its longest side to the River with the NW & SE Corners cutt off. It is near half a Mile in length & about Two thirds of that in breadth taking in the Common and Scite of the College[1] which is a detached part on the NE side. It is a most Charming little Town where numbers of Gentlemen of Fortune have fixt their abode of retirement. The Place called the Common is a very spacious Square in the Front of the College on all sides of which Houses are built & building.

The Structure of the College is a square of three sides built of Brick in the manner of our English Colleges; except that it is open at the Corners. The side to Common is open. The Side to the North E is called Harvard College, The Side to the S is Called Stoughton College & that to the SW Massachusetts College. On the outside of this Square is a very good Lodge for the President and Pretty modern built Chappel & a Printing House. There is a very good Library in the College furnished with several thousand of books encreasing by Donations every day.

To the Southward of Cape Ann, a long Hook of a Promontory called CAPE COD, takes up again the Line of Coast. The Promontory itself is high Land & rises with steep upright cliffs on the east side to Seaward. The Long Low neck of land by which this is joined to the Main seems to have been formed by the Coil and Recoil of the Tides, rolling up Silt and Sand at the Thread of their least Force. In the Barb (if I may so express myself) of this Hook, is Cape-Cod Harbour. This Promontory forms One of the Counties of the Province now State Massachusetts, and is called *Barnstable County*.[2] It circumscribes Barnstable-Bay.[3] Many and various Alterations have been made, and are continually making on the East Coast at the Back of this Promontory: And a long Point of Sand has been formed into solid Marsh Land within these Forty Years, at the South Point of it. Let those who are curious in the Process

D a 3

---

[1]Now Harvard University.

[2]Present Plymouth and Barnstable Counties, Massachusetts.

[3]Cape Cod Bay.

of the Operations of Nature, watch the Progress of George's Sand. From the Inquiries I made, and the Answers I got, I think that will in some Years, and perhaps not many hence, form into another Sable Island. Its southern Point is now at Low Water with a strong off Shore Wind visibly a Shoal.

Barnstable-bay[1] is nearly circular of a Diameter of 30 miles. Having thriving populous Towns, inhabited by numbers of Fishermen, on its Shores on every side. On the SW side is a convenient Harbour of the most pleasing aspect, from the number of farms & settlements on yᵉ rising hills which surround it, is situated the Town of Plymouth. This was the First Settlement made by the Adventurers, under the New-England Charter, called the Plymouth Company. The Scite of the Town is on the West side of a Cove fenced off from the main bay by a long point of Land & is a Place of no inconsiderable share of Business. I have been told that it is a sweet pretty Town. It so happened that I never was at it which I have more than once regretted.

E a 3   Going round this Promontory South, and then West, the Islands NANTUCKETT [Nantucket] and MARTHA'S VINEYARD present themselves. The First is a Settlement of Whalers and Fishers, on a hilly, sandy, bare Island, which could give Subsistence to no other Species of Being. So improved, it swarms with Inhabitants; and is become so considerable in its Interest and Property, as to form One of the Counties of the Massachusetts, by the Name of *Nantuckett* [Nantucket] *County*.

E a 2   Martha's Vineyard is a very peculiar Spot of Ground, a triangular Plain of fine Meadow Land, hemmed in North West and North East by two hilly rocky Sides. This also swarms with Inhabitants, and is a Settlement of Consideration sufficient to have been formed into One of the Counties of the same State, by the Name of *Duke's County*.

E a 1   Hence rounding to the North, and passing by Elizabeth's Islands and Buzzard's Bay, on the North East, one comes to Naragenset [Narragansett] Bay and Rhode Island, the District of New England which forms the united Colony of RHODE ISLAND AND PROVIDENCE PLANTATION. The Land round this Bay is high and hilly; and through the Middle of Rhode-Island, from South to North, runs a hilly elevated Ridge.

[1]Cape Cod Bay.

SECT. IV.

Of the Western Division

"THE Land, South-westward of Hudson's River, may be considered as divided into a Number of Stages. The first Object worthy Regard, in this Part, is a Rief, or Vein of Rocks, of the Talky[1] or Isinglassy Kind, some Two or Three, or Half a Dozen Miles broad; rising generally some small Matter higher than the adjoining Land; and extending from New-York City, South-westerly by the Lower Falls of Delaware, Schuylkill, Susquehanna, Gun-Powder, Patapsco, Potomack [Potomac], Rapahannock [Rappahannock], James River, and Roanoak [Roanoke]. This was the antient maritime Boundary of America, and forms a very regular Curve. The Land between this Rief and the Sea, and from the Navesink Hills[a] South-westward as far as this Map Extends, and probably to the Extremity of Georgia, may be denominated the *Lower Plains*, and consists of Soil washed down from above, and Sand accumulated from the Ocean. Where these Plains are not penetrated by Rivers, they are a white Sea-Sand, about 20 Feet deep, and perfectly barren, as no Mixture of Soil helps to enrich them. But the Borders of the Rivers, which descend from the Uplands, are rendered fertile by the Soil washed down with the Floods, and mixed with the Sand gathered from the Sea. The Substratum of Sea Mud, Shells, and other foreign Subjects, is a perfect Confirmation of this Supposition. And hence it is, that for 40 or 50 Miles Inland, and all the Way from the Navesinks to Cape Florida, all is a perfect Barren, where the Wash from the Upland has not enriched the Borders of the Rivers; or some Ponds and Defiles have not furnished proper Support for the Growth of White Cedars."[2]

As I have now added to this Edition a Map of the Southern Colonies,[3] I shall in this topographical Description take a more extensive view of this Tract of Lands which lyes between yᵉ Hills & the Sea-line. This Tract may be stiled (taking up the Name which the Dutch gave to those parts of it which they possessed) *New-Netherlands*. Or as it seems to

Margin notes:
The Western Series

a F c

First Stage, or Lower Plains

Description of the Lower Plains Continued

---

[1]Talc.
[2]Quoted from Evans' *Analysis*, pp. 6-7; reprinted in Gipson's *Lewis Evans*, pp. 150-51.

[3][Pownall's note for revised and enlarged edition] See [Map] at the End of the work.

have arisen above the Sea by Accretion of Soil both from Sea and Land,
It may very well be a Name given under the Circumstances, be called
Zealand. This Tract is in general very Sandy & like all other half-formed
land full of Swamps & bogs. The Natural Vegetation of the Sandy Parts
is most of the Species of Pines & Cedars. In the more Southern Parts,
those of South Carolina & Georgia, The Palm Palmetta, Opuntia & a
variety of other Shrubs. Where the Soil of the Hills or Mould, is become
incorporated with the original sand as it is in the interval lands on the
banks of Rivers, the vegetation is of live-oaks & Poplars white & yellow,
Black walnut, Sycamore, Elm & Myrtle bushes & some sort of spiny
grass. There are Swamps in which The Cedar Tree has for ages been
growing and dyeing with perpetual Succession. The old ones lyeing as
they fall, uncorrupted at yᵉ bottom while the young ones Grow up between them. These The Inhabitants call Cedar Swamps. They are a kind
of Mine of Timber, almost inexhaustible. I remember to have seen in
New Jersey a pretty large park belonging to Col. Schyeler[1] with all its
fences entirely formed with whole unsawed logs of this Swamp Cedar.
In other swamps which are marshy no Tree or Shrub but Fresh-water
Marsh Grass, wild oates & Southward, a Species of Cane, grow; these
are said to be good food for Horses & Cattle. These latter Swamps when
properly banked & slusced become Rice Lands. The Botanists, & particularly the ingenious Mʳ William Gerard de Brahm[2] give long lists of
the Trees & Shrubs which form the natural vegetation of these parts;
but as I said before being myself no Botanist I must for these particulars
referr to them.

On the sides of the Rivers which run through these Netherlands,
the land lyes low. The Soil is generally of a very rich black mould with a
Foundation of Clay. And in both its natural & cultured powers capable
of every vegetation.

The very barren sands from New Jersey to Florida are capable by
Culture of having a power of Vegetation given to them, as the Settlers,
in different parts, by different culture suited to those parts, have found.
These Netherlands are not intirely of this barren or unmixt Sandy Soil.
There are Parts which Partake of Mould loam & clay & in these Parts
the natural Vegetation is of Oak, Beech, Birch, Poplar, Black walnut &c.
But there is a circumstance of Vegetation worth particular notice. This

[1]Peter Schuyler (1710-1762) younger son of Arent Schuyler who discovered and first operated the famous Schuyler copper mines. John O. Raum, *The History of New Jersey* (Phila., J. E. Potter, 1877), I, 237.

[2]In 1764 William Gerard de Brahm was appointed surveyor general for the Southern Department in North America.

is a kind of Moss[1] which is peculiar to the Trees of this Tract of Land. It grows upon & hangs down from the branches of the trees to a very great length, which I remember to have given occasion to a joke passed upon a credulous note-taking traveller under a ridiculous description of the Peruke tree which perhaps may sometime or other appear in some publication. Of the Circumstance & Thing itself take the Description of M[r] de Brahm in his report[2] to the Lord of Trade. There seems to be a line which nature has drawn that marks this Zealand. "It spreads (says He) nearly parrallel with the Sea Coast as farr back in the Country as the Trees are hung with a kind of Moss.[3] This Moss grows to the length of three yards: When baked in ovens or when hanging long on the trees it assumes the likeness, & almost the nature, of long black horse hair; & is used to stuff saddles & mattrasses[4] by y[e] common inhabitants. As long as it is fresh on y[e] Trees in winter Horses & Cattle seem fond to feed on it. This Moss is no longer mett with in the Woods where the Air may be supposed to be impregnated with the Marine-exhalations. Through All y[e] Tract betwixt this Line & the Sea the Air may be called *Sea Air*, the Country within it Landwards may be said to have *fresh-Air*. Within this Line the Country begins to rise & becomes more particularly proper for European Culture."

To give some general Idea of the Shape of This Tract beginning from the point of Sandy-hoek [hook] at y[e] Mouth of Hudson's River & running back South westerly in an irregular Curve so as to include the Promontary of East Florida, it may be said to be of the Shape of a Harp.

The Country within or Interior to this Natural Demarkation begins to rise in hills. The first Ridge seems to be a Vein of Clay, "some Three or Four Miles wide; which is a coarse Fullers Earth, and excellently fitted, with a proper Portion of Loom, to make Bricks of."[5] Next with this is the vein of Isinglassy sand. This is not equally visible in all parts.

A Vein of Clay

"From this Rief of Rocks, over which all the Rivers fall, to that Chain of broken Hills, called the South Mountain, there is a Distance of 50, 60, or 70 Miles of very uneven Ground, rising sensibly as you ad-

[1]Spanish moss.

[2]De Brahm spent 20 years, 1751-1771, collecting materials for his "Report of the General Survey in the Southern District of North America." This is a detailed account of the topography, towns, fortifications, inhabitants, flora and fauna of the Southern colonies. British Museum. King's Manuscripts, 210-11. Photostat in Library of Congress. Calendared in the Charles M. Andrews and Francis G. Davenport

Guide to the Manuscript Materials for the History of the United States to 1783, in the British Museum ... (Washington, D.C., Carnegie Institution of Washington, 1908), p. 27.

[3]Spanish Moss.

[4]This moss is still used for this purpose and for other upholstering.

[5]Quoted from Evans' *Analysis* p. 7; reprinted in Gipson's *Lewis Evans*, p. 151.

Second Stage,
or the
Upland

vance further inland and may be denominated the *Upland*. This consists of Veins of different Kinds of Soil and Substrata, some Scores of Miles in Length; and in some Places overlaid with little Ridges and Chains of Hills.''[1] There is a peculiar Stratum of Soil runs in the same Direction with the last through this Stage. The People of the Country call it *Red Shell Land*. It appears to me to be a Species of red Marl, although where it is dug up, or turned up with the Plough, it rises in slaty Kind of Lamina, and seems stony, yet it soon dissolves in the Air, and is excellent Wheat Land. When it has been tilled for many Years, so that it begins to fail in its Fertility, if the Husbandman sets his Plough a little deeper, so as to turn up a fresh Layer, this, mixed with the old worn Top, gives fresh Power of Vegetation to it.

The First Place in which this Stratum appears, as far as I have been able to learn, is in the Red Mountains,[2] West of Winnipissiocket [Winnepesaukee] Lake: As running in a Vein, the First Appearance of it is on the West Side of the Range of Mountains which run on the East Side of Connecticut River, and beginning at Hertford [Hartford], runs 10 Miles South West to Farmington, then Six Miles West to Penthorn,[3] then South West to the Mountains. It appears again in New Jersey, at Schuyler's Mines,[4] runs thence to Brunswick, and spreading goes across the Jerseys, over the high Ridge on which Prince-Town [Princeton] stands. I am told it continues in the same general Direction across Pennsylvania, but I had not the Means of pursuing it.

Lime Stone is found almost every where in the upper Parts of this Stage, and it is the general Dressing that the Husbandmen use.

There is found to the Northward of Newark in New-Jersey, an exceeding good Fire Stone, which stands well.

The Soap Stone is found about the Delaware River; and the Asbestos in many Parts of this Stage.

There are in New Jersey Two Copper Mines, One at Col. Schyler's[5] on the Passaick [Passaic] River, a very fruitful one of rich Ore; the Water obstructed the Working of it for some Time: a worse Perplexity about the Title since his Death hath stopped its being worked. It was said that there was Silver mixed in with this Ore,[6] it certainly sold as Ore

[1]Quoted from Evans' *Analysis*, p. 7; reprinted in Gipson's *Lewis Evans*, p. 151.
[2]East of Center Harbor, New Hampshire.
[3]Not identified.
[4]John Schuyler's Copper Mines in Bergen Co., New Jersey. John, fourth son of Arent Schuyler,

inherited these mines from his father. *N. J. Archives*, *op. cit.*, XII, 588.
[5]John Schuyler.
[6]"Four ounces of silver to each hundred weight of Cupreous Metal," J. L. Bishop, *History of American Manufacturers from 1608-1806*. (Phila., Edward Young & Co., 1864), I, 546.

at a great Price.[1] The other is at Mr. Stevens[2] on the upper Part of the Raritan. There is certainly now and then little Grains of native pure Gold found in this Ore, I have had some of it. This sold for 60£ and 62£ Sterling a Ton in 1754, Schyler's for above 70£ Sterling.

I have not heard of any Lead anywhere as yet found on the South or East Side the Mountains; there are several Appearances of it on the West Side. The French worked a Lead Mine in the Oïilinois [Illinois] Country.[3]

"The Declivity of the Whole gives Rapidity to the Streams; and our violent Gusts of Rain have washed it all into Gullies, and carried down the Soil to enrich the Borders of the Rivers in the *Lower Plains*. These Inequalities render Half the Country not easy capable of Culture, and impoverish it, where torn up with the Plough, by daily washing away the richer Mould that covers the Surface.

"The *South* Mountain[4] is not in Ridges like the *Endless* Mountains,[5] but in small, broken, steep, stony Hills; nor does it run with so much Regularity. In some Places it gradually degenerates to Nothing, not to appear again for some Miles, and in others spreads several Miles in Breadth."[6] It runs in more regular Ridges through Virginia under the Name of the Blue Ridge Pignut and South Mountain; after it has passed the Maryland, it spreads in more regular Hills, the North Ridges of which trending North for about 13 Miles approach near to the Kittatinny Ridge; but resuming again the main Course the Hills of this Mountain range along between Yellow Breeches and Conawegy [Conewaga] Creeks to the River Susquehanna opposite to the Mouth of Swataro [Swatara] Creek, and continue North East, under the Names of the Flying and Oley Hills,[7] through Pennsylvania to the Delaware: Its southern Ridge runs off East North East by Hanover to Susquehanna,

Third Stage, or Piemont

[1]Yield of copper was 80 percent and sold for £40 per ton. *Ibid.*

[2]John Stevens (1715?-1792). Stevens' Copper Mines were at Rocky Hill, Hunterdon County, New Jersey. New Jersey, *Archives, op. cit.*, XI, 526n. George Washington wrote his "Farewell Address to the American Army, Nov. 2, 1783" at Rocky Hill. George Washington, *Writings* . . . edited by John C. Fitzpatrick. (Washington, Gov't. Printing Office, 1931-44), XXVII, 222.

[3]Joseph Schlarman, *From Quebec to New Orleans* . . . (Belleville, Ill., Buechler Publishing Co., 1929), pp. 204-207.

[4][Pownall's note] This Mountain in its several Ridges as it crosses New Jersey, Pennsylvania, Maryland, and Virginia so abounds with Iron Ore

that it might not improperly be called the *Iron Mountain*.

[5]Allegheny Mountains. For description and extent read Lewis Evans' "Remarks on the Endless Mountain &c," printed on his *Map of Pennsylvania, New Jersey, New York and the Three Delaware Counties, 1749, op. cit.*

[6]Quoted from Evans' *Analysis*, p. 7; reprinted in Gipson's *Lewis Evans*, p. 151.

[7][Pownall's note] So called from the innumerable Flights of Turkeys on them.

"The Oley Hills are a continuation of the South Mountain and terminate at Reading." William Reichel, *Memorials of the Moravian Church* (Philadelphia, J. B. Lippincott & Co., 1870), p. 75.—Ed.

where Pequa [Pequea] Creek falls into it, and thence to Trenton. In New Jersey the northern Hills narrow and rise again into the Form of a Ridge, and it is called Mescapetcung [Musconetong]; and in New York the Highlands. Between this Range and the Kittatinny Mountains, as they run through Pennsylvania, lies the Vale of Talpahockin [Tulpehockin], One of the great rich Vales of Pennsylvania. In New Jersey and New York almost the whole Vale is a great Swamp or drowned Lands. Money alone has been wanting for the general Draining of these Lands. Whenever they are drained, this Tract will become One of the richest in America. The southern Part of this Tract as it passes through New Jersey is elevated Upland, but not Ranges of Hills. There are amongst the Hills into which this Mountain spreads itself, between the Susquehanna and Scuylkill [Schuylkill] Rivers, to a Breadth from 15 to 30 Miles, several Valleys. A Succession of such, divided from each other by little hilly Branchings of the main Hills, run from Wright's Ferry[1] on the Susquehanna to the Swedes Ford near Norriton [Norristown] on the Scuylkill [Schuylkill], some Two Miles broad, some more. The Lands are of a Limestone good farming Soil. Every Farmer has a Limekiln burnt for the dressing of his Land, and they raise a great deal of Wheat. The Sides of the Hills are covered with Woods: The Timber in general Oak, Chesnut, and Hickory. The First Valley which the Road from Philadelphia to Lancaster passes through runs from the Swedes Ford to the Middle Branch of Brandy-wine Creek, and is about Two Miles wide: Hence the Road runs slanting over Three Ascents and Three Rivulets about 13 Miles, and comes to a Second Valley which runs along the South Side of the Range called *Welsh Mountains* to Lancaster: Hence it continues in a Bosom of gently swelling Hills to Wright's Ferry[2] on the Susquehanna. These Successions of Valleys appeared to me as I rode along them the most charming of Landscapes. The Bottoms of the Vales were full of cultured Farms, with Houses, such as Yeomanry, not Tenants, live in: These were busked up with Gardens, and with Peach and Apple Orchards all round them, and with every convenience and Enjoyment that Property and Plenty could give to Peace and Liberty. My Heart felt an Overflowing of Benevolence at the Sight of so much and such real Happiness. "Between the South Mountain and the higher Chain of the Endless Mountains (often for Distinction called the North Mountain,[a] and in some Places the Kittatinni[b] [Kittatinny], and Pequil-

Ffe

aHK bCc

[1] John Wright, justice of the peace of Lancaster County and keeper of a ferry at present Columbia, Pennsylvania.   [2] *Ibid.*

Hitherto unpublished material in Pownall's own handwriting equals a third of the work published in 1776.

Some Extracts from my Travelling Journal as I passed through the Jersey and Pensylvania will give a kind of View of the Country — a view which in a country that is by its progress of settlement & cultivation changing every day will become in this short space a matter of curiosity & antiquity rather a painting of what it was, than of what perhaps it is — The Topography however remains the same.

In Going from New York to the Jerseys you pass in a Shallop over across the bay to Staten Island. The Road, if you are going to Elizabeth Town, was about six miles along the north side of this Island. At the End a Ferry conveys one over the sound to Elizabeth Town — A Township which knows no bounds & has been perpetually engaged in Laws about them, The Scite of the Town is laid by Lotts running in strait lines so that whatever houses are built in consequence of this Plan the Streets, if they may be so called, for they have & appearance of wide Country Roads, are all in right line. The Town Part is large The Houses Good & Handsome It looks more like a collection of

in[e] [Pequea]) there is a Valley[1] of pretty even good Land, some Eight, c F e 10 or 20 Miles wide, which is the most considerable Quantity of valuable Land the English are possessed of; and runs through New Jersey, Pennsylvania, Maryland, and Virginia. It has yet obtained no general Name, but may properly enough be called *Piemont*, from its Situation. Besides Conveniencies always attending good Land, this Valley is every where enriched with Lime Stone."[2]

On the East Side of the Mountains, next the European Settlements, there are some,[3] but very few, and those thin Beds of Coal: There are some Brackish Licks or Springs, but no Salt Springs. On the West Side, both these abound every where.

Some Extracts from my Travelling Journal[4] as I passed through the Jerseys and Pensylvania will give a kind of View of the Country—A View which in a Country whose Face is by its hasty advancing progress of settlement & Cultivation changing everyday will become in this short space a matter of curiosity & a record of antiquity rather painting what it was, than what perhaps it is. The Topography however remains the same.

In Going from New York to the Jerseys You pass in a Shallop across the bay[5] to Staten Island about 12 miles. The Road, if you are going to Elizabeth Town, runs about six miles along the north side of the Island. At the End a Ferry conveys one over the sound to Elizabeth Town—A Township which knows no bounds & has been perpetually engaged in Law about them.[6] The Scite of the Town is laid by Lotts ranging in strait lines so that whatever Houses are built in consequence of this Plan the Streets, if they may be so called, for they have y[e] appearance of wide Country Roads, are all in right line. The Town Part is large. The Houses Good & Handsome. It looks more like a Collection of the Country Places of a rich & thriving Germany than a Town. It has the usual Publick Edifices which are all large & Spacious. My First excursion into the Jersies was to see Col. Schyelers[7] Copper Mine & Place, & the Passaïck [Passaic] Falls. From [New] Brunswick to Newark a pleasant ride of six Miles along a level way with picturesque hills on the left & an open bay on the right. This is a neat Country Town of the same sort as the last. There is an English Church & Congregation here. Col. Peter Schye-

[1]Cumberland or Great Valley. Henry F. Walling, *New Topographical Atlas of the State of Pennsylvania* . . . (Phila., Stedman, Brown & Lyon, 1782), p. 5.

[2]Quoted from Evans' *Analysis*, p. 7; reprinted in Gipson's *Lewis Evans*, p. 151.

[3][Pownall's note] One at the Falls of James River.

[4]Pownall made this trip in 1754. See page 105 this work.

[5]New York Bay.

[6]For documents concerning boundary controversies see New Jersey *Archives, op. cit.*, VI, 205-15; XIX, 403-05.

[7]John Schuyler's copper mines in Bergen County, New Jersey.

ler's Park is of 750 Acres of Land enclosed with fences made of Cedar Logs such are taken out of the Cedar Swamps which are frequent in this Province. Col. John Schyelers, at whose Place[1] the Copper Mines are, is 2 miles & quarter higher up the River. His Park contains 680 Acres & has in it three hundred head of Deer. Between the high Lands of Bergen a narrow Ridge which Forms the West side of N York bay & Hudson river & the East Side of Bergen bay to the rising hills west of Second River. The Bay & its salt marshes is a Flatt of about 5 miles long & 2 wide. These are not yet embanked. From yᵉ Top of the Fire Engine[2] at Schyeler's One has a view over all this Country of Staten Island & Part of Long Island an Extensive & Varied Prospect of Bays & Islands. I have mentioned the Mine & Copper before. The Settlements on this River being Dutch & what we English call towns, are there called Neighbourhoods. The Roads run along the Banks of the river which is a clear & smooth one up to the Rift at Aquacinock.[3] The Country being cleared only round the settlements has a natural Sylvan beauty which our Nobility & Gentry are at such great expence to procure by Planting & Dressing their Places. From Schyelers to Second-river[4] Neighbourhood 2 miles & a half: To Aquacinock[5] 6: Thence to Weisel[6] 6: Thence to the long bridge over the Passaick [Passaic] River 2: Thence to the Falls one.

A sloop drawing Ten feet of water can Navigate up the Passaick [Passaic] to a rift about 2 miles below Aquacinock Church.

When the Dutch satt down at New Amsteldam [Amsterdam] & Crossed yᵉ North River to penetrate into yᵉ Country not knowing the names given by Indians to the rivers which they Cross'd the Hackinsaeg [Hackinsack] being the first & parallel to the Passaik [Passaic] then They called these, The First & Second Rivers; names which they are still called by.

The Falls of Passaik [Passaic] are a very curious natural Phenomenon. The River running round the Back of a Rocky Cliff, which by

[1]Belleville, a suburb of Newark, New Jersey. John Raum, *The History of New Jersey . . . op. cit.,* I, 241.

[2]Steam engine brought to Schuyler's copper mine from Europe by Josiah Hornblower on Sept. 9, 1753. New Jersey *Archives, op. cit.,* XII, 535n.

[3]Acquackanonck, probably present Passaic River. Thomas Gordon, *A Gazetteer of the State of New Jersey . . .* (Trenton, Daniel Fenton, 1834), p. 92. Present 139-153 River Drive, Passaic, New Jersey, is the site of early Acquackanonk Landing. Federal Writers' Project, New Jersey, *New Jersey, a Guide to its Present and Past* (N.Y., The Viking Press, 1939), p. 348.

[4]Belleville, New Jersey.

[5]Present Passaic, New Jersey. Federal Writers' Project. New Jersey, *op. cit.,* p. 346.

[6]Weasel, an early settlement extending nearly four miles along the right bank of the Passaic near Paterson, New Jersey. Thomas Gordon, *op. cit.,* p. 262. Present Passaic, New Jersey. Federal Writers' Project. New Jersey, *ibid.,* p. 346.

some Accident has been shattered & riven from Top to Bottom about 90 feet, turns short round & Tumbles head long with an Inconceivable force & Velocity down this horrid chasm foaming with its hoarse stunning roar at its base more like something combustible than Water. There is a lesser Chasm on the right side of this Through which a Column of Water shoots directly across the great fall & has a peculiar effect & appearance. The Rocks on the left hand of this great Chasm is a Steep Cliff the Rocks of which are riven in two Places from top to bottom. I measured their height with a pack thread & stone, &, as near as I could regulate my measure, they were 90 feet high. I jump'd across one of these Chasms to go to the Cliff: & when I had done it, my head so turned; my heart misgave me; and It required an effort of mind to go back again. I think of it now with dread. I made upon the Spott a drawing of this, from a coloured copy, which P. Sandby made of it an Engraving has been given to the Publick.[1]

The next journey which I shall transcribe, so far as it relates to the nature of the Country & its settlements is from Elizabeth Town to Easton on ye Delaware River & to Bethlehem on the Leigh [Lehigh] River, a Branch of the Delaware. From Elizabeth Town to Woodbridge 10 miles; from Woodbridge to [New] Brunswick 12. The road runs in many Parts through woods in several places not unlike Sherwood Forest. To about 4 miles beyond Woodbridge the road keeps on ye flatt ground & then begins to rise up the Hilly Country & the red Marly soil. From the Tops of these, one has a view of the Raritan River & of the Pine-land country beyond it.

[New] Brunswick stands on the SW side of the Raritan about 12 miles from the mouth of it. It consists of 134 Houses, an English Church,[2] a Dutch Church & a Presbyterian Church.

Its Navigation consists Cheifly of Boats sloop-riggd of about 40 Ton, & about 30 in number, which make each, once a week at least, a trip to New York with the produce of the Country, Also Two Schooners which go on ye same errand to Rhode-Island, a Snow & a large Schooner of 140 tons which go to West Indies. The Soil here a red Marl, hence to Mr Steven's Copper Mine.[3] The Mine is in a hill NE of his House. From the Top of this Hill there is a pleasing Prospect of a fine settled Vale

[1]"A View of the Falls on the Passaic or Second River in the Province of New Jersey.... Sketched on the Spot by His Excellency Governor Pownall. Painted and Engraved by Paul Sandby." Scenographia Americana, *op. cit.*

[2]Christ Protestant Episcopal Church, on Neilson Street in present New Brunswick, is on the site of the original eighteenth century church. Federal Writers' Project. New Jersey, *op. cit.*, p. 309.

[3]John Stevens' Copper Mine at Rocky Hill, Hunterdon County, New Jersey.

bounded by Mountains which at 5.7. & 10 Miles distance run round it. It is a Vale in respect of these high mountains but lyes varied by lesser vallies & ranges of gently swelling hills. From hence to the Forks of this River Through the Woods all the Way Cheifly White oak & Walnut or Hickory Some few Chestnuts. To Potterstown: hence to Allen's[1] & Turners[2] Iron Workes. Hence five miles to the old Furnace called The Union.[3] Crost the Raritan & Spruce run. The Country between this Place & Mr. Stevens[4] lyes thru Ridges of Mountains & between them for 5, 8 or 10 miles a Vale-like Country of alternate rising hills & Vallies, then again Ridges of Mountains & Alternate Vales of the like Sort but mostly in Woods unclear'd & looks when one casts one's Eye down from the high ground like a long rolling Sea of Woods.

We rode late in the Ev'ning from the New Furnace[5] to the Union.[6] It growing dark & the road being but a mere track through the Woods, we had much trouble to see our way & was on y⁰ point of being benighted & began to form our Ideas of sleeping in the Woods. At This Moment we heard a Trio of French-Horns playing a pleasing meloncholly Tune. The Reader may imagine this must have been pleasant under these circumstances, if it had not been good musick. It struck me then a Stranger in y⁰ Country like, & was really like, an Incident in a Romance. We followed the Sound & our Horses found the way which led us to the Dwellings about the Mines. As we approached We found our Concert was performed by an old German & his two Sons sitting at the Door of their Cottage thus amusing themselves in peace & happiness at the close of the Ev'ning after their day's labour. What pleasure must this Old Man, escaped from the Sovereign Tyranny of his European Lords & while here—placida â compôstus pace quiescit—feel in the Contrast: And yet I thought the melancholly of the Musick had a retrospective regrett of his Native Country. I asked him. He said No & yet I thought he felt yes; so are we formed. We were most hospitably received & treated & I never lay in a neater more cleanly comfortable bed in my Life.

From hence our rode led over large hills & vales to the Hickory Tavern[7] 8 miles through the woods, oaks Hickory & some

[1]William Allen (1704-1780), prominent Philadelphian, mayor of the city and chief justice of the Supreme Court of Pennsylvania.

[2]Joseph Turner of Philadelphia. New Jersey *Archives*, VII, 560.

[3]Owned and operated by William Allen and Joseph Turner. *Ibid.*

[4]John Stevens' Copper Mines were at Rocky Hill, Hunterdon County, New Jersey.

[5]Not identified.

[6][Pownall's note for revised and enlarged edition] These are the great Iron Works.

[7]On the road to Easton and the Moravian settlements. In 1759 Hickory Tavern was advertised "To be Lett or sold by Colonel John Hackett at Union Iron Works and Anthony White in New Brunswick." New Jersey *Archives, op. cit.*, XX, 316.

Chestnut, on the banks of the runs in yᵉ vallies. Some very tall Poplars.

Hence to Johnson's Mill[1] through woods of the same kind, 5 miles. Passed by the beginnings of some settlements only three in yᵉ whole way. We ford the Rivulet at the head of the mill dam: thence West northerly three miles to the Pohatcung [Pohatcong] Creek, on which stands Kitchen's Mill[2] over a high level land. This Mill stands about 3 miles (up yᵉ river) from yᵉ Delaware river. The wood still the same.

The road led hence N & by W over the ends of Ridges of mountains, whose Wood was cheifly oak, 5 miles to a new-settled Town Called Philipsburg [Phillipsburg]. This Town Plott as laied out contained 100 acres & consisted (1754) of 14 Houses.

Hence Ferry over the Delaware at the Forks to another new settled Town called Easton. First began in 1752 under the Care of Mʳ Parson's[3] a very uncommonly ingenious Man. A Man having no views in life, but Quietude & Retirement, but engaged in this business of settling & running this Sweet Settlement.

The Scite of the Town is at the Point of the Forks of the River Delaware. Having that River in its front; The West branch or Leighy [Lehigh] River on its left; & a small rivulet on its right: It was a Flat Point of Land on pretty elevated banks surrounded on all sides with high hills.

The Plott of the town was that of a square laid out in strait Streets crossing each other at right angles: Four running directly east & west parallel to each a four like streets running north & south with an open Square in the Center. The Street running directly from the River was called Spring-garden Street, Northampton Street, Ferry Street, the name of the other I have forgotten.[4] The Cross Streets were Front street, Fermer[5] Street, Pomfret[6] street & Hamilton[7] Street. Alas! these great names, the relatives of the Penns, fixt as a mark of boasted honor on this property remain now only as objects of regret & humiliation. The side of each square of buildings crossed by these streets was 480 feet.[8] Each Lott was 60 feet front by 230 deep. The settlers paied for this seven shil-

---

[1]Samuel Johnston's Mills on the Musconctung River. New Jersey *Archives, op. cit.,* XXIV, 527-28; XXXV, 225.

[2]Samuel Kitchen's Mills in Amwell Township, Hunterdon County, New Jersey. New Jersey *Archives,* XXX, 285; XXXIV, 290.

[3]William Parsons (—d. 1757), Surveyor General for Pennsylvania and founder of Easton, Pennsylvania.

[4]Lehigh Street, Easton, Pennsylvania.

[5]Now Second Street.

[6]Now Third Street.

[7]Now Fourth Street.

[8][Pownall's note for revised and enlarged edition] There were already 36 houses built in 1754 when I was there.

lings sterling per annum quitt rent to the Proprietor Penn. The Whole contained about 100 acres.

I was politely, it now enough to say hospitably entertained & most comfortably lodged by Mr Parsons at his new house, a pretty neat habitation very compleatly furnished.

I went from hence about five o'clock in the afternoon of the next day, rode along a pathway road under the shade of woods so that although it was a very hott day we were very little incommoded & arrived at Bethlehem about sunsett. Coming out from amidst a wilderness of woods through which I had been travelling some daies all at once at the top of a hill & viewing hence this cultivated populous settlement & its cluster of College like buildings large & spacious all of stone; with the grounds all around planted with orchards; & varied with tillage in all its forms of culture; & border'd on the banks of the river on which it lyes & of the rivulet which runns thro' it which rich & green meadows My Eye was struck with unexpected pleasure. The Place itself makes a delightfull landskip but found, & thus seen in the center of a wilderness, derives unusual beauty from the contrast & surprise with which it presents itself. I made here a Sketch[1] of it after a drawing from which an engraving has been made & published.

The Distance of Bethlehem from Easton is 12 miles the ground between hilly all ye way but fine land. At about four miles from Easton I observed we were riding through a wood of Young Saplings, resembling a young planted wood rising near some of our fine new-made places in England. This was the first time that this circumstance in the Course of vegitation had mett my Observation: and I was totally at a loss to account for it. I state my doubts to Mr Parsons,[2] who accompanied me to Bethlehem. He could not but look down upon my ignorance but with great good breeding said He did wonder to find that this circumstance was new to a person, who was born, & had always lived, in a world clear'd of its woods. He should have been more surprised at my inattention, if this circumstance had escaped my observation. As I could never have had in the old world an opportunity of examining this matter as to its fact, it was natural that I should be at a loss in reasoning about the State of the fact. He that had spent his life in the woods & had been conversant with the nature of their existence, had studied their vegitable life. He observed that every soil produced its natural race of vegitable

---

[1]"A View of Bethlehem, the great Moravian Settlement in the Province of Pennsylvania. Sketched on the Spot by his Excellency Gov. Pownall, Painted and Engraved by Paul Sandby." In *Scenographia Americana, op. cit.*

[2]William Parsons.

inhabitants; that each individual tree had & went through all the periods of life from youth through adultness & sunk by old age to death as men do: that their life was liable to defects in health & to disease which went to loss of life, that this was not only so in the individual but that the woods were liable to epidemical endemial maladies like the race of man; that such when they happened would lay waste whole tracts of country, that when this happened, if any change of circumstances made any change of the nature of the soil either for the better or the worse Quite a different race of Trees would spring up, if no change was made then Trees of the same sort would spring in succession to those which had dyed there as was the case in the present instance. But that an instance of the former case had occurred to him some years prior to ye present when he was surveying in the Valley beyond the Kittatiny Mountains. He found a whole tract of Country full of Loggs of Pine trees lyeing along the ground so as almost to Cover it the boles of trees which once grown on it, but were now dead. That a young Wood was growing amongst these, a young vegitation of quite a different Race; that to the former inhabitants the Pines, Oakes & Hickory were coming up in succession. That in many parts, of America, in the as yet uncultured parts, especially on the banks of rivers, where a new soil had accumulated many feet above the old, & what one may call the original soil,—Trees of a very different species were growing from those which by digging were found lyeing on a different stratum of soil beneath the present face of the earth.

The next Day in the morning I waited on Bishop Spanenberg[1] [Spangenberg], Superintendant general of the Outward & Inward, the Temporal & Spiritual Oeconomy of the Moravians throughout all America. He received me with that address & politeness which is peculiar only to Men of the first fashion in the great world and treated me while I staid in these settlements, with attentions that could only derive to me who had no right to them from a benevolence that could alone exceed his politeness.

These Settlements, which I will describe both as to the Farms as also as to the peculiar Community which occupied them consisted of about 10,000 acres of Good Land.

The Community settled on them was of those People, who stile themselves the *Unitas Fratrum*,[2] & who being Emigrants from Moravia

[1]Augustus Gottlieb Spangenberg (1704-1792), bishop in the Moravian Church at Bethlehem, Pennsylvania, 1744 to 1750, when he was replaced by Bishop John Nitschmann.

[2]From the original Bohemian name meaning Brethren's Church. Joseph Levering, *A History of Bethlehem, Pennsylvania, 1741-1892* (Bethlehem, Pa., Times Publishing Co., 1903), p. 7, 8n.

are called Moravians, but named in their original settlement under Count Zinzendorf[1] Hereen-huters.[2] They are a Society of Christians, obeying, rather than what can be stiled governed by, an Episcopalian Hierarchy both as to their Temporal as well as Spiritual Interests. They hold that their Episcopacy hath preserved its succession pure & uninterrupted from the first ages of Christianity preserving the faith also pure incorrupted without mixture or connection with the Government or the Doctrines of the Church of Rome. They cannot therefore as they do not call themselves, be called Protestants or a reformed Church. They hold however pretty much in a catholick spirit, the same principles as the reformed Churches. The Church & Legislature of England have acknowledged them as being what they profess themselves to be in their Episcopalian Succession.

They have adopted in the litteral sense some expressions of the Holy Scriptures; and have adopted the idea of a Society found'd on a Community of Property & Labour;[3] without attending to that distribution of property & the paying taxes there from which Christ referred to when he saied render unto Caesar the things which are Caesars & unto God the things which are Gods. Be their Opinions on this point what they may; be they right or wrong, I am rather apt to think from what little I understand that the *Model of their Community* will be rather sooner found in Plato's Republick than in the Gospel of Christ or the Doctrines of his Apostles.

However such is their Doctrine & such is their Actual Establishment. Under This *Oconomy* (here I use their own peculiar term) they possess & Cultivate near 10,000 Acres of Land comprised in six Farms. viz Bethlehem,[4] Nazareth,[5] Gnadenhüt,[6] Christian-sprung,[7] Gnadenthall,[8] and Vriedenthall.[9] The Title to which is vested in David Nitchman

[1] Nicolaus Ludwig, Count von Zinzendorf (1700-1760).

[2] From village of Herrnhüt, Germany, first place of worship for the six leaders in the Moravian Church (1724). Levering, *op. cit.*, p. 22.

[3] The co-operative plan was not a part of the religious belief of the Moravians in America, but was adopted as an expedient in order to build a self-sustaining mission in Pennsylvania. By 1761 the mission had reached its goal and the cooperative plan was abolished. Information given to the editor by Dr. S. H. Gapp, Archivist, Archives of the Moravian Church, Bethlehem, Pennsylvania. However, it was not until 1814 that the oil mill, the tobacco factory, and the slaughterhouse, all run as community enterprises were given up; the grist mill continued to be used by the community until 1825; and it was not until 1837 that the remaining business enterprises conducted by the Moravian Church in Bethlehem were sold. Warren N. Nonnemaker, "The Moravian Church in the United States during the Middle Period, 1812-1860" (Master's Thesis, Lehigh University, 1935), pp. 9, 13, and 16. For many years, Mr. Nonnemaker was principal of the Moravian Preparatory School in Bethlehem.

[4] Bethlehem. The deed for land on "The Allen Tract" was dated Apr. 2, 1741. On Christmas Eve, Dec. 24, 1741, the community was named Bethlehem by mutual consent of the religious congregation. Levering, *op. cit.*, p. 61, 79.

[Nitschmann][1] in trust for the use of the Unitas Fratrum. Writing from my Journal I speak of it as it was when I was there in the year 1754, & as it had long subsisted, I think about 14 years.[2]

The Principle which they hold out as the spirit which animates & unites them into one body in Christian Love to each other & to the United Community, the Unitas Fratrum, as members & the Body of Christ of which Body Christ is the Head. The Spirit which actuates the Oconomy is an Authority, rather than power, founded in an opinion that the Bishops, Deacons, Ministers, Spiritual Labourers, & Superintendants who administer the Spiritual & Direct the Temporal Matters of the Society are the visible Deputies being the Successors on Earth of the Apostles & Disciples of Christ.

The Model of the *Unitas Fratrum* as raised on this Basis was called their Oconomy and as the animal Oconomy of Man consists of an Union of Soul & Body each having their respective powers form & operation; so here The Oconomy of this *Unitas* had a Spiritual & Temporal Form. Bishop Spanenberg [Spangenberg] was the Intendant general throughout all America both of the Spiritual & Temporal Oconomy. He had under him two other Bishops—Mr Beler[3] [Boehler] & Mr Hale[4] [Heyl]. Under these were Ministers to administer the ordinances & to preach. They were sent out itinerant into various parts to preach as the Bishops & Synod should direct. There were also Deacons who preached who Baptised who were the Spiritual Labourers. There were also Schoolmasters & Catechists. Their Church Service was conducted by an established Liturgy. Their Psalmody & Hymns were accompanied with Musick of every sort. The Temporal Oconomy was superintended by Temporal Oconomists Temporal Deacons & their Assistants. The Deacons managed the whole of their Property & Revenue. They directed

---

[5]Nazareth (Ten miles north of Bethlehem). Deeded to Count Zinzendorf, May 11, 1740, by Wm. Allen. *Ibid.*, p. 44.

[6]Gnadenhütten (Habitation of Grace). On the Lehigh at the mouth of Mahoning Creek. The first 15 settlers left Bethlehem, June 13, 1746 to found this new Moravian settlement. *Ibid.*, p. 193.

[7]Christian Sprung (Christian's Spring). Was known as Albrecht's Brunn but officially named Christian's Brunn, Aug. 4, 1749. *Ibid.*, p. 190.

[8]Gnadenthal (Grace Dale). Settlement began Jan. 13, 1745. *Ibid.*, p. 190.

[9]Friedensthal (Vale of Peace). The mill was built in 1750, but the dwelling was not occupied until April 27, 1751. On that date the community was given its official name—Friedensthal. William C. Reichel, *Friedensthal and its stockaded mill . . . 1749-1767* (Nazareth, Pa., Whitfield House, 1877), pp. 7, 8.

[1]Bishop David Nitschmann, Sr. (1696-1772), first bishop of the Unitas Fratrum in America and the official founder of its first American Settlement.

[2]Founded in 1741.

[3]Peter Boehler (1712-1775), was consecrated bishop in the Moravian Church in 1748 and was acting superintendent of the Moravian Church in America, 1742-44.

[4]Matthew Gottfried Heyl (1705-1787), bishop of the Moravian Church for 30 years. Moravian Historical Society. *Transactions of . . .* (Nazareth, Pa., Whitfield House, 1876-date), VII, 243, no. 110.

the Supply & Consumption & Had the Care of all the personalty & Stock. Mr Lawatsch[1] was, under Bishop Spanenberg [Spangenberg], first Deacon & Superintendant for Temporal affairs; Treasurer & Auditor. The Persons who were members of this Society & composed this settlement were, in 1754, 910 individuals. They were considered & considered themselves as one Family. This family was divided into seperate classes, which were called *Choirs*. These choirs were not only thus distinguished for orders sake but lived seperately from each other & never mett but at Chapel. They had each Choir—seperate houses, even the Children were seperated from the parents & were nursed in their own choir, at first at Bethlehem & afterwards at Nazareth. These Choirs were: 1. The Choir of Infants who had Nurses & every other necessary attendant appointed to the care of them. 2. The Choirs of Children, that is of Boys & of Girls, in two seperate choirs. These had proper persons appointed to attend their nurture & Education. 3. The Choir of single men. 4. The Choir of Single Women and 5. The Choir of Married People. They had four Distinct Houses for these at Bethlehem & a fifth at Nazareth. These Houses were all Spacious large buildings of Stone plain but neat & handsome. The House for the Choir of single men was a long Building of four stories high, beside the base story. The first was assigned to the offices, the second was the Refrectory, one very long room the whole length of the building. The next, the Dormitory another long room of the same kind. The highest story another long room of the same sort which was the Vestiary for here their Cloathing was deposited. Each individual had two suits one for summer & one other for Winter annually. They all wore the same habit without distinction. The Apartments for the single Women were in a quadrangle open on one side to the South. The East & West sides were appropriated for the appartments, the North side was the Chapell. The Infants were in a House by themselves with their nurses. And the Married Couples had seperate lodgings in another House by themselves each in seperate lodgings, & accommodated to that state of life. The two Houses of the Single Men & Single Women had each a Garden & Orchard seperate & distinct, also each a laundry seperate. For none of these individuals were ever sufferrd to meet unless such as the Bishops & Ministers had destined for marriage with each other.

[1]Rev. Andrew Anthony Lawatsch, a principal elder in the Moravian Church in Bethlehem, was ordained in the Moravian Church in Marienborn, Germany, in 1745 and came to America in 1752. "Clergy of the American province of the Unitas Fratrum," I, 67. Manuscript in Moravian Archives, Bethlehem, Pennsylvania.

As the Property & its Produce was, as I have marked above Common to the whole Community & governed by the oconomy as above described: so was the Labor. The Deacons & their Assistants distributed & directed the individual each to that branch of buisness or that line of labour for which he was best calculated, or best understood. The Produce of which Common Labor, in each branch, was carried to the common Stock. Besides the Farm labourers in which both women as well men worked, There were, when I was there the Following Trades carried on by the Fratres at this Settlement. Saddle-tree maker, Sadler, Glover, Shoemaker, Stocking-weavers, 4 frames going, Button maker Taylor & Women Taylor, Hatter, Ribband-weavers, Linnen-weavers, 6 looms in work, Woollen-weavers, three looms at work, Wool-comber, Dyer, Fuller, Dresser, Tanner, Currier, Skinner, Butcher, Miller, Chandler, Oil-maker, Baker, Cooper, Joiner, Carpenter, Mason, Glazier, Brick maker Stone Cutter Turner Potter Stovemaker Wheelwright Blacksmith, Gunsmith Nail-Maker Lock-smith, Pewterer, Tinman Silver-smith, Clockmaker Harnes-maker, Hemp dresser, Boat-builder, Surgeon, Apothecary. These Artificers & Manufacturers had each seperate appartments & shops to themselves. Although this Community of Property Labour Supply & Consumption thus took place in general: Yet those of the Brethern who chose to live seperate & to keep their property & Labor distinct & to themselves were at liberty to do so. Those who partook of the Common supply, were bound to contribute their common labour to the raising & making of it, & è contra those who gave their labor to the common stock partook in all things of the Common Supply under the direction & distribution of the common Oconomy. Many however who were members of the Spiritual Oeconomy & of the Church; as to outward matter & Oconomy held possessed & actuated their own private property & oconomy distinct within themselves & to themselves of which were many, cheifly of the married People.

About ten miles N. of Bethlehem the Society had another noble Farm of 6000 acres of land called Nazareth, at which all the Children who were brought up as the Children of the Family, were nursed and educated from 18 months old to three Years. It was worked in the ordinary labour of the Farm by 30 couple of the married Choir. The Hay & Corn harvest was gotten in by Labourers sent from the other Choirs for the time under the superintendence & direction of the Deacons or Assistants. They had a little Farm of 60 Acres called Gnaden-hüt[ten] at an Indian town about 28 miles off Bethlehem where they had a Grist & Saw Mill. They told me they had Baptised 100 Indians at this place.[1]

They had another most noble farm & Settlement begun in 1748 Called Christian-sprung of — acres worked by 40 Brethern sent from the Single Mens choir & two couples from the Married Choir. The Familys Brewhouse Distillery, Dairy & Saw Mills were. Here first I saw some trout that would come to the edge of ye water & take bread out of one's hand, here first also I saw that sort of dairy called a spring-house.

There was another fine farm adjoining to this called Gnadenthall, begun in 1746, & worked by 14 couple sent from the married Choir.

About two miles from Nazareth there was another little Farm of about 300 acres purchased in 1749 & settled in 1750 & in great forwardness of Culture. This was worked by 6 Couple of the married Choir. This was called Vriedenthall. I dined here & was entertained at Dinner by a very good Harper. I thought a fine one. I'm sure 'twas pleasant & novel such thus removed from ye cultured world. One of finest Grist-Mills at this place that I ever saw in America, the mill at Trentown [Trenton][2] excepted. Every one of these Farms had large houses & round them Peach & Apple orchard planted with the best of Fruit as also gardens.

I forgott to mention The Grist Mills, Fulling mills, Oil-mills, & other mills which performed various operations at Bethlehem.

As this Curious Settlement was an instance existing in fact & actuating the plan of Plato's Utopeia, I could not in the description of this New World, which is rising intirely on an experimental System, avoid describing it. But apart the singlarity of its System of Community, The Fineness of its Settlements & Farms did of themselves deserve a special notice. I Confine myself to the description of ye Facts & enter not into reasoning about the System.

My Tour led me hence back to Easton & thence between 40 & 50 miles through the woods & over one ridge of mountains, & over to Trenton a Pretty good Town in the Jerseys on the banks of the river Delaware just below the falls.[3] It consisted at this time of 100 Houses & one of the finest mills working 4 pair of Horses, that I ever saw. It is the

[1] In 1754 the mission at Gnadenhütten numbered 137 Indians. Reichel, *Memorials . . . op. cit.*, p. 34n.

[2] The William Trent Mill, a two story stone structure built in 1690 on the site of the Mahlon Stacy Mill (1680). The building stood until carried away by flood waters in 1843. John Raum, *History of the city of Trenton, New Jersey . . .* (Trenton, N. J., W. T. Nicholson & Co., 1871), p. 234.

[3] At Trenton, New Jersey. "Known from earliest settlement as the Falls." Federal Writers' Project, New Jersey, *op. cit.*, p. 398.

Barcadore of the upper Country produce which goes down hence upon the Delaware to Philadelphia. The Articles sent from hence are, Wheat flour, Pipe-staves, Iron, Flax, Hemp &c. There were 8 schallops belonging to this town which plyed & were constantly employed in the navigation between this town & Philadelphia. There was a Plating mill here.[1] There are here an English Church[2] a Presbyterian[3] and a Quaker meeting.[4] The Majority of the Inhabitants are Quakers.

Before I quitt this town on my Way to Philadelphia I will mark the course of the road between [New] Brunswick & Trentown [Trenton] & the nature of the land & Country of Jersey in the settled Parts. A little to the East of [New] Brunswick that is, between that & Woodbridge begins the red marly stratum. Going west from [New] Brunswick the road rises up a country of swelling hills but at about 7 miles from [New] Brunswick begins to mount the ridge of the high lands of the Jerseys & runs along that ridge to Kingstown [Kingston], Prince [Princeton] & Maidenhead. As the road runs along this high ridge, one looks over to the left the low flatt Country of New Jersey. At the foot of this high ridge hilly ground which forms the foreground of a pleasing landskip, spangled thick which Gentleman's Houses & rich Farmers Places seen amongst the woods as if standing at the upper end of long spacious avenues of clear'd & cultured ground consisting of orchards of Peaches & Apples Growing in regular rows as also Cherry holly Wheat land, Flax & Hemp lands Pasture & Meadows below & beyond this foreground one looks over the great extensive level flatt of Sandy Pine land interspersed with Cedars away to the *Navesink*. The road was all the way from [New] Brunswick to Trenton through a continued succession of Plantations so that one is never out of sight of a House, except when the road runs through the little woods & Coppices which make part of each Plantation. A Farm or Plantation consists of a Good neat House, &, if it stands on a convenient run of water, of a mill also; it is generally busked upon each side or behind with an Apple & a Peach orchard. It hath generally a farm yard joining to it with a good barn, a hay rick, a Cyder press & mill a Corn Shed Hogsties & Cow-yard, with fields of English Grass, Indian Corn, Wheat, Buckwheat mostly belted round with woods. One rides thus through a kind of Garden the whole way.

[1]The only plating mill in New Jersey. Located at west end of Trenton and owned by Benjamin Yard of Hunterdon County. New Jersey *Archives, op. cit.,* VII, 558; X, 31.

[2]On the present site of St. Michael's Protestant Episcopal Church, 140 N. Warren St., Trenton.

Federal Writers' Project, New Jersey, *op. cit.,* p. 409.

[3]On the present site of the First Presbyterian Church, 114 E. State Street. *Ibid.*

[4]The Old Friends Meeting House, corner of E. Hanover and Montgomery Sts., Trenton. This Meeting House, built in 1739, is still standing. *Ibid.*

A very large & well built College has been erected at Princetown [Princeton] the highest & most healthy tract of Land in this rout.

On September 3 I left Trenton cross over the Delaware by a ferry[1] about a furlong broad into Pennsylvania. Thence through woods all the way 10 miles to Bristol. Bristol stands upon the west side, northerly, of a pretty circular bason near ¾ of a mile broad, & a mile & ¼ long. Opposite to this bearing South easterly sitts Burlington on the Banks on the Jersey side, Bristol had then 60 houses, three bake-houses for biscuit, a Meeting. Employ'd in its intercourse with Philadelphia, a Sloop & two Shallops. Burlington has 130 houses a Church & a Quaker Meeting, has one Biscuit Baking-house employs a shallop & two passage boats has a very pretty street right up from the river. Two neat Market-houses, & Court house being a Market Town. From Bristol through woods still, to a Ferry over a Creek,[2] from hence 4 miles to another Creek[3] & Ferry, where is a good tavern called Widow Amos's:[4] Hence 4 miles through pretty good settlements the land along most of this latter way the Isinglas soil. Hence 8 miles to Frankfort; & 5 to Philadelphia.

Fourth Stage, or the Endless Mountains

"The *Endless Mountains*,[5] so called from a Translation of the Indian Name bearing that Signification, come next in Order. They are not confusedly scattered, and in lofty Peaks over-topping one another, but stretch in long uniform Ridges, scarce Half a Mile perpendicular in any Place above the intermediate Vallies. Their Name is expressive of their Extent, though, no Doubt, not in a literal Sense. In some Places,

d J k

as the Head of Ronoak[d] [Roanoke], one would be induced to imagine he had found their End, but let him look a little on, and he will find them again spread in new Branches, of no less Extent than what first

Allegheny Mountains e F h

presented themselves. The *further* Chain, or Allegeny Ridge of Mountains,[e] keeps mostly on a Parallel with the *Isinglassy* Rief, and terminates in a rough stony Piece of Ground at the Head of Ronoak [Roanoke]

f D c

and New River.[f] The more Easterly Chains, as they run further Southward, trend also more and more Westerly; which is the Reason that the *Upland* and *Piemont* Valley are so much wider in Virginia than farther Northward. This South-westerly Trending of the hither Chains brings them to meet the Allegeny Mountain, and in several Places to intersect

[1]Thomas Hooton was keeper of Trenton Ferry in 1750. New Jersey *Archives, op. cit.,* XII, 679-80.
[2]Mill Creek. See "Wm. Scull's Map of Pennsylvania . . . 1770," *op. cit.* Not shown on modern maps.
[3]Neshaminy Creek. *Ibid.*
[4]On Neshaminy Creek. *Ibid.*
[5]Read Lewis Evans' description of the Endless Mountains, printed on his *Map* of 1749.

it, and form new Series of Mountains; as is the Case I believe, of the
Ouasioto."g1   g J a

They certainly do end to the Northward and North East, at the
hKaats Kill [Catskill] Mountains, and at the iBrimston [Brimstone] and   h C d
Oneida Ridge, which lie South of Mohawks River. The Triangular   i B d e
Mountainous Tract of kCouchsackrage, [Couxsachrage] lying between   k D e
the Mohawks and St. Lawrence Rivers and Lake Champlin, [Cham-
plain] and the Range of Mountains on the East Side Hudson River, are
distinct and different Ranges of Country.

"There are many Chains of the Endless Mountains, which, had
they come to my Knowledge, might have filled several Places which lie
vacant in the Map."2 [Several of these are inserted in the present
Edition.] "But so far as we are acquainted with them, we observe that
each Chain consists of a particular Kind of Stone, and each different
from the rest; and these Differences continue for their whole Extent, as
far as I can learn. When I crossed them I was not apprehensive of this,
and omitted enumerating their Species. Some of the Chains are single
narrow Ridges, as the Kittatinni [Kittatinny]; some spread Two or
Three Miles broad on the Top; some steep on one Side, and extending
with a long Slope on the other; and the steeper they are, the more
rocky; but they are every where woody where there is Soil proper and
sufficient to supporr the Trees. Towards the further Chains North-
eastward, the Mountains consist of rich Land, and in some Places are
but as large broad Banks, which take Two or Three Miles to cross."3

Many of these Chains consist of several Ridges, one main Ridge,
and a Number of lesser ones, and sometimes with irregular Hills at their
Foot in the Vale. Where any of those Chains so spread, they meet and
sometimes cross each other; sometimes lesser Branches or Spurs shoot
out from the main Ridges, and these also generally end by irregular Hills.

"In the Way to Ohio, by Franks Town,4 after you are past the   E h
Allegeny [Allegheny] Mountain, the Ground is rough in many Places, and
continues, so to the River. Hereabouts the Lawrel [Laurel] Hill springs
from the Mountain, and continues though not large, in a very regular

---

1Renamed Cumberland Mountains in honor of the
Duke of Cumberland, by Dr. Thomas Walker of
Virginia in 1748. J. G. M. Ramsey, *Annals of
Tennessee* . . . (Kingsport, Tenn., Kingsport Press,
1926), pp. 65-66. This quotation is from Evans'
Analysis, pp. 7-8; reprinted in Gipson's *Lewis Evans*,
pp. 151-52.

2Quoted from Evans' *Analysis*, p. 8; reprinted in
Gipson's *Lewis Evans*, p. 152.

3*Ibid.*

4The Old Delaware and Shawnee Town (1731)
Assunepachla. Named Frank's Town by early
Indian Traders. Charles A. Hanna, *The Wilderness
Trail* . . . (N.Y., G. P. Putnam's Sons, 1911), I, 259.
Near present site of Hollidaysburg, Blair Co.,
Pennsylvania.

k F h

Land
among the
Mountains

Chain, I believe, to the Ouasioto Mountain.[1] For though the Allegeny [Allegheny] Mountain is the most Westerly, on the West Branch of Susquehanna,[k] it is far from being so, back of Virginia.

"Except the further Ridges, as just now mentioned, there is but little good Land in the Mountains; to be sure not one Tenth Part is capable of Culture; and what small Matter is so, consists of extreme rich Soil, in Lawns, on the River Edges, being so much rich Mud subsided there; and commonly gathered above Falls, formerly in drowned Land, and now drained by the Rivers wearing Channels through the Rocks,[2] which, like Dams, held up the Waters at each respective Fall."

The Cherokee or Apalachian [Appalachian] Mountain on the Back of the Carolinas & Northwestern parts of Georgia, although in like manner rocky & gravelly are yet well cloathed with Forest Trees & Shrubs. The Bay Cypress Cedar & Laurel, The Oak, Chestnut, Mulberry, Maple, Hickory, Acasia [Acacia], Walnut, Plumbtree [Plum] & vine both the Cluster & fox-grape. The vallies have a soil rich to a degree beyond what manure can produce on poorer cultured lands: the sides of yᵉ ridges of the Mountains are bare the tops, where not clear'd of their natural Vegetation, are yet covered with a good coating of Soil. The Ridges in many parts are four or five hundred feet high & almost impracticably steep & not more than from six to twelve feet wide; in some places they are so narrow that two horses loaded cannot pass each other & yet it is necessary in most places to continue the road along these ridges untill a proper descent offerrs itself. But bad are yᵉ best: And in general These descents are not only difficult almost to impracticability for Pack-horses but in many instances attended with imminent risque & danger. The Vallies here also, as has been observed of other Parts of these Mountains, are very deep & narrow in general, & liable to Flood: Yet in their Climate the most delightfull & beneficial Settlements may be established in them.

Amidst the Detail of these dry Descriptions, it may perhaps relieve and amuse the Reader to insert some Observations and Opinions which I found in and extracted from Mr. Evans's Journal.[3]

a E f

"The Stones in all Parts of these Mountains are full of Sea Shells: It is not in the loose Stones scattered through the Vales that these Shells abound only, but they are found at the Tops of the Mountains also. I saw some mixed with the rocky Base of a high Mountain; in ᵃWishoôchon

---

[1]Cumberland Mountain.
[2]Here ends this quotation from Evans' *Analysis*, pp. 8-9; reprinted in Gipson's *Lewis Evans*, pp. 152-53.

[3]From the *Journal* of 1743, part of which is printed in *Appendix* of this work. Gipson, *op. cit.*, p. 3.

[Wissahickon] Creek I found a soft Stone Five or Six Feet long, as full of all Sorts of Shells as if they were kneaded into a lump of brown Clay: There was all the Variety that could be imagined, and many that had never before come under my Observation, many that I could not imagine to exist in Nature as the Shells of any Animal, particularly a large Escolop with Corbels, as fine as those of Cockles. I was almost disposed to pronounce this a Lusus Naturae, but I have since found that Sort of Shell, and many other of the Sorts which I saw here, in a Bed of Soil more than 30 Feet under Ground in Virginia. The Observations also which I had an Opportunity of making at Moor's Mill[1] near London Town,[2] in Maryland, shewed me how ill imagined any such Idea was. This Place is not far from the Sea Side, the Earth had been dug from an adjoining Bank for a Mill-dam; at the Top I found the Shells mixed with a loose Sand; at Three or Four Feet deep they were inclosed in a sandy Clay; and at Four or Five Feet deeper, the Clay was gradually hardened into a loose Kind of Stone, in which were mixed Shells, many resembling the Specimens which we had before observed in the Mountains. This Instance of the Soil hardening by Degrees from a loose Sand to an indifferent Stone in the Space of Eight or 10 Feet, where there could be no Doubt but that the Shells were genuine, and where the Shells were actually of the same Sort as those which I had observed in the Mountains, convinced me that those Shells of the Mountains were real, and had been mixed with and finally incrusted in the Stones where they were found, by the same Process as here appeared in its several Gradations.

"Various Systems and Theories of the present Earth have been devised in order to account for this Phaenomenon. One System supposes that the Whole of this Continent, the highest Mountains themselves, as they now appear, were formerly but one large Plain, inclining with a considerable Slant towards the Sea; that this has been worn into its present Appearance of Ridges, with Vales between them, by the Rains of the Heavens and Waters of the Earth washing away the Soil from the upper Parts, and carrying it down to Seawards. That the Soil thus carried down and lodged in various Places hath in a Series of Ages

[1]Dr. George Walker and Jonathan Hanson built two water-mills *ca.* 1711 and 1733 respectively. These mills were later called Moore's Mills. *Maryland Historical Magazine* (Baltimore, 1906-date), XVI, (1921), 216n. They were located near Jones Falls. See Warner & Hanna's *Plan of the City and Environs of Baltimore respectfully dedicated to the Mayor City Council, & Citizens thereof, by the Pro-* *prietors, 1801.* [Baltimore, 1801.]

[2]London Town was on the south bank of the South River, about four miles from Annapolis. In 1923 one brick mansion used as Anne Arundel County home was all that remained to mark the site of this once thriving town. *Maryland Historical Magazine, ibid.,* XVIII (1923), 254.

formed the lower Plains of the Jerseys, Pennsylvania, Maryland, Virginia, and the Carolinas. The most material Arguments to support this Hypothesis are, that the very Tops of the Mountains on the western Side, though much higher than those bordering on the English Pale, consist yet of extraordinary rich Land, but that towards our Side the Soil of the very Vales as well as of the Mountains is thin and stony, and the Rock almost bare as if the Earth had been swept away off from them. The Downfall of Waters from the Melting of the Snow, the Rains, and the swollen Springs is such amongst the Mountains, and the Discharge from thence so great, that the Freshes on the Susquehanna River, where it is a Mile broad, rise 20 Feet, though they are discharged with a violent and precipitate Current. These Freshes carry down with them immense Quantities of Soil which they begin to drop as the Velocity of their Course slackens in gliding over the lower Plains, and which they finally lodge in Bars and Islands at the Mouths of the Rivers where they meet the Sea.[1] Thus have been many very extensive Countries formed at the Mouths of all the great Rivers in the World, and thus at the several Mouths of the many great Rivers ranging so near one another along this Coast may that long continued Range of flat Country, which is herein before called the *Lower Plains*, be formed. And if we suppose this Operation to have begun immediately at the carrying off of the Waters of the Deluge when the Earth was in a State of Fluidity, and to have continued in Operation ever since, the Effects will not appear more than natural. This Hypothesis accounts for all the Appearances which are observed, and all the Peculiarities which are found on the lower Plains of America, such as the Nature of the difference Layers of Strata of which they consist, for the Sea Shells and Fish Bones being found at 30 and 40 Feet deep, and probably deeper, if examined for the various Logs, and especially for the Caedar Swamps and Pine Bogs, which are perfect Mines of Timber.

"But we must have recourse to some other Explanation in order to account for the Situation of the Shells on the Tops of the Mountains.

"It is easy to shew the Earth and Sea *may* assume one another's Places, but positively to assert *how that hath actually happened* in Times past, is hazardous; we know what an immense Body of Water is contained in the great Lakes at the Top of the Country, and that this is

---

[1][Pownall's note] I will here transcribe an Extract from a Letter of Monsieur Vaudreuil, the Governor of Louisiana, dated September 28, 1752. There is infinite Difficulty, says he, in settling towards the Mouth of the River Mississippi, on account of the immense Expence in Banking against the Inundations of the Sea and Land-floods. I am against settling it as yet; and for waiting until the Ground be more and more raised by the Accretion of Soil; as it hath been *Three Feet* in the Space of 15 Years.

damm'd and held up by Ridges of Rocks: Let us suppose these Ridges broken down by any natural Accident, or that in a long Course of Ages a Passage may be worn through them, the Space occupied by the Water would be drained: This Part of America, disburthened of such a Load of Waters, would of course rise, as the immediate Effect of the shifting of the Center of Gravity in the Globe at once or by Degrees, much or little, accordingly as the Operation of such Event had Effect on that Center. The directly opposite Part of the Earth would, as Part of the same Effect, sink and become depressed, and liable to be deluged without any apparent Reason discoverable in those Parts for such a Change. There is no Doubt but that many such Accidents have happened in the World before it became settled in its present Condition and State. That there have happened some such Accidents, by which the general Body of the Land of America hath been raised, we have Reason to collect from the Chinese Chorography, called Quang-yn-ki,[1] which describes Tshaossanas in Corea [Korea], which is now divided from it by the Gulf Leao Tong, where the Sea has encroached so much that the Mountain Kiesheshang, which was formerly Part of the Continent, is now near 500 Leagues off at Sea. If the Land of China became thus much depressed by the Change of the Center of Gravity of the Earth, those Parts of America which lie nearly in an opposite Meridian would be equally raised. No doubt many partial Deluges have happened from such Causes, the Reason of which, for want of Knowledge is what had passed on the opposite Side of the Globe, could never be explained. Some such Changes may have come gradually and advanced by such slow Degrees, as that in a Period of a few Ages would not be perceptible; History therefore could take no Notice of them.

"We know from Observation how much higher the Atlantic Ocean is than the Pacific, and how it is piled up against the American Coast on the western Shore of the Gulf of Mexico, driven thither by the Trade Winds and Attraction of the Moon and Sun. Let us suppose it possible that a Passage might be forced through the Isthmus of Darien[2] or some other Part of America between the Tropics; these Waters then would pour down from this Height and be discharged through this Passage, instead of running back through the Gulf of Florida; the Height of the Atlantic would be lower between the Tropics, and the Level of the Pacific Ocean would rise; the Center of Gravity of the Earth would

[1] "Kuang-yü chi, is a geography of the Empire in 24 books, written by Lŭh Ying-yâng about the commencement of the 17th century." Alexander Wylie, *Notes on Chinese Literature* . . . (Shanghai, Presbyterian Mission Press, 1922), p. 59.
[2] Panama.

shift, and there would be few Places on the Earth but what would perceive the Effect, although none would be able to conceive the Cause, that did not know the particular Event of this Passage being opened." Suppose now that the Bahama and Caribbee Islands were once (which they certainly appear to be) an Isthmus (like that of Darien) the Continuation of the Apalachian [Appalachian] Mountains and the Al-a-Bah'ma[1] Country; that what is now the Gulph of Mexico was a most extensive Plain, and that some such Accident as is above supposed did actually happen by the Breaking of the Sea through this Chain of Land into this Plain now the Great Gulf, that Part of the Globe actually becoming depressed, the opposite Point would be raised. "I have mentioned, says Evans, these different Systems as they occurr'd to me on viewing the various Phaenomena which meet our Eye in the Mountains; for the Information of those who are curious in enquiring into the System of our World; but I have neither pursued the Investigation with that Attention, nor explained them with that Closeness of Reasoning which I might have done had I been interested about them; I shall therefore beg the Reader to make Choice of that Hypothesis which he likes best and thinks most probable; for my own Part I can conclude on neither singly." The Editor[2] here will take up this Subject where Lewis Evans hath left it, and add One more Hypothesis or Theory to the many with which the Learned have been amused.

Mons' Buffon Modestly as a first step introduces his Theory of ye Formation of the Planets by the name of *Simple Conjectures*[3] but adds as ye next step that shall give it a much greater degree of probability that anyone of all the Theories which have been formed on the same subject can assume.

A mere Globe of Mud wherein all ye Parts remained in an indigested state of Fluidity which yet could not properly be called Water. I sufferr not my imagination to conceive by any theory What that Process of Nature was which first collected into a Globe these concentring particles because there is nothing even in analogy much less in experience to give ye least grounds to such Theory: But from analogy of what is now passing in the region of Worlds I can suppose this Chaotic Globe (as well as the rest of the Planets) to have been in every circumstance Just what the Comets now are. These Comets impressed with a pro-

[1]The Appalachian range terminates in the Al-a-Bah-ma or northern Alabama. The terrain slopes gradually to the Gulf of Mexico.

[2]Thomas Pownall.

[3]Georges Louis Leclerc, comte de Buffon (1707-1788), *Natural history, general and particular* . . . Translated into English . . . (3d ed., London, A. Strahan, 1791), I, 59-96.

jectile motion & in the progress of that motion coming with the Sphere of attraction of some those Immense bodies which at rest or nearly so acquire a parabolic & by degrees an elliptic course, in extremly excentric Orbits. Many of these may be supposed as Sr Isaac Newton thinks,[1] to accede nearer & nearer in a spiral Orbit to ye Center of their courses & so finally to fall into those Suns or Globes of Fire which first Attracted them. He states some appearance which seem to favor this Idea And then suggests that these Wandering Chaotick Globes do thus become a supply or alimentary fuel to ye Burning Globes or Suns. But although He supposes that this may be the Case with some of these Comets yet he supposes, & even shows by calculating the trajectory of their Course that being first attracted into parabolic, they do finally revolve in Elliptick Orbits round their respective Suns or rather round ye Center of Gravity of the System into which they have fallen. In General They make their Revolutions in extreme excentric Orbits, in all Directions, & all plains of courses. Had the Use, or final cause, which Sr Isaac Newton ascribes[2] to them is that with their vapours (raised from them by the heat of the Sun & dispersed through the System) they supply & replenish the Planets with moisture & Spirit, which is continually through Vegitation & Putrefaction consuming & growing deficient in the Planets.

Those who in their Perihelia approach nearly to ye sun must be so vitrifyed beyond all remaining Capacity of Vegitation may be supposed to be in ye first class who became fuel to ye Suns. The other whose orbits are more remote from that Center & who scarce descend nearer than ye Orbit of Jupiter is or of ye second of Chaotick Globes of Mud. While in the state of Cometts they are not unusefull to ye System into which they have been attracted & may finally by a concurrence of Positions & a Combination of different lines of Attraction becomes planets of the Secondary kind that is Sattellites at least. Perhaps the Primary Planets where at first something of the kind, receiving these Globes of Sulpher mediately by some second cause unknown to our limited Capacities a simple projectile Force such we see with that thus moving forward &

---

[1][Pownall's note for revised and enlarged edition] "Cometa qui anno 1680 apparuit, minus distabat a Sole in Perihelio suo quam parte sexta diametri Solis; & propter summam velocitatem in vicinia illa, & densitatem aliquam Atmosphaerae Solis, resistentiam nonnullam sentire debuit, & aliquantulum retardari & propius ad Solem accedere: & Singulus revolutionibus accedendo ad Solem, incidet is tandem in corpus Solis." Isaac Newton, *Philosophiae Naturalis Principia Mathematica*, Book III, Prop., 42, Prob., 22.

[2][Pownall's note for revised and enlarged edition] "ex quorum exhalationibus & vaporibus condensatis, quicquid liquoris per vegetationem & putrefactionem consumitur & in terram aridam convertitur, continuo suppleri & refici possit . . . Porro suspicor Spiritum illum, qui Aeris nostri pars minima est sed subtilissima & optima, & ad rerum omnium vitam requiritur, ex Cometis praecipue venire." Newton *op. cit.*, Prop., 41, Prob., 21.

what we call the shooting Starrs shoot forward Coming within the Sphere of attraction of some Starr or Sun acquired first a parabolic & by degrees an elliptic course round that Sun as the Center of its motion.

Viewing this Earth as it is, not as learned Theorists suppose it should have been, or was, at first made: Examining with attentive Investigation of Facts, the actual State & progress of its Existence: Analysing the Operations which Heat and Moisture, Vegetation, Corruption, and a continued Process of Exsiccation have on it, in its ordinary Course of Existence: Viewing the Effects of Earthquakes and Volcanoes, I am led, by a Combination of all the Ideas which these Objects offer, up to that State of this Globe which I conceive to have been *its original State*, and from thence I can, as I persuade myself, trace it through every Progress of its changing Existence. From the Manner in which the Land hath been continually encreasing upon the Waters of the Globe from its first Appearance, I traced back my Ideas to the Viewing This Planet in the First Stage of its Existence as *a mere Globe of Mud:* that as the earthy Parts subsided and began to concrete into Sand, or Clay, or Stone; this Globe, then became *an aqueous Planet*, & was the proper Habitation for the Inhabitants of that Element only: that in Time as the Planet, in the natural and ordinary Operations of the Power of Nature, directed by the great Creator, dried, the Land appeared; and was seperated from the Waters: As soon as it was thus emerged above the Face of the Waters, It began to vegetate. That such Animals then, as the advancing Vegetation became a proper Habition for, were created and came into Being; the Fowls of the Air first, and every creeping Thing, and the Beasts of the Field in the next Progress. That when this Earth had advanced so forward in the Melioration of Being as to become a proper Seat and Habitation for Man, then in this last State of the Planet, the Human Race was brought into Being; at first, *a mere Sylvan Animal* of the Woods. Having thus pursued this Theory (for I call it no other) by the Analysis and Combination of my philosophic Ideas, I proceed to examine it by the actual Account which our Holy Scripture give us of it.

I find therein that the First State of this Globe is there described just as my Ideas led me to conceive of it: There was a Firmament in the Midst of the Waters, which divided the Waters from the Waters, *those which were under the Firmament*, and those which were above it; the Latter were called the Heavens, the Former were this Planet. The next Progress of Creation was the Exsiccation of this aqueous Planet, so that dry Land appeared, and was called Earth. The next is, that the Earth began to vegetate Grass first, Shrubs next, and Trees next, whose Seed were in themselves. As these Waters and this Earth were prepared for Reception and Sustenance of their respective Inhabitants, the Waters brought forth abundantly the moving Creature that hath Life; the Fowl also multiplied, and every creeping Thing on the Earth; the Beast next after his Kind. The last Stage of this Process the Divine Creator allotted to the Production of Man, to whom he gave *every Herb bearing Seed*, and *every Tree in which is Fruit, to be to him for Meat*. He dwelt in a Paradise, and did not work the Land; nor gain his Food by the Sweat of his Brow. That was (as we are taught) a Curse which he afterward entailed upon himself, through an Ambition of being wise above what was ordained for him. Thus say the Indians, speaking to The European Land-workers You take a deal of Pains to spoil a good World.

That the literal Style of the Apologue describes the Process of the advancing Existence of this Planet and its Inhabitants by a Series of *Days*,[1] and that my Idea must suppose a Series of Ages makes no Difference; the Process is the same, a Myriad of Years in the Sight of God are but as one Day. As according to this Idea of mine, the Waters must naturally, and, as according to the Account in our Holy Scripture, they did actually cover the Whole of the Globe before the Earth appeared, and as its Appearance was gradually by a natural Separation, I never was surprized or thought it any extraordinary Circumstance which required the Supposition of some extraordinary Cause to account for it, that Shells and Marine Skeletons should be found on the highest Mountains, I should think it extraordinary and rather be surprized if they were not. If you will trust Nature or believe the Scriptures you will find that they have been from the Creation, and are a Proof, *not of the Deluge*, but of the Truth of the philosophic Account of the Creation given in the Book of Genesis.

But to return, from this Digression of Amusement and Speculation, to Business, the Analysis proceeds to describe the Fifth or Upper Stage which lies North West on the Back of the western Division. The northern Part of this may be considered as one great LEVEL PLAIN continuing as yet in its original State. Although it is the most elevated Tract at the Top of all this Country, yet it is occupied by a Mass of Waters which lies on its Face in Five great Lakes;[2] the Lands and Country bordering on these Lakes slope gently towards, and many Streams run hence into, them.[3]

Vide Memoire presented to the D. of Cumberland, Appendix to Administration of the Colonies

[1][Pownall's note] I am told that the Word used in the Original signifies not Days but Periods.

[2]The Great Lakes.

[3][Pownall's note] These Parts of the Map here

Lake Ontario
C f g h j

"Ontario or Cataraqui, or *The beautiful Lake*, is a Mass of fresh Water, very deep, and has a moderate steep Bank and gravelly Shore along the South Side: The Rivers which fall into it are apt to be sometimes barred at the Entrances. This, like the Mediterranean, the Caspian, and other large invasated Waters, has a small Rising and Fall-

Its Tides

ing of the Water like Tides, some 12 or 18 Inches perpendicular[1] occasioned by the Changes in the State of the Atmosphere; rising higher, as the Weight of the incumbent Air is less, and falling, as it becomes greater. This Lake is best fitted for the Passage of Batteaux and Canoes, along the South Side, the other having several Rocks near the Surface of the Water; but the Middle is every where safe for Shipping. The Snow is deeper on the South Side of this Lake than any other Place in these Parts, but the Lake does not freeze in the severest Winter out of Sight of

The Streight
of Niágara
a C D j
Portage

Land. The Streight of Oghniágara[a] [Niagara], between the Lake Ontario and Erie, is easily passable some Five or Six Miles with any Ships, or 10 Miles in all with Canoes; then you are obliged to make a Portage up Three pretty sharp Hills about Eight Miles, where there is now cut a pretty good Cartway. This Portage is made to avoid that stupendous

Falls

Fall of Oghniágara [Niagara][2] which in one Place precipitates headlong 25 or 26 Fathoms, and continues for Six or Seven Miles more to tumble in little Falls, and run with inconceivable Rapidity. And indeed the Streight for a Mile or Two is so rapid above the Fall, that it is not safe venturing near it. They embark again at the Fishing Battery,[3] and thence to Lake Erie it is 18 Miles, and the Stream so swift, that the stiffest Gale is scarce sufficient to stem it in a Ship; but it is easily passed in Canoes, where the Current here, as in all other Places, is less rapid along the Shore.

Lake Erie
b D E j K l
m n o

"Lake *Erie*[b] has a sandy Shore on the North Side, and in many Places such on the other, especially towards the South East Part. The Weather and Climate of this is far more moderate than that of Ontario." On account of the Sands the Navigation running amidst crooked Channels is perplex'd and difficult.

Streight of
St. Clair
c C D o

"The Streight St. Clair,[c4] as far as Fort Pontchartrain,[5] is passable

---

described are not pretended to be laid down accurately. Future Discoveries will give local Precision. We here only mean to exhibit a Sketch not a Plan.

[1][Pownall's note] Partially also as the Wind setts.

[2][Pownall's note] Vide Peter Calm's Account of it, published at the End of Bartram's Journal. Bartram, *op. cit.*, pp. 79-94.—Ed.

[3]Fishing or Fisher's Battery, the site of Fort Schlosser on the Niagara, was located at the Carry-

ing Place about a mile above the Falls. *N.Y.C.D.*, VI, 608; X, 731n; Orsamus Marshall, *The Niagara Frontier; Embracing Sketches of its Early History* . . . (Buffalo, printed for private circulation by Joseph Warren & Co., 1865), p. 22.

[4]St. Clair River.

[5]French fort, built in 1701 on Lake St. Clair by Antoine de la Mothe Cadillac. Present site Detroit, Mich. *N.Y.C.D.*, *op. cit.*, IX, 671n.

in a Ship with a pretty moderate Gale, but from the upper Side of the Little Lake[1] to Lake Huron on the Channel is intricate, but deep enough, and the Stream to be stemm'd with a stiff Gale.

"The Lake Huron communicates with Lake Michigan or Illinois by a Streight[d2] that is wide, and the Current running sometimes in, and sometimes out, by reason of the small Runs which fall into this latter Lake, scarce supplying what is dissipated in Exhalations.

Lake Huron
d Missilima-kinack

"Mineami [Maumee] River,[e] *Sandusky,*[f] *Cayahóga*[g] [Cuyahoga], and *Cherâge,*[h3] fine Rivers, navigable a good Way with Shallops, fall into the South Side of Lake Erie. Though the Bank on this Side is about Eight or Ten Feet high, and dry enough in most Places; the Land a little Way back is generally wet and swampy, by reason of these Rivers wanting sufficient Descent, or better Channels made to drain it.

e E n
f E m
g E l
h E k
Rivers on the South Side of Lake Erie.

"The Great and Little *Sèneca* Rivers[i] are the most considerable Waters that fall into the South Side of Lake Ontario, but neither navigable with Shallops, save about Half a Mile in the former, and Two or Three Miles in the latter. Their Falls over the Edge of the elevated Plains, are the Causes of these Obstructions. But after you are gone up the Little Seneca River above the Three Falls, and the Great Seneca River, about Half a Mile above the Mouth of Onondaga River, they are both very slow and deep. The latter is best laid down in the Map, for I have had an Opportunity of viewing it myself from Onondaga downwards, and thence upwards I have been favoured with the Observations of Mr. Bleecher."[4]

On the South of Lake Ontario
i C e
C g

This Ocean of Waters, has but one Embouchure through the Canada River,[5] and the Issue of it is a Stream which bears no Proportion to the immeasurable Mass of Waters. These Lakes are found to have retired from Parts which seem to have been their former Shores, and decrease. There may be, in the Course of Nature, Accidents which may lay some of these Lakes quite dry, when they would become great Plains.

The southern Parts of this upper Stage lie as one extensive broad Bosom of a Vale more than 1500 Miles long, containing a Wilderness of Waters, which all fall into and drain through the Channel of the River Messachibee [Mississippi], which signifies *the Father of Rivers,* into the

Messasiippi River

---

[1]Lake St. Clair.
[2]Mackinac Straits.
[3]Cherage or Racoon River, later known as the Grand River. Hanna, *op. cit.,* I, 336. The Grand River empties into Lake Erie at Painesville, Ohio.

[4]John Rutger Bleeker. This quotation is from Evans' *Analysis,* pp. 17-18; reprinted in Gipson's *Lewis Evans,* pp. 161-62.
[5]St. Lawrence River.

Gulf of Mexico; the East Side of this great Vale descends from the End-less Mountains[1] in gently swelling Hills: The Parts of this Country to the North East of the Kiskamenitas [Kiskiminetas] Creek were, when the First Edition of this Map was published, very little known; nor can I learn that they are much more at present unless to some Land-jobbers,[2] whose Interest it is to keep their Knowledge secret. I have however an Opportunity of giving the Reader a pretty accurate Account of that Part of it which is contained between the Ohio River and the Allegehenny [Allegheny] Mountains on the North West and South East, and the Monongahela and Great Kanawa [Kanawha] Rivers North East and South West. I extract it from the Journal of a second Tour made by Mr. Gist in 1761,[3] for the express Purpose of examining those Lands.

G i
G h

To begin with the Youghiogeny [Youghiogheny] and its Branches: The Valleys on the Branches or Springs which form the Middle Forks,[4] are but narrow at its Head; but there are about 2000 Acres of good farm-ing Land on the Hills about the largest Branch. As one approaches Lawrel-hill [Laurel],[5] the Undergrowth towards and over this Hill is so abundant in Lawrel Thickets that the Traveller must cut his Way through them: The Lands of the Country through which the Youghio-geny [Youghiogheny] runs are broken and stony, but rich and well timbered; in some Parts, as on a Creek called Lawrel [Laurel] Creek, rocky and mountainous.

From the Mountains[6] to Monongahêla, about 15 Miles in the Line of Gist's Rout, the first Five Miles are good level farming Land with fine Meadows; the Timber White Oak and Hickory. The same Kind of Land holds South to the upper Branches[7] or Forks of this River 10 Miles, and about the same Distance North to where the Youghiogeny [Youghio-gheny] falls into it;[8] the Lands for about Eight Miles along the same Course of the River on each Side, though hilly, are richer and better timbered; the Growth Walnuts, Locust, Poplars, the Sugar Trees or Sweet Maple. The Bottoms or Intervals by the River Side are about One Mile wide, in some Places Two Miles. For several Miles more down the River on the East Side the Intervals are very rich, and a Mile wide:

[1]Allegheny Mountains.

[2]Probably refers to the Ohio Company of Virginia.

[3]1751. Christopher Gist, in the employ of the Ohio Company of Virginia, began this second journey July 26, 1751. The *Journal* of his second journey was first published in 1893. Christopher Gist. *Journals of* . . . [ed.] by William M. Darlington.

(Pittsburgh, J. R. Weldin & Co., 1893), pp. 67-79.

[4]Castleman's River. Gist (Darlington edition), *op. cit.*, p. 138.

[5]A ridge of the Allegheny Mountains.

[6]Laurel Ridge, a ridge of the Alleghenies.

[7]Monongahela and Cheat Rivers unite in southern Pennsylvania near the Maryland border.

[8]At McKeesport, Pennsylvania.

The Upland, which he examined for Eight or 10 Miles East, extraordinary rich and well timbered. The Intervals on the West Side are not above 100 Yards wide; the Upland on this Side the River, both up and down it, rich Soil and full of the Sugar Tree.

He next examined the Lands in several Courses forming, to speak generally, a South West Course, first up by some Branches of the Monongahêla, and then across the Heads of several Rivers[1] which run into the Ohio till he struck the great Kanâwa [Kanawha] River: He found the Land in general hilly but rich, rocky in some Places yet not poor; the Timber Walnut, Ash, and Sugar Trees. The Intervals on the Borders of the Creeks in some Places 200 Yards, in others a Quarter of a Mile broad. When he came within about 21 Miles of the Kanâwa [Kanawha], he crossed over a high Ridge of Pine Land which was but poor Soil, but descending thence the Land became pretty much the same as before.

The Kanâwa [Kanawha] 79 Poles wide; the Intervals on its Borders a Mile wide and very rich; further up the River a Mile and Half wide, and full of lofty Timber.

He went from the Kanâwa [Kanawha] on a West North West Course or thereabout[2] to the Ohio, and returned up the South East Side of that River by a North East Course by Le Fort's [Torts] Creek,[3] Little Kanâwa [Kanawha], or Buffalo Creek; Fishing or Nawmissippi [Naumissippia] Creek;[4] Weeling [Wheeling] Creek; and the Two Upper Creeks,[5] and thence East and South East to his old Camp on the Monongahêla. The Borders or Intervals on the Ohio a Mile, and in some Places a Mile and Half wide; the Land rich and good, but the Upland in general broken hilly Land: He met with Coal in some Places. He examined the Land up the Creeks as these, which we should think great Rivers, are called, and found the Face of the Country the same, rich

G k
and
H l

[1]Shurtees, Fishing or Little Conhaway, and Lawawlaconin Creeks. Manuscript map showing Christopher Gist's first and second tours to the Ohio. Great Britain Public Records Office. Colonial Office. *Maps, Virginia*, no. 13. Photostat, courtesy of Howard N. Eavenson, Pittsburgh, Pennsylvania.
On modern maps: Shurtees (Chartiers), Fishing (Little Kanawha), and Lawawlaconin (Pond Creek, Wood County, W. Va.). Gist (Darlington edition), *op. cit.*, p. 145.
[2]"N 45 W 4 M W 7 M, to a high hill [Kanawha Ridge] from whence We could see the River Ohio." Gist (Darlington edition), *op. cit.*, pp. 75, 144.
[3]A creek which flows from the east and empties into the Ohio a short distance above the mouth of the Great Kanawha. Manuscript map showing Christopher Gist's *First and Second Journey, 1750-52*. Great Britain Public Records Office. Colonial Office. *Maps, Virginia*, no. 13, courtesy of Howard N. Eavenson.
[4]Apparently Mr. Pownall has confused names of creeks mentioned by Christopher Gist. Little Kanawha, Naumissippia, and Fishing Creek are one and the same. Gist (Darlington edition), *op. cit.*, pp. 76, 145.
[5]Buffalo Creek and Cross Creek, Ohio County, West Virginia. Gist (Darlington edition), *op. cit.*, p. 146.

Intervals and good farming Land on the Uplands. This whole Country abounds with Game, as Bear, Elk, Deer, Turkeys, and in one Place he killed a black Fox.[1]

This Country is now settling fast, and will soon be better known.

The Triangular Tract of Land at the Head of this great Vale, and between the Mississippi, the Ohio, and Lake Erie (as that Lake is vulgarly called) the Country of the Ilinois [Illinois], is the finest Spot of Earth upon the Globe, swelling with moderate Hills, but no Mountains, watered by the finest Rivers, and of the most delightful Climate; the Soil, as appears from the Woods with which it is cloathed, is of the most abundant Fruitfulness in Vegetation. It abounds with Coal; and there are Multitudes of Salt Springs in all Parts of it. There are Mines of Iron, Copper, and Lead. Wild Rye grows here also spontaneously.[2]

Parts executed without actual Surveys appear less accurate in the Map.

"The Map in the *Ohio*, and its Branches, as well as the Passes through the Mountains Westward, is laid down by the Information of Traders, and others who have resided there, and travelled them for many Years together. Hitherto[3] there have not been any Surveys made of them, except the Road[4] which goes from Shippensburg round Parnel's Knob[5] and by Ray's Town, over the Allegeny [Allegheny] Mountains. For this Reason I have particularly endeavoured to give these Parts, which are done from Computations, another Appearance than those among the Settlements, where I had actual Surveys to assist me; lest the Reader be deceived by an Appearance of Accuracy, where it was impossible to attain it."[6]

In the present Edition[7] of this Map 1776, I have, by peck'd Lines, drawn a supposed Course of these lower Parts of the River Ohio, so as to

[1]Here ends the account taken from Christopher Gist's *Second Journal*.

[2]Information from George Mercer. See page 26 this work.

[3]Before 1755, the date of Lewis Evans' *Analysis*.

[4]This road, laid out in 1755 by George Croghan and his assistants, was requested by General Braddock, in preparation for his campaign against Fort Duquesne in 1755. The road began south of Shippensburg and followed an old Indian trail and traders' path. Albert Volwiler, *George Croghan and the Westward Movement, 1741-1782* (Cleveland, Ohio, Arthur H. Clark Co., 1926), pp. 91-92.

[5]Parnell's Knob is near the foot of the Tuscarora Valley. Uriah J. Jones, *History of the Early Settlement of the Juniata Valley* . . . (Phila., Henry B. Ashmead, 1856), I, 154.

[6]Quoted from Evans' *Analysis*, p. 10; reprinted in Gipson's *Lewis Evans*, p. 154.

[7][Pownall's note] None of the Parts of the Map West or North West of the Ohio are presumed to be other than such a Sketch as shall give a general Idea. Every new Map may correct the last before it, and yet be no more than a Sketch at best. We must wait for Observations and Surveys in our future Knowledge of this Country, in order to give an actual Map. There is none such yet: nor are there any Materials as yet from which any such Map can be compiled, whatever may be pretended. In Justice to Mr. Lewis Evans's Industry, I will venture to say none as yet can give a better Idea of those Parts than this Map has done, not even those done by the French while they had Possession and commanded in these Parts.

coincide in general with the Courses of Gist's Journal,[1] and the Observations of Latitude found in Capt. Gordon's Journal.[2]

"The Pass through the Mountains from Pennsylvania, by Shamokin[3] The Author's
to Onondaga[4] and Oswego, is from my own Observations, and well Route to
Oswego
deserves Regard; because I had a pretty good Instrument for observing
the Latitude, and minutely noted all our Courses, and am well accustomed to form a Judgment of travelling Distance. Mr. William
Franklin's Journal to Ohio[5] has been my principal Help in ascertaining
the Longitude of the Fork[6] of Ohio and Monaungáhela [Monongahela];
but however I must not omit mentioning that the Latitude of this Latitude of
Fork is laid down from the Observation[7] of Colonel Fry, and is at least Fort
du Quesne
10 Miles more Northerly than I would otherwise have thought it was.
The River from hence downward is agreed by all who have gone down Ohio not
it, to be in general pretty strait, nor can its Curves be indeed con- very crooked.
siderable where it is confined in a Manner by a Chain of little Hills,
from the last-mentioned Fork[8] to 10 Miles below the Falls.[9] Mr. Joseph
Dobson[10] gave me an Account of the Distances from Creek to Creek
as they fall in, and of the Islands, Rifts, and Falls all the Way from the
Fork to Sioto [Scioto]; and Mr. Alexander Maginty [McGinty][11] and
Mr. Alexander Lowry [Lowrey][12] gave me the rest to the Falls, as well
as confirmed the others. The River from the Fork upwards is mostly
from Mr. John Davison;[13] but that Part from Canawagy [Conewango]

[1]Christopher Gist's *Journal.* See pages 171-200 this work.

[2]Captain Harry Gordon, British army officer and chief engineer of the Western Department in 1766. His *Journal* is an account of his journey "down the Ohio to the Illinois, down the Mississippi to New Orleans, and from thence to Mobile and Pensacola," undertaken under official orders in 1766. The *Journal* is printed in Newton Mereness, ed., *Travels in the American Colonies . . .* (New York, Macmillan, 1916), pp. 457-58.

[3]Since it was the residence of Allummapees, the "king" of the Delawares, and Shikellamy, deputy of Iroquois, Shamokin was regarded as the Indian capital of Pennsylvania. Present site of Sunbury, Pennsylvania.

[4]Onondaga, chief village of the Onondagas, and capital of the League of the Iroquois or Six Nations. On present site of Syracuse, New York. In 1743 Lewis Evans accompanied John Bartram on his trip from Philadelphia to Onondago, Oswego, and Lake Ontario. Bartram, *op. cit.,* p. 9.

[5]Unfortunately Wm. Franklin's "Journal" is not extant. Gipson, *op. cit.,* p. 57.

[6]At present Pittsburgh, Pennsylvania.

[7]Col. Fry's "Observation of Latitude from Shannopin's Town, June 16, 1752" was communicated to Pennsylvania Provincial Council by William West. Printed in *Colonial Records of Pennsylvania,* V, 761.

[8]At present Pittsburgh, Pennsylvania.

[9]At Louisville, Kentucky, a limestone ledge extends across the Ohio River and forms rapids of about three miles. In this distance the river falls 26 feet. In 1825-1830 locks were built so that boats could proceed uninterrupted down the river. Writers' program, Kentucky. *Louisville, a Guide to the Falls City . . .* (N.Y., M. Barrows and Company, 1940), p. 9.

[10]Factor at Fort Pitt for the Philadelphia firm, Baynton, Wharton, and Morgan. Hanna, *op. cit.,* II, 234-235.

[11]Licensed Indian trader on the Ohio taken captive by the French January 26, 1753. Hanna, *op. cit.,* II, 253.

[12]Alexander Lowrey (1723-1805). A trader on the Ohio after 1744. Hanna, *op. cit.,* II, 335.

[13]Pennsylvania Indian trader. Interpreter for

General
Situations

to the Head is entirely by guess, for I have no other Information of it, than that it heads with the Cayúga Branch of Susquehanna. The Routs across the Country, as well as the Situation of Indian Villages, trading Places, the Creeks that fall into Lake Erie, and other Affairs relating to Ohio and its Branches, are from a great Number of Informations of Traders and others, and especially of a very intelligent Indian called *The Eagle*,[1] who had a good Notion of Distances, Bearings, and Delineating." Indeed all the Indians have this Knowledge to a very great Degree of practical Purpose. They are very attentive to the Positions of the Sun and Stars, and on the Lakes can steer their Course by them. The different Aspects which the Hills exhibit on the North Side, from that which the South has impressed on their Eyes, suggest, habitually, at the Moment, in every Spot, an almost intuitive Knowledge of the Quarters of the Heavens which we, mechanically, mark by the Compass. This, at the first Blush, may appear incredible to some; but it may be explained even to the most incredulous. Can any, the most inattentive Observer, be at a Loss to pronounce, in a Moment, which is the North or South Side of any Building in the Country. The same Difference between the South or North Aspect of a Mountain or a Hill, or even a Tree, is equally striking to the Attention of an Indian; and is much more strongly marked by that Accuracy with which he views these Objects; he sees it instantly, and has, from Habit, this Impression continually on his Mind's Eye, and will mark his Courses as he runs, more readily than most Travellers who steer by the Compass. The Ranges of the Mountains, the Courses of the Rivers, the Bearings of the Peaks, the Knobs and Gaps in the Mountains, are all Land Marks, and picture the Face of the Country on his Mind. The Habit of travelling mark to him the Distances, and he will express accurately from these distinct Impressions, by drawing on the Sand a Map which would shame many a Thing called a Survey. When I have been among them at Albany, and enquiring of them about the Country, I have sat and

Detroit

seen them draw such. "The Situation of *Detroit* is chiefly determined by the Computation of its Distance from Fort Niagara by Mr. Maginty,[2] and its Bearing and Distance from the Mouth of Sandusky.

"I must not omit my Acknowledgment to Mr. William West[3] for

---

George Washington at Venango in 1753, and at Logstown Conference in 1754. Hanna, *op. cit.*, II, 330.

[1]Not identified.

[2]Alexander McGinty, who was captured by the

French in 1753, was taken to Montreal via Detroit and Niagara. Hanna, *op. cit.*, II, 255-56.

[3]An Indian trader on the Ohio in 1753 and Pennsylvania Commissioner at the Lancaster Conference with the Indians in 1756. *Colonial Records of Pennsylvania*, V, 761; VII, 96.

several valuable Notes about Potomack [Potomac], the Forks of Ohio, and Parts adjacent; nor to Richard Peters,[1] Esq; for the great Chearfulness he assisted me with in this Composition. As for the Branches of Ohio, which head in the New Virginia,[2] I am particularly obliged to Dr. Thomas Walker,[3] for the Intelligence of what Names they bear, and what Rivers they fall into Northward and Westward; but this Gentleman being on a Journey[4] when I happened to see him, had not his Notes, whereby he might otherwise have rendered those Parts more perfect. But the Particulars of these and many other Articles relating to the Situation of Places, I must defer till I deliver an Account of the several Rivers and Creeks, their Navigation, Portages, and Lands thereon."[5]

Assistance given the Author

A brief Description of the most considerable RIVERS, *in the* WESTERN DIVISION

"The Face of the Country, as already represented, determines the Nature of the Rivers. The flat Country (or *Lower Plains*) which lies between the Falls and the Sea, is every where interwoven with the most beautiful Bays, Rivers, and Creeks, navigable for all Sorts of Vessels; and is the Reason of so many fine Creeks spreading on every Side, from the Bays of Chesopeak [Chesapeake] and Delaware. For, as the Land has no Declivity, the Flux and Reflux of the Sea contribute to so wide extended Navigation. All the Creeks on Delaware, the Verges of the Sounds, which extend along the Sea-coast, and some Creeks in Virginia, and towards the Head of Chesopeak [Chesapeake] on the West Side, are bordered with Salt Marshes, some a Mile or Two wide. The First Settlers of America, for the Sake of the Grass for the Winter Support of their Cattle, fixing their Habitations along these Places, being infested

All the Rivers and Creeks navigable in the Lower Plains.

Salt Marshes

---

[1]Richard Peters (1704-1776), prominent Pennsylvanian, secretary of the Land Office, rector of Christ (Episcopal) Church, Philadelphia, and secretary of the Provincial Council of Pennsylvania, 1743-1762.

[2][Pownall's note] So called for Distinction-sake, that Part of Virginia South East of the Ouasioto [Cumberland] Mountains, and on the Branches of Green Briar, New River, and Holston River.

[3]Thomas Walker (1715-1794). *Journal of an Exploration in the Spring of the Year 1750 . . . with a*

Preface by William Cabell Rives. (Boston, Little, Brown, and Company, 1888). About one-half of this book consists of a biography of Dr. Walker.

[4]Dr. Walker, while serving as commissary to the Virginia troops in Braddock's army, visited Philadelphia early in the year 1755. *Ibid.*, p. 16. Lewis Evans, a resident of Philadelphia, may have conferred with him at that time.—Ed.

[5]Quoted from Evans' *Analysis*, pp. 10-11; reprinted in Gipson's *Lewis Evans*, pp. 154-55.

with Muskitoes and Intermitting Fevers, gave the Foundation for supposing America unhealthy. The Rest of Chesopeak [Chesapeake] Bay, and its Branches, is almost all a clean, gravelly, steep, dry Bank; and, were it not for the Scarcity of Fresh Water in some Parts of the Eastern Shore, would be as pleasant a Country as Imagination could well represent.

"The Isinglass Vein already described,[1] though broken at New-York, to let the Tide through into Hudson's [Hudson] River, to a far greater Distance than any other River on this Coast, continues still North-eastward, but with less Uniformity, over the West End of Long-Island and the Connecticut Shore, appearing but here and there, by reason of its being overlaid with the Ridges which terminate here.[2]

Delaware River
a D d E d

b B d F d

c F e

d E d

Leghei-wachsein
E d

"Delaware River,[3] from the Head to Cushietunk,[a4] though not obstructed with Falls, has not been improved to any Inland Navigation, by reason of the Thinness of the Settlements that Way. From Cushietunk to Trenton Falls,[b5] are Fourteen considerable Rifts, yet all passable in the long flat Boats[6] used in the Navigation of these Parts; some carrying 500 or 600 Bushels of Wheat. The greatest Number of the Rifts are from Easton[c] downward. And those Fourteen Miles above Easton, another just below Well's Ferry,[7] and that at Trenton, are the worst. The Boats seldom come down but with Freshes, especially from the Minnesinks:[d8] The Freight thence to Philadelphia is 8d. a Bushel for Wheat, and 3s. a Barrel for Flour. From the Forks, and other Places below, 20s. a Ton for Pig Iron, 7d. a Bushel for Wheat, 2s. 6d. a Barrel for Flour. This River, above Trenton, has no Branches worth mentioning for Conveniency of Navigation; *Legheiwacsein*[e] [Lackawaxen] has not a Hundredth Part so much Water as Delaware has at the Mouth of it. This Creek takes the general Course laid down in the Map. But as

[1]Pages 93, 94 this work.

[2]Quoted from Evans' *Analysis*, pp. 16-17; reprinted in Gipson's *Lewis Evans*, pp. 160-61.

[3][Pownall's note] Called by the Natives *Petuxat*; and by the Dutch *South River*, correlative to that at New York called *North River*.

[4]A mountain range north and parallel to the Tuscarora Mountains in northeastern Pennsylvania shown on Pownall's map. Cushichtun Mountain. *W. Scull's, Map of Pennsylvania, op. cit.*

[5]At Trenton, New Jersey.

[6][Pownall's note] These Boats are made like Troughs, square above, the Heads and Sterns sloping a little fore and aft; generally 40 or 50 Feet long, Six or Seven Feet wide, and Two Feet Nine Inches

or Three Feet deep, and draw 20 or 22 Inches Water, when loaden.

These boats known as Durham boats were developed to carry bulk products over the rifts in the Delaware River. They followed the pattern of Indian canoes and could be rowed, poled, or sailed. *Steelways* (N.Y. American Iron and Steel Institute), I (1947), no. 13, p. 28.—Ed.

[7]Near Raven Rock, Bucks County, Pennsylvania.

[8]The Minisink lands, formerly the home of the Minisink, a clan of the Delaware tribe, are on both sides of the Delaware at the Water Gap. The eastern townships in Monroe and Pike Counties, Pennsylvania. Hanna, *op. cit.*, I, 91.

Mr. Edward Scull,[1] to whom I am obliged for many Observations in the Course of my Map, has lately laid out some great Tracts of Land on this Creek, and given me an Account of it, since the Engraving of that Part, I shall here deliver a few Particulars, to avert some public Disputes that have been about it. From the Mouth to the Fork the Course Its Fork is S. 70° W. about Twelve Miles in a strait Line, the Creek crooked and rapid. There the Two Branches are nearly of a Bigness, the Southern The Southern one rather the largest. Half a Mile above the Fork, the South Branch, or Branch
Three great Wallanpaupack [Wallenpaupack], tumbles about Thirty Feet per- Falls pendicularly; and a little Way higher are Two other Falls, not quite so large. From the Fork to the Proprietaries Tract,[2] it is S 60 W. Four or Five Miles, the Channel pretty strait. Thence for Ten Miles taken in a strait Line, the Course is S. 56 W. by Compass, the Stream crooked and very gentle. By the Range of the Hills, this Branch continues much the same Direction to its Source. The Northern Branch of Legheiwacsein The Northern [Lackawaxen] divides again into Two Branches, at about a Mile and a Branch
forks again Quarter above the Mouth, where each is about large enough to turn an under-shot Grist Mill. Three Quarters of a Mile higher is a great Pine Swamp, through which both Branches come. Mr. Scull[3] thinks that these Branches, whose general Course is about N.W. do not at most extend above Fifteen Miles; and that all the Waters this Way are confined to the lower Side of the great Chains of Mountains, which extend from about the Station Point[4] to Susquehanna about Whioming [Wyoming].[5]

"The *West* Branch[f6] of Delaware is but inconsiderable, compared f The West with the North-eastern Branch, into which it falls at Easton. Above the Branch F e Tuscarora Hills at Gnadenhutten it is divided into little Creeks, and no Part goes North-westward of the Cushietunk Mountains. Delaware has no other Branches on the West Side between the Station Point and Easton worth the mentioning; the Country being drained by little Runs and Creeks.

"Schuylkill is a fine Branch, up which the Tide runs Five Miles

---

[1]In 1749 Edward Scull was commissioned by the Proprietaries of Pennsylvania to survey the lands on the Lackawaxen, which had been sold to them by the Five Nations in 1748. *Colonial Records of Pennsylvania*, V, 489-90.

[2]See "Map of the Indian Walking Purchase, 1737, by Lewis Evans," frontispiece in Gipson, *op. cit.*

[3]Edward Scull.

[4]The Station fixed as the terminating point on the branch of the Delaware farthest north in 41° 40′ north latitude. New Jersey *Archives, op. cit.*, VIII, 20-22.

[5]A section of the Susquehanna Valley about 100 miles due west of New York City. This valley extends about 20 miles from Lackawanna Gap to Nanticoke Gap. First important Indian territory and later the scene of the Connecticut-Pennsylvania land controversy. In the vicinity of the present city of Wilkesbarre, Pennsylvania. See also Pownall's *note* 4, p. 130.

[6]Lehigh River.

Schuykill
Philadelphia

above Philadelphia, where there is an impassable Fall; and Three Miles higher another not much better. Thence to Reading is a fine gliding Current easy set against, as the Bottom is gravelly and even; and at Seasons not very dry, would furnish 15 or 16 inches Water all the Way."[1]

A Conversation passing one day in 1755 at M[r] Allen's[2] The Cheif-Justice of Pensylvania [Pennsylvania], on the uncommon Event of such a Town as Philadelphia arising, amidst a wilderness, in so short a time, & becoming so fine & populous a City as we all saw it. I addressed myself on the subject to his Mother then at table. The Old Lady told me that she who now lived to see this great Town with near Thirty thousand inhabitants in it, enjoying every comfort & elegance & even luxury that the first town in Europe could offerr, had seen the beginning of it; & what was more rememberd well when she lived with her Parents in New-Jersey, & when this Country now Pensylvania [Pennsylvania] was a Wilderness, to have heard them mention the period that to her it was merely talked of *as a Report*, That a Society of the Friends (so the people called Quakers are properly denominated) at the head of which Friend Penn was, did intend to transport themselves to America, & to make an Establishment somewhere about the Swedes upper settlements. That any Person should live to see any Object brought forward from speculation & realized in so extraordinary a manner is so singular an Anecdote in the History of Man, that I dare say my inserting it here will to whomsoever reads it, as it did to me who heard it, suggest matter & Views of curious disquisition into the powers of man, & the operations of Human Society, when founded in *natural* & established on *true* principles; & when conducted in the spirit of peace by the vigour of Liberty.

Susquehanna
River, its
upper Parts
navigable.
g G d p F f
i F f
k F f

"Susquehanna River is navigable with Canoes, quite from the Lakes at the Head[g] to the Falls at Conewega [Conewago];[p3] nor is there any Fall till that Three Miles below Whioming [Wyoming].[i4] A Quarter of a Mile below Nescopeki [Nescopek][k] is another; both passable up or

[1]Quoted from Evans' *Analysis*, pp. 20-22; reprinted in Gipson's *Lewis Evans*, pp. 164-66.
[2]William Allen.
[3]The Conewago comes into the Susquehanna near York Haven, Pennsylvania.
[4][Pownall's note] This Place and the District is now settled by a populous Colony, which swarmed and came forth from Connecticut. The People of Connecticut say, that their Charter and the Grant of Lands under it was prior to that of Pennsylvania; that the Grant of Lands to them extended within the Latitudes of their Grant (except where possessed

by other Powers at that Time) to the South Seas. They allow New York and New Jersey to have been so possessed at the Time of their Grant, but say, that their Right emerges again at the West Boundary of those Provinces. Mr. Penn, and the People of Pennsylvania who have taken Grants under him say, that this District is in the very Heart of the Province Pennsylvania. On this State of Claims the Two Colonies are in *actual War*, which they have not even remitted against each other here, although united in Arms against Great Britain 1775.
See also *note 5*, p. 129.

down with Safety. The Water thence to Samokin [Shamokin][11] is generally pretty gentle. Thence to Conewega [Conewago] are several troublesome Falls, but all passable downward with Safety in Freshes. Conewega [Conewago] is the only Fall which tumbles headlong in this River. Below this are Three or Four others, which are passable only with Freshes. By reason of so many bad Falls this River has not yet any Inland Navigation; nor is it indeed capable of any from Conewega [Conewago] downwards. Its considerable Branches are, Owege,[m] Tohiccon or Cayuga,[2] Senaghse, or West Branch, Juniata, Swatara, Conewega [Conewago], Codorus,[3] Constoga [Conestoga]. *Tohiccon*[n] promises well for a good Navigation with Canoes to the Head of Ohio River, as it is a fine large Branch, and the Stream pretty moderate. The *West* Branch[o] is shallow and rapid, and has scarce a Fall worth the mentioning, and not one impassable. It is passable only when the Rains raise it; and then to the Path[p4] leading from Franks Town to Ohio, where a Portage of Forty Miles makes this Way a Communication with that River. Juniata,[q] as it is obstructed with short Falls, is gentle and pretty deep in the intermediate Places, and may be improved for the Carriage of Goods almost to Franks Town.[5] Swatara,[r] Conewega [Conewago], Codorus,[6] and Conestoga, some Centuries hence will, no Doubt, be improved to good Account.

"Chesopeak [Chesapeake] may be justly esteemed the Bay of Susquehanna; and as such we may reckon all the Creeks and Rivers from Potomack [Potomac] upwards, as so many Branches of it. The many Portages from the Creeks of this Bay to those of Delaware, are become already very useful, and in future Ages will be more so. Several are pointed out in the Map: And it may also be observed here, that the Road at each is extremely level and good; and Vessels of different Magnitude come up to the Portages.

"Large Sloops can come up to Snow Hill on *Pokomoke* [Pocomoke], the Portage is Five Miles from thence to Senepuxen Sound,[7] where Ships may come. If the Marylanders ever intend a direct Passage through their own Colony to the Sea, here an Attempt would be most likely to succeed.

l F f
Conewega the only impassable Falls

m E e

n Tohiccon E f Its considerable Branches.

o West Branch F f

p F h

q Juniata F f

r Swatara &c F f

Chesopeak Bay Many Portages between its Creeks and those of Delaware

Portages from Pokomoke H e

[1]On present site of Sunbury, Pennsylvania.

[2]Chemung River, New York. Paul A. W. Wallace, *Conrad Weiser . . . Friend of Colonist and Mohawk* (Philadelphia, University of Pennsylvania Press, 1945), p. 157.

[3]Codorus Creek flows into Creitz Creek at York, Pennsylvania. Creitz Creek empties into the Susquehanna near Columbia.

[4]For full description of the Frankstown Path read Hanna, *op. cit.*, I, 247-273.

[5]Near present Hollidaysburg, Pennsylvania.

[6]A tributary of Creitz Creek in the vicinity of York, Pennsylvania.

[7]Sinepuxent Bay.

"Shallops may go up *Nanticoke* River, near Twenty Miles into Delaware Colony;[u] the Portage from this River to Indian River is Thirteen Miles, and to Broad[1] Creek Twelve.

"*Choptank*[w] is navigable with Shallops to the Bridge, about Six or Seven Miles within Delaware Colony; and the Portage thence to Motherkill[2] is Fifteen Miles.

"From *Chester* River[x] to Salisbury[3] on Duck Creek,[4] the Portage is Thirteen Miles. And from Sassefras[5] there is another Portage to the same Place Thirteen Miles also.

"From *Frederick*[6] on Sassefras, where good Ships can come, there is a Portage to Cantwell's Bridge[7] on Apoquinimy [Appoquinimink] Fourteen Miles.

"From *Bohemia*,[8] where large Flats or small Shallops can come, there is a Portage[9] of Eight Miles to Cantwell's Bridge. This is the most frequented of any between the Waters of Delaware and Chesopeak [Chesapeake]. All these Creeks which lead into Delaware will receive large Shallops, but no larger Vessels.

"From the *Head of Elk*, where Shallops can come, the Portage is Twelve Miles to Christeen Bridge.[10] And it is about the same Distance to Omelanden Point,[11] a fast Landing on Delaware River, Three or Four Miles below Newcastle. This latter Portage has not been occupied since these Parts came last under the Dominion of the English.

"*Potomack* [Potomac] is navigable with large Shipping to Alexandria, and for Shallops Fourteen Miles more to the Falls; the Portage thence is Six Miles by a good Waggon Road. Boats[12] shaped like those of Delaware, and of something less Dimensions, may go up to the North Mountain without Obstruction, save at the Rift, or Falls, in the South Mountain,[y] which however is passable. The River runs through the

[1]Broadkill Creek, Delaware.
[2]Murderkill River, Delaware. Federal Writers' Project. Delaware, *op. cit.*, pp. 345-46.
[3]Duck Creek Village, Delaware. *Ibid.*, p. 376.
[4]Present Smyrna River. *Ibid.*, p. 477.
[5]Sassafras River, Delaware.
[6]On northern bank of Sassafras River opposite Georgetown, Delaware. Herman Böÿe. *A Map of the State of Virginia Constructed in Conformity to Law from the late Surveys authorized by the Legislature ... 1825. Corrected by order of the Executive 1859.* [1859]. Not located on modern maps.
[7]Present Odessa, Delaware. *Ibid.*, pp. 340-41.

[8]Probably at the junction of Great and Little Bohemia Creeks. In the latter part of the seventeenth century Caspar and Ephriam Herman lived here on Bohemian Manor. *Ibid.*, p. 475.
[9]This portage or road from the Herman estate to Cantwell's Bridge, near Odessa, was in use as early as 1679. *Ibid.*
[10]Present Christiana, Delaware. Federal Writers' Project. Delaware. *Ibid.*, pp. 483-84.
[11]Probably at present Leipsic, Delaware. The first village, founded in 1723, was called *Fast Landing. Ibid.*, pp. 477-78.
[12]Durham boats.

North Mountain without any Fall; and from thence to Will's Creek,[z1] z G h
there are Three or Four Rifts passable with Canoes or Batteaux, when
the Water is not very low. The Inland Navigation by this River is
scarce begun; but one may foresee that it will become in Time the most
important in America, as it is likely to be the sole Passage from Ohio to
the Ocean. The North Branch is scarce passable with Canoes beyond
the Shawane Fields,[2] some Three or Four Miles above Will's Creek. The Portage from
Portage from this Branch to Ohio is yet unsettled, by reason of the bad Will's Creek
Roads and Hills. But as at this Time, it may be an Object of Enquiry, to Youghiogani
some Account of the Ground will not be unacceptable. From Will's Creek
the Ground is very stony for the greater Part of the Allegeny [Allegheny]
Mountain;[a] but not so much so from the Shawane Fields.[3] The Moun- a G h
tain, though pretty stony, may have a good Waggon Road made over it.
On the North West Side of this Chain of Hills there is all along a great
Deal of swampy Ground, which is a considerable Obstruction to a
direct Passage; but yet manageable by taking some little Compass round.
From this Westward you cross Two Branches[4] of Youghiogani [Youghio-
gheny]: the greater,[5] which is the most Westerly, at Three Miles above
the Joining of the Three Forks, or Turkey Foot.[b6] And the Three Forks b G j
are Three Miles above the Lawrel [Laurel] Hill, through which Youghio- Ohiopyle
gani [Youghiogheny] precipitates by a great Fall[7] of near Thirty Feet, Falls.
and continues to run with great Rapidity for Two or Three Miles
further. At this Time to go from the Crossing[8] to Youghiogani [Youghio-
gheny] below the Falls, they are obliged to go by the Meadows,[9] there
cross Lawrel [Laurel] Hill, and return again Northward, and by that
Means take near Thirty Miles to reach the navigable Water of this
River; whereas if a Road could be made near the Fall, Fifteen or Twenty
Miles might be saved in the Way to Fort du Quesne.[10] There is a good
Ford through Youghiogani [Youghiogheny], and the Ground all the Way

[1]At Cumberland, Maryland.

[2]Shawnee Fields on the Potomac on the flat lands
now in part occupied by the west side of the city of
Cumberland. Hanna, *op. cit.*, I, 157.

[3]*Ibid.*

[4]The two branches, Main, or south branch (i.e.
Youghiogheny River proper) and Castlemans River
rise in Virginia and Maryland respectively.

[5]Main or south branch.

[6]Present Confluence, Somerset County, Pennsyl-
vania. Here the third or Pennsylvania branch,
Laurel Hill Creek which rises in Somerset County,
Pennsylvania, meets the other two branches of the
Youghiogheny.

[7]Ohiopyle Falls in Fayette County, Pennsylvania.

[8]Great Crossing. An historic marker marks this
site, a bridge near Addison, Pennsylvania, on highway U.S. Route 40.

[9]Great Meadows, the site of Fort Necessity. A
Virginia fort was built and commanded by George
Washington in 1754. The reconstructed Fort, and
State Historical Museum are at Great Meadows near
Uniontown, Pennsylvania.

[10]Fort Duquesne (1754-58). French fort built at
the confluence of the Allegheny and Monongahela
Rivers. On present site of Pittsburgh, Pennsylvania.

good and sound; and a Road may easily be made along it. Lawrel [Laurel] Hill, though small, is a Ridge very hard to cross, by reason of its Steepness; but at the Meadows is the best Pass we know of yet towards Virginia; there a Waggon, which would require four Horses to travel with, may be drawn up by Six. Probably a Pass may also be found for Wheel Carriages to the North of the Falls; and if there should, it would much improve the Portage between Potomack [Potomac] and Youghiogani [Youghiogheny], and reduce it to Fifty Miles, whereas it is now but little short of Seventy. If we have the good Fortune of being Masters of Ohio, the Navigation of Youghiogani [Youghiogheny] will be of Importance, since it is passable with flat bottomed Boats, capable of carrying Four or Five Tons, from the Mouth to the Foot of the Rift below the Falls. A Horse Path may be conducted in Six or Seven Miles, without much Expence, from the great Crossing[1] to the Head of navigable Water. From this to Fort du Quesne[2] you may go down in a Day, but it requires at least Three to return up the Stream."[3]

The following very curious and very interesting Account of the Communications betwixt the Waters of the European present Settlements and the Waters of Ohio, I received from Lieutenant Governor Mercer,[4] which I give to the Reader in his own Words:

"During the last War[5] on the Ohio most of the heavy and bulky Commodities were landed at George Town[6] on Potomack [Potomac] River, and conveyed thence in Waggons to Conogochieg [Conecocheague],[7] where they were embarked on Batteaux and Canoes, and were landed at Fort Cumberland;[8] from Fort Cumberland they were conveyed in Waggons to the Monongahela at the Mouth of Red Stone Creek,[9] and there put on board Batteaux, which conveyed them to Pitsburg [Pittsburgh]; the Distance from Fort Cumberland to the Mouth of Red Stone Creek is 73 Miles, and was generally performed in Three Days; each Waggon with Four Horses carried 22 Cwt. and were allowed 9s. Sterling per Day; but it was afterwards known that a good Waggon Road might be made from Fort Cumberland on the North Branch of the Potomack [Potomac] to a Branch of the Youghiog[h]eny,

Lawrel Hill G j

Youghiogani Navigable to Falls

[1]Near present Addison, Pennsylvania.
[2]On present site of Pittsburgh, Pennsylvania.
[3]Quoted from Evans' *Analysis*, pp. 22-24; reprinted in Gipson's *Lewis Evans*, pp. 166-68.
[4]George Mercer.
[5][Pownall's note for revised and enlarged edition] The Warr of 1755.

[6]Georgetown, District of Columbia, is the head of navigation on the Potomac River.
[7]On present site of Williamsport, Maryland.
[8]Fort Cumberland, built in 1754 as Fort Mt. Pleasant, by Colonel James Innes, and renamed Fort Cumberland, in 1755. William H. Lowdermilk. *History of Cumberland, (Maryland)* ... (Washington, D.C., James Anglim, 1878), pp. 89-94.
[9]Present Brownsville, Pennsylvania.

which would not exceed 40 Miles. The Troops left in Garrison at Pitsburg [Pittsburgh] after the Conclusion of the Indian War received very large Supplies of Provision, &c. from the Inhabitants of the South Branch of Potomack [Potomac] in Virginia, who cleared a Waggon Road and found a good Pass through the Mountains to Cheat River, a Branch of the Monongahela, about 50 Miles above the Mouth of Red Stone Creek, and found a good and speedy Conveyance thence by Water to Pitsburg [Pittsburgh]. The Distance from the Waters of the South Branch of the Potomack [Potomac] to Cheat River is only 20 Miles, and Col. Wilson[1] has erected good Grist and Saw Mills on Cheat River: These Circumstances are known to all the Officers who served in that Quarter last War. And since the War some Persons in Virginia, in particular Mr. John Balleneine [Ballendine],[2] who is a good Mechanick, has explored these Waters and the several natural Advantages they offer; and is of Opinion, nay has proved, that for less than 40,000£. Locks,[3] &c. might be formed at the Falls both of Potomack [Potomac] and James Rivers, which would render those Rivers navigable at all Seasons of the Year for the largest Barges now used on the Thames, nay even of Barges of 200 Tons, as from his general Observations of those Rivers, particularly of Potomack [Potomac], at the Falls of which he has remarkable fine Mills and a Forge,[4] and was also Proprietor of a Furnace[5] for Iron Ore near the Mouth of the Shannandoah [Shenandoah] for many Years, that they never would have less than Four Feet Water in the driest Seasons; and from an actual Survey[6] he assures me that the Waters of James River and of those of the Kenhawa [Kanawha] are no more than Four Miles distant, and that the Waters of the Kenhawa [Kanawha] are also navigable, and together with those of the South Branch might be made completely so for the Expence above mentioned.

"Though in Search of the *Head of Potomac*, the King's and Lord Fairfax's Commissioners determined the *North* to be the main Branch; yet it is very well known, that the *South* Branch is navigable 40 Miles up with Batteaux. And as it was not clear to me that the true Head of Potomac was at the Place those Gentlemen determined it, I have

[marginal note: H j]

[marginal note: South Branch of Potomac]

[1]Not identified.

[2]John Ballendine—(d. 1785?), owner of iron furnaces in colonial Virginia.

[3]The *James River Company*, incorporated for the purpose of improving navigation of the James River was probably an outgrowth of the Ballendine interests. Virginia Laws, statutes, etc. *The Statutes at Large . . . of Virginia . . .* published by William W.

Hening. (Richmond, printed for the editor by George Cochran, 1823), XI, 450-62.

[4]John Ballendine's mills and forge were at Westham, near Richmond, Virginia. Virginia *Calendar of Virginia State Papers . . .* , edited by Wm. P. Palmer, (Richmond, R. F. Walker, 1875), I, 364.

[5]Probably Buckingham forge. *Ibid.*

[6]Not located.

not laid down the western Side of Maryland, which should be a Meridian drawn from the Head of Potomac to the Pennsylvania Line. If the Affair is candidly examined, it will probably be determined, that the South Branch is the most considerable. If so, the Head of the North Branch will not be the western Extremity of Maryland, though it now is of Lord Fairfax's Grant.[1] Very hilly and swampy Ground prevents a Portage by any tolerable Road from the South Branch to Monaungáhela [Monongahela].[a] As this latter River is fine and gentle some Use may in future Times be made of it, either in a Communication with Green Briar [Greenbrier] or Potomac; for it is passable with Flats a great Way above Red Stone Creek, and interrupted with one impassable Fall only.[2]

"Shanedore [Shenandoah] is a fine Branch of Potomac, but its Inland Navigation is yet inconsiderable; but, in future Time, it will no doubt be improved to a good Account.

"Rapahannock[b] [Rappahannock], *York River*,[b] *Matapany*[b] [Mattapony], and *Pamúnky*[b] [Pamunkey] though of excellent Marine Navigation, are but inconsiderable above the *Lower Plains;* their Branches being confined below the South Mountain, and impassable with the slightest Inland Craft.

"James River is scarce inferior to any in excellent Navigation for Marine as well as Inland Craft. The Tide runs up to the foot of the Falls,[3] a distance if measured in right line about 110 Miles, 140 & more as the Water winds. Marine Vessels of great Burthen go up to these Falls, or near them. At Jamestown the river is about 2½ Miles broad, at Richmond which is on the banks of the River a little below the falls it is about half a Mile broad. Its lower Falls being near Six Miles long, and tumbling in little short Cascades, are intirely impassable. The River thence upward to an impassable Fall[4] in the South Mountain is excellently fitted for large Boats[5] like those already described in Delaware.

a Monaunga-hela G j

Shanedore G g

b Rapa-hannock York River, Matapany and Pamunky J f J g

[1]In 1733 Lord Fairfax petitioned the Crown to have the bounds of his grant in Virginia finally settled. The survey was made in 1736 and a map was made in duplicate to show the bounds of the Northern Neck of Virginia, Lord Fairfax's grant. Read "Proceedings of the Commissioners to Lay out the Bounds of the Northern Neck," in William Byrd's *History of the Dividing Line and Other Tracts . . .* (Richmond, Va., 1866), II, 83-139.
One copy of the map is now in the Public Records Office, London, and the other* is in possession of the Darlington Memorial Library, University of Pitts-

burgh. *A Map of the Northern Neck in Virginia; The Territory of the Right Honourable Lord Fairfax; Situate between the Rivers Potomack and Rappahanock, according to a late Survey; Drawn in the Year 1737 by Wm. Mayo.*

[2]In this paragraph Pownall's quotation from Evans' *Analysis* is almost paraphrase.

[3]At Richmond, Virginia.

[4]Balcony Falls. Blair Niles, *The James, from Iron Gate to the Sea* (N.Y., Farrar & Rinehart, [c1945]), p. 6. Near Glasgow, Virginia.

[5][Pownall's note] Generally 30 or 40 Feet Long,

And it is passable with lighter Craft much further, and would not require above 40 or 50 Miles Portage to the Branches of Kanhawa [Kanawha] River. But this however is not improveable to Ohio; for Kanhawa [Kanawha] has an impassable Fall[1] in a Ridge, which is impassable for Man or Beast by Land. But its opening a Passage to the New Virginia[2] is a very great Advantage.

Kanhawa River

"Roanoak [Roanoke], which falls into Albemarle Sound, beyond the Bounds of this Map, is barred at the Entrance, so as not to receive such large Ships as it would otherwise bear. It is passable with Shallops to the Falls.[c3] From thence upwards it is generally placid and wide, and in some Places interrupted with little Rifts and Falls, none of which, that I have heard of, impassable. It is liable to very great Freshes, and has not been yet improved to any Inland Navigation; for the People on its Branches, Holstein [Holston][4] River,[d] Yadkin,[e5] and New River,[f6] turn hitherto all their Commerce into James River. There is no River more likely to be of Importance in the future Navigation of the Inland Parts this Way than Roanoak [Roanoke], because it hath good Depth of Water, and extends right into the Country.

Roanoak River

c K k

d K l
e K g
f J k

"There are many other Creeks and Rivers in the Settlements that are obscured by the superior Excellence of these already described, which would well deserve Description, if I were to give a Detail of any particular Colony.

"The little Acquaintance that the Public has had with the River OHIO, will be a sufficient Apology for my entering into a more minute Detail of it and its Branches than of any other already described.

Ohio

"From the Head,[g] which interlocks with the Cayuga Branch[7] of Susquehanna to Canawagy,[h8] I have little Knowledge, but suppose, from the Evenness of the Land, that it may afford good Inland Navigation in future Ages. From Canawagy[9] to Chartier's Old Town,[i10] the

From the Head to Canawagúng
g E j   h E g
Thence to Chartier's
i F j

Three or Four Feet broad, and drawing empty 10 to 12 Inches Water, and when loaded about 18 Inches. Durham boats.

[1]Kanawha Falls, about two miles below the junction of the New and Gauley Rivers, which forms the Great Kanawha River. George W. Atkinson, *History of Kanawha County* ... (Charleston, printed at the office of the West Virginia Journal, 1876), p. 10. In Fayette County, West Virginia.

[2]Kentucky.

[3]Roanoke Rapids.

[4]Holston is a tributary of the Tennessee River.

[5]Yadkin is a tributary of the Peedee River.

[6]New River is a tributary of the Great Kanawha River.

[7]Chemung River, N.Y.

[8]Conewango or Connewango, a Seneca Indian town that stood on the site of present Warren, Pennsylvania. This Indian town was destroyed by Colonel Brodhead in 1781. Hodge, *op. cit.*, I, 338.

[9]Present site, Warren, Pennsylvania.

[10]A Shawnee town on the Allegheny near the present site of Tarentum, Pennsylvania. The town was named for Peter Chartier, the French-Shawnee Indian trader. Hanna, *op. cit.*, I, 269, 307.

River is all along sufficiently moderate, and always deep enough for Canoes and Batteaux, which do not draw above 15 Inches Water; nor is it obstructed with any remarkable Rifts or Falls, save at a sharp Bent[1] some Miles below Licking Creek,[2] where the Water rushes on a Rock with great Violence;[k] and at Toby's Falls,[13] which is a Rift passable with Safety on the West Side. In this Part of the River are several Fording-places, but they are more rare as you come lower down. That at Char-tier's Old Town[m4] is the best; which, as soon as the Rock appears above Water, is passable close above it. At Shanoppens[n5] [Shanoppin's] is an-other in very dry Times, and the lowest down the River. This Part, which is very crooked, has seldom been navigated by our People, be-cause the great Number of Horses necessary to carry their Goods to Ohio, serve also to carry them there from Place to Place; and the little Game that Way makes it but little frequented.

"The Navigation from Chartier's Old Town,[o6] all the Way down to the Falls,[p7] has been hitherto performed in very large wooden Canoes,[8] which they make of great Length better fitted to steer against a rapid stream; they are navigated down by Two Men, and upwards by Four at least. From Chartier's to the Lower Shawane Town,[9] they are in the Spring about Four Days in going down with the Freshes; for then they let the Canoe drive in the Night; but towards the End of Summer, when the Water is low, and less swift, they usually spend 10 or 12 Days; but at moderate Seasons the Passage is performed in Six or Eight. In returning, they take often 30 or 40 Days, though double handed, and seldom less than 20. Supposing we go down the River from Chartier's, the Water is pretty moderate till you come to Sweep Chimney Island,[10]

Side notes:
A Sharp Bent below Licking Creek
k E j
l F j
Fords

m
at Chartier's Old Town F j
n at Shanoppens. F j

Navigation from Chartier's Old Town to the Falls o F j
p J r

Small Rifts

[1]Probably Brady's Bend, Armstrong County, Pennsylvania.

[2]Present East Sandy Creek which flows into the Allegheny River five miles south of Franklin, Pennsylvania. Howard N. Eavenson, *The First Century and a Quarter of American Coal Industry.* (Pittsburgh, Pa., Privately printed, Koppers Building, 1942), p. 21.

[3]Toby Creek, present Clarion River. Hanna, *op. cit.,* I, 213-14. Probably near Parker's Landing on the Allegheny River at the mouth of the Clarion River.

[4]See *note* 10, page 137.

[5]A Delaware town on the Allegheny River about two miles above its junction with the Monongahela, at present Pittsburgh, Pennsylvania. Since this town, the home of Chief Shanopin, was on the path from the east to the Ohio country, it was much frequented by traders. Hodge, *op. cit.,* II, 526-27.

[6]Near present site of Tarentum, Pennsylvania.

[7]Louisville, Kentucky.

[8][Pownall's note] Generally 30 or 40 Feet long, Three or Four Feet broad, and drawing empty 10 or 12 Inches Water, and when loaded about 18 inches.

[9]This Shawnee town was just below the mouth of the Scioto until about 1750 when it was carried off by a flood and rebuilt on the opposite side of the river near the present site of Portsmouth, Ohio. Hodge, *op. cit.,* I, 777.

[10]Probably Nine Mile Island. E. L. Babbitt, *The Allegheny Pilot . . .* (Freeport, Pa., E. L. Babbitt, 1855), p. 53.

between Dick's[1] and Pine Creek,[2] where it is very rapid. It generally happens that where the River is confined to narrower Bounds by Islands it is more rapid, yet not so but Canoes may be easily set against it. At Fort du Quesne, at Paul's Island,[3] Five Miles lower, and at a Flat between that and Logs Town, the Water is pretty rapid; as it is also at a small Island[4] between that and Beaver Creek. These are, however, inconsiderable; nor are those Places just below Beaver Creek and at a Flat a little above the upper End of the Pipe Hills[5] much more worthy Regard. At *Hart's Rock*q[6] the River makes a quick Bend round a rocky Point, and a very sharp Rippling, where the Boatmen are obliged to wade and haul up near the Rock, the South East Side being full of Quicksands. At Weeling [Wheeling] Island,r[7] Muskingum Islands8[8] (a little Way above a fine Branch of that Name) and at Beaty's Island,[9] the Current is pretty rapid. At Three or Four Miles above the big Bent[10] is a considerable Rift called *Le Tart's Falls*,b[11] where the Water is so rapid that they are obliged to haul the Canoes with Ropes in coming up for near a Furlong along the South East Side. From this to the Lower Shawane Town,[12] at the Mouth of Sioto [Scioto], is no Obstruction worth mentioning."[13] The Ohio, as I learn from Capt. Gordon's Journal of 1766,[14] from 50 Miles above Muskingum to the North of Sioto [Scioto], is most beautiful, and interspersed with Numbers of Islands covered with the most stately Timber, with several long straight Reaches, one of which is 16 Miles and an Half long. "And the Stream thence downward to the Falls is still more gentle, and better fitted for Vessels drawing

q Hart's Rock
F k

r F k   s G l

Le Tart's
Fall
b H m

[1]Probably Deer Creek, which flows into the Allegheny River near Oakmont, Pennsylvania. Not located on modern maps.

[2]Pine Creek flows into the Allegheny River at Etna, a suburb of Pittsburgh, Pennsylvania.

[3][Pownall's note] Here are some Places mentioned, too inconsiderable to be laid down in this Map.

Paul's Island may be present Neville's Island, about six miles below Pittsburgh.—Ed.

[4]Crow's Island, 24 miles below Pittsburgh, is between Logstown and Big Beaver Creek. *The Navigator* . . . [by Zadok Cramer] (10th ed., Pittsburgh, Cramer & Spear, 1818), p. 70.

[5]Lewis Evans' *Map* of 1755 indicated that Pipe Hills are on both banks of the Ohio River above the mouth of Wheeling Creek. Pipe Hill is about 6 miles below Wheeling. "Fourth Rout down the Ohio." In William Smith, *Historical Account of Bouquet's Expedition Against the Ohio Indians* (Cincinnati, O., Robert Clarke & Co., 1868), p. 151.

[6]Present site of Smith's Ferry, Beaver County, Pennsylvania. Hanna, *op. cit.*, I, 207.

[7][Pownall's note] Above this there are Two remarkable Creeks, called, by the Traders, the Two Upper Creeks, which like Twins run about 30 Miles parallel to each other, and within Three Miles Distance, with a very rich Mesopatamia between them.

[8]Muskingum Island is three miles below the mouth of the Muskingum River. *Cramer's Navigator* (1818), *op. cit.*, p. 85.

[9]Not identified.

[10]The Great Bend in the Ohio.

[11]Also written Le Tort's Falls.

[12]Near present site of Portsmouth, Ohio.

[13]Quoted from Evans' *Analysis*, pp. 24-26; reprinted in Gipson's *Lewis Evans*, pp. 168-70.

[14]Extracts from Captain Harry Gordon's *Journal* are printed in Appendix IV of this book.

greater Depth of Water."[1] These Falls don't deserve that Name, as I am taught by Capt. Gordon's Journal, as the Stream on the North Side has no sudden Pitch, but only runs rapid over the Ledge of a Flat Limestone Rock; several Boats passed it in the driest Season of the Year, unloading One-third of their Freight, they passed on the North Side, where the Carrying-place is Three Quarters of a Mile long. On the South East Side it is about Half that Distance, and is reckoned the safest Passage for those who are unacquainted, but it is the most tedious, as during Part of the Summer and Fall they drag their Boats

c The Falls of Ohio J r

over the flat Rock. "The Fall is about Half a Mile rapid Water,[c] which however is passable, by wading and dragging the Canoe against the Stream, when lowest; and with still greater Ease when the Water is raised a little.

Great Floods

"Ohio, as the Winter Snows are thawed, by the Warmth or Rains in the Spring, rises in vast Floods, in some Places exceeding 20 Feet in Height, but scarce any where over-flowing its high and upright Banks. These Floods continue of some Height for at least a Month or Two, being guided in the Time by the late or early Breaking up of the Winter. The Stream is then too rapid to be stemmed upwards by Sailing or Rowing, and too deep for Setting,[2] but excellently fitted for large Vessels going down. Then Ships of 100 or 200 Tons may go from Fort du Quesne to the Sea with Safety; these Floods reducing the Falls, Rifts, and Shallows to an entire Equality with the rest of the River.

"Ohio carries a great Uniformity of Breadth, gradually increasing

d F j

from Two or Three Furlongs at the Forks[d] to near a Mile, as you go lower down; and spreading to Two Miles or more, where damm'd by

e J r
Navigation below the Falls

the Rief of Rocks, which make the Falls.[e] Thence to Mississippi its Breadth, Depth, and easy Current, equalling any River in Europe, except the Danube, affording there the finest Navigation for large sailing Vessels; but however in great Freshes it is full rapid to stem, without a good Breeze. And there is scarce any Gale stiff enough to stem the Falls, when deep enough to pass in Freshes. Upon the Whole, the

Navigation to Chartier's F j

Navigation of this River may be divided into Four Parts: 1. From Canawagy [Conewango] to Chartier's Old Town,[3] in Batteaux, capable of carrying about Three or Four Tons, and drawing 12 Inches Water.

[1]Quoted from Evans' *Analysis*, p. 26; reprinted in Gipson's *Lewis Evans*, p. 170.

[2][Pownall's note] By the known Laws of Mechanics, a Man Setting a Boat over a firm hard Bottom has twice the Advantage of the like Strength employed in Rowing. In Rowing, the Water being moveable, receives Half the Motion; While in Setting, the Boat receives the Whole.

[3]From present Warren to Tarentum, Pennsylvania.

2. From Chartier's to the Pig Bent,[1] in Flats, like those used in Delaware,[2] or larger; bearing 18 or 20 Tons. These Two Parts must be performed in long flat-bottomed Boats, as better fitted for Setting in shallow Water and rapid Streams. 3. From the Big Bent [Great Bend] to the Falls, in Shallops or Schooners of 10 or 15 Tons. As these are made for sailing and working to Windward, they must have sharp Bottoms and deep Keels; and though made broader than the Flats, they will not admit such great Lengths, and therefore not capable of so large Burdens. 4. From the Falls[3] to Mississippi thence to the Sea is only fitted for light Canoes or Batteaux against the Stream; but for any Vessels downwards, when the Floods are not so high as to overflow the adjoining wide extended Flats. Hence, in Process of Time, large Ships may be built upon Ohio, and sent off to Sea with the heavy Produce of the Country, and sold with the Cargoes.

    "OHIO has a great many *Branches*, which furnish good Navigation to the adjacent Parts; the most remarkable I intend to enumerate.

    "Canawagy[b] [Conewango], when raised with Freshes, is passable with Bark Canoes, or little Batteaux, to a little Lake at its Head; from which there is a Portage of 20 Miles to Lake Erie, at the Mouth of a little Creek called Jadághque.[4] This Portage is but little frequented, because Canawagy [Conewango] is too shallow in the Summer for the lightest Craft.

    "Bughaloons[c5] is not navigable, and noted only for large Meadows, as the Word signifies in the Delaware Indian Language.

    "Toranadaghkoa, French Creek, or Riviere le Bieuf,[d] is noted for its furnishing the nearest Passage to Lake Erie. It is navigable with Canoes to the French Fort by a very crooked Channel; the Portage thence to another Fort on Lake Erie called *Presqu' Isle*,[6] from an adjoining Peninsula, is 15 Miles; this Way the French come from Canada to Ohio. *Licking Creek*[7] and *Lacomick*[8] have no Navigation; but the former has Plenty of Coals.

    "Toby's Creek[9] is passable with Bark Canoes a good Way up

Margin notes:
To the
Big Bent
H m
To the Falls

To the
Mississippi;
thence to
the Sea

b Canawagy.
E j
Portage to
Lake Erie

c Bughaloons.
E j

d Riviere le
Bieuf. E j
Portage to
Lake Erie.
Licking
Creek, &c.
E j

Toby's Creek
E j

---

[1]From present Tarentum to the Great Bend in the Ohio, the vicinity of Le Tort's Falls.

[2]See *note* 6, p. 128.

[3]At Louisville, Kentucky.

[4]Probably Lake Chautauqua and Chautauqua Creek.

[5]Present Brokenstraw Creek. M. H. Deardorff, "Zeisberger's Allegheny River Indian Towns: 1767-1770." In *Pennsylvania Archaeologist* (Phila., Society for Pennsylvania Archaeology, 1930-), XVI (1946), no. 1, p. 18.

[6]French fort built in 1753. On present site of Erie, Pennsylvania.

[7]East Sandy Creek.

[8]Sandy Creek which flows from the west into the Allegheny River at the Indian Bend, Venango County, Pennsylvania.

[9]Clarion River. Hanna, *op. cit.*, I, 214.

towards the West Branch of Susquehanna; and a pretty short Portage may probably be found between them.

Moghul-
bughkitum
F j
"Moghulbughkitum[1] is passable also a good Way towards the same Branch, and will probably furnish a good Portage also.

Kish-
keminetas
F j
"Kishkeminetas [Kiskiminetas] is passable with Canoes 40 or 50 Miles, and good Portages will probably be found between it and Juniata and Potomac. It has Coal and Salt.

Monaunga-
hela F j
"Monaungahela [Monongahela] is a very large Branch, at whose Junction with Ohio stands Fort du Quesne. It is deep and gentle, and passable with large Batteaux beyond Redstone Creek, and still farther with lighter Craft. At Six Miles from the Mouth it divides into Two

Youghigani
F j
Branches; the Northernmost Youghiogani [Youghiogheny], passable with good Batteaux to the Foot of the Rift at Lawrel [Laurel] Hill. The Portage from this to Potamac has been already mentioned.

Sorts of Land
on Ohio
above Fort
du Quesne.
"The *Soil* along these Parts of Ohio and its eastern Branches, though but little broken with high Mountains, is none of the best; consisting in general of low dry Ridges of White Oak and Chesnut Land, with very rich interval low Meadow Ground. Here and there are Spots of fine White Pines, and in many Places great Extents of poor Pitch Pines. The Land from the back Part of the Endless Mountains, Westward to Ohio, and from Fort du Quesne upward, is of these Sorts. The same little broken Chain of Hills, which borders it here, near the River Side, continues South-westerly, till it ends at 10 Miles below the Falls; keeping at some 10 or 15 Miles from the general Course of the River all the Way down."

Capt. Gordon's Journal gives the following a Description of this Part of the Country: From the Falls to about 155 Miles and Three Quarters it is very hilly, the Course of the River very winding and narrow, and but very few Spots of level Land on the Sides of the River. The Hills are mostly stony and steep, but from the great Herds of Buffaloes which we saw on the Beaches of the River, and on the Islands into which they came, there must be good Pasture. After this the ridgy Ground ends, the Country then grows flat, and the River, whose Bed widens, is divided by Islands. The Navigation is good from the Falls, but where the flat Country begins Boats must keep the principal Channel, which is on the Right Hand going down.

e Beaver
Creek F K
"Beaver Creek[e] is navigable with Canoes only. At Kishkuskes[2]

---

[1] Probably Mahoning Creek.
[2] An Indian village of mixed Delaware and Iro-quois, which from 1753 to 1770 was on the banks of Beaver Creek near New Castle, Lawrence County, Pennsylvania. Hodge, *op. cit.*, I, 737.

[Kuskuskies], about 16 Miles up, Two Branches[1] spread opposite Ways; one interlocks with French Creek and Cherâge,[2] the other Westward with Muskingum and Cayahôga [Cuyahoga]; on this are many Salt Springs, about 35 Miles above the Forks; it is canoable about 20 Miles farther. The eastern Branch is less considerable, and both are very slow, spreading through a very rich level Country, full of Swamps and Ponds, which prevent a good Portage that might otherwise be made to Caya-hóga [Cuyahoga]; but will, no doubt, in future Ages, be fit to open a Canal between the Waters of Ohio and Lake Erie.

"Muskingum[f] is a fine gentle River, confined within high Banks that prevent its Floods from damaging the surrounding Land." It is 250 Yards wide at its Confluence with the Ohio. "It is passable with large Batteaux to the Three Logs [Legs],[3] and with small Ones to a little Lake at its Head, without any Obstruction from Falls or Rifts. From hence to Cayahoga [Cuyahoga] is a Portage[a] a Mile long. *Cayhahoga* [Cuyahoga], the Creek that leads from this Portage to Lake Erie, is muddy and mid-dling swift, but no where obstructed with Falls or Rifts. As this has fine Land, wide extended Meadows, lofty Timber, Oak and Mulberry fitted for Shipbuilding, Walnut, Chesnut, and Poplar for domestic Services, and furnishes the shortest and best Portage between Ohio and Lake Erie; and its Mouth is sufficient to receive good Sloops from the Lake: It will in Time become a Place of Consequence. *Muskingum*, though so wide extended in its Branches, spreads all in most excellent Land, abounding in good Springs and Conveniencies, particularly adapted for Settlements remote from Marine Navigation, as Coal, Clay, and Free-stone. In 1748 a Coal Mine, opposite Lamenshikola[4] Mouth, took Fire, and kept burning above a Twelve-month, where great Quantities are still left. Near the same Place is excellent Whetstone; and about Eight Miles higher up the River is Plenty of white and blue Clay for Glass Works and Pottery. Though the Quantity of good Land on Ohio, and its Branches, is vastly great, and the Conveniencies attending it so like-wise; we may esteem that on Muskingum the Flower of it all.

"Hockhocking[a5] is passable with Batteaux Seventy or Eighty

f Muskingum
G l

a Portage to
Cayahoga
F f
Cayahoga
E m
Its conse-
quence
Muskingum

a
Hockhocking
G m

[1]Shenango Creek interlocks with French Creek and the Grand River, the Mahoning with Musk-ingum and Cuyahoga Rivers. Hanna, *op. cit.*, I, 342.

[2]Grand River in Ohio. *Ibid.*

[3][Pownall's note] The Forks at which the Tus-caroras dwelt should have been placed 15 Miles North of the Three Logs [Legs].

Three Legs, an Indian town, abandoned before

1764, was located at the mouth of Big Stillwater Creek. Hanna, *op. cit.*, II, 188. Stillwater River is a tributary of the Tuscarawa River.—Ed.

[4]Probably Sandy Creek, Stark County, Ohio. Not located on contemporary (excepting Evans' *Map*) or modern maps.

[5]Also spelled *Hocking*.

Miles up; it has fine rich Land, and vast grassy Meadows, high Banks, and seldom overflows. It has Coals about Fifteen Miles up, and some Knowls of Freestone.

b
Big Canhawa
H m

"Big Canhawa[b] [Kanawha] falls into Ohio on the South East Side, and is so considerable a Branch, that it may, by Persons coming up Ohio on that Side, be mistaken for the main River. It is slow for Ten Miles, to the little broken Hills, and the Land very rich; as it is for about the same Breadth along Ohio, all the Way from the Pipe Hills[1] to the Falls.[2] After Ten Miles up Canhawa [Kanawha], the Land is hilly, the Water pretty rapid, for Fifty or Sixty Miles further to the Falls, to

Its Falls impassible H m

which Boats may go. This is a very remarkable Fall, not for its great Height, but for coming through a Mountain now thought impassable for Man or Beast, and is itself impassable. But no Doubt Foot or Horse Paths will be found when a greater Number of People make the Search, and under less Inconveniencies than our Travellers are at present. By reason of the Difficulty of passing the Ouasioto Mountains,[3] I thought them a very natural Boundary between Virginia and Ohio in these Parts; and for that Reason made them the Bounds of the Colours (in the coloured Maps) not that there is any Difference of Right between one

Its branches

Side and the other. *Louisa*, *New River*, and *Green Briar* [Greenbrier] are fine large Branches of Canhawa [Kanawha]; which in future Times will be of Service for the Inland Navigation of New Virginia,[4] as they interlock with Monaungahela [Monongahela], Potomack [Potomac], James River, Ronoak [Roanoke] and the Cuttawa River.[5]

c Totteroy
H n

d J n

"Totteroy[c6] falls into Ohio on the same Side, and is passable with Boats to the Mountains. It is long, and has not many Branches, interlocks with Red Creek, or Clinch's [Clinch] River[d] (a Branch of Cuttawa).[7] It has below the Mountains, especially for Fifteen Miles from the Mouth, very good Land. And here is a visible Effect of the Difference of Climate from the upper Parts of Ohio. Here the large Reed, or Carolina Cane, grows in Plenty, even upon the Upland, and the Severity of the Winter does not kill them; so that Travellers this Way are not obliged to

e J r

provide any Winter Support for their Horses. And the same holds all the Way down Ohio, especially on the South East Side to the Falls,[e8] and thence on both Sides.

[1]On both sides of the Ohio River above Wheeling Creek.
[2]At Louisville, Kentucky.
[3]Cumberland Mountains.
[4]Kentucky.

[5]Tennessee River. Donald Davidson, *The Tennessee*, (N.Y. Rinehart & Company, Inc., [1946-48]), I, 39.
[6]Big Sandy River, Kentucky.
[7]Tennessee River.
[8]At Louisville, Kentucky.

"Great Salt Lick Creek[f1] is remarkable for fine Land. Plenty of Buffaloes, Salt Springs, White Clay, and Limestone. Canoes may come up to the Crossing of the War Path, or something higher, without a Fall. The Salt Springs hurt its Water for Drinking, but the Number of fresh Springs near it make sufficient Amends.

f Great
Salt Lick
Creek H p

"Kentucke[g] [Kentucky] is larger than the foregoing, has high Clay Banks, abounds in Cane and Buffaloes, and has also some very large Salt Springs. It has no Limestone yet discovered, but some other fit for building. Its Navigation is interrupted with Shoals, but passable with Canoes to the Gap,[2] where the War Path[3] goes through the Ouasioto[4] Mountain. This Gap[k] I point out in the Map, as a very important Pass, and it is truly so, by reason of its being the only Way passable with Horses, from Ohio Southward, for 300 or 400 Miles Extent. And if the Government has a Mind to preserve the Country back of Carolina, is should be looked to in Time.

g Kentucke
J p

k An impor-
tant Pass thro'
Ouasioto
Mountain
J o

"As we go further down Ohio, the Distance from the Ouasioto Mountains[5] to the River becomes more considerable. The Land, from the little broken Hills to the Mountains, is of a middling Kind, and consists of different Veins and Stratas; and though everywhere as good as any Part of the English Settlements, falls far short of that on the other Side of Ohio, or between the little Hills and the River. These Hills[b] are small, and seem only the Brink of a rising Stage of Land, and dividing the rich Plains of Ohio from the Upland, bordering on the Ouasioto Mountains. They terminate at Ten Miles below the Falls; indeed a little Spur extended from their Side is that Limestone Reach that Ohio ripples over at the Falls.

b The little
Hills South
of Ohio
J q to F j

"Now to return to the other Side of Ohio. *Sioto* [Scioto] is a large gentle River, bordered with rich Flats, which it overflows in the Spring; spreading then above Half a Mile in Breadth, though when confined to its Banks it is scarce a Furlong wide.[6] If it floods early, it scarce retires within its Banks in a Month, or is fordable in a Month or Two more. The Land is so level, that in the Freshes of Ohio the Back-water runs Eight Miles up. Opposite the Mouth of this River is the Lower Shawane Town,[i7] removed from the other Side, which was One of the most noted

Sioto H o

i Lower
Shawane
Town. H o

---

[1]Probably Licking River which flows into the Ohio at Newport, Kentucky.

[2]Cumberland Gap.

[3]Catawba or Great Warriors' Trail. Hanna, *op. cit.*, II, 119.

[4]Cumberland Mountains.

[5]*Ibid.*

[6][Pownall's note] The Latitude of its Mouth 38° 22'. I have marked the Error of its being placed too high in the Map. Muskingum is in Evans's Map placed in its general Run much too far to the West; I have in some Measure corrected it in this Edition.

[7]Site of present Portsmouth, Ohio.

Places of English Trade with the Indians. This River, besides vast Extents of good Land, is furnished with Salt on an Eastern Branch, and Red Bole on Necunsia Skeintat. The Stream is very gentle, and passable with large Batteaux a great Way up, and with Canoes near 200 Miles to a Portage near the Head, where you carry over good Ground Four Miles to Sanduski [Sandusky]. *Sanduski*[k] [Sandusky] is a considerable River, abounding in level rich Land, its Stream gentle all the Way to the Mouth, where it will receive considerable Sloops. This River is an important Pass, and the French have secured it as such; the Northern Indians cross the Lake here from Island to Island,[1] land at Sanduski [Sandusky], and go by a direct Path[1] to the Lower Shawane Town, and thence to the Gap of Ouasioto,[2] in their Way to the Cuttawas [Catawba] Country. This will, no Doubt, be the Way that the French will take from *Detroit* to *Moville* [Mobile],[3] unless the English will be advised to secure it, now that it is in their Power.

k Sanduski, F n, an Important Place

E n

"Little Mineami [Miami] River[m] is too small to be gone far with Canoes. It has much fine Land, and some Salt Springs; its high Banks, and middling Current, prevent its overflowing much the surrounding Land.

m Little Mineami River H p

"Great Mineami [Miami] River, Assereniet, or Rocky River,[n] has a very stony Channel, a swift Stream, but no Falls. It has several large Branches, passable with Canoes a great Way; one[o][4] extending Westward towards the Quiaaghtena River;[5] another[6] towards a Branch of Mineami [Maumee] River (which runs into Lake Erie) to which there is a Portage, and a Third[7] has a Portage to the West Branch of Sanduski [Sandusky]; besides Mad Creek, where the French have lately established themselves. A Vein of elevated Land, here and there a little stony, which begins in the Northern Part of the Peninsula, between the Lakes Erie, Huron, and Michigan, extends across the Lake Mineami [Maumee] River, below the Fork, and Southward along the Rocky River,[8] to Ohio; and is the Reason of this River's being stony, and the Grounds rising a little higher than the adjacent Plains. It is, like all the Land on this River, very rich, and would scarce have been perceived, had not the River worn the Channel down to the Rocks which lie beneath.

n Rocky River G p o H q

"Quiaaghtena River, called by the French *Ouabach* [Wabash],

Quiaaghtena River. G r

[1]Catawba or Great Warriors' Path.
[2]Cumberland Gap.
[3]Founded by the French in 1702. Schlarman, *op. cit.*, p. 118.
[4]Whitewater River.
[5]Wabash River.
[6]Loramic Creek which flows into the Miami River near Lockington, Shelby County, Ohio.
[7]Great Miami River proper.
[8]Great Miami River.

though that is truly the Name of its South-Eastern Branch, is very large, and furnishes a fine Navigation; but whether interrupted with Rifts or Falls, I am not informed, but probably it is not, as the Lands round are fine level Flats, of vast Extent. The *Western League of Indians*,[1] known to themselves by the general Name of WELINIS, corruptly called by the French *Ilinois* [Illinois] (frequently distinguished by us, according to the several Tribes[2] or Nations that it consists of; as the Piancashas [Piankashaws], Wawiaghtas [Weas], Piques [Picts], Tawightawis [Twightwees], and Mineamis [Miamis]) are seated from this River to Sioto [Scioto]; and were permitted, about Sixteen Years ago, to settle there by the express Leave of the Confederates. *Present State of the Welinis*

"Into the Western End of Lake Erie falls Mineami [Maumee] River, a considerable Stream, navigable with Canoes to the Portages, which lead to the Quiaaghtena[3] and Rocky River,[4] interrupted with Three considerable Rifts below the Forks: But however it is an important River, because of the Portages it furnishes South-Westward."[5] *Mineami River E o*

I shall close this Account of the natural State of the Country with some Considerations on the Nature of its Climate.

The principal Circumstances on which singly and combined the Nature of the Climate of any Country depends, are, 1st. the Aspect of the given Horizon, as constituted and situated to *receive*, and 2dly The Nature of the Soil as constituted to *retain* the heat of the Sun: a Third is the Nature of the Atmosphere which is in the longest Continuance of Contact with this Horizon.

1st. If this Globe of Earth had One uniform plain Surface, the nearer Approach to, or greater Elongation from the Equator which any Country had (*caeteris paribus*) the greater or lesser Degree of Heat its Climate would partake of, because the more directly, or more obliquely that the Rays of the Sun strike any Surface, the greater or the lesser must the Reverberation of Heat be, as the Angle of Reflection is more acute or more obtuse: The more or less also will the Atmosphere in Contact with this Land be heated by this Reverberation; but as this is

[1] "A confederacy of Algonquin tribes, occupying S. Wisconsin, N. Illinois, and sections of Iowa and Missouri, comprising the Cahokia, Kaskaskia, Michigamea, the Moingwena, Peoria, and Tamaroa." Hodge, *op. cit.*, I, 597.

[2] The Piankashaw and Wea were subtribes of the Miami, but later became separate people. In 1854 the remnants of these tribes joined the Illinois which at that time were known as the Peoria or Kaskaskia. Hodge, *op. cit.*, II, 240, 925. Miamis and Twight-

wees were considered one and the same. The English usually designated the Miamis as Twightwees. *Ibid.*, I, 852-53. Of the Picts little is known excepting that they lived in the vicinity of the Miami village, Pickawillany (present Piqua, Ohio). *Ibid.*, II, 242.

[3] Wabash River.

[4] Great Miami River.

[5] Quoted from Evans' *Analysis*, pp. 26-31; reprinted in Gipson's *Lewis Evans*, pp. 170-75.

not the Case of the Surface of the Earth, a thousand other collateral Circumstances interfere with and break this Rule. As the Surface of the Earth is broken with numberless Irregularities, wherever the Inclination of the given Horizon lies different from the general Horizon of the Globe, it counteracts this general Effect: If on the North of the Equator it slopes Southward, or on the South of the Equator slopes Northward, so as to extend its general Plain nearer at right Angles with the Rays of the Sun than the spherick Plain of its Latitude would have been, it will receive and retain more heat in proportion than belongs to that Latitude. Hence the intense Heat of the southern Parts of Persia, and of those Parts which we call the East Indies. Hence also, principally, though other Circumstances may concur in the Cause, is the Climate of North America hotter than in the same Latitudes in Europe. Hence also, in Part it happens, that the Regions in North America, in the upper Stages, are not so liable to Heat as those in the lower Plains, though in the same Latitude. If on the contrary the given Horizon slopes from the Sun's Place, the Heat in the lower Latitudes will be more moderate, which is the Case of France and Germany compared with the Countries of the same Latitude in America, and in the higher Latitudes the Country will suffer more rigorous Cold. This latter is the Case of Siberia, the Plain of whose Horizon being in a high North Latitude slopes from the high Tartar Plains Northward; hence the more than natural Rigour of the Climate; hence the unfruitful and inhospitable Nature of its Soil.

2. Some Surfaces and some Soils (other Circumstances remaining alike) are more formed to create a Reverberation of Heat and to retain it. A sandy Soil soon heats, and also retains its Heats. A Surface uneven and irregular Hills and deep Vales, and even that which is broken with Mountains (if those be not too high, as explained below) reflecting the Rays of the Sun a thousand Ways, and occasioning them to cross each other constantly in all Directions, creates a stronger Reverberation of local Heat than is found in any extended Plain. A Country cloathed with Woods, which shade the Earth from the Action of the Sun, will always (taking in the whole Region) be colder than a Country cleared of those Woods; and the Air which lies in Contact with it, or passes over it, will be always colder. As these Regions become cleared of these Woods, are dried and cultured, that Part of the Climate which depends on this Circumstance always meliorates in Proportion. This has been found to be the Case with Gaul and Germany. This Effect was sensibly felt, and very early observed, by some of the First Settlers in North

America; some of the very earliest written Accounts which I have seen relate this Circumstance very particularly, and Men of Observation in that Country have in every successive Age marked the Progress of this Melioration.

There is another Circumstance, which indeed does not much enter into the Case of the Climate of North America, but is amongst these general Propositions worth Notice. It is this:

The longer the Portion is of any given Period of Time, in which the Sun shines in any Horizon, the hotter in that Season will the Region of that Horizon be. Hence the intense Heat of the latter End of Summer in Russia.

3. The Air or Atmosphere can be acted upon by the Reverberation of the Sun's Rays, and be heated only in Proportion to its greater Density near the Earth, and in Proportion to the Continuity of Contact which it hath with the heated Parts of the Earth. The Earth also in Proportion to this more continued Contact amongst its Parts, in the general Level of the Surface, receives and retains more Heat than it does in the higher mountainous discontinued Parts above that Level. From these Two Circumstances combined it arises, that in the very high Mountains, even under the Equator, the Cold is intense; and at a certain Elevation above the general Level of the Globe, so rigorous and intense as to put a Stop to all Vegetation.

The Atmosphere will also be heated or chilled according to the Nature of the Particles which attracted by it are mixed and suspended in it, whether they be aqueous, or whether nitrous or sulphureous Salts, and according to the Fixation, Fermentation, or Precipitation of these Particles.

The Regions covered with great Lakes of fresh Water, but more especially the Region of the main Ocean, the component Parts of whose Mass are in perpetual Motion, are in general warmer than, although in hot Seasons and Climates never so hot as, the Body of the Land: It retains however a more equable Heat while the Heat of the Land changes from one Degree of Heat to an opposite one of Cold.

The general Currents of the Air, and the Nature of the Vapours which may be mixed with them, must depend greatly on the Position which these different Portions of the Globe have in respect of each other in any Region. In Summer, and in other Seasons when the Land is heated, the Winds which blow from Sea must prevail; in Winter, when the Land is chilled, and while the Sea retains its usual Warmth, the Wind will blow from Land to Sea, and more or less violent in Proportion to the Contrast. The Position of these Regions in respect to the general Currents of the Atmosphere and of the Ocean operate greatly in forming the Courses of the Seasons, and the Nature of the Climate.

These Principles, thus laid down and explained, I will proceed to state the Facts. The Climate of the Continent at large, or rather of that Portion of North America which is contained within the Limits of this Map, may be thus stated.

Its Seasons are *Summer*, Autumn, or what the Americans more expressively call *The Fall*, and *Winter*. The Transition from the Locking up of all Vegetation in Winter to the sudden Burst of it again to Life at the Beginning of the Summer, excludes that progressive Season which in the more moderate Climate of Europe we call Spring.

The Season begins to break soon after the Fall of the Leaf, and temporary cold Rains and Sleets of Snow fall in November, the North West Winds begin, and towards Christmas Winter in all its Rigour sets in; the Ground is covered with Snow, the Frost is settled, the Sky becomes clear and one continued Expanse of Azure, with constant Sunshine; temporary Blasts and Storms are at Intervals Exceptions to this. Towards April the Currents of the Air begin to change to North, and round to North East, and the Season of hazy, foggy, and rainy Squalls from North East begin towards the latter End of April in some Parts, towards the Beginning of May in others. The Frost breaks up, the Snow melts, and within a Week or 10 Days after, the Woods and the Orchards are in the full Glow of Bloom. About the Middle of September the Mornings and Evenings begin to grow cool, and from that Time to the Beginning of the Winter Season it is the Climate of Paradise.

To give a Description of the Climate of New England, which Part is now first published and added to this Map, I shall transcribe that Account which Dr. Douglas[1] gives, as he, during a long Residence therein, did, with a peculiar scientific Attention observe it. "In New England generally the falling Weather is from North East to South East in Winter: If the Wind is North of East, Snow; if South of East, Rain. The North East Storms are of the greatest Continuance; the South East are the most violent. A North West freezing Wind backing to the South West, if reverberated, proves the most intense cold Weather. Our great Rains are in August about Two Months after the Summer Solstice; and our great Snows about Two Months after the Winter Solstice. In falling Weather the further the Wind is from the East the finer and drier is the Snow; the further South from the East the more humid and fleaky. When

[1]Dr. William Douglass.

the Wind gets South of South East it turns to Rain. The Winds from West South West to North North West are dry Winds, fit for dry curing of Salt-fish; further North they are damp and soft, as coming from the Ocean; further South are from the hot Latitudes, and Sun-burn the Fish. Our intense hot Days are with the Wind from South to West South West; from North to East North East our most chilly Weather. The dry Winds are from West to North North West, all other Winds carry more or less. From the Middle of October begin, and about the Middle of April leave off, Chamber Fires. Our Seasons as to Temper of the Weather may be reckoned as follows: Winter, from the Winter Solstice to the Spring Equinox: Spring, from said Equinox to Summer Solstice. Summer, from said Summer Solstice to Winter Equinox; and Autumn from thence to Winter Solstice." I have as above ventured to differ from this Division of the Doctor's[1] having divided the Seasons into Winter, Summer, and Fall; in his next Paragraph he seems to be sensible of this Division: "At the End of August the Symptoms of approaching Winter begin to appear, we call it the *Fall* of the Year," as the Leaves begin to fall.

Lewis Evans, in a Map of Pennsylvania, New Jersey, and New York, which he published in 1749, says, "That at Philadelphia, by many Years Observations, the Extremes of the Barometer were 28 59 and 30 78. And that by One Year's Observation, which was not remarkable either for Heat or Cold, Farenheit's Pocket Thermometer was from 14 to 84."

The Courses and the Nature of the Winds are in this Region exactly what from the above Principles one might pronounce them to be. In Winter generally, and taking the Year through for near Half the Period, the Land Winds blow, that is, the Course of the Air is from the colder Region of a shaded uncultivated Land, to the milder Region of the Sea: These Land Winds are the West and North West Winds. These Winds are always dry, and in the Winter Season intensely cold. These Land Winds in very dry Weather are endued with a strong Power of Attraction, and absorb the Vapours of the Inland Waters of the Country, and create, as they approach towards the lower Plains, very thick Fogs, which intercept the direct Rays of Light, so that the luminous Object of the Sun appears as red as Blood; there are various other Phaenomena attendant on this State of Refraction. These Vapours are greatly heated by the Sun, and greatly heat the Air; in consequence of this, when these Fogs are dissipated, the most intense Heat succeeds them. If they last

[1]Dr. William Douglass.

till Evening before they are dissipated, they are frequently followed by Thunder Gusts. As the West and North West Winds are steady and equable, the South West are unsettled and squally. The North Winds are the Carriers of Sleet, both Snow and Rain. The North East when it takes to blow, as it does at the Season between the Breaking-up of Winter and the Commencement of Summer, is settled Cold, and blows hard, with continued Rains; and to the Northward, as for Example, on the Coasts of Nova Scotia, and often on the Coast of New England, when it does not bring Rain, it drives in thick and fixed Fogs before it. The East Winds are warm, but not settled under a fixed Characteristic as to wet or dry. The South East are warm and wet.

I cannot close these Observations without transcribing from Lewis Evans's Map of Pennsylvania, New York, and New Jersey, printed at Philadelphia 1749, the following curious, at that Time novel and very curious, philosophic Propositions; not only as they point to very ingenious Experiments, but as they shew what Progress *He* had made in that singular Branch of Philosophy, *Electricity*, at a Period when even the first Philosophers were but Empirics in it.

"All our Storms, says he, begin to Leeward; thus a North East Storm will be a Day sooner in Virginia than in Boston.

"Thunder never happens but by the Meeting of Sea and Land Clouds, the Sea Clouds coming, *freighted with Electricity*, meeting and others less so, the Equilibrium is restored by *Snaps of Lightening*; and the more opposite the Winds and the larger and compacter the Clouds, the more dreadful are these Shocks: The Sea Clouds thus suddenly bereft of that universal Element of Repellancy, contract, and their Waters gush down in Torrents."

His Philosophy here is not perfectly just, though it contains very shrewd leading Theorems, of which, with a true and painful philosophic Course of Experiments, Dr. Franklin[1] elicited the real Truth.

I did intend to have continued this Paper with a Description of the ORIGINAL INDIGENOUS INHABITANTS,

> Haec Nemora Indigenae fauni Nymphaeque tenebant
> Gensque Virûm truncis et duro robore Nati
> Queîs nec *Mos nec Cultus* erat, nec jungere Tauros
> Aut Componere Opes nôrant, aut parcere parto,
> Sed Rami atque asper victu *Venatus* alebat.

I should have inserted a List of the Tribes or Nations both in the northern and southern District marking their Dwellings. This Part

---

[1]Benjamin Franklin (1706-1790).

would contain a Description of their Nature, their System of Life, and Mode of Subsistence; of the Progress they have made, and of the Point in which they are found as to Society, Communion, and Government; as to their Manners in the Individual, the Family, the Tribe; as to the general Spirit by which they regulate themselves when considered as a Nation. But although I have many Materials, and these nearly arranged, yet I cannot at present find either Leisure or Spirits to undertake this Part. On this Head therefore I will take the Liberty at present to refer the Reader, who may be desirous of seeing something on this Subject, to those Parts of° *the Administration of the Colonies*[1] where these Matters are treated of, so far as respects the general Subject of that Treatise. c Vol. 1 Ch 7

I had also proposed to have given an Account of this Country IN ITS SETTLED AND CULTIVATED STATE, containing an Account of the Mode[2] of Settling, and a Detail of the Nature, Progress, and Completion of these Settlements; of the Produce of this cultivated Continent in the Three different Regions into which the Nature of this Produce divides it; of the internal forensic, and external commercial Value of these Products; of the Nature of the Inhabitancy of the Country, and of the great Towns; of the Spirit and Character in Religion, Manners, and Government of each Province and Colony: And finally, from my Journals, a portrayed Description of the Country as one sees it in travelling through it. The wretched State of Confusion and Ruin into which it has fallen, compared with the happy State in which I saw it, is, I own, a View that my Eye and Heart turn away from; nor can I bear the Retrospect, which the very reading over my Journals opens to me. If I live, and have Leisure, when I may see their happier Days of Peace and good Government return again, most likely I shall insert these Matters in some future Edition of this Work.

[1]By Thomas Pownall. *Op. cit.*
[2][Pownall's note for revised and enlarged edition] Nullas Germanorum populis urbes habitari, satis notum est: ne pati quidem inter se junctas sedes. Colunt discreti ac diversi, ut fons, ut campus, ut nemus placuit. Tacitus De Germania, xvi.

APPENDIX

NUMBER I.

The Account[1] of CAPT. ANTHONY VAN SCHAICK[2] *of the Ground between the Entrance of Lake Champlain at Crown Point, and the Mouth of Otter Creek.*

I WAS commmissioned by Lieutenant Governor Phipps,[3] of the Massachuset's [Massachusetts] Bay, to go to Canada to exchange and procure the redemption of prisoners. I set out from Albany on the 28th of January, 1752. I have been at Crown Point six several Times. I have heard people talk with one another from Fort Saint Frederick to the opposite shore, without any difficulty of making each other hear, and I do think it is at most 700 yards across. The bay on the west side of Fort St. Frederick does at the upper end trend to the eastward, so that from the head of it to *the drowned lands*, there is a short carrying-place, over which the Indians carry when they come from Canada with smuggled beaver. From Fort Saint Frederick I went over the ice (it being froze) across the lake, to a point about two miles on the east side of the lake, there I landed on the banks, thence due east about three-fourths of a mile, and struck a meadow of about 150 yards across which trended in the same direction as the lake to the mouth of Otter Creek. I followed this Meadow, which, as it approached to Otter Creek, become *drowned land* more and more flooded, till, as it approached the Creek, it became all water, and a river: that the mouth of Otter Creek, where it empties itself, is a large bay.[4] To the east of this drowned land is a ridge of high land, that comes down to this bay, but sloped away before it comes to the water; for at the banks there is low land for about 60 yards. As near as I can guess from hence, that is to say, this point, to the opposite side of this bay, or mouth of Otter Creek, is near a mile. The land on the opposite side all low marshy land.

ANTHONY VAN SCHAICK.

[1]The original manuscript of this account is in the Henry E. Huntingdon Library. LO 432.

[2]Captain of a company of New York militia, who was taken prisoner by the French before October, 1748 and was not exchanged until June 26, 1750. For the next few years he acted as interpreter and officer appointed to exchange and redeem prisoners held in New France. In 1756 he was commissioned as Captain of a company of Rangers. *N.Y.C.D.*, VI, 492, 495; X, 211-15.

[3]Spencer Phips (1685-1757), member of the Council of Massachusetts and Lieutenant Governor of the colony from 1732 to 1757. Shirley, *op. cit.*, I, 489n.

[4]Baye des Vasseaux. "William Brassier. A Survey

NUMBER II.

CAPTAIN ANTHONY VAN SCHAICK'S JOURNAL.[1] 1756.

I LEFT Fort Edward August 18th, about 12 o'clock; travelled north three miles; came to the falls on Hudson's River; steered N.N.E. pine woods; the soil indifferent; travelled about two miles; there halted; very good road; continued the same course two miles more; came to the head of the brook which empties itself at Ford Edward; the soil very good; the woods, oak, maple, beech, and hemlock; the country full of coves and ridges, but easy to be avoided; there encamped.

19th, set off about seven o'clock; travelled one mile and a half N.E. by E. the soil rich, the country level; the woods beech in general; turned E. about four miles more; came to Fort Ann; there encamped; Wood Creek being very low, not above 15 inches of water, but its banks pleasant, about 10 feet high, about 20 or 25 feet across, goosebury bushes on the banks.

20th, Left Fort Ann early in the morning; travelled one mile; came to Fork's Creek,[2] about half a mile from the mouth thereof; travelled down to the mouth, where its course is E. by N. for about half a mile, then turns N. is about 30 feet wide; the country level; the soil exceeding rich; the wood, maple, beech, bass wood; this kind of land about a mile wide, one place with another, on each side; its banks about 10 feet perpendicular; steered straight north about four miles; came to the foot of a mountain which ranges due north; strove to go round it to the westward, but the men seemed discouraged, ascended the mountain, then travelled due north about six miles; discovered two more ridges of mountains ranging the same course, with two intervals between them which seemed to be pretty level at the bottom; it being near four miles from top to top; but the eastmost mountain running farthest north; there encamped near the top of the mountain, by a pleasant spring.

---

of Lake Champlain including Lake George, Crown Point and St. John . . ." In Jeffery's *American Atlas, op. cit.,* map no. 18.

Now Kellogg Bay, Lake Champlain.

[1]On August 13, 1756, Captain Anthony Van Schaick received his commission from Lord Loudoun to organize a Company of Rangers. Manuscript in the Henry E. Huntingdon Library. LO 1400.

Although the Company was never completed this *Journal* is an account of a scouting trip made under the Warrant. The original manuscript of this account is in the Henry E. Huntingdon Library. LO 1663.

[2]Located and named on Brassier, *A Survey of Lake Champlain, op. cit.* Located but not named on modern maps.

The first
Narrows,
vide fig. 11
in the map.

21st, Set off due east about two miles and a half; came to Wood Creek; travelled about one mile and a half along Wood Creek; there was about 20 feet water in the Creek; and it was about 50 feet wide; travelled along the Creek about a quarter of a Mile; here a spur of the mountain runs quite close to the Creek side, and forms the banks; but by cutting 30 yards through this, a road may be made, if thought more convenient. This part of Wood Creek is a very good situation for a bridge, having good footing for the heads of a bridge, and being not more than 40 or 50 feet across, and it being good travelling on the east side, which leads to the place noticed below, the general course being N.E. by N. about three miles: fell in with Col. Fitch's[1] Tracks, coming from the south west end of South Bay, continued our course along Wood Creek five miles more, the passage of the river being stopped up with trees for about a quarter of a mile, felled down by the French last War,[2] forms a kind of dam, which must be cut before any canoes or batteaux can pass; came to Montour's[3] river, which stands into Wood Creek out of E. by N. travelled about two miles more; encamped.

The 22d, Set off; travelled about two miles and a half, came to the Falls which run N.N.E. where there is a good place for a fort, followed the river for near a mile, then turned west to the top of a mountain, between Wood Creek and South Bay, which mountain terminates in a perpendicular at its north point, beneath which there is a triangle of flat hemlock woods, of about half a mile wide, at the north point of which there is a triangle of reeds and water weeds of about four acres, then the channel of Wood Creek and South Bay meet. This is the seventh time I have been at South Bay by different ways, and have endeavoured to find a way by which a carriage, or at least a horse might go, but could never find any such.

ANTHONY VAN SCHAICK.

[1]Lieutenant-colonel Eliezer Fitch of the first regiment, Connecticut Provincials. This regiment was raised to serve under the general command of John Winslow in his expedition against Crown Point in 1756. Connecticut (Colony), *Public Records of . . . .* Edited by Charles J. Hoadly (Hartford, Case, Lockwood & Brainard Co., [etc.], 1850-90), X, 470-71.

[2]Terminated by the Treaty of Aix la Chapelle, Oct. 7, 1748.

[3]Probably East Creek, present Poultney River.

NUMBER III.

CAPTAIN HOBBS'S ACCOUNT[1] OF THE WAY FROM NO. 4, Db IN NEW HAMPSHIRE, TO THE MOUTH OF OTTER CREEK.

FROM No. 4,[2] up the river,[3] on the east side about a mile, to avoid crossing Black River; then cross the river, deep still water, good landing on the banks, to the northward of north west to the foot of a mountain called Ascoudne [Ascutney] about two miles, the land white oak and pine, sandy and of course full of gullies, at the foot of the mountain, struck into the Indian road, which followed to Otter Creek: left the mountain to the northward; the land much the same but more inclined to oak and beech, tolerable level, steered about W.N.W. four days and came to Otter Creek, the land pretty much the same till I came towards Otter Creek, when it inclined more to beech, and the sugar-maple tree: called it then 60 miles, but do not think it is so much, thence down the river, on each side of which interval, land about a mile wide, and continued after this sort to the Great Falls.[4] I am very confident a good waggon road may be made hitherto. I crossed below the Falls, the water about knee deep: from the Falls down the west side, to the mouth two days. Rough land, no sharp hills, or pitches nor rocky. The road I kept was between the interval land on Otter Creek, and the swamp meadow that runs down the east side of Lake Champlain, upon the up land, which is a ridge, that runs between these quite down the lake; the interval land below the Falls being wet rushy drowned lands. The second time I went down this river, just before I came to the Falls I turned away east, and left a big mountain on the left hand to the west, followed an Indian path, till I struck a river that falls into Otter Creek, then went on the east side. Rough bad travelling.

A little fortified post on Connecticut River, so numbered and called.

HUMPHREY HOBBS.

Albany, *Sept.* 18*th*, 1756.

[1]The manuscript of this account is in the Henry E. Huntingdon Library. LO 1839.
[2]Present Charlestown, New Hampshire.

[3]The Connecticut River.
[4]Unidentified. Four separate falls are indicated on Brassier, *A Survey of Lake Champlain, op. cit.*

157

NUMBER IV.

EXTRACTS FROM THE JOURNAL OF CAPTAIN HARRY GORDON, CHIEF ENGINEER IN THE WESTERN DEPARTMENT IN NORTH AMERICA, WHO WAS SENT FROM FORT PITT ON THE RIVER OHIO, DOWN THE SAID RIVER, &c. TO ILINOIS, IN 1766.[1]

Now Pitsburg F j

JUNE the 18th, 1766, embarked at Fort Pitt,[2] on the River Ohio, and arrived at the Mingo[3] Town, 71 miles, on the 19th. The country between these two Places is broken, with many high ridges or hills; the vallies narrow, and the course of the river plunged from many high grounds which compose its banks. When the water is high, you go with moderate rowing from six to seven miles an hour.

G 1

The 23d, arrived at the mouth of Muskingum River, in latitude 39° 19′. Muskingum is 250 yards wide, at its confluence with the Ohio, and navigable for batteauxs 150 up: it runs through a very pleasant and extremely fertile country. Killed several buffaloes between the Mingo Town and Muskingum; but the first we met with were about 100 miles below Fort Pitt, which is distant from Muskingum 161 miles.

H n

The 29th, arrived at the mouth[4] of the Scioto 366 miles; navigation good at all seasons without the least obstruction from the Mingo Town, 71 miles and a half from Fort Pitt, and indeed very little from the mouth[5] of Big Beaver Creek, which is 29 miles and a quarter from Fort Pitt. The Ohio River from 50 miles above Muskingum to Scioto is most beautiful, and interspersed with numbers of islands of different sizes, covered with the most stately timber; with several long reaches, one of which is 16 miles and a half, inclosed with the finest trees of various verdures, which afford a noble and inchanting prospect. A glorious vista found on one of these islands, is terminated by two small hills, shaped like sugar-loaves, of very easy ascent, from whence you may see all this magnificient variety.

[1]Captain Harry Gordon's "Journal" (1766) is printed in Clarence W. Alvord, ed., *The New Regime*, 1765-1767 (Springfield, Illinois State Historical Library, 1916), pp. 290-311; Newton Mereness, ed., *op. cit.*, pp. 464-89. Extracts and abridged versions are printed in various other places.

[2]Fort Pitt (1758-91) an English fort built at the forks of the Ohio. Present site of Pittsburgh, Pennsylvania.

[3]Present site of Mingo [Junction], Jefferson Co., Ohio. Hanna, *op. cit.*, II, 141.

[4]Present site of Portsmouth, Ohio.

[5]Near present Beaver, Pennsylvania.

The rivers Hockhocking [Hocking] and Canhawa [Kanawha],[1] fall Gm&Hn
into the Ohio in this space, beside many others of a smaller size. Up the
Big Cahawa [Great Kanawha], the western Indians penetrate into the
Cherokee country.[2] It is a fine large river, and navigable by report,
100 miles towards the southward. The country on the Ohio, &c. is every
where pleasant, with large level spots of the richest land, remarkably
healthy. One general remark of this nature may serve for the whole
tract of the globe, comprehended between the western skirts of the
Allegany [Allegheny] Mountains, beginning at Fort Ligonier,[3] thence Fh
bearing south westerly to the distance of 500 miles opposite the Ohio
Falls,[4] then crossing them northerly to the heads of the rivers that empty
themselves into the Ohio; thence east along the ridge[5] that separates the
lakes and Ohio's streams to French Creek,[6] which is opposite to the
above-mentioned Fort Ligonier northerly. This country may, from a
proper knowledge, be affirmed to be the most healthy (as no sort of
chronic disorder ever prevailed in it) the most pleasant, the most
commodious, and most fertile spot of earth known to European people.

The latitude of Scioto is 38° 22'. Remained here till the 8th of July. Jo

The 16th of July, encamped opposite to the Great Lick,[7] 390 miles;[8]
it is five miles distance south of the river. The extent of the muddy part
of the Lick is three-fourths of an acre.

The Ohio continues to be narrow from Fort Pitt to within 100
miles of the Falls; its breadth seldom exceeds 500 yards, and is confined
by rising grounds, which cause many windings, although the reaches are
sometimes from two to four miles long; the largest and most beautiful
(as has been already mentioned) is above the Scioto, and is 16 miles and
a half. The Ohio, 100 miles above the Falls, widens to 700 yards in

---

[1]Little Kanawha. Mereness, op. cit., p. 465n.

[2]The Cherokees in early time held the whole mountain region of the southern Alleghenies in southern West Virginia, western North & South Carolina, northern Georgia, eastern Tennessee and north eastern Alabama, and claimed the land as far north as the Ohio River. Hodge, op. cit., I, 245.

[3]In 1758 Captain Harry Gordon, in preparation for General John Forbes' expedition against Fort Duquesne, built Fort Ligonier at Loyalhanning. Western Pennsylvania Historical Magazine (Pittsburgh, Historical Society of Western Pennsylvania, 1918-date), XVII (1934), 265. On present site of Ligonier, Pennsylvania.

[4]At present Louisville, Kentucky.

[5]A ridge of high lands that determine the course

which the streams run from east to west across the entire state. Benson J. Lossing, A Pictorial Description of Ohio . . . (New York, Ensings & Thayer, 1849), pp. 12-13. The ridge ranges E.N.E. from the northern part of Darke to Trumbull County. Mereness, op. cit., p. 466n.

[6]In northwestern Pennsylvania.

[7]Big Bone Lick in the valley of Bone Lick Creek in Boone County, Kentucky, one and one-half miles east of Hamilton on the Ohio River. Richard H. Collins, History of Kentucky (Covington, Collins & Co., 1874), II, 51.

[8]Here Mr. Pownall has confused the distance of Big Bone Lick and Big Buffalo Lick. Captain Gordon's table of miles from Fort Pitt gives 560¼ and 390 miles respectively.

many places, and contains a great number of islands. The grounds diminish generally in height, and the country is not so broken. Some of the banks are, at times, overflowed by freshes; and there is scarce any place from Fort Pitt to the Falls, where a good road may not be made along the banks of the river, and horses employed in drawing up bilanders against the stream, which is gentle, except in freshes. The height of the banks permit them every where to be settled; and they are not subject to crumble away.

H q

The little and big Mineami [Little and Great Miami] rivers fall in between the Scioto on the north side, and the Licking Creek and Kentucke [Kentucky] on the south side.

There are many good encampments on the islands, and one in particular very remarkable, and safe, opposite to the Big Lick.

H r

The waters at the Falls were low; it being the summer. They do not, however, deserve the name of Falls, as the stream on the north side has no sudden pitch, but only runs rapid over the ledge of a flat limestone rock, which the Author of Nature put here to keep up the waters of the higher Ohio, and to be the cause of that beautiful stillness of the river's course above.

This bed or dam is made almost flat and smooth to resist less the current, which would soon get the better of greater resistance; but as it is subject to wear, there is enough of it, being two miles wide, and its length in the country unknown.

Several boats passed it at the very driest season of the year, when the waters are at the lowest by unloading one-third of their freight. They passed on the north-side, where the carrying-place is three-fourths of a mile long; and on the south-east side it is about half that distance, and is reckoned the safest passage for these who are unacquainted, but it is the most tedious; as, during part of the summer, and fall, they must drag their *boats* over the flat rock.

For all the remaining part of this journal the reader must refer to the little sketch on the west side of the map.

The heat by day is by no means intense, and the coolness of the nights always required a blanket even in their tents. Notwithstanding the distance from Port Pitt is 682 miles, the latitude is not much southerly; the Falls being 38° 8′.

Westerly and south-west winds generally blow, and will greatly assist the navigation up the river Ohio.

The 23d July left the Falls, and encamped the 31st on a large island[1] opposite to the mouth of the Wabash, which is 317 miles and a half below the Falls, and 999 Miles and a half from Fort Pitt.

[1]Wabash Island.

From the Falls to about half this distance of 317 miles and a half, the country is very hilly; the course of the river very winding and narrow, and but very few spots of level land on the sides of the river. The hills are mostly stoney and steep; but from the great herds of buffalo, we observed on the beaches of the river and islands into which they come for air, and coolness in the heat of the day, there must be good pasturage.

The ridgy ground ends 837 miles below Fort Pitt; the country then grows flat, and the river, whose bed widens, is often divided by islands.

The navigation is good from the Falls; but where the flat country begins, boats must keep the *principal channel*, which is on the *right hand* going down.

The Wabash is marked by a large island,[1] round which boats may go most times of the year. The end of the fork of the two rivers,[2] the Ohio and Wabash, is narrow, and overflowed; a mile and a half upwards the ground is higher. Very large herds of buffaloes are frequently seen in this country.

The river Wabash, at its confluence with the Ohio, is 306 yards wide, and it discharges a great quantity of a muddy kind of water into the Ohio. It is navigable 300 or 400 miles upwards, but boats smaller than 33 feet long and seven feet wide, the size they then had, should be used on it, as there is no great depth of water in the summer and fall. Latitude of Wabash 37′ 41°.[3] The country between the course of this river and the Missisippi is in general flat, open, and of a rich luxuriant soil; that on the banks of the Ohio is level, and in many places hereabouts overflows.

The 2d August, in the evening, left Wabash, stopped next morning near the Saline,[4] or Salt Run; of which any quantity of good salt may be made here.

From hence Indians were sent to the Ilinois [Illinois], to notify our intended visit to that place.

The 6th of August, halted at Port Massiac [Fort Massac],[5] formerly a French post, 120 miles below the mouth of the Wabash, and eleven

[1]Wabash Island.

[2]"Here ends the Indiana territory, and the Illinois Commences." Cramer, *op. cit.*, p. 117.

[3]That is 37° 41′.

[4]Saline River. Around the mouth of this river grew the chief pioneer trading center for salt on the lower Ohio. Thomas Hutchins, *The Courses of the Ohio River* . . . ed. by Beverly Bond (Cincinnati, Historical and Philosophical Society of Ohio, 1942), p. 68, *note* 37.

[5]Fort Ascension, renamed Fort Massac, was built in 1757, abandoned by the French in 1764, and rebuilt and occupied by a United States garrison during the 1794 campaign. Clarence Alvord and Clarence E. Carter, editors, *The Critical Period, 1763-1765* (Springfield, Ill., Illinois State Historical Library, 1915), p. 3n. On the present site of Metropolis, Illinois. Schlarman, *op. cit.*, p. 342.

miles below the mouth of the Cherokee river.[1] The country 25 miles from the Wabash begins again to be mountainous, being the north-west end of the Apalachian [Appalachian] mountains, which entirely terminate a small distance from the river northerly. They are here between 50 and 60 miles across, and are scarpt, rocky precipices, below them no more high lands to be seen to the westward as far as those that border on the Mexican provinces. The French fixed a post here,[2] to secure their traders against the Cherokees; and it would be proper for the English to have one on the same spot, to prevent an illicit trade being carried on up the Wabash.

Hunters from this fort, may get any quantity of buffaloes, and salt from the Saline, with very little trouble or expense.

The river Ohio is here,[3] that is, from the entrance[4] of the Cherokee river,[5] between 700 and 800 yards wide. There is no proper spot for a post nearer the Cherokee river above, or on the Missisippi [Mississippi] below, but this; as the grounds on the banks of the Ohio begin to be very low. The current of the river towards the Missisippi is very still, and may be easily ascended, if affairs are any ways doubtful at or near the Ilinois [Illinois].

The 7th, we arrived at the fork[6] of the Ohio, in latitude 36° 43'. The gentle Ohio is pushed back by the impetuous stream of the Missisippi [Mississippi], where the muddy white water of the latter, is to be seen above 200 yards up the former. Examined the ground for several miles within the fork: it is an aggregation of mud and dirt, interspersed with marsh, and some ponds of water, and is in high times of the Missisippi [Mississippi] overflowed, which is the case with the other sides of both the Ohio and it. The mouth of the Ohio is 1164 miles from Fort Pitt.

The 9th and 10th of August, stayed at the mouth of the Ohio. The 10th, began to ascend the Missisippi [Mississippi], whose rapid stream had broke through the country, and divided it every where with a number of islands. The low lands on each side continue eight leagues upwards, when it becomes broken, and small ridges appear the rest of the way to Kuskuskies [Kaskaskia]:[7] there are many islands in this distance, some of which are entirely rock.

[1]Tennessee River.
[2]Fort Massac.
[3]*Ibid.*
[4]Near Paducah, Kentucky.
[5]Tennessee River.
[6]At present Cairo, Illinois.

[7]Indian village, *Kaskaskia*, was located at the mouth of Kaskaskia River near the site of the present town of Kaskaskia, Randolph County, Illinois. The Kaskaskias, a tribe of the Illinois, lived here from about 1700 to 1832. This tribe with remnants of the Weas and Piankashaws are now known officially as the Peorias. Hodge, *op. cit.*, I, 662.

The island of La Tour[1] is six leagues below the Kuskuskies [Kaskaskia] river, which is 31 leagues from the fork of the Ohio.

The principal stream of the Missisippi [Mississippi] is from 500 to 700 yards wide, but it is scarcely ever to be seen together, and some small parts are above a mile distant from one another. The principal stream likewise often shifts, as well as the depth of the channel, which make the pilotage of the river difficult, and boats often get aground in ascending, when endeavouring to avoid the rapid current.

The 19th, in the morning, arrived at the small river of the Kuskuskies [Kaskaskia], 80 yards wide at its mouth; it is deep; carries five feet water up to the village, which is two leagues from the mouth of the river, and is said to be navigable 50 leagues further up. The high grounds before-mentioned skirt along the south side of the Kuskuskies [Kaskaskia] River, come opposite to the village, and continue along northerly, in a chain nearly parallel to the east branch of the Missisippi [Mississippi], at the distance of two or three miles from it. The space between is level, mostly open, and of the richest kind of soil, in which the inhabitants of the Ilinois [Illinois] raise their grain, &c.

The Kuskuskies [Kaskaskia] village is on the plain; it consists of 80 houses, well built, mostly of stone, with gardens, and large lots. The inhabitants generally live well, and have large stocks of cattle and hogs.

The road to Fort Chartres[2] is along the plain, passing in some places near the chain of rocky height above-mentioned. The distance to the front is 18 miles. The road passes through the Indian village of the Keskesquois [Kaskaskias],[3] of fifteen cabbins; also, through a French one, called Prairi de Roché [Prairie du Rocher],[4] in which are 14 families: this last is three miles from Fort Chartres; between which is the village

[1] Unidentified.

[2] The new Fort Chartres, built near the site of the first fort, was completed in 1755. By the terms of the Treaty of Peace of 1763 it came into British possession in 1765, and was renamed Fort Cavendish. The fort was abandoned and destroyed by the British in 1772. Lawrence H. Gipson, The British Empire Before the American Revolution (New York, Alfred A. Knopf, 1936-), IV, 145; Alvord, The New Regime, op. cit., p. 123n. The foundation of Fort Chartres has been cleared and repaired and the powder magazine has been restored. These remains and exact reproductions of other parts of the fort may be viewed in the Illinois Fort Chartres State Park, located four miles from Prairie du Rocher, Illinois. Federal Writers' Project. Illinois, Illinois, A Descriptive and Historical Guide ... (Chicago, A. C. McClurg & Co., 1939), p. 496.

[3] It is interesting to note that in addition to the French and Indian village of Kaskaskia, there was also a small Indian village in this vicinity.

[4] Founded about 1725 on lands granted to Pierre Dugué Boisbriant, builder of the first Fort Chartres. Gipson, The British Empire, op. cit., IV, 124. For location of Prairie de Roche and other French and Indian establishments in the Illinois Country see: "Plan des Differents Villages Francois dans le Pays des Illynois...." Op. cit., map opposite page 126. This early French village was on the present site of Prairie du Rocher, Randolph County, Illinois.

called l'Etablissement,[1] mostly deserted, and the inhabitants removed to Misaini [Misère],[2] on the west branch[3] of the river, a little higher up[4] the Kuskuskies [Kaskaskia].

The 20th of August, arrived at Fort Chartres, which is well imagined and finished. It has four bastions of stone masonry, designed defensible against musquetry. The barracks are also of masonry, commodious and elegant. The fort is large enough to contain 400 men, but may be defended by one third of that number against Indians.

Visited Kyashshie [Cahokia],[5] 45 miles distant from Fort Chartres, and is the uppermost settlement on our side. In this rout we pass l'petit village,[6] five miles from Fort Chartres, formerly inhabited by 12, but now by one family only. The abandoned houses are most of them well built, and are left in good order. The ground is excellent for grain, and a sufficiency cleared for 100 men.

At Kyaboshie [Cahokia] are 40 families of French, who live well, and so might three times the number, as there is a great quantity of clear land near it: there are likewise 20 cabbins of the Periorie [Peoris] Indians left here; the rest, and best part of them, are removed to the French side, two miles below Point Court [Pain Court].[7] Wheat thrives better here than at Kuskuskies [Kaskaskia], owing, probably, to its being more northerly by near a degree.

The village of Point Court [Pain Court] is pleasantly situated on a high bank, which forms the western bank of the Missisippi; it is three miles higher up than Kyaboskie [Cahokia], has already 50 families, chiefly supported from thence. At this place, found Mr. Le Clef,[8] the principal Indian trader, (he resides here) who takes such good measures, that the whole trade of the Missouri, that of the Missisippi [Mississippi] northward, and that of the nations near le Baye,[9] Lake Machigan

[1]Nouvelle Chartres, later called Cavendish, a village around Fort Chartres. Alvord, *The New Regime*, *op. cit.*, pp. 154n, 298.

[2]Ste. Genevieve, on the west bank of the Mississippi nearly opposite Kaskaskia. Gipson, *op. cit.*, map opposite page 126. This ancient village was situated, on what was once the river's bank, about three miles below the present town of Ste. Genevieve, Missouri. Writers' Program. Missouri, *Missouri, a Guide to the "Show Me" State* (New York, Duell, Sloan and Pearce (1941), p. 521.

[3]According to the official copy, "on the bank" not "on the west branch." Great Britain. Public Record Office, C. O. 5: 85/128.

[4]"than" not "up." *Ibid.*

[5]The Indian town on the present site of Cahokia, near the southern limits of East St. Louis, Illinois. In 1721 this town was second in importance among the Illinois. Hodge, *op. cit.*, I, 185.

[6]St. Philippe, founded about 1725 on lands granted to Philippe Francois Renault. Gipson, *The British Empire*, *op. cit.*, IV, 124. This village was probably near the present site of Renault, Monroe County, Illinois.

[7]A French village or trading post founded early in 1764 by Pierre Laclede Liguest on the present site of St. Louis, Missouri. Pain Court was the nickname for Laclede's settlement.

[8]Pierre Laclede Liguest, the founder of St. Louis. Alvord, *The Critical Period*, *op. cit.*, p. 127n.

[9]Green Bay, Wisconsin. Alvord, *The New Regime*, *op. cit.*, index *Green Bay*.

[Michigan] and Saint Josepho [Joseph],[1] by the Ilinois [Illinois] River, is entirely brought to him. He is sensible and clever; has a good education; is very active, and will give us some trouble before we get the parts of this trade that belong to us into our hands. Our possession of the Ilinois [Illinois] is only useful to us at present in one respect; it shews the Indian nations our superiority over the French, to whom they can thence perceive we give law; this is dearly bought to us, by the expence and inconvenience of supporting it. The French carry on the trade all around us by land and water. First, up the Missisippi [Mississippi], and to the lakes by Ouisconsia [Wisconsin], Foxes,[2] Chicegou [Chicago] and Ilinois [Illinois] Rivers. Secondly, up the Ohio to the Wabash Indians; and even the small quantity of skins and furrs that the Kuskuskies [Kaskaskias] and Picarias [Peoris] (who are also on our side) get by hunting, is carried under our nose to Misere[3] and Pain Court.[4]

A garrison at the Ilinois [Illinois] River, and a post at le Baye,[5] will partly prevent the first; and one at Massiac [Massac] will, as has been said, stop their intercourse with the people on the Wabash, who consist of several nations.

Cooped up at Fort Chartres only, we make a foolish figure; hardly have the dominion of the country, or as much credit with the inhabitants as to induce them to give us any thing for money, while our neighbours have plenty on trust.

The French have large boats of 20 tons, rowed with 20 oars, which will go in *seventy odd days* from New Orleans to the Ilinois [Illinois]. These boats go to the Ilinois [Illinois] twice a year, and are not half loaded on their return: was there any produce worth sending to market, they could carry it at no great expence. They, however, carry lead, the produce of a mine[6] on the French side of the river, which yields but a small quantity, as they have not hands to work it. These boats, in times of the floods, which happen only in May and June, go down to New Orleans from the Ilinois [Illinois] in 14 and 16 days.

Distances from Fort Pitt in Latitude 40° 26′ to the Mouth of the Ohio, in Latitude 36° 43′, taken by Captain Harry Gordon, Chief Engineer in America, on his Passage down the River Ohio, undertaken by Order in 1766; together with the Latitude of some of the most remarkable Places which he took at the same Time, viz.

[1]Potawatomis lived on St. Joseph River near the south end of Lake Michigan. A French Mission was established there in 1688. The inhabitants were known as St. Joseph Indians. Hodge, *op. cit.*, II, 412.

[2]Fox River in Wisconsin and Fox River in Illinois.

[3]Ste. Genevieve.

[4]St. Louis.

[5]Green Bay, Wisconsin.

[6]Near Ste. Genevieve, Missouri. Alvord, *The Critical Period*, *op. cit.*, p. 210.

	Latitude	Miles	Miles
Logg's Town – – – – – – – – – – –		–	18½
Big Beaver Creek – – – – – – – –		10¾	29¼
Little Beaver Creek – – – – – – – –		12¾	42
Yellow Creek – – – – – – – – –		10½	52
Mingo Town – – – – – – – – – –		19¾	71½
Two Creeks – – – – – – – – – –		–	72¼
Long Reach – – – – – – – – – –		51	123¼
End of Long Reach – – – – – – – –		14¾	138
Muskingum Run – – – – – – –	39° 16′	23	161
Little Kanhawa River – – – – – –		12¾	172¾
Hockhocking River – – – – – – – –		13¼	126
Big Kanhawa River – – – – – – –		80¼	266¼
Big Guyandot – – – – – – – – –		41¾	308
Big Sandy Creek – – – – – – – –		13	321
Scioto River – – – – – – – – –	38° 22′	45	366
Big Buffalo Lick, one mile eastward of the Ohio – – – – – – – – – –		24	390
Large Island, divided by a gravelly beach – –		20½	410½
Little Mineami River – – – – – – – –		81¾	492¼
Licking Creek – – – – – – – – – –		8	500¼
Great Mineami River – – – – – – – –		26¾	527½
The place where the elephant's bones were found – – – – – – – – –		32¾	560¼
Kentucké River – – – – – – – – –		44¼	604½
The Falls – – – – – – – – – – –	38° 8′	77½	682
Where the Low Country begins – – – –		155¾	837¾
Beginning of the Five Islands – – – – –		37¾	875¼
Large river on the east side – – – – –		27	902¼
Very large island in the middle of the river – – – – – – – – – – –		58	690¼ [1]
Wabash River – – – – – – – – –		38¾	999½
Big rock and cave on the west side – – – –		42¾	1042¼
Shawana River – – – – – – – – –		52½	1094¾
Cherokee River – – – – – – – – –		13	1107¾
Fort Massiac – – – – – – – – – –		11	1118¾
The mouth of the Ohio River – – – –	36° 43′	46	1164

[1] 990¼

NUMBER V.

EXTRACT FROM MR. LEWIS EVAN'S JOURNAL. 1743.

OUR journey[1] from Philadelphia, for about seventy miles, was through the English and Dutch settlements to the Blue Mountains.[2] The way we took was up the Schuyl-kill River; and we crossed it to the west, about four miles above Monotawny [Manatawny] Creek. Then by a new road over the Flyeing-hills[3] into Tulpohoocking [Tulpehocken] Vale,[4] which is a very beautiful and healthy bottom, extending under different names from Hudson's River to Georgia, about two hundred miles short of Apalachy [Apalachicola] Bay. It is generally eight, ten, or twelve miles broad; bounded on the S.E. by the Flyeing-hills, on the N.W. by the Blue or Apalachian [Appalachian] Mountains. This south-eastern ridge is called in New York the Highlands; in New Jersey, Mascapetcunk [Musconetcong]; in Pennsylvania the Oley Hills and Flyeing-hills; in Virginia the Blue Ridge.

The reader, who is curious in the knowledge of this new country, may on this subject refer to J. Bartram's journal of the same journey, published by Whiston and White, London, 1751 F f

Tulpohoocking [Tulpehocken] is settled by High-Dutchers,[5] who have fine plantations; raise great quantity of wheat, and manufacture it into very fine flour, which they bring in the spring and fall seventy or eighty miles to Philadelphia.

About twenty-four miles west of the waggon-ford over Schuyllkill, is the passage[6] through the first ridge of the Kittocktinny [Kittatinny] Mountains: it is easily known by its lying west of the bluff head[7] of a mountain: it is also a mile of ascent, and as much descent and steep.

---

[1]Lewis Evans and John Bartram accompanied Conrad Weiser on his mission to the Six Nations at Onondaga for William Gooch, lieutenant governor of Virginia. The attack of Virginians upon Indians of the Six Nations who had penetrated into the Shenandoah Valley threatened to disturb the peace between the Six Nations and the Virginians. Conrad Weiser, the trusted Indian interpreter of Pennsylvania was sent to confer with the Iroquois and thus prevent the conflict. A conflict with Virginia would involve Pennsylvania as well. It was not the Six Nations but the Shawnee under French influence who were expected to use the ruse of loyalty to the Six Nations as an excuse to attack all white men. Wallace, *op. cit.*, pp. 145-54.

[2]A range of the Alleghenies called Kittatinny or Blue Mountains.

[3]A continuation of South Mountain which terminates at Reading, Pennsylvania.

[4]Tulpehocken or Lebanon Valley. Between Kittatinny and South Mountains. Reading is the eastern and Harrisburg the western entrance to the valley. Wallace, *op. cit.*, p. 36.

[5]Germans who emigrated, for the most part, from southern Germany. In contrast to Low German the dialect of the inhabitants of the Lowlands.

[6]Great Swatara Gap in Lebanon County. Reichel, *Memorials, op. cit.*, p. 80n.

[7]Named Thurnstein by Conrad Weiser. *Ibid.*, p. 82. Present Peters Mountain. *Pennsylvania Magazine of History and Biography, op. cit.*, II (1878), 426n.

From the top of this pass we have a view of a vale ten miles across, varied here and there with swelling hills, some of them appearing at a distance like clear land, but they are covered with dwarf oak, in about elbow or shoulder high: these oaks bear acorns, and the best gall nuts of any we have. Count Zinzindorff [Zinzendorf] gave this vale the name of *Saint Anthony's Wilderness;*[1] and designs, as Mr. Conrad Weisar [Weiser][2] tells me, to bring over some Germans to settle it. The soil is but poor and ordinary, except on the Swartaro [Swatara] Creek; and there is at present no practicable road over the mountain, by which it may communicate with the settled part of the province. The vegetation is at present chiefly of spruce fir, white oak, and some pine: the native wood grass grows here in great abundance, but this always dies with the first frost.

In this St. Anthony's Wilderness, we crossed the branches of the *Swartaro* [Swatara] Creek. At the conflux of two of these branches, is a small Indian settlement, of five Delaware families. The westernmost branch of the Swartaro [Swatara] comes through a ridge of the Kittock-tinny [Kittatinny] Mountains. Along the eastern banks of this creek, we passed through the first ridge of these mountains, and in one-third of a mile more we crost it to the left: we then passed upon a stony reach, and over two or three rugged barren mountains, covered with only hurtleberries, dwarf-oak, and a few pitch-pines; in six miles more, we went down a very stony deep descent to Lawrel [Laurel] Creek,[3] a rivulet, which falls into Kind Creek, about eight miles lower down. On the north sides of Lawrel [Laurel] and Kind Creeks, is a pleasant and fruitful valley two or three miles wide, varies here and there with most beautiful groves of white-pines and white oak. This would make a pretty settlement.

We came in fifteen miles travel, west along this valley, to the strait by which Kind Creek passes to the north, through one of the ridges of the mountains, into another little pleasant valley. We pass along the banks of this creek for four miles more; then leaving this creek on our left hand, the path led us through a narrow pass between two mountains, where grew the tallest white pines that I ever saw; I will not hazard my judgement to what height I guessed them to be, because it is

[1]Location of St. Anthony's Wilderness. Wallace, *op. cit.*, map opposite p. 139.

[2]Conrad Weiser (1696-1760), Pennsylvania colonial Indian agent, interpreter, and official representative of the colony at many Indian conferences. In

1741 Mr. Weiser was named a justice of the peace for Lancaster County, and, in 1752 at the time of the erection of Berks County, he was made its first justice of the peace, and from 1752 to 1760 served as the first president judge of the county.

[3]Present Pine Creek. Wallace, *op. cit.*, p. 155.

F f

so incredible. I going out, had time to measure them, and when I returned I had lost my triangle.

A mile beyond this gap we passed by a path, or Indian road, led N.W. directly over the mountains to *Shamokin;*[1] but this is little frequented, on account of the great steeps over which it leads. Passing thence three miles, along a continued slant of shrub and white-oak, we came to more ridges: our path led us up some of these, and along the tops of others for twelve miles; we then came to a creek which falls into the Susquahanna [Susquehanna] River, and has at its confluence an island in the mouth of it. This creek is called Moxenay [Mahanoy], and hath some old Indian fields on its banks, and near it.

It is now the Scite of Sunbury, the county town of Northumberland county, 1775

We crossed this creek, and came along a rich border, about two miles to the Susquahanna [Susquehanna] River. This river is here about a mile and a half wide, is full of islands, and glides with a bright and easy current over a stony and gravelly bottom, and may be easily forded. Passing up along the east side of this river, we came under a high peaked mountain, here we struck off to the right, and for twelve months[2] our path led us over several ordinary hills, and across several vales, not much better, to a hill just above Shamokin: in one of these we saw the appearance of an iron mine. Descending this hill, it was so steep, we were obliged to hold the horse which carried our baggage, both by the head and tail, to prevent his tumbling head-long: at the bottom we crossed the creek[3] on which Shamokin is, and came to the town.

This Indian town is a settlement or dwelling-place of Delaware Indians, situate on the confluence of two main branches of the Susquahanna [Susquehanna] River. Its latitude is 40° 45'. Here are about *** wigwaums,[4] or Indian huts, lying pretty near together, and many more scattered here and there, over a very fruitful spot of ground, of about seven or eight hundred acres. This is encompassed with the river on one side, and enclosed in by the mountains on the other. The freshes of the river, which run with great impetuosity, generally when they come down lay the land under water, although it lies 15 or 20 feet higher than the common surface of the river.

F f

"*The observations and reflections which Lewis Evans made in his passage through these mountains,[5] called by the Indians by a name which imports Endless Mountains, to Goosberry-hill, the westernmost ridge of*

D e

[1]Present site of Sunbury, Pennsylvania.
[2]Miles.
[3]Shamokin Creek.
[4]There were eight cabins in Shamokin at this time. Bartram, *op. cit.*, p. 14.

[5]The northerly continuation of the Allegheny Mountains terminates in Tioga County, New York. Franklin B. Hough, *Gazetteer of the State of New York* (Albany, N.Y., Andrew Boyd, 1872), p. 650.

them are either marked in the map or inserted in the analysis, where a general description of these mountains is given."

D e   From Goosberry-hill, travelling N.N.E. through a most beautiful and fruitful country about eight and forty miles, we reached the first town[1] of the Onondâga Indians. This country is varied with pleasant swelling knolls, brooks and little lakes. In its vegitation it abounds with sweet-maple, linden, birch, elm, white pines and spruce in some places; and with gooseberry under-woods on the north side of all the hills.

      At twenty-five miles we passed between a lake,[2] at the head of one of the lesser branches of *the Susquahanna* [Susquehanna], and a mountain called by the Indians *Onugareckny*.[3] From this lake canoes may go down the Susquahanna [Susquehanna] to the settlements of

D e   Pennsylvania with a fresh. On this mountain the Indians, as their tradition says, first found Indian corn or maize, tobacco, squashes and pompions.

      In 18 miles further travel, we passed over a mountain, which we called Table Mountain.[4] This is the height of the land, for on the other side of it, the rivers run north and west, and fall into the lakes.

D e   In 10 miles further travel down this hill, we came to the great council-residence of the *Five Nation Confederacy* at Onondada [Onondaga].[5] This stands upon a creek to S.W. of a little lake of the same name. On the sides of this lake are salt springs, very strongly impregnated with that mineral, so that bushes on the margins hang glittering with the salt like splendid icicles.

      This lake,[6] which is about five miles long, and a mile and a half broad, falls at the N.W. into the Seneca River. This river having

C e   received the waters of this lake, holds on its waters in a slow still stream for about ten miles northerly. The river which comes W. from the Oheyda [Oneida] Lake joins it, and they hold on in the same still way a little further, and then, with rapids and over-falls tumble into the great Lake Ontario by Oswêgo.

C e   Oswêgo is rather a collection of trading huts, built for the residence of the Indian traders during the mart, or trading season, than a fixt habitation of settlers. It consists of about seventy logg-houses, in two rows, forming a street, on the west shore of the river, at its mouth. The fort stood at the point next the Lake. The latitude of this place is 43° 22'.

---

[1]Cachiadachse. Wallace, *op. cit.*, p. 159.
[2]One of the Tully Lakes. Wallace, *op. cit.*, p. 158.
[3]Not identified.
[4]Onondaga West Hill. Joshua Clark, *Onondaga; or*

Reminiscences of Earlier and Later Times . . . (Syracuse, Stoddard and Babcock, 1849), I, 323.
[5]Present site of Syracuse, New York.
[6]Onondaga Lake.

NUMBER VI.

A JOURNAL.[1]

OF Christopher Gist's[2] journey, began from Col. Cresap's,[3] at the *old town*[4] *on Potomack* [Potomac] *river, Maryland,* October 31, 1750, continued *down the Ohio,* within 15 *miles of the Falls*[5] *thereof;* and from thence to *Roanoak* [Roanoke] *river in North Carolina,* where he arrived May 19, 1751; undertaken on the account of the Ohio company,[6] and by the instructions of their committee.

Instructions given Mr. Christopher Gist by the committee of the Ohio company, the 11th day of September 1750.

You are to go out as soon as possible to the westward of the great mountains, and carry with you such a number of men as you think necessary, in order to search out and discover the lands upon the *river Ohio* (and other adjoining branches of the *Missisippi* [Mississippi]) down as low as the *great Falls* thereof.

You are particularly to observe the ways and passes through all the mountains you cross, and take an exact account of the soil, quality, and product of the land; the width and depth of the rivers, and the several falls belonging to them; together with the courses and bearings of the rivers and mountains as near as you conveniently can: You are also to observe what nations of Indians inhabit there, their strength and numbers, who they trade with, and in what commodities they deal.

When you find a large quantity of good level land, such as you think will suit the company, you are to measure the breadth of it, in three or four different places, and take the courses of the river and mountains on which it binds, in order to judge the quantity; you are to fix the beginning and bounds in such a manner, that they may be easily found again

Margin notes: Old town G h — Gist's instructions — To discover the nations of Indians, and their trade.

---

[1]This *Journal* was edited by Wm. Darlington in 1893. Christopher Gist, "*Journals with Historical, Geographical, and Ethnological notes . . .* " by William M. Darlington (Pittsburgh, J. R. Weldin & Co., 1893).

[2]See *note 2, p. 26.*

[3]Thomas Cresap (1700?-1790?), Indian trader and agent, and member of the Ohio Company of Virginia. For biographical sketch read Kenneth Bailey, *The Ohio Company of Virginia* ... (Glendale,

California, The Arthur H. Clark Company, 1939), pp. 46-49.

[4]Located on the north bank of the Potomac opposite Green Spring, Maryland. Gist, *Journals* (Darlington ed.), *op. cit.,* p. 90; Scull's Map of Pennsylvania (1770), *op. cit.*

[5]Falls in the Ohio at Louisville, Kentucky.

[6]Ohio Company of Virginia. Christopher Gist was an agent for this company.

by your description; the nearer in the land lies the better, provided it be good and level, but we had rather go quite down the Missisippi [Mississippi] than take mean broken land. After finding a large body of good level land, you are not to stop, but proceed farther as low as the falls of the Ohio, that we may be informed of that navigation; and you are to take an exact account of all the large bodies of good level land in the same manner as above directed, that the company may the better judge where it will be most convenient for them to take theirs.

You are to note all the bodies of good land as you go along, though there is not a sufficient quantity for the Company's grant; but you need not be so particular in the mensuration of that, as in the large bodies.

You are to draw as good a plan as you can of the country you pass through, and take an exact and particular journal of all your proceedings, and make a true report thereof to the Ohio company.

In compliance with my instructions from the committee of the Ohio company, bearing date the 11th day of September 1750.

Wednesday, October 31, 1750. Set out from Col. Cresap's,[1] at the *Old Town on Potomack* [Potomac] *river, in Maryland,* and went along an old Indian path,[2] N. 30 d. E. about 11 miles.

Thursday, November 1. N. 1 m. N. 30 d. E. 3 m. Here I was taken sick and stayed all night.

Friday 2. N. 30 d. E. 6 m. Here I was so bad that I was not able to proceed any farther that night, but grew better in the morning.

Saturday 3. N. 3 m.[3] to *Juniatta* [Juniata], a large branch of Susquahanna [Susquehanna], where I stayed all night.

Sunday 4th. Crossed *Juniatta* [Juniata] and went up it S. 55 d. W. about 16 min.[4]

Monday 5th. Continued the same course S. 55 d. W. 6 m. to the top of a *large mountain, called the Allegany* [Allegheny] *Mountain;* here our path turned, and we went N. 45 d. W. 6 m. and encamped.

Tuesday 6, Wednesday 7, and Thursday 8, had snow, and such bad weather that we could not travel; but I killed a young bear, so that we had provision enough.

To examine the Navigation of the Ohio to the Falls.

To note all the bodies of good land

To draw a plan of the country, and keep a journal

Gist begins his journey

Old town

G h

Juniatta

Allegany Mountains

[1]Thomas Cresap.

[2]"Gist's route from Old Town lay by the Warrior's Path along the base of the Great Warrior Mountain now known as Tussey Mountain, on the eastern side, passing through the present district of Flintstone, Allegheny County, Maryland, and the townships of Southampton, Monroe, and Providence, in Bedford County, Pennsylvania, reaching the Juniata at the Warrior's Gap, near the village of Bloody Run [Everett], Pennsylvania, eight miles east of the present town of Bedford." Gist (Darlington edition), *op. cit.,* p. 90.

[3]Eight miles not three miles. *Ibid.,* p. 32.

[4]"Miles" not "minutes." Here Pownall has interpreted "M" to be minutes not miles.

Friday 9th. Set out N. 70 d. W. about 8 min.[1] Here I crossed a creek of *Susquahanna* [Susquehanna],[2] and it raining hard, I went into an old Indian cabbin,[3] where I stayed all night.

Saturday, November 10. Rain and snow all day, but cleared away in the evening.

Sunday 11th. Set out late in the morning, N. 70 d. W. 6 m. crossing two forks of a creek[4] of Susquahanna [Susquehanna]; here the way being bad, I encamped and killed a turkey. F j

Monday 12th. Set out N. 45 d. W. 8 m. and crossed a great *Laurel mountain*. Laurel Mountain

Tuesday 13th. Rain and snow.

Wednesday 14th. Set out N. 45 d. W. 6 m. to *Loylhannon*,[5] an old Indian town on a creek of the Ohio, called *Kiskeminetas* [Kiskiminetas], then N. 1 m. N.W. 1 m. to an Indian camp on the said creek. Loylhannon Kiskeminetas F j

Thursday 15. The weather being bad, and I unwell, stayed here all day. The Indian, to whom this camp belonged, spoke good English, and directed me the way to his town, which is called *Shanoppin*;[6] he said it was about sixty miles, and a pretty good way.

Friday 16th. Set out S. 70 d. W. 10 m.

Saturday 17th. The same course (S 70 d. W) 15 m. to an old Indian camp.[7]

Sunday 18th. I was very sick, and sweated myself according to the Indian custom, in a sweat-house, which gave me ease, and my fever abated.

Monday 19th. Set out early in the morning the same course, (S. 70 d. W.) travelled very hard about twenty miles to a small Indian town of the Delawares, called *Shanoppin* [Shannopin], *on the S.E. side of the river Ohio*,[8] where we rested and got corn for our horses. F j Shannoppin's Town

Tuesday 20th. I was unwell, and stayed in this town to recover myself. While I was here I took an opportunity to set my compass privately, and took the distance across the river; for I understood it was dangerous to let a compass be seen: *the Ohio is 76 poles wide here.* There Width of the Ohio

[1]"Miles" not "minutes."

[2]The path led across Stoney Creek near Stoyestown, Somerset County, Pennsylvania. This creek is a tributary of the Allegheny not the Susquehanna River. Gist (Darlington edition), *op. cit.*, p. 91.

[3]Cabin of Kickeney Paulin, a Delaware minor chief. Hanna, *op. cit.*, I, 282.

[4]Quemahoning, a branch of Stoney Creek. Gist (Darlington edition), *op. cit.*, p. 91.

[5]Loyalhanna, on the present site of Ligioner, Pennsylvania. Hanna, *op. cit.*, I, 269.

[6]On the site of present twelfth ward, Pittsburgh, Pennsylvania.

[7]Cockey or Cock Eye's Cabin on Bushy Run, Westmoreland County, Pennsylvania. Gist (Darlington edition), p. 92.

[8]Allegheny River. In early time the French considered the Allegheny River the Ohio; the English often did likewise.

are about twenty families in this town. *The land in general from Potomack* [Potomac] *to this place is mean, stony, and broken, with here and there good spots upon the creeks and branches, but no body of it.*

Land mean

Land good

Saturday 24th. Set out from *Shanoppin* [Shannopin], and swam our horses across the *Ohio*, and went down the river S. 75 d. W. 4 m. N. 75 d. W. 7 m. W. 2 m. the land from Shanoppin [Shannopin] is good along the river, but the bottoms not broad: at a distance from the river good land for farming, covered with small white and red oaks, and tolerable level: fine runs for mills, &c.

F k
Logg's Town.
Land very rich.

Sunday 25th. Down the river W. 3 m. N.W. 5 m. to *Loggs Town* [Logstown]:[1] the lands for these last eight miles very rich, the bottoms above a mile wide, but on the S.E. side scarce a mile, the hills high and steep. In the town I found scarce any body but a parcel of reprobate Indian traders, the chief of the Indians being out hunting; here I was informed, that George Croghan[2] and Andrew Montour,[3] who were sent upon an embassy[4] from Pennsylvania to the Indians, were passed about a week before me. The people here enquiring my business; and, because I did not readily inform them, began to suspect me, saying, I was come to settle the Indian lands, and that I should never go home again safe. I found this discourse was like to be of ill consequence, so pretended to speak very slightingly of what they had said, and enquired for [George] Croghan (who is a mere idol among his countrymen, the Irish traders) and Andrew Montour, the interpreter for Pennsylvania; and told them I had a message to deliver the Indians from the king, by order of the president of Virginia, and for that reason wanted to see Mr. Montour. This made them all pretty easy (being afraid to interrupt the king's message) and obtained me quiet and respect among them; otherwise, I doubt not, they would have contrived some evil against me. I immediately wrote to Mr. Croghan by one of the traders people.

F k
Great Beaver Creek

Monday 26th. Though I was unwell, I preferred the woods to such company; and set out from Loggs Town [Logstown][5] down the river N.W. 6 m. to *Great Beaver Creek*, where I met one Burny Curran,[6] a

[1]Logstown, on the north bank of the Ohio River about 18 miles below Pittsburgh and near the present site of Economy, Pennsylvania. Hanna, *op. cit.*, I, 289.

[2]George Croghan (—— d. 1782). Famous Indian trader, land speculator, and deputy Indian agent under Sir Wm. Johnson.

[3]Andrew Montour, noted Indian interpreter. For sketch of his life read Hanna, *op. cit.*, I, 223-46.

[4]George Croghan and Andrew Montour were sent

to the Ohio Country with a small present for the Twightwees; and to inform the Indians that a present prepared for them by the government of Pennsylvania would be distributed at Logstown in the spring of 1751. *Colonial Records of Pennsylvania*, *op. cit.*, V, 496-98, 517-24.

[5]See *note* 1, this page.

[6]Barnaby Curran, an Indian trader. Curran, at one time, was employed by Hugh Parker for the Ohio Company and was later a guide to George

trader for the Ohio company, and we continued together as far as
Muskingum.[1] The bottoms upon the river below Loggs Town [Logstown]
are very rich, but narrow; the high land pretty good, but not very rich;
the land upon Beaver Creek of the same kind. From this place we left
the Ohio to the S.E. and travelled across the country.

Tuesday 27th. Set out from the E. side of *Beaver Creek*, N.W. 6 m. Land very
W. 4 m. upon these two last courses very good high land, and not much good.
broken, fit for farming.

Wednesday 28th. Rained, and we could not travel.

Thursday 29th. W. 6 m. through good land; the same course continued 6 m. farther, through very broken land: here I found myself
pretty well recovered, and being in want of provision, went out and
killed a deer.

Friday 30. Set out S. 45 d. W. 12 m. crossed the last branch of
Beaver Creek,[2] where one of Curran's[3] men and myself killed twelve
turkeys.

Saturday, December 1st. N. 45 d. W. 10 m.[4] the land high and
tolerable good.

Sunday 2d. N. 45 d. W. 8 m.[5] the same sort of land, but near the
creeks bushy, and very full of thorns.

Monday 3d. Killed a deer, and stayed in our camp all day.

Tuesday 4th. Set out late S. 45 d. W. about 4 m. here I killed three
fine fat deer; so that tho' we were eleven in company, we had great
plenty of provisions.

Wednesday 5th. Set out down the side of a creek, called *Elk's Eye* F 1
Creek,[6] S. 70 d. W. 6 m. good land, but void of timber; meadows upon Elk's Eye
the creek, and fine runs for mills. Creek
No timber.

Thursday 6th. Rained all day, so that we were obliged to continue
in our camp.

Friday 7th. Set out S.W. 8 min.[7] crossing *Elk's Eye Creek* to a
town of the Ottawa's,[8] a nation of French Indians; an old Frenchman, Ottawa's
Town

Washington on his trip to Venango in 1753. Hanna,
op. cit., II, 330.

[1]Muskingum or Conchake, a Wyandot town at the
forks of the Muskingum River. Near the present site
of Coshocton, Ohio. *Ibid.*, II, 188, 268.

[2]West branch of Little Beaver Creek in southern
Columbiana County, Ohio. Gist (Darlington edition), *op. cit.*, p. 103.

[3]Barnaby Curran.

[4]To a point near present Hanover, Columbiana

County, Ohio. Gist (Darlington edition), *ibid.*, p. 103.

[5]To a point near Bayard, Columbiana County,
Ohio. *Ibid.*

[6]Big Sandy Creek, a tributary of the Tuscawaras
River. *Ibid.*

[7]Miles.

[8]At the junction of the Big Sandy and Tuscawaras
Rivers near the present town of Bolivar, Ohio. Fort
Laurens, in Revolutionary times, was located here.
Gist (Darlington edition), *op. cit.*, pp. 103-05.

named Mark Coonce,[1] who had married an Indian woman of the Six Nations, lived here. The Indians were all out hunting; the old man was civil to me; but after I was gone to my camp, upon his understanding I came from Virginia, he called me the Big Knife.[2] There are not above six or eight families belonging to this town.

Saturday 8th. Stayed in the town.

Sunday 9th. Set out down the *Elk's Eye Creek* S. 45 d. W. 6 m. to *Margaret's Creek*,[3] a branch of *Elk's Eye Creek*.

Margaret's
Creek

Monday 10th. The same course S. 45 d. W. 2 m. to a large creek.

Tuesday 11th. The same course twelve miles; killed two deer.

Wednesday 12th. The same course eight miles; encamped by the side of *Elk's Eye Creek*.

Thursday 13. Rained all day.

F M
Muskingum
Lands broken
Wiandots
divided.

Friday 14th. Set out W. 5 m. to *Muskingum*,[4] a town of the Wiandots [Wyandots]. The land upon *Elk's Eye Creek* is in general very broken, the bottoms narrow. The Wiandots [Wyandots][5] or little Mingoes are divided between the French and English; one half of them adhere to the first; and the other half are firmly attached to the latter: the town of Muskingum consists of about one hundred families; when we came within sight of it, we perceived English colours hoisted on the king's house, and at George Croghan's,[6] upon enquiring the reason, I was informed, that the French had lately taken several English traders;[7] and that Mr. Croghan had ordered all the white men to come into this town,[8] and had sent expresses to the traders of the lower towns, and among the Picqualinees [Pickawillanys]; and the Indians had sent to their people to come to council about it.

Saturday 15, and Sunday 16. Nothing remarkable happened.

Monday 17. Two traders belonging to Mr. Croghan came into town,

[1]Probably Macoonce or Maconce, a French interpreter at Saguin's (Seguin's) trading house on the Cuyahoga River. Hanna, *op. cit.*, I, 333-34.

[2]Assarigoa, or Long Knife, was the Iroquois name for the Virginians.

[3]Present Sugar Creek which empties into the Tuscarawas River at Dover, Ohio. Gist (Darlington edition), *op. cit.*, p. 105.

[4]See *note* 1, p. 175.

[5]A dependent people who, in order to escape destruction by the Iroquois in 1639, gained refuge with the Huron Confederation. Hodge, *op. cit.*, I, 584.

[6]George Croghan had a trading post at Muskingum. Gist (Darlington edition), *op. cit.*, p. 108.

[7]The four English traders were Luke Irwin [Erwin] of Philadelphia, Joseph Fortiner [Faulkner] of New York, Thomas Bourke [Burk] of Lancaster, and George Pathon [John Pattin] of Wilmington. All were traders, licensed in Philadelphia. For full details read "Extract of the interrogatories of the four English traders, taken upon the territories of France." In *The Conduct of the Late Ministry, or A Memorial; Containing a Summary of Facts with their Vouchers, in Answer to The Observations, sent by the English Ministry, to the Courts of Europe* ... (London, W. Bizet, 1757), pp. 92-106.

[8]Muskingum.

and informed us, that two[1] of his people were taken by forty Frenchmen, and twenty French Indians, who had carried them, with seven horse-loads of skins, to a new fort[2] that the French were building on one of the branches of Lake Erie.

Tuesday 18th. I acquainted Mr. Croghan and Andrew Montour with my business with the Indians, and talked much of a regulation of trade, with which they were pleased, and treated me very well. *Talk of a regulation in the trade.*

Wednesday 19th to Monday 24th. Nothing remarkable.

Tuesday 25th. This being Christmas-day, I intended to read prayers; but after inviting some of the white men, they informed each other of my intentions; and being of several different persuasions, and few of them inclined to hear any good, they refused to come: but one Thomas Burney, a black-smith, who is settled there, went about and talked to them, and then several of them came; and Andrew Montour invited several of the well-disposed Indians who came freely. By this time the morning was spent, and I had given over all thoughts of them; but seeing them come, to oblige all and offend none, I stood up and said, Gentlemen, I have no design or intention to give offence to any particular sect or religion; but as our king indulges us all in a liberty of conscience, and hinders none of you in the exercise of your religious worship, so it would be unjust in you to endeavour to stop the propagation of his. The doctrine of salvation, faith and good works, is what I only propose to treat of, as I find it extracted from the homilies of the church of England, which I then read to them in the best manner I could; and after I had done, the interpreter told the Indians what I had read, and that it was the true faith which the great King, and his church, recommended to his children: the Indians seemed well pleased, and came up to me, and returned me their thanks, and then invited me to live among them, and gave me a name in their language, Annosannoah: the interpreter told me this was the name of a good man that had formerly lived among them, and their King said that must be always my name, for which I returned them thanks; but, as to living among them, I excused myself by saying, I did not know whether the governor would give me leave; and if he did, the French would come and carry me away, as they had done the English traders; to which they answered, I might bring great guns and make a fort, that they had now left the French, and

Christmas-day, Gist proposes to read prayers.

Indians attend

Gist reads prayers

Indians much pleased, give him an Indian name;

desire a fort to be built;

[1]Probably two of the four traders mentioned in *note* 7, p. 176.

[2]Probably "Fort Sandoski, which is a small Pallisadoed Fort, with about 20 Men lying on the South side of Lake Erie, and was built the latter end of the Year 1750." "A Journal or Account of the Capture of John Pattin." *Pennsylvania Magazine, op. cit.*, LXV (1941), 427.

were very desirous of being instructed in the principles of Christianity, that they liked me very well, and wanted me to marry them after the christian manner, and baptize their children; and then, they said, they would never desire to return to the French, or suffer them or their priests to come near them more; for they loved the English, but had seen little religion among them. Some of their great men came and wanted me to baptize their children, for as I had read to them, and appeared to talk about religion, they took me to be a minister of the gospel; upon which I desired Mr. Montour,[1] the interpreter, to tell them that no minister could venture to baptize any children, until those that were to be sureties for them, were well instructed in the faith themselves; and that was according to the great King's religion, in which he desired his children should be instructed, and we dare not do it in any other way than by law established; but I hoped, if I could not be admitted to live among them, that the great King would send them proper ministers to exercise that office among them, at which they seemed well pleased; and one of them went and brought me his book, which was a kind of alma-nack contrived for them by the French, in which the days of the week were so marked, that by moving a pin every morning, they kept a pretty exact account of the time, to shew me that he understood me, and that he and his family always observed the Sabbath day.

Wednesday 26th. This day a woman, who had been long a pris-oner, and had deserted, being retaken, and brought into the town on Christmas Eve, was put to death in the following manner. They car-ried her without the town, and let her loose; and when she attempt-ed to run away, the persons appointed for that purpose, pursued her, and struck her on the ear, on the right side of her head, which beat her flat on her face to the ground; they then stuck her several times through the back with a dart, to the heart, scalped her, and threw the scalp in the air, and another cut off her head. Thus the dismal spectacle lay till the evening, and then Barney [Barnaby] Curran de-sired leave to bury her, which he and his men, and some of the Indians did, just at dark.

Thursday 27th to Thursday, January 3d, 1775 [1750-51]. Nothing remarkable happened in the town.

Friday 4th, one Taaf,[2] an Indian trader, came to town from near Lake Erie, and informed us that the Wiandots [Wyandots][3] had advised

[1]Andrew Montour.
[2]Michael Teaffe (Taffe) was associated in the Indian trade with William Trent, Robert Callendar, and George Croghan. Volwiler, *op. cit.*, p. 39.
[3]Wyandots or Hurons.

him to keep clear of the Outawais [Ottawas] (a nation of Indians firmly attached to the French, living near the lakes) and told him that the branches of the lakes were claimed by the French; but that all the branches of the Ohio belong to them, and their brothers the English; and that the French had no business there, and that it was expected that the other part of the Wiandots [Wyandots] would desert the French, and come over to the English interest, and join their brethren on Elk's Eye Creek, and build a strong fort and town there.

Saturday 5th. The weather still continuing bad, I stayed in the town to recruit my horses; and though corn was very dear among the Indians, I was obliged to feed them well, or run the risque of losing them, as I had a great way to travel.

Wednesday 9th. The wind southerly, and the weather something warmer: This day came into town two traders from among the Pic-qualinnees [Pickawillany] (a tribe of the Tawightwis [Twightwees]) and brought news that another English trader[1] was also taken prisoner by the French; and that three French soldiers had deserted and come over to the English, and surrendered themselves to some of the traders of the Pick town;[2] and that the Indians would have put them to death, to revenge their taking our traders, but as the French had surrendered themselves to the English, they would not let the Indians hurt them; but had ordered them to be sent under the care of three of our traders, and delivered at this town[3] to George Croghan.

Traders protect three French deserters from the Indians.

Thursday, January the 10th. Wind still at South, and warm.

Friday 11th. This day came into town an Indian from near the lakes, and confirmed the news we had heard.

Saturday 12th. We sent away our people towards the lower town,[4] intending to follow them the next morning; and this evening we went into council in the Wiandot [Wyandot] king's house; The council had been put off a long time, expecting some of their great men in, but few of them came; and this evening some of the king's council being a little disordered with liquor, no business could be done, but we were desired to come next day.

Sunday 13th. No Business done.

Monday 14th. This day George Croghan, by the assistance of Andrew Montour, acquainted the king and council of this nation

[1]Probably John Pattin who was taken captive by the French in November, 1750.

[2]Picktown (Pickawillany), an important trading center on the Great Miami River near the present site of Piqua, Miami County, Ohio, Hodge, *op. cit.*, II, 242.

[3]Muskingum.

[4]An Indian town on White Woman's Creek.

Acquaints
the Indians
the king had
sent them a
present, and
invites them
to come
down to
receive it.
Indians
would not
give an
answer till a
full council
should
assemble.

(presenting them four strings of wampum) that the great King over the water, their Roggony (father) had sent, under the care of the governor of Virginia, their brother, a large present of goods, which were now landed safe in Virginia; and that the governor had sent me to invite them to come and see him, and partake of their father's charity, to all his children on the branches of Ohio.

In answer to which one of the chiefs stood up and said, "That their king and all of them, thanked their brother the governor of Virginia, for his care, and me for bringing them the news; but they could not give an answer, until they had a full, or general council of the several nations of Indians, which could not be till next spring; and so the king and council shaking hands with us, we took our leave."

F m
White
Woman's
Creek

Tuesday 15th. We left *Muskingum* and went W. 5 m. to the *White Woman's Creek*,[1] on which is a small town.[2] This white woman was taken away from New England, when she was not above ten years old, by the French Indians. She is now upwards of fifty, has an Indian husband and several children, her name is Mary Harris;[3] she still remembers they used to be very religious in New England, and wonders how the white men can be so wicked as she has seen them in these woods.

G m
Licking
Creek
Land rich
but broken
Salt ponds.

Wednesday 16th. Set out S.W. 25 m. to *Licking Creek*,[4] the land from *Muskingum* to this place, rich but broken. *Upon the North side of Licking Creek, about six miles from the mouth, are several salt licks, or ponds, formed by little streams or drains of water, clear, but of a bluish colour, and salt taste. The traders and Indians boil their meat in this water, which if proper care be not taken, will sometimes make it too salt to eat.*

Thursday 17th. Set out W. 5 m. S.W. 15 m. to a great swamp.

Friday 18th. Set out from the great swamp S.W. 15 m.

G n
Hockhocking
Town

Saturday 19th. W. 15 m. to *Hochocking*,[5] a small town with only four or five Delaware families.[6]

G n
Maguck
Town

Sunday 20th. The snow began to grow thin, and the weather warmer. Set out from *Hockhocking* S. 5 m. then W. 5 m. then S.W. 5 m. to

[1]Walhonding River. Henry Howe, *Historical Collections of Ohio . . .* (Cincinnati, Derby, Bradley & Co., 1848), pp. 115-16.

[2]White Woman's Town.

[3]Mary Harris was taken captive at Deerfield, Massachusetts on February 29, 1704. John Williams, *The Redeemed Captive returning to Zion: or, A Faithful History of Remarkable Occurrences in the Captivity and Deliverance of Mr. John Williams . . .* (6th ed., Boston, Samuel Hall, 1795), p. 108.

[4]Present Licking River, Ohio.

[5]Hockhocking, on present site of Lancaster, Fairfield County, Ohio. Gist (Darlington edition), *op. cit.*, p. 116.

[6]Near the beginning of the eighteenth century the Delawares who occupied a greater part of New Jersey, Delaware, eastern Pennsylvania, and New York were subdued by the Iroquois. After this time they gradually moved westward and in 1751, a group was invited by the Hurons or Wyandots to settle on the Muskingum and other streams in eastern Ohio. Hodge, *op. cit.*, I, 385.

Maguck,[1] a little Delaware town of about ten families, by the north side of a plain, or clear field, about five miles in length, N.E. and S.W. and two miles broad, with a small rising in the middle, which gives a fine prospect over the whole plain, and a large creek on the north side of it, called *Sioto Creek* [Scioto River]; all the way from *Licking Creek*[2] to this place, is fine, rich, level land, with large meadows and fine clover bottoms, with spacious plains, covered with wild rye; the wood chiefly large walnuts and hiccories, here and there mixed with poplars, cherry-trees, and sugar-trees.

Land very rich, with fine meadows and variety of fine timber

Monday 21st to Wednesday 23d. Stayed in the *Maguck town*.

Thursday 24th. Set out from *Maguck town*, S. about 15 m. through fine, rich, level land, to a small town called *Hurricane Tom's*,[3] consisting of about five or six Delaware Families, on the S.W. of *Sioto Creek* [Scioto River].

G n
Hurricane Tom's Town

Friday 25th. The creek being very high, and full of ice, we could not ford, and were obliged to go down it on the S.E. side, S.E. 4 m. to the *Salt Lick Creek*;[4] *about a mile up this creek, on the south side is a very large salt lick, the streams which run into this lick are very salt, and, though clear, leave a bluish sediment: the Indians and traders make salt for their horses of this water, by boiling it; it has at first a bluish colour, and somewhat bitter taste, but upon being dissolved in fair water, and boiled the second time, it comes to tolerably pure salt.*

Land rich and level.
H n
Salt Lick Creek
Salt springs Indians make salt.

Saturday 26th. Set out S. 2 m. S.W. 14 m.

Sunday 27th. S. 12 m. to a small Delaware town,[5] of about twenty families, on the S.E. side of *Sioto Creek* [Scioto River]. We lodged at the house of an Indian, whose name was Windaughalah,[6] a great man, and chief of this town, and much in the English interest; he entertained us very kindly, and ordered a negro man that belonged to him, to feed our horses well: this night it snowed, and in the morning, *though the snow was six or seven inches deep, the wild rye*[7] *appeared very green and flourishing through it*, and our horses had very fine feeding.

Wild rye appears above the snow, which was 6 or 7 inches deep.

Monday 28th. We went into council with the Indians of this town,

[1]Located between Scippo Creek and the Scioto River, about three and one-half miles south of present Circleville, Pickaway County, Ohio. *Ibid.* For "Map of the Ancient Shawanoese Towns, on the Pickaway Plain" see Howe, *op. cit.*, p. 402.

[2]Licking River.

[3]Harrickintom's Town located below the present Chillicothe, Ohio, and opposite the mouth of Paint Creek. Gist (Darlington edition), *op. cit.*, pp. 118-19.

[4]Present Salt Creek which flows into the Scioto River in southeastern Ross County, Ohio. Gist (Darlington edition), *op. cit.*, p. 119.

[5]Situated on the east branch of the Scioto in present Clay Township, Scioto County, Ohio. Gist (Darlington edition), *op. cit.*, p. 119.

[6]Windaughulah, or The Council Door, a celebrated Delaware chief who represented the Delawares and Wyandots at several conferences in Pennsylvania. *Ibid.*, pp. 119-20.

[7]See page 26, this work.

and after the interpreter had informed them of his instructions[1] from the governor of Pennsylvania, and given them some cautions in regard to the French, they returned for answer as follows: The speaker, with four strings of wampum in his hand, stood up, and addressing himself to the governor of Pennsylvania, said, "Brothers, we the Delawares, return you our hearty thanks for the news you have sent us, and we assure you, we will not hear the voice of any other nation; for we are to be directed by you, our brothers, the English, and by none else; we shall be very glad to hear what our brothers have to say to us at the Logg's town [Logstown] in the spring; and do assure you of our hearty good will and love to our brothers, we present you with these four strings of wampum." This is the last town of the Delawares to the westward. The Delaware Indians, by the best accounts I could gather, consist of about five hundred fighting men, all firmly attached to the English interest: they are not properly a part of the Six Nations, but are scattered about among most of the Indians upon the Ohio, and some of them among the Six Nations,[2] from whom they have leave to hunt upon their lands.

Tuesday 29th. Set out S.W. 5 m. to the mouth of *Sioto Creek* [Scioto River], opposite to the *Shawane town;*[3] here we fired our guns to alarm the traders, who soon answered, and came and ferried us over. The land, about the mouth of *Sioto Creek* [Scioto River], is rich, but broken, fine bottoms upon the river and creek. The *Shawane town* is situate on both sides of the Ohio, just below the mouth of *Sioto Creek* [Scioto River], and contains about three hundred men; there are about forty Houses on the south side of the river, and about a hundred on the north side, with a kind of state house of about ninety feet long, with a light cover of bark, in which they hold their councils: the Shawanes [Shawnee] are not a part of the Six Nations, but were formerly at variance with them, though now reconciled; they are great friends to the English, who once protected them from the fury of the Six Nations, which they gratefully remember.

Wednesday 30th. We were conducted into council, where George Croghan delivered sundry speeches from the government of Pennsylvania to the chiefs[4] of this nation; in which he informed them, "That two prisoners[5] who had been taken by the French, and had made their escape

---

[1]See *note* 4, p. 174.

[2]Iroquois Confederacy. Six Nations consisting of the tribes of the Cayugas, Mohawks, Oneidas, Onondagas, Senecas, and Tuscaroras. Known as the Five nations until the admission of the Tuscaroras in 1722.

[3]Lower Shawnee Town.

[4]Takentoa, Molsinoughkio, and Nynickenowea, Piankashaw and Wea chiefs. *Colonial Records of Pennsylvania, op. cit.,* V, 523.

[5]Morris Turner and Ralph Kilgore. *Ibid.,* 482-84.

from the French officer at Lake Erie, as he was carrying them toward
Canada, brought news that the French offered a large sum of money to
any who would bring to them the said Croghan, and Andrew Montour
alive, or if dead, their scalps; and that the French also threatened those
Indians and the Wiandots [Wyandots] with war in the spring. The same
person farther said, that they had seen twenty French canoes, loaded
with stores, for a new fort[1] they designed on the south side Lake Erie."
Mr. Croghan also informed them, that several of our traders had been
taken, and advised them to keep their warriors at home, until they could
see what the French intended, which he doubted not would appear in
the spring. Then Andrew Montour informed this nation, as he had done   Acquaints the
the Wiandots [Wyandots] and the Delawares, "That the King of Great   Indians the
Britain had sent them a large present of goods in company with the Six   king had
Nations, which was under the care of the governor of Virginia, who had   present
sent me out to invite them to come and see him, and partake of their
father's present next summer." To which we received this answer, Big
Hanoahansa[2] their speaker, taking in his hand the several strings of
wampum, which had been given by the English, said, "These are the   Indians
speeches received by us from your great men. From the beginning of our   answer
friendship, all that our brothers the English have told us has been good
and true, for which we return our hearty thanks; then taking up four
other strings of wampum in his hand, he said; Brothers, I now speak the
sentiments of all our people. When first our forefathers the English met
our brothers, they found what our brothers the English told them to be
true, and so have we; we are but a small people, but it is not to us only
that you speak, but to all nations: we shall be glad to hear what our
brothers will say to us at the Logg's town [Logstown] in the spring; and
we hope that the friendship now subsisting between us and our brothers
will last as long as the sun shines or the moon gives light. We hope that
our children will hear and believe what our brothers say to them as we
have always done; and to assure you of our hearty good-will towards
you our brothers, we present you with these four strings of wampum."
After the council was over, they had much talk about sending a guard
with us to the Picqualinnee [Pickawillany] town (these are a tribe of
the Tawightwis [Twightwees])[3] which was reckoned near 200 miles; but
after a long consultation, their king being sick, they came to no deter-
mination about it.

[1]Probably Presqu' Isle.   [3]Miamis.
[2]Big Hominy, a Shawnee Chief. Hanna, *op. cit.*,
II, 139.

Appendix
page 185
Resolves to
go to the
Tawightwis

Thursday 31st, to Monday February 11th. Stayed in the *Shawane*[1] *town*. While I was here the Indians had a very extraordinary festival, at which I was present, and which I have exactly described at the end of my journal. As I had particular instructions from the president of Virginia to discover the strength and number of some Indian nations to the westward, who had lately revolted from the French, and had some messages to deliver them from him, I resolved to set out for the *Tawightwi town*.[2]

Tuesday 12th. Having left my boy to take care of my horses in the *Shawane town*, and supplied myself with a fresh horse to ride, I set out with my old company, viz. George Croghan, Andrew Montour, Robert Kallendar [Callendar], and a servant to carry our provision, &c. N.W. 10 m.

Wednesday 13th. The same course, N.W. about 35 m.

Thursday 14th. The same course about 30 m.

Friday 15th. The same course 15 m. we met with nine Shawane [Shawnee] Indians coming from one of the Picqualinnee [Pickawillany] towns, where they had been to council; they told us there were fifteen more of them behind at the Tawightwi [Twightwee] town, waiting for the arrival of the Wawiaghtas[3] (a tribe of the Tawightwis [Twightwees]) who were to bring with them a Shawane [Shawnee] woman and child to deliver to their men that were behind. This woman, they informed us, was taken prisoner last fall by some of the Wawiaghta warriors through a mistake, which was like to have engaged those nations in war.

G o
Little
Mineami
river.
G p
Big Mineami
river.
Tawightwi
town. Land
very rich,
with fine
meadows and
streams,
variety of
timber, and
abundance of
game. The
Ohio abounds
with fish.

Saturday 16th. Set out the same course, N.W. about 35 m. to the *little Mineami* [Miami] *river or creek*.[4]

Sunday 17th. Crossed the *little Mineami*[5] [Miami], and altered our course S.W. 25 m. to the *big Mineami* [Great Miami] *river*, opposite to the *Tawightwi* [Twightwee] town. All the land from the *Shawane* [Shawnee][6] *town* to this place (except the first twenty miles, which is broken) is fine rich level land, well timbered, with large walnut, ash, sugar-trees, cherry-trees, &c. well watered with a great number of little streams and rivulets; full of beautiful natural meadows, covered with wild rye, blue grass, and clover; and abounds with turkeys, deer, elks, and most sorts of game, particularly buffaloes, thirty or forty of which are frequently seen feeding in one meadow; in short, it wants nothing

[1]Lower Shawnee Town.
[2]Pickawillany.
[3]Wea, a subtribe of the Miami.

[4]Mad River not the Little Miami River. Gist (Darlington edition), *op. cit.*, p. 123.
[5]*Ibid.*
[6]Lower Shawnee Town.

but cultivation to make it a most delightful country. The Ohio and all the large branches are said to be full of fine fish of several kinds, particularly a sort of cat-fish[1] of a prodigious size; but as I was not there at a proper season, I had not an opportunity of seeing any of them. The traders had always reckoned it 200 miles from the *Shawane* [Shawnee] *town*[2] to the *Tawightwi* [Twightwee] *town;*[3] but by my computation, I could make it no more than 150. The *Mineami* [Miami] *river* being high, we were obliged to make a raft of logs to transport our goods and saddles, and swim our horses over: after firing a few guns and pistols, and smoak- ing in the warriors pipe, who came to invite us to the town, according to their custom of inviting and welcoming strangers, and great men, we entered the town with English colours before us, and were kindly re- ceived by their king, who invited us into his own house, and set our colours upon the top of it. The firing of the guns held about a quarter of an hour, and then all the white men and traders that were there came and welcomed us to the *Tawightwi* [Twightwee] *town. This town is situate on the N.W. side of the big Mineami* [Miami] *river, about 150 miles from the mouth thereof;* it consists of about four hundred families, and is daily increasing; it is accounted one of the strongest Indian towns upon this part of the continent. The Tawightwis [Twightwee] are a very numerous people, consisting of many different tribes, under the same form of government; each tribe has a particular chief, or king, one of which is chosen indifferently out of any tribe to rule the whole nation, and is vested with greater authorities than any of the others. They are accounted the most powerful nation to the westward of the English settlements, and much superior to the Six Nations with whom they are now in amity. Their strength and numbers are not thoroughly known, as they have but lately traded with the English, and indeed have very little trade among them; they deal in much the same commodities as the northern Indians: there are other nations or tribes still farther to the westward daily coming in to them; and it is thought their power and interest reaches to the westward of the Missisippi, if not across the continent; they are at present very well affected to the English, and seem fond of an alliance with them; they formerly lived on the farther side of the Wabash, and were in the French interest, who supplied them with some few trifles, at a most exorbitant price; they were called by the French Mineamis [Miamis], but they have now revolted from them, and

Smoak the pipe of peace.

Is kindly received by the Tawightwi king

Remarks on the Tawightwi town and nation

[1][Pownall's note]. The editor has seen them of 60 pounds weight.

[2]Lower Shawnee Town.

[3]Pickawillany, near present site of Piqua, Ohio.

left their former habitations, for the sake of trading with the English, and notwithstanding all the artifices the French have used, they have not been able to recall them. After we had been some time in the king's house, Mr. Montour told him that we wanted to speak with him, and the chiefs of this nation this evening, upon which we were invited into the long house, and having taken our places, Mr. Montour began as follows.

Montour tells the king he had come on business to him.
Montour speaks to the Tawightwis.

"Brothers the Tawightwis [Twightwees][1] as we have been hindered by the high waters, and some business with our other Indian brothers, no doubt our long stay has caused some trouble among our brothers here, therefore we now present you with two strings of wampum, to remove all the trouble of your hearts, and clear your eyes that you may see the sun shine clear, for we have a great deal to say to you; and would have you send for one of your friends that can speak the Mohickan [Mahican] or Mingo tongue[2] well, that we may understand each other thoroughly, as we have a great deal of business to do." The Mohickons [Machican][3] are a small tribe, who most of them speak English, and are also well acquainted with the language of the Tawightwis [Twightwee], and they with theirs. Mr. Montour then proceeded to deliver them a message from the Wiandots [Wyandots] and Delawares as follows.

Speech from the Wiandots and Delawares to the Tawightwis

"Brothers the Tawightwis [Twightwees], this comes by our brothers the English, who are coming with good news to you. We hope you will take care of them, and all our brothers, the English, who are trading among you. You made a road for our brothers the English to come and trade among you, but it is now very foul, great logs are fallen across it, and we would have you be strong, like men, and have one heart with us, and make the road clear, that our brothers the English may have free course and recourse between you and us. In the sincerity of our hearts we send you these four strings of wampum." To which they gave their usual Yo Ho. They then said they wanted some tobacco to smoak with us, and that to-morrow they would send for their interpreter.

Monday 18th. We walked about, and viewed the fort, which wanted some repairs, and the trader's men helped them to bring logs to line the inside.

Tuesday 19th. We gave their kings and great men some cloaths, paint, and shirts, and they were busy dressing and preparing themselves for the council. The weather grew warm, and the creeks began to lower very fast.

[1]Miamis.

[2]Refers to Algonquin language. Hodge, *op. cit.*, I, 786, 867.
[3]Mingoes.

Wednesday 20th. About twelve o'clock we were informed that some of the foreign tribes were coming, upon which proper persons were ordered to meet them, and conduct them to the town, and then we were invited into the long house: after we had been seated about a quarter of an hour, four Indians, two from each tribe, who had been sent before to bring the long pipe, and to inform us that the rest were coming, came in and informed us, that their friends had sent those pipes that we might smoak the calumet pipe of peace with them, and that they intended to do the same with us.

Thursday 21st. We were invited again into the long house (where Mr. Croghan made them) with the foreign tribes, a present to the value of one hundred pounds Pennsylvania money, and delivered all our speeches to them, at which they seemed well pleased, and said they would take time and consider well what we had said to them. Croghan delivers a present and messages.

Friday 22d. Nothing remarkable happened.

Saturday 23d. In the afternoon there was an alarm, which caused great confusion and running about among the Indians; upon enquiring the reason of this stir, they told us, it was occasioned by six Indians that came to war against them from the southward, three of them Cuttawas [Catawbas], and three Shawanes [Shawnee]; these were some of the Shawanes [Shawnee] who had formerly deserted from the other part of the nation, and now lived to the southward: towards night there was a report spread in town, that four Indians, and four hundred French, were on their march and just by the town, but soon after the messenger who brought the news said, there were only four French Indians coming to council, and that they bid him say so, only to see how the English would behave themselves, but as they had behaved themselves like men, he now told the truth.

Sunday, February 24th. This morning the four French Indians came into town and were kindly received by the town Indians. They marched in under French colours, and were conducted into the long house, and after they had been in about a quarter of an hour, the council sat, and we were sent for, that we might hear what the French had to say. The *Piankasha* [Piankeshaw] king,[1] who was at that time the principal man, and commander in chief of the *Tawightwis* [Twightwee], said he would have the English colours set up in this council, Four French Indians come in

[1]LaDemoiselle, or Old Briton, famous Miami chief who founded Pickawillany about 1748. This village was the center of English influence in this region, until 1752, when it was destroyed by Indians under French command. Chief Demoiselle was killed in battle and afterwards the enemy boiled his body and ate it. Gipson, *The British Regime, op. cit.,* IV, 177, 222-23.

as well as the French; to which we answered he might do as he thought fit; after we were seated opposite to the French ambassadors,

French present to the Indians
one of them said he had a present to make them, so a place was prepared, as they had before done for our present, between them and us, and then their speaker stood up and laid his hands upon two keggs of brandy that held about seven quarts each, and a roll of Tobacco of about ten pounds weight, then taking two strings of wampum in his hand, he said, "What he had to deliver them was from their father (meaning the French king) and he desired that they would hear what he was about to say." Then he laid the two strings of wampum upon the keggs, and taking up four other strings of black and white wampum, he said,

French speech
"That their father, remembering his children, had sent them two keggs of milk,[1] and some tobacco, and that he had now made a clear road for them, to come and see him and his officers, and pressed them very much to come and see him." Then he took another string of wampum in his hand, and said, "Their father would now forget all little differences that had been between them, and desired them not to be of two minds, but to let him know their minds freely, for he would send for them no

Piankasha king's reply to the French
more." To which the *Piankasha* [Piankeshaw] king replied, it was true their father had sent for them several times, and said the road was clear, but he understood it was made foul and bloddy, and by them. We, said he, have cleared a road for our brothers the English, and your fathers have made it bad, and have taken some of our brothers prisoners, which we look upon as done to us," and he turned short about, and went out of council. After the French ambassador had delivered his message, he went into one of the private houses, and endeavoured much to prevail on some Indians there, and was seen to cry and lament, which was, as he said, for the loss of that nation.

Wawiaghta speech
Monday 25th. This day we received a speech from the *Wawiaghtas*[2] and *Piankashas* [Piankeshaws], two tribes of the *Tawightwis* [Twightwees], one of the chiefs of the former spoke, "Brothers, we have heard what you have said to us by the interpreter, and we see you take pity upon our poor wives and children, and have taken us by the hand into the great chain of friendship, therefore we present you with these two bundles of skins, to make *shoes* for your people, and this pipe to smoak in, to assure you our hearts are good and true towards you our brothers, and we hope that we shall all continue in true love and friendship with one another, as people with one head and one heart ought to do. You

[1]Brandy.
[2]Weas, a subtribe of the Miamis.

have pitied us, as you always did the rest of our Indian brothers. We hope the pity you have always shewn, will remain as long as the sun gives light, and on our side you may depend upon sincere and true friendship towards you, as long as we have strength." This person stood up and spoke with the air and gesture of an orator.

Tuesday 26th. The *Tawightwis* [Twightwees] delivered the following answer to the four Indians sent by the French. The Captain of the warriors stood up, and taking some strings of black and white wampum in his hand, he spoke with a fierce tone, and very warlike air: "Brothers the *Owtawais* [Ottawas],[1] you are always differing with the French yourselves, and yet you listen to what they say, but we will let you know by these four strings of wampum that we will not hear any thing they say to us, or do any thing they bid us do." Then the same speaker, with six strouds, two matchcoats, and a string of black wampum (I understood the goods were in return for the milk[2] and tobacco) directed his speech to the French and said, "Fathers you desire that we will speak our minds from our hearts, which I am going to do. You have often desired we should go home to you, but I tell you it is not our home, for we have made a road as far as the sea, to the sun rising, and have been taken by the hand by our brothers, *the English, the Six Nations, the Delawares, Shawanes* [Shawnee], *and Wiandots* [Wyandots], and we assure you that is the road we will go; and as you threaten us with war in the spring,[3] we tell you if you are angry we are ready to receive you, and resolve to die here, before we will go to you, and that you may know this is our mind, we send you this string of black wampum." After a short pause the same speaker spoke again thus; "Brothers, the *Owtawais* [Ottawas] you hear what I say, tell that to your fathers the French, for that is our mind, and we speak it from our hearts."

Wednesday February 27th. This day they took down the French colours, and dismissed the four French Indians, so they took their leave of the town, and set off for the French fort.[4]

Thursday 28th. The cryer of the town, came by the king's order, and invited us to the long house, to see the *warriors feather-dance:*[5] it

Marginal notes:
Tawightwi's reply to the French speech

Refuse to go among the French, and say they have joined the English, &c.

Tell them they are ready for war.

Indian feather dance

---

[1] Friends and allies of the French. Hodge, *op. cit.*, II, 169.

[2] Brandy. See p. 188, this work.

[3] The Ottawa and Chippewa under the command of Langlade did attack and destroy Pickawillany in June, 1752. For a concise account of this attack read Gipson's *The British Empire, op. cit.*, IV, 222-23.

[4] French Fort Miami on the present site of Fort Wayne, Indiana. Gist (Darlington edition), *op. cit.*, p. 126.

[5] "Tcitahaia, popularly known as the 'feather dance' because the dancers have canes in their hands with feathers fastened at the ends. This is distinctly a peace dance." U. S. Bureau of Ethnology, *Annual Report of the Bureau of Ethnology to the Secretary of Smithsonian Institution*, 1924-25 (Washington, Government Printing Office, 1928), XLII, 609.

was performed by three dancing masters who were painted all over of various colours, with long sticks in their hands, upon the ends of which, are fastened long feathers of swans, and other birds, neatly woven in the shape of a fowl's wing; in this disguise they performed many antick tricks, waving their sticks and feathers about with great skill, to imitate the flying and fluttering of birds, keeping exact time with their musick; while they are dancing, some of the warriors strike a post, upon which the musick and dancers cease, and the warrior gives an account of his atchievements in war, and when he has done, throws down some goods as a recompence to the performers and musicians, after which they proceed in their dance as before, till another warrior strikes the post, and so on as long as they think fit.

Tawightwi's speech to the governor of Pennsylvania

Friday, March 1st. We received the following speech from the *Tawightwis* [Twightwees]. The speaker stood up, and addressing himself as to the governor of Pennsylvania, with two strings of wampum in his hand, he said, "Brothers, our hearts are glad that you have taken notice of us; and surely, brothers, we hope, that you will order a smith to settle here to mend our guns and hatchets: your kindness makes us so bold as to ask this request. You told us our friendship should last as long, and be as the greatest mountain. We have considered well, and all our great kings and warriors are come to a resolution, never to give heed to what the French say to us, but always to hear and believe what you, our brothers, say to us. Brothers, we are obliged to you for your kind invitation to receive a present at the Logg's town [Logstown], but as our foreign tribes are not yet come, we must wait for them, but you may depend we will come as soon as our women have planted corn, to hear what our brothers will say to us. Brothers, we present you with this bundle of skins, as we are but poor, to be for shoes for you on the road, and we return you our hearty thanks for the cloaths which you have put upon our wives and children."

We then took our leaves of the kings and chiefs, and they ordered that a small party of Indians should go with us as far as *Hockhocking;* but as I had left my boy and horses at the *Lower Shawane town*, I was obliged to go by myself, or to go sixty or seventy miles out of my way, which I did not care to do; so we all came over the *Mineami* [Miami] *River* together this evening, but Mr. Croghan and Mr. Montour, went over again and lodged in the town, I stayed on this side at one Robert Smith's, a trader, where we had left our horses. Before the French Indians had come into town, we had drawn articles of peace and alliance between the

English and *Wawiaghtas*[1] and *Piankashas* [Piankashaws], the indentures were signed, sealed, and delivered on both sides, and as I drew them I took a copy. The land upon the great *Mineami* [Miami] *River* is very rich, level, and well timbered, some of the finest meadows that can be: the Indians and traders assure me that it holds as good, and, if possible better, to the westward as far as the *Wabash*, which is accounted 100 miles, and quite up to the head of the *Mineami* [Miami] *River*, which is sixty miles above the *Tawightwi* [Twightwee] *town*, and down the said river quite to the *Ohio*, which is reckoned 150 miles. The grass here grows to a great height in the clear fields, of which there are a great number, and the bottoms are full of white clover, wild rye, and blue grass.

Articles of peace between the English and Wawiaghtas and Piankashas.
Land on the great Mineami river very fine, and the same for several miles on the Wabash, &c. Many clear fields with fine grass. White clover, wild rye, and blue grass.

Saturday 2d. George Croghan, and the rest of our company, came over the river; we got our horses, and travelled about 35 m. to *Mad Creek*, this is a place where some English traders had been taken prisoners[2] by the French.

Sunday 3d. We parted, they for *Hockhocking*, and I for the *Shawane* [Shawnee] *town*;[3] and as I was quite alone, and knew that the French Indians had threatened us, and would probably pursue, or lie in wait for us, I left the path, and went to the southwestward, down the little *Mineami* [Miami] *river* or *creek*, where I had fine travelling, through rich land and beautiful meadows, in which I could sometimes see forty or fifty buffaloes feeding at once. The little *Mineami* [Miami] *river* or *creek* continued to run through the middle of a fine meadow, about a mile wide, very clear, like an old field, and not a bush in it. I could see the buffaloes in it about two miles off. I travelled this day about thirty miles.

Land on little Mineami river very fine. Large herds of buffaloes.

Monday 4th. This day I heard several guns, but was afraid to examine who fired them, lest they might be some of the French Indians; so I travelled through the woods about 30 m. just at night I killed a fine barren cow buffaloe, and took out her tongue, and a little of the best of her meat. The land still level, rich, and well timbered with oak, walnut, ash, locust, and sugar-trees.

Land very fine and well timbered.

Tuesday 5th. I travelled about 30 miles.

Wednesday 6th. I travelled about thirty miles and killed a fat bear.

Thursday 7th. Set out with my horse load of bear, and travelled about 30 m. This afternoon I met a young man, a trader, and we en-

---

[1]Weas, a subtribe of the Miamis.

[2]In 1750 Morris Turner and Ralph Kilgore were taken prisoners at this place which is about seven miles west of Springfield, Clarke County, Ohio. Gist (Darlington edition), *op. cit.*, pp. 126-27.

[3]Lower Shawnee Town, on the present site of Portsmouth, Ohio.

camped together that night; he happened to have some bread with him, and I had plenty of meat, so we fared very well.

Shawane town

Friday 8th. Travelled about 30 m. and arrived at night at the *Shawane* [Shawnee] *town*. All the Indians, as well as the white men, came out to welcome my return to their town, being very glad that all things were rightly settled in the *Mineami* [Miami] country; they fired upwards of 150 guns in the town, and made an entertainment on account of the peace with the western Indians. On my return from the *Tawightwi* [Twightwee], to the *Shawane* [Shawnee] *town*, I did not keep an exact account of course or distance, for as the land thereabout was much the same, and the situation of the country was sufficiently described in my journey to the *Tawightwi* [Twightwee] *town*, I thought it unnecessary, but have, notwithstanding, laid down my track pretty nearly in my plot.

Saturday 9th. In the *Shawane* [Shawnee] *town* I met with one of the Mingoe [Mingo] chiefs, who had been down at the falls of Ohio, so that we did not see him as we went up. I informed him of the king's present, and the invitation down to Virginia; he told me that there was a party of French Indians hunting at the falls, and if I went they would kill or carry me away prisoner to the French, for it was certain they would not let me pass; however as I had a great inclination to see the Falls, and the lands on the east side the Ohio, I resolved to venture as far as possible.

Sunday 10th. Stayed in the town and prepared for my departure.

Ohio at the Shawane town ¾ mile wide, very deep, and a gentle current.

Tuesday 12th. I got my horses over the river,[1] and after breakfast, my boy and I got ferried over. The Ohio is near three quarters of a mile wide at the Shawane [Shawnee] town, and is very deep and smooth.

Wednesday 13th. We set out S. 45d. W. down the river, on the S.E. side 8 m. then S. 10 m. here I met two men belonging to Robert Smith at whose house I lodged on this side the *Mineami* [Miami] *river*, and one Hugh Crawford;[2] the said Robert Smith had given me an order upon these men, for two of the teeth of a large beast,[3] which they were bringing from towards the Falls of Ohio, one of which I brought in and delivered to the Ohio company. Robert Smith informed me that about seven years ago, these teeth, and the bones of three large beasts, one of which was somewhat smaller than the other two, *were found in a salt lick*[4] *or spring, upon a small creek, which runs into the south side of the*

Three very large car- casses of beasts found on the Ohio

[1]Meaning Ohio River.

[2]Distinguished Indian trader and soldier. Gist (Darlington edition), *op. cit.*, pp. 128-29.

[3]The early explorers found bones, tusks, and teeth, remains of the mammoth that inhabited this region, in the valley of Big Bone Creek in Boone County, Kentucky. Collins, *op. cit.*, II, 51-52; Gist (Darlington edition), *op. cit.*, pp. 129-30.

[4]Big Bone Lick, Boone County, Kentucky.

Ohio, about fifteen miles below the mouth of the great Mineami river, and twenty above the Falls of Ohio; he assured me that the rib bones of the largest of those beasts, were eleven feet long, and the scull bone six feet across the forehead, and the other bones in proportion, and that there were several teeth there, some of which he called horns, and said they were upwards of five feet long, and as much as a man could well carry; that he had hid one in a branch at some distance from the place, lest the French Indians should carry it away. The tooth which I brought in, for the Ohio company, was a jaw tooth, of better than four pounds weight, it appeared to be the farthest tooth in the jaw, and looked like fine ivory, when the outside was scraped off. I also met with four *Shawane* [Shawnee] Indians coming up the river in their canoes, who informed me that there were about sixty French Indians encamped at the Falls.

Thursday 14th. I went down the river S. 15 m. the land upon this side the Ohio chiefly broken, and the bottoms but narrow.

Friday 15th. S. 5 m. S.W. 10 m. to a creek[1] that was so high that we could not get over that night.

Saturday 16th. S. 45d. W. about 35 m.

Sunday 17th. The same course 15 m. then N. 45 d. W. 5 m.

Monday 18th. N. 45 d. W. 5 m. then S.W. 20 m. to the *lower salt lick creek,*[2] which Robert Smith and the Indians told me was about 15 miles above the *Falls of Ohio;* the land still hilly, the salt lick here much the same with those before described. This day we heard several guns, which made me imagine the French Indians were not moved, but were still hunting and firing thereabouts; we also saw some traps newly set, and the footsteps of some Indians, plain on the ground, as if they had been there the day before. I was now much troubled that I could not comply with my instructions, and was once resolved to leave the boy and horses, and go privately on foot to view the Falls; but the boy being a poor hunter, was afraid he would starve if I was long from him, and there was also great danger lest the French Indians should come upon our horses tracks, or hear their bells, and as I had seen good land enough, I thought perhaps I might be blamed for venturing so far, in such dangerous times, so I concluded not to got to the Falls, but travelled away to the southward, till we were over the *little Cuttawa river.*[3] *The Falls of Ohio,* by the best information I could get, are not very

Rib bones 11 feet Scull bone 6 feet across

Teeth 5 feet long

Tooth Gist brought above 4 pounds in weight

Land broken, bottoms narrow
10

Lower salt lick 15 miles from the falls of the Ohio
J P

Afraid to go to the falls.

Little Cuttawa river
Falls of Ohio described

[1]"Probably the Licking River at the Lower Blue Licks," Gist (Darlington edition), *op. cit.,* p. 130. The Licking River flows into the Ohio at Newport, Kentucky.

[2]Salt River, Kentucky.

[3]Kentucky River. Gist crossed the Kentucky River near the present site of Frankfort, Kentucky. Gist (Darlington edition), *op. cit.,* pp. 130-31.

steep; on the S.E. side there is a bar of sand at some distance from the shore, the water between the bar and the shore, is not above three feet deep, and the stream moderately strong: the Indians frequently pass safely in their canoes, through this passage, but are obliged to take great care as they go down, lest the current, which is much the strongest on the N.W. side, should draw them that way, which would be very dangerous, as the water on that side runs with great rapidity, over several ledges of rocks. The waters below the Falls, as they say, is about six fathoms deep, and the river continues without any obstruction, till it empties itself into the Missisippi, which is accounted upwards of 400 miles. The Ohio, near the mouth, is said to be very wide, and the land upon both sides very rich, and in general very level all the way from the Falls. After I had determined not to go to the Falls, we turned from salt lick creek, to a ridge of mountains that made towards the [Little] *Cuttawa river*,[1] and from the top of the mountain, we saw a fine level country S.W. as far as our eyes could behold; and it was a very clear day. We then went down the mountain, and set out S. 20 d. W. about 5 m. through rich level land, covered with small walnut, sugar-trees, red-buds, &c.

Tuesday 19th. We set out south, and crossed several creeks, all running to the S.W. at about twelve miles came to the *little Cuttawa river*, we were obliged to go up it about a mile to an island which was the shoalest place we could find to cross[2] at: we then continued our course in all about thirty miles, through rich level land, except about two miles, which was broken and indifferent: this level is about thirty five miles broad, and as we came up the side of it along the branches of the *little Cuttawa*,[3] we found it about 150 miles long, and how far towards the S.W. we could not tell, but imagined it held as far as the *great Cuttawa river*,[4] which would be upwards of 100 miles more, and appeared much broader that way, than here, as I could discern from the tops of the mountains.

Wednesday 20th. We did not travel. I went up to the top of a mountain to view the country: To the S.E. it looked very broken, and mountainous, but to the eastward and S.W. it appeared very level.

Thursday 21st. Set out S. 45 d. E. 15 m. S. 5 m. here I found a place[5] where the stones shined like high coloured brass; the heat of the

---

400 miles from the falls to the Mississippi Ohio wide Lands very rich.

Lands on the Cuttawa river rich, and level, for a great distance. Great Cuttawa river.

Finds a kind of borax.

[1]Kentucky River.

[2]Gist crossed the Kentucky River in the vicinity of present Frankfort, Kentucky. Gist (Darlington edition), *op. cit.*, p. 130.

[3]Kentucky River.

[4]Tennessee River.

[5]On the Kentucky River near the mouth of the Red River. Gist (Darlington edition), *op. cit.*, p. 133.

sun drew out of them a kind of borax, or salt petre, only something sweeter, some of which I brought in to the Ohio Company, though I believe it was nothing but a sort of sulphur.

Friday 22d. S.E. 12 m. I killed a fat bear, and was taken sick that night.

Saturday 23d. I stayed here, and sweated after the Indian manner, which helped me.

Sunday 24th. Set out E. 2 m. N.E. 3 m. N. 1 m. E. 2 m. S.E. 5 m. E. 2 m. N. 2 m. S.E. 7 m. to a small creek,[1] where we encamped, in a place where we had but poor food for our horses, and both we and they were very much wearied. The reason of our making so many short courses was, we were driven by a branch of the *little Cuttawa river,*[2] whose banks were so exceeding steep, that it was impossible to ford it, into a ledge of rocky laurel mountains, which was almost impassable.

Monday 25th. Set out S.E. 12 m. N. 2 m. E. 1 m. S. 4 m. S.E. 2 m. we killed a buck elk here, and took out his tongue to carry with us.

Tuesday 26th. Set out S.E. 10 m. S.W. 1 m. S.E. 1 m. S.W. 1 m. S.E. 1 m. S.W. 1 m. S.E. 5 m. killed two buffaloes, and took out their tongues, and encamped. These two days we travelled through rocks and mountains, full of laurel thickets, which we could hardly creep through, without cutting our way.

Laurel thickets J o

Wednesday 27th. Our horses and selves were so tired, that we were obliged to stay this day to rest, for we were unable to travel: *On all the branches of the little Cuttawa river was great plenty of fine coal,* some of which I brought in to the Ohio company.

Plenty of fine coal on the Cuttawa J o

Thursday 28th. Set out S.E. 15 m. crossing several creeks of the *little Cuttawa river; the land still full of coal, and black slate.*

Coal and slate

Friday 29th. The same course S.E. about 12 m. the land still mountainous.

Saturday 30th. Stayed to rest our horses. I went on foot, and found a passage through the mountains, to another creek, or a fork of the same creek, that we were upon.

Sunday 31st. The same course S.E. 15 m. killed a buffaloe, and encamped.

Monday, April 1st. Set out the same course about 20 m. part of the way we went along a path up the side of a little creek, at the head of which, was a gap in the mountains,[3] then our path went down another

[1]North fork of the Kentucky River. Gist (Darlington edition), *op. cit.,* p. 133.
[2]Kentucky River.

[3]Pound or Stony Gap near Whitesburg, Letcher County, Kentucky. Gist (Darlington edition), *op. cit.,* p. 134.

creek[1] to a lick, *where blocks of coal about eight or ten inches square lay upon the surface of the ground;* here we killed a bear, and encamped.

Tuesday 2d. Set out S. 2 m. S.E. 1 m. N.E. 3 m. killed a buffaloe.

Wednesday 3d. S. 1 m. S.W. 3 m. E. 3 m. S.E. 2 m. to a small creek,[2] on which was a large warrior's camp that would contain seventy or eighty warriors; their captain's name or title was the crane,[3] as I knew by his picture or arms painted on a tree.

Thursday 4th. I stayed here all day to rest our horses: I plotted down our courses, and found I had still near 200 miles home upon a straight line.

Friday 5th. Rained, and we staid at the warrior's camp.

Saturday 6th. We went along the warrior's road S. 1 m. S.E. 3 m. S. 2 m. S.E. 3 m. E. 3 m. killed a bear.

Sunday 7th. Set out E. 2 m. N.E. 1 m. S.E. 1 m. S. 1 m. W. 1 m. S.W. 1 m. S. 1 m. S.E. 2 m. S. 1 m.

Monday 8th. S. 1 m. S.E. 1 m. E. 3 m. S.E. 1 m. E. 3 m. N.E. 2 m. N. 1 m. E. 1 m. N. 1 m. E. 2 m. and encamped on a small laurel creek.

Tuesday 9th, and Wednesday 10th. The weather being bad, we did not travel these two days, the country being still rocky, mountainous, and full of laurel thickets; the worst travelling[4] I ever saw.

Thursday 11th. We travelled several courses near 20 miles, but in the afternoon, as I could see from the top of a mountain the place we came from, I found we had not come upon a straight line more than N. 65 d. E. 10 m.

Friday 12th. Set out through very difficult ways E. 5 m. to a small creek.

Saturday 13th. The same course E. upon a straight line; though the way we were obliged to travel was near twenty miles: here we killed two bears, the way still rocky and mountainous.

Sunday 14th. As food was very scarce in these barren mountains, we were obliged to move for fresh feeding for our horses; in climbing up the clifts and rocks this day, two of our horses fell down, and were much hurt, and a paroquet, which I had got from the Indians on the other side of the Ohio, where there are a great number, died of a bruise he got by the fall; though it was but a trifle, I was much concerned at losing him,

Marginal notes: Blocks of coal eight inches square, on the surface of the earth. / Country mountainous, with laurel thickets / Paroquets on the Ohio

[1]Pound Creek fork of the Big Sandy River. *Ibid.*
[2]Indian Creek, the middle fork of Big Sandy River. Gist (Darlington edition), *op. cit.*, p. 134.
[3]This must have been a camp of the Miami tribe, for the crane is the totem of the Miamis. Hodge, *op. cit.*, I, 852.
[4]Gist was traveling through the country that has been called the Switzerland of Virginia. This territory in and around Tazewell County, Virginia has the appearance of a "tossed bed of mountains." Edward A. Pollard, *The Virginia Tourist* . . . (Philadelphia, J. B. Lippincott & Co., 1870), pp. 155-56.

as he was perfectly tame, and had been very brisk all the way, and I had still corn enough left to feed him. In the afternoon I left the horses, and went all the way down the creek, and found such a precipice, and such laurel thickets that we could not pass, and the horses were not able to go up the mountain, till they had rested a day or two.

Monday 15th. We cut a passage through the laurels better than two miles; as I was climbing up the rocks, I got a fall which hurt me much. This afternoon we wanted provision. I killed a bear.

Cut a passage thro' a laurel thicket two miles.

Tuesday 16th. Thunder and rain, in the morning we set out N. 25 d. E. 3 m.

Wednesday 17th. This day I went to the top of a mountain to view the way, and found it so bad that I did not care to engage in it, but rather chose to go out of the way, and keep down along the side of a creek, till I could find a branch or run, on the other side to go up.

Thursday 18th. Set out down the creek's side, N. 3 m. then the creek, turning N.W. I was obliged to leave it, and go up a ridge N.E. 1 m. E. 2 m. S.E. 2 m. N.E. 1 m. to the fork of a river.

Friday 19th. Set out down the run N.E. 2 m. E. 2 m. S.E. 2 m. N. 20 d. E. 2 m. E. 2 m. up a large run.

Saturday 20th. Set out S.E. 10 m. E. 4 m. over a small creek. We had such bad travelling down this creek, that we had like to have lost one of our horses.

Sunday 21st. Stayed to rest our horses.

Monday 22d. Rained all day, we could not travel.

Tuesday 23d. Set out E. 8 m. along a ridge of mountains,[1] then S.E. 5 m. E. 3 m. S.E. 4 m. and encamped among very steep mountains.

Wednesday 24th. S.E. 4 m. through steep mountains and thickets, E. 6 m.

Thursday 25th. E. 5 m. S.E. 1 m. N.E. 2 m. S.E. 2 m. E. 1 m. then S. 2 m. E. 1 m. killed a bear.

Friday 26th. Set out S.E. 2 m. here it rained so hard we were obliged to stop.

Saturday 27th, to Monday 29th. These three days it continued rainy and bad weather, so that we could not travel. All the way from Salt Lick creek to this place,[2] the branches of the little Cuttawa were so high that we could not pass them, which obliged us to go over the heads

[1]Along the New Garden ridge dividing Buchanan and Russell Counties, Virginia. Gist (Darlington edition), *op. cit.*, p. 134.

[2]In Baptist Valley, Tazewell Co. Gist traveled the valley of the Clinch River, on the south side of the ridge dividing the heads of the Big Sandy from the Clinch River. Gist thought the Clinch River was the Kentucky. *Ibid.*

of them, through a continued ledge of almost inaccessible mountains, rocks, and laurel thickets.

Blue Stone river J l

Tuesday 30th. Fair weather, set out E. 3 m. S.E. 8 m. E. 2 m. to a *little river or creek which falls into the Big Kanhawa* [Kanawha], *called Blue Stone*, where we encamped and had good feeding for our horses.

Remarkable rock J l

Wednesday, May 1st. Set out N. 75 d. E. 10 m. and killed a buffaloe; then went up a very high mountain,[1] upon the top of which was a rock sixty or seventy feet high, and a cavity in the middle, into which I went, and found there was a passage through it, which gradually ascended to the top, with several holes in the rock, which let in the light; when I got to the top of this rock, I could see a prodigious distance, and could plainly discover where the Big Kanhawa [Kanawha] river broke through the next high mountain.[2] I then came down and continued my course N. 75 d. E. 6 m. farther, and encamped.

Thursday 2d, and Friday 3d. These two days it rained, and we staid at our camp, to take care of some provision we had killed.

Saturday 4th. This day our horses ran away, and it was late before we got them, so we could not travel far; we went N. 75 d. E. 4 m.

Sunday 5th. Rained all day.

Monday 6th. Set out through very bad ways E. 3 m. N.E. 6 m. over a bad laurel creek E. 4 m.

Big Kanhawa, or New River. J k

Kanhawa 200 yards wide, deep, with many falls. Bottoms rich but narrow: high land broken.

Tuesday 7th. Set out E. 10 m. to the *Big Kanhawa* [Kanawha] *or new river*, and got over half of it to a *large island*, where we lodged all night.

Wednesday 8th. We made a raft of logs, and crossed the other half of the river, and went up it S. 2 m. *The Kanhawa* [Kanawha] *or new river* (*by some called Wood's river*) where I crossed it, which was about eight miles above the mouth of the *Blue Stone river*, is better than 200 yards wide, and pretty deep, but full of rocks and falls. The bottoms upon it, and *Blue Stone river* are very rich, but narrow; the high land broken.

Thursday 9. Set out E. 13 m. to a large Indian warrior's camp, where we killed a bear, and staid all night.

Friday 10th. Set out E. 4 m. S.E. 3 m. S. 3 m. through mountains covered with ivy, and laurel thickets.

Saturday 11th. Set out S. 2 m. S.E. 5 m. to a creek, and a meadow where we let our horses feed, then S.E. 2 m. S. 1 m. S.E. 2 m. to a very

---

[1] A high peak in Mercer County, Virginia. Gist (Darlington edition), *op. cit.*, p. 135.

[2] The Big Kanawha River breaks through the mountains below the mouth of Greenbrier River, in Raleigh County, West Virginia.

high mountain, upon the top of which was a lake or pond[1] about three quarters of a mile long N.E. and S.W. and a quarter of a mile wide, the water fresh and clear, and a clean gravelly shore about ten yards wide with a fine meadow, and six fine springs in it; then S. about 4 m. to a branch of the Kanhawa called *Sinking Creek*.[2]

J k
A lake on the top of a mountain

Sunday 12th. Stayed to rest our horses, and dry some meat we had killed.

Monday 13th. Set out S.E. 2 m. E. 1 m. S.E. 3 m. S. 12 m. to one Richard Hall's,[3] in Augusta county; this man is one of the farthest settlers to the westward up the new river.

R. Hall the farthest settler to the west of new river.

Tuesday 14th. Stayed at Richard Hall's, and wrote to the president of Virginia,[4] and the Ohio company, to let them know I should be with them by the 15th day of June.

Wednesday 15th. Set out from Richard Hall's S. 16 m.

Thursday 16th. The same course S. 22 m. and encamped at *Beaver Island Creek*,[5] *a branch of the Kanhawa* [Kanawha], opposite to the head of *Roanoak* [Roanoke].

K k
Beaver Island creek

Friday 17th. Set out S.W. 3 m. then S. 9 m. to the dividing line between Carolina and Virginia, where I stayed all night. The land from Richard Hall's to this place is broken.

Line between North Carolina and Virginia.

Saturday 18th. Set out S. 20 m. to my own house on the *Yadkin river*; when I came there, I found all my family gone, for the Indians had killed five people in the winter near that place, which frightened my wife and family away to *Roanoak* [Roanoke], about 35 miles nearer in among the inhabitants, which I was informed of by an old man I met near the place.

Gist arrives at his own house, on the Yadkin river.

Sunday 19th. Set out for *Roanoak* [Roanoke], and as we had now a path, we got there the same night, where I found all my family well.

CHRISTOPHER GIST.

[1]Salt Pond, a lake of pure fresh water located on top of Salt Pond Mountain, about 16 miles from Christianburg, Montgomery County, Virginia. Pollard, *op. cit.*, p. 146. At present this lake is called Mountain Lake.

[2]In Giles County, Virginia.

[3]Near Christianburg, Montgomery County, Virginia. Gist (Darlington edition), *op. cit.*, p. 136.

[4]Thomas Lee (1690-1751), member and later president of the Virginia Council, Virginia's commissioner to the Indian treaty at Lancaster in 1744, and member of the Ohio Company of Virginia.

[5]Now called Reed Island Creek in Carroll County, Virginia.

Shawane
festival.
Indian
marriages
dissolved.

An account of the Festival at the Shawane [Lower Shawnee] Town mentioned in my Journal, page 184. In the evening a proper officer made a public proclamation, that all the Indian marriages were dissolved, and a public feast was to be held for the three succeeding days after, in which the women (as their custom was) were again to choose their husbands.

The next morning early the Indians breakfasted, and after spent the day in dancing, till the evening, when a plentiful feast was prepared; after feasting, they spent the night in dancing.

The same way they passed the two next days till the evening, the men dancing by themselves, and then the women in turns round fires, and dancing in their manner in the form of the figure 8, about 60 or 70 of them at a time. The women, the whole time they danced, sung a song in their language, the chorus of which was,

I am not afraid of my husband;
I will choose what man I please.

Singing those lines alternately.

Indian
women
choose
husbands.

The third day, in the evening, the men, being about 100 in number, danced in a long string, following one another, sometimes at length, at other times in a figure of 8 quite round the fort, and in and out of the long house, where they held their councils, the women standing together as the men danced by them; and as any of the women liked a man passing by, she stepped in, and joined in the dance, taking hold of the man's stroud, whom she chose, and then continued in the dance, till the rest of the women stepped in, and made their choice in the same manner; after which the dance ended, and they all retired to consummate.

N.B. This was given to me by colonel [George] Mercer,[1] agent to the Ohio Company, and now lieutenant-governor of North Carolina.

[1]See *note* 5, p. 26.

FINIS

BIBLIOGRAPHY

GENERAL REFERENCE WORKS
(Not cited in footnotes)

Dictionary of American Biography . . . . New York, C. Scribner's Sons, 1928-44. 21 vols.

Dictionary of National Biography . . . . London, Smith Elder & Co., 1885-1901. 66 vols.

The Encyclopaedia Americana . . . . New York, The Encyclopaedia Americana Corporation, 1924. 30 vols.

The Encyclopaedia Britannica. New York, 14th ed., Encyclopaedia Britannica, Inc., [c1929]. 24 vols.

Lippincott's Pronouncing Gazetteer. A Complete Pronouncing Gazetteer or Geographical Dictionary of the World. Philadelphia, J. B. Lippincott & Co., 1856. 2 vols.

Lossing, Benson J. . . . *Harper's Encyclopaedia of United States History* . . . . New York, Harper & Brothers, [c1905]. 10 vols.

Rand McNally Commercial Atlas and Marketing Guide. Chicago, 56th ed., Rand McNally & Co., 1925.

U.S. Geological Survey. *Topographic Maps of the United States.*

BIBLIOGRAPHIES

MANUSCRIPT

Great Britain. Board of Trade and Plantations. "List of Maps, Plans, &c belonging to the Right Hon[ble] the Lords Commissioners for Trade and Plantations Under the Care of Francis Aegidius Assiotti, Draughtsman, 1780." Public Records Office. CO 326/15.

PRINTED

Andrews, Charles, comp. *Guide to the Manuscript Materials for the History of the United States to 1783, in the British Museum, in Minor London Archives, and in the Libraries of Oxford and Cambridge.* By Charles M. Andrews and Frances G. Davenport. Washington, The Carnegie Institution of Washington, 1908. (Carnegie Institution of Washington. *Publication* No. 90.)

Sabin, Joseph [and others]. *A Dictionary of Books Relating to America, From its Discovery to the Present Time.* New York, J. Sabin [etc.], 1868-1936. 29 vols.

U.S. Library of Congress. Division of Maps. *A List of Geographical Atlases in the Library of Congress, with Bibliographical Notes.* Compiled Under the Direction of Philip Lee Phillips. Washington, Government Printing Office, 1909-20. 4 vols.

—— *List of Maps of America in the Library of Congress, preceded by a List of Works Relating to Cartography.* By P. Lee Phillips. Washington, Government Printing Office, 1901.

Wylie, Alexander. *Notes on Chinese Literature.* Shanghai, Presbyterian Mission Press, 1922.

SOURCE MATERIAL

MANUSCRIPTS

"The Account of Captain Anthony Van Schaick, of the Ground between the Enterance of Lake Champlain at Crown Point & the Mouth of Otter Creek." Photostat from Henry E. Huntington Library and Art Gallery, San Marino, Calif. LO 432.

"Capt. Hobbs' and Lieut. Kennedy's Account of the River Kennebeck & the Carrying Place to the River Chaudiere. Septemb[r] 17th 1756." Photostat from Henry E. Huntington Library and Art Gallery, San Marino, Calif. LO 1824.

"Capt. Hobbs' Account of the Way from No. 4, in New Hampshire, to the Mouth of Otter Creek. Sept. 18, 1756." Photostat from Henry E. Huntington Library and Art Gallery, San Marino, Calif. LO 1839.

"Clergy of the American Province of the Unitas Fratrum," I, 67. Manuscript in the Moravian Archives. These Archives are housed in the Moravian Archives Building, Bethlehem, Pa.

"Commission to Anthony Van Schaick from Lord Loudoun to organize a Company of Rangers." Photostat from Henry E. Huntington Library and Art Gallery, San Marino, Calif. LO 1400.

"Massachusetts Archives," CXVI, 17. The Massachusetts Archives are housed in the Secretary of State's Office, State House, Boston, Mass.

"Report of the General Survey in the Southern District of North America." British Museum. King's Manuscripts. Nos. 210-211. This report is in transcript and photostat form in the Library of Congress.

"To his Excellency the R^t Honble The Earl of Loudoun, Commander in Chief &c, &c, &c." Letter from Anthony Van Schaick to Lord Loudoun. Photostat from Henry E. Huntington Library and Art Gallery, San Marino, Calif. LO 1663.

PRINTED DOCUMENTS

American Archives: Fourth Series, Containing a Documentary History of the English Colonies in North America, from the King's Message to Parliament, of March 7, 1774, to the Declaration of Independence by the United States. Washington, Published by M. St. Clair Clarke and Peter Force, 1837-1846. 6 vols.

Connecticut (Colony). *The Public Records of the Colony of Connecticut [1636-1776]*. . . . Transcribed and published, in accordance with a resolution of the General Assembly. Hartford, Press of the Case Lockwood & Brainard Company [etc.], 1850-90. 15 vols.

Documents Relating to the Colonial History of New Jersey. . . . v. p., v. pub., 1880-1929. 33 vols. (*Archives of the State of New Jersey, First series*, Vols. I-XXXIII.)

Documents Relative to the Colonial History of the State of New York. . . . Albany, Weed, Parsons and Company, printers, 1853-87. 15 vols.

Great Britain (1760-1820). George III. House of Commons. *Debates of the House of Commons in the Year 1774, of the Bill for Making More Effective Provision for the Government of the Province of Quebec.* Drawn from the Notes of Sir Henry Cavendish. With a Map of Canada, Copied from the Second Edition of Mitchell's Map of North America Referred to in the Debates. London, Ridgay, 1839.

Massachusetts (Colony) Statutes. *Acts and Laws, Passed by the Great and General Court or Assembly of Their Majesties Province of Massachusetts Bay in New England. Begun at Boston the Eighth Day of June, 1692. And Continued by Adjournment, Unto Wednesday the Twelfth Day of October Following*. . . . Boston, Benjamin Harris, 1692.

Pennsylvania (Colony). General Assembly. House of Representatives. *Votes and Proceedings of the House of Representatives of the Province of Pennsylvania . . . from 15th Day of October, 1774 to September 30, 1758.* Philadelphia, Henry Miller, 1774. Vol. IV. There are six volumes in this set, each published separately.

Pennsylvania (Colony). Provincial Council. *Minutes of the Provincial Council from its organization to the Termination of the Proprietary*

Government. Philadelphia [etc.], Jo[seph] Severns & Co. [etc.], 1852-54. 16 vols.

Pennsylvania Archives. First series. Philadelphia, Joseph Severns & Co., 1852-1856. 12 vols.

U.S. Treaties, etc. *Treaties and Other International Acts of the United States of America.* Hunter Miller, ed. . . . Washington, Government Printing Office, 1931-42. Vols. II-VII. 6 vols. Vol. I not published.

Virginia. *Calendar of Virginia State Papers and Other Manuscripts. . . . Preserved in the Capitol at Richmond.* Arranged and edited by William P. Palmer. Richmond, R. F. Walker [etc.], 1875-93. 11 vols.

Virginia. Laws, Statutes, etc. *The Statutes at Large; Being a Collection of All the Laws of Virginia from the First Session of the Legislature, in the Year 1619.* By William Waller Hening. v. p., v. pub., 1809-1823. 13 vols.

OTHER PRINTED SOURCES

Alvord, Clarence, ed. *The Critical Period, 1763-1765.* Edited with Introduction and Notes by Clarence Walworth Alvord and Clarence Edwin Carter. Springfield, Ill., The Trustees of the Illinois State Historical Library, 1915. (*Collections* of the Illinois State Historical Library. Vol. X, "British" series, Vol. I.)

———— *The New Regime, 1765-1767.* Edited with Introduction and Notes by Clarence Walworth Alvord and Clarence Edwin Carter. Springfield, Ill., Illinois State Historical Library, 1916. (*Collections* of the Illinois State Historical Library. Vol. XI, "British" series, Vol. II.)

American Philosophical Society, Philadelphia. *Transactions of. . . .* Philadelphia, William and Thomas Bradford, 1769-1809. First series. 6 vols.

Babbitt, E. L. *The Allegheny Pilot.* Freeport, Pa., E. L. Babbitt, 1855.

Bartram, John. *Observations on the Inhabitants, Climate, Soil, Rivers, Productions, Animals, and Other Matters Worthy of Notice . . . . To Which is Annex'd a Curious Account of the Cataracts at Niagara.* By Peter Kalm. London, Printed for J. Whiston and B. White, 1751.

Buffon, George Louis Leclerc, comte de. *Natural History, General and Particular. . . .* Translated into English . . . by William Smellis . . . . London, 3rd ed., A. Strahan [etc.], 1791. 9 vols.

Byrd, William. *History of the Dividing Line, and Other Tracts.* From the Papers of William Byrd, of Westover, in Virginia, Esquire. Richmond, Va., 1866. 2 vols. (*Historical Documents from the Old Dominion*, Nos. 2-3.)

Champlain, Samuel de. *The Works of*. . . . Reprinted, translated and annotated by Six Canadian Scholars Under the General Editorship of H. G. Biggar. . . . Toronto, The Champlain Society, 1922-36. 6 vols. (The *Publications* of the Champlain Society. New Series.)

Charlesvoix, Pierre Francois Xavier de. *History and General Description of New France*. By Rev. P. F. X. de Charlevoix. Translated with notes by John Gilmary Shea. . . . New York, J. G. Shea, 1866-72. 6 vols.

Colles, Christopher. *A Survey of the Roads of United States of America, 1789*. [New York, 1789.]

Conduct of the late Ministry: or, A Memorial: Containing a Summary of Facts with Their Vouchers, in Answer to the Observations, Sent by the English Ministry to the Courts of Europe. . . . London, W. Bizet, 1757.

Connecticut. Secretary of State. *Register and Manual of the State of Connecticut, 1939*. Hartford, The State, 1939.

Cramer, Zadok. *The Navigator*. . . . Pittsburgh, 10th ed., Cramer & Spear, 1818.

Douglass, William. *A Summary, Historical and Political of the First Planting Progressive Movements, and Present State of the British Settlements in North America; With Some Transient Accounts of the Bordering French and Spanish Settlements*. Boston, New England, printed: London, Reprinted for R. Baldwin, 1755. 2 vols.

Drake, Samuel Gardner, ed. *The Old Indian Chronicle; Being a Collection of Exceeding Rare Tracts Written and Published in the Time of King Philip's War, by Persons Residing in the Country; to Which are now Added an Introduction and Notes by Samuel G. Drake*. Boston, S. A. Drake, 1867.

Dwight, Timothy. *Travels in New England and New York*. London, Printed for W. Baynes and Son [etc.], 1823. 4 vols.

Evans, Lewis. *Geographical, Historical, Political, Philosophical and Mechanical Essays. The First, Containing an Analysis of a General Map of the Middle British Colonies in America*. . . . Philadelphia, B. Franklin, and D. Hall, 1755.

Evans, Lewis. *Geographical, Historical, Political, Philosophical and Mechanical Essays. Number II Containing a Letter Representing the Impropriety of Sending Forces to Virginia*. . . . *Published in the New York Mercury, No. 178, January 5, 1756, With an Answer to so*

Much Thereof as Concerns the Public. Philadelphia, Printed for the Author, 1756. Reprinted in Lawrence H. Gipson's *Lewis Evans*.... Philadelphia, Historical Society of Pennsylvania, 1939.

Gage, Thomas. *The Correspondence of General Thomas Gage*.... Compiled and Edited by Clarence Edwin Carter.... New Haven, Yale University Press; London, H. Milford, Oxford University Press, 1931-33. 2 vols. (*Yale Historical Publications. Manuscripts and Edited Texts*, Nos. 11-12.)

Galbreath, Charles B., ed. *Expeditions of Céloron to the Ohio Country in 1749*.... Columbus, Ohio, The F. J. Heer Printing Co., 1921. (Republished with additions from the *Ohio Archaeological and Historical Quarterly*, October, 1920.)

Gist, Christopher. *Christopher Gist's Journals with Historical, Geographical, and Ethnological Notes and Biographies of his Contemporaries, by William M. Darlington*. Pittsburgh, J. R. Weldin & Co. 1893.

Hutchins, Thomas. *The Courses of the Ohio River taken by Lt. T. Hutchins Anno 1766 and Two Accompanying Maps*. Beverly W. Bond, Jr., ed. Cincinnati, Historical and Philosophical Society of Ohio, 1942. (*Publications* of the Historical and Philosophical Society of Ohio.)

Johnson, Sir William. *The Papers of Sir William Johnson*. Prepared for Publication by the Division of Archives and History.... Albany, The University of the State of New York, 1921-39. 9 vols.

Kalm, Per. *Travels in North America*.... Translated into English by John Reinhold Forster. London, Printed for the Editor, 1770-71. 3 vols.

Le Page Du Pratz. *Histoire de la Louisiane, Contenant la Découverte de ce Vaste Pays; sa Description Géographique; un Voyage dans les Terres: l'Histoire Naturelle: les Moeurs, Coûtumes & Religion des Naturels, avec leurs Origines*.... Paris, De Bure, 1758. 3 vols.

Maine Historical Society. *Collections*.... First series. Portland, The Society, 1831-37. 10 vols.

Mereness, Newton D., ed. *Travels in the American Colonies*. New York, The Macmillan Company, 1916.

Moravian Historical Society. *Transactions*.... Nazareth, Whitfield House, 1876-date. Published irregularly.

Pownall, Thomas. *The Administration of the Colonies*. London, 2nd ed., R. Dodsley, 1765.

Royal Society of London. *Philosophical Transactions*.... First series. London, The Society, 1665-1885. Nos. 270-272 (1701); 385 (1724).

Shirley, William. *Correspondence of William Shirley, Governor of Massachusetts and Military Commander in America, 1731-1760*. Charles Henry Lincoln, ed. New York, The Macmillan Company, 1912. 2 vols.

Smith, William. *Historical Account of Bouquet's Expedition Against the Ohio Indians*. Cincinnati, Ohio, Robert Clarke & Co., 1868. "Ohio Valley Historical Series," No. 1.

Stark, Caleb. *Memoir and Official Correspondence of Gen. John Stark, With Notices of Several Other Officers of the Revolution. Also a Biography of Capt. Phineas Stevens and of Col. Robert Rogers, With Account of His Service in America during the "Seven Years War."* Concord [N.H.], G. P. Lyon, 1860.

Strahlenberg, John Philip von. *An Historico-geographical Description of the North and Eastern Parts of Europe and Asia; but More Particularly of Prussia, Siberia and Great Tartary. . . .* Now Faithfully Translated into English. . . . London, Printed for Innys and R. Mansby, 1738.

Walker, Thomas. *Journal of an Exploration in the Spring of the Year 1750 . . . with a Preface by William Cabell Rives*. Boston, Little, Brown, and Company, 1888.

Washington, George. *The Writings of. . . . From the Original Manuscript Sources, 1745-1799*. Prepared under the direction of the U.S. George Washington Bicentennial Commission and published by authority of Congress; John C. Fitzpatrick, ed. Washington, Government Printing Office, [1931-44]. 39 vols.

Williams, John. *The Redeemed Captive Returning to Zion: or, A Faithful History of Remarkable Occurrences in the Captivity and Deliverance of Mr. John Williams. . . .* The Sixth Edition. Boston, Samuel Hall, 1795.

ATLASES

SOURCE MATERIAL

The Atlantic Neptune, Published for the Use of the Royal Navy of Great Britain, by Joseph F. W. Des Barres. . . . Under the Directions of the Right Hon[ble] the Lords Commissioners of the Admiralty. [London, 1774-1781.] 3 vols.

Jefferys, Thomas, engr. *The American Atlas. . . .* London, R. Sayer & J. Bennett, 1776.

Jefferys, Thomas, engr. *A General Topography of North America and the West Indies*. London, for R. Sayer & T. Jefferys, 1768.

Sayer, Robert and J. Bennett. *The American Military Pocket Atlas of the British Colonies; Especially Those Which Now Are, or Probably May Be the Theatre of War. Taken Principally From the Actual Surveys and Judicious Observations of Engineers De Brahm and Romans; Cook, Jackson and Collet; Maj. Holland, and Other Officers, Employed in His Majesty's Fleets and Armies*. London, for R. Sayer and J. Bennett, [1776].

SECONDARY MATERIAL

Walling, Henry F. *New Topographical Atlas of the State of Pennsylvania* .... By Henry F. Walling and A. W. Gray. Philadelphia, Stedman Brown & Lyon, 1872.

MAPS

SOURCE MATERIAL

1722   *The Town of Boston in New England by Cap* John Bonner, 1722*. Engraven and Printed by Fra: Dewing, Boston N.E. 1722. Sold by Cap*t* John Bonner and Will*m* Price against y*e* Town House. Reproduction in Shurtleff's. . . *Boston*.

1735   *To the Merchants of London Trading to Virginia & Maryland This Mapp of the Bay of Chesepeack, with the Rivers Potomack, Potapsco, North East, and Part of Chester*. London, W. Beitts and E. Baldwin, 1755. Photostat in New York Public Library.

1737   *Map of the Indian Walking Purchase, 1737, by Lewis Evans*. Frontispiece in Lawrence Gipson's *Lewis Evans*. . . .

1737   "A Map of the Northern Neck in Virginia; The Territory of the Right Honourable Thomas Lord Fairfax; Situate betwixt the Rivers Potomack and Rappahanock, According to a Late Survey; Drawn in the Year 1737 by W*m* Mayo." Manuscript Map in the Darlington Memorial Library, University of Pittsburgh.

1739   *A Map of Part of the Province of Pennsylvania and of the Counties of New Castle, Kent and Sussex on Delaware: Showing the Temporary Limits of the Jurisdiction of Pennsylvania and Maryland, Fixed According to an Order of His Majesty in Coun-*

cil dated the 25th Day of May in the Year 1738. Surveyed in the Year 1739. Reproduction in *Pennsylvania Archives*, Vol. I.

1749 *A Map of Pensilvania, New Jersey, New York, and the Three Delaware Counties: by Lewis Evans, 1749.* L. Herbert, sculp. Philadelphia, L. Evans, 1749.

1750- "Map of Albany County With the Country of the Five Nations."
1770? By Jno R. Bleecker. Manuscript Map in the New York Historical Society, New York, N.Y.

1751 *A Map of the Most Inhabited Part of Virginia Containing the Whole Province of Maryland With Part of Pensilvania, New Jersey and North Carolina.* Drawn by Joshua Fry and Peter Jefferson in 1751. Printed for Robt. Sayer at No. 53 in Fleet Street & Thos. Jefferys at the Corner of St. Martins Lane, Charing Cross, London.

1752 *A Map of Pensilvania, New Jersey, New York and the Three Delaware Counties: By Lewis Evans,* 1749. The Second Edition. July 1752. Reproduction in Gipson's *Lewis Evans....*

1753 *Plan of the British Dominions of New England in North America Composed from Actual Surveys.* By Dr. William Douglas. Engraved by R. W. Seale, London, 1753.

1753? *Map. Virginia.* [A sketch showing the Courses of Christopher Gist's First and Second Tours] MSS. Great Britain. Public Records Office, Colonial Office. Maps, Virginia, No. 13. (Photostat, courtesy of Howard N. Eavenson.)

1755 *A General Map of the Middle British Colonies, in America: ... By Lewis Evans. 1755.* Engraved by Ja⁸ Turner in Philadelphia. Published According to Act of Parliament, by Lewis Evans, June 23, 1755. And Sold by R. Dodsley, in Pall-Mall, London, & by the Author in Philadelphia.

1755 [Sir William] *Johnson's Map of Lake George and Vicinity.* Printed in Sir William Johnson's *Papers*, II, Map opposite p. 422.

1755 *A Map of the British and French Dominions in North America, with the Roads, Distances, Limits, and Extent of the Settlements. . . .* By Jnº Mitchell. London, Printed for Jefferys & Faden, Feb. 13th, 1755.

1758 *A General Map of the Middle British Colonies in America: viz. Virginia, Maryland, Delaware, Pensilvania. . . . By Lewis Evans. Corrected and Improved in the Addition of the Line of Forts on the Back Settlements.* By Thomas Jefferys. [London], R. Sayer & T. Jefferys, 1758.

1759   *To the Honourable Thomas Penn and Richard Penn, this Map of the Improved Part of the Province of Pennsylvania is Humbly Dedicated by Nicholas Scull* . . . . Philadelphia, Engraved by J. Turner, and printed by J. Davis for the Author, 1759.

1762   *A Survey of Lake Champlain including Lake George, Crown Point and St. John. Surveyed by Order of His Excellency Major General S*ʳ *Jeffery Amherst* . . . . By William Brassier, Draughtsman, 1762. London; Printed for Robᵗ Sayer & Jnᵒ Bennett . . . , Aug. 5ᵗʰ 1776. In Jeffery's *American Atlas,* No. 18.

Before 1764   *Plan des Différents Villages François dans le Pays des Illynois avec une Partie de la Riviere Mississipi et des Confluents des Fleuves Missouri et Illinois.* Printed in Lawrence H. Gipson's *The British Empire* . . . , IV, Map opposite p. 126.

1768   *Map of the Frontiers of the Northern Colonies with the Boundary Line Established Between Them and the Indians at the Treaty Held by S*ʳ *Will Johnson at Fort Stanwix in Nov'r 1768. Corrected and Improved from Evans' Map.* By Guy Johnson, Agt. for Indian Affairs. Printed in Sir William Johnson's *Papers* . . . , VI, Map opposite p. 450.

1770   *A New and Accurate Map of Virginia Wherein Most of the Counties Are Laid Down From Actual Surveys. With a Concise Account of the Number of Inhabitants, the Trade, Soil, and Produce of that Province.* By John Henry. Engraved by Thomas Jefferys, Geographer to the King. London, February, 1770. Published According to Act of Parliament for the Author, by Thoˢ Jefferys at the Corner of St. Martins Lane in the Strand. Reproduction in Abernethy's *Western Lands.* . . .

1770   *To the Honorable Thomas Penn and Richard Penn, esquires, True and Absolute Proprietors and Governors of the Province of Pennsylvania and the Territories Thereunto Belonging and to the Honorable John Penn, Esquire, Lieutenant Governor of the Same. This Map of the Province of Pennsylvania is Humbly Dedicated by Their Most Obedient Serv't W. Scull.* Henry Dawkins Sculp't. Philadelphia, James Nevil, for the Author, April 1st, 1770.

1770   *A Plan of the West Line or Parallel of Latitude Which is the Boundary Between the Provinces of Maryland and Pennsylvania.* Engraved by J. Smither, 1770. Title from: Great Britain. Board of Trade and Plantations, *List of Maps.* . . .

1773- 1774?   "A Plan of a Survey made to Explore the Country for a Road Between Connecticut River and St. Francis." [By Hugh Finlay, anon.] MSS in Library of Congress. Division of Maps.

1774 *A Map of the Most Inhabited Part of New England Containing the Provinces of Massachusets Bay and New Hampshire With the Colonies of Conecticut and Rhode Island Divided into Counties and Townships.* [By J. Green, anon.] November 29th, 1774. Published According to Act by Tho⁸ Jefferys. In Jefferys' *American Atlas* . . . , Nos. 15-16.

1776 *A General Map of the Southern British Colonies in America* . . . . By B. Romans. London, Printed for R. Sayer and J. Bennett, 15th Octʳ 1776.

1776 *A Map of the Province of New York, Reduc'd From the Large Scale Drawings of That Province, Compiled From Actual Surveys by Order of His Excellency William Tryon.* By Claude Joseph Sauthier . . . . Engraved by William Faden, 1776. London, Wᵐ Faden, 1776. Reprinted by U.S. Constitution Sesquicentennial Convention under the Title: *New York at the Time of the Ratification of the Constitution from 1776 and 1787 originals in the Library of Congress at Washington.*

1776 *To His Excellency Sir Henry Moore . . . This Plan of the City of New York and its Environs, Survey'd and Laid Down: Is Most Humbly Dedicated by His Excellency's Most obedt. Humble Servant, B. Ratzer, Lieut. in His Majesty's 60th or Royal American Regt. . . . Plan of the City of New York in North America: Surveyed in The Years 1766 & 1767.* London, W. Faden & Jefferys, 1776.

1777 *The Province of New Jersey, Divided Into East and West, Commonly Called the Jerseys. Drawn From the Survey Made in 1769 by Order of the Commissioners Appointed to Settle the Partition Line Between the Provinces of New York & New Jersey by Bernard Ratzer, and From Another Large Survey of the Northern Parts by Gerard Barker.* Engraved by Wᵐ Faden. London, W. Faden, Dec. 1, 1777. In William Faden's *North American Atlas* . . . , No. 22.

1779 *A Chorographical Map of the Province of New York, Divided Into Counties, Manors, etc. Compiled From Actual Surveys Deposited in the Patent Office at New York by Order of General William Tryon.* By Claude Joseph Sauthier. London, W. Faden. Jan. 1, 1779. In Jefferys' *American Atlas* . . . , No. 17½.

1784 *A Topographical Map of the Province of New Hampshire Surveyed by Mr. Thomas Wright and Others.* Author, S. Holland, London,

1784. Printed for William Faden, Mar. 1, 1784. Title from:
Great Britain. Board of Trade and Plantations, *List of Maps....*

1801 *Warner & Hanna's Plan of the City and Environs of Baltimore Respectfully Dedicated to the Mayor, City Council, and Citizens Thereof by the Proprietors, 1801.* [Baltimore, 1801.]

1859 *A Map of the State of Virginia. Constructed in Conformity to Law from the Late Surveys, Authorized by the Legislature.* By Herman Böyë. Corrected by Order of the Executive, 1859. n.p., n. pub., [1859].

SECONDARY MATERIAL

"A Map of the Site of the Battle of Lake George, September 8th, 1755. In Caldwell, Warren County, N.Y." From the *Fifth Annual Report of the Society for the Preservation of Scenic and Historic Places and Objects.* Albany: 1900. Reprinted in Sir William Johnson's *Papers,* II, Map opposite p. 2.

"Map of the Ancient Shawanoese Towns, on the Pickaway Plain." Howe's *Historical Collections of Ohio,* p. 402.

"Original Elbow District, Mass., 1716-1752." Compiled by E. B. Gates. Temple's *History of the Town of Palmer,* Map No. 1.

"Trails, Military Roads and Forts from Albany to Crown Point, 1750-1780." Prepared by R. J. Brown formerly Warren County engineer under supervision of James A. Holden. Sir William Johnson's *Papers,* I, opposite p. 896.

"Vandalia as Originally Plotted on Evans' Map." Abernethy's *Western Lands...,* Map opposite p. 39.

VIEWS

MANUSCRIPT

"A View of the Cohoes or Great Falls on the Mohawk River." Pen and Ink Sketch. Library of Congress. Division of Maps.

ENGRAVINGS

Scenographia Americana; or, A Collection of Views in North America and the West Indies. Neatly Engraved by Messrs. Sandby, Grignion, Rooker, Canot, Elliot, and Others; From Drawings On the Spot, by

Several Officers of the British Navy & Army.... London, Printed for John Bowles, Robert Sayer, Thomas Jefferys, Carington Bowles & Henry Packer, 1768. A List of engravings executed from Governor Pownall's sketches mentioned in this work is as follows:

"A View of Bethlehem, the Great Moravian Settlement in the Province of Pennsylvania. ..."

"A View of Hudson's River at the Entrance of What is Called the Topan Sea. ..."

"A View of Hudson's River of the Pakepsey and the Catts-kill Mountains from Sopos Island. ..."

"A View of the Falls on the Passaic or Second River in the Province of New Jersey. ..."

"A View of the Great Cohoes Falls on the Mohawk River; the Fall About Seventy Feet; the River Near a Quarter of a Mile Broad. ..."

SECONDARY MATERIAL

Abernethy, Thomas Perkins. *Western Lands and the American Revolution*. New York, London, D. Appleton-Century Co., Inc., 1937. (University of Virginia, Institute for Research in the Social Sciences. *Institute Monograph*, No. 25.)

Atkinson, George. *History of Kanawha County, from its Organization in 1789 Until the Present Time....* Charleston, printed at the office of the West Virginia Journal, 1876.

Bailey, Kenneth P. *The Ohio Company of Virginia and the Westward Movement 1748-1792....* Glendale, California, The Arthur H. Clark Company, 1939.

Baldwin, Leland D. *Pittsburgh, the Story of a City*. [Pittsburgh], University of Pittsburgh Press, 1939.

Barber, John Warner. *History and Antiquities of New Haven, Conn., from the Earliest Settlement to the Present Time....* New Haven, J. W. Barber, 1831.

Benton, Nathaniel S. *A History of Herkimer County, Including the Upper Mohawk Valley, from the Earliest Period to the Present Time*. Albany, J. Munsell, 1856.

Bining, Arthur Cecil. *British Regulation of the Colonial Iron Industry*. Philadelphia, Ph.D. Dissertation, University of Pennsylvania, 1933.

Bishop, John L. *A History of American Manufactures, from 1608 to 1860 ... Comprising Annals of the Industry of the United States in*

Machinery, Manufactures and Useful Arts. Philadelphia, E. Young & Co.; London, S. Low, Son & Co., 1864. 2 vols.

Boynton, Edward C. *History of West Point*. London, Sampson Low, Son & Marston, 1864.

Carrier, Lyman. *The Beginnings of Agriculture in America*. New York, McGraw Hill, 1923.

Clark, Joshua V. H. *Onondaga; or, Reminiscences of Earlier and Later Times; Being a Series of Historical Sketches Relative to Onondaga....* Syracuse, Stoddard and Babcock, 1849. 2 vols.

Collins, Lewis. *History of Kentucky. Revised, Enlarged ... and Brought Down to the Year 1874.* . . . Covington, Ky., Collins & Co., 1874. 2 vols.

Davidson, Donald. *The Tennessee. . . .* New York, Toronto, Rinehart & Co., Inc., [1946-1948]. 2 vols. "Rivers of America" series.

Eavenson, Howard N. *The First Century and a Quarter of American Coal Industry*. Pittsburgh, Pa., Privately printed, 1942.

Federal Writers' Project. Delaware. *Delaware, a Guide to the First State*. New York, The Viking Press, 1938. "American Guide Series."

Federal Writers' Project. Illinois. *Illinois, a Descriptive and Historical Guide....* Chicago, A. C. McClurg & Co., 1939. "American Guide Series."

Federal Writers' Project. Maine. *Maine, 'A Guide Down East.'* Boston, Houghton Mifflin Co., 1937. "American Guide Series."

Federal Writers' Project. Massachusetts. *Massachusetts: a Guide to Its Places and People*. Boston, Houghton Mifflin Co., 1937. "American Guide Series."

Federal Writers' Project. New Hampshire. *New Hampshire, a Guide to the Granite State*. Boston, Houghton Mifflin Co., 1938. "American Guide Series."

Federal Writers' Project. New Jersey. *New Jersey, a Guide to its Past and Present*. New York, The Viking Press, 1939. "American Guide Series."

Federal Writers' Project. Rhode Island. *Rhode Island, a Guide to the Smallest State*. Boston, Houghton Mifflin Co., 1937. "American Guide Series."

Gipson, Lawrence Henry. *The British Empire Before the American Revolution: Provincial Characteristics and Sectional Tendencies in the Era Preceding the American Crisis....* Caldwell, Idaho, The Caxton Printers; New York, Alfred A. Knopf, 1936-date. 6 vols., all published to date.

Gipson, Lawrence Henry. *Lewis Evans, by Lawrence Henry Gipson: to Which is Added Evans' A Brief Account of Pennsylvania, Together with Facsimiles of His Geographical, Political, Philosophical and Mechanical Essays, Numbers I and II . . . Also Facsimiles of Evans' Maps.* Philadelphia, The Historical Society of Pennsylvania, 1939.

Gordon, Thomas F. *A Gazetteer of the State of New Jersey.* Trenton, Daniel Fenton, 1834.

Hanna, Charles A. *The Wilderness Trail; or, The Ventures and Adventures of the Pennsylvania Traders on the Allegheny Path, with Some New Annals of the Old West, and the Records of Some Strong Men and Some Bad Ones.* New York, London, G. P. Putnam's Sons, 1911. 2 vols.

Hard, Walter. *The Connecticut.* New York, Rinehart & Co., [c1947]. "Rivers of America" series.

Hodge, Frederick, ed. *Handbook of American Indians North of Mexico.* Washington, Government Printing Office, 1907-10. 2 vols. (Smithsonian Institution. Bureau of Ethnology. *Bulletin* 30.)

Hough, Franklin B. *Gazetteer of the State of New York, Embracing a Comprehensive Account of the History and Statistics of the State. . . .* Albany, N.Y., A. Boyd, 1872.

Howe, Henry. *Historical Collections of Ohio.* Cincinnati, Derby, Bradley & Co., 1848.

Jones, Uriah. *History of the Early Settlement of the Juniata Valley.* Philadelphia, H. B. Ashmead, 1856.

Levering, Joseph M. *A History of Bethlehem, Pennsylvania, 1741-1892, With Some Account of Its Founders, and Their Early Activity in America. . . .* Bethlehem, Pa., Times Publishing Co., 1903.

Loescher, Burt Garfield. *The History of Rogers Rangers. . . .* San Francisco, [The Author], 1946-date. Vol. I, all published to date.

Lossing, Benson J., comp. *A Pictorial Description of Ohio.* New York, Ensigns & Thayer, 1849.

Lowdermilk, William H. *History of Cumberland (Maryland) From the Time of the Indian Town, Caiuctucuc, in 1728, up to the Present Day, Embracing an Account of Washington's First Campaign, and Battle of Fort Necessity, Together With a History of Braddock's Expedition.* Washington, D.C., J. Anglis, 1878.

Marshall, Orsamus. *The Niagara Frontier. Embracing Sketches of Its Early History, and Indian, French and English Local Names.* Read before the Buffalo Historical Society, February 27th, 1865. [Buffalo], 1881. (Buffalo Historical Society. *Publications.*)

Maryland Historical Magazine. Baltimore, The Society, 1906-date. 43 vols.

Massachusetts Historical Society. *Collections*. Second series, Boston, John Eliot, 1814-23. 10 vols.

—— *Proceedings*. Boston, The Society, 1791-date. 67 vols.

Morgan, Lewis H. *League of the Ho-dá-sau-nee, or Iroquois*. Rochester, Sage & Brothers, 1851.

Niles, Blair. *The James, from Iron Gate to the Sea*. New York, Farrar & Rinehart, [c1945]. "Rivers of America" series.

Nonnemaker, Warren N. "The Moravian Church in the United States during the Middle Period, 1812-1860." M. A. Thesis, Lehigh University, 1935.

Palmer, Peter S. *History of Lake Champlain, From Its First Exploration by the French in 1609, to the Close of the Year 1814*. Albany, J. Munsell, 1866.

Pennsylvania Archaeologist. Philadelphia, Society for Pennsylvania Archaeology, 1930-date. 18 vols.

Pennsylvania Magazine of History and Biography. Philadelphia, Publication Fund of the Historical Society of Pennsylvania, 1877-date. 47 vols.

Pollard, Edward A. *The Virginia Tourist*. Philadelphia, J. B. Lippincott & Co., 1870.

Pownall, Charles. *Thomas Pownall. . . . Governor of Massachusetts Bay, Author of the Letters of Junius, With a Supplement Comparing the Colonies of Kings George III and Edward VII. . . .* London, H. Stevens, Son, & Stiles, [c1908].

Ramsey, J. G. M. *Annals of Tennessee. . . .* [Kingsport, Tenn.], Kingsport Press, 1926.

Raum, John O. *History of the City of Trenton, New Jersey, Embracing a Period of Nearly Two Hundred Years. . . .* Trenton, W. T. Nicholson & Co., 1871.

—— *The History of New Jersey, from its Earliest Settlement to the Present Time. . . .* Philadelphia, J. E. Potter and Company, [1877]. 2 vols.

Reichel, William C. *Friedensthal and Its Stockaded Mill. A Moravian Chronicle, 1749-1767*. Nazareth, Pa., printed for the Society, 1877. (Moravian Historical Society. *Transactions*, Vol. II.)

Reichel, William C., ed. *Memorials of the Moravian Church*. Philadelphia, J. B. Lippincott & Co., 1870. Vol. I, all published.

Schlarman, Joseph. *From Quebec to New Orleans*. Belleville, Ill., Buechler Publishing Co., 1929.

Schuyler, George E. *Colonial New York; Philip Schuyler and His Family*. New York, C. Scribner's Sons, 1885. 2 vols.

Shurtleff, Nathaniel B. *A Topographical and Historical Description of Boston*. Boston, 3rd ed., Published by Order of the Common Council, 1891.

Simms, Jeptha. *History of Schoharie County, and Border Wars of New York*. Albany, Munsell & Tanner, 1845.

Steelways. New York, American Iron and Steel Institute, 1947-date. 2 vols.

Stevens, Henry N. *Lewis Evans, His Map of the Middle English Colonies in America*. London, 3rd ed., H. Stevens, Son & Stiles, 1924.

Temple, Josiah H. *History of the Town of Palmer, Massachusetts, Early Known as the Elbow Tract: Including Records of the Plantation, District and Town, 1716-1889*. [Springfield], published by the town of Palmer, 1889.

Thompson, Jeanette R. *History of the Town of Stratford, New Hampshire, 1773-1925*. ... Concord, N. H., The Rumford Press, 1925.

U.S. Bureau of American Ethnology. *Annual Reports of the Bureau of Ethnology to the Secretary of Smithsonian Institution*. Washington, U.S. Government Printing Office, 1879/80 - 1930/31. Forty-eight reports in 54 vols.

Valentine's Manual of Old New York, 1924. Edited by Henry Collins Brown. New York, Gracie Mansion, [c1923]. (Museum of the City of New York. *Yearbook*.)

Volwiler, Albert T. *George Croghan and the Westward Movement, 1741-1782*. Cleveland, The Arthur H. Clark Company, 1926. (Early Western Journals, No. 3.)

Wallace, Paul A. W. *Conrad Weiser, 1696-1760, Friend of Colonist and Mohawk*. Philadelphia; University of Pennsylvania Press, 1945.

Watson, John Fanning. *Annals of Philadelphia* .... Philadelphia, For Sale by Uriah Hunt, 1830.

Watson, John F. *Annals and Occurrences of New York City and State in the Olden Time*. Philadelphia, H. F. Anners, 1846.

Williamson, William D. *The History of the State of Maine; From its First Discovery, A.D. 1602, to the Separation, A.D. 1820, inclusive*. Hallowell, [Me.], Glazier, Masters & Co., 1832. 2 vols.

Western Pennsylvania Historical Magazine. Pittsburgh, Published by the Historical Society of Western Pennsylvania, 1918-date. 30 vols.

Writers' Program. Kentucky. *Louisville: a Guide to the Falls City* .... New York, M. Barrows & Company, Inc., 1940. "American Guide Series."

Writers' Program. Missouri. *Missouri, a Guide to the "Show Me" State* .... New York, Duell, Sloan and Pearce, [c1941]. "American Guide Series."

Yale University. *Historical Register of Yale University, 1701-1937.* New Haven, Conn., Yale University, 1939.

INDEX

The additions and corrections listed in this index under the heading, Pownall, Thomas, *Topographical Descriptions* revised (1949), are new material, never before published.

Creek printed, 157; Journal used by Pownall, 50, 74

Hockhocking [Hocking] River (Ohio), 159, 180*n*, 190; coal, 144; description, 143-44; distance from Fort Pitt, 166; freestone, 144

Hoek. *See* Sandy Hook.

Hog Island (Me.), 73

Holland, Samuel, 7, 8, 9, 19; observations, 19-20; survey of land route between St. Francis and Connecticut Rivers, 17, 52, 54; surveys Boston coast, 85

Holliston, Mass., 61

Holliston Ridge, 64

Holliston Township, Mass., 60

Hollowell, Benjamin. *See* Hallowell, Benjamin.

Holly trees, New York, 41

Holston [Holstein] River, 137

Holt Island (Me.), 70

Holyoke [Holy Oaks], Mt. (Mass.), 57

Homer, quotation from, 41

Hope, Mt. (R.I.), 64

Hopkington Ridge, 64

Hopkinton, Mass., 61

Hopkinton Township, Mass., 60

Hoppin Brook (Mass.), 63*n*

Hornbeam trees, Massachusetts, 164

Hornblower, Josiah, 98

Horsneck, Conn., 58

Hospital Island (Boston), 85

Housatonic [Hoosatonick] Mountains (Conn.), 53

Housatonic [Hoosatonick] River (Conn.), 53. *See also* Stratford River.

Howard, John, 74

Hoxton, Walter, *Chart of Chesapeake Bay*, 21

Hubert, Madam, experiments on native and foreign silk worms in Louisiana, 28

Hudson River (N.Y.), 1, 8, 9, 32, 37, 41, 91; boundary of New England, 18; called North River by the Dutch, 33; description, 32, 35, 38-40; depth, 45, 46; single channel, 47; Taconic Range parallel, 47; transportation, 45; trees, 35, 47, 155

Hull Island (Boston), 84

Hunter, Fort (N.Y.), 34

Hurd's River (N.H.), 55

Huron, Lake, 121

Illinois [Welenis], Western League of Indians, 147

Illinois Country, boundary on Ohio River, 161*n*; grain raising, 163, 164; French and Indian trade, 164-65; lead mine, 95; wild rye, 26

Illinois [Ilinois] River, 165

Indian River (Del.), 132

Indian trade, in the Illinois Country, monopolized by the French, 164-65

Indiana Territory, boundary on Ohio River, 161*n*

Indians, their sense of direction, 126. *See also* under names of individual tribes.

Interval lands, 23; along Mohawk River, 33-34

Ipswich River (Mass.), 63, 83

Iron ore, Connecticut, 67*n*; New England, 67; Ohio Country, 124; Taconic Mountains, 67*n*

Iroquois Confederacy. *See* Six Nations.

Isinglass. *See* Talc.

Isle au Haut. *See* Holt Island.

Jamaica, L.I., 23

James, Cape. *See* Cape Henlopen.

James River (Va.), 91, 144; description and navigation, 30, 136-37

James River Company, 135*n*

Jamestown, Va., 136

Jefferson, Peter, 20. *See also* Fry and Jefferson.

Jefferys, Thomas, 8; piracy of Evans' *Map*, 10-11

Jefferys, William, 8

Johnson, Guy, *Map of the Frontiers of the Northern Colonies* (1768), 5*n*

Johnson, Samuel, mill in New Jersey, 101

Johnson, Sir William, "Map of Lake George and Vicinity", 17

Juniata River (Pa.), 131; C. Gist camps, 172

Kanawha [Cahawa, Canhawa, Conhawa, Kanâwa, Kenhawa] (Great) River, 135, 198; bottoms fertile but narrow, 123, 198; description, 123, 144; distance from Fort Pitt, 166; falls, 137; navigation, 159; pass through mountains, 198*n*

Kanawha (Little) River, 123*n*, 159; distance from Fort Pitt, 166

Kankusker Bay (Lake George), 48

Kaskaskia [Kuskuskies] (Ill.), Indian village, 162*n*, 163

Kaskaskia River (Ill.), 163

Kaskaskias [Keskesquois], Indian tribe of the Illinois or Western League of Indians, 162*n*, 163

Kayaderosseras [Kaiaderossoras], 38

Kellog, Mr., 18

Kellogg Bay. *See* Baye des Vasseaux.

Kennebec [Kenebaëg, Kenebec] River (Me.), 19, 20, 62, 73; communication with Penobscot River, 80; description, 74-78; route to Quebec, described, 74-77

Kennebunk River (Me.), 79

Kennedy, Samuel, "Journal", used by Pownall, 74

Kensington, Conn., 57, 59

Kentucky, buffaloes, 145; clay, 145. *See also* New Virginia.

Kentucky River, 145, 160; distance from Fort Pitt, 166. *See also* Cuttawa (Little) River.

Kickeney Paulin, C. Gist stays at cabin, 173

Kilgore, Ralph, 182*n*, 191*n*

Kind Creek (Pa.), 168

TWO THOUSAND COPIES OF THIS BOOK WERE PRINTED

FOR THE UNIVERSITY OF PITTSBURGH PRESS

ON SPECIAL WHITE ANTIQUE BOOK VELLUM FINISH

FROM MONOTYPE CASLON OLD STYLE

BY THE EDDY PRESS CORPORATION

PITTSBURGH, PENNSYLVANIA

S0-BBW-944

D'accord! 1

LANGUE ET CULTURE DU MONDE FRANCOPHONE

VISTA®
HIGHER LEARNING

Boston, Massachusetts

On the cover: View of the Louvre from the clock at Musée d'Orsay, Paris, France

Publisher: José A. Blanco
Editorial Development: Megan Moran, Sharla Zwirek
Project Management: Brady Chin, Sally Giangrande, Rosemary Jaffe, Faith Ryan
Rights Management: Annie Pickert Fuller, Ashley Poreda
Technology Production: Jamie Kostecki, Reginald Millington, Sonja Porras, Paola Ríos Schaaf
Design: Radoslav Mateev, Gabriel Noreña, Andrés Vanegas
Production: Sergio Arias, Oscar Díez

Student Text ISBN: 978-1-68005-784-3
Teacher's Edition ISBN: 978-1-68005-785-0
Library of Congress Control Number: 2017949781

1 2 3 4 5 6 7 8 9 TC 22 21 20 19 18 17

Printed in Canada

Contents

Scope & Sequence: D'accord! 1A & 1B

1A

Unit/Lesson	Contextes	Structures	Culture/Panorama
Unité 1 Salut!			
Leçon 1A	Greetings and goodbyes Introductions and expressions of courtesy	Nouns and articles Numbers 0–60	Greetings and manners
Leçon 1B	People and things around the classroom	Subject pronouns and the verb **être** Adjective agreement	French identity and diversity **Le monde francophone**
Unité 2 Au lycée			
Leçon 2A	Academic life	Present tense of regular **-er** verbs Forming questions and expressing negation	French school life
Leçon 2B	Everyday activities	Present tense of **avoir** Telling time	**Le bac** **La France**
Unité 3 La famille et les copains			
Leçon 3A	Family, friends, and pets	Descriptive adjectives Possessive adjectives	Families in France
Leçon 3B	Descriptive adjectives Occupations	Numbers 61–100 Prepositions of location and disjunctive pronouns	Relationships **La Suisse** **La Belgique**
Unité 4 Au café			
Leçon 4A	Places and activities around town	The verb **aller** Interrogative words	Popular leisure activities
Leçon 4B	Going to a **café**	The verbs **prendre** and **boire**; Partitives Regular **-ir** verbs	**Café** culture **Le Québec**

1B

Unit/Lesson	Contextes	Structures	Culture/Panorama
Reprise			
	A brief overview of the contexts and grammar from Level 1A		
Unité 5 Les loisirs			
Leçon 5A	Leisure activities	The verb **faire** and the expression **il faut** Irregular **-ir** verbs	Soccer in France
Leçon 5B	Weather Seasons and months	Numbers 101 and higher Spelling-change **-er** verbs	Public spaces in France **L'Afrique de l'Ouest** **L'Afrique centrale**
Unité 6 Les fêtes			
Leçon 6A	Parties and celebrations Stages of life	Demonstrative adjectives The **passé composé** with **avoir**	**Le carnaval**
Leçon 6B	Clothing and colors	Indirect object pronouns Regular and irregular **-re** verbs	Fashion **Le Maroc** **L'Algérie** **La Tunisie**
Unité 7 En vacances			
Leçon 7A	Travel and transportation	The **passé composé** with **être** Direct object pronouns	Tahiti
Leçon 7B	Hotels and accommodations	Adverbs and the verbs **dire**, **écrire**, and **lire** The **imparfait**	Vacations **La Polynésie française** **L'Asie du Sud-Est**
Unité 8 Chez nous			
Leçon 8A	Parts of the house Furniture	The **passé composé** vs. the **imparfait** (Parts 1 and 2) The verb **vivre**	Housing in the Francophone world
Leçon 8B	Household chores	The **passé composé** vs. the **imparfait** (Summary) The verbs **savoir** and **connaître**	Household interiors **Paris** **L'Île-de-France**

1	Unit/Lesson	Contextes	Structures	Culture/Panorama
	Unité 1 Salut!			
	Leçon 1A	Greetings and goodbyes Introductions and expressions of courtesy	Nouns and articles Numbers 0–60	Greetings and manners
	Leçon 1B	People and things around the classroom	Subject pronouns and the verb **être** Adjective agreement	French identity and diversity **Le monde francophone**
	Unité 2 Au lycée			
	Leçon 2A	Academic life	Present tense of regular **-er** verbs Forming questions and expressing negation	French school life
	Leçon 2B	Everyday activities	Present tense of **avoir** Telling time	**Le bac** **La France**
	Unité 3 La famille et les copains			
	Leçon 3A	Family, friends, and pets	Descriptive adjectives Possessive adjectives	Families in France
	Leçon 3B	Descriptive adjectives Occupations	Numbers 61–100 Prepositions of location and disjunctive pronouns	Relationships **La Suisse** **La Belgique**
	Unité 4 Au café			
	Leçon 4A	Places and activities around town	The verb **aller** Interrogative words	Popular leisure activities
	Leçon 4B	Going to a **café**	The verbs **prendre** and **boire;** Partitives Regular **-ir** verbs	**Café** culture **Le Québec**
	Unité 5 Les loisirs			
	Leçon 5A	Leisure activities	The verb **faire** and the expression **il faut** Irregular **-ir** verbs	Soccer in France
	Leçon 5B	Weather Seasons and months	Numbers 101 and higher Spelling-change **-er** verbs	Public spaces in France **L'Afrique de l'Ouest** **L'Afrique centrale**
	Unité 6 Les fêtes			
	Leçon 6A	Parties and celebrations Stages of life	Demonstrative adjectives The **passé composé** with **avoir**	**Le carnaval**
	Leçon 6B	Clothing and colors	Indirect object pronouns Regular and irregular **-re** verbs	Fashion **Le Maroc** **L'Algérie** **La Tunisie**
	Unité 7 En vacances			
	Leçon 7A	Travel and transportation	The **passé composé** with **être** Direct object pronouns	Tahiti
	Leçon 7B	Hotels and accommodations	Adverbs and the verbs **dire, écrire,** and **lire** The **imparfait**	Vacations **La Polynésie française** **L'Asie du Sud-Est**
	Unité 8 Chez nous			
	Leçon 8A	Parts of the house Furniture	The **passé composé** vs. the **imparfait** (Parts 1 and 2) The verb **vivre**	Housing in the Francophone world
	Leçon 8B	Household chores	The **passé composé** vs. the **imparfait** (Summary) The verbs **savoir** and **connaître**	Household interiors **Paris** **L'Île-de-France**

2	Unit/Lesson	Contextes	Structures	Culture/Panorama
	Reprise			
		Review of Level 1 vocabulary	Review of Level 1 grammar	Summer vacation activities
	Unité Préliminaire Chez nous			
	Leçon PA	Parts of the house Furniture	The **passé composé** vs. **the imparfait** (Parts 1 and 2) The verb **vivre**	Housing in the Francophone world
	Leçon PB	Household chores	The **passé composé** vs. **the imparfait** (Summary) The verbs **savoir** and **connaître**	Household interiors **Paris** **L'Île-de-France**
	Unité 1 La nourriture			
	Leçon 1A	Food and meals	The verb **venir**, the **passé récent**, and time expressions The verbs **devoir, vouloir, pouvoir**	French gastronomy and the **Guide Michelin**
	Leçon 1B	Dining Specialty food shops	Comparatives and superlatives of adjectives and adverbs Double object pronouns	French meals **La Normandie** **La Bretagne**
	Unité 2 La santé			
	Leçon 2A	Parts of the body Daily routine	Reflexive verbs Reflexives: **Sens idiomatique**	Healthcare in France
	Leçon 2B	Health, maladies, and remedies	The **passé composé** and **imparfait** of reflexive verbs The pronouns **y** and **en**	**La sécurité sociale** **La Nouvelle-Aquitaine** **L'Occitanie**
	Unité 3 La technologie			
	Leçon 3A	Computers and electronics	Prepositions with the infinitive Reciprocal verbs	Technology
	Leçon 3B	Cars and driving	The verbs **ouvrir** and **offrir** **Le conditionnel**	Cars in France **Provence-Alpes-Côte d'Azur** **La Corse**
	Unité 4 En ville			
	Leçon 4A	Errands	**Voir, croire, recevoir,** and **apercevoir** Negative/affirmative expressions	Small shops
	Leçon 4B	Giving and getting directions	**Le futur simple** Irregular stems in the **futur simple**	French cities and towns **Les Pays de la Loire** **Le Centre-Val de Loire**
	Unité 5 L'avenir et les métiers			
	Leçon 5A	At the office Making phone calls	**Le futur simple** with **quand** and **dès que** The interrogative pronoun **lequel**	Phones in France
	Leçon 5B	Professions	**Si** clauses Relative pronouns **qui, que, dont, où**	Unions and strikes **L'Auvergne-Rhône-Alpes** **La Bourgogne-Franche-Comté**
	Unité 6 L'espace vert			
	Leçon 6A	Environmental concerns	Demonstrative pronouns The subjunctive (Part 1)	The ecological movement in France
	Leçon 6B	Nature	The subjunctive (Part 2) Comparatives and superlatives of nouns	National parks **Le Grand Est** **Les Hauts-de-France**
	Unité 7 Les arts			
	Leçon 7A	Performance arts	The subjunctive (Part 3) Possessive pronouns and **être à (quelqu'un)**	Theater in France
	Leçon 7B	Literary arts TV and movies	The subjunctive (Part 4) Review of the subjunctive	Haitian painting **La France d'outre-mer**

3

Lesson	Contextes	Structures	Imaginez/Culture	Film/Littérature
Reprise				
	Review of Levels 1 and 2 vocabulary	Review of Levels 1 and 2 grammar		
Leçon 1 Ressentir et vivre				
	Relationships	Spelling-change verbs The irregular verbs **être, avoir, faire,** and **aller** Forming questions	**Les États-Unis** **Les francophones d'Amérique**	**Court métrage:** *Tout le monde dit je t'aime* (**France**) **Littérature:** *Il pleure dans mon cœur* de Paul Verlaine
Leçon 2 Habiter en ville				
	Towns and cities	Reflexive and reciprocal verbs Descriptive adjectives and adjective agreement Adverbs	**La France** **Rythme dans la rue: La fête de la Musique**	**Court métrage:** *J'attendrai le suivant* (**France**) **Littérature:** *Tout bouge autour de moi* de Dany Laferrière
Leçon 3 L'influence des médias				
	News and media	The **passé composé** with **avoir** The **passé composé** with **être** The **passé composé** vs. the **imparfait**	**Le Québec** **Guy Laliberté, un homme hors du commun**	**Court métrage:** *Le Technicien* (**Canada**) **Littérature:** *99 Francs* de Fréderic Beigbeder
Leçon 4 La valeur des idées				
	Human rights Politics	The **plus-que-parfait** Negation and indefinite adjectives and pronouns Irregular **-ir** verbs	**Les Antilles** **Haïti, soif de liberté**	**Court métrage:** *L'hiver est proche* (**France**) **Littérature:** *Discours sur la misère* de Victor Hugo
Leçon 5 La société en évolution				
	Diversity Social change	Partitives The pronouns **y** and **en** Order of pronouns	**L'Afrique de l'Ouest** **Le numérique fait bouger les écoles africaines**	**Court métrage:** *Samb et le commissaire* (**Suisse**) **Littérature:** *Le marché de l'espoir* de Ghislaine Sathoud
Leçon 6 Les générations que bougent				
	Families Stages of life	The subjunctive: impersonal expressions; will, opinion, and emotion Demonstrative pronouns Irregular **-re** verbs	**L'Afrique du Nord et le Liban** **Jour de mariage**	**Court métrage:** *De l'autre côté* (**Algérie/France**) **Littérature:** *La logique des grands* de Olivier Charneux
Leçon 7 À la recherche du progrès				
	Technology and inventions The sciences	The comparative and superlative of adjectives and adverbs The **futur simple** The subjunctive with expressions of doubt and conjunctions; the past subjunctive	**La Belgique, la Suisse, et le Luxembourg** **CERN: À la découverte d'un univers particulier**	**Court métrage:** *Le Manie-Tout* (**France**) **Littérature:** *Solitude numérique* de Didier Daeninckx
Leçon 8 S'évader et s'amuser				
	Leisure activities Sports	Infinitives Prepositions with geographical names The **conditionnel**	**L'océan Indien** **La Réunion, île intense**	**Court métrage:** *Le ballon prisonnier* (**France**) **Littérature:** *Le football* de Sempé-Goscinny
Leçon 9 Perspectives de travail				
	At the office Banking and finances	Relative pronouns The present participle Irregular **-oir** verbs	**L'Afrique Centrale** **Des Africaines entrepreneuses**	**Court métrage:** *Bonne nuit Malik* (**France**) **Littérature:** *Les tribulations d'une caissière* de Anna Sam
Leçon 10 Les richesses naturelles				
	Nature The environment	The past conditional The future perfect **Si** clauses	**La Polynésie française, la Nouvelle-Calédonie, l'Asie** **Les richesses du Pacifique**	**Court métrage:** *L'homme qui plantait des arbres* (**Québec, Canada**) **Littérature:** *Baobab* de Jean-Baptiste Tati-Loutard

Traditional
sequence of study

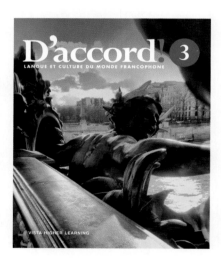

Year 1

Year 2

Year 3

- Sequenced instruction builds interpretive, interpersonal, and presentational communication skills
- Consistent pedagogy enables a seamless transition from year to year

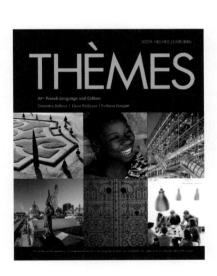

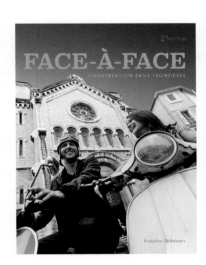

AP®   Advanced

- Focus on personalized language learning enhances the student experience
- A single technology portal built specifically for world language education—vhlcentral

Alternate
sequence of study

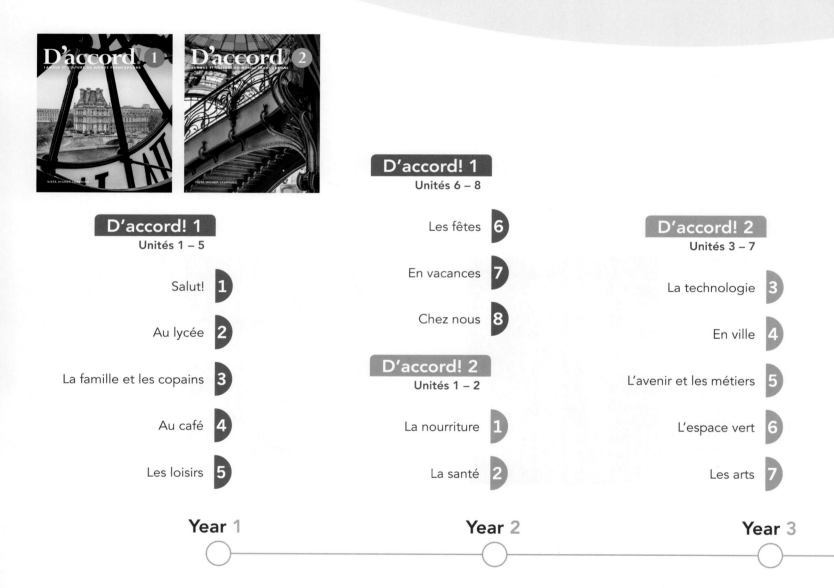

D'accord! 1
Unités 6 – 8

D'accord! 1
Unités 1 – 5

Les fêtes **6**

D'accord! 2
Unités 3 – 7

Salut! **1**

En vacances **7**

La technologie **3**

Au lycée **2**

Chez nous **8**

En ville **4**

La famille et les copains **3**

D'accord! 2
Unités 1 – 2

L'avenir et les métiers **5**

Au café **4**

La nourriture **1**

L'espace vert **6**

Les loisirs **5**

La santé **2**

Les arts **7**

Year 1

Year 2

Year 3

Are you considering a different pace that better accommodates the breadth and depth of the program? Then consider this alternative sequence of study successfully used in schools across the country.

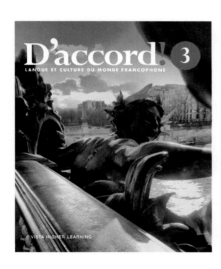

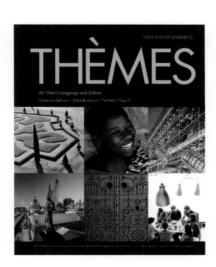

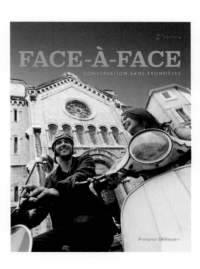

Year 4   AP®   Advanced

Pace **D'accord!** 1 and 2 over three years to give you the flexibility you desire for your program. And no matter which sequence of study you choose, vhlcentral is always there to support instruction and learning.

D'accord! PRIME vs. D'accord! Supersite

At Vista Higher Learning, we recognize that classrooms and districts across the country are implementing technology at varying rates. That's why we offer two levels of technology with **D'accord! Prime** or **Supersite**. The program's flexibility makes it a good fit for any curriculum or infrastructure—both today and for years to come.

For the **Teacher**

COMPONENT	WHAT IS IT?	PRIME	Supersite
Teacher's Edition	Teacher support for core instruction	•	•
Activity Pack (with Answer Key)	Supplementary activities for levels 1 and 2, including: • Additional structured language practice • Additional activities using authentic sources • Communication activities for practicing interpersonal speaking • Lesson review activities	•	•
Audio and Video Scripts	Scripts for all audio and video selections: • Textbook audio • *Cahier de l'élève* audio • Testing Program audio • Video Virtual Chat scripts • *Roman-photo*, *Le Zapping*, and *Flash culture* • Grammar Tutorials	•	•
Cahier de l'élève Teacher's Edition	Workbook with overprinted answers		•
Digital Image Bank	Images and maps from the text to use for presentation in class, plus a bank of illustrations to use with the Instructor-Created Content tool	•	•
Grammar Presentation Slides	Grammar presentation reformatted in PowerPoint	•	•
I Can Worksheets	Unit Objectives broken down by section and written in student-friendly "I Can" statement format	•	•
Implementation Guides	In-depth support for every stage of instruction—from planning and implementation, to assessment and remediation	•	•
Index to AP® Themes and Contexts	Overview chart showing where you can explore the various themes and contexts with students		•
Learning Templates	Pre-built syllabi that provide you with flexible options to suit your On-level and Above-level classes	•	
Lesson Plans	Editable block and standard schedules	•	•
Middle School Activity Pack (with Answer Key)	Hands-on vocabulary and grammar practice designed for younger learners, but effective for kinesthetic instruction for levels 1A, 1B, and 1	•	•
Pacing Guides	Guidelines for how to cover the level's instructional material for a variety of scenarios (standard, block, etc.)	•	•
Program Audio	Audio files for all textbook and *Cahier* audio activities	•	•
Teacher's DVD Set	*Roman-photo/Flash culture* DVD, Teacher Resources DVD	•	•
Testing Program (with Answer Key)	Quizzes, tests, and exams; includes IPAs with grading rubrics	•	•
Testing Program Audio	Audio to accompany all tests and exams	•	•

For the **Student**

COMPONENT	WHAT IS IT?	PRIME	Supersite
Student Edition	Core instruction for students	•	•
Cahier de l'élève	Student workbook with listening and writing practice		•
Audio-synced Readings	Audio to accompany all *Lecture* selections	•	•
Dictionary	Easy digital access to dictionary	•	•
eBook	Downloadable Student Edition		•
eCompanion	Online version of the Student Edition	•	
Enhanced Diagnostics	Embedded assessment activities provide immediate feedback to students	•	
Flash culture Video	Young broadcasters from the French-speaking world share cultural aspects of life	•	•
Grammar Tutorials	Animated tutorials pair lesson concepts with fun examples and interactive questions that check for understanding		•
Grammar Tutorials with Diagnostics	Interactive tutorials featuring embedded quick checks and multi-part diagnostics with real-time feedback and remediation	•	
Learning Progression	Unique learning progression logically contextualizes lesson content	•	
Le Zapping Video	Authentic TV clips from across the French-speaking world	•	•
My Vocabulary	A variety of tools to practice vocabulary	•	•
News and Cultural Updates	Monthly posting of authentic resource links with scaffolded activities	•	•
Online Information Gap Activities	Student pairs work synchronously to record a conversation as they negotiate for meaning to complete a task	•	
Partner Chat Activities	Pairs of students work synchronously to record a conversation in the target language	•	•
Personalized Study Plan	Personalized prescriptive pathway highlights areas where students need more practice	•	
Practice Tests with Diagnostics	Students get feedback on what they need to study before a test or exam	•	•
Pronunciation Tutorials	Interactive presentation of French pronunciation and spelling with Speech Recognition	•	
Roman-photo Video	Engaging storyline video	•	•
Speech Recognition	Innovative technology analyzes students' speech and provides real-time feedback	•	
vText	Virtual interactive textbook for browser-based exploration		•
Video Virtual Chat Activities	Students create simulated conversations by responding to questions delivered by video recordings of native speakers	•	•
Vocabulary Hotspots	Vocabulary presentation with embedded audio	•	•
Vocabulary Spotlights	Automated spotlighting on images with audio	•	
Vocabulary Tutorials (Interactive)	Lesson vocabulary taught in a cyclical learning sequence—Listen & repeat, Match, Say it—with Speech Recognition and diagnostics	•	
Web-enhanced Readings	Dynamic presentation with audio		•

Student-Directed Learning

To effectively learn a new language, students need opportunities for meaningful practice—both inside and outside of the classroom. **D'accord! Prime** provides students with the interactive tools and engaging content they need to stay motivated and on track throughout the school year.

D'accord! Prime is unique in its organization and delivery of lesson content. Each color-coded strand features a progression that contextualizes the learning experience for students by breaking lesson content into comprehensible chunks.

Teacher-Driven Technology

D'accord! Prime allows your unique teaching style to shine through. Use the powerful Assignment Wizard to build courses quickly and easily to meet the needs of each classroom. With this program, you'll have the time and flexibility to create and incorporate your own activities, videos, assignments, and assessments. Adding your own voice is easy—and your students will hear your unique accent loud and clear.

With integrated content, comprehensive resources, and innovative tools, **D'accord! Prime** online provides everything you need to engage students and support language learning—all while making instruction easier.

A powerful setup wizard lets you customize your course settings, copy previous courses to save time, and create your all-in-one gradebook. Grades for teacher-created assignments (pop-quizzes, class participation, etc.) can be incorporated for a true, up-to-date cumulative grade.

Convenient options for grading include spot-checking, student-by-student, and question-by-question approaches. Plus, in-line editing tools and voice comments provide additional opportunities for targeted feedback.

Administer pre-built online quizzes and tests or develop your own—such as open-ended writing prompts or chat activities. You can also add your own text reference, image reference, or word bank to a section of a test.

Tailor your course to fit your needs. Create your own open-ended video Partner Chat activities, add video or outside resources, and modify existing content with personalized notes.

Explore and Learn

Explore and Learn activities engage students, so they can actively learn and build confidence in a safe online environment. With these low-stakes assignments, students receive credit for participation, not performance.

Explore

Explore interactive presentations activate students' prior knowledge and connect them with the material they are about to learn.

Contextes Explore features a multimodal presentation with audio, text, illustrations, and contemporary photos that immerses students in an engaging learning environment.

Contextes Spotlights capture and focus students' attention on key vocabulary from the lesson.

Roman-photo Explore mini video clips in an easy-to-follow storyboard format set the context for the entire episode.

Structures Explore features carefully designed charts and diagrams that call out key grammatical structures as well as additional active vocabulary. Audio and point-of-use photos from the Vocabulary Tutorials and *Roman-photo* episode provide additional context.

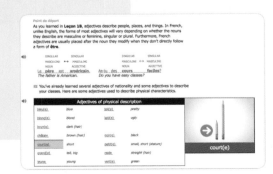

Learn

Learn activities shift from receptive to interactive, inviting students to be active participants and take ownership of their learning. Embedded quick checks give students immediate feedback, without grading or demotivating them.

Vocabulary Tutorials feature a cyclical learning sequence that optimizes comprehension and retention:

- **Listen & repeat:** How does the word look and sound?

- **Match:** Which picture represents the word?

- **Say it:** Do you recognize the picture? Do you know how to say the word?

Audio hints and cognate/false cognate icons help students understand and remember new vocabulary.

Speech Recognition, embedded in the Vocabulary Tutorials, Pronunciation Tutorials, and *Roman-photo*, identifies student utterances in real time and objectively determines whether a student knows the word.

This innovative technology increases student awareness of pronunciation through low-stakes production practice.

Pronunciation Tutorials require students to engage with the material via interactive quick checks throughout each tutorial.

Real-time feedback via embedded Speech Recognition gives students an opportunity to reflect on their language patterns and increases their awareness of pronunciation for more effective speaking and listening skills.

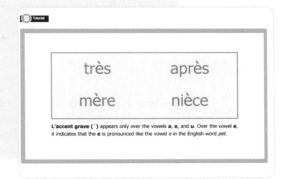

Culture à la loupe features a dynamic web-enhanced presentation of the reading with audio to engage 21st-century learners.

Practice

Practice activities are carefully scaffolded—moving from discrete to open-ended—to support students as they acquire new language. This purposeful progression develops students' confidence and skills as they master new vocabulary and structures.

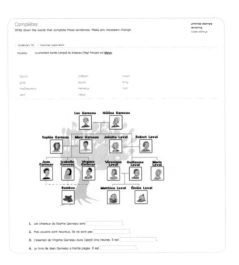

Communicate

Communicate activities provide opportunities for students to develop their oral skills and build confidence. Scaffolded activities expand on the three modes of communication: interpretive, interpersonal, and presentational.

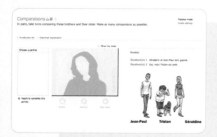

Online Information Gap activities engage student partners in interpersonal communication as they negotiate meaning to solve a real-world task. They also provide opportunities for students to learn how to ask for clarification, request information, and use circumlocution or paraphrasing when faced with misunderstandings.

Self-check

Self-check activities enable students to gauge their performance every step of the way. These low-stakes activities feature real-time feedback and personalized remediation that highlights areas where students may need more practice.

Évaluation personnelle is a self-check activity that provides students with low-stakes diagnostic opportunities for each vocabulary and grammar section. Depending on their performance, students are provided with opportunities for review.

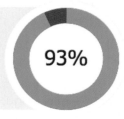

Assessment

A variety of formative and summative assessments allow for varied and ongoing evaluation of student learning and progress. Tailor these assessments to meet the needs of your students.

Épreuve diagnostique is a multi-question practice test in the *Révision* section of each B lesson that provides students with a low-stakes opportunity for assessing their knowledge of the vocabulary and grammar points covered in each unit.

A **Personalized Study Plan** highlights areas where students need additional support and recommends remediation activities for completion prior to the unit test.

World-Readiness Standards
for Learning Languages

D'accord! blends the underlying principles of the *ACTFL Proficiency Guidelines and the World-Readiness Standards for Learning Languages* with features and strategies tailored specifically to build students' language and cultural competencies.

The *Standards* are organized into five goal areas, often called the Five C's: Communication, Cultures, Connections, Comparisons, and Communities. As **D'accord!** takes a communicative approach to the teaching and learning of French, the Communication goal is central to instruction. For example, the diverse formats used in *Communication* activities engage students in communicative exchanges, providing and obtaining information, and expressing feelings and emotions.

The Cultures goal is most evident in the *Culture*, *Le Zapping*, *Flash culture*, and *Panorama* sections, but **D'accord!** also weaves in culture throughout, exposing students to the multiple facets of practices, products, and perspectives of the French-speaking world. In keeping with the Connections goal, students can connect with other disciplines such as geography, history, fine arts, and science in the *Panorama* section; they can acquire information and recognize distinctive cultural viewpoints in the non-literary and literary texts of the *Lecture* sections.

The *Structures* sections feature clear explanations that reflect the Comparisons goal. Students can work toward the Connections and Communities goal when they do the *Culture* and *Panorama* sections' *Sur Internet activities.* Key Standards are called out in the Teacher's Edition wrap.

THE FIVE C'S OF FOREIGN LANGUAGE LEARNING	
Communication	Understand and be understood: read and listen to understand the French-speaking world, converse with others, and share your thoughts clearly through speaking and writing.
Cultures	Experience French-speaking cultures through their own viewpoints, in the places, objects, behaviors, and beliefs important to the people who live them.
Connections	Apply what you learn in your French course to your other studies; apply what you know from other courses to your French studies.
Comparisons	Discover in which ways the French language and French-speaking cultures are like your own—and how they differ.
Communities	Engage with French-speaking communities locally, nationally, and internationally both in your courses and beyond—for life.

Adapted from ACTFL's *Standards for Foreign Language Learning in the 21st Century*

Six-step
instructional design

D'accord! is built around Vista Higher Learning's proven six-step instructional design. Each unit is organized into color-coded strands that present new material in clear, comprehensible, and communicative ways. With a focus on personalization, authenticity, cultural immersion, and the seamless integration of text and technology, language learning comes to life in ways that are meaningful to each and every student.

1 **Context**
Provide students with a place to start. Let them share their own experiences with and about the unit topic.

2 **Vocabulary**
Give students a new linguistic code to express what they already know and experience in the context of the unit theme.

3 **Media**
Once students see that French is a tool for expressing their own ideas, media helps them relate their own experiences to those of native speakers.

4 **Culture**
Bring students into the experience of contemporary French-speaking culture as seen from the perspective of those living it.

5 **Structure**
The formal presentation of relevant grammar and scaffolded, personalized activities help students leverage grammar as a tool for building confidence, fluency, and accuracy.

6 **Synthesis**
Pulling everything together, students integrate context, personal experience, communication tools, and cultural products, perspectives, and practices.

Beginning with the
student in mind

Pour commencer
jump-starts the unit, allowing students to use the French they know to talk about the photo.

All units open with images that provide visual context for the unit theme.

La famille et les copains

Pour commencer
- Qui (*Who*) est sur la photo?
  a. des amis b. une famille c. une classe
- Combien de personnes y a-t-il?
  a. deux b. trois c. quatre
- Où (*Where*) sont-ils?
  a. une cantine b. un café c. un parc

At-a-glance content summaries provide an overview of the vocabulary, grammar, and cultural topics covered in the unit.

Each unit includes two lessons and an end-of-unit **Savoir-faire** section.

Setting the stage
for communication

You will learn how to...
highlights the communicative goals and real-life tasks students will be able to carry out in French by the end of each lesson.

Theme-related vocabulary is introduced through full-color, expansive illustrations and easy-to-use reference lists.

Mise en pratique starts the lesson's activity sequence with controlled practice.

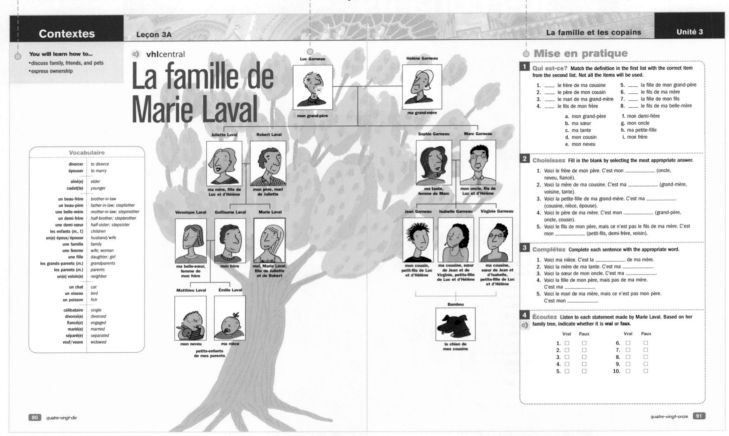

Engaging students in
active communication

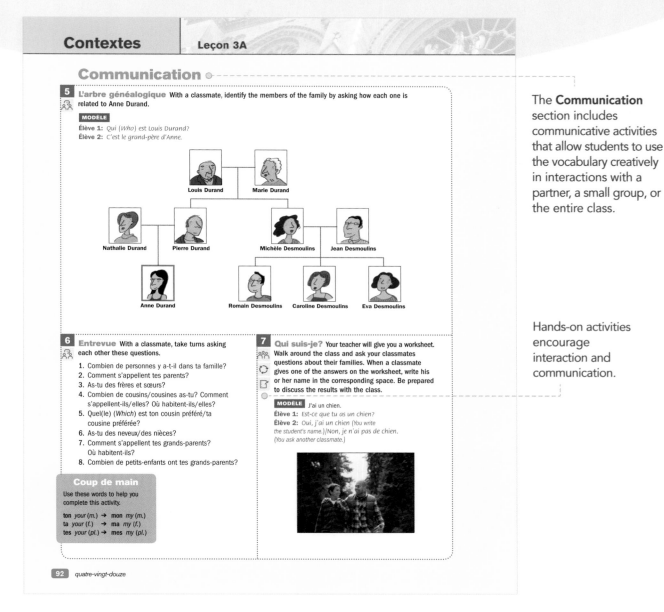

Contextes | Leçon 3A

Communication

5 L'arbre généalogique With a classmate, identify the members of the family by asking how each one is related to Anne Durand.

MODÈLE
Élève 1: Qui (*Who*) est Louis Durand?
Élève 2: C'est le grand-père d'Anne.

6 Entrevue With a classmate, take turns asking each other these questions.

1. Combien de personnes y a-t-il dans ta famille?
2. Comment s'appellent tes parents?
3. As-tu des frères et sœurs?
4. Combien de cousins/cousines as-tu? Comment s'appellent-ils/elles? Où habitent-ils/elles?
5. Quel(le) (*Which*) est ton cousin préféré/ta cousine préférée?
6. As-tu des neveux/des nièces?
7. Comment s'appellent tes grands-parents? Où habitent-ils?
8. Combien de petits-enfants ont tes grands-parents?

Coup de main
Use these words to help you complete this activity.

ton *your (m.)* → mon *my (m.)*
ta *your (f.)* → ma *my (f.)*
tes *your (pl.)* → mes *my (pl.)*

7 Qui suis-je? Your teacher will give you a worksheet. Walk around the class and ask your classmates questions about their families. When a classmate gives one of the answers on the worksheet, write his or her name in the corresponding space. Be prepared to discuss the results with the class.

MODÈLE J'ai un chien.
Élève 1: Est-ce que tu as un chien?
Élève 2: Oui, j'ai un chien (*You write the student's name.*)/Non, je n'ai pas de chien. (*You ask another classmate.*)

92 quatre-vingt-douze

The **Communication** section includes communicative activities that allow students to use the vocabulary creatively in interactions with a partner, a small group, or the entire class.

Hands-on activities encourage interaction and communication.

Video Virtual Chats Students create simulated conversations by responding to questions delivered by video recordings of native speakers. Students benefit from non-verbal and articulatory cues—essential for production and pronunciation.

Authenticity
in pronunciation and spelling

Les sons et les lettres presents the rules of French pronunciation and spelling.

The last activity features illustrative sayings and proverbs to practice the pronunciation or spelling point in an entertaining cultural context.

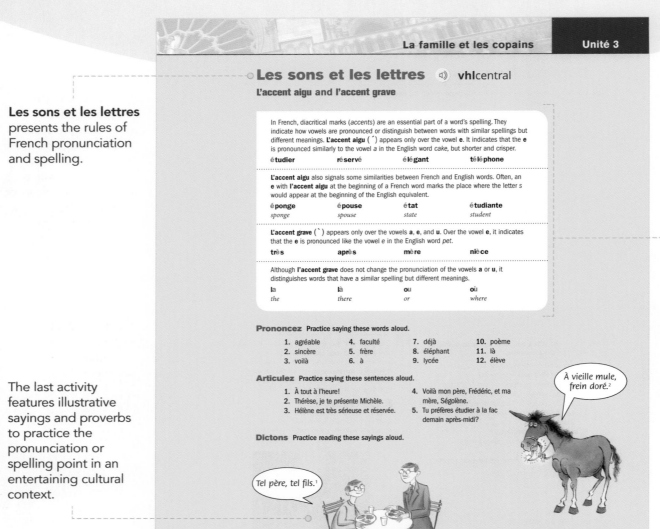

La famille et les copains — Unité 3

Les sons et les lettres — vhlcentral
L'accent aigu and l'accent grave

In French, diacritical marks (*accents*) are an essential part of a word's spelling. They indicate how vowels are pronounced or distinguish between words with similar spellings but different meanings. **L'accent aigu** (´) appears only over the vowel **e**. It indicates that the **e** is pronounced similarly to the vowel *a* in the English word *cake*, but shorter and crisper.

| é**tudier** | ré**servé** | élé**gant** | té**lé**phone |

L'accent aigu also signals some similarities between French and English words. Often, an **e** with **l'accent aigu** at the beginning of a French word marks the place where the letter *s* would appear at the beginning of the English equivalent.

| é**ponge** | é**pouse** | é**tat** | é**tudiante** |
| *sponge* | *spouse* | *state* | *student* |

L'accent grave (`) appears only over the vowels **a**, **e**, and **u**. Over the vowel **e**, it indicates that the **e** is pronounced like the vowel *e* in the English word *pet*.

| trè**s** | aprè**s** | mè**re** | niè**ce** |

Although **l'accent grave** does not change the pronunciation of the vowels **a** or **u**, it distinguishes words that have a similar spelling but different meanings.

| la | là | ou | où |
| *the* | *there* | *or* | *where* |

Prononcez Practice saying these words aloud.

1. agréable
2. sincère
3. voilà
4. faculté
5. frère
6. à
7. déjà
8. éléphant
9. lycée
10. poème
11. là
12. élève

Articulez Practice saying these sentences aloud.

1. À tout à l'heure!
2. Thérèse, je te présente Michèle.
3. Hélène est très sérieuse et réservée.
4. Voilà mon père, Frédéric, et ma mère, Ségolène.
5. Tu préfères étudier à la fac demain après-midi?

Dictons Practice reading these sayings aloud.

À vieille mule, frein doré.[2]

Tel père, tel fils.[1]

[1] Like father, like son.
[2] For an old mule, a golden bit.

quatre-vingt-treize 93

An abundance of model words and phrases focus students' attention on the target sounds and letters.

Media bridges
language and culture

Follow characters through all the levels of **D'accord!**

Roman-photo storyline video brings lesson vocabulary and grammar to life. Students experience local life with a group of students living in Aix-en-Provence, France.

Products, practices, and perspectives are featured in every episode.

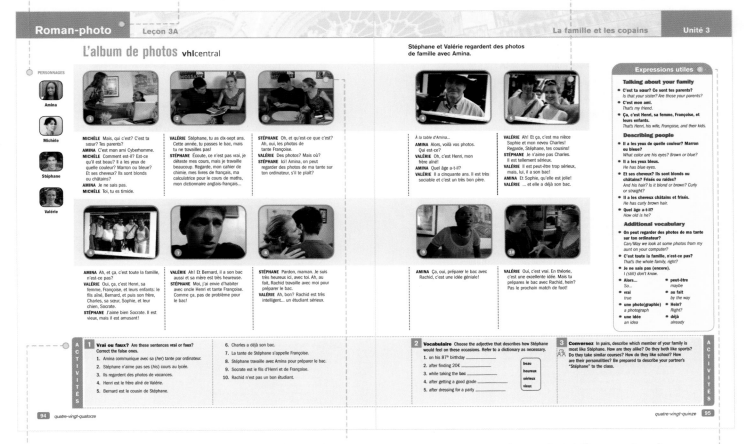

Activities feature comprehension questions, communicative tasks, and research-based tasks.

The easy-to-follow storyboard sets the context for the video, while the dialogue boxes reinforce the lesson's vocabulary and preview the language structures that will be covered later in the lesson.

Expressions utiles organizes the most important words and expressions from the episode by language function, showing how students can apply them in real, practical ways.

Roman-photo Episodes bridge language and culture, providing a glimpse into everyday life in the French-speaking world. Each dramatic segment presents and reviews vocabulary and structures in accurate cultural contexts for effective training in both comprehension and personal communication.

Culture
presented in context

Culture à la loupe explores a topic related to the lesson theme with in-depth cultural information on related products, practices, and perspectives.

Le français quotidien presents familiar words and phrases related to the lesson's theme that are used in everyday spoken French.

Portrait features Francophone personalities, places, and customs that are of interest to students.

Coup de main boxes provide handy, on-the-spot language or cultural information that supports student learning.

Le monde francophone continues the exploration of the lesson's cultural theme, featuring information about various regions of the Francophone world.

Comprehension activities solidify learning.

Sur Internet features additional cultural explorations online.

News and Cultural Updates provide real-world connections to language and culture via authentic articles and videos. From online newspaper articles to TV news segments, each source is chosen for its age-appropriate content, currency, and high interest to students. All selections include scaffolded pre-, during-, and post-reading and viewing activities for a wide range of learning abilities.

Grammar
as a tool not a topic

The **Structures** sections include two grammar points per lesson, each with an explanation and practice activities.

Carefully designed charts and diagrams call out key grammatical structures and forms, as well as important related vocabulary.

Assign **Vérifiez** activities online to give students practice with discrete grammar concepts before they move on to the main practice sequence.

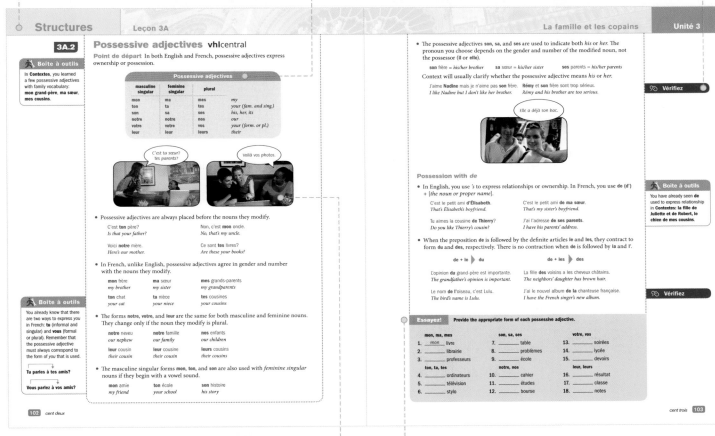

Photos from the **Roman-photo** show the grammar in context.

Essayez! offers students their first comprehensive practice of each new grammar point.

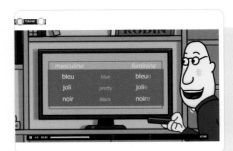

Animated Grammar Tutorials feature guided instruction with interspersed quick checks to keep students on track and ensure comprehension. *Le professeur* provides a humorous, engaging, and relatable twist to grammar instruction.

Carefully scaffolded activities

- - **Mise en pratique** includes contextualized, sequenced activities that practice all the forms and structures in the grammar presentation.

- - **Communication** features pair and group activities for interpersonal and presentational communicative practice.

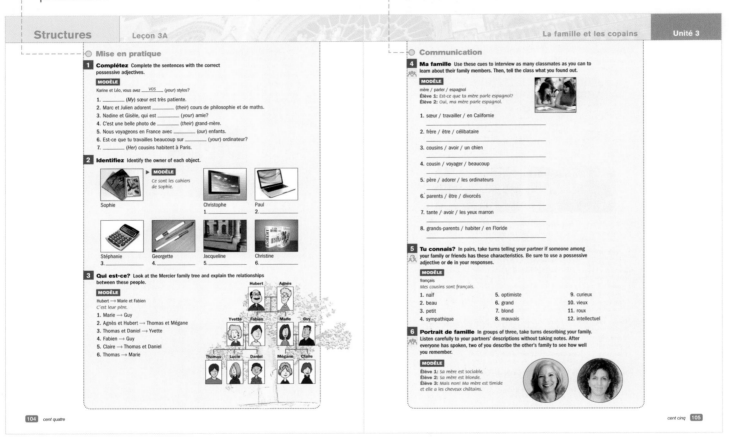

Mise en pratique

1 Complétez Complete the sentences with the correct possessive adjectives.

MODÈLE
Karine et Léo, vous avez ___vos___ (your) stylos?

1. _____ (My) sœur est très patiente.
2. Marc et Julien adorent _____ (their) cours de philosophie et de maths.
3. Nadine et Gisèle, qui est _____ (your) amie?
4. C'est une belle photo de _____ (their) grand-mère.
5. Nous voyageons en France avec _____ (our) enfants.
6. Est-ce que tu travailles beaucoup sur _____ (your) ordinateur?
7. _____ (Her) cousins habitent à Paris.

2 Identifiez Identify the owner of each object.

▶ **MODÈLE**
Ce sont les cahiers de Sophie.

Sophie

Christophe
1. _____

Paul
2. _____

Stéphanie
3. _____

Georgette
4. _____

Jacqueline
5. _____

Christine
6. _____

3 Qui est-ce? Look at the Mercier family tree and explain the relationships between these people.

MODÈLE
Hubert → Marie et Fabien
C'est leur père.

1. Marie → Guy
2. Agnès et Hubert → Thomas et Mégane
3. Thomas et Daniel → Yvette
4. Fabien → Guy
5. Claire → Thomas et Daniel
6. Thomas → Marie

Communication

4 Ma famille Use these cues to interview as many classmates as you can to learn about their family members. Then, tell the class what you found out.

MODÈLE
mère / parler / espagnol
Élève 1: Est-ce que ta mère parle espagnol?
Élève 2: Oui, ma mère parle espagnol.

1. sœur / travailler / en Californie
   _____
2. frère / être / célibataire
   _____
3. cousins / avoir / un chien
   _____
4. cousin / voyager / beaucoup
   _____
5. père / adorer / les ordinateurs
   _____
6. parents / être / divorcés
   _____
7. tante / avoir / les yeux marron
   _____
8. grands-parents / habiter / en Floride
   _____

5 Tu connais? In pairs, take turns telling your partner if someone among your family or friends has these characteristics. Be sure to use a possessive adjective or de in your responses.

MODÈLE
français
Mes cousins sont français.

1. naïf
2. beau
3. petit
4. sympathique
5. optimiste
6. grand
7. blond
8. mauvais
9. curieux
10. vieux
11. roux
12. intellectuel

6 Portrait de famille In groups of three, take turns describing your family. Listen carefully to your partners' descriptions without taking notes. After everyone has spoken, two of you describe the other's family to see how well you remember.

MODÈLE
Élève 1: Sa mère est sociable.
Élève 2: Sa mère est blonde.
Élève 3: Mais non! Ma mère est timide et elle a les cheveux châtains.

104   cent quatre

cent cinq   105

Partner Chat activities enable students to work in pairs to synchronously record a conversation in the target language to complete a specific activity. This collaboration facilitates spontaneous and creative communication in a safe environment.

Targeted review
and recycling

Révision activities integrate the lesson's two grammar points with previously learned vocabulary and structures, providing consistent, built-in review and recycling as students progress through the text.

Interpersonal activities encourage students to demonstrate proficiency with the lesson's vocabulary and grammar.

Révision

1 Expliquez In pairs, take turns randomly calling out one person from column A and one from column B. Your partner will explain how they are related.

MODÈLE

Élève 1: *ta sœur et ta mère*
Élève 2: *Ma sœur est la fille de ma mère.*

A	B
1. sœur	a. cousine
2. tante	b. mère
3. cousins	c. grand-père
4. frère	d. neveux
5. père	e. oncle

2 Les yeux de ma mère List seven physical or personality traits that you share with other members of your family. Be specific. Then, in pairs, compare your lists and be ready to present your partner's list to the class.

MODÈLE

Élève 1: *J'ai les yeux bleus de mon père et je suis fier/fière comme (like) mon grand-père.*
Élève 2: *Moi, je suis impatient(e) comme ma mère.*

3 Les familles célèbres In groups of four, play a guessing game. Imagine that you belong to one of these famous families or one of your choice. Take turns describing your new family to the group. The first person who guesses which family you belong to and where you fit in is the winner.

> La famille Addams
> La famille Kardashian
> Les familles de *Modern Family*
> La famille Weasley
> La famille Simpson

4 La famille idéale Walk around the room to survey your classmates. Ask them to describe their ideal family. Record their answers. Then, in pairs, compare your results.

MODÈLE

Élève 1: *Comment est ta famille idéale?*
Élève 2: *Ma famille idéale est petite, avec deux enfants et beaucoup de chiens et de chats.*

5 Le casting A casting director is looking for actors to star in a new comedy about a strange family. In pairs, role-play a conversation between the casting director and an agent in which you discuss possible actors to play each character, based on these illustrations.

MODÈLE

Élève 1 (**agent**): *Pour la mère, il y a Émilie. Elle est rousse et elle a les cheveux courts.*
Élève 2 (**casting director**): *Ah, non. La mère est brune et elle a les cheveux longs. Avez-vous une actrice brune?*

La famille

le fils   la fille   le père   la mère   le cousin

Les acteurs et les actrices

Michelle   Patrick
Annick
Julie
Laurent
Stéphane   Robert   Émilie

6 Les différences Your teacher will give you and a partner each a similar drawing of a family. Identify and name the six differences between your picture and your partner's.

MODÈLE

Élève 1: *La mère est blonde.*
Élève 2: *Non, la mère est brune.*

Authentic media and listening
for interpretive communication

Le Zapping presents authentic video clips from around the Francophone world connected to the language, vocabulary, and theme of the lesson.

À l'écoute builds students' listening skills with a recorded conversation or narration.

La famille et les copains **Unité 3**

Le Zapping

vhlcentral

Préparation Answer these questions.

1. Les parents sont-ils généreux? Comment? Qu'est-ce qu'ils donnent à leurs enfants?
2. Êtes-vous généreux/généreuse? Comment? Qu'est-ce que vous donnez à vos ami(e)s?

Pages d'Or

The **Pages d'Or** of Belgium offer a range of services that connect businesses with potential customers. Technology is the principal means used by **Pages d'Or** to reach a wide customer base. The **Pages d'Or** website, downloadable PDFs, smartphone and tablet applications, and digital television listings allow consumers to find businesses quickly for the services they need.

publicité ad **Pages d'Or** Golden Pages **je décrocherais la Lune** I would give you the moon

Publicité°: Pages d'Or°

–Pour toi, je décrocherais la Lune°.

Vocabulaire utile

combien	how much
une grue	crane
c'est bien trouvé	now that's a good choice

Compréhension Answer these questions.

1. Qui (Who) sont les deux personnes dans la publicité?
2. Pourquoi l'homme téléphone-t-il pour obtenir (to obtain) une grue?
3. Comment trouve-t-il le numéro de téléphone?

Conversation In small groups, discuss the following.

1. Utilisez le vocabulaire de cette leçon pour décrire les parents idéaux.
2. Décrivez les méthodes que vous utilisez pour trouver le cadeau (gift) idéal pour les personnes que vous aimez.

Application Tell about a time when you used an outside resource to do something special for someone to show him or her how much you cared. Use as much French as you can in your presentation.

cent sept **107**

The scaffolded activity sequence engages students by helping them to understand and apply what they have seen.

La famille et les copains **Unité 3**

À l'écoute
vhlcentral

STRATÉGIE

Asking for repetition/ Replaying the recording

Sometimes it is difficult to understand what people say, especially in a noisy environment. During a conversation, you can ask someone to repeat by asking **Comment?** (What?) or **Pardon?** (Pardon me?). In class, you can ask your teacher to repeat by saying, **Répétez, s'il vous plaît** (Repeat, please). If you don't understand a recorded activity, you can simply replay it.

To help you practice this strategy, you will listen to a short paragraph. Ask your teacher to repeat it or replay the recording, and then summarize what you heard.

Préparation

Based on the photograph, where do you think Suzanne and Diane are? What do you think they are talking about?

À vous d'écouter

Now you are going to hear Suzanne and Diane's conversation. Use **R** to indicate adjectives that describe Suzanne's boyfriend, Robert. Use **E** for adjectives that describe Diane's boyfriend, Édouard. Some adjectives will not be used.

____ brun	____ optimiste
____ laid	____ intelligent
____ grand	____ blond
____ intéressant	____ beau
____ gentil	____ sympathique
____ drôle	____ patient

Compréhension

Identifiez-les Whom do these statements describe?

1. Elle a un problème avec un garçon. _____
2. Il ne parle pas à Diane. _____
3. Elle a de la chance. _____
4. Ils parlent souvent. _____
5. Il est sympa. _____
6. Il est timide. _____

Vrai ou faux? Indicate whether each sentence is **vrai** or **faux**, then correct any false statements.

1. Édouard est un garçon très patient et optimiste.
2. Diane pense que Suzanne a de la chance.
3. Suzanne et son petit ami parlent de tout.
4. Édouard parle souvent à Diane.
5. Robert est peut-être un peu timide.
6. Suzanne parle de beaucoup de choses avec Robert.

cent vingt-cinq **125**

Stratégie and **Préparation** prepare students for the listening passage.

À vous d'écouter guides students through the recorded passage, and **Compréhension** checks their understanding of what they heard.

Le Zapping clips are a great tool for exposing students to target language discourse. This authentic input provides evidence of the correct formulations of the language so that students can form hypotheses about how it works.

Perspective through **geography**

Panorama presents interesting details about Francophone countries and regions.

Maps point out major cities, rivers, and other geographical features while captioned images provide a glimpse into the featured locations.

Art, history, and daily life are brought to life using vivid language and photos.

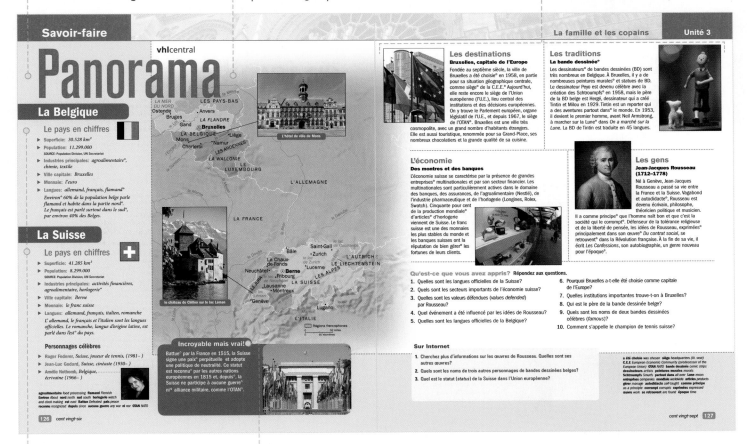

Interesting key facts about the featured location(s) demonstrate the diversity of the Francophone world.

Incroyable mais vrai! highlights an "Isn't that cool?" fact about the featured place or its people.

An **Interactive Map** points out major cities and geographical features and situates the country or region in the context of its immediate surroundings and the world.

Reading skills
developed in context

Avant la lecture presents valuable reading strategies and pre-reading activities.

Context-based readings pull all the unit elements together.

Après la lecture activities include comprehension checks and post-reading expansion exercises.

Graphic organizers, photos, and other visual elements support reading comprehension.

Lecture readings provide students with an opportunity to listen to native speakers as audio-sync highlighting of sentences guides their eyes and makes content more salient.

Writing skills
developed in context

Stratégie boxes provide strategies for preparation and execution of the writing task related to the unit's theme.

Après l'écriture provides post-writing tasks and problem-solving exercises for pairs or groups.

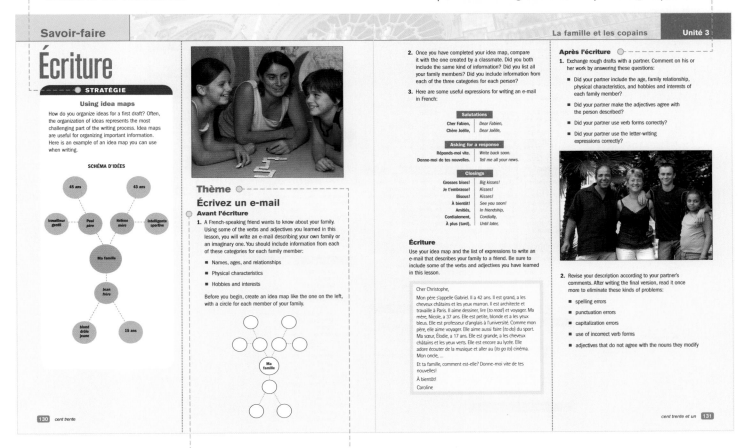

Avant l'écriture includes step-by-step tasks and problem-solving exercises for pairs or groups.

Thème describes the writing topic and includes suggestions for approaching it.

Vocabulary as a reference
and study tool

Vocabulaire summarizes all the active vocabulary in the unit.

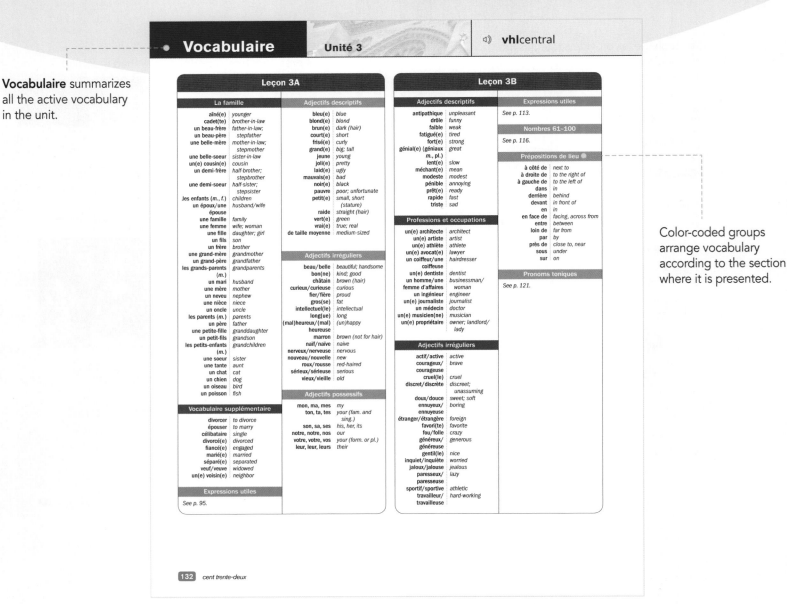

Vocabulaire — Unité 3 — ◀)) **vhl**central

Leçon 3A

La famille

aîné(e)	younger
cadet(te)	brother-in-law
un beau-frère	father-in-law;
un beau-père	stepfather
une belle-mère	mother-in-law; stepmother
une belle-sœur	sister-in-law
un(e) cousin(e)	cousin
un demi-frère	half-brother; stepbrother
une demi-sœur	half-sister; stepsister
les enfants (m., f.)	children
un époux/une épouse	husband/wife
une famille	family
une femme	wife; woman
une fille	daughter; girl
un fils	son
un frère	brother
une grand-mère	grandmother
un grand-père	grandfather
les grands-parents (m.)	grandparents
un mari	husband
une mère	mother
un neveu	nephew
une nièce	niece
un oncle	uncle
les parents (m.)	parents
un père	father
une petite-fille	granddaughter
un petit-fils	grandson
les petits-enfants (m.)	grandchildren
une sœur	sister
une tante	aunt
un chat	cat
un chien	dog
un oiseau	bird
un poisson	fish

Vocabulaire supplémentaire

divorcer	to divorce
épouser	to marry
célibataire	single
divorcé(e)	divorced
fiancé(e)	engaged
marié(e)	married
séparé(e)	separated
veuf/veuve	widowed
un(e) voisin(e)	neighbor

Expressions utiles

See p. 95.

Adjectifs descriptifs

bleu(e)	blue
blond(e)	blond
brun(e)	dark (hair)
court(e)	short
frisé(e)	curly
grand(e)	big; tall
jeune	young
joli(e)	pretty
laid(e)	ugly
mauvais(e)	bad
noir(e)	black
pauvre	poor; unfortunate
petit(e)	small, short (stature)
raide	straight (hair)
vert(e)	green
vrai(e)	true; real
de taille moyenne	medium-sized

Adjectifs irréguliers

beau/belle	beautiful; handsome
bon(ne)	kind; good
châtain	brown (hair)
curieux/curieuse	curious
fier/fière	proud
gros(se)	fat
intellectuel(le)	intellectual
long(ue)	long
(mal)heureux/(mal)heureuse	(un)happy
marron	brown (not for hair)
naïf/naïve	naïve
nerveux/nerveuse	nervous
nouveau/nouvelle	new
roux/rousse	red-haired
sérieux/sérieuse	serious
vieux/vieille	old

Adjectifs possessifs

mon, ma, mes	my
ton, ta, tes	your (fam. and sing.)
son, sa, ses	his, her, its
notre, notre, nos	our
votre, votre, vos	your (form. or pl.)
leur, leur, leurs	their

Leçon 3B

Adjectifs descriptifs

antipathique	unpleasant
drôle	funny
faible	weak
fatigué(e)	tired
fort(e)	strong
génial(e) (géniaux m., pl.)	great
lent(e)	slow
méchant(e)	mean
modeste	modest
pénible	annoying
prêt(e)	ready
rapide	fast
triste	sad

Professions et occupations

un(e) architecte	architect
un(e) artiste	artist
un(e) athlète	athlete
un(e) avocat(e)	lawyer
un coiffeur/une coiffeuse	hairdresser
un(e) dentiste	dentist
un homme/une femme d'affaires	businessman/woman
un ingénieur	engineer
un(e) journaliste	journalist
un médecin	doctor
un(e) musicien(ne)	musician
un(e) propriétaire	owner; landlord/lady

Adjectifs irréguliers

actif/active	active
courageux/courageuse	brave
cruel(le)	cruel
discret/discrète	discreet; unassuming
doux/douce	sweet; soft
ennuyeux/ennuyeuse	boring
étranger/étrangère	foreign
favori(te)	favorite
fou/folle	crazy
généreux/généreuse	generous
gentil(le)	nice
inquiet/inquiète	worried
jaloux/jalouse	jealous
paresseux/paresseuse	lazy
sportif/sportive	athletic
travailleur/travailleuse	hard-working

Expressions utiles

See p. 113.

Nombres 61–100

See p. 116.

Prépositions de lieu ●

à côté de	next to
à droite de	to the right of
à gauche de	to the left of
dans	in
derrière	behind
devant	in front of
en	in
en face de	facing, across from
entre	between
loin de	far from
par	by
près de	close to, near
sous	under
sur	on

Pronoms toniques

See p. 121.

Color-coded groups arrange vocabulary according to the section where it is presented.

leur/leurs ◀)

My Vocabulary enables students to identify, practice, and retain individualized vocabulary for each lesson.

Students can print bilingual word lists. They can also create personalized word lists.

Interactive Flashcards featuring the French word or expression (with audio) and the English translation are available for fast and effective review and practice.

Learning to Use Your **Teacher's Edition**

D'accord! offers you a comprehensive, thoroughly developed Teacher's Edition (TE). It features student text pages overprinted with answers to all activities with discrete responses. Each page also contains annotations for most activities that were written to complement and support varied teaching styles, to extend the already rich contents of the student textbook, and to save you time in class preparation and course management.

In the Teacher Wrap

- **Section Goals** summarize what students will learn and practice in each section

- **Key Standards** list the ACTFL standards that are met in each section

- **Suggestions** offer ideas for working with on-page materials, carrying out specific activities, and presenting new vocabulary or grammar

- **Expansions** present ways to expand or vary the activities on the page

- **TELL Connections** offer suggestions for incorporating the Teacher Effectiveness for Language Learning framework to define and focus on the skills, behaviors, and professional growth of world language educators

- **21st Century Skills** incorporate the Partnership for 21st Century Skills framework to identify and classify skills that high school students need to meet today's workplace requirements

- **Pre-AP®** activity suggestions offer ways for students to work with the materials on the page in a way that prepares them for advanced study

- **Communication Icons** indicate activities that engage students in one of the three different modes of communication:

    Interpretive communication Exercises that target students' reading or listening skills and assess their comprehension

    Presentational communication Ideas and contexts that require students to produce a written or verbal presentation in the target language

    Interpersonal communication Activities that provide students with opportunities to carry out language functions in simulated real-life contexts or engage in personalized communication with others

    Pre-AP is a registered trademark of the College Board, which was not involved in the production of, and does not endorse, this product.

 Please visit **vhlcentral.com** for additional teaching support.

Differentiation

Knowing how to appeal to learners of different abilities and learning styles will allow you to foster a positive teaching environment and motivate all your students. Here are some strategies for creating inclusive learning environments. Point-of-use expansion activities and ideas for differentiation are also provided in your Teacher Wrap.

Learners with Special Needs

Learners with special needs include students with attention priority disorders or learning disabilities, slower-paced learners, at-risk learners, and English-language learners. Some inclusion strategies that work well with such students are:

Clear Structure By teaching concepts in a predictable order, you can help students organize their learning. Encourage students to keep outlines of materials they read, classify words into categories such as colors, or follow prewriting steps.

Frequent Review and Repetition Preview material to be taught and review material covered at the end of each lesson. Pair proficient learners with less proficient ones to practice and reinforce concepts. Help students retain concepts through continuous practice and review.

Multi-sensory Input and Output Use visual, auditory, and kinesthetic tasks to add interest and motivation, and to achieve long-term retention. For example, vary input with the use of audio recordings, video, guided visualization, rhymes, and mnemonics.

Additional Time Consider how physical limitations may affect participation in special projects or daily routines. Provide additional time and recommended accommodations.

Different Learning Styles

Visual Learners learn best by seeing, so engage them in activities and projects that are visually creative. Encourage them to write down information and think in pictures as a long-term retention strategy; reinforce their learning through visual displays such as diagrams, videos, and handouts.

Auditory Learners best retain information by listening. Engage them in discussions, debates, and role-playing. Reinforce their learning by playing audio versions of texts or reading aloud passages and stories. Encourage them to pay attention to voice, tone, and pitch to infer meaning.

Kinesthetic Learners learn best through moving, touching, and doing hands-on activities. Involve such students in skits and dramatizations; to infer or convey meaning, have them observe or model gestures and facial expressions.

Best Practices

The creators of **D'accord!** understand that there are many different approaches to successful language teaching and that no one method works perfectly for all teachers or all learners. These strategies and tips may be applied to any language-teaching method.

Maintain the Target Language

As much as possible, create an immersion environment by using French to *teach* French. Encourage the exclusive use of the target language in your classroom, employing visual aids, mnemonics, circumlocution, or gestures to complement what you say. Encourage students to perceive meaning directly through careful listening and observation, and by using cognates and familiar structures and patterns to deduce meaning.

Cultivate Critical Thinking

Prompt students to reflect, observe, reason, and form judgments in French. Engaging students in activities that require them to compare, contrast, predict, criticize, and estimate will help them to internalize the language structures they have learned.

Encourage Use of Circumlocution

Prompt students to discover various ways of expressing ideas and of overcoming potential blocks to communication through the use of circumlocution and paraphrasing.

Engage all students

Learning French isn't all about grammar and memorization. **D'accord!** provides multiple ways to get students excited about the language and culture of the Francophone world.

Make It Personal

- Find out why students decided to learn French. Is it to speak to relatives? To interact with Francophone friends on social media? To learn more about a particular element of French culture, film, or literature? Keep students motivated by helping them see how individual tasks lead to the larger goal of communicating with French-speaking people. Take the time to explore (and expand on) the **Culture** and **Panorama** sections to engage students with daily life and geography, as well as fine and performing arts.

- Have students talk about themselves! The Teacher's Edition interpersonal communication annotations point out activities where students ask each other questions about their own lives. Personalizing the discussion helps keep students engaged with the material they are practicing in French.

Get Students Talking

Look for icons calling out pair and group work. Some great speaking activities include:

Virtual and Partner Chat activities:

- Offer opportunities for spoken production beyond the face-to-face classroom

- Help reduce students' affective filter and build confidence

- Provide a recorded portfolio of students' spoken work that can be easily graded

Info Gap activities: Give students these worksheets either electronically or in print, and have them work to get information from a partner.

Textbook Activity Worksheets: Get the whole class on their feet to participate in classroom activities, such as surveys, using the language they just learned.

Take Advantage of Multimedia

For students:

- Are your students on YouTube every minute of their free time? Engage them with the video selections in **Le Zapping**.

- Do your students want to study abroad in a Francophone area? Get them engaged with the **Roman-photo** series featuring David, an American studying abroad in Aix-en-Provence. Younger students are fascinated by what older students are doing, so the situations with university students should hold their interest.

- Make learning vocabulary engaging and effective for students with **My Vocabulary** online. They can study the vocabulary for each lesson or customize flashcard banks to study only those words they need to learn for an upcoming quiz. The flashcard tool is ideal for student self-study of vocabulary.

- Provide a humorous, engaging, and relatable approach to gammar instruction with the **Grammar Tutorials** online. They feature guided instruction to keep students on track and ensure comprehension.

For teachers:

- Assign or use the audio-enabled **Vocabulary Presentations** online to give students an interactive experience while they hear the new terms spoken by a native speaker of French.

- Use the **Digital Image Bank** to enliven your own digital or print activities.

- Have students follow along in their text as the selections in **Lecture** are read aloud by a native French speaker.

- Keep grammar instruction focused by using the **Grammar Slides**. Breaking up the instructional points into slides helps make the lesson more digestible.

- Don't forget to use the summaries of the **Roman-photo** to reinforce grammar instruction.

Assessment

As you use the **D'accord!** program, you can employ a variety of assessments to evaluate progress. The program provides comprehensive, discrete answer assessments, as well as more communicative assessments that elicit open-ended, personalized responses.

Testing Program

The **D'accord!** Testing Program offers quizzes for each vocabulary and grammar section, Lesson and Unit tests with listening comprehension, Cumulative Exams, Optional Test Sections, IPAs with rubrics for every unit, oral testing suggestions with grading rubrics, audio scripts for listening comprehension activities, and all answer keys. The quizzes, tests, and exams may be administered online or printed for in-class assessment, and may be customized by adding, eliminating, or moving items according to your classroom and student needs.

Portfolio Assessment

Portfolios can provide further valuable evidence of your students' learning. They are useful tools for evaluating students' progress in French and also suggest to students how they are likely to be assessed in the real world. Since portfolio activities often comprise classroom tasks that you would assign as part of a lesson or as homework, you should think of the planning, selecting, recording, and interpreting of information about individual performance as a way of blending assessment with instruction.

You may find it helpful to refer to portfolio contents, such as drafts, essays, and samples of presentations when writing student reports and conveying the status of a student's progress to his or her parents.

Ask students regularly to consider which pieces of their own work they would like to share and help them develop criteria for selecting representative samples. Prompt students to choose a variety of media to demonstrate development in all four language skills.

Self-assessment

Students can assess their own progress by using "I Can" (or "Can-Do") Statements. The templates provided may be customized to guide student learning within and between units, and to train students to assess their progress.

Integrated Performance Assessments

IPAs give students a real-life task that makes sense to them and engages their interest. To complete the task, students progress through the three modes of communication: they read, view, and listen for information (interpretive mode); they talk and write with classmates and others on what they have experienced (interpersonal mode); and they share formally what they have learned (presentational mode). A critical step in administering the IPA is to define and share rubrics with students before beginning the task so they are aware of what successful performance should look like.

Strategies for Differentiating Assessment

Adjust Questions Direct complex or higher-level questions to students who are equipped to answer them adequately and modify questions for students with greater needs. Always ask questions that elicit thinking, but keep in mind the students' abilities.

Provide Tiered Assignments Assign tasks of varying complexity depending on individual student needs.

Promote Flexible Grouping Encourage movement among groups of students so that all learners are appropriately challenged. Group students according to interest, oral proficiency levels, or learning styles.

Adjust Pacing Pace the sequence and speed of assessments to suit your students' needs. Time advanced learners to challenge them and allow slower-paced learners more time to complete tasks or to answer questions.

The **Vista Higher Learning** Story

Your Specialized Foreign Language Publisher

Independent, specialized, and privately owned, Vista Higher Learning was founded in 2000 with one mission: to raise the teaching and learning of world languages to a higher level. This mission is based on the following beliefs:

- It is essential to prepare students for a world in which learning another language is a necessity, not a luxury.
- Language learning should be fun and rewarding, and all students should have the tools they need to achieve success.
- Students who experience success learning a language will be more likely to continue their language studies both inside and outside the classroom.

With this in mind, we decided to take a fresh look at all aspects of language instructional materials. Because we are specialized, we dedicate 100 percent of our resources to this goal and base every decision on how well it supports language learning.

That is where you come in. Since our founding, we have relied on the invaluable feedback of language teachers and students nationwide. This partnership has proved to be the cornerstone of our success, allowing us to constantly improve our programs to meet your instructional needs.

The result? Programs that make language learning exciting, relevant, and effective through:

- unprecedented access to resources
- a wide variety of contemporary, authentic materials
- the integration of text, technology, and media
- a bold and engaging textbook design

By focusing on our singular passion, we let you focus on yours.

The Vista Higher Learning Team

www.vistahigherlearning.com

D'accord!

LANGUE ET CULTURE DU MONDE FRANCOPHONE

VISTA®
HIGHER LEARNING

Boston, Massachusetts

On the cover: View of the Louvre from the clock at Musée d'Orsay, Paris, France

Publisher: José A. Blanco

Editorial Development: Megan Moran, Sharla Zwirek

Project Management: Brady Chin, Sally Giangrande, Rosemary Jaffe, Faith Ryan

Rights Management: Annie Pickert Fuller, Ashley Poreda

Technology Production: Jamie Kostecki, Reginald Millington, Sonja Porras, Paola Ríos Schaaf

Design: Radoslav Mateev, Gabriel Noreña, Andrés Vanegas

Production: Sergio Arias, Oscar Díez

Student Text ISBN: 978-1-68005-784-3
Library of Congress Control Number: 2017949781

1 2 3 4 5 6 7 8 9 TC 22 21 20 19 18 17

Printed in Canada

D'accord! 1

LANGUE ET CULTURE DU MONDE FRANCOPHONE

Table of Contents

Contextes

Roman-photo

Table of Contents

Table of Contents

Le monde francophone

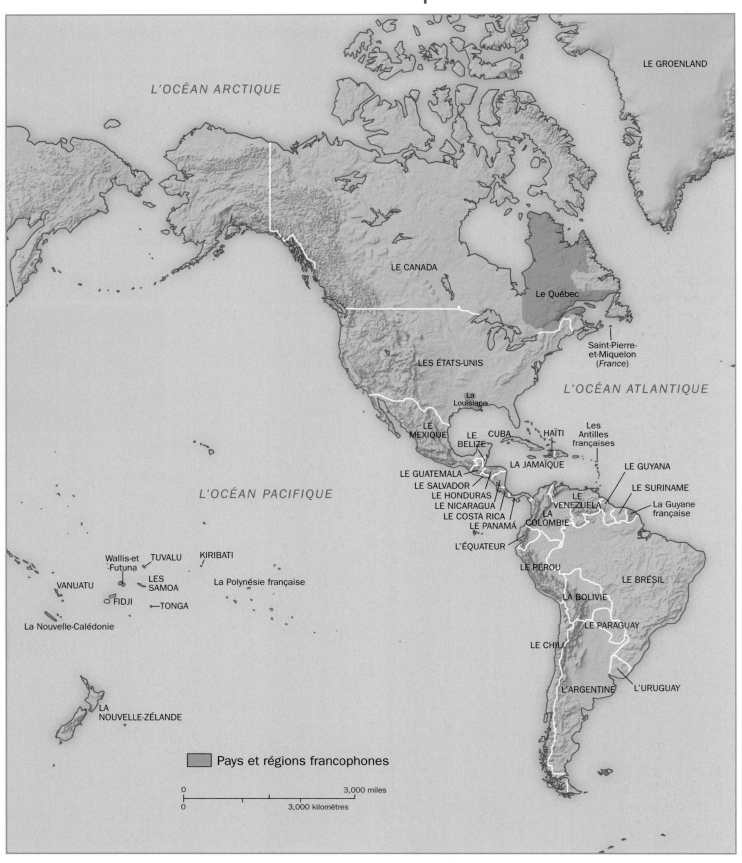

L'OCÉAN ARCTIQUE

LE GROENLAND

LE CANADA

Le Québec

LES ÉTATS-UNIS

Saint-Pierre-
et-Miquelon
(*France*)

L'OCÉAN ATLANTIQUE

La
Louisiane

LE
MEXIQUE

LE
BELIZE

CUBA

HAÏTI

Les
Antilles
françaises

LA JAMAÏQUE

LE GUYANA

LE GUATEMALA

LE SALVADOR

LE HONDURAS

LE NICARAGUA

LE COSTA RICA

LE PANAMÁ

LE
VENEZUELA

LE SURINAME

La Guyane
française

LA
COLOMBIE

L'OCÉAN PACIFIQUE

L'ÉQUATEUR

LE PÉROU

LE BRÉSIL

Wallis-et-
-Futuna

TUVALU

KIRIBATI

VANUATU

LES
SAMOA

FIDJI

TONGA

La Polynésie française

LA BOLIVIE

LE PARAGUAY

La Nouvelle-Calédonie

LE CHILI

L'ARGENTINE

L'URUGUAY

LA
NOUVELLE-ZÉLANDE

Pays et régions francophones

0   3,000 miles

0   3,000 kilomètres

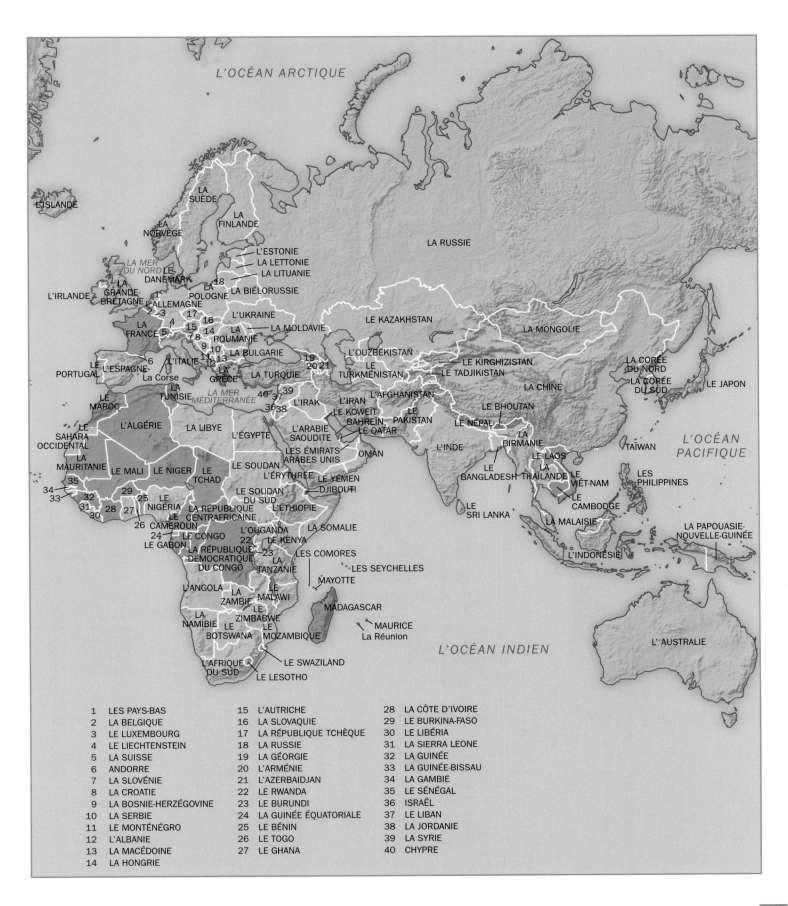

L'OCÉAN ARCTIQUE

L'ISLANDE

LA SUÈDE

LA NORVÈGE

LA FINLANDE

L'ESTONIE
LA LETTONIE
LA LITUANIE

LA RUSSIE

LA MER DU NORD

LE DANEMARK

L'IRLANDE

LA GRANDE-BRETAGNE

LA POLOGNE

LA BIÉLORUSSIE

18

1 L'ALLEMAGNE

2 3

L'UKRAINE

LE KAZAKHSTAN

LA MONGOLIE

4

17 16

5

15 14

LA FRANCE

7 8

LA MOLDAVIE

LA ROUMANIE

9 10

L'OUZBÉKISTAN

LE KIRGHIZISTAN

LA CORÉE DU NORD

6

L'ITALIE

11 13

LA BULGARIE

19

20 21

LE TURKMÉNISTAN

LE TADJIKISTAN

LA CHINE

LA CORÉE DU SUD

LE JAPON

LE PORTUGAL

L'ESPAGNE

12

LA GRÈCE

LA TURQUIE

L'AFGHANISTAN

La Corse

LA TUNISIE

LA MER MÉDITERRANÉE

39

L'IRAK

L'IRAN

LE BHOUTAN

40 37

LE KOWEÏT

LE NÉPAL

LE MAROC

36 38

BAHREÏN

LE PAKISTAN

LA BIRMANIE

TAÏWAN

L'OCÉAN PACIFIQUE

LE SAHARA OCCIDENTAL

L'ALGÉRIE

LA LIBYE

L'ÉGYPTE

L'ARABIE SAOUDITE

LE QATAR

L'INDE

LA MAURITANIE

LES ÉMIRATS ARABES UNIS

OMAN

LE MALI

LE NIGER

LE TCHAD

LE SOUDAN

L'ÉRYTHRÉE

LE YÉMEN

LE BANGLADESH

LE LAOS

LA THAÏLANDE

LE VIÊT-NAM

LES PHILIPPINES

35

LE SOUDAN DU SUD

DJIBOUTI

34

33

29

25 LE NIGÉRIA

L'ÉTHIOPIE

LE SRI LANKA

LE CAMBODGE

31

32

28 27

LA RÉPUBLIQUE CENTRAFRICAINE

30

LA MALAISIE

LA PAPOUASIE-NOUVELLE-GUINÉE

26 LE CAMEROUN

24 LE CONGO

LE GABON

L'OUGANDA

LE KENYA

22

LA SOMALIE

L'INDONÉSIE

LA RÉPUBLIQUE DÉMOCRATIQUE DU CONGO

23

LA TANZANIE

LES COMORES

LES SEYCHELLES

L'ANGOLA

LA ZAMBIE

LE MALAWI

MAYOTTE

LA NAMIBIE

LE ZIMBABWE

MADAGASCAR

LE BOTSWANA

LE MOZAMBIQUE

MAURICE

La Réunion

L'OCÉAN INDIEN

L'AUSTRALIE

L'AFRIQUE DU SUD

LE SWAZILAND

LE LESOTHO

1	LES PAYS-BAS	15	L'AUTRICHE	28	LA CÔTE D'IVOIRE
2	LA BELGIQUE	16	LA SLOVAQUIE	29	LE BURKINA-FASO
3	LE LUXEMBOURG	17	LA RÉPUBLIQUE TCHÈQUE	30	LE LIBÉRIA
4	LE LIECHTENSTEIN	18	LA RUSSIE	31	LA SIERRA LEONE
5	LA SUISSE	19	LA GÉORGIE	32	LA GUINÉE
6	ANDORRE	20	L'ARMÉNIE	33	LA GUINÉE-BISSAU
7	LA SLOVÉNIE	21	L'AZERBAIDJAN	34	LA GAMBIE
8	LA CROATIE	22	LE RWANDA	35	LE SÉNÉGAL
9	LA BOSNIE-HERZÉGOVINE	23	LE BURUNDI	36	ISRAËL
10	LA SERBIE	24	LA GUINÉE ÉQUATORIALE	37	LE LIBAN
11	LE MONTÉNÉGRO	25	LE BÉNIN	38	LA JORDANIE
12	L'ALBANIE	26	LE TOGO	39	LA SYRIE
13	LA MACÉDOINE	27	LE GHANA	40	CHYPRE
14	LA HONGRIE				

L'Amérique du Nord et du Sud

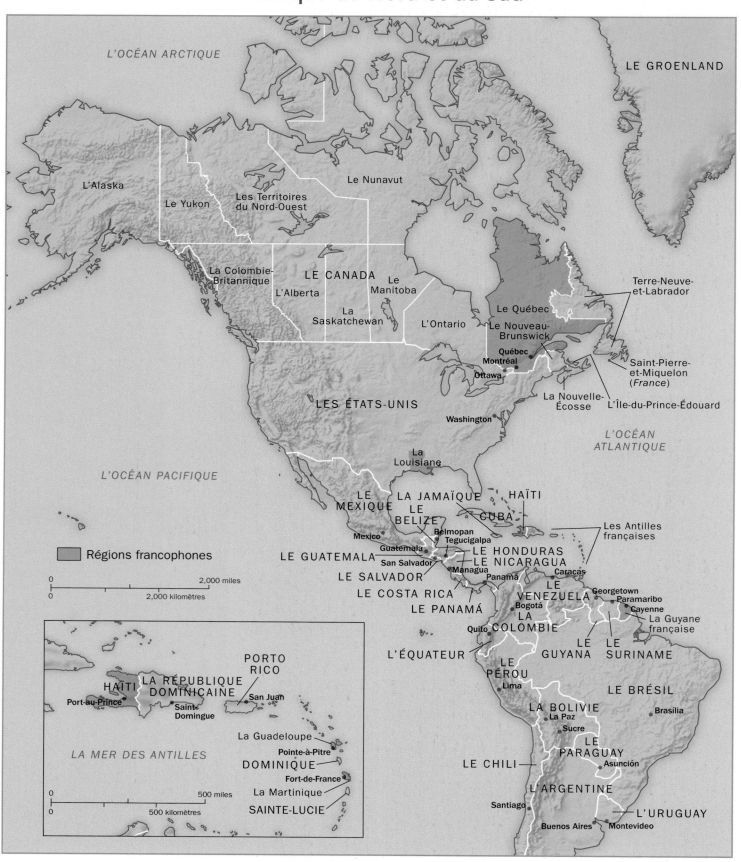

L'OCÉAN ARCTIQUE

LE GROENLAND

L'Alaska

Le Nunavut

Le Yukon

Les Territoires
du Nord-Ouest

La Colombie-
Britannique

LE CANADA

Le Manitoba

Terre-Neuve-
et-Labrador

L'Alberta

La
Saskatchewan

Le Québec

L'Ontario

Le Nouveau-
Brunswick

Saint-Pierre-
et-Miquelon
(France)

Québec
Montréal
Ottawa

La Nouvelle-
Écosse

L'Île-du-Prince-Édouard

LES ÉTATS-UNIS

Washington

L'OCÉAN
ATLANTIQUE

La
Louisiane

L'OCÉAN PACIFIQUE

LE
MEXIQUE

LA JAMAÏQUE

HAÏTI

LE
BELIZE

CUBA

Les Antilles
françaises

Mexico

Belmopan
Tegucigalpa

Régions francophones

Guatemala

LE HONDURAS

0   2,000 miles
0   2,000 kilomètres

LE GUATEMALA

San Salvador

LE NICARAGUA

Managua

Caracas

Georgetown

LE SALVADOR

Panamá

LE COSTA RICA

LE
VENEZUELA

Paramaribo
Cayenne

LE PANAMÁ

Bogotá

LA
COLOMBIE

La Guyane
française

Quito

L'ÉQUATEUR

LE
GUYANA

LE
SURINAME

PORTO
RICO

LE
PÉROU

HAÏTI

LA RÉPUBLIQUE
DOMINICAINE

Lima

LE BRÉSIL

Port-au-Prince

San Juan

LA BOLIVIE

Brasília

Saint
Domingue

La Paz

LA MER DES ANTILLES

La Guadeloupe

Sucre

Pointe-à-Pitre

LE
PARAGUAY

DOMINIQUE

LE CHILI

Asunción

0   500 miles
0   500 kilomètres

Fort-de-France

La Martinique

L'ARGENTINE

SAINTE-LUCIE

Santiago

L'URUGUAY

Buenos Aires
Montevideo

La France

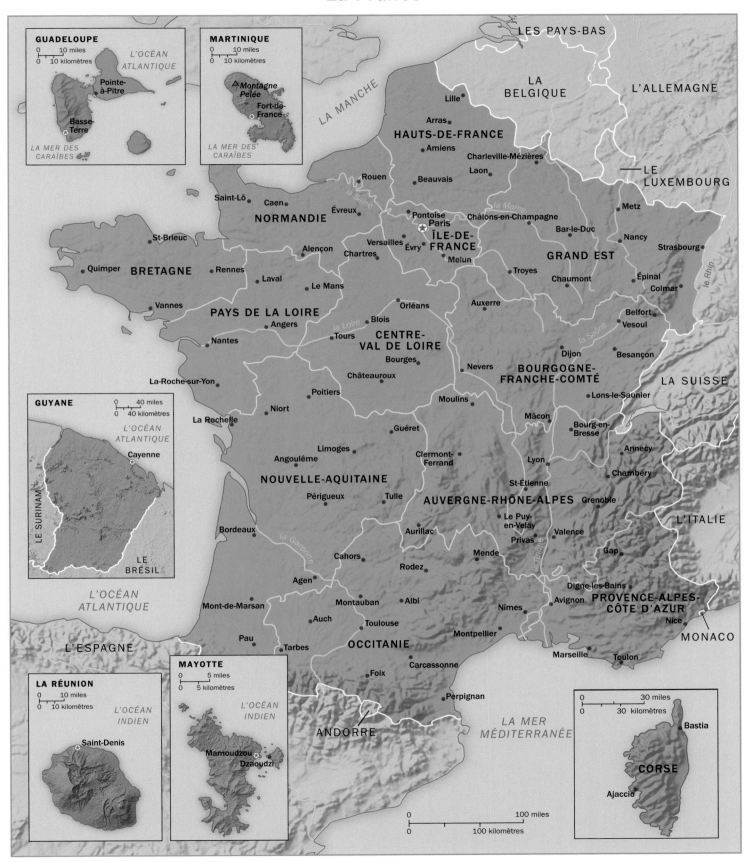

GUADELOUPE
0 10 miles
0 10 kilomètres
L'OCÉAN ATLANTIQUE
Pointe-à-Pitre
Basse-Terre
LA MER DES CARAÏBES

MARTINIQUE
0 10 miles
0 10 kilomètres
△ Montagne Pelée
Fort-de-France
LA MER DES CARAÏBES

LES PAYS-BAS
LA BELGIQUE
L'ALLEMAGNE
LE LUXEMBOURG
LA MANCHE
Lille
Arras
HAUTS-DE-FRANCE
Amiens
Charleville-Mézières
Laon
Beauvais
Rouen
la Seine
Charleville-Mézières
Metz
la Marne
Saint-Lô
Caen
NORMANDIE
Évreux
Pontoise
Paris
Châlons-en-Champagne
Bar-le-Duc
Nancy
St-Brieuc
Versailles
Évry
ÎLE-DE-FRANCE
Melun
GRAND EST
Strasbourg
le Rhin
Quimper
BRETAGNE
Rennes
Alençon
Chartres
Troyes
Chaumont
Épinal
Colmar
Vannes
Laval
Le Mans
Belfort
Vesoul
PAYS DE LA LOIRE
Angers
Orléans
Blois
la Loire
Auxerre
la Saône
Dijon
Besançon
Nantes
Tours
CENTRE-VAL DE LOIRE
Bourges
Nevers
BOURGOGNE-FRANCHE-COMTÉ
La-Roche-sur-Yon
Châteauroux
Moulins
Lons-le-Saunier
LA SUISSE

GUYANE
0 40 miles
0 40 kilomètres
L'OCÉAN ATLANTIQUE
Cayenne
LE SURINAM
LE BRÉSIL
Poitiers
Niort
Guéret
Mâcon
Bourg-en-Bresse
Annecy
La Rochelle
Limoges
Clermont-Ferrand
Lyon
Chambéry
Angoulême
NOUVELLE-AQUITAINE
St-Étienne
Grenoble
L'ITALIE
L'OCÉAN ATLANTIQUE
Périgueux
Tulle
AUVERGNE-RHÔNE-ALPES
Le Puy-en-Velay
Valence
Gap
Bordeaux
Aurillac
Privas
la Garonne
Cahors
Rodez
Mende
le Rhône
Digne-les-Bains
Agen
PROVENCE-ALPES-CÔTE D'AZUR
L'ESPAGNE
Mont-de-Marsan
Montauban
Albi
Nîmes
Avignon
Nice
MONACO

MAYOTTE
0 5 miles
0 5 kilomètres
L'OCÉAN INDIEN
Mamoudzou
Dzaoudzi

LA RÉUNION
0 10 miles
0 10 kilomètres
L'OCÉAN INDIEN
Saint-Denis

Auch
Toulouse
Montpellier
Marseille
Toulon
Pau
Tarbes
OCCITANIE
Carcassonne
Foix
Perpignan
ANDORRE
LA MER MÉDITERRANÉE

0 30 miles
0 30 kilomètres
Bastia
CORSE
Ajaccio

0 100 miles
0 100 kilomètres

L'Europe

0 — 500 miles
0 — 500 kilomètres

Pays francophones

LA MER DE BARENTS

LA MER DE NORVÈGE

L'ISLANDE
Reykjavik

LA SUÈDE

LA FINLANDE
Helsinki

LA NORVÈGE
Oslo
Stockholm

Tallinn
L'ESTONIE

LA RUSSIE

Moscou

LA MER BALTIQUE

Riga
LA LETTONIE

LA MER DU NORD

LE DANEMARK
Copenhague

LA LITUANIE
Vilnius

LA RUSSIE

Minsk

L'IRLANDE
Dublin

LA GRANDE BRETAGNE

LES PAYS-BAS
La Haye

Berlin

LA BIÉLORUSSIE

Londres

Bruxelles
LA BELGIQUE

L'ALLEMAGNE

Varsovie

LA POLOGNE

Kiev

L'UKRAINE

L'OCÉAN ATLANTIQUE

Paris

Luxembourg
LE LUXEMBOURG

Prague

LA RÉPUBLIQUE TCHÈQUE

LA SLOVAQUIE

L'AUTRICHE

Bratislava
Vienne
Budapest

LA MOLDAVIE
Chisinau

LE LIECHTENSTEIN

Berne
LA SUISSE

LA HONGRIE

LA ROUMANIE

LA MER NOIRE

LA FRANCE

Ljubljana
LA SLOVÉNIE

Zagreb

Belgrade

Bucarest

LA CROATIE

LA BOSNIE-HERZÉGOVINE

LA SERBIE

LA BULGARIE

Monte Carlo

Andorre-la-Vieille

L'ITALIE

Sarajevo

Podgorica
LE MONTÉNÉGRO

Sofia
Skopje

LE PORTUGAL

ANDORRE

MONACO

La Corse

Rome

Tirana

LA MACÉDOINE

LA TURQUIE

Madrid

L'ESPAGNE

L'ALBANIE

LA GRÈCE

Lisbonne

La Sardaigne

Athènes

Nicosie

La Sicile

CHYPRE

MALTE
La Valette

LA MER MÉDITERRANÉE

LE MAROC

LA TUNISIE

L'ALGÉRIE

LA LIBYE

L'ÉGYPTE

L'Afrique

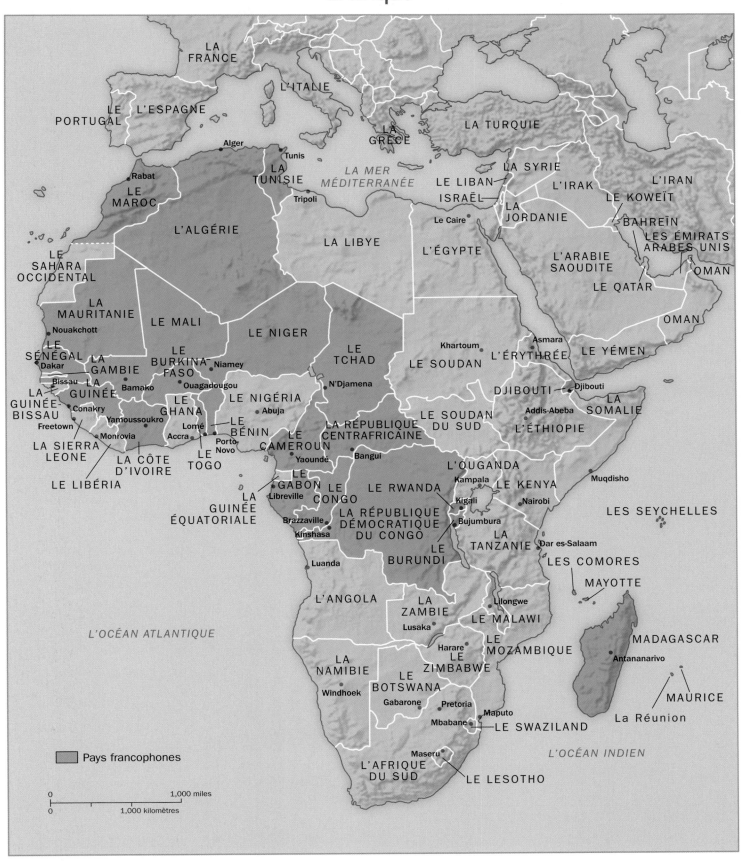

LA FRANCE

L'ITALIE

LE PORTUGAL   L'ESPAGNE

LA GRÈCE

LA TURQUIE

Alger

Tunis

LA TUNISIE

LA MER MÉDITERRANÉE

LA SYRIE

L'IRAN

Rabat

Tripoli

LE LIBAN

LE KOWEÏT

LE MAROC

ISRAËL

LA JORDANIE

BAHREÏN

L'ALGÉRIE

LA LIBYE

L'ÉGYPTE

LES ÉMIRATS ARABES UNIS

Le Caire

L'ARABIE SAOUDITE

OMAN

LE SAHARA OCCIDENTAL

LE QATAR

OMAN

LA MAURITANIE

LE MALI

LE NIGER

Nouakchott

Khartoum

Asmara

LE YÉMEN

LE SÉNÉGAL

LA GAMBIE

LE BURKINA-FASO

LE TCHAD

L'ÉRYTHRÉE

Dakar

Niamey

LE SOUDAN

Bissau

LA GUINÉE

Bamako

Ouagadougou

N'Djamena

DJIBOUTI

Djibouti

LA GUINÉE-BISSAU

Conakry

LE GHANA

LE NIGÉRIA

Abuja

LE SOUDAN DU SUD

Addis-Abeba

LA SOMALIE

Yamoussoukro

Lomé

LE BÉNIN

LA RÉPUBLIQUE CENTRAFRICAINE

L'ÉTHIOPIE

Freetown

Accra

LE CAMEROUN

LA SIERRA LEONE

Monrovia

Porto-Novo

Bangui

LA CÔTE D'IVOIRE

LE TOGO

Yaoundé

L'OUGANDA

LE LIBÉRIA

LE GABON

LE CONGO

LE RWANDA

Kampala

LE KENYA

Muqdisho

Libreville

Kigali

Nairobi

LES SEYCHELLES

LA GUINÉE ÉQUATORIALE

Brazzaville

LA RÉPUBLIQUE DÉMOCRATIQUE DU CONGO

Bujumbura

Kinshasa

LE BURUNDI

LA TANZANIE

Dar es-Salaam

LES COMORES

Luanda

MAYOTTE

L'ANGOLA

LA ZAMBIE

Llongwe

L'OCÉAN ATLANTIQUE

Lusaka

LE MALAWI

MADAGASCAR

Harare

LE MOZAMBIQUE

Antananarivo

LA NAMIBIE

LE ZIMBABWE

LE BOTSWANA

Windhoek

MAURICE

Gabarone

Pretoria

La Réunion

Maputo

Mbabane

LE SWAZILAND

□ Pays francophones

Maseru

L'OCÉAN INDIEN

L'AFRIQUE DU SUD

LE LESOTHO

0   1,000 miles

0   1,000 kilomètres

L'Asie et l'Océanie

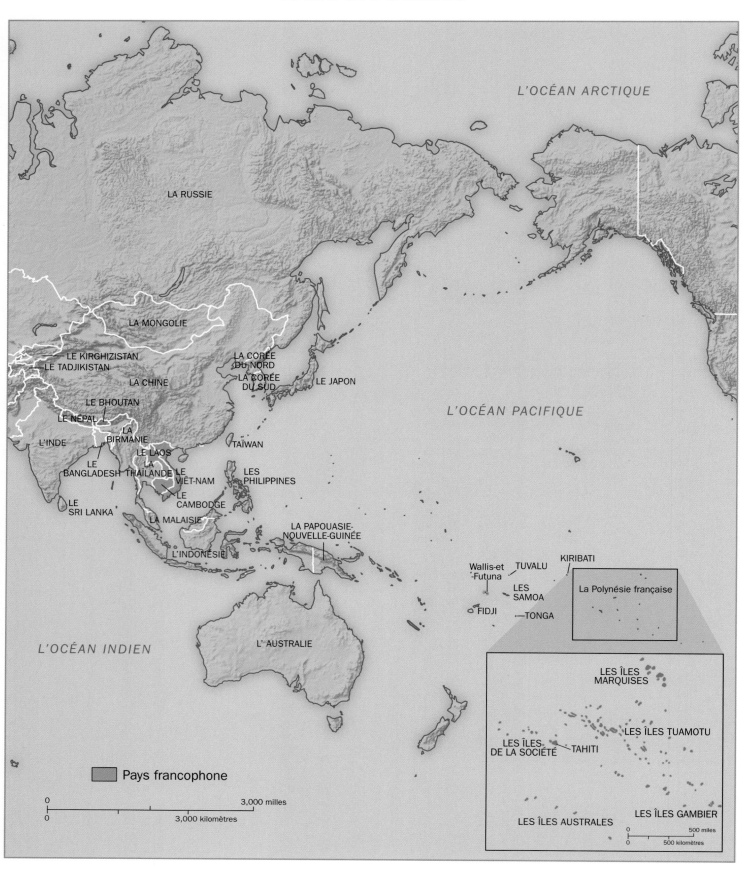

L'OCÉAN ARCTIQUE

LA RUSSIE

LA MONGOLIE

LE KIRGHIZISTAN
LE TADJIKISTAN

LA CHINE

LA CORÉE
DU NORD
LA CORÉE
DU SUD

LE JAPON

L'OCÉAN PACIFIQUE

LE BHOUTAN
LE NÉPAL
L'INDE
LA
BIRMANIE
LE LAOS
LE
BANGLADESH
LA
THAÏLANDE
LE
VIÊT-NAM
LES
PHILIPPINES
TAÏWAN

LE
SRI LANKA
LE
CAMBODGE
LA MALAISIE

L'INDONÉSIE

LA PAPOUASIE-
NOUVELLE-GUINÉE

Wallis-et-
Futuna
TUVALU
KIRIBATI

LES
SAMOA

FIDJI
TONGA

La Polynésie française

L'OCÉAN INDIEN

L' AUSTRALIE

LES ÎLES
MARQUISES

LES ÎLES TUAMOTU

LES ÎLES
DE LA SOCIÉTÉ
TAHITI

Pays francophone

LES ÎLES AUSTRALES
LES ÎLES GAMBIER

| 0 | | 3,000 milles |
| 0 | | 3,000 kilomètres |

| 0 | | 500 miles |
| 0 | | 500 kilomètres |

Roman-photo video program

Fully integrated with your textbook, the **Roman-photo** video series contains 36 dramatic episodes—one for each lesson in Levels 1 and 2, and 6 episodes in the **Reprise** lesson in Level 3. The episodes present the adventures of four college students who are studying in the south of France at the Université Aix-Marseille. They live in apartments above and near Le P'tit Bistrot, a café owned by Valérie Forestier. The videos tell their story and the story of Madame Forestier and her teenage son, Stéphane.

The **Roman-photo** dialogues in the printed textbook are an abbreviated version of the dramatic version of the video episodes. Therefore, each **Roman-photo** section in the text can used as a preparation before you view the corresponding video episode, as post-viewing reinforcement, or as a stand-alone section.

Each episode in Levels 1 and 2 features the characters using the vocabulary and grammar you are studying, as well as previously taught language. Each episode ends with a **Reprise** segment, which features the key language functions and grammar points used in the episode. The first four episodes in the Level 3 **Reprise** lesson review the topics and structures from Levels 1 and 2. The final two episodes bring you up-to-date on the lives of the characters.

The cast

Here are the main characters you will meet when you watch **Roman-photo**:

Of Senegalese heritage
Amina Mbaye

From Washington, D.C.
David Duchesne

From Paris
Sandrine Aubry

From Aix-en-Provence
Valérie Forestier

Of Algerian heritage
Rachid Kahlid

And, also from Aix-en-Provence
Stéphane Forestier

Flash culture video program

For one lesson in each unit, a **Flash culture** segment allows you to experience the sights and sounds of the French-speaking world and the daily life of French speakers. Each segment is from two-to-three minutes long and is correlated to your textbook in one **Culture** section in each unit.

Hosted by narrators Csilla and Benjamin, these segments of specially shot footage transport you to a variety of venues: schools, parks, public squares, cafés, stores, cinemas, outdoor markets, city streets, festivals, and more. They also incorporate mini-interviews with French speakers in various walks of life: for example, family members, friends, students, and people in different professions.

The footage was filmed taking special care to capture rich, vibrant images that will expand your cultural perspectives with information directly related to the content of your textbook. In addition, the narrations were carefully written to reflect the vocabulary and grammar covered in **D'accord!**

Le Zapping

Authentic TV clips from around the French-speaking world connect the vocabulary and theme of each unit. These clips include commercials, newscasts, short films, and TV shows.

Publicité de PagesJaunes

Je souhaiterais° une pièce montée° s'il te plaît.

The French-speaking World

Do you know someone who speaks French? Chances are you do! More than 2 million Americans speak French or one of its varieties at home, and it is the second most common language in some states. It is the official language of more than twenty-five countries and an official language of the European Union and United Nations. English and French are the only two languages that are spoken on every continent of the world.

The Growth of French

Have you ever heard someone say that French is a Romance language? This doesn't mean it's romantic—although some say it is the language of love!—but that it is derived from Latin, the language of the Romans. Gaul, a country largely made up of what is now France and Belgium, was absorbed into the Roman Empire after the Romans invaded Gaul in 58 B.C. Most Gauls began speaking Latin. In the third century, Germanic tribes including the Franks invaded the Roman territories of Western Europe. Their language also influenced the Gauls. As the Roman empire collapsed in the fifth century, people in outlying regions and frontiers were cut off from Rome. The Latin spoken by each group was modified more and more over time. Eventually, the language that was spoken in Paris became the standard for modern-day French.

The French-speaking World

Speakers of French
(approx. 228 million worldwide)

- America and the Caribbean 7%
- Asia and Oceania 1%
- Europe 47%
- North Africa and the Middle-East 12%
- Sub-Saharan Africa and the Indian Ocean 33%

Source: Organisation internationale de la Francophonie

French in the United States

1500   **1600**   **1700**

1534
Jacques Cartier claims territories for France as he explores the St. Lawrence river, and the French establish fur-trading posts.

1600s
French exploration continues in the Great Lakes and the Mississippi Valley. La Salle takes the colony of Louisiana for France in 1682.

1685–1755
The Huguenots (French Protestants) form communities in America. French Acadians leave Nova Scotia and settle in northern New England and Louisiana.

French in the United States

French came to North America in the 16th and 17th centuries when French explorers and fur traders traveled through what is now America's heartland. French-speaking communities grew rapidly when the French Acadians were forced out of their Canadian settlement in 1755 and settled in New England and Louisiana. Then, in 1803, France sold the Louisiana territory to the United States for 80 million francs, or about 15 million dollars. Overnight, thousands of French people became citizens of the United States, bringing with them their rich history, language, and traditions.

This heritage, combined with that of the other French populations that have immigrated to the United States over the years, as well as U.S. relations with France in World Wars I and II, has led to the remarkable growth of French around the country. It is one of the most commonly spoken languages in the U.S., and there are significant populations in Louisiana, Maine, New Hampshire, and Vermont who speak French or one of its varieties.

You've made a popular choice by choosing to take French in school; it is the second most commonly taught foreign language in classrooms throughout the country! Have you heard people speaking French in your community? Chances are that you've come across an advertisement, menu, or magazine that is in French. If you look around, you'll find that French can be found in some pretty common places. Depending on where you live, you may see French on grocery items such as juice cartons and cereal boxes. In some large cities, you can see French language television broadcasts on stations such as TV5Monde. When you listen to the radio or download music from the Internet, some of the most popular choices are French artists who perform in French. French and English are the only two official languages of the Olympic Games. More than 20,000 words in the English language are of French origin. Learning French can create opportunities within your everyday life.

1800   **1900**   **2000**

1803
The United States purchases Louisiana, where Cajun French is widely spoken.

1980s
Nearly all high schools, colleges, and universities in the United States offer courses in French as a foreign language. It is the second most commonly studied language.

2011
In the U.S., French is one of the languages most commonly spoken at home, with over 2 million speakers.

Why Study French?

Connect with the World

Learning French can change how you view the world. While you learn French, you will also explore and learn about the origins, customs, art, music, and literature of people all around the world. When you travel to a French-speaking country, you'll be able to converse freely with the people you meet. And whether here in the U.S. or abroad, you'll find that speaking to people in their native language is the best way to bridge any culture gap.

Learn an International Language

There are many reasons for learning French, a language that has spread to many parts of the world and has along the way embraced words and sounds of languages as diverse as Latin, Arabic, German, and Celtic. The French language, standardized and preserved by the Académie française since 1634, is now among the most commonly spoken languages in the world. It is the second language of choice among people who study languages other than English in North America.

Understand the World Around You

Knowing French can also open doors to communities within the United States, and it can broaden your understanding of the nation's history and geography. The very names Delaware, Oregon, and Vermont are French in origin. Just knowing their meanings can give you some insight into the history and landscapes for which the states are known. Oregon is derived from a word that means "hurricane," which tells you about the windy weather; and Vermont comes from a phrase

City Name	Meaning in French
Bel Air, California	"beautiful air"
Boise, Idaho	"wooded"
Des Moines, Iowa	"of the monks"
Montclair, New Jersey	"bright mountain"

meaning "green mountain," which is why its official nickname is The Green Mountain State. You've already been speaking French whenever you talk about these states!

Explore Your Future

How many of you are already planning your future careers? Employers in today's global economy look for workers who know different languages and understand other cultures. Your knowledge of French will make you a valuable candidate for careers abroad as well as in the United States. Doctors, nurses, social workers, hotel managers, journalists, businesspeople, pilots, flight attendants, and many other kinds of professionals need to know French or another foreign language to do their jobs well.

Expand Your Skills

Studying a foreign language can improve your ability to analyze and interpret information and help you succeed in many other subject areas. When you begin learning French, much of your studies will focus on reading, writing, grammar, listening, and speaking skills. You'll be amazed at how the skills involved with learning how a language works can help you succeed in other areas of study. Many people who study a foreign language claim that they gained a better understanding of English and the structures it uses. French can even help you understand the origins of many English words and expand your own vocabulary in English. Knowing French can also help you pick up other related languages, such as Portuguese, Spanish, and Italian. French can really open doors for learning many other skills in your school career.

How to Learn French

Start with the Basics!

As with anything you want to learn, start with the basics and remember that learning takes time!

Vocabulary Every new word you learn in French will expand your vocabulary and ability to communicate. The more words you know, the better you can express yourself. Focus on sounds and think about ways to remember words. Use your knowledge of English and other languages to figure out the meaning of and memorize words like **téléphone**, **l'orchestre**, and **mystérieux**.

Grammar Grammar helps you put your new vocabulary together. By learning the rules of grammar, you can use new words correctly and speak in complete sentences. As you learn verbs and tenses, you will be able to speak about the past, present, or future; express yourself with clarity; and be able to persuade others with your opinions. Pay attention to structures and use your knowledge of English grammar to make connections with French grammar.

Culture Culture provides you with a framework for what you may say or do. As you learn about the culture of French-speaking communities, you'll improve your knowledge of French. Think about a word like **cuisine** and how it relates to a type of food as well as the kitchen itself. Think about and explore customs observed at **le Réveillon de la Saint-Sylvestre** (New Year's Eve) or **le Carnaval** (or **Mardi Gras**, "fat Tuesday") and how they are similar to celebrations you are familiar with. Observe customs. Watch people greet each other or say good-bye. Listen for sayings that capture the spirit of what you want to communicate!

Listen, Speak, Read, and Write

Listening Listen for sounds and for words you can recognize. Listen for inflections and watch for key words that signal a question such as **comment** (*how*), **où** (*where*), or **qui** (*who*). Get used to the sound of French. Play French pop songs or watch French movies. Borrow books on CD from your local library, or try to attend a meeting with a French language group in your community. Download a podcast in French or watch a French newscast online. Don't worry if you don't understand every single word. If you focus on key words and phrases, you'll get the main idea. The more you listen, the more you'll understand!

Speaking Practice speaking French as often as you can. As you talk, work on your pronunciation, and read aloud texts so that words and sentences flow more easily. Don't worry if you don't sound like a native speaker, or if you make some mistakes. Time and practice will help you get there. Participate actively in French class. Try to speak French with classmates, especially native speakers (if you know any), as often as you can.

Reading Pick up a French-language newspaper or a magazine on your way to school, read the lyrics of a song as you listen to it, or read books you've already read in English translated into French. Use reading strategies that you know to understand the meaning of a text that looks unfamiliar. Look for cognates, or words that are related in English and French, to guess the meaning of some words. Read as often as you can, and remember to read for fun!

Writing It's easy to write in French if you put your mind to it. Memorize the basic rules of how letters and sounds are related, practice the use of diacritical marks, and soon you can probably become an expert speller in French! Write for fun—make up poems or songs, write e-mails or instant messages to friends, or start a journal or blog in French.

Tips for Learning French

- **Listen** to French radio shows, often available online. Write down words you can't recognize or don't know and look up the meaning.

- **Watch** French TV shows or movies. Read subtitles to help you grasp the content.

- **Read** French-language newspapers, magazines, websites, or blogs.

- **Listen** to French songs that you like— anything from a a jazzy pop song by Zaz to an old French ballad by Edith Piaf. Sing along and concentrate on your pronunciation.

- **Seek** out French speakers. Look for neighborhoods, markets, or cultural centers where French might be spoken in your community. Greet people, ask for directions, or order from a menu at a French restaurant in French.

- **Pursue** language exchange opportunities in your school or community. Try to join language clubs or cultural societies, and explore opportunities for studying abroad or hosting a student from a French-speaking country in your home or school.

Practice, practice, practice!

Seize every opportunity you find to listen, speak, read, or write French. Think of it like a sport or learning a musical instrument— the more you practice, the more you will become comfortable with the language and how it works. You'll marvel at how quickly you can begin speaking French and how the world that it transports you to can change your life forever!

- **Connect** your learning to everyday experiences. Think about naming the ingredients of your favorite dish in French. Think about the origins of French place names in the U.S., like Baton Rouge and Fond du Lac, or of common English words and phrases like **café**, **en route**, **fiancé**, **matinée**, **papier mâché**, **petite**, and **souvenir**.

- **Use** mnemonics, or a memorizing device, to help you remember words. Make up a saying in English to remember the order of the days of the week in French (L, M, M, J, V, S, D).

- **Visualize** words. Try to associate words with images to help you remember meanings. For example, think of a **pâté** or **terrine** as you learn the names of different types of meats and vegetables. Imagine a national park and create mental pictures of the landscape as you learn names of animals, plants, and habitats.

- **Enjoy** yourself! Try to have as much fun as you can learning French. Take your knowledge beyond the classroom and find ways to make your learning experience your very own.

Common Names

Get started learning French by using a French name in class. You can choose from the lists on these pages, or you can find one yourself. How about learning the French equivalent of your name? The most popular French names for girls are Emma, Léa, Chloé, Manon, and Inès. The most popular French names for boys are Nathan, Lucas, Enzo, Léo, and Louis. Is your name, or that of someone you know, in the French top five?

More Boys' Names	More Girls' Names
Thomas	Lola
Gabriel	Zoé
Théo	Alice
Hugo	Louise
Maxime	Camille
Alexandre	Océane
Antoine	Marie
Adam	Sarah
Quentin	Clara
Clément	Lilou
Nicolas	Laura
Alexis	Julie
Romain	Mathilde
Raphaël	Lucie
Valentin	Anaïs
Noah	Pauline
Julien	Margot
Paul	Lisa
Baptiste	Eva
Tom	Justine
Jules	Maéva
Arthur	Jade
Benjamin	Juliette
Mohamed	Charlotte
Mathis	Émilie

The top five names for boys:	The top five names for girls:
Nathan	Emma
Lucas	Léa
Enzo	Chloé
Léo	Manon
Louis	Inès

Useful French Expressions

The following expressions will be very useful in getting you started learning French. You can use them in class to check your understanding, and to ask and answer questions about the lessons. Learn these ahead of time to help you understand direction lines in French, as well as your teacher's instructions. Remember to practice your French as often as you can!

Expressions utiles	Useful expressions
Allez à la page 2.	Go to page 2.
Alternez les rôles.	Switch roles.
À tour de rôle...	Take turns...
À voix haute	Aloud
À votre/ton avis	In your opinion
Après une deuxième écoute...	After a second listen...
Articulez.	Enunciate.; Pronounce carefully.
Au sujet de, À propos de	Regarding/about
Avec un(e) partenaire/ un(e) camarade de classe	With a partner/a classmate
Avez-vous/As-tu des questions?	Do you have any questions?
Avez-vous/As-tu fini/ terminé?	Are you done?/Have you finished?
Chassez l'intrus.	Choose the item that doesn't belong.
Choisissez le bon mot.	Choose the right word.
Circulez dans la classe.	Walk around the classroom.
Comment dit-on ____ en français?	How do you say ____ in French?
Comment écrit-on ____ en français?	How do you spell ____ in French?

Expressions utiles	Useful expressions
Corrigez les phrases fausses.	Correct the false statements.
Créez/Formez des phrases...	Create/Form sentences...
D'après vous/Selon vous...	According to you...
Décrivez les images/ dessins...	Describe the images/ drawings...
Désolé(e), j'ai oublié.	I'm sorry, I forgot.
Déterminez si...	Decide whether...
Dites si vous êtes/Dis si tu es d'accord ou non.	Say if you agree or not.
Écrivez une lettre/ une phrase.	Write a letter/a sentence.
Employez les verbes de la liste.	Use the verbs from the list.
En utilisant...	Using...
Est-ce que vous pouvez/tu peux choisir un(e) autre partenaire/ quelqu'un d'autre?	Can you please choose... another partner/someone else?
Êtes vous prêt(e)?/ Es-tu prêt(e)?	Are you ready?
Excusez-moi, je suis en retard.	Excuse me for being late.
Faites correspondre...	Match...
Faites les accords nécessaires.	Make the necessary agreements.

Expressions utiles	Useful expressions
Félicitations!	Congratulations!
Indiquez le mot qui ne va pas avec les autres.	Indicate the word that doesn't belong.
Indiquez qui a dit…	Indicate who said…
J'ai gagné!/Nous avons gagné!	I won!/We won!
Je n'ai pas/Nous n'avons pas encore fini.	I/We have not finished yet.
Je ne comprends pas.	I don't understand.
Je ne sais pas.	I don't know.
Je ne serai pas là demain.	I won't be here tomorrow.
Je peux continuer?	May I continue?
Jouez le rôle de…/ la scène…	Play the role of…/ the scene…
Lentement, s'il vous plaît.	Slowly, please.
Lisez…	Read…
Mettez dans l'ordre…	Put in order…
Ouvrez/Fermez votre livre.	Open/Close your books.
Par groupes de trois/ quatre…	In groups of three/four…
Partagez vos résultats…	Share your results…
Posez-vous les questions suivantes.	Ask each other the following questions.
Pour demain, faites…	For tomorrow, do…

Expressions utiles	Useful expressions
Pour demain, vous allez/tu vas faire…	For tomorrow you are going to do…
Prononcez.	Pronounce.
Qu'est-ce que ____ veut dire?	What does ____ mean?
Que pensez-vous/ penses-tu de…	What do you think about…
Qui a gagné?	Who won?
…qui convient le mieux.	…that best completes/is the most appropriate.
Rejoignez un autre groupe.	Get together with another group.
Remplissez les espaces.	Fill in the blanks.
Répondez aux questions suivantes.	Answer the following questions.
Soyez prêt(e)s à…	Be ready to…
Venez/Viens au tableau.	Come to the board.
Vous comprenez?/ Tu comprends?	Do you understand?
Vous pouvez nous expliquer/m'expliquer encore une fois, s'il vous plaît?	Could you explain again, please?
Vous pouvez répéter, s'il vous plaît?	Could you repeat that, please?
Vrai ou faux?	True or false?

Acknowledgments

On behalf of its authors and editors, Vista Higher Learning expresses its sincere appreciation to the many educators nationwide who reviewed materials from **D'accord!** Their input and suggestions were vitally helpful in forming and shaping the program in its final, published form.

We also extend a special thank you to Mayanne Wright, Stephen Adamson, and Séverine Champeny, whose hard work was central to bringing **D'accord!** to fruition.

We are especially grateful to Norah Jones, for her continued support and feedback regarding all aspects of the text.

Reviewers

Rachel Safier Albino
  Saint Francis High School
  Mountain View, CA

Erin Austin
  Poudre High School
  Fort Collins, CO

Rebecca Barck
  The Bryn Mawr School
  Baltimore, MD

Jennifer Barnhill
  The Archer School for Girls
  Los Angeles, CA

Michael Battle
  Saint Francis High School
  Mountain View, CA

Mary Bell
  St Mary's Episcopal School
  Memphis, TN

Morgan Benz
  Drew School
  San Francisco, CA

Marie France Bernard
  Carrollton School of the Sacred Heart
  Miami, FL

Joyce Besserer
  Brookfield Academy
  Brookfield, WI

Cree Bol
  Polaris Expeditionary School
  Fort Collins, CO

Greta Brewer
  West Boca High School
  Boca Raton, FL

Kari Bridenbaugh
  Rocky Mountain High School
  Fort Collins, CO

Bradey Bulk
  Wilmington Friends School
  Wilmington, DE

Chantal Cassan
  St Andrew's Episcopal School
  Potomac, MD

Christi Castenson
  West Aurora High School
  Aurora, IL

Anna Maria Cherubin
  Eleanor Roosevelt High School
  Greenbelt, MD

Ines du Cos de La Hitte
  Sierra Canyon School
  Chatsworth, CA

Amaris Cuchanski
  Falmouth Academy
  Falmouth, MA

Isabelle Daly
  Ranney School
  Tinton Falls, NJ

Silvana Dessi-Olive
  The Blake School
  Minneapolis, MN

Michele Diament
  Collins Hill High School
  Suwanee, GA

Catherine Douglas
  Xaverian Brothers High School
  Westwood, MA

Parthena Draggett
  Community School of Naples
  Naples, FL

Jillian Eilert
  Avon High School
  Avon, IN

Erin Feltman
  Timberline High School
  Olympia, WA

Kristine Finnegan
  Kempsville High School
  Virginia Beach, VA

Mary Beth Fischer
  Kinard Core Knowledge Middle School
  Fort Collins, CO

Kimberly Fogelson
  Dominion High School
  Sterling, VA

Acknowledgments

Kevin Giggy
Mitchell High School
Mitchell, IN

Lee Holcomb
Inspire School of Arts & Sciences
Chico, CA

Anne Jackson
Holy Innocents Episcopal School
Atlanta, GA

Debra Jukich
Mead High School
Longmont, CO

Kimberley Jurawan
The Benjamin School
Palm Beach Gardens, FL

Catalina Keilhauer
The Madeira School
McLean, VA

Benjamin Lizotte
St. John's High School
Shrewsbury, MA

Jean Mari Hernandez Lopez
Westtown School
West Chester, PA

Sabrina Maggio
Marist High School
Chicago, IL

Miranda Markland
Preston Middle School
Fort Collins, CO

Michelle Martin
Brebeuf Jesuit Preparatory School
Indianapolis, IN

Patricia Massey
Potomac Falls High School
Potomac Falls, VA

Thomas Michaud
Nichols School
Buffalo, NY

Caron Morton
Suncoast Community High School
Riviera Beach, FL

Nadine Paulsen
Archbishop Mitty High School
San Jose, CA

Marilyn Payton
St. John XXIII College Preparatory
Katy, TX

Rebecca Philippone
Greene High School
Greene, NY

Sarah du Plessis
Hopkins School
New Haven, CT

Tom Pozen
Saint Ignatius College Prep
Chicago, IL

Meghan Primm
Mill Creek High School
Hoschton, GA

Carolyn Quinby
Terra Linda High School
San Rafael, CA

Philippe Radelet
Benjamin Franklin High School
New Orleans, LA

Caroline Ridenour
Heritage Christian School
North Hills, CA

Donna Romanick
Pope John XXIII High School
Sparta, NJ

Tracy Rucker
Louisville Collegiate School
Louisville, KY

Katherine Saxby
Orinda Academy
Orinda, CA

Sarah Sexton
Fossil Ridge High School
Fort Collins, CO

Ellen Spence
Beavercreek High School
Beavercreek, OH

Suzanne Stluka
The New School of Northern Virginia
Fairfax, VA

Maggie Strahl
Bishop Fenwick High School
Franklin, OH

Cammie Williams
William Byrd High School
Vinton, VA

Pachao Yajcherthao
The Blake School
Minneapolis, MN

Valerie Yoshimura
The Archer School for Girls
Los Angeles, CA

Salut!

Pour commencer
- What are these people saying?
  a. Excusez-moi. b. Bonjour! c. Merci.
- How many people are there in the photo?
  a. une personne b. deux personnes
  c. trois personnes
- What do you think is an appropriate title for the person on the left?
  a. Monsieur b. Madame c. Mademoiselle

Unit Goals
Leçon 1A
In this lesson, students will learn:
- terms for greetings, farewells, and introductions
- expressions of courtesy
- the French alphabet and the names of accent marks
- about shaking hands and **bises**
- more about greetings and farewells through specially shot video footage
- gender of nouns
- articles (definite and indefinite)
- the numbers 0–60
- the expression **il y a**
- about the **Institut national de prévention et d'éducation pour la santé**

Leçon 1B
In this lesson, students will learn:
- terms to identify people
- terms for objects in the classroom
- rules for silent letters
- about France's multicultural society
- subject pronouns
- the present tense of **être**
- **c'est** and **il/elle est**
- adjective agreement
- some descriptive adjectives and adjectives of nationality
- to listen for familiar words

Savoir-faire
In this section, students will learn:
- cultural, linguistic, and historical information about the Francophone world
- to recognize cognates
- strategies for writing in French
- to write a telephone/address book

 21ˢᵗ Century Skills

Initiative and Self-Direction
Students can monitor their progress online using the activities and assessments on vhlcentral.com.

Pour commencer
- b. Bonjour!
- b. deux personnes
- c. Mademoiselle

SUPPORT FOR BACKWARD DESIGN

Unité 1 **Essential Questions**
1. How do people greet one another?
2. How do people make introductions?
3. In what parts of the world do people speak French?

Unité 1 **Integrated Performance Assessment**
Before teaching the chapter, review the Integrated Performance Assessment (IPA) and its accompanying scoring rubric provided in the Testing Program. Use the IPA to assess students' progress toward proficiency targets at the end of the chapter.
IPA Context: You and your classmates want to attend an event in honor of the **Journée Internationale de la Francophonie**. In anticipation of meeting people from the French-speaking world, you and a partner will practice greeting French speakers from a variety of countries.

FORUMS

Forums on vhlcentral.com allow you and your students to record and share audio messages.
Use Forums for presentations, oral assessments, discussions, directions, etc.

You will learn how to...
- greet people in French
- say good-bye

◁)) **vhl**central

Ça va?

GEORGES Ça va, Henri?
HENRI Oui, ça va très bien, merci. Et vous, comment allez-vous?
GEORGES Je vais bien, merci.

PAUL Merci!
JEAN Il n'y a pas de quoi.

Vocabulaire

Bonsoir.	Good evening.; Hello.
À bientôt.	See you soon.
À demain.	See you tomorrow.
Bonne journée!	Have a good day!
Au revoir.	Good-bye.
Comme ci, comme ça.	So-so.
Je vais bien/mal.	I am doing well/badly.
Moi aussi.	Me too.
Comment t'appelles-tu? *(fam.)*	What is your name?
Je vous/te présente... *(form./fam.)*	I would like to introduce (name) to you.
De rien.	You're welcome.
Excusez-moi. *(form.)*	Excuse me.
Excuse-moi. *(fam.)*	Excuse me.
Merci beaucoup.	Thanks a lot.
Pardon.	Pardon (me).
S'il vous plaît. *(form.)*	Please.
S'il te plaît. *(fam.)*	Please.
Je vous/t'en prie. *(form./fam.)*	You're welcome.; It's nothing.
Monsieur (M.)	Sir (Mr.)
Madame (Mme)	Ma'am (Mrs.)
Mademoiselle (Mlle)	Miss
ici	here
là	there
là-bas	over there

MARIE À plus tard, Guillaume!
GUILLAUME À tout à l'heure, Marie!

JACQUES Bonjour, Monsieur Boniface. Je vous présente Thérèse Lemaire.
M. BONIFACE Bonjour, Mademoiselle.
THÉRÈSE Enchantée.

2 deux

Mise en pratique

Attention!

In French, people can be addressed formally or informally. Use the **tu/toi** forms with close friends, family, or children. Use the **vous** forms with groups, a boss, adults, or someone you do not know, unless they ask you to use **tu**.

MARC Bonjour, je m'appelle Marc, et vous, comment vous appelez-vous?
ANNIE Je m'appelle Annie.
MARC Enchanté.

1 Chassez l'intrus Circle the word or expression that does not belong.

1. a. Bonjour.
   b. Bonsoir.
   c. Salut.
   d. Pardon. *(circled)*
2. a. Bien.
   b. Très bien.
   c. De rien. *(circled)*
   d. Comme ci, comme ça.
3. a. À bientôt.
   b. À demain.
   c. À tout à l'heure.
   d. Enchanté. *(circled)*
4. a. Comment allez-vous?
   b. Comment vous appelez-vous? *(circled)*
   c. Ça va?
   d. Comment vas-tu?

5. a. Pas mal. *(circled)*
   b. Excuse-moi.
   c. Je vous en prie.
   d. Il n'y a pas de quoi.
6. a. Comment vous appelez-vous?
   b. Je vous présente Dominique.
   c. Enchanté.
   d. Comment allez-vous? *(circled)*
7. a. Pas mal.
   b. Très bien.
   c. Mal.
   d. Et vous? *(circled)*
8. a. Comment allez-vous?
   b. Comment vous appelez-vous?
   c. Et toi? *(circled)*
   d. Je vous en prie.

2 Écoutez Listen to each of these questions or statements and select the most appropriate response.

1.	Enchanté. ☐		Je m'appelle Thérèse. ☑
2.	Merci beaucoup. ☐		Je vous en prie. ☑
3.	Comme ci, comme ça. ☑		De rien. ☐
4.	Bonsoir, Monsieur. ☑		Moi aussi. ☐
5.	Enchanté. ☑		Et toi? ☐
6.	Bonjour. ☐		À demain. ☑
7.	Pas mal. ☑		Pardon. ☐
8.	Il n'y a pas de quoi. ☑		Moi aussi. ☐
9.	Enchanté. ☐		Très bien. Et vous? ☑
10.	À bientôt. ☑		Mal. ☐

3 Conversez Madeleine is introducing her classmate Khaled to Libby, an American exchange student. Complete their conversation, using a different expression from **CONTEXTES** in each blank. *Answers will vary.*

MADELEINE (1) ___Bonjour/Salut___ !
KHALED Salut, Madeleine. (2) ___Comment vas-tu?/ Comment ça va___?
MADELEINE Pas mal. (3) ___Et toi, comment vas-tu?/ Et toi, ça va___?
KHALED (4) ___Je vais (très) bien/ (Très) bien___, merci.
MADELEINE (5) ___Je te présente___ Libby. Elle est de (*She is from*) Boston.
KHALED (6) ___Enchanté___, Libby. (7) ___Je m'appelle___ Khaled.
(8) ___Comment vas-tu/Ça va___?
LIBBY (9) ___Je vais (très) bien/ Ça va (très) bien___, merci.
KHALED Oh, là, là. Je vais rater (*I am going to miss*) le bus. À bientôt.
MADELEINE (10) ___Au revoir/À bientôt___.
LIBBY (11) ___Au revoir/À bientôt___.

SOPHIE Bonjour, Catherine!
CATHERINE Salut, Sophie!
SOPHIE Ça va?
CATHERINE Oui, ça va bien, merci. Et toi, comment vas-tu?
SOPHIE Pas mal.

4 Suggestions
- Before beginning the activity, encourage students to use as many different words and expressions as they can from the **Vocabulaire** on page 2 rather than repeating the same expressions in each conversation.
- Have a few volunteers write their conversations on the board. Ask the class to identify, correct, and explain any errors.

4 Virtual Chat You can also assign **Conversation 1** and **Conversation 2** on vhlcentral.com. Students record individual responses that appear in your gradebook.

4 Expansions
- Have students look at the photo, identify the conversation it most likely corresponds to (**Conversation 1**), and explain their reasoning. Point out that nearly all formal greetings are accompanied by a handshake. Tell the class that they will learn more about gestures used in greetings in the **Culture** section of this lesson.
- Have students rewrite **Conversation 1** in the formal register, and **Conversations 2** and **3** in the informal register.

5 Suggestions
- Before beginning this activity, ask students if they would use **tu** or **vous** in each situation.
- If class time is limited, assign a specific situation to each pair.
- Call on volunteers to act out their conversations for the class.

6 Suggestion Have two volunteers read the **modèle** aloud. Remind students to use **vous** when addressing more than one classmate at a time.

Activity Pack For additional activities, go to the Activity Pack in the Resources section of vhlcentral.com.

Communication

4 Discutez With a partner, complete these conversations. Then act them out. Answers will vary.

Conversation 1 Salut! Je m'appelle François. Et toi, comment t'appelles-tu?

_____

Ça va?

_____

Conversation 2 _____

Comme ci, comme ça. Et vous?

_____

Bon (*Well*), à demain.

_____

Conversation 3 Bonsoir, je vous présente Mademoiselle Barnard.

_____

Enchanté(e).

_____

Très bien, merci. Et vous?

_____

5 C'est à vous! How would you greet these people, ask them for their names, and ask them how they are doing? With a partner, write a short dialogue for each item and act it out. Pay attention to the use of **tu** and **vous**. Answers will vary.

1. **Madame Colombier**   2. **Mademoiselle Estèves**

3. **Monsieur Marchand**   4. **Marie, Guillaume et Geneviève**

6 Présentations Form groups of three. Introduce yourself, and ask your partners their names and how they are doing. Then, join another group and take turns introducing your partners. Answers will vary.

MODÈLE

Élève 1: *Bonjour. Je m'appelle Fatima. Et vous?*
Élève 2: *Je m'appelle Fabienne.*
Élève 3: *Et moi, je m'appelle Antoine. Ça va?*
Élève 1: *Ça va bien, merci. Et toi?*
Élève 3: *Comme ci, comme ça.*

EXPANSION

Using Categories Read some sentences to the class and ask if they would use them with another student of the same age or an older person they do not know. Examples: **1. Je te présente Guillaume.** (student) **2. Merci beaucoup, Monsieur.** (older person) **3. Comment vas-tu?** (student) **4. Bonjour, professeur _____.** (older person) **5. Comment vous appelez-vous?** (older person)

TEACHING OPTIONS

Mini-conversations Have students circulate around the classroom and conduct mini-conversations in French with other students, using the words and expressions they learned on pages 2–3. As students are carrying out the activity, move around the room, monitoring their work and offering assistance if requested.

Les sons et les lettres vhlcentral

The French alphabet

The French alphabet is made up of the same 26 letters as the English alphabet. While they look the same, some letters are pronounced differently. They also sound different when you spell.

lettre		exemple	lettre		exemple	lettre		exemple
a	(a)	**a**dresse	j	(ji)	**j**ustice	s	(esse)	**s**pécial
b	(bé)	**b**anane	k	(ka)	**k**ilomètre	t	(té)	**t**able
c	(cé)	**c**arotte	l	(elle)	**l**ion	u	(u)	**u**nique
d	(dé)	**d**essert	m	(emme)	**m**ariage	v	(vé)	**v**idéo
e	(e)	r**e**belle	n	(enne)	**n**ature	w	(double vé)	**w**agon
f	(effe)	**f**ragile	o	(o)	**o**live	x	(iks)	**x**ylophone
g	(gé)	**g**enre	p	(pé)	**p**ersonne	y	(i grec)	**y**oga
h	(hache)	**h**éritage	q	(ku)	**q**uiche	z	(zède)	**z**éro
i	(i)	**i**nnocent	r	(erre)	**r**adio			

Notice that some letters in French words have accents. You'll learn how they influence pronunciation in later lessons. Whenever you spell a word in French, include the name of the accent after the letter. For double letters, use **deux: ss = deux s.**

accent	nom	exemple	orthographe
´	*accent aigu*	**identité**	I-D-E-N-T-I-T-E-accent aigu
`	*accent grave*	**problème**	P-R-O-B-L-E-accent grave-M-E
ˆ	*accent circonflexe*	**hôpital**	H-O-accent circonflexe-P-I-T-A-L
¨	*tréma*	**naïve**	N-A-I-tréma-V-E
¸	*cédille*	**ça**	C-cédille-A

L'alphabet Practice saying the French alphabet and example words aloud.

Ça s'écrit comment? Spell these words aloud in French.

1. judo
2. yacht
3. forêt
4. zèbre
5. existe
6. clown
7. numéro
8. français
9. musique
10. favorite
11. kangourou
12. parachute
13. différence
14. intelligent
15. dictionnaire
16. alphabet

Dictons Practice reading these sayings aloud.

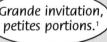

Grande invitation, petites portions.[1]

 Tout est bien qui finit bien.[2]

Lundi   *Mardi*

[1] Great boast, small roast.
[2] All's well that ends well.

cinq **5**

Section Goals
In this section, students will learn about:
- the French alphabet and how it contrasts with the English alphabet
- the names of the letters
- the names of the accent marks

Key Standards
4.1

Suggestions
- Model the pronunciation of the French alphabet and the example words. Have students repeat.
- Point out that vowel sounds can have many different pronunciations when combined with other vowels or when spelled with accents, particularly the **e**.
- Point out the different diacritical marks and model their pronunciation. For a detailed explanation of **l'accent aigu** and **l'accent grave**, see **Leçon 3A**, page 93. For an explanation of **l'accent circonflexe**, **le tréma**, and **la cédille**, see **Leçon 3B**, page 111.
- Draw attention to any posters, signs, or maps in the classroom. Point out individual letters, and ask the class to identify them in French.
- Tell students that the words **yacht** and **clown** are pronounced very differently than one would expect. Model their pronunciation for students to repeat.
- Have students work on the **Ça s'écrit comment?** activity in pairs.
- The explanation and exercises are available on vhlcentral.com. You may want to play them in class so students hear French speakers other than yourself.

Interpretive Listening Practice
Read aloud for students the following tongue twister: **Je suis ce que je suis, et si je suis ce que je suis, qu'est-ce que je suis?** Ask them what sounds they hear, and which French letters make those sounds.

EXPANSION

Mini-dictée Do a dictation activity in which you spell out a list of words in French to the class. Spell each word twice to allow students sufficient time to write. After you have finished, write your list on the board or project it on a transparency and have students check their work.

EXPANSION

Making Friends Tell students to greet two classmates that they haven't met yet, ask each person his or her name, and ask the person to spell the last name as they write it down. Tell them to verify the spelling with the person to make sure it is correct. Before beginning the activity, write this question on the board and model the pronunciation: **Comment s'écrit** _last name_?

Section Goals

In this section, students will learn functional phrases for making introductions and speaking on the telephone through comprehensible input.

Key Standards

1.2, 2.1, 2.2, 4.1, 4.2

Video Synopsis Sandrine buys a magazine at Monsieur Hulot's newsstand. At **Le P'tit Bistrot**, Rachid introduces David, his American friend, to Sandrine and Amina. Madame Forestier (Valérie), who owns the café, gets a phone call from her son's high school French teacher because he didn't do well on his French exam. Stéphane tells Rachid to introduce David to his mother so he can avoid talking to her.

Suggestions

- Have students cover the French captions and guess the plot based only on the video stills. Write their predictions on the board.
- Have students volunteer to read the characters' parts in the **Roman-photo** aloud. Then have them get together in groups of eight to act out the episode.
- After students have read the **Roman-photo**, quickly review their predictions, and ask them which ones were correct.
- Point out that 100 centimes = 1 euro, the monetary unit of the European Union, which includes France.

Au café   vhlcentral

PERSONNAGES

Amina

David

Monsieur Hulot

Michèle

Rachid

Sandrine

Stéphane

Valérie

Au kiosque...
SANDRINE Bonjour, Monsieur Hulot!
M. HULOT Bonjour, Mademoiselle Aubry! Comment allez-vous?
SANDRINE Très bien, merci! Et vous?
M. HULOT Euh, ça va. Voici 45 (quarante-cinq) centimes. Bonne journée!
SANDRINE Merci, au revoir!

À la terrasse du café...
AMINA Salut!
SANDRINE Bonjour, Amina. Ça va?
AMINA Ben... ça va. Et toi?
SANDRINE Oui, je vais bien, merci.
AMINA Regarde! Voilà Rachid et... un ami?

RACHID Bonjour!
AMINA ET SANDRINE Salut!
RACHID Je vous présente un ami, David Duchesne.
SANDRINE Je m'appelle Sandrine.
DAVID Enchanté.

STÉPHANE Oh, non! Madame Richard! Le professeur de français!
DAVID Il y a un problème?

STÉPHANE Oui! L'examen de français! Présentez-vous, je vous en prie!

VALÉRIE Oh... l'examen de français! Oui, merci, merci Madame Richard, merci beaucoup! De rien, au revoir!

ACTIVITÉS

1 Vrai ou faux? Decide whether each statement is **vrai** or **faux**.

1. Sandrine va (*is doing*) bien. Vrai.
2. Sandrine et Amina sont (*are*) amies. Vrai.
3. David est français. Faux.
4. David est de Washington. Vrai.
5. David présente Rachid à Sandrine et Amina. Faux.
6. Stéphane est étudiant à l'université. Faux.
7. Il y a un problème avec l'examen de sciences politiques. Faux.
8. Amina, Rachid et Sandrine sont (*are*) à Paris. Faux.
9. Michèle est au P'tit Bistrot. Vrai.
10. Madame Richard est le professeur de Stéphane. Vrai.
11. Valérie va mal. Vrai.
12. Rachid a (*has*) cours de français dans 30 minutes. Faux.

TEACHING OPTIONS

Au café Before showing the video episode, have students brainstorm greetings and other expressions that they might hear in an episode in which some of the characters meet each other for the first time.

EXPANSION

Extra Practice Play the episode once and tell the class to listen for basic greetings. After the video is over, have students recall the greetings they heard and write them on the board. Show the episode again and ask the class to write down all of the courtesy expressions that they hear, including ways to say *pleased to meet you*.

Les étudiants se retrouvent (*meet*) au café.

DAVID Et toi..., comment t'appelles-tu?
AMINA Je m'appelle Amina.
RACHID David est un étudiant américain. Il est de Washington, la capitale des États-Unis.
AMINA Ah, oui! Bienvenue à Aix-en-Provence.
RACHID Bon..., à tout à l'heure.
SANDRINE À bientôt, David.

À l'intérieur (inside) du café...
MICHÈLE Allô. Le P'tit Bistrot. Oui, un moment, s'il vous plaît. Madame Forestier! Le lycée de Stéphane.
VALÉRIE Allô. Oui. Bonjour, Madame Richard. Oui. Oui. Stéphane? Il y a un problème au lycée?

RACHID Bonjour, Madame Forestier. Comment allez-vous?
VALÉRIE Ah, ça va mal.
RACHID Oui? Moi, je vais bien. Je vous présente David Duchesne, étudiant américain de Washington.

DAVID Bonjour, Madame. Enchanté!
RACHID Ah, j'ai cours de sciences politiques dans 30 (trente) minutes. Au revoir, Madame Forestier. À tout à l'heure, David.

Expressions utiles

Introductions

- **David est un étudiant américain. Il est de Washington.**
  David is an American student. He's from Washington.
- **Présentez-vous, je vous en prie!**
  Introduce yourselves, please!
- **Il/Elle s'appelle...**
  His/Her name is...
- **Bienvenue à Aix-en-Provence.**
  Welcome to Aix-en-Provence.

Speaking on the telephone

- **Allô.**
  Hello.
- **Un moment, s'il vous plaît.**
  One moment, please.

Additional vocabulary

- **Regarde! Voilà Rachid et... un ami?**
  Look! There's Rachid and... a friend?
- **J'ai cours de sciences politiques dans 30 (trente) minutes.**
  I have political science class in thirty minutes.
- **Il y a un problème au lycée?**
  Is there a problem at the high school?
- **Il y a...**   **euh**
  There is/are...   *um*
- **Il/Elle est**   **bon**
  He/She is...   *well; good*
- **Voici...**   **centimes**
  Here's...   *cents*
- **Voilà...**
  There's...

A C T I V I T É S

2 **Complétez** Fill in the blanks with the words from the list. Refer to the video scenes as necessary.

1. _____Bienvenue_____ à Aix-en-Provence.
2. Il est de Washington, la _____capitale_____ des États-Unis.
3. _____Voici_____ 45 (quarante-cinq) centimes. Bonne journée!
4. J'_____ai_____ cours de sciences politiques.
5. David _____est_____ un étudiant américain.

ai	est
bienvenue	voici
capitale	

3 **Conversez** In groups of three, write a conversation where you introduce an exchange student to a friend. Be prepared to present your conversation to the class.

sept 7

Successful Language Learning Tell your students that their conversational skills will grow more quickly as they learn each lesson's **Expressions utiles**. This feature is designed to teach phrases that will be useful in conversation, and it will also help students understand key phrases in each **Roman-photo**.

Expressions utiles
- Tell students that all the items in **Expressions utiles** are active vocabulary for which they are responsible. Model the pronunciation of the words and expressions and have the class repeat.
- As you work through the list, point out examples of nouns with indefinite articles (**un étudiant, un moment, un ami, un problème**). Tell students that nouns and articles will be formally presented in the **Structures** section.

1 Suggestion Have students correct the false statements.

2 Expansion Tell students to write three additional fill-in-the-blank statements based on the **Roman-photo**. Then have them exchange papers with a classmate and complete the sentences.

 PRE-AP®

3 Interpersonal Speaking Have volunteers act out their conversations for the class or another group.

21st Century Skills

3 Collaboration If you have access to students in a Francophone country, ask them to write a conversation as described in Activity 3 for your students to act out.

 TELL Connection

Learning Experience 6 *Why:* Language happens within culture. *What:* Provide time for students to reflect on their own cultural behaviors and products, and then compare them with those in the video.

EXPANSION

Extra Practice Choose four or five lines of the **Roman-photo** to use as a dictation. Read each line twice, pausing after each line so that students have time to write. Have students check their own work by comparing it with the **Roman-photo** text.

Cultural Comparison Have students make observations about the places and people that they saw in the video. Ask what was surprising

EXPANSION

or different about any of the scenes or the characters' mannerisms. Did they notice anything different about the way that the American student, David, introduced himself compared to the others?

Point out that greeting friends, family members, and loved ones with a kiss on both cheeks is not unique to the French-speaking world. This custom is common throughout Europe and in other parts of the world.

7

AP® Theme: Families and Communities
Context: Friendship and Love

Section Goals

In this section, students will:
- learn about gestures used with greetings
- learn some familiar greetings and farewells
- learn some tips about good manners in different Francophone countries
- read about Aix-en-Provence
- view authentic cultural footage

Key Standards

2.1, 2.2, 3.1, 3.2, 4.2

21st Century Skills

Global Awareness
Students will gain perspectives on the Francophone world to develop respect and openness to other cultures.

Culture à la loupe

Avant la lecture Ask students how they greet their friends, family members, fellow students, and people they meet for the first time. Ask them for some examples of regional variations in greetings in the United States (e.g., Howdy, Hiya, Yo).

Lecture
- Ask students what information the map on this page shows. (It shows the number of kisses traditionally given by region.)
- Explain that **faire la bise** does not actually mean to kiss another's cheek, but rather to kiss parallel to the other person's face, so that physical contact is limited to a grazing of cheeks.

Après la lecture Have students compare French and American greetings or any other method of greeting with which they are familiar.

1 Expansion Have students work in pairs. Tell them to role-play the situations in items 1–6. Example: 1. Students give each other four kisses because they are in northwestern France.

---

vhlcentral | *Flash culture*

CULTURE À LA LOUPE

La poignée de main ou la bise?

French friends and relatives usually exchange a kiss (la bise) on alternating cheeks whenever they meet and again when they say good-bye. Friends of friends may also kiss on the cheek when introduced, even though they have just met. This is particularly true among students and young adults. It is normal for men of the same family to exchange **la bise**; otherwise, men generally greet one another with a handshake (**la poignée de main**). As the map shows, the number of kisses varies from place to place in France. In some regions, two kisses (one on each cheek) is the standard while in others, people may exchange as many as four kisses. Whatever the number, each kiss is accompanied by a slight kissing sound.

Unless they are also friends, business acquaintances and coworkers usually shake hands each time they meet and do so again upon leaving. A French handshake is brief and firm, with a single downward motion.

Coup de main

If you are not sure whether you should shake hands or kiss someone, or if you don't know which side to start on, you can always follow the other person's lead.

Combien de *How many*

Combien de° bises?

A C T I V I T É S

1 **Vrai ou faux?** Indicate whether each statement is **vrai** or **faux**. Correct any false statements.

1. In northwestern France, giving four kisses is common. Vrai.
2. Business acquaintances usually kiss one another on the cheek. Faux. They usually shake hands.
3. French people may give someone they've just met **la bise**. Vrai.
4. **Bises** exchanged between French men at a family gathering are common. Vrai.
5. In a business setting, French people often shake hands when they meet each day and again when they leave. Vrai.
6. When shaking hands, French people prefer a long and soft handshake. Faux. A French handshake is brief and firm.
7. The number of kisses given can vary from one region to another. Vrai.
8. It is customary for kisses to be given silently. Faux. Each kiss is accompanied by a slight kissing sound.

EXPANSION

La bise Tell students that, although people in some social circles in the United States commonly kiss each other on the cheek once, this is not common practice in France. It could be considered impolite to give only one **bise** since the other person would be waiting for the second kiss. In some regions of France and Switzerland, people may even give three **bises**, but just one is rare.

TEACHING OPTIONS

Using Games Divide the class into two teams. Indicate one team member at a time, alternating teams. Give situations in which people greet each other. Students should say if the people should greet each other with **la poignée de main** or **la bise**. Examples: female friends (**la bise**); male and female business associates (**la poignée de main**). Give a point for each correct answer. The team with the most points at the end wins.

Le français quotidien
- Model the pronunciation of each expression and have students repeat.
- Tell students to list all the situations they can think of in which they could use these expressions. Then have them compare their lists in pairs or small groups.

LE FRANÇAIS QUOTIDIEN

Les salutations

À la prochaine!	*Until next time!*
À plus!	*See you later!*
Ciao!	*Bye!*
Coucou!	*Hi there!/Hey!*
Pas grand-chose.	*Nothing much.*
Quoi de neuf?	*What's new?*
Rien de nouveau.	*Nothing new.*

AP® **Theme:** Families and Communities **Context:** Customs and Ceremonies

LE MONDE FRANCOPHONE

Les bonnes manières

In the francophone world, making an effort to speak in French is important. Respecting cultural norms and using polite expressions, such as **excusez-moi**, **s'il vous plaît**, and **merci**, goes a long way when conversing with locals.

Dos and don'ts in the francophone world:

France Always greet shopkeepers upon entering a store and say good-bye upon leaving.

Cambodia Greet others traditionally with your palms together and raised in front of you.

French Polynesia/Tahiti Shake hands with everyone in a room, unless the group is large.

Vietnam Remove your hat in the presence of older people and monks to show respect.

Ivory Coast Avoid making eye contact, as it is considered rude to stare.

PORTRAIT

Aix-en-Provence: ville d'eau, ville d'art°

Aix-en-Provence is a lively university town that welcomes international students. Its main boulevard, **le cours Mirabeau**, is great for people-watching or just relaxing in a sidewalk café. One can see many beautiful fountains, traditional and ethnic restaurants, and the daily vegetable and flower market among the winding, narrow streets of **la vieille ville** (*old town*).

Aix is also well-known for its dedication to the arts, hosting numerous cultural festivals every year such as **le Festival International d'Art Lyrique**, and **Aix en Musique**. For centuries, artists have been drawn to Provence for its natural beauty and its unique quality of light. Paul Cézanne, artist and native son of Provence, spent his days painting the surrounding countryside.

Paris
★
LA FRANCE
Aix-en-Provence •

ville d'eau, ville d'art *city of water, city of art*

AP® **Theme:** Families and Communities **Context:** Customs and Ceremonies

 Sur Internet

What behaviors are socially unacceptable in French-speaking countries?

Go to **vhlcentral.com** to find more information related to this **Culture** section and to watch the corresponding **Flash culture** video.

Portrait Mention that Aix-en-Provence is often referred to simply as Aix. Ask students why they think Aix is called **ville d'eau, ville d'art** in the title. Tell them that the Romans made Aix famous for its thermal baths.

Le monde francophone Ask students which dos and don'ts in the Francophone world should be followed in the Anglophone world, too. Have the class think of logical reasons for following each custom or social convention. Example: In French Polynesia and Tahiti, greeting everybody in the room expresses connection.

Sur Internet Point out to students that they will find supporting activities and information at **vhlcentral.com**.

🌙 **21ˢᵗ Century Skills**

Information and Media Literacy: Sur Internet Students access and critically evaluate information from the Internet.

3 Suggestion Before beginning this activity, ask students if they would use **tu** or **vous** in each situation. Remind them to use appropriate gestures and manners.

Flash culture Tell students that they will learn more about greetings and farewells in French by watching a variety of real-life images narrated by Csilla. You can use the activities in the video manual in class to reinforce this **Flash culture** or assign them as homework.

---

2 **Les bonnes manières** In which places might these behaviors be particularly offensive?

1. making direct eye contact
   Ivory Coast
2. greeting someone with a **bise** when introduced
   Cambodia
3. wearing a hat in the presence of older people
   Vietnam
4. failing to greet a salesperson
   France
5. failing to greet everyone in a room
   French Polynesia/Tahiti

3 **À vous** With a partner, practice meeting and greeting people in French in various social situations.

1. Your good friend from Provence introduces you to her close friend.
2. You walk into your neighborhood bakery.
3. You arrive for an interview with a prospective employer.

A C T I V I T É S

EXPANSION

Cultural Activity Have students choose one of these topics to research on the Internet: **Aix-en-Provence, le Festival International d'Art Lyrique, Aix en Musique,** or **Paul Cézanne**. Tell them to come to the next class with printouts of two photos illustrating their topic and a sentence or two about each photo. Divide the class into groups of three or four students so that

TEACHING OPTIONS

they can present the material to one another while looking at the images.

Mini-skits Have students work in groups of three or four. Tell them to create an informal conversation using the expressions in **Le français quotidien** and appropriate gestures. Have a few groups act out their conversations for the class.

Section Goals

In this section, students will learn:
• gender and number of nouns
• definite and indefinite articles

Key Standards
4.1, 5.1

Suggestions: Scaffolding
• Present **Point de départ**. Give examples of people (**professeur**), places (**café**), things (**examen**), and ideas (**problème**). Present nouns for people in context. Examples: **Anne est l'amie de Paul. Paul est l'ami d'Anne. M Dupin est professeur et Mme Anglin est professeur aussi.** Explain that **étudiant(e)** *usually* refers to a college student, while **élève** (presented in **Leçon 1B**), refers to high school or younger students.
• Use photos, drawings, or actual items to present the nouns for objects. Tell students that they should memorize each noun's gender.
• Follow the Rapid Drill and/or the Using Games suggestion.
• Present the final two points on p. 10 by writing on the board: **professeur, professeurs, étudiante, étudiantes, bureau, bureaux, animal, animaux.** Have students indicate the singular and plural nouns and explain how the plurals are formed. Then have students repeat the words after you to emphasize the silent **-s** and **-x**.
• Present the first point on p. 11.
• Have students complete the **Vérifiez** activity on vhlcentral.com.
• Remind students that they are responsible for learning all new vocabulary in **Structures**.

1A.1

Nouns and articles vhlcentral

Point de départ A noun designates a person, place, or thing. As in English, nouns in French have number, meaning they are singular or plural. However, nouns in French also have gender, meaning they are either masculine or feminine.

masculine singular	masculine plural	feminine singular	feminine plural
le café	**les cafés**	**la bibliothèque**	**les bibliothèques**
the café	*the cafés*	*the library*	*the libraries*

• You can't guess the gender of a noun unless it refers to a person. In this case, nouns that designate a male are usually masculine and nouns that designate a female are usually feminine.

masculine		feminine	
l'acteur	*the actor*	l'actrice	*the actress*
l'ami	*the (male) friend*	l'amie	*the (female) friend*
le chanteur	*the (male) singer*	la chanteuse	*the (female) singer*
l'étudiant	*the (male) student*	l'étudiante	*the (female) student*
le petit ami	*the boyfriend*	la petite amie	*the girlfriend*

• There are exceptions to the rule above. Sometimes a masculine noun or a feminine noun can refer to either a male or a female. Here are two.

un professeur
a (male or female) teacher, professor

une personne
a (male or female) person

• The genders of nouns that refer to objects and ideas, however, have to be memorized.

masculine		feminine	
le bureau	*the office; desk*	la chose	*the thing*
le lycée	*the high school*	la différence	*the difference*
l'examen	*the test, exam*	la librairie	*the bookstore*
l'objet	*the object*	la littérature	*literature*
l'ordinateur	*the computer*	la sociologie	*sociology*
le problème	*the problem*	l'université	*the university*

• You can make many nouns plural by adding -s.

	singular		plural	
masculine noun	l'objet	*the object*	les objets	*the objects*
feminine noun	la télévision	*the television*	les télévisions	*the televisions*

• For nouns that end in **-eau** in the singular, add **-x** to the end to make it plural. For most nouns ending in **-al**, drop the **-al** and add **-aux**.

le bureau	les bureaux	l'animal	les animaux
the office	*the offices*	*the animal*	*the animals*

🏃 Boîte à outils

As you learn new nouns, study them with their corresponding articles. This will help you remember their gender.

🏃 Boîte à outils

The final **-s** in the plural form of a noun is not pronounced. Therefore **ami** and **amis** sound the same. You can determine whether the word you're hearing is singular or plural by the article that comes before it.

🎧 Vérifiez

EXPANSION

Rapid Drill Write ten singular nouns on the board. In a rapid-response drill, call on students to give the appropriate gender. Examples: **bureau** (masculine), **télévision** (feminine). You may also do this activity without writing the words on the board.

TEACHING OPTIONS

Using Games Divide the class into groups of three to four students. Bring in photos or magazine pictures, point to various objects or people, and say the French word without saying the article. Call on groups to indicate the person's or object's gender. Give a point for each correct answer. Deduct a point for each wrong answer. The group with the most points at the end wins.

- When you have a group composed of males and females, use the masculine plural noun.

les amis
the (male, or male and female) friends

les étudiants
the (male, or male and female) students

Definite and indefinite articles

- The words **le**, **la**, **l'** and **les** you've seen in front of nouns are called definite articles. They all correspond to the word *the*, the only form of the definite article in English. In French, the definite article you use depends on the number and gender of the noun it goes with. For singular nouns, it also depends if they begin with a consonant or vowel sound.

	singular noun beginning with a consonant		singular noun beginning with a vowel sound		plural noun	
masculine	le tableau	*the painting/ blackboard*	l'ami	*the (male) friend*	les cafés	*the cafés*
feminine	la librairie	*the bookstore*	l'université	*the university*	les télévisions	*the televisions*

- Indefinite articles can also be used before nouns. In English, the singular forms are *a/an* and the plural form is *some*. In French, the masculine singular form is **un**, the feminine singular form is **une**, and the plural form is **des**. Unlike in English, the indefinite article **des** cannot be omitted in French.

	singular		plural	
masculine	un instrument	*an instrument*	des instruments	*(some) instruments*
feminine	une table	*a table*	des tables	*(some) tables*

- Use **c'est** followed by a singular article and noun or **ce sont** followed by a plural article and noun to identify people and objects.

Qu'est-ce que **c'est**?
What is that?

C'est une librairie.
It's a bookstore.

Ce sont des bureaux.
Those are offices.

🏃 **Boîte à outils**

In English, you sometimes omit the definite article when making general statements.

I love French.

Literature is difficult.

In French, you must always use the definite article in such cases.

J'adore le français.

La littérature est difficile (*difficult*).

Essayez! Select the correct article for each noun.

le, la, l' ou les?

1. _le_ café
2. _la_ bibliothèque
3. _l'_ acteur
4. _l'_ amie
5. _les_ problèmes
6. _le_ lycée
7. _les_ examens
8. _la_ littérature

un, une ou des?

1. _un_ bureau
2. _une_ différence
3. _un_ objet
4. _des_ amis
5. _des_ amies
6. _une_ université
7. _un_ ordinateur
8. _des_ tableaux

Mise en pratique

1 Les singuliers et les pluriels Make the singular nouns plural, and the plural nouns singular.

1. l'actrice   les actrices
2. les lycées   le lycée
3. les différences   la différence
4. la chose   les choses
5. le bureau   les bureaux
6. le café   les cafés
7. les librairies   la librairie

8. les étudiantes   l'étudiante
9. les acteurs   l'acteur
10. l'ami   les amis
11. l'université   les universités
12. les tableaux   le tableau
13. le problème   les problèmes
14. les bibliothèques   la bibliothèque

2 Le lycée Complete the sentences with an appropriate word from the list. Don't forget to provide the definite articles.   Answers may slightly vary. Suggested answers below.

| bibliothèque | examen | ordinateurs | sociologie |
| bureau | lycée | petit ami | |

1. À (a) ____la bibliothèque____, les tableaux et (b) ____les ordinateurs____ sont (are) modernes.
2. Marc, c'est (c) ____le petit ami____ de (of) Marie. Marc étudie (studies) la littérature.
3. Marie étudie (d) ____la sociologie____. (e) ____Le lycée____ de Marie et Marc s'appelle Henri IV.
4. Sylvie étudie pour (for) (f) ____l'examen____ de français.

3 Les mots Find ten words (mots) hidden in this word jumble. Then, provide the corresponding indefinite articles.   une actrice; une amie; des bureaux; un café; une chose; un lycée; des objets; des ordinateurs; une librairie; un tableau

Communication

4 **Qu'est-ce que c'est?** In pairs, take turns identifying the item(s) in each image.

▶ **MODÈLE**

Élève 1: *Qu'est-ce que c'est?*

Élève 2: *C'est un ordinateur.*

1. _Ce sont des tables._   2. _Ce sont des étudiants._

3. _C'est un tableau._   4. _Ce sont des télévisions._   5. _C'est une bibliothèque._   6. _C'est un café._

5 **Identifiez** In pairs, take turns providing a category for each item.

MODÈLE

Michigan, UCLA, Rutgers, Duke
Ce sont des universités.

1. saxophone   C'est un instrument.
2. Sheldon, Penny, Leonard, Rajesh, Howard   Ce sont des amis.
3. SAT   C'est un examen.
4. Library of Congress   C'est une bibliothèque.
5. Jennifer Lawrence, Marion Cotillard, Emma Watson, Sophie Turner   Ce sont des actrices.
6. Beyoncé, Bruno Mars   Ce sont des chanteurs.

6 **Le français** Your partner gets French words mixed up. Correct your partner as he or she points to various people and objects in the illustration and names them. When you're done, switch roles. Answers will vary.

MODÈLE

Élève 1: *C'est une personne.*

Élève 2: *Non, c'est un objet.*

7 **Pictogrammes** In groups of four, someone draws a person, object, or concept for the others to guess. Whoever guesses correctly draws next. Continue until everyone has drawn at least once. Answers will vary.

4 **Suggestion** Before beginning this activity, have students identify the items in the photos. Then read the **modèle** aloud with a volunteer. Remind them that **Ce sont** is used with plural nouns.

5 **Expansion** Have students work in pairs. Tell them to write two more items for the activity. Example: PSAT, ACT (**Ce sont des examens.**) Then have volunteers read their items aloud, while the rest of the class guesses the category.

5 **Virtual Chat** You can also assign activity 5 on vhlcentral.com. Students record individual responses that appear in your gradebook.

7 **Suggestions**
• Before beginning the activity, remind students that they must choose something the class knows how to say in French, and that to guess what the picture is, they should say: **C'est un(e) _____?** or **Ce sont des _____?**
• Tell students they will learn more about **c'est/ce sont** later in the unit.

Activity Pack For additional activities, go to the Activity Pack in the Resources section of vhlcentral.com.

TEACHING OPTIONS

Pairs Have pairs jot down a mix of ten singular and plural nouns, without their articles. Have them exchange their lists with another pair. Each pair then has to write down the appropriate definite and indefinite articles for each item. After pairs have finished, have them exchange lists and correct them.

EXPANSION

Extra Practice To challenge students, slowly read aloud a short passage from a novel, story, poem or newspaper article written in French, preferably one with a large number of nouns and articles. As a listening exercise, have students write down every noun and article they hear, even unfamiliar ones.

Section Goals

In this section, students will learn:
- the numbers 0–60
- the expression **il y a**

Key Standards
4.1, 5.1

Suggestions: Scaffolding
- Introduce numbers by asking students how many of them can count to ten in French. Hold up varying numbers of fingers and ask students to shout out the corresponding number in French.
- Consider demonstrating how the French count numbers on their fingers, starting with the thumb for *one*; the thumb and index finger for *two*; the thumb, index, and middle fingers for *three*; and so on. Ask if other cultures have a different way of counting with their fingers.
- Go through the numbers, modeling the pronunciation of each and having students repeat them. Write individual numbers on the board and call on students to say each number as you point to it. Then follow the Using Games suggestion below.
- Review the agreement rules. Then write 1, 21, 31, 41, or 51 followed by a masculine or feminine noun and have students write out the number.

1A.2

Numbers 0–60 vhlcentral

Point de départ Numbers in French follow patterns, as they do in English. First, learn the numbers **0–30**. The patterns they follow will help you learn the numbers **31–60**.

Numbers 0–30					
0–10		**11–20**		**21–30**	
0	zéro				
1	un	**11**	onze	**21**	vingt et un
2	deux	**12**	douze	**22**	vingt-deux
3	trois	**13**	treize	**23**	vingt-trois
4	quatre	**14**	quatorze	**24**	vingt-quatre
5	cinq	**15**	quinze	**25**	vingt-cinq
6	six	**16**	seize	**26**	vingt-six
7	sept	**17**	dix-sept	**27**	vingt-sept
8	huit	**18**	dix-huit	**28**	vingt-huit
9	neuf	**19**	dix-neuf	**29**	vingt-neuf
10	dix	**20**	vingt	**30**	trente

- When counting a series of numbers, use **un** for *one*.

  un, deux, trois, quatre...
  one, two, three, four...

- When *one* is followed by a noun, use **un** with a masculine noun and **une** with a feminine noun.

  un objet   **une** télévision
  an/one object   *a/one television*

- The number **21** (**vingt et un**) follows a different pattern than the numbers **22–30**. When **vingt et un** precedes a feminine noun, add **-e** to the end of it: **vingt et une**.

  vingt et un objets   **vingt et une** choses
  twenty-one objects   *twenty-one things*

- The numbers **31–39**, **41–49**, and **51–59** follow the same pattern as the numbers **21–29**.

Numbers 31–60					
31–34		**35–38**		**39, 40, 50, 60**	
31	trente et un	**35**	trente-cinq	**39**	trente-neuf
32	trente-deux	**36**	trente-six	**40**	quarante
33	trente-trois	**37**	trente-sept	**50**	cinquante
34	trente-quatre	**38**	trente-huit	**60**	soixante

- As with the number **21**, add an **-e** to **trente et un**, **quarante et un**, and **cinquante et un** when used before a feminine noun.

  trente et **un** objets   trente et **une** choses
  thirty-one objects   *thirty-one things*

  cinquante et **un** objets   cinquante et **une** choses
  fifty-one objects   *fifty-one things*

14   *quatorze*

DIFFERENTIATION

For Kinesthetic Learners Assign ten students a number from 0–60 and line them up in front of the class. Call out one of the numbers at random and have the student assigned to that number take a step forward. When two students have stepped forward, ask them to repeat their numbers. Then ask individuals to add (say: **plus**) or subtract (say: **moins**) the two numbers.

EXPANSION

Using Games Hand out Bingo cards with B-I-N-G-O across the top of five columns. The 25 squares underneath will contain random numbers. From a hat, draw letters and numbers and call them out in French. The first student that can fill in a number in each one of the lettered columns yells "Bingo!" and wins.

Il y a and *Combien de...?*

- Use **il y a** to say *there is* or *there are* in French.

  Il y a un ordinateur dans le bureau.
  There is a computer in the office.

  Il y a des tables dans le café.
  There are tables in the café.

  Il y a une table dans le café.
  There is one table in the café.

  Il y a dix-huit objets sur le bureau.
  There are eighteen objects on the desk.

Il y a deux amies.

Il y a trois étudiants.

- In most cases, the indefinite article (**un**, **une**, or **des**) or a number is used with **il y a**, rather than the definite article (**le**, **la**, **l'**, or **les**).

  Il y a un professeur de biologie américain.
  There's an American biology teacher.

  Il y a des étudiants français et anglais.
  There are French and English students.

- Use the expression **il n'y a pas de/d'** followed by a noun to express *there isn't a...* or *there aren't any....* Note that no article (definite or indefinite) is used in this case. Use **de** before a consonant sound and **d'** before a vowel sound.

before a consonant

before a vowel sound

  Il n'y a pas de tables dans le café.
  There aren't any tables in the café.

  Il n'y a pas d'ordinateur dans le bureau.
  There isn't a computer in the office.

- Use **combien de/d'** to ask how many of something there are.

  Il y a **combien de tables**?
  How many tables are there?

  Il y a **combien d'ordinateurs**?
  How many computers are there?

  Il y a **combien de librairies**?
  How many bookstores are there?

  Il y a **combien d'étudiants**?
  How many students are there?

⟨⟩ Vérifiez

Essayez! Write out or say the French word for each number below.

1. 15 _quinze_
2. 6 _six_
3. 22 _vingt-deux_
4. 5 _cinq_
5. 12 _douze_

6. 8 _huit_
7. 30 _trente_
8. 21 _vingt et un_
9. 1 _un_
10. 17 _dix-sept_

11. 44 _quarante-quatre_
12. 14 _quatorze_
13. 38 _trente-huit_
14. 56 _cinquante-six_
15. 19 _dix-neuf_

quinze **15**

Suggestions: Scaffolding

- Before presenting **il y a**, review numbers by assigning each student a number at random that they must remember. When finished, have the student assigned **un** say his or her number aloud, then **deux, trois,** etc. Help anyone who struggles with his or her number.
- Review the variable forms of **un** and **une**, **vingt et un**, and **vingt et une**, giving examples of each. Examples: **vingt et un étudiants, vingt et une personnes**.
- Present **il y a** by pointing out various singular and plural objects in the room. Then use **il n'y a pas de/d'** to state what is not in the room. Finally, ask students yes/no questions about objects and people in the room using **il y a**. Example: **Il y a des ordinateurs? (Non, il n'y a pas d'ordinateurs.)**
- Ask questions like the following: **Il y a combien d'élèves dans la classe? (Il y a seize élèves dans la classe.)**
- Assign **Vérifiez** on vhlcentral.com to check students' understanding of **il y a/il n'y a pas de/d'**.

Essayez! Have students write four more numbers from 0–60. Tell them to exchange papers with a classmate and write the numbers as words.

DIFFERENTIATION

For Kinesthetic Learners Give ten students a card with a number from 0–60. (You may want to assign numbers in fives to simplify the activity.) The card must be visible to the other students. Then call out simple math problems (addition or subtraction) involving the assigned numbers. When the first two numbers are called, each student steps forward. The student whose assigned number completes the math problem has five seconds to join them.

EXPANSION

My School Ask questions about your school and the town or city in which it is located. Examples: **Il y a combien de professeurs de français? Il y a combien de professeurs d'anglais? Il y a combien de bibliothèques à _____?** Encourage students to guess the number if they don't know it.

1 Suggestion Once students have filled in the missing numbers, have volunteers read each series aloud.

1 Expansion Ask the class to list the prime numbers (**les nombres premiers**) up to 30. Explain that a prime number is any number that can only be divided by itself and 1. Prime numbers to 30 are: 1, 2, 3, 5, 7, 11, 13, 17, 19, 23, 29.

2 Suggestion Help students form complete sentences using **Il y a** when answering. Example: **Il y a douze mois dans une année.**

2 Expansion For additional practice, give students these items. **7. jours: semaine (sept) 8. jours: novembre (trente) 9. minutes: heure** (*hour*) **(soixante) 10. saisons** (*seasons*): **année (quatre)**

3 Expansion Write on the board three more telephone numbers for real places in town with their area codes, using double digits as in the activity. Call on volunteers to read the numbers aloud. Permit students to say the digits one by one if the numbers exceed 60.

Mise en pratique

1 Logique Provide the number that completes each series. Then, write out the number in French.

MODÈLE

2, 4, __6__, 8, 10; __six__

1. 9, 12, __15__, 18, 21; __quinze__
2. 15, 20, __25__, 30, 35; __vingt-cinq__
3. 2, 9, __16__, 23, 30; __seize__
4. 0, 10, 20, __30__, 40; __trente__
5. 15, __17__, 19, 21, 23; __dix-sept__
6. 29, 26, __23__, 20, 17; __vingt-trois__
7. 2, 5, 9, __14__, 20, 27; __quatorze__
8. 30, 22, 16, 12, __10__; __dix__

2 Il y a combien de...? Provide the number that you associate with these pairs of words.

MODÈLE

lettres: l'alphabet vingt-six

1. mois (*months*): année (*year*) douze
2. états (*states*): USA cinquante
3. semaines (*weeks*): année cinquante-deux
4. jours (*days*): octobre trente et un
5. âge: le vote dix-huit
6. Noël (*Christmas*): décembre vingt-cinq

3 Numéros de téléphone Your mother left behind a list of phone numbers to call today. Now she calls you and asks you to read them off. (Note that French phone numbers are read as double, not single, digits.)

MODÈLE

Le bureau, c'est le zéro un, vingt-trois, quarante-cinq, vingt-six, dix-neuf.

1. *bureau: 01.23.45.26.19*

2. *bibliothèque: 01.47.15.54.17*
La bibliothèque, c'est le zéro un, quarante-sept, quinze, cinquante-quatre, dix-sept.

3. *café: 01.41.38.16.29*
Le café, c'est le zéro un, quarante et un, trente-huit, seize, vingt-neuf.

4. *librairie: 01.10.13.60.23*
La librairie, c'est le zéro un, dix, treize, soixante, vingt-trois.

5. *lycée: 01.58.36.14.12*
Le lycée, c'est le zéro un, cinquante-huit, trente-six, quatorze, douze.

EXPANSION

Rapid Drill Say numbers aloud at random and have students hold up the appropriate number of fingers. Then reverse the drill; hold up varying numbers of fingers at random and ask students to shout out the corresponding number in French.

DIFFERENTIATION

For Visual Learners Hold up or point to classroom objects and ask how many there are. Since students will not know the names of many items, a simple number will suffice to signal comprehension. Ex: **Il y a combien de dictionnaires? Deux**.

Communication

4 **Contradiction** Thierry is describing the new café in the neighborhood, but Paul contradicts everything he says. In pairs, act out the roles using words from the list. Be sure to pay attention to whether the word is singular (use **un/une**) or plural (use **des**). *Answers will vary.*

MODÈLE

Élève 1: *Dans (In) le café, il y a des tables.*
Élève 2: *Non, il n'y a pas de tables.*

actrices	professeurs
bureau	tableau
étudiants	tables
ordinateur	télévision

5 **Au Lycée** Nathalie's little brother wants to know everything about her school. In pairs, take turns acting out the roles.

MODÈLE

bibliothèques: 3
Élève 1: *Il y a combien de bibliothèques?*
Élève 2: *Il y a trois bibliothèques.*

1. professeurs: 22   Il y a vingt-deux professeurs.
2. étudiants dans (in) la classe de français: 15   Il y a quinze étudiants dans la classe de français.
3. télévision dans la classe de sociologie: 0   Il n'y a pas de télévision dans la classe de sociologie.
4. ordinateurs dans la bibliothèque: 8   Il y a huit ordinateurs dans la bibliothèque.
5. employés dans la librairie du lycée: 1   Il y a un employé dans la librairie.
6. tables dans la cantine (*cafeteria*): 50   Il y a cinquante et une tables dans la cantine.
7. tableaux dans la bibliothèque: 21   Il y a vingt et un tableaux dans la bibliothèque.
8. personne dans le bureau: 1   Il y a une personne dans le bureau.

6 **Choses et personnes** In groups of three, make a list of ten things or people that you see or don't see in the classroom. Use **il y a** and **il n'y a pas de**, and specify the number of items you can find. Then, compare your list with that of another group. *Answers will vary.*

MODÈLE

Élève 1: *Il y a un étudiant français.*
Élève 2: *Il n'y a pas de télévision.*
Élève 3: *Il y a...*

4 **Suggestion** Have two volunteers read the **modèle** aloud. Remind students that they shouldn't use any article (definite or indefinite) after **Il n'y a pas de/d'**.

4 **Partner Chat** You can also assign Activity 4 on vhlcentral.com. Students work in pairs to record the activity online. The pair's recorded conversation will appear in yourgradebook.

5 **Suggestion** Have two volunteers read the **modèle** aloud. Remind students to use **combien d'** before a noun that begins with a vowel sound.

6 **Expansion** After groups have compared their answers, convert the statements into questions. Example: **Il y a combien d'étudiants?**

Activity Pack For additional activities, go to the Activity Pack in the Resources section of vhlcentral.com.

EXPANSION

Extra Practice Ask questions about your school and the town or city in which it is located. Examples: **Il y a combien de professeurs de français? Il y a combien de professeurs d'anglais? Il y a combien de bibliothèques? Il y a combien de lycées à _____?** Encourage students to guess the number if they don't know it.

DIFFERENTIATION

For Visual Learners Divide the class into pairs. Give half of the pairs magazine pictures that contain images of familiar words or cognates. Give the other half written descriptions of the pictures, using **il y a**. Ex: **Il y a deux instruments sur la photo**. Have pairs circulate around the room to match the descriptions with the corresponding pictures.

Révision

1 Des lettres In pairs, take turns choosing nouns. One partner chooses only masculine nouns, while the other chooses only feminine. Slowly spell each noun for your partner, who will guess the word. Find out who can give the quickest answers. *Answers will vary.*

2 Le pendu In groups of four, play hangman (**le pendu**). Form two teams of two partners each. Take turns choosing a French word or expression you learned in this lesson for the other team to guess. Continue to play until your team guesses at least one word or expression from each category. *Answers will vary.*

1. un nom féminin
2. un nom masculin
3. un nombre entre (*number between*) 0 et 30
4. un nombre entre 31 et 60
5. une expression

3 C'est... Ce sont... Doug is spending a week in Paris with his French e-mail pal, Marc. As Doug points out what he sees, Marc corrects him sometimes. In pairs, act out the roles. Doug should be right half the time. *Answers will vary.*

MODÈLE
Élève 1: *C'est une bibliothèque?*
Élève 2: *Non, c'est une librairie.*

1. C'est une bibliothèque./ Ce sont des élèves/étudiants.
4. Ce sont des acteurs.

2. C'est un café.
5. C'est un professeur. / Ce sont des élèves/étudiants.

3. C'est une actrice.
6. Ce sont des amies.

4 Les présentations In pairs, introduce yourselves. Together, meet another pair. One person per pair should introduce him or herself and his or her partner. Use the items from the list in your conversations. Switch roles until you have met all of the other pairs in the class. *Answers will vary.*

ami	élève
c'est	ami(e)
ce sont	professeur

5 S'il te plaît You need help finding your way and so you ask your partner for assistance. He or she gives you the building (**le bâtiment**) and room (**la salle**) number and you thank him or her. Then, switch roles and repeat with another place from the list. *Answers will vary.*

MODÈLE
Élève 1: *Pardon... l'examen de sociologie, s'il te plaît?*
Élève 2: *Ah oui... bâtiment E, salle dix-sept.*
Élève 1: *Merci beaucoup!*
Élève 2: *De rien.*

Bibliothèque .... Bâtiment C Salle 11
Bureau de Mme Girard .... Bâtiment A Salle 35
Bureau de M. Brachet .... Bâtiment J Salle 42
Bureau de M. Grondin .... Bâtiment H Salle 59
Examen de français .... Bâtiment B Salle 46
Examen d'anglais .... Bâtiment E Salle 24
Examen de sociologie .... Bâtiment E Salle 17
Salle de télévision .... Bâtiment F Salle 33
Salle des ordinateurs .... Bâtiment D Salle 40

6 Mots mélangés You and a partner each have half the words of a wordsearch (**des mots mélangés**). Pick a number and a letter and say them to your partner, who must tell you if he or she has a letter in the corresponding space. Do not look at each other's worksheet. *Answers will vary.*

vhlcentral

AP® **Theme:** Global Challenges
Context: Health Issues

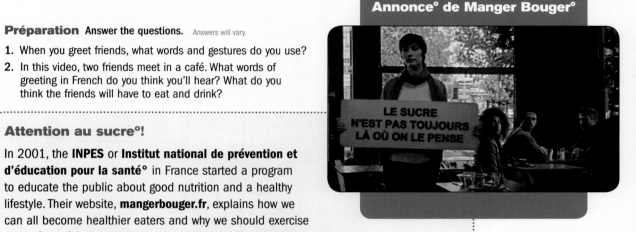

Annonce° de Manger Bouger°

LE SUCRE
N'EST PAS TOUJOURS
LÀ OÙ ON LE PENSE

Préparation Answer the questions. Answers will vary.

1. When you greet friends, what words and gestures do you use?
2. In this video, two friends meet in a café. What words of greeting in French do you think you'll hear? What do you think the friends will have to eat and drink?

Attention au sucre°!

In 2001, the **INPES** or **Institut national de prévention et d'éducation pour la santé°** in France started a program to educate the public about good nutrition and a healthy lifestyle. Their website, **mangerbouger.fr**, explains how we can all become healthier eaters and why we should exercise more. One of their campaigns also raises public awareness about eating excess fat, salt, or sugar. To get the message across, the ads present foods that are rich in one of these ingredients in a new and surprising context. This particular commercial starts when two friends meet in a coffee shop.

Annonce *Ad* **Manger Bouger** *Eat Move* **sucre** *sugar* **santé** *health*

Vocabulaire utile

je sors juste	*I just left*
le ciné	*movie theater*
deux cafés	*two coffees*
t'as vu quoi?	*what did you see?*
drôle	*funny*

 Compréhension Answer the questions.

1. Indicate the word or phrase in each pair that you heard the friends say.
   Bonjour / (Salut)
   Ça va? / (Comment allez-vous?)
   Oui, et vous? / (Oui, et toi?)
2. What gestures did the friends use in greeting? kisses on the cheeks
3. What did they order? coffee

 Conversation In groups of three, answer these questions.
Answers will vary.

1. What does the waiter bring with the coffees? What does the ketchup stand for? Can you explain why?
2. Besides the ketchup, what else seems out of place in this scene?

 Application Imagine that a friend of one of the women arrives at the café. In groups of three, role-play a scene in which the new friend is properly introduced and orders something to eat or drink.

dix-neuf **19**

Section Goals

In this section, students will learn and practice vocabulary related to:
- objects in the classroom
- identifying people

Key Standards

1.1, 1.2, 4.1

Suggestions
- Introduce vocabulary for classroom objects, such as **un cahier, une carte, un dictionnaire, un stylo**. Hold up or point to an object and say: **C'est un stylo.**
- Hold up or point to an object and ask either/or questions. Examples: **C'est un crayon ou un stylo? C'est une porte ou une fenêtre?**
- Using either objects in the classroom or the digital image for this page, point to items or people and ask questions, such as **Qu'est-ce que c'est? Qui est-ce? C'est un stylo? C'est un professeur?**
- Have students pick up or point out objects you name. You might want to teach them the expression **Montrez-moi un/une ____.**

You will learn how to...
- identify yourself and others
- ask yes/no questions

◁) **vhl**central

En classe

Vocabulaire

Qui est-ce?	*Who is it?*
Quoi?	*What?*
une calculatrice	*calculator*
une montre	*watch*
une porte	*door*
un résultat	*result*
une salle de classe	*classroom*
un(e) camarade de classe	*classmate*
une classe	*class (group of students)*
un copain/ une copine (*fam.*)	*friend*
un(e) élève	*pupil, student*
une femme	*woman*
une fille	*girl*
un garçon	*boy*
un homme	*man*

EXPANSION

Making Lists Have students work in pairs and take an inventory of all the people and items in the classroom. Tell them to write their list in French using the expression **Il y a ____**. After students have finished, tell them to compare their list with another pair's list to see if they are the same.

TEACHING OPTIONS

Using Games Divide the class into teams. Then, in English, say the name of a classroom object and ask one of the teams to provide the French equivalent. If the team provides the correct term, it gets a point. If not, the second team gets a chance to give the correct term. Alternate giving items to the two teams. The team with the most points at the end of the game wins.

Mise en pratique

1 **Chassez l'intrus** Circle the word that does not belong.

1. étudiants, élèves, (professeur)
2. un stylo, un crayon, (un cahier)
3. un livre, un dictionnaire, (un stylo)
4. un homme, (un crayon,) un garçon
5. une copine, (une carte,) une femme
6. une porte, une fenêtre, (une chaise)
7. une chaise, (un professeur,) une fenêtre
8. (un crayon,) une feuille de papier, un cahier
9. une calculatrice, une montre, (une copine)
10. une fille, (un sac à dos,) un garçon

2 **Écoutez** Listen to Madame Arnaud as she describes her French classroom, then check the items she mentions.

1. une porte ☑
2. un professeur ☐
3. une feuille de papier ☐
4. un dictionnaire ☑
5. une carte ☑
6. vingt-quatre cahiers ☐
7. une calculatrice ☐
8. vingt-sept chaises ☑
9. une corbeille à papier ☑
10. un stylo ☑

3 **C'est...** Work with a partner to identify the items you see in the image.

MODÈLE

Élève 1: *Qu'est-ce que c'est?*
Élève 2: *C'est un tableau.*

1. un tableau
2. une porte
3. un crayon/stylo
4. un livre
5. une calculatrice
6. un stylo/crayon
7. une feuille (de papier)
8. un bureau
9. un dictionnaire
10. une corbeille à papier
11. une chaise
12. un professeur

une carte

une chaise

vingt et un **21**

4 Virtual Chat You can also assign Activity 4 on vhlcentral.com. Students record an open-ended response that appears in your gradebook.

4 Expansion For additional practice, point to different students' desks that have objects on them and ask: **Qu'est ce qu'il y a sur le bureau de ____?** You might also ask: **Qu'est-ce qu'il y a sur mon bureau?**

5 Suggestion Before beginning the activity, have a few volunteers demonstrate what students should do using the **modèle**.

6 Suggestion Before beginning the activity, remind students that to guess what the drawing represents, they should say: **C'est un(e) ____?** or **Ce sont des ____?**

7 Suggestions
• Divide the class into pairs and distribute the Info Gap Handouts from the Activity Pack. Give students ten minutes to complete the activity.
• Have two volunteers read the **modèle** aloud.

7 Expansion Have students describe the people and objects in the photo using **Il y a.**

Successful Language Learning Remind the class that errors are a natural part of language learning. Point out that it is impossible to speak "perfectly" in any language. Emphasize that their spoken and written French will improve if they practice.

Activity Pack For additional activities, go to the Activity Pack in the Resources section of vhlcentral.com.

Communication

4 Qu'est-ce qu'il y a dans mon sac à dos? Make a list of six different items that you have in your backpack, then work with a partner to compare your answers. Answers will vary.

Dans mon (*my*) sac à dos, il y a...

1. _____
2. _____
3. _____
4. _____
5. _____
6. _____

Dans le sac à dos de ____*nom*____, il y a...

1. _____
2. _____
3. _____
4. _____
5. _____
6. _____

5 Qu'est-ce que c'est? Point at eight different items around the classroom and ask a classmate to identify them. Write your partner's responses on the spaces provided below. Answers will vary.

MODÈLE

Élève 1: *Qu'est-ce que c'est?*
Élève 2: *C'est un stylo.*

1. _____
2. _____
3. _____
4. _____

5. _____
6. _____
7. _____
8. _____

6 Pictogrammes Play pictionary as a class.
Answers will vary.
• Take turns going to the board and drawing words you learned on pp. 20–21.
• The person drawing may not speak and may not write any letters or numbers.
• The person who guesses correctly in French what the **grand(e) artiste** is drawing will go next.
• Your teacher will time each turn and tell you if your time runs out.

7 Sept différences Your teacher will give you and a partner two different drawings of a classroom. Do not look at each other's worksheet. Find seven differences between your picture and your partner's by asking each other questions and describing what you see. Answers will vary.

MODÈLE

Élève 1: *Il y a une fenêtre dans ma (my) salle de classe.*
Élève 2: *Oh! Il n'y a pas de fenêtre dans ma salle de classe.*

TEACHING OPTIONS

Using Games Divide the class into two teams. Put labels of classroom vocabulary in a box. Alternating between teams, one person picks a label out of the box without showing it to anyone. This person must place the label on the correct person or object in the classroom and say the word aloud. Each player is allowed only 15 seconds and one guess per turn. Award a point for a correct response. If a player is incorrect, the next player on the opposing team may "steal" the point by placing the label on the correct person or object. The team with the most points at the end of the game wins.

Les sons et les lettres 🔊 **vhl**central

Silent letters

Final consonants of French words are usually silent.

| françai~~s~~ | spor~~t~~ | vou~~s~~ | salu~~t~~ |

An unaccented **-e** (or **-es**) at the end of a word is silent, but the preceding consonant is pronounced.

| français~~e~~ | américain~~e~~ | orang~~es~~ | japonais~~es~~ |

The consonants **-c**, **-r**, **-f**, and **-l** are usually pronounced at the ends of words. To remember these exceptions, think of the consonants in the word **ca**r**e**f**u**l.

| par**c** | bonjou**r** | acti**f** | anima**l** |
| la**c** | professeu**r** | naï**f** | ma**l** |

Prononcez Practice saying these words aloud.

1. traditionnel
2. étudiante
3. généreuse
4. téléphones
5. chocolat
6. Monsieur
7. journalistes
8. hôtel
9. sac
10. concert
11. timide
12. sénégalais
13. objet
14. normal
15. importante

Articulez Practice saying these sentences aloud.

1. Au revoir, Paul. À plus tard!
2. Je vais très bien. Et vous, Monsieur Dubois?
3. Qu'est-ce que c'est? C'est une calculatrice.
4. Il y a un ordinateur, une table et une chaise.
5. Frédéric et Chantal, je vous présente Michel et Éric.
6. Voici un sac à dos, des crayons et des feuilles de papier.

Dictons Practice reading these sayings aloud.

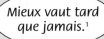

Mieux vaut tard que jamais.[1]

Aussitôt dit, aussitôt fait.[2]

[1] Better late than never.
[2] No sooner said than done.

vingt-trois **23**

Section Goals

In this section, students will learn about:
- silent letters
- a strategy for remembering which consonants are pronounced at the end of words

Key Standards
4.1

Suggestions
- Write the sentences below on the board or a transparency. Then say each sentence and ask students which letters are silent. Draw a slash through the silent letters as students say them. **Qui est-ce? C'est Gilbert. Il est français. Qu'est-ce que c'est? C'est un éléphant.**
- Work through the example words. Have students repeat each word after you.
- Tell students that the final consonants of a few words that end in **c, r, f,** or **l** are silent. Examples: **porc** (*pork*), **blanc** (*white*), **nerf** (*nerve*), **gentil** (*nice*), and the modern pronunciation of **monsieur**.
- Point out that the letters **-er** at the end of a word are pronounced like the vowel sound in *say*. Examples: **cahier** and **papier**.
- Explain that numbers are exceptions to pronunciation rules. When counting, some final consonants are pronounced. Have students compare the pronunciation of the following: **six, sept, huit; six cahiers, sept stylos, huit crayons**.
- Tell students that the final consonants of words borrowed from other languages are often pronounced. Examples: **snob, autobus,** and **club**.
- The explanations and exercises are recorded on the Teacher's Resource DVD and are available on vhlcentral.com. You may want to play them in class so students hear French speakers other than yourself.

EXPANSION

Pronunciation Write on the board or an overhead transparency a list of words that have silent letters. Call on volunteers to spell each word in French and then pronounce it. Examples: **art**, **comment**, **sont**, **est**, **intelligent**, **sac à dos**, and **résultat**.

TEACHING OPTIONS

Reading Aloud Working in groups of three or four, have students practice pronunciation by reading the vocabulary words aloud on pages 20–21. Circulate among the groups and model correct pronunciation as needed. When they have finished, ask them if they discovered any exceptions to the pronunciation rules. (**cahier, papier**)

Les copains vhlcentral

PERSONNAGES

Amina

David

Michèle

Stéphane

Touriste

Valérie

À la terrasse du café...
VALÉRIE Alors, un croissant, une crêpe et trois cafés.
TOURISTE Merci, Madame.
VALÉRIE Ah, vous êtes... américain?
TOURISTE Um, non, je suis anglais. Il est canadien et elle est italienne.
VALÉRIE Moi, je suis française.

À l'intérieur du café...
VALÉRIE Stéphane!!!
STÉPHANE Quoi?! Qu'est-ce que c'est?
VALÉRIE Qu'est-ce que c'est! Qu'est-ce que c'est! Une feuille de papier! C'est l'examen de maths! Qu'est-ce que c'est?
STÉPHANE Oui, euh, les maths, c'est difficile.

VALÉRIE Stéphane, tu es intelligent, mais tu n'es pas brillant! En classe, on fait attention au professeur, au cahier et au livre! Pas aux fenêtres. Et pas aux filles!
STÉPHANE Oh, oh, ça va!!

À la table d'Amina et de David...
DAVID Et Rachid, mon colocataire? Comment est-il?
AMINA Il est agréable et très poli... plutôt réservé mais c'est un étudiant brillant. Il est d'origine algérienne.

DAVID Et toi, Amina. Tu es de quelle origine?
AMINA D'origine sénégalaise.
DAVID Et Sandrine?

AMINA Sandrine? Elle est française.
DAVID Mais non... Comment est-elle?
AMINA Bon, elle est chanteuse, alors elle est un peu égoïste. Mais elle est très sociable. Et charmante. Mais attention! Elle est avec Pascal.
DAVID Pfft, Pascal, Pascal...

A C T I V I T É S

1 **Identifiez** Indicate which character would make each statement: Amina (A), David (D), Michèle (M), Sandrine (S), Stéphane (St), or Valérie (V).

1. Les maths, c'est difficile. St
2. En classe, on fait attention au professeur! V
3. Michèle, les trois cafés sont pour les trois touristes. V
4. Ah, Madame, du calme! M

5. Ma mère est très impatiente! St
6. J'ai (*I have*) de la famille au Sénégal. A
7. Je suis une grande chanteuse! S
8. Mon colocataire est très poli et intelligent. D
9. Pfft, Pascal, Pascal... D
10. Attention, David! Sandrine est avec Pascal. A/V

Amina, David et Stéphane passent la matinée (*spend the morning*) au café.

Au bar...
VALÉRIE Le croissant, c'est pour l'Anglais, et la crêpe, c'est pour l'Italienne.
MICHÈLE Mais, Madame. Ça va? Qu'est-ce qu'il y a?
VALÉRIE Ben, c'est Stéphane. Des résultats d'examens, des professeurs... des problèmes!

MICHÈLE Ah, Madame, du calme! Je suis optimiste. C'est un garçon intelligent. Et vous, êtes-vous une femme patiente?
VALÉRIE Oui... oui, je suis patiente. Mais le Canadien, l'Anglais et l'Italienne sont impatients. Allez! Vite!

VALÉRIE Alors, ça va bien?
AMINA Ah, oui, merci.
DAVID Amina est une fille élégante et sincère.
VALÉRIE Oui! Elle est charmante.
DAVID Et Rachid, comment est-il?
VALÉRIE Oh! Rachid! C'est un ange! Il est intelligent, poli et modeste. Un excellent camarade de chambre.

DAVID Et Sandrine? Comment est-elle?
VALÉRIE Sandrine?! Oh, là, là. Non, non, non. Elle est avec Pascal.

Expressions utiles

Describing people

● **Vous êtes/Tu es américain?**
You're American?

● **Je suis anglais. Il est canadien et elle est italienne.**
I'm English. He's Canadian, and she's Italian.

● **Et Rachid, mon colocataire? Comment est-il?**
And Rachid, my roommate (in an apartment)? What's he like?

● **Il est agréable et très poli... plutôt réservé mais c'est un étudiant brillant.**
He's nice and polite... rather reserved, but a brilliant student.

● **Tu es de quelle origine?**
What's your heritage?

● **Je suis d'origine algérienne/sénégalaise.**
I'm of Algerian/Senegalese heritage.

● **Elle est avec Pascal.**
She's with (dating) Pascal.

● **Rachid! C'est un ange!**
Rachid! He's an angel!

Asking questions

● **Ça va? Qu'est-ce qu'il y a?**
Are you OK? What is it?/What's wrong?

Additional vocabulary

● **Ah, Madame, du calme!**
Oh, ma'am, calm down!

● **On fait attention à...**
One pays attention to...

● **Mais attention!**   ● **alors**
But watch out!   *so*

● **Allez! Vite!**   ● **mais**
Go! Quickly!   *but*

● **Mais non...**   ● **un peu**
Of course not...   *a little*

vingt-cinq **25**

Expressions utiles

● Model the pronunciation of the **Expressions utiles** and have students repeat after you.
● Point out forms of the verb **être** and adjective agreement in the captions and in the **Expressions utiles**. Tell students that this material will be formally presented in the **Structures** section.
● Ask a few questions based on the **Expressions utiles**. Examples: **Et _____, vous êtes américain(e) [canadien(ne)/ italien(ne)]? Ça va? Qu'est-ce qu'il y a?**

1 Expansion For additional practice, read these items aloud or write them on the board.
11. Je suis optimiste. (Michèle)
12. Je suis anglais. (le touriste)
13. Rachid! C'est un ange! (Valérie)

2 Expansion Write the following adjectives on the board and ask students which video character they describe.
1. sénégalais(e) (Amina)
2. algérien(ne) (Rachid)
3. français(e) (Sandrine, Stéphane, Valérie, Michèle)
4. charmant(e) (Sandrine)
5. réservé (Rachid)

---

2 Complétez Use words from the list to describe these people in French. Refer to the video scenes and a dictionary as necessary.

1. Michèle always looks on the bright side. __optimiste__
2. Rachid gets great grades. __intelligent__
3. Amina is very honest. __sincère__
4. Sandrine thinks about herself a lot. __égoïste__
5. Sandrine has a lot of friends. __sociable__

égoïste	
intelligent	
optimiste	
sincère	
sociable	

3 Conversez In pairs, choose the words from this list you would use to describe yourselves. What personality traits do you have in common? Be prepared to share your answers with the class.

brillant	modeste
charmant	optimiste
égoïste	patient
élégant	sincère
intelligent	sociable

A C T I V I T É S

EXPANSION

Mini-dictée Choose four or five lines of the **Roman-photo** to use as a dictation. Read each line twice, pausing after each line so that students have time to write. Have students check their own work by comparing it with the **Roman-photo** text.

EXPANSION

Practicing Improvisation Have students work in pairs. Tell them to look at video stills 2–3 and 6–8, and choose a situation to ad-lib. Assure them that it is not necessary to follow or memorize the **Roman-photo** word for word. Students should be creative while getting the general meaning across with the vocabulary and expressions they know.

AP® **Theme:** Personal and Public Identities
Context: Multiculturalism

Section Goals

In this section, students will:
- learn about France's multicultural society
- learn some familiar terms for identifying people
- read about official languages in some Francophone countries
- read about Marianne, a symbol of the French Republic

Key Standards
2.1, 2.2, 3.1, 3.2, 4.2

21st Century Skills

Global Awareness
Students will gain perspectives on the Francophone world to develop respect and openness to other cultures.

Culture à la loupe
Avant la lecture Have students discuss what their idea of a typical French person is.

Lecture
- Point out the regions where Provençal (**Provence**), Breton (**Bretagne**), and Basque (**Pays basque**) are spoken on the map of France in the frontmatter.
- Explain that there are other regional languages not mentioned in the text: Alsatian, Caribbean Creole, Catalan, Corsican, Dutch, Gascon, Lorraine German dialect, and Occitan.

Après la lecture Ask students what facts in this reading are interesting or surprising to them.

1 Expansion For additional practice, give students these items. 11. There are several official languages in France. (**Faux.** French is the only official language.) 12. South Africans represent a significant immigrant population in France. (**Faux.** North and West Africans represent significant immigrant populations.) 13. There are more immigrants in France from both Italy and Spain than from Tunisia. (**Vrai.**)

---

vhlcentral

CULTURE À LA LOUPE

Qu'est-ce qu'un Français typique?

What is your idea of a typical Frenchman? Do you picture a man wearing a **béret**? How about French women? Are they all fashionable and stylish? Do you picture what is shown in these photos? While real French people fitting one aspect or another of these cultural stereotypes do exist, rarely do you find individuals who fit all aspects.

France is a multicultural society with no single, national ethnicity. While the majority of French people are of Celtic or Latin descent, France has significant North and West African (e.g., Algeria, Morocco, Senegal) and Asian (e.g., Vietnam, Laos, Cambodia) populations as well. Long a **terre d'accueil°**, France today has over eleven million foreigners and immigrants. Even as France has maintained a strong concept of its culture through the preservation of its language, history, and traditions, French culture has been ultimately enriched by the contributions of its immigrant populations. Each region of the country also has its own traditions, folklore, and, often, its own language. Regional languages, such as Provençal, Breton, and Basque, are still spoken in some areas, but the official language is, of course, French.

| Immigrants in France, by country of birth ||
COUNTRY NAME	NUMBER OF PEOPLE
Other European countries	811,421
Algeria	748,034
Morocco	692,923
Sub-Saharan Africa	655,460
Portugal	599,333
Other Asian countries	447,149
Italy	292,592
Spain	245,077
Turkey	248,159
Tunisia	251,220
Cambodia, Laos, Vietnam	127,641
UK	152,786

terre d'accueil *a land welcoming of newcomers*

A C T I V I T É S

1 Vrai ou faux? Indicate whether each statement is **vrai** or **faux**. Correct the false statements.

1. Cultural stereotypes are generally true for most people in France.
   Faux. Rarely do you find individuals who fit all aspects of a stereotype.
2. People in France no longer speak regional languages.
   Faux. Regional languages are still spoken in some areas.
3. Many immigrants from North Africa live in France. Vrai.
4. More immigrants in France come from Portugal than from Morocco. Faux. More immigrants come from Morocco.

5. Algerians and Moroccans represent the largest immigrant populations in France. Vrai.
6. Immigrant cultures have little impact on French culture.
   Faux. French culture has been enriched by immigrant cultures.
7. Because of immigration, France is losing its cultural identity.
   Faux. France has maintained its culture.
8. French culture differs from region to region. Vrai.
9. Most French people are of Anglo-Saxon heritage.
   Faux. The majority of French people are of Celtic or Latin descent.
10. For many years, France has received immigrants from many countries. Vrai.

26 *vingt-six*

Le français quotidien
- Point out that this vocabulary is very familiar. These words are usually used in informal conversations among young people.
- Model the pronunciation of each term and have students repeat.

LE FRANÇAIS QUOTIDIEN

Les gens

ado (*m./f.*)	adolescent, teen
bonhomme (*m.*)	fellow
gars (*m.*)	guy
mec (*m.*)	guy
minette (*f.*)	young woman, sweetie
nana (*f.*)	young woman, girl
pote (*m.*)	buddy
type (*m.*)	guy

AP® **Theme:** Personal and Public Identities **Context:** Language and Identity

LE MONDE FRANCOPHONE

Les langues

Many francophone countries are multilingual, some with several official languages.

Switzerland German, French, Italian, and Romansh are all official languages. German is spoken by about 64% of the population and French by about 23%. Italian and Romansh speakers together account for about 8% of the country's population.

Belgium There are three official languages: French, Dutch, and German. Wallon, the local variety of French, is used by one-third of the population. Flemish, spoken primarily in the north, is used by roughly two-thirds of Belgians.

Morocco Classical Arabic is the official language, but most people speak the Moroccan dialect of Arabic. Berber is spoken by about 15 million people, and French remains Morocco's unofficial third language.

PORTRAIT

AP® **Theme:** Personal and Public Identities
Context: Beliefs and Values

Marianne

Marianne, a young woman wearing a soft, conical cap or helmet, is a symbol that embodies the French Republic. She represents fundamental French values, expressed in the national motto: **liberté**, **égalité°**, **fraternité°**. Her image first appeared in the late 18th century during the French Revolution, when the name Marie-Anne came to represent "the people." Later, the Republic adopted her as the official symbol on its seal. However, Marianne's origins date back to ancient Rome. At that time, democracy was often represented by a woman's face and freedom was symbolized by the conical Phrygian cap. Over time, Marianne has become the most widely used symbol of France. Sculptures of Marianne appear in every town hall across the country and variations of her image appear on everything from official government documents to postage stamps.

égalité equality **fraternité** brotherhood

Sur Internet

What countries are former French colonies?

Go to **vhlcentral.com** to find more information related to this **Culture** section.

2 **Complétez** Provide responses to these questions.

1. ___Marianne___ is a symbol of France.
2. ___Liberté, égalité, fraternité___ is the motto of the French Republic.
3. The Phrygian bonnet symbolizes ___freedom___.
4. The French term ___ado___ refers to a person aged 15 or 16.
5. ___Flemish___ is spoken by roughly two-thirds of Belgians.

3 **Et les Américains?** What might a comic-book character based on a "typical American" be like? With a partner, brainstorm a list of stereotypes to create a profile for such a character. Compare the profile you create with your classmates'. Do they fairly represent Americans? Why or why not?

A C T I V I T É S

EXPANSION

Cultural Comparison Have students compare **Marianne** and the French values **liberté**, **égalité**, **fraternité** to symbols and values in the United States. Discuss where these things come from and which values the two countries have in common.

EXPANSION

Les langues Have students research official and non-official languages in other Francophone countries or areas, and report on their findings.

1B.1   Subject pronouns vhlcentral and the verb *être*

Point de départ The subject of a sentence is the person or thing that performs the action. The verb expresses the action.

SUBJECT ⟷ VERB
Le professeur parle français.
The teacher speaks French.

Subject pronouns

• Subject pronouns replace a noun that is the subject of a sentence.

SUBJECT PRONOUN ⟷ VERB
Il parle français.
He speaks French.

Boîte à outils

In English, you sometimes use the pronoun *it* to replace certain nouns.
The exam is long.
It is long.

In French, there is no equivalent neuter pronoun. You must use **il** or **elle** depending on the gender of the noun it is replacing.
L'examen est long.
Il est long.

French subject pronouns				
	singular		**plural**	
first person	je	*I*	nous	*we*
second person	tu	*you (fam.)*	vous	*you*
	vous	*you (form.)*		
third person	il	*he/it (masc.)*	ils	*they (masc., masc. + fem.)*
	elle	*she/it (fem.)*		
	on	*one*	elles	*they (fem.)*

• Use **tu** for informal address and **vous** for formal. **Vous** is also the plural form of *you*, both informal and formal.

Comment vas-**tu**?
How's it going?

Comment allez-**vous**?
How are you?

Comment t'appelles-**tu**?
What's your name?

Comment vous appelez-**vous**?
What is/What are your name(s)?

• The subject pronoun **on** refers to people in general, just as the English subject pronouns *one*, *they*, or *you* sometimes do. **On** can also mean *we* in casual speech. **On** always takes the same verb form as **il** and **elle**.

En France, **on** parle français.
In France, they speak French.

On est au café.
We are at the coffee shop.

• Use the pronoun **ils** when replacing a noun or nouns that refer to a mixed group of males and females.

Rémy et Marie dansent très bien.
Ils dansent très bien.
They dance very well.

M. et Mme Diop sont de Dakar.
Ils sont de Dakar.
They are from Dakar.

Vérifiez

The verb *être*

- **Être** (*to be*) is an irregular verb. Its conjugation (set of forms for different subjects) does not follow a pattern. The form **être** is called the infinitive. It does not have a subject.

être (to be)			
je suis	*I am*	nous sommes	*we are*
tu es	*you are*	vous êtes	*you are*
il/elle est	*he/she/it is*	ils/elles sont	*they are*
on est	*one is*		

- The -s of the subject pronoun **vous** is pronounced like *z* in the phrase **vous êtes**.

  Vous êtes à Paris.   **Vous êtes** M. Leclerc? Enchantée.
  You are in Paris.   *Are you Mr. Leclerc? Pleased to meet you.*

C'est and *il/elle* est

- You learned in **Leçon 1A** to use **c'est** and its plural form **ce sont** plus a noun to identify who or what someone or something is. Remember to use an article before the noun.

  C'est un téléphone.   **Ce sont** des photos.
  That's a phone.   *Those are pictures.*

- You can also use the expressions **c'est** and **ce sont** followed by proper nouns to identify someone, but don't use an article before the names.

  C'est Amina.   **Ce sont** Amélie et Anne.
  That's Amina.   *That's Amélie and Anne.*

- Use **il/elle est** and **ils/elles sont** to refer to someone or something previously mentioned.

  La bibliothèque? **Elle est** moderne.   Nathalie et Félix? **Ils sont** intelligents.
  The library? It's modern.   *Nathalie and Félix? They are intelligent.*

- Use the phrases **il/elle est** and **ils/elles sont** to tell someone's profession or relationship. Note that in French, you do not use an article before the profession.

  Voilà M. Richard. **Il est** acteur.   **Elles sont** amies.
  There's Mr. Richard. He's an actor.   *They are friends.*

 Vérifiez

Essayez!   Fill in the blanks with the correct forms of the verb *être*.

1. Je ___suis___ ici.
2. Ils ___sont___ intelligents.
3. Tu ___es___ étudiante.
4. Nous ___sommes___ à Québec.
5. Vous ___êtes___ Mme Lacroix?
6. Marie ___est___ chanteuse.

Suggestions: Scaffolding
- Ask students what they remember about how to use **C'est** and **Ce sont**. Go over the two points pertaining to their use. Then go over the point about using **il/elle est** and **ils/elles sont**.
- Contrast the uses of **c'est/ce sont** and **il(s)/elle(s) est/sont** by explaining that **c'est/ce sont** is most often followed by a noun and **il(s)/elle(s) est/sont** is most often followed by an adjective. Give several examples: **C'est une amie. Elle est super! C'est un ordinateur. Il est petit** (*little*). Tell students that there are exceptions: **C'est très bien. Elle est chanteuse.** Have students do the Extra Practice activity below, and then complete the **Vérifiez** activity on vhlcentral.com.

Essayez! Have students create additional simple sentences using the verb **être**.

EXPANSION

Video Replay the video episode, having students focus on subject pronouns and the verb **être**. Ask them to write down as many examples of sentences that use forms of **être** as they can. Stop the video where appropriate to ask comprehension questions about what the characters said.

EXPANSION

Extra Practice Have pairs of students introduce each other to the class. They should begin by saying **C'est... Il/Elle est...** Assist them with unfamiliar vocabulary as necessary.

1 Suggestions
• Before students begin the activity, present the disjunctive pronouns **moi** and **toi**. Tell them that these pronouns are used after the word **et** (*and*). Explain that **moi** plus another person corresponds to the subject pronoun **nous** while **toi** plus another person corresponds to **vous**.
• Have students work on this activity in pairs. Tell them to switch roles for items 5–8.

2 Suggestion To check students' answers, call on volunteers to read the sentences aloud or write them on the board.

3 Suggestions
• Before beginning the activity, have students quickly identify the items or people in the photos.
• When going over answers, have them explain why they chose each structure.

Mise en pratique

1 **Clarifications** Pascal asks Odile to clarify what he thinks he heard. Complete her responses with the correct subject pronoun.

MODÈLE

Chantal? _____Elle_____ est étudiante.

1. Les professeurs? ___Ils___ sont en Tunisie.
2. Charles? ___Il___ est ici.
3. Moi? ___Je___ suis chanteuse.
4. Nadège et moi? ___Nous___ sommes au lycée.
5. Toi (*You*)? Oui, ___tu___ es un ami.
6. L'ordinateur? ___Il___ est dans la bibliothèque.
7. Annie et Claire? ___Elles___ sont là.
8. Lucien et toi? ___Vous___ êtes copains.

2 **Où sont-ils?** Thérèse wants to know where all her friends are. Tell her by completing the sentences with the appropriate subject pronouns and the correct forms of **être**.

MODÈLE

Sylvie / au café
Elle est au café.

1. Georges / au lycée   Il est au lycée.
2. Marie et moi / dans (*in*) la salle de classe   Nous sommes dans la salle de classe.
3. Christine et Anne / à la bibliothèque   Elles sont à la bibliothèque.
4. Richard et Vincent / là-bas   Ils sont là-bas.
5. Véronique, Marc et Anne / à la librairie   Ils sont à la librairie.
6. Jeanne / au bureau   Elle est au bureau.
7. Hugo et Isabelle / au lycée   Ils sont au lycée.
8. Martin / au bureau   Il est au bureau.

3 **Identifiez** Describe these photos using **c'est, ce sont, il/elle est,** or **ils/elles sont.**

1. ___C'est___ un acteur.   2. ___Il est___ ici.   3. ___Elles sont___ copines.

4. ___Elle est___ chanteuse.   5. ___Elle est___ là.   6. ___Ce sont___ des montres.

EXPANSION

Extra Practice Write cognates on the board and ask students to identify the professions of famous people. Ex: **acteur/actrice, président(e), artiste, pianiste**. Say: **Brad Pitt? (Il est acteur.) Beyoncé? (Elle est chanteuse.)**

TEACHING OPTIONS

Game Make up a list of simple sentences containing the verb **être** and write individual words on index cards. Distribute 3 or 4 cards to each student. As you read a sentence, the students holding the cards with each of the words must stand up in front of the class and arrange themselves into the sentence, so that the class can read the sentence and all forms are correct.

Communication

4 **Assemblez** In pairs, take turns using the verb **être** to combine elements from both columns. Talk about yourselves and people you know.

MODÈLE

Tu es sincère.

	A	B
Singulier:		
	Je	agréable
	Tu	d'origine française
	Mon (*My*, masc.) prof	difficile (*difficult*)
	Mon/Ma (*My*, fem.)	élève
	camarade de classe	sincère
	Mon cours	sociable
	_____	_____
Pluriel:		
	Nous	agréables
	Mes (*My*) profs	copains/copines
	Mes camarades	difficiles
	de classe	élèves
	Mes cours	sincères

5 **Qui est-ce?** In pairs, identify who or what is in each picture. If possible, use **il/elle est** or **ils/elles sont** to add something else about each person or place. Answers will vary.

▶ **MODÈLE**

C'est Céline Dion. Elle est chanteuse.

1. _____

2. _____

3. _____

4. _____

5. _____

6. _____

6 **On est comment?** In pairs, take turns describing these famous people using the phrases **C'est**, **Ce sont**, **Il/Elle est**, or **Ils/Elles sont** and words from the box.

professeur(s)	actrice(s)	chanteuse(s)
chanteur(s)	adorable(s)	pessimiste(s)
optimiste(s)	timide(s)	acteur(s)

1. Justin Bieber
2. Taylor Swift et Adèle
3. Michelle Obama
4. Leonardo DiCaprio
5. Tina Fey et Will Ferrell
6. Anne Hathaway

7 **Enchanté** You and your brother are in a local bookstore. You run into one of his classmates, whom you've never met. In a brief conversation, introduce yourselves, ask one another how you are, and say something about yourselves using a form of **être**. Answers will vary.

---

4 **Suggestions**
- Before students complete the activity, go over the adjectives to make sure they know their meaning. Tell them to refer to the list of adjectives on p. 32 if needed.
- Tell students to add two questions of their own to the list and to jot down notes during their interviews.

5 **Suggestion** Tell students to write down their descriptions. After they have completed the activity, call on volunteers to read their descriptions.

6 **Partner Chat** You can also assign Activity 6 on vhlcentral.com. Students work in pairs to record the activity online. The pair's recorded conversation will appear in your gradebook.

7 **Suggestion** Have volunteers act out their conversations for the class.

Activity Pack For additional activities, go to the Activity Pack in the Resources section of vhlcentral.com.

TEACHING OPTIONS

Small Groups Working in small groups, have students write sentences about people in the classroom using **être**. Tell them to use as many different conjugations as they can. Allow five minutes to complete the activity, then call on groups to write their best sentences on the board for the class to correct.

EXPANSION

Extra Practice Bring in pictures of people and objects and ask students to describe them using **c'est, ce sont, il/elle est,** or **ils/elles sont**.

31

Section Goals

In this section, students will learn:
- forms, agreement, and position of adjectives
- some descriptive adjectives
- adjectives of nationality

Key Standards

4.1, 5.1

Suggestions: Scaffolding

- Present **Point de départ** and adjectives using TPR. Have students repeat adjectives after you. Explain that **sympathique** does not mean *sympathetic* except in medical terms. Act out behaviors and have students call out the corresponding adjective.
- Have students read the point on making adjectives feminine and masculine. Write different adjectives on the board and have students identify their gender and number, or if they can't tell.
- Explain that the **e** added to an adjective is silent, but the final consonant is pronounced. Have students repeat adjective pairs after you: **charmant/charmante**, **patient/patiente**, etc.
- Point out that in English most adjectives come before the noun, but in French they come after the noun. Write sentences like **C'est un examen difficile.** on the board, circle the adjective, and draw an arrow pointing to the noun. Then have students work in pairs to write two sentences modeled after examples in the textbook. Have them write their sentences on the board for the class to check.
- Have students complete the **Vérifiez** activity on vhlcentral.com.

1B.2

Adjective agreement **vhl**central

Point de départ Adjectives are words that describe people, places, and things. They are often used with the verb **être** to point out the qualities of nouns or pronouns.

*Le cours est **difficile**.*

*Je suis **optimiste**.*

- Many adjectives in French are cognates; that is, they have the same or similar spellings and meanings in French and English.

Cognate descriptive adjectives

agréable	*pleasant*	intelligent(e)	*intelligent*
amusant(e)	*fun*	intéressant(e)	*interesting*
brillant(e)	*brilliant*	occupé(e)	*busy*
charmant(e)	*charming*	optimiste	*optimistic*
désagréable	*unpleasant*	patient(e)	*patient*
différent(e)	*different*	pessimiste	*pessimistic*
difficile	*difficult*	poli(e)	*polite*
égoïste	*selfish*	réservé(e)	*reserved*
élégant(e)	*elegant*	sincère	*sincere*
impatient(e)	*impatient*	sociable	*sociable*
important(e)	*important*	sympathique	*nice*
indépendant(e)	*independent*	(sympa)	
		timide	*shy*

- In French, most adjectives agree in number and gender with the nouns they modify. To make many adjectives feminine, you add **-e** to the masculine form. If the adjective already ends in an unaccented **-e**, you add nothing.

MASCULINE SINGULAR		FEMININE SINGULAR
patient	⟶	patiente
optimiste	⟶	optimiste

Henri est **élégant** et **agréable**.
Henri is elegant and pleasant.

Carole est **élégante** et **agréable**.
Carole is elegant and pleasant.

- To make most adjectives plural, add **-s**.

	SINGULAR	ADD -s	PLURAL
MASCULINE	patient	⟶	patient**s**
FEMININE	patiente	⟶	patiente**s**

MASC./FEM. SINGULAR	ADD -s	MASC./FEM. PLURAL
optimiste	⟶	optimiste**s**

Marc et David sont **intelligents** et **sociables**.
Marc and David are intelligent and sociable.

Anne et Claire sont **intelligentes** et **sociables**.
Anne and Claire are intelligent and sociable.

🏃 **Boîte à outils**

Use the masculine plural form of an adjective to describe a group composed of masculine and feminine nouns: **Henri et Patricia sont élégants.**

🔊 **Vérifiez**

EXPANSION

Extra Practice Have pairs of students write sentences using adjectives such as **intelligent(e), optimiste, sociable**. When they have finished, ask volunteers to dictate their sentences to you while you write them on the board. After you have written a sentence and corrected any errors, ask volunteers to suggest a sentence that uses the antonym of the adjective.

TEACHING OPTIONS

Using Games Divide the class into two teams and have them line up. Point to a member from each team and give a certain form of an adjective (Ex: **patients**). Then name another form that you want students to provide (Ex: feminine singular) and have them race to the board. The first student who writes the correct form earns one point for his or her team. Deduct one point for each wrong answer. The team with the most points at the end wins.

- French adjectives are usually placed after the noun they modify when they don't directly follow a form of **être**.

Ce sont des **élèves brillantes**.
They're brilliant students.

Bernard est un homme **agréable et poli**.
Bernard is a pleasant and polite man.

- Here are some adjectives of nationality. For some of them, you add -**ne** to the masculine form to make them feminine: **algérienne, canadienne, italienne, vietnamienne**.

Adjectives of nationality

algérien(ne)	*Algerian*	japonais(e)	*Japanese*
allemand(e)	*German*	marocain(e)	*Moroccan*
anglais(e)	*English*	martiniquais(e)	*from Martinique*
américain(e)	*American*	mexicain(e)	*Mexican*
canadien(ne)	*Canadian*	québécois(e)	*from Quebec*
espagnol(e)	*Spanish*	sénégalais(e)	*Senegalese*
français(e)	*French*	suisse	*Swiss*
italien(ne)	*Italian*	vietnamien(ne)	*Vietnamese*

- The first letter of adjectives of nationality is not capitalized as it is in English.

Il est **américain**.
He is American.

Elle est **française**.
She is French.

- Adjectives like **sénégalais** that already end in -**s**, have the same masculine singular and plural forms. However, you must add an -**s** to the feminine form to make it plural.

	SINGULAR		PLURAL
MASCULINE	sénégalais	⟶	sénégalais
		BUT	
FEMININE	sénégalaise	⟶	sénégalaises

- To ask someone's nationality or heritage, use **Quelle est ta/votre nationalité?** or **Tu es/ Vous êtes de quelle origine?** Note that the adjectives following **nationalité** and **origine** are feminine. This is because both nouns are feminine.

Quelle est votre nationalité?
What is your nationality?

Je suis de nationalité canadienne.
I'm Canadian.

Je suis canadien.
I'm Canadian.

Tu es de quelle origine?
What is your heritage?

Je suis d'origine italienne.
I'm of Italian heritage.

Vérifiez

Essayez! Write in the correct forms of the adjectives.

1. Marc est ___timide___ (timide).
2. Ils sont ___anglais___ (anglais).
3. Elle adore la littérature ___française___ (français).
4. Ce sont des actrices ___suisses___ (suisse).
5. Marie est ___mexicaine___ (mexicain).
6. Les actrices sont ___impatientes___ (impatient).
7. Elles sont ___réservées___ (réservé).
8. Il y a des universités ___importantes___ (important).
9. Christelle est ___amusante___ (amusant).
10. Les élèves sont ___polis___ (poli) en cours.
11. Mme Castillion est très ___occupée___ (occupé).
12. Luc et moi, nous sommes ___sincères___ (sincère).

EXPANSION

Extra Practice Have students collect several interesting pictures of people from magazines or newspapers. Have them prepare a description of one of the pictures ahead of time. Invite them to show the pictures to the class and then give their descriptions orally without indicating which picture they are talking about. The class will guess which of the pictures is being described.

EXPANSION

Extra Practice Do a quick class survey to find out how many nationalities are represented in your class. As students respond, write the nationality and number of students on the board. Ask: **Combien d'élèves sont d'origine américaine? Mexicaine? Vietnamienne?** If students ask, clarify that the gender of the adjective of nationality agrees with the word **origine**, which is feminine.

- Present adjectives of nationality referring to a world map. State the country and then the nationality, giving both the masculine and feminine form. Have students repeat after you.
- Go over capitalization and how to make masculine adjectives of nationality feminine and plural. Explain that adjectives of nationality can be used as nouns as well. Examples: **La femme anglaise est réservée. L'Anglaise est réservée.** Point out that nouns of nationality are capitalized, while adjectives of nationality are not.
- Use pictures and the names of celebrities to practice adjectives of nationality. Examples: **Le prince William est canadien? (Non, il est anglais.) Julia Roberts est française? (Non, elle est américaine.)**
- Model how to ask someone's nationality and how to answer. Then assign a nationality to each student and ask: **Quelle est votre/ta nationalité?** Then, have students ask each other their nationalities.
- Assign **Vérifiez** activity. Check. Assign **Essayez!** for homework. Remind students to watch the Grammar Tutorial to review.

33

Mise en pratique

1 **Nous aussi!** Jean-Paul is bragging about himself, but his younger sisters Stéphanie and Gisèle believe they have the same characteristics. Give their responses.

MODÈLE

Je suis amusant.
Nous aussi, nous sommes amusantes.

1. Je suis intelligent. ___Nous aussi, nous sommes intelligentes.___
2. Je suis sincère. ___Nous aussi, nous sommes sincères.___
3. Je suis élégant. ___Nous aussi, nous sommes élégantes.___
4. Je suis patient. ___Nous aussi, nous sommes patientes.___
5. Je suis sociable. ___Nous aussi, nous sommes sociables.___
6. Je suis poli. ___Nous aussi, nous sommes polies.___
7. Je suis charmant. ___Nous aussi, nous sommes charmantes.___
8. Je suis optimiste. ___Nous aussi, nous sommes optimistes.___

2 **Les nationalités** You are with a group of students from all over the world. Indicate their nationalities according to the cities they come from.

MODÈLE

Monique est de (*from*) Paris.
Elle est française.

1. Les amies Fumiko et Keiko sont de Tokyo. Elles sont japonaises.
2. Hans est de Berlin. Il est allemand.
3. Juan et Pablo sont de Guadalajara. Ils sont mexicains.
4. Wendy est de Londres. Elle est anglaise.
5. Jared est de San Francisco. Il est américain.
6. Francesca est de Rome. Elle est italienne.
7. Aboud et Moustafa sont de Casablanca. Ils sont marocains.
8. Jean-Pierre et Mario sont de Québec. Ils sont québécois.

3 **Voilà Mme...** Your parents are having a party and you point out different people to your friend. Use one of the adjectives you just learned each time. Answers will vary.

MODÈLE

Voilà M. Duval. Il est sénégalais.
C'est un ami.

M. Duval
Catherine et Jeanne
M. Forestier
Georges et Denise
Mme Malbon

Communication

4 **Interview** Interview someone to see what he or she is like. In pairs, play both roles. Are you compatible as friends? Answers will vary.

MODÈLE

pessimiste
Élève 1: *Tu es pessimiste?*
Élève 2: *Non, je suis optimiste.*

1. impatient
2. modeste
3. timide
4. sincère
5. égoïste
6. sociable
7. indépendant
8. amusant

5 **Ils sont comment?** In pairs, take turns describing each item below. Tell your partner whether you agree (**C'est vrai**) or disagree (**C'est faux**) with the descriptions. Answers will vary.

MODÈLE

Daniel Radcliffe
Élève 1: *C'est un acteur désagréable.*
Élève 2: *C'est faux. Il est charmant.*

1. Beyoncé et Céline Dion
2. les étudiants de Harvard
3. Usher
4. la classe de français
5. le président des États-Unis (*United States*)
6. Tom Hanks et George Clooney
7. le prof de français
8. Steven Spielberg
9. notre (*our*) lycée
10. Amanda Seyfried et Amy Adams

Coup de main

Use **c'est** or **ce sont** instead of **il/elle est** and **ils/elles sont** when you have an adjective qualifying the noun that follows.

C'est un professeur intelligent.
He is an intelligent teacher.

Ce sont des actrices élégantes.
Those are elegant actresses.

Use **il/elle est** and **ils/elles sont** when followed directly by an adjective.

Il est intelligent.
He is intelligent.

Elles sont élégantes.
They are elegant.

6 **Au café** You and two classmates are talking about your new teachers, each of whom is very different from the other two. In groups of three, create a dialogue in which you greet one another and describe your teachers. Answers will vary.

4 **Suggestions**
• Have students add two more qualities to the list that are important to them.
• After students have completed the activity, ask them if they are compatible and to explain why or why not.

4 **Virtual Chat** You can also assign Activity 4 on vhlcentral.com. Students record individual responses that appear in your gradebook.

5 **Suggestion** Present the information in **Coup de main**. Then ask students to explain why **c'est** is used by **Élève 1** and **il est** is used by **Élève 2**.

5 **Expansion** Have small groups brainstorm names of famous people, places, and things not found in the activity and write them in a list. Tell them to include some plural items. Then ask the groups to exchange lists and describe the people, places, and things on that list.

6 **Suggestion** Encourage students to ask each other questions about their teachers during the conversation.

Activity Pack For additional activities, go to the Activity Pack in the Resources section of vhlcentral.com.

EXPANSION

Extra Practice Write each descriptive adjective in Activity 4 on two cards or slips of paper and put them in two separate piles in random order. Hand out one card to each student. Tell students they have to find the person who has the same adjective as they do. Example: **Élève 1: Tu es optimiste? Élève 2: Oui, je suis optimiste./Non, je suis sociable**. For variation, this activity can also be used to practice adjectives of nationality.

EXPANSION

Extra Practice As a rapid-response drill, say the name of a country and have students respond with the appropriate adjective of nationality. For variation, have students write the adjective on the board or tell them to spell the adjective after they say it.

Révision

1 Interpersonal Speaking
Have pairs act out their conversations for the rest of the class.

1 Partner Chat You can also assign Activity 1 on vhlcentral.com. Students work in pairs to record the activity online. The pair's recorded conversation will appear in your gradebook.

2 Suggestion Before students begin to make corrections on their classmates' papers, tell them to check the following: correct use of articles and subject pronouns, subject-verb agreement, and adjective agreement.

3 Expansion Have students repeat the activity and describe their differences this time.

4 Suggestion Because this is the first activity in which the **Feuilles d'activités** are used, explain to students that they must approach their classmates with their paper in hand and ask questions following the **modèle**. When they find someone who answers affirmatively, that student signs his or her name.

5 Expansion Have a few volunteers read their descriptions aloud. Then ask the class to point out the differences between the various descriptions.

6 Suggestions
• Give students ten minutes to complete the activity.
• Have two volunteers read the **modèle** aloud.

---

1 **Festival francophone** With a partner, act out a conversation between two people from the list. They are meeting for the first time at a francophone festival so they should use **vous**. Then, choose two other people and repeat. *Answers will vary.*

Angélique, Sénégal

Abdel, Algérie

Laurent, Martinique

Sylvain, Suisse

Hélène, Canada

Daniel, France

Mai, Viêt-Nam

Nora, Maroc

2 **Tu ou vous?** How would the conversations between the people in **Activité 1** be different if they were students at your school? Write out the conversation. Then, exchange papers with another pair of students for correction. Act out the corrected version of the conversation. *Answers will vary.*

3 **En commun** Tell your partner the name of a friend. Then, use adjectives to say what you and the friend have in common. Share with the class what you learned about your partner and his or her friend. *Answers will vary.*

MODÈLE

Charles est un ami. Charles et moi, nous sommes amusants.
Nous sommes patients aussi.

---

4 **Comment es-tu?** Your teacher will give you a worksheet. Survey as many classmates as possible to ask if they would use the adjectives listed to describe themselves. Then, decide which two students in the class are most similar. *Answers will vary.*

MODÈLE

Élève 1: *Tu es sociable?*
Élève 2: *Non. Je suis timide.*

Adjectifs	Noms
1. timide	Éric
2. impatient(e)	
3. optimiste	
4. réservé(e)	
5. charmant(e)	
6. poli(e)	
7. agréable	
8. amusant(e)	

5 **Mes camarades de classe** Write a brief description of the students in your French class. What are their names? What are their personalities like? What is their heritage? Use all the French you have learned so far. Write at least eight sentences. Remember, be complimentary! *Answers will vary.*

6 **Les descriptions** Your teacher will give you one set of drawings of eight people and a different set to your partner. Each person in your drawings has something in common with a person in your partner's drawings. Find out what it is without looking at your partner's sheet. *Answers will vary.*

MODÈLE

Élève 1: *Jean est à la bibliothèque.*
Élève 2: *Gina est à la bibliothèque.*
Élève 1: *Jean et Gina sont à la bibliothèque.*

TEACHING OPTIONS

Mini-skits 👥 Have students work in groups of three or four. Tell them to prepare a skit on any situation they wish, provided that they use material presented in this lesson. Possible situations can include meeting at a café (as in **Roman-photo**), meeting in between classes, and introducing friends to teachers. Remind them to use as many adjectives as possible. Encourage students to have fun with the skit and be creative.

EXPANSION

Interview As a follow-up to Activity 4 and to practice **vous**, have students ask you yes/no questions. First, have them guess your nationality. Example: **Vous êtes français(e)?** Then have them ask you about your personality. Example: **Vous êtes impatient(e)?**

À l'écoute vhlcentral

STRATÉGIE

Listening for words you know

You can get the gist of a conversation by listening for words and phrases you already know.

🔊 To help you practice this strategy, listen to this sentence and make a list of the words you have already learned.

_____ _____

_____

Préparation

Look at the photograph. Where are these people? What are they doing? In your opinion, do they know one another? Why or why not? What do you think they're talking about?

🔊 À vous d'écouter

As you listen, indicate the items you associate with Hervé and those you associate with Laure and Lucas.

HERVÉ	LAURE ET LUCAS
la littérature	la littérature
le café	le café
l'examen	l'examen
le bureau	le bureau
la sociologie	la sociologie
la librairie	la librairie
la bibliothèque	la bibliothèque
le lycée	le lycée
le tableau	le tableau
l'université	l'université

Compréhension

Vrai ou faux? Based on the conversation you heard, indicate whether each of the following statements is **vrai** or **faux**.

	Vrai	Faux
1. Lucas and Hervé are good friends.	☐	☑
2. Hervé is preparing for an exam.	☑	☐
3. Laure and Lucas know each other from school.	☑	☐
4. Hervé is on his way to the library.	☐	☑
5. Lucas and Laure are going to a café.	☑	☐
6. Lucas studies literature.	☐	☑
7. Laure is in high school.	☐	☑
8. Laure is not feeling well today.	☐	☑

Présentations It's your turn to get to know your classmates. Using the conversation you heard as a model, select a partner you do not know and introduce yourself to him or her in French. Follow the steps below.

- Greet your partner.
- Find out his or her name.
- Ask how he or she is doing.
- Introduce your partner to another student.
- Say good-bye.

Section Goals

In this section, students will:
- learn to listen for known vocabulary
- listen to sentences containing familiar and unfamiliar vocabulary
- listen to a conversation and complete several activities

Key Standards
1.2, 2.1

21ˢᵗ Century Skills

Critical Thinking and Problem Solving
Students practice aural comprehension as a tool to negotiate meaning in French.

Stratégie
Script Je vous présente une amie, Juliette Lenormand. Elle est élève dans mon lycée.
Teacher Resources DVD

Successful Language Learning Tell your students that many people feel nervous about their ability to comprehend a foreign language. Tell them to follow the advice in the **Stratégie** sections to lessen anxiety.

TELL Connection

Performance & Feedback 5
Why: Using multiple assessment measures that culminate in performance will accurately reflect how language skills are gained and used. _What:_ Help students understand and measure each step toward proficiency in this segment: thinking strategically, practicing a strategy before applying it, completing scaffolded activities that lead to better performance.

À vous d'écouter
Script
HERVÉ: Salut, Laure! Ça va?
LAURE: Bonjour, Hervé. Ça va bien. Et toi?
HERVÉ: Pas mal, merci.
LAURE: Je te présente un copain de l'université.
Lucas, Hervé. Hervé, Lucas.

LUCAS: Enchanté.
H: Bonjour, Lucas. Comment vas-tu?
LU: Très bien, merci.
LA: Qu'est-ce que tu fais, Hervé?
H: Je vais à la librairie pour acheter un livre sur la littérature.
LA: Pour un examen?

H: Oui, pour un examen. Et vous?
LA: Nous, on va au café.
H: Alors, à plus tard.
LA: Oui, salut.
LU: Au revoir, Hervé.
H: À bientôt.
Teacher Resources DVD

Savoir-faire

vhl central

Panorama

Le monde francophone

Pays et régions francophones

Les pays en chiffres°

 Organisation internationale de la Francophonie

▶ Nombre de pays° où le français est langue° officielle: *29*

▶ Nombre de pays où le français est parlé°: *plus de° 60*

▶ Nombre de francophones dans le monde°: *274.000.000 (deux cent soixante-quatorze millions)*
SOURCE: Organisation internationale de la Francophonie

Villes capitales

▶ **Algérie:** *Alger*
▶ **Cameroun:** *Yaoundé*
▶ **France:** *Paris*
▶ **Guinée:** *Conakry*
▶ **Haïti:** *Port-au-Prince*
▶ **Laos:** *Vientiane*
▶ **Mali:** *Bamako*
▶ **Rwanda:** *Kigali*
▶ **Seychelles:** *Victoria*
▶ **Suisse:** *Berne*

Francophones célèbres

▶ Marie Curie, *Pologne, scientifique, prix Nobel en chimie et physique (1867–1934)*

▶ René Magritte, *Belgique, peintre° (1898–1967)*

▶ Ousmane Sembène, *Sénégal, cinéaste° et écrivain° (1923–2007)*

▶ Jean Reno, *Maroc, acteur (1948–)*

▶ Céline Dion, *Québec, chanteuse (1968–)*

▶ Marie-José Pérec, *Guadeloupe (France), athlète (1968–)*

chiffres *numbers* **pays** *countries* **langue** *language* **parlé** *spoken* **plus de** *more than* **monde** *world* **peintre** *painter* **cinéaste** *filmmaker* **écrivain** *writer* **sur** *on* **comme** *such as* **l'OTAN** *NATO* **Jeux** *Games* **deuxième** *second* **enseignée** *taught* **Heiva** *an annual Tahitian festival*

L'AMÉRIQUE DU NORD

L'EUROPE
LA FRANCE

L'ASIE

L'OCÉAN ATLANTIQUE

L'AFRIQUE

L'OCÉAN PACIFIQUE

L'AMÉRIQUE DU SUD

0 — 3,000 miles
0 — 3,000 kilomètres

PAYS FRANCOPHONES EN ASIE

LE LAOS
LE CAMBODGE
L'OCÉAN INDIEN
LE VIÊT-NAM

LA POLYNÉSIE FRANÇAISE

L'OCÉAN PACIFIQUE
Les îles Marquises
Les îles de la Société
Les îles Tuamotu
Tahiti
Les îles Australes
Les îles Gambier

0 — 500 miles
0 — 500 kilomètres

Incroyable mais vrai!

La langue française est une des rares langues à être parlées sur° cinq continents. C'est aussi la langue officielle de beaucoup d'organisations internationales comme° l'OTAN°, les Nations unies, l'Union européenne, et aussi les Jeux° Olympiques! Le français est la deuxième° langue enseignée° dans le monde, après l'anglais.

AP® Theme: Personal and Public Identities
Context: Language and Identity

La société

Le français au Québec

Au Québec, province du Canada, le français est la langue officielle, parlée par° 80% (quatre-vingts pour cent) de la population. Les Québécois, pour° préserver l'usage de la langue, ont° une loi° qui oblige l'affichage° en français dans les lieux° publics. Le français est aussi la langue co-officielle du Canada: les employés du gouvernement doivent° parler anglais et français.

AP® Theme: Personal and Public Identities
Context: Language and Identity

Les destinations

Haïti, première République noire

En 1791, un ancien esclave°, Toussaint Louverture, mène° une rébellion pour l'abolition de l'esclavage en Haïti, ancienne colonie française. Après avoir gagné° le combat, Toussaint Louverture se proclame gouverneur de l'île d'Hispaniola (Haïti et Saint-Domingue) et abolit l'esclavage. Il est plus tard° capturé par l'armée française et renvoyé° en France. Son successeur, Jean-Jacques Dessalines, lui-même° ancien esclave, vainc° l'armée en 1803 et proclame l'indépendance d'Haïti en 1804. C'est la première République noire du monde° et le premier pays occidental° à abolir l'esclavage.

Les destinations

AP® Theme: Personal and Public Identities
Context: Language and Identity

La Louisiane

Ce territoire au sud° des États-Unis a été nommé° «Louisiane» en l'honneur du Roi° de France Louis XIV. En 1803 (mille huit cent trois), Napoléon Bonaparte vend° la colonie aux États-Unis pour 15 millions de dollars, pour empêcher° son acquisition par les Britanniques. Aujourd'hui° en Louisiane, entre 150.000 et 200.000 personnes parlent° le français cajun. La Louisiane est connue° pour sa° cuisine cajun, comme° le jambalaya, ici sur° la photo.

AP® Theme: Personal and Public Identities
Context: Language and Identity

Les traditions

La Journée internationale de la Francophonie

LE POUVOIR DES MOTS

Chaque année°, l'Organisation internationale de la Francophonie (O.I.F.) coordonne la Journée internationale de la Francophonie. Dans plus de° 100 (cent) pays et sur cinq continents, on célèbre la langue française et la diversité culturelle francophone avec des festivals de musique, de gastronomie, de théâtre, de danse et de cinéma. Le rôle principal de l'O.I.F. est la promotion de la langue française et la défense de la diversité culturelle et linguistique du monde francophone.

Qu'est-ce que vous avez appris? Complete the sentences.

1. __Ousmane Sembène__ est un cinéaste africain.

2. __274 millions__ de personnes parlent français dans le monde.

3. __L'Organisation internationale de la Francophonie__ est responsable de la promotion de la diversité culturelle francophone.

4. Les employés du gouvernement du Canada parlent __anglais et français__.

5. En 1791, __Toussaint Louverture__ mène la rébellion pour l'abolition de l'esclavage en Haïti.

6. Haïti proclame son indépendance en __1804__.

7. Le nom «Louisiane» vient du (comes from the) nom de __Louis XIV__.

8. Plus de 100 pays célèbrent __la Journée internationale de la Francophonie__.

9. Le français est parlé sur __cinq__ continents.

10. En 1803, Napoléon Bonaparte vend __la Louisiane__ aux États-Unis.

Sur Internet

1. Les États-Unis célèbrent la Journée internationale de la Francophonie. Faites (Make) une liste de trois événements (events) et dites (say) où ils ont lieu (take place).

2. Trouvez des informations sur un(e) chanteur/chanteuse francophone célèbre aux États-Unis. Citez (Cite) trois titres de chanson (song titles).

parlée par spoken by **pour** in order to **ont** have **loi** law **affichage** posting **lieux** places **doivent** must **ancien esclave** former slave **mène** leads **Après avoir gagné** After winning **plus tard** later **renvoyé** sent back **lui-même** himself **vainc** defeats **du monde** in the world **pays occidental** Western country **au sud** in the South **a été nommé** was named **Roi** King **vend** sells **empêcher** to prevent **Aujourd'hui** Today **parlent** speak **connue** known **sa** its **comme** such as **sur** in **Chaque année** Each year **Dans plus de** In more than

---

Suggestion Tell students they are not expected to understand every word in the texts. Suggest they look for cognates to help them understand the gist of each section.

Le français au Québec Since Jacques Cartier first arrived in Gaspé and claimed the land for the French king in 1534, the people of Quebec have maintained their language and culture, despite being outnumbered and surrounded by English speakers. French became an official language of Canada in 1867.

Haïti, première République noire Haitian Creole and French are the two official languages of Haiti. The grammar of Haitian Creole is similar to languages of West Africa and other Caribbean creoles. Distribute examples of Haitian Creole and have students compare the language with French.

La Louisiane The early settlers of Louisiana came from France and Acadia (now Nova Scotia and adjacent areas) during the seventeenth and eighteenth centuries. The Acadian settlers were descendents of French Canadians who were exiled from Acadia by the English and eventually settled in the bayou region. Cajun French evolved over time borrowing terms from American Indian, German, English, African, and Spanish speakers.

La Journée internationale de la Francophonie
- The members of **l'Organisation internationale de la Francophonie** comprise 63 states and governments (notice the organization's symbol on page 38). The celebrations in the various Francophone regions take place throughout the month of March.

21st Century Skills

Information and Media Literacy: Sur Internet Students access and critically evaluate information from the Internet.

Using Maps Have students work in pairs. Tell them to look at the maps in the frontmatter and make a list of the Francophone countries and capitals that do not appear in the section **Villes capitales**. Point out that they need to find eighteen countries.

Cultural Comparison Ask students if they know of any places in the United States where people speak two languages or they can see bilingual signs.

Cultural Comparison In groups of three, have students compare **la Journée internationale de la Francophonie** to a cultural celebration held in their town, city, or region. Tell them to discuss the purpose of each celebration, the reasons why people attend them, and the types of events or activities that are part of the celebration.

Savoir-faire

Lecture vhlcentral

Avant la lecture

STRATÉGIE

Recognizing cognates

Cognates are words that share similar meanings and spellings in two or more languages. When reading in French, it's helpful to look for cognates and use them to guess the meaning of what you're reading. However, watch out for false cognates. For example, **librairie** means *bookstore*, not *library*, and **coin** means *corner*, not *coin*. Look at this list of French words. Can you guess the meaning of each word?

important	banque
pharmacie	culture
intelligent	actif
dentiste	sociologie
décision	fantastique
télévision	restaurant
médecine	police

Examinez le texte

Briefly look at the document. What kind of information is listed? In what order is it listed? Where do you usually find such information? Can you guess what this document is?

Mots apparentés

Read the list of cognates in the **Stratégie** box again. How many cognates can you find in the reading selection? Are there additional cognates in the reading? What are they? Can you guess their English equivalents?

Devinez

In addition to using cognates and words you already know, you can also use context to guess the meaning of words you do not know. Find the following words in the reading selection and try to guess what they mean. Compare your answers with those of a classmate.

horaires	lundi	ouvert	soirs	tous

40 *quarante*

Carnet d'adresses

Carnet d'adresses

Recherche ▶

A B C D E F G H I J K L

☑ **DAMERY Jean-Claude**
dentiste
✉ 18, rue des Lilas   02 38 23 45 46
45000 Orléans

☐ **Café de la Poste**
Ouvert° tous les jours°, de 7h00° à 22h00
✉ 25, place de la Poste   02 38 27 18 00
45000 Orléans

☐ **Librairie Balzac**
Horaires: 9h00–12h00 et 14h00–18h00
✉ 18, route de Lorient   02 38 18 60 36
45000 Orléans

☐ **DANTEC Pierre-Henri**
médecin généraliste
✉ 23, rue du Lac   02 38 47 34 20
45000 Orléans

☑ **Banque du Centre**
Ouvert de 9h00 à 17h00 du lundi° au vendredi°
✉ 17, boulevard Giroud   02 38 58 35 00
45000 Orléans

Dîner vendredi 8h00
Restaurant du Chat qui dort

Après la lecture

Où aller? Tell where each of these people should go based on what they need or want to do.

MODÈLE

Camille's daughter is starting high school.
Lycée Molière

1. Mrs. Leroy needs to deposit her paycheck.
   Banque du Centre

2. Laurent would like to take his girlfriend out for a special dinner.
   Restaurant du Chat qui dort

3. Marc has a toothache.
   DAMERY Jean-Claude, dentiste

4. Céleste would like to go see a play tonight.
   Théâtre de la Comédie

5. Pauline's computer is broken.
   Messier et fils, Réparations ordinateurs et télévisions

6. Mr. Duchemin needs to buy some aspirin for his son.
   Pharmacie Vidal

7. Jean-Marie needs a book on French history but he doesn't want to buy one.
   Bibliothèque municipale

8. Noémie thinks she has the flu.
   DANTEC Pierre-Henri, médecin généraliste

9. Mr. and Mrs. Prudhomme want to go out for breakfast this morning.
   Café de la Poste

10. Jonathan wants to buy a new book for his sister's birthday.
    Librairie Balzac

Notre annuaire With a classmate, select three of the listings from the reading and use them as models to create similar listings in French advertising places or services in your area.

MODÈLE

Restaurant du Chat qui dort
Ouvert tous les soirs pour le dîner
Horaires: 19h00 à 23h00
29, avenue des Rosiers
45000 Orléans
02 38 45 35 08

Always Good Eats Restaurant
Ouvert tous les jours
Horaires: 6h00 à 19h00
1250 9th Avenue
San Diego, CA 92108
224-0932

Où aller? Go over the activity with the class. If students have trouble inferring the answer to any question, help them identify the cognate or provide additional context clues.

Notre annuaire
- Before beginning the activity, have students brainstorm places and services in the area, and write a list on the board. You might also want to bring in a few local telephone books for students to use as references for addresses and phone numbers.
- You may wish to have students include e-mail addresses (**les adresses e-mail**) and websites (**les sites web**) in their lists.

21ˢᵗ Century Skills

Creativity and Innovation
Ask students to research and prepare a presentation on ten common false cognates in French, inspired by the information on these two pages.

TELL Connection

Collaboration 1 *Why:* When students, their families, and school personnel understand how languages share common features and words, the usefulness of lifelong language learning becomes apparent. *What:* Help students understand the nature of cognates by using the ones in this section. Have students share their knowledge with others at school and at home, and find examples on their own.

Messier et fils°
Réparations ordinateurs et télévisions
56, boulevard Henri IV   02 38 44 42 59
45000 Orléans

Théâtre de la Comédie
11, place de la Comédie   02 38 45 32 11
45000 Orléans

Pharmacie Vidal
45, rue des Acacias   02 38 13 57 53
45000 Orléans

Restaurant du Chat qui dort°
Ouvert tous les soirs pour le dîner / Horaires: 19h00 à 23h00
29, avenue des Rosiers   02 38 45 35 08
45000 Orléans

Bibliothèque municipale
Place de la gare   02 38 56 43 22
45000 Orléans

Lycée Molière
15, rue Molière   02 38 29 23 04
45000 Orléans

11:29 AM

Contacts   Éditer

P Q R S T U V W X Y Z

Ouvert *Open* **tous les jours** *every day* **7h00 (sept heures)** *7:00* **lundi** *Monday*
vendredi *Friday* **fils** *son(s)* **Chat qui dort** *Sleeping cat*

Écriture

STRATÉGIE

Writing in French

Why do we write? All writing has a purpose. For example, we may write a poem to reveal our innermost feelings, a letter to provide information, or an essay to persuade others to accept a point of view. Proficient writers are not born, however. Writing requires time, thought, effort, and a lot of practice. Here are some tips to help you write more effectively in French.

DO

- ▶ Write your ideas in French.
- ▶ Organize your ideas in an outline or graphic organizer.
- ▶ Decide what the purpose of your writing will be.
- ▶ Use grammar and vocabulary you know.
- ▶ Use your textbook for examples of style, format, and expressions in French.
- ▶ Use your imagination and creativity to make your writing more interesting.
- ▶ Put yourself in your reader's place to see if your writing is interesting and/or meets the reader's need.

DON'T

- ▶ Translate your ideas from English to French.
- ▶ Repeat what is in the textbook or on a web page.
- ▶ Use a bilingual dictionary until you have learned how to use one effectively.

Thème
Faites une liste!
Avant l'écriture

1. Imagine that several students from a French-speaking country will be spending a year at your school. Put together a list of people and places that might be useful and of interest to them. Your list should include:

   - Your name, address, phone number(s) (home and/or cell), and e-mail address

   - The names of four other students in your French class, their addresses, phone numbers, and e-mail addresses

   - Your French teacher's name, phone number(s), and e-mail address

   - Your school library's phone number and hours

   - The names, addresses, and phone numbers of three places near your school where students like to go

 2. Interview your classmates and your teacher to find out the information you need to include. Use the following questions and write down their responses.

Informal	Formal
Comment t'appelles-tu?	Comment vous appelez-vous?
Quel est ton numéro de téléphone?	Quel est votre numéro de téléphone?
Quelle est ton adresse e-mail?	Quelle est votre adresse e-mail?

3. Find out the addresses, telephone numbers, and e-mail addresses/URLs of three places in your community that a group of students from a French-speaking country would enjoy visiting. They could be a library, a store, a skate park, a restaurant, a theater, or a city park. Write them down.

Écriture

Write your complete list, making sure it includes all the required information for:

- you
- four classmates
- your teacher
- the school library
- three places around town

Après l'écriture

1. Exchange your list with a partner's. Comment on his or her work by answering these questions.

- Did your partner include the correct number of people and places?
- Did your partner include the required information for each?

NOM: _Madame Smith (professeur de français)_ ☎

ADRESSE: _Compton School_ ✉

NUMÉRO DE TÉLÉPHONE: _512-645-3458 (bureau)_
NUMÉRO DE PORTABLE: _512-919-0040_
ADRESSE E-MAIL: _absmith@yahoo.com_
NOTES: _—_

NOM: _Skate World_
ADRESSE: _8970 McNeil Road_

NUMÉRO DE TÉLÉPHONE: _512-658-0349_
NUMÉRO DE PORTABLE: _—_
ADRESSE E-MAIL: _skate@skateworld.com_
NOTES: _—_

2. Edit your partner's work, pointing out any spelling or content errors. You can use these editing symbols:

- ℘ delete
- ∧ insert letter or word(s) written in margin
- | replace letter or word(s) with one(s) in margin
- ≡ change to uppercase
- / change to lowercase
- ∿ transpose (switch) indicated letters or words

Now look at this model of what an edited draft looks like:

> o   N̶m: Sally Wagner
> é   Télé̶phone: 655–8888
>   A̶Dresse e-ma̶il: sally@uru.edu
>
>   Nom: Madame̶ Nancy smith
> Téléphone: ̶655–8090
>
>   Adresse e-mail: nsmith@uru.edu

3. Revise your list according to your partner's comments and corrections. After writing the final version, read it one more time to eliminate these kinds of problems:

- spelling errors
- punctuation errors
- capitalization errors
- use of incorrect verb forms
- use of incorrect adjective agreement
- use of incorrect definite and indefinite articles

Key Standards

4.1

Suggestions

- Tell students that this is active vocabulary for which they are responsible and that it will appear on tests and exams.
- Tell them that an easy way to study from **Vocabulaire** is to cover up the French half of each section, leaving only the English equivalents exposed. They can then quiz themselves on the French items. To focus on the English equivalents of the French entries, they simply reverse this process.

21st Century Skills

Creativity and Innovation

Ask students to prepare a list of three products or perspectives they learned about in this unit to share with the class. Consider asking them to focus on the **Culture** and **Panorama** sections.

21st Century Skills

Leadership and Responsibility: Extension Project

If you have access to students in a Francophone country, have students decide on three questions they want to ask the partner class related to this unit's topic. Based on the responses they receive, work as a class to explain to the partner class one aspect of their responses that surprised the class and why.

Leçon 1A

Bonjour et au revoir

À bientôt.	See you soon.
À demain.	See you tomorrow.
À plus tard.	See you later.
À tout à l'heure.	See you later.
Au revoir.	Good-bye.
Bonne journée!	Have a good day!
Bonjour.	Good morning.; Hello.
Bonsoir.	Good evening.; Hello.
Salut!	Hi!; Bye!

Comment ça va?

Ça va?	What's up?; How are things?
Comment allez-vous? (form.)	How are you?
Comment vas-tu? (fam.)	How are you?
Comme ci, comme ça.	So-so.
Je vais bien/mal.	I am doing well/ badly.
Moi aussi.	Me too.
Pas mal.	Not badly.
Très bien.	Very well.

Expressions de politesse

De rien.	You're welcome.
Excusez-moi. (form.)	Excuse me.
Excuse-moi. (fam.)	Excuse me.
Il n'y a pas de quoi.	It's nothing; You're welcome.
Je vous en prie. (form.)	Please.; You're welcome.
Merci beaucoup.	Thank you very much.
Monsieur (M.)	Sir (Mr.)
Madame (Mme)	Ma'am (Mrs.)
Mademoiselle (Mlle)	Miss
Pardon.	Pardon (me).
S'il vous/te plaît. (form./fam.)	Please.

Les présentations

Comment vous appelez-vous? (form.)	What is your name?
Comment t'appelles-tu? (fam.)	What is your name?
Enchanté(e).	Delighted.
Et vous/toi? (form./fam.)	And you?
Je m'appelle...	My name is...
Je vous/te présente... (form./fam.)	I would like to introduce (name) to you.

Expressions utiles

See p. 7.

Le campus

une bibliothèque	library
un café	café
une librairie	bookstore
un lycée	high school
une université	university
une différence	difference
un examen	exam, test
la littérature	literature
un problème	problem
la sociologie	sociology
un bureau	desk; office
un ordinateur	computer
une table	table
un tableau	blackboard; painting
la télévision	television
une chose	thing
un instrument	instrument
un objet	object

Les personnes

un(e) ami(e)	friend
un(e) étudiant(e)	student
un(e) petit(e) ami(e)	boyfriend/ girlfriend
une personne	person
un acteur/une actrice	actor
un chanteur/une chanteuse	singer
un professeur	teacher, professor

Numbers 0–60

See p. 14.

Identifier

c'est/ce sont	it's/they are
Combien...?	How much/ many...?
ici	here
là	there
là-bas	over there
Il y a...	There is/are...
Qu'est-ce que c'est?	What is it?
voici	here is/are
voilà	here is/are

Leçon 1B

En classe

une salle de classe	classroom
un dictionnaire	dictionary
un livre	book
un résultat	result
une carte	map
une chaise	chair
une fenêtre	window
une horloge	clock
une porte	door
un cahier	notebook
une calculatrice	calculator
une corbeille (à papier)	wastebasket
un crayon	pencil
une feuille de papier	sheet of paper
une montre	watch
un sac à dos	backpack
un stylo	pen

Les personnes

un(e) camarade de classe	classmate
une classe	class (group of students)
un copain/une copine (fam.)	friend
un(e) élève	pupil, student
une femme	woman
une fille	girl
un garçon	boy
un homme	man

Identifier

Qui est-ce?	Who is it?
Quoi?	What?

Expressions utiles

See p. 25.

Subject pronouns

je	I
tu	you
il	he/it (masc.)
elle	she/it (fem.)
on	one
nous	we
vous	you
ils	they (masc.)
elles	they (fem.)

Être

je suis	I am
tu es	you are
il/elle est	he/she/it is
on est	one is
nous sommes	we are
vous êtes	you are
ils/elles sont	they are

Descriptive adjectives

agréable	pleasant
amusant(e)	fun
brillant(e)	brilliant
charmant(e)	charming
désagréable	unpleasant
différent(e)	different
difficile	difficult
égoïste	selfish
élégante(e)	elegant
impatient(e)	impatient
important(e)	important
indépendant(e)	independent
intelligent(e)	intelligent
intéressant(e)	interesting
occupé(e)	busy
optimiste	optimistic
patient(e)	patient
pessimiste	pessimistic
poli(e)	polite
réservé(e)	reserved
sincère	sincere
sociable	sociable
sympathique (sympa)	nice
timide	shy

Adjectives of nationality

algérien(ne)	Algerian
allemand(e)	German
américain(e)	American
anglais(e)	English
canadien(ne)	Canadian
espagnol(e)	Spanish
français(e)	French
italien(ne)	Italian
japonais(e)	Japanese
marocain(e)	Moroccan
martiniquais(e)	from Martinique
mexicain(e)	Mexican
québécois(e)	from Quebec
sénégalais(e)	Senegalese
suisse	Swiss
vietnamien(ne)	Vietnamese

Au lycée

Pour commencer

- Which room at school is pictured?
  a. la bibliothèque   b. la salle de classe
  c. le café
- What are the students looking at?
  a. un cahier   b. un professeur   c. un livre
- How do the students look in this photo?
  a. intelligents   b. sociables   c. impatients
- Which item is not visible in the photo?
  a. une table   b. une fenêtre
  c. un ordinateur

Unit Goals

Leçon 2A

In this lesson, students will learn:
- terms for academic subjects
- to express likes and dislikes
- about liaisons
- about French high schools and the Canadian French immersion program
- the present tense of regular -er verbs
- about spelling changes in **-cer** and **-ger** verbs
- to ask questions and express negation
- about a typical school day in a French **collège**

Leçon 2B

In this lesson, students will learn:
- terms for talking about schedules and when things happen
- to pronounce the French **r**
- about **le bac** and higher education in France
- more about university life through specially shot video footage
- the present tense of **avoir**
- some expressions with **avoir**
- to tell time
- to listen for cognates

Savoir-faire

In this section, students will learn:
- cultural, economic, geographical, and historical information about France
- to use text formats to predict content
- to brainstorm before writing
- to write a personal description

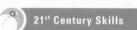
21st Century Skills

Initiative and Self-Direction
Students can monitor their progress online using the activities and assessments on vhlcentral.com.

Pour commencer
- **b. la salle de classe**
- **b. un professeur**
- **a. intelligents**
- **b. une fenêtre**

SUPPORT FOR BACKWARD DESIGN

Unité 2 **Essential Questions**
1. How do students talk about their classes and school life?
2. How do people ask and answer questions about their daily activities?
3. How is school in France the same as, and different from, school in the U.S.?

Unité 2 **Integrated Performance Assessment**
Before teaching the chapter, review the Integrated Performance Assessment (IPA) and its accompanying scoring rubric provided in the Testing Program. Use the IPA to assess students' progress toward proficiency targets at the end of the chapter.
IPA Context: A French student exchange program wants to evaluate the class offerings at your school to see if it would be a good place to send French students. You and your classmates need to create a brochure for your school to attract exchange students.

FORUMS

Forums on vhlcentral.com allow you and your students to record and share audio messages. Use Forums for presentations, oral assessments, discussions, directions, etc.

Section Goals

In this section, students will learn and practice vocabulary related to:
• academic subjects
• places around school
• expressing likes and dislikes

Key Standards

1.1, 1.2, 4.1

Suggestions

• Have students look at the new vocabulary and identify cognates. Say the words and have students repeat after you and guess the meaning. Point out that the words **lettres** and **note** are **faux amis** in this context.

• Call students' attention to the pronunciation of **ps** in **psychologie**.

• Point out that abbreviations such as **sciences po** are common. For more examples, see **Le français quotidien** on page 53.

• To review classroom objects and practice new vocabulary, show items and ask what courses they might be used for. Example: **Un dictionnaire, c'est pour quel cours?**

• Explain that many of the adjectives students learned for nationalities in **Leçon 1B** are also used for languages and language classes. Examples: **le cours de français (d'anglais, d'italien, d'espagnol)**

• Introduce vocabulary for expressing likes and dislikes by talking about your own. Use facial and hand gestures to convey meaning. Examples: **J'adore la littérature française. J'aime bien l'histoire. Je n'aime pas tellement la biologie. Je déteste l'informatique.**

You will learn how to...
▪ talk about your classes
▪ ask questions and express negation

◁)) **vhl**central

Les cours

Vocabulaire

J'aime bien...	I like...
Je n'aime pas tellement...	I don't like... very much
être reçu(e) à un examen	to pass an exam
l'art (*m.*)	art
l'éducation physique (*f.*)	physical education
la gestion	business administration
les lettres (*f.*)	humanities
la philosophie	philosophy
les sciences (politiques / po) (*f.*)	(political) science
une bourse	scholarship, grant
une cantine	cafeteria
un cours	class, course
un devoir; les devoirs	homework
un diplôme	diploma, degree
l'école (*f.*)	school
les études (supérieures) (*f.*)	(higher) education; studies
le gymnase	gymnasium
une note	grade
difficile	difficult
facile	easy
inutile	useless
utile	useful
surtout	especially; above all

46 *quarante-six*

TEACHING OPTIONS

Oral Practice Ask students questions using the new vocabulary words. Examples: **La physique, c'est facile ou difficile? L'informatique est utile ou inutile?**

Brainstorming Have them brainstorm adjectives that can describe their courses and write them: **facile, difficile, utile, intéressant, amusant, agréable,** and **important**. Ask students to

EXPANSION

describe various courses. Example: **Le cours de chimie est difficile.**

Using Games Divide the class into teams. Say the name of a course in English and ask one team to say it in French. If the team is correct, it gets a point. If not, the other team gets a chance to say it and "steal" the point. Alternate giving words to the two teams.

Mise en pratique

1 Associez Which classes, activities, or places do you associate with these words? Not all items in the second column will be used.

_d_	**1.** manger (*to eat*)	a. les mathématiques
_e_	**2.** un ordinateur	b. la physique
_i_	**3.** le français	c. l'histoire
_a_	**4.** une calculatrice	d. une cantine
_f_	**5.** le sport	e. l'informatique
_h_	**6.** Socrate	f. l'éducation physique
_b_	**7.** E=MC²	g. la biologie
_c_	**8.** Napoléon	h. la philosophie
		i. les langues étrangères
		j. l'art

2 Écoutez Aurélie and Hassim are discussing their classes. Indicate who likes each of the following classes. For one class, you will indicate both Aurélie and Hassim.

	Aurélie	Hassim
1. l'informatique	✓	
2. l'économie	✓	
3. la chimie	✓	
4. l'histoire		✓
5. la géographie		✓
6. la psychologie		✓
7. la gestion	✓	
8. les langues étrangères	✓	✓

3 Qu'est-ce que j'aime? Read each statement and indicate whether you think it is **vrai** or **faux**. Compare your answers with a classmate's. Do you agree? Why? Answers will vary.

	Vrai	Faux
1. C'est facile d'être reçu à l'examen de mathématiques.	☐	☐
2. Je déteste manger à la cantine.	☐	☐
3. Je vais recevoir (*receive*) une bourse; c'est très utile.	☐	☐
4. L'art, c'est inutile.	☐	☐
5. Avoir (*To have*) un diplôme du lycée, c'est facile.	☐	☐
6. La chimie, c'est un cours difficile.	☐	☐
7. Je déteste les lettres.	☐	☐
8. Les notes sont très importantes.	☐	☐
9. Je n'aime pas tellement les études.	☐	☐
10. J'adore les langues étrangères.	☐	☐

les langues étrangères (f.)

l'économie (f.)

l'histoire (f.)

La Révolution française

la psychologie

1 Expansion Have students brainstorm a list of famous people that they associate with the following fields: **la physique** (Isaac Newton, Albert Einstein); **l'informatique** (Bill Gates, Mark Zuckerberg). Then have the class guess the field associated with each of the following people: Louis Pasteur (**la biologie**), Adam Smith (**l'économie**).

2 Script AURÉLIE: Bonjour, Hassim. Comment ça va?
HASSIM: Bien. Et toi?
A: Pas mal, merci.
H: Tu aimes le cours d'informatique?
A: Oui, j'adore et j'aime bien l'économie et la chimie aussi.
H: Moi, je n'aime pas tellement l'informatique, c'est difficile. J'aime l'histoire, la géographie et la psychologie. C'est très intéressant.
A: Tu aimes la gestion?
H: Ah non, je déteste!
A: Mais c'est très utile!
H: Mais non! Les langues, oui, sont utiles. J'aime bien l'italien.
A: Oui, j'adore l'italien, moi aussi!
H: Bon, à tout à l'heure, Aurélie!
A: Oui, à bientôt!
Teacher Resources DVD

2 Suggestion Tell students to focus their listening on three things: the person speaking, the school subject, and if the person speaking likes or dislikes the subject.

3 Suggestion Tell students that the expression **C'est** + *adjective*, which means *It's* + *adjective*, is used to make a general comment about the information that precedes or follows the expression. Have them find examples in the **Roman-photo**.

3 Expansion Take a class survey of students' responses and tally the results on the board. Ask students on which questions they agree. You might want to introduce the expression **être d'accord**, which will be presented in the **Roman-photo** later in this lesson.

Margin notes (left column)

4 Suggestion Before doing this activity, complete a similar exchange; scramble the order of the sentences and write them on the board or on a transparency. Tell students to put the sentences in order to make a logical conversation.

5 Suggestion Have several volunteers write their captions on the board for the class to correct.

6 Suggestion Have students look these people up online if they are not familiar with them.

6 Partner Chat You can also assign Activity 6 on vhlcentral.com. Students work in pairs to record the activity online. The pair's recorded conversation will appear in your gradebook.

PRE-AP®

6 Interpersonal Speaking For additional practice, have students ask each celebrity one or two questions, such as **Comment allez-vous, Monsieur Einstein?** or **Quelle est votre nationalité?**

7 Suggestions
- Read the **modèle** aloud with a volunteer. Then distribute the **Feuilles d'activités** from the Activity Pack.
- Have volunteers share their findings with the class.

21st Century Skills

7 Collaboration
If you have access to students in a Francophone country, ask them to conduct a similar survey to find out about their opinions on the subjects they study in school. Then, ask groups of students to read their counterparts' answers and prepare a comparison of the preferences of both classes.

Activity Pack For additional activities, go to the **Activity Pack** in the **Resources** section of vhlcentral.com.

Communication

4 Conversez In pairs, fill in the blanks according to your own situations. Then, act out the conversation for the class. Answers will vary. Suggested answers:

Élève A: ___Salut/Bonjour___, comment ça va?
Élève B: _Ça va (très) bien/Pas mal_. Et toi?
Élève A: _Ça va (très) bien/Pas mal_, merci.
Élève B: Est-ce que tu aimes le cours de _chimie/physique/biologie..._?

Élève A: J'adore le cours de _chimie/physique/biologie..._
Élève B: Moi aussi. Tu aimes _l'économie/la géographie/ l'histoire..._?
Élève A: Non, j'aime mieux (*better*) _l'économie/la géographie/. l'histoire..._
Élève B: Bon, à bientôt.
Élève A: À _tout à l'heure/bientôt/ plus tard..._

5 Qu'est-ce que c'est? Write a caption for each image, stating where the students are and how they feel about the classes they are attending. Then, in pairs, take turns reading your captions for your partner to guess about whom you are talking. Answers will vary. Suggested answers.

MODÈLE
C'est le cours de français.
Le français est facile.

1. C'est le cours d'informatique. Je déteste l'informatique.

2. Être reçu à l'examen / Avoir le diplôme du lycée est difficile.

3. C'est la philosophie. J'adore la philosophie.

4. C'est le cours de chimie. La chimie est facile.

5. C'est le cours d'éducation physique / la cantine. Je n'aime pas tellement...

6. C'est un devoir de mathématiques. $x^2 + 7x + 12$ J'aime bien...

6 Vous êtes... Imagine what subjects these famous people liked and disliked as students. In pairs, take turns playing the role of each one and guessing the answer. Answers will vary.

MODÈLE
Élève 1: *J'aime la physique et la chimie, mais je n'aime pas tellement les cours d'économie.*
Élève 2: *Vous êtes Albert Einstein!*

- Albert Einstein
- Louis Pasteur
- Oprah Winfrey
- Abraham Lincoln
- Tony Parker
- Le docteur Phil
- Bill Gates
- Picasso

7 Sondage Your teacher will give you a worksheet to conduct a survey (**un sondage**). Go around the room to find people that study the subjects listed. Ask what your classmates think about their subjects. Keep a record of their answers to discuss with the class. Answers will vary.

MODÈLE
Élève 1: *Jean, est-ce que tu étudies (do you study) la chimie?*
Élève 2: *Oui. J'aime bien la chimie. C'est un cours utile.*

EXPANSION

Using Games To teach students about famous French people, play a game of Concentration. Divide the class into two teams. Write names of courses or people on index cards and tape them face down on the board. Have students match courses with an expert in the field. Examples: **l'art/**Claude Monet and **la philosophie/**Jean-Paul Sartre. As students turn over a card, they must read it aloud. If a player has a match, that player's

TEACHING OPTIONS

team collects those cards. When all the cards have been matched, the team with the most cards wins.

Oral Practice To practice expressing likes and dislikes, ask students yes/no and either/or questions. Examples: **Vous aimez bien la psychologie? Vous détestez la géographie? Vous adorez les lettres ou les sciences?**

Les sons et les lettres 🔊 vhlcentral

Liaisons

Consonants at the end of French words are generally silent but are usually pronounced when the word that follows begins with a vowel sound. This linking of sounds is called a liaison.

À tou͜t à l'heure!   **Comment͜ allez-vous?**

An **s** or an **x** in a liaison sounds like the letter **z**.

les͜ étudiants   **trois͜ élèves**   **six͜ élèves**   **deux͜ hommes**

Always make a liaison between a subject pronoun and a verb that begins with a vowel sound; always make a liaison between an article and a noun that begins with a vowel sound.

nous͜ aimons   **ils͜ ont**   **un͜ étudiant**   **les͜ ordinateurs**

Always make a liaison between **est** (a form of **être**) and a word that begins with a vowel or a vowel sound. Never make a liaison with the final consonant of a proper name.

Robert͟ est͜ anglais.   **Paris͟ est͜ exceptionnelle.**

Never make a liaison with the conjunction **et** (*and*).

Carole e͟t Hélène   **Jacques e͟t Antoinette**

Never make a liaison between a singular noun and an adjective that follows it.

un cours͟ horrible   **un instrument͟ élégant**

Prononcez Practice saying these words and expressions aloud.

1. un examen
2. des étudiants
3. les hôtels
4. dix acteurs
5. Paul et Yvette
6. cours important
7. des informations
8. les études
9. deux hommes
10. Bernard aime
11. chocolat italien
12. Louis est

Articulez Practice saying these sentences aloud.

1. Nous aimons les arts.
2. Albert habite à Paris.
3. C'est un objet intéressant.
4. Sylvie est avec Anne.
5. Ils adorent les deux universités.

Dictons Practice reading these sayings aloud.

Les amis de nos amis sont nos amis.[1]

Un hôte non invité doit apporter son siège.[2]

[1] Friends of our friends are our friends.
[2] An uninvited guest must bring his own chair.

Section Goals

In this section, students will learn about liaisons.

Key Standards
4.1

Suggestions
- Model the pronunciation of each phrase and have students repeat. Explain the liaison for each case.
- Point out expressions with liaison in **Contextes** or ask students to find them. Have them repeat after you. Example: **les études**.
- Ask students to provide expressions from **Leçons 1A–1B** that contain a liaison. Examples: **les États-Unis** and **Comment allez-vous?**
- Write the sentences in **Articulez** on the board or a transparency. Have students listen to the recording and tell you where they hear liaisons. Alternately, have students write the sentences on a sheet of paper, draw lines linking letters that form liaisons, and cross out silent final consonants.
- The explanation and exercises are available on vhlcentral.com. You may want to play them in class so students practice listening to French speakers other than yourself.

Dictons Tell students to pronounce the liaison between **n** and **in** in **non invité**. Have students compare the saying **«Un hôte non invité doit apporter son siège»** with its literal translation. Ask what they think it means figuratively. (Possible answer: People who show up unexpectedly have no right to complain about the service.) Ask: What do the two sayings in this section reveal about French culture?

EXPANSION

Liasons Dictate the following phrases, saying each one at least two times. Then write them on the board or on a transparency and have students check what they wrote. **1. dix-huit étudiants 2. les élèves 3. un cours utile 4. les études supérieures 5. les langues étrangères**

EXPANSION

Mini-dictée Here are additional sentences with liaisons to use for oral practice or dictation. **1. Robert et Alex sont anglais. 2. C'est un film très intéressant. 3. Il y a trois élèves. 4. C'est un restaurant italien.**

49

Section Goals

In this section, students will learn functional phrases for talking about their courses.

Key Standards

1.2, 2.1, 2.2, 4.1, 4.2

Video Recap: Leçon 1B
Before doing this **Roman-photo**, review the previous one.
1. Le cours d'histoire est difficile pour Stéphane, n'est-ce pas? (Non, les maths et le français sont difficiles pour Stéphane.)
2. Comment est Sandrine? (égoïste, sociable et charmante)
3. De quelle origine est Amina? (sénégalaise) Et Rachid? (algérienne)
4. Comment est Amina? (charmante, sincère et élégante)
5. Comment est Rachid? (intelligent, poli, modeste, réservé et brillant)

Video Synopsis Rachid and Antoine discuss their political science class. As they are walking, David joins them, and Rachid introduces him. Then Antoine leaves. When the two roommates get to Rachid's car, Sandrine and Amina are waiting for them. The girls ask David about school and his classes. Later, at **Le P'tit Bistrot**, Stéphane joins the four friends and they continue their discussion about classes. Stéphane hates all of his courses.

Suggestions

• Have students predict what they think the episode will be about. Record predictions on the board.
• Have students work in groups of six. Tell them to choose a role and read the **Roman-photo** conversation aloud. Ask one or two groups to act out the conversation for the class.
• After students have read the **Roman-photo**, review their predictions and ask which ones were correct. Then ask a few questions to guide them in summarizing this episode.

Trop de devoirs! vhlcentral

PERSONNAGES

Amina

Antoine

David

Rachid

Sandrine

Stéphane

ANTOINE Je déteste le cours de sciences po.
RACHID Oh? Mais pourquoi? Je n'aime pas tellement le prof, Monsieur Dupré, mais c'est un cours intéressant et utile!
ANTOINE Tu crois? Moi, je pense que c'est très difficile, et il y a beaucoup de devoirs. Avec Dupré, je travaille, mais je n'ai pas de bons résultats.

RACHID Si on est optimiste et si on travaille, on est reçu à l'examen.
ANTOINE Toi, oui, mais pas moi! Toi, tu es un étudiant brillant! Mais moi, les études, oh là là.
DAVID Eh! Rachid! Oh! Est-ce que tu oublies ton coloc?

RACHID Pas du tout, pas du tout. Antoine, voilà, je te présente David, mon colocataire américain.
DAVID Nous partageons un des appartements du P'tit Bistrot.
ANTOINE Le P'tit Bistrot? Sympa!

SANDRINE Salut! Alors, ça va l'université française?
DAVID Bien, oui. C'est différent de l'université américaine, mais c'est intéressant.
AMINA Tu aimes les cours?
DAVID J'aime bien les cours de littérature et d'histoire françaises. Demain, on étudie *Les Trois Mousquetaires* d'Alexandre Dumas.

SANDRINE J'adore Dumas. Mon livre préféré, c'est *Le Comte de Monte-Cristo*.
RACHID Sandrine! S'il te plaît! *Le Comte de Monte-Cristo*?
SANDRINE Pourquoi pas? Je suis chanteuse, mais j'adore les classiques de la littérature.
DAVID Donne-moi le sac à dos, Sandrine.

Au P'tit Bistrot...
RACHID Moi, j'aime le cours de sciences po, mais Antoine n'aime pas Dupré. Il pense qu'il donne trop de devoirs.

A C T I V I T É S

1 **Vrai ou faux?** Choose whether each statement is **vrai** or **faux**.

1. Rachid et Antoine n'aiment pas le professeur Dupré. Vrai.
2. Antoine aime bien le cours de sciences po. Faux.
3. Rachid et Antoine partagent (*share*) un appartement. Faux.
4. David et Rachid cherchent (*look for*) Amina et Sandrine après (*after*) les cours. Vrai.
5. Le livre préféré de Sandrine est *Le Comte de Monte-Cristo*. Vrai.

6. L'université française est très différente de l'université américaine. Vrai.
7. Stéphane aime la chimie. Faux.
8. Monsieur Dupré est professeur de maths. Faux.
9. Antoine a (*has*) beaucoup de devoirs. Vrai.
10. Stéphane adore l'anglais. Faux.

TEACHING OPTIONS

Trop de devoirs! Before showing the video episode, have students brainstorm some expressions people might use when talking about their classes and teachers.

TEACHING OPTIONS

Regarder la vidéo Download and print the videoscript and white out ten words or expressions in order to create a master for a cloze activity. Hand out the photocopies and tell students to fill in the missing words as they watch the video episode. You may want to show the episode twice if students have difficulty with the activity. Then have students compare their answers in small groups.

Antoine, David, Rachid et Stéphane parlent (*talk*)
de leurs (*their*) cours.

RACHID Ah... on a rendez-vous avec
Amina et Sandrine. On y va?
DAVID Ah, oui, bon, ben, salut,
Antoine!
ANTOINE Salut, David. À demain,
Rachid!

SANDRINE Bon, Pascal, au revoir,
chéri.
RACHID Bonjour, chérie. Comme
j'adore parler avec toi au téléphone!
Comme j'adore penser à toi!

STÉPHANE Dupré? Ha! C'est Madame
Richard, mon prof de français. Elle,
elle donne trop de devoirs.
AMINA Bonjour, comment ça va?
STÉPHANE Plutôt mal. Je n'aime
pas Madame Richard. Je déteste
les maths. La chimie n'est pas
intéressante. L'histoire-géo,
c'est l'horreur. Les études, c'est
le désastre!

DAVID Le français, les maths, la
chimie, l'histoire-géo... mais on
n'étudie pas les langues étrangères
au lycée en France?
STÉPHANE Si, malheureusement!
Moi, j'étudie l'anglais. C'est une
langue très désagréable! Oh, non,
non, ha, ha, c'est une blague, ha,
ha. L'anglais, j'adore l'anglais. C'est
une langue charmante....

Expressions utiles

Talking about classes

● **Tu aimes les cours?**
Do you like the classes?

● **Antoine n'aime pas Dupré.**
Antoine doesn't like Dupré.

● **Il pense qu'il donne trop de devoirs.**
He thinks he gives too much homework.

● **Tu crois? Mais pourquoi?**
You think? But why?

● **Avec Dupré, je travaille, mais je n'ai pas
de bons résultats.**
*With Dupré, I work, but I don't get good
results (grades).*

● **Demain, on étudie** *Les Trois Mousquetaires.*
Tomorrow we're studying The Three
Musketeers.

● **C'est mon livre préféré.**
It's my favorite book.

Additional vocabulary

● **On a rendez-vous (avec des ami(e)s).**
We're meeting (friends).

● **Comme j'adore...**
How I love...

● **parler au téléphone**
to talk on the phone

● **C'est une blague.**
It's a joke.

● **Si, malheureusement!**
Yes, unfortunately!

● **On y va? / On y va.**
Are you ready? / Let's go.

● **Eh!**
Hey!

● **pas du tout**
not at all

● **chéri(e)**
darling

ACTIVITÉS

2 **Complétez** Match the people in the second column with the
verbs in the first. Refer to a dictionary, the dialogue, and the video
stills as necessary. Use each option once.

b/e **1.** travailler — a. Sandrine is very forgetful.
c **2.** partager — b. Rachid is very studious.
a **3.** oublier — c. David can't afford his own apartment.
b/e **4.** étudier — d. Amina is very generous.
d **5.** donner — e. Stéphane needs to get good grades.

3 **Conversez** In this episode, Rachid, Antoine, David, and Stéphane
talk about the subjects they are studying. Get together with a partner.
Do any of the characters' complaints or preferences remind you of your
own? Whose opinions do you agree with? Whom do you disagree with?

51

AP® Theme: Contemporary Life
Context: Education

vhlcentral | *Flash culture*

CULTURE À LA LOUPE

Au lycée

What is high school like in France? At the end of middle school (**le collège**), French students begin three years of high-school study at the **lycée.** Beginning in **seconde** (10th grade), students pass into **première** (11th grade), and end with **terminale** (12th grade).

The **lycée** experience is quite different from American high school. For example, the days are much longer: often from 8:00 am until 5:00 pm. On Wednesdays, classes typically end at noon. Students in some **lycées** may also have class on Saturday morning. French schools do not offer organized sports after school, like American schools do, but students who want to play an organized sport can join **l'Association sportive scolaire.** Every public **lycée** must offer this option to its students. All such extra-curricular activities take place after school hours or on Wednesday afternoons.

Grades are based on a 20-point scale, with 10 being the average grade. As students advance in their studies, it becomes harder for them to achieve a grade of 16/20 or even 14/20. A student can receive a below-average score in one or more courses and still advance to the next level as long as their overall grade average is at least 10/20.

Another important difference is that French students must begin a specialization while in high school, at the end of the **classe de seconde.** That choice is likely to influence the rest of their studies and, later, their job choice. While they can change their mind after the first trimester of **première,** by then students are already set on a course towards the **baccalauréat** or **bac,** the exit exam that concludes their **lycée** studies.

Système français de notation

NOTE FRANÇAISE	NOTE AMÉRICAINE	%	NOTE FRANÇAISE	NOTE AMÉRICAINE	%
0	F	0	11	B-	82
2	F	3	12	B+	88
3	F	8	13	A-	93
4	F	18	14	A	95
5	F	28	15	A	96
6	F	38	16	A+	98
7	D-	60	17	A+	98
8	D-	65	18	A+	99
9	D+	68	19	A+	99
10	C	75	20	A+	100

ACTIVITÉS

1 **Vrai ou faux?** Indicate whether each statement is **vrai** or **faux.** Correct the false statements.

1. The **lycée** comes after **collège.**
   Vrai.
2. It takes 4 years to complete **lycée.**
   Faux. It takes three years.
3. The grade order in the **lycée** is **terminale**, **première**, and lastly **seconde.**
   Faux. The order is **seconde**, **première**, **terminale.**
4. **Lycées** never have classes on Saturday.
   Faux. Some **lycées** have classes Saturday mornings.
5. French students have class from Monday to Friday all day long.
   Faux. Wednesdays are typically half days.

6. French students have to specialize in a field of study while in high school.
   Vrai.
7. French students begin their specialization in **première.**
8. The French grading system resembles the US grading system.
   Faux. The American grading system is based on 100 points.
9. The highest grade that a French student can get is 20/20.
   Vrai.
10. To obtain a grade of 20/20 is common in France.
    Faux. A grade of 20/20 is very rare.

Section Goals

In this section, students will:
- learn about **le lycée** in France
- learn some familiar terms for talking about academic courses
- learn about high school in the Francophone world
- read about French immersion in Canadian schools

Key Standards

2.1, 2.2, 3.1, 3.2, 4.2

Culture à la loupe
Avant la lecture Have the class brainstorm and make a list of the most important characteristics of high school life in the United States.

Lecture
- Draw students' attention to the box **Système français de notation.** Point out that in France, a grade of 10 is a passing grade and therefore not the equivalent of a 50 in the American system.
- Explain that French students rarely get praise from teachers. While American teachers are trained to encourage students for effort, the French typically reserve praise for only truly excellent work.
- Explain that while the French school day is longer, students have longer breaks and lunch periods (up to 1.5 hours for lunch).

Après la lecture Have small groups compare French and American high schools. Tell them to make a list of the similarities and differences. Then ask several groups to read their lists to the class.

Flash culture Tell students that they will learn more about classes and school life in the video narrated by Benjamin. As they watch the video, have them jot down in French at least three examples of people or things they saw. You can also use the activities in the video manual in class or assign them as homework.

EXPANSION

Numbers To review numbers and the alphabet, have students take turns making true/false statements about the French and American grading systems based on the information in the chart. Write on the board: a plus sign = **plus**; a minus sign = **moins.** Example: **Un vingt en France est un A plus plus plus plus plus plus aux États-Unis. (Vrai.).**

DIFFERENTIATION

For Visual Learners Working in groups of three, have students describe the photos on these pages. Tell them to create as many sentences in French as they can. Then have volunteers read their descriptions to the class.

LE FRANÇAIS QUOTIDIEN

Les cours

être fort(e) en...	to be good at
être nul(le) en...	to stink at
sécher un cours	to skip a class
potasser	to cram
piger	to get it
l'emploi du temps	class schedule
l'histoire-géo	history-geography
les maths	math
la philo	philosophy
le prof	teacher
la récré(ation)	break

LE MONDE FRANCOPHONE

Le lycée

Le «lycée» n'existe pas partout°.

En Afrique francophone, on utilise° les termes de *lycée* et de *baccalauréat*.

En Belgique, le lycée public s'appelle une *école secondaire* ou un *athénée*. Un lycée privé° s'appelle un *collège*. Le bac n'existe pas°.

En Suisse, les lycées s'appellent *gymnases, écoles préparant à la maturité* ou *écoles de culture générale*. Les élèves reçoivent° un certificat du secondaire II.

partout *everywhere* on utilise *one uses* privé *private* n'existe pas *does not exist* reçoivent *receive*

PORTRAIT

AP® **Theme:** Contemporary Life
Context: Education

Immersion française au Canada

English and French are the official languages of Canada, but not necessarily of each province. In fact, New Brunswick is the only province that is officially bilingual. Only 17.4% of Canadians speak French and English. However, there is an immersion program that encourages bilingualism: Canadian students in elementary school through high school can choose to take their classes in French. This means that for 3 years or more, all their classes are conducted in French. In New Brunswick, 32% of students take part in this program. Although the majority of people in Quebec province are **francophone**, there is also a large community of English-speakers, and 22% of students take part in the French immersion program there.

Sur Internet

AP® **Theme:** Contemporary Life
Context: Education

Quelle (*Which*) **spécialisation choisiriez-vous** (*would you choose*)?

Go to **vhlcentral.com** to find more information related to this **Culture** section and to watch the corresponding **Flash culture** video.

---

2 Complétez Complete each statement.

1. English and French are the official languages of _____Canada_____.
2. Students can begin an immersion program in __elementary__ school.
3. Immersion programs in Canada last for ___three___ or more years.
4. ___New Brunswick___ is the only province that is officially bilingual.
5. In Switzerland, **les lycées** are called __gymnases__.

3 Les cours Research what classes are taught in **lycée** and how long each class is. How does this compare to your class schedule? You may search in your library or online.

A C T I V I T É S

Section Goals

In this section, students will learn:
- the present tense of regular -er verbs
- spelling changes in -cer and -ger verbs

Key Standards

4.1, 5.1

Suggestions: Scaffolding
- Tell students that they have been using verbs from the start: **Comment t'appelles-tu?**, **il y a**, forms of **être**, etc. Then, present **Point de départ** and the meanings of common -er verbs.
- Model forms of **parler** indicating different people: **Je parle français. Anne parle français aussi. Nous parlons français.**
- Use the Grammar Slide showing the conjugations of **parler** to introduce the idea of a "boot verb." Trace a line around **je, tu, il/elle/on**, and **ils/elles**, forming the shape of a boot. Tell students that the verb forms inside the "boot" are pronounced alike.
- Follow the Extra Practice Suggestion, p. 55. Then assign the **Vérifiez** activity on vhlcentral.com.
- Present points discussing verbs of preference. Create sentences with **j'aime…** and **j'adore…** followed by infinitives or nouns. Ask students if they like different activities and things. Examples: **Vous aimez voyager? Vous aimez l'informatique?** Then assign the second **Vérifiez** activity.

2A.1

Present tense of regular -er verbs   vhlcentral

Point de départ The largest group of infinitives in French end in **-er**. To form the present tense of regular -er verbs, drop the **-er** from the infinitive and add the corresponding endings for the different subject pronouns. This chart demonstrates how to conjugate regular -er verbs.

parler (to speak)	
je parle	nous parlons
tu parles	vous parlez
il/elle/on parle	ils/elles parlent

- The English translation of the French verb forms in the present tense depends on the context of the sentence.

> Éric et Nadine **parlent** français.
> *Éric and Nadine speak French.*
> *Éric and Nadine are speaking French.*
> *Éric and Nadine do speak French.*

- Here are some other common **-er** verbs.

Common *-er* verbs			
adorer	to love; to adore	habiter (à)	to live (in)
aimer	to like; to love	manger	to eat
aimer mieux	to prefer (to like better)	oublier	to forget
arriver	to arrive	partager	to share
chercher	to look for	penser (que/qu'…)	to think (that…)
commencer	to begin, to start	regarder	to look (at)
dessiner	to draw; to design	rencontrer	to meet
détester	to hate	retrouver	to meet up with; to find (again)
donner	to give	travailler	to work
étudier	to study	voyager	to travel

🏃 Boîte à outils

Unlike the English *to look for*, the French verb **chercher** requires no preposition before the noun that follows it.

Nous cherchons les stylos.
We are looking for the pens.

◎ Vérifiez

- Note that **je** becomes **j'** when it appears before a verb that begins with a vowel sound.

> **J'habite** à Bruxelles.   **J'étudie** la psychologie.
> *I live in Brussels.*   *I study psychology.*

Verbs of preference

- The verbs **adorer**, **aimer**, and **détester** can be followed by a noun or an infinitive. When followed by a noun, use the definite article to tell what someone loves, likes, prefers, or hates.

> J'aime mieux **l'**art.   Marine déteste **les** devoirs.
> *I prefer art.*   *Marine hates homework.*

- When the verbs **adorer**, **aimer**, and **détester** are followed by another verb to say that you like (or hate, etc.) to do something, only the first verb is conjugated. The second verb remains in the infinitive form.

◎ Vérifiez

> Ils **adorent travailler** ici.   Ils **détestent étudier** ensemble.
> *They love working here.*   *They hate to study together.*

54   *cinquante-quatre*

EXPANSION

Questions Ask students questions, using **étudier, manger,** and **parler**. Students should answer in complete sentences.
Ex: —_____, tu étudies le français? —Oui, j'étudie le français.
—Vous mangez beaucoup? —Qui mange plus?

EXPANSION

Pairs Ask students to create a two-column chart with the heads **J'adore…** and **Je déteste…** Have them complete the chart with five things they love and hate doing. Ex: **J'adore manger des pizzas. Je déteste dessiner.** Assist them with unfamiliar vocabulary as necessary. Have students share their sentences with the class.

Verbs with spelling changes

Verbs ending in -ger (**manger**, **partager**, **voyager**) and -cer (**commencer**) have a spelling change in the **nous** form. All the other forms are the same as regular -er verbs.

manger
je mange
tu manges
il/elle/on mange
nous mangeons
vous mangez
ils/elles mangent

commencer
je commence
tu commences
il/elle/on commence
nous commençons
vous commencez
ils/elles commencent

Nous **voyageons** avec une amie.
We are traveling with a friend.

Nous **commençons** les devoirs.
We're starting our homework.

Vous **mangez** à la cantine.
You eat at the cafeteria.

Vous **commencez** l'examen.
You are starting the test.

Commands

- If you want to tell someone what to do, you use commands. Like English, you drop the subject pronoun and use the present tense form of the verb. The **nous** and **vous** command forms are identical to those of the present tense.

  Parlez français!
  Speak French!

  Travaillons!
  Let's work!

- The **tu** command form of -er verbs drops the -s from the present tense form.

  Tu regardes le tableau.
  You are looking at the board.

  ▶ **Regarde** le tableau!
  Look at the board!

- The command forms of **être** are irregular: **sois, soyons, soyez.**

  Sois patient!
  Be patient!

  Soyez utiles!
  Be useful!

  Soyons optimistes.
  Let's be optimistic.

 Boîte à outils

The spelling change in the **nous** form is made in order to maintain the same sound that the **c** and the **g** make in the infinitives **commencer** and **manger.**

 Vérifiez

Essayez! Complete the sentences with the correct present tense forms of the verbs.

1. Je ___parle___ (parler) français en classe.
2. Nous ___habitons___ (habiter) près de (*near*) l'école.
3. Ils ___aiment___ (aimer) le cours de sciences politiques.
4. Vous ___mangez___ (manger) en classe?!
5. Le cours ___commence___ (commencer) à huit heures (*at eight o'clock*).
6. Marie-Claire ___cherche___ (chercher) un stylo.
7. Nous ___partageons___ (partager) un crayon en cours de maths.
8. Tu ___étudies___ (étudier) l'économie.
9. Les élèves ___voyagent___ (voyager) en France.
10. Nous ___adorons___ (adorer) parler italien.

1 Suggestion Go over the answers quickly in class, then ask several pairs of students to act out the conversation and add at least two lines of their own at the end.

2 Suggestion To check students' answers, have volunteers write the sentences on the board and read them aloud.

2 Expansion For additional practice, change the subjects of the sentences and have students restate or write the sentences. Examples: **1. Tu (Tu oublies le devoir de littérature.) 2. Chantal (Chantal commence les problèmes de maths.) 3. Je (Je rencontre des amis au lycée.) 4. Les élèves (Les élèves détestent travailler.) 5. Nous (Nous cherchons un cours facile.) 6. Pascale (Pascale arrive avec des dictionnaires.)**

3 Expansion Have students add additional sentences to the captions below the drawings. Example: **1. Il étudie l'histoire. Il y a un examen.**

3 Expansion Have students redo the activity using **aimer** + [*infinitive*] to tell what Stéphanie's friends like to do after school. Ex: **Nathalie aime aller à la bibliothèque.**

Mise en pratique

1 **Complétez** Complete the conversation with the correct forms of the verbs.

ARTHUR   Tu (1) ___parles___ (parler) bien français!

OLIVIER   Mon ami Marc et moi, nous (2) ___retrouvons___ (retrouver) un professeur de français et nous (3) ___étudions___ (étudier) ensemble. Et toi, tu (4) ___aimes___ (aimer) les langues?

ARTHUR   Non, j' (5) ___aime___ (aimer) l'art. Je (6) ___dessine___ (dessiner) bien et j' (7) ___adore___ (adorer) l'art moderne. Marc et toi, vous (8) ___habitez___ (habiter) à Paris?

2 **Phrases** Form sentences using the words provided. Conjugate the verbs and add any necessary words.

1. je / oublier / devoir de littérature   J'oublie le devoir de littérature.
2. nous / commencer / problèmes de maths   Nous commençons les problèmes de maths.
3. vous / rencontrer / amis / au / lycée   Vous rencontrez des amis au lycée.
4. Hélène / détester / travailler   Hélène déteste travailler.
5. tu / chercher / cours / facile   Tu cherches un cours facile.
6. élèves / arriver / avec / dictionnaires   Les élèves arrivent avec des dictionnaires.

3 **Après l'école** Say what Stéphanie and her friends are doing after (**après**) school. Answers may vary.

 ▶ **MODÈLE**
Nathalie cherche un livre.

1. André ___travaille___ à la bibliothèque.

2. Édouard ___retrouve___ Caroline au café.

3. Jérôme et moi, nous ___dessinons___.

4. Julien et Audrey ___parlent___ avec Simon.

5. Robin et toi, vous ___voyagez___ avec la classe.

6. Je ___mange___.

4 **Le verbe logique** Complete the following sentences logically with the correct form of an **–er** verb. Suggested answers.

1. La chimie, c'est très difficile. Je ___déteste___ !
2. Qu'est-ce que tu ___cherches___ dans le sac à dos?
3. Nous ___mangeons___ souvent (*often*) à la cantine.
4. Tristan et Irène ___oublient___ toujours (*always*) les clés (*keys*).
5. Le film ___commence___ dans dix minutes.
6. Yves et toi, vous ___pensez___ que Martine est charmante?
7. M. et Mme Legrand ___habitent___ à Paris.
8. On n'aime pas ___regarder___ la télévision.

Communication

5 Activités In pairs, tell your partner which of these activities you and your best friend both do. Then, share your partner's answers with the class. Answers will vary.

MODÈLE

To your partner: *Nous parlons au téléphone, nous...*
To the class: *Ils/Elles parlent au téléphone, ils/elles...*

manger à la cantine	étudier une langue étrangère
oublier les devoirs	commencer les devoirs
retrouver des amis à la cantine	arriver en classe
travailler	voyager

6 Les études In pairs, take turns asking your partner if he or she likes one academic subject or another. If you don't like a subject, mention one you do like. Then, use **tous** (*m.*)/**toutes** (*f.*) **les deux** (*both of us*) to tell the class what subjects both of you like or hate. Answers will vary.

MODÈLE

Élève 1: *Tu aimes la chimie?*
Élève 2: *Non, je déteste la chimie. J'aime mieux les langues.*
Élève 1: *Moi aussi... Nous adorons tous/toutes les deux les langues.*

7 Un sondage In groups of three, survey your partners to find out how frequently they do certain activities. First, prepare a chart with a list of eight activities. Then take turns asking your partners how often they do each one, and record each person's response.

MODÈLE

Élève 1: *Moi, je dessine rarement. Et toi?*
Élève 2: *Moi aussi, je dessine rarement.*
Élève 3: *Moi, je dessine parfois.*

Activité	souvent	parfois	rarement
dessiner		Sara	David Clara
voyager	Clara David Sara		

Coup de main

To express yourself with greater accuracy, use these adverbs: **assez** (enough), **d'habitude** (usually), **de temps en temps** (from time to time), **parfois** (sometimes), **quelquefois** (sometimes), **rarement** (rarely), **souvent** (often), **toujours** (always). Place the adverbs after the verb.

8 Adorer, aimer, détester In small groups, use commands to give each other advice about how to succeed at school. Use the verbs below and tell each other how often to do these things. How many different pieces of advice can you give? Answers will vary.

MODÈLE

Sois toujours patient(e) avec tes camarades de classe.

arriver	oublier les devoirs
chercher	parler
commencer	partager
être	regarder
étudier	retrouver
manger	travailler

5 Suggestion Encourage students to personalize the information and to add additional information. Examples: **étudier** *a different subject*, **travailler dans** *a place*, and **regarder la télé.**

5 Partner Chat You can also assign Activity 5 on vhlcentral.com. Students work in pairs to record the activity online. The pair's recorded conversation will appear in your gradebook.

6 Suggestion Before beginning the activity, tell students to jot down a list of academic subjects that they can ask their partner about and to note their partner's responses. Examples: **Il/Elle aime** or **Il/Elle déteste.**

7 Suggestion Present the adverbs in **Coup de main** before students begin the activity. Tell them they should add these words to their vocabulary lists.

7 Expansion Have students share with the class which activity most people in their group do often and which one most do rarely.

8 Suggestion Refer students to the **Coup de main** box for adverbs.

Activity Pack For additional activities, go to the **Activity Pack** in the **Resources** section of vhlcentral.com.

EXPANSION

Game Divide the class into two teams. Choose one team member at a time to go to the board, alternating between teams. Say an infinitive and a subject pronoun. The person at the board must write and say the correct present tense form. Example: **parler: vous (vous parlez).** Give a point for each correct answer. The team with the most points at the end of the game wins.

EXPANSION

Questions Prepare eight questions. Write their answers on the board in random order. Then read your questions aloud, having students match the question to the appropriate answer. Make sure that only one of the possible answers corresponds logically to the question you ask. Example: **Pourquoi déteste-t-il les maths? (Le prof est désagréable.)**

57

2A.2

Forming questions and **vhl**central expressing negation

Point de départ You have learned how to make affirmative statements in French. Now you will learn how to form questions and make negative statements.

Forming questions

 Boîte à outils

Use questions with rising intonation and tags mainly when speaking. Use **est-ce que** when speaking and writing.

- There are several ways to ask a question in French. The simplest and most informal way is to make a statement but with rising intonation. In writing, simply put a question mark at the end.

  Vous habitez à Bordeaux?
  You live in Bordeaux?

  Tu aimes le cours de français?
  You like French class?

- A second way is to place the phrase **Est-ce que...** directly before a statement. If the next word begins with a vowel sound, use **Est-ce qu'**. Questions with **est-ce que** are somewhat informal.

  Est-ce que vous parlez français?
  Do you speak French?

  Est-ce qu'il aime dessiner?
  Does he like to draw?

Vérifiez

- A third way is to end a statement with a tag question, such as **n'est-ce pas?** (*isn't that right?*), **non?** (*no?*) or **d'accord?** (*OK?*). This type of question is informal.

  Nous mangeons bientôt, **n'est-ce pas**?
  We eat soon, don't we?

  On commence bientôt, **d'accord**?
  We're starting soon, OK?

 Boîte à outils

Use questions with inversion in writing and when you speak formally. Note that **D'accord!** uses this style of questioning in the majority of its activities, because it is preferred in many academic and business situations. Therefore, it is important to have plenty of practice.

- A fourth way is to invert the subject pronoun and the verb and place a hyphen between them. If the verb ends in a vowel and the subject pronoun is **il**, **elle**, or **on**, insert -t- between the verb and the pronoun. Inversion is considered more formal.

  Vous parlez français.
  You speak French.
  ▶
  Parlez-vous français?
  Do you speak French?

  Il mange à la cantine.
  He eats in the cafeteria.
  ▶
  Mange-t-il à la cantine?
  Does he eat in the cafeteria?

Only subject pronouns can be inverted. If the subject is a noun, you need to add the corresponding pronoun to invert with the verb.

  Les élèves mangent à la cantine.
  The students are eating in the cafeteria.
  ▶
  Les élèves mangent-**ils** à la cantine ?
  Are the students eating in the cafeteria?

  Nina arrive demain.
  Nina arrives tomorrow.
  ▶
  Nina arrive-**t-elle** demain?
  Does Nina arrive tomorrow?

The inverted form of **il y a** is **y a-t-il**. **C'est** becomes **est-ce**.

  Y a-t-il une horloge dans la classe?
  Is there a clock in the class?

  Est-ce le professeur de lettres?
  Is he the humanities professor?

- Use **pourquoi** to ask *why?* Use **parce que** (**parce qu'** before a vowel sound) to answer *because*.

  Pourquoi retrouves-tu Sophie ici?
  Why are you meeting Sophie here?

  Parce qu'elle habite près d'ici.
  Because she lives near here.

Vérifiez

Expressing negation

- To make a sentence negative in French, place **ne** (**n'** before a vowel sound) before the conjugated verb and **pas** after it.

  Je **ne** dessine **pas** bien.
  I don't draw well.

  Elles **n'**étudient **pas** la chimie.
  They don't study chemistry.

- In the construction [*conjugated verb + infinitive*], **ne** (**n'**) comes before the conjugated verb and **pas** after it.

  Abdel **n'**aime **pas** étudier.
  Abdel doesn't like to study.

  Vous **ne** détestez **pas** travailler?
  You don't hate to work?

- In questions with inversion, place **ne** before the inversion and **pas** after it.

  Abdel **n'**aime-t-il **pas** étudier?
  Doesn't Abdel like to study?

  Ne détestez-vous **pas** travailler?
  Don't you hate to work?

- You already know how to use the expression **moi aussi** (*me too*) to express agreement. Here are some other expressions to express agreement and disagreement.

Expressions of agreement and disagreement

oui	*yes*	**(mais) non**	*no (but of course not)*
bien sûr	*of course*	**pas du tout**	*not at all*
moi/toi non plus	*me/you neither*	**peut-être**	*maybe, perhaps*

  Vous aimez manger à la cantine?
  Do you like to eat in the cafeteria?

  Non, pas du tout.
  No, not at all.

- Use **si** instead of **oui** to contradict a negative question.

  Ne parles-tu pas à Daniel?
  Aren't you talking to Daniel?

  Si!
  Yes (I am)!

⟲ Vérifiez

Essayez! Make questions out of these statements. Use **est-ce que/qu'** in items 1–5 and inversion in 6–10.

Statement	Question
1. Vous mangez à la cantine.	*Est-ce que vous mangez à la cantine?*
2. Ils adorent les devoirs.	Est-ce qu'ils adorent les devoirs?
3. La biologie est difficile.	Est-ce que la biologie est difficile?
4. Tu travailles.	Est-ce que tu travailles?
5. Elles cherchent le prof.	Est-ce qu'elles cherchent le prof?
6. Vous arrivez demain.	*Arrivez-vous demain?*
7. L'élève oublie le livre.	L'élève oublie-t-il/elle le livre?
8. Il y a deux salles de classe.	Y a-t-il deux salles de classe?
9. Ils n'habitent pas à Québec.	N'habitent-ils pas à Québec?
10. C'est le professeur d'art.	Est-ce le professeur d'art?

59

Mise en pratique

1 **L'inversion** Restate the questions using inversion.

1. Est-ce que vous parlez espagnol? Parlez-vous espagnol?
2. Est-ce qu'il étudie à Paris? Étudie-t-il à Paris?
3. Est-ce qu'ils voyagent avec des amis? Voyagent-ils avec des amis?
4. Est-ce que tu aimes les cours de langues? Aimes-tu les cours de langues?
5. Est-ce que le professeur parle anglais? Le professeur parle-t-il anglais?
6. Est-ce que les élèves aiment dessiner? Les élèves aiment-ils dessiner?

2 **Les questions** Ask the questions that correspond to the answers. Use **est-ce que/qu'** and inversion for each item.

MODÈLE

Nous habitons loin (*far away*).
Est-ce que vous habitez loin? / Habitez-vous loin?

1. Il mange à la cantine. Est-ce qu'il mange à la cantine? / Mange-t-il à la cantine?
2. J'oublie les examens. Est-ce que tu oublies les examens? / Oublies-tu les examens?
3. François déteste les maths. Est-ce que François déteste les maths? / François déteste-t-il les maths?
4. Nous adorons voyager. Est-ce que vous adorez voyager? / Adorez-vous voyager?
5. Les cours ne commencent pas demain. Est-ce que les cours ne commencent pas demain? / Les cours ne commencent-ils pas demain?
6. Les élèves arrivent en classe. Est-ce que les élèves arrivent en classe? / Les élèves arrivent-ils/elles en classe?

3 **Complétez** Complete the conversation with the correct questions for the answers given. Act it out with a partner. Suggested answers

MYLÈNE Salut, Arnaud. Ça va?

ARNAUD Oui, ça va. Alors (*So*)... (1) __Tu aimes les cours?__

MYLÈNE J'adore le cours de sciences po, mais je déteste l'informatique.

ARNAUD (2) __Pourquoi est-ce que tu détestes l'informatique?__

MYLÈNE Parce que le prof est très strict.

ARNAUD (3) __Il y a des élèves sympathiques, n'est-ce pas?__

MYLÈNE Oui, il y a des élèves sympathiques... Et demain? (4) __Tu retrouves Béatrice?__

ARNAUD Peut-être, mais demain je retrouve aussi Dominique.

MYLÈNE (5) __Tu cherches une petite amie?__

ARNAUD Pas du tout!

Communication

4 **Au café** In pairs, take turns asking each other questions about the drawing. Use verbs from the list. Answers will vary.

MODÈLE

Élève 1: *Monsieur Laurent parle à Madame Martin, non?*
Élève 2: *Mais non. Il n'aime pas parler.*

arriver	dessiner	manger	partager
chercher	étudier	oublier	rencontrer

5 **Questions** You and your partner want to get to know each other better. Take turns asking each other questions. Modify or add elements as needed. Some answers will vary.

MODÈLE aimer / l'art
Élève 1: *Est-ce que tu aimes l'art?*
Élève 2: *Oui, j'adore l'art./ Non, je n'aime pas l'art.*

1. détester / devoirs   Est-ce que tu détestes les devoirs?

2. étudier / avec / amis   Est-ce que tu étudies avec des amis?

3. penser qu'il y a / cours / intéressant / au lycée   Est-ce que tu penses qu'il y a des cours intéressants au lycée?

4. cours de sciences / être / facile   Est-ce que les cours de sciences sont faciles?

5. aimer mieux / biologie / ou / physique   Est-ce que tu aimes mieux la biologie ou la physique?

6. retrouver / copains / à la cantine   Est-ce que tu retrouves des copains à la cantine?

6 **Confirmez** In groups of three, confirm whether the statements are true of your school. Correct any untrue statements by making them negative. Answers will vary.

MODÈLE

Les profs sont désagréables.
Pas du tout, les profs ne sont pas désagréables.

1. Les cours d'informatique sont inutiles.

2. Il y a des élèves de nationalité allemande.

3. Nous mangeons une cuisine excellente à la cantine.

4. Tous (*All*) les élèves étudient à la bibliothèque.

5. Le cours de chimie est facile.

6. Nous adorons le gymnase.

---

4 Suggestion Tell students to vary the method of asking questions instead of always using a tag question as in the **modèle**.

5 Suggestions
• Have two volunteers read the **modèle** aloud.
• After students have completed the activity, ask volunteers to report what they learned about their partner.

6 Suggestion Encourage students to use as many expressions indicating agreement or disagreement as they can.

6 Expansion Have groups write three additional true/false statements about your school. Ask several groups to read their statements and have the class respond to them. Encourage students to respond with **Mais oui!** or **Mais non!** where appropriate.

Activity Pack For additional activities, go to the **Activity Pack** in the **Resources** section of vhlcentral.com.

EXPANSION

Have students write six sentences containing two parts connected by the word **mais** (*but*). The first part of the sentence should be affirmative and the second part negative. Ex: **J'aime la biologie mais je n'aime pas les maths**. Encourage students to share their sentences in small groups.

EXPANSION

Video Replay the video episode, having students focus on the different forms of questions used. Tell them to write down each question they hear. Stop the video where suitable to give students time to write and to discuss what was heard.

Révision

Key Standards
1.1

1 Partner Chat You can also assign Activity 1 on vhlcentral.com. Students work in pairs to record the activity online. The pair's recorded conversation will appear in your gradebook.

1 Suggestion Discuss which elements of each class students should describe: the items and people in the room and what the students are doing. Model a few statements before students begin.

2 Suggestion Have two volunteers read the **modèle** aloud.

3 Suggestion As students share their responses with the class, make a list of their likes and dislikes on the board under the headings **Nous aimons** and **Nous n'aimons pas.**

4 Suggestion Tell students they may use adjectives that are not in the list.

5 Suggestion Before beginning the activity, have the class decide on names for the people in the drawings. Also have them brainstorm possible relationships between the people, for example, strangers meeting for the first time.

6 Suggestion Divide the class into pairs and distribute the Info Gap Handouts from the Activity Pack. Give students ten minutes to complete the activity.

6 Expansion Have pairs compare their answers with another pair to confirm the people's likes and dislikes. Then ask a few groups to share some of their sentences with the class

1 Des styles différents In pairs, describe these two very different classes. Then, tell your partner which class you prefer and why. Answers will vary.

2 Les activités In pairs, discuss whether these expressions apply to both of you. React to every answer you hear. Answers will vary.

MODÈLE

Élève 1: *Est-ce que tu étudies le week-end?*
Élève 2: *Non! Je n'aime pas étudier le week-end.*
Élève 1: *Moi non plus. J'aime mieux étudier le soir.*

1. adorer la cantine
2. aimer le cours d'art
3. étudier à la bibliothèque
4. manger souvent (*often*) des sushis
5. oublier les devoirs
6. parler espagnol
7. travailler le soir
8. voyager souvent

3 Le lycée In pairs, prepare ten questions inspired by the list and what you know about your school. Together, survey as many classmates as possible to find out what they like and dislike. Answers will vary.

MODÈLE

Élève 1: *Est-ce que tu aimes étudier à la bibliothèque?*
Élève 2: *Non, pas du tout. J'aime mieux étudier...*

bibliothèque	élève	cantine
bureau	gymnase	salle de classe
cours	librairie	salle d'ordinateurs

4 Pourquoi? Survey as many classmates as possible to find out if they like these subjects and why. Ask what adjective they would pick to describe them. Tally the most popular answers for each subject. Answers will vary.

MODÈLE

Élève 1: *Est-ce que tu aimes la philosophie?*
Élève 2: *Pas tellement.*
Élève 1: *Pourquoi?*
Élève 2: *Parce que c'est trop difficile.*

1. la biologie
2. la chimie
3. l'histoire
4. l'éducation physique
5. l'informatique
6. les langues
7. les mathématiques
8. la psychologie

a. agréable
b. amusant
c. désagréable
d. difficile
e. facile
f. important
g. inutile
h. utile

5 Les conversations In pairs, act out a short conversation between the people shown in each drawing. They should greet each other, describe what they are doing, and discuss their likes or dislikes. Choose your favorite skit and role-play it for another pair. Answers will vary.

MODÈLE

Élève 1: *Bonjour, Aurélie.*
Élève 2: *Salut! Tu travailles, non?*

6 Les portraits Your teacher will give you and a partner a set of drawings showing the likes and dislikes of eight people. Discuss each person's tastes. Do not look at each other's worksheet. Answers will vary.

MODÈLE

Élève 1: *Sarah n'aime pas travailler.*
Élève 2: *Mais elle adore manger.*

EXPANSION

Writing Practice Have students write a brief paragraph describing the activities they like or don't like to do. Collect the descriptions and read a few of them to the class. Have the class guess who wrote each description by asking: **Est-ce que c'est...?**

TEACHING OPTIONS

Video Expansion Tell students to turn to the **Roman-photo** on pages 50–51 and write five comprehension questions based on the dialogue. Then have them get together in groups of three or four, and take turns asking and answering each other's questions.

vhlcentral

AP® **Theme:** Contemporary Life
Context: Education

Section Goals
In this section, students will:
• read about French schools
• watch a video about a typical day in a French **collège**
• complete activities based on the video

Key Standards
1.2, 2.1, 3.2, 4.2

Préparation Answer the following questions. Answers will vary.

1. How do you get to and from school?
2. How many classes do you take?
3. How is middle or high school different from elementary school?
4. What functions does student government serve in your school?

L'âge de classe: la journée° d'un collégien

After French students finish **l'école élémentaire**, they attend **collège°** for four years. In their first year of **collège**, which is called **sixième°**, students adjust to their new school, schedule, and classes. Unlike in elementary school, they study a variety of subjects with different **professeurs** throughout the day. **Collégiens** study subjects like **français**, **maths**, **histoire-géo**, and **sciences**, and they also have opportunities to participate in sports and extracurricular activities. In the video, Arthur shows what his school day is like so that students transitioning from elementary school to **collège** have an idea of what to expect from their new school and schedule.

vie *life* **collégien** *middle-school student* **journée** *day* **collège** *middle school* **sixième** *sixth grade*

Vidéo de Tout le Bas-Rhin

...la vie° d'un collégien°.

Vocabulaire utile

un car	*bus*
une carte	*card*
une déléguée de classe	*student council representative*
une matière	*subject*
dur	*hard*

 Compréhension Select the word or phrase that matches each description.

> un car   une carte   la vie d'un collégien   une déléguée de classe   une matière

1. Arthur's mission is to describe this to students entering **collège**.
   la vie d'un collégien
2. Arthur and his friends travel to school in this.
   un car
3. This is what Arthur shows to the driver when he gets on the bus.
   une carte
4. This is Margot's role in student government.
   une déléguée de classe
5. In **collège**, students have a different **prof** for each one of these.
   une matière

 Conversation Discuss the following topics with a partner, then share your thoughts with the class. Answers will vary.

1. Compare Arthur's school transportation to your own. What are the advantages of each?
2. Compare your weekday schedule with Arthur's. How are they similar?

Application With a partner, prepare a presentation about a typical day at your school for a group of exchange students. Include information about school transportation, schedule, lunch time, and after-school activities.

Préparation Tell students they will watch the first minute and a half of the video and that these questions will help them understand what they will see now and prepare them for watching the rest of the video in later units.

L'âge de classe: la journée d'un collégien You may wish to explain to students that the levels of **collège** are called **sixième**, **cinquième**, **quatrième**, and **troisième**, and that the levels of **lycée** are **seconde**, **première**, and **terminale**. You might also mention that near the end of **collège**, students reflect on their interests and skills to decide whether they should choose traditional or technical studies in **lycée**.

Compréhension Have students work in pairs and write down their answers. Then show the video again so they can check and revise their answers if necessary.

Application Have students create a visual aid for their presentation.

⭐ **TELL Connection**

Learning Experience 5 *Why:* Relevant authentic media engages student interest. *What:* Introduce authentic media at the introductory level, modifying and personalizing tasks as needed, and use selected portions of the media over a period of time.

TEACHING OPTIONS

Using Video The video in its entirety is about 10 minutes long. For this unit, have students watch the video from the beginning until 1:41. Have them watch it several times, focusing on a different aspect each time: images they see, cognates and language they recognize, facial expressions and gestures, etc. Return to this video to show additional segments as students learn about different types of classes, personality types, sports, foods and eating, and daily routines in other units. Have students use their new vocabulary and grammar to describe what they see and hear in different portions of the video. You might also show this first segment again with later segments so students can note their progress in understanding what they hear. Later in the year, you may also wish to have students repeat the presentation in **Application** in French.

63

Section Goals

In this section, students will learn and practice vocabulary related to:
• talking about schedules
• the days of the week
• sequencing events

Key Standards

1.1, 1.2, 4.1

Suggestions
• Write days of the week across the board and present them like this: **Aujourd'hui, c'est _____. Demain, c'est _____. Après-demain, c'est _____?**
• Write the following questions and answers on the board, explaining their meaning:
—**Quel jour sommes-nous?**
—**Nous sommes _____.**
—**C'est quel jour demain?**
—**Demain, c'est _____.**
—**C'est quand l'examen?**
—**L'examen est _____.**
Ask students the questions.
• Tell students Monday is the first day of the week in France.
• Point out that days of the week are masculine and lowercase.
• Explain the differences between **le matin/la matinée, le soir/la soirée,** and **le jour/la journée.** Use them in sentences to contrast units of time versus duration. Example: **J'ai cours le matin.** (*I have class in the morning.*) **J'étudie toute la matinée.** (*I study all morning.*)
• Introduce new vocabulary using the digital image for this page. Give the student a name, for example, Henri. Ask students picture-based questions. Examples: **Quel jour Henri assiste-t-il au cours d'économie? Il assiste au cours d'économie le matin ou le soir? Quels jours visite-t-il Paris avec Annette?**
• Point out that **visiter** is used with places, not people.

Contextes

Leçon 2B

◁)) **vhl**central

You will learn how to...
▪ say when things happen
▪ discuss your schedule

Une semaine au lycée

Vocabulaire	
demander	to ask
échouer	to fail
écouter	to listen (to)
enseigner	to teach
expliquer	to explain
trouver	to find; to think
Quel jour sommes-nous?	What day is it?
un an	year
une/cette année	a/this year
après	after
après-demain	day after tomorrow
un/cet après-midi	an/this afternoon
aujourd'hui	today
demain (matin/ après-midi/soir)	tomorrow (morning/ afternoon/evening)
un jour	day
une journée	day
un/ce matin	a/this morning
la matinée	morning
un mois/ce mois-ci	month/this month
une/cette nuit	a/this night
une/cette semaine	a/this week
un/ce soir	an/this evening
une soirée	evening
un/le/ce week-end	a/the/this weekend
dernier/dernière	last
premier/première	first
prochain(e)	next

semaine

| lundi | mardi | mercredi | jeudi | vendredi |

matin

assister au cours d'économie

passer l'examen de maths

après-midi

préparer l'examen de maths

téléphoner à Marc

soir

dîner en famille

Attention!

Use the masculine definite article **le** + [*day of the week*] when an activity is done on a weekly basis. Omit **le** when it is done on a specific day.

Le prof enseigne le lundi.
The teacher teaches on Mondays.

Je passe un examen lundi.
I'm taking a test on Monday.

samedi | dimanche

visiter Paris avec une amie

rentrer à la maison

Mise en pratique

1 Écoutez You will hear Lorraine describing her schedule. Listen carefully and indicate whether the statements are **vrai** or **faux** for her.

		Vrai	Faux
1.	Il y a quatre cours chaque (*each*) jour.	☑	☐
2.	Le cours de chimie est le mardi et le jeudi.	☐	☑
3.	Le cours d'histoire est le lundi, le mercredi et le vendredi.	☑	☐
4.	Le cours d'informatique est le mardi et le jeudi matin.	☑	☐
5.	Les cours d'art et de mathématiques sont le mardi et le jeudi après-midi.	☑	☐
6.	Lorraine trouve les mathématiques difficiles.	☑	☐
7.	Le professeur de mathématiques explique bien.	☐	☑
8.	Lorraine rentre à la maison le soir.	☐	☑
9.	Lorraine regarde la télévision, écoute de la musique ou téléphone à ses amies le soir.	☑	☐
10.	Le week-end, Lorraine aime être à la maison.	☐	☑

2 La classe de Mme Arnaud Complete this paragraph by selecting the correct verb from the list below. Make sure to conjugate the verb. Some verbs will not be used.

demander	expliquer	rentrer
écouter	passer un examen	travailler
enseigner	préparer	trouver
étudier	regarder	visiter

Madame Arnaud (1) ___travaille___ au lycée. Elle (2) ___enseigne___ le français. Elle (3) ___explique___ les verbes et la grammaire aux élèves. Le vendredi, en classe, les élèves (4) ___regardent___ une vidéo en français ou (*or*) (5) ___écoutent___ de la musique française. Ce week-end, ils (6) ___étudient/travaillent___ pour (*for*) (7) ___préparer___ l'examen très difficile de lundi matin. Je/J' (8) ___travaille/étudie___ beaucoup pour ce cours, mais mes (*my*) amis et moi, nous (9) ___trouvons___ la classe sympa.

3 Quel jour sommes-nous? Complete each statement with the correct day of the week.

1. Aujourd'hui, c'est ___Answers will vary.___.
2. Demain, c'est ___Answers will vary.___.
3. Après-demain, c'est ___Answers will vary.___.
4. Le week-end, c'est ___le samedi et le dimanche___.
5. Le premier jour de la semaine en France, c'est ___le lundi___.
6. Les jours du cours de français sont ___Answers will vary.___.
7. Mon (*My*) jour préféré de la semaine, c'est ___Answers will vary.___.
8. Je travaille à la bibliothèque ___Answers will vary.___.

---

1 Script Cette année au lycée, j'assiste aux cours de chimie et d'anglais le lundi, le mercredi et le vendredi matin et aux cours d'histoire et de sport l'après-midi. Le mardi et le jeudi, j'assiste aux cours d'informatique et de français le matin et aux cours d'art et de mathématiques l'après-midi. Je déteste les mathématiques. Le professeur n'explique pas bien et je trouve le cours difficile. Après l'école, je rentre à la maison. J'aime étudier l'après-midi. Le soir, je regarde la télévision, j'écoute de la musique ou je téléphone à mes amies. Le week-end, j'adore visiter Paris avec la famille!
Teacher Resources DVD

1 Suggestions
- Before playing the recording, have students read the statements and identify the expressions that describe when things occur. Examples: **le soir**, **le week-end**, and **le jeudi matin**.
- Go over the answers with the class. If students have difficulty, replay the recording.

2 Expansion Have pairs write original sentences about Madame Arnaud and her class using the verbs that weren't in this paragraph. Ask volunteers to read their sentences aloud.

PRE-AP®

2 Presentational Speaking Ask students to use the paragraph on Madame Arnaud as a model to write a short paragraph about one of their current teachers. Then, ask them to make a brief presentation to the class.

3 Expansions
- Give these items for more practice. **9. Le jour après lundi, c'est ____. 10. Il n'y a pas de cours de français le ____.**
- Have students repeat items 1–4 from the perspective of a different day of the week.

DIFFERENTIATION

For Kinesthetic Learners Create a schedule for an imaginary student using the whole class. Assign each day of the week to a different student and assign each of the remaining students a different activity. As you describe the schedule, students arrange themselves as a page in a weekly day-planner, starting with the day of the week and then each activity you mention. Example: **Le lundi matin, j'assiste au cours. L'après-midi, j'étudie la chimie. Le soir, je dîne en famille.**

EXPANSION

Writing Practice Have students write a paragraph similar to the one in **Activité 2** describing your French class or a different class. They should use as many verbs from the list as possible. Ask volunteers to read their paragraph aloud.

Communication

4 Suggestion Before doing this activity, you may want to write a short list of musical genres on the board for item 5. Also tell students that **quand** means *when*.

4 Expansions
• Have volunteers report what they learned about their classmate.
• To practice the **nous** forms, ask students what they have in common with their partner.

4 Virtual Chat You can assign Activity 4 on vhlcentral.com. Students record individual responses that appear in your gradebook.

5 Suggestion Tell students to switch roles after completing the conversation so that both students have the opportunity to ask and answer questions.

6 Suggestions
• Distribute the **Feuilles d'activités** from the Activity Pack. Have two volunteers read the **modèle** aloud. Make sure students understand the directions.
• Have students repeat the activity with a different partner.

7 Suggestion To save time in class, assign the written part of this activity the day before as homework.

Activity Pack For additional activities, go to the **Activity Pack** in the **Resources** section of vhlcentral.com.

4 Conversez Interview a classmate. Answers will vary.

1. Quel jour sommes-nous?
2. Quand (*When*) est le prochain cours de français?
3. Quand rentres-tu à la maison?
4. Est-ce que tu prépares un examen cette semaine?
5. Est-ce que tu écoutes la radio? Quel genre de musique aimes-tu?
6. Quand téléphones-tu à des amis?
7. Est-ce que tu regardes la télévision l'après-midi ou (*or*) le soir?
8. Est-ce que tu dînes dans un restaurant ce mois-ci?

5 Le premier jour You make a new friend in your French class and want to know what his or her class schedule is like this semester. With a partner, prepare a conversation to perform for the class where you: Answers will vary.

• ask his or her name
• ask what classes he or she is taking
• ask at which times of day (morning or afternoon) he or she has French class
• ask at which times of day (morning or afternoon) he or she has English and History classes

6 Bataille navale Your teacher will give you a worksheet. Choose four spaces on your chart and mark them with a battleship. In pairs, create questions by using the subjects in the first column and the verbs in the first row to find out where your partner has placed his or her battleships. Whoever "sinks" the most battleships wins. Answers will vary.

MODÈLE
Élève 1: *Est-ce que Luc et Sabine téléphonent à Jérôme?*
Élève 2: *Oui, ils téléphonent à Jérôme.*
(if you marked that square)
Non, ils ne téléphonent pas à Jérôme.
(if you didn't mark that square)

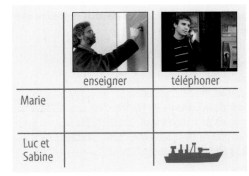

	enseigner	téléphoner
Marie		
Luc et Sabine		🚢

7 Le week-end Write a schedule to show what you do during a typical weekend. Use the verbs you know. Compare your schedule with a classmate's, and talk about the different activities that you do and when. Be prepared to discuss your results with the class.
Answers will vary.

	Moi	Nom
Le vendredi soir 🌙		
Le samedi matin ☀		
Le samedi après-midi ☀		
Le samedi soir 🌙		
Le dimanche matin ☀		
Le dimanche après-midi ☀		
Le dimanche soir 🌙		

Using Games Play a memory game in which the first player says one activity he or she does on a particular day of the week. The next player repeats what the first person said, then adds what he or she does on the following day. The third player must remember what the first two people said before saying what he or she does on the next day. Continue until the end of a week. If someone makes a mistake, then choose another student to continue.

Oral Practice Have students work in groups of three. Tell them to take turns asking and answering what days of the week different TV shows are on. Example: **Quel(s) jour(s) est la série *CSI*?**

Les sons et les lettres 🔊 vhlcentral

The letter r

The French **r** is very different from the English *r*. The English *r* is pronounced by placing the tongue in the middle and toward the front of the mouth. The French **r** is pronounced in the throat. You have seen that an **-er** at the end of a word is usually pronounced **-ay**, as in the English word *way*, but without the glide sound.

| chant**er** | mang**er** | expliqu**er** | aim**er** |

In most other cases, the French **r** has a very different sound. Pronunciation of the French **r** varies according to its position in a word. Note the different ways the **r** is pronounced in these words.

| **r**ivière | litté**r**ature | o**r**dinateu**r** | devoi**r** |

If an **r** falls between two vowels or before a vowel, it is pronounced with slightly more friction.

| **r**are | ga**r**age | Eu**r**ope | **r**ose |

An **r** sound before a consonant or at the end of a word is pronounced with slightly less friction.

| po**r**te | bou**r**se | ado**r**e | jou**r** |

Prononcez Practice saying these words aloud.

1. crayon
2. professeur
3. plaisir
4. différent
5. terrible
6. architecture
7. trouver
8. restaurant
9. rentrer
10. regarder
11. lettres
12. réservé
13. être
14. dernière
15. arriver
16. après

Articulez Practice saying these sentences aloud.

1. Au revoir, Professeur Colbert!
2. Rose arrive en retard mardi.
3. Mercredi, c'est le dernier jour des cours.
4. Robert et Roger adorent écouter la radio.
5. La corbeille à papier, c'est quarante-quatre euros!
6. Les parents de Richard sont brillants et très agréables.

Dictons Practice reading these sayings aloud.

Quand le renard prêche, gare aux oies.[2]

Qui ne risque rien n'a rien.[1]

[1] Nothing ventured, nothing gained.
[2] When the fox preaches, watch your geese.

soixante-sept **67**

Section Goals

In this section, students will learn about the letter **r**.

Key Standards
4.1

Suggestions

- Model the pronunciation of words and expressions with **r** from **Contextes**. Then have students repeat. Examples: **regarder, préparer un examen**, etc.
- Explain that the French **r** has more in common with a **k** sound than it does with the English *r*. The **k** sound is produced when the back of the tongue touches the soft palate. The French **r** is produced a bit farther back in the mouth with the back of the tongue and the uvula.
- Model the pronunciation of each example word and have students repeat.
- Ask students to provide words or expressions from previous lessons that contain the letter **r**. Examples: **au revoir**, **très bien**, **professeur**, and **merci**.
- The explanation and exercises are available on vhlcentral.com. You may want to play them in class so students hear French speakers other than yourself.

Dictons Ask students if they can think of an English saying that is similar to **«Quand le renard prêche, gare aux oies.»** (*Don't let a fox guard the hen house.*)

EXPANSION

Mini-dictée Dictate five familiar words with the **r** in different places, saying each one at least two times. Examples: **librairie**, **résultat**, **jour**, **chercher**, and **montre**. Then write them on the board or a transparency and have students check their spelling.

EXPANSION

Mini-dictée Use these sentences with the letter **r** for additional oral practice or dictation. **1. Renée regarde un garçon américain. 2. Le grand-père de Grégoire est réservé. 3. Je travaille le mercredi après-midi et le vendredi soir. 4. Nous trouvons le cours d'histoire très intéressant.**

Section Goals

In this section, students will learn functional phrases for talking about their schedules and classes and telling time.

Key Standards

1.2, 2.1, 2.2, 4.1, 4.2

Section Goals

In this section, students will learn functional phrases for talking about their schedules and classes and telling time.

Key Standards

1.2, 2.1, 2.2, 4.1, 4.2

Video Recap: Leçon 2A
Before doing this **Roman-photo**, review the previous one with this activity.

1. Comment est-ce que Rachid trouve le cours de sciences po? (intéressant et utile)
2. Comment s'appelle le colocataire de Rachid? (David)
3. Comment est-ce que David trouve l'université française? (C'est différent de l'université américaine, mais c'est intéressant.)
4. Quels cours est-ce que David aime? (littérature et histoire françaises)
5. Stéphane a des problèmes dans quels cours? (français, maths, chimie et histoire-géo)

Video Synopsis At **Le P'tit Bistrot**, Rachid, Sandrine, Amina and David discuss their schedules. Astrid arrives; she is supposed to study with Stéphane. While she waits, Astrid talks about **le bac** and how Stéphane never does his homework. Rachid and Astrid decide to go to the park because they think Stéphane is there. At the park, Astrid and Stéphane argue. When Stéphane complains about his problems at school, Rachid offers to help him study.

Suggestions

• Have volunteers play the roles of Rachid, Sandrine, Amina, David, and Astrid in the scenes that match video stills 1–5.
• Have the class predict what will happen in scenes 6–10. Write predictions on the board.
• Read remaining scenes correcting the predictions. Ask questions to help students summarize this episode.

On trouve une solution vhlcentral

AP® **Theme:** Contemporary Life
Context: Education

PERSONNAGES

Amina

Astrid

David

Rachid

Sandrine

Stéphane

À la terrasse du café...
RACHID Alors, on a rendez-vous avec David demain à cinq heures moins le quart pour rentrer chez nous.
SANDRINE Aujourd'hui, c'est mercredi. Demain... jeudi. Le mardi et le jeudi, j'ai cours de chant de trois heures vingt à quatre heures et demie. C'est parfait!
AMINA Pas de problème. J'ai cours de stylisme...

AMINA Salut, Astrid!
ASTRID Bonjour.
RACHID Astrid, je te présente David, mon (my) coloc américain.
DAVID Alors, cette année, tu as des cours très difficiles, n'est-ce pas?

ASTRID Oui? Pourquoi?
DAVID Ben, Stéphane pense que les cours sont très difficiles.
ASTRID Ouais, Stéphane, il assiste au cours, mais... il ne fait pas ses (his) devoirs et il n'écoute pas les profs. Cette année est très importante, parce que nous avons le bac...
DAVID Ah, le bac...

Au parc...
ASTRID Stéphane! Quelle heure est-il? Tu n'as pas de montre?
STÉPHANE Oh, Astrid, excuse-moi! Le mercredi, je travaille avec Astrid au café sur le cours de maths...
ASTRID Et le mercredi après-midi, il oublie! Tu n'as pas peur du bac, toi!

STÉPHANE Tu as tort, j'ai très peur du bac! Mais je n'ai pas envie de passer mes (my) journées, mes soirées et mes week-ends avec des livres!
ASTRID Je suis d'accord avec toi, Stéphane! J'ai envie de passer les week-ends avec mes copains... des copains qui n'oublient pas les rendez-vous!

RACHID Écoute, Stéphane, tu as des problèmes avec ta (your) mère, avec Astrid aussi.
STÉPHANE Oui, et j'ai d'énormes problèmes au lycée. Je déteste le bac.
RACHID Il n'est pas tard pour commencer à travailler pour être reçu au bac.
STÉPHANE Tu crois, Rachid?

A C T I V I T É S

1 Vrai ou faux? Choose whether each statement is **vrai** or **faux**.

1. Le mardi et le mercredi, Sandrine a (has) cours de chant. Faux.
2. Le jeudi, Amina a cours de stylisme. Vrai.
3. Astrid pense qu'il est impossible de réussir (pass) le bac. Faux.
4. La famille de David est allemande. Faux.
5. Le mercredi, Stéphane travaille avec Astrid au café sur le cours de maths. Vrai.

6. Stéphane a beaucoup de problèmes. Vrai.
7. Rachid est optimiste. Vrai.
8. Stéphane dîne chez Rachid samedi. Faux.
9. Le sport est très important pour Stéphane. Vrai.
10. Astrid est fâchée (angry) contre Stéphane. Vrai.

TEACHING OPTIONS

On trouve une solution Write the title **On trouve une solution** on the board. Ask the class: Who has a problem in the video? What is it? Then ask the class to predict how the problem will be solved.

TEACHING OPTIONS

Regarder la vidéo Show the video episode and have students give you a play-by-play description of the action. Write their descriptions on the board. Then show the episode again so students can add more details to the description.

Les amis organisent des rendez-vous.

RACHID C'est un examen très important que les élèves français passent la dernière année de lycée pour continuer en études supérieures.

DAVID Euh, n'oublie pas, je suis de famille française.

ASTRID Oui, et c'est difficile, mais ce n'est pas impossible. Stéphane trouve que les études ne sont pas intéressantes. Le sport, oui, mais pas les études.

RACHID Le sport? Tu cherches Stéphane, n'est-ce pas? On trouve Stéphane au parc! Allons-y, Astrid.

ASTRID D'accord. À demain!

RACHID Oui. Mais le sport, c'est la dernière des priorités. Écoute, dimanche prochain, tu dînes chez moi et on trouve une solution.

STÉPHANE Rachid, tu n'as pas envie de donner des cours à un lycéen nul comme moi!

RACHID Mais si, j'ai très envie d'enseigner les maths...

STÉPHANE Bon, j'accepte. Merci, Rachid. C'est sympa.

RACHID De rien. À plus tard!

Expressions utiles

Talking about your schedule

- **Alors, on a rendez-vous demain à cinq heures moins le quart pour rentrer chez nous.**
  So, we're meeting tomorrow at quarter to five to go home (our home).
- **J'ai cours de chant de trois heures vingt à quatre heures et demie.**
  I have voice (singing) class from three-twenty to four-thirty.
- **J'ai cours de stylisme de deux heures à quatre heures vingt.**
  I have fashion design class from two o'clock to four-twenty.
- **Quelle heure est-il?** • **Tu n'as pas de montre?**
  What time is it?   *You don't have a watch?*

Talking about school

- **Nous avons le bac.**
  We have the bac.
- **Il ne fait pas ses devoirs.**
  He doesn't do his homework.
- **Tu n'as pas peur du bac!**
  You're not afraid of the bac!
- **Tu as tort, j'ai très peur du bac!**
  You're wrong, I'm very afraid of the bac!
- **Je suis d'accord avec toi.**
  I agree with you.
- **J'ai d'énormes problèmes.**
  I have big/enormous problems.
- **Tu n'as pas envie de donner des cours à un(e) lycéen(ne) nul(le) comme moi.**
  You don't want to teach a high school student as bad as myself.

Useful expressions

- **C'est parfait!**
  That's perfect!
- **Allons-y!**
  Let's go!
- **D'accord.**
  OK./All right.
- **Ouais.**
  Yeah.
- **C'est sympa.**
  That's nice/fun.

2 **Répondez** Answer these questions. Refer to the video scenes and use a dictionary as necessary. You do not have to answer in complete sentences. Answers will vary.

1. Où (*Where*) est-ce que tu as envie de voyager?

2. Est-ce que tu as peur de quelque chose? De quoi?

3. Qu'est-ce que tu dis (*say*) quand tu as tort?

3 **À vous!** With a partner, describe someone you know whose personality, likes, or dislikes resemble those of Rachid or Stéphane.

MODÈLE

*Paul est comme (*like*) Rachid... il est sérieux.*

A C T I V I T É S

soixante-neuf **69**

Expressions utiles

- Model the pronunciation of the **Expressions utiles** and have students repeat after you.
- As you work through the list, point out forms of **avoir**, idiomatic expressions with **avoir**, and expressions for telling time. Tell students that these concepts will be formally presented in **Structures**.
- Respond briefly to questions about **avoir** and reinforce correct forms, but do not expect students to produce them consistently at this time.
- Ask students a few questions based on the **Expressions utiles**. Examples: **Tu as cours de chant aujourd'hui? Tu as cours de sport?**
- Have students scan the video-still captions for phrases or sentences that show a sequence of time or events. Examples: **Aujourd'hui, c'est mercredi. Demain jeudi, ...**

1 **Suggestion** After students have completed the activity, review their answers and clarify as needed.

1 **Expansion** Have students correct the false statements to make them true.

2 **Expansion** For additional practice, ask these questions. **4. Où est-ce que tu as envie de dîner? 5. À qui est-ce que tu as envie de téléphoner? 6. Est-ce que tu as peur de regarder des films d'horreur?**

3 **Suggestion** Before beginning the activity, tell pairs to brainstorm and write a list of adjectives or phrases that describe Rachid and Stéphane.

TEACHING OPTIONS

Skits Working in groups of three, have students create a short skit similar to the scenes in video stills 6–10 in which one of the students forgets to show up for a study session or a meeting. Give students ten minutes to prepare, then call on groups to perform their skits for the class.

TEACHING OPTIONS

Oral Practice Have students work in pairs. Tell them to create two-line conversations using as many of the **Expressions utiles** as they can. Example:
—**Alors, on a rendez-vous à cinq heures?**
—**Ouais! C'est parfait!**

69

vhlcentral   CULTURE À LA LOUPE

Le bac

The three years of **lycée** culminate in a high stakes exam called the **baccalauréat** or **bac**. Students begin preparing for this exam by the end of **seconde** (10ᵗʰ grade), when they must decide the type of **bac** they will take. This choice determines their coursework during the last two years of **lycée**; for example, a student who plans to take the **bac S** will study mainly physics, chemistry, and math. Most students take **le bac économique et social (ES)**, **le bac littéraire (L)**, or **le bac scientifique (S)**. Others, though, choose to follow a more technical path, for example **le bac sciences et technologies de l'industrie et du développement durable (STI2D)**, **le bac sciences et technologies de la santé et du social (ST2S)**, or **le bac sciences et technologies du management et de la gestion (STMG)**. There is even a **bac technique** for hotel management and music/dance!

The **bac** has both oral and written sections, which are weighted differently according to the type of **bac**. This means that, for example, a bad grade on the math section would lower a

student's grade significantly on a **bac S** but to a lesser degree on a **bac L**. In all cases, the highest possible grade is 20/20. If a student's overall score on the **bac** is below 10/20 (the minimum passing grade) but above 8/20, he/she can take the **rattrapage**, or make-up exam. If the student fails again, then he/she can **redoubler**, or repeat the school year and take the **bac** again.

Students usually go to find out their results with friends and classmates just a few days after they take the exam. This yearly ritual is full of emotion: it's common to see groups of students frantically looking for their results posted on bulletin boards at the **lycée**. Over 80% of students successfully pass the **bac** every year, granting them access to France's higher education system.

Students can pass the **bac** with:	
18/20 - 20/20	mention Très bien et félicitations du jury
16/20 - 18/20	mention Très bien
14/20 - 16/20	mention Bien
12/20 - 14/20	mention Assez bien
10/20 - 12/20	no special mention

Coup de main

In French, a superscript ᵉ following a numeral tells you that it is an ordinal number. It is the equivalent of a -ᵗʰ after a numeral in English: 10ᵉ (**dixième**) = 10ᵗʰ.

A C T I V I T É S

1 Vrai ou faux? Indicate whether each statement is **vrai** or **faux**. Correct the false statements.

1. The **bac** is an exam that students take at the end of **terminale**.
   Vrai.
2. The **bac** has only oral exams.
   Faux. It also has written exams.
3. The highest possible grade on the **bac** is 20/20.
   Vrai.
4. Students decide which **bac** they will take at the beginning of **terminale**.
   Faux. Students must decide which bac they will take by the end of seconde.
5. Most students take the **bac technique**.
   Faux. Most students take le bac ES, le bac L, or le bac S.

6. All the grades of the **bac** are weighted equally.
   Faux. The different sections are weighted differently in each bac.
7. A student with an average grade of 14.5 on the **bac** receives his diploma with **mention Bien**.
   Vrai.
8. A student who fails the **bac** but has an overall grade of 8/20 can take a make-up exam.
   Vrai.
9. A student who fails the **bac** and the **rattrapage** cannot repeat the year.
   Faux. He can repeat the year and attempt the bac again.
10. Passing the **bac** enables students to register for college or to apply for the **grandes écoles**.
    Vrai.

LE FRANÇAIS QUOTIDIEN

Les examens

assurer/cartonner (à un examen)	to ace (an exam)
bachoter	to cram for the *bac*
bosser	to work hard
une moyenne	an average
rater (un examen)	to fail (an exam)
réviser	to study, to review
un(e) surveillant(e)	a proctor
tricher	to cheat

LE MONDE FRANCOPHONE

L'immersion française

Voici quelques° lycées du monde où les élèves suivent leurs cours° en français.

Aux États-Unis École franco-américaine de Chicago, École franco-américaine de San Diego, Lycée français de La Nouvelle-Orléans, Lycée franco-américain de New York, The French-American School of Minneapolis

Au Canada Collège Stanislas à Montréal, Lycée français de Toronto

Au Maroc Lycée André Malraux de Rabat

À Madagascar Lycée français de Tananarive

Au Viêt-nam Lycée Français International Marguerite Duras de Hô-Chi-Minh-Ville

quelques *some* suivent leurs cours *take their classes*

PORTRAIT

AP® **Theme:** Contemporary Life **Context:** Education

Les études supérieures en France

After taking the **bac**, students continuing their studies have several choices. The highest achieving students often enroll in a **classe préparatoire**, which prepares them for the entrance tests to the **grandes écoles**. The **grandes écoles** are France's most prestigious and elite institutions of higher learning. The best known are **l'ENA (École nationale d'administration), Polytechnique, HEC (École des hautes° études commerciales) et Sciences Po (Institut des sciences politiques).** Other students choose **une école spécialisée**, such as a business or jounalism school. These establishments offer a highly specialized course of study and degree. Another option is enrolling in **l'université**. University students begin classes in their chosen field of study in their first year. University studies generally take three to four year to complete, or longer for a doctorate.

haute *higher-level*

Sur Internet

AP® **Theme:** Contemporary Life
Context: Education

Quel (*Which*) bac aimeriez-vous (*would you like*) passer?

Go to **vhlcentral.com** to find more information related to this **Culture** section.

---

2 **Les études supérieures en France** What kind of higher education might these students seek? Write the school types in French.

1. a future journalist une école spécialisée
2. an outstanding student une grande école
3. a foreign language student l'université
4. a business student une école spécialisée
5. a chemistry student l'université

3 **Et les cours?** In French, name two courses you might take in preparation for each of these **baccalauréat** exams. Answers will vary. Possible answers shown.

1. un bac L
   le français et la philosophie
2. un bac STMG
   la biologie et la psychologie
3. un bac ES
   l'économie et la sociologie
4. un bac STI2D
   la physique et les maths

A C T I V I T É S

2B.1

Present tense of *avoir* vhlcentral

Point de départ The verb **avoir** (*to have*) is used frequently. You will have to memorize each of its present tense forms because they are irregular.

Present tense of *avoir*			
j'ai	*I have*	nous avons	*we have*
tu as	*you have*	vous avez	*you have*
il/elle/on a	*he/she/it/one has*	ils/elles ont	*they have*

On a rendez-vous avec David demain.

Cette année, nous avons le bac.

- Liaison is required between the final consonants of **on, nous, vous, ils,** and **elles** and the first vowel of forms of **avoir** that follow them. When the final consonant is an **-s,** pronounce it as a z before the verb forms.

On a un prof sympa.
We have a nice teacher.

Vous avez deux stylos.
You have two pens.

Nous avons un cours d'art.
We have an art class.

Elles ont un examen de psychologie.
They have a Psychology exam.

- Keep in mind that an indefinite article, whether singular or plural, usually becomes **de/d'** after a negation.

J'ai **un** cours difficile.
I have a difficult class.

Je n'ai pas **de** cours difficile.
I don't have a difficult class.

Il a **des** examens.
He has exams.

Il n'a pas **d'**examens.
He does not have exams.

- The verb **avoir** is used in certain idiomatic or set expressions where English generally uses *to be* or *to feel*.

Expressions with *avoir*

avoir... ans	*to be... years old*	avoir froid	*to be cold*
avoir besoin (de)	*to need*	avoir honte (de)	*to be ashamed (of)*
avoir de la chance	*to be lucky*	avoir l'air	*to look like, to seem*
		avoir peur (de)	*to be afraid (of)*
avoir chaud	*to be hot*	avoir raison	*to be right*
avoir envie (de)	*to feel like*	avoir sommeil	*to be sleepy*
		avoir tort	*to be wrong*

In the expression **avoir l'air** + [*adjective*], the adjective does not change to agree with the subject. It is always masculine singular, because it agrees with **air**. Examples:

Elle a l'air charmant.
She seems charming.

Ils ont l'air content.
They look happy.

Il a chaud.

Ils ont froid.

Elle a sommeil.

Il a peur.

- The expressions **avoir besoin de**, **avoir honte de**, **avoir peur de**, and **avoir envie de** can be followed by either a noun or a verb.

  J'**ai besoin d'**une calculatrice.
  I need a calculator.

  J'**ai besoin d'**étudier.
  I need to study.

- The command forms of **avoir** are irregular: **aie, ayons, ayez.** Place **ne** and **pas** around the command to make it negative.

  Aie un peu de patience.
  Be a little patient.

  N'**ayez** pas peur.
  Don't be afraid.

Essayez!   Complete the sentences with the correct forms of **avoir**.

1. La température est de 35 degrés Celsius. Nous __avons__ chaud.
2. En Alaska, en décembre, vous __avez__ froid.
3. Martine __a__ envie de danser.
4. Ils __ont__ besoin d'une calculatrice pour le devoir.
5. Est-ce que tu __as__ peur des insectes?
6. Sébastien pense que je travaille aujourd'hui. Il __a__ raison.
7. J' __ai__ cours d'économie le lundi.
8. Mes amis voyagent beaucoup. Ils __ont__ de la chance.
9. Mohammed __a__ deux cousins à Marseille.
10. Vous __avez__ un grand appartement.

1 Suggestions
- Before students complete the activity, review forming questions with **avoir** using inversion. Write statements on the board and have students write the questions. Examples: **Martine a cours le lundi matin. (Martine a-t-elle cours le lundi matin?) Vous avez une montre. (Avez-vous une montre?)**
- This activity can be done in pairs. Tell students to alternate asking and answering the questions.

2 Expansion For each drawing, ask students how many people there are, their names, and their ages. Example: **Combien de personnes y a-t-il sur le dessin numéro 1? Comment s'appellent les personnes sur le dessin numéro 2? Quel âge a _____?**

3 Suggestion This activity can be done orally or in writing, in pairs or groups.

Mise en pratique

1 On a... Use the correct forms of **avoir** to form questions from these elements. Use inversion and provide an affirmative or negative answer as indicated.

MODÈLE

tu / un examen (oui)
As-tu un examen? Oui, j'ai un examen.

1. nous / un dictionnaire (oui)   Avons-nous un dictionnaire? Oui, nous avons un dictionnaire.
2. Luc / un diplôme (non)   Luc a-t-il un diplôme? Non, il n'a pas de diplôme.
3. elles / des montres (non)   Ont-elles des montres? Non, elles n'ont pas de montres.
4. vous / des copains (oui)   Avez-vous des copains? Oui, j'ai/nous avons des copains.
5. Thérèse / un téléphone (oui)   Thérèse a-t-elle un téléphone? Oui, elle a un téléphone.
6. Charles et Jacques / une calculatrice (non)   Charles et Jacques ont-ils une calculatrice? Non, ils n'ont pas de calculatrice.
7. on / un examen (non)   A-t-on un examen? Non, on n'a pas d'examen.
8. tu / des livres de français (non)   As-tu des livres de français? Non, je n'ai pas de livres de français.

2 C'est évident Describe these people using expressions with **avoir**.

1. J' ___ai besoin d'___ étudier.   2. Vous ___avez froid___.

3. Tu ___as honte___.   4. Elles ___ont sommeil___.

3 Assemblez Use the verb avoir and combine elements from the two columns to create sentences about yourself, your class, and your school. Make any necessary changes or additions.   Answers will vary.

A	B
Je	cours utiles
Le lycée	bonnes notes
Les profs	professeurs brillants
Mon (*My*) petit ami	ami(e) mexicain(e) / anglais(e) / canadien(ne) / vietnamien(ne)
Ma (*My*) petite amie	élèves intéressants
Nous	cantine agréable
	cours d'informatique

Communication

4 Besoins Your teacher will give you a worksheet. Ask different classmates if they need to do these activities. Find at least one person to answer **Oui** and at least one to answer **Non** for each item. *Answers will vary.*

MODÈLE

regarder la télé

Élève 1: *Tu as besoin de regarder la télé?*
Élève 2: *Oui, j'ai besoin de regarder la télé.*
Élève 3: *Non, je n'ai pas besoin de regarder la télé.*

Activités	Oui	Non
1. regarder la télé	Anne	Louis
2. étudier ce soir		
3. passer un examen cette semaine		
4. retrouver des amis demain		
5. travailler à la bibliothèque		
6. commencer un devoir important		
7. téléphoner à un(e) copain/copine ce week-end		
8. parler avec le professeur		

5 C'est vrai? Interview a classmate by transforming each of these statements into a question. Be prepared to report the results of your interview to the class.

MODÈLE J'ai deux ordinateurs.

Élève 1: *Tu as deux ordinateurs?*
Élève 2: *Non, je n'ai pas deux ordinateurs.*

1. J'ai peur des examens.
2. J'ai seize ans.
3. J'ai envie de visiter Montréal.
4. J'ai un cours de biologie.
5. J'ai sommeil le lundi matin.
6. J'ai un(e) petit(e) ami(e) égoïste.

6 Interview You are talking to a school counselor. Answer his or her questions. In pairs, practice the scene and role-play it for the class. *Answers will vary.*

1. Qu'est-ce que (*What*) vous avez envie d'étudier?
2. Est-ce que vous avez d'excellentes notes?
3. Est-ce que vous avez souvent besoin d'aide (*help*) avec les devoirs?
4. Est-ce que vous mangez à la cantine?
5. Est-ce que vous avez un ordinateur?
6. Est-ce que vous retrouvez des amis au lycée?
7. Est-ce que vous écoutez de la musique?
8. Est-ce que vous avez des cours le soir?

soixante-quinze **75**

---

4 Suggestions
- Have three volunteers read the **modèle** aloud. Then distribute the **Feuilles d'activités**, found in the Activity Pack on vhlcentral.com.
- Have students add at least two activities of their own.

5 Suggestion Have two volunteers read the **modèle** aloud. Remind students that an indefinite article becomes **de (d')** if it follows **avoir** in the negative.

5 Virtual Chat You can assign Activity 5 on vhlcentral.com. Students record individual responses that appear in your gradebook.

6 Suggestions
- Remind students to do the interview twice so each person asks and answers the questions.
- Ask volunteers to summarize their partners' responses. Record the responses on the board as a survey (**un sondage**) about the class' characteristics. Then ask questions like this: **Combien d'élèves dans la classe ont envie d'étudier la physique?**

6 Virtual Chat You can assign Activity 6 on vhlcentral.com. Students record individual responses that appear in your gradebook.

Activity Pack For additional activities, go to the **Activity Pack** in the **Resources** section of vhlcentral.com.

EXPANSION

Game Divide the class into two teams. Choose one team member at a time to go to the board, alternating between teams. Say a subject pronoun. The person at the board must write and say the correct form of **avoir**. Example: **elle (elle a)**. Give a point for each correct answer. The team with the most points at the end of the game wins.

TEACHING OPTIONS

For Visual Learners Bring in magazine photos or illustrations showing people holding different items. As you show the images, ask students to raise their hands and say what the people in the images are holding. Ex: **Il a un café, elle a un livre**.

2B.2

Telling time   vhlcentral

Point de départ You use the verb **être** with numbers to tell time.

- There are two ways to ask what time it is.

  Quelle heure est-il?
  What time is it?

  Quelle heure avez-vous/as-tu?
  What time do you have?

🏃 Boîte à outils

In English, you often leave out the word *o'clock* when telling time. You might say "The class starts at eleven" or "I arrive at seven." In French, however, you must always include the word **heure(s)**.

- To tell time on the hour, use a *number* + **heures**. Use **une heure** for one o'clock.

Il est **six heures**.   Il est **une heure**.

- To tell the time from the hour to the half-hour, add the number of minutes past the hour. To say it is fifteen minutes past the hour, use **et quart**. To say it is thirty minutes past the hour, use **et demie**.

Il est quatre heures **cinq**.   Il est onze heures **vingt**.

Il est une heure **et quart**.   Il est sept heures **et demie**.

- To tell the time from the half hour to the hour, use **moins** (*minus*) and subtract the number of minutes or the portion of an hour from the next hour.

Il est trois heures **moins dix**.   Il est une heure **moins le quart**.

- To say at what time something happens, use the preposition **à**.

  Le cours commence **à neuf heures moins vingt**.
  The class starts at 8:40.

  Nous avons un examen **à une heure**.
  We have a test at one o'clock.

🔊 Vérifiez

Section Goals

In this section, students will learn:
- to tell time
- some time expressions
- the 24-hour system of telling time

Suggestions: Scaffolding
- To prepare for telling time, review the meanings of **il est** and numbers 0–60.
- Use a paperplate clock to introduce: **Il est sept heures (huit heures, neuf heures…)**.
- Explain to students that **heures** refers to *hours* when telling time, but can also mean *o'clock*.
- Next, introduce: **Il est _____ heure(s) cinq, dix, et quart**, and **et demie**.
- Using a paper plate clock, display various times on the hour. Ask: **Quelle heure est-il?**
- Introduce and explain: **Il est _____ heure(s) moins cinq, moins dix, moins le quart**, and **moins vingt**. Repeat the procedure above using your movable-hands clock.
- Present the information about liaison in the first two bullets on p. 76. Read the examples and have students repeat.
- Expansion: Explain that the French view times of day differently from Americans. In France, they say «**bonjour**» until about 4:00 or 5:00 p.m. After that, they use the greeting «**bonsoir**». They say «**bonne nuit**» only when going to sleep.

EXPANSION

Extra Practice Give half the class slips of paper with clock faces depicting certain times. Give the corresponding times written out in French to the other half of the class. Have students circulate around the room to match their times. To increase difficulty, include duplicates of each time with **du matin** or **du soir** on the written-out times and a sun or a moon on the clock faces.

TEACHING OPTIONS

Game Divide the class into two teams. Write two city names on the board. (Ex: **Detroit** and **Des Moines**) Check that students know the time difference and then list a time underneath the first city. (Ex: **7:30 a.m.**) Point to the first member of each team and ask: **Il est sept heures et demie à Detroit. Quelle heure est-il à Des Moines?** The first student to write the correct time in French earns a point for his or her team.

- **Liaison** occurs between numbers and the word **heure(s)**. Final **-s** and **-x** in **deux, trois, six,** and **dix** are pronounced like a z. The final **-f** of **neuf** is pronounced like a *v*.

  Il est **deux heures**.   Il est **neuf heures** et quart.
  It's two o'clock.   *It's 9:15.*

- You do not usually make a **liaison** between the verb form **est** and a following number that starts with a vowel sound.

  Il est onze heures.   Il est une heure vingt.   Il est huit heures et demie.
  It's eleven o'clock.   *It's 1:20.*   *It's 8:30.*

Expressions for telling time

À quelle heure?	(At) what time/ When?	midi	noon
de l'après-midi	in the afternoon	minuit	midnight
du matin	in the morning	pile	sharp, on the dot
du soir	in the evening	presque	almost
en avance	early	tard	late
en retard	late	tôt	early
		vers	about

  Il est **minuit** à Paris.   Il est six heures **du soir** à New York.
  It's midnight in Paris.   *It's six o'clock in the evening in New York.*

- The 24-hour clock is often used to express official time. Departure times, movie times, and store hours are expressed this way. Official time is also becoming more popular in everyday conversation. Only numbers are used to tell time this way. Expressions like **et demie, moins le quart,** etc. are not used.

  Le train arrive à **dix-sept heures six**.   Le film est à **vingt-deux heures trente-sept**.
  The train arrives at 5:06 p.m.   *The film is at 10:37 p.m.*

J'ai cours de trois heures vingt à quatre heures et demie.

Stéphane! Quelle heure est-il?

- When writing the time in French using numbers, the hour and minutes are separated by the letter **h**, which stands for **heure(s)**, while in English a colon is used.

  3:25 = **3h25**   11:10 = **11h10**   5:15 = **5h15**   9:30 p.m. = **21h45**

Essayez! Complete the sentences by writing out the correct times according to the cues.

1. (1:00 a.m.) Il est ___une heure___ du matin.
2. (2:50 a.m.) Il est ___trois heures moins dix___ du matin.
3. (8:30 p.m.) Il est ___huit heures et demie___ du soir.
4. (10:08 a.m.) Il est ___dix heures huit___ du matin.
5. (7:15 p.m.) Il est ___sept heures et quart___ du soir.
6. (12:00 p.m.) Il est ___midi___ .
7. (4:05 p.m.) Il est ___quatre heures cinq___ de l'après-midi.
8. (4:45 a.m.) Il est ___cinq heures moins le quart___ du matin.
9. (3:20 a.m.) Il est ___trois heures vingt___ du matin.
10. (12:00 a.m.) Il est ___minuit___ .

soixante-dix-sept **77**

Suggestions: Scaffolding
- Model the pronunciation of the time expressions in the box and have students repeat. Point out that a.m. and p.m. are not used in France or most Francophone regions. Instead, they use **du matin**, **de l'après midi**, and **du soir**.
- Tell students that **et demi(e)** agrees in gender with the noun it follows, but not in number. After **midi** and **minuit**, both **et demi** and **et demie** are accepted.
- Have students complete the **Vérifiez** activity on time expressions.
- Explain the use of the 24-hour clock. Have students practice saying times this way by adding 12. Have students complete the **Vérifiez** activity.

Essayez! For additional practice, give students these items.
11. 6:20 p.m.   12. 9:10 a.m.
13. 2:15 p.m.   14. 10:35 a.m.
15. 11:15 a.m.   16. 9:55 p.m.

🏃 Boîte à outils

In French, there are no words for *a.m.* and *p.m.* You can use **du matin** for *a.m.*, **de l'après-midi** from noon until about 6 p.m., and **du soir** from about 6 p.m. until midnight. When you use the 24-hour clock, it becomes obvious whether you're referring to *a.m.* or *p.m.*

🖇 Vérifiez

À noter

As you learned in **Leçon 1A**, when you say 21, 31, 41, etc. in French, the *one* agrees with the gender of the noun that follows. Therefore, **21h00** is **vingt et une heures**.

🖇 Vérifiez

EXPANSION

Extra Practice Draw a large clock face on the board with its numbers but without the hands. Say a time and ask a volunteer to come up and draw the hands to indicate that time. The rest of the class verifies whether or not the person has written the correct time, saying: **Il/Elle a raison/tort.** Repeat this procedure a number of times.

TEACHING OPTIONS

Video Play the video episode again to give students additional input on telling time and the verb **avoir**. Pause the video where appropriate to discuss how time or **avoir** were used and to ask comprehension questions. Example: **Est-ce que Stéphane a peur de parler à Astrid? (Mais non, il a peur du bac.)**

Mise en pratique

1 **Quelle heure est-il?** Give the time shown on each clock or watch.

MODÈLE
Il est quatre heures et quart de l'après-midi.

1. <u>Il est midi/minuit et demi(e).</u>
2. <u>Il est une heure du matin.</u>
3. <u>Il est huit heures dix.</u>
4. <u>Il est onze heures moins le quart.</u>

5. <u>Il est deux heures douze.</u>
6. <u>Il est sept heures cinq.</u>
7. <u>Il est quatre heures moins cinq.</u>
8. <u>Il est minuit moins vingt-cinq.</u>

2 **À quelle heure?** Find out when you and your friends are going to do certain things.

MODÈLE
À quelle heure est-ce qu'on étudie? (about 8 p.m.)
On étudie vers huit heures du soir.

À quelle heure...

1. ...est-ce qu'on arrive au café? (at 10:30 a.m.) On arrive au café à dix heures et demie du matin.
2. ...est-ce que vous parlez avec le professeur? (at noon) Nous parlons avec le professeur à midi.
3. ...est-ce que tu travailles? (late, at 11:15 p.m.) Je travaille tard, à onze heures et quart du soir.
4. ...est-ce qu'on regarde la télé? (at 9:00 p.m.) On regarde la télé à neuf heures du soir.
5. ...est-ce que Marlène et Nadine mangent? (around 1:45 p.m.) Elles mangent vers deux heures moins le quart de l'après-midi.
6. ...est-ce que le cours commence? (very early, at 8:20 a.m.) Il commence très tôt, à huit heures vingt du matin.

3 **Départ à...** Tell what each of these times would be on a 24-hour clock.

MODÈLE
Il est trois heures vingt de l'après-midi.
Il est quinze heures vingt.

1. Il est dix heures et demie du soir. Il est vingt-deux heures trente.
2. Il est deux heures de l'après-midi. Il est quatorze heures.
3. Il est huit heures et quart du soir. Il est vingt heures quinze.
4. Il est minuit moins le quart. Il est vingt-trois heures quarante-cinq.
5. Il est six heures vingt-cinq du soir. Il est dix-huit heures vingt-cinq.
6. Il est trois heures moins cinq du matin. Il est deux heures cinquante-cinq.
7. Il est six heures moins le quart de l'après-midi. Il est dix-sept heures quarante-cinq.
8. Il est une heure et quart de l'après-midi. Il est treize heures quinze.
9. Il est neuf heures dix du soir. Il est vingt et une heures dix.
10. Il est sept heures quarante du soir. Il est dix-neuf heures quarante.

---

1 **Expansion** At random, say the times shown and have students say the number of the clock or watch described. Example: **Il est sept heures cinq. (C'est le numéro six.)**

2 **Suggestion** Read the **modèle** aloud with a volunteer. Working in pairs, have students take turns asking and answering the questions.

3 **Expansion** Create a train schedule and write it on the board or use photocopies of a real one. Ask students questions based on the schedule. Example: **À quelle heure est le train Paris-Bordeaux le vendredi soir?**
• Have students write out the time in numbers.

EXPANSION

Pairs Have student pairs take turns telling each other what time their classes are this semester/trimester/term. Example: **J'ai un cours à _____ heures**…. For each time given, the other student draws a clock face with the corresponding time. The first student verifies if the clock is correct.

EXPANSION

Pairs Have students work with a partner to create an original conversation in which they: (1) greet each other appropriately, (2) ask for the time, (3) ask what time a particular class is, and (4) say goodbye. Have pairs role-play their conversations for the class.

Communication

4 **Télémonde** Look at this French TV guide. In pairs, ask questions about program start times. Answers will vary.

MODÈLE

Élève 1: À quelle heure commence Télé-ciné sur Antenne 4?
Élève 2: Télé-ciné commence à dix heures dix du soir.

dessins animés	cartoons
feuilleton télévisé	soap opera
film policier	detective film
informations	news
jeu télévisé	game show

VENDREDI

Antenne 2	Antenne 4	Antenne 5
15h30 Pomme d'Api (dessins animés)	**14h00** Football: match France-Italie	**18h25** Montréal: une ville à visiter
17h35 Reportage spécial: le sport dans les lycées	**19h45** Les informations	**19h30** Des chiffres et des lettres (jeu télévisé)
20h15 La famille Menet (feuilleton télévisé)	**20h30** Concert: orchestre de Nice	**21h05** Reportage spécial: les Sénégalais
21h35 Télé-ciné: L'inspecteur Duval (film policier)	**22h10** Télé-ciné: Une chose difficile (comédie dramatique)	**22h05** Les informations

5 **Où es-tu?** In pairs, take turns asking where (**où**) your partner usually is on these days at these times. Choose from the places listed. Answers will vary.

MODÈLE

Élève 1: Où es-tu samedi à midi?
Élève 2: Le samedi à midi, je suis à la cantine.

au lit (*bed*)	chez moi (*at home*)
à la cantine	
à la bibliothèque	chez mes copains
en ville (*town*)	au lycée
au parc	au restaurant
en cours	

1. Le samedi: à 8h00 du matin; à midi; à minuit
2. En semaine: à 9h00 du matin; à 3h00 de l'après-midi; à 7h00 du soir
3. Le dimanche: à 4h00 de l'après-midi; à 6h30 du soir; à 10h00 du soir
4. Le vendredi: à 11h00 du matin; à 5h00 de l'après-midi; à 11h00 du soir

6 **Le suspect** Someone at your school is a suspect in a crime. You and a partner are detectives. Keeping a log of the person activities, use the 24-hour clock to say what he or she is doing when. Answers will vary.

MODÈLE

À vingt-deux heures trente-trois, il parle au téléphone.

4 Suggestion Before starting this activity, have students read the TV guide, point out cognates, and predict their meaning. Provide examples for non-cognate categories so students can guess their meaning. Examples: **dessins animés, feuilleton télévisé**, and **jeu télévisé**.

4 Expansion Have pairs ask each other additional questions based on the TV guide. Examples: **Est-ce qu'il y a un reportage à vingt heures dix?** (Non, les reportages sont à dix-sept heures trente-cinq et à vingt et une heures cinq.) **J'ai envie de regarder le film policier. À quelle heure est-il?** (Le film policier est à vingt et une heures trente-cinq.)

5 Suggestion Role-play the model with a student, then call on volunteers to model a second conversation.

6 Expansion After completing the activity, ask students if the suspect has an alibi at certain times. Tell them to respond using the information on their logs. Example: **Le suspect a-t-il un alibi à vingt-trois heures?** (Oui, à vingt-trois heures il étudie avec un ami.)

Activity Pack For additional activities, go to the **Activity Pack** in the **Resources** section of vhlcentral.com.

EXPANSION

Small Groups Have students work in groups of three. Tell them to take turns asking what time various TV shows start and answering. Example: **À quelle heure est *Big Bang Theory*?** (**C'est à vingt heures.**) Remind students to use the 24-hour system when talking about TV shows.

TEACHING OPTIONS

Small Groups Have small groups prepare skits. Students can choose any situation they wish, provided that they use material presented in the **Contextes** and **Structures** sections. Possible situations include: describing classes and schedules and discussing likes and dislikes.

Révision

1 J'ai besoin de... In pairs, take turns saying which items you need. Your partner will guess why you need them. How many times did each of you guess correctly? Answers will vary.

MODÈLE

Élève 1: *J'ai besoin d'un cahier et d'un dictionnaire pour demain.*
Élève 2: *Est-ce que tu as un cours de français?*
Élève 1: *Non. J'ai un examen d'anglais.*

un cahier	un livre de physique
une calculatrice	une montre
une carte	un ordinateur
un dictionnaire	un stylo
une feuille de papier	un téléphone

2 Université d'été Imagine you are attending a special summer program at a university to gain extra credits. You need to register for one language class, a science class, and an elective of your choice. Take turns deciding what classes want to take. Your partner will tell you the days and times so you can set up your schedule. Answers will vary.

MODÈLE

Élève 1: *J'ai besoin d'un cours de maths, peut-être «Initiation aux maths».*
Élève 2: *C'est le mardi et le jeudi après-midi, de deux heures à trois heures et demie.*
Élève 1: *J'ai aussi besoin d'un cours de langue...*

Les cours	Jours et heures
Allemand	mardi, jeudi; 14h00-15h30
Biologie II	mardi, jeudi; 9h00-10h30
Chimie générale	lundi, mercredi; 11h00-12h30
Espagnol	lundi, mercredi; 11h00-12h30
Gestion	mercredi; 13h00-14h30
Histoire des États-Unis	jeudi; 12h15-14h15
Initiation à la physique	lundi, mercredi; 12h00-13h30
Initiation aux maths	mardi, jeudi; 14h00-15h30
Italien	lundi, mercredi; 12h00-13h30
Japonais	mardi, jeudi; 9h00-10h30
Les philosophes grecs	lundi; 15h15-16h45
Littérature moderne	mardi; 10h15-11h15

3 Les cours Your partner will tell you what classes he or she is currently taking. Make a list, including the times and days of the week. Then, talk to as many classmates as you can to find two students who have the exact same schedule as your partner. Answers will vary.

4 On y va? Walk around the room and find at least one classmate who feels like doing each of these activities with you. For every affirmative answer, record the name of your classmate and agree on a time and date. Do not speak to the same classmate twice. Answers will vary.

MODÈLE

Élève 1: *Tu as envie de retrouver des amis avec moi?*
Élève 2: *Oui, pourquoi pas? Samedi, à huit heures du soir, peut-être?*
Élève 1: *D'accord!*

chercher un café sympa	regarder la télé
manger à la cantine	retrouver des amis
écouter de la musique	travailler à la bibliothèque
étudier le français cette semaine	visiter un musée

5 Au téléphone In pairs, prepare a conversation in which you and your partner discuss your classes, the days and times they meet, and what you like and dislike about them. Then, role-play the conversation for the class. Answers will vary.

MODÈLE

Élève 1: *J'ai cours de chimie à dix heures et demie.*
Élève 2: *Je n'ai pas de cours de chimie cette année.*
Élève 1: *Aimes-tu les sciences?*
Élève 2: *Oui, mais...*

6 La semaine de Patrick Your teacher will give you and a partner different incomplete pages from Patrick's day planner. Do not look at each other's worksheet while you complete your own. Answers will vary.

MODÈLE

Élève 1: *Lundi matin, Patrick a cours de géographie à dix heures et demie.*
Élève 2: *Lundi, il a cours de sciences po à deux heures de l'après-midi.*

À l'écoute vhlcentral

Préparation

Based on the photograph, who and where do you think Marie-France and Dominique are? Do you think they know each other well? Where are they probably going this morning? What do you think they are talking about?

🔊 À vous d'écouter

 Listen to the conversation and list any cognates you hear. Listen again and complete the highlighted portions of Marie-France's schedule.

28 OCTOBRE	lundi		
8H00	*jogging*	14H00	
8H30		14H30	maths
9H00	biologie	15H00	
9H30		15H30	
10H00		16H00	
10H30	informatique	16H30	*rentrer à la maison*
11H00		17H00	
11H30		17H30	*étudier*
12H00	cantine	18H00	
12H30		18H30	
13H00	histoire	19H00	*téléphoner à papa*
13H30		19H30	*en famille:* dîner

Compréhension

👥 Vrai ou faux? Indicate whether each statement is **vrai** or **faux**.

1. D'après Marie-France, la biologie est facile.
   Vrai.

2. Marie-France adore l'informatique.
   Faux.

3. Marie-France mange avec des copains à midi.
   Vrai.

4. Marie-France a trois cours cet après-midi.
   Faux.

5. Marie-France aime les maths.
   Vrai.

6. Monsieur Meyer est professeur d'histoire.
   Faux.

7. Monsieur Meyer donne des devoirs difficiles.
   Vrai.

8. Dominique dîne avec Marie-France ce soir.
   Vrai.

👥 Votre emploi du temps With a partner, discuss the classes you're taking. Be sure to say when you have each one, and give your opinion of at least three courses.

M: Dis, est-ce que tu as envie de dîner avec ma famille et moi ce soir?
D: Oui, avec plaisir. À quelle heure?
M: À sept heures et demie.

D: Bon, d'accord. À ce soir.
M: Salut.
Teacher Resources DVD

Panorama

vhlcentral

La France

Le pays en chiffres

▶ **Superficie:** 549.000 km² (*cinq cent quarante-neuf mille kilomètres carrés°*)

▶ **Population:** 64.395.000 (*soixante-quatre millions trois cent quatre-vingt-quinze mille*)
SOURCE: INSEE

▶ **Industries principales:** *agro-alimentaires°, assurance°, banques, énergie, produits pharmaceutiques, produits de luxe, télécommunications, tourisme, transports*

La France est le pays° le plus° visité du monde° avec plus de° 83 millions de touristes chaque° année. Son histoire, sa culture et ses monuments–plus de 43.000 (quarante-trois mille)–et musées–plus de 1.200 (mille deux cents)–attirent° des touristes d'Europe et de partout° dans le monde.

▶ **Villes principales:** *Paris, Lille, Lyon, Marseille, Toulouse*

▶ **Monnaie°:** *l'euro*
La France est un pays membre de l'Union européenne dont la monnaie est l'euro.

Français célèbres

▶ **Jeanne d'Arc,** *héroïne française (1412–1431)*

▶ **Émile Zola,** *écrivain° (1840–1902)*

▶ **Pierre-Auguste Renoir,** *peintre° (1841–1919)*

▶ **Claude Debussy,** *compositeur et musicien (1862–1918)*

▶ **Camille Claudel,** *sculptrice (1864–1943)*

▶ **Claudie André-Deshays,** *médecin, première astronaute française (1957–)*

carrés *square* agro-alimentaires *food processing* assurance *insurance* pays *country* le plus *the most* monde *world* plus de *more than* chaque *each* attirent *attract* partout *everywhere* Monnaie *Currency* écrivain *writer* peintre *painter* élus à vie *elected for life* Depuis *Since* mots *words* courrier *mail* pont *bridge*

LE ROYAUME-UNI

LA MER DU NORD

LA MANCHE

LA BELGIQUE

L'ALLEMAGNE

LES ARDENNES

LE LUXEMBOURG

Lille
Rouen
Le Havre
Caen
le Mont-St-Michel
Versailles · **Paris**
Strasbourg
LES VOSGES
la Seine
la Marne
le Rhin
Rennes
Nantes
la Loire
Bourges
la Saône
LE JURA
LA SUISSE
Poitiers
Limoges
Lyon
L'ITALIE
Clermont-Ferrand
LES ALPES
Bordeaux
la Garonne
LE MASSIF CENTRAL
le Rhône
Aix-en-Provence
MONACO
Toulouse
Nîmes
Marseille
LES PYRÉNÉES
LA CORSE
ANDORRE
LA MER MÉDITERRANÉE
L'ESPAGNE

L'OCÉAN ATLANTIQUE

LA FRANCE

un bateau-mouche sur la Seine

le château de Chenonceau

le pont° du Gard

0 ____ 100 miles
0 ____ 100 kilomètres

Incroyable mais vrai!

Être «immortel», c'est réguler et défendre le bon usage du français! Les académiciens de l'Académie française sont élus à vie° et s'appellent les «Immortels». Depuis° 1635 (mille six cent trente-cinq), ils décident de l'orthographe correcte des mots° et publient un dictionnaire. Attention, c'est «courrier° électronique», pas «e-mail»!

La géographie

L'Hexagone

Surnommé° «Hexagone» à cause de° sa forme géométrique, le territoire français a trois fronts maritimes: l'océan Atlantique, la mer° Méditerranée et la Manche°; et quatre frontières° naturelles: les Pyrénées, les Ardennes, les Alpes et le Jura. À l'intérieur du pays°, le Massif central et les Vosges ponctuent° un relief composé de vastes plaines et de forêts. La Loire, la Seine, la Garonne, le Rhin et le Rhône sont les fleuves° principaux de l'Hexagone.

AP® Theme: Contemporary Life
Context: Travel

La technologie

Le Train à Grande Vitesse

Le chemin de fer° existe en France depuis° 1827 (mille huit cent vingt-sept). Aujourd'hui, la SNCF (Société nationale des chemins de fer français) offre la possibilité aux voyageurs de se déplacer° dans tout° le pays et propose des tarifs° avantageux aux élèves et aux moins de 25 ans°. Le TGV (Train à Grande Vitesse°) roule° à plus de 300 (trois cents) km/h (kilomètres/ heure) et emmène° les voyageurs jusqu'à° Londres et Bruxelles.

AP® Theme: Beauty and Aesthetics   **Context:** Performing Arts

Les arts

Le cinéma, le 7ᵉ art!

L'invention du cinématographe par les frères° Lumière en 1895 (mille huit cent quatre-vingt-quinze) marque le début° du «7ᵉ (septième) art». Le cinéma français donne naissance° aux prestigieux César° en 1976 (mille neuf cent soixante-seize), à des cinéastes talentueux comme° Jean Renoir, François Truffaut et Luc Besson, et à des acteurs mémorables comme Brigitte Bardot, Catherine Deneuve, Olivier Martinez et Audrey Tautou.

L'économie

L'industrie

Avec la richesse de la culture française, il est facile d'oublier que l'économie en France n'est pas limitée à l'artisanat°, à la gastronomie ou à la haute couture°. En fait°, la France est une véritable puissance° industrielle et se classe° parmi° les économies les plus° importantes du monde. Ses° activités dans des secteurs comme la construction automobile (Peugeot, Citroën, Renault), l'industrie aérospatiale (Airbus) et l'énergie nucléaire (Électricité de France) sont considérables.

Qu'est-ce que vous avez appris? Complete these sentences.

1. _Camille Claudel_ est une sculptrice française.
2. Les Académiciens sont élus _à vie_.
3. Pour «e-mail», on utilise aussi l'expression _courrier électronique_.
4. À cause de sa forme, la France s'appelle aussi _«l'Hexagone»_.
5. La _SNCF_ offre la possibilité de voyager dans tout le pays.
6. Avec le _TGV_, on voyage de Paris à Londres.
7. Les _frères Lumière_ sont les inventeurs du cinéma.
8. _Answers will vary._ est un grand cinéaste français.
   Possible answer: Jean Renoir
9. La France est une grande puissance _industrielle_.
10. Électricité de France produit (*produces*) _l'énergie nucléaire_.

Sur Internet

1. Cherchez des informations sur l'Académie française. Faites (*Make*) une liste de mots ajoutés à la dernière édition du dictionnaire de l'Académie française.

2. Cherchez des informations sur l'actrice Catherine Deneuve. Quand a-t-elle commencé (*did she begin*) sa (*her*) carrière? Trouvez ses (*her*) trois derniers films.

Surnommé *Nicknamed* **à cause de** *because of* **mer** *sea* **Manche** *English Channel* **frontières** *borders* **pays** *country* **ponctuent** *punctuate* **fleuves** *rivers* **chemin de fer** *railroad* **depuis** *since* **se déplacer** *travel* **dans tout** *throughout* **tarifs** *fares* **moins de 25 ans** *people under 25* **Train à Grande Vitesse** *high speed train* **roule** *rolls, travels* **emmène** *takes* **jusqu'à** *all the way to* **frères** *brothers* **début** *beginning* **donne naissance** *gives birth* **César** *equivalent of the Oscars in France* **comme** *such as* **artisanat** *craft industry* **haute couture** *high fashion* **En fait** *In fact* **puissance** *power* **se classe** *ranks* **parmi** *among* **les plus** *the most* **Ses** *Its*

Le Train à Grande Vitesse
- The first **TGV** service was from Paris to Lyon in 1981. Since then, its service has expanded. The high speed system includes over 2,000 kilometers of track connecting most of France's largest cities.
- Have students look at the photo and compare the **TGV** to the trains they have traveled on or seen in the United States. Then have them figure out the speed of the **TGV** in miles per hour (1 km = 0.62 mile). (300 km/h = 186 mph)

Le cinéma, le 7e art!
- Each year the members of **l'Académie des Arts et Techniques du Cinéma** choose the actors, actresses, directors, and others involved in film-making to receive the **César** awards for their outstanding achievements. The ceremony was named after the artist who designed the award trophies.
- The six traditional arts are **architecture**, **sculpture**, **peinture** (painting), **littérature**, **musique**, and **danse**.

L'industrie
- The craft industry, **l'artisanat**, can be found throughout France. Using traditional methods that are centuries old, French artisans craft products, such as pottery and figurines, but also work as bakers, carpenters, confectioners, butchers, or masons. Each region's products reflect the history and culture of that particular area.
- Bring in some French craft items or magazine photos of items to show the class.

21ˢᵗ Century Skills

Information and Media Literacy: Sur Internet
Students access and critically evaluate information from the Internet.

EXPANSION

Using Games Create categories for the newly learned information on France: **Géographie, Français célèbres, Technologie,** etc. Make index cards with a question on one side and category on the other. Tape cards to the board under the appropriate categories with questions face down. Teams take turns picking a card and answering the question. Give a point for each right answer. The team with the most points at the end wins.

EXPANSION

Cultural Comparison Distribute a list in French of the award categories for the **César** from the website of **l'Académie des Arts et Techniques du Cinéma** (www.lescesarducinema. com). Ask if the same categories exist for the Oscars. Show students pictures of a **César** and an Oscar. Have them compare the trophies.

Section Goals

In this section, students will:
- learn to use text formats to predict content
- read a brochure for a French language school

Key Standards
1.2, 2.1, 3.2, 5.2

PRE-AP®

Interpretive Reading
Ask students to discuss these questions in small groups: What clues can the format of a document provide about what content you can expect? What kind of document does this reading present? What can you predict about this reading from its format?

Stratégie
Tell students that many documents have easily identifiable formats that can help them predict the content. Have them look at the document in the **Stratégie** box and ask them to identify the recognizable elements:
- days of the week
- times
- classes

Ask what kind of document it is. (a student's weekly schedule)

Examinez le texte Have students look at the headings and ask them what type of information is contained in **École de français (pour étrangers) de Lille**. (lists of courses by level and specialization, a list of supplementary activities, and a list of types of housing available) Then ask students what types of documents contain these elements. (brochures)

Mots apparentés
- In pairs, have students scan the brochure, identify cognates, and guess their meanings.
- Ask students what this document is and its purpose. (It's a brochure. It's advertising a French language and culture immersion program. Its purpose is to attract students.)

Lecture vhlcentral

Avant la lecture

STRATÉGIE

Predicting content through formats

Recognizing the format of a document can help you to predict its content. For instance, invitations, greeting cards, and classified ads follow an easily identifiable format, which usually gives you a general idea of the information they contain. Look at the text and identify it based on its format.

	lundi	mardi	mercredi	jeudi	vendredi
8h30	biologie	littérature	biologie	littérature	biologie
9h00					
9h30	anglais	anglais	anglais	anglais	anglais
10h00					
10h30	maths	histoire	maths	histoire	maths
11h00					
11h30	français		français		français
12h00					
12h30					
1h00	art	économie	art	économie	art

If you guessed that this is a page from a student's schedule, you are correct. You can now infer that the document contains information about a student's weekly schedule, including days, times, and activities.

Examinez le texte
Briefly look at the document. What is its format? What kind of information is given? How is it organized? Are there any visuals? What kind? What type(s) of documents usually contain these elements?

Mots apparentés
As you have already learned, in addition to format, you can use cognates to help you predict the content of a document. With a classmate, make a list of all the cognates you find in the reading selection. Based on these cognates and the format of the document, can you guess what this document is and what it's for?

ÉCOLE DE FRANÇAIS
(pour étrangers°) DE LILLE

COURS DE FRANÇAIS POUR TOUS°	COURS DE SPÉCIALISATION
Niveau° débutant°	Français pour enfants°
Niveau élémentaire	Français des affaires°
Niveau intermédiaire	Droit° français
Niveau avancé	Français pour le tourisme
Conversation	Culture et civilisation
Grammaire française	Histoire de France
	Art et littérature
	Arts culinaires

26, place d'Arsonval • 59000 Lille
Tél. 03.20.52.48.17 • Fax. 03.20.52.48.18 • www.efpelille.fr

EXPANSION

Schedules Have students write a friend's or family member's weekly schedule as homework. Tell them to label the days of the week in French and add notes for that person's appointments and activities. In class, ask students questions about the schedules they wrote. Examples: **Quel cours est-ce que _____ a aujourd'hui? Combien de jours est-ce que _____ travaille cette semaine?**

EXPANSION

Cultural Activity Ask students what aspects of this school they find appealing or interesting: **Qu'est-ce que vous trouvez intéressant à l'école?** Jot down their responses on the board. Then do a quick class survey to find out which aspect is the most appealing.

Programmes de 2 à 8 semaines,
4 à 8 heures par jour
Immersion totale
Professeurs diplômés

le Musée des Beaux-Arts, Lille

GRAND CHOIX° D'ACTIVITÉS SUPPLÉMENTAIRES

- Excursions à la journée dans la région
- Visites de monuments et autres sites touristiques
- Sorties° culturelles (théâtre, concert, opéra et autres spectacles°)
- Sports et autres activités de loisir°

HÉBERGEMENT°

- En cité universitaire°
- Dans° une famille française
- À l'hôtel

pour étrangers *for foreigners* tous *all* Niveau *Level* débutant *beginner* enfants *children* affaires
business Droit *Law* choix *choice* Sorties *Outings* spectacles *shows* loisir *leisure* hébergement
lodging cité universitaire *university dormitories (on campus)* Dans *In*

Après la lecture

Répondez Select the correct response or completion to each question or statement, based on the reading selection.

1. C'est une brochure pour...
   - a. des cours de français pour étrangers.
   - b. une université française.
   - c. des études supérieures en Belgique.

2. «Histoire de France» est...
   - a. un cours pour les professeurs diplômés.
   - b. un cours de spécialisation.
   - c. un cours pour les enfants.

3. Le cours de «Français pour le tourisme» est utile pour...
   - a. une étudiante qui (*who*) étudie les sciences po.
   - b. une femme qui travaille dans un hôtel.
   - c. un professeur d'administration et gestion.

4. Un étudiant étranger qui commence le français assiste probablement à quel (*which*) cours?
   - a. Cours de français pour tous, Niveau avancé
   - b. Cours de spécialisation, Art et littérature
   - c. Cours de français pour tous, Niveau débutant

5. Quel cours est utile pour un homme qui parle assez bien français et qui travaille dans l'économie?
   - a. Cours de spécialisation, Français des affaires
   - b. Cours de spécialisation, Arts culinaires
   - c. Cours de spécialisation, Culture et civilisation

6. Le week-end, les étudiants...
   - a. passent des examens.
   - b. travaillent dans des hôtels.
   - c. visitent la ville et la région.

7. Les étudiants qui habitent dans une famille...
   - a. ont envie de rencontrer des Français.
   - b. ont des bourses.
   - c. ne sont pas reçus aux examens.

8. Un étudiant en histoire va aimer...
   - a. le cours de droit français.
   - b. les visites de monuments et de sites touristiques.
   - c. les activités sportives.

Complétez Complete these sentences.

1. Le numéro de téléphone est le ___03.20.52.48.17___.

2. Le numéro de fax est le ___03.20.52.48.18___.

3. L'adresse de l'école est ___26, place d'Arsonval, 59000 Lille___

4. L'école offre des programmes de français de ___2 à 8___ semaines et de ___4 à 8 heures___ par jour.

Répondez Go over the answers with the whole class or have students check their answers in pairs.

Complétez For additional practice, give students these items.
5. L'école est à ____. (Lille)
6. L'adresse Internet de l'école est ____. (www.efpelille.fr)
7. «Grammaire française» est un cours de ____. (français pour tous) 8. Les professeurs de l'école sont ____. (diplômés)
9. On habite en cité universitaire, ____ ou à l'hôtel. (dans une famille française)

Suggestion Encourage students to record unfamiliar words and phrases that they learn in **Lecture** in their notebooks.

21st Century Skills

Creativity and Innovation
Ask students to prepare a presentation on the ideal language school inspired by the information on these two pages.

Écriture

STRATÉGIE

Brainstorming

How do you find ideas to write about? In the early stages of writing, brainstorming can help you generate ideas on a specific topic. You should spend ten to fifteen minutes brainstorming and jotting down any ideas about the topic that occur to you. Whenever possible, try to write down your ideas in French. Express your ideas in single words or phrases, and jot them down in any order. While brainstorming, do not worry about whether your ideas are good or bad. Selecting and organizing ideas should be the second stage of your writing. Remember that the more ideas you write down while brainstorming, the more options you will have to choose from later when you start to organize your ideas.

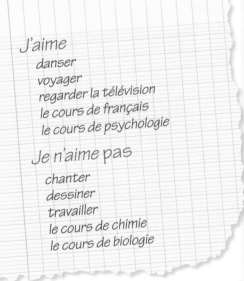

J'aime
danser
voyager
regarder la télévision
le cours de français
le cours de psychologie

Je n'aime pas
chanter
dessiner
travailler
le cours de chimie
le cours de biologie

Thème
Une description personnelle
Avant l'écriture

1. You will be writing a description of yourself to post on a website in order to find a francophone e-pal. Your description should include:

- your name and where you are from

- the name of your school and where it is located

- the courses you are currently taking

- some of your likes and dislikes

- where you work if you have a job

- any other information you would like to include

Begin by using a chart like this one to brainstorm information about your likes and dislikes.

J'aime	Je n'aime pas

2. Now fill out this chart to organize the content of your description. Include the information you brainstormed about your likes and dislikes.

Je m'appelle...	(name).
Je suis...	(where you are from).
J'étudie...	(names of classes) à/au/à la (name of school) à (city).
Je ne travaille pas./ Je travaille à/au/ à la/chez...	(place where you work).
J'aime...	(activities you like).
Je n'aime pas...	(activities you dislike).

Écriture

Use the information from the second chart to write a paragraph describing yourself. Make sure you include all the information from the chart in your paragraph. Use the structures provided for each topic.

Bonjour!

Je m'appelle Stacy Adams. Je suis de Rochester. J'étudie le français, les maths, l'anglais, la géographie et la biologie au lycée à New York. Je travaille à la bibliothèque le samedi. J'aime parler avec des amis, écouter de la musique et voyager. Je n'aime pas le sport...

Après l'écriture

1. Exchange a rough draft of your description with a partner. Comment on his or her work by answering these questions:

- Did your partner include all the necessary information (at least five facts)?

- Did your partner use the structures provided in the chart?

- Did your partner use the vocabulary of the unit?

- Did your partner use the grammar of the unit?

2. Revise your description according to your partner's comments. After writing the final version, read it one more time to eliminate these kinds of problems:

- spelling errors

- punctuation errors

- capitalization errors

- use of incorrect verb forms

- use of incorrect adjective agreement

- use of incorrect definite and indefinite articles

EVALUATION

Criteria

Content Includes all the information mentioned in the six bulleted items in the description of the task.
Scale: 1 2 3 4 5

Organization Organizes the description similarly to the model provided.
Scale: 1 2 3 4 5

Accuracy Uses **j'aime/je n'aime pas**, regular **-er** verbs, and negation patterns correctly. Words are spelled correctly and adjectives agree with the nouns they modify.
Scale: 1 2 3 4 5

Creativity Includes additional information that is not specified in the task and makes an effort to create longer sentences with a number of items.
Scale: 1 2 3 4 5

Scoring
Excellent	18–20 points
Good	14–17 points
Satisfactory	10–13 points
Unsatisfactory	< 10 points

21st Century Skills

Social and Cross-cultural Skills
Remind your students their description will be read by someone from a different culture so it is important to offer specific details on issues such as geographic location, schedules, or leisure activities.

 TELL Connection

Professionalism 3 *Why:* Professional development progresses by reflecting on and growing best practices. *What:* Before assigning this writing activity, review your own experience with process writing, peer review, and using rubrics. Then help students to better understand the impact of these practices on writing success.

Écriture Before students begin writing, give them some transition words they may want to incorporate into their descriptions. Words and expressions such as **mais**, **ou**, and **et** can be used to make sentences longer and to make transitions between them.

Après l'écriture Once students have written their descriptions, choose several among those and ask the authors for their permission to read them aloud. As you read each one, see if the class can guess whom it is describing, based on the likes, dislikes, and other information included.

Suggestion Tell students that an easy way to study from **Vocabulaire** is to cover up the French half of each section, leaving only the English equivalents exposed. They can then quiz themselves on the French items. To focus on the English equivalents of the French entries, they simply reverse this process.

21ˢᵗ Century Skills

Creativity and Innovation
Ask students to prepare a list of three products or perspectives they learned about in this unit to share with the class. Consider asking them to focus on the **Culture** and **Panorama** sections.

21ˢᵗ Century Skills

Leadership and Responsibility Extension Project
If you have access to students in a Francophone country, have students decide on three questions they want to ask the partner class related to this unit's topic. Based on the responses they receive, work as a class to explain to the partner class one aspect of their responses that surprised the class and why.

Leçon 2A

Les cours

l'art (*m.*)	art
la biologie	biology
la chimie	chemistry
l'économie (*f.*)	economics
l'éducation physique (*f.*)	physical education
la géographie	geography
la gestion	business administration
l'histoire (*f.*)	history
l'informatique (*f.*)	computer science
les langues (étrangères) (*f.*)	(foreign) languages
les lettres (*f.*)	humanities
les mathématiques (maths) (*f.*)	mathematics
la philosophie	philosophy
la physique	physics
la psychologie	psychology
les sciences (politiques/po) (*f.*)	(political) science
une bourse	scholarhip, grant
la cantine	cafeteria
un cours	class, course
un devoir; les devoirs	homework
un diplôme	diploma, degree
l'école (*f.*)	school
les études (supérieures) (*f.*)	(higher) education; studies
le gymnase	gymnasium
une note	grade

Adjectifs et adverbes

difficile	difficult
facile	easy
inutile	useless
utile	useful
surtout	especially; above all

Vocabulaire supplémentaire

J'adore...	I love...
J'aime bien...	I like...
Je n'aime pas tellement...	I don't like... very much.
Je déteste...	I hate...
être reçu(e) à un examen	to pass an exam

Expressions utiles

See p. 51.

Verbes

adorer	to love; to adore
aimer	to like; to love
aimer mieux	to prefer
arriver	to arrive
chercher	to look for
commencer	to begin, to start
dessiner	to draw; to design
détester	to hate
donner	to give
étudier	to study
habiter (à)	to live (in)
manger	to eat
oublier	to forget
parler (au téléphone)	to speak (on the phone)
partager	to share
penser (que/qu')	to think (that)
regarder	to look (at), to watch
rencontrer	to meet
retrouver	to meet up with; to find (again)
travailler	to work
voyager	to travel

Des questions et des opinions

bien sûr	of course
d'accord	OK, all right
Est-ce que/qu'...?	Question phrase
(mais) non	no (but of course not)
moi/toi non plus	me/you neither
ne... pas	no, not
n'est-ce pas?	isn't that right?
oui/si	yes
parce que	because
pas du tout	not at all
peut-être	maybe, perhaps
Pourquoi?	Why?

Leçon 2B

Les cours

assister à	to attend
demander	to ask
dîner	to have dinner
échouer	to fail
écouter	to listen (to)
enseigner	to teach
expliquer	to explain
passer un examen	to take an exam
préparer	to prepare (for)
rentrer (à la maison)	to return (home)
téléphoner à	to telephone
trouver	to find; to think
visiter	to visit (a place)

Expressions de temps

Quel jour sommes-nous?	What day is it?
un an	a year
une/cette année	one/this year
après	after
après-demain	day after tomorrow
un/cet après-midi	an/this afternoon
aujourd'hui	today
demain (matin/ après-midi/soir)	tomorrow (morning/ afternoon/ evening)
un jour	a day
une journée	a day
(le) lundi, mardi, mercredi, jeudi, vendredi, samedi, dimanche	(on) Monday(s), Tuesday(s), Wednesday(s), Thursday(s), Friday(s), Saturday(s), Sunday(s)
un/ce matin	a/this morning
la matinée	morning
un mois/ce mois-ci	a month/this month
une/cette nuit	a/this night
une/cette semaine	a/this week
un/ce soir	an/this evening
une soirée	an evening
un/le/ce week-end	a/the/this weekend
dernier/dernière	last
premier/première	first
prochain(e)	next

Expressions utiles

See p. 69.

Expressions avec *avoir*

avoir	to have
avoir... ans	to be... years old
avoir besoin (de)	to need
avoir chaud	to be hot
avoir de la chance	to be lucky
avoir envie (de)	to feel like
avoir froid	to be cold
avoir honte (de)	to be ashamed (of)
avoir l'air	to look like, to seem
avoir peur (de)	to be afraid (of)
avoir raison	to be right
avoir sommeil	to be sleepy
avoir tort	to be wrong

L'heure

Quelle heure est-il?	What time is it?
Quelle heure avez-vous/as-tu?	What time do you have?
Il est... heures.	It is... o'clock.
une heure	one o'clock
et quart	fifteen minutes past the hour
et demie	thirty minutes past the hour
moins dix	ten minutes before the hour
moins le quart	fifteen minutes before the hour
À quelle heure?	(At) what time/ when?
de l'après-midi	in the afternoon
du matin	in the morning
du soir	in the evening
en avance	early
en retard	late
midi	noon
minuit	midnight
pile	sharp, on the dot
presque	almost
tard	late
tôt	early
vers	about

La famille et les copains

Unit Goals

Leçon 3A

In this lesson, students will learn:
- words for family members and marital status
- some words for pets
- usage of **l'accent aigu** and **l'accent grave**
- about the French family
- more about families and friends through specially shot video footage
- descriptive adjectives
- possessive adjectives
- about the Belgian company **Pages d'Or**

Leçon 3B

In this lesson, students will learn:
- words for some professions and occupations
- more descriptive adjectives
- usage of **l'accent circonflexe**, **la cédille**, and **le tréma**
- about different types of friendships and relationships
- the numbers 61–100
- some prepositions of location
- disjunctive pronouns
- to ask for repetition in oral communication

Savoir-faire

In this section, students will learn:
- historical and cultural information about **la Belgique** and **la Suisse**
- to use visuals and graphic elements to predict content
- to use idea maps to organize information
- to write an informal e-mail

 **21st Century Skills**

Initiative and Self-Direction
Students can monitor their progress online using the activities and assessments on vhlcentral.com.

Pour commencer
- b. une famille
- c. quatre
- c. un parc

Pour commencer
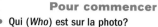
- Qui (*Who*) est sur la photo?
  a. des amis b. une famille c. une classe
- Combien de personnes y a-t-il?
  a. deux b. trois c. quatre
- Où (*Where*) sont-ils?
  a. une cantine b. un café c. un parc

SUPPORT FOR BACKWARD DESIGN

Unité 3 **Essential Questions**
1. How do people describe their families and family members?
2. How do people talk about how they spend their time?
3. How has the structure of the French family evolved?

Unité 3 **Integrated Performance Assessment**
Before teaching the chapter, review the Integrated Performance Assessment (IPA) and its accompanying scoring rubric provided in the Testing Program. Use the IPA to assess students' progress toward proficiency targets at the end of the chapter.
IPA Context: You and your classmates are spending spring vacation in France, and the coordinator of the trip needs to place you with host families. You will choose from characters introduced in the Roman-photo. Decide which person is the best host for your classmate. Then, present your recommendation to the class.

 FORUMS
Forums on vhlcentral.com allow you and your students to record and share audio messages. Use Forums for presentations, oral assessments, discussions, directions, etc.

Section Goals

In this section, students will learn and practice vocabulary related to:
- family members
- some pets
- marital status

Key Standards

1.1, 1.2, 4.1

Suggestions

- Use the digital image for this page. Point out that the family tree is drawn from the point of view of Marie Laval. Describe the different family relationships, and have students repeat vocabulary after you. Then have students refer to the family tree to answer questions about it. Example: **Comment s'appelle la mère de Marie?**
- Point out the meanings of plural family terms so students understand that the masculine plural forms can refer to mixed groups of males and females: **les enfants** *male children; male and female children* **les cousins** *male cousins; male and female cousins* **les petits-enfants** *male grandchildren; male and female grandchildren*
- Point out the difference in meaning between the noun **mari** (*husband*) and the adjective **marié(e)** (*married*).
- Personalize active lesson vocabulary with questions and gestures. Ask: **Comment s'appelle votre frère?** Ask a different student: **Comment s'appelle le frère de _____?** Work your way through various family relationships.

You will learn how to...
- discuss family, friends, and pets
- express ownership

AP® Theme: Families and Communities
Context: Family Structures

◁)) **vhl**central

La famille de Marie Laval

Luc Garneau
mon grand-père

Vocabulaire

divorcer	to divorce
épouser	to marry
aîné(e)	elder
cadet(te)	younger
un beau-frère	brother-in-law
un beau-père	father-in-law; stepfather
une belle-mère	mother-in-law; stepmother
un demi-frère	half-brother; stepbrother
une demi-sœur	half-sister; stepsister
les enfants (*m., f.*)	children
un(e) époux/épouse	husband/wife
une famille	family
une femme	wife; woman
une fille	daughter; girl
les grands-parents (*m.*)	grandparents
les parents (*m.*)	parents
un(e) voisin(e)	neighbor
un chat	cat
un oiseau	bird
un poisson	fish
célibataire	single
divorcé(e)	divorced
fiancé(e)	engaged
marié(e)	married
séparé(e)	separated
veuf/veuve	widowed

Juliette Laval
ma mère, fille de Luc et d'Hélène

Robert Laval
mon père, mari de Juliette

Véronique Laval
ma belle-sœur, femme de mon frère

Guillaume Laval
mon frère

Marie Laval
moi, Marie Laval, fille de Juliette et de Robert

Matthieu Laval
mon neveu

Émilie Laval
ma nièce

petits-enfants de mes parents

EXPANSION

Family Tree Draw your own family tree on a transparency or the board and label it with names. Ask students questions about it. Examples: **Est-ce que _____ est ma sœur ou ma tante? Comment s'appelle ma grand-mère? _____ est le neveu ou le frère de _____? Qui est le grand-père de _____?** Help them identify the relationships between members. Then invite them to ask you questions.

EXPANSION

Les noms de famille français Ask for a show of hands to see if any students' last names are French in origin. Examples: names that begin with **Le____** or **La____** such as **Leblanc** or **Larose**, or even names such as **Fitzgerald** or **Fitzpatrick** (**Fitz-** = **fils de**). Ask these students what they know about their French heritage or family history.

Mise en pratique

1 Qui est-ce?
Match the definition in the first list with the correct item from the second list. Not all the items will be used.

1. __d__ le frère de ma cousine
2. __g__ le père de mon cousin
3. __a__ le mari de ma grand-mère
4. __e__ le fils de mon frère
5. __c__ la fille de mon grand-père
6. __i__ le fils de ma mère
7. __h__ la fille de mon fils
8. __f__ le fils de ma belle-mère

a. mon grand-père
b. ma sœur
c. ma tante
d. mon cousin
e. mon neveu
f. mon demi-frère
g. mon oncle
h. ma petite-fille
i. mon frère

2 Choisissez
Fill in the blank by selecting the most appropriate answer.

1. Voici le frère de mon père. C'est mon __oncle__ (oncle, neveu, fiancé).
2. Voici la mère de ma cousine. C'est ma __tante__ (grand-mère, voisine, tante).
3. Voici la petite-fille de ma grand-mère. C'est ma __cousine__ (cousine, nièce, épouse).
4. Voici le père de ma mère. C'est mon __grand-père__ (grand-père, oncle, cousin).
5. Voici le fils de mon père, mais ce n'est pas le fils de ma mère. C'est mon __demi-frère__ (petit-fils, demi-frère, voisin).

3 Complétez
Complete each sentence with the appropriate word.

1. Voici ma nièce. C'est la __petite-fille__ de ma mère.
2. Voici la mère de ma tante. C'est ma __grand-mère__.
3. Voici la sœur de mon oncle. C'est ma __tante__.
4. Voici la fille de mon père, mais pas de ma mère. C'est ma __demi-sœur__.
5. Voici le mari de ma mère, mais ce n'est pas mon père. C'est mon __beau-père__.

4 Écoutez
Listen to each statement made by Marie Laval. Based on her family tree, indicate whether it is **vrai** or **faux**.

	Vrai	Faux		Vrai	Faux
1.	☑	☐	6.	☐	☑
2.	☐	☑	7.	☐	☑
3.	☑	☐	8.	☑	☐
4.	☐	☑	9.	☑	☐
5.	☐	☑	10.	☑	☐

Family tree (left column)

Hélène Garneau
ma grand-mère

Sophie Garneau
ma tante, femme de Marc

Marc Garneau
mon oncle, fils de Luc et d'Hélène

Jean Garneau
mon cousin, petit-fils de Luc et d'Hélène

Isabelle Garneau
ma cousine, sœur de Jean et de Virginie, petite-fille de Luc et d'Hélène

Virginie Garneau
ma cousine, sœur de Jean et d'Isabelle, petite-fille de Luc et d'Hélène

Bambou
le chien de mes cousins

Successful Language Learning
Tell students that it isn't necessary to understand every word they hear in French. They will feel less anxious if they listen for general meaning.

1 Suggestion Mention that adjectives such as **beau** and **petit** in hyphenated family terms must agree in gender. Exceptions: **la grand-mère, la demi-sœur**.

2 & 3 Suggestion Some students may struggle to "see" the relationships. Suggest that they use the family tree to "trace" the connections with their finger as they read and complete the activities.

4 Script
1. Marc est mon oncle.
2. Émilie est la nièce de Véronique.
3. Jean est le petit-fils d'Hélène.
4. Robert est mon grand-père.
5. Luc est le père de Sophie.
6. Isabelle est ma tante.
7. Matthieu est le fils de Jean.
8. Émilie est la fille de Guillaume.
9. Juliette est ma mère.
10. Virginie est ma cousine.
Teacher Resources DVD

4 Suggestion Review the names of each family member before beginning the activity. You may also wish to review their relationships to each other.

4 Expansion Play Marie's statements again, stopping at the end of each. Where the statements are true, have students repeat. Where the statements are false, have students correct them by referring to Marie Laval's family tree.

TELL Connection

Environment 1 *Why:* Support a positive learning environment. *What:* Using official information about your students' backgrounds, plan activities that reflect and respect their family experiences.

EXPANSION

Using Games As a class or group activity, have students state the relationship between people on Marie Laval's family tree. Their classmates will guess which person on the family tree they are describing. Example: **C'est la sœur de Jean et la fille de Sophie. (Isabelle ou Virginie)** Take turns until each member of the class or group has had a chance to state a relationship.

EXPANSION

My Family Tree Have students draw their own family tree as homework. Tell them to label each position on the tree with the appropriate French term and the person's name. Also tell them to write five fill-in-the-blank statements based on their family tree. Examples: **Je suis la fille de ____. Mon frère s'appelle ____.** In the next class, have students exchange papers with a classmate and complete the activity.

5 Suggestion Use the digital image for this activity.

6 Suggestion Tell students to jot down their partner's responses.

6 Expansion After they have finished the interview, ask students questions about their partner's answers. Examples: **Combien de personnes y a-t-il dans la famille de ____? Comment s'appellent les parents de ____?**

6 Virtual Chat You can also assign Activity 6 on vhlcentral.com. Students record individual responses that appear in your gradebook.

PRE-AP®

6 Interpersonal Speaking Have students prepare by reading the questions in advance. Ask them to write two additional questions about their partner's family and include them as part of their interview.

7 Suggestion Have two volunteers read the **modèle**. Then distribute the **Feuilles d'activités** from the Activity Pack.

7 Expansion After students have finished, ask yes/no questions. Example: **Est-ce que ____ a un chien?**

Activity Pack For additional activities, go to the Activity Pack in the Resources section of vhlcentral.com.

Communication

5 L'arbre généalogique With a classmate, identify the members of the family by asking how each one is related to Anne Durand. *Answers will vary.*

MODÈLE
Élève 1: *Qui (Who) est Louis Durand?*
Élève 2: *C'est le grand-père d'Anne.*

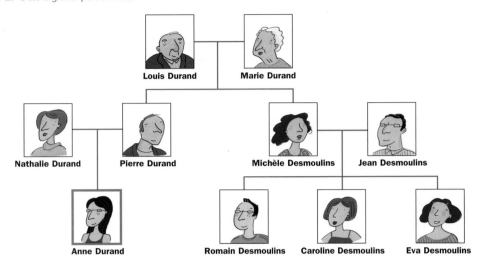

6 Entrevue With a classmate, take turns asking each other these questions. *Answers will vary.*

1. Combien de personnes y a-t-il dans ta famille?
2. Comment s'appellent tes parents?
3. As-tu des frères et sœurs?
4. Combien de cousins/cousines as-tu? Comment s'appellent-ils/elles? Où habitent-ils/elles?
5. Quel(le) (Which) est ton cousin préféré/ta cousine préférée?
6. As-tu des neveux/des nièces?
7. Comment s'appellent tes grands-parents? Où habitent-ils?
8. Combien de petits-enfants ont tes grands-parents?

Coup de main

Use these words to help you complete this activity.

ton *your (m.)* → mon *my (m.)*
ta *your (f.)* → ma *my (f.)*
tes *your (pl.)* → mes *my (pl.)*

7 Qui suis-je? Your teacher will give you a worksheet. Walk around the class and ask your classmates questions about their families. When a classmate gives one of the answers on the worksheet, write his or her name in the corresponding space. Be prepared to discuss the results with the class. *Answers will vary.*

MODÈLE J'ai un chien.
Élève 1: *Est-ce que tu as un chien?*
Élève 2: *Oui, j'ai un chien (You write the student's name.)/Non, je n'ai pas de chien. (You ask another classmate.)*

DIFFERENTIATION

For Visual Learners Have students bring in some family photos. In pairs, tell them to take turns pointing to people in their partner's photo and asking who it is. Example: **Qui est-ce? (C'est mon/ma ____ .)** Model a few examples. If necessary, write the question and a sample response on the board.

DIFFERENTIATION

For Kinesthetic Learners Make a family tree using the whole class. Have each student write the family designation you assign him or her on a note card, then arrange students as in a family tree with each one displaying the note card. Then, ask questions about relationships. Examples: **Qui est la mère de ____ ? Comment s'appelle l'oncle de ____ ?** Give students the opportunity to ask questions by switching roles with them.

Les sons et les lettres 🔊 vhlcentral

L'accent aigu and l'accent grave

In French, diacritical marks (*accents*) are an essential part of a word's spelling. They indicate how vowels are pronounced or distinguish between words with similar spellings but different meanings. **L'accent aigu** (´) appears only over the vowel **e**. It indicates that the **e** is pronounced similarly to the vowel *a* in the English word *cake*, but shorter and crisper.

étudier	**r**é**serv**é	é**l**é**gant**	**t**é**l**é**phone**

L'accent aigu also signals some similarities between French and English words. Often, an **e** with **l'accent aigu** at the beginning of a French word marks the place where the letter *s* would appear at the beginning of the English equivalent.

éponge	**é**pouse	**é**tat	**é**tudiante
sponge	*spouse*	*state*	*student*

L'accent grave (`) appears only over the vowels **a**, **e**, and **u**. Over the vowel **e**, it indicates that the **e** is pronounced like the vowel *e* in the English word *pet*.

tr**è**s	apr**è**s	m**è**re	ni**è**ce

Although **l'accent grave** does not change the pronunciation of the vowels **a** or **u**, it distinguishes words that have a similar spelling but different meanings.

la	là	ou	où
the	*there*	*or*	*where*

Prononcez Practice saying these words aloud.

1. agréable
2. sincère
3. voilà
4. faculté
5. frère
6. à
7. déjà
8. éléphant
9. lycée
10. poème
11. là
12. élève

Articulez Practice saying these sentences aloud.

1. À tout à l'heure!
2. Thérèse, je te présente Michèle.
3. Hélène est très sérieuse et réservée.
4. Voilà mon père, Frédéric, et ma mère, Ségolène.
5. Tu préfères étudier à la fac demain après-midi?

Dictons Practice reading these sayings aloud.

À vieille mule, frein doré.[2]

Tel père, tel fils.[1]

[1] Like father, like son.
[2] For an old mule, a golden bit.

quatre-vingt-treize **93**

Section Goals

In this section, students will learn about:
- l'accent aigu
- l'accent grave
- a strategy for recognizing cognates

Key Standards

4.1

Suggestions

- Write **é** on the board. Tell students to watch your mouth as you pronounce the sound. Explain that when **é** appears at the beginning of a word, the corners of your mouth are slightly turned up and your tongue is low behind your bottom teeth. Have students repeat **é** after you several times.
- Write words and/or French names from the Laval family with **l'accent aigu** on the board. Pronounce each word as you point to it and have students repeat it after you. Examples: **époux**, **célibataire**, **fiancé**, **séparé**, **Émilie**, and **Véronique**.
- Give students some sample sentences with **la**, **là**, **ou**, or **où** and ask them what the words mean to demonstrate how context clarifies meaning. Examples: **1. Où est la fille? 2. La fille est là. 3. Est-ce que Sophie est la tante ou la grand-mère de Marie Laval?**
- Ask students to provide more examples of words they know with these accents.
- The explanation and exercises are available on vhlcentral.com. You may want to play them in class so students hear French speakers besides yourself.

Dictons Explain to students that the saying **«À vieille mule, frein doré»** applies to a situation in which someone tries to sell something old by dressing it up or decorating it. For example, to have a better chance at selling an old car, give it a new paint job.

EXPANSION

Mini-dictée Here are additional sentences to use for extra practice with **l'accent aigu** and **l'accent grave**. **1. Étienne est mon frère préféré. 2. Ma sœur aînée est très occupée avec les études. 3. André et Geneviève sont séparés. 4. Vous êtes marié ou célibataire? 5. Éric et Sabine sont fiancés.**

TEACHING OPTIONS

Using Games Have a spelling bee using words with **l'accent aigu** and/or **l'accent grave** from **Leçon 3A** or previous lessons. Divide the class into two teams. Call on one team member at a time, alternating between teams. Give a point for each correct answer. The team with the most points at the end of the game wins. Before students begin, remind them that they must indicate the accent marks in the words. Give them an example: **très T-R-E accent grave-S**.

Section Goals

In this section, students will learn functional phrases for talking about their families and describing people through comprehensible input.

Key Standards

1.2, 2.1, 2.2, 4.1, 4.2

Video Recap: Leçon 2B
Before doing this **Roman-photo**, review the previous one with this activity.
1. Comment s'appelle la copine de Stéphane? (Astrid)
2. Qu'est-ce qu'elle pense de Stéphane? (Answers will vary. **Elle pense qu'il n'est pas sérieux, qu'il ne fait pas ses devoirs et qu'il n'écoute pas en classe.**)
3. Qui téléphone à Sandrine? (Pascal)
4. Comment Stéphane prépare-t-il le bac? (Il étudie les maths avec Rachid.)

Video Synopsis

Michèle wants to know what Amina's friend, Cyberhomme, looks like. Valérie describes her brother's family as she, Stéphane, and Amina look at their photos. Valérie keeps pointing out all the people who have their **bac** because she thinks Stéphane is not studying enough to pass his **bac**. To ease his mother's mind, Stéphane finally tells her that Rachid is helping him study.

Suggestions

- Ask students to read the title, glance at the video stills, and predict what they think the episode will be about. Record their predictions.
- Have students work in groups of four. Tell them to choose a role and read the **Roman-photo** conversation aloud.
- After students have read the **Roman-photo**, quickly review their predictions and ask them which ones were correct. Then ask a few questions to help guide students in summarizing this episode.

L'album de photos vhlcentral

PERSONNAGES

Amina

Michèle

Stéphane

Valérie

MICHÈLE Mais, qui c'est? C'est ta sœur? Tes parents?
AMINA C'est mon ami Cyberhomme.
MICHÈLE Comment est-il? Est-ce qu'il est beau? Il a les yeux de quelle couleur? Marron ou bleue? Et ses cheveux? Ils sont blonds ou châtains?
AMINA Je ne sais pas.
MICHÈLE Toi, tu es timide.

VALÉRIE Stéphane, tu as dix-sept ans. Cette année, tu passes le bac, mais tu ne travailles pas!
STÉPHANE Écoute, ce n'est pas vrai, je déteste mes cours, mais je travaille beaucoup. Regarde, mon cahier de chimie, mes livres de français, ma calculatrice pour le cours de maths, mon dictionnaire anglais-français...

STÉPHANE Oh, et qu'est-ce que c'est? Ah, oui, les photos de tante Françoise.
VALÉRIE Des photos? Mais où?
STÉPHANE Ici! Amina, on peut regarder des photos de ma tante sur ton ordinateur, s'il te plaît?

AMINA Ah, et ça, c'est toute la famille, n'est-ce pas?
VALÉRIE Oui, ça, c'est Henri, sa femme, Françoise, et leurs enfants: le fils aîné, Bernard, et puis son frère, Charles, sa sœur, Sophie, et leur chien, Socrate.
STÉPHANE J'aime bien Socrate. Il est vieux, mais il est amusant!

VALÉRIE Ah! Et Bernard, il a son bac aussi et sa mère est très heureuse.
STÉPHANE Moi, j'ai envie d'habiter avec oncle Henri et tante Françoise. Comme ça, pas de problème pour le bac!

STÉPHANE Pardon, maman. Je suis très heureux ici, avec toi. Ah, au fait, Rachid travaille avec moi pour préparer le bac.
VALÉRIE Ah, bon? Rachid est très intelligent... un étudiant sérieux.

A C T I V I T É S

1 **Vrai ou faux?** Are these sentences **vrai** or **faux**? Correct the false ones.

1. Amina communique avec sa (*her*) tante par ordinateur. Faux. Elle communique avec Cyberhomme.
2. Stéphane n'aime pas ses (*his*) cours au lycée. Vrai.
3. Ils regardent des photos de vacances. Faux. Ils regardent les photos de tante Françoise.
4. Henri est le frère aîné de Valérie. Vrai.
5. Bernard est le cousin de Stéphane. Vrai.

6. Charles a déjà son bac. Vrai.
7. La tante de Stéphane s'appelle Françoise. Vrai.
8. Stéphane travaille avec Amina pour préparer le bac. Faux. Il travaille avec Rachid.
9. Socrate est le fils d'Henri et de Françoise. Faux. C'est le chien d'Henri et de Françoise.
10. Rachid n'est pas un bon étudiant. Faux. C'est un étudiant sérieux.

TEACHING OPTIONS

L'album de photos Before students view the video episode **L'album de photos**, ask them to brainstorm a list of things someone might say when describing his or her family photos.

TEACHING OPTIONS

Extra Practice Play the first half of the video episode and have students describe what happened. Write their observations on the board. Then ask them to guess what will happen in the second half of the episode. Write their ideas on the board. Play the entire video episode; then help the class summarize the plot.

Stéphane et Valérie regardent des photos
de famille avec Amina.

À la table d'Amina...

AMINA Alors, voilà vos photos.
Qui est-ce?

VALÉRIE Oh, c'est Henri, mon
frère aîné!

AMINA Quel âge a-t-il?

VALÉRIE Il a cinquante ans. Il est très
sociable et c'est un très bon père.

VALÉRIE Ah! Et ça, c'est ma nièce
Sophie et mon neveu Charles!
Regarde, Stéphane, tes cousins!

STÉPHANE Je n'aime pas Charles.
Il est tellement sérieux.

VALÉRIE Il est peut-être trop sérieux,
mais, lui, il a son bac!

AMINA Et Sophie, qu'elle est jolie!

VALÉRIE ... et elle a déjà son bac.

AMINA Ça, oui, préparer le bac avec
Rachid, c'est une idée géniale!

VALÉRIE Oui, c'est vrai. En théorie,
c'est une excellente idée. Mais tu
prépares le bac avec Rachid, hein?
Pas le prochain match de foot!

Expressions utiles

Talking about your family

- **C'est ta sœur? Ce sont tes parents?**
  Is that your sister? Are those your parents?

- **C'est mon ami.**
  That's my friend.

- **Ça, c'est Henri, sa femme, Françoise, et leurs enfants.**
  That's Henri, his wife, Françoise, and their kids.

Describing people

- **Il a les yeux de quelle couleur? Marron ou bleue?**
  What color are his eyes? Brown or blue?

- **Il a les yeux bleus.**
  He has blue eyes.

- **Et ses cheveux? Ils sont blonds ou châtains? Frisés ou raides?**
  And his hair? Is it blond or brown? Curly or straight?

- **Il a les cheveux châtains et frisés.**
  He has curly brown hair.

- **Quel âge a-t-il?**
  How old is he?

Additional vocabulary

- **On peut regarder des photos de ma tante sur ton ordinateur?**
  Can/May we look at some photos from my aunt on your computer?

- **C'est toute la famille, n'est-ce pas?**
  That's the whole family, right?

- **Je ne sais pas (encore).**
  I (still) don't know.

- **Alors...**
  So...
- **peut-être**
  maybe

- **vrai**
  true
- **au fait**
  by the way

- **une photo(graphie)**
  a photograph
- **Hein?**
  Right?

- **une idée**
  an idea
- **déjà**
  already

---

2 Vocabulaire Choose the adjective that describes how Stéphane would feel on these occasions. Refer to a dictionary as necessary.

1. on his 87th birthday _____ vieux
2. after finding 20€ _____ heureux
3. while taking the **bac** _____ sérieux
4. after getting a good grade _____ heureux
5. after dressing for a party _____ beau

> beau
> heureux
> sérieux
> vieux

3 Conversez In pairs, describe which member of your family is most like Stéphane. How are they alike? Do they both like sports? Do they take similar courses? How do they like school? How are their personalities? Be prepared to describe your partner's "Stéphane" to the class.

quatre-vingt-quinze **95**

Expressions utiles

- Point out the possessive adjectives and descriptive adjectives in the captions and the **Expressions utiles**. Tell students that this material will be formally presented in the **Structures** section. Do not expect students to produce the forms correctly at this time.

- Model the pronunciation of the **Expressions utiles** and have students repeat them.

- To practice new vocabulary, ask students to describe their classmates' eyes and hair and tell their age. Examples:
  _____ a les yeux de quelle couleur? Marron ou bleue? Avez-vous les yeux bleus? _____ a-t-il/elle les cheveux blonds ou châtains? Qui a les cheveux blonds/châtains dans la classe? Est-ce que les cheveux de _____ sont frisés ou raides? _____, quel âge-a-t-il/elle?

1 Expansion For additional practice, give students these items. **11. Valérie n'aime pas son frère, Henri. (Faux.) 12. Stéphane aime les gens très sérieux. (Faux.) 13. Stéphane et Rachid préparent le prochain match de foot. (Faux.)**

2 Suggestion Before students begin the activity, you might want to introduce the adjectives in the word list using pictures or the people and text in the video stills, rather than having students look them up in the dictionary.

2 Expansion Have students describe Rachid, Charles, and Henri using the adjectives in the word list. At this point, avoid asking students to describe people that would require a feminine or plural form of these adjectives.

3 Suggestion If time is limited, this activity may be assigned as a written composition for homework.

3 Partner Chat You can also assign Activity 3 on vhlcentral.com. Students work in pairs to record the activity online. The pair's recorded conversation will appear in your gradebook.

EXPANSION

Valérie's Family Tree Working in pairs, have students draw a family tree based on Valérie's description of her brother's family. Tell them to use the family tree on pages 90-91 as a model. Remind them to include Valérie and Stéphane. Then have them get together with another pair of students and compare their drawings.

EXPANSION

Writing Questions Have students write four questions about Henri's family based on the conversation and video still #6. Then have them get together in groups of three and take turns asking and answering each other's questions. Examples: **Combien de personnes y a-t-il dans la famille d'Henri? Comment s'appelle le fils aîné? Combien de frères a Sophie?**

AP® Theme: Families and Communities
Context: Family Structures

Section Goals

In this section, students will:
- learn about different types of families in France
- learn some informal terms for family members
- find out when Mother's Day and Father's Day are celebrated in various French-speaking regions
- read about Yannick Noah and his family
- view authentic video footage

Key Standards

2.1, 2.2, 3.1, 3.2, 4.2

Culture à la loupe

Avant la lecture
- Have students look at the photo and describe the family there. Ask: **La famille est-elle traditionnelle ou non-conventionnelle? (Elle est traditionnelle.)**
- Tell students to scan the reading, identify the cognates, and guess their meanings.

Lecture Point out the statistics chart. Tell students that this data refers to Metropolitan France. Ask them what information this chart shows. (The percentages of different types of French households by age group.) Ask students to name the types of households.

Après la lecture
- Ask students what facts about families in France are new or surprising to them.
- Have students compare French and American families. Ask: **Est-ce qu'il y a des similitudes (similarities) entre la famille française et la famille américaine? Et des différences?**

1 Suggestion If students have difficulty filling in the blanks, provide them with a word bank.

---

vhlcentral | *Flash culture*   CULTURE À LA LOUPE

La famille en France

Comment est la famille française? Est-elle différente de la famille américaine? La majorité des Français sont-ils mariés, divorcés ou célibataires?

Il n'y a pas de réponse simple à ces questions. Les familles françaises sont très diverses. Le mariage est toujours° très populaire: la majorité des hommes et des femmes sont mariés. Mais attention!

Les nombres° de personnes divorcées et de personnes célibataires augmentent chaque° année.

La structure familiale traditionnelle existe toujours en France, mais il y a des structures moins traditionnelles, comme les familles monoparentales, où° l'unique parent est divorcé, séparé ou veuf. Il y a aussi des familles recomposées, c'est-à-dire qui combinent deux familles, avec un beau-père, une belle-mère, des demi-frères et des demi-sœurs. Certains couples choisissent° le Pacte Civil de Solidarité (PACS), qui offre certains droits° et protections aux couples non-mariés. Depuis 2013, la France autorise également le mariage entre personnes de même sexe.

Géographiquement, les membres d'une famille d'immigrés peuvent° habiter près ou loin° les uns des autres°. Mais en général, ils préfèrent habiter les uns près des autres parce que l'intégration est parfois° difficile. Il existe aussi des familles d'immigrés séparées entre° la France et le pays d'origine.

Alors, oubliez les stéréotypes des familles en France. Elles sont grandes et petites, traditionnelles et non-conventionnelles; elles changent et sont toujours les mêmes°.

> **Coup de main**
>
> Remember to read decimal places in **French** using the French word **virgule** (*comma*) where you would normally say *point* in English. To say *percent*, use **pour cent**.
>
> **64,3%** soixante-quatre virgule trois pour cent
>
> *sixty-four point three percent*

toujours *still* **nombres** *numbers* **chaque** *each* **où** *where* **choisissent** *choose* **droits** *rights* **peuvent** *can* **près ou loin** *near or far from* **les uns des autres** *one another* **parfois** *sometimes* **entre** *between* **mêmes** *same* **tranche** *bracket*

La situation familiale des Français
(par tranche° d'âge)

ÂGE	CÉLIBATAIRE	EN COUPLE SANS ENFANTS	EN COUPLE AVEC ENFANTS	PARENT D'UNE FAMILLE MONOPARENTALE
< 25 ans	8%	3,5%	1,3%	0,4%
25–29 ans	1,9%	16,8%	49,4%	5,9%
30–44 ans	17%	17%	54%	9,4%
45–59 ans	23%	54%	17,9%	3,9%
> 60 ans	38%	54,3%	4,7%	2,9%

SOURCE: INSEE

ACTIVITÉS

1 Complétez Provide logical answers, based on the reading.

1. Si on regarde la population française d'aujourd'hui, on observe que les familles françaises sont très ___diverses___.
2. Le ___mariage___ est toujours très populaire en France.
3. La majorité des hommes et des femmes sont ___mariés___.
4. Le nombre de Français qui sont ___célibataires___ augmente.
5. Dans les familles ___monoparentales___, l'unique parent est divorcé, séparé ou veuf.
6. Il y a des familles qui combinent ___deux___ familles.
7. Le ___PACS___ offre certains droits et protections aux couples qui ne sont pas mariés.
8. Les immigrés aiment ___habiter___ les uns près des autres.
9. Oubliez les ___stéréotypes___ des familles en France.
10. Les familles changent et sont toujours ___les mêmes___.

EXPANSION

La famille française Explain to students that the concept of family is changing in France. In the past, extended families (grandparents, parents, and children) often lived in the same dwelling. Today fewer grandparents live with their children, and the number of traditional nuclear families (mother, father, and children) as well as non-traditional families is increasing.

In spite of these changes, family life is still an important social institution in French culture. When people say **la famille**, the majority of them are referring to their extended family. Most holidays are spent with family, and college students often choose a university near their home so that they can spend the weekends with their family.

LE FRANÇAIS QUOTIDIEN

La famille

un **frangin**	brother
une **frangine**	sister
maman	Mom
mamie	Nana, Grandma
un **minou**	kitty
papa	Dad
papi	Grandpa
tata	Auntie
tonton	Uncle
un **toutou**	doggy

AP® Theme: **Contemporary Life** Context: **Holidays and Celebrations**

LE MONDE FRANCOPHONE

Les fêtes et la famille

Les États-Unis ont quelques fêtes° en commun avec le monde francophone, mais les dates et les traditions de ces fêtes diffèrent d'un pays° à l'autre°. Voici deux fêtes associées à la famille.

La Fête des mères

En France le dernier° dimanche de mai ou le premier° dimanche de juin

En Belgique le deuxième° dimanche de mai

À l'île Maurice le dernier dimanche de mai

Au Canada le deuxième dimanche de mai

La Fête des pères

En France le troisième° dimanche de juin

En Belgique le deuxième° dimanche de juin

Au Canada le troisième dimanche de juin

quelques fêtes *some holidays* pays *country* autre *other* dernier *last* premier *first* deuxième *second* troisième *third*

PORTRAIT

Les Noah

Dans° la famille Noah, le sport est héréditaire. À chacun son° sport: pour° Yannick, né° en France, c'est le tennis; pour son père, Zacharie, né à Yaoundé, au Cameroun, c'est le football°; pour son fils, Joakim, né aux États-Unis, c'est le basket-ball. Yannick est champion junior à Wimbledon en 1977 et participe aux championnats° du Grand Chelem° dans les années 1980. Son fils, Joakim, est un joueur° de basket-ball aux États-Unis. Il gagne° la finale du *Final Four NCAA* en 2006 et en 2007 avec les Florida Gators. Il est aujourd'hui joueur professionnel avec les Chicago Bulls. Le sport est dans le sang° chez les Noah!

Dans *In* **À chacun son** *To each his* **pour** *for* **né** *born* **football** *soccer* **championnats** *championships* **Chelem** *Slam* **joueur** *player* **gagne** *wins* **sang** *blood*

 Sur Internet

Yannick Noah: célébrité du tennis et... de la musique?

Go to **vhlcentral.com** to find more cultural information related to this **Culture** section. Then watch the corresponding **Flash culture**.

---

2 **Vrai ou faux?** Indicate if these statements are **vrai** or **faux**.

1. Le tennis est héréditaire chez les Noah.   Faux.
2. Zacharie Noah est né au Cameroun.   Vrai.
3. Zacharie Noah était (*was*) un joueur de basket-ball.   Faux.
4. Yannick gagne à l'US Open.   Faux.
5. Joakim joue (*plays*) pour les Lakers.   Faux.
6. Le deuxième dimanche de mai, c'est la Fête des mères en Belgique et au Canada.   Vrai.

3 **À vous...** With a partner, write six sentences describing another celebrity family whose members all share a common field or profession. Be prepared to share your sentences with the class.

A
C
T
I
V
I
T
É
S

Le français quotidien Point out that these words are commonly used in informal conversations with family members, children, and close friends.

Portrait Show the class a photo of Yannick Noah. Ask: **Qui est-ce? Comment s'appelle-t-il?** Ask students what they know about him. Explain that thanks to his active involvement in charity work, Noah is often referred to as **Tonton Yannick**.

Le monde francophone Explain that Mother's Day and Father's Day did not originate in France. The first **Journée des mères** took place in France in 1926; it became an official holiday, **la Fête des mères,** in 1950.

2 Suggestion Have students correct the false statements.

2 Expansion Have students write three more true/false statements based on **Portrait** and **Le monde francophone**. Then have them work in groups of three and take turns reading their statements while the other group members respond **vrai** or **faux**.

3 Expansion Have students work in pairs to create a brief conversation in which they talk about their families and pets, using vocabulary in **Le français quotidien**. Example: **Est-ce que tu as un minou? Non, mais ma tata, elle a des minous.** Remind students that this level of language is only appropriate in informal conversations.

Flash culture Tell students that they will learn more about family and friends by watching a video narrated by Csilla. Show the video segment, then have students jot down in French at least three people or things they saw. You can also use the activities in the video manual in class to reinforce this **Flash culture** or assign them as homework.

21ˢᵗ Century Skills

Information and Media Literacy: Sur Internet Students access and critically evaluate information from the Internet.

EXPANSION

Les fêtes et la famille Explain to students that many countries around the world have a special day to honor mothers. **La Fête des mères** and **la Fête des pères** are celebrated somewhat similarly in France, Belgium, and Canada to the way Mother's Day and Father's Day are celebrated in the United States. Children create cards, write poems, and make handicrafts in school to give to their parents on these holidays. Older sons and daughters often give a small gift. On **l'Île Maurice**, they do not officially celebrate Father's Day. In other Francophone regions, such as North and West Africa, there is no official holiday for either Mother's or Father's Day.

Section Goals

3A.1

Descriptive adjectives vhlcentral

Point de départ As you learned in **Leçon 1B**, adjectives describe people, places, and things. In French, the forms of most adjectives vary depending on whether the nouns they describe are masculine or feminine, singular or plural. Furthermore, French adjectives are usually placed after the noun they modify when they don't directly follow a form of **être**.

SINGULAR MASCULINE NOUN ⟷ SINGULAR MASCULINE ADJECTIVE

Le **père** est **américain**.
The father is American.

PLURAL MASCULINE NOUN ⟷ PLURAL MASCULINE ADJECTIVE

As-tu des **cours faciles**?
Do you have easy classes?

• You've already learned several adjectives of nationality as well as some adjectives to describe someone's personality and your classes. Here are some adjectives to describe physical characteristics.

Adjectives of physical description			
bleu(e)	*blue*	**joli(e)**	*pretty*
blond(e)	*blond*	**laid(e)**	*ugly*
brun(e)	*dark (hair)*	**marron**	*brown (not for hair)*
châtain	*brown (hair)*	**noir(e)**	*black*
court(e)	*short*	**petit(e)**	*small, short (stature)*
grand(e)	*tall, big*	**raide**	*straight (hair)*
jeune	*young*	**vert(e)**	*green*

• In the examples below, the adjectives agree in number and gender with the subjects they describe. Remember that, in general, you add **-e** to make an adjective feminine, unless it already ends in an unaccented **-e**. You add **-s** to make an adjective plural, unless it already ends in an **-s**.

L'examen est **long**.
The exam is long.

Elle est **blonde** et **petite**.
She is blond and short.

Les tableaux sont **laids**.
The paintings are ugly.

Éva et Julie sont **jeunes** et **jolies**.
Éva and Julie are young and pretty.

• The adjective **marron** is invariable; in other words, it does not agree in gender and number with the noun it modifies. The adjective **châtain** is almost exclusively used to describe hair color.

Mon neveu a les **yeux marron**.
My nephew has brown eyes.

Ma nièce a les **cheveux châtains**.
My niece has brown hair.

• Use the expression **de taille moyenne** to describe someone or something of medium size.

Victor est un homme **de taille moyenne**.
Victor is a man of medium height.

C'est une université **de taille moyenne**.
It's a medium-sized university.

Vérifiez

Some irregular adjectives

masculine singular	feminine singular	masculine plural	feminine plural	
beau	belle	beaux	belles	*beautiful; handsome*
bon	bonne	bons	bonnes	*good; kind*
fier	fière	fiers	fières	*proud*
gros	grosse	gros	grosses	*fat*
heureux	heureuse	heureux	heureuses	*happy*
intellectuel	intellectuelle	intellectuels	intellectuelles	*intellectual*
long	longue	longs	longues	*long*
naïf	naïve	naïfs	naïves	*naive*
roux	rousse	roux	rousses	*red-haired*
vieux	vieille	vieux	vieilles	*old*

À noter

In **Leçon 1B**, you learned that if the masculine singular form of an adjective already ends in **-s (sénégalais)**, you don't add another one to form the plural. The same is also true for words that end in **-x (roux, vieux).**

- The forms of the adjective **nouveau** (*new*) follow the same pattern as those of **beau.**

MASCULINE PLURAL
J'ai trois **nouveaux** stylos.
I have three new pens.

FEMININE SINGULAR
Tu aimes la **nouvelle** horloge?
Do you like the new clock?

- Other adjectives that follow the pattern of **heureux** are **curieux** (*curious*), **malheureux** (*unhappy*), **nerveux** (*nervous*), and **sérieux** (*serious*).

Vérifiez

Position of certain adjectives

- Unlike most French adjectives, certain ones are placed *before* the noun they modify. These include: **beau, bon, grand, gros, jeune, joli, long, nouveau, petit,** and **vieux.**

J'aime bien les **grandes** familles.
I like large families.

Joël est un **vieux** copain.
Joël is an old friend.

- Other adjectives that are also generally placed before a noun are: **mauvais(e)** (*bad*), **pauvre** (*poor* as in *unfortunate*), **vrai(e)** (*true, real*).

Ça, c'est un **pauvre** homme.
That is an unfortunate man.

C'est une **vraie** catastrophe!
This is a real disaster!

Boîte à outils

When **pauvre** and **vrai(e)** are placed after the noun, they have a slightly different meaning: **pauvre** means *poor* as in *not rich,* and **vrai(e)** means *true.*

Ça, c'est un homme pauvre.
That is a poor man.

C'est une histoire vraie.
This is a true story.

- When placed before a *masculine singular noun that begins with a vowel sound,* these adjectives have a special form.

beau	▶	bel	▶	un **bel** appartement
vieux		vieil		un **vieil** homme
nouveau		nouvel		un **nouvel** ami

- The plural indefinite article **des** changes to **de** when the adjective comes before the noun.

ADJECTIVE BEFORE NOUN
J'habite avec **de bons amis**.
I live with good friends.

ADJECTIVE AFTER NOUN
J'habite avec **des amis sympathiques**.
I live with nice friends.

Vérifiez

Essayez!   Provide all four forms of the adjectives.

1. grand   *grand, grande, grands, grandes*
2. nerveux   nerveux, nerveuse, nerveux, nerveuses
3. roux   roux, rousse, roux, rousses
4. bleu   bleu, bleue, bleus, bleues
5. naïf   naïf, naïve, naïfs, naïves
6. gros   gros, grosse, gros, grosses
7. long   long, longue, longs, longues
8. fier   fier, fière, fiers, fières

Suggestions: Scaffolding
- Teach students the irregular adjectives in semantic pairs. **Example: Anne a les cheveux longs, mais Paul a les cheveux courts.** Have students repeat feminine and masculine forms after you. Point out patterns, such as **-eux/-euse** and **-el/-elle.**
- Do a written drill to practice gender and number of the irregular adjectives, then have students complete the **Vérifiez** activity.
- Present the points about the position of adjectives. Teach students the mnemonic device **BAGS** (beauty, age, goodness, size) to help them remember which adjectives generally precede the nouns they modify. Give examples for each category: beauty (**beau, joli**), age (**jeune, vieux**), goodness (**bon, mauvais**), size (**grand, petit**).
- Give students scrambled sentences to practice adjective placement. Examples: **famille/une/grande/j'ai (J'ai une grande famille.) garçon/est/sympa/un/David (David est un garçon sympa.)** Have students complete the **Vérifiez** activity.

Essayez! Suggest that students watch the Grammar Tutorial before completing the activity.

TELL Connection

Learning Tools 2 *Why:* Use available technologies to expand students' experiences. *What:* Ask students to find images of people on websites from the French-speaking world, and write about them using descriptive adjectives. Guide students to recognize and describe the wide variety of ethnicities of the Francophone world.

EXPANSION

Extra Practice Have students brainstorm and make a list of adjectives in French that describe their ideal friend (**Mon copain idéal/Ma copine idéale**). Tell them to rank each adjective in terms of its importance to them. Then take a quick class survey to find out what the most important and least important qualities are in the ideal friend. Tally the results on the board.

EXPANSION

Extra Practice Have pairs of students write sentences using adjectives such as **jeune, grand, joli,** and **petit.** When they have finished, ask volunteers to dictate their sentences to you to write on the board. After you have written a sentence and corrected any errors, ask volunteers to suggest a sentence that uses the antonym of the adjective.

1 & **2** Suggestions
- Before students begin the activities, review the four different forms of the adjectives used in each item or follow the game suggestion, p. 101.
- To check students' work, have volunteers write their sentences on the board and read them aloud.

1 Expansion Have students restate the answers, except #3, #7, #8 and #9, using the phrase **les deux** to practice plural forms. Example: **1. Les deux sont curieux.**

2 Expansion For additional practice, change the adjective(s) and have students restate or write the sentences. Examples: **1. bon (Elle a de bons amis.) 2. beau (Elle habite dans un bel appartement.) 3. agréable (Son mari a un travail agréable.) 4. bon (Ses filles sont de bonnes étudiantes.) 5. indépendant/élégant (Christine est indépendante et élégante.) 6. fier (Son mari est un homme fier.) 7. poli (Elle a des collègues polis.) 8. joli/intelligent (Sa secrétaire est une jolie fille intelligente.) 9. beau (Elle a de beaux chiens.) 10. américain (Ses voisins sont américains.)**

Mise en pratique

1 **Ressemblances** Family members often look and behave alike. Describe these family members.

MODÈLE

Caroline est intelligente. Elle a un frère.
Il est intelligent aussi.

1. Jean est curieux. Il a une sœur. Elle est curieuse aussi.
2. Carole est blonde. Elle a un cousin. Il est blond aussi.
3. Albert est gros. Il a trois tantes. Elles sont grosses aussi.
4. Sylvie est fière et heureuse. Elle a un fils. Il est fier et heureux aussi.
5. Christophe est vieux. Il a une demi-sœur. Elle est vieille aussi.
6. Martin est laid. Il a une petite-fille. Elle est laide aussi.
7. Sophie est intellectuelle. Elle a deux grands-pères. Ils sont intellectuels aussi.
8. Céline est naïve. Elle a deux frères. Ils sont naïfs aussi.
9. Anne est belle. Elle a cinq neveux. Ils sont beaux aussi.
10. Anissa est rousse. Elle a un mari. Il est roux aussi.

2 **Une femme heureuse** Complete these sentences about Christine. Remember: some adjectives precede and some follow the nouns they modify.

MODÈLE

Christine / avoir / trois enfants (beau)
Christine a trois beaux enfants.

1. Elle / avoir / des amis (sympathique)
   Elle a des amis sympathiques.

2. Elle / habiter / dans un appartement (nouveau)
   Elle habite dans un nouvel appartement.

3. Son *(Her)* mari / avoir / un travail (bon)
   Son mari a un bon travail.

4. Ses *(Her)* filles / être / des étudiantes (sérieux)
   Ses filles sont des étudiantes sérieuses.

5. Christine / être / une femme (heureux)
   Christine est une femme heureuse.

6. Son mari / être / un homme (beau)
   Son mari est un bel homme.

7. Elle / avoir / des collègues amusant(e)s
   Elle a des collègues amusant(e)s.

8. Sa *(Her)* secrétaire / être / une fille (jeune/intellectuel)
   Sa secrétaire est une jeune fille intellectuelle.

9. Elle / avoir / des chiens (bon)
   Elle a de bons chiens.

10. Ses voisins / être (poli)
    Ses voisins sont polis.

Communication

3 **Descriptions** In pairs, take turns describing these people and things using the expressions **C'est** or **Ce sont**.

Answers will vary.

MODÈLE

C'est un cours difficile.

1. _____   2. _____   3. _____

4. _____   5. _____   6. _____

4 **Comparaisons** In pairs, take turns comparing these brothers and their sister. Make as many comparisons as possible, then share them with the class. Answers will vary.

MODÈLE

Géraldine et Jean-Paul sont grands mais Tristan est petit.

Jean-Paul   **Tristan**   **Géraldine**

5 **Qui est-ce?** Choose the name of a classmate. Your partner must guess the person by asking up to 10 **oui** or **non** questions. Then, switch roles. Answers will vary.

MODÈLE

Élève 1: *C'est un homme?*
Élève 2: *Oui.*
Élève 1: *Il est de taille moyenne?*
Élève 2: *Non.*

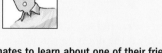

6 **Les bons copains** Interview two classmates to learn about one of their friends, using these questions. Your partners' answers will incorporate descriptive adjectives. Be prepared to report to the class what you learned. Answers will vary.

- Est-ce que tu as un(e) bon(ne) copain/copine?
- Comment est-ce qu'il/elle s'appelle?
- Quel âge est-ce qu'il/elle a?
- Comment est-ce qu'il/elle est?
- Il/Elle est de quelle origine?
- Quels cours est-ce qu'il/elle aime?
- Quels cours est-ce qu'il/elle déteste?

3 **Expansion** Students could also describe an image and have their partner guess which one they are describing. Example: **Élève 1:** Elles sont belles. **Élève 2:** C'est la photo numéro un!

4 **Expansion** To practice negation, have students say what the people in the drawings are not. Example: **Géraldine et Jean-Paul ne sont pas petits.**

4 **Partner Chat** You can also assign Activity 4 on vhlcentral.com. Students work in pairs to record the activity online. The pair's recorded conversation will appear in your gradebook.

5 **Suggestions**
- Before students begin the activity, review when to use **C'est/Ce sont** and **Il/Elle est, Ils/Elles sont.**
- This activity can also be done in small groups or with the whole class.

6 **Suggestions**
- To model this activity, have students respond as you ask the interview questions. Tell them to invent answers, where necessary.
- Tell students to take notes during their interviews. Suggest they create some kind of graphic organizer, such as a table with labeled rows and columns, to record their notes.
- If time is limited, have students write a description of one of their classmates' friends as written homework.

Activity Pack For additional activities, go to the **Activity Pack** in the **Resources** section of vhlcentral.com.

EXPANSION

Extra Practice Prepare short descriptions of five easily recognizable people. Write their names on the board in random order. Tell students to write your descriptions as you dictate them. Then have them match the description to the appropriate name. Example: **Elle est jeune, brune, athlétique et intellectuelle. (Serena Williams)**

TEACHING OPTIONS

Game Divide the class into two teams. Call on one team member at a time, alternating between teams. Give a certain form of an adjective and name another form that the person must say and write on the board. Example: **beau**; feminine plural (**belles**). Give a point for each correct answer. The team with the most points at the end of the game wins.

Section Goals

In this section, students will learn:
- possessive adjectives
- to express possession and relationships with **de**

Key Standards

4.1, 5.1

Suggestions: Scaffolding
- Introduce the concept of possessive adjectives. Ask volunteers questions, such as: **Est-ce que votre mère est heureuse? Comment est votre oncle préféré?** Point out the possessive adjectives in questions and responses.
- List the possessive adjectives on the board. Use each with a noun to illustrate agreement. Point out that all possessive adjectives agree in number with the noun they modify, but that all singular possessives must agree in gender and number. Examples: **son cousin, sa cousine, ses cousin(e)s; leur cousin, leur cousine, leurs cousin(e)s.** Also point out that **mon, ton,** and **son** are used before feminine singular nouns beginning with a vowel sound or silent **h**. Examples: **mon épouse, ton idée, son université.**
- Have students give the plural or singular of possessive adjectives with nouns. Say: **Donnez le pluriel: mon élève, ton examen, notre cours.** Say: **Donnez le singulier: mes sœurs, nos frères, leurs chiens, ses enfants.**
- Have students complete the **For Visual Learners** activity.

3A.2

Boîte à outils

In **Contextes**, you learned a few possessive adjectives with family vocabulary: **mon grand-père, ma sœur, mes cousins.**

Boîte à outils

You already know that there are two ways to express *you* in French: **tu** (informal and singular) and **vous** (formal or plural). Remember that the possessive adjective must always correspond to the form of *you* that is used.

Tu parles à tes amis?

Vous parlez à vos amis?

Possessive adjectives vhlcentral

Point de départ In both English and French, possessive adjectives express ownership or possession.

Possessive adjectives			
masculine singular	**feminine singular**	**plural**	
mon	ma	mes	*my*
ton	ta	tes	*your (fam. and sing.)*
son	sa	ses	*his, her, its*
notre	notre	nos	*our*
votre	votre	vos	*your (form. or pl.)*
leur	leur	leurs	*their*

C'est ta sœur? Tes parents?

Voilà vos photos.

- Possessive adjectives are always placed before the nouns they modify.

C'est **ton** père?   Non, c'est **mon** oncle.
Is that your father?   *No, that's my uncle.*

Voici **notre** mère.   Ce sont **tes** livres?
Here's our mother.   *Are these your books?*

- In French, unlike English, possessive adjectives agree in gender and number with the nouns they modify.

mon frère   **ma** sœur   **mes** grands-parents
my brother   *my sister*   *my grandparents*

ton chat   **ta** nièce   **tes** cousines
your cat   *your niece*   *your cousins*

- The forms **notre, votre,** and **leur** are the same for both masculine and feminine nouns. They change only if the noun they modify is plural.

notre neveu   **notre** famille   **nos** enfants
our nephew   *our family*   *our children*

leur cousin   **leur** cousine   **leurs** cousins
their cousin   *their cousin*   *their cousins*

- The masculine singular forms **mon, ton,** and **son** are also used with *feminine singular* nouns if they begin with a vowel sound.

mon amie   **ton** école   **son** histoire
my friend   *your school*   *his story*

TEACHING OPTIONS

Video Replay the video episode, having students focus on possessive adjectives. Tell them to write down each one they hear with the noun it modifies. Afterward, ask the class to describe Valérie and Stéphane's family. Remind them to use definite articles and **de** if necessary.

DIFFERENTIATION

For Visual Learners Ask students to bring photos of their families (including pets) to the class. In small groups, each student will describe his/her family members (pointing at the photos) using both possessive and descriptive adjectives. Bring your own photos and visit the small groups to share with your students and check their work.

- The possessive adjectives **son**, **sa**, and **ses** are used to indicate both *his* or *her*. The pronoun you choose depends on the gender and number of the modified noun, not the possessor (**il** or **elle**).

     son frère = *his/her brother*   **sa** sœur = *his/her sister*   **ses** parents = *his/her parents*

Context will usually clarify whether the possessive adjective means *his* or *her*.

> J'aime **Nadine** mais je n'aime pas **son** frère.   **Rémy** et **son** frère sont trop sérieux.
> *I like Nadine but I don't like her brother.*   *Rémy and his brother are too serious.*

Elle a déjà son bac.

◯◯ **Vérifiez**

Possession with *de*

- In English, you use *'s* to express relationships or ownership. In French, you use **de** (**d'**) + [*the noun or proper name*].

> C'est le petit ami **d'Élisabeth**.   C'est le petit ami **de ma sœur**.
> *That's Élisabeth's boyfriend.*   *That's my sister's boyfriend.*
>
> Tu aimes la cousine **de Thierry**?   J'ai l'adresse **de ses parents**.
> *Do you like Thierry's cousin?*   *I have his parents' address.*

- When the preposition **de** is followed by the definite articles **le** and **les**, they contract to form **du** and **des**, respectively. There is no contraction when **de** is followed by **la** and **l'**.

     de + le ▶ **du**   **de + les** ▶ **des**

> L'opinion **du** grand-père est importante.   La fille **des** voisins a les cheveux châtains.
> *The grandfather's opinion is important.*   *The neighbors' daughter has brown hair.*
>
> Le nom **de l'**oiseau, c'est Lulu.   J'ai le nouvel album **de la** chanteuse française.
> *The bird's name is Lulu.*   *I have the French singer's new album.*

◯◯ **Vérifiez**

Boîte à outils

You have already seen **de** used to express relationship in **Contextes**: **la fille de Juliette et de Robert, le chien de mes cousins**.

Essayez!   **Provide the appropriate form of each possessive adjective.**

mon, ma, mes
1. _mon_ livre
2. _ma_ librairie
3. _mes_ professeurs

ton, ta, tes
4. _tes_ ordinateurs
5. _ta_ télévision
6. _ton_ stylo

son, sa, ses
7. _sa_ table
8. _ses_ problèmes
9. _son_ école

notre, nos
10. _notre_ cahier
11. _nos_ études
12. _notre_ bourse

votre, vos
13. _vos_ soirées
14. _votre_ lycée
15. _vos_ devoirs

leur, leurs
16. _leur_ résultat
17. _leur_ classe
18. _leurs_ notes

Suggestions: Scaffolding
- To introduce possession with **de**, write the following phrases in a list on the board: **l'ordinateur de Monique, l'ordinateur d'Alain, l'ordinateur du professeur, les ordinateurs des professeurs.** Explain the use of the contractions **d'**, **du** (**de + le**), and **des** (**de + les**). Then, have students complete the **Vérifiez** activity.
- Review all concepts by asking students questions such as these: **C'est mon stylo? C'est votre amie? Ce sont leurs devoirs? C'est sa feuille de papier? Ce sont nos livres de français? C'est l'ordinateur de ____? C'est le sac à dos de ____?**

Essayez! Have students create sentences using these phrases. Examples: **C'est mon livre. Mes professeurs sont patients.**

TELL Connection

Professionalism 4 *Why:* Challenging concepts require creative and collaborative approaches. *What:* Research how colleagues compare and contrast the ways French and English express possession with adjectives. Use what you learn to supplement your own approach to provide students with different ways of understanding this concept.

EXPANSION

Pairs To practice plural possessive adjectives, have pairs describe the family on pages 90–91 from the point of view of Luc and Hélène Garneau. Encourage them to include descriptive adjectives and be creative in their sentences. You might want to introduce the term **les arrière-petits-enfants** (*great-* *grandchildren*) for this activity. Examples: **Juliette et Marc sont nos enfants. Juliette est blonde, mais Marc est brun. Juliette et son époux, Robert, ont trois enfants. Leurs enfants s'appellent Véronique, Guillaume et Marie.**

Mise en pratique

1 Complétez Complete the sentences with the correct possessive adjectives.

MODÈLE

Karine et Léo, vous avez ___VOS___ (*your*) stylos?

1. ___Ma___ (*My*) sœur est très patiente.
2. Marc et Julien adorent ___leurs___ (*their*) cours de philosophie et de maths.
3. Nadine et Gisèle, qui est ___votre___ (*your*) amie?
4. C'est une belle photo de ___leur___ (*their*) grand-mère.
5. Nous voyageons en France avec ___nos___ (*our*) enfants.
6. Est-ce que tu travailles beaucoup sur ___ton___ (*your*) ordinateur?
7. ___Ses___ (*Her*) cousins habitent à Paris.

2 Identifiez Identify the owner of each object.

▶ **MODÈLE**

Ce sont les cahiers de Sophie.

Sophie

Christophe

1. C'est la télévision de Christophe.

Paul

2. C'est l'ordinateur de Paul.

Stéphanie

3. C'est la calculatrice de Stéphanie.

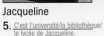

Georgette

4. Ce sont les stylos de Georgette.

Jacqueline

5. C'est l'université/la bibliothèque/le lycée de Jacqueline.

Christine

6. Ce sont les dictionnaires de Christine.

3 Qui est-ce? Look at the Mercier family tree and explain the relationships between these people.

MODÈLE

Hubert → Marie et Fabien
C'est leur père.

1. Marie → Guy   C'est sa femme.
2. Agnès et Hubert → Thomas et Mégane   Ce sont leurs grands-parents.
3. Thomas et Daniel → Yvette   Ce sont ses fils.
4. Fabien → Guy   C'est son beau-frère.
5. Claire → Thomas et Daniel   C'est leur cousine.
6. Thomas → Marie   C'est son neveu.

Hubert   Agnès

Yvette   Fabien   Marie   Guy

Thomas   Lucie   Daniel   Mégane   Claire

Communication

4 **Ma famille** Use these cues to interview as many classmates as you can to learn about their family members. Then, tell the class what you found out.

Answers will vary.

MODÈLE

mère / parler / espagnol
Élève 1: *Est-ce que ta mère parle espagnol?*
Élève 2: *Oui, ma mère parle espagnol.*

1. sœur / travailler / en Californie

_____

2. frère / être / célibataire

_____

3. cousins / avoir / un chien

_____

4. cousin / voyager / beaucoup

_____

5. père / adorer / les ordinateurs

_____

6. parents / être / divorcés

_____

7. tante / avoir / les yeux marron

_____

8. grands-parents / habiter / en Floride

_____

5 **Tu connais?** In pairs, take turns telling your partner if someone among your family or friends has these characteristics. Be sure to use a possessive adjective or **de** in your responses. Answers will vary.

MODÈLE

français
Mes cousins sont français.

1. naïf	5. optimiste	9. curieux
2. beau	6. grand	10. vieux
3. petit	7. blond	11. roux
4. sympathique	8. mauvais	12. intellectuel

6 **Portrait de famille** In groups of three, take turns describing your family. Listen carefully to your partners' descriptions without taking notes. After everyone has spoken, two of you describe the other's family to see how well you remember. Answers will vary.

MODÈLE

Élève 1: *Sa mère est sociable.*
Élève 2: *Sa mère est blonde.*
Élève 3: *Mais non! Ma mère est timide et elle a les cheveux châtains.*

cent cinq **105**

4 Suggestion Have two volunteers read the **modèle**. Explain to students that they use the cues to create the questions.

4 Expansion To practice asking questions with the formal *you* forms, tell students that they are going to interview a French teacher about his or her family. Then have students restate the questions.

5 Expansion Have students take notes on what their partner says and share them with the rest of the class. Example:
Élève 1: Mon cousin est beau.
Élève 2: Son cousin est beau.

5 Virtual Chat You can also assign Activity 5 on vhlcentral.com. Students record individual responses that appear in your gradebook.

6 Suggestion Before students begin the activity, tell them to make a list of the family members they plan to describe. Call on three volunteers to read the **modèle**. Explain that one student will describe his or her own family (using **mon, ma, mes**) and then the other two will describe the first student's family (using **son, sa, ses**).

Activity Pack For additional activities, go to the **Activity Pack** in the **Resources** section of vhlcentral.com.

TEACHING OPTIONS

Small Groups Give small groups three minutes to brainstorm how many words they can associate with the phrases **notre lycée** and **notre cours de français**. Have them model their responses on **Dans notre cours, nous avons un(e)/des _____** and **Notre lycée est _____**. Have the groups share their associations with the rest of the class.

EXPANSION

Extra Practice To practice **votre** and **vos,** have students ask you questions about your family. Examples: **Comment s'appellent vos parents? Est-ce que vous avez des enfants? Comment s'appellent-ils? Est-ce que vous avez des neveux ou des nièces? Comment s'appellent-ils?**

Révision

1 Expliquez In pairs, take turns randomly calling out one person from column A and one from column B. Your partner will explain how they are related. Answers will vary.

MODÈLE

Élève 1: *ta sœur et ta mère*
Élève 2: *Ma sœur est la fille de ma mère.*

A	B
1. sœur	a. cousine
2. tante	b. mère
3. cousins	c. grand-père
4. frère	d. neveux
5. père	e. oncle

2 Les yeux de ma mère List seven physical or personality traits that you share with other members of your family. Be specific. Then, in pairs, compare your lists and be ready to present your partner's list to the class. Answers will vary.

MODÈLE

Élève 1: *J'ai les yeux bleus de mon père et je suis fier/fière comme (like) mon grand-père.*
Élève 2: *Moi, je suis impatient(e) comme ma mère.*

3 Les familles célèbres In groups of four, play a guessing game. Imagine that you belong to one of these famous families or one of your choice. Take turns describing your new family to the group. The first person who guesses which family you belong to and where you fit in is the winner. Answers will vary.

> La famille Addams
> La famille Kardashian
> Les familles de *Modern Family*
> La famille Weasley
> La famille Simpson

4 La famille idéale Walk around the room to survey your classmates. Ask them to describe their ideal family. Record their answers. Then, in pairs, compare your results. Answers will vary.

MODÈLE

Élève 1: *Comment est ta famille idéale?*
Élève 2: *Ma famille idéale est petite, avec deux enfants et beaucoup de chiens et de chats.*

5 Le casting A casting director is looking for actors to star in a new comedy about a strange family. In pairs, role-play a conversation between the casting director and an agent in which you discuss possible actors to play each character, based on these illustrations. Answers will vary.

MODÈLE

Élève 1 (agent): *Pour la mère, il y a Émilie. Elle est rousse et elle a les cheveux courts.*
Élève 2 (casting director): *Ah, non. La mère est brune et elle a les cheveux longs. Avez-vous une actrice brune?*

La famille

le fils   la fille   le père   la mère   le cousin

Les acteurs et les actrices

Michelle   Patrick
Annick
Julie
Laurent
Émilie
Stéphane   Robert

6 Les différences Your teacher will give you and a partner each a similar drawing of a family. Identify and name the six differences between your picture and your partner's.

MODÈLE

Élève 1: *La mère est blonde.*
Élève 2: *Non, la mère est brune.*

Le Zapping

vhlcentral

AP® **Theme:** Science and Technology
Context: Social Impact of Technology

 Préparation Answer these questions. Answers will vary.

1. Les parents sont-ils généreux? Comment? Qu'est-ce qu'ils donnent à leurs enfants?

2. Êtes-vous généreux/généreuse? Comment? Qu'est-ce que vous donnez à vos ami(e)s?

Pages d'Or

The **Pages d'Or** of Belgium offer a range of services that connect businesses with potential customers. Technology is the principal means used by **Pages d'Or** to reach a wide customer base. The **Pages d'Or** website, downloadable PDFs, smartphone and tablet applications, and digital television listings allow consumers to find businesses quickly for the services they need.

publicité *ad* **Pages d'Or** *Golden Pages* **je décrocherais la Lune** *I would give you the moon*

 Compréhension Answer these questions. Some answers will vary.

1. Qui (*Who*) sont les deux personnes dans la publicité?
C'est un père et son fils.
2. Pourquoi l'homme téléphone-t-il pour obtenir (*to obtain*) une grue?
Il aime beaucoup son fils.
3. Comment trouve-t-il le numéro de téléphone?
Il cherche dans les Pages d'Or.

 Conversation In small groups, discuss the following.
Answers will vary.

1. Utilisez le vocabulaire de cette leçon pour décrire les parents idéaux.

2. Décrivez les méthodes que vous utilisez pour trouver le cadeau (*gift*) idéal pour les personnes que vous aimez.

Publicité°: Pages d'Or°

—Pour toi, je décrocherais la Lune°.

Vocabulaire utile

combien	*how much*
une grue	*crane*
c'est bien trouvé	*now that's a good choice*

 Application Tell about a time when you used an outside resource to do something special for someone to show him or her how much you cared. Use as much French as you can in your presentation.

Section Goals

In this section, students will:
• read about the **Pages d'Or** of Belgium
• watch a commercial for their information services
• answer questions about the commercial and the **Pages d'Or**

Key Standards
1.1, 1.2, 1.3, 2.2, 4.2

Pages d'Or
Have students compare and contrast the **Pages d'Or** to the Yellow Pages. Have them visit each company's website and ask them to compare the range of services each offers.

PRE-AP®

Audiovisual Interpretive Communication Previewing Strategy
Have students look at the screen shot and predict what they will see in the video. Ask: **Pourquoi le garçon est-il heureux? (Il regarde la lune.) Qui prononce la citation? (La mère ou le père du garçon.) Quels mots (*words*) pensez-vous entendre (*hear*) dans la vidéo? (maman, papa, lune, nuit, téléphone, ordinateur)**

Vidéo
Have students watch the video once without sound to focus on images and once with sound to focus on language.

Compréhension Have students write their answers. Then show the video again so that they can check their answers.

Conversation
Write on the board the students' descriptions of the ideal parents. Determine the three most common answers and discuss why it is so important for a good parent to have these particular skills.

EXPANSION

Les Pages d'Or Obtaining a business telephone listing has come a long way since the printed phone book. The **Pages d'Or** website offers customers an attractive and user-friendly interface for finding a specific number, of course. However, its services go a great deal beyond that. Depending on the time of year, for instance, the site might provide lists of seasonal tasks that people typically need to accomplish around that time. A selection of categories not only reminds the user that it is spring and time to plant a new garden, but also provides links to business throughout Belgium for starting the job.

107

Section Goals

In this section, students will learn and practice vocabulary related to:
- professions and occupations
- character traits and some emotional states

Key Standards

1.1, 1.2, 4.1

Suggestions

- Use magazine pictures to introduce occupations. As you show each picture identify the occupation and write it on the board. Example: **Il/Elle est architecte.**
- To introduce the adjectives, pantomime the emotions or character traits using facial expressions and/or body language. Example: **Je suis triste.** (Make a sad face.) Then ask a few students if they feel or are the same way. Example: _____, **êtes-vous triste aujourd'hui?**
- Point out that **paresseux** and **travailleur** follow the patterns of **généreux** and **coiffeur**, respectively, to form the feminine **paresseuse** and **travailleuse**. Then have students find other patterns for making adjectives feminine. Examples: **intellectuel(le), cuel(le); actif/active, sportif/ sportive, naïf/naïve; heureux/ heureuse, généreux/généreuse.**
- Point out that the masculine noun **médecin** is also used to refer to a female doctor. The expression **une femme médecin** is also common.
- Use the digital image for this page. Ask students yes/no or either/or questions using the new vocabulary. Examples: **Est-ce que la petite fille est drôle? (Non, elle n'est pas drôle.) Le petit garçon est-il heureux ou triste? (Il est triste.)**

You will learn how to...
- describe people
- talk about occupations

◁) **vhl**central

Comment sont-ils?

Vocabulaire

actif/active	active
antipathique	unpleasant
courageux/courageuse	courageous, brave
cruel(le)	cruel
doux/douce	sweet; soft
ennuyeux/ennuyeuse	boring
étranger/étrangère	foreign
faible	weak
favori(te)	favorite
fou/folle	crazy
généreux/généreuse	generous
génial(e) (géniaux pl.)	great
gentil(le)	nice
lent(e)	slow
méchant(e)	mean
modeste	modest, humble
pénible	tiresome
prêt(e)	ready
sportif/sportive	athletic
un(e) architecte	architect
un(e) artiste	artist
un(e) athlète	athlete
un(e) avocat(e)	lawyer
un(e) dentiste	dentist
un homme/une femme d'affaires	businessman/woman
un ingénieur	engineer
un(e) journaliste	journalist
un médecin	doctor

108 *cent huit*

DIFFERENTIATION

For Kinesthetic Learners Have students play a miming game in groups of four or five. Tell them that each person should think of an adjective presented in this lesson and act out the word. The first person to guess correctly acts out the next one. Example: **Es-tu fatigué(e)?** Then have each group pick out the best mime. Ask students to act out their mimes while the class guesses what they are doing.

EXPANSION

Word Association Say the French term for a profession, for example, **un médecin**. Tell students to write down as many words as possible, especially the new adjectives, that they associate with this job. Then call on volunteers to read their lists as you write the words on the board, or have students compare their lists in pairs.

Mise en pratique

la coiffeuse (coiffeur m.)

Il est drôle.

un musicien (musicienne f.)

1 **Les célébrités** Match these famous people with their professions. Not all of the professions will be used.

h	1. Oprah Winfrey	a.	médecin
e	2. Claude Monet	b.	journaliste
d	3. Paul Mitchell	c.	musicien(ne)
a	4. Dr. Phil C. McGraw	d.	coiffeur/coiffeuse
i	5. Serena Williams	e.	artiste
b	6. Katie Couric	f.	architecte
c	7. Beethoven	g.	avocat(e)
f	8. Frank Lloyd Wright	h.	homme/femme d'affaires
		i.	athlète
		j.	dentiste

2 **Les contraires** Complete each sentence with the opposite adjective.

1. Ma grand-mère n'est pas cruelle, elle est _douce/gentille_.
2. Mon frère n'est pas travailleur, il est _paresseux_.
3. Mes cousines ne sont pas faibles, elles sont _fortes_.
4. Ma tante n'est pas drôle, elle est _ennuyeuse_.
5. Mon oncle est un bon athlète. Il n'est pas lent, il est _rapide_.
6. Ma famille et moi, nous ne sommes pas antipathiques, nous sommes _sympathiques_.
7. Mes parents ne sont pas méchants, ils sont _gentils/doux_.
8. Mon oncle n'est pas heureux, il est _triste_.

3 **Écoutez** You will hear descriptions of three people. Listen carefully and indicate whether the statements about them are **vrai** or **faux**.

Nora   Ahmed   Françoise

		Vrai	Faux
1.	L'architecte aime le sport.	☐	☑
2.	L'artiste est paresseuse.	☐	☑
3.	L'artiste aime son travail.	☑	☐
4.	Ahmed est médecin.	☐	☑
5.	Françoise est gentille.	☑	☐
6.	Nora est avocate.	☐	☑
7.	Nora habite au Québec.	☐	☑
8.	Ahmed est travailleur.	☑	☐
9.	Françoise est mère de famille.	☑	☐
10.	Ahmed habite avec sa femme.	☐	☑

---

1 **Suggestion** To check students' answers, tell them to form complete sentences using the verb **être**. Example: **Oprah Winfrey est une femme d'affaires.** You might also have students include the person's nationality. Example: **Claude Monet est un artiste français.**

1 **Expansion** Have students provide additional names of famous people for each profession listed. Example: **Henri Matisse est un artiste.**

2 **Suggestion** Before students begin the activity, do a quick drill to review the feminine and plural forms of the adjectives in **Contextes**.

3 **Script** NORA: Moi, c'est Nora. J'ai 27 ans. Je suis artiste. Je suis mexicaine et j'habite à Paris. Je ne suis pas paresseuse. Je suis active, sportive et sympa. J'adore les animaux et l'art, bien sûr!
AHMED: Moi, je m'appelle Ahmed. J'ai 30 ans. Je suis architecte. Je suis discret, travailleur et un peu jaloux. Je ne suis pas sportif; je trouve le sport ennuyeux. J'habite avec mes parents au Québec.
FRANÇOISE: Moi, c'est Françoise. J'ai 51 ans. Je suis médecin. Je suis généreuse et gentille. Je travaille dans un hôpital. J'ai deux enfants, une fille et un fils. Les deux sont étudiants à l'université.
Teacher Resources DVD

3 **Suggestions**
- Have students take notes as they listen. Tell them to note characteristics, profession, and family members for each person.
- Pause the recording after each person speaks to allow students to jot down notes and/or review the questions.

Communication

4 Les professions In pairs, say what the real professions of these people are. Alternate reading and answering the questions.

MODÈLE

Élève 1: *Est-ce que Sabine et Sarah sont femmes d'affaires?*
Élève 2: *Non, elles sont avocates.*

1. Est-ce que Louis est architecte?
   Non, il est dentiste.

2. Est-ce que Jean est professeur?
   Non, il est coiffeur.

3. Est-ce que Juliette est ingénieur?
   Non, elle est journaliste.

4. Est-ce que Charles est médecin?
   Non, il est homme d'affaires.

5. Est-ce que Pauline est musicienne?
   Non, elle est architecte.

6. Est-ce que Jacques et Brigitte sont avocats?
   Non, ils sont athlètes.

7. Est-ce qu'Édouard est dentiste?
   Non, il est artiste.

8. Est-ce que Martine et Sophie sont dentistes?
   Non, elles sont musiciennes.

5 Conversez Interview a classmate. Your partner should answer **pourquoi** questions with **parce que** (*because*). Answers will vary.

1. Quel âge ont tes parents? Comment sont-ils?
2. Quelle est la profession de tes parents?
3. Qui est ton/ta cousin(e) préféré(e)? Pourquoi?
4. Qui n'est pas ton/ta cousin(e) préféré(e)? Pourquoi?
5. As-tu des animaux de compagnie (*pets*)? Quel est ton animal de compagnie favori? Pourquoi?
6. Qui est ton professeur préféré? Pourquoi?
7. Qui est gentil dans la classe?
8. Quelles professions aimes-tu?

Coup de main

Here are some useful question words:

Comment? *How/What?*
Quel(le)(s)? *Which/What?*
Qui? *Who?*
Pourquoi? *Why?*

6 Portrait Write a description of yourself and your best friend. Include details such as age, physical characteristics, and personality traits for both you and your friend. After your classmates share their descriptions, discuss in small groups who you would like to get to know better based on common interests. Answers will vary.

7 Quelle surprise! Imagine that it is fifteen years from now, you are working in your chosen profession, and you have just run into a former classmate from high school. With a partner, prepare a conversation where you: Answers will vary.
• greet each other
• ask what each other's professions are
• ask about marital status and for a description of your significant others
• ask if either of you have children, and if so, for a description of them

Les sons et les lettres 🔊 vhlcentral

L'accent circonflexe, la cédille, and le tréma

L'accent circonflexe (^) can appear over any vowel.

p**â**té	pr**ê**t	a**î**né	dr**ô**le	cro**û**ton

L'accent circonflexe is also used to distinguish between words with similar spellings but different meanings.

m**û**r	mur	s**û**r	sur
ripe	*wall*	*sure*	*on*

L'accent circonflexe indicates that a letter, frequently an **s**, has been dropped from an older spelling. For this reason, **l'accent circonflexe** can be used to identify French cognates of English words.

hospital → h**ô**pital   *forest* → for**ê**t

La cédille (¸) is only used with the letter **c**. A **c** with a **cédille** is pronounced with a soft **c** sound, like the *s* in the English word *yes*. Use a **cédille** to retain the soft **c** sound before an **a**, **o**, or **u**. Before an **e** or an **i**, the letter **c** is always soft, so a **cédille** is not necessary.

gar**ç**on	fran**ç**ais	**ç**a	le**ç**on

Le tréma (¨) is used to indicate that two vowel sounds are pronounced separately. It is always placed over the second vowel.

égo**ï**ste	na**ï**ve	No**ë**l	Ha**ï**ti

Prononcez Practice saying these words aloud.

1. naïf
2. reçu
3. châtain
4. âge
5. français
6. fenêtre
7. théâtre
8. garçon
9. égoïste
10. château

Articulez Practice saying these sentences aloud.

1. Comment ça va?
2. Comme ci, comme ça.
3. Vous êtes française, Madame?
4. C'est un garçon cruel et égoïste.
5. J'ai besoin d'être reçu à l'examen.
6. Caroline, ma sœur aînée, est très drôle.

Dictons Practice reading these sayings aloud.

Impossible n'est pas français.[1]

Plus ça change, plus c'est la même chose.[2]

[1] There's no such thing as "can't". (lit. *Impossible is not French.*)
[2] The more things change, the more they stay the same.

Section Goals

In this section, students will learn about:
- l'accent circonflexe
- la cédille
- le tréma
- a strategy for recognizing cognates

Key Standards

4.1

Suggestions
- Write the words **pâté, prêt, aîné, drôle,** and **croûton** on the board. Model the pronunciations and have students repeat. Explain that **l'accent circonflexe** can appear over any vowel. Repeat using examples with **la cédille** and **le tréma**.
- Have volunteers write **hôpital** and **forêt** on the board. Ask students what each means in English. As they respond, insert an **s** in the appropriate place above the French word. Then write these words and have students guess their meaning: **arrêter** (*to arrest*), **bête** (*beast*), **coûte** (*cost*), **île** (*isle, island*), and **Côte d'Ivoire** (*Ivory Coast*).
- Model the pronunciation of **mûr, mur,** and **sûr, sur**. Give students sentences with **mûr, mur, sûr,** or **sur** and ask them what the words mean based on the context. Examples: **1. Une grande carte est sur le mur. 2. J'ai raison; je suis sûr. 3. Les tomates ne sont pas mûres.**
- Write **comme ça** on the board and have students pronounce the words. Ask why **ça** needs **la cédille** and **comme** does not.
- The explanation and exercises are available on vhlcentral.com. You may want to play them in class so students hear French speakers besides yourself.

Dictons «Impossible n'est pas français» is a quote from Napoléon Bonaparte (1769–1821).

DIFFERENTIATION

For Visual Learners Write on the board the names of French personalities. Pronounce them and have the class repeat after you. Then show students each celebrity's photo and say his or her name. Show the photos a second time and ask the class to call out each name. Examples: **François Mitterrand (ancien président), Marie Laforêt (chanteuse), Jérôme Rothen (footballeur), Loïc Herbreteau (cycliste)**

EXPANSION

Synthesizing Have students work in pairs. Tell them to write three sentences using as many words as possible on this page with **l'accent circonflexe, la cédille,** and **le tréma**. Encourage students to be creative and even humorous. Then ask volunteers to share their sentences with the class.

On travaille chez moi! vhlcentral

PERSONNAGES

Amina

David

Rachid

Sandrine

Stéphane

Valérie

SANDRINE Alors, Rachid, où est David?

Un portable sonne (a cell phone rings)...

VALÉRIE Allô.

RACHID Allô.

AMINA Allô.

SANDRINE C'est Pascal! Je ne trouve pas mon téléphone!

AMINA Il n'est pas dans ton sac à dos?

SANDRINE Non!

RACHID Ben, il est sous tes cahiers.

SANDRINE Non plus!

AMINA Il est peut-être derrière ton livre... ou à gauche.

SANDRINE Mais non! Pas derrière! Pas à gauche! Pas à droite! Et pas devant!

RACHID Non! Il est là... sur la table. Mais non! La table à côté de la porte.

SANDRINE Ce n'est pas vrai! Ce n'est pas Pascal! Numéro de téléphone 06.62.70.94.87. Mais qui est-ce?

DAVID Sandrine? Elle est au café?

RACHID Oui... pourquoi?

DAVID Ben, j'ai besoin d'un bon café, oui, d'un café très fort. D'un espresso! À plus tard!

RACHID Tu sais, David, lui aussi, est pénible. Il parle de Sandrine. Sandrine, Sandrine, Sandrine.

RACHID ET STÉPHANE C'est barbant!

STÉPHANE C'est ta famille? C'est où?

RACHID En Algérie, l'année dernière chez mes grands-parents. Le reste de ma famille — mes parents, mes sœurs et mon frère, habitent à Marseille.

STÉPHANE C'est ton père, là?

RACHID Oui. Il est médecin. Il travaille beaucoup.

RACHID Et là, c'est ma mère. Elle, elle est avocate. Elle est très active... et très travailleuse aussi.

ACTIVITÉS

1 Identifiez Indicate which character would make each statement. The names may be used more than once. Write **D** for David, **R** for Rachid, **S** for Sandrine, and **St** for Stéphane.

1. J'ai envie d'être architecte. _St_

2. Numéro de téléphone 06.62.70.94.87. _S_

3. David est pénible. _R_

4. Stéphane! Tu n'es pas drôle! _S_

5. Que c'est ennuyeux! _St_

6. On travaille chez moi! _R_

7. Sandrine, elle est tellement pénible. _St_

8. Sandrine? Elle est au café? _D_

9. J'ai besoin d'un café très fort. _D_

10. C'est pour ça qu'on prepare le bac. _R_

Sandrine perd (*loses*) son téléphone.
Rachid aide Stéphane à préparer le bac.

STÉPHANE Qui est-ce? C'est moi!

SANDRINE Stéphane! Tu n'es pas drôle!

AMINA Oui, Stéphane. C'est cruel.

STÉPHANE C'est génial...

RACHID Bon, tu es prêt? On travaille chez moi!

À l'appartement de Rachid et de David...

STÉPHANE Sandrine, elle est tellement pénible. Elle parle de Pascal, elle téléphone à Pascal... Pascal, Pascal, Pascal! Que c'est ennuyeux!

RACHID Moi aussi, j'en ai marre.

STÉPHANE Avocate? Moi, j'ai envie d'être architecte.

RACHID Architecte? Alors, c'est pour ça qu'on prépare le bac.

Rachid et Stéphane au travail...

RACHID Allez, si *x* égale 83 et *y* égale 90, la réponse, c'est...

STÉPHANE Euh... 100?

RACHID Oui! Bravo!

Expressions utiles

Making complaints

- **Sandrine, elle est tellement pénible.**
  Sandrine is so tiresome.
- **J'en ai marre.**
  I'm fed up.
- **Tu sais, David, lui aussi, est pénible.**
  You know, David, he's tiresome, too.
- **C'est barbant!/C'est la barbe!**
  What a drag!

Reading numbers

- **Numéro de téléphone 06.62.70.94.87 (zéro six, soixante-deux, soixante-dix, quatre-vingt-quatorze, quatre-vingt-sept).**
  Phone number 06.62.70.94.87.
- **Si *x* égale 83 (quatre-vingt-trois) et *y* égale 90 (quatre-vingt-dix)...**
  If x equals 83 and y equals 90...
- **La réponse, c'est 100 (cent).**
  The answer is 100.

Expressing location

- **Où est le téléphone de Sandrine?**
  Where is Sandrine's telephone?
- **Il n'est pas dans son sac à dos.**
  It's not in her backpack.
- **Il est sous ses cahiers.**
  It's under her notebooks.
- **Il est derrière son livre, pas devant.**
  It's behind her book, not in front.
- **Il est à droite ou à gauche?**
  Is it to the right or to the left?
- **Il est sur la table à côté de la porte.**
  It's on the table next to the door.

---

2 Vocabulaire Refer to the video stills and dialogues to match these people and objects with their locations.

- a/c/e **1.** sur la table
- a **2.** pas sous les cahiers
- b/c/e **3.** devant Rachid
- b **4.** au café
- a/f **5.** à côté de la porte
- d **6.** en Algérie

- a. le téléphone de Sandrine
- b. Sandrine
- c. l'ordinateur de Rachid
- d. la famille de Rachid
- e. le café de Rachid
- f. la table

3 Écrivez In pairs, write a brief description in French of one of the video characters. Do not mention the character's name. Describe his or her personality traits, physical characteristics, and career path. Be prepared to read your description aloud to your classmates, who will guess the identity of the character.

ACTIVITÉS

cent treize **113**

AP® Theme: Families and Communities
Context: Friendship and Love

CULTURE À LA LOUPE

L'amitié

Section Goals

In this section, students will:
- learn to distinguish between different types of friendships
- learn some commonly used adjectives to describe people
- learn about marriage in the Francophone world
- read about the Cousteau family

Key Standards
2.1, 2.2, 3.1, 3.2, 4.2

 21st Century Skills

Global Awareness
Students will gain perspectives on the Francophone world to develop respect and openness to other cultures.

Culture à la loupe
Avant la lecture
- Introduce the reading topic by asking: **Avez-vous beaucoup de copains? Combien d'amis avez-vous? De quoi parlez-vous avec vos copains? Et avec vos amis?**
- Have students look at the photos and describe the people.
- Tell students to scan the reading, identify the cognates, and guess their meanings.

Lecture
- Point out that **un(e) petit(e) ami(e)** is the main term for boyfriend and girlfriend, but **mon ami(e)** or **mon copain/ma copine** alone without **petit(e)** can also imply a romantic relationship.
- Tell students that it is not uncommon to hear people describe their significant others as **fiancé(e)** even if they are not officially engaged.

Après la lecture Have students identify some differences in French and American dating customs.

1 Expansion Have students write two more true/false statements. Then tell them to exchange their papers with a classmate and complete the activity.

Pour les Français, l'amitié° est une valeur sûre. En effet, plus de 95% d'entre eux estiment° que l'amitié est importante pour leur équilibre personnel°, et les amis sont considérés par beaucoup comme une deuxième famille.

Quand on demande aux Français de décrire leurs amis, ils sont nombreux à dire que ceux-ci leur ressemblent. On les choisit selon son milieu°, ses valeurs, sa culture ou son mode de vie°.

Pour les Français, l'amitié ne doit pas être confondue° avec le copinage. Les copains, ce sont des personnes que l'on voit de temps en temps, avec lesquels on passe un bon moment, mais qu'on ne considère pas comme des personnes proches. Il peut s'agir de relations professionnelles ou de personnes qu'on fréquente° dans le cadre d'une activité commune: clubs sportifs, associations, etc. Quant aux° «vrais» amis, les Français disent en avoir seulement entre cinq et six.

Pour 6 Français sur 10, le facteur le plus important en amitié est la notion d'entraide°: on est prêt à presque tout pour aider ses amis. Viennent ensuite la fidélité et la communication. Mais attention, même si on se confie à ses amis en cas de problèmes, les amis ne sont pas là pour servir de psychologues.

Les Français considèrent aussi que l'amitié prend du temps et qu'elle est fragile. En effet, l'éloignement° et le manque de temps° peuvent lui nuire°. Mais c'est la trahison° que les Français jugent comme la première cause responsable de la fin d'une amitié.

Coup de main

To ask *what is* or *what are*, you can use **quel** and a form of the verb **être**. The different forms of **quel** agree in gender and number with the nouns to which they refer:

Quel/Quelle est...?
What is...?

Quels/Quelles sont...?
What are...?

amitié *friendship* **estiment** *consider* **équilibre personnel** *personal well-being* **milieu** *background, social standing* **mode de vie** *lifestyle* **confondue** *confused* **fréquente** *see* **Quant aux** *As for* **entraide** *mutual assistance* **éloignement** *distance* **manque de temps** *lack of time* **nuire** *to be detrimental* **trahison** *disloyalty*

A C T I V I T É S

1 **Vrai ou faux?** Are these statements **vrai** or **faux**?

1. Un copain est un très bon ami. Faux.
2. En général, les Français ont des amis très différents d'eux. Faux.
3. Les Français ont plus d'amis que (*than*) de copains. Faux.
4. On a une relation très solide avec un ami. Vrai.
5. Les Français pensent qu'on doit (*should*) toujours aider ses amis. Vrai.
6. Un ami écoute quand on a un problème. Vrai.

7. Pour les Français, rester amis est toujours facile. Faux.
8. Les amis sont là pour servir de psychologues si nécessaire. Faux.
9. Les Français pensent que les amis sont comme une deuxième famille. Vrai.
10. Une trahison peut détruire (*can destroy*) une amitié. Vrai.

TEACHING OPTIONS

Using Categories In small groups, have students draw a chart with three columns. Tell them to label the columns with the three main types of relationships between people: fellow students or coworkers (**les copains, les collègues**); intimate, platonic friends (**les amis**); and people that are boyfriend and girlfriend (**un[e] petit[e] ami[e]**). Then have students list at least five adjectives in each column in French that apply to the people in that type of relationship. Tell them that they can use adjectives from the reading or others that they know. Examples: **normal**, **ordinaire**, **intime**, **personnel**, **établi**, **profond**, **stable**, **solide**, and **éphémère**. When students have finished, ask different groups to read their lists of adjectives and compile the results on the board.

LE FRANÇAIS QUOTIDIEN

Pour décrire les gens

bête	*stupid*
borné(e)	*narrow-minded*
canon	*good-looking*
coincé(e)	*inhibited*
cool	*relaxed*
dingue	*crazy*
malin/maligne	*clever*
marrant(e)	*funny*
mignon(ne)	*cute*
zarbi	*weird*

LE MONDE FRANCOPHONE

Le mariage: Qu'est-ce qui est différent?

En France Les mariages sont toujours à la mairie°, en général le samedi après-midi. Beaucoup de couples vont° à l'église° juste après. Il y a un grand dîner le soir. Tous les amis et la famille sont invités.

Au Maroc Les amis de la mariée lui appliquent° du henné sur les mains°.

En Suisse Il n'y a pas de *bridesmaids* comme aux États-Unis mais il y a deux témoins°. En Suisse romande, la partie francophone du pays°, les traditions pour le mariage sont assez° similaires aux traditions en France.

mairie *city hall* **vont** *go* **église** *church* **lui appliquent** *apply* **henné sur les mains** *henna to the hands* **témoins** *witnesses* **pays** *country* **assez** *rather*

PORTRAIT

Les Cousteau

AP® Theme: Global Challenges
Context: Environmental Issues

Jacques-Yves Cousteau

L'océan est une passion pour les trois générations Cousteau. Le grand-père, Jacques-Yves (1910–1997), surnommé° le «Commandant Cousteau», a consacré sa vie° à l'exploration du monde sous-marin° et à sa préservation. Ses voyages télévisés à bord de son bateau° la *Calypso* l'ont rendu° célèbre partout dans le monde°. Ses fils Philippe et Jean-Michel ont continué ses efforts. Jean-Michel est le fondateur de l'association *Ocean Futures Society*, qui est dédiée à la protection des océans et à l'éducation. Même° les petits-enfants, Alexandra et Philippe Jr., ont hérité de la volonté de sauver° la planète. Ils défendent des causes environnementales avec leur organisation *Earth Echo International*.

Philippe, Jr.

Alexandra

surnommé *nicknamed* **consacré sa vie** *dedicated his life* **monde sous-marin** *underwater world* **bateau** *boat* **l'ont rendu** *made him* **partout dans le monde** *around the world* **Même** *Even* **ont hérité de la volonté de sauver** *inherited the desire to save*

Sur Internet

Quand ils sortent (*go out*), **où vont** (*go*) **les jeunes couples français?**

Go to **vhlcentral.com** to find more cultural information related to this **Culture** section.

---

2 **Les Cousteau** Complete these statements with the correct information.

1. La passion de la famille Cousteau est _____l'océan_____.

2. Les trois générations Cousteau ont dédié leur vie à l'exploration et à la __préservation/protection__ du monde sous-marin.

3. Le Commandant Cousteau est célèbre grâce à (*thanks to*) __ses voyages télévisées (à bord de la Calypso)__.

4. __Alexandra et Philippe, Jr.__ sont les petits-enfants du Commandant Cousteau.

3 **Comment sont-ils?** Look at the photos of the Cousteau family. With a partner, take turns describing each person in detail in French. How old do you think they are? What do you think their personalities are like? Do you see any family resemblances?

ACTIVITÉS

cent quinze **115**

Le français quotidien Have students work in pairs and take turns describing their friends or classmates using these words.

Portrait Show the class a photo of Jacques-Yves Cousteau. Ask: **Qui est-ce? Comment s'appelle-t-il? Quelle est sa profession?** Repeat the questions with photos of his two sons and two grandchildren. Then have students search online for more information about the Cousteau family. Have them find out what contributions each member has made to science, scuba diving, and to the protection of the environment, and report to the class.

Le monde francophone Ask students which difference they find most surprising and why. Then explain that not everyone in these countries follows these customs. As in the United States, wedding traditions often depend on the couple's religion.

21st Century Skills

Information and Media Literacy Students access and critically evaluate information from the Internet.

2 **Expansion** To check students' answers, have them work in pairs and take turns asking the questions that would elicit each statement and responding with the completed sentence.

3 **Expansions**
- Give students these dates of birth and have them calculate each person's age: Jean-Michel (1938), Philippe, Jr. (1980), Alexandra (1976).
- Philippe Cousteau, **père**, was a daring adventurer and explorer like his father, Jaques-Yves. He began scuba diving at age 4 and worked with his father much of his life. He died in an airplane crash in 1979 before the birth of his son Philippe, Jr.

EXPANSION

Le mariage: Qu'est-ce qui est différent? Share the following additional information about wedding customs or traditions with students.
- A traditional Moroccan wedding ceremony lasts from four to seven days. After the couple exchanges vows, the bride walks around the exterior of her new home three times.

- In Belgium, wedding invitations are traditionally printed on two sheets of paper—one sheet is from the bride's family and the other sheet is from the groom's family. The two sheets of paper symbolize the union of two families.

3B.1

Numbers 61–100 vhlcentral

Boîte à outils

Study tip: To say numbers **70–99**, remember the arithmetic behind them. For example, **quatre-vingt-douze (92)** is **4 (quatre)** x **20 (vingt)** + **12 (douze)**.

Numbers 61–100

61–69		80–89	
61	soixante et un	80	quatre-vingts
62	soixante-deux	81	quatre-vingt-un
63	soixante-trois	82	quatre-vingt-deux
64	soixante-quatre	83	quatre-vingt-trois
65	soixante-cinq	84	quatre-vingt-quatre
66	soixante-six	85	quatre-vingt-cinq
67	soixante-sept	86	quatre-vingt-six
68	soixante-huit	87	quatre-vingt-sept
69	soixante-neuf	88	quatre-vingt-huit
		89	quatre-vingt-neuf

70–79		90–100	
70	soixante-dix	90	quatre-vingt-dix
71	soixante et onze	91	quatre-vingt-onze
72	soixante-douze	92	quatre-vingt-douze
73	soixante-treize	93	quatre-vingt-treize
74	soixante-quatorze	94	quatre-vingt-quatorze
75	soixante-quinze	95	quatre-vingt-quinze
76	soixante-seize	96	quatre-vingt-seize
77	soixante-dix-sept	97	quatre-vingt-dix-sept
78	soixante-dix-huit	98	quatre-vingt-dix-huit
79	soixante-dix-neuf	99	quatre-vingt-dix-neuf
		100	cent

- Numbers that end in the digit **1** are not usually hyphenated. They use the conjunction **et** instead.

  trente et un   cinquante et un   soixante et un

- Note that **81** and **91** are exceptions:

  quatre-vingt-un   quatre-vingt-onze

- The number **quatre-vingts** ends in -s, but there is no -s when it is followed by another number.

  quatre-vingts   quatre-vingt-cinq   quatre-vingt-dix-huit

Essayez! What are these numbers in French?

1. 67 _soixante-sept_
2. 75 _soixante-quinze_
3. 99 _quatre-vingt-dix-neuf_
4. 70 _soixante-dix_
5. 82 _quatre-vingt-deux_
6. 91 _quatre-vingt-onze_
7. 66 _soixante-six_
8. 87 _quatre-vingt-sept_
9. 80 _quatre-vingts_
10. 60 _soixante_

Le français vivant
- Call on a volunteer to read the catalogue page aloud. Point out the prices in euros.
- Ask students: **Combien d'objets y a-t-il sur la photo?**

Le français vivant

As-tu envie d'être

ingénieur, musicien, architecte, professeur?

le sac à dos 70€

le bureau 96€

la calculatrice 61€

la chaise 82€

Tu as besoin d'une calculatrice intelligente, d'un beau bureau, d'une chaise confortable et d'un bon sac à dos.

Tu trouves tout dans le Catalogue AAZ!

Identifiez Scan this catalogue page, and identify the instances where the numbers 61–100 are used. Answers will vary.

 Questions Answers will vary.

1. Qui sont les personnes sur la photo?
2. Où (*Where*) est-ce qu'elles habitent?
3. Qu'est-ce qu'elles ont dans leur maison?
4. Quels autres (*other*) objets trouve-t-on dans le Catalogue AAZ? (Imaginez.)
5. Quels sont leurs prix (*prices*)?

Mise en pratique

1 Les numéros de téléphone Write down these phone numbers, then read them aloud in French.

MODÈLE

C'est le zéro un, quarante-trois, soixante-quinze, quatre-vingt-trois, seize.
01.43.75.83.16

1. C'est le zéro deux, soixante-cinq, trente-trois, quatre-vingt-quinze, zéro six.
02.65.33.95.06

2. C'est le zéro un, quatre-vingt-dix-neuf, soixante-quatorze, quinze, vingt-cinq.
01.99.74.15.25

3. C'est le zéro cinq, soixante-cinq, onze, zéro huit, quatre-vingts.
05.65.11.08.80

4. C'est le zéro trois, quatre-vingt-dix-sept, soixante-dix-neuf, cinquante-quatre, vingt-sept.
03.97.79.54.27

5. C'est le zéro quatre, quatre-vingt-cinq, soixante-neuf, quatre-vingt-dix-neuf, quatre-vingt-onze.
04.85.69.99.91

6. C'est le zéro un, vingt-quatre, quatre-vingt-trois, zéro un, quatre-vingt-neuf.
01.24.83.01.89

7. C'est le zéro deux, quarante et un, soixante et onze, douze, soixante.
02.41.71.12.60

8. C'est le zéro quatre, cinquante-huit, zéro neuf, quatre-vingt-dix-sept, treize.
04.58.09.97.13

2 Les maths Read these math problems, then write out each answer in words.

MODÈLE

$65 + 3 =$ _soixante-huit_

1. $70 + 15 =$ quatre-vingt-cinq
2. $82 + 10 =$ quatre-vingt-douze
3. $76 + 3 =$ soixante-dix-neuf
4. $88 + 12 =$ cent
5. $40 + 27 =$ soixante-sept

6. $67 + 6 =$ soixante-treize
7. $43 + 54 =$ quatre-vingt-dix-sept
8. $78 + 5 =$ quatre-vingt-trois
9. $70 + 20 =$ quatre-vingt-dix
10. $64 + 16 =$ quatre-vingts

3 Comptez Write out the missing number in the following patterns.

1. 62, 64, 66, ... 70   soixante-huit
2. 80, 84, 88, ... 96   quatre-vingt-douze
3. 40, 50, 60, ... 80   soixante-dix
4. 81, 83, 85, ... 89   quatre-vingt-sept

5. 90, 85, 80, ... 70   soixante-quinze
6. 55, 57, 59, ... 63   soixante-et-un
7. 100, 93, 86, ... 72   soixante-dix-neuf
8. 99, 96, 93, ... 87   quatre-vingt-dix

---

1 Expansions
• Model the question: **Quel est ton numéro de téléphone?** Then have students circulate around the room asking each other their phone numbers. Tell them to write the person's number next to his or her name and have the person verify it.
• Dictate actual phone numbers to the class and tell them to write the numerals. Examples: your office number, the school's number, etc.

2 Suggestion To go over the answers, have students read each math problem aloud while a volunteer writes them on the board for the class to check.

2 Expansion Have each student write five more addition or subtraction problems. Then have students work in pairs and take turns reading their problems aloud while the other person says the answer.

3 Expansion Tell students to write three additional series of numbers. Then have them exchange papers with a classmate and take turns reading the series and filling in the numbers.

DIFFERENTIATION

For Kinesthetic Learners Write number patterns on cards (one number per card) and distribute them among the class. Begin a number chain by calling out **the first three numbers in the pattern.** Ex: **vingt-cinq, cinquante, soixante-quinze.** The students holding these cards have five seconds to get up and stand in front of the class. The rest of the class continues by calling out the numbers in the pattern for the students to join the

EXPANSION

chain. Continue until the chain is broken or complete; then begin a new pattern.

Extra Practice Write the beginning of a series of numbers on the board and have students continue the sequence out loud. Ex: **50, 55, 60...** or **77, 80, 83, 86...**

Communication

4 **Questions indiscrètes** With a partner, take turns asking how old these people are. *Answers will vary.*

M. Hubert
Mme Hubert
M. Moreau
Mme Moreau
M. Durand
Mme Durand

MODÈLE

Élève 1: *Madame Hubert a quel âge?*
Élève 2: *Elle a 70 ans.*

5 **Qui est-ce?** Interview as many classmates as you can in five minutes to find out the name, relationship, and age of their oldest family member. Identify the student with the oldest family member to the class. *Answers will vary.*

MODÈLE

Élève 1: *Qui est le plus vieux (the oldest) dans ta famille?*
Élève 2: *C'est ma tante Julie. Elle a soixante-dix ans.*

6 **Fournitures scolaires** Take turns playing the role of a store employee ordering the school supplies (**fournitures scolaires**) below. Tell how many of each item you need. Your partner will write down the number of items ordered. Switch roles when you're done. *Answers will vary.*

MODÈLE

Élève 1: *Vous avez besoin de combien de crayons?*
Élève 2: *J'ai besoin de soixante-dix crayons.*

1. _____
2. _____
3. _____
4. _____

5. _____
6. _____
7. _____
8. _____

4 Expansion To review descriptive adjectives, have students describe the people in the drawing.

4 Virtual Chat You can also assign Activity 4 on vhlcentral.com. Students record individual responses that appear in your gradebook.

5 Suggestions
• Have two volunteers read the **modèle**.
• You may wish to provide a few supplementary terms for family members, such as **l'arrière-grand-mère** and **l'arrière-grand-père**.
• Ask various students to identify the person who has the oldest family member from their interviews. Continue until students identify the oldest person among all the families.

6 Suggestion Tell students that they should choose a number between 60–100 for each item. After all items are complete, have students read back their list to their partner to check accuracy.

Activity Pack For additional activities, go to the **Activity Pack** in the **Resources** section of vhlcentral.com.

EXPANSION

Extra Practice Ask students to write down their phone numbers on a slip of paper. Collect the papers. Tell students to say **«C'est mon numéro de téléphone!»** when they hear their number. Then proceed to read the numbers aloud at random.

TEACHING OPTIONS

Game Play a game of Bingo. Have students draw a square on a sheet of paper with three horizontal and three vertical rows. Tell them to write nine different numbers between 61–100 in the boxes. Explain that they should cross out the numbers as they hear them and that they should say "Bingo!" if they have three numbers in a horizontal, vertical, or diagonal row. Then call out numbers at random and write them down to verify.

119

Section Goals

In this section, students will learn:
- prepositions of location
- disjunctive pronouns

Key Standards
4.1, 5.1

Suggestions: Scaffolding

- Ask students what the prepositions **à**, **en**, and **de** mean and where they have seen them before. (**à bientôt**, **à** + *time*, **être de**, **en classe**, etc.) Then, present **Point de départ**.
- Present the prepositions of location by placing an object, perhaps a stuffed animal, in different locations. Then go over remaining bullet points on this page.
- Remind students that they may need to use the contractions **du** and **des**.
- Take a book or other object and place it in various locations in relation to your desk or a student's desk as you ask individual students about its location. Examples: **Où est le livre? Est-ce qu'il est derrière le bureau? Quel objet est à côté du livre?** Work through various locations, eliciting all prepositions of location. Have students complete the **Vérifiez** activity.
- Note: The Grammar Tutorial discusses using the prepositions **à** and **en** with geographical locations, but the textbook will not be focusing on this concept here. If you wish to teach these prepositions, point out that **à** is used before cities to indicate *in* or *to*, **en** is used before continents, feminine countries and masculine countries beginning with a vowel sound, **au** is used before masculine singular countries, and **aux** before masculine plural countries. **D'accord! 3** will cover this topic in greater detail.

3B.2 Prepositions of location and vhlcentral disjunctive pronouns

Point de départ You have already learned expressions in French containing prepositions like **à**, **de**, and **en**. Prepositions of location describe the location of something or someone, often in relation to something or someone else.

Prepositions of location

à côté de	*next to*	**en face de**	*facing, across from*
à droite de	*to the right of*	**entre**	*between*
à gauche de	*to the left of*	**loin de**	*far from*
dans	*in*	**près de**	*close to, near*
derrière	*behind*	**sous**	*under*
devant	*in front of*	**sur**	*on*
en	*in*		

La librairie est **derrière** le lycée
The bookstore is behind the high school.

Ma maison est **loin de** la ville.
My house is far from town.

- When a preposition of location ends in **de** and is followed by **le** and **les**, remember that it contracts to form **du** and **des** respectively. There is no change when **de** is followed by **la** or **l'**.

  La cantine est **à côté du** gymnase.
  The cafeteria is next to the gym.

  Notre chien aime manger **près des** fenêtres.
  Our dog likes to eat near the windows.

  Ils sont **à gauche de** la bibliothèque.
  They're in front of the library.

  Le café est **à droite de** l'hôtel.
  The café is to the right of the hotel.

- You can further modify prepositions of location by using intensifiers, such as **tout** (*very, really*) and **juste** (*just, right*).

  Ma sœur habite **juste en face de** l'université.
  My sister lives right across from the university.

  Le lycée est **juste derrière** son appartement.
  The high school is just behind his apartment.

  Eva travaille **tout près de la** librairie.
  Eva works really close to the bookstore.

  La librairie est **tout à côté du** café.
  The bookstore is right next to the café.

- You may use a preposition without the word **de** *if it is not followed by a noun.*

  Ma sœur habite **juste à côté**.
  My sister lives right next door.

  Elle travaille **tout près**.
  She works really close by.

🏃 Boîte à outils

You can also use the prepositions **derrière** and **devant** without a following noun.

Le chien habite derrière.
The dog lives out back.

However, a noun must always follow the prepositions **dans**, **en**, **entre**, **par**, **sous**, and **sur**.

∿ Vérifiez

Il n'est pas sous les cahiers.

Pas derrière! Pas à droite!

EXPANSION

Extra Practice Ask where different students are in relation to one another. Example:___ , où est ___? (Il/Elle est à côté de [à droite de, à gauche de, derrière] ___.)

TEACHING OPTIONS

For Kinesthetic Learners On the board, write a number of prepositions, such as **à droite de**, **derrière**, and **entre**. Have students pass around an object. Each time the object gets moved, ask a volunteer to describe where it is using a preposition. Ex: **Le livre est à droite de Marie. Le livre est entre le stylo et le dictionnaire.**

- The preposition **chez** has no exact English equivalent. It expresses the idea of *at* or *to someone's house* or *place*.

  Louise étudie **chez Arnaud**.
  Louise is studying at Arnaud's.

  Laurent est **chez sa cousine**.
  Laurent is at his cousin's.

- The preposition **chez** is also used to express the idea of *at* or *to a professional's office* or *business*.

  chez le docteur
  at the doctor's

  chez la coiffeuse
  to the hairdresser's

On travaille chez moi!

Stéphane est chez Rachid.

Disjunctive pronouns

When you want to use a pronoun after any type of preposition, you need to use what is called a disjunctive pronoun, not a subject pronoun.

Disjunctive pronouns			
singular		**plural**	
je → moi		nous → nous	
tu → toi		vous → vous	
il → lui		ils → eux	
elle → elle		elles → elles	

Maryse travaille **à côté de moi**.
Maryse is working next to me.

Nous pensons **à toi**.
We're thinking about you.

Tu as besoin **d'elle** aujourd'hui?
Do you need her today?

J'aime mieux dîner **chez vous**.
I prefer to have dinner at your house.

Voilà ma cousine Lise, **devant nous**.
There's my cousin Lise, in front of us.

Vous n'avez pas peur **d'eux**.
You're not afraid of them.

∽ Vérifiez

Essayez! **Complete each sentence with the equivalent of the expression in parentheses.**

1. La librairie est ___derrière___ (*behind*) la cantine.

2. J'habite ___près de___ (*close to*) leur lycée.

3. Le laboratoire est ___à côté de___ (*next to*) ma résidence.

4. Tu retournes ___chez___ (*to the house of*) tes parents ce week-end?

5. La fenêtre est ___en face de___ (*across from*) la porte.

6. Mon sac à dos est ___sous___ (*under*) la chaise.

7. Ses crayons sont ___sur___ (*on*) la table.

8. Votre ordinateur est ___dans___ (*in*) la corbeille!

9. Il n'y a pas de secrets ___entre___ (*between*) amis.

10. Le professeur est ___devant___ (*in front of*) les élèves.

cent vingt et un **121**

Suggestions: Scaffolding

- Write the following in a column on the board and explain each usage of **chez**: chez + *person's name or person* (**chez Rachid, chez des amis**); **chez** + *professional's office or business* (**chez le docteur**); and **chez** + *disjunctive pronoun* (**chez toi**).

- Model the pronunciation of the disjunctive pronouns and have students repeat them. Explain that these pronouns are used in prepositional phrases. Examples: **1. Ma famille vient** (*comes*) **souvent chez moi. 2. Je suis en face de toi.** Then ask volunteers for examples.

- Compare sentences with subject pronouns and disjunctive pronouns to help students understand when to use each. On the board, write: **Mon ami est français. ____ parle français. Je travaille chez ____ le week-end.** Ask students to fill in the blanks. Highlight that the first blank, which precedes a verb, requires a subject pronoun while the second, which follows a preposition, must be filled with a disjunctive pronoun. Give other examples.

- Point out the disjunctive pronouns are also used with conjunctions, such as **et** and **ou: toi et moi, elle ou lui**.

Essayez! Have students write three more fill-in-the-blank sentences describing where certain objects are located in their family's house or apartment. Then tell them to exchange papers with a classmate and complete the sentences.

DIFFERENTIATION

For Kinesthetic Learners Have one student start with a small beanbag or rubber ball. You call out another student identified only by his or her location with reference to other students. Example: **C'est la personne derrière ___.** The student with the beanbag or ball has to throw it to the student identified. The latter student must then throw the object to the next person you identify.

EXPANSION

Video Show the video episode again to give students more input using prepositions and disjunctive pronouns. Stop the video where appropriate to discuss how the prepositions of location and disjunctive pronouns were used. Ask comprehension questions.

Suggestion To check students' answers, have them work in pairs and take turns asking the completed questions and answering them in the affirmative or negative.

Suggestion Before students begin the activity, have them identify the people, places, and other objects in the drawing. Example: **Il y a un oiseau.**

Expansion Have students create additional sentences about the location of the people or objects in the drawing. To practice negation, have students describe where the people and other objects are not located. Example: **La famille n'est pas devant la bibliothèque.**

Mise en pratique

1 **Où est ma montre?** Claude has lost her watch. Choose the appropriate prepositions to complete her friend Pauline's questions.

MODÈLE

Elle est (*à gauche du* / entre le) livre?

1. Elle est (sur / entre) le bureau? sur
2. Elle est (chez / derrière) la télévision? derrière
3. Elle est (entre / dans) le lit et la table? entre
4. Elle est (dans / sous) la chaise? sous

5. Elle est (sur / à côté de) la fenêtre? à côté de
6. Elle est (près du / entre le) sac à dos? près du
7. Elle est (devant / sur) la porte? devant
8. Elle est (dans / sous) la corbeille? dans

2 **Complétez** Look at the drawing, and complete these sentences with the appropriate prepositions. Suggested answers

MODÈLE

Nous sommes _chez_ nos cousins.

1. Nous sommes __devant__ la maison de notre tante.
2. Michel est __loin de__ Béatrice.
3. __Entre__ Jasmine et Laure, il y a le petit cousin, Adrien.
4. Béatrice est __à côté de/à droite de__ Jasmine.
5. Jasmine est tout __près de__ Béatrice.
6. Michel est __derrière__ Laure.
7. Un oiseau est __sur__ la maison.
8. Laure est __à gauche/à côté d'__ Adrien.

Michel   Laure   Adrien   Jasmine   Béatrice

3 **Où est-on?** Tell where these people, animals, and things are in relation to each other. Replace the second noun or pronoun with the appropriate disjunctive pronoun. Answers will vary. Possible answers:

▶ **MODÈLE**
Alex / Anne
Alex est à droite d'elle.

1. _____
2. _____

3. _____   4. _____   5. _____   6. _____

1. l'oiseau / je   L'oiseau est loin de moi.
2. le chien / Gabrielle et Emma   Le chien est entre elles.
3. le monument / tu   Le monument est en face de toi.

4. l'ordinateur / Ousmane   L'ordinateur est devant lui.
5. Mme Fleury / Max et Élodie   Mme Fleury est derrière eux.
6. les enfants / la grand-mère   Les enfants sont près d'elle.

TEACHING OPTIONS

Extra Practice Have students make labels for objects in the classroom using the prepositional expressions they have learned in this lesson. Have them place the labels as they tell where the objects are located. Example: **La carte est à côté de la fenêtre.**

DIFFERENTIATION

For Visual Learners Bring in magazine photos or illustrations showing people or objects in different locations. As you show the images to the class, ask the students where the people or objects are located. They should use prepositions in their answers. Ex: **La femme est sous l'arbre; le chat est à droite de la maison.**

Communication

4 **Où est l'objet?** In pairs, take turns asking where these items are in the classroom. Use prepositions of location. Answers will vary.

MODÈLE la carte

Élève 1: *Où est la carte?*
Élève 2: *Elle est devant la classe.*

1. l'horloge
2. l'ordinateur
3. le tableau
4. la fenêtre
5. le bureau du professeur
6. ton livre de français
7. la corbeille
8. la porte

5 **Qui est-ce?** Choose someone in the room. The rest of the class will guess whom you chose by asking yes/no questions that use prepositions of location. Answers will vary.

MODÈLE

Est-ce qu'il/elle est à côté de toi?
Est-ce qu'il/elle est entre Jean-Pierre et Suzanne?

6 **S'il vous plaît...?** A tourist stops someone on the street to ask where certain places are located. In pairs, play these roles using the map to locate the places. Answers will vary.

MODÈLE

Élève 1: *La banque, s'il vous plaît?*
Élève 2: *Elle est en face de l'hôpital.*

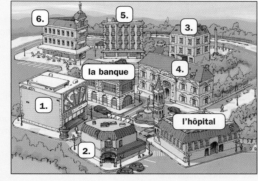

1. le cinéma Ambassadeur
2. le restaurant Chez Marlène
3. la librairie Antoine
4. le lycée Camus
5. l'hôtel Royal
6. le café de la Place

7 **Ma ville** In pairs, take turns telling your partner where the places below are located in your town or neighborhood. Correct your partner when you disagree. Answers will vary.

MODÈLE

la banque
La banque est tout près du cinéma.

1. le café
2. la librairie
3. le lycée
4. le gymnase
5. l'hôtel
6. la bibliothèque
7. l'hôpital
8. le restaurant italien

4 Suggestion Have two volunteers read the **modèle** aloud. Remind students to pay attention to the gender of the nouns when responding.

4 Expansion For additional practice, give students these items if they are present in the classroom. **9. le dictionnaire de français 10. la calculatrice 11. les examens**

5 Suggestion To continue this activity, allow the student who guessed the correct person to choose another person and have the class ask the student yes/no questions.

6 Suggestion Before students begin this activity, make sure they understand that the numbers on the illustration correspond to the places on the list. Have two volunteers read the **modèle** aloud.

6 Virtual Chat You can also assign Activity 6 on vhlcentral.com. Students record individual responses that appear in your gradebook.

7 Suggestion Students could even draw a rough map of the town based on their partner's description. They should first situate your school before they draw the other places.

Activity Pack For additional activities, go to the **Activity Pack** in the **Resources** section of vhlcentral.com.

TEACHING OPTIONS

Small Groups In groups of three or four, have students think of a city or town within a 100-mile radius of your school. They need to figure out how many miles away it is and what other cities or towns are nearby (**La ville est près de...**) and write a description. Then have them get together with another group and read their descriptions. The other group has to guess which city or town is being described.

EXPANSION

Extra Practice Have students look at the world maps in the frontmatter at the beginning of this book, or use the digital images. Make true/false statements about the locations of various countries. Examples: **1. La Chine est près des États-Unis. (Faux.) 2. Le Luxembourg est entre la France et l'Allemagne. (Vrai.)** For variation, you can make statements or ask true/false questions about the location of various cities in France.

123

Révision

1 Le basket These college basketball rivals are competing for the title. In pairs, predict the missing playoff scores. Then, compare your predictions with those of another pair. Be prepared to share your predictions with the class. *Answers will vary.*

1. Ohio State 76, Michigan _____
2. Florida _____, Florida State 84
3. Stanford _____, UCLA 79
4. Purdue 81, Indiana _____
5. Duke 100, Virginia _____
6. Kansas 95, Colorado _____
7. Texas _____, Oklahoma 88
8. Kentucky 98, Tennessee _____

2 La famille d'Édouard In pairs, take turns describing the members of Édouard's family and where they are in relationship to one another in the photo. *Answers will vary.*

MODÈLE

Le père d'Édouard est derrière sa mère. Il est gentil et drôle.

Édouard

3 La ville In pairs, take turns describing the location of a building (**un bâtiment**) somewhere in your town or city. Your partner must guess which building you are describing in three tries. Keep score to determine the winner after several rounds.

MODÈLE *Answers will vary.*

Élève 1: *C'est un bâtiment entre la banque et le lycée.*
Élève 2: *C'est l'hôpital?*
Élève 1: *C'est ça!*

4 C'est quel numéro? You are looking up phone numbers for your grandmother who needs help from several professionals. Take turns role-playing by asking and answering questions using the phone numbers below. *Answers will vary.*

MODÈLE

Élève 1: *Je cherche un artiste.*
Élève 2: *C'est le zéro quatre...*

Profession	Numéro de téléphone
architecte	04.70.65.74.92
artiste	04.76.72.63.85
coiffeuse	04.61.84.79.64
professeur d'anglais	04.06.99.90.82
avocat	04.25.86.66.93
dentiste	04.42.75.99.80
médecin	04.15.61.88.91
ingénieur	04.57.68.96.81
journaliste	04.33.70.83.97

5 À la librairie In pairs, role-play a customer at a bookstore and a clerk who points out where supplies are located. Then, switch roles. Each turn, the customer picks four items from the list. Use the drawing to find the supplies. *Answers will vary.*

MODÈLE

Élève 1: *Je cherche des stylos.*
Élève 2: *Ils sont à côté des cahiers.*

des cahiers	un dictionnaire
une calculatrice	un iPhone®
une carte	du papier
des crayons	un sac à dos

6 Trouvez Your teacher will give you and your partner each a drawing of a family picnic. Ask each other questions to find out where all of the family members are located. *Answers will vary.*

MODÈLE

Élève 1: *Qui est à côté du père?*
Élève 2: *Le neveu est à côté du père.*

À l'écoute vhlcentral

STRATÉGIE

Asking for repetition/ Replaying the recording

Sometimes it is difficult to understand what people say, especially in a noisy environment. During a conversation, you can ask someone to repeat by asking **Comment?** (*What?*) or **Pardon?** (*Pardon me?*). In class, you can ask your teacher to repeat by saying, **Répétez, s'il vous plaît** (*Repeat, please*). If you don't understand a recorded activity, you can simply replay it.

To help you practice this strategy, you will listen to a short paragraph. Ask your teacher to repeat it or replay the recording, and then summarize what you heard.

Préparation

Based on the photograph, where do you think Suzanne and Diane are? What do you think they are talking about?

À vous d'écouter

Now you are going to hear Suzanne and Diane's conversation. Use **R** to indicate adjectives that describe Suzanne's boyfriend, Robert. Use **E** for adjectives that describe Diane's boyfriend, Édouard. Some adjectives will not be used.

_E_	brun	_R_	optimiste
___	laid	_E_	intelligent
_E_	grand	___	blond
_E_	intéressant	_E_	beau
_E_	gentil	_E_	sympathique
_R_	drôle	_R_	patient

Compréhension

Identifiez-les Whom do these statements describe?

1. Elle a un problème avec un garçon. _Diane_
2. Il ne parle pas à Diane. _Édouard_
3. Elle a de la chance. _Suzanne_
4. Ils parlent souvent. _Suzanne et Robert_
5. Il est sympa. _Robert_
6. Il est timide. _Édouard_

Vrai ou faux? Indicate whether each sentence is **vrai** or **faux**, then correct any false statements.

1. Édouard est un garçon très patient et optimiste.
   Faux. Robert est très patient et optimiste.

2. Diane pense que Suzanne a de la chance.
   Vrai.

3. Suzanne et son petit ami parlent de tout.
   Vrai.

4. Édouard parle souvent à Diane.
   Faux. Édouard ne parle pas à Diane.

5. Robert est peut-être un peu timide.
   Faux. Édouard est peut-être un peu timide.

6. Suzanne parle de beaucoup de choses avec Robert.
   Vrai.

cent vingt-cinq **125**

Section Goals

In this section, students will:
• learn to ask for repetition in oral communication
• listen to and summarize a short paragraph
• listen to a conversation and complete several activities

Key Standards
1.2, 2.1

21st Century Skills

Critical Thinking and Problem Solving
Students practice aural comprehension as a tool to negotiate meaning in French.

Stratégie
Script Bonjour, je m'appelle Christine Dupont. Je suis médecin et mère de famille. Mon mari, Richard, est ingénieur. Il est intelligent et très drôle aussi. Nous avons trois enfants charmants: deux fils et une fille. Les garçons sont roux et notre fille est blonde. Notre fils aîné, Marc, a 17 ans. Le cadet, Pascal, a 15 ans. Leur petite sœur, Véronique, a 12 ans.
Teacher Resources DVD

Préparation Before students do the activity, tell them to look at the photo and describe what they see. Ask students to justify their responses based on visual clues in the photo.

Suggestion To check students' answers for the **À vous d'écouter** activity, have them work in pairs and take turns asking and answering questions using the adjectives listed. Example:
Est-ce que Robert est brun?
Non, Édouard est brun.

À vous d'écouter
Script
SUZANNE: Salut, Diane. Est-ce que ça va?
DIANE: Oh, comme ci, comme ça. J'ai un petit problème. Ce n'est pas grand-chose, mais…
S: Quel genre de problème?
D: Tu sais que j'aime bien Édouard.

S: Oui.
D: Le problème, c'est qu'il ne me parle pas!
S: Il t'aime bien aussi. Il est peut-être un peu timide?
D: Tu crois? …Il est si beau! Grand, brun… Et puis, il est gentil, très intelligent et aussi très intéressant. Et Robert et toi, comment ça va?
S: Euh… plutôt bien. Robert est sympa. Je l'aime

beaucoup. Il est patient, optimiste et très drôle.
D: Vous parlez souvent?
S: Oui. Nous parlons deux à trois heures par jour. Nous parlons de beaucoup de choses! De nos cours, de nos amis, de nos familles… de tout.
D: C'est super! Tu as de la chance.
Teacher Resources DVD

vhlcentral

Panorama

La Belgique

Le pays en chiffres

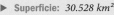

▶ **Superficie:** *30.528 km²*

▶ **Population:** *11.299.000*
SOURCE: Population Division, UN Secretariat

▶ **Industries principales:** *agroalimentaire°, chimie, textile*

▶ **Ville capitale:** *Bruxelles*

▶ **Monnaie:** *l'euro*

▶ **Langues:** *allemand, français, flamand°*

Environ° 60% de la population belge parle flamand et habite dans la partie nord°. Le français est parlé surtout dans le sud°, par environ 40% des Belges.

La Suisse

Le pays en chiffres

▶ **Superficie:** *41.285 km²*

▶ **Population:** *8.299.000*
SOURCE: Population Division, UN Secretariat

▶ **Industries principales:** *activités financières, agroalimentaire, horlogerie°*

▶ **Ville capitale:** *Berne*

▶ **Monnaie:** *le franc suisse*

▶ **Langues:** *allemand, français, italien, romanche*

L' allemand, le français et l'italien sont les langues officielles. Le romanche, langue d'origine latine, est parlé dans l'est° du pays.

Personnages célèbres

▶ **Roger Federer,** *Suisse, joueur de tennis, (1981–)*

▶ **Jean-Luc Godard,** *Suisse, cinéaste (1930–)*

▶ **Amélie Nothomb,** *Belgique, écrivaine (1966–)*

agroalimentaire *food processing* **flamand** *Flemish* **Environ** *About* **nord** *north* **sud** *south* **horlogerie** *watch and clock making* **est** *east* **Battue** *Defeated* **paix** *peace* **reconnu** *recognized* **depuis** *since* **aucune guerre** *any war* **ni** *nor* **OTAN** *NATO*

L'hôtel de ville de Mons

le château de Chillon sur le lac Léman

LA MER DU NORD · Ostende · Bruges · Gand · LA FLANDRE · Anvers · LES PAYS-BAS · Bruxelles · LA BELGIQUE · Mons · Charleroi · Liège · Namur · LES ARDENNES · LA WALLONIE · LE LUXEMBOURG · L'ALLEMAGNE · LA FRANCE · Bâle · Zurich · Saint-Gall · L'AUTR · LE LIECHTEN · La Chaux-de-Fonds · Neuchâtel · Berne · Fribourg · Lucerne · LES ALPES · LE JURA · Lausanne · LA SUISSE · Montreux · Genève · Lugano · L'ITALIE · le lac de Constance · le lac de Zurich · le lac de Neuchâtel · le lac Léman · le Tessin · le lac Majeur · le lac de Côme · le Rhin · le Danube · la Meuse · le Lys · l'Escaut · la Sambre · la Marne · le Doubs · le Rhône · la Loire

Régions francophones
0 — 50 milles
0 — 50 kilomètres

Incroyable mais vrai!

Battue° par la France en 1515, la Suisse signe une paix° perpétuelle et adopte une politique de neutralité. Ce statut est reconnu° par les autres nations européennes en 1815 et, depuis°, la Suisse ne participe à aucune guerre° ni° alliance militaire, comme l'OTAN°.

AP® Theme: Contemporary Life
Context: Travel

Les destinations

Bruxelles, capitale de l'Europe

Fondée au septième siècle, la ville de Bruxelles a été choisie° en 1958, en partie pour sa situation géographique centrale, comme siège° de la C.E.E.° Aujourd'hui, elle reste encore le siège de l'Union européenne (l'U.E.), lieu central des institutions et des décisions européennes. On y trouve le Parlement européen, organe législatif de l'U.E., et depuis 1967, le siège de l'OTAN°. Bruxelles est une ville très cosmopolite, avec un grand nombre d'habitants étrangers. Elle est aussi touristique, renommée pour sa Grand-Place, ses nombreux chocolatiers et la grande qualité de sa cuisine.

AP® Theme: Beauty and Aesthetics
Context: Literature

Les traditions

La bande dessinée°

Les dessinateurs° de bandes dessinées (BD) sont très nombreux en Belgique. À Bruxelles, il y a de nombreuses peintures murales° et statues de BD. Le dessinateur Peyo est devenu célèbre avec la création des Schtroumpfs° en 1958, mais le père de la BD belge est Hergé, dessinateur qui a créé Tintin et Milou en 1929. Tintin est un reporter qui a des aventures partout dans° le monde. En 1953, il devient le premier homme, avant Neil Armstrong, à marcher sur la Lune° dans *On a marché sur la Lune*. La BD de Tintin est traduite en 45 langues.

L'économie

AP® Theme: Global Challenges
Context: Economic Issues

Des montres et des banques

L'économie suisse se caractérise par la présence de grandes entreprises° multinationales et par son secteur financier. Les multinationales sont particulièrement actives dans le domaine des banques, des assurances, de l'agroalimentaire (Nestlé), de l'industrie pharmaceutique et de l'horlogerie (Longines, Rolex, Swatch). Cinquante pour cent de la production mondiale° d'articles° d'horlogerie viennent de Suisse. Le franc suisse est une des monnaies les plus stables du monde et les banques suisses ont la réputation de bien gérer° les fortunes de leurs clients.

Les gens

AP® Theme: Global Challenges
Context: Economic Issues

Jean-Jacques Rousseau (1712–1778)

Né à Genève, Jean-Jacques Rousseau a passé sa vie entre la France et la Suisse. Vagabond et autodidacte°, Rousseau est devenu écrivain, philosophe, théoricien politique et musicien. Il a comme principe° que l'homme naît bon et que c'est la société qui le corrompt°. Défenseur de la tolérance religieuse et de la liberté de pensée, les idées de Rousseau, exprimées° principalement dans son œuvre° *Du contrat social*, se retrouvent° dans la Révolution française. À la fin de sa vie, il écrit *Les Confessions*, son autobiographie, un genre nouveau pour l'époque°.

Qu'est-ce que vous avez appris? Répondez aux questions.

1. Quelles sont les langues officielles de la Suisse?
   L'allemand, le français et l'italien.
2. Quels sont les secteurs importants de l'économie suisse?
   Le secteur financier, l'agroalimentaire, l'industrie pharmaceutique et l'horlogerie.
3. Quelles sont les valeurs défendues (*values defended*) par Rousseau? La tolérance religieuse et la liberté de pensée.
4. Quel événement a été influencé par les idées de Rousseau?
   La Révolution française.
5. Quelles sont les langues officielles de la Belgique?
   Le flamand, le français et l'allemand.

6. Pourquoi Bruxelles a-t-elle été choisie comme capitale de l'Europe? Pour sa situation géographique centrale en Europe.
7. Quelles institutions importantes trouve-t-on à Bruxelles?
   Le Parlement européen et le siège de l'OTAN.
8. Qui est le père de la bande dessinée belge?
   C'est Hergé.
9. Quels sont les noms de deux bandes dessinées célèbres (*famous*)?
   Tintin et les Schtroumpfs.
10. Comment s'appelle le champion de tennis suisse?
    Roger Federer.

Sur Internet

1. Cherchez plus d'informations sur les œuvres de Rousseau. Quelles sont ses autres œuvres?
2. Quels sont les noms de trois autres personnages de bandes dessinées belges?
3. Quel est le statut (*status*) de la Suisse dans l'Union européenne?

a été choisie *was chosen* **siège** *headquarters (lit. seat)* **C.E.E** *European Economic Community (predecessor of the European Union)* **OTAN** *NATO* **bande dessinée** *comic strips* **dessinateurs** *artists* **peintures murales** *murals* **Schtroumpfs** *Smurfs* **partout dans** *all over* **Lune** *moon* **entreprises** *companies* **mondiale** *worldwide* **articles** *products* **gérer** *manage* **autodidacte** *self-taught* **comme principe** *as a principle* **corrompt** *corrupts* **exprimées** *expressed* **œuvre** *work* **se retrouvent** *are found* **époque** *time*

Bruxelles, capitale de l'Europe
Tell students that the **Union Européenne** is a political and economic union among 28 European countries. Member countries share a common currency, the **euro**, and citizens of one member country may travel, work, or live in another member country. **L'OTAN**, or NATO (North Atlantic Treaty Organization), is an international military organization that provides mutual defence for members against external threats.

La bande dessinée
• In Brussels, one can learn about the creation and history of Belgian comic strips, such as Tintin, at the **Centre Belge de la Bande Dessinée**.
• *The Smurfs* was an American TV show in the 1980s. Ask students if they have ever heard of this cartoon or seen reruns of *The Smurfs*. Suggest they watch an episode in French of **Les Schtroumpfs** online and compare it to the American program.

Des montres et des banques
• Have students look at the photo and describe what they see. Then ask: **Connaissez-vous** (*Are you familiar with*) **les montres Swatch ou Rolex? Pourquoi ces montres sont-elles populaires?**
• Tell students that Swiss banks are known for their confidentiality and secrecy. The identity of account owners is highly protected.

Jean-Jacques Rousseau
Rousseau's writings have shaped people's views of society, family values, and political and ethical thinking. His writings have particularly influenced people's attitudes toward freedom of expression.

 21st Century Skills

Information and Media Literacy
Go to vhlcentral.com to complete the **Sur Internet** activity associated with **Panorama** for additional practice accessing and using culturally authentic sources.

EXPANSION

Cultural Comparison Working in small groups, have students compare Brussels with New York or Washington D.C. Tell them to list similarities and differences in a two-column chart under the headings **Similitudes** and **Différences**. Call on volunteers to read their lists. You may wish to assign a different American city to each group.

EXPANSION

Les montres suisses Watches, clocks, and alarm clocks manufactured in Switzerland must carry the designation "Swiss made" or "Swiss." A lot of technical expertise goes into fitting very complex mechanisms into small casings. A typical luxury watch usually has over 300 parts. One of the most complex luxury watches in the world is Calibre 89 by Patek Philippe, which contains 1,728 parts.

127

Lecture vhlcentral

Avant la lecture

STRATÉGIE

Predicting content from visuals

When you are reading in French, be sure to look for visual clues to help you understand the content and purpose of what you are reading. Photos and illustrations, for example, will often give you a good idea of the main points in the reading. You may also find helpful visuals that summarize large amounts of information. These visuals include bar graphs, pie charts, flow charts, lists of percentages, and other diagrams.

Le Top 10 des chiens de race°
le berger° allemand
le berger belge
le golden retriever
le Staffordshire terrier américain
le berger australien
le Staffordshire bull terrier
le labrador
le cavalier King Charles
le chihuahua
le bouledogue français

Examinez le texte

Take a quick look at the visual elements of the article and make a list of the information you expect to find. Then, compare your list with a classmate's. Are your lists the same or are they different? Discuss your lists and make any changes needed to produce a final list of ideas.

race *breed* **berger** *shepard*

Fido

Les Français adorent les animaux. Plus de la moitié° des foyers en France ont un chien, un chat ou un autre animal de compagnie°. Les chiens sont particulièrement appréciés et intégrés dans la famille et la société françaises.

Qui possède un chien en France et pourquoi? Souvent°, la présence d'un chien en famille suit l'arrivée° d'enfants, parce que les parents pensent qu'un chien contribue positivement à leur développement. Il est aussi commun de trouver deux chiens ou plus dans le même° foyer.

Les chiens sont d'excellents compagnons. Leurs maîtres° sont moins seuls° et déclarent avoir moins de stress. Certaines personnes possèdent un chien pour faire plus d'exercice

en famille

physique. Et il y a aussi des personnes qui possèdent un chien parce qu'elles en ont toujours eu un° et n'imaginent pas une vie° sans° chien.

Les chiens ont parfois° les mêmes droits° que les autres membres de la famille, et parfois des droits spéciaux. Bien sûr, ils accompagnent leurs maîtres pour les courses en ville° et les promenades dans le parc, et ils entrent même dans certains magasins°. Ne trouvez-vous pas parfois un bouledogue ou un labrador avec son maître dans un restaurant?

En France, il n'est pas difficile d'observer que les chiens ont une place privilégiée au sein de° la famille.

Pourquoi avoir un animal de compagnie?

RAISON	CHIENS	CHATS	OISEAUX	POISSONS
Pour l'amour des animaux	61,4%	60,5%	61%	33%
Pour avoir de la compagnie	43,5%	38,2%	37%	10%
Pour s'occuper°	40,4%	37,7%	0%	0%
Parce que j'en ai toujours eu un	31,8%	28,9%	0%	0%
Pour le bien-être° personnel	29,2%	26,2%	0%	0%
Pour les enfants	23,7%	21,3%	30%	48%

Plus de la moitié *More than half* **animal de compagnie** *pet* **Souvent** *Often* **suit l'arrivée** *follows the arrival* **même** *same* **maîtres** *owners* **moins seuls** *less lonely* **en ont toujours eu un** *have always had one* **vie** *life* **sans** *without* **parfois** *sometimes* **droits** *rights* **courses en ville** *errands in town* **magasins** *stores* **au sein de** *in the heart of* **s'occuper** *keep busy* **Parce que j'en ai toujours eu un** *Because I've always had one* **bien-être** *well-being*

Après la lecture

Vrai ou faux? Indicate whether these items are **vrai** or **faux**, based on the reading.

	Vrai	Faux
1. Les chiens accompagnent leurs maîtres pour les promenades dans le parc.	☑	☐
2. Parfois, les chiens accompagnent leurs maîtres dans les restaurants.	☑	☐
3. Le chat n'est pas un animal apprécié en France.	☐	☑
4. Certaines personnes déclarent posséder un chien pour avoir plus d'exercice physique.	☑	☐
5. Certaines personnes déclarent posséder un chien pour avoir plus de stress.	☐	☑
6. En France, les familles avec enfants n'ont pas de chien.	☐	☑

Fido en famille Choose the correct response according to the article.

1. Combien de foyers en France ont au moins (*at least*) un animal de compagnie?
   a. 20%–25%
   b. 40%–45%
   c. 50% ou plus

2. Pourquoi est-ce une bonne idée d'avoir un chien?
   a. pour la protection
   b. pour trouver des amis
   c. pour la compagnie

3. Que pensent les familles françaises de leurs chiens?
   a. Les chiens sont plus importants que les enfants.
   b. Les chiens font partie (*are part*) de la famille.
   c. Le rôle des chiens est limité aux promenades.

4. À quel moment les Français adoptent-ils un chien?
   a. juste après le mariage
   b. après un divorce
   c. à l'arrivée des enfants

5. Y a-t-il des familles avec plus d'un chien?
   a. non
   b. oui
   c. Ce n'est pas indiqué dans l'article.

Mes animaux In groups of three, say why you own or someone you know owns a pet. Give one of the reasons listed in the table on the left or a different one. Use the verb **avoir** and possessive adjectives.

MODÈLE

Mon grand-père a un chien pour son bien-être personnel.

Vrai ou faux? Have students correct the false statements and check their answers with a partner.

Fido en famille Go over the answers with the class. Ask students to read the corresponding line(s) of the text that contain(s) the answer to each question.

Suggestion Encourage students to record unfamiliar words and phrases that they learn in **Lecture** in their notebooks.

Expansions
- Ask students to describe their pets. If they don't own a pet, then tell them to describe someone else's pet. Example: **Mon chat s'appelle Tyler. Il est très gentil avec tout le monde. Il est noir et c'est un bon copain.**
- Write these headings on the board: **animaux de compagnie, chiens, chats, oiseaux, poissons**, and **autres animaux**. Do a quick class survey to find out how many have pets in general and how many have dogs, cats, birds, fish, and other animals. Record the results on the board. Then ask them why they have a pet. If students need help expressing their reasons, tell them to look at the reasons in the chart on this page.

Mes animaux Ask students to report their partners' answers to the class.

21st Century Skills

Creativity and Innovation
Ask students to prepare a presentation on the ideal pet inspired by the information on these two pages.

EXPANSION

Cultural Comparison Have students work in pairs or groups of three. Tell them to draw a two-column chart and write the headings **Similitudes** (*Similarities*) and **Différences** (*Differences*). Then, tell them to list the similarities and differences between the French and American attitudes toward dogs based on the facts in the reading and what they know about Americans and their pets. Allow students to use their books for this activity. After pairs have completed their charts, call on volunteers to read their lists. Ask the class if they agree or disagree with the similarities and differences.

Section Goals

In this section, students will:
- learn to use idea maps to organize information
- learn to write an informal e-mail in French

Key Standards

1.3, 3.1, 5.1

Stratégie Tell students that they might find it helpful to use a mind mapping application or paper note cards to create idea maps. Either method will allow them to rearrange ideas and experiment with organization. Remind students to write their ideas in French, since they may not have the vocabulary or structures for some English terms they generate.

 PRE-AP®

Interpersonal Writing
Introduce the common salutations and closings used in informal e-mails in French. Point out the difference between **cher** (masculine) and **chère** (feminine). Model the pronunciation to show students that the two words sound the same.

 **TELL Connection**

Planning 3 *Why:* Meaningful contexts and clear performance targets engage students and promote proficiency. *What:* Provide opportunities for students to experiment with different types of idea maps. Assist them in understanding writing rubrics and modifying them so that they clearly reflect performance objectives and levels of possible achievement.

Interpersonal Writing Introduce the common salutations and closings used in informal letters in French. Point out the difference between **cher** (masculine) and **chère** (feminine). Model the pronunciation to show students that the two words sound the same.

Écriture

STRATÉGIE

Using idea maps

How do you organize ideas for a first draft? Often, the organization of ideas represents the most challenging part of the writing process. Idea maps are useful for organizing important information. Here is an example of an idea map you can use when writing.

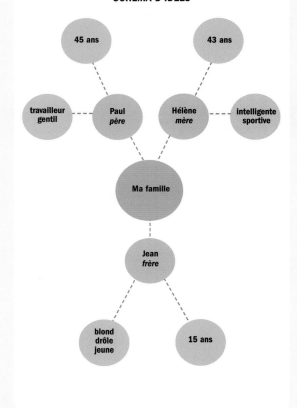

SCHÉMA D'IDÉES

Thème

Écrivez un e-mail

Avant l'écriture

1. A French-speaking friend wants to know about your family. Using some of the verbs and adjectives you learned in this lesson, you will write an e-mail describing your own family or an imaginary one. You should include information from each of these categories for each family member:

   - Names, ages, and relationships

   - Physical characteristics

   - Hobbies and interests

   Before you begin, create an idea map like the one on the left, with a circle for each member of your family.

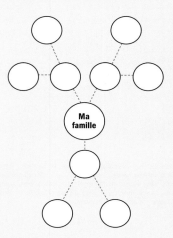

EXPANSION

Avant l'écriture Remind students that they used a word web to brainstorm ideas in Unit 2. Tell them that an idea map is similar, but that it links various ideas to a central topic and breaks those ideas down into smaller categories. Point out the colors used in the idea map on page 130 and how they are used to group similar levels of information.

Help students create an outline for a typical e-mail: a salutation, an introductory paragraph, a second paragraph with the family description, a third paragraph with a request for a response, a closing, and a signature. Tell students their introductory paragraph should include an inquiry into how the person is doing, along with a similar comment about themselves.

2. Once you have completed your idea map, compare it with the one created by a classmate. Did you both include the same kind of information? Did you list all your family members? Did you include information from each of the three categories for each person?

3. Here are some useful expressions for writing an e-mail in French:

Salutations	
Cher Fabien,	*Dear Fabien,*
Chère Joëlle,	*Dear Joëlle,*

Asking for a response	
Réponds-moi vite.	*Write back soon.*
Donne-moi de tes nouvelles.	*Tell me all your news.*

Closings	
Grosses bises!	*Big kisses!*
Je t'embrasse!	*Kisses!*
Bisous!	*Kisses!*
À bientôt!	*See you soon!*
Amitiés,	*In friendship,*
Cordialement,	*Cordially,*
À plus (tard),	*Until later,*

Écriture

Use your idea map and the list of expressions to write an e-mail that describes your family to a friend. Be sure to include some of the verbs and adjectives you have learned in this lesson.

> Cher Christophe,
>
> Mon père s'appelle Gabriel. Il a 42 ans. Il est grand, a les cheveux châtains et les yeux marron. Il est architecte et travaille à Paris. Il aime dessiner, lire (*to read*) et voyager. Ma mère, Nicole, a 37 ans. Elle est petite, blonde et a les yeux bleus. Elle est professeur d'anglais à l'université. Comme mon père, elle aime voyager. Elle aime aussi faire (*to do*) du sport. Ma sœur, Élodie, a 17 ans. Elle est grande, a les cheveux châtains et les yeux verts. Elle est encore au lycée. Elle adore écouter de la musique et aller au (*to go to*) cinéma. Mon oncle, ...
>
> Et ta famille, comment est-elle? Donne-moi vite de tes nouvelles!
>
> À bientôt!
>
> Caroline

Après l'écriture

1. Exchange rough drafts with a partner. Comment on his or her work by answering these questions:

- Did your partner include the age, family relationship, physical characteristics, and hobbies and interests of each family member?

- Did your partner make the adjectives agree with the person described?

- Did your partner use verb forms correctly?

- Did your partner use the letter-writing expressions correctly?

2. Revise your description according to your partner's comments. After writing the final version, read it once more to eliminate these kinds of problems:

- spelling errors

- punctuation errors

- capitalization errors

- use of incorrect verb forms

- adjectives that do not agree with the nouns they modify

Key Standards

4.1

Suggestion Tell students that an easy way to study from **Vocabulaire** is to cover up the French half of each section, leaving only the English equivalents exposed. They can then quiz themselves on the French items. To focus on the English equivalents of the French entries, they simply reverse this process.

21st Century Skills

Creativity and Innovation
Ask students to prepare a list of three products or perspectives they learned about in this unit to share with the class. Consider asking them to focus on the **Culture** and **Panorama** sections.

21st Century Skills

Leadership and Responsibility Extension Project
If you have access to students in a Francophone country, have students decide on three questions they want to ask the partner class related to this unit's topic. Based on the responses they receive, work as a class to explain to the partner class one aspect of their responses that surprised the class and why.

Leçon 3A

La famille

aîné(e)	younger
cadet(te)	brother-in-law
un beau-frère	father-in-law; stepfather
un beau-père	stepfather
une belle-mère	mother-in-law; stepmother
une belle-sœur	sister-in-law
un(e) cousin(e)	cousin
un demi-frère	half-brother; stepbrother
une demi-sœur	half-sister; stepsister
les enfants (m., f.)	children
un époux/une épouse	husband/wife
une famille	family
une femme	wife; woman
une fille	daughter; girl
un fils	son
un frère	brother
une grand-mère	grandmother
un grand-père	grandfather
les grands-parents (m.)	grandparents
un mari	husband
une mère	mother
un neveu	nephew
une nièce	niece
un oncle	uncle
les parents (m.)	parents
un père	father
une petite-fille	granddaughter
un petit-fils	grandson
les petits-enfants (m.)	grandchildren
une sœur	sister
une tante	aunt
un chat	cat
un chien	dog
un oiseau	bird
un poisson	fish

Vocabulaire supplémentaire

divorcer	to divorce
épouser	to marry
célibataire	single
divorcé(e)	divorced
fiancé(e)	engaged
marié(e)	married
séparé(e)	separated
veuf/veuve	widowed
un(e) voisin(e)	neighbor

Expressions utiles

See p. 95.

Adjectifs descriptifs

bleu(e)	blue
blond(e)	blond
brun(e)	dark (hair)
court(e)	short
frisé(e)	curly
grand(e)	big; tall
jeune	young
joli(e)	pretty
laid(e)	ugly
mauvais(e)	bad
noir(e)	black
pauvre	poor; unfortunate
petit(e)	small, short (stature)
raide	straight (hair)
vert(e)	green
vrai(e)	true; real
de taille moyenne	medium-sized

Adjectifs irréguliers

beau/belle	beautiful; handsome
bon(ne)	kind; good
châtain	brown (hair)
curieux/curieuse	curious
fier/fière	proud
gros(se)	fat
intellectuel(le)	intellectual
long(ue)	long
(mal)heureux/(mal)heureuse	(un)happy
marron	brown (not for hair)
naïf/naïve	naive
nerveux/nerveuse	nervous
nouveau/nouvelle	new
roux/rousse	red-haired
sérieux/sérieuse	serious
vieux/vieille	old

Adjectifs possessifs

mon, ma, mes	my
ton, ta, tes	your (fam. and sing.)
son, sa, ses	his, her, its
notre, notre, nos	our
votre, votre, vos	your (form. or pl.)
leur, leur, leurs	their

Leçon 3B

Adjectifs descriptifs

antipathique	unpleasant
drôle	funny
faible	weak
fatigué(e)	tired
fort(e)	strong
génial(e) (géniaux m., pl.)	great
lent(e)	slow
méchant(e)	mean
modeste	modest
pénible	annoying
prêt(e)	ready
rapide	fast
triste	sad

Professions et occupations

un(e) architecte	architect
un(e) artiste	artist
un(e) athlète	athlete
un(e) avocat(e)	lawyer
un coiffeur/une coiffeuse	hairdresser
un(e) dentiste	dentist
un homme/une femme d'affaires	businessman/woman
un ingénieur	engineer
un(e) journaliste	journalist
un médecin	doctor
un(e) musicien(ne)	musician
un(e) propriétaire	owner; landlord/lady

Adjectifs irréguliers

actif/active	active
courageux/courageuse	brave
cruel(le)	cruel
discret/discrète	discreet; unassuming
doux/douce	sweet; soft
ennuyeux/ennuyeuse	boring
étranger/étrangère	foreign
favori(te)	favorite
fou/folle	crazy
généreux/généreuse	generous
gentil(le)	nice
inquiet/inquiète	worried
jaloux/jalouse	jealous
paresseux/paresseuse	lazy
sportif/sportive	athletic
travailleur/travailleuse	hard-working

Expressions utiles

See p. 113.

Nombres 61–100

See p. 116.

Prépositions de lieu

à côté de	next to
à droite de	to the right of
à gauche de	to the left of
dans	in
derrière	behind
devant	in front of
en	in
en face de	facing, across from
entre	between
loin de	far from
par	by
près de	close to, near
sous	under
sur	on

Pronoms toniques

See p. 121.

Au café

Unit Goals

Leçon 4A

In this lesson, students will learn:
- names for places around town
- terms for activities around town
- to pronounce oral vowels
- about pastimes of young French people and **le verlan**
- the verb **aller** and to express future actions with it
- the preposition **à** and contractions with it
- interrogative words
- about a French Youtuber and his collaboration with **PagesJaunes**

Leçon 4B

In this lesson, students will learn:
- terms for food items at a café
- expressions of quantity
- to pronounce nasal vowels
- about the role of the café in France and the cafés of North Africa
- more about cafés and food items through specially shot video footage
- the present tense of **prendre** and **boire**
- the formation and use of partitive articles
- regular **-ir** verbs
- to listen for the gist in oral communication

Savoir-faire

In this section, students will learn:
- cultural and historical information about the province of **Québec** in Canada
- to scan a text to improve comprehension
- to add details in French to make writing more interesting

 21ˢᵗ Century Skills

Initiative and Self-Direction
Students can monitor their progress online using the activities and assessments on vhlcentral.com.

Pour commencer
- a. **neuf heures du matin**
- b. **des boissons**
- a. **boire**

Pour commencer
- Quelle heure est-il, à votre avis?
  a. neuf heures du matin b. midi
  c. dix heures du soir
- Qu'est-ce qu'il y a sur la table?
  a. des sandwiches b. des boissons
  c. de la soupe
- Qu'est-ce que ces garçons ont envie de faire?
  a. boire b. manger c. partager

SUPPORT FOR BACKWARD DESIGN

Unité 4 Essential Questions
1. How do people talk about pastimes and weekend activities?
2. How do people order food in a café and discuss eating habits?
3. What role does the café play in life in the Francophone world?

Unité 4 Integrated Performance Assessment
Before teaching the chapter, review the Integrated Performance Assessment (IPA) and its accompanying scoring rubric provided in the Testing Program. Use the IPA to assess students' progress toward proficiency targets at the end of the chapter.
IPA Context: You will listen to two candidates for student council talk about their plans and interests, then discuss with a partner which person would make a better candidate. Finally, you will describe your ideal candidate to the class.

 FORUMS

Forums on vhlcentral.com allow you and your students to record and share audio messages. Use Forums for presentations, oral assessments, discussions, directions, etc.

You will learn how to...
- say where you are going
- say what you are going to do

🔊 **vhl**central

Où allons-nous?

Vocabulaire

danser	to dance
explorer	to explore
fréquenter	to frequent; to visit
inviter	to invite
nager	to swim
patiner	to skate
une banlieue	suburbs
un bureau	office; desk
un centre commercial	shopping center, mall
un centre-ville	city/town center, downtown
un cinéma (ciné)	movie theater, movies
un endroit	place
un grand magasin	department store
un gymnase	gym
un hôpital	hospital
un lieu	place
un magasin	store
un marché	market
un musée	museum
un parc	park
une piscine	pool
un restaurant	restaurant
une ville	city, town

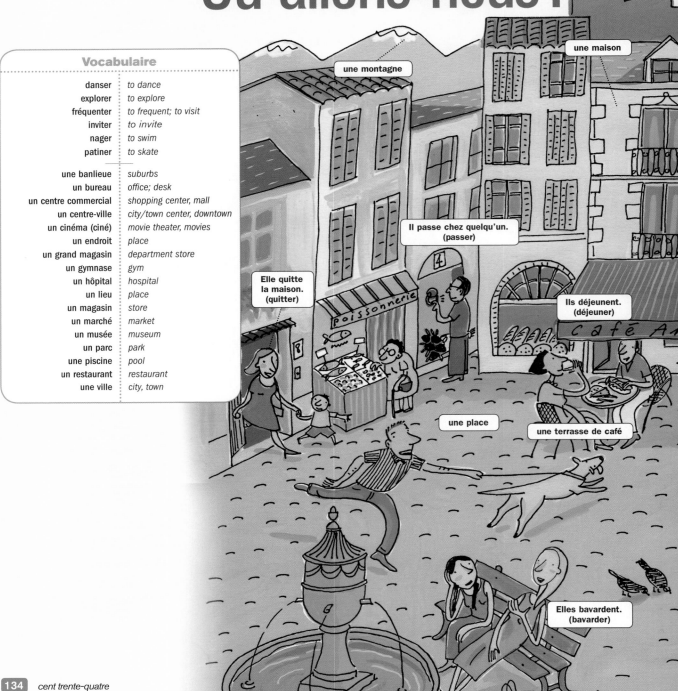

une montagne

une maison

Il passe chez quelqu'un. (passer)

Elle quitte la maison. (quitter)

Ils déjeunent. (déjeuner)

une place

une terrasse de café

Elles bavardent. (bavarder)

une église

une épicerie

e u r o m a r c h é

JOURNAUX

un kiosque

Il dépense de l'argent (*m.*).
(dépenser)

Attention!

Remember that nouns that end in –al have an irregular plural. Replace –al with –aux.

un hôpital ➜ deux hôpitaux

À (*to, at*) before le or les makes these contractions:
à + le = au   à + les = aux
le musée ➜ au musée
les endroits ➜ aux endroits
À does NOT contract with l' or la.

Mise en pratique

1 **Associez** Quels lieux associez-vous à ces activités?

1. nager ___une piscine___
2. acheter (*to buy*) un jean ___un (*grand*) magasin, un centre commercial___
3. dîner ___un restaurant___
4. travailler ___un bureau___
5. habiter ___une maison___
6. épouser ___une église___
7. voir (*to see*) un film ___un cinéma___
8. acheter des fruits ___un marché, une épicerie___

2 🔊 **Écoutez** Djamila parle de sa journée à son amie Samira. Écoutez la conversation et mettez (*put*) les lieux de la liste dans l'ordre chronologique. Il y a deux lieux en trop (*extra*).

___3___ a. à l'hôpital
___8___ b. à la maison
___1___ c. à la piscine
___5___ d. au centre commercial
___6___ e. au cinéma
___NA___ f. à l'église
___2___ g. au musée
___7___ h. au bureau
___NA___ i. au parc
___4___ j. au restaurant

Coup de main

Note that the French **Je vais à...** is the equivalent of the English *I am going to...*

3 **Logique ou illogique** Lisez chaque phrase et déterminez si l'action est **logique** ou **illogique**. Corrigez si nécessaire. Suggested answers

	Logique	Illogique
1. Maxime invite Delphine à une épicerie.	☐	☑
Maxime invite Delphine au musée.		
2. Caroline et Aurélie bavardent au marché.	☑	☐
3. Nous déjeunons à l'épicerie.	☐	☑
Nous déjeunons au restaurant.		
4. Ils dépensent beaucoup d'argent au centre commercial.	☑	☐
5. Vous explorez une ville.	☑	☐
6. Vous escaladez (*climb*) un kiosque.	☐	☑
Vous escaladez une montagne.		
7. J'habite en banlieue.	☑	☐
8. Tu danses dans un studio.	☑	☐

1 **Expansion**
- For additional practice, give students these items.
  9. chanter (une église)
  10. manger (un restaurant/un café) 11. dessiner (un musée)
- Do this activity in reverse. Name places and have students say what activities can be done there.

2 **Script** DJAMILA: Allô, Samira. Comment ça va?
SAMIRA: Très bien, et toi?
D: Aujourd'hui, très bien, mais alors demain, quelle journée!
S: Comment ça?
D: Eh bien… demain matin, je vais à la piscine avec mon frère, Hassan, à 8h00. À 10h00, je vais au musée Rodin avec ma classe. À 11h00, je passe un moment avec grand-mère à l'hôpital. À midi, je vais au restaurant Chez Benoît, près de la place Carnot. L'après-midi, je vais au centre commercial et au cinéma voir le dernier film de Jean Reno. Pour terminer, à 17h00, je vais au bureau de maman pour travailler un peu et nous rentrons à la maison ensemble.
S: Quel programme! Bon, courage Djamila et à bientôt.
D: Merci, bonne soirée.
Teacher Resources DVD

2 **Suggestion** Before beginning the activity, present contractions with **à**, then have students read the list of places and the **Coup de main**.

3 **Suggestion** Tell students to write their corrections. Then have volunteers write their sentences on the board.

3 **Expansion** For additional practice, give students these items. **9. Vous dansez au magasin. (illogique) 10. Je nage au musée. (illogique) 11. Madame Ducharme habite dans une maison. (logique)**

DIFFERENTIATION

For Kinesthetic Learners Have students represent various stores and places in town by giving them signs to hold. Ask them where one does various activities. Examples: **Où est-ce qu'on regarde un film/mange/nage?** The student with the appropriate sign should step forward and answer. Examples: **On regarde un film au cinéma. On mange au restaurant. On nage à la piscine.**

EXPANSION

Oral Practice Ask students about their favorite places. Tell them to use generic place names in front of proper nouns, such as **le parc Zilker** and **le musée du Louvre**. Ask: **Quel est votre restaurant/musée préféré?**

Communication

4 Suggestion Have two volunteers read the **modèle** aloud.

4 Expansion After completing the activity, have students share their partners' opinions with the rest of the class.

5 Suggestion Divide the class into pairs and distribute the Info Gap Handouts from the Activity Pack. Give students ten minutes to complete the activity.

PRE-AP®

6 Interpersonal Writing: Suggestion
Tell students that they should use the salutation **chère** if they are writing to a female. Remind them to include expressions of time, such as **le lundi après-midi** and **le samedi soir** in their letters.

Successful Language Learning Remind students that it's important to proofread their work. Have them brainstorm a checklist of potential errors, for example, accents, adjective agreement, and subject-verb agreement. Tell students to add grammar points to their checklists as they learn new structures and make mistakes.

21st Century Skills

Technology Literacy
Ask students to prepare a digital presentation on an ideal town. They should include a map of the city showing its layout.

Interpersonal Communication Practice In pairs, have students take turns telling where they go each day of the week. Example: **Le lundi, je vais au lycée pour étudier. Après, je vais au parc. Je joue au foot et je bavarde avec mes amis. Et toi?**

Activity Pack For additional activities, go to the **Activity Pack** in the **Resources** section of vhlcentral.com.

---

4 Conversez Avec un(e) partenaire, échangez vos opinions sur ces activités. Utilisez un élément de chaque colonne dans vos réponses. Answers will vary.

MODÈLE
Élève 1: Moi, j'adore bavarder au restaurant, mais je déteste parler au musée.
Élève 2: Moi aussi, j'adore bavarder au restaurant. Je ne déteste pas parler au musée, mais j'aime mieux bavarder au parc.

Opinion	Activité	Lieu
adorer	bavarder	au bureau
aimer (mieux)	danser	au centre commercial
ne pas tellement aimer	déjeuner	au centre-ville
détester	dépenser de l'argent	au cinéma
	étudier	au gymnase
	inviter	au musée
	nager	au parc
	parler	à la piscine
	patiner	au restaurant

5 La journée d'Anne Votre professeur va vous donner, à vous et à votre partenaire, une feuille d'activités. À tour de rôle, posez-vous des questions pour compléter vos feuilles respectives. Utilisez le vocabulaire de la leçon. Attention! Ne regardez pas la feuille de votre partenaire. Answers will vary.

MODÈLE
Élève 1: À 7h30, Anne quitte la maison. Qu'est-ce qu'elle fait ensuite (do next)?
Élève 2: À 8h00, elle…

Anne

6 Une lettre Écrivez une lettre à un(e) ami(e) dans laquelle (in which) vous décrivez vos activités de la semaine. Utilisez les expressions de la liste. Answers will vary.

bavarder	passer chez quelqu'un
déjeuner	travailler
dépenser de l'argent	quitter la maison
étudier	un centre commercial
manger au restaurant	un cinéma

Cher Paul,

Comment vas-tu? Pour (For) moi, tout va bien. Je suis très actif/active. Je travaille beaucoup et j'ai beaucoup d'amis. En général, le samedi, après les cours, je déjeune chez moi et l'après-midi, je bavarde avec mes amis…

DIFFERENTIATION

For Kinesthetic Learners On a sheet of paper, have students write down six places they like to go and what they like to do there. Tell them to circulate around the room trying to find other students who also like to go to those places or do those things. Remind them to jot down the names of people who share something in common with them. Then have them report what they have in common with their classmates.

TEACHING OPTIONS

Ideal Town Have small groups plan and design an ideal town or neighborhood. Have them draw the plan, label each place, and list fun activities to do at each one. One person from each group should present the plan to the class. Hold a secret vote and give prizes for the best plan in various categories, such as **le plus amusant**, **le plus créatif**, and **le plus réaliste**.

Les sons et les lettres 🔊 vhlcentral

Oral vowels

French has two basic kinds of vowel sounds: oral vowels, the subject of this discussion, and nasal vowels, presented in **Leçon 4B**. Oral vowels are produced by releasing air through the mouth. The pronunciation of French vowels is consistent and predictable.

In short words (usually two-letter words), **e** is pronounced similarly to the *a* in the English word *about*.

| l**e** | qu**e** | c**e** | d**e** |

The letter **a** alone is pronounced like the *a* in *father*.

| l**a** | ç**a** | m**a** | t**a** |

The letter **i** by itself and the letter **y** are pronounced like the vowel sound in the word *bee*.

| ic**i** | l**i**vre | st**y**lo | l**y**cée |

The letter combination **ou** sounds like the vowel sound in the English word *who*.

| v**ou**s | n**ou**s | **ou**blier | éc**ou**ter |

The French **u** sound does not exist in English. To produce this sound, say *ee* with your lips rounded.

| t**u** | d**u** | **u**ne | ét**u**dier |

Prononcez Répétez les mots suivants à voix haute.

1. je
2. chat
3. fou
4. ville
5. utile
6. place
7. jour
8. triste
9. mari
10. active
11. Sylvie
12. rapide
13. gymnase
14. antipathique
15. calculatrice
16. piscine

Articulez Répétez les phrases suivantes à voix haute.

1. Salut, Luc. Ça va?
2. La philosophie est difficile.
3. Brigitte est une actrice fantastique.
4. Suzanne va à son cours de physique.
5. Tu trouves le cours de maths facile?
6. Viviane a une bourse universitaire.

Dictons Répétez les dictons à voix haute.

Qui va à la chasse perd sa place.[1]

Plus on est de fous, plus on rit.[2]

[1] He who steps out of line loses his place.
[2] The more the merrier.

Section Goals

In this section, students will learn about oral vowels.

Key Standards

4.1

Suggestions

- Model the pronunciation of each vowel sound. Have students watch the shape of your mouth, then repeat the sound after you. Pronounce each of the example words and have students repeat them.
- Tell students that an unaccented **e** at the end of a word is silent, but will cause a consonant that precedes it to be pronounced. Example: **petit/petite**.
- Contrast the pronunciation of words containing **u** and **ou**. Examples: **vous/vu** and **tous/tu**.
- Tell students that this lesson focuses mainly on single oral vowels and that they will learn more about letter combinations like **ou** in other lessons.
- Dictate five familiar words containing oral vowels to the class, repeating each one at least two times. Then write them on the board or on a transparency and have students check their spelling.

Dictons Ask students if they can think of a saying in English that is similar to **«Qui va à la chasse perd sa place.»** (*You snooze, you lose.*)

🔅 **TELL Connection**

Professionalism 2 *Why:* Maintain and improve your own language skills while developing those of your students. *What:* Use the audio for **Les sons et les lettres** and other media provided to keep your ear and pronunciation sharp and to model life-long learning.

EXPANSION

Using Games Have a spelling bee using vocabulary words from **Unités 1–3** that contain oral vowel sounds. Pronounce each word, use it in a sentence, and then say the individual word again. Tell students that they must spell the words in French and include the diacritical marks.

EXPANSION

Mini-dictée Use these sentences with oral vowels for additional practice or dictation. **1. Madame Duclos et son mari sont séparés. 2. Marianne prépare le bac. 3. Tu aimes mieux le parc ou le gymnase? 4. Coralie nage à la piscine.**

Star du cinéma vhlcentral

PERSONNAGES

Amina

David

Pascal

Sandrine

À l'épicerie...
DAVID Juliette Binoche? Pas possible! Je vais chercher Sandrine!

Au café...
PASCAL Alors, chérie, tu vas faire quoi de ton week-end?
SANDRINE Euh, demain je vais déjeuner au centre-ville.
PASCAL Bon... et quand est-ce que tu vas rentrer?
SANDRINE Euh, je ne sais pas. Pourquoi?

PASCAL Pour rien. Et demain soir, tu vas danser?
SANDRINE Ça dépend. Je vais passer chez Amina pour bavarder avec elle.
PASCAL Combien d'amis as-tu à Aix-en-Provence?
SANDRINE Oh, Pascal...
PASCAL Bon, moi, je vais continuer à penser à toi jour et nuit.

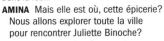

DAVID Mais l'actrice! Juliette Binoche!
SANDRINE Allons-y! Vite! C'est une de mes actrices préférées! J'adore le film *Chocolat*!
AMINA Et comme elle est chic! C'est une vraie star!
DAVID Elle est à l'épicerie! Ce n'est pas loin d'ici!

Dans la rue...
AMINA Mais elle est où, cette épicerie? Nous allons explorer toute la ville pour rencontrer Juliette Binoche?
SANDRINE C'est là, l'épicerie Pierre Dubois, à côté du cinéma?
DAVID Mais non, elle n'est pas à l'épicerie Pierre Dubois, elle est à l'épicerie près de l'église, en face du parc.

AMINA Et combien d'églises est-ce qu'il y a à Aix?
SANDRINE Il n'y a pas d'église en face du parc!
DAVID Bon, hum, l'église sur la place.
AMINA D'accord, et ton église sur la place, elle est ici au centre-ville ou en banlieue?

A C T I V I T É S

1 **Vrai ou faux?** Indiquez pour chaque phrase si l'affirmation est **vraie** ou **fausse**.
1. David va chercher Pascal. *Faux.*
2. Sandrine va déjeuner au centre-ville. *Vrai.*
3. Pascal va passer chez Amina. *Faux.*
4. Pascal va continuer à penser à Sandrine jour et nuit. *Vrai.*
5. Pascal va bien. *Vrai.*

6. Juliette Binoche est une des actrices préférées de Sandrine. *Vrai.*
7. Les amis cherchent l'épicerie Pierre Dubois. *Faux.*
8. L'épicerie est en banlieue. *Faux.*
9. Il n'y a pas d'église en face du parc. *Vrai.*
10. Juliette Binoche fréquente le P'tit Bistrot. *Faux.*

David et les filles à la recherche de (*in search of*) leur actrice préférée

SANDRINE Oui. Génial.
Au revoir, Pascal.
AMINA Salut, Sandrine. Comment
va Pascal?
SANDRINE Il va bien, mais il
adore bavarder.

DAVID Elle est là, elle est là!
SANDRINE Mais, qui est là?
AMINA Et c'est où, «là»?
DAVID Juliette Binoche! Mais non,
pas ici!
SANDRINE ET AMINA Quoi? Qui? Où?

Devant l'épicerie...
DAVID C'est elle, là! Hé, JULIETTE!
AMINA Oh, elle est belle!
SANDRINE Elle est jolie, élégante!
AMINA Elle est... petite?
DAVID Elle, elle... est... vieille?!?

AMINA Ce n'est pas du tout
Juliette Binoche!
SANDRINE David, tu es complètement
fou! Juliette Binoche, au
centre-ville d'Aix?
AMINA Pourquoi est-ce qu'elle ne
fréquente pas le P'tit Bistrot?

Expressions utiles

Talking about your plans

● **Tu vas faire quoi de ton week-end?**
What are you doing this weekend?

● **Je vais déjeuner au centre-ville.**
I'm going to have lunch downtown.

● **Quand est-ce que tu vas rentrer?**
When are you coming back?

● **Je ne sais pas.**
I don't know.

● **Je vais passer chez Amina.**
I am going to Amina's (house).

● **Nous allons explorer toute la ville.**
We're going to explore the whole city.

Additional vocabulary

● **C'est une de mes actrices préférées.**
She's one of my favorite actresses.

● **Comme elle est chic!**
She is so chic!

● **Ce n'est pas loin d'ici!**
It's not far from here!

● **Ce n'est pas du tout...**
It's not... at all.

● **Ça dépend.**
It depends.

● **Pour rien.**
No reason.

● **Vite!**
Quick!, Hurry!

---

2 **Questions** À l'aide (*the help*) d'un dictionnaire, choisissez le bon mot pour chaque question.

1. (Avec qui, Quoi) Sandrine parle-t-elle au téléphone?
2. (Où, Parce que) Sandrine va-t-elle déjeuner?
3. (Qui, Pourquoi) Pascal demande-t-il à Sandrine quand elle va rentrer?
4. (Combien, Comment) d'amis Sandrine a-t-elle?
5. (Combien, À qui) Amina demande-t-elle comment va Pascal?
6. (Quand, Où) est Juliette Binoche?

3 **Écrivez** Pensez à votre acteur ou actrice préféré(e) et préparez un paragraphe où vous décrivez son apparence, sa personnalité et sa carrière. Comment est-il/elle? Dans quel(s) (*which*) film(s) joue-t-il/elle? Si un jour vous rencontrez cet acteur/cette actrice, qu'est-ce que vous allez lui dire (*say to him or her*)?

ACTIVITÉS

Expressions utiles

● Model the pronunciation of the **Expressions utiles** and have students repeat after you.

● As you work through the list, point out forms of **aller** and the interrogative words. Tell students that these concepts will be formally presented in **Structures**.

● Point out that, like the English verb *to go*, the verb **aller** is used to express future actions.

● Write **je vais** and **tu vas** on the board. Ask students the questions in the **Expressions utiles** and have them respond. Examples: **Tu vas faire quoi de ton week-end? Quand est-ce que tu vas rentrer?**

● Have students scan the video-still captions for interrogative words that are not in the list and read the sentences. Examples: **combien de, comment, qui, où,** and **pourquoi.**

1 **Suggestion** Have students correct the false statements on the board: **1. David va chercher Sandrine. 3. Sandrine va passer chez Amina. 7. Ils cherchent l'épicerie près de l'église, en face du parc. 8. L'épicerie est au centre-ville. 10. Juliette Binoche ne fréquente pas le P'tit Bistro.**

1 **Expansion** For additional practice, give students these items. **11. Juliette Binoche est vieille. (Faux. Elle n'est pas vieille.) 12. Amina pense que Juliette Binoche est chic. (Vrai.)**

2 **Expansion**

● For additional practice, give students these items. **7. (Qui, Comment) est-ce que David voit (*see*) à l'épicerie? (Qui) 8. (Pourquoi, Comment) est Juliette Binoche? (Comment) 9. (Quand, Où) est-ce que Pascal va penser à Sandrine? (Quand)**

● Have students answer the questions.

3 **Suggestion** Have students exchange papers for peer editing. Remind them to pay particular attention to adjective agreement and subject-verb agreement.

Juliette Binoche Juliette Binoche (1964–), often referred to by the French press simply as "La Binoche", was born in Paris. In addition to being an actress, she is a poster designer and avid painter. Her first film was *Liberty Belle* (1983). She has now acted in more that 40 films. She won a César for "Best actress" in *Bleu* (1983) and an Oscar for "Best Supporting Actress" in

TEACHING OPTIONS

The English Patient (1996). *Chocolat* (2000) is the film version of the novel *Chocolat* by Joanne Harris.

Skits Working in groups of three, have students create a short skit similar to the scenes in video stills 5–10 in which someone thinks they have seen a famous person. Give students ten minutes to prepare, then call on groups to perform their skits for the class.

AP® **Theme:** Contemporary Life
Context: Leisure and Sports

vhlcentral

CULTURE À LA LOUPE

Les passe-temps des jeunes Français

Comment est-ce que les jeunes occupent leur temps libre° en France? Si la télévision a été pendant longtemps° un des passe-temps préféré, aujourd'hui près de° 60% (pour cent) des jeunes disent être plus attachés à° leur *smartphone*. En effet, ils sont 68% à ne jamais sortir sans leur portable, et ils veulent être connectés partout°. Les médias jouent donc un rôle très important dans leur vie, surtout les réseaux sociaux° qu'ils utilisent pour communiquer avec leurs amis et leurs proches°. Les portables sont aussi considérés très pratiques pour télécharger° et écouter de la musique, surfer sur Internet, jouer à des jeux° vidéo ou regarder des films.

Les activités culturelles, en particulier le cinéma, sont aussi très appréciées: en moyenne°, les jeunes y° vont une fois° par semaine. Ils aiment également° la littérature et l'art: presque° 50% des jeunes visitent des musées ou des monuments historiques chaque année et plus de° 40% vont au théâtre ou à des concerts. Un jeune sur cinq° joue d'un instrument de musique ou chante°, et environ 20% d'entre eux° pratiquent une activité artistique, comme la danse, le théâtre, la sculpture, le dessin° ou la peinture°. La photographie et la vidéo sont aussi très appréciées.

Quant à° la pratique sportive, elle concerne près de 90% des jeunes Français, qui font partie de clubs ou s'entraînent entre copains.

Beaucoup de jeunes Français sont aussi membres de la Maison des Jeunes et de la Culture (MJC) de leur ville. Les MJC proposent des activités culturelles, sportives et des cours et ateliers° dans de nombreux domaines.

Et bien sûr, comme tous les jeunes, ils aiment aussi tout simplement se détendre° et bavarder avec des amis, le plus souvent dans un des nombreux cafés du centre-ville.

temps libre *free time* **a été pendant longtemps** *has for a long time been* **près de** *close to* **attachés à** *fond of* **partout** *everywhere* **réseaux sociaux** *social networks* **proches** *people close to them* **télécharger** *download* **jeux** *games* **en moyenne** *on average* **y** *there* **fois** *time* **également** *also* **presque** *almost* **plus de** *more than* **Un... sur cinq** *One . . . in five* **chante** *sings* **d'entre eux** *of them* **dessin** *drawing* **peinture** *painting* **Quant à** *As for* **ateliers** *workshops* **se détendre** *relax* **les** *them* **Sortir** *Go out* **Lire** *Read* **Échanger** *Exchange* **Faire une sortie** *Go on ... outing*

Loisirs les plus populaires en France	
(% des Français qui les° pratiquent)	
Écouter de la musique	87%
Regarder la télévision	84%
Sortir° avec des amis	82%
Lire° un magazine ou un journal	80%
Échanger° à distance	77%
Écouter la radio	74%
Surfer sur Internet	69%
Regarder une vidéo	66%
Aller au cinéma	63%
Faire une sortie° culturelle	58%

SOURCE: Ipsos in France for the Centre National du Livre. The survey was conducted in France, by telephone on 1,012 people (aged 15 y.o. and more), from February 3rd to 11th, 2015.

A C T I V I T É S

1 Vrai ou faux? Indiquez si les phrases sont **vraies** ou **fausses**.

1. Les portables sont rarement utilisés pour écouter de la musique. Faux.
2. Les jeunes Français n'utilisent pas Internet. Faux.
3. Les musées sont des lieux appréciés pour les loisirs. Vrai.
4. Les réseaux sociaux ne sont pas très utilisés pour communiquer entre amis. Faux.
5. Les jeunes Français n'aiment pas pratiquer d'activités artistiques. Faux.

6. Le sport n'est pas important dans la vie des jeunes. Faux.
7. Les jeunes Français regardent moins la télévision aujourd'hui. Vrai.
8. En général, les Français aiment les médias. Vrai.
9. Les jeunes aiment mieux regarder la télé que (*than*) d'aller au cinéma. Vrai.
10. Dans les MJC, on peut faire une grande variété d'activités. Vrai.

AP® Theme: Personal and Public Identities
Context: Language and Identity

LE FRANÇAIS QUOTIDIEN

Le verlan

En France, on entend parfois° des jeunes parler en **verlan**. En verlan, les syllabes des mots sont inversées°:

l'envers° → vers–l'en → verlan.

Voici quelques exemples:

français	verlan	anglais
louche	chelou	*shady*
café	féca	*café*
mec	keum	*guy*
femme	meuf	*woman*

parfois *sometimes* **inversées** *inverted* **l'envers** *the reverse*

AP® Theme: Contemporary Life Context: Leisure and Sports

LE MONDE FRANCOPHONE

Où passer le temps

Voici quelques endroits typiques où les jeunes francophones aiment se restaurer° et passer du temps.

En Afrique de l'Ouest

Le maquis Commun dans beaucoup de pays° d'Afrique de l'Ouest°, le maquis est un restaurant où on peut manger à bas prix°. Situé en ville ou en bord de route°, le maquis est typiquement en plein air°.

Au Sénégal

Le tangana Le terme «tang» signifie «chaud» en wolof, une des langues nationales du Sénégal. Le tangana est un lieu populaire pour se restaurer. On trouve souvent les tanganas au coin de la rue°, en plein air, avec des tables et des bancs°.

se restaurer *have something to eat* **pays** *countries* **Ouest** *West*
à bas prix *inexpensively* **en bord de route** *on the side of the road*
en plein air *outdoors* **coin de la rue** *street corner* **bancs** *benches*

PORTRAIT

Le parc Astérix

AP® Theme: Contemporary Life
Context: Leisure and Sports

Situé° à 30 kilomètres de Paris, en Picardie, le parc Astérix est le premier parc à thème français. Le parc d'attractions°, ouvert° en 1989, est basé sur la bande dessinée° française, *Astérix le Gaulois*. Création de René Goscinny et d'Albert Uderzo, Astérix est un guerrier gaulois° qui lutte° contre l'invasion des Romains. Au parc Astérix, il y a des montagnes russes°, des petits trains et des spectacles, tous° basés sur les aventures d'Astérix et de son meilleur ami, Obélix. Une des attractions, *le Tonnerre° de Zeus*, est la plus grande° montagne russe en bois° d'Europe.

Situé *Located* **parc d'attractions** *amusement park*
ouvert *opened* **bande dessinée** *comic strip* **guerrier**
gaulois *Gallic warrior* **lutte** *fights* **montagnes russes** *roller*
coasters **tous** *all* **Tonnerre** *Thunder* **la plus grande** *the*
largest **en bois** *wooden*

Albert Uderzo

Sur Internet

Comment sont les parcs d'attractions dans les autres pays francophones?

Go to **vhlcentral.com** to find more information related to this **Culture** section.

---

2 **Compréhension** Complétez les phrases.

1. Le parc Astérix est basé sur Astérix le Gaulois, une bande dessinée.
2. Astérix le Gaulois est une création de René Goscinny et d'Albert Uderzo.
3. Le parc Astérix est près de la ville de Paris.
4. Astérix est un guerrier gaulois.
5. En verlan, on peut passer du temps avec ses copains au féca.
6. Au Sénégal, les jeunes aiment passer du temps au tangana.

3 **Vos activités préférées** Posez des questions à trois ou quatre de vos camarades de classe à propos de leurs activités favorites. Comparez vos résultats avec ceux (*those*) d'un autre groupe.

A C T I V I T É S

Sidebar (right column)

Le français quotidien Model the pronunciation of each term and have students repeat it. Ask students what language or jargon in English is similar to **verlan**. (pig latin)

Portrait Point out Astérix and Obélix in the photo. If possible, bring in an Astérix comic strip to show the students.

Le monde francophone Have students read the text. Then ask a few comprehension questions. Examples: **1. Pourquoi les jeunes fréquentent-ils les maquis et les tanganas? (pour manger et passer le temps) 2. On trouve les maquis en ville ou en bord de route? (les deux) Et les tanganas? (Ils sont souvent au coin d'une rue.) 3. On mange à l'intérieur ou en plein air dans le maquis et le tangana? (en plein air)**

21ˢᵗ Century Skills

Information and Media Literacy: Sur Internet Students access and critically evaluate information from the Internet.

2 Expansion For additional practice, give students these items. **7. Le parc Astérix est le premier _____ à thème français. (parc) 8. Astérix lutte (*fights*) contre les _____. (Romains) 9. Au parc Astérix, il y a des montagnes _____. (russes) 10. L'ami d'Astérix s'appelle _____. (Obélix)**

3 Expansion Do a quick class survey to find out how many students like each activity and which one is the most popular. Tally the results on the board. Example: **Combien d'élèves surfent sur Internet?**

21ˢᵗ Century Skills

Flexibility and Adaptability Remind students to include input from all team members when comparing answers with other teams.

EXPANSION

Le verlan Write on the board: **1. une bande 2. la musique 3. le métro 4. manger 5. bonjour 6. fou.** Have students work in pairs. Tell them to copy the words and write the equivalents in **verlan**. Answers: **1. une deban 2. la siquemu/sicmu 3. le tromé 4. géman 5. jourbon 6. ouf**

EXPANSION

Le parc Astérix Some other popular attractions at the park are **La Galère** (a giant swinging ship), **Les Chaises Volantes** (flying chairs), **Le Cheval de Troie** (the Trojan horse), and **Transdemonium** (a ghost train through a castle dungeon). Have students take a virtual tour of the park by going to **www.parcasterix.fr.**

141

4A.1 The verb *aller* **vhl**central

Point de départ In **Leçon 1A**, you saw a form of the verb **aller** (*to go*) in the expression **ça va.** Now you will use this verb to talk about going places and to express actions that take place in the immediate future.

aller			
je vais	*I go*	**nous allons**	*we go*
tu vas	*you go*	**vous allez**	*you go*
il/elle/on va	*he/she/it/one goes*	**ils/elles vont**	*they go*

- The verb **aller** is irregular. Only the **nous** and **vous** forms resemble the infinitive.

Tu **vas** souvent au cinéma?
Do you go to the movies often?

Je **vais** à la piscine.
I'm going to the pool.

Nous **allons** au marché le samedi.
We go to the market on Saturdays.

Vous **allez** au parc aussi?
Are you going to the park too?

Le futur proche

- The present tense of **aller** can be used with the infinitive form of another verb to tell what is going to happen. This construction is called **le futur proche** (*the immediate future*).

Nous **allons déjeuner** sur la terrasse.
We're going to eat lunch on the terrace.

Je **vais partager** la pizza avec ma copine.
I'm going to share the pizza with my friend.

Marc et Julie **vont explorer** le centre-ville.
Marc and Julie are going to explore the city center.

Elles **vont retrouver** Guillaume à la cantine.
They're going to meet Guillaume at the cafeteria.

Demain, je vais déjeuner au centre-ville.

Et quand est-ce que tu vas rentrer?

- To negate an expression in **le futur proche**, place **ne/n'** before the conjugated form of **aller** and **pas** after it.

Je **ne vais pas** oublier la date.
I'm not going to forget the date.

Tu **ne vas pas** manger au café?
Aren't you going to eat at the café?

Nous **n'allons pas** quitter la maison.
We're not going to leave the house.

Ousmane **ne va pas** retrouver Salima au parc.
Ousmane is not going to meet Salima at the park.

- Note that **le futur proche** can be used with the infinitive of **aller** to mean *going to go (somewhere)*.

Elle **va aller** à la piscine.
She's going to go to the pool.

Vous **allez aller** au gymnase ce soir?
Are you going to go to the gym tonight?

The preposition *à* and prepositions with place names

- The preposition **à** can be translated in various ways in English: *to, in, at*. When followed by the definite article **le** or **les**, the preposition **à** and the definite article contract into one word.

  à + le ▸ au

  Nous allons **au** magasin.
  We're going to the store.

  à + les ▸ aux

  Ils parlent **aux** profs.
  They're talking to the teachers.

- The preposition **à** does not contract with **la** or **l'**.

  à + la ▸ à la

  Je rentre **à la** maison.
  I'm going back home.

  à + l' ▸ à l'

  Il va **à l'**épicerie.
  He's going to the grocery store.

- The preposition **à** often indicates a physical location, as with **aller à** and **habiter à**. However, it can have other meanings depending on the verb used.

Verbs with the preposition *à*			
commencer à + [*infinitive*]	to start (doing something)	penser à	to think about
parler à	to talk to	téléphoner à	to phone (someone)

  Elle va **parler au** professeur.
  She's going to talk to the teacher.

  Il **commence à travailler** demain.
  He starts working tomorrow.

 Vérifiez

- In general, **à** is used to mean *at* or *in,* whereas **dans** is used to mean *inside* or *within.* When learning a place name in French, learn the preposition that accompanies it.

Prepositions with place names			
à la maison	*at home*	dans la maison	*inside the house*
à Paris	*in Paris*	dans Paris	*within Paris*
en ville	*in town*	dans la ville	*within the town*
sur la place	*in the square*	à/sur la terrasse	*on the terrace*

  Tu travailles **à la maison**?
  Are you working at home?

  On mange **dans la maison**.
  We'll eat in the house.

Vérifiez

Essayez!

Utilisez la forme correcte du verbe aller. Pour les phrases 2–6, utilisez aussi la forme correcte de la préposition à et l'article défini.

1. Comment ça ___*va*___ ?
2. Tu ___*vas à la*___ piscine pour nager.
3. Ils ___*vont au*___ centre-ville.
4. Nous ___*allons*___ bavarder ___*au*___ parc.
5. Vous ___*allez*___ aller ___*au*___ restaurant ce soir?
6. Elle ___*va*___ aller ___*à l'*___ église dimanche matin.
7. Ce soir, je ___*vais*___ faire mes devoirs.
8. On ne ___*va*___ pas passer par l'épicerie cet après-midi.

Suggestions: Scaffolding
- Have students complete the Extra Practice activity, p. 142.
- Bring in pictures of people dressed for different activities. Describe them to the class using the verb **aller**. Example: Showing a picture of a swimmer, say: **Il/Elle va à la piscine.** Then explain the contractions **à + le = au** and **à + les = aux**.
- Present verbs with the preposition **à**. Point out that **commencer à** is the only one followed by an infinitive. The other verbs are followed by nouns. Tell students that, when followed by another verb (in the infinitive), **penser** doesn't take a preposition. Example: **Je pense aller au parc après les cours.** Have students work in pairs to write two sentences for each verb. Call on volunteers to share sentences for the class to correct. Then have students complete the second **Vérifiez** activity.
- Model the pronunciation of the list of prepositions with places. Tell students that they should memorize these phrases. Ask students questions using the prepositions with places. Example: **Vous dînez à la maison ou en ville?**
- Have students complete the third **Vérifiez** activity.

TELL Connection

Planning 7 *Why:* Planning to use French at least 90% of the time at all stages of instruction promotes language proficiency. *What:* Plan how to use visuals, mime, and other tools to guide student understanding and application of new grammatical concepts without resorting to English.

Essayez! Before students complete **Essayez!**, have them watch the Grammar Tutorial for review.

EXPANSION

Extra Practice Have students make a list of activities for their next school break using the verb **aller**. If they don't have plans yet, they can make something up. Ask them to share their lists with a classmate. Then, each pair should share their classmate's plans with the class. Example: **Il/Elle va voyager en Afrique.** Encourage them to mention activities they have in common so they use **nous**: **Nous allons nager à la piscine.**

DIFFERENTIATION

For Kinesthetic Learners Invent gestures to pantomime some activities taught in **Leçon 4B**. Examples: **nager**: *move arms as if swimming*; **bavarder**: *make talking gestures with hands*; **dépenser de l'argent**: *turn pockets inside out.* Signal individuals to gesture appropriately as you cue activities by saying: **Nous allons…** or **On va….**

Mise en pratique

1 Samedi prochain Voici ce que (*what*) vous et vos amis faites (*are doing*) aujourd'hui. Indiquez que vous allez faire les mêmes (*same*) choses samedi prochain.

MODÈLE

Je nage.
Samedi prochain aussi, je vais nager.

1. Paul bavarde avec ses copains. Samedi prochain aussi, Paul va bavarder avec ses copains.
2. Nous dansons. ... nous allons danser.
3. Je dépense de l'argent dans un magasin. ... je vais dépenser de l'argent dans un magasin.
4. Luc et Sylvie déjeunent au restaurant. ... Luc et Sylvie vont déjeuner au restaurant.
5. Vous explorez le centre-ville. ... vous allez explorer le centre-ville.
6. Tu patines. ... tu vas patiner.
7. Amélie nage à la piscine. ... Amélie va nager à la piscine.
8. Lucas et Sabrina téléphonent à leurs grands-parents. ... Lucas et Sabrina vont téléphoner à leurs grands-parents.

2 Questions parentales Votre père est très curieux. Écrivez les questions qu'il pose. Utilisez la forme correcte du verbe **aller** et de la préposition nécessaire.

MODÈLE

tes frères / piscine
Tes frères vont à la piscine?

1. tu / cinéma / ce soir   Tu vas au cinéma ce soir?
2. tes amis et toi, vous / café   Tes amis et toi, vous allez au café?
3. ta mère et moi, nous / ville / vendredi   Ta mère et moi, nous allons en ville vendredi?
4. ton ami(e) / souvent / marché   Ton ami(e) va souvent au marché?
5. je / musée / avec toi / demain   Je vais au musée avec toi demain?
6. tes amis / parc   Tes amis vont au parc?
7. on / église / dimanche   On va à l'église dimanche?
8. tes amis et toi, vous / parfois / gymnase   Tes amis et toi, vous allez parfois au gymnase?

3 Où vont-ils? Indiquez où vont les personnages.   Answers will vary.

▶ **MODÈLE**

Henri va au cinéma.

Henri

1. tu

2. nous

3. Paul et Luc

4. vous

_____ _____ _____ _____

Communication

4 Activités du week-end Avec un(e) partenaire, assemblez les éléments des colonnes pour poser des questions. Rajoutez (*Add*) d'autres éléments utiles. Answers will vary.

MODÈLE

Élève 1: *Est-ce que tu vas déjeuner aves tes copains?*
Élève 2: *Oui, je vais déjeuner avec mes copains.*

A	B	C	D
ta sœur	aller	voyager	professeur
vous		aller	cinéma
tes copains		déjeuner	piscine
nous		bavarder	centre
tu		nager	commercial
ton petit ami		parler	café
ta petite amie		inviter	parents
tes		téléphoner	copains
grands-parents		visiter	petit(e) ami(e)
		patiner	camarades de classe
			musée
			cousin(e)s

5 Le grand voyage Vous avez gagné (*have won*) un voyage. Par groupes de trois, expliquez à vos camarades ce que vous allez faire pendant (*during*) le voyage. Vos camarades vont deviner (*to guess*) où vous allez. Answers will vary.

MODÈLE

Élève 1: *Je vais visiter le musée du Louvre.*
Élève 2: *Est-ce que tu vas aller à Paris?*

6 À Deauville Votre professeur va vous donner, à vous et à votre partenaire, un plan (*map*) de Deauville. Posez-vous des questions pour découvrir (*to find out*) où va chaque membre de la famille de votre liste. Attention! Ne regardez pas la feuille de votre partenaire. Answers will vary.

MODÈLE

Élève 1: *Où va Simon?*
Élève 2: *Il va au kiosque.*

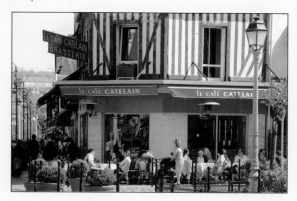

4 Suggestion Have two volunteers read the **modèle**. Remind students that they can answer in the negative. Encourage them to expand on their answers. Examples: **Oui, je vais déjeuner avec mes copains au Petit Croissant./Non, je ne vais pas déjeuner avec mes copains, mais je vais aller au centre commercial avec ma mère.**

4 Partner Chat You can also assign Activity 4 on vhlcentral.com. Students work in pairs to record the activity online. The pair's recorded conversation will appear in your gradebook.

5 Suggestion Have two volunteers read the **modèle**. Encourage students to choose famous places in the Francophone world.

6 Suggestions
• Tell students that Deauville is a fashionable seaside resort in Normandy frequented by the rich and famous.
• Divide the class into pairs and distribute the Info Gap Handouts found in the Activity Pack on vhlcentral.com. Give students ten minutes to complete the activity.

Activity Pack For additional activities, go to the **Activity Pack** in the **Resources** section of vhlcentral.com.

TEACHING OPTIONS

Extra Practice Do a quick substitution drill to practice **aller**. Write a sentence on the board and have students read it aloud. Then say a new subject and have students repeat the sentence, substituting the new subject. Examples: **1. Tu vas à l'hôpital. (nous, mon frère, vous, mes parents, je) 2. Il va aller au kiosque. (je, Claudine, nous, tu, les enfants, vous)**

TEACHING OPTIONS

Game Divide the class into four-member teams. Using the immediate future, each team will write a description of tomorrow's events for a well-known fictional character. Teams take turns reading and/or writing the description on the board without giving the character's name. The other teams will guess the identity. Each correct guess earns a point. If a team fools the others, it earns two points. The team with the most points wins.

4A.2 Interrogative words vhlcentral

Section Goals

In this section, students will learn interrogative words.

Key Standards

4.1, 5.1

Suggestions: Scaffolding

- Review how to form questions using **est-ce que** and inversion.
- Have students identify the interrogative words they know. Examples: **comment?**, **combien?**, **pourquoi?**, **qui?**, and **quel(s)/quelle(s)?** Model the pronunciation of the new words and have students repeat.
- Go over the three ways to form questions presented in bullets 1–2.
- Present bullet 3, pointing out the parts of speech of each word in the examples. Write sentences on the board and have students identify whether **qui** is the object or subject of the sentence. Examples: **Qui est ton ami?** (subject) **Qui écoutes-tu?** (object)
- Present bullets 4–5. Ask students questions using **quand, à quelle heure,** and **qu'est-ce que.** Examples: **Quand est-ce que vous travaillez? À quelle heure dînez-vous? Qu'est-ce que vous regardez à la télé ce soir?**

Point de départ In **Leçon 2A**, you learned four ways to ask yes or no questions in French. However, many questions seek information that can't be provided by a simple yes or no answer.

- Use these words with **est-ce que** or inversion to ask for more specific information.

Interrogative words			
à quelle heure?	*at what time?*	**quand?**	*when?*
combien (de)?	*how many?; how much?*	**que/qu'...?**	*what?*
		quel(le)(s)?	*which?; what?*
comment?	*how?; what?*	**(à/avec/pour)**	*(to/with/for)*
où?	*where?*	**qui?**	*who(m)?*
pourquoi?	*why?*	**quoi?**	*what?*

À qui est-ce que tu penses?
Who are you thinking about?

Combien de villes **y a-t-il** en Suisse?
How many cities are there in Switzerland?

Pourquoi est-ce que tu danses?
Why are you dancing?

Que vas-tu manger?
What are you going to eat?

- Another way to ask questions with most interrogative words is by placing them after a verb. This kind of formulation is very informal but very common.

Tu t'appelles **comment**?
What's your name?

Tu habites **où**?
Where do you live?

- When the question word **qui** (*who*) is the subject of a sentence, it is followed directly by a verb in the third person singular.

Qui invite Patrice à dîner?
Who is inviting Patrice to dinner?

Qui n'aime pas danser?
Who doesn't like to dance?

When the question word **qui** (*whom*) is the object of a sentence, it is followed by **est-ce que** plus a subject and verb or an inverted subject and verb.

Qui est-ce que tu regardes?
Who are you looking at?

Qui regardes-tu?
Who are you looking at?

- Although **quand?** and **à quelle heure?** can both be translated as *when?*, they are not interchangeable in French. Use **quand** to ask about a day or date and **à quelle heure** to ask about a specific time of day.

Quand est-ce que le cours commence?
When does the class start?

Il commence **le lundi 28 août**.
It starts Monday, August 28.

À quelle heure est-ce qu'il commence?
At what time does it begin?

Il commence **à dix heures et demie**.
It begins at 10:30.

- The question word **que/qu'** (*what*) used with **est-ce que** or with inversion is always the object of the sentence. This means that a subject and verb must follow it.

Que regardons-nous?
What are we looking at?

Que pensez-vous visiter?
What are you planning to visit?

Qu'est-ce que tu vas manger?
What are you going to eat?

Qu'est-ce que Sandrine étudie?
What is Sandrine studying?

Boîte à outils

If a question word is followed immediately by the verb **être**, don't use **est-ce que**.

Où est mon sac à dos?
Where is my backpack?

Comment est ta petite amie?
What's your girlfriend like?

À noter

Refer to **Structures 2A.2** to review how to answer a question with **pourquoi** using **parce que/qu'**.

DIFFERENTIATION

For Kinesthetic Learners Read aloud a series of statements and questions, including tag questions (which were introduced in **Leçon 2A**). Have students raise their right hand when they hear a statement or their left hand when they hear a question.

TEACHING OPTIONS

Pairs Give pairs of students five minutes to write original questions using as many interrogative words as they can. Can any pair come up with questions using all the interrogative words?

- The question word **quoi?** also means *what*? Use it after a preposition followed by **est-ce que** or inversion instead of **que/qu'** or **qu'est-ce que**. You can also use **quoi** after the verb in informal questions when there is no preposition.

  À quoi pensez-vous?
  What are you thinking about?

  De quoi est-ce qu'il parle?
  What is he talking about?

  Elle étudie **quoi**?
  What does she study?

  Tu regardes **quoi**?
  What are you looking at?

- Use **Comment?** or **Pardon?** to indicate that you don't understand what's being said. You may also use **Quoi?** but only in informal situations with friends.

  Vous allez voyager cette année?
  Are you going to travel this year?

  Comment?
  I beg your pardon?

The interrogative adjective *quel(le)(s)*

- The interrogative adjective **quel** means *what* or *which*. The form of **quel** varies in gender and number with the noun it modifies.

The interrogative adjective *quel(le)(s)*				
	singular		**plural**	
masculine	Quel	*restaurant?*	Quels	*cours?*
feminine	Quelle	*montre?*	Quelles	*filles?*

  Quel restaurant aimes-tu?
  Which restaurant do you like?

  Quelle montre a-t-il?
  What watch does he have?

  Quels cours commencent à dix heures?
  What classes start at ten o'clock?

  Quelles filles vont à la cantine?
  Which girls are going to the cafeteria?

- **Quel** is always linked to a noun. It is used either directly before a noun or before the verb **être** followed by a noun.

  Quelles amies invites-tu?
  What friends are you inviting?

  Quel est ton numéro de téléphone?
  What is your phone number?

  Quelle heure est-il?
  What time is it?

  Quels sont tes cours préférés?
  What are your favorite classes?

Vérifiez

Boîte à outils

You can also use a form of **quel** as an exclamation.
Quel beau garçon!
What a handsome boy!
Quelles grandes maisons!
What big houses!

Vérifiez

Essayez!　　**Donnez les mots (*words*) interrogatifs.**

1. _Comment_ allez-vous?
2. _Qu'_ est-ce que vous allez faire (*do*) après le cours?
3. Le cours commence à _quelle_ heure?
4. _Pourquoi_ est-ce que tu ne travailles pas?
5. Avec _qui_ est-ce qu'on va au cinéma ce soir?
6. _Combien_ d'élèves y a-t-il?
7. _Quels_ musées vas-tu visiter?
8. _Quand_ est-ce que tes parents arrivent?
9. _Qui_ n'aime pas voyager?
10. _Où_ est-ce qu'on dîne ce soir?
11. De _quoi_ parlez-vous?
12. _Quel_ est ton restaurant préféré?

cent quarante-sept **147**

---

1 **Suggestion** Have one student ask the question and call on another student to answer it.

1 **Expansion** Have students compare their answers with a classmate's.

2 **Suggestion** Have one student say the question and call on another student to answer it.

3 **Suggestion** Before beginning the activity, point out that there is more than one way to form some of the questions. Have students work in pairs. Tell them to take turns asking and answering the questions.

Mise en pratique

1 **Le français familier** Utilisez l'inversion pour reformuler les questions.

MODÈLE

Tu t'appelles comment?
Comment t'appelles-tu?

1. Tu habites où? Où habites-tu?
2. Le film commence à quelle heure? À quelle heure le film commence-t-il?
3. Il est quelle heure? Quelle heure est-il?
4. Tu as combien de frères? Combien de frères as-tu?
5. Le prof parle quand? Quand le prof parle-t-il?
6. Vous aimez quoi? Qu'aimez-vous?
7. Elle téléphone à qui? À qui téléphone-t-elle?
8. Il étudie comment? Comment étudie-t-il?
9. Il y a combien d'enfants? Combien d'enfants y a-t-il?
10. Elle aime qui? Qui aime-t-elle?

2 **La paire** Trouvez la paire et formez des phrases complètes. Utilisez chaque (*each*) option une seule fois (*only once*). Answers may vary.

1. À quelle heure d
2. Comment f
3. Combien de g
4. Avec qui h
5. Où b
6. Pourquoi c
7. Qu' a
8. Quelle e

a. est-ce que tu regardes?
b. habitent-ils?
c. est-ce que tu habites dans le centre-ville?
d. est-ce que le cours commence?
e. heure est-il?
f. vous appelez-vous?
g. villes est-ce qu'il y a aux États-Unis?
h. parlez-vous?

3 **La question** Vous avez les réponses. Quelles sont les questions? Some answers will vary.

MODÈLE

Il est midi.
Quelle heure est-il?

1. Les cours commencent à huit heures. À quelle heure est-ce que les cours commencent?
2. Stéphanie habite à Paris. Où est-ce que Stéphanie habite?
3. Julien danse avec Caroline. Avec qui est-ce que Julien danse?
4. Elle s'appelle Julie. Comment s'appelle-t-elle?
5. Laetitia a deux chiens. Combien de chiens Laetitia a-t-elle?
6. Elle déjeune dans ce restaurant parce qu'il est à côté de son bureau. Pourquoi déjeune-t-elle dans ce restaurant?
7. Nous allons bien, merci. Comment allez-vous?
8. Je vais au marché mardi. Quand est-ce que tu vas au marché?
9. Simon aime danser. Qui aime danser?
10. Brigitte pense à ses études. À quoi Brigitte pense-t-elle?

DIFFERENTIATION

For Auditory Learners Prepare eight questions and answers. Write only the answers on the board in random order. Then read the questions aloud and have students identify the appropriate answer. Ex: **À quelle heure est le cours de français? (à neuf heures).**

EXPANSION

Pairs Have student pairs script an interview with a famous person, using as many interrogative words as possible. Have them present their interviews to the class. To make sure listeners pay attention and are involved, ask the pair presenting the interview not to say the name of the interviewee so the rest of the class can try to guess who he/she is.

Communication

4 **Questions et réponses** À tour de rôle, posez une question à un(e) partenaire au sujet de chaque (*each*) thème de la liste. Posez une seconde question basée sur sa réponse. Answers will vary.

MODÈLE

Élève 1: *Où est-ce que tu habites?*
Élève 2: *J'habite au centre-ville.*
Élève 1: *Pourquoi est-ce que tu habites au centre-ville?*

Thèmes

- où vous habitez
- ce que vous faites (*do*) le week-end
- à qui vous téléphonez
- combien de frères et sœurs vous avez
- les endroits que vous fréquentez avec vos copains
- comment sont vos camarades de classe
- quels cours vous aimez

5 **La montagne** Par groupes de quatre, lisez (*read*) avec attention la lettre de Céline. Fermez votre livre. Une personne du groupe va poser une question basée sur l'information donnée. La personne qui répond pose une autre question au groupe, etc. Answers will vary.

Bonjour. Je m'appelle Céline. J'ai 17 ans. Je suis grande, mince et sportive. J'habite à Grenoble dans une maison agréable. Je suis en première. J'adore la montagne.

Tous les week-ends, je vais skier à Chamrousse avec mes trois amis Alain, Catherine et Pascal. Nous skions de midi à cinq heures. À six heures, nous prenons un chocolat chaud à la terrasse d'un café ou nous allons manger des crêpes dans un restaurant. Nous allons au cinéma tous ensemble.

6 **Le week-end** Avec un(e) partenaire, posez-vous des questions pour savoir (*know*) où vous allez aller ce (*this*) week-end. Utilisez **le futur proche**. Posez beaucoup de questions pour avoir tous les détails sur les projets (*plans*) de votre partenaire.

MODÈLE

Élève 1: *Où est-ce que tu vas aller samedi?*
Élève 2: *Je vais aller au centre commercial.*
Élève 1: *Avec qui?*

4 Suggestion Have two volunteers read the **modèle** aloud. Tell students to jot down their partner's responses.

4 Partner Chat You can also assign Activity 4 on vhlcentral.com. Students work in pairs to record the activity online. The pair's recorded conversation will appear in your gradebook.

5 Suggestion Circulate among the groups, providing help where necessary. You might want to have one person in each group keep the book open to verify answers.

6 Suggestion Tell students to jot down notes on their partner's plans. Have them report to the class what their partners will be doing next weekend in as much detail as possible.

Activity Pack For additional activities, go to the **Activity Pack** in the **Resources** section of vhlcentral.com.

Révision

Key Standards

1.1

1 Suggestion Model the activity with a volunteer by asking questions about **le café**. Tell students to jot down notes during the interviews. Encourage them to add other places to the list.

2 Suggestion Photocopy and distribute a page from a French day planner so that students can make a note of the activities in the appropriate place. To review telling time, tell students to say the time at which they do the activities as well as the day.

3 Suggestion Before beginning the activity, have students make a list of possible activities for the weekend.

4 Suggestion Before beginning the activity, give students a few minutes to make a list of possible activities in their hometown to discuss.

4 Partner Chat You can also assign Activity 4 on vhlcentral.com. Students work in pairs to record the activity online. The pair's recorded conversation will appear in your gradebook.

5 Suggestion Have two volunteers read the **modèle** aloud. Then have students brainstorm places they could go and things they could do in each city. Write their suggestions on the board.

5 Partner Chat You can also assign Activity 5 on vhlcentral.com. Students work in pairs to record the activity online.

6 Expansion Call on volunteers to read their descriptions aloud and have the class compare them.

---

1 **En ville** Par groupes de trois, interviewez vos camarades. Où allez-vous en ville? Quand ils mentionnent un endroit de la liste, demandez des détails (quand? avec qui? pourquoi? etc.). Présentez les réponses à la classe. Answers will vary.

le centre commercial	le musée
le cinéma	le parc
le gymnase	la piscine
le marché	le restaurant

2 **La semaine prochaine** Voici votre agenda (*day planner*). Parlez de votre semaine avec un(e) partenaire. Mentionnez trois activités associées au lycée, trois activités d'un autre type et deux activités à faire en groupe. Answers will vary.

MODÈLE

Lundi, je vais préparer un examen, mais mardi, je vais au centre commercial.

	L	M	M	J	V	S	D
8h30							
9h00							
9h30							
10h00							
10h30							
11h00							
11h30							
12h00							
12h30							

3 **Le week-end** Par groupes de trois, posez-vous des questions sur vos projets (*plans*) pour le week-end prochain. Donnez des détails. Mentionnez des activités qu'on fait (*does*) avec des amis. Answers will vary.

MODÈLE

Élève 1: *Quels projets avez-vous pour ce week-end?*
Élève 2: *Nous allons au marché samedi.*
Élève 3: *Et nous allons au cinéma dimanche.*

4 **Ma ville** Votre partenaire passe une semaine chez vous. Parlez des activités dans votre ville que vous et votre partenaire ont envie de faire. Ensuite (*Then*), comparez vos projets (*plans*) avec ceux (*those*) d'un autre groupe. Answers will vary.

MODÈLE

Élève 1: *Samedi, on va au centre-ville.*
Élève 2: *Nous allons dépenser de l'argent!*

5 **Où passer un long week-end?** Vous et votre partenaire avez la possibilité de passer un long week-end à Montréal ou à La Nouvelle-Orléans, mais vous préférez chacun(e) (*each one*) une ville différente. Présentez votre conversation à la classe. Answers will vary.

MODÈLE

Élève 1: *À Montréal, on va aller dans les librairies!*
Élève 2: *Oui, mais à La Nouvelle-Orléans, je vais aller à des concerts de musique cajun!*

Montréal

- le jardin (*garden*) botanique
- le musée des Beaux-Arts
- le parc du Mont-Royal
- le Vieux-Montréal

La Nouvelle-Orléans

- le Café du Monde
- la cathédrale Saint-Louis
- la route des plantations
- le vieux carré, quartier (*neighborhood*) français

6 **La semaine de Martine** Votre professeur va vous donner, à vous et à votre partenaire, des informations sur la semaine de Martine. Attention! Ne regardez pas la feuille de votre partenaire. Answers will vary.

MODÈLE

Lundi matin, Martine va dessiner au parc.

PRE-AP®

Interpersonal Speaking Invite a native French speaker to class. Before the person arrives, have students prepare a list of questions that they would like to ask this person. For example, they could ask about the person's job, family, leisure-time activities, weekend plans, and the places he or she frequents. Have students use their questions to interview the person.

TEACHING OPTIONS

Writing Practice Give pairs three minutes to write as many questions as they can using interrogative words. Then have them get together with another pair and take turns asking and answering the questions.

vhlcentral

AP® **Theme:** Contemporary Life
Context: Advertising and Marketing

Préparation Répondez aux questions suivantes. Answers will vary.

1. Aimez-vous cuisiner (*to cook*)? Où allez-vous pour acheter (*to buy*) de la nourriture (*food*)?

2. Achetez-vous des desserts, ou préférez-vous les préparer vous-même (*yourself*)?

Un tuto° original

Bons plans, réservations en ligne, des tutos originaux—PagesJaunes est beaucoup plus qu'un annuaire°. C'est un site de services. Dans sa campagne publicitaire «*Don't do it yourself*», PagesJaunes travaille en partenariat° avec FastGoodCuisine, nom professionnel du Youtuber cuisinier° Charles Gilles-Compagnon. Ensemble, ils présentent un tuto à «comment ne pas faire soi-même°». Le tuto a un grand succès grâce au° charme et à la célébrité de FastGoodCuisine. Avec plus d'un million de followers, cette star d'Internet réinvente la notion du fast-food en proposant des tutos créatifs, des interviews de grands chefs et des recettes simples, bonnes et saines°.

souhaiterais *would like* **une pièce montée** *tiered/layered dessert* **tuto** *tutorial* **annuaire** *phone book* **en partenariat** *in partnership* **cuisinier** *cook* **ne pas faire soi-même** *not to do it yourself* **grâce au** *thanks to* **saines** *healthy*

Publicité de PagesJaunes

Je souhaiterais° une pièce montée° s'il te plaît.

Vocabulaire utile

une astuce	*trick, tip*
les choux (*m.*)	*light, puffed pastries*
une étape	*step*
goûter	*to taste*
une pâtisserie	*bakery*

Compréhension Indiquez l'ordre des évènements (*events*) de la vidéo.

___2___ FastGoodCuisine dit bonjour à Guillaume.

___5___ FastGoodCuisine goûte un chou.

___1___ FastGoodCuisine va à la pâtisserie.

___3___ FastGoodCuisine demande une pièce montée.

___4___ FastGoodCuisine va en terrasse.

___6___ FastGoodCuisine et Guillaume prennent une photo.

Conversation À deux, répondez aux questions. Answers will vary.

1. Utilisez-vous l'Internet pour apprendre (*to learn*) de nouvelles activités? Quels types d'activités?

2. Pour quelles activités ou tâches (*tasks*) avez-vous besoin d'un professionnel? Pourquoi?

Application Pensez à un service pour lequel (*for which*) vous avez besoin d'un professionnel. Cherchez sur Internet deux personnes ou compagnies dans votre région qui offrent ce service. Notez les adresses, les numéros de téléphone, les prix (*prices*) et les critiques. Ensuite, préparez une représentation graphique des deux compagnies et présentez-la à la classe. Quelle compagnie préférez-vous? Pourquoi?

cent cinquante et un **151**

Section Goals

In this section, students will learn and practice vocabulary related to:
• foods and beverages
• eating at a café or restaurant

Key Standards

1.1, 1.2, 4.1

Suggestions

• Use the digital image for this page. Ask students to describe where the scene takes place and what people are doing. Have students identify items they know.
• Have students look at the new vocabulary and identify the cognates.
• Model the pronunciation of the words and have students repeat after you. Then ask students a few questions about the people in the drawing. Examples: **Qui a faim? Que mange l'homme? Qui a soif?**
• Point out the menu in the illustration. Explain the difference between **un menu** and **une carte**. Ask students what **soupe du jour** and **plat du jour** mean. Then ask: **Combien coûte le plat du jour? Et la soupe du jour?**
• Tell students that a 15% tip is usually included in the price of a meal in a café or restaurant. If the service is particularly good, it is customary to leave a little bit extra.
• Present quantities by using food or other items and making comparisons. Example: **J'ai quelques bonbons** (taking 3 from a bag). **Maintenant, j'ai plusieurs bonbons** (taking several). **Et maintenant, j'ai tous les bonbons** (taking the whole bag).

You will learn how to...
▪ order food and beverages
▪ ask for your check

◀)) **vhl**central

J'ai faim!

Vocabulaire

apporter	to bring, to carry
coûter	to cost
Combien coûte(nt)...?	How much is/are...?
une baguette	baguette (long, thin loaf of bread)
le beurre	butter
des frites (f.)	French fries
un fromage	cheese
le jambon	ham
un pain (de campagne)	(country-style) bread
un sandwich	sandwich
une boisson (gazeuse)	(soft) (carbonated) drink/beverage
un chocolat (chaud)	(hot) chocolate
une eau (minérale)	(mineral) water
un jus (d'orange, de pomme, etc.)	(orange, apple, etc.) juice
le lait	milk
une limonade	lemon soda
un thé (glacé)	(iced) tea
(pas) assez (de)	(not) enough (of)
beaucoup (de)	a lot (of)
d'autres	others
un morceau (de)	piece, bit (of)
un peu (plus/moins) (de)	a little (more/less) (of)
plusieurs	several
quelque chose	something; anything
quelques	some
tous (m. pl.)	all
tout (m. sing.)	all
tout le/tous les (m.)	all the
toute la/toutes les (f.)	all the
trop (de)	too many/much (of)
un verre (de)	glass (of)

Labels in illustration: un serveur (serveuse f.); le prix; une bouteille d'eau; l'addition (f.); une soupe; les croissants (m.); Elle laisse un pourboire. (laisser); Il a faim.

Menu du jour: soupe du jour 3.50€; plat du jour 12€

EXPANSION

Food and Drink Write **le matin**, **à midi**, and **le soir** on the board or on a transparency. Then ask students when they prefer to have various foods and beverages. Example: **Préférez-vous manger des frites le matin ou à midi?** Other items you can mention are **un éclair**, **un sandwich**, **une soupe**, and **un croissant**.

EXPANSION

Categories Have students work in pairs. Tell them to classify the foods and drinks under the headings **Manger** and **Boire** (*To drink*). After pairs have completed the activity, tell them to compare their lists with another pair and to resolve any differences.

1 Expansion For additional practice, give students these items. **9. beaucoup de, un verre de, assez de, un peu de (un verre de) 10. le café, le jus, le thé, le chocolat chaud (le jus) 11. l'addition, le prix, le serveur, le pourboire (le serveur)**

2 Suggestion You may wish to introduce words for other types of containers, such as **une assiette, un bol,** and **un paquet.**

2 Expansion For additional practice, give students these items. **9. lait (une bouteille de/un verre de) 10. beurre (un morceau de)**

3 Script SERVEUR: Bonjour, Monsieur! Vous désirez? ANDRÉ: Bonjour! Combien coûtent les sandwichs? S: Ça dépend. Un sandwich au jambon coûte 4€, mais un sandwich au jambon avec du fromage et des frites coûte 7,50€. A: Et combien coûte un café? S: Un café coûte 2,50€ et un café au lait coûte 5,50€. A: Y a-t-il d'autres boissons? S: Bien sûr, il y a du jus d'orange, des boissons gazeuses, de la limonade et de l'eau. A: Je n'ai pas beaucoup d'argent sur moi, mais j'ai très faim. J'ai envie d'un sandwich au jambon, s'il vous plaît. Et comme je n'ai pas très soif, alors un café au lait, s'il vous plaît. S: Très bien, Monsieur. A: Excusez-moi, c'est combien? S: C'est 9,50€. A: Voici. Merci et bonne journée! S: Merci, Monsieur, au revoir. Oh là là! Pas de pourboire! *Teacher Resources DVD*

3 Suggestion Have students correct the false items.

Mise en pratique

Attention!

To read prices in French, say the number of euros (**euros**) followed by the number of cents (**centimes**). French decimals are marked with a comma, not a period.

8,10€ = huit euros dix (centimes)

1 **Chassez l'intrus** Trouvez le mot qui ne va pas avec les autres.

1. un croissant, le pain, le fromage, une baguette
2. une limonade, un jus de pomme, un jus d'orange, le beurre
3. des frites, un sandwich, le sucre, le jambon
4. le jambon, un éclair, un croissant, une baguette
5. l'eau, la boisson, l'eau minérale, la soupe
6. l'addition, un chocolat, le pourboire, coûter
7. apporter, d'autres, plusieurs, quelques
8. un morceau, une bouteille, un verre, une tasse

2 **Reliez** Choisissez les expressions de quantité qui correspondent le mieux (*the best*) aux produits.

MODÈLE

un morceau de baguette

une bouteille de	une tasse de
un morceau de	un verre de

1. un verre d'/une bouteille d' eau
2. un morceau de sandwich
3. un morceau de fromage
4. une tasse de chocolat
5. une tasse de café
6. un verre de/une bouteille de jus de pomme
7. une tasse de thé
8. un verre de limonade

3 **Écoutez** Écoutez la conversation entre André et le serveur du café Gide, et décidez si les phrases sont **vraies** ou **fausses.**

	Vrai	Faux
1. André n'a pas très soif.	☑	☐
2. André n'a pas faim.	☐	☑
3. Au café, on peut commander (*one may order*) un jus d'orange, une limonade, un café ou une boisson gazeuse.	☑	☐
4. André commande un sandwich au jambon avec du fromage.	☐	☑
5. André commande une tasse de chocolat.	☐	☑
6. André déteste le lait.	☐	☑
7. André n'a pas beaucoup d'argent.	☑	☐
8. André ne laisse pas de pourboire.	☑	☐

Il a soif.

le sucre

le thé

une tasse

Il mange quelque chose. (manger)

un café

un éclair

TEACHING OPTIONS

Using Games Write these categories on the board: **Boissons froides / chaudes** and **Nourriture froide / chaude.** Toss a beanbag to a student at random and call out a category. The student has four seconds to name a food or beverage that fits the category. He or she then tosses the beanbag to another student and calls out a category. Players who cannot think of an item in time or repeat an item are eliminated. The last person standing wins.

EXPANSION

Oral Practice For additional practice, ask students questions about their food and drink preferences. Examples: **Préférez-vous le thé ou le chocolat? Le lait ou l'eau minérale? Le jus d'orange ou le jus de pomme? Le jambon ou le fromage? Les sandwichs ou les éclairs? La soupe ou les frites? Les baguettes ou les croissants?**

4 Suggestion Tell students that in conversation, the word **euro** is often omitted when giving prices that contain whole euros and cents. Example: **10,50€ = dix, cinquante.**

5 Suggestion Tell students to jot down notes during their interviews. Then have volunteers report their findings to the class.

5 Virtual Chat You can also assign Activity 5 on vhlcentral.com. Students record individual responses that appear in your gradebook.

6 Suggestion Distribute photocopies of actual café menus for students to use or have students base their conversation on the menu in **Activité 4.**

21st Century Skills

Productivity and Accountability
Provide students with the oral testing rubric found in the Teacher Resources on vhlcentral.com. Ask them to keep these strategies in mind as they prepare their oral exchanges.

7 Suggestion Divide the class into pairs and distribute the Info Gap Handouts from the Activity Pack.

TELL Connection

Collaboration 5 *Why:* Support students' understanding and appreciation of French products, practices, and perspectives. *What:* Connect with local, regional, or online francophone communities to share their food and dining experiences with your students.

Communication

4 Combien coûte...? Regardez la carte et, à tour de rôle, demandez à votre partenaire combien coûte chaque élément. Répondez par des phrases complètes.

MODÈLE
Élève 1: *Combien coûte un sandwich?*
Élève 2: *Un sandwich coûte 3,50€.*

1. Combien coûtent les frites? Les frites coûtent 2€.
2. Combien coûte une boisson gazeuse? Une boisson gazeuse coûte 2€.
3. Combien coûte une limonade? Une limonade coûte 1,75€.
4. Combien coûte une bouteille d'eau? Une bouteille d'eau coûte 2€.
5. Combien coûte une tasse de café? Une tasse de café coûte 3€.
6. Combien coûte une tasse de thé? Une tasse de thé coûte 2,50€.
7. Combien coûte un croissant? Un croissant coûte 1€.
8. Combien coûte un éclair? Un éclair coûte 1,95€.

5 Conversez Interviewez un(e) camarade de classe. Answers will vary.

1. Qu'est-ce que tu aimes boire (*drink*) quand tu as soif? Quand tu as froid? Quand tu as chaud?
2. Quand tu as faim, est-ce que tu manges un sandwich? Qu'est-ce que tu aimes manger?
3. Est-ce que tu aimes le café ou le thé? Combien de tasses est-ce que tu aimes boire par jour?
4. Comment est-ce que tu aimes le café? Avec du lait? Avec du sucre? Noir (*Black*)?
5. Comment est-ce que tu aimes le thé? Avec du lait? Avec du sucre? Nature (*Black*)?
6. Dans ta famille, qui aime le thé? Et le café?
7. Est-ce que tu aimes les boissons gazeuses ou l'eau minérale?
8. Quand tu manges avec ta famille dans un restaurant, est-ce que vous laissez un pourboire au serveur/à la serveuse?

6 Au restaurant Avec deux partenaires, écrivez une conversation entre deux client(e)s et leur serveur/ serveuse. Préparez-vous à jouer (*perform*) la scène devant la classe. Answers will vary.

Client(e)s

- Demandez des détails sur le menu et les prix.
- Choisissez des boissons et des plats (*dishes*).
- Demandez l'addition.

Serveur/Serveuse

- Parlez du menu et répondez aux questions.
- Apportez les plats et l'addition.

Coup de main

Vous désirez?
What can I get you?

Je voudrais...
I would like...

C'est combien?
How much is it/this/that?

7 Sept différences Votre professeur va vous donner, à vous et à votre partenaire, deux feuilles d'activités différentes. Posez-vous des questions pour trouver les sept différences. Attention! Ne regardez pas la feuille de votre partenaire.

MODÈLE
Élève 1: *J'ai deux tasses de café.*
Élève 2: *Oh, j'ai une tasse de thé!*

EXPANSION

Using Games Divide the class into two teams. At the same time, give one person on each team a set of scrambled words that form a sentence about foods and/or beverages. The first person to unscramble the words and write the sentence on the board correctly scores a point for his or her team. The team with the most points at the end of the game wins.

DIFFERENTIATION

For Visual Learners To review vocabulary, bring in pictures or magazine photos of the foods and drinks listed. Ask students to identify the items. Example: **Qu'est-ce que c'est? (C'est ____.)** Or you can make false statements about the pictures and have students correct them. Example: **C'est un(e) ____, n'est-ce pas? (Non, c'est ____.)** When plural, remind students to say **Ce sont ____.**

Les sons et les lettres 🔊 vhlcentral

Nasal vowels

In French, when vowels are followed by an **m** or an **n** in a single syllable, they usually become nasal vowels. Nasal vowels are produced by pushing air through both the mouth and the nose.

The nasal vowel sound you hear in **français** is usually spelled **an** or **en**.

an	fr**an**çais	**en**chanté	**en**f**an**t

The nasal vowel sound you hear in **bien** may be spelled **en**, **in**, **im**, **ain**, or **aim**. The nasal vowel sound you hear in **brun** may be spelled **un** or **um**.

exam**en**	améric**ain**	l**un**di	parf**um**

The nasal vowel sound you hear in **bon** is spelled **on** or **om**.

t**on**	all**on**s	c**om**bien	**on**cle

When **m** or **n** is followed by a vowel sound, the preceding vowel is not nasal.

image	**in**utile	**am**i	**am**our

Prononcez Répétez les mots suivants à voix haute.

1. blond
2. dans
3. faim
4. entre
5. garçon
6. avant
7. maison
8. cinéma
9. quelqu'un
10. différent
11. amusant
12. télévision
13. impatient
14. rencontrer
15. informatique
16. comment

Articulez Répétez les phrases suivantes à voix haute.

1. Mes parents ont cinquante ans.
2. Tu prends une limonade, Martin?
3. Le Printemps est un grand magasin.
4. Lucien va prendre le train à Montauban.
5. Pardon, Monsieur, l'addition s'il vous plaît!
6. Jean-François a les cheveux bruns et les yeux marron.

Dictons Répétez les dictons à voix haute.

> *L'appétit vient en mangeant.*[1]

> *N'allonge pas ton bras au-delà de ta manche.*[2]

[1] Appetite comes from eating.

[2] Don't bite off more than you can chew. (lit. Don't stretch your arm out farther than your sleeve.)

Section Goals
In this section, students will learn about nasal vowels.

Key Standards
4.1

Suggestions
• Model the pronunciation of each nasal vowel sound and have students repeat after you. Then pronounce each of the example words and have students repeat them.
• Tell students that when an **m** or an **n** is followed by an unaccented **e** at the end of a word, the preceding vowel is not nasalized. Have them compare these words: **un/une**, **brun/brune**, and **faim/femme**.
• Ask students to provide more examples of words they know with nasal vowels. Examples: **croissant**, **boisson**, **jambon**, **inviter**, **quand**, **dépenser**, and **danser**.
• Dictate five simple sentences with words containing nasal vowels to the class, repeating each one at least two times. Then write them on the board or on a transparency and have students check their spelling.

Dictons Ask students if they can think of a saying in English that is similar to **«L'appétit vient en mangeant.»** (*The more one has, the more one wants.*)

EXPANSION

Tongue Twisters Teach students these French tongue-twisters that contain nasal vowel sounds. **1. Son chat chante sa chanson. 2. Un chasseur sachant chasser sait chasser sans son chien de chasse. 3. Dans la gendarmerie, quand un gendarme rit, tous les gendarmes rient dans la gendarmerie.**

EXPANSION

Mini-dictée Use these sentences with nasal vowels for additional practice or dictation. **1. Raymond mange un sandwich au jambon. 2. Martin invite ses cousins au restaurant. 3. Tante Blanche a soixante-cinq ans. 4. Mon oncle Quentin a envie de danser.**

155

Section Goals

In this section, students will learn functional phrases for ordering foods and drinks and talking about food through comprehensible input.

Key Standards

1.2, 2.1, 2.2, 4.1, 4.2

Video Recap: Leçon 4A
Before doing this **Roman-photo**, review the previous one with this activity.

1. David pense qu'il y a une femme célèbre à l'épicerie. Qui est-ce? (Juliette Binoche)
2. À qui Sandrine parle-t-elle au téléphone? (à Pascal)
3. Les jeunes trouvent-ils facilement l'épicerie? (non)
4. Comment est la femme à l'épicerie? (belle, jolie, élégante, petite et vieille)
5. En réalité, qui est la femme? (quelqu'un qui travaille à l'épicerie)

Video Synopsis As the four friends approach **Le P'tit Bistrot**, Amina and Sandrine are hungry and want to go eat. Rachid and David decide to go back to their apartment. Valérie tells Amina and Sandrine what she is serving for lunch that day, and they place their order. Michèle makes a mistake on a customer's check, and Valérie serves the wrong food and drinks to Amina and Sandrine.

Suggestions

• Ask students to read the title, glance at the video stills, and predict what the episode will be about. Record their predictions.
• Have students volunteer to read the characters' parts in the **Roman-photo** aloud.
• After reading the **Roman-photo**, review students' predictions and ask them which ones are correct. Then help them summarize this episode.

L'heure du déjeuner **vhl**central

PERSONNAGES

Amina

David

Michèle

Rachid

Sandrine

Valérie

Près du café...
AMINA J'ai très faim. J'ai envie de manger un sandwich.
SANDRINE Moi aussi, j'ai faim, et puis j'ai soif. J'ai envie d'une bonne boisson. Eh, les garçons, on va au café?

RACHID Moi, je rentre à l'appartement étudier pour un examen de sciences po. David, tu vas au café avec les filles?
DAVID Non, je rentre avec toi. J'ai envie de dessiner un peu.
AMINA Bon, alors, à tout à l'heure.

Au café...
VALÉRIE Bonjour, les filles! Alors, ça va, les études?
AMINA Bof, ça va. Qu'est-ce qu'il y a de bon à manger, aujourd'hui?
VALÉRIE Eh bien, j'ai une soupe de poisson maison délicieuse! Il y a aussi des sandwichs jambon-fromage, des frites... Et, comme d'habitude, j'ai des éclairs, euh...

VALÉRIE Et pour toi, Amina?
AMINA Hmm... Pour moi, un sandwich jambon-fromage avec des frites.
VALÉRIE Très bien, et je vous apporte du pain tout de suite.
SANDRINE ET AMINA Merci!

Au bar...
VALÉRIE Alors, pour la table d'Amina et Sandrine, une soupe du jour, un sandwich au fromage... Pour la table sept, une limonade, un café, un jus d'orange et trois croissants.
MICHÈLE D'accord! Je prépare ça tout de suite. Mais Madame Forestier, j'ai un problème avec l'addition de la table huit.

VALÉRIE Ah, bon?
MICHÈLE Le monsieur ne comprend pas pourquoi ça coûte onze euros cinquante. Je ne comprends pas non plus. Regardez.
VALÉRIE Ah, non! Avec tout le travail que nous avons cet après-midi, des problèmes d'addition aussi?!

ACTIVITÉS

1 Identifiez Trouvez à qui correspond chacune (*each*) des phrases. Écrivez **A** pour Amina, **D** pour David, **M** pour Michèle, **R** pour Rachid, **S** pour Sandrine et **V** pour Valérie.

__M__ 1. Je ne comprends pas non plus.
__V__ 2. Vous prenez du jus d'orange uniquement le matin.
__S__ 3. Tu bois de l'eau aussi?
__M__ 4. Je prépare ça tout de suite.
__A__ 5. Je ne bois pas de limonade.
__S__ 6. Je vais apprendre à préparer des éclairs.
__D__ 7. J'ai envie de dessiner un peu.
__V__ 8. Je vous apporte du pain tout de suite.
__R__ 9. Moi, je rentre à l'appartement étudier pour un examen de sciences po.
__A__ 10. Qu'est-ce qu'il y a de bon à manger, aujourd'hui?

156   *cent cinquante-six*

TEACHING OPTIONS

L'heure du déjeuner Before viewing the video, have students work in pairs and write a list of words and expressions that they might hear in a video episode entitled **L'heure du déjeuner**.

TEACHING OPTIONS

Regarder la vidéo Show the video episode and tell students to check off the words or expressions they hear on their lists. Then show the episode again and have students give you a play-by-play description of the action. Write their descriptions on the board.

Amina et Sandrine déjeunent au café.

SANDRINE Oh, Madame Forestier, j'adore! Un jour, je vais apprendre à préparer des éclairs. Et une bonne soupe maison. Et beaucoup d'autres choses.
AMINA Mais pas aujourd'hui. J'ai trop faim!
SANDRINE Alors, je choisis la soupe et un sandwich au fromage.

VALÉRIE Et comme boisson?
SANDRINE Une bouteille d'eau minérale, s'il vous plaît. Tu bois de l'eau aussi? Avec deux verres, alors.

VALÉRIE Ah, ça y est! Je comprends! La boisson gazeuse coûte un euro vingt-cinq, pas un euro soixante-quinze. C'est noté, Michèle?
MICHÈLE Merci, Madame Forestier. Excusez-moi. Je vais expliquer ça au monsieur. Et voilà, tout est prêt pour la table d'Amina et Sandrine.
VALÉRIE Merci, Michèle.

À la table des filles...
VALÉRIE Voilà, une limonade, un café, un jus d'orange et trois croissants.
AMINA Oh? Mais Madame Forestier, je ne bois pas de limonade!
VALÉRIE Et vous prenez du jus d'orange uniquement le matin, n'est-ce pas? Ah! Excusez-moi, les filles!

Expressions utiles

Talking about food

- **Moi aussi, j'ai faim, et puis j'ai soif.**
  Me too, I am hungry, and I am thirsty as well.
- **J'ai envie d'une bonne boisson.**
  I feel like having a nice drink.
- **Qu'est-ce qu'il y a de bon à manger, aujourd'hui?**
  What looks good on the menu today?
- **Une soupe de poisson maison délicieuse.**
  A delicious homemade fish soup.
- **Je vais apprendre à préparer des éclairs.**
  I am going to learn (how) to prepare éclairs.
- **Je choisis la soupe.**
  I choose the soup.
- **Tu bois de l'eau aussi?**
  Are you drinking water too?
- **Vous prenez du jus d'orange uniquement le matin.**
  You only have orange juice in the morning.

Additional vocabulary

- **On va au café?**
  Shall we go to the café?
- **Bof, ça va.**
  So-so.
- **comme d'habitude**
  as usual
- **Le monsieur ne comprend pas pourquoi ça coûte onze euros cinquante.**
  The gentleman doesn't understand why this costs 11,50€.
- **Je ne comprends pas non plus.**
  I don't understand either.
- **Je prépare ça tout de suite.**
  I am going to prepare this right away.
- **Ça y est! Je comprends!**
  That's it! I get it!
- **C'est noté?**
  Understood?/Got it?
- **Tout est prêt.**
  Everything is ready.

---

2 Mettez dans l'ordre Numérotez les phrases suivantes dans l'ordre correspondant à l'histoire.

   5   a. Michèle a un problème avec l'addition.
   3   b. Amina prend (*gets*) un sandwich jambon-fromage.
   1   c. Sandrine dit qu'elle (*says that she*) a soif.
   2   d. Rachid rentre à l'appartement.
   4   e. Valérie va chercher du pain.
   6   f. Tout est prêt pour la table d'Amina et Sandrine.

3 Conversez Au moment où Valérie apporte le plateau (*tray*) de la table sept à Sandrine et Amina, Michèle apporte le plateau de Sandrine et Amina à la table sept. Avec trois partenaires, écrivez la conversation entre Michèle et les client(e)s et jouez-la devant la classe.

ACTIVITÉS

Expressions utiles
- Model the pronunciation of the **Expressions utiles** and have students repeat after you.
- As you work through the list, point out the forms of the verbs **prendre** and **boire** and the partitive articles. Tell students that these verbs and the partitive articles will be formally presented in the **Structures** section.
- Ask students questions about foods and beverages using the vocabulary in the **Expressions utiles**. Examples: **Vous prenez du jus d'orange uniquement le matin? Quand est-ce que vous avez envie de boire de l'eau?**

1 Expansion
- For additional practice, give students these items. **11. Le monsieur ne comprend pas pourquoi ça coûte 11,50€. (M) 12. J'ai faim et puis j'ai soif. (S) 13. Mais pas aujourd'hui. J'ai trop faim! (A) 14. Non, je rentre avec toi. (D)**
- Write these adverbial expressions on the board: **non plus, aussi,** and **tout de suite.** Have students create sentences with them.

2 Suggestion Have students work in groups of six. Write each sentence on a strip of paper. Make a set of sentences for each group, then distribute them to students. Tell them to read their sentences aloud and arrange them in the proper order.

2 Expansion Have students create sentences to fill in the missing parts of the story.

PRE-AP®

3 Interpersonal Speaking: Suggestion
Before doing this activity, have the class brainstorm vocabulary and expressions they might use in this activity and write their ideas on the board.

EXPANSION

Mini-dialogues Have students work in pairs. Tell them to combine sentences in **Expressions utiles** with other words and expressions they know to create mini-dialogues. Example:
—**Qu'est-ce qu'il y a de bon aujourd'hui?**
—**Il y a une soupe de poisson maison délicieuse.**

PRE-AP®

Interpersonal Speaking Ask volunteers to ad-lib the **Roman-photo** episode for the class. Tell them that it is not necessary to memorize the episode or to stick strictly to its content. They should try to get the general meaning across with the vocabulary and expressions they know, and they should also feel free to be creative. Give them time to prepare.

AP® **Theme:** Contemporary Life
Context: Leisure and Sports

Section Goals

In this section, students will:
• learn about the role of the café in French life
• learn some terms for describing how people eat and drink
• learn about some common snacks in different Francophone countries
• read about the cafés of North Africa
• view authentic cultural footage

Key Standards
2.1, 2.2, 3.1, 3.2, 4.2

21st Century Skills

Global Awareness
Students will gain perspectives on the Francophone world to develop respect and openness toward others and to interact appropriately and effectively with citizens of Francophone cultures.

Culture à la loupe

Avant la lecture Have students look at the photo and describe what they see.

Lecture Point out that you can order a drink or food at the counter (**le comptoir**) and pay less than sitting at a table. Sitting on the **terrasse** is even more expensive in some places. The menu posted outside a café usually indicates the different **tarifs**.

Après la lecture Ask students what aspects of French cafés they find interesting.

1 Suggestion Have students correct the false statements.

---

vhlcentral | *Flash culture*   CULTURE À LA LOUPE

Le café français

À Toute Heure

Quiches.................12,50€
Pâtisseries............4,50€
Omelettes..............9,25€
Thé.........................5,00€
Glaces ....7,50€
Café.......................4,50€
Cappuccino...........7,00€
Chocolat chaud ....5,50€

Le café est une partie importante de la culture française. Les Français adorent passer du temps° à la terrasse des cafés. C'est un des symboles de l'art de vivre° à la française.

On peut aller au café à tout moment de la journée: le matin, pour prendre un café et manger un croissant, le midi pour déjeuner entre copains ou avec des collègues, et le soir après les cours ou le travail pour boire quelque chose et se détendre° entre amis.

Il y a de très célèbres° cafés à Paris: «Les Deux Magots» ou le «Café de Flore» par exemple, dans le quartier° de Saint-Germain. Ils sont connus° parce que c'était le rendez-vous des intellectuels et des écrivains°, comme Jean-Paul Sartre, Simone de Beauvoir et Albert Camus, après la Deuxième Guerre mondiale°.

Le premier café français, le Procope, a ouvert° ses portes à Paris en 1686. C'était° un lieu° pour boire du café, qui était une boisson exotique à l'époque°. On pouvait° aussi manger un sorbet dans des tasses en porcelaine. Benjamin Franklin et Napoléon Bonaparte fréquentaient le Procope.

a ouvert *opened* **C'était** *It was* **lieu** *place* **à l'époque** *at the time* **pouvait** *could* **fréquentaient** *used to frequent* **passer du temps** *spending time* **vivre** *living* **en lisant** *while reading* **se détendre** *to relax* **célèbres** *famous* **quartier** *neighborhood* **connus** *known* **écrivains** *writers* **Deuxième Guerre mondiale** *World War II*

1 **Vrai ou faux?** Indiquez si les phrases sont **vraies** ou **fausses**.

1. Le premier café parisien date des années 1686. Vrai.
2. Le café était (*was*) une boisson courante (*common*) dans les années 1600. Faux.
3. Napoléon Bonaparte et Benjamin Franklin sont d'anciens clients du Procope. Vrai.
4. Le café est une partie importante de la culture française. Vrai.
5. Les Français n'aiment pas les terrasses des cafés. Faux.

6. Le matin, les Français prennent du jambon et du fromage. Faux.
7. Les Français mangent rarement au café à midi. Faux.
8. Les Français se retrouvent souvent avec leurs amis au café. Vrai.
9. «Les Deux Magots» et le «Café de Flore» sont deux cafés célèbres à Paris. Vrai.
10. Les intellectuels français fréquentent les cafés après la Première Guerre mondiale. Faux.

EXPANSION

Cultural Comparison Have students work in groups of three and compare French cafés to the cafés they know about. Tell them to list the similarities and differences in a two-column chart under the headings **Similitudes** and **Différences**. After completing their charts, have two groups get together and compare their lists.

DIFFERENTIATION

For Visual Learners Have students look at the **À Toute Heure** menu. Ask them what they are having and how much it costs. Examples: **Qu'est-ce que vous prenez? Combien coûte le chocolat chaud?** Alternatively, this activity can be done in pairs.

LE FRANÇAIS QUOTIDIEN

J'ai faim!

avoir les crocs	to be hungry
avoir un petit creux	to be slightly hungry
boire à petites gorgées	to sip
bouffer	to eat
dévorer	to devour
grignoter	to snack on
mourir de faim	to be starving
siroter	to sip (with pleasure)

LE MONDE FRANCOPHONE

Des spécialités à grignoter

Voici quelques spécialités à grignoter dans les pays et régions francophones.

En Afrique du Nord la merguez (saucisse épicée°) et le makroud (pâtisserie° au miel° et aux dattes)

En Côte d'Ivoire l'aloco (bananes plantains frites°)

En France le pan-bagnat (sandwich avec de la salade, des tomates, des œufs durs° et du thon°) et les crêpes (pâte° cuite° composée de farine°, d'œufs et de lait, de forme ronde)

À la Martinique les accras de morue° (beignets° à la morue)

Au Québec la poutine (frites avec du fromage fondu° et de la sauce)

Au Sénégal le chawarma (de la viande°, des oignons et des tomates dans du pain pita)

saucisse épicée *spicy sausage* pâtisserie *pastry* miel *honey* frites *fried* œufs durs *hard-boiled eggs* thon *tuna* pâte *batter* cuite *cooked* farine *flour* morue *cod* beignets *fritters* fondu *melted* viande *meat*

PORTRAIT

Les cafés nord-africains

AP® Theme: Families and Communities
Context: Customs and Ceremonies

Comme en France, les cafés ont une grande importance culturelle en Afrique du Nord. C'est le lieu où les amis se rencontrent pour discuter° ou pour jouer aux cartes° ou aux dominos. Les cafés ont une variété de boissons, mais la boisson typique, au café comme à la maison, est le thé à la menthe°. Il a peu de caféine, mais il a des vertus énergisantes et il favorise la digestion. En général, ce sont les hommes qui le° préparent. C'est la boisson qu'on vous sert° quand vous êtes invité, et ce n'est pas poli de refuser!

pour discuter *to chat* jouer aux cartes *play cards* menthe *mint* le *it* on vous sert *you are served*

AP® Theme: Families and Communities
Context: Customs and Ceremonies

Sur Internet

Comment prépare-t-on le thé à la menthe au Maghreb?

Go to **vhlcentral.com** to find more information related to this **Culture** section and to watch the corresponding **Flash culture** video.

ACTIVITÉS

2 Compréhension Complétez les phrases.
1. Quand on a un peu soif, on a tendance à (*tends to*) boire à petites gorgées.
2. On aime jouer aux cartes ou rencontrer des amis pour discuter dans les cafés nord-africains.
3. Le thé à la menthe est la boisson typique de l'Afrique du Nord.
4. Il n'est pas poli de refuser une tasse de thé en Afrique du Nord.
5. Si vous aimez les frites, vous allez aimer la poutine au Québec.

3 Un café francophone Par groupes de quatre, préparez une liste de suggestions pour un nouveau café francophone: noms pour le café, idées (*ideas*) pour le menu, prix, heures, etc. Indiquez où le café va être situé et qui va fréquenter ce café.

EXPANSION

Oral Practice Have students work in pairs. Tell them to take turns stating that they like one of the specialties in the list **Des spécialités à grignoter** at their house. The other person should guess where they live based on the snack named. Example: **Élève 1:** Chez moi, on aime les accras de morue. **Élève 2:** Alors tu habites à la Martinique, n'est-ce pas?

EXPANSION

True/False Have students write five true/false statements based on the information in the **J'ai faim!** and **Des spécialités à grignoter** sections. Then tell them to exchange papers with a classmate and complete the activity. Remind them to verify their answers.

Side margin

Le français quotidien Model the pronunciation of each term and have students repeat it. Then ask questions based on the vocabulary. Examples: **Avez-vous les crocs? Vous mangez quoi quand vous avez les crocs? Vous dévorez votre déjeuner?**

Portrait The mint tea served in North Africa is a mixture of green tea (often imported from China) and spearmint leaves that is sweetened heavily with sugar. It is served in small glasses, not cups.

Le monde francophone Have students read the text. Tell them to choose a specialty they would like to eat from the list. Then ask: **Quelle spécialité préférez-vous manger? Pourquoi?** Students might then find recipes for the food specialties and prepare them for the class to taste.

2 Expansion Have students write three more fill-in-the-blank statements based on **Portrait** and **Le monde francophone**. Then have them work in groups of three and take turns reading their statements while the other group members respond.

3 Expansion Have groups present their suggestions to the class. Then have the class discuss the role that the country's culture played in forming their ideas. For example, did it affect the name, the hours of operation, the menu, or the prices?

Flash culture Tell students that they will learn more about French cafés by watching a video narrated by Benjamin. Show the video segment, then have students jot down at least three examples of things they see. You can also use the activities in the video manual in class to reinforce this **Flash culture** or assign them as homework.

 21st Century Skills

Information and Media Literacy: Sur Internet Students access and critically evaluate information from the Internet.

159

Section Goals

In this section, students will learn:
- the verbs **prendre**, **apprendre**, and **comprendre**
- the verb **boire**
- partitive articles

Key Standards

4.1, 5.1

Suggestions: Scaffolding

- Point out that **prendre** means *to have* when saying what one is having to eat or drink, but it cannot be used to express possession. For possession, **avoir** must be used.
- Point out to students that all the singular forms of **prendre** sound the same. Make sure that students pronounce the **n** sound in **prennent**.
- Ask students if they can think of any English words related to **apprendre** (*apprentice*) and **comprendre** (*comprehend*).
- Ask students questions to elicit the different forms of **prendre**, **apprendre**, and **comprendre**. Examples: **Comprenez-vous bien cette leçon? Vous prenez le déjeuner à quelle heure?** Then, have students complete the first **Vérifiez** activity.
- Work through the forms of **boire**, asking students what they drink most often or rarely. Model a response by first saying what you drink: **Je bois souvent _____. Qu'est-ce que vous buvez?**
- Write the conjugation of **boire** on the board with the singular forms in one column and the plural forms in another column. Draw a line around the forms that have **oi**. Tell students that **boire** is a "boot verb."
- Have students complete the second **Vérifiez** activity.

4B.1

The verbs *prendre* and *boire*; Partitives

vhlcentral

Point de départ The verbs **prendre** (*to take, to have food or drink*) and **boire** (*to drink*), like **être, avoir,** and **aller,** are irregular.

> Je prends la soupe et un sandwich au fromage.

> Je ne bois pas de limonade.

prendre			
je prends	*I take*	**nous prenons**	*we take*
tu prends	*you take*	**vous prenez**	*you take*
il/elle/on prend	*he/she/it/one takes*	**ils/elles prennent**	*they take*

Brigitte **prend** le métro le soir.
Brigitte takes the subway in the evening.

Nous **prenons** un café chez moi.
We are having a coffee at my house.

- The forms of the verbs **apprendre** (*to learn*) and **comprendre** (*to understand*) follow the same pattern as that of **prendre**.

Tu ne **comprends** pas l'espagnol?
Don't you understand Spanish?

Elles **apprennent** beaucoup.
They're learning a lot.

Boîte à outils

You can use the construction **apprendre à** + [*infinitive*] to mean *to learn to do something*. Example: **J'apprends à nager.** *I'm learning to swim.*

Vérifiez

> Je ne comprends pas non plus.

> Un jour, je vais apprendre à préparer des éclairs.

boire			
je bois	*I drink*	**nous buvons**	*we drink*
tu bois	*you drink*	**vous buvez**	*you drink*
il/elle/on boit	*he/she/it/one drinks*	**ils/elles boivent**	*they drink*

Ton père **boit** un jus d'orange.
Your father is drinking an orange juice.

Vous **buvez** un chocolat chaud, M. Dion?
Are you drinking hot chocolate, Mr. Dion?

Je **bois** toujours du lait.
I always drink milk.

Nous ne **buvons** pas de café.
We don't drink coffee.

Vérifiez

EXPANSION

Extra Practice On the board, write a list of sentences containing the verbs **prendre** and **boire**, and partitives. Ask your students to say the same sentences out loud using different subjects. Example: **Je prends de la limonade à la cantine (Nous). (Nous prenons de la limonade à la cantine).**

EXPANSION

Interview Have pairs of students interview each other about what they eat and drink in certain situations (**le matin, dans un restaurant...**). Ask them to report to the class about their partners. Ex: **Il/Elle boit du chocolat chaud le matin.** They should also mention common habits in order to use **nous.** Ex: **Nous buvons du jus d'orange le matin.**

Partitives

- Partitive articles in French express *some* or *any*. To form the partitive, use the preposition **de** followed by a definite article. Although the words *some* and *any* are often omitted in English, the partitive must always be used in French.

masculine singular	feminine singular	singular noun beginning with a vowel
du thé	de la limonade	de l'eau

Je bois **du** thé chaud.	Tu bois **de la** limonade?	Elle prend **de l'**eau?
I drink (some) hot tea.	*Are you drinking (any) lemon soda?*	*Is she having (some) water?*

- Partitive articles are used with non-count nouns (nouns whose quantity cannot be expressed by a number). For count nouns, use definite articles.

PARTITIVE NON-COUNT
ARTICLE   NOUN
Tu prends **du** pain tous les jours.
You have (some) bread every day.

INDEFINITE COUNT
ARTICLE   NOUN
Tu prends **une** banane, aussi.
You have a banana, too.

- The article **des** also means *some*. It is the plural form of the indefinite article, not the partitive. This means it is used with nouns you can count.

PARTITIVE
ARTICLE
Vous prenez **de la** limonade.
You're having (some) lemon soda.

INDEFINITE
ARTICLE
Nous prenons **des croissants**.
We're having (some) croissants.

- As with the indefinite articles, the partitives **du**, **de la**, and **de l'** become **de** (meaning *not any*) in a negative sentence.

Est-ce qu'il y a **du** lait?	Non, il n'y a pas **de** lait.
Is there (any) milk?	*No, there isn't (any) milk.*
Prends-tu **de la** soupe?	Non, je ne prends pas **de** soupe.
Will you have (some) soup?	*No, I'm not having (any) soup.*

À noter

The partitives follow the same pattern of contraction as the possessive **de** + [*definite article*] you learned in **Structures 3A.2: du, de la, de l'**.

Boîte à outils

Partitives are used to say that you want *some* of an item, whereas indefinite articles are used to say that you want *a whole item* or *several whole items*.
Tu prends de la pizza?
(part of a whole pizza)
Tu prends une pizza?
(a whole pizza)

Vérifiez

Essayez!   Complétez les phrases. Utilisez la forme correcte du verbe entre parenthèses et l'article qui convient.

1. Ma sœur __prend__ (prendre) __des__ éclairs.
2. Tes parents __boivent__ (boire) __du__ café?
3. Louise ne __boit__ (boire) pas __de__ thé.
4. Est-ce qu'il y __a__ (avoir) __du__ sucre?
5. Nous __buvons__ (boire) __de la__ limonade.
6. Non, merci. Je ne __prends__ (prendre) pas __de__ frites.
7. Vous __prenez__ (prendre) __un__ taxi?
8. Nous __prenons__ (prendre) __de l'__ eau.

1 Suggestion Tell students that they will need to decide whether to use the partitive or indefinite article in their sentences. After they complete the activity, have them explain their choices.

2 Suggestion Have students ask the questions, then call on other individuals to answer them. Examples: **Oui, on prend ____. Non, on ne prend pas de/d' ____.**

2 Suggestion You may want to point out that it is sometimes possible to use either a partitive or an indefinite article. The choice depends on whether the speaker interprets the noun as count (e.g., a glass of iced tea, a bottle of mineral water) or non-count (e.g., some iced tea, some mineral water).

3 Suggestion This activity can also be done in pairs. One person should say the sentence and the other person responds. Remind students to switch roles after items 1–3.

Mise en pratique

1 Au café Indiquez l'article correct.

MODÈLE

Avez-vous __du__ lait froid?

1. Prenez-vous __du/un__ thé glacé?
2. Je voudrais __une__ baguette, s'il vous plaît.
3. Elle prend __un__ croissant.
4. Nous ne prenons pas __de__ sucre dans le café.
5. Tu ne laisses pas __de__ pourboire?
6. Vous mangez __des__ frites.
7. Zeina commande __une__ boisson gazeuse.
8. Voici __de l'/une__ eau minérale.
9. Nous mangeons __du__ pain.
10. Je ne prends pas __de__ fromage.

2 Des suggestions Laurent est au café avec des amis et il fait (*makes*) des suggestions. Que suggère-t-il?

▶ **MODÈLE**

On prend du jus d'orange?

1. On prend de la limonade? 2. On prend de l'eau minérale? 3. On prend du thé? 4. On prend des sandwichs?

3 Au restaurant Alain est au restaurant avec toute sa famille. Il note les préférences de tout le monde. Utilisez le verbe indiqué et un article indéfini.

MODÈLE

Oncle Lucien aime bien le café. (prendre) *Il prend un café.*

1. Marie-Hélène et papa adorent le thé. (prendre)
   Ils prennent un thé.
2. Tu adores le chocolat chaud. (boire)
   Tu bois un chocolat chaud.
3. Vous aimez bien le jus de pomme. (prendre)
   Vous prenez un jus de pomme.
4. Mes nièces aiment la limonade. (boire)
   Elles boivent une limonade.
5. Tu aimes les boissons gazeuses. (prendre)
   Tu prends une boisson gazeuse.
6. Vous adorez le café. (boire)
   Vous buvez un café.

EXPANSION

Small Groups Have students work in groups of three. Ask them to imagine they are at a restaurant and they will tell the class what each of them is having. They should use the verbs **prendre** and **boire**, and partitives. Remind them to include plural pronouns (**nous, ils/elles**) in their sentences. Example: **Je prends de la soupe; John et Annie prennent de la pizza; ils boivent du…**

DIFFERENTIATION

For Visual Learners Bring in pictures or magazine photos of people consuming food, drink, or taking various things. Have students describe what the people in the pictures are doing using **boire**, **prendre**, and partitive articles.

Communication

4 Échanges Posez les questions à un(e) partenaire. Answers will vary.

1. Qu'est-ce que tu bois quand tu as très soif?
2. Qu'est-ce que tu apprends au lycée?
3. Quelles langues est-ce que tes parents comprennent?
4. Est-ce que tu bois beaucoup de café? Pourquoi?
5. Qu'est-ce que tu prends à manger à midi?
6. Quelle langue est-ce que ton/ta meilleur(e) ami(e) apprend?
7. Où est-ce que tu prends tes repas (*meals*)?
8. Qu'est-ce que tu bois le matin? À midi? Le soir?

5 Je bois, je prends Votre professeur va vous donner une feuille d'activités. Circulez dans la classe pour demander à vos camarades s'ils prennent rarement, une fois (*once*) par semaine ou tous les jours la boisson ou le plat (*dish*) indiqués. Écrivez (*Write*) les noms sur la feuille, puis présentez vos réponses à la classe. Answers will vary.

MODÈLE

Élève 1: *Est-ce que tu bois du café?*
Élève 2: *Oui, je bois du café une fois par semaine. Et toi?*

Boisson ou plat	rarement	une fois par semaine	tous les jours
1. café		Didier	
2. fromage			
3. thé			
4. soupe			
5. chocolat chaud			
6. jambon			

6 Après les cours Des amis se retrouvent au café. Par groupes de quatre, jouez (*play*) les rôles d'un(e) serveur/serveuse et de trois clients. Utilisez les mots de la liste et présentez la scène à la classe. Answers will vary.

addition	chocolat chaud	frites
avoir faim	coûter	prix
avoir soif	croissant	sandwich
boisson	eau minérale	soupe
éclair	jambon	limonade

4 Virtual Chat You can also assign Activity 4 on vhlcentral.com. Students record individual responses that appear in your gradebook.

5 Suggestion Have two volunteers read the **modèle** aloud. Then distribute the **Feuilles d'activités** found in the Activity Pack on vhlcentral.com.

6 Suggestions
- Bring in a few props, such as cups, bottles, and plates, for students to use in their role-plays.
- Have volunteers perform their role-plays for the class.

EXPANSION

Extra Practice Write this activity on the board. Tell students to add the missing words and form complete sentences.
1. Marc / boire / eau / et / prendre / sandwich / jambon
2. Solange / prendre / soupe / et / boire / boisson gazeuse
3. Nous / boire / café / lait / et / prendre / éclairs
4. Henri et Paul / prendre / hot-dogs / et / frites
5. Anne / prendre / soupe / poisson / et / verre / thé glacé

PRE-AP®

Interpersonal Speaking Have students look back at the **Roman photo** on pages 156–157. Have them ask and answer questions about what the characters are eating, drinking, taking and learning. They should use the verbs **prendre**, **apprendre** and **boire**, and partitives.

163

Section Goals

In this section, students will learn regular **-ir** verbs.

Key Standards

4.1, 5.1

Suggestions: Scaffolding

- Present **Point de départ**. Model the pronunciation of the forms of **finir** and have students repeat them. Call students' attention to the **-iss-** in the plural forms.
- Introduce the other **-ir** verbs by narrating actions you mime. Then ask a series of questions using the verbs. Begin by saying what time you finish teaching today and asking students what time they finish classes. Examples: **Aujourd'hui, je finis d'enseigner à cinq heures. Et vous, à quelle heure finissez-vous les cours?** Then ask students to ask a classmate: **Et toi, à quelle heure finis-tu, aujourd'hui?** Continue this type of questioning using the other verbs.
- Tell students that many **-ir** verbs are derived from adjectives, such as **grand**, **rouge**, **gros**, or **vieux**.
- Present the information on command forms. To practice, give students a situation and have them state an appropriate command. Examples: **Je suis gros. (Maigrissez!) Qu'est-ce qu'on choisit? Les éclairs ou les croissants? (Choisissons les éclairs!)**

Essayez! For additional practice, give students these items. **9. Comment _____ (réagir)-vous quand vous avez peur? (réagissez) 10. Vos grands-parents _____ (vieillir) ensemble. (vieillissent)**

4B.2

Regular *-ir* verbs vhlcentral

Point de départ In **Leçon 2A**, you learned the forms of **-er** verbs in the present tense. Now you will learn the forms for verbs that end in **-ir**. They follow a different pattern.

finir	
je finis	nous finissons
tu finis	vous finissez
il/elle/on finit	ils/elles finissent

Je **finis** mes devoirs.
I'm finishing my homework.

Alain et Chloé **finissent** leurs sandwichs.
Alain and Chloé are finishing their sandwiches.

- Here are some other verbs that follow the same pattern as **finir**.

Other regular *-ir* verbs			
choisir	to choose	réfléchir (à)	to think (about), to reflect (on)
grandir	to grow		
grossir	to gain weight	réussir (à)	to succeed (in doing something)
maigrir	to lose weight		
obéir (à)	to obey	rougir	to blush
réagir	to react	vieillir	to grow old

Je **choisis** un chocolat chaud.
I choose a hot chocolate.

Vous **réfléchissez** à ma question?
Are you thinking about my question?

🏃 Boîte à outils

Use the constructions **finir de** + [*infinitive*] and **choisir de** + [*infinitive*] to mean *to finish doing* and *to choose to do something*.

Je finis de manger.
I'm finishing eating.

Nous choisissons de rester ici.
We choose to stay here.

À noter

In **Leçon 2A**, you learned the phrase **être reçu(e) à un examen**. You can also use the phrase **réussir un examen** to mean *to pass a test or exam*.

Une minute... je réfléchis.

Je choisis un sandwich.

- Like for **-er** verbs, use present tense verb forms to give commands. However, do not drop the **-s** in the **tu** form.

Réagis vite!	**Obéissez**.	**Réfléchissons** bien.	Ne **rougis** pas.
React quickly!	*Obey.*	*Let's think well.*	*Don't blush.*

Essayez!   Complétez les phrases.

1. Quand on ne mange pas beaucoup, on __maigrit__ (maigrir).
2. Il __réussit__ (réussir) son examen.
3. Vous __finissez__ (finir) vos devoirs?
4. Lundi prochain nous __finissons__ (finir) le livre.
5. Les enfants __grandissent__ (grandir) très vite (*fast*).
6. Vous __choisissez__ (choisir) le fromage?
7. Ils n' __obéissent__ (obéir) pas à leur parents.
8. Je __réfléchis__ (réfléchir) beaucoup à ce problème.

EXPANSION

Video Replay the **Roman-photo**. Have students listen for **-ir** verbs and write down those they hear. Afterward, write the verbs on the board and ask their meanings. Have students write original sentences using each verb.

EXPANSION

Questions Ask students questions using **-ir** verbs in the present and also with the **futur proche**. Examples: **Quand allez-vous finir le lycée? Réussissez-vous vos examens?**

Le français vivant
• Model a sample interchange for one of the situations before students begin the activity.
• Ask volunteers to share their responses with the class.
• Have students act out a scene in which they order from the café menu. Encourage them to use as many **-ir** verbs as possible. Ask volunteers to perform their scene for the class.

Le français vivant

Café du Marché

Formule petit-déjeuner simple   **7,50€**

boisson chaude + croissant + jus de fruits (au choix°) ou boisson chaude + mini-baguette avec du beurre + jus de fruits (au choix)

✱✱✱

Formule petit-déjeuner complet   **9,50€**

boisson chaude + croissant jambon-fromage + jus de fruits (au choix)

Boissons

Café .... 2,50€	
Café déca .... 3,00€	
Café crème .... 4,50€	
Chocolat chaud ..... 5,00€	Eau minérale .... 3,50€
Thé .... 4,50€	Jus de fruits .... 4,80€
	Limonade .... 4,80€

au choix *your choice of*

Répondez Avec un(e) partenaire, discutez de la carte et de ces (*these*) situations. Utilisez des verbes en **-ir.**

1. Je prends quatre croissants.
2. J'ai très faim.
3. Je ne mange pas beaucoup.
4. Je ne commande pas encore.
5. J'ai très soif.

2 Suggestion Go over the correct answers with the class. Then ask two volunteers to act out the conversation.

3 Expansion Have students create additional sentences using these verbs with different subjects.

Mise en pratique

1 **On fait quoi?** Choisissez la forme correcte du verbe en **-ir**.

1. Nous (finissons / grandissons) nos devoirs avant le dîner.
2. Ursula (choisis / choisit) un croissant.
3. Eva et Léo (rougissent / réussissent) à faire un gâteau.
4. Omar (réfléchit / réfléchis) à ses problèmes.
5. Nous essayons de ne pas (grandir / grossir).
6. Tu manges une salade parce que tu essaies de (vieillir / maigrir)?

2 **Au restaurant** Complétez le dialogue avec la forme correcte du verbe entre parenthèses.

SERVEUR Vous désirez?

MARC Nous (1) _____réfléchissons_____ (réfléchir) encore.

FANNY Je pense savoir ce que je veux (*know what I want*).

SERVEUR Que (2) _____choisissez_____ (choisir)-vous, Mademoiselle?

FANNY Je (3) _____choisis_____ (choisir) un hamburger avec des frites. Et toi?

MARC Euh... je (4) _____réfléchis_____ (réfléchir). La soupe ou la salade, je pense... Oui, je prends la salade.

SERVEUR Très bien. Je vous apporte ça tout de suite (*right away*).

FANNY Tu n'as pas très faim?

MARC Non, pas trop. Et je suis au régime (*on a diet*). J'ai besoin de (5) _____maigrir_____ (maigrir) un peu.

FANNY Tu (6) _____réussis_____ (réussir) déjà. Ton jean est trop grand. Tu n'as pas envie de partager mon éclair?

MARC Mais non! Je vais (7) _____grossir_____ (grossir)!

FANNY Alors, je (8) _____finis_____ (finir) l'éclair.

3 **Complétez** Complétez les phrases avec la forme correcte des verbes de la liste. N'utilisez les verbes qu'une seule fois.

choisir	maigrir
finir	obéir
grandir	rougir
grossir	vieillir

1. Nous _____choisissons_____ l'endroit où nous allons déjeuner.
2. Corinne _____rougit_____ quand elle a honte.
3. Mes frères cadets _____grandissent_____ encore. Ils sont déjà (*already*) très grands!
4. Vous ne mangez pas assez et vous _____maigrissez_____.
5. Nous _____obéissons_____ aux profs.
6. Sylvie _____finit_____ ses études cette année.
7. Mes grands-parents _____vieillissent_____.
8. Quand on mange beaucoup de chocolat, on _____grossit_____.

TEACHING OPTIONS

Pairs Give pairs of students five minutes to write a conversation in which they use as many expressions with regular **-ir** verbs as they can in a logical manner. Have pairs perform their conversations for the class.

EXPANSION

Pairs Have pairs of students role-play an interview with a movie star. Ask them to use as many **-ir** verbs as possible in their interview. Allow sufficient time to plan and practice; they can review previous lesson vocabulary if needed. After completing the activity, ask a few pairs to introduce their characters and perform the interview for the class.

Communication

4 **Ça, c'est moi!** Avec un(e) partenaire, complétez les phrases suivantes pour parler de vous-même.

1. Je ne finis jamais (de)...
2. Je grossis quand...
3. Je maigris quand...
4. Au restaurant, je choisis souvent...
5. Je réfléchis quelquefois (*sometimes*) à...
6. Je réussis toujours (à)...

5 **Assemblez** Avec un(e) partenaire, assemblez les éléments des trois colonnes pour créer des phrases. *Answers will vary.*

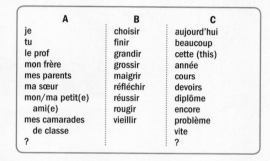

A	B	C
je	choisir	aujourd'hui
tu	finir	beaucoup
le prof	grandir	cette (*this*)
mon frère	grossir	année
mes parents	maigrir	cours
ma sœur	réfléchir	devoirs
mon/ma petit(e)	réussir	diplôme
ami(e)	rougir	encore
mes camarades	vieillir	problème
de classe		vite
?		?

6 **Votre vie au lycée** Posez ces questions à un(e) partenaire puis présentez vos réponses à la classe. *Answers will vary.*

1. Pendant ce semestre, dans quel cours réussis-tu le mieux (*best*)?
2. Comment est-ce que tu choisis un/une ami(e)?
3. En général, est-ce que tu réussis aux examens de français? Comment trouves-tu les examens?
4. Est-ce que tu maigris ou grossis au lycée? Pourquoi?
5. À quelle heure est-ce que tes cours finissent le vendredi? Que fais-tu (*do you do*) après les cours?
6. Comment tes parents réagissent-ils quand tu réussis tes examens?
7. Quand fais-tu tes devoirs? À quelle heure finis-tu tes devoirs?

7 **Qui...?** Posez (*Ask*) des questions pour trouver une personne dans la classe qui fait ces (*does these*) choses.

MODÈLE
Élève 1: *Est-ce que tu rougis facilement?*
Élève 2: *Non, je ne rougis pas facilement.*

1. rougir facilement (*easily*)
2. réagir vite
3. obéir à ses parents
4. finir toujours ses devoirs
5. choisir bien sa nourriture (*food*)

---

4 **Suggestion** Call on volunteers to share their information with the rest of the class.

4 **Partner Chat** You can also assign Activity 4 on vhlcentral.com. Students work in pairs to record the activity online. The pair's recorded conversation will appear in your gradebook.

5 **Suggestion** Give students five minutes to write as many sentences as they can using **–ir** verbs. Then have volunteers read some of their sentences aloud or write them on the board.

7 **Suggestion** Remind students to ask and answer questions using complete sentences. Have them write the name of the person they find for each question. Follow up with questions about what they found out. Example: **Qui finit toujours ses devoirs?**

EXPANSION

Extra Practice Have students restate these sentences using **-ir** verbs. **1.** Mes tantes sont moins jeunes qu'avant (*than before*). **2.** Cédric est moins gros qu'avant. **3.** Nous sommes plus grands qu'avant. **4.** Vous pensez beaucoup. **5.** Je termine le lycée.

EXPANSION

Extra Practice Have students write fill-in-the-blank or dehydrated sentences for each of the **-ir** verbs. Then tell them to exchange papers with a partner and complete the activity. Remind students to verify their answers.

Révision

1 **Suggestion** Before students begin the activity, have them describe the images.

1 **Partner Chat** You can also assign Activity 1 on vhlcentral.com. Students work in pairs to record the activity online. The pair's recorded conversation will appear in your gradebook.

2 **Suggestions**
- Tell students to jot down notes during their interviews.
- Have students report some of their findings to the rest of the class.

21ˢᵗ Century Skills

3 **Collaboration**
If you have access to students in a Francophone country, ask them to provide some names for the café and some prices for your students to use as they create their own café.

4 **Suggestion** Have volunteers state one difference until all options are exhausted.

5 **Suggestion** Have pairs perform dialogs for the class.

5 **Partner Chat** You can also assign Activity 5 on vhlcentral.com. Students work in pairs to record the activity online. The pair's recorded conversation will appear in your gradebook.

6 **Suggestion** Divide the class into pairs and distribute the Info Gap Handouts from the Activity Pack. Give students ten minutes to complete the activity.

---

1 **Ils aiment apprendre** À tour de rôle, demandez à votre partenaire pourquoi il/elle apprend les activités suivantes. Donnez à votre partenaire une réponse logique à ses questions. *Answers will vary.*

MODÈLE

Élève 1: *Pourquoi est-ce que tu apprends à travailler sur l'ordinateur?*
Élève 2: *J'apprends parce que j'aime les ordinateurs.*

1.

4.

2.

5.

3.

6.

2 **Quelle boisson?** À tour de rôle, interviewez deux personnes pour découvrir ce qu' (*to find out what*) elles boivent dans les occasions suivantes. Utilisez des articles partitifs dans vos réponses. *Answers will vary.*

1. au café
2. au cinéma
3. en classe
4. le dimanche matin
5. le matin très tôt
6. quand il/elle passe des examens
7. quand il/elle a très soif
8. quand il/elle étudie toute la nuit

3 **Notre café** Vous et votre partenaire allez créer une carte pour un café français. Choisissez le nom du café et huit boissons. Pour chaque (*each*) boisson, inventez deux prix, un pour le comptoir (*bar*) et un pour la terrasse. Comparez votre café au café d'un autre groupe. *Answers will vary.*

4 **La terrasse du café** Avec un(e) partenaire, trouvez au minimum quatre différences entre les deux dessins. Ensuite, écrivez (*write*) un paragraphe sur ces trois personnages en utilisant (*by using*) des verbes en **–ir**. *Answers will vary.*

MODÈLE

Élève 1: *Mylène prend une limonade.*
Élève 2: *Mylène prend de la soupe.*

Patrick   Mylène   Djamel

5 **Dialogue** Avec un(e) partenaire, créez un dialogue avec les éléments de la liste. *Answers will vary.*

choisir	du chocolat
grossir	de l'eau minérale
maigrir	un sandwich au jambon
réagir	des frites
réfléchir (à)	de la soupe
réussir (à)	du jus de pomme

6 **La famille Arnal au café** Votre professeur va vous donner, à vous et à votre partenaire, des photos de la famille Arnal. Posez-vous des questions pour savoir qui prend quoi. Attention! Ne regardez pas la feuille de votre partenaire. *Answers will vary.*

MODÈLE

Élève 1: *Qui prend un sandwich?*
Élève 2: *La grand-mère prend un sandwich.*

PRE-AP®

Presentational Writing ←🗣→ Have students write a brief story about some friends who go to a café and what happens when they are there. Tell students that the story can be real or imaginary. Encourage them to be creative.

EXPANSION

Questions Have students write five questions that they would like to ask you using the verbs **apprendre**, **comprendre**, **boire**, **prendre**, and **-ir** verbs. Then allow each student the opportunity to ask you one question.

À l'écoute vhlcentral

STRATÉGIE

Listening for the gist

Listening for the general idea, or gist, can help you follow what someone is saying even if you can't hear or understand some of the words. When you listen for the gist, you try to capture the essence of what you hear without focusing on individual words.

🔊 To help you practice this strategy, you will listen to three sentences. Jot down a brief summary of what you hear.

Préparation

Regardez la photo. Combien de personnes y a-t-il? Où sont Charles et Gina? Qu'est-ce qu'ils vont manger? Boire? Quelle heure est-il? Qu'est-ce qu'ils vont faire (to do) cet après-midi?

🔊 À vous d'écouter

Écoutez la conversation entre Charles, Gina et leur serveur. Écoutez une deuxième fois (a second time) et indiquez quelles activités ils vont faire.

- ✓ 1. acheter un livre
- ✓ 2. aller à la librairie
- ____ 3. aller à l'église
- ✓ 4. aller chez des grands-parents
- ____ 5. boire un coca
- ✓ 6. aller au cinéma
- ✓ 7. dépenser de l'argent
- ____ 8. étudier
- ✓ 9. manger au restaurant
- ✓ 10. manger un sandwich

Compréhension

 Un résumé Complétez ce résumé (summary) de la conversation entre Charles et Gina avec des mots et expressions de la liste.

aller au cinéma	un croissant
aller au gymnase	une eau minérale
aller au musée	faim
avec son frère	un jus d'orange
café	manger au restaurant
chez ses grands-parents	du pain
des copains	soif

Charles et Gina sont au (1) ____café____. Charles va boire (2) ____une eau minérale____. Gina n'a pas très (3) ____faim____. Elle va manger (4) ____un croissant____. Cet après-midi, Charles va (5) ____aller au gymnase____. Ce soir, il va (6) ____manger au restaurant____ avec (7) ____des copains____. Cet après-midi, Gina va peut-être (8) ____aller au musée____. Ce soir, elle va manger (9) ____chez ses grands-parents____. À neuf heures et demie, elle va (10) ____aller au cinéma____ avec Charles.

Et vous? Avec un(e) camarade, discutez de vos projets (plans) pour ce week-end. Où est-ce que vous allez aller? Qu'est-ce que vous allez faire (to do)?

cent soixante-neuf **169**

Section Goals

In this section, students will:
- learn to listen for the gist
- listen to and summarize a short paragraph
- listen to a conversation and complete several activities

Key Standards

1.2, 2.1

Stratégie

Script Aujourd'hui, c'est dimanche. Ce matin, Marie va aller au café avec une copine. Cet après-midi, elle va aller au centre commercial et ce soir, elle va aller danser.
Teacher Resources DVD

À vous d'écouter

Script CHARLES: Alors, Gina, où est-ce que tu vas cet après-midi? Au centre-ville pour du shopping?
GINA: Eh bien, oui. Je cherche un livre pour mon frère. Je vais aller à la librairie Monet, près de l'hôpital. Il y a beaucoup de livres intéressants là-bas.
C: Et après, où vas-tu?
G: Euh... Je vais peut-être aller au musée.
SERVEUR: Bonjour. Vous désirez?
C: Pour moi, un sandwich au jambon et une eau minérale, s'il vous plaît.
S: Pour le sandwich, de la baguette ou du pain de campagne?
C: De la baguette, s'il vous plaît.
S: Très bien. Et pour vous, Mademoiselle?
G: Euh... Je ne sais pas... euh... un café, s'il vous plaît. Et un croissant. Je n'ai pas très faim ce midi.
S: D'accord. Merci.
G: Et toi, tu vas où cet après-midi?
C: Je vais aller au gymnase avec Pierre. Et ce soir, je vais manger au restaurant avec des copains et après, on va aller au cinéma.
G: Ah oui? Où ça? En banlieue, près du centre commercial?
C: Non, dans le centre-ville, près du parc. Tu as envie d'y aller?
G: Au restaurant, non. Je vais manger chez mes grands-parents ce soir, mais au cinéma, oui, pourquoi pas. À quelle heure?
C: Ben, je passe chez toi après le restaurant, vers neuf heures et demie, d'accord?
G: D'accord.
C: Excusez-moi, Monsieur, l'addition, s'il vous plaît.
S: Voilà.
Teacher Resources DVD

169

Savoir-faire

vhlcentral

Panorama

Le Québec

La province en chiffres

▶ **Superficie:** *1.667.441 km²*

▶ **Population:** *8.263.600*
SOURCE: Statistique Canada

▶ **Industries principales:** *agriculture, exploitation forestière°, hydroélectricité, industrie du bois (papier), minerai° (fer°, cuivre°, or°)*

▶ **Villes principales:** *Montréal, Québec, Trois-Rivières*

▶ **Langues:** *anglais, français*

Le français parlé par les Québécois a une histoire très intéressante. La population française qui s'installe° au Québec en 1608 est composée en majorité de Français du nord-ouest de la France. Ils parlent tous leur langue régionale, comme le normand ou le breton. Beaucoup d'entre eux parlent aussi le français de la cour du roi°, langue qui devient la langue commune de tous les Québécois. Assez isolés du reste du monde francophone et ardents défenseurs de leur langue, les Québécois continuent à parler un français considéré plus pur même° que celui° des Français.

▶ **Monnaie:** *le dollar canadien*

Québécois célèbres

▶ **Justin Trudeau**, *premier ministre du Canada (1971–)*

▶ **Céline Dion**, *chanteuse (1968–)*

▶ **Guy Laliberté**, *fondateur du Cirque du Soleil (1959–)*

▶ **Leonard Cohen**, *poète, romancier, chanteur (1934–2016)*

▶ **Julie Payette**, *astronaute (1963–)*

▶ **Georges St-Pierre**, *pratiquant d'arts martiaux mixtes (1981–)*

exploitation forestière *forestry* **minerai** *ore* **fer** *iron* **cuivre** *copper* **or** *gold* **s'installe** *settles* **cour du roi** *king's court* **même** *even* **celui** *that* **traîneau à chiens** *dogsled* **loger** *house* **Bonhomme** *Snowman (mascot of the carnival)* **longueur** *long* **hauteur** *high* **largeur** *wide*

un traîneau à chiens°

□ Région francophone

LA BAIE D'HUDSON

LA MER DU LABRADOR

Kangiqsujuaq

Inukjuak

LE QUÉBEC

TERRE-NEUVE-ET-LABRADOR

LE CANADA

Chisasibi

Labrador City

La Tabatière

la ville de Trois-Rivières

le Saint-Laurent

L'ÎLE-DU-PRINCE-ÉDOUARD

Québec

Trois-Rivières

LE NOUVEAU-BRUNSWICK

L'ONTARIO
Ottawa

Montréal

LA NOUVELLE-ÉCOSSE

Toronto
le lac Ontario

LES ÉTATS-UNIS

0 ____ 200 miles
0 ____ 200 kilomètres

le Stade olympique, Montréal

L'OCÉAN ATLANTIQUE

Incroyable mais vrai!

Chaque année, pour le carnaval d'hiver de la ville de Québec, 15 personnes travaillent pendant deux mois à la construction d'un immense palais de glace pour loger° le Bonhomme° Carnaval. L'architecture et la taille du palais changent chaque année, mais il mesure parfois jusqu'à 50 mètres de longueur°, 20 m de hauteur° et 20 m de largeur°.

AP® Theme: Personal and Public Identities
Context: Nationalism and Patriotism

La société

Un Québec indépendant

Pour des raisons politiques, économiques et culturelles, un grand nombre de Québécois, surtout les francophones, luttent°, depuis les années soixante, pour un Québec indépendant du Canada. Ils forment le mouvement souverainiste° et font des efforts pour conserver l'identité culturelle québécoise. Ces Canadiens francophones ont pris° le nom de Québécois pour montrer leur «nationalisme». Les séparatistes ont perdu° deux référendums en 1980 et en 1995, mais aujourd'hui, l'indépendance est une idée toujours d'actualité°.

Les destinations

Montréal

Montréal, deuxième ville francophone du monde après Paris, est située sur une île du fleuve° Saint-Laurent et présente une ambiance américano-européenne. Elle a été fondée° en 1642 et a l'énergie d'un centre urbain moderne et le charme d'une vieille ville de style européen. Ville cosmopolite et largement bilingue de 1,8 million d'habitants, elle attire° beaucoup de touristes et accueille° de nombreux étudiants dans ses quatre universités. La majorité des Montréalais, 65,7%, est de langue maternelle française; 12,5% parlent l'anglais et 21,8% une autre langue. Pourtant°, 51,9% de la population montréalaise peuvent communiquer en français et en anglais.

La musique

AP® Theme: Beauty and Aesthetics
Context: Music

Le festival de jazz de Montréal

Le Festival International de Jazz de Montréal est parmi° les plus prestigieux du monde. Avec 1.000 concerts, dont° plus de 600 donnés gratuitement en plein air°, le festival attire 3.000 artistes de 30 pays, et plus de 2 millions de spectateurs. Le centre-ville, fermé à la circulation, se transforme en un village musical. De grands noms internationaux comme Miles Davis, Ella Fitzgerald, Dizzy Gillespie ou Pat Metheny sont venus au festival, ainsi que° des jazzmen locaux.

L'histoire

La ville de Québec

Capitale de la province de Québec, la ville de Québec est la seule° ville d'Amérique au nord du Mexique qui a conservé ses fortifications. Fondée par l'explorateur français Samuel de Champlain en 1608, Québec est située sur un rocher°, au bord du fleuve Saint-Laurent. Elle est connue° en particulier pour sa vieille ville, son carnaval d'hiver et le château Frontenac. Les plaines d'Abraham, où les Britanniques ont vaincu° les Français en 1759 pour prendre le contrôle du Canada, servent aujourd'hui de vaste parc public. De nombreux étudiants de l'Université Laval profitent° du charme de cette ville francophone.

Qu'est-ce que vous avez appris? Répondez aux questions.

1. Quelle langue devient (*becomes*) la langue commune des Québecois?
   Le français de la cour du roi.
2. Quel est le nom d'une chanteuse québecoise célèbre?
   Céline Dion.
3. Pour quel évènement est-ce qu'on construit (*build*) un palais de glace à la ville de Québec?
   Pour le carnaval d'hiver.
4. Le palais est-il identique chaque année?
   Non, son architecture change chaque année.
5. Que désire le mouvement souverainiste pour le Québec?
   Un Québec indépendant.

6. Quelles sont les deux langues principales parlées à Montréal?
   Le français et l'anglais.
7. En quoi se transforme le centre-ville de Montréal pour le festival de jazz?
   En village musical.
8. Qui chantent ou jouent du jazz au festival?
   De grands noms internationaux et des musiciens locaux.
9. Au bord de quel fleuve (*river*) se trouvent Montréal et la ville de Québec?
   Le fleuve Saint-Laurent.
10. Qui est le fondateur de la ville de Québec?
    Samuel de Champlain.

Sur Internet

1. Quelles sont quelques-unes des expressions qui sont particulières au français des Québécois?

2. Quels sont les autres grands festivals du Québec? Quand ont-ils lieu?

3. Cherchez plus d'informations sur le carnaval d'hiver de Québec. Le palais de glace a-t-il toujours été fait (*been made*) de glace?

luttent *fight* **souverainiste** *in support of sovereignty for Quebec* **ont pris** *took* **ont perdu** *lost* **d'actualité** *current, relevant* **fleuve** *river* **fondée** *founded* **attire** *attracts* **accueille** *welcomes* **Pourtant** *However* **parmi** *among* **dont** *of which* **en plein air** *outside* **ainsi que** *as well as* **seule** *only* **rocher** *rock* **connue** *known* **ont vaincu** *defeated* **profitent** *take advantage of, benefit from*

Un Québec indépendant
- The **Québec** flag and its saying **«Je me souviens»**, which appears on **Québec** license plates, are symbols of **Québec**'s nationalism and reflect its French heritage.
- Ask students: **Quels sont les avantages et les inconvénients d'un Québec indépendant?**

Montréal Montreal's name is derived from the name of the mountain on which it is built, Mont-Royal. Due to the fur trade, Montreal grew rapidly in the eighteenth century. The majority of the population was French until around 1830. Between 1830 and 1865, the British became the majority as a result of immigration. Today, Montreal is one of Canada's chief ports.

Le festival de jazz de Montréal The festival has taken place for over 35 years. It is a non-profit event; any surplus funds are used to promote local and international jazz year round.

La ville de Québec
- The historic district of Old Quebec has been designated a World Heritage City by UNESCO. **Vieux Québec** is surrounded by 4.6 kilometers (3 miles) of ramparts. Inside the walls are museums, shops, restaurants, buildings, churches, monuments, museums, and **la Citadelle**.

 21st Century Skills

Information and Media Literacy: Sur Internet
Students access and critically evaluate information from the Internet.

EXPANSION

Using Games Create categories for the information on Quebec, for example, **Québécois célèbres, La ville de Québec, Montréal**, and **Culture**. For each category, make index cards with a question on one side. Tape the cards to the board under the appropriate category. Divide the class into two teams, and have them take turns selecting a card and answering the question.

EXPANSION

Teams receive a point for each correct answer. The team with the most points at the end of the game wins.

Writing Practice Have students work in pairs. Tell them to make a list of reasons why a tourist should visit Quebec and Montreal. After students have completed their lists, call on volunteers to read one item from their list until all options are exhausted.

Lecture vhlcentral

Avant la lecture

STRATÉGIE

Scanning

Scanning involves glancing over a document in search of specific information. For example, you can scan a document to identify its format, to find cognates, to locate visual clues about the document's content, or to find specific facts. Scanning allows you to learn a great deal about a text without having to read it word-for-word.

Examinez le texte

Regardez le texte et indiquez huit mots apparentés (*cognates*) que vous trouvez. Answers may vary.

1. Chocolat
2. Sandwich
3. Accès Internet
4. Omelette
5. Salade
6. Tarte
7. Soupe
8. Snack

Trouvez

Regardez le document. Indiquez si les informations suivantes sont présentes dans le texte.

✓ 1. une adresse
___ 2. le nombre de tables
___ 3. un plat du jour (*daily special*)
✓ 4. de l'accès Internet
✓ 5. les noms des propriétaires
___ 6. des prix réduits (*reduced*) pour les jeunes
___ 7. de la musique *live*
✓ 8. les heures d'ouverture (*business hours*)
✓ 9. un numéro de téléphone
___ 10. une librairie à l'intérieur

Décrivez

Regardez les photos. Écrivez un paragraphe pour décrire (*describe*) le café. Comparez votre paragraphe avec le paragraphe d'un(e) camarade.

Café Le connecté 🔊

- **Ouvert° du lundi au samedi, de 7h00 à 20h00**
- **Snack et restauration rapide**
- **Wi-Fi haut débit° et sécurisé**

Café Le connecté

MENU

PETIT-DÉJEUNER° FRANÇAIS	12,00€	**PETIT-DÉJEUNER ANGLAIS**	15,00€
Café, thé, chocolat chaud ou lait Pain, beurre et confiture° Orange pressée		Café, thé, chocolat chaud ou lait Œufs° (au plat° ou brouillés°), bacon, toasts Orange pressée	
VIENNOISERIES°	3,00€		
Croissant, pain au chocolat, brioche°, pain aux raisins		**DESSERTS**	
		Tarte aux fruits	7,50€
		Banana split	8,40€
SANDWICHS ET SALADES			
Sandwich (jambon ou fromage; baguette ou pain de campagne)	7,50€	**AUTRES SÉLECTIONS CHAUDES**	
		Frites	4,30€
Croque-monsieur°	8,80€	Soupe à l'oignon	8,00€
Salade verte°	6,20€	Omelette au fromage	8,50€
		Omelette au jambon	8,50€
BOISSONS CHAUDES			
Café/Déca	3,80€	**BOISSONS FROIDES**	
Grand crème	5,50€	Eau minérale non gazeuse	3,00€
Chocolat chaud	5,80€	Eau minérale gazeuse	3,50€
Thé	5,50€	Jus de fruits (orange...)	5,80€
Lait chaud	4,80€	Soda, limonade	5,50€
		Café, thé glacé°	5,20€
Propriétaires: Bernard et Marie-Claude Fouchier			

- **Le connecté, le café préféré des étudiants**

- **Wi-Fi gratuit° avec consommation ou 3€ de l'heure en connection**

24, place des Terreaux
69001 LYON
Tél. 04.72.45.87.90
www.leconnecte.fr

Place des Terreaux
★
Rue d'Algérie
Rue Paul Chenavard
Musée des
Beaux-Arts
de Lyon
Rue de Constantine

Situé en face du musée des Beaux-Arts

Ouvert *Open* **haut débit** *high speed* **Petit-déjeuner** *Breakfast* **confiture** *jam*
Viennoiseries *Breakfast pastries* **brioche** *a light, slightly-sweet bread*
Croque-monsieur *Grilled sandwich with cheese and ham* **verte** *green*
Œufs *Eggs* **au plat** *fried* **brouillés** *scrambled* **glacé** *iced* **gratuit** *free*

Après la lecture

Répondez Répondez aux questions par des phrases complètes.

1. Quand est-ce qu'on peut (*can*) aller au café?
On peut aller au café du lundi au samedi de 7h00 à 20h00.

2. Qui adore ce café?
Les étudiants adorent ce café.

3. Combien coûte l'accès Internet?
C'est gratuit avec consommation ou 3€ de l'heure en connection.

4. Comment est la connection wi-fi?
Le wi-fi est haut débit et sécurisé.

5. Quelles sont les deux boissons gazeuses? Combien coûtent-elles?
L'eau minérale gazeuse coûte 3,50€. Un soda coûte 5,50€.

6. Combien de desserts sont proposés?
Deux desserts sont proposés.

Choisissez Indiquez qui va prendre quoi. Écrivez des phrases complètes. *Answers may vary. Possible answers provided.*

MODÈLE

Julie a soif. Elle n'aime pas les boissons gazeuses. Elle a 6 euros.
Julie va prendre un jus d'orange.

1. Lise a froid. Elle a besoin d'une boisson chaude. Elle a 4 euros et 90 centimes.
Lise va prendre un café.

2. Nathan a faim et soif. Il a 15 euros.
Nathan va prendre un croque-monsieur et un soda.

3. Julien va prendre un plat chaud. Il a 8 euros et 80 centimes.
Julien va prendre une omelette au jambon.

4. Lola a chaud et a très soif. Elle a 5 euros et 75 centimes.
Lola va prendre un thé glacé.

5. Marina va prendre une boisson gazeuse. Elle a 4 euros et 20 centimes.
Marina va prendre une eau minérale gazeuse.

6. Ève va prendre un dessert. Elle n'aime pas les bananes. Elle a 8 euros.
Ève va prendre une tarte aux fruits.

L'invitation Avec un(e) camarade, jouez (*play*) cette scène: vous invitez un ami à déjeuner au café Le connecté. Parlez de ce que vous allez manger et boire. Puis (*Then*), discutez de vos activités de l'après-midi et du soir.

Répondez Go over the answers with the class.

Choisissez Have students write two more situations similar to those in the activity. Then tell them to exchange papers with a partner, write the answers, and verify the answers.

L'invitation Before beginning the activity, tell students that they only have 20€ to spend at the **Café Le connecté**.

 21st Century Skills

Creativity and Innovation
Ask students to prepare a presentation on the ideal café for students, inspired by the information on these two pages.

TELL Connection

Learning Tools 3 *Why:* Authentic materials and quality facsimiles provide perspectives behind the products and practices of francophone cultures. *What:* Have students research cafés in the United States and in a variety of francophone cultures and comment on the perspectives reflected by their services and products.

Écriture

STRATÉGIE

Adding details

How can you make your writing more informative or more interesting? You can add details by answering the "W" questions: Who? What? When? Where? Why? The answers to these questions will provide useful and interesting details that can be incorporated into your writing. You can use the same strategy when writing in French. Here are some useful question words that you have already learned:

(À/Avec) Qui?	À quelle heure?
Quoi?	Où?
Quand?	Pourquoi?

Compare these two sentences.

> Je vais aller nager.

> Aujourd'hui, à quatre heures, je vais aller nager à la piscine du parc avec mon ami Paul, parce que nous avons chaud.

While both sentences give the same basic information (the writer is going to go swimming), the second, with its detail, is much more informative.

Thème

Un petit mot

Avant l'écriture

1. Vous passez un an en France et vous vivez (*are living*) dans une famille d'accueil (*host family*). C'est samedi, et vous allez passer la journée en ville avec des amis. Écrivez un petit mot (*note*) pour informer votre famille de vos projets (*plans*) pour la journée.

2. Choisissez cinq activités que vous allez faire (*to do*) avec vos amis aujourd'hui.

Activité 1:
Activité 2:
Activité 3:
Activité 4:
Activité 5:

3. Complétez ce tableau pour organiser vos idées.
Répondez à toutes les questions.

	Activité 1	Activité 2	Activité 3	Activité 4	Activité 5
Qui?					
Quoi?					
Quand?					
Où?					
Comment?					
Pourquoi?					

4. Comparez votre tableau à celui (*to the one*) d'un(e)
partenaire. Avez-vous tous les deux cinq activités? Avez-
vous des informations dans toutes les colonnes? Avez-
vous répondu à toutes les questions?

Écriture

Écrivez la note à votre famille d'accueil. Référez-vous au
tableau que vous avez complété et incluez toutes les
informations. Utilisez les verbes **aller**, **boire** et **prendre**,
et le vocabulaire de l'unité. Organisez vos idées de
manière logique.

> *Chère famille,*
> *Aujourd'hui, je vais visiter*
> *la ville avec Xavier et*
> *Laurent, deux élèves belges*
> *du lycée…*

Après l'écriture

1. Échangez votre tableau et votre note avec ceux (*the ones*)
d'un(e) partenaire. Faites des commentaires sur son
travail (*work*) d'après (*according to*) ces questions:

- Votre partenaire a-t-il/elle inclus dans la note toutes
  les informations du tableau?

- A-t-il/elle correctement (*correctly*) utilisé le vocabulaire
  de l'unité?

- A-t-il/elle utilisé la forme correcte des verbes **aller**,
  boire et **prendre**?

- A-t-il/elle présenté ses informations de manière logique?

2. Corrigez (*Correct*) votre note d'après les commentaires
de votre partenaire. Relisez votre travail pour éliminer
ces problèmes:

- des fautes (*errors*) d'orthographe

- des fautes de ponctuation

- des fautes de conjugaison

- des fautes d'accord (*agreement*) des adjectifs

cent soixante-quinze **175**

EVALUATION

Criteria
Content Contains a greeting,
describes the five planned
activities, answers the questions:
qui? quoi? quand? où? pourquoi?,
and includes supporting detail
without redundancy.
Scale: 1 2 3 4 5

Organization Organizes the note
into a salutation, a description,
and a signature.
Scale: 1 2 3 4 5

Accuracy Uses forms of **aller**
and places in town correctly.
Spells words, conjugates
verbs, and modifies adjectives
correctly throughout. Avoids
redundant language.
Scale: 1 2 3 4 5

Creativity Includes additional
information that is not included
in the task, mentions more than
five activities and/or includes a
closing (not shown
in the model).
Scale: 1 2 3 4 5

Scoring
Excellent	18–20 points
Good	14–17 points
Satisfactory	10–13 points
Unsatisfactory	< 10 points

21ˢᵗ Century Skills

**Productivity and
Accountability**
Provide the rubric to students
before they hand their work in for
grading. Ask students to make
sure they have met the highest
standard possible on the rubric
before submitting their work.

TELL Connection

Learning Experience 2 *Why:*
Clear and simple performance
objectives encourage and equip
students. *What:* Before students
begin writing, explain how the
Evaluation Criteria contribute to
the quality of their final product
and how to check their progress
against the rubric. Modify,
as desired, to ensure student
understanding and ownership
of each step toward achieving
their writing goals.

EXPANSION

Écriture Ask for other details that could be added, such as
departure and return times, activities in the town, the town's
name and the students' ages. Finally, have students analyze
these extra details to see which are useful for the note's
message and which are extraneous or redundant.

Show students how to avoid redundancies by combining similar
sentences. Compare **Je vais en ville**. **Je vais avec mes amis.**
Je vais lundi matin. with **Je vais en ville avec mes amis lundi
matin.** Tell them to look for ways to condense language when
they edit their work.

Key Standards
4.1

Suggestion Tell students that an easy way to study from **Vocabulaire** is to cover up the French half of each section, leaving only the English equivalents exposed. They can then quiz themselves on the French items. To focus on the English equivalents of the French entries, they simply reverse this process.

 21st Century Skills

Creativity and Innovation
Ask students to prepare a list of three products or perspectives they learned about in this unit to share with the class. Consider asking them to focus on the **Culture** and **Panorama** sections.

21st Century Skills

Leadership and Responsibility: Extension Project
If you have access to students in a Francophone country, have students decide on three questions they want to ask the partner class related to this unit's topic. Based on the responses they receive, work as a class to explain to the partner class one aspect of their responses that surprised the class and why.

Leçon 4A

Dans la ville

un bureau	office; desk
un centre commercial	shopping center, mall
un cinéma (ciné)	movie theater, movies
une église	church
une épicerie	grocery store
un grand magasin	department store
un gymnase	gym
un hôpital	hospital
un kiosque	kiosk
un magasin	store
une maison	house
un marché	market
un musée	museum
un parc	park
une piscine	pool
une place	square; place
un restaurant	restaurant
une terrasse de café	café terrace
une banlieue	suburbs
un centre-ville	city/town center, downtown
un endroit	place
un lieu	place
une montagne	mountain
une ville	city, town

Activités

bavarder	to chat
danser	to dance
déjeuner	to eat lunch
dépenser de l'argent (m.)	to spend money
explorer	to explore
fréquenter	to frequent; to visit
inviter	to invite
nager	to swim
passer chez quelqu'un	to stop by someone's house
patiner	to skate
quitter la maison	to leave the house

Expressions utiles

See p. 139.

Verbes

aller	to go
commencer à + [infinitive]	to start (doing something)
parler à	to talk to
penser à	to think about
téléphoner à	to phone (someone)

Prepositions

à [+ definite article]	to, in, at
dans	inside; within
à la maison	at home
à Paris	in Paris
en ville	in town
sur la place	in the square
dans la maison	inside the house
dans Paris	within Paris
dans la ville	within the town
à/sur la terrasse	on the terrace

Les questions

à quelle heure?	at what time?
à qui?	to whom?
avec qui?	with whom?
combien (de)?	how many?; how much?
comment?	how?; what?
où?	where?
parce que	because
pour qui?	for whom?
pourquoi?	why?
quand?	when?
quel(le)(s)?	which?; what?
que/qu'...?	what?
qui?	who?; whom?
quoi?	what?

Leçon 4B

À table

avoir faim	to be hungry
avoir soif	to be thirsty
manger quelque chose	to eat something
une baguette	baguette (long, thin loaf of bread)
le beurre	butter
un croissant	croissant (flaky, crescent-shaped roll)
un éclair	éclair (pastry filled with cream)
des frites (f.)	French fries
un fromage	cheese
le jambon	ham
un pain (de campagne)	(country-style) bread
un sandwich	sandwich
une soupe	soup
le sucre	sugar
une boisson (gazeuse)	(soft/carbonated) drink/beverage
un café	coffee
un chocolat (chaud)	(hot) chocolate
une eau (minérale)	(mineral) water
un jus (d'orange, de pomme, etc.)	(orange, apple, etc.) juice
le lait	milk
une limonade	lemon soda
un thé (glacé)	(iced) tea

Expressions de quantité

(pas) assez (de)	(not) enough (of)
beaucoup (de)	a lot (of)
d'autres	others
une bouteille (de)	bottle (of)
un morceau (de)	piece, bit (of)
un peu (plus/moins) (de)	little (more/less) (of)
plusieurs	several
quelque chose	something; anything
quelques	some
une tasse (de)	cup (of)
tous (m. pl.)	all
tout (m. sing.)	all
tout (tous) le/les (m.)	all the
toute(s) la/les (f.)	all the
trop (de)	too many/much (of)
un verre (de)	glass (of)

Au café

apporter l'addition (f.)	to bring the check/bill
coûter	to cost
laisser un pourboire	to leave a tip
Combien coûte(nt)...?	How much is/are...?
un prix	price
un serveur/une serveuse	server

Expressions utiles

See p. 157.

Verbes

apprendre	to learn
boire	to drink
choisir	to choose
comprendre	to understand
finir	to finish
grandir	to grow
grossir	to gain weight
maigrir	to lose weight
obéir	to obey
prendre	to take; to have
réagir	to react
réfléchir (à)	to think (about), to reflect (on)
réussir (à)	to succeed (in doing something)
rougir	to blush
veillir	to grow old

Les loisirs

Pour commencer
- Qui est sur la photo?
- Quel sport pratique-t-elle?
- Pensez-vous qu'elle aime le sport?
- Et vous, vous aimez le sport? Quel(s) sport(s) pratiquez-vous?

Unit Goals

Leçon 5A

In this lesson, students will learn:
- terms for sports and leisure activities
- adverbs of frequency
- about intonation
- about **le football**
- more about sports and leisure activities through specially shot video footage
- the verb **faire**
- expressions with **faire**
- the expression **il faut**
- irregular **-ir** verbs
- about the UNSS and sports in France

Leçon 5B

In this lesson, students will learn:
- terms for seasons and months
- weather expressions
- to tell the date
- differences between open and closed vowels
- about public gardens and parks in the Francophone world
- the numbers 101 and higher
- **-er** verbs with spelling changes
- to listen for key words in oral communication

Savoir-faire

In this section, students will learn:
- cultural and historical information about West Africa and Central Africa
- to skim a text
- to use a French-English dictionary

21st Century Skills

Initiative and Self-Direction
Students can monitor their progress online using the activities and assessments on vhlcentral.com.

Pour commencer
- **C'est une joueuse/une athlète.**
- **Elle pratique le football.**
- **Oui, je pense qu'elle aime le sport.**
- Answers will vary

SUPPORT FOR BACKWARD DESIGN

Unité 5 Essential Questions
1. How do people talk about sports and other pastimes?
2. How do people talk about the weather?
3. How do people discuss and plan a vacation?

Unité 5 Integrated Performance Assessment
Before teaching the chapter, review the Integrated Performance Assessment (IPA) and its accompanying scoring rubric provided in the Testing Program. Use the IPA to assess students' progress toward proficiency targets at the end of the chapter.
IPA Context: Six students from your French class will be chosen to spend a week in Montreal. Students will be chosen in pairs based on their presentation to the selection committee.

FORUMS

Forums on vhlcentral.com allow you and your students to record and share audio messages. Use Forums for presentations, oral assessments, discussions, directions, etc.

Section Goals

In this section, students will learn and practice vocabulary related to:
• sports and leisure activities
• adverbs of frequency

Key Standards

1.1, 1.2, 4.1

Suggestions

• Have students look over the new vocabulary, covering the translations. Guide them to notice the numerous cognates for sports terms. See how many words students know without looking at the English.
• Use the digital image for this page to describe what people are doing. Examples: **Ils jouent au football. Elles jouent au tennis.** Encourage students to add their remarks.
• Teach students the expression **aider quelqu'un à... (étudier, bricoler, travailler)**. Pointing to the person toward the right helping his injured friend, say: **Il aide son copain à marcher.**
• Point out the differences between the words **un jeu, jouer, un joueur,** and **une joueuse.**
• Ask students closed-ended questions about their favorite activities: **Vous préférez jouer au tennis ou aller à la pêche? Aller à un spectacle ou jouer au golf?**
• Call out sports and other activities from this section and have students classify them as either **un sport** or **un loisir.** List them on the board in two columns.

You will learn how to...

▪ talk about activities
▪ tell how often and how well you do things

🔊 **vhl**central

Le temps libre

Vocabulaire

aller à la pêche	*to go fishing*
bricoler	*to tinker; to do odd jobs*
désirer	*to want*
jouer (à/de)	*to play*
pratiquer	*to play regularly, to practice*
skier	*to ski*
le baseball	*baseball*
le cinéma	*movies*
le foot(ball)	*soccer*
le football américain	*football*
le golf	*golf*
un jeu	*game*
un loisir	*leisure activity*
un passe-temps	*pastime, hobby*
un spectacle	*show*
un stade	*stadium*
le temps libre	*free time*
le volley(-ball)	*volleyball*
une/deux fois	*one/two time(s)*
par jour, semaine, mois, an, etc.	*per day, week, month, year, etc.*
déjà	*already*
encore	*again, still*
jamais	*never*
longtemps	*long time*
maintenant	*now*
parfois	*sometimes*
rarement	*rarely*
souvent	*often*

les joueuses (f.)

un match de tennis (m.)

Elle marche. (marcher)

le sport

une équipe

les joueurs (m.)

Il joue au foot. (jouer)

Il gagne. (gagner)

les cartes (f.)

une bande dessinée (B.D.)

EXPANSION

Brainstorming Have students give their opinions about activities in **Contextes**. Brainstorm pairs of adjectives that apply to activities and write them on the board or on a transparency. Examples: **agréable/désagréable, intéressant/ennuyeux, utile/ inutile, génial/nul, facile/difficile.** Then ask questions like these: **Le football, c'est intéressant ou c'est ennuyeux? Les échecs, c'est facile ou difficile?**

TEACHING OPTIONS

Using Games Play a game of **Jacques a dit** (*Simon says*) using the activities in this section. Tell students to mime each activity only if they hear the words **Jacques a dit.** If a student mimes an activity not preceded by **Jacques a dit,** he or she is eliminated from the game. The last person standing wins. You might want students to take turns calling out activities.

Attention!

Use **jouer à** with games and sports.

Elle joue aux cartes/au baseball.
She plays cards/baseball.

Use **jouer de** with musical instruments.

Vous jouez de la guitare/du piano.
You play the guitar/piano.

le basket(-ball)

Il aide le joueur.
(aider)

Il chante.
(chanter)

Il indique.
(indiquer)

les échecs (m.)

Mise en pratique

1 **Remplissez** Choisissez dans la liste le mot qui convient (*the word that fits*) pour compléter les phrases. N'oubliez pas de conjuguer les verbes.

aider	jeu	pratiquer
bande dessinée	jouer	skier
bricoler	marcher	sport
équipe		

1. Notre __équipe__ joue un match cet après-midi.
2. Le solitaire est un __jeu__ de cartes.
3. Mon livre préféré, c'est une __bande dessinée__ de Tintin, *Le sceptre d'Ottokar*.
4. J'aime __jouer__ aux cartes avec ma grand-mère.
5. Pour devenir (*To become*) champion de volley, je __pratique__ tous les jours.
6. Le dimanche, nous __marchons__ beaucoup, environ (*about*) cinq kilomètres.
7. Mon __sport__ préféré, c'est le foot.
8. Mon père __aide__ mon frère à préparer son match de tennis.
9. J'aime bien __skier__ dans le Colorado.
10. Il faut réparer la table, mais je n'aime pas __bricoler__.

2 **Écoutez** Écoutez Sabine et Marc parler de leurs passe-temps préférés. Dans le tableau suivant, écrivez un **S** pour Sabine et un **M** pour Marc pour indiquer s'ils pratiquent ces activités **souvent**, **parfois**, **rarement** ou **jamais**. Attention, une activité n'est pas utilisée.

Activités	Souvent	Parfois	Rarement	Jamais
1. le golf				M
2. le tennis	M	S		
3. les cartes				
4. le basket	S	M		
5. le spectacle	M		S	
6. le cinéma	M, S			
7. chanter	S			
8. aller à la pêche			M	S

3 **Les loisirs** Utilisez un élément de chaque colonne pour former huit phrases au sujet des loisirs de ces personnes. N'oubliez pas les accords (*agreements*). Answers will vary.

Personnes	Activités	Fréquence
Je	jouer aux échecs	maintenant
Ma sœur	chanter	parfois
Mes parents	jouer au tennis	rarement
Christian	gagner le match	souvent
Sandrine et Cédric	skier	déjà
Les élèves	regarder un spectacle	une fois par semaine
Élise	jouer au basket	une fois par mois
Mon ami(e)	aller à la pêche	encore

cent soixante-dix-neuf **179**

1 **Suggestions**
- To review **-er** verb forms, conjugate on the board one of the verbs from the list.
- Tell students to use each item in the word box only once.

2 **Script** SABINE: Bonjour, Marc, comment ça va?
MARC: Pas mal. Et toi?
S: Très bien, merci. Est-ce que tu joues au golf?
M: Non, jamais. Je n'aime pas ce sport. Je préfère jouer au tennis. En général, je joue au tennis trois fois par semaine. Et toi?
S: Moi? Jouer au tennis? Oui, parfois, mais j'aime mieux le basket. C'est un sport que je pratique souvent.
M: Ah le basket, je n'aime pas tellement. Je joue parfois avec des amis, mais ce n'est pas mon sport préféré. Le soir, j'aime bien aller au spectacle ou au cinéma. Et toi, qu'est-ce que tu aimes faire le soir?
S: Oh, je vais rarement au spectacle mais j'adore aller au cinéma. J'y vais très souvent.
M: C'est quoi, ton passe-temps préféré?
S: Mon passe-temps préféré, c'est le chant. J'aime chanter tous les jours.
M: Moi, j'adore aller à la pêche quand j'ai du temps libre, mais ce n'est que très rarement.
S: La pêche? Oh, moi, jamais. Je trouve ça ennuyeux.
Teacher Resources DVD

2 **Expansion** Have students tell a partner how often they, themselves, do these activities.

3 **Suggestion** Ask volunteers to write one of their sentences on the board, making sure to have one example sentence for each of the verbs listed in this activity.

3 **Expansion** Ask students how frequently they do each of the activities listed. Encourage them to use as many different adverbial expressions as possible.

EXPANSION

Making Associations Call out names of famous athletes and have students say: **Ils jouent au __sport__**. Examples: Brittany Lang, Arnold Palmer (**golf**), David Beckham, Zinédine Zidane (**football**), Serena Williams, Roger Federer (**tennis**), Antonio Brown, Luke Kuechly (**football américain**), Tony Parker, Kawhi Leonard (**basket-ball**), and Babe Ruth, Mark McGwire (**baseball**).

TEACHING OPTIONS

Using Games Write each of the words or expressions in **Activité 3** on an index card. Label three boxes **Personnes**, **Activités**, and **Fréquence**. Then place the cards in their respective boxes. Divide the class into two teams. Students take turns drawing one card from each box. Each player has five seconds to form a sentence using all of the words on the three cards. If they do not make a mistake, they score a point for their team.

Communication

4 Suggestion Follow up this activity by asking students about their partners' favorite sports and activities. Examples: **Est-ce que ____ est sportif/sportive? Quel sport pratique-t-il/elle? Combien de fois par mois est-ce que ____ va au cinéma?**

4 Expansion Have students conduct an informal survey by circulating around the room and asking these questions to five other students. Tell them to write down all of the responses for each question. As a class, share and compare students' findings.

4 Virtual Chat You can also assign Activity 4 on vhlcentral.com. Students record individual responses that appear in your gradebook.

5 Suggestion Have two volunteers read the **modèle** aloud. Then distribute the **Feuilles d'activités** from the Activity Pack.

5 Expansion Tally the results of the survey to determine the most and least popular activities among your students.

6 Partner Chat You can also assign Activity 6 on vhlcentral.com. Students work in pairs to record the activity online. The pair's recorded conversation will appear in your gradebook.

PRE-AP®

7 Interpersonal Writing: Strategy Have students exchange letters with a classmate. Remind them to begin the letter with **Chère** if they are writing to a woman.

Successful Language Learning Suggest that students use mnemonic devices to memorize vocabulary. Examples: Use alliteration for interrogative words like **qui**, **quand**, and **quoi**. Group words in categories, such as team sports (**football, basket-ball, volley-ball**) versus those that are usually played one-on-one (**échecs, cartes, tennis**). Learn word "families," such as **un jeu, jouer, un joueur,** and **une joueuse**.

---

4 **Répondez** Avec un(e) partenaire, posez les questions et répondez à tour de rôle. Answers will vary.

1. Quel est votre loisir préféré?
2. Quel est votre sport préféré à la télévision?
3. Êtes-vous sportif/sportive? Si oui, quel sport pratiquez-vous?
4. Qu'est-ce que vous désirez faire (*to do*) ce week-end?
5. Combien de fois par mois allez-vous au cinéma?
6. Que faites-vous (*do you do*) quand vous avez du temps libre?
7. Est-ce que vous aidez quelqu'un? Qui? À faire quoi? Comment?
8. Quel est votre jeu de société (*board game*) préféré? Pourquoi?

5 **Sondage** Votre professeur va vous donner une feuille d'activités. Circulez dans la classe et demandez à vos camarades s'ils pratiquent les activités sur la feuille et si oui (*if so*), à quelle fréquence. Quelle est l'activité la plus pratiquée (*the most practiced*) de la classe? Answers will vary.

MODÈLE
aller à la pêche
Élève 1: Est-ce que tu vas à la pêche?
Élève 2: Oui, je vais parfois à la pêche.

Activités	Noms	Fréquence
1. aller à la pêche	François	parfois
2. jouer au tennis		
3. jouer au foot		
4. skier		

6 **Conversez** Avec un(e) partenaire, écrivez une conversation au sujet de vos loisirs. Utilisez les mots intérrogatifs dans la liste et le vocabulaire de la leçon. Présentez votre travail à la classe. Answers will vary.

MODÈLE
Élève 1: Que fais-tu (*do you do*) comme sport?
Élève 2: Je joue au volley.
Élève 1: Tu joues souvent?
Élève 2: Oui, trois fois par semaine, avec mon amie Julie. C'est un sport que j'adore. Et toi, quel est ton passe-temps préféré?

Avec qui?	Pourquoi?
Combien de fois par...?	Quand?
Comment?	Quel(le)(s)?
Où?	Quoi?

7 **La lettre** Écrivez une lettre à un(e) ami(e) au sujet de vos loisirs. Dites ce que vous faites (*do*), quand, avec qui et à quelle fréquence.

Cher Marc,

Pendant (*During*) mon temps libre, j'aime bien jouer au basket et au tennis. J'aime gagner, mais ça n'arrive pas souvent! Je joue au tennis avec mes amis deux fois par semaine, le mardi et le vendredi, et au basket le samedi. J'adore les films et je vais souvent au cinéma avec ma sœur ou mes amis. Le soir...

EXPANSION

Making Comparisons Give students five minutes to jot down a description of their typical weekend, including what they do, where they go, and with whom they spend time. Circulate among the class to help with unfamiliar vocabulary. Then have volunteers share their information with the rest of the class. The class decides whether or not each volunteer represents a "typical" student.

TEACHING OPTIONS

Using Games Play a game of **Dix questions**. Ask a volunteer to think of a sport, activity, person, or place from the vocabulary drawing or list. Other students get one chance to ask a yes/no question and make a guess until someone guesses the word. Limit attempts to 10 questions per word. You may want to write some phrases on the board to cue students' questions.

Les sons et les lettres 🔊 vhlcentral

Intonation

In short, declarative sentences, the pitch of your voice, or intonation, falls on the final word or syllable.

Nathalie est française.   **Hector joue au football.**

In longer, declarative sentences, intonation rises, then falls.

À trois heures et demie, j'ai sciences politiques.

In sentences containing lists, intonation rises for each item in the list and falls on the last syllable of the last one.

Martine est jeune, blonde et jolie.

In long, declarative sentences, such as those containing clauses, intonation may rise several times, falling on the final syllable.

Le samedi, à dix heures du matin, je vais au centre commercial.

Questions that require a yes or no answer have rising intonation. Information questions have falling intonation.

C'est ta mère?   **Est-ce qu'elle joue au tennis?**

Quelle heure est-il?   **Quand est-ce que tu arrives?**

Prononcez Répétez les phrases suivantes à voix haute.

1. J'ai dix-neuf ans.
2. Tu fais du sport?
3. Quel jour sommes-nous?
4. Sandrine n'habite pas à Paris.
5. Quand est-ce que Marc arrive?
6. Charlotte est sérieuse et intellectuelle.

Articulez Répétez les dialogues à voix haute.

1. —Qu'est-ce que c'est?
   —C'est un ordinateur.
2. —Tu es américaine?
   —Non, je suis canadienne.
3. —Qu'est-ce que Christine étudie?
   —Elle étudie l'anglais et l'espagnol.
4. —Où est le musée?
   —Il est en face de l'église.

Dictons Répétez les dictons à voix haute.

Si le renard court, le poulet a des ailes.[1]

Petit à petit, l'oiseau fait son nid.[2]

[1] Though the fox runs, the chicken has wings.
[2] Little by little, a bird builds its nest.

Section Goals

In this section, students will learn about using intonation.

Key Standards
4.1

Suggestions
• Model the intonation of each example sentence and have students repeat it after you.
• Remind students that information questions contain question words: **qui**, **qu'est-ce que**, **quand**, **comment**, **pourquoi**, etc. Remind students that the question word is not always the first word of the sentence. Examples: **À qui parles-tu? Ils arrivent quand?**
• Contrast the intonation of various types of declarative sentences (short, long, and those containing lists).
• Point out that the sentences without question words in the **Prononcez** activity (all except items 3 and 5) can be changed from a question to a statement and vice-versa simply by changing the intonation.

Dictons
• Ask students if they can think of sayings in English that are similar to **«Petit à petit, l'oiseau fait son nid.»** (*Slow and steady wins the race.*)
• Have students discuss the meaning of **«Si le renard court, le poulet a des ailes.»**

⭐ **TELL Connection**

Learning Tools 3 *Why:* Provide students with a variety of authentic input to gain insight into cultural perspectives and practices. *What:* Proverbs are one of the authentic perspective elements in each unit, joining media, readings, internet searches, and extended listening.

EXPANSION

Intonation Here are some sentences to use for additional practice with intonation: **1. Il a deux frères? 2. Il a deux frères. 3. Combien de frères est-ce qu'il a? 4. Vous jouez au tennis? 5. Vous jouez au tennis. 6. Avec qui est-ce que vous jouez au tennis?** Make sure students hear the difference between declarative and interrogative statements.

TEACHING OPTIONS

Using Games Divide the class into small groups. Pronounce ten phrases based on those in the examples and in **Prononcez**. Have students silently pass one piece of paper, numbered 1–10, around their group. Members of each group take turns recording whether the statements are declarative or interrogative. Collect the papers, one per group, when you finish saying the phrases. The group with the most correct answers wins.

Au parc vhlcentral

AP® Theme: Contemporary Life
Context: Leisure and Sports

PERSONNAGES

David

Rachid

Sandrine

Stéphane

DAVID Oh là là… On fait du sport aujourd'hui!
RACHID C'est normal! On est dimanche. Tous les week-ends à Aix, on fait du vélo, on joue au foot…
SANDRINE Oh, quelle belle journée! Faisons une promenade!
DAVID D'accord.

DAVID Moi, le week-end, je sors souvent. Mon passe-temps favori, c'est de dessiner la nature et les belles femmes. Mais Rachid, lui, c'est un grand sportif.
RACHID Oui, je joue au foot très souvent et j'adore.

RACHID Tiens, Stéphane! Déjà? Il est en avance.
SANDRINE Salut.
STÉPHANE Salut. Ça va?
DAVID Ça va.
STÉPHANE Salut.
RACHID Salut.

STÉPHANE Pfft! Je n'aime pas l'histoire-géo.
RACHID Mais, qu'est-ce que tu aimes alors, à part le foot?
STÉPHANE Moi? J'aime presque tous les sports. Je fais du ski, de la planche à voile, du vélo… et j'adore nager.
RACHID Oui, mais tu sais, le sport ne joue pas un grand rôle au bac.

RACHID Et puis, les études, c'est comme le sport. Pour être bon, il faut travailler!
STÉPHANE Ouais, ouais.
RACHID Allez, commençons. En quelle année Napoléon a-t-il…

SANDRINE Dis-moi David, c'est comment chez toi, aux États-Unis? Quels sont les sports favoris des Américains?
DAVID Euh… chez moi? Beaucoup pratiquent le baseball ou le basket et surtout, on adore regarder le football américain. Mais toi, Sandrine, qu'est-ce que tu fais de tes loisirs? Tu aimes le sport? Tu sors?

A C T I V I T É S

1 **Les événements** Mettez ces (*these*) événements dans l'ordre chronologique.

___10___ **a.** David dessine un portrait de Sandrine.

___6___ **b.** Stéphane se plaint (*complains*) de ses cours.

___4___ **c.** Rachid parle du match de foot.

___9___ **d.** David complimente Sandrine.

___2___ **e.** David mentionne une activité que Rachid aime faire.

___7___ **f.** Sandrine est curieuse de savoir (*to know*) quels sont les sports favoris des Américains.

___5___ **g.** Stéphane dit (*says*) qu'il ne sait (*knows*) pas s'il va gagner son prochain match.

___3___ **h.** Stéphane arrive.

___1___ **i.** David parle de son passe-temps favori.

___8___ **j.** Sandrine parle de sa passion.

182 *cent quatre-vingt-deux*

Les amis parlent de leurs loisirs.

RACHID Alors, Stéphane, tu crois que tu vas gagner ton prochain match?
STÉPHANE Hmm, ce n'est pas garanti! L'équipe de Marseille est très forte.
RACHID C'est vrai, mais tu es très motivé, n'est-ce pas?
STÉPHANE Bien sûr.

RACHID Et, pour les études, tu es motivé? Qu'est-ce que vous faites en histoire-géo en ce moment?
STÉPHANE Oh, on étudie Napoléon.
RACHID C'est intéressant! Les cent jours, la bataille de Waterloo...

SANDRINE Bof, je n'aime pas tellement le sport, mais j'aime bien sortir le week-end. Je vais au cinéma ou à des concerts avec mes amis. Ma vraie passion, c'est la musique. Je désire être chanteuse professionnelle.

DAVID Mais tu es déjà une chanteuse extraordinaire! Eh! J'ai une idée. Je peux faire un portrait de toi?
SANDRINE De moi? Vraiment? Oui, si tu insistes!

Expressions utiles

Talking about your activities

- **Qu'est-ce que tu fais de tes loisirs? Tu sors?**
  What do you do in your free time? Do you go out?
- **Le week-end, je sors souvent.**
  On weekends I often go out.
- **J'aime bien sortir.**
  I like to go out.
- **Tous les week-ends, on/tout le monde fait du sport.**
  Every weekend, people play/everyone plays sports.
- **Qu'est-ce que tu aimes alors, à part le foot?**
  What else do you like then, besides soccer?
- **J'aime presque tous les sports.**
  I like almost all sports.
- **Je peux faire un portrait de toi?**
  Can/May I do a portrait of you?
- **Qu'est-ce que vous faites en histoire-géo en ce moment?**
  What are you doing in history-geography at this moment?
- **Les études, c'est comme le sport. Pour être bon, il faut travailler!**
  Studies are like sports. To be good, you have to work!
- **Faisons une promenade!**
  Let's take a walk!

Additional vocabulary

- **Dis-moi.**
  Tell me.
- **Tu sais.**
  You know.
- **Ce n'est pas garanti!**
  It's not guaranteed!
- **Vraiment?**
  Really?
- **Bien sûr.**
  Of course.
- **Tiens.**
  Hey, look./Here you are.

---

2 **Questions** Choisissez la traduction (*translation*) qui convient pour chaque activité. Essayez de ne pas utiliser de dictionnaire. Combien de traductions y a-t-il pour le verbe **faire**?

- c 1. faire du ski
- d 2. faire une promenade
- b 3. faire du vélo
- a 4. faire du sport

- a. to play sports
- b. to go biking
- c. to ski
- d. to take a walk

3 **À vous!** David et Rachid parlent de faire des projets (*plans*) pour le week-end, mais les loisirs qu'ils aiment sont très différents. Ils discutent de leurs préférences et finalement choisissent une activité qu'ils vont pratiquer ensemble (*together*). Avec un(e) partenaire, écrivez la conversation et jouez la scène devant la classe.

ACTIVITÉS

Expressions utiles
- Draw attention to the forms of the verb **faire** and irregular **-ir** verbs in the captions, in the **Expressions utiles** box, and as they occur in your conversation with students. Tell students that this material will be presented in **Structures**.
- Respond briefly to questions about **faire** and irregular **-ir** verbs. Reinforce correct forms, but do not expect students to produce them consistently at this time.
- Work through the **Expressions utiles** by asking students about their activities. As you do, respond to the content of their responses and ask other students questions about their classmates' answers. Example: **Qu'est-ce que vous faites de vos loisirs? Vous sortez?**
- Remind students that the **nous** form of a verb can be used to say *Let's...* Example: **Faisons une promenade!** = *Let's take a walk!*

1 **Suggestion** Form several groups of eight students. Write each of these sentences on individual strips of paper and distribute them among the students in each group. Make a set of sentences for each group. Have students read their sentences aloud in the correct order.

1 **Expansion** Have students make sentences to fill in parts of the story not mentioned in this activity.

2 **Suggestion** Remind students that **faire** has several English translations.

3 **Suggestion** Remind students of expressions like **On...?** for suggesting activities and **D'accord** and **Non, je préfère...** for accepting or rejecting suggestions. As students write their scenes, circulate around the room to help with unfamiliar vocabulary and expressions.

EXPANSION

Mini-conversations Have pairs of students create two-line mini-conversations using as many **Expressions utiles** as they can. Example: —**Qu'est-ce que tu aimes alors, à part le foot?** —**J'aime presque tous les sports.**
Then have them use the vocabulary in this section to talk about their own activities and those of their friends and family.

PRE-AP®

Interpersonal Speaking Ask volunteers to ad-lib the **Roman-photo** episode for the class. Assure them that it is not necessary to memorize the episode or to stick strictly to its content. They should try to get the general meaning across with the vocabulary and expressions they know. Encourage creativity. Give them time to prepare. You may want to assign this as homework and do it the next class period as a review activity.

AP® Theme: Contemporary Life
Context: Leisure and Sports

vhlcentral | Flash culture

CULTURE À LA LOUPE

Le football

Le football est le sport le plus° populaire dans la majorité des pays° francophones. Tous les quatre ans°, des centaines de milliers de° fans, ou «supporters», regardent la Coupe du Monde°: le championnat de foot(ball) le plus important du monde. En 1998 (mille neuf cent quatre-vingt-dix-huit), l'équipe de France gagne la Coupe du Monde, en 2006 (deux mille six), elle perd en finale contre l'Italie et en 2016 (deux mille seize), contre le Portugal.

Le Cameroun a aussi une grande équipe de football. «Les Lions Indomptables°» gagnent la médaille d'or° aux Jeux Olympiques de Sydney en 2000. En 2007, l'équipe camerounaise est la première équipe africaine à être dans le classement mondial° de la FIFA (Fédération Internationale de Football Association). Certains «Lions» jouent dans les clubs français et européens.

En France, il y a deux ligues professionnelles de vingt équipes chacune°. Ça fait° quarante équipes professionnelles de football pour un pays plus petit que° le Texas! Certaines équipes, comme le Paris Saint-Germain («le PSG») ou l'Olympique de Marseille («l'OM»), ont beaucoup de supporters.

Les Français, comme les Camerounais, adorent regarder le football, mais ils sont aussi des joueurs très sérieux: aujourd'hui en France, il y a plus de 17.000 (dix-sept mille) clubs amateurs de football et plus de deux millions de joueurs.

Nombre° de membres des fédérations sportives en France

Football	2.002.400
Tennis	1.103.500
Judo-jujitsu	634.900
Basket-ball	536.900
Rugby	447.500
Golf	414.200
Natation°	304.000
Ski	136.100
Vélo°	119.200
Danse	84.000

SOURCE: Ministère de la Jeunesse et des Sports

le plus *the most* pays *countries* Tous les quatre ans *Every four years* centaines de milliers de *hundreds of thousands of* Coupe du Monde *World Cup* Indomptables *Untamable* or *gold* classement mondial *world ranking* chacune *each* Ça fait *That makes* un pays plus petit que *a country smaller than* Nombre *Number* Natation *Swimming* Vélo *Cycling*

ACTIVITÉS

1 Vrai ou faux? Indiquez si ces phrases sont **vraies** ou **fausses**.

1. Le football est le sport le plus populaire en France. Vrai.
2. La Coupe du Monde a lieu (*takes place*) tous les deux ans. Faux.
3. En 1998, l'équipe de France gagne la Coupe du Monde. Vrai.
4. Le Cameroun gagne une médaille de football aux Jeux Olympiques de Sydney. Vrai.
5. L'équipe du Cameroun est la première équipe africaine à être au classement mondial de la FIFA. Vrai.

6. Certains «Lions Indomptables» jouent dans des clubs français et européens. Vrai.
7. En France, il y a vingt équipes professionnelles de football. Faux.
8. L'Olympique de Marseille est un célèbre stade de football. Faux.
9. Les Français aiment jouer au football. Vrai.
10. Les Français n'aiment pas du tout les sports individuels. Faux.

Section Goals

In this section, students will:
• learn about a popular sport
• learn sports terms
• learn names of champions from French-speaking regions
• read about two celebrated French athletes
• view authentic video footage

Key Standards
2.1, 2.2, 3.1, 3.2, 4.2

21st Century Skills

Global Awareness
Students will gain perspectives on the Francophone world to develop respect and openness to other cultures.

Culture à la loupe

Avant la lecture Before opening their books, ask students to call out as many sports-related words as they can remember in French. Ask them to name the most popular sports in the United States and those that they associate with the Francophone world.

Lecture
• Point out the chart and ask students what information it shows.
• Make sure your class understands that **le football américain** is *football* and **le foot** is *soccer*.

Après la lecture Have students prepare a list of questions with **jouer** and frequency expressions to ask a classmate. Example:
Élève 1: Est-ce que tu joues parfois au football? Élève 2: Non, je joue rarement au football.

1 Expansion Ask these additional true/false statements.
11. En France, le basket-ball est plus populaire que la natation. (Vrai.) 12. On fait moins de rugby que de ski en France. (Faux.) 13. L'équipe de foot de Marseille est très populaire. (Vrai.)

EXPANSION

Writing Practice Provide groups of three students with a list of words that are relevant to **Le football** like **gagner**, **longtemps**, **courir** from the **Leçon 5A** vocabulary list. Ask them to work together to create sentences about the reading by incorporating the lexical items you have prompted. Example: **gagner (En 1998, la France gagne la Coupe du Monde.)** Answers will vary in an open-ended activity like this, but remind the class to stick to learned material. Follow up by creating a column on the board for each word that you prompted so students can share sentences they consider successful. After at least one student has written a response for each word, correct the sentences as a class.

LE FRANÇAIS QUOTIDIEN

Le sport

arbitre (*m./f.*)	referee
ballon (*m.*)	ball
coup de sifflet (*m.*)	whistle
entraîneur/-euse	coach
maillot (*m.*)	jersey
terrain (*m.*)	playing field
hors-jeu	off-side
marquer	to score

LE MONDE FRANCOPHONE

Des champions

Voici quelques champions olympiques récents.

Algérie Taoufik Makhloufi, athlétisme°, argent°, Rio de Janeiro, 2016

Burundi Francine Niyonsaba, athlétisme, argent, Rio de Janeiro, 2016

Cameroun Françoise Mbango Etone, athlétisme, or°, Pékin, 2008

Canada Alexandre Bilodeau, ski acrobatique, or, Sochi, 2014

France Teddy Riner, judo, or, Rio de Janeiro, 2016

Maroc Mohammed Rabii, boxe, bronze, Rio de Janeiro, 2016

Suisse Dominique Gisin, ski alpin, or, Sochi, 2014

Tunisie Oussama Mellouli, natation, or, Londres, 2012

athlétisme *track and field* **argent** *silver* **or** *gold*

PORTRAIT

AP® **Theme:** Contemporary Life
Context: Leisure and Sports

Zinédine Zidane et Laura Flessel

Zinédine Zidane, ou «Zizou», est un footballeur français. Né° à Marseille de parents algériens, il joue dans différentes équipes françaises. Nommé trois fois «Joueur de l'année» par la FIFA (la Fédération Internationale de Football Association), il gagne la Coupe du Monde avec l'équipe de France en 1998 (mille neuf cent quatre-vingt-dix-huit). Il est aujourd'hui entraîneur du Real Madrid, en Espagne°.

Née à la Guadeloupe, Laura Flessel commence l'escrime à l'âge de sept ans. Après plusieurs titres° de championne de Guadeloupe, elle va en France pour continuer sa carrière. En 1991, à 20 ans, elle est championne de France et cinq ans plus tard, elle est double championne olympique à Atlanta en 1996. En 2007 (deux mille sept), elle gagne aussi la médaille d'or aux Championnats d'Europe en individuel. Et en 2017, elle devient ministre des Sports du gouvernement français.

Né *Born* **Espagne** *Spain* **plusieurs titres** *several titles* **porte-drapeau** *flag bearer*

Sur Internet

AP® **Theme:** Contemporary Life
Context: Leisure and Sports

Qu'est-ce que le «free-running»?

Go to **vhlcentral.com** to find more information related to this **Culture** section and to watch the corresponding **Flash culture** video.

---

2 **Zinédine ou Laura?** Indiquez de qui on parle.

1. <u>Zinédine</u> est de France métropolitaine.
2. <u>Laura</u> est née à la Guadeloupe.
3. <u>Zinédine</u> gagne la Coupe du Monde pour la France en 1998.
4. <u>Laura</u> est championne de France en 1991.
5. <u>Laura</u> est double championne olympique en 1996.
6. <u>Zinédine</u> a été trois fois joueur de l'année.

3 **Une interview** Avec un(e) partenaire, préparez une interview entre un(e) journaliste et un(e) athlète que vous aimez. Jouez la scène devant la classe. Est-ce que vos camarades peuvent deviner (*can guess*) le nom de l'athlète?

A C T I V I T É S

Sidebar (right column)

Le français quotidien You might extend this list to include **le poteau de but** (*goalpost*), **le coup d'envoi** (*kickoff*), **un penalty** (*penalty kick*), and **une faute** (*foul*).

Portrait Zinédine Zidane became the most expensive player in the history of soccer when Real Madrid acquired him for the equivalent of about $66 million American dollars. «Zizou» also made history as Christian Dior's first male model. Laura Flessel is a left-handed fencer called «**la Guêpe**» (*Wasp*) because of her competitive and dangerous attack.

Le monde francophone Model the pronunciation of names and places in this box. Then ask students if they know of any other athletes from the Francophone world.

2 Expansion Continue the activity with additional fill-in-the-blank statements such as these.
7. _____ est entraîneur pour une équipe espagnole. (Zinédine)
8. _____ est le porte-drapeau aux Jeux Olympiques de 2012. (Laura)

3 Expansion Have students prepare five sentences in the first person for homework, describing themselves as a well-known athlete. Ask students to introduce themselves to the class. The class tries to guess the presenter's identity.

Flash culture Tell students that they will learn more about sports and leisure activities by watching a video narrated by Csilla. Show the video, and then have students close their eyes and describe from memory what they saw. Write their descriptions on the board. You can also use the activities in the video manual in class to reinforce this **Flash culture** or assign them as homework.

21ˢᵗ Century Skills

Information and Media Literacy: Sur Internet Students access and critically evaluate information from the Internet.

EXPANSION

Des champions Look at the maps of the world in the beginning of the book to remind students where Francophone countries featured in **Le monde francophone** are located. Ask students to pick one of the athletes from this list to research for homework. They should come to the next class with five French sentences about that athlete's life and career. You may want to have students bring an image from the Internet of the athlete they chose to research. Collect the photos and gather different images of the same athlete. Have students who researched the same champion work together as a group to present that athlete while the rest of the class looks at the images they found.

5A.1

The verb *faire* and expression *il faut* **vhl**central

Point de départ Like other commonly used verbs, the verb **faire** (*to do, to make*) is irregular in the present tense.

faire (to do, to make)	
je fais	nous faisons
tu fais	vous faites
il/elle/on fait	ils/elles font

Il ne **fait** pas ses devoirs.
He doesn't do his homework.

Qu'est-ce que vous **faites** ce soir?
What are you doing this evening?

Tes parents **font**-ils quelque chose vendredi?
Are your parents doing anything Friday?

Nous **faisons** une sculpture dans mon cours d'art.
We're making a sculpture in my art class.

On fait du sport aujourd'hui!

Qu'est-ce que vous faites en histoire-géo?

- Use the verb **faire** in these idiomatic expressions. Note that it does not always translate into English as *to do* or *to make*.

Expressions with *faire*			
faire de l'aérobic	to do aerobics	faire de la planche à voile	to go wind-surfing
faire attention (à)	to pay attention (to)	faire une promenade	to go for a walk
faire du camping	to go camping		
faire du cheval	to go horseback riding	faire une randonnée	to go for a hike
faire la connaissance de...	to meet (someone) for the first time	faire du ski	to go skiing
		faire du sport	to play sports
faire la cuisine	to cook	faire un tour (en voiture)	to go for a walk (drive)
faire de la gym	to work out		
faire du jogging	to go jogging	faire du vélo	to go bike riding

Tu **fais** souvent **du sport**?
Do you play sports often?

Nous **faisons attention** en classe.
We pay attention in class.

Elles **font du camping**.
They go camping.

Yves **fait la cuisine**.
Yves is cooking.

Je **fais de la gym**.
I'm working out.

Faites-vous **une promenade**?
Are you going for a walk?

- Make sure to learn the correct article with each **faire** expression that calls for one. For **faire** expressions requiring a partitive or indefinite article (**un, une, du, de la**), the article is replaced with **de** when the expression is negated.

Elles font **de la** gym trois fois par semaine.
They work out three times a week.

Elles ne font pas **de** gym le dimanche.
They don't work out on Sundays.

Fais-tu **du** ski?
Do you ski?

Non, je ne fais pas **de** ski.
No, I don't ski.

- Use **faire la connaissance de** before someone's name or another noun that identifies a person you do not know.

Je vais enfin **faire la connaissance de Martin**.
I'm finally going to meet Martin.

Je vais **faire la connaissance des joueurs**.
I'm going to meet the players.

The expression *il faut*

Pour être bon, il faut travailler!

Il ne faut pas regarder la télé.

- When followed by a verb in the infinitive, the expression **il faut...** means *it is necessary to...* or *one must...*

Il faut faire attention en cours de maths.
It is necessary to pay attention in math class.

Il ne faut pas manger après dix heures.
One must not eat after 10 o'clock.

Faut-il laisser un pourboire?
Is it necessary to leave a tip?

Il faut gagner le match!
We must win the game!

🔊 **Vérifiez**

🏃 **Boîte à outils**

The infinitive of **faut** is **falloir**. **Falloir** is an irregular impersonal verb, which means that it only has one conjugated form in every tense: the third person singular. The verbs **pleuvoir** (*to rain*) and **neiger** (*to snow*), which you will learn in **Leçon 5B**, work the same way.

🔊 **Vérifiez**

Essayez! Complétez chaque phrase avec la forme correcte du verbe **faire** au présent.

1. Tu _____fais_____ tes devoirs le samedi?
2. Vous ne ___faites___ pas attention au professeur.
3. Nous ___faisons___ du camping.
4. Ils ___font___ du jogging.
5. On ___fait___ une promenade au parc.
6. Il ___fait___ du ski en montagne.
7. Je ___fais___ de l'aérobic.
8. Elles ___font___ un tour en voiture.
9. Est-ce que vous ___faites___ la cuisine?
10. Nous ne ___faisons___ pas de sport.
11. Je ne ___fais___ pas de planche à voile.
12. Irène et Sandrine ___font___ une randonnée avec leurs copines.

Suggestions: Scaffolding
- Go over the first two bullets on this page. Then ask students if they do the various activities, when, how often, with whom, and where. Examples: **Faites-vous du vélo? Quand/Combien de fois par semaine/Avec qui/Où faites-vous du vélo?** Check comprehension of other students by asking questions, such as: **Quand Laura fait-elle du vélo?**
- Have students complete the first **Vérifiez** activity.
- Explain that **il faut** is a very common expression in French even though its English translations are not as widely used in everyday language.
- Consider explaining to students that the negative form of the expression, **il ne faut pas**, is most often used to mean *one must not* rather than *it is not necessary.*
- Have students complete the second **Vérifiez** activity.

Essayez!
- Draw students' attention to the use of **de** in items 10 and 11.
- Have students check each other's answers.

TEACHING OPTIONS

Game Divide the class into two teams. Pick one team member at a time to go to the board, alternating between teams. Give a subject pronoun that the team member must write and say aloud with the correct form of **faire**. Example: **vous (vous faites)**. Give a point for each correct answer. The game ends when all students have had a chance to go to the board. The team with the most points at the end of the game wins.

EXPANSION

Extra Practice Have students study the captions from **Roman-photo**. In small groups, tell them to think of additional phrases containing **faire** expressions and **il faut** that the characters would likely say. Write the main characters' names on the board in a row and have volunteers put their ideas underneath. Ask what can be concluded about each character. Example: **Rachid donne beaucoup de conseils.**

Mise en pratique

1 Chassez l'intrus Quelle activité ne fait pas partie du groupe?

1. a. faire du jogging   b. faire une randonnée   c. faire de la planche à voile
2. a. faire du vélo   b. faire du camping   c. faire du cheval
3. a. faire une promenade   b. faire la cuisine   c. faire un tour
4. a. faire du sport   b. faire de la gym   c. faire la connaissance
5. a. faire ses devoirs   b. faire du ski   c. faire du camping
6. a. faire la cuisine   b. faire du sport   c. faire de l'aérobic

2 Que font-ils? Regardez les dessins. Que font les personnages?

▶ **MODÈLE**

Julien fait du jogging.

Julien

1. Je
Je fais du cheval.

2. tu
Tu fais de la planche à voile.

3. Anne
Anne fait de l'aérobic.

4. Louis et Paul
Louis et Paul font du camping.

5. Vous
Vous faites la cuisine.

6. Denis
Denis fait du ski.

7. Nous
Nous faisons une randonnée.

8. Elles
Elles font du vélo.

3 La paire Faites correspondre (*Match*) les éléments des deux colonnes et rajoutez (*add*) la forme correcte du verbe **faire**.

1. Elle aime courir (*to run*), alors elle... e. fait du jogging.
2. Ils adorent les animaux. Ils... d. font du cheval.
3. Quand j'ai faim, je... b. fais la cuisine.
4. L'hiver, vous... g. faites du ski.
5. Pour marcher, nous... f. faisons une promenade.
6. Tiger Woods... a. fait du golf.

a. du golf.
b. la cuisine.
c. les devoirs.
d. du cheval.
e. du jogging.
f. une promenade.
g. du ski.
h. de l'aérobic.

Communication

4 Ce week-end Que faites-vous ce week-end? Avec un(e) partenaire, posez les questions à tour de rôle. *Answers will vary.*

MODÈLE

tu / jogging
Élève 1: Est-ce que tu fais du jogging ce week-end?
Élève 2: Non, je ne fais pas de jogging. Je fais du cheval.

1. tu / le vélo *Est-ce que tu fais du vélo ce week-end?*
2. tes amis / la cuisine *Est-ce que tes amis font la cuisine ce week-end?*
3. ton/ta meilleur(e) ami(e) et toi, vous / le jogging *Est-ce que ton/ta meilleur(e) ami(e) et toi, vous faites du jogging ce week-end?*
4. toi et moi, nous / une randonnée *Est-ce que toi et moi, nous faisons une randonnée ce week-end?*
5. tu / la gym *Est-ce que tu fais de la gym ce week-end?*
6. ton/ta camarade de classe / le sport *Est-ce que ton/ta camarade de classe fait du sport ce week-end?*
7. on / faire de la planche à voile *Est-ce qu'on fait de la planche à voile ce week-end?*
8. tes parents et toi, vous / un tour au parc *Est-ce que tes parents et toi, vous faites un tour au parc ce week-end?*

5 De bons conseils À tour de rôle, posez des questions à votre partenaire qui va vous donner de bon conseils (*advice*). Utilisez les éléments de la liste dans vos questions. Ensuite, présentez vos idées à la classe. *Answers will vary.*

MODÈLE

Élève 1: Qu'est-ce qu'il faut faire pour avoir de bonnes notes?
Élève 2: Il faut étudier jour et nuit.

être en pleine forme (*great shape*)	avoir de bonnes notes
avoir de l'argent	gagner une course (*race*)
avoir beaucoup d'amis	bien manger
être champion de ski	réussir aux examens

6 Les sportifs Votre professeur va vous donner une feuille d'activités. Faites une enquête sur le nombre d'élèves qui pratiquent certains sports et activités dans votre classe. Présentez les résultats à la classe. *Answers will vary.*

MODÈLE

Élève 1: Est-ce que tu fais du jogging?
Élève 2: Oui, je fais du jogging.

Sport	Nom
1. jogging	Carole
2. vélo	
3. planche à voile	
4. cuisine	
5. camping	
6. cheval	
7. aérobic	
8. ski	

cent quatre-vingt-neuf **189**

5A.2

Irregular -ir verbs **vhl**central

Point de départ You already know how to conjugate regular **-ir** verbs. However, some of the most commonly used **-ir** verbs are irregular in their conjugation.

- **Sortir** is used to express leaving a room or a building. It also expresses the idea of going out, as with friends or on a date.

sortir	
je sors	nous sortons
tu sors	vous sortez
il/elle/on sort	ils/elles sortent

Tu **sors** souvent avec tes copains?
Do you go out often with your friends?

Quand **sortez**-vous?
When are you going out?

Mon frère n'aime pas **sortir** avec Chloé.
My brother doesn't like to go out with Chloé.

Mes parents ne **sortent** pas lundi.
My parents aren't going out Monday.

- Use the preposition **de** after **sortir** when the place someone is leaving is mentioned.

L'élève **sort de** la salle de classe.
The student is leaving the classroom.

Nous **sortons du** restaurant vers vingt heures.
We're leaving the restaurant around 8:00 p.m.

Le week-end, je sors souvent.

Ils partent pour la fac.

- **Partir** is generally used to say someone is leaving a large place such as a city, country, or region. Often, a form of **partir** is accompanied by the preposition **pour** and the name of a destination.

partir	
je pars	nous partons
tu pars	vous partez
il/elle/on part	ils/elles partent

À quelle heure **partez**-vous?
At what time are you leaving?

Nous **partons** à midi.
We're leaving at noon.

Je **pars pour** l'Algérie.
I'm leaving for Algeria.

Ils **partent pour** Genève demain.
They're leaving for Geneva tomorrow.

190 *cent quatre-vingt-dix*

Suggestion: Scaffolding

- Go over other irregular **-ir** verbs, pointing out that they are all in the same grammatical "verb family" as **sortir** and **partir**. Note that all verbs of this type have two stems: **sortir**: singular stem **sor-** and plural stem **sort-**. Point out that **courir** does not follow exactly the same pattern as the other verbs in the singular forms. Do a Rapid Drill as described on p. 190 to practice all verbs and their forms.
- Follow the suggestion for Kinesthetic Learners. Then ask students simple questions using the verbs. Examples: **Combien d'heures dormez-vous par nuit? Pensez-vous que les roses sentent bon? Qu'est-ce que votre restaurant préféré sert?**

Essayez! Give these items for additional practice, having students choose which **-ir** verb(s) to use. **9.** J'adore ____. (courir) Je ____ vingt à trente kilomètres par semaine. (cours) **10.** Les enfants ne ____ pas parce qu'ils ne sont pas fatigués. (dorment) **11.** Qu'est-ce qu'on ____ au café en face de chez toi? (sert) **12.** Merci pour les fleurs. Elles ____ très bon. (sentent)

Culture Practice Give students the words to the traditional French children's song **Frère Jacques**. Have them identify the **-ir** verb in the lyrics, then sing the song together as a class.

Other irregular -ir verbs

	dormir *(to sleep)*	servir *(to serve)*	sentir *(to feel)*	courir *(to run)*
je	dors	sers	sens	cours
tu	dors	sers	sens	cours
il/elle/on	dort	sert	sent	court
nous	dormons	servons	sentons	courons
vous	dormez	servez	sentez	courez
ils/elles	dorment	servent	sentent	courent

Rachid dort.

Nous courons.

Elles **dorment** jusqu'à midi.
They sleep until noon.

Je **sers** du fromage à la fête.
I'm serving cheese at the party.

- **Sentir** can mean *to feel, to smell,* or *to sense.*

Je **sens** que l'examen va être difficile.
I sense that the exam is going to be difficult.

Ça **sent** bon!
That smells good!

Vous **sentez** le parfum?
Do you smell the perfume?

Ils **sentent** sa présence.
They feel his presence.

Vous **courez** vite!
You run fast!

Nous **servons** du thé glacé.
We are serving iced tea.

Essayez! Complétez les phrases avec la forme correcte du verbe.

1. Nous __sortons__ (sortir) vers neuf heures.
2. Je __sers__ (servir) des boissons gazeuses aux invités.
3. Tu __pars__ (partir) quand pour le Canada?
4. Nous ne __dormons__ (dormir) pas en cours.
5. Ils __courent__ (courir) tous les week-ends.
6. Tu fais la cuisine? Ça __sent__ (sentir) bon.
7. Vous __sortez__ (sortir) avec des copains ce soir.
8. Elle __part__ (partir) pour Dijon ce week-end.

DIFFERENTIATION

For Kinesthetic Learners Tell students that they will act out the appropriate gestures when you say what certain people in the class are doing. Examples: ____ **dort.** (The student gestures sleeping.) ____ **et** ____ **courent.** (The two students indicated run in place briefly.) Repeat verbs and vary forms as much as possible.

EXPANSION

Extra Practice Dictate sentences like these to the class, saying each one twice and pausing between. **1.** Je pars pour la France la semaine prochaine. **2.** Mon copain et moi, nous sortons ce soir. **3.** Les élèves ne dorment jamais en classe. **4.** La fleur sent bon. **5.** Tu cours vite. **6.** Que servez-vous au restaurant? Advise students to pay attention to the verbs.

Mise en pratique

1 Choisissez Monique et ses amis aiment bien sortir. Choisissez la forme correcte des verbes **partir** ou **sortir** pour compléter la description de leurs activités.

1. Samedi soir, je _____sors_____ avec mes copains.
2. Mes copines Magali et Anissa _____partent_____ pour New York.
3. Nous _____sortons_____ du cinéma.
4. Nicolas _____part_____ pour Dakar vers dix heures du soir.
5. À midi, vous _____partez_____ pour l'aéroport.
6. Je _____pars_____ pour le Maroc dans une semaine.
7. Tu _____sors/pars_____ avec ton ami ce week-end.
8. Olivier et Bernard _____sortent_____ tard du bureau.
9. Lucien et moi, nous _____partons_____ pour l'Algérie.
10. Thomas _____sort_____ du stade à deux heures de l'après-midi.

2 Votre temps libre Utilisez les éléments des colonnes pour décrire (*describe*) le temps libre de votre famille et de vos amis. Answers will vary.

A	B	C
je	(ne pas) courir	jusqu'à (*until*) midi
mon frère	(ne pas) dormir	tous les week-ends
ma sœur	(ne pas) partir	tous les jours
mes parents	(ne pas) sortir	souvent
mes cousins		rarement
mon meilleur ami		jamais
ma meilleure amie		une (deux, etc.) fois
mes copains		par jour/ semaine
?		

3 Descriptions Complétez les phrases avec la forme correcte d'un verbe en **-ir**.

1. Véronique /  / tard   Véronique dort tard.

2. je / / sandwichs   Je sers des sandwichs.

3. les enfants / / le chocolat chaud   Les enfants sentent le chocolat chaud.

4. nous / / souvent   Nous courons souvent.

5. tu / / de l'hôpital   Tu sors de l'hôpital.

Communication

4 **La question** Vincent parle au téléphone avec sa mère. Vous entendez (*hear*) ses réponses, mais pas les questions. À tour de rôle, reconstruisez leur conversation. Answers will vary.

MODÈLE

<u>Comment vas-tu?</u> Ça va bien, merci.

1. _____ Oui, je sors ce soir.
2. _____ Je sors avec Marc et Audrey.
3. _____ Nous partons à six heures.
4. _____ Oui, nous allons jouer au tennis.
5. _____ Après, nous allons au restaurant.
6. _____ Nous sortons du restaurant à neuf heures.
7. _____ Marc et Audrey partent pour Nice le week-end prochain.
8. _____ Non. Moi, je pars dans deux semaines.

5 **Indiscrétions** Votre partenaire est curieux/curieuse et désire savoir (*to know*) ce que vous faites chez vous. Répondez à ses questions. Answers will vary.

1. Jusqu'à (*Until*) quelle heure dors-tu le week-end?
2. Dors-tu après les cours? Pourquoi?
3. À quelle heure sors-tu le samedi soir?
4. Avec qui sors-tu le samedi soir?
5. Est-ce que tu sors souvent avec des copains pendant la semaine?
6. Que sers-tu quand tu as des copains à la maison?
7. Pars-tu bientôt en vacances (*vacation*)? Où?

6 **Dispute** Laëtitia est très active. Son petit ami Bertrand ne sort pas beaucoup, alors ils ont souvent des disputes. Avec un(e) partenaire, jouez les deux rôles. Utilisez les mots et les expressions de la liste. Answers will vary.

dormir	partir
faire des promenades	un passe-temps
	sentir
faire un tour (en voiture)	sortir
	rarement
par semaine	souvent

---

4 Expansion Ask students to imagine they are on the telephone and a classmate can overhear them. Have students write three answers to say in front of a partner who will guess the questions. Example: **Non, maman, on ne sort pas trop souvent. Je fais mes devoirs tous les soirs. (Tu ne sors pas trop souvent avec tes copains?)**

5 Suggestion Remind students to answer in complete sentences.

5 Virtual Chat You can also assign Activity 5 on vhlcentral.com. Students record individual responses that appear in your gradebook.

6 Suggestion Have a couple of volunteer pairs act out their conversations for the class.

Activity Pack For additional activities, go to the **Activity Pack** in the **Resources** section of vhlcentral.com.

TEACHING OPTIONS

Game Divide the class into two teams. Announce an infinitive and a subject pronoun. Example: **dormir**; **elle**. At the board, have the first member of Team A say and write down the given subject and the conjugated form of the verb. If the team member answers correctly, Team A gets one point. If not, give the first member of Team B the same example. The team with the most points at the end of the game wins.

EXPANSION

Small Groups Have small groups of students create a short story in the present tense or a conversation in which they logically mention as many verb forms as possible of **sortir**, **partir**, **dormir**, **servir**, **sentir**, and **courir**. If the class is advanced, add **mentir**. Call on groups to tell their story to the class or act out their conversation. Have students vote on the best story or conversation.

193

Révision

1 **Au parc** C'est dimanche. Avec un(e) partenaire, décrivez les activités de tous les personnages. Comparez vos observations avec les observations d'un autre groupe pour compléter votre description. Answers will vary.

2 **Mes habitudes** Avec un(e) partenaire, parlez de vos habitudes de la semaine. Que faites-vous régulièrement? Utilisez tous les mots de la liste. Answers will vary.

MODÈLE

Élève 1: Je fais parfois de la gym le lundi. Et toi?
Élève 2: Moi, je fais parfois la cuisine le lundi.

parfois le lundi	souvent à midi
le mercredi à midi	toujours le vendredi
le jeudi soir	tous les jours
le vendredi matin	trois fois par semaine
rarement le matin	une fois par semaine

3 **Mes vacances** Parlez de vos prochaines vacances (*vacation*) avec un(e) partenaire. Mentionnez cinq de vos passe-temps habituels en vacances et cinq nouvelles activités que vous allez essayer (*to try*). Comparez votre liste avec la liste de votre partenaire, puis présentez les réponses à la classe. Answers will vary.

4 **Que faire ici?** Avec un(e) partenaire, trouvez au minimum quatre choses à faire dans chaque (*each*) endroit. Quel endroit préférez-vous et pourquoi? Parlez de vos préférences avec la classe. Answers will vary.

MODÈLE

Élève 1: À la campagne, on fait des randonnées à cheval.
Élève 2: Oui, et il faut marcher.

1. à la campagne

3. au parc

2. à la plage

4. au gymnase

5 **Le conseiller** Un(e) conseiller/conseillère au lycée suggère des stratégies à un(e) élève pour l'aider (*help him or her*) à préparer les examens. Avec un(e) partenaire, jouez les deux rôles. Answers will vary.

MODÈLE

Élève 1: Qu'est-ce qu'il faut faire pour réussir les examens?
Élève 2: Il faut faire tous les devoirs.

6 **Quelles activités?** Votre professeur va vous donner, à vous et à votre partenaire, deux feuilles d'activités différentes pour le week-end. À tour de rôle, interviewez votre partenaire pour compléter les feuilles. Attention! Ne regardez pas la feuille de votre partenaire. Answers will vary.

MODÈLE

Élève 1: Est-ce que tu fais une randonnée dimanche après-midi?
Élève 2: Oui, je fais une randonnée dimanche après-midi.

AP® Theme: Contemporary Life
Context: Leisure and Sports

vhl central

Reportage de Canal 32

...une vingtaine° de ligues sportives étaient présentes...

Préparation Répondez aux questions. Answers will vary.

1. Qu'est-ce que vous aimez faire pendant votre temps libre?
2. Quel est le rôle du sport dans votre vie?

Jeux régionaux de la jeunesse à Troyes

En France, les associations sportives offrent des activités physiques aux collégiens et lycéens, surtout le mercredi, parce que beaucoup d'écoles sont fermées° l'après-midi. L'UNSS, ou l'Union nationale du sport scolaire, dont le but° est de mettre en avant° la valeur éducative du sport, est ouverte° à tous les élèves français. Au travers de ses° compétitions locales, régionales et nationales, le comité régional olympique et sportif et l'UNSS offrent aux jeunes la possibilité de découvrir° des sports qu'ils n'ont pas l'habitude de° pratiquer dans leurs associations sportives. Les jeunes athlètes peuvent se découvrir de nouvelles passions sportives, et les organisateurs peuvent détecter de jeunes talents pour l'avenir°, de futurs sportifs qui pourraient° un jour aller aux Jeux olympiques.

une vingtaine *around twenty* fermées *closed* dont le but *whose goal* mettre en avant *showcase* ouverte *open* Au travers de ses *Through its* découvrir *discover* n'ont pas l'habitude de *don't usually* avenir *future* pourraient *could*

Vocabulaire utile

l'athlétisme (*m.*)	track and field
l'aviron (*m.*)	rowing, crew
conquis(e)	won over
le mot d'ordre	key word
le plaisir	pleasure, enjoyment
le vivier	recruiting ground

Compréhension Répondez aux questions.

1. Combien d'élèves participent aux jeux de Troyes? plus de mille
2. Quels sports sont mentionnés? le football, l'athlétisme, le golfe, le judo et l'aviron
3. Avec quelle fréquence les jeux de Troyes ont-ils lieu (*take place*)? tous les deux ans

Conversation En petits groupes, discutez des questions suivantes. Answers will vary.

1. Quel est le rôle du sport dans la vie des jeunes? De quelle manière (*How*) les activités physiques sont-elles importantes pour eux?
2. Quel est le rôle du gouvernement (régional ou national) dans les sports et compétitions dans votre pays? De quelle manière le rôle du gouvernement est-il différent en France?

Application En petits groupes, faites des recherches sur une association ou compétition sportive destinée aux jeunes dans votre région ou pays. Quels sports et activités sont offerts? Est-ce que la participation est gratuite (*free*)? Présentez vos recherches à la classe.

Section Goals

In this section, students will:
- read about the UNSS and sports in France
- watch a report about the UNSS games in Troyes
- complete activities based on the video and reading

Key Standards

1.1, 1.2, 1.3, 2.2, 3.2, 4.1, 5.2

Préparation Ask students when and where they play individual and team sports.

Jeux régionaux de la jeunesse à Troyes Ask students these comprehension questions: **Comment les jeunes Français commencent-ils un sport? (avec des associations sportives) Qu'est-ce que l'UNSS offre aux jeunes? (la possibilité de pratiquer des sports variés et de participer aux compétitions)**

PRE-AP®

Audiovisual Interpretive Communication Tell students to use what they already know about sports and competitions to help them understand the video. Have them note what is familiar and any questions they have. Then discuss with the class.

Conversation Ask students if they find it unusual to not have sports at school. Point out that cultural practices of one culture may seem strange to people from other cultures.

Application Ask students to make a chart or graph to summarize the similarities and differences between their findings and the information in the video.

EXPANSION

Presentational Writing with Cultural Comparison Have students research youth athletic organizations and associations in other parts of the francophone world. How do they compare to those in France? What resources do they have or lack? Finally, how do these approaches compare to their own experiences? Have students write a paragraph answering these questions.

EXPANSION

Recycling Ask students to watch the segment of the **Zapping** video in **Unité 2** that focuses on sports (4:38–5:39). Ask them how Arthur's experience with sports compares to what they learned here. You may also ask them to reflect on how their comprehension has improved since the first time they saw this video.

195

Section Goals

In this section, students will learn and practice vocabulary related to:
• the weather
• seasons and dates

Key Standards

1.1, 1.2, 4.1

Suggestions

• Use the digital image for this page to present new vocabulary. Then describe the weather in places around the world. Example: **Aujourd'hui à Chicago, il pleut et il fait du vent.**
• Tell students that most weather expressions use the verb **faire**, but **neiger** and **pleuvoir** stand alone. Point out that they are only used in the third person singular.
• Point out that the expressions **avoir froid** and **avoir chaud** refer to people, but **faire froid** and **faire chaud** describe weather. Bring in photos that include people to illustrate this distinction.
• Mention to students that **temps** in this context means *weather*, not *time*.
• Using magazine photos of weather conditions and seasons, describe each image. Show photos again one at a time. Then ask: **En quelle saison sommes-nous? Quel temps fait-il?**
• Present how to ask and state the date using a calendar. Write the formula **C'est le** + [**chiffre**] + [**mois**] on the board. Explain that the first of the month is **le premier** + [**mois**]. Then point to a day on the calendar and ask students the date. Tell them when your birthday is, indicating the date on the calendar. Then ask students when their birthdays are.

You will learn how to...
▪ talk about seasons and the date
▪ discuss the weather

◁)) **vhl**central

Quel temps fait-il?

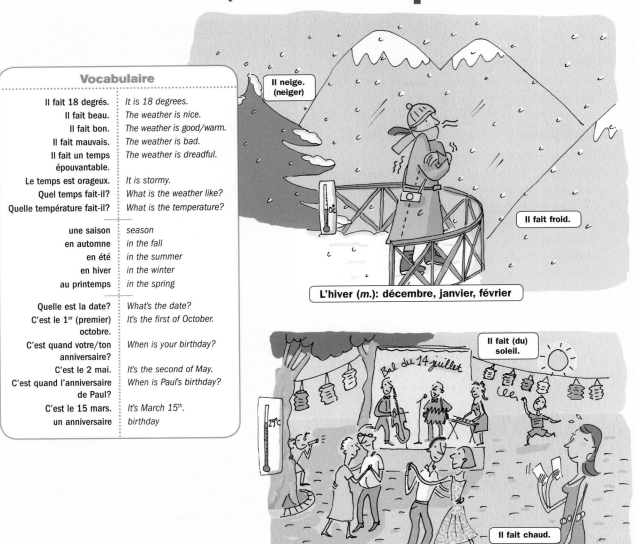

Vocabulaire

Il fait 18 degrés.	*It is 18 degrees.*
Il fait beau.	*The weather is nice.*
Il fait bon.	*The weather is good/warm.*
Il fait mauvais.	*The weather is bad.*
Il fait un temps épouvantable.	*The weather is dreadful.*
Le temps est orageux.	*It is stormy.*
Quel temps fait-il?	*What is the weather like?*
Quelle température fait-il?	*What is the temperature?*
une saison	*season*
en automne	*in the fall*
en été	*in the summer*
en hiver	*in the winter*
au printemps	*in the spring*
Quelle est la date?	*What's the date?*
C'est le 1ᵉʳ (premier) octobre.	*It's the first of October.*
C'est quand votre/ton anniversaire?	*When is your birthday?*
C'est le 2 mai.	*It's the second of May.*
C'est quand l'anniversaire de Paul?	*When is Paul's birthday?*
C'est le 15 mars.	*It's March 15ᵗʰ.*
un anniversaire	*birthday*

Il neige. (neiger)

Il fait froid.

L'hiver (*m.*): décembre, janvier, février

Il fait (du) soleil.

Bal du 14 juillet

29°C

Quelle est la date d'aujourd'hui? C'est le 14 juillet.

Il fait chaud.

L'été (*m.*): juin, juillet, août

196 *cent quatre-vingt-seize*

Attention!

In France and in most of the Francophone world, temperature is given in Celsius. Convert from Celsius to Fahrenheit with this formula: F = (C x 1.8) + 32. Convert from Fahrenheit to Celsius with this formula: C = (F − 32) x 0.56.

11°C = 52°F   78°F = 26°C

Il pleut. (pleuvoir)

un parapluie

un imperméable

Le printemps (m.): mars, avril, mai

Le temps est nuageux.

Il fait frais.

13°C

Il fait du vent.

L'automne (m.): septembre, octobre, novembre

Mise en pratique

1 Les fêtes et les jours fériés
Indiquez la date et la saison de chaque fête et jour férié (*holiday*).

	Date	Saison
1. la fête nationale française	le 14 juillet	l'été
2. l'indépendance des États-Unis	le 4 juillet	l'été
3. Poisson d'avril (*April Fool's Day*)	le 1er avril	le printemps
4. Noël	le 25 décembre	l'hiver
5. la Saint-Valentin	le 14 février	l'hiver
6. le Nouvel An	le 1er janvier	l'hiver
7. Halloween	le 31 octobre	l'automne
8. l'anniversaire de Washington	le 22 février	l'hiver

2 Quel temps fait-il?
Répondez aux questions par des phrases complètes. *Answers will vary.*

1. Quel temps fait-il en été?
2. Quel temps fait-il en automne?
3. Quel temps fait-il au printemps?
4. Quel temps fait-il en hiver?
5. Où est-ce qu'il neige?
6. Quel est votre mois préféré de l'année? Pourquoi?
7. Quand est-ce qu'il pleut où vous habitez?
8. Quand est-ce que le temps est orageux où vous habitez?

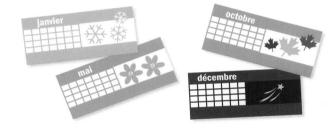

janvier

octobre

mai

décembre

3 Écoutez
Écoutez le bulletin météorologique et répondez aux questions suivantes.

	Vrai	Faux
1. C'est l'été.	☐	☑
2. Le printemps commence le 21 mars.	☑	☐
3. Il fait 11 degrés vendredi.	☑	☐
4. Il fait du vent vendredi.	☐	☑
5. Il faut utiliser le parapluie et l'imperméable vendredi.	☐	☑
6. Il va faire soleil samedi.	☐	☑
7. Il ne va pas faire chaud samedi.	☑	☐
8. Il va faire un temps épouvantable dimanche.	☑	☐

---

1 Suggestions
- Remind students to give the date in the correct order (day before month) and to include **le** before the day.
- Point out that the day always precedes the month in French when the date is written with numbers. Examples: **14 avril 2011, 14/04/2011**

1 Expansion Using this year's calendar, have students find the dates of these holidays. **9. la fête du travail aux États-Unis 10.** *Thanksgiving* **11.** *Easter* (**Pâques**) **12.** *Memorial Day* You may ask students to look up dates of other secular celebrations or religious holidays from various faiths. Answers will vary from year to year.

2 Suggestions
- Have students work in pairs or small groups to answer these questions.
- Tell students they may also encounter the phrase **à l'automne**, meaning *in the fall*. For other seasons, make sure they know to use **en** before those starting with a vowel sound and **au** with **printemps**, as it starts with a consonant.

3 Script Aujourd'hui, vendredi 21 mars, nous commençons le printemps avec une température de 11 degrés; il n'y a pas de vent, mais il y a quelques nuages. Votre météo du week-end: samedi, il ne va pas faire soleil; il va faire frais avec une température de 13 degrés; dimanche, encore 13 degrés, mais il va faire un temps épouvantable; il va pleuvoir toute la journée, alors, n'oubliez pas votre parapluie et votre imperméable! *Teacher Resources DVD*

3 Suggestion You may wish to pause the audio after the weather for each day is given to allow students time to answer corresponding questions.

TELL Connection

Environment 1 *Why:* Students come from diverse backgrounds. *What:* Involve students in describing weather and holidays based on their own personal experience.

EXPANSION

Le calendrier républicain During the French Revolution, the official calendar was changed. The New Year began on September 22 (the autumnal equinox), and the year was divided into 30-day months named as follows: **Vendémiaire** (*Vintage*), **Brumaire** (*Mist*), **Frimaire** (*Frost*), **Nivôse** (*Snow*), **Pluviôse** (*Rain*), **Ventôse** (*Wind*), **Germinal** (*Seed time*), **Floréal** (*Flower*), **Prairial** (*Meadow*), **Messidor** (*Harvest*), **Thermidor** (*Heat*), and **Fructidor** (*Fruits*).

TEACHING OPTIONS

Using Games Have students take turns guessing another student's birthday. He or she responds by saying **avant** or **après** until someone guesses correctly. The class then tries to guess the winning student's birthday. Play several rounds of this game to give all students as many opportunities as possible to guess.

Communication

4 Conversez Interviewez un(e) camarade de classe. Answers will vary.

1. C'est quand ton anniversaire? C'est quand l'anniversaire de ton père? Et de ta mère?
2. En quelle saison est ton anniversaire? Quel temps fait-il?
3. Quelle est ta saison préférée? Pourquoi? Quelles activités aimes-tu pratiquer?
4. En quelles saisons utilises-tu un parapluie et un imperméable? Pourquoi?
5. À quel moment de l'année es-tu en vacances? Précise les mois. Pendant (*During*) quels mois de l'année préfères-tu voyager? Pourquoi?
6. À quelle période de l'année étudies-tu? Précise les mois.
7. Quelle saison détestes-tu? Pourquoi?
8. Quand est l'anniversaire de mariage de tes parents?

5 Une lettre Vous avez un(e) correspondant(e) (*pen pal*) en France qui va vous rendre visite (*to visit you*). Écrivez (*Write*) une lettre à votre ami(e) où vous décrivez (*describe*) le temps qu'il fait à chaque saison et les activités que vous pouvez (*can*) faire. Comparez votre lettre avec la lettre d'un(e) camarade de classe. Answers will vary.

Cher Thomas,

Ici à Boston, il fait très froid en hiver et il neige souvent. Est-ce que tu aimes la neige? Moi, j'adore parce que je fais du ski tous les week-ends.

Et toi, tu fais du ski? ...

6 Quel temps fait-il en France? Votre professeur va vous donner, à vous et à votre partenaire, deux feuilles d'activités différentes. Travaillez ensemble pour compléter les feuilles. Attention! Ne regardez pas la feuille de votre partenaire.

MODÈLE
Élève 1: *Quel temps fait-il à Paris?*
Élève 2: *À Paris, le temps est nuageux et la température est de dix degrés.*

7 La météo Préparez avec un(e) camarade de classe une présentation où vous: Answers will vary.

- mentionnez le jour, la date et la saison.
- présentez la météo d'une ville francophone.
- présentez les prévisions météo (*weather forecasts*) pour le reste de la semaine.
- préparez une affiche pour illustrer votre présentation.

La météo d'Haïti en juillet — Port-au-Prince

samedi 23	dimanche 24	lundi 25
27°C	35°C	37°C
☀	⛅	⛈
soleil	nuageux	orageux

Aujourd'hui samedi, c'est le 23 juillet.
C'est l'été. Il va faire soleil...

Les sons et les lettres ◄)) vhlcentral

Open vs. closed vowels: Part 1

You have already learned that **é** is pronounced like the vowel *a* in the English word *cake*. This is a closed **e** sound.

| étudiant | agréable | nationalité | enchanté |

The letter combinations **–er** and **–ez** at the end of a word are pronounced the same way, as is the vowel sound in single-syllable words ending in **–es**.

| travailler | avez | mes | les |

The vowels spelled **è** and **ê** are pronounced like the vowel in the English word *pet*, as is an **e** followed by a double consonant. These are open **e** sounds.

| répète | première | pêche | italienne |

The vowel sound in *pet* may also be spelled **et**, **ai**, or **ei**.

| secret | français | fait | seize |

Compare these pairs of words. To make the vowel sound in *cake*, your mouth should be slightly more closed than when you make the vowel sound in *pet*.

| mes mais | ces cette | théâtre thème |

Prononcez Répétez les mots suivants à voix haute.

1. thé
2. lait
3. belle
4. été
5. neige
6. aider
7. degrés
8. anglais
9. cassette
10. discret
11. treize
12. mauvais

Articulez Répétez les phrases suivantes à voix haute.

1. Hélène est très discrète.
2. Céleste achète un vélo laid.
3. Il neige souvent en février et en décembre.
4. Désirée est canadienne; elle n'est pas française.

Dictons Répétez les dictons à voix haute.

Qui sème le vent récolte la tempête.²

Péché avoué est à demi pardonné.¹

¹ An offense admitted is half pardoned.
² You reap what you sow. (lit. He who sows the wind reaps a storm.)

Section Goals
In this section, students will learn about open and closed vowels.

Key Standards
4.1

Suggestions
• Model the pronunciation of these open and closed vowel sounds and have students watch the shape of your mouth, then repeat each sound after you. Then pronounce each of the example words and have students repeat them.
• Mention words and expressions from the **Vocabulaire** on page 196 that contain the open and closed vowels presented on this page. Alternately, ask students to recall such vocabulary. Then have them repeat after you. Examples: **février**, **Il fait frais**, etc. See if a volunteer is able to recall any expression from previous lessons. Examples: **seize**, **vélo**, **aérobic**.
• Dictate five familiar words containing the open and closed vowels presented on this page, repeating each one at least two times. Then write them on the board or on a transparency and have students check and correct their spelling.
• Remind students that **ai** and **ei** are nasalized when followed by **m** or **n**. Compare the following words: **français** / **faim**, **seize** / **hein**.
• Point out that, unlike English, there is no diphthong or glide in these vowel sounds. To illustrate this, contrast the pronunciation of the English word *may* with that of the French word **mai**.

EXPANSION

Extra Practice Here are some sentences to use for additional practice with these open and closed vowel sounds. **1. Il fait soleil. 2. En janvier, il neige et il fait mauvais. 3. Toute la journée, j'aide ma mère. 4. Didier est français, mais Hélène est belge.**

EXPANSION

Using Games Have a spelling bee using words that contain the two open and closed vowel sounds featured on this page. Pronounce each word, use it in a sentence, and then say the individual word again. Tell students that they must spell the words in French and include all diacritical marks.

199

Section Goals

In this section, students will learn functional phrases for talking about seasons, the weather, and birthdays through comprehensible input.

Key Standards

1.2, 2.1, 2.2, 4.1, 4.2

Video Recap: Leçon 5A
Before doing this **Roman-photo**, review the previous one with this activity.

1. Où sont les jeunes dans cet épisode? (Ils sont au parc.)
2. Que font Rachid et Stéphane? (Ils jouent au football.)
3. Qu'est-ce que Stéphane étudie? (l'histoire-géo, Napoléon)
4. Qu'est-ce que Sandrine aime faire de ses loisirs? (aller au cinéma ou à des concerts)

Video Synopsis Rachid and Stéphane are in the park playing soccer. They talk about the weather. Meanwhile, David is sketching Sandrine at his apartment. They talk about the weather in Washington and things they like to do. Sandrine tells David that Stéphane's 18th birthday is next Saturday and invites him to the surprise party. Rachid arrives home and admires the portrait. Sandrine offers to make them all dinner.

Suggestions
- Ask students to predict what the episode will be about.
- Have students make a list of vocabulary they expect to see in an episode about weather and seasons.
- Ask students to read the **Roman-photo** conversation in groups of four. Ask one or two groups to present their dramatic readings to the class.
- Quickly review the predictions and confirm the correct ones.

Quel temps! vhlcentral

PERSONNAGES

David

Rachid

Sandrine

Stéphane

Au parc...
RACHID Napoléon établit le Premier Empire en quelle année?
STÉPHANE Euh... mille huit cent quatre?
RACHID Exact! On est au mois de novembre et il fait toujours chaud.
STÉPHANE Oui, il fait bon!... dix-neuf, dix-huit degrés!

RACHID Et on a chaud aussi parce qu'on court.
STÉPHANE Bon, allez, je rentre faire mes devoirs d'histoire-géo.
RACHID Et moi, je rentre boire une grande bouteille d'eau.

RACHID À demain, Stéph! Et n'oublie pas: le cours du jeudi avec ton professeur, Monsieur Rachid Kahlid, commence à dix-huit heures, pas à dix-huit heures vingt!
STÉPHANE Pas de problème! Merci et à demain!

SANDRINE Et puis, en juillet, le Tour de France commence. J'aime bien le regarder à la télévision. Et après, c'est mon anniversaire, le 20. Cette année, je fête mes vingt et un ans. Tous les ans, pour célébrer mon anniversaire, j'invite mes amis et je prépare une super soirée. J'adore faire la cuisine, c'est une vraie passion!
DAVID Ah, oui?

SANDRINE En parlant d'anniversaire, Stéphane célèbre ses dix-huit ans samedi prochain. C'est un anniversaire important. ...On organise une surprise. Tu es invité!
DAVID Hmm, c'est très gentil, mais... Tu essaies de ne pas parler deux minutes, s'il te plaît? Parfait!

SANDRINE Pascal! Qu'est-ce que tu fais aujourd'hui? Il fait beau à Paris?
DAVID Encore un peu de patience! Allez, encore dix secondes... Voilà!

A C T I V I T É S

1 **Qui?** Identifiez les personnages pour chaque phrase. Écrivez **D** pour David, **R** pour Rachid, **S** pour Sandrine et **St** pour Stéphane

1. Cette personne aime faire la cuisine. S
2. Cette personne sort quand il fait froid. D
3. Cette personne aime le Tour de France. S
4. Cette personne n'aime pas la pluie. S

5. Cette personne va boire de l'eau. R
6. Ces personnes ont rendez-vous tous les jeudis. R, St
7. Cette personne fête son anniversaire en janvier. D
8. Ces personnes célèbrent un joli portrait. D, R, S
9. Cette personne fête ses dix-huit ans samedi prochain. St
10. Cette personne prépare des crêpes pour le dîner. S

Quel temps! Before showing the video, show students individual photos illustrating various weather conditions and have them write their own captions.
Ask volunteers to write their captions on the board.

Regarder la vidéo Download and print the videoscript found on vhlcentral.com, and white out months, seasons, weather-related expressions, and other new vocabulary items. Distribute the scripts for pairs or groups to complete as cloze paragraphs as they watch the video.

Les anniversaires à travers (*through*) les saisons

À l'appartement de David et de Rachid...

SANDRINE C'est quand, ton anniversaire?

DAVID Qui, moi? Oh, c'est le quinze janvier.

SANDRINE Il neige en janvier, à Washington?

DAVID Parfois... et il pleut souvent à l'automne et en hiver.

SANDRINE Je déteste la pluie. C'est pénible. Qu'est-ce que tu aimes faire quand il pleut, toi?

DAVID Oh, beaucoup de choses! Dessiner, écouter de la musique. J'aime tellement la nature, je sors même quand il fait très froid.

SANDRINE Moi, je préfère l'été. Il fait chaud. On fait des promenades.

RACHID Oh là là, j'ai soif! Mais... qu'est-ce que vous faites, tous les deux?

DAVID Oh, rien! Je fais juste un portrait de Sandrine.

RACHID Bravo, c'est pas mal du tout! Hmm, mais quelque chose ne va pas, David. Sandrine n'a pas de téléphone dans la main!

SANDRINE Oh, Rachid, ça suffit! C'est vrai, tu as vraiment du talent, David. Pourquoi ne pas célébrer mon joli portrait? Vous avez faim, les garçons?

RACHID ET DAVID Oui!

SANDRINE Je prépare le dîner. Vous aimez les crêpes ou vous préférez une omelette?

RACHID ET DAVID Des crêpes... Miam!

Expressions utiles

Talking about birthdays

- **Cette année, je fête mes vingt et un ans.**
  This year, I celebrate my twenty-first birthday.
- **Pour célébrer mon anniversaire, je prépare une super soirée.**
  To celebrate my birthday, I plan a great party.
- **Stéphane célèbre ses dix-huit ans samedi prochain.**
  Stéphane celebrates his eighteenth birthday next Saturday.
- **On organise une surprise.**
  We are planning a surprise.

Talking about hopes and preferences

- **Tu essaies de ne pas parler deux minutes, s'il te plaît?**
  Could you try not to talk for two minutes, please?
- **J'aime tellement la nature, je sors même quand il fait très froid.**
  I like nature so much, I go out even when it's very cold.
- **Moi, je préfère l'été.**
  Me, I prefer summer.
- **Vous aimez les crêpes ou vous préférez une omelette?**
  Do you like crêpes or do you prefer an omelette?

Additional vocabulary

- **encore un peu**
  a little more
- **Quelque chose ne va pas.**
  Something's not right/working.
- **Allez.**
  Come on.
- **main**
  hand
- **Ça suffit!**
  That's enough!
- **Miam!**
  Yum!

---

2 **Faux!** Toutes ces phrases contiennent une information qui est fausse. Corrigez chaque phrase. Answers will vary. Suggested answers below.

1. Stéphane a dix-huit ans. Stéphane a dix-sept ans.

2. David et Rachid préfèrent une omelette. Ils préfèrent des crêpes.

3. Il fait froid et il pleut. Il fait beau/bon.

4. On n'organise rien (*anything*) pour l'anniversaire de Stéphane.
On organise une surprise pour l'anniversaire de Stéphane.

5. L'anniversaire de Stéphane est au printemps.
L'anniversaire de Stéphane est en automne.

6. Rachid et Stéphane ont froid.
Ils ont chaud.

3 **Conversez** Parlez avec vos camarades de classe pour découvrir (*find out*) qui a l'anniversaire le plus proche du vôtre (*closest to yours*). Qui est-ce? Quand est son anniversaire? En quelle saison? Quel mois? En général, quel temps fait-il le jour de son anniversaire?

A C T I V I T É S

Expressions utiles

- Draw attention to numbers 101 and higher and spelling-change **-er** verbs in the video-still captions, in the **Expressions utiles** box, and as they occur in your conversation with students.
- Have students scan the video-still captions and the **Expressions utiles** box for expressions related to hopes and preferences.
- Ask students about their own preferences. You might ask questions like: **Vous préférez l'été ou l'hiver? l'automne ou le printemps? janvier ou juillet? regarder la télé ou aller au cinéma?** For a more challenging activity, follow up by asking **Pourquoi?**

1 Expansion
- Continue the activity with more statements like these. **11. Cette personne fête son anniversaire samedi prochain. (St) 12. Cette personne parle souvent au téléphone. (S) 13. Cette personne aime écouter de la musique. (D)**
- Assign one of the four main characters in this episode to a small group. Each group should write a brief description of their character's likes, dislikes, and preferences.

2 Suggestion Have students correct false statements on the board.

2 Expansion Give these additional false items for extra practice. **7. Sandrine n'aime pas parler au téléphone (Elle aime beaucoup parler au téléphone.) 8. Stéphane et Rachid étudient la psychologie aujourd'hui. (Ils étudient l'histoire-géo.) 9. Sandrine n'aime pas regarder la télé. (Elle aime bien regarder la télé.) 10. Sur son portrait, Sandrine a un téléphone dans la main. (Elle n'a pas de téléphone dans la main.)**

3 Suggestion Brainstorm questions students might ask to find the person whose birthday is closest to their own. Once they have found that person, ask volunteers to tell the class what they learned about their partner.

AP® Theme: Beauty and Aesthetics
Context: Contributions to World Artistic Heritage, Ideals of Beauty

CULTURE À LA LOUPE

Les jardins publics français

Dans toutes les villes françaises, la plupart° du temps au centre-ville, on trouve des jardins° publics. Les jardins à la française ou jardins classiques sont très célèbres° depuis° le 17e (dix-septième) siècle°. Les jardins de Versailles, créés° pour Louis XIV, le roi° Soleil, vont être copiés par toutes les cours° d'Europe. Dans le jardin à la française, l'ordre et la symétrie dominent: Il faut dompter° la nature «sauvage». La perspective et l'harmonie donnent une notion de grandeur absolue. De façon° très symbolique, la géométrie présente un monde° ordré où le contrôle règne°. Il y a beaucoup de châteaux qui ont de très beaux jardins.

À Paris, le jardin des Tuileries et le jardin du Luxembourg sont deux jardins publics de style classique. Il y a des parterres de fleurs° extraordinaires avec de savants° agencements° de couleurs. Dans les deux jardins, il n'y a pas de bancs° mais des chaises, où on peut° se reposer tranquillement à l'endroit de son choix, sous un arbre° ou près d'un bassin°. Il y a aussi deux grands parcs à côté de Paris: le bois° de Vincennes, qui a un zoo, et le bois de Boulogne, qui a un parc d'attractions° pour les enfants.

En général, les villes de France sont très fleuries°. Il y a même° des concours° pour la ville la plus° fleurie. Le concours des villes et villages fleuris a lieu° depuis 1959. Il est organisé pour promouvoir° le développement des espaces verts dans les villes.

Le bois de Vincennes et le bois de Boulogne	
VINCENNES	**BOULOGNE**
• une superficie° totale de 995 hectares	• une superficie totale de 863 hectares
• un zoo de 15 hectares	• un jardin d'acclimation°
• 19 km de sentiers pour les promenades à cheval et à vélo	• 95 km d'allées
• 32 km d'allées pour le jogging	• une cascade° de 10 mètres de large° et 14 mètres de haut°
• la Ferme° de Paris, une ferme de 5 hectares	• deux hippodromes°

Coup de main

In France and in most other countries, units of measurement are different than those used in the United States.

1 hectare = *2.47 acres*

1 kilomètre = *0.62 mile*

1 mètre = *approximately 1 yard (3 feet)*

la plupart *most* **jardins** *gardens, parks* **célèbres** *famous* **depuis** *since* **siècle** *century* **créés** *created* **roi** *king* **cours** *courts* **dompter** *to tame* **façon** *way* **monde** *world* **règne** *reigns* **parterres de fleurs** *flower beds* **savants** *clever* **agencements** *schemes* **bancs** *benches* **peut** *can* **arbre** *tree* **bassin** *fountain, pond* **bois** *forest, wooded park* **parc d'attractions** *amusement park* **fleuries** *decorated with flowers* **même** *even* **concours** *competitions* **la plus** *the most* **a lieu** *takes place* **promouvoir** *to promote* **superficie** *area* **Ferme** *Farm* **jardin d'acclimation** *playground/amusement park* **cascade** *waterfall* **de large** *wide* **de haut** *high* **hippodromes** *horse racetracks*

Section Goals

In this section, students will:
• learn about French public gardens
• learn terms for activities practiced in parks
• learn names of public gardens and parks in various French-speaking regions
• read about cycling in France

Key Standards

2.1, 2.2, 3.1, 3.2, 4.2

21st Century Skills

Global Awareness
Students will gain perspectives on the Francophone world to develop respect and openness to other cultures.

Culture à la loupe

Avant la lecture Take a poll of students to find out how many of them have visited towns with public parks.

Lecture
• Point out the chart comparing **Le bois de Vincennes et le bois de Boulogne**. Ask students what information is shown. Have them compare details about the two parks.
• Look at a detailed map of Paris with the class, so students visualize where **le bois de Vincennes** and **le bois de Boulogne** are located. Introduce **le jardin des Plantes**, **le parc Monceau** and **le parc des Buttes Chaumont**.

Après la lecture Have students think of parks in the United States. Have them compare the roles and levels of popularity between French and American parks.

1 Suggestion Tell students to use vocabulary from the text to answer the questions. Challenge them to use complete sentences.

1 Expansion Continue the activity with additional questions:
11. Quelles activités y a-t-il pour les adultes au bois de Boulogne?
12. Quels sports peut-on pratiquer à Vincennes? 13. Dans quel parc trouve-t-on une cascade?

A C T I V I T É S

1 **Répondez** Répondez aux questions.

1. Où trouve-t-on, en général, des jardins publics?
   Au centre-ville.
2. Les jardins de Versailles sont créés pour quel roi?
   Louis XIV.
3. Qu'est-ce qui domine dans le jardin à la française?
   L'ordre et la symétrie.
4. Quelle est la fonction de la perspective et de l'harmonie?
   Donner une notion de grandeur absolue.
5. Qu'est-ce qu'il y a dans le jardin des Tuileries?
   Des parterres de fleurs, de savants agencements de couleurs et des chaises.

6. Qu'est-ce qu'il y a au jardin du Luxembourg pour se reposer (to rest)?
   Des chaises.
7. Quels deux grands parcs y a-t-il à côté de Paris?
   Le bois de Vincennes et le bois de Boulogne.
8. Que peut-on (can one) faire au bois de Vincennes?
   Aller au zoo.
9. Comment les villes françaises sont-elles en général?
   Très fleuries.
10. Pourquoi les concours de villes et villages fleuris sont-ils organisés?
    Pour promouvoir le développement des espaces verts dans les villes.

EXPANSION

Les jardins publics français Explain the longstanding reputations of **le bois de Vincennes** and **le bois de Boulogne**. **Le bois de Vincennes** was a working-class destination. **Le bois de Boulogne** was a place where the well-heeled hoped to be seen. **Marie-Antoinette** lived in **le château de Bagatelle**, which she commissioned at the western end of **le bois de Boulogne**.

There is no longer a socio-economic status attached to either of these green spaces, but many Parisians are familiar with their reputations.

LE FRANÇAIS QUOTIDIEN

Ça bouge° aux parcs!

flâner	to stroll, wander
faire de la luge	to sled
faire de la raquette	to snowshoe
faire du cerf-volant	to fly a kite
faire du patin à glace	to ice-skate
faire une balade	to go for a walk
jouer à la pétanque	to play **pétanque** (a lawn bowling game)
promener son chien	to walk one's dog
pique-niquer	to picnic

Ça bouge *Things are moving*

LE MONDE FRANCOPHONE

Des parcs publics

Voici quelques parcs publics du monde francophone.

Bruxelles, Belgique
le bois de la Cambre 123 hectares, un lac° avec une île° au centre

Casablanca, Maroc
le parc de la Ligue Arabe des palmiers°, un parc d'attractions pour enfants, des cafés et restaurants

Québec, Canada
le parc des Champs de Batailles («Plaines d'Abraham») 107 hectares, 6.000 arbres°

Tunis, Tunisie
le parc du Belvédère 110 hectares, un zoo de 13 hectares, 230.000 arbres (80 espèces° différentes), situé° sur une colline°

lac *lake* **île** *island* **palmiers** *palm trees* **arbres** *trees* **espèces** *species* **situé** *located* **colline** *hill*

PORTRAIT   **AP® Theme:** Contemporary Life   **Context:** Leisure and Sports

Les Français et le vélo

Tous les étés, la course° cycliste du Tour de France attire° un grand nombre de spectateurs, Français et étrangers, surtout lors de° son arrivée sur les Champs-Élysées, à Paris. C'est le grand événement° sportif de l'année pour les amoureux du cyclisme. Les Français adorent aussi faire du vélo pendant° leur temps libre. Beaucoup de clubs organisent des randonnées en vélo de course° le week-end. Pour les personnes qui préfèrent le vélo tout terrain (VTT)°, il y a des sentiers° adaptés dans les parcs régionaux et nationaux. Certaines agences de voyages proposent aussi des vacances «vélo» en France ou à l'étranger°.

course *race* **attire** *attracts* **lors de** *at the time of* **événement** *event* **pendant** *during* **vélo de course** *road bike* **vélo tout terrain (VTT)** *mountain biking* **sentiers** *paths* **à l'étranger** *abroad*

le Tour de France sur les Champs-Élysées

AP® Theme: Contemporary Life
Context: Leisure and Sports

Sur Internet

Qu'est-ce que Jacques Anquetil, Eddy Merckx et Bernard Hinault ont en commun?

Go to **vhlcentral.com** to find more information related to this **Culture** section.

ACTIVITÉS

2 **Vrai ou faux?** Indiquez si les phrases sont **vraies** ou **fausses**.

1. Les Français ne font pas de vélo. *Faux.*
2. Les membres de clubs de vélo font des promenades le week-end. *Vrai.*
3. Les agences de voyages offrent des vacances «vélo». *Vrai.*
4. On utilise un VTT quand on fait du vélo sur la route. *Faux.*
5. Le Tour de France arrive sur les Champs-Élysées à Paris. *Vrai.*

3 **Les parcs publics** Comment sont les parcs publics dans votre région? Avec un(e) partenaire, choisissez un parc et utilisez les expressions du **français quotidien** pour le décrire (*describe it*) à vos camarades de classe. Qu'est-ce qu'on trouve dans le parc? Quelles activités fait-on dans le parc? Vos camarades peuvent-ils deviner (*can they guess*) de quel parc vous parlez?

EXPANSION

Des parcs publics Assign a Francophone country to several students in class. Have everyone do individual research on gardens or a park in the country he or she has been assigned. Students should be prepared to present their findings about the park in at least three clear sentences in French and an image from the Internet, if possible.

EXPANSION

Les Français et le vélo Bring in an example of Francophone music or film about cycling. For example, play the song **Mon vélo est blanc** by Anne Sylvestre. Screen part of the Belgian film **Le vélo de Ghislain Lambert**. There are also scenes with Charlotte Gainsbourg riding a bicycle in **La petite voleuse**.

Section Goals

In this section, students will learn:
- numbers 101 and higher
- mathematical terms

Key Standards

4.1, 5.1

Suggestions: Scaffolding

- Review numbers 0–100. Write a number on the board and have students state what it is. Then ask questions that call for a number in the answer. Examples: **Combien d'élèves y a-t-il dans la classe? Quel âge avez-vous? Quel âge a votre grand-mère? Anne a trois crayons. J'ai quatre boîtes de vingt crayons. Combien de crayons avons-nous? (quatre-vingt-trois)**
- Write on the board: **quatre cents élèves, neuf cents personnes, deux mille livres, onze millions de voyageurs.** Help students deduce the meanings of the numbers.
- Model pronunciation of example numbers. Write other three-to seven-digit numbers on the board and have students read them.
- Go over the example sentences containing **cent, mille,** and **million** and the rules for agreement.
- Point out that a space may be used instead of a period to indicate thousands and millions.
- Go over the bullet points about writing the year. Write several years on the board and have students read them aloud and write them out.

5B.1

Numbers 101 and higher   **vhl**central

Numbers 101 and higher	
101 cent un	**800** huit cents
125 cent vingt-cinq	**900** neuf cents
198 cent quatre-vingt-dix-huit	**1.000** mille
200 deux cents	**1.100** mille cent
245 deux cent quarante-cinq	**2.000** deux mille
300 trois cents	**5.000** cinq mille
400 quatre cents	**100.000** cent mille
500 cinq cents	**550.000** cinq cent cinquante mille
600 six cents	**1.000.000** un million
700 sept cents	**8.000.000** huit millions

- Note that French uses a period, rather than a comma, to indicate thousands and millions.

Agreement with *cent*, *mille*, and *million*

- The word **cent**, when used in multiples of one hundred, takes a final **-s**. However, if followed by another number, **cent** drops the **-s**.

J'ai **quatre cents** bandes dessinées. *I have 400 comic books.*	*but*	Cette bibliothèque a **neuf cent vingt** livres. *This library has 920 books.*
Il y a **cinq cents** animaux dans le zoo. *There are 500 animals in the zoo.*	*but*	Nous allons inviter **trois cent trente-huit** personnes. *We're going to invite 338 people.*

- The word **mille** is invariable. It never takes an **-s**.

Mille personnes habitent le village. *One thousand people live in the village.*	**Onze mille** étudiants sont inscrits. *Eleven thousand students are registered.*

- The word **million** takes an **s** when used in multiples of one million. **Million** and **millions** are followed by **de/d'** when used before a noun.

Un million de personnes sont ici. *One million people are here.*	Il y a **seize millions d'habitants** dans la capitale. *There are 16,000,000 inhabitants in the capital.*

Writing out years

- When writing out years, the word **mille** is often shortened to **mil**.

    mil huit cent soixante-cinq
    eighteen (hundred) sixty-five

- In French, years before 2000 may be written out in two ways. Notice that in English, the word *hundred* can be omitted, but in French, the word **cent** is required.

mil neuf cent treize *one thousand nine hundred (and) thirteen*	*or*	**dix-neuf cent treize** *nineteen (hundred) thirteen*

À noter

Cent and **mille** do *not* take the number **un** before them to mean *one hundred* and *one thousand*.

EXPANSION

Extra Practice Ask students to work in pairs. One student thinks of a number between 100 and 1000 and writes it down without showing it to his/her partner, who should guess what the number is. The first student uses the expressions **plus** and **moins** to help the other guess the number.

TEACHING OPTIONS

Game Ask for two volunteers and station them at opposite ends of the board so neither one can see what the other is writing. Say a number for them to write on the board. If both students are correct, continue to give numbers until one writes an incorrect number. The winner continues on to play against another student.

Mathematical terms

- You can talk about mathematical operations both formally and informally.

Mathematical terms		
	informal	formal
plus	et	plus
minus	moins	moins
multiplied by	fois	multiplié par
divided by	sur	divisé par
equals	font	égale

110 et 205 font 315
110 + 205 = 315

60 fois 3 font 180
60 × 3 = 180

999 sur 9 font 111
999 ÷ 9 = 111

110 plus 205 égale 315
110 + 205 = 315

60 multiplié par 3 égale 180
60 × 3 = 180

999 divisé par 9 égale 111
999 ÷ 9 = 111

À noter

Activities in **D'accord!** primarily use informal mathematical terms.

- In French, a comma (**une virgule**) is used instead of a decimal point and a period (**un point**) is used instead of a comma to indicate thousands and millions.

5.419,32   **cinq mille quatre cent dix-neuf virgule trente-deux**
5,419.32   *five thousand four hundred nineteen point thirty-two*

- The expression **pour cent** (*percent*) is two words, not one.

    Le magasin offre une réduction de cinquante **pour cent**.
    The store is offering a fifty percent discount.

Vérifiez

Essayez! Écrivez les nombres en toutes lettres. (*Write out the numbers.*)

1. 10.000 _dix mille_
2. 620 six cent vingt
3. 365 trois cent soixante-cinq
4. 42.000 quarante-deux mille
5. 1.392.000 un million trois cent quatre-vingt-douze mille
6. 171 cent soixante et onze
7. 200.000.000 deux cents millions
8. 480 quatre cent quatre-vingts
9. 1.789 mille sept cent quatre-vingt-neuf
10. 400 quatre cents
11. 8.000.000 huit millions
12. 5.053 cinq mille cinquante-trois

Suggestion: Scaffolding
- Write the numerical version of the math problems on the board. Read them to students using the informal set of mathematical terms. Tell students these are the terms they will see used in **D'accord!**. Then read the problems again using the formal terms.
- You may also want to teach your students these mathematical terms:
  la différence *difference*
  le produit *product*
  le quotient *quotient*
  la somme *sum*
- Present the last two bullets. Then write several math problems on the board. Have students read and solve them. Have students complete the Extra Practice activity, p. 205.
- Assign the **Vérifiez** activity.

Successful Language Learning Tell students that to count from 101–199, they should say **cent** followed by 1–99. So, 101: **cent un**, 102: **cent deux**, 103: **cent trois**, and so forth up to 199: **cent quatre-vingt-dix-neuf**. Tell them to use the same strategy after **deux cents**, **trois cents**, etc.

Essayez! Have students write four more numbers and exchange papers with a classmate, who will write out the numbers. If students struggle to complete the activity, have them watch the Grammar Tutorial.

 TELL Connection

Performance & Feedback 2
Why: Immediate and practical performance feedback facilitates learning and builds confidence in self-diagnostics and remediation. *What:* Use the presentation of mathematical equations to provide students with real-world and practical-application use of numbers. Add to the ones here and on vhlcentral.com to provide regular, periodic practice of this important cross-disciplinary skill.

TEACHING OPTIONS

Extra Practice Have small groups of students work together to create a worksheet consisting of five math word problems for their classmates to complete. Have students take turns reading problems to the class or one of the other small groups, who, in turn, will solve the problems. Have groups include an answer key with their worksheets.

DIFFERENTIATION

For Kinesthetic Learners Divide the class into groups of ten. Give a flashcard with a number from 0–9 to each person in each group. If one group is smaller, distribute extra numbers to group members, as needed, so some students have more than one card. Call out a three- to nine-digit number in which none of the digits is repeated. Students arrange themselves, showing their flashcard(s) to reflect the number. Repeat with other numbers.

205

Mise en pratique

1 Quelle adresse? Écrivez les adresses.

MODÈLE

cent deux, rue Lafayette
102, rue Lafayette

1. deux cent cinquante-deux, rue de Bretagne ___252, rue de Bretagne___
2. quatre cents, avenue Malbon ___400, avenue Malbon___
3. cent soixante-dix-sept, rue Jeanne d'Arc ___177, rue Jeanne d'Arc___
4. cinq cent quarante-six, boulevard St.-Marc ___546, boulevard St. Marc___
5. six cent quatre-vingt-huit, avenue des Gaulois ___688, avenue des Gaulois___
6. trois cent quatre-vingt-douze, boulevard Micheline ___392, boulevard Micheline___
7. cent vingt-cinq, rue des Pierres ___125, rue des Pierres___
8. trois cent quatre, avenue St.-Germain ___304, avenue St. Germain___

2 Les maths Faites les additions et écrivez les réponses.

MODÈLE

200 + 300 =
Deux cents plus trois cents font cinq cents.

1. 5.000 + 3.000 = ___Cinq mille plus trois mille font huit mille.___
2. 650 + 750 = ___Six cent cinquante plus sept cent cinquante font mille quatre cents.___
3. 2.000.000 + 3.000.000 = ___Deux millions plus trois millions font cinq millions.___
4. 4.400 + 3.600 = ___Quatre mille quatre cents plus trois mille six cents font huit mille.___
5. 155 + 310 = ___Cent cinquante-cinq plus trois cent dix font quatre cent soixante-cinq.___
6. 7.000 + 3.000 = ___Sept mille plus trois mille font dix mille.___
7. 9.000.000 + 2.000.000 = ___Neuf millions plus deux millions font onze millions.___
8. 1.250 + 2.250 = ___Mille deux cent cinquante plus deux mille deux cent cinquante font trois mille cinq cents.___

3 Quand? Regardez les dates et dites quand ces événements culturels ont lieu (*take place*).

1661 — Le Nôtre commence les jardins de Versailles
1783 — Premier vol d'une montgolfière
1895 — Invention du Cinématographe
1903 — Premier Tour de France
1943 — Publication du Petit Prince
1980 — Invention du Minitel
2012 — The Artist gagne 4 Oscars
2017 — Disneyland Paris fête ses 25 ans

1. Le jardinier Le Nôtre commence les jardins de Versailles. Il commence les jardins de Versailles en mille six cent soixante et un.
2. Le premier vol d'une Montgolfière, un ballon à air chaud, a lieu. Le premier vol d'une montgolfière, un ballon à air chaud, a lieu en mille sept cent quatre-vingt-trois.
3. Avec l'invention du Cinématographe, le cinéma est né (*born*). Avec l'invention du Cinématographe, le cinéma est né en mille huit cent quatre-vingt-quinze.
4. Le premier Tour de France a lieu. Le premier Tour de France a lieu en mille neuf cent trois.
5. Antoine de Saint-Exupéry publie *Le Petit Prince*. Antoine de Saint-Exupéry publie Le Petit Prince en mille neuf cent quarante-trois.
6. On invente le Minitel, un précurseur de l'Internet. On invente le Minitel, un précurseur de l'Internet, en mille neuf cent quatre-vingts.
7. Le film français, *The Artist*, gagne quatre Oscars. Le film français, The Artist, gagne quatre Oscars en deux mille douze.
8. Disneyland Paris fête ses 25 ans. Disneyland Paris fête ses 25 ans en deux mille dix-sept.

Communication

4 Combien d'habitants? À tour de rôle, demandez à votre partenaire combien d'habitants il y a dans chaque ville d'après (*according to*) les statistiques.

> **MODÈLE**
>
> Dijon: 153.003
> **Élève 1:** *Combien d'habitants y a-t-il à Dijon?*
> **Élève 2:** *Il y a cent cinquante-trois mille trois habitants.*

1. Toulouse: 466.219 ___Il y a quatre cent soixante-six mille deux cent dix-neuf habitants.___
2. Abidjan: 6.783.906 ___Il y a six millions sept cent quatre-vingt-trois mille neuf cent six habitants.___
3. Lyon: 509.233 ___Il y a cinq cent neuf mille deux cent trente-trois habitants.___
4. Québec: 516.620 ___Il y a cinq cent seize mille six cent vingt habitants.___
5. Marseille: 864.323 ___Il y a huit cent soixante-quatre mille trois cent vingt-trois habitants.___
6. Papeete: 26.244 ___Il y a vingt-six mille deux cent quarante-quatre habitants.___
7. Dakar: 2.682.158 ___Il y a deux millions six cent quatre-vingt-deux mille cent cinquante huit habitants.___
8. Nice: 346.251 ___Il y a trois cent quarante-six mille deux cent cinquante et un habitants.___

5 Combien ça coûte? Vous regardez un catalogue avec un(e) ami(e). À tour de rôle, demandez à votre partenaire le prix des choses.

> ▶ **MODÈLE**
>
> **Élève 1:** *Combien coûte l'ordinateur?*
> **Élève 2:** *Il coûte mille huit cents euros.*

1. É1: ... la montre?
É2: Elle ... quatre cent trente-deux ...

2. É1: ... les dictionnaires?
É2: Ils ... cent seize ...

3. É1: ... le sac à dos?
É2: Il ... cent dix-huit ...

4. É1: ... le vélo?
É2: Il ... six cent soixante-quinze ...

6 Dépensez de l'argent Vous et votre partenaire avez 100.000€. Décidez quels articles de la liste vous allez prendre. Expliquez vos choix à la classe. Answers will vary.

> **MODÈLE**
>
> **Élève 1:** *On prend un rendez-vous avec Brad Pitt parce que c'est mon acteur favori.*
> **Élève 2:** *Alors, nous avons encore (still) 50.000 euros. Prenons les 5 jours à Paris pour pratiquer le français.*

un ordinateur... 2.000€	des vacances à Tahiti... 7.000€
un rendez-vous avec Brad Pitt... 50.000€	un vélo... 1.000€
un rendez-vous avec Rihanna... 50.000€	une voiture de luxe... 80.000€
5 jours à Paris... 8.500€	un dîner avec Justin Bieber... 45.000€
un séjour ski en Suisse... 4.200€	un jour de shopping... 10.000€
une montre 6.800€	un bateau (*boat*)... 52.000€

4 Expansion Write on the board some well-known American cities and the city or town where your school is located. Ask students: **Combien d'habitants...?** Have them guess the number. Then write the accurate number next to each city. Have students come to the board to write out the populations in French.

5 & 6 Suggestions
• Before beginning each activity, make sure students know the vocabulary.
• Do the **modèles** with a volunteer to make sure students understand the activities.

6 Partner Chat You can also assign Activity 6 on vhlcentral.com. Students work in pairs to record the activity online. The pair's recorded conversation will appear in your gradebook.

Activity Pack For additional activities, go to the **Activity Pack** in the **Resources** section of vhlcentral.com.

TEACHING OPTIONS

Game Ask students to stand up to create a number chain. The first student states the number 25. The next student says 50. Students continue the chain, using multiples of 25. If a student misses the next number in sequence, he or she must sit down. Continue play until only one student is left standing. If a challenge is required to break a tie, play the game with multiples of 30.

TEACHING OPTIONS

Extra Practice Ask students to make a list of nine items containing the following: a variety of plural and singular nouns, three numerals in the hundreds, three in the thousands, and three in the millions. Once lists are completed, have students exchange them and read the items off their partners' lists aloud. Partners should listen for the correct number and any agreement errors.

Section Goals

In this section, students will learn **-er** verbs with spelling changes.

Key Standards

4.1, 5.1

Suggestions: Scaffolding

- Model the pronunciation of all forms of **acheter** and **espérer**. Have students practice the difference between closed **é** and open **è**.
- Go over the conjugations of all three verbs. Guide students to notice that, like regular **-er** verbs, spelling-change **-er** verbs are "boot verbs."
- Point out that infinitives often follow forms of **espérer**. Example: **Il espère gagner.**
- Ask questions using verbs from this section, encouraging student responses. Examples: **Où est-ce que vous achetez du pain? Quelle saison préférez-vous: l'été ou l'hiver? Combien de SMS envoyez-vous par jour?** Have students provide both oral and written responses.

5B.2

Spelling-change -er verbs vhlcentral

Point de départ Some **-er** verbs with regular endings have spelling changes in the verb stem.

- For many infinitives with an unaccented **e** in the next-to-last syllable, the **e** changes to **è** in all forms but **nous** and **vous**.

acheter (to buy)

j'achète	nous achetons
tu achètes	vous achetez
il/elle/on achète	ils/elles achètent

Où est-ce que tu **achètes** des skis?
Where do you buy skis?

Achetez-vous une nouvelle maison?
Are you buying a new house?

Ils **achètent** beaucoup sur Internet.
They buy a lot on the Internet.

Je n'**achète** pas de lait.
I'm not buying any milk.

- For infinitives with an **é** in the next-to-last syllable, the **é** changes to **è** in all forms but **nous** and **vous**.

espérer (to hope)

j'espère	nous espérons
tu espères	vous espérez
il/elle/on espère	ils/elles espèrent

Elle **espère** arriver tôt aujourd'hui.
She hopes to arrive early today.

Espérez-vous faire la connaissance de Joël?
Are you hoping to meet Joël?

Nos profs **espèrent** avoir de bons élèves en classe.
Our teachers hope to have good students in class.

J'**espère** avoir de bonnes notes.
I hope I get good grades.

🏃 Boîte à outils

Use a conjugated form of **espérer** + [*infinitive*] to mean *to hope to do something.*

Tu espères jouer au golf samedi.
You hope to play golf on Saturday.

- For infinitives ending in **-yer**, the **y** changes to **i** in all forms except **nous** and **vous**.

envoyer (to send)

j'envoie	nous envoyons
tu envoies	vous envoyez
il/elle/on envoie	ils/elles envoient

J'**envoie** une lettre.
I'm sending a letter.

Nous **envoyons** des bandes dessinées aux enfants.
We're sending the kids comic books.

Tes amis **envoient** beaucoup d'e-mails.
Your friends send lots of e-mails.

Salima **envoie** un message à ses parents.
Salima is sending a message to her parents.

Elle achète quelque chose.

Ils répètent.

EXPANSION

Extra Practice Write a pattern sentence on the board. Ex: **Elle envoie une lettre.** Have students write down the model, and then dictate a list of subjects (Ex: **Pascal, nous, mon frère**), pausing after each one to allow students to write a complete sentence using the model verb. Ask volunteers to write their sentences down on the board.

EXPANSION

Extra Practice Ask students to prepare five questions containing spelling-change **-er** verbs and interview one of their classmates. Ex: **Élève 1: Est-ce-que tu préfères l'hiver ou l'été? Élève 2: Je préfère l'été**.

- The change of **y** to **i** is optional in verbs whose infinitives end in **-ayer**.

Comment est-ce que tu **payes**?
How do you pay?

Je **paie** avec une carte de crédit.
I pay with a credit card.

Other spelling change -er verbs

like espérer		like acheter	
célébrer	to celebrate	amener	to bring (someone)
considérer	to consider	emmener	to take (someone)
posséder	to possess, to own	**like envoyer**	
préférer	to prefer	employer	to use, to employ
protéger	to protect	essayer (de + [inf.])	to try (to)
répéter	to repeat; to rehearse	nettoyer	to clean
		payer	to pay

Je préfère l'été. Il fait chaud.

Tu essaies de ne pas parler?

- Note that the **nous** and **vous** forms of the verbs presented in this section have no spelling changes.

Vous **achetez** des sandwichs aussi.
You're buying sandwiches, too.

Nous **espérons** partir à huit heures.
We hope to leave at 8 o'clock.

Nous **envoyons** les enfants à l'école.
We're sending the children to school.

Vous **payez** avec une carte de crédit.
You pay with a credit card.

Essayez!

Complétez les phrases avec la forme correcte du verbe.

1. Les bibliothèques _emploient_ (employer) beaucoup d'étudiants.
2. Vous _répétez_ (répéter) les phrases en français.
3. Nous _payons_ (payer) assez pour les livres.
4. Mon frère ne _nettoie_ (nettoyer) pas son bureau.
5. Est-ce que tu _espères_ (espérer) gagner?
6. Vous _essayez_ (essayer) parfois d'arriver à l'heure.
7. Tu _préfères_ (préférer) prendre du thé ou du café?
8. Elle _emmène_ (emmener) sa mère au cinéma.
9. On _célèbre_ (célébrer) une occasion spéciale.
10. Les parents _protègent_ (protéger) leurs enfants?

Boîte à outils

Amener is used when you are bringing someone to the place where you are.

J'amène ma nièce chez moi.
I'm bringing my niece home.

Emmener is used when you are taking someone to a different location from where you are.

J'emmène ma grand-mère à l'hôpital.
I'm taking my grandmother to the hospital.

À noter

Use **apporter** instead of **amener** when you are bringing an object instead of a person or animal.

Qui apporte les cartes?
Who's bringing the cards?

Suggestions: Scaffolding
- Go over the meanings of the verbs. Note the number of cognates. Make sure students understand that **amener** and **emmener** are only used for people. Ask: What verbs would you use to say *to take* and *to bring* objects? (**prendre**; **apporter**).
- Consider going over the constructions **essayer de** + [*infinitive*] and **essayer de ne pas** + [*infinitive*] with students and giving some examples.
- Follow the Game suggestion, p. 209. Then have students prepare questions using spelling-change **-er** verbs and interview a partner. See Extra Practice suggestion, p. 208.

Essayez! For additional drills with spelling-change **-er** verbs for the whole class or those who need extra practice, do this activity orally and on the board with different subjects.

Mise en pratique

1 **Passe-temps** Chaque membre de la famille Desrosiers a son passe-temps préféré. Utilisez les éléments pour dire comment ils préparent leur week-end.

MODÈLE

Tante Manon fait une randonnée. (acheter / sandwichs)
Elle achète des sandwichs.

1. Nous faisons du vélo. (essayer / vélo) Nous essayons le vélo.
2. Christiane aime chanter. (répéter) Elle répète.
3. Les filles jouent au foot. (espérer / gagner) Elles espèrent gagner.
4. Vous allez à la pêche. (emmener / enfants) Vous emmenez les enfants.
5. Papa fait un tour en voiture. (nettoyer / voiture) Il nettoie la voiture.
6. Mes frères font du camping. (préférer / partir tôt) Ils préfèrent partir tôt.
7. Ma petite sœur va à la piscine. (essayer de / plonger (*to dive*)) Elle essaie de plonger.
8. Mon grand-père aime la montagne. (préférer / faire une randonnée) Il préfère faire une randonnée.
9. J'adore les chevaux. (espérer / faire du cheval) J'espère faire du cheval.
10. Mes parents vont faire un dessert. (acheter / fruits) Ils achètent des fruits.

2 **Que font-ils?** Dites ce que font les personnages. Answers will vary.

▶ **MODÈLE**

Il achète une baguette.

acheter

1. envoyer

2. payer

3. répéter

4. nettoyer

3 **Invitation au cinéma** Avec un(e) partenaire, jouez les rôles de Halouk et de Thomas. Ensuite, présentez la scène à la classe.

THOMAS J'ai envie d'aller au cinéma.

HALOUK Bonne idée. Nous (1) _____emmenons_____ (emmener, protéger) Véronique avec nous?

THOMAS J' (2) _____espère_____ (acheter, espérer) qu'elle a du temps libre.

HALOUK Peut-être, mais j' (3) _____envoie_____ (envoyer, payer) des e-mails tous les jours et elle ne répond pas.

THOMAS Parce que son ordinateur ne fonctionne pas. Elle (4) _____préfère_____ (essayer, préférer) parler au téléphone.

HALOUK D'accord. Alors toi, tu (5) _____achètes_____ (acheter, répéter) les tickets et moi, je vais chercher Véronique.

Communication

4 **Questions** À tour de rôle, posez des questions à un(e) partenaire. Answers will vary.

1. Qu'est-ce que tu achètes pour la fête des mères?
2. Qu'est-ce que tu achètes tous les mois?
3. Comment célèbres-tu l'anniversaire de ton/ta meilleur(e) ami(e)?
4. Est-ce que toi et ton/ta camarade de classe partagez vos livres?
5. Est-ce que tu possèdes un vélo?
6. Qui nettoie ta chambre?
7. À qui est-ce que tu envoies des e-mails?
8. Qu'est-ce que tu espères faire cet été?
9. Qu'est-ce que tu préfères faire le vendredi soir?
10. Quand tu vas au cinéma, est-ce que tu emmènes quelqu'un? Qui?
11. Est-ce que ta famille célèbre une occasion spéciale cet (*this*) été? Quand?
12. Aimes-tu essayer de nouveaux plats de cuisine (*food dishes*)?

5 **Réponses affirmatives** Votre professeur va vous donner une feuille d'activités. Trouvez au moins deux camarades de classe qui répondent oui à chaque question. Et si vous aussi, vous répondez oui aux questions, écrivez votre nom. Answers will vary.

MODÈLE

Élève 1: Est-ce que tu achètes tes livres sur Internet?
Élève 2: Oui, j'achète mes livres sur Internet.

Questions	Noms
1. acheter ses livres sur Internet	Virginie, Éric
2. posséder un ordinateur	
3. envoyer des lettres à ses grands-parents	
4. célébrer une occasion spéciale demain	

6 **E-mail à l'oncle Marcel** Xavier va écrire un e-mail à son oncle pour raconter (*to tell*) ses activités de la semaine prochaine. Il prépare une liste des choses qu'il veut dire (*wants to say*). Avec un(e) partenaire, écrivez son e-mail. Answers will vary.

- lundi: emmener maman chez le médecin
- mercredi: envoyer notes à Anne
- jeudi: répéter rôle Roméo et Juliette
- vendredi: célébrer anniversaire papa
- vendredi: essayer faire gym
- samedi: parents acheter voiture

---

4 Expansion Have students write two more questions containing spelling-change -er verbs that they would like to ask their partner.

4 Virtual Chat You can also assign Activity 4 on vhlcentral.com. Students record individual responses that appear in your gradebook.

5 Suggestion Call on two volunteers to read the **modèle** aloud. Then distribute the **Feuilles d'activités** found in the Activity Pack on vhlcentral.com.

6 Expansion Have students think of a family member or friend to whom they would likely write an e-mail. Tell them to first list at least five ideas using as many spelling-change -er verbs as possible. Then have them write an e-mail of at least five sentences.

Activity Pack For additional activities, go to the **Activity Pack** in the **Resources** section of vhlcentral.com.

DIFFERENTIATION

For Auditory Learners Ask students to write a short paragraph using as many spelling-change -er verbs as possible. In pairs, have students dictate their paragraph to each other. Tell them to check each other's work for accuracy.

TEACHING OPTIONS

Small Groups Have small groups write dehydrated sentences with only subjects and infinitives. Examples: **1.** tu / **amener** / **???** **2. Sylvie et Véronique** / **espérer** / **???** Tell groups to switch with another group, who will form a complete sentence by conjugating the verb and inventing an appropriate ending. Ask for volunteers to write one of their group's sentences on the board.

Révision

Key Standards
1.1

1 Expansion Have students write a story about their preferred sport modeled on the paragraph in this activity.

2 Suggestion Have pairs get together to form groups of four to review each others' sentences. Have students explain any corrections or suggested changes.

3 Suggestion Encourage students to choose places from the French-speaking world that they have learned about in **Culture** and **Panorama** sections.

3 Expansion Have students create more questions based on those in the activity to ask their partner. Guide the class to ask about where the partner hopes or prefers to go for various vacations throughout the year. Students may combine reusing weather conditions described in the box and using additional weather descriptions.

4 Suggestion Go over the model with students. Point out there is only one commission price per purchase, even if the trip is purchased for two people.

5 Suggestion Ask for volunteers to do the **modèle** and auction off a few more items to set further examples.

6 Suggestions
- Divide the class into pairs and distribute the Info Gap Handouts from the Activity Pack. Give students ten minutes to complete the activity.
- Act out the **modèle** with a student volunteer playing the role of **Élève 2**.

1 Le basket Avec un(e) partenaire, utilisez les verbes de la liste pour compléter le paragraphe.

| acheter | considérer | envoyer | essayer | préférer |
| amener | employer | espérer | payer | répéter |

Je m'appelle Stéphanie et je joue au basket. Je/J'
(1) __amène__ toujours (*always*) mes parents avec moi aux matchs le samedi. Ils (2) __considèrent__ que les filles sont de très bonnes joueuses. Mes parents font aussi du sport. Ma mère fait du vélo et mon père (3) __espère__ gagner son prochain match de foot! Le vendredi matin, je/j' (4) __envoie__ un e-mail à ma mère pour lui rappeler (*remind her of*) le match. Mais elle n'oublie jamais! Ils ne/n' (5) __achètent__ pas de tickets pour les matchs, parce que les parents des joueurs ne/n' (6) __paient__ pas. Nous (7) __essayons__ toujours d'arriver une demi-heure avant le match, parce que maman et papa (8) __préfèrent, espèrent__ s'asseoir (*to sit*) tout près du terrain (*court*). Ils sont tellement fiers!

2 Que font-ils? Avec un(e) partenaire, parlez des activités des personnages et écrivez une phrase par illustration. Answers will vary.

1. _____ 2. _____ 3. _____

4. _____ 5. _____ 6. _____

3 Où partir? Avec un(e) partenaire, choisissez cinq endroits intéressants à visiter où il fait le temps indiqué sur la liste. Ensuite, répondez aux questions. Answers will vary.

| Il fait chaud. | Il fait soleil. | Il fait du vent. | Il neige. | Il pleut. |

1. Où essayez-vous d'aller cet été? Pourquoi?
2. Où préférez-vous partir cet hiver? Pourquoi?
3. Quelle est la première destination que vous espérez visiter? La dernière? Pourquoi?
4. Qui emmenez-vous avec vous? Pourquoi?

4 Quelle générosité! Imaginez que vous pouvez (*can*) payer un voyage aux membres de votre famille et à vos amis. À tour de rôle, choisissez un voyage et donnez à votre partenaire la liste des personnes qui partent. Votre partenaire va vous donner le prix à payer. Answers will vary.

MODÈLE
Élève 1: *J'achète un voyage de dix jours dans les Pays de la Loire à ma cousine Pauline et à mon frère Alexandre.*
Élève 2: *D'accord. Tu paies deux mille cinq cent soixante-deux euros.*

Voyages	Prix par personne	Commission
Dix jours dans les Pays de la Loire	1.250€	62€
Deux semaines de camping	660€	35€
Sept jours au soleil en hiver	2.100€	78€
Trois jours à Paris en avril	500€	55€
Trois mois en Europe en été	10.400€	47€
Un week-end à Nice en septembre	350€	80€
Une semaine à la montagne en juin	990€	66€
Une semaine à la neige	1.800€	73€

5 La vente aux enchères Par groupes de quatre, organisez une vente aux enchères (*auction*) pour vendre les affaires (*things*) du professeur. À tour de rôle, un(e) élève joue le rôle du vendeur/de la vendeuse et les autres élèves jouent le rôle des enchérisseurs (*bidders*). Vous avez 5.000 euros et toutes les enchères (*bids*) commencent à cent euros. Answers will vary.

MODÈLE
Élève 1: *J'ai le cahier du professeur. Qui paie cent euros?*
Élève 2: *Moi, je paie cent euros.*
Élève 1: *Qui paie cent cinquante euros?*

6 À la bibliothèque Votre professeur va vous donner, à vous et à votre partenaire, deux feuilles d'activités différentes. Posez-vous des questions pour compléter les feuilles. Attention! Ne regardez pas la feuille de votre partenaire. Answers will vary.

MODÈLE
Élève 1: *Est-ce que tu as le livre «Candide»?*
Élève 2: *Oui, son numéro de référence est P, Q, deux cent soixante-six, cent quarante-sept, cent dix.*

PRE-AP®

Interpersonal Speaking Have students write a conversation between two friends. One tries to convince the other to go out. The other makes excuses to not go. Students should include as many spelling-change **-er** verbs and weather expressions as possible. Example: **Élève 1: Faisons une randonnée! Élève 2: Mais je nettoie ma chambre. Élève 1: Mais il fait beau. Élève 2: Il va pleuvoir plus tard.**

EXPANSION

Using Lists Ask students to imagine they are going on an extended trip. Have them make a list of at least five things they are to do (buy things, take someone somewhere, send mail, etc.) before leaving. Examples: **Je vais acheter un nouveau parapluie. J'espère envoyer une carte d'anniversaire.**

À l'écoute vhlcentral

STRATÉGIE

Listening for key words

By listening for key words (**mots-clés**) or phrases, you can identify the subject and main ideas of what you hear, as well as some of the details.

🔊 To practice this strategy, you will listen to a short paragraph. Jot down the key words that help you identify the subject of the paragraph and its main ideas.

Préparation

Regardez l'image. Où trouve-t-on ce type d'image? Manque-t-il des éléments (*Is anything missing*) sur cette carte? Faites une liste de mots-clés qui vont vous aider à trouver ces informations quand vous allez écouter la météo (*the forecast*).

🔊 À vous d'écouter

Écoutez la météo. Puis, écoutez une deuxième fois et complétez le tableau. Écrivez un **X** pour indiquer le temps qu'il fait dans chaque ville et notez la température.

Ville	☀	⛅	☁	🌧	💨	❄	Température
Paris			X				8°C
Lille				X			6°C
Strasbourg						X	5°C
Brest			X				10°C
Lyon				X			9°C
Bordeaux		X					11°C
Toulouse	X						12°C
Marseille			X				12°C
Nice					X		13°C

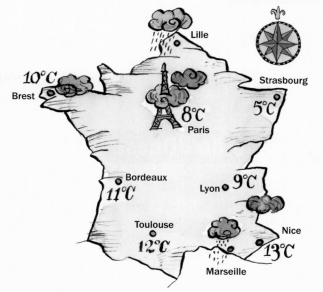

Compréhension

Probable ou improbable? Indiquez si ces (*these*) phrases sont probables ou improbables, d'après la météo d'aujourd'hui.

	Probable	Improbable
MODÈLE		
Ève va nager à Strasbourg.		✓
1. Lucie fait du vélo à Lille.		✓
2. Il fait froid à Strasbourg.	✓	
3. Émilien joue aux cartes à la maison à Lyon.	✓	
4. À Lyon, on a besoin d'un imperméable.		✓
5. Jérome et Yves jouent au golf à Bordeaux.	✓	
6. Il fait un temps épouvantable à Toulouse.		✓
7. Il va neiger à Marseille.		✓
8. Nous allons nager à Nice cet après-midi.		✓

Quelle ville choisir? Imaginez qu'aujourd'hui vous êtes en France. Décidez dans quelle ville vous avez envie de passer la journée. Pourquoi? Décrivez le temps qu'il fait et citez des activités que vous allez peut-être faire.

MODÈLE

J'ai envie d'aller à Strasbourg parce que j'aime l'hiver et la neige. Aujourd'hui, il fait froid et il neige. Je vais faire une promenade en ville et après, je vais boire un chocolat chaud au café.

deux cent treize **213**

Section Goals

In this section, students will:
- learn to listen for key words
- listen to a short paragraph and note the key words
- answer questions based on the content of a recorded weather forecast

Key Standards

1.2, 2.1

21ˢᵗ Century Skills

Critical Thinking and Problem Solving
Students practice aural comprehension as a tool to negotiate meaning in French.

Stratégie
Script Qu'est-ce que je fais quand j'ai du temps libre? Eh bien, l'hiver, j'aime faire du ski. Au printemps et en automne, quand il fait bon, je fais du vélo et du cheval. Et l'été, je fais de la planche à voile.
Teacher Resources DVD

Préparation Have students look at the map and describe what they see. Guide them to think about expressions that are commonly mentioned during a weather forecast. Ask them to brainstorm and write a list of as much weather-related vocabulary as they can in five minutes.

À vous d'écouter
Script Mesdames, Mesdemoiselles, Messieurs, bonjour et bienvenue sur Radio Satellite. Il est 10h00 et voici la météo. Aujourd'hui, sur la capitale, des nuages toute la journée. Eh oui, il fait frais à Paris ce matin, avec une température maximale de huit degrés. À Lille, on va avoir un temps épouvantable. Il fait froid avec six degrés seulement et il va pleuvoir tout l'après-midi et toute la soirée. À Strasbourg, il fait cinq degrés et il neige encore. Il fait assez frais à Brest, avec dix degrés et beaucoup de nuages. À Lyon, il fait neuf degrés aussi avec un temps très orageux, alors ne sortez pas sans votre parapluie! À Bordeaux, il fait bon, onze degrés

et quelques nuages. Toulouse va avoir du soleil toute la journée et il va faire douze degrés. À Marseille, la température est de douze degrés maintenant, mais il va pleuvoir dans l'après-midi. Sur la Côte d'Azur, il fait treize degrés à Nice, et il y a beaucoup de vent. Bonne journée!
Teacher Resources DVD

Savoir-faire

vhlcentral

Panorama

un marché en Afrique

L'Afrique de l'Ouest

La région en chiffres

▶ **Bénin:** *(10.880.000 habitants), Porto Novo*
▶ **Burkina-Faso:** *(18.106.000), Ouagadougou*
▶ **Côte d'Ivoire:** *(22.702.000), Yamoussoukro*
▶ **Guinée:** *(12.609.000), Conakry*
▶ **Mali:** *(17.600.000), Bamako*
▶ **Mauritanie:** *(4.068.000), Nouakchott*
▶ **Niger:** *(19.899.000), Niamey*
▶ **Sénégal:** *(15.129.000), Dakar*
▶ **Togo:** *(7.305.000), Lomé*
SOURCE: Population Division, UN Secretariat

L'Afrique centrale

La région en chiffres

▶ **Burundi:** *(11.179.000), Bujumbura*
▶ **Cameroun:** *(23.344.000), Yaoundé*
▶ **Congo:** *(4.620.000), Brazzaville*
▶ **Gabon:** *(1.725.000), Libreville*
▶ **République centrafricaine:** *(4.900.000), Bangui*
▶ **République démocratique du Congo (R.D.C.):** *(77.267.000), Kinshasa*
▶ **Rwanda:** *(11.610.000), Kigali*
▶ **Tchad:** *(14.037.000), N'Djamena*

Personnes célèbres

▶ Sonia Rolland, *Rwanda, actrice et réalisatrice (1981–)*

▶ Djimon Hounsou, *Bénin, acteur (1964–)*

▶ Françoise Mbango-Etone, *Cameroun, athlète olympique (1976–)*

Terre *Earth* **plus ancien** *oldest* **En plus de** *On top of* **abrite** *houses* **paysages** *landscapes* **les plus actifs** *the most active*

214   *deux cent quatorze*

la ville d'Abidjan

la place des Artistes à Kinshasa

LA TUNISIE
LE MAROC
L'ALGÉRIE
LA LIBYE
LE SAHARA OCCIDENTAL
LE SAHARA
LA MAURITANIE
⊛ **Nouakchott**
LE MALI
LE NIGER
LE TCHAD
LE SÉNÉGAL
⊛ **Dakar**
LA GAMBIE
LE BURKINA-FASO
⊛ **Niamey**
LE SOUDAN
LA GUINÉE
Bamako
⊛ **Ouagadougou**
N'Djamena
LA GUINÉE-BISSAU
⊛ **Conakry**
LE GHANA
LE BÉNIN
LE NIGÉRIA
LA SIERRA LEONE
Yamoussoukro
LE TOGO
⊛ **Lomé**
⊛ **Porto Novo**
LE CAMEROUN
LA RÉPUBLIQUE CENTRAFRICAINE
LE SOUDAN DU SUD
LA CÔTE D'IVOIRE
⊛ **Bangui**
LE LIBÉRIA
⊛ **Yaoundé**
L'OUGANDA
LE GOLFE DE GUINÉE
⊛ **Libreville**
LE RWANDA
LA GUINÉE ÉQUATORIALE
LE GABON
LE CONGO
⊛ **Kigali**
L'OCÉAN ATLANTIQUE
⊛ **Brazzaville**
Bujumbura
LA RÉPUBLIQUE DÉMOCRATIQUE DU CONGO
LA TANZANIE
⊛ **Kinshasa**
LE BURUNDI
L'ANGOLA
LA ZAMBIE

□ Pays francophones

0   500 miles
0   500 kilomètres

Incroyable mais vrai!

Où se trouve le paradis des hippopotames sur Terre°? Dans les rivières du plus ancien° parc d'Afrique, le parc national des Virunga, en République démocratique du Congo. En plus de° ses 20.000 hippopotames, le parc abrite° une biodiversité exceptionnelle due à la variété de ses paysages°, dominés par les deux volcans les plus actifs° du continent.

Les gens
AP® Theme: Global Challenges
Context: Human Rights

Bineta Diop, la «vice-présidente» des femmes (Sénégal) (1950–)

Bineta Diop a appris de sa mère, Maréma Lo, une féministe pour le parti de Léopold Sédar Senghor au Sénégal, l'importance de la cause féminine, et elle dédie sa vie professionnelle à cette cause. En 1996, elle fonde une ONG° à Genève, Femmes Africa Solidarité, pour essayer d'encourager la solidarité entre femmes. Avec l'aide d'importantes avocates africaines, elle crée aussi un protocole pour les droits° de la femme qui naîtra° au Mozambique en 2003. Depuis janvier 2014, elle est l'envoyée spéciale pour les femmes, la paix et la sécurité à la Commission de l'Union Africaine, l'organisation principale des pays d'Afrique. Pas étonnant donc que le magazine *Times* la° nomme en 2011 l'une des cent personnalités les plus influentes au monde°!

La musique
AP® Theme: Beauty and Aesthetics
Context: Music

Le reggae ivoirien

Alpha Blondy

La Côte d'Ivoire est un des pays d'Afrique où le reggae africain est le plus développé. Ce type de reggae se distingue du reggae jamaïcain par les instruments de musique utilisés et les thèmes abordés°. En fait, les artistes ivoiriens incorporent souvent des instruments traditionnels d'Afrique de l'Ouest et les thèmes sont souvent très politiques. Alpha Blondy, par exemple, est le plus célèbre des chanteurs ivoiriens de reggae et fait souvent des commentaires sociopolitiques. Le chanteur Tiken Jah Fakoly critique la politique occidentale et les gouvernants africains, et Ismaël Isaac dénonce les ventes d'armes° dans le monde. Le reggae ivoirien est chanté en français, en anglais et dans les langues africaines.

Les lieux
AP® Theme: Global Challenges
Context: Environmental Issues

Les parcs nationaux du Cameroun

Avec la forêt, la savane et la montagne dans ses réserves et parcs nationaux, le Cameroun présente une des faunes et flores les plus riches et variées d'Afrique. Deux cent quarante empreintes° de dinosaures sont fossilisées au site de dinosaures de Manangia, dans la province du Nord. Les différentes réserves du pays abritent°, entre autres, éléphants, gorilles, chimpanzés, antilopes et plusieurs centaines d'espèces de reptiles, d'oiseaux et de poissons. Le parc national Korup est une des plus anciennes forêts tropicales du monde. Il est connu surtout récemment pour une liane°, découverte là-bas, qui pourrait avoir un effet sur la guérison° de certains cancers et du VIH°.

Les traditions
AP® Theme: Beauty and Aesthetics   Context: Visual Arts

Les masques du Gabon

Les masques gabonais exposés° aujourd'hui dans les musées européens ont inspiré de grands artistes du vingtième siècle, comme Matisse et Picasso. Pourtant, ces masques ne sont pas à l'origine de simples décorations ou objets d'art. Ce sont des objets rituels, utilisés par les différents groupes ethniques et sociétés initiatiques du Gabon. Chaque° société produit ses propres° masques; ils ont donc des formes très variées. Les masques sont le plus souvent° portés par les hommes, dans des cérémonies et rituels de groupe. Leurs matériaux et apparences sont très symboliques. Ils sont surtout faits de bois°, mais aussi de plumes°, de raphia° ou de peaux°, et ils ont des formes anthropomorphiques, zoomorphiques ou abstraites.

Qu'est-ce que vous avez compris? Répondez aux questions.

1. Qui est Françoise Mbango-Etone?
   C'est une athlète olympique de Cameroun.
2. Où est le paradis des hippopotames sur Terre?
   Il est dans le parc des Virunga, en République démocratique du Congo.
3. À quoi Bineta Diop dédie-t-elle sa vie professionnelle?
   Elle dédie sa vie professionnelle à la cause féminine.
4. Que fait Bineta Diop depuis 2014?
   Elle est l'envoyée spéciale pour les femmes, la paix et la sécurité à la Commission de l'Union Africaine.
5. Qu'est-ce qui distingue le reggae de Côte d'Ivoire du reggae jamaicain?
   Les instruments de musique et les thèmes des chansons.
6. Dans quelle langue est-ce qu'on chante le reggae en Côte d'Ivoire?
   On chante le reggae en français, en anglais et dans les langues africaines.
7. Qu'a-t-on trouvé sur le site de Manangia?
   On a trouvé des empreintes de dinosaures.
8. Où trouve-t-on une importante plante médicinale?
   On trouve cette plante dans le parc national Korup.
9. Quels artistes ont été inspirés par les masques du Gabon?
   Picasso et Matisse ont été inspirés par ces masques.
10. Pour quelles occasions porte-on les masques du Gabon?
    On porte les masques dans des cérémonies et rituels de groupe.

Sur Internet

1. Cherchez plus d'information sur le parc national Korup. Pourquoi sa biodiversité est-elle considérée comme une des plus riches de l'Afrique?

2. Écoutez des chansons (*songs*) de reggae ivoirien. Quels sont leurs thèmes?

3. Trouvez des exemples de masques du Gabon. Aimez-vous leurs styles? Pourquoi ou pourquoi pas?

ONG *NGO* **droits** *rights* **naîtra** *will be born* **la** *her*
personnalités les plus influentes au monde *most*
influential personalities in the world **abordés** *dealt with*
ventes d'armes *weapons sales* **empreintes** *footprints*
abritent *provide a habitat for, shelter* **liane** *vine* **guérison** *cure*
VIH *HIV* **exposés** *exhibited* **Chaque** *Each* **propres** *own*
le plus souvent *most often* **bois** *wood* **plumes** *feathers*
raphia *raffia* **peaux** *skins*

Bineta Diop
- As a special envoy, Bineta Diop works to protect women and children in conflict situations, to involve women in peace processes, and prevent armed conflict.
- Explain that an NGO (non-governmental organization) is a non-profit, voluntary group that performs a service or humanitarian function.

Le reggae ivoirien Traditional African musical instruments include talking drums, djembe, balafone, kora, bolon, daro, and the gourd rattle. Have students find examples of these online.

Les parcs nationaux du Cameroun Ask students: **Quelles espèces d'animaux peut-on voir dans les réserves du Cameroun? (éléphants, gorilles, chimpanzés, antilopes, reptiles, oiseaux et poissons)**

Les masques du Gabon The Gabonese use masks in rituals to praise their ancestors and mark important life events. They also use them to show cultural identity, for protection, and to promote fertility. Discuss with students how masks are used in their culture(s): **Pour quelles occasions utilse-t-on des masques? Pourquoi utilise-t-on les masques?**

 21st Century Skills

Information and Media Literacy Go to vhlcentral.com to complete the Sur Internet activity associated with **Panorama** for additional practice accessing and using culturally authentic sources.

EXPANSION

Léopold Sédar Senghor Léopold Sédar Senghor (1906–2001) was a poet and politician. He led his native Senegal in its fight for independence and became the country's first president in 1960. He is also a founding father of a literary movement called **la Négritude**. This African and Caribbean movement called on writers to cast aside colonial influence to embrace their own cultural heritage, traditions, history and belief and use them in the modern world. Examples of this can be seen in poems where the traditional values of closeness to nature and constant contact with ancestors are featured. Have students read one of Senghor's poems online and report on the themes and values highlighted in the poem.

215

Lecture vhlcentral

Avant la lecture

STRATÉGIE

Skimming

Skimming involves quickly reading through a document to absorb its general meaning. This allows you to understand the main ideas without having to read word for word. When you skim a text, look at its title and subtitles and read the first sentence of each paragraph.

Examinez le texte

Regardez rapidement le texte. Quel est le titre (*title*) du texte? En combien de parties le texte est-il divisé? Quels sont les titres des parties? Maintenant, regardez les photos. Quel est le sujet de l'article?

Catégories

Dans le texte, trouvez trois mots ou expressions qui représentent chaque catégorie. Answers will vary. Suggested answers below.

les loisirs culturels

| musique classique | cinéma africain | musée des Beaux-Arts |

les activités sportives

| golf | ski | tennis |

les activités de plein air (*outdoor*)

| camping | randonnées | équitation |

Trouvez

Regardez le document. Indiquez si vous trouvez ces informations.

_____ 1. où manger cette semaine
_____ 2. le temps qu'il va faire cette semaine
__✓__ 3. où aller à la pêche
_____ 4. des prix d'entrée (*entrance*)
__✓__ 5. des numéros de téléphone
__✓__ 6. des sports
__✓__ 7. des spectacles
_____ 8. des adresses

CETTE SEMAINE À MONTRÉAL ET DANS LA RÉGION

ARTS ET CULTURE

Festivals et autres manifestations culturelles à explorer:

- Festival de musique classique, samedi de 16h00 à 22h00, à la Salle de concerts Richelieu, à Montréal
- Festival du cinéma africain, dans tous les cinémas de Montréal
- Journée de la bande dessinée, samedi toute la journée, à la Librairie Rochefort, à Montréal
- Festival de reggae, dimanche tout l'après-midi, à l'Espace Lemay, à Montréal

Spectacle à voir°
- *La Cantatrice chauve*, pièce° d'Eugène Ionesco, samedi et dimanche à 20h00, au Théâtre du Chat Bleu, à Montréal

À ne pas oublier°
- Le musée des Beaux-Arts de Montréal, avec sa collection de plus de° 30.000 objets d'art du monde entier°

SPORTS ET JEUX

- L'Académie de golf de Montréal organise un grand tournoi° le mois prochain. Pour plus d'informations, contactez le (514) 846-1225.

- Tous les dimanches, le Club d'échecs de Montréal organise des tournois d'échecs en plein air° dans le parc Champellier. Pour plus d'informations, appelez le (514) 846-1085.

- Skiez! Passez la fin de semaine dans les Laurentides° ou dans les Cantons-de-l'Est!

- Et pour la famille sportive: essayez le parc Lafontaine, un centre d'amusement pour tous qui offre: volley-ball, tennis, football et baseball.

PASSIONNÉ° DE PÊCHE?
N'OUBLIEZ PAS LES NOMBREUX
LACS° OÙ LA PÊCHE EST AUTORISÉE.

EXPLORATION

Redécouvrez la nature grâce à° ces activités à ne pas manquer°:

Visite du parc national de la Jacques-Cartier°
- Camping
- Promenades et randonnées
- Observation de la faune et de la flore

Région des Laurentides et Gaspésie°
- Équitation°
- Randonnées à cheval de 2 à 5 jours en camping

voir *see* **pièce (de théâtre)** *play* **À ne pas oublier** *Not to be forgotten* **plus de** *more than* **du monde entier** *from around the world* **tournoi** *tournament* **en plein air** *outdoor* **Laurentides** *region of eastern Quebec* **Passionné** *Enthusiast* **lacs** *lakes* **grâce à** *thanks to* **à ne pas manquer** *not to be missed* **la Jacques-Cartier** *the Jacques-Cartier river in Quebec* **Gaspésie** *peninsula of Quebec* **Équitation** *Horseback riding*

Après la lecture

Répondez Répondez aux questions avec des phrases complètes.

1. Citez deux activités sportives qu'on peut pratiquer à l'extérieur.
   Answers will vary.

2. À quel jeu est-ce qu'on joue dans le parc Champellier?
   On joue aux échecs dans le parc Champellier.

3. Où va peut-être aller un passionné de lecture et de dessin?
   Un passionné de lecture et de dessin va peut-être aller à la Journée de la bande dessinée.

4. Où pratique-t-on des sports d'équipe?
   On pratique des sports d'équipe au parc Lafontaine.

5. Où y a-t-il de la neige au Québec en cette saison?
   Il y a de la neige dans les Laurentides et dans les Cantons-de-l'Est.

6. Si on aime beaucoup la musique, où peut-on aller?
   On peut aller au Festival de musique classique ou au Festival de reggae.

Suggestions Lucille passe une année dans un lycée du Québec. Ce week-end, elle invite sa famille à explorer la région. Choisissez une activité à faire ou un lieu à visiter que chaque membre de sa famille va aimer.

MODÈLE

La sœur cadette de Lucille adore le ski.
Elle va aimer les Laurentides et les Cantons-de-l'Est.

1. La mère de Lucille est artiste.
   Elle va aimer le musée des Beaux-Arts de Montréal.

2. Le frère de Lucille joue au volley-ball à l'université.
   Il va aimer le parc Lafontaine.

3. La sœur aînée de Lucille a envie de voir un film sénégalais.
   Elle va aimer le Festival du cinéma africain.

4. Le grand-père de Lucille joue souvent aux échecs.
   Il va aimer les tournois d'échecs en plein air dans le parc Champellier.

5. La grand-mère de Lucille est fan de théâtre.
   Elle va aimer *La Cantatrice chauve* au Théâtre du Chat Bleu.

6. Le père de Lucille adore la nature et les animaux, mais il n'est pas très sportif.
   Answers will vary. Possible answer: Il va aimer les promenades dans le parc national de la Jacques-Cartier.

Une invitation Vous allez passer le week-end au Québec. Qu'est-ce que vous allez faire? Par groupes de quatre, discutez des activités qui vous intéressent (*that interest you*) et essayez de trouver trois ou quatre activités que vous avez en commun. Attention! Il va peut-être pleuvoir ce week-end, alors ne choisissez pas (*don't choose*) uniquement des activités de plein air!

deux cent dix-sept 217

Répondez Present these as items 7–10. **7. Où peut-on voir des films africains?** (On peut voir des films africains dans tous les cinémas de Montréal.) **8. Combien d'objets d'art y a-t-il au musée des Beaux-Arts de Montréal?** (Il y a plus de 30.000 objets d'art.) **9. Quels sports pratique-t-on au parc Lafontaine?** (On propose le volley-ball, le tennis, le football et le baseball.) **10. Si on aime beaucoup les animaux et les fleurs, où peut-on aller?** (On peut aller au parc national de la Jacques-Cartier.)

Suggestions Ask students to write about three more members of Lucille's family. They should model their sentences after the ones in the activity, saying what each person enjoys doing. Then have students read their sentences to a partner. The partner will come up with a suggested activity or place to visit that will suit each person.

Une invitation Give students a couple of minutes to review the **Vocabulaire** on page 178, **Expressions utiles** on page 183, and Expressions with **faire** on page 186. Add activities, such as **faire du surf des neiges, prendre des photos, faire des arts martiaux,** and **faire du skateboard.**

Expansion Have one or two groups act out their conversation from **Une invitation** for the rest of the class. Before the groups begin, have the listeners in the class write a list of ten activities that they think will be mentioned in each of the presentations. As students listen, have them check off on their list the activities they hear.

21st Century Skills

Creativity and Innovation Ask students to prepare a presentation on the ideal weekend in a city like Montreal, inspired by the information on these two pages.

EXPANSION

True-False Statements Give students true or false statements about the **Lecture.** Example: **On peut faire des randonnées à cheval au parc national de la Jacques-Cartier.** (Faux. On peut faire des randonnées à cheval en Région des Laurentides et Gaspésie.)

TEACHING OPTIONS

Writing Practice Ask students to go through the selection and locate all of the activities that require the usage of **faire.** (Encourage them to use their dictionaries, if necessary.) Then have them write sentences saying whether or not they like doing those activities. Example: **Activités avec faire: faire du vélo, faire de l'équitation,** etc. **J'aime faire du vélo. Je n'aime pas faire d'équitation.**

217

Écriture

STRATÉGIE

Using a dictionary

A common mistake made by beginning language learners is to use the dictionary as the ultimate resource for reading, writing, and speaking. While it is true that the dictionary is a useful tool that can provide valuable information about vocabulary, using the dictionary correctly requires that you understand the elements of each entry.

If you glance at a French-English dictionary, you will notice that the format is similar to that of an English dictionary. The word is listed first, usually followed by its pronunciation. Then come the definitions, organized by parts of speech. Sometimes, the most frequently used meanings are listed first.

To find the best word for your needs, you should refer to the abbreviations and the explanatory notes that appear next to the entries. For example, imagine that you are writing about your pastimes. You want to write *I want to buy a new racket for my match tomorrow*, but you don't know the French word for *racket*.

In the dictionary, you might find an entry like this one:

> **racket** n 1. boucan; 2. raquette (sport)

The abbreviation key at the front of the dictionary says that *n* corresponds to **nom** (*noun*). Then, the first word you see is **boucan**. The definition of **boucan** is *noise or racket,* so **boucan** is probably not the word you want. The second word is **raquette**, followed by the word *sport*, which indicates that it is related to **sports**. This detail indicates that the word **raquette** is the best choice for your needs.

Thème

Écrire une brochure

Avant l'écriture

1. Choisissez le sujet de votre brochure:

   A. Vous travaillez à la Chambre de Commerce de votre région. Elle vous demande de créer (*asks you to create*) une petite brochure sur le temps qu'il fait dans votre région aux différentes saisons de l'année pour des hommes et femmes d'affaires francophones en visite. Pour chaque saison, décrivez le temps, les endroits qu'il faut visiter pendant cette (*during that*) saison et les activités culturelles et sportives à faire.

   B. Vous avez une réunion familiale pour décider où aller en vacances cette année. Choisissez un lieu de vacances où vous avez envie d'aller et créez une brochure pour montrer à votre famille pourquoi il faut y aller (*go there*). Décrivez la météo (*the weather*) de l'endroit et indiquez les différentes activités culturelles et sportives qu'on peut y faire.

   C. Vous passez un semestre dans le pays francophone de votre choix (*of your choice*). Deux élèves de votre cours de français ont aussi envie de visiter ce pays. Créez une petite brochure pour partager vos impressions du pays. Présentez le pays, donnez des informations sur le temps et décrivez vos activités préférées dans ce pays.

2. Choisissez le sujet de votre brochure et pensez au vocabulaire utile à son écriture. Utilisez le tableau (*chart*) pour noter tous les mots (*words*) en français qui vous viennent à l'esprit (*you can think of*). Ensuite (*Next*), regardez le tableau. Avez-vous besoin d'autres mots? Ajoutez-les (*Add them*) en anglais.

3. Cherchez les mots en anglais dans le dictionnaire. N'oubliez pas d'utiliser la procédure de **Stratégie**. Ajoutez les mots au tableau.

Mots en français (de moi)	Mots en anglais	Équivalent français des mots en anglais

Écriture

Utilisez le vocabulaire du tableau pour créer votre brochure. N'oubliez pas de penser à un titre (*title*). Ensuite, créez des sections et donnez-leur (*them*) aussi un titre, comme **Printemps, Été, …; Ville, Campagne (Countryside), …; France, Tunisie, …** Vous pouvez (*can*) utiliser des photos pour illustrer.

Après l'écriture

1. Échangez votre brochure avec celle (*the one*) d'un(e) partenaire. Répondez à ces questions pour commenter son travail.

- Votre partenaire a-t-il/elle couvert (*did cover*) le sujet?

- A-t-il/elle donné (*did give*) un titre à la brochure et aux sections?

- S'il (*If there*) y a des photos, illustrent-elles le texte?

- Votre partenaire a-t-il/elle utilisé (*did use*) le vocabulaire approprié?

- A-t-il/elle correctement conjugué (*did conjugate*) les verbes?

2. Corrigez votre brochure d'après (*according to*) les commentaires de votre partenaire. Relisez votre travail pour éliminer ces problèmes:

- des fautes (*errors*) d'orthographe

- des fautes de ponctuation

- des fautes de conjugaison

- des fautes d'accord (*agreement*) des adjectifs

- un mauvais emploi (*use*) de la grammaire

deux cent dix-neuf **219**

EVALUATION

Criteria

Content Contains all the information included in the subject description the student chose.
Scale: 1 2 3 4 5

Organization Follows a typical brochure organization with a major head, text, and at least one visual.
Scale: 1 2 3 4 5

Accuracy Uses possessive and descriptive adjectives and modifies them accordingly. Spells words and conjugates verbs correctly throughout.
Scale: 1 2 3 4 5

Creativity The student includes additional information that is not included in the task, adds extra features to the brochure such as bulleted lists and boxed text, and/or spends extra time on design and presentation.
Scale: 1 2 3 4 5

Scoring

Excellent	18–20 points
Good	14–17 points
Satisfactory	10–13 points
Unsatisfactory	< 10 points

21ˢᵗ Century Skills

Productivity and Accountability
Provide the rubric to students before they hand their work in for grading. Ask students to make sure they have met the highest standard possible on the rubric before submitting their work.

EXPANSION

Avant l'écriture Group students who have chosen to work on the same brochures and encourage them to share their ideas and personalized vocabulary from step 2 before they begin writing. As a group, have them brainstorm additional vocabulary they may need to look up before they begin writing.

Before students begin writing, have the class discuss some of the features that are typically found in brochures, such as headings, schedules, lists, boxed/highlighted text, photos, graphics, and other visuals. Bring in some brochures for students to analyze before they create their own.

Key Standards

4.1

Suggestion Tell students that an easy way to study from **Vocabulaire** is to cover up the French half of each section, leaving only the English equivalents exposed. They can then quiz themselves on the French items. To focus on the English equivalents of the French entries, they simply reverse this process.

21st Century Skills

Creativity and Innovation
Ask students to prepare a list of three products or perspectives they learned about in this unit to share with the class. Consider asking them to focus on the **Culture** and **Panorama** sections.

21st Century Skills

Leadership and Responsibility: Extension Project
If you have access to students in a Francophone country, have students decide on three questions they want to ask the partner class related to this unit's topic. Based on the responses they receive, work as a class to explain to the partner class one aspect of their responses that surprised the class and why.

Leçon 5A

Activités sportives et loisirs

aider	to help
aller à la pêche	to go fishing
bricoler	to tinker; to do odd jobs
chanter	to sing
désirer	to want; to desire
gagner	to win
indiquer	to indicate
jouer (à/de)	to play
marcher	to walk (person); to work (thing)
pratiquer	to practice; to play (a sport)
skier	to ski
une bande dessinée (B.D.)	comic strip
le baseball	baseball
le basket(-ball)	basketball
les cartes (f.)	cards
le cinéma	movies
les échecs (m.)	chess
une équipe	team
le foot(ball)	soccer
le football américain	football
le golf	golf
un jeu	game
un joueur/une joueuse	player
un loisir	leisure activity
un match	game
un passe-temps	pastime, hobby
un spectacle	show
le sport	sport
un stade	stadium
le temps libre	free time
le tennis	tennis
le volley(-ball)	volleyball

La fréquence

une/deux fois	one/two time(s)
par jour, semaine, mois, an, etc.	per day, week, month, year, etc.
déjà	already
encore	again; still
jamais	never
longtemps	a long time
maintenant	now
parfois	sometimes
rarement	rarely
souvent	often

Expressions utiles

See p. 183.

faire

faire	to do, to make
je fais, tu fais, il/elle/on fait, nous faisons, vous faites, ils/elles font	

Expressions with *faire*

faire de l'aérobic	to do aerobics
faire attention (à)	to pay attention (to)
faire du camping	to go camping
faire du cheval	to go horseback riding
faire la connaissance de...	to meet (someone) for the first time
faire la cuisine	to cook
faire de la gym	to work out
faire du jogging	to go jogging
faire de la planche à voile	to go windsurfing
faire une promenade	to go for a walk
faire une randonnée	to go for a hike
faire du ski	to go skiing
faire du sport	to play sports
faire un tour (en voiture)	to go for a walk (drive)
faire du vélo	to go bike riding

Il faut...

il faut...	it is necessary to...; one must...

Verbes irréguliers en *-ir*

courir	to run
dormir	to sleep
partir	to leave
sentir	to feel; to smell; to sense
servir	to serve
sortir	to go out, to leave

Leçon 5B

Le temps qu'il fait

Il fait 18 degrés.	It is 18 degrees.
Il fait beau.	The weather is nice.
Il fait bon.	The weather is good/warm.
Il fait chaud.	It is hot (out).
Il fait (du) soleil.	It is sunny.
Il fait du vent.	It is windy.
Il fait frais.	It is cool.
Il fait froid.	It is cold.
Il fait mauvais.	The weather is bad.
Il fait un temps épouvantable.	The weather is dreadful.
Il neige. (neiger)	It is snowing. (to snow)
Il pleut. (pleuvoir)	It is raining. (to rain)
Le temps est nuageux.	It is cloudy.
Le temps est orageux.	It is stormy.
Quel temps fait-il?	What is the weather like?
Quelle température fait-il?	What is the temperature?
un imperméable	rain jacket
un parapluie	umbrela

Les saisons, les mois, les dates

une saison	season
l'automne (m.)/à l'automne	fall/in the fall
l'été (m.)/en été	summer/in the summer
l'hiver (m.)/en hiver	winter/in the winter
le printemps (m.)/au printemps	spring/in the spring
janvier	January
février	February
mars	March
avril	April
mai	May
juin	June
juillet	July
août	August
septembre	September
octobre	October
novembre	November
décembre	December
Quelle est la date?	What's the date?
C'est le 1er (premier) octobre.	It's the first of October.
C'est quand votre/ton anniversaire?	When is your birthday?
C'est le 2 mai.	It's the second of May.
C'est quand l'anniversaire de Paul?	When is Paul's birthday?
C'est le 15 mars.	It's March 15th.
un anniversaire	birthday

Expressions utiles

See p. 201.

Numbers 101 and higher

See p. 204.

Mathematical terms

et	plus
divisé par	divided by
égale	equals
fois	times
font	equals
moins	minus
multiplié par	multiplied by
plus	plus
sur	divided by

Verbes

acheter	to buy
amener	to bring (someone)
célébrer	to celebrate
considérer	to consider
emmener	to take (someone)
employer	to use
envoyer	to send
espérer	to hope
essayer (de + inf.)	to try (to)
nettoyer	to clean
payer	to pay
posséder	to possess, to own
préférer	to prefer
protéger	to protect
répéter	to repeat; to rehearse

Les fêtes

Pour commencer
- Combien de personnes y a-t-il sur la photo?
  Quel âge ont-ils, à votre avis?
- Qu'est-ce qu'ils fêtent aujourd'hui?
- Qu'est-ce qu'ils vont manger, du fromage ou
  un dessert?
- Et vous, organisez-vous souvent des fêtes?
  Pour quelles occasions?

Unit Goals
Leçon 6A
In this lesson, students will learn:
- terms for parties and
  celebrations
- terms for the stages of life
- more differences between
  open and closed vowels
- about **carnaval** and France's
  Bastille Day
- more about festivals and
  holiday celebrations through
  specially shot video footage
- demonstrative adjectives
- the **passé composé** with **avoir**
- some irregular past participles
- about a Christmas market
  in Paris

Leçon 6B
In this lesson, students will learn:
- terms for clothing, shopping,
  and colors
- more about open and
  closed vowels
- about fashion in France
- indirect object pronouns
- more uses of disjunctive
  pronouns
- the present tense and **passé
  composé** of regular and
  irregular **-re** verbs
- to listen for linguistic cues in
  oral communication

Savoir-faire
In this section, students will learn:
- cultural, geographical, and
  historical information about
  Algeria, Morocco, and Tunisia
- to recognize word families
- how to report an interview

 **21ˢᵗ Century Skills**

Initiative and Self-Direction
Students can monitor their
progress online using the
activities and assessments
on vhlcentral.com.

Pour commencer
- **Il y a trois personnes. Ils ont
  peut-être quinze ou seize ans.**
- **Ils fêtent l'anniversaire de
  la fille.**
- **Ils vont manger un dessert.**
- Answers will vary.

SUPPORT FOR BACKWARD DESIGN

Unité 6 **Essential Questions**
1. How do people talk about
   celebrating life events?
2. How do people talk about
   shopping and describe clothing?
3. How do people talk about events
   in the past?

Unité 6 **Integrated Performance Assessment**
Before teaching the chapter, review the Integrated Performance Assessment (IPA) and
its accompanying scoring rubric provided in the Testing Program. Use the IPA to assess
students' progress toward proficiency targets at the end of the chapter.
IPA Context: You recently met a new acquaintance from Quebec who just moved to your town.
Your new friend wants to know about the most important or fun celebration in your area. With a
partner, you record a short video to describe this celebration to your new friend and compare it
to a popular celebration in Quebec.

 FORUMS

Forums on vhlcentral.com
allow you and your
students to record and
share audio messages.
Use Forums for presentations,
oral assessments, discussions,
directions, etc.

Section Goals

In this section, students will learn and practice vocabulary related to:
- parties and celebrations
- stages of life and interpersonal relationships

Key Standards
1.1, 1.2, 4.1

Suggestions
- Have students look over the new vocabulary and identify the cognates. Examples: **organiser, fiancé(e), mariage,** and **divorce.**
- Describe what people are doing in the drawing using the digital image for this page. Follow up with simple questions based on your narrative.
- Point out the banner and the cake in the illustration. Ask students what **Bon anniversaire** and **Joyeux anniversaire** mean. (*Happy birthday*)
- Point out the similarities and differences between these related words: **aimer, ami(e), l'amitié, un amour, amoureux,** and **amoureuse.**

⊛ TELL Connection

Environment 4 *Why:* A culture-rich environment supports language use. *What:* Support the unit theme by having students help create **décor** for a party; you may need to give students additional terms in French to support class discussion of the **décor** they create.

You will learn how to...
- talk about celebrations
- talk about the stages of life

◁)) **vhl**central

Surprise!

Vocabulaire

faire une surprise (à quelqu'un)	to surprise (someone)
fêter	to celebrate
organiser une fête	to organize a party
une fête	party; celebration
un jour férié	holiday
l'amitié	friendship
l'amour	love
le bonheur	happiness
un(e) fiancé(e)	fiancé
des jeunes mariés (m.)	newlyweds
un rendez-vous	date; appointment
l'adolescence (f.)	adolescence
l'âge adulte (m.)	adulthood
un divorce	divorce
l'enfance (f.)	childhood
une étape	stage
la jeunesse	youth
un mariage	marriage; wedding
la mort	death
la naissance	birth
la vie	life
la vieillesse	old age
prendre sa retraite	to retire
tomber amoureux/ amoureuse	to fall in love
ensemble	together

Labels on illustration: les invitées (f.), les invités (m.), l'hôte (m.), l'hôtesse (f.), le gâteau, la glace, les biscuits (m.), les bonbons (m.), les desserts (m.), les glaçons (m.)

EXPANSION

Les fêtes Point out that, in addition to celebrating birthdays, many people in French-speaking cultures celebrate **la fête,** or saint's day, which is based upon their given name. Bring in a French calendar that has the names of **fêtes** and have students find their own saint's day. You may need to help students find the name that most closely resembles their own.

EXPANSION

Writing Practice Have students write three fill-in-the-blank sentences based on the drawing above, using the new vocabulary. Then have each student exchange papers with a classmate and complete the sentences. Remind them to verify their answers.

BON ANNIVERSAIRE, MARC!

la surprise
le couple
le cadeau

Mise en pratique

1 **Chassez l'intrus** Indiquez le mot ou l'expression qui n'appartient pas (*doesn't belong*) à la liste.

1. l'amour, tomber amoureux, un fiancé, un divorce
2. un mariage, un couple, un jour férié, une fiancée
3. un biscuit, un glaçon, un dessert, un gâteau
4. la retraite, l'amitié, le bonheur, l'amour
5. la vieillesse, la naissance, l'enfance, la jeunesse
6. faire la fête, un hôte, des invités, une étape
7. fêter, un cadeau, la vie, une surprise
8. la glace, l'âge adulte, la mort, l'adolescence

2 **Écoutez** Écoutez la conversation entre Anne et Nathalie. Indiquez si les affirmations sont **vraies** ou **fausses**.

	Vrai	Faux
1. Jean-Marc va prendre sa retraite dans six mois.	☐	☑
2. Nathalie a l'idée d'organiser une fête pour Jean-Marc.	☐	☑
3. Anne va acheter un gâteau.	☑	☐
4. Nathalie va apporter de la glace.	☐	☑
5. La fête est une surprise.	☑	☐
6. Nathalie va envoyer les invitations par e-mail.	☑	☐
7. La fête va avoir lieu (*take place*) dans le bureau d'Anne.	☐	☑
8. La maison d'Anne n'est pas belle.	☐	☑
9. Tout le monde va donner des idées pour le cadeau.	☑	☐
10. Les invités vont acheter le cadeau.	☐	☑

3 **Associez** Faites correspondre les mots et expressions de la colonne de gauche avec les définitions de la colonne de droite. Notez que tous les éléments ne sont pas utilisés. Ensuite (*Then*), avec un(e) partenaire, donnez votre propre définition de quatre expressions de la première colonne. Votre partenaire doit deviner (*must guess*) de quoi vous parlez.

b 1. la naissance
n/a 2. l'enfance
c 3. l'adolescence
n/a 4. l'âge adulte
e 5. tomber amoureux
a 6. un jour férié
g 7. le mariage
f 8. le divorce
h 9. prendre sa retraite
d 10. la mort

a. C'est une date importante, comme le 4 juillet aux États-Unis.
b. C'est la fin de l'étape prénatale.
c. C'est l'étape de la vie pendant laquelle (*during which*) on va au lycée.
d. C'est un événement très triste.
e. C'est soudain (*suddenly*) aimer une personne.
f. C'est le futur probable d'un couple qui se dispute (*fights*) tout le temps.
g. C'est un jour de bonheur et de célébration de l'amour.
h. C'est quand une personne décide de ne plus travailler.

deux cent vingt-trois **223**

1 **Expansion** Have students create one or two additional items using at least three of the new vocabulary words in each one. Collect their papers and write some of the items on the board.

2 **Script** ANNE: Nathalie, je vais organiser une fête pour Jean-Marc. Il va prendre sa retraite dans un mois. Ça va être une surprise. Je vais acheter un gâteau.
NATHALIE: Oh, et moi, qu'est-ce que je fais pour aider, Anne? J'apporte des biscuits?
A: Oui, c'est une bonne idée. Il faut aussi trouver un cadeau original.
N: D'accord, mais je vais avoir besoin d'un peu de temps pour y penser.
A: Qu'est-ce qu'on fait pour les invités?
N: Pour faire une vraie surprise à Jean-Marc, il faut être discrètes. Je propose d'envoyer un e-mail à tout le monde. En plus, comme ça, c'est rapide.
A: Et qu'est-ce qu'on fait pour la décoration?
N: Pourquoi ne pas fêter sa retraite chez toi? Ta maison est belle, et on n'a pas besoin de beaucoup de décoration.
A: Oui, pourquoi pas! Maintenant, il ne reste plus qu'à trouver un cadeau. Pourquoi est-ce qu'on ne demande pas aux autres de donner des idées par e-mail?
N: Oui, et quel beau cadeau pour Jean-Marc si tout le monde participe et donne un peu d'argent!
Teacher Resources DVD

2 **Suggestion** Play the conversation again, stopping at the end of each sentence that contains the answer to one of these items. Have students verify true statements and correct the false ones.

3 **Suggestion** Have volunteers share their definitions with the class.

DIFFERENTIATION

For Visual Learners Write vocabulary words on index cards. On another set of cards, draw or paste pictures to match or demonstrate each term. Tape them face down on the board in random order. Divide the class into two teams. Then play a game of concentration, matching words with pictures. When a player has a match, his/her team collects those cards. When all the cards have been matched, the team with the most cards wins.

TEACHING OPTIONS

Opposites Say vocabulary words aloud and have students write or say opposite terms. Examples: **la jeunesse (la vieillesse)**, **le divorce (le mariage)**, **la naissance (la mort)**, **séparé (ensemble)**, and **enfant (adulte)**.

Communication

4 Le mot juste Complétez les phrases par le mot illustré. Faites les accords nécessaires. Ensuite (*Then*), avec deux personnes, créez (*create*) une phrase pour laquelle (*for which*) vous illustrez trois mots de **CONTEXTES**. Échangez votre phrase avec celle d'un autre groupe et résolvez le rébus (*puzzle*).

1. Caroline est une amie d' __enfance__ . Je vais lui faire une __surprise__ samedi.

   C'est son anniversaire.

2. Marc et Sophie sont inséparables. Ils sont toujours __ensemble__ . C'est le bonheur et

   le grand __amour__ .

3. Les __invités__ aiment beaucoup les desserts: un __gâteau__ au chocolat

   et des __bonbons__ .

4. Les (jeunes) mariés __ ont beaucoup de __cadeaux__ .

5. La __naissance__ de ma sœur est un grand __bonheur__ pour mes parents.

5 Sept différences Votre professeur va vous donner, à vous et à votre partenaire, deux feuilles d'activités différentes. À tour de rôle, posez-vous des questions pour trouver les sept différences entre les illustrations de l'anniversaire des jumeaux (*twins*) Boniface. Attention! Ne regardez pas la feuille de votre partenaire.

MODÈLE

Élève 1: *Sur mon image, il y a trois cadeaux. Combien de cadeaux y a-t-il sur ton image?*
Élève 2: *Sur mon image, il y a quatre cadeaux.*

6 C'est la fête! Vous avez envie d'organiser une fête! Avec un(e) partenaire, écrivez une conversation au sujet de la préparation de cette fête. N'oubliez pas de répondre aux questions suivantes. Ensuite (*Then*), jouez (*act out*) votre dialogue devant la classe. Answers will vary.

1. Quand allez-vous organiser la fête?
2. Qui vont être les invités?
3. Où la fête va-t-elle avoir lieu (*take place*)?
4. Qu'allez-vous manger? Qu'allez-vous boire?
5. Qui va apporter quoi?
6. Qui est responsable de la musique? De la décoration?
7. Qu'allez-vous faire pendant (*during*) la fête?
8. Qui va nettoyer après la fête?

Les sons et les lettres ◀)) vhlcentral

Open vs. closed vowels: Part 2

The letter combinations **au** and **eau** are pronounced like the vowel sound in the English word *coat*, but without the glide heard in English. These are closed **o** sounds.

chaud	aussi	beaucoup	tableau

When the letter **o** is followed by a consonant sound, it is usually pronounced like the vowel in the English word *raw*. This is an open **o** sound.

homme	téléphone	ordinateur	orange

When the letter **o** occurs as the last sound of a word or is followed by a *z* sound, such as a single **s** between two vowels, it is usually pronounced with the closed **o** sound.

trop	héros	rose	chose

When the letter **o** has an **accent circonflexe**, it is usually pronounced with the closed **o** sound.

drôle	bientôt	pôle	côté

Prononcez Répétez les mots suivants à voix haute.

1. rôle
2. porte
3. dos
4. chaud
5. prose
6. gros
7. oiseau
8. encore
9. mauvais
10. nouveau
11. restaurant
12. bibliothèque

Articulez Répétez les phrases suivantes à voix haute.

1. En automne, on n'a pas trop chaud.
2. Aurélie a une bonne note en biologie.
3. Votre colocataire est d'origine japonaise?
4. Sophie aime beaucoup l'informatique et la psychologie.
5. Nos copains mangent au restaurant marocain aujourd'hui.
6. Comme cadeau, Robert et Corinne vont préparer un gâteau.

Dictons Répétez les dictons à voix haute.

La fortune vient en dormant.[2]

Tout nouveau, tout beau.[1]

[1] Shiny and new.

[2] Fortune comes while you sleep.

Section Goals
In this section, students will learn more about open and closed vowels.

Key Standards
4.1

Suggestions
• Model the pronunciation of each open and closed vowel sound. Have students watch the shape of your mouth, then repeat the sound after you. Pronounce each of the example words and have students repeat them.
• Remind students that **o** is sometimes nasalized when followed by a single **m** or **n**. Compare the following words: **bon, nom,** and **bonne, homme**.
• Ask students to provide more examples of words from this lesson or previous lessons with these vowel sounds. Examples: **cadeau, gâteau, hôte, octobre,** and **beau**.
• Dictate five familiar words containing the open and closed vowels presented here, repeating each one at least two times. Then write them on the board or on a transparency and have students check their spelling.

Dictons Ask students if they can think of sayings in English that are similar to **«La fortune vient en dormant.»** (*Good things come to those who wait. Patience is a virtue.*)

EXPANSION

Mini-dictée Use these sentences with open and closed vowel sounds for additional practice or dictation. **1. Octobre est en automne. 2. Est-ce qu'il fait mauvais aujourd'hui? 3. En août, il fait beau, mais il fait chaud. 4. Aurélie est aussi drôle que Paul.**

EXPANSION

Tongue Twister Teach students this French tongue-twister that contains a variety of vowel sounds. **Paul se pèle au pôle dans sa pile de pulls et polos pâles. Pas plus d'appel de la poule à l'Opel que d'opale dans la pelle à Paul.**

Les cadeaux vhlcentral

AP® Theme: Contemporary Life
Context: Holidays and Celebrations

PERSONNAGES

 Amina
 Astrid
 Rachid
 Sandrine
 Valérie
 Vendeuse

À l'appartement de Sandrine...
SANDRINE Allô, Pascal? Tu m'as téléphoné? Écoute, je suis très occupée, là. Je prépare un gâteau d'anniversaire pour Stéphane... Il a dix-huit ans aujourd'hui... On organise une fête surprise au P'tit Bistrot.

SANDRINE J'ai fait une mousse au chocolat, comme pour ton anniversaire. Stéphane adore ça! J'ai aussi préparé des biscuits que David aime bien.

SANDRINE Quoi? David!... Mais non, il n'est pas marié. C'est un bon copain, c'est tout!... Désolée, je n'ai pas le temps de discuter. À bientôt.

RACHID Écoute, Astrid. Il faut trouver un cadeau... un *vrai* cadeau d'anniversaire.
ASTRID Excusez-moi, Madame. Combien coûte cette montre, s'il vous plaît?
VENDEUSE Quarante euros.
ASTRID Que penses-tu de cette montre, Rachid?
RACHID Bonne idée.

VENDEUSE Je fais un paquet cadeau?
ASTRID Oui, merci.
RACHID Eh, Astrid, il faut y aller!
VENDEUSE Et voilà dix euros. Merci, Mademoiselle, bonne fin de journée.

Au café...
VALÉRIE Ah, vous voilà! Astrid, aide-nous avec les décorations, s'il te plaît. La fête commence à six heures. Sandrine a tout préparé.
ASTRID Quelle heure est-il? Zut, déjà? En tout cas, on a trouvé des cadeaux.
RACHID Je vais chercher Stéphane.

A C T I V I T É S

1 **Vrai ou faux?** Indiquez si ces (*these*) affirmations sont vraies ou fausses.
1. Sandrine prépare un gâteau d'anniversaire pour Stéphane. Vrai.
2. Sandrine est désolée parce qu'elle n'a pas le temps de discuter avec Rachid. Faux.
3. Pour aider Sandrine, Valérie va apporter les desserts. Vrai.
4. Rachid ne comprend pas la blague. Vrai.
5. Rachid et Astrid trouvent un cadeau pour Valérie. Faux.
6. Rachid n'aime pas l'idée de la montre pour Stéphane. Faux.
7. La fête d'anniversaire pour Stéphane commence à huit heures. Faux.
8. Sandrine va chercher Stéphane. Faux.
9. Amina a apporté de la glace au chocolat. Vrai.
10. Les parents d'Amina vont passer l'été en France. Vrai.

Tout le monde prépare la surprise pour Stéphane.

VALÉRIE Oh là là! Tu as fait tout ça pour Stéphane?!

SANDRINE Oh, ce n'est pas grand-chose.

VALÉRIE Tu es un ange! Stéphane va bientôt arriver. Je t'aide à apporter ces desserts?

SANDRINE Oh, merci, c'est gentil.

Dans un magasin...

ASTRID Eh Rachid, j'ai eu une idée géniale... Des cadeaux parfaits pour Stéphane. Regarde! Ce matin, j'ai acheté cette calculatrice et ces livres.

RACHID Mais enfin, Astrid, Stéphane n'aime pas les livres.

ASTRID Oh, Rachid, tu ne comprends rien. C'est une blague.

AMINA Bonjour! Désolée, je suis en retard!

VALÉRIE Ce n'est pas grave. Tu es toute belle ce soir!

AMINA Vous trouvez? J'ai acheté ce cadeau pour Stéphane. Et j'ai apporté de la glace au chocolat aussi.

VALÉRIE Oh, merci! Il faut aider Astrid avec les décorations.

ASTRID Salut, Amina. Ça va?

AMINA Oui, super. Mes parents ont téléphoné du Sénégal ce matin! Ils vont passer l'été ici. C'est le bonheur!

Expressions utiles

Talking about celebrations

- **J'ai fait une mousse au chocolat, comme pour ton anniversaire.**
  I made a chocolate mousse, (just) like for your birthday.

- **J'ai aussi préparé des biscuits que David aime bien.**
  I have also prepared some cookies that David likes.

- **Je fais un paquet cadeau?**
  Shall I wrap the present?

- **En tout cas, on a trouvé des cadeaux.**
  In any case, we have found some presents.

- **Et j'ai apporté de la glace au chocolat.**
  And I brought some chocolate ice cream.

Talking about the past

- **Tu m'as téléphoné?**
  Did you call me?

- **Tu as fait tout ça pour Stéphane?!**
  You did all that for Stéphane?!

- **J'ai eu une idée géniale.**
  I had a great idea.

- **Sandrine a tout préparé.**
  Sandrine prepared everything.

Pointing out things

- **Je t'aide à apporter ces desserts?**
  Can I help you to carry these desserts?

- **J'ai acheté cette calculatrice et ces livres.**
  I bought this calculator and these books.

- **J'ai acheté ce cadeau pour Stéphane.**
  I bought this present for Stéphane.

Additional vocabulary

- **Ce n'est pas grave.**
  It's okay./No problem.
- **Tu ne comprends rien.**
  You don't understand a thing.
- **désolé(e)**
  sorry
- **discuter**
  to talk
- **zut**
  darn

---

2 **Le bon mot** Choisissez le bon mot entre **ce** (*m.*), **cette** (*f.*) et **ces** (*pl.*) pour compléter les phrases. Attention, les phrases ne sont pas identiques aux dialogues!

1. Je t'aide à apporter _ce_ gâteau?

2. Ce matin, j'ai acheté _ces_ calculatrices et _ce_ livre.

3. Rachid ne comprend pas _cette_ blague.

4. Combien coûtent _ces_ montres?

5. À quelle heure commence _cette_ classe?

3 **Imaginez** Avec un(e) partenaire, imaginez qu'Amina soit (*is*) dans un grand magasin et qu'elle téléphone à Valérie pour l'aider à choisir le cadeau idéal pour Stéphane. Amina propose plusieurs possibilités de cadeaux et Valérie donne son avis (*opinion*) sur chacune d'entre elles (*each of them*).

A C T I V I T É S

Expressions utiles
- Model the pronunciation of the **Expressions utiles** and have students repeat them.
- As you work through the list, point out forms of the **passé composé** and demonstrative adjectives. Tell students that these grammar structures will be formally presented in the **Structures** section.
- Respond briefly to questions about the **passé composé** and demonstrative adjectives. Reinforce correct forms, but do not expect students to produce them consistently at this time.
- Say some of the **Expressions utiles** and have students react to them. Examples: 1. J'ai eu une idée géniale! (Ah oui? Quelle est votre idée?) 2. Sandrine a tout préparé. (Oh, c'est gentil!)

1 **Expansion** Have students correct the false sentences: **2. Elle n'a pas le temps de discuter avec Pascal. 5. Ils trouvent un cadeau pour Stéphane. 6. Rachid aime l'idée de la montre pour Stéphane. 7. Elle commence à six heures. 8. Rachid va chercher Stéphane.**

2 **Suggestion** Before beginning the activity, point out the gender of each demonstrative adjective given. Tell students that demonstrative adjectives must agree with the noun they modify.

2 **Expansion** For additional practice, give students these items. **6. Je t'aide à apporter ____ desserts? (ces) 7. Tu es très belle ____ soir. (ce) 8. Mes parents ont téléphoné du Sénégal ____ matin. (ce)**

3 **Suggestion** If time is limited, assign students the roles of Valérie or Amina and tell them to prepare for homework a list of possible questions or responses according to their role. Then allow partners a few minutes to work together before presenting their conversations.

EXPANSION

Les cadeaux Point out the question **Je fais un paquet cadeau?** Explain that many stores gift wrap items free of charge, especially small items. The wrapping is often a simple sack sealed with a small ribbon and a sticker, which usually bears the name of the store.

EXPANSION

L'étiquette Point out some basic etiquette regarding gifts in France. For example, if invited to eat at someone's house, one should not bring a dish to eat because the host or hostess most certainly will have planned the entire menu. Instead, choose candy or flowers.

AP® **Theme:** Contemporary Life
Context: Holidays and Celebrations

vhlcentral | *Flash culture*

CULTURE À LA LOUPE

Le carnaval

Tous les ans, beaucoup de pays° et de régions francophones célèbrent le carnaval. Cette tradition est l'occasion de fêter la fin° de l'hiver et l'arrivée° du printemps. En général, la période de fête commence la semaine avant le Carême° et finit le jour du Mardi gras. Le carnaval demande très souvent des mois de préparation. La ville organise des défilés° de musique, de masques, de costumes et de chars fleuris°. La fête finit souvent par la crémation du roi° Carnaval, personnage de papier qui représente le carnaval et l'hiver.

Certaines villes et certaines régions sont réputées° pour leur carnaval: Nice, en France, la ville de Québec, au Canada, La Nouvelle-Orléans, aux États-Unis, et la Martinique. Chaque ville a ses traditions particulières. La ville de Nice, lieu du plus grand° carnaval français, organise une grande bataille de fleurs° où des jeunes, sur des chars, envoient des fleurs aux spectateurs. À Québec, le climat intense transforme le carnaval en une célébration de l'hiver. Le symbole officiel

le roi du carnaval de Nice

de la fête est le «Bonhomme» (de neige°) et les gens font du ski, de la pêche sous la glace° ou des courses de traîneaux à chiens°. À la Martinique, le carnaval continue jusqu'au° mercredi des Cendres°, à minuit: les gens, tout en noir et blanc°, regardent la crémation de Vaval, le roi Carnaval. Le carnaval de La Nouvelle-Orléans est célébré avec de nombreux bals° et défilés costumés. Ses couleurs officielles sont l'or°, le vert° et le violet.

pays *countries* **fin** *end* **arrivée** *arrival* **Carême** *Lent* **défilés** *parades*
chars fleuris *floats decorated with flowers* **roi** *king* **réputées** *famous*
plus grand *largest* **bataille de fleurs** *flower battle* **«Bonhomme» (de neige)** *snowman*
pêche sous la glace *ice-fishing* **courses de traîneaux à chiens** *dogsled races*
jusqu'au *until* **mercredi des Cendres** *Ash Wednesday* **noir et blanc** *black and white*
bals *balls (dances)* **or** *gold* **vert** *green* **reine** *queen* **a eu lieu** *took place* **pendant** *during*

Le carnaval en détail

Martinique	Chaque ville choisit une reine°.
Nice	La première bataille de fleurs a eu lieu° en 1876. Chaque année, on envoie entre 80.000 et 100.000 fleurs aux spectateurs.
La Nouvelle-Orléans	Il y a plus de 70 défilés pendant° le carnaval.
la ville de Québec	Le premier carnaval a eu lieu en 1894.

A C T I V I T É S

1 Compréhension Répondez aux questions.

1. En général, quel est le dernier jour du carnaval?
   le Mardi gras
2. Dans quelle ville des États-Unis est-ce qu'on célèbre le carnaval?
   La Nouvelle-Orléans
3. Où a lieu le plus grand (*largest*) carnaval français?
   à Nice
4. Qu'est-ce que les jeunes envoient aux spectateurs du carnaval de Nice?
   des fleurs
5. Quel est le symbole officiel du carnaval de Québec?
   le «Bonhomme»

6. Que fait-on pendant (*during*) le carnaval de Québec?
   On pratique des activités d'hiver.
7. Quand est-ce que le carnaval de la Martinique finit?
   le mercredi des Cendres
8. Comment s'appelle le roi du carnaval à la Martinique?
   Vaval
9. Comment est-ce qu'on célèbre le carnaval à La Nouvelle-Orléans?
   avec des bals et des défilés
10. Quelles sont les couleurs officielles du carnaval de La Nouvelle-Orléans?
    l'or, le vert et le violet

LE FRANÇAIS QUOTIDIEN

Les vœux

À votre santé!	To your health!
Bonne année!	Happy New Year!
Bravo! Félicitations!	Bravo! Congratulations!
Joyeuses fêtes!	Have a good holiday!
Meilleurs vœux!	Best wishes!
Santé!	Cheers!
Tous mes vœux de bonheur!	All the best!

AP® Theme: Contemporary Life   Context: Holidays and Celebrations

LE MONDE FRANCOPHONE

Fêtes et festivals

Voici d'autres fêtes et festivals francophones.

En Côte d'Ivoire
La fête des Ignames (plusieurs dates) On célèbre la fin° de la récolte° des ignames°, une ressource très importante pour les Ivoiriens.

Au Maroc
La fête du Trône (le 30 juillet) Tout le pays honore le roi° avec des parades et des spectacles.

À la Martinique/À la Guadeloupe
La fête des Cuisinières (en août) Les femmes défilent° en costumes traditionnels et présentent des spécialités locales qu'elles ont préparées pour la fête.

Dans de nombreux pays
L'Aïd el-Fitr C'est la fête musulmane° de la rupture du jeûne° à la fin du Ramadan.

fin *end* **récolte** *harvest* **ignames** *yams* **roi** *king* **défilent** *parade* **musulmane** *Muslim* **jeûne** *fast*

PORTRAIT

Le 14 juillet

AP® Theme: Contemporary Life
Context: Holidays and Celebrations

Le 14 juillet 1789, sous le règne° de Louis XVI, les Français se sont rebellés contre° la monarchie et ont pris° la Bastille, une forteresse utilisée comme prison. Cette date est très importante dans l'histoire de France parce qu'elle représente le début de la Révolution.
Le 14 juillet symbolise la fondation de la République française et a donc° été sélectionné comme date de la Fête nationale. Tous les ans, il y a un grand défilé° militaire sur les Champs-Élysées, la plus grande° avenue parisienne. Partout° en France, les gens assistent à des défilés et à des fêtes dans les rues°. Le soir, il y a de nombreux bals populaires° où les Français dansent et célèbrent cette date historique. Le soir, on assiste aux feux d'artifices° traditionnels.

règne *reign* **se sont rebellés contre** *rebelled against* **ont pris** *stormed* **donc** *therefore* **défilé** *parade* **la plus grande** *the largest* **Partout** *Everywhere* **rues** *streets* **bals populaires** *public dances* **feux d'artifices** *fireworks*

Sur Internet

Qu'est-ce que c'est, la fête des Rois?

Go to **vhlcentral.com** to find more information related to this **Culture** section and to watch the corresponding **Flash culture** video.

---

2 Les fêtes Complétez les phrases.

1. Le 14 juillet 1789 est la date ___du début de la Révolution française___
2. Aujourd'hui, le 14 juillet est la ___Fête nationale de la République française___
3. En France, le soir du 14 juillet, il y a ___des bals populaires et___
4. À plusieurs dates, les Ivoiriens fêtent ___des feux d'artifices___ ___la fin de la récolte des ignames___
5. Au Maroc, il y a un festival au mois de ___juillet___
6. Dans les pays musulmans, l'Aïd el-Fitr célèbre ___la fin du Ramadan___

3 Faisons la fête ensemble! Vous êtes en vacances dans un pays francophone et vous invitez un(e) ami(e) à aller à une fête ou à un festival francophone avec vous. Expliquez à votre partenaire ce que vous allez faire. Votre partenaire va vous poser des questions.

A
C
T
I
V
I
T
É
S

Le français quotidien
- Point out that the expression **«Tous mes vœux de bonheur!»** is used primarily at weddings. You might also teach the expression **Bonne chance!** (*Good luck!*)
- Have students identify whether they would use these expressions at **une fête d'anniversaire, une réception de mariage**, or **un anniversaire de mariage**.

Portrait If possible, bring in a photo of the Bastille. Then have students look at a map of Paris. Point out that the military parade begins at **Charles de Gaulle-Étoile** and ends at the **Place de la Concorde**. During the French Revolution, the **Place de la Concorde** was known as the **Place de la Révolution** because so many executions took place there, including the execution of Louis XVI on January 21, 1793.

Le monde francophone Point out that Ramadan, celebrated during the ninth month of the Islamic lunar year, is a special time during which Muslims fast and focus on prayer, purification, and charitable acts.

2 Expansion For additional practice, give students these items. **7. La Bastille était** (*was*) **une forteresse utilisée comme _____ avant la Révolution.** (prison) **8. Le défilé militaire pour le 14 juillet a lieu sur _____.** (les Champs-Élysées)

3 Suggestion Before beginning the activity, have students choose a holiday or festival to discuss.

Flash culture Tell students that they will learn more about French festivals and holiday celebrations by watching a variety of real-life images narrated by Benjamin. Show the video segment, and then have students jot down at least three examples of things they saw. You can also use the activities in the video manual in class to reinforce this **Flash culture** or assign them as homework.

EXPANSION

Cultural Comparison First, ask students: **Quel jour férié aux États-Unis correspond au 14 juillet en France?** (la fête de l'indépendance américaine, le 4 juillet) Then have them work in small groups and compare the two holidays. Tell them to make a list of the similarities (**Similitudes**) and differences (**Différences**) in French. Have groups read their lists to the class.

EXPANSION

Le 14 juillet Explain that a Bastille Day celebration would not be complete without a rendering of France's national anthem, *La Marseillaise*, composed by Claude-Joseph Rouget de Lisle in 1792. Bring the lyrics and a recording of the song for students to listen to. Alternatively, you can have students go to **www.marseillaise.org** to hear the song or read the lyrics.

229

6A.1 **Demonstrative adjectives** **vhl**central

Point de départ To identify or point out a noun with the French equivalent of *this/these* or *that/those*, use a demonstrative adjective before the noun. In French, the form of the demonstrative adjective depends on the gender and number of the noun that it goes with.

Demonstrative adjectives			
	singular		**plural**
	Before consonant	Before vowel sound	
masculine	**ce** café	**cet** éclair	**ces** cafés, **ces** éclairs
feminine	**cette** surprise	**cette** amie	**ces** surprises, **ces** amies

Ce copain organise une fête.
That friend is planning a party.

Cette glace est excellente.
This ice cream is excellent.

Cet hôpital est trop loin du centre-ville.
That hospital is too far from downtown.

Je préfère **ces** cadeaux.
I prefer those gifts.

Combien coûte cette montre?

J'ai ce cadeau pour Stéphane.

● Note that the forms of **ce** can refer to a noun that is near (*this/these*) or far (*that/those*). The meaning will usually be clear from context.

Ce dessert est délicieux.
This dessert is delicious.

Ils vont aimer **cette** surprise.
They're going to like this surprise.

Joël préfère **cet** éclair.
Joël prefers that éclair.

Ces glaçons sont pour la limonade.
Those ice cubes are for the lemon soda.

La maison Julien

Pour toutes ces occasions...

pour célébrer tout ce bonheur...

nous pensons à tous les détails.

In this section, students will learn:
• demonstrative adjectives
• to use -ci and -là to specify demonstratives

Key Standards

4.1, 5.1

Suggestions: Scaffolding
• Go over the introduction in **Point de départ**. Then point to a book on your desk. Say: **Ce livre est sur mon bureau.** Point to a sheet of paper next to the book. Say: **Cette feuille de papier est à côté du livre.** Then point to an object in front of you and say: **Cet objet est devant moi.**
• Present the rest of **Point de départ** and bullet 1. Point out that the masculine singular demonstrative adjective has two forms. Say the following words and have students give the demonstrative: **garçon, homme, biscuit, ordinateur, cadeau,** and **examen**.
• Point out that there is only one plural demonstrative adjective in French, regardless of gender: **ces**.
• Have students identify the demonstrative adjectives in the ad for **La maison Julien**. Ask them what type of store it is.
• Hold up pictures or point to one or more objects and have students state the appropriate demonstrative adjective and the noun. Examples: **ces livres, ce stylo, cette calculatrice.**

Extra Practice Ask students to make a list of objects they have in their backpacks. They can consult the dictionary for any unknown vocabulary. Once they have completed their lists, ask them to take each object out of their backpacks and show it to the class identifying it with a demonstrative adjective and any additional description. Ex: **Ce livre, ici, est mon dictionnaire de français. Ce stylo est mon stylo préféré.**

For Visual Learners In preparation for this activity, students will form groups of 4 and write descriptions of themselves. Then they will stand in pairs in front of the class, one pair at a different corner of the classroom. They will take turns describing their classmates using demonstrative adjectives and the expressions **ci** and **là** according to their location. Example: **Ce garçon-ci est américain. Cette fille-là a les cheveux roux.**

- To make it especially clear that you're referring to something near versus something far, add **-ci** or **-là**, respectively, to the noun following the demonstrative adjective.

ce couple**-ci**	**ces** biscuits**-ci**
this couple (here)	*these cookies (here)*
cette invitée**-là**	**ces** fêtes**-là**
that guest (there)	*those parties (there)*

- Use **-ci** and **-là** in the same sentence to contrast similar items.

On prend **cette glace-ci**, pas **cette glace-là**.
We'll have this ice cream, not that ice cream.

J'aime **ce** cadeau**-ci** mais je préfère **ce** cadeau**-là**.
I like this gift, but I prefer that gift.

Tu achètes **ce fromage-ci** ou **ce fromage-là**?
Are you buying this cheese or that cheese?

Nous achetons **ces** bonbons-ci et Isabelle achète **ce** gâteau**-là**.
We're buying these candies, and Isabelle is buying that cake.

J'aime bien **cette robe-ci**.
I like this dress.

Je n'aime pas **ces chaussures-là**.
I don't like those shoes.

Essayez!　　**Complétez les phrases avec la forme correcte de l'adjectif démonstratif.**

1. __Cette__ glace au chocolat est très bonne!
2. Qu'est-ce que tu penses de ____ce____ cadeau?
3. __Cet__ homme-là est l'hôte de la fête.
4. Tu préfères ___ces___ biscuits-ci ou ___ces___ biscuits-là?
5. Vous aimez mieux ___ce___ dessert-ci ou ___ce___ dessert-là?
6. __Cette__ année-ci, on va fêter l'anniversaire de mariage de nos parents en famille.
7. Tu achètes ___cet___ éclair-là.
8. Vous achetez ___cette___ montre?
9. __Cette__ surprise va être géniale!
10. ___Cet___ invité-là est antipathique.
11. Ma mère fait ___ces___ gâteaux pour mon anniversaire.
12. __Cette__ robe coûte 100 euros.
13. ___Cet___ exercice est très difficile pour les enfants.

231

Mise en pratique

1 **Monsieur Parfait** Juste avant la fête, l'hôte fait le tour de la salle et donne son opinion. Complétez ce texte avec **ce, cette** ou **ces**.

Mmm! (1) _____Cette_____ glace est parfaite. Ah! (2) _____Ces_____ gâteaux sont magnifiques,
(3) _____ces_____ biscuits sont délicieux et j'adore (4) _____ces_____ chocolats. Bah!
(5) _____Ces_____ bonbons sont originaux, mais pas très bons. Ouvrez (*Open*) (6) _____cette_____ bouteille.
(7) _____Ce_____ café sur (8) _____cette_____ table sent très bon. (9) _____Cette_____ plante a besoin d'eau.
(10) _____Ce_____ tableau n'est pas droit (*straight*)! Oh là là! Arrangez (11) _____ces_____ chaises autour de
(*around*) (12) _____ces_____ trois tables!

2 **Magazine** Vous regardez un vieux magazine. Complétez les phrases.

▶ **MODÈLE**

Ce cheval est très grand.

1. __Ce gâteau__ au chocolat et __cette glace__ sont délicieux.

2. __Cette fille__ aime beaucoup __ces bonbons__.

3. __Ces jeunes mariés__ sont très heureux.

4. __Cet homme__ va prendre sa retraite.

5. __Ce couple__ n'est plus (*no longer*) ensemble.

6. __Ces enfants__ adorent le chocolat chaud!

7. __Ce garçon__ est très méchant.

8. __Cette plage__ est absolument super!

3 **Remplacez** Remplacez les noms au singulier par des noms au pluriel et vice versa. Faites tous les autres changements nécessaires.

MODÈLE

J'aime mieux ce dessert.
J'aime mieux ces desserts.

1. Ces glaces au chocolat sont délicieuses. Cette glace au chocolat est délicieuse.
2. Ce gâteau est énorme. Ces gâteaux sont énormes.
3. Ces biscuits ne sont pas bons. Ce biscuit n'est pas bon.
4. Ces invitées sont gentilles. Cette invitée est gentille.
5. Ces hôtes parlent japonais. Cet hôte parle japonais.
6. Cette fille est allemande. Ces filles sont allemandes.
7. Maman achète ces imperméables pour Julie. Maman achète cet imperméable pour Julie.
8. Ces bonbons sont délicieux. Ce bonbon est délicieux.

Communication

4 **Comparez** Avec un(e) partenaire, regardez les illustrations. À tour de rôle, comparez les personnages et les objets. Answers will vary.

> **MODÈLE**
>
> **Élève 1:** *Comment sont ces hommes?*
> **Élève 2:** *Cet homme-ci est petit et cet homme-là est grand.*

1.   2.   3.   4.

5 **Préférences** Demandez à votre partenaire ses préférences, puis donnez votre opinion. Employez des adjectifs démonstratifs et présentez vos réponses à la classe. Answers will vary.

> **MODÈLE**
>
> **Élève 1:** *Quel film est-ce que tu aimes?*
> **Élève 2:** *J'aime bien* Star Wars.
> **Élève 1:** *Moi, je n'aime pas du tout ce vieux film.*

acteur/actrice	passe-temps
chanteur/chanteuse	restaurant
dessert	saison
film	sport
magasin	ville
?	?

6 **Invitation** Nathalie est au supermarché avec sa soeur. Elles organisent une fête, mais elles ne sont pas d'accord sur ce qu'elles vont acheter. Avec un(e) partenaire, jouez les rôles. Answers will vary.

> **MODÈLE**
>
> **Élève 1:** *On achète cette glace-ci?*
> **Élève 2:** *Je n'aime pas cette glace-ci. Je préfère cette glace-là!*
> **Élève 1:** *Mais cette glace-là coûte dix euros!*
> **Élève 2:** *D'accord! On prend cette glace-ci.*

7 **Quelle fête!** Vous êtes à la fête d'un(e) voisin(e) et il y a des personnes célèbres (*famous*). Avec un(e) partenaire, faites une liste des célébrités présentes et puis parlez d'elles. Employez des adjectifs démonstratifs. Answers will vary.

> **MODÈLE**
>
> **Élève 1:** *Qui est cet homme-ci?*
> **Élève 2:** *Ça, c'est Justin Timberlake. Il est sympa, mais cet homme-là est vraiment génial.*
> **Élève 1:** *Oui, c'est...*

4 Suggestion Have two volunteers read the **modèle** aloud. Remind students to take turns asking and answering the questions.

4 Virtual Chat You can also assign Activity 4 on vhlcentral.com. Students record individual responses that appear in your gradebook.

5 Suggestion Have two volunteers read the **modèle** aloud. Tell students to add at least two items of their own to the list.

6 Suggestion Before beginning the activity, have students brainstorm items they might buy for the party and write them on the board.

Activity Pack For additional activities, go to the Activity Pack in the Resources section of vhlcentral.com.

EXPANSION

Game Divide the class into two teams. Choose one team member at a time to go to the board, alternating between teams. Say a noun. The person at the board must write and say the noun with the correct demonstrative adjective. Example: **fille (cette fille).** Give a point for each correct answer. The team with the most points at the end of the game wins.

EXPANSION

Extra Practice Hold up or point to various classroom objects. Tell students to write down all forms of demonstrative adjectives that could apply. Example: **chaise (cette chaise, ces chaises, cette chaise-ci, cette chaise-là, ces chaises-ci, ces chaises-là).**

Section Goals

In this section, students will learn:
- the **passé composé** with **avoir**
- some irregular past participles

Key Standards

4.1, 5.1

Suggestions: Scaffolding
- Quickly review the present tense of **avoir**. Then brainstorm with the class a list of **-er** and **-ir** verbs they have learned. Include **-er** verbs with spelling changes.
- Introduce the **passé composé** by describing what you did yesterday. Include adverbs commonly used to indicate past actions, such as **hier** and **hier soir**. Examples: **Hier, j'ai enseigné deux cours de français. Hier soir, j'ai téléphoné à un(e) ami(e) et j'ai écouté de la musique.** Each time you say a **passé composé** form write it on the board.
- Go over **Point de départ** and the first four bullet points. Do a rapid drill to practice conjugations of **-er** verbs.
- Present the last two points on p. 234. Write the **passé composé** conjugations for **finir** on the board. Read them aloud and have students repeat. Have students provide past participles for the **-ir** verbs they brainstormed earlier that are conjugated with **avoir**. Do a rapid drill to practice conjugations of **-ir** verbs.
- Have students complete the **Vérifiez** activity.

6A.2

The *passé composé* with *avoir* **vhl**central

Point de départ French uses two main tenses to talk about past events: the **passé composé** and the **imparfait**. In this lesson, you will learn how to use the **passé composé** to express actions that began and ended in the past.

- The **passé composé** has three possible translations in English and is composed of two parts: the *auxiliary verb* (present tense of **avoir** or **être**) and the *past participle* of the main verb. Most verbs in French take **avoir** as the auxiliary verb in the **passé composé**.

  AUXILIARY   PAST
  VERB   PARTICIPLE

  Nous **avons fêté**.
  We celebrated.
  We have celebrated.
  We did celebrate.

- The past participle of a regular **-er** verb is formed by replacing the **-er** ending of the infinitive with **-é**.

infinitive	past participle
fêt**er**	fêt**é**
oubli**er**	oubli**é**
cherch**er**	cherch**é**

Boîte à outils

The **passé composé** has three English equivalents. Example: **Nous avons parlé**. = *We spoke. We have spoken. We did speak.*

- Most regular **-er** verbs are conjugated in the **passé composé** as shown below for the verb **parler**.

parler au passé composé	
j'ai parlé	nous avons parlé
tu as parlé	vous avez parlé
il/elle/on a parlé	ils/elles ont parlé

- The past participles of **-er** verbs with spelling changes in the present tense do not have spelling changes in the **passé composé**.

  Laurent a **acheté** le cadeau.   Vous avez **envoyé** des bonbons.
  Laurent bought a gift.   *You sent the candies.*

- The past participle of most regular and irregular **-ir** verbs is formed by replacing the **-ir** ending with **i**. These include such verbs as **choisir**, **finir**, **grandir**, **obéir**, and **réussir** as well as **dormir**, **servir**, and **sentir**.

  Nous avons **fini** le gâteau.   Sylvie a **dormi** jusqu'à dix heures.
  We finished the cake.   *Sylvie slept until 10 o'clock.*

- The adverbs **hier** (*yesterday*) and **avant-hier** (*the day before yesterday*) are used often with the **passé composé**.

  Hier, Marie **a retrouvé** ses amis au stade.   Ses parents **ont téléphoné** avant-hier.
  Marie met her friends at the stadium yesterday.   *Her parents called the day before yesterday.*

Vérifiez

EXPANSION

Rapid Drill As a rapid-response drill, call out subject pronouns and have students respond with the correct form of **avoir**. Examples: **tu (as)** and **vous (avez)**. Then reverse the drill; say the forms of **avoir** and have students give the subject pronouns.

EXPANSION

Extra Practice Ask students to make a list of things they did yesterday using the **passé composé**. Encourage them to memorize their lists. Call out one student to tell the whole class what he or she did and another one to write the sentences on the board in the third person singular. Example: **Élève 1** says **J'ai fait mes devoirs**. **Élève 2** writes **Elle a fait ses devoirs**.

- The past participles of many common verbs are irregular. You will need to memorize them.

Some irregular past participles			
apprendre	appris	être	été
avoir	eu	faire	fait
boire	bu	pleuvoir	plu
comprendre	compris	prendre	pris
courir	couru	surprendre	surpris

Nous avons **bu** de la limonade.
We drank lemonade.

Ils ont **été** très en retard.
They were very late.

- The **passé composé** of **il faut** is **il a fallu**; that of **il y a** is **il y a eu**.

Il a fallu passer par le supermarché.
It was necessary to stop by the supermarket.

Il y a eu deux fêtes hier soir.
There were two parties last night.

Negation and asking questions with the *passé composé*

- To make a verb negative in the **passé composé**, place **ne/n'** and **pas** around the conjugated form of **avoir**.

On **n'a pas** fêté mon anniversaire.
We didn't celebrate my birthday.

Elles **n'ont pas** servi de biscuits hier.
They didn't serve any cookies yesterday.

- There are three ways to ask yes or no questions in the **passé composé**: simply add a question mark and use rising intonation, add **est-ce que** in front of the subject, or invert the subject pronoun and the conjugated form of **avoir**. For the subject pronouns **il(s)**, **elle(s)**, and **on**, you will need to insert a **t** between the conjugated from of **avoir** and the subject pronoun.

Elles ont acheté du fromage hier?
Did they buy the cheese yesterday?

Est-ce que tu as mangé les biscuits?
Did you eat the cookies?

Avez-vous fêté votre anniversaire?
Did you celebrate your birthday?

Luc **a-t-il** aimé son cadeau?
Did Luc like his gift?

Boîte à outils

Some verbs, like **aller**, **sortir**, and **tomber**, use **être** instead of **avoir** to form the **passé composé**. You will learn more about these verbs in **Leçon 7A**.

Vérifiez

Essayez! Indiquez les formes du passé composé des verbes.

1. j' _ai commencé, je n'ai pas servi_ (commencer, ne pas servir)
2. tu _____ (donner, finir) tu as donné, tu as fini
3. on _____ (parler, ne pas dormir) on a parlé, on n'a pas dormi
4. nous _____ (adorer, choisir) nous avons adoré, nous avons choisi
5. vous _____ (ne pas employer, grossir) vous n'avez pas employé, vous avez grossi
6. elles _____ (espérer, sentir) elles ont espéré, elles ont senti
7. je _____ (avoir, ne pas faire) j'ai été, je n'ai pas fait
8. tu _____ (être, boire) tu as été, tu as bu
9. il _____ (ne pas comprendre, courir) il n'a pas compris, il a couru

Reformulez ces phrases en questions.

1. Tu as payé 10 euros pour le gâteau. _Est-ce que tu as payé 10 euros pour le gâteau? As-tu payé 10 euros pour le gâteau?_
2. Il a oublié les boissons. Est-ce qu'il a oublié les boissons? A-t-il oublié les boissons?
3. Vous avez grossi. Est-ce que vous avez grossi? Avez-vous grossi?

Suggestions: Scaffolding
- Present the points on irregular past participles and **il a fallu** and **il y a eu**. Drill irregular verbs. Call out a subject and an infinitive, and have students give the conjugation. Have students complete the **Vérifiez** activity.
- Present the points on negation and asking questions. Write statements on the board and have students make them negative and convert them into questions. Examples: **Elle a fait ses devoirs. (Elle n'a pas fait ses devoirs. Est-ce qu'elle a fait ses devoirs? A-t-elle fait ses devoirs?)**
- Model and engage students in simple interchanges. Example: **J'ai bu du café ce matin. Avez-vous bu du café?**
- Have students complete **Essayez!** Suggest that students watch the Grammar Tutorial to review concepts for homework.

Essayez! For additional practice, have students create complete sentences orally or in writing using the subjects and verbs given.

EXPANSION

Pairs Working in pairs, have students tell each other two things they did last week, two things their best friend did, and two things they did together. Then have each student get together with another classmate and report what the first person told him or her.

EXPANSION

Small Groups Divide the class into groups of five. Give each group a list of verbs, including some with irregular past participles. The first student chooses a verb from the list and gives the **je** form. The second student gives the **tu** form, and so on. Students work their way down the list, alternating who chooses the verb.

1 Suggestion Before beginning the activity, review the past participles of the verbs in parentheses.

1 Expansion Ask follow-up questions about Laurent's weekend. Examples: **1. Qu'est-ce qu'ils ont mangé? 2. Qui a acheté une montre? 3. Qui a pris une glace à la terrasse d'un café? 4. Qu'est-ce que ses parents ont célébré? 5. Quand est-ce que Laurent et sa famille ont eu sommeil?**

2 Suggestion To check answers, have one student ask the question and call on another student to answer it. This activity can also be done in pairs.

3 Expansion For additional practice, give students these items. **9. parler à ses parents (Stéphane) 10. boire du café (toi et ton copain)**

3 Suggestion Before beginning this activity, call on volunteers to give the past participles of verbs listed.

Mise en pratique

1 Qu'est-ce qu'ils ont fait? Laurent parle de son week-end en ville avec sa famille. Complétez ses phrases avec le **passé composé** du verbe correct.

1. Nous _____avons mangé_____ (nager, manger) des escargots.
2. Papa _____a acheté_____ (acheter, apprendre) une nouvelle montre.
3. J' _____ai pris_____ (prendre, oublier) une glace à la terrasse d'un café.
4. Vous _____avez essayé_____ (enseigner, essayer) un nouveau restaurant.
5. Mes parents _____ont célébré_____ (dessiner, célébrer) leur anniversaire de mariage.
6. Ils _____ont fait_____ (fréquenter, faire) une promenade.
7. Ma sœur _____a bu_____ (boire, nettoyer) un chocolat chaud.
8. Le soir, nous _____avons eu_____ (écouter, avoir) sommeil.

2 Pas encore Un copain pose des questions pénibles. Écrivez ses questions puis donnez des réponses négatives.

MODÈLE

inviter vos amis (vous)
Vous avez déjà invité vos amis? Non, nous n'avons pas encore invité nos amis.

1. écouter mon CD (tu) — Tu as déjà écouté mon CD? Non, je n'ai pas encore écouté ton CD.
2. faire ses devoirs (Matthieu) — Matthieu a déjà fait ses devoirs? Non, il n'a pas encore fait ses devoirs.
3. courir dans le parc (elles) — Elles ont déjà couru dans le parc? Non, elles n'ont pas encore couru dans le parc.
4. parler aux profs (tu) — Tu as déjà parlé aux profs? Non, je n'ai pas encore parlé aux profs.
5. apprendre les verbes irréguliers (André) — André a déjà appris les verbes irréguliers? Non, il n'a pas encore appris les verbes irréguliers.
6. être à la piscine (Marie et Lise) — Marie et Lise ont déjà été à la piscine? Non, elles n'ont pas encore été à la piscine.
7. emmener Yassim au cinéma (vous) — Vous avez déjà emmené Yassim au cinéma? Non, nous n'avons pas encore emmené Yassim au cinéma.
8. avoir le temps d'étudier (tu) — Tu as déjà eu le temps d'étudier? Non, je n'ai pas encore eu le temps d'étudier.

Coup de main

Adverbs, such as **déjà**, **encore**, **bien**, **mal**, and **beaucoup** are placed between the auxiliary verb or **pas** and the past participle.

Tu as *déjà* mangé?
(Have you already eaten?)

Non, je n'ai pas *encore* mangé.
(No, I haven't eaten yet.)

3 La semaine Assemblez les éléments des colonnes pour expliquer ce que (*what*) tout le monde (*everyone*) a fait cette semaine. Answers will vary.

A	B	C
je	acheter	bonbons
Luc	apprendre	café
mon prof	boire	cartes
Sylvie	enseigner	l'espagnol
mes parents	étudier	famille
mes copains et moi	faire	foot
tu	jouer	glace
vous	manger	jogging
?	parler	les maths
	prendre	promenade
	regarder	vélo
	?	?

EXPANSION

Interviews Ask student pairs to prepare an interview about what they did yesterday. Encourage them to ask follow-up questions if possible, and to use affirmative and negative responses. Ask a few pairs to present their interviews to the class. Ex: **Élève 1: Qu'est-ce que tu as fait hier soir? Élève 2: J'ai fait mes devoirs de maths. Élève 1: Tu as déjà fait les devoirs d'anglais? Élève 2: Non, je n'ai pas encore fait les devoirs d'anglais.**

EXPANSION

Small Groups Have students work in small groups and talk about what they have already done/haven't done yet this school year. Encourage them to find similarities and differences among them. Once they have spoken for a few minutes, ask them to stop and share their responses with the whole class. Ex: **J'ai déjà acheté un nouvel ordinateur. Anne et moi, nous avons déjà visité le musée.**

Communication

4   L'été dernier Vous avez passé l'été dernier avec deux amis, mais vos souvenirs (*memories*) diffèrent. Par groupes de trois, utilisez les expressions de la liste et imaginez le dialogue.

Answers will vary.

MODÈLE

Élève 1: *Nous avons fait du cheval tous les matins.*
Élève 2: *Mais non! Moi, j'ai fait du cheval. Vous deux, vous avez fait du jogging.*
Élève 3: *Je n'ai pas fait de jogging. J'ai dormi!*

acheter	essayer	faire une promenade
courir	faire du cheval	jouer au foot
dormir	faire du jogging	jouer aux cartes
emmener	faire la fête	manger

5   Vendredi soir Vous et votre partenaire avez assisté à une fête vendredi soir. Parlez de la fête à tour de rôle. Qu'est-ce que les invités ont fait? Quelle a été l'occasion?   Answers will vary.

6   Qu'est-ce que tu as fait? Avec un(e) partenaire, posez-vous les questions à tour de rôle. Ensuite, présentez vos réponses à la classe.   Answers will vary.

1. As-tu fait la fête samedi dernier? Où? Avec qui?

2. Est-ce que tu as célébré une occasion importante cette année? Quelle occasion?

3. As-tu organisé une fête? Pour qui?

4. Qui est-ce que tu as invité à ta dernière fête?

5. Qu'est-ce que tu as fait pour fêter ton dernier anniversaire?

6. Est-ce que tu as préparé quelque chose à manger pour une fête ou un dîner? Quoi?

7   Ma fête Votre partenaire a organisé une fête le week-end dernier. Posez sept questions pour avoir plus de détails sur la fête. Ensuite, alternez les rôles.   Answers will vary.

MODÈLE

Élève 1: *Pour qui est-ce que tu as organisé la fête samedi dernier?*
Élève 2: *Pour ma sœur.*

4 Suggestion Have three volunteers read the **modèle** aloud. Encourage students to be creative.

5 Suggestion Before beginning the activity, have students describe what people are doing in the present tense.

6 Suggestion Tell students to jot down notes on their partner's responses and to add two of their own questions to the list.

6 Virtual Chat You can also assign Activity 6 on vhlcentral.com. Students record individual responses that appear in your gradebook.

7 Suggestion Have students brainstorm a list of questions before they begin the activity.

Activity Pack For additional activities, go to the Activity Pack in the Resources section of vhlcentral.com.

DIFFERENTIATION

For Kinesthetic Learners Working in groups of three, have students write three sentences in the **passé composé**, each with a different verb. After they have finished, have each group mime its sentences for the class. When someone guesses the mimed action, the group writes the sentence on the board.

EXPANSION

Extra Practice For homework, have students write a paragraph about what they did yesterday or last weekend. Then, in class, have them exchange papers with a classmate and peer edit each other's work.

Révision

1 L'année dernière et cette année Décrivez vos dernières fêtes de Thanksgiving à votre partenaire. Utilisez les verbes de la liste. Parlez aussi des projets (*plans*) de votre famille pour le prochain Thanksgiving. *Answers will vary.*

MODÈLE

Élève 1: *L'année dernière, nous avons fêté Thanksgiving chez mes grands-parents. Cette année, nous allons manger au restaurant.*

Élève 2: *Moi, j'ai fait la fête avec toute la famille l'année dernière. Cette année, nous allons visiter New York avec ma tante.*

aller	donner	fêter	préparer
acheter	dormir	manger	regarder
boire	faire	prendre	téléphoner

2 Ce musée, cette ville Faites une liste de cinq lieux (villes, musées, restaurants, etc.) que vous avez visités. Avec un(e) partenaire, comparez vos listes. Utilisez des adjectifs démonstratifs dans vos phrases. *Answers will vary.*

MODÈLE

Élève 1: *Ah, tu as visité Bruxelles. Moi aussi, j'ai visité cette ville. Elle est belle.*

Élève 2: *Tu as mangé au restaurant La Douce France. Je n'aime pas du tout ce restaurant!*

3 La fête Vous et votre partenaire avez préparé une fête avec vos amis. Vous avez acheté des cadeaux, des boissons et des snacks. À tour de rôle, parlez de ce qu'il y a sur l'illustration. *Answers will vary.*

MODÈLE

Élève 1: *J'aime bien ces biscuits-là.*

Élève 2: *Moi, j'ai apporté cette glace-ci.*

4 Enquête Qu'est-ce que vos camarades ont fait de différent dans leur vie? Votre professeur va vous donner une feuille d'activités. Parlez à vos camarades pour trouver une personne différente pour chaque expérience, puis écrivez son nom. *Answers will vary.*

MODÈLE

Élève 1: *As-tu déja parlé à une actrice?*

Élève 2: *Oui! Une fois, j'ai parlé à Jennifer Lawrence!*

Expérience	Noms
1. parler à un(e) acteur/actrice	Julien
2. passer une nuit entière sans dormir	
3. dépenser plus de $100 pour de la musique en une fois	
4. faire la fête un lundi soir	
5. courir cinq kilomètres ou plus	
6. faire une surprise à un(e) ami(e) pour son anniversaire	

5 Conversez Avec un(e) partenaire, imaginez une conversation entre deux ami(e)s qui ont mangé dans un restaurant le week-end dernier. À tour de rôle, racontez: *Answers will vary.*

- où ils ont mangé
- les thèmes de la conversation
- qui a parlé de quoi
- qui a payé
- la date du prochain dîner

6 Magali fait la fête Votre professeur va vous donner, à vous et à votre partenaire, deux feuilles d'activités différentes. Attention! Ne regardez pas la feuille de votre partenaire. *Answers will vary.*

MODÈLE

Élève 1: *Magali a parlé avec un homme. Cet homme n'a pas l'air intéressant du tout!*

Élève 2: *Après, ...*

Le Zapping

vhlcentral

AP® **Theme:** Contemporary Life
Context: Holidays and Celebrations

Préparation Répondez aux questions suivantes. *Answers will vary.*

1. Quelles fêtes célébrez-vous? Quelles fêtes sont les plus (*the most*) importantes dans votre famille ou votre communauté?

2. Comment sont ces célébrations? Décrivez les repas, la musique, les activités, les décorations et les vêtements qu'on porte.

Reportage de ResoNews

C'est du pain d'épices artisanal°.

Les marchés de Noël

Les marchés de Noël ont commencé en Europe centrale, dans des pays comme l'Allemagne, l'Autriche et la Suisse. En France on ne les trouvait qu'°en Alsace. Mais depuis° quelques années, ces marchés sont arrivés° dans d'autres régions ou villes, et en particulier, à Paris.

La ville a plusieurs marchés de Noël pendant les fêtes, mais celui° des Champs-Élysées est situé sur l'avenue la plus célèbre° de la capitale. Ses nombreux petits chalets° vendent toutes sortes de produits et de sa grande roue°, on a une belle vue panoramique de l'avenue.

artisanal *handcrafted* **ne les trouvait qu'** *only found them* **depuis** *since* **sont arrivés** *arrived* **celui** *the one* **la plus célèbre** *the most famous* **chalets** *cabins* **grande roue** *Ferris wheel*

Vocabulaire utile

le pain d'épices	*gingerbread*
de la présence	*people (in attendance)*
faible	*weak, underwhelming*
un conseil	*piece of advice*
un sapin de Noël	*Christmas tree*
un bilan	*assessment*
mitigé	*mixed*
la féerie	*wonder*

 Compréhension Répondez aux questions. *Answers will vary. Sample answers shown.*

1. Quels éléments dans la vidéo indiquent qu'on fête Noël?
le Père Noël, les cadeaux, les gateaux, les bonbons, les décorations, le temps (l'hiver), la neige
2. Quelles activités sont mentionnées ou filmées dans la vidéo?
le patinage, acheter des cadeaux, manger, monter dans la grande roue, faire de la photo
3. Qu'est-ce qu'on achète sur le marché de Noël des Champs-Élysées? du pain d'épices, un sapin, de la nourriture

 Conversation En petits groupes, répondez aux questions. *Answers will vary.*

1. Partagez vos réponses aux questions de **Préparation**. En quoi ces célébrations se ressemblent-elles? Comment sont-elles différentes?

2. Quels éléments du marché de Noël de la vidéo ressemblent-ils aux éléments d'une fête célébrée dans votre communauté? Décrivez les points communs et les différences.

 Application Préparez une présentation écrite ou orale dans laquelle (*in which*) vous décrivez et illustrez les activités, les objets et d'autres éléments d'une fête importante dans votre communauté ou votre tradition.

Section Goals

In this section, students will:
• read about Christmas markets
• watch a video about the Christmas market on the Champs-Élysées in Paris
• discuss different aspects of holidays

Key Standards

1.1, 1.2, 1.3, 2.1, 2.2, 3.2, 4.2, 5.2

Préparation Before beginning this activity, discuss with students the ways holiday experiences vary from person to person.

Les marchés de Noel Have students locate on a map the countries and regions mentioned in the reading. Ask: What do they think these areas have in common? Have students predict what they expect to see in the video based on the reading and photo.

Video Play the video once without sound and have students note the objects and activities they see. Play the video again with sound and have them listen for cognates and vocabulary from the chapter.

Conversation Have groups note their ideas in a chart to better compare information. Then have groups share their findings to create a class chart. What patterns do they see? Why do they think these patterns exist?

TELL Connection

Collaboration 3 *Why:* Communities support student engagement by respecting heritage. *What:* Research students' heritage background with administration; engage heritage students to share cultural products, practices, and perspectives on the topic.

PRE-AP®

Interpersonal Speaking Have students create a short questionnaire in French to find out about the holidays people celebrate and the traditions associated with those holidays. Suggest that they adapt questions from **Le Zapping** activities. Tell students to administer their questionnaire to students in other French classes at their school or in their area, French speakers in their community, or online. Have students present or publish their findings.

EXPANSION

Cultural Presentation Have students work with a partner to research a holiday from the Francophone world. Tell them to find out what the holiday celebrates, when it is celebrated, and any special traditions associated with it. Have students present their findings orally to the class, in a written report, or using technology or media.

Section Goals

In this section, students will learn and practice vocabulary related to:
• clothing and accessories
• shopping
• colors

Key Standards

1.1, 1.2, 4.1

Suggestions

• Use the digital image for this page. Point out clothing items in the store and describe what the people in the illustration are wearing. Examples: **Cette femme porte une robe. Ce tee-shirt est bon marché.**

• After presenting the new vocabulary, briefly describe what you and some of the students are wearing.

• Have students name one item of clothing they are wearing today. Then ask: **Qu'est-ce que _____ porte? De quelle couleur est _____?**

• Tell students that the word **taille** is used to talk about *clothing sizes*. **Pointure** refers to *shoe sizes*. To ask a person's size, they should say: **Quelle taille/pointure faites-vous?** To respond, they should say: **Je fais...**

• Point out the title of this lesson. Tell students that **chic** is an invariable adjective.

• Tell students that the verb **porter** means *to wear* or *to carry*. The verb **mettre** (*to put on*) is presented on page 253.

You will learn how to...
▪ describe clothing
▪ offer and accept gifts

🔊 **vhl**central

Très chic!

Vocabulaire

aller avec	to go with
un anorak	ski jacket, parka
une chaussette	sock
une chemise (à manches courtes/longues)	shirt (short-/long-sleeved)
un chemisier	blouse
un gant	glove
un jean	jeans
une jupe	skirt
un manteau	coat
un pantalon	pants
un pull	sweater
un sous-vêtement	underwear
une taille	clothing size
un tailleur	(woman's) suit; tailor
un tee-shirt	tee shirt
un vendeur/une vendeuse	salesman/saleswoman
des vêtements (m.)	clothing
De quelle couleur...?	In what color...?
des soldes (m.)	sales
chaque	each
large	loose; big
serré(e)	tight

un chapeau (chapeaux *pl.*)

un maillot de bain

cher (chère *f.*)

une cravate

une ceinture

une robe

un short

des baskets (*f.*)

un sac à main

Il porte un costume. (porter)

des chaussures (*f.*)

violet (violette *f.*)

rose

gris (grise *f.*)

vert (verte *f.*)

noir (noire *f.*)

jaune

orange

bleu (bleue *f.*)

marron

blanc (blanche *f.*)

rouge

TEACHING OPTIONS

Using Games Have students stand. Toss a beanbag to a student at random and say the name of a sport, place, or activity. The person has four seconds to name a clothing item or accessory that goes with it. That person then tosses the beanbag to another student and says a sport, place, or activity. Students who cannot think of an item in time or repeat an item that has already been mentioned are eliminated. The last person standing wins.

EXPANSION

Oral Practice Review the weather and seasons by asking students what they wear in various circumstances. Examples: **Que portez-vous quand il fait chaud/quand il fait frais/quand il neige/au printemps/en hiver?**

Mise en pratique

Les vêtements Choisissez le mot qui ne va pas avec les autres.

1. des baskets, [une cravate,] une chaussure
2. un jean, un pantalon, [une jupe]
3. un tailleur, un costume, [un short]
4. [des lunettes,] un chemisier, une chemise
5. [un tee-shirt,] un pull, un anorak
6. une casquette, [une ceinture,] un chapeau
7. un sous-vêtement, une chaussette, [un sac à main]
8. une jupe, une robe, [une écharpe]

2 **Écoutez** Guillaume prépare ses vacances d'hiver (*winter vacation*). Indiquez quels vêtements il va acheter pour son voyage.

	Oui	Non
1. des baskets	☑	☐
2. un maillot de bain	☐	☑
3. des chemises	☐	☑
4. un pantalon noir	☑	☐
5. un manteau	☑	☐
6. un anorak	☐	☑
7. un jean	☑	☐
8. un short	☐	☑
9. un pull	☐	☑
10. une robe	☐	☑

Guillaume

3 **De quelle couleur?** Indiquez de quelle(s) couleur(s) sont ces choses.

MODÈLE

l'océan
Il est bleu.
la statue de la Liberté
Elle est verte.

1. le drapeau français _Il est bleu, blanc et rouge._
2. les dollars américains _Ils sont verts._
3. les pommes (*apples*) _Answers will vary. Elles sont rouges, vertes ou jaunes._
4. le soleil _Il est jaune._
5. la nuit _Elle est noire._
6. le zèbre _Il est blanc et noir._
7. la neige _Elle est blanche._
8. les oranges _Elles sont orange._
9. le café _Il est marron ou noir._
10. les bananes _Elles sont jaunes._

Attention!

Note that the adjectives **orange** and **marron** are invariable; they do not vary in gender or number to match the noun they modify. J'aime l'anorak **orange**.

Il porte des chaussures **marron**.

des lunettes (de soleil) (*f.*)

une casquette

une écharpe

un blouson

bon marché

---

1 Expansion

- For additional practice, give students these items. **9. un sac à main, une ceinture, une robe (une robe) 10. un pull, un gant, un tee-shirt (un gant) 11. un pantalon, un blouson, un anorak (un pantalon) 12. des chaussettes, des baskets, un chapeau (un chapeau)**
- Have students create one or two additional items using at least three new vocabulary words in each one. Collect their papers and write some of the items on the board.

2 Script Bonjour! Je m'appelle Guillaume. Je vais aller en Suisse pour mes vacances d'hiver. J'ai besoin d'acheter un manteau parce qu'il va faire froid. J'ai déjà acheté un pull gris. J'ai aussi un bel anorak bleu qui est un peu vieux, mais chaud. Pour faire des randonnées, j'ai besoin d'un jean et de nouvelles baskets. Pour aller en boîte, je vais acheter un pantalon noir qui va aller avec toutes mes chemises: j'ai des chemises de toutes les couleurs, des chemises à manches longues, à manches courtes. Bien sûr, je ne vais pas avoir besoin d'un short parce qu'il ne va pas faire chaud. *Teacher Resources DVD*

2 Expansion Play the recording again. Ask students why Guillaume is not going to buy the items marked **Non**. Example: **Pourquoi Guillaume ne va-t-il pas acheter un maillot de bain? (parce qu'il va faire froid en Suisse)**

3 Expansion

- Point out items in the classroom and have students tell what color they are. Examples: **le tableau, ce sac à dos,** and **mon stylo**.
- Have students name items of various colors. Example: **Nommez** (*Name*) **quelque chose de rouge. (le chemisier de ____)**

DIFFERENTIATION

For Kinesthetic Learners Play a game of **Jacques a dit** (*Simon says*). Write **asseyez-vous** and **levez-vous** on the board and model them by sitting and standing as you say them. Start by saying: **Jacques a dit: Si vous portez un jean noir, levez-vous.** Students wearing black jeans stand up and remain standing until further instruction. Work through various items of clothing. Give instructions without saying **Jacques a dit…** once in a while.

TEACHING OPTIONS

Vacations Divide the class into small groups. Assign each group a season and a vacation destination. Have groups brainstorm a list of items to pack and write a brief explanation for each item. You might want to have groups write two lists, one for a girl and one for a boy.

4 Suggestion Tell students to write their descriptions. Then have volunteers write a description on the board for each picture.

4 Expansion Have students describe what they are wearing in detail, including accessories and colors of each item.

5 Suggestion Remind students to include greetings and other polite expressions in their role-plays. Have volunteers perform their role-plays for the rest of the class.

6 Expansion Take a quick class survey to find out students' clothing preferences. Tally the results on the board.

6 Virtual Chat You can also assign Activity 6 on vhlcentral.com. Students record individual responses that appear in your gradebook.

7 Suggestion Have a volunteer read the **modèle** aloud, and have students practice appropriate intonation for their oral descriptions before presenting to the class.

Activity Pack For additional activities, go to the Activity Pack in the Resources section of vhlcentral.com.

21ˢᵗ Century Skills

Technology Literacy
As a variant to Activity 7, ask students to prepare a digital presentation of their fashion show.

Communication

4 Qu'est-ce qu'ils portent? Avec un(e) camarade de classe, regardez les images et à tour de rôle, décrivez ce que les personnages portent. *Answers will vary.*

MODÈLE
Elle porte un maillot de bain rouge.

1.   2.   3.   4.

5 On fait du shopping Avec deux partenaires, préparez une conversation. Deux client(e)s et un vendeur/une vendeuse sont dans un grand magasin. Les client(e)s sont invité(e)s à un événement (*event*) très chic, mais ils ou elles n'ont pas envie de dépenser beaucoup d'argent. *Answers will vary.*

Client(e)s
- Décrivez l'événement auquel (*to which*) vous êtes invité(e)s.
- Parlez des vêtements que vous cherchez, de vos couleurs préférées, de votre taille. Trouvez-vous le vêtement trop large, trop serré, etc.?
- Demandez les prix et dites si vous trouvez que c'est cher, bon marché, etc.

Vendeur/Vendeuse
- Demandez les tailles, préférences, etc. des client(e)s.
- Répondez à toutes les questions de vos client(e)s.
- Suggérez des vêtements appropriés.

Coup de main
To compare French and American sizes, see the chart on p. 246.

6 Conversez Interviewez un(e) camarade de classe. *Answers will vary.*
1. Qu'est-ce que tu portes l'hiver? Et l'été?
2. Qu'est-ce que tu portes pour aller au lycée?
3. Qu'est-ce que tu portes pour aller à la plage (*beach*)?
4. Qu'est-ce que tu portes pour faire une randonnée?
5. Qu'est-ce que tu portes pour aller en ville?
6. Qu'est-ce que tu portes quand il pleut?
7. Quelle est ta couleur préférée? Pourquoi?
8. Qu'est-ce que tu portes pour aller dans un restaurant très élégant?
9. Où est-ce que tu achètes tes vêtements? Pourquoi?
10. Est-ce que tu prêtes (*lend*) tes vêtements à tes ami(e)s?

7 Défilé de mode Votre classe a organisé un défilé de mode (*fashion show*). Votre partenaire est mannequin (*model*) et vous représentez la marque (*brand*) de vêtements. Pendant que votre partenaire défile, vous décrivez à la classe les vêtements qu'il ou elle porte. Après, échangez les rôles. *Answers will vary.*

MODÈLE
Et voici la charmante Julie, qui porte les modèles de la dernière collection H&M®: une chemise à manches courtes et un pantalon noir, ensemble idéal pour sortir le soir. Ses chaussures blanches vont parfaitement avec l'ensemble. Cette collection H&M est très à la mode et très bon marché.

PRE-AP®

Presentational Writing Have students write a paragraph about a real or imaginary vacation they plan to take and the clothing they will take with them. Tell them to include what kind of weather they expect at their destination and any weather-specific clothing they will need. Ask volunteers to share their paragraphs with the class.

EXPANSION

Writing Practice Have students write descriptions of an article of clothing or a complete outfit that best describes them without indicating who they are. Collect the papers and read the descriptions aloud. The rest of the class has to guess who wrote each one.

Les sons et les lettres 🔊 vhlcentral

Open vs. closed vowels: Part 3

The letter combination **eu** can be pronounced two different ways, open and closed. Compare the pronunciation of the vowel sounds in these words.

che**veu**x	ne**veu**	h**eu**re	meill**eu**r

When **eu** is followed by a pronounced consonant, it has an open sound. The open **eu** sound does not exist in English. To pronounce it, say **è** with your lips only slightly rounded.

p**eu**r	j**eu**ne	chant**eu**r	b**eu**rre

The letter combination **œu** is usually pronounced with an open **eu** sound.

s**œu**r	b**œu**f	**œu**f	ch**œu**r

When **eu** is the last sound of a syllable, it has a closed vowel sound, similar to the vowel sound in the English word *full*. While this exact sound does not exist in English, you can make the closed **eu** sound by saying **é** with your lips rounded.

d**eu**x	bl**eu**	p**eu**	mi**eu**x

When **eu** is followed by a z sound, such as a single **s** between two vowels, it is usually pronounced with the closed **eu** sound.

chant**eu**se	génér**eu**se	séri**eu**se	curi**eu**se

Prononcez Répétez les mots suivants à voix haute.

1. leur
2. veuve
3. neuf
4. vieux
5. curieux
6. acteur
7. monsieur
8. coiffeuse
9. ordinateur
10. tailleur
11. vendeuse
12. couleur

Articulez Répétez les phrases suivantes à voix haute.

1. Le professeur Heudier a soixante-deux ans.
2. Est-ce que Matthieu est jeune ou vieux?
3. Monsieur Eustache est un chanteur fabuleux.
4. Eugène a les yeux bleus et les cheveux bruns.

Dictons Répétez les dictons à voix haute.

Qui vole un œuf, vole un bœuf.[1]

Les conseilleurs ne sont pas les payeurs.[2]

[2] Those who give advice are not the ones who pay the price.
[1] He who steals an egg would steal an ox.

Section Goals

In this section, students will learn about additional open and closed vowel sounds.

Key Standards

4.1

Suggestions

- Model the pronunciation of each open and closed vowel sound. Have students watch the shape of your mouth, then repeat each sound after you. Pronounce each of the example words and have students repeat them.
- Point out that the final r in **monsieur** is not pronounced, unlike in other words, such as **ordinateur** and **acteur**.
- Point out that the letters **o** and **e** together are usually written as the single character **œ**.
- Ask students to provide more examples of words from this lesson or previous lessons with these vowel sounds. Examples: **tailleur, vendeuse, ordinateur, feuille,** and **chanteuse.**
- Dictate five familiar words containing the open and closed vowels presented in this section to the class, repeating each one at least two times. Then write them on the board or on a transparency and have students check their spelling.

Dictons Ask students to explain the two sayings in their own words.

⏺ **TELL Connection**

Learning Tools 4 *Why:* Tracking and documenting student performance allows you to demonstrate their growth and encourage them to furhter growth. *What:* Use vhlcentral.com recording activities to benchmark student accuracy in replicating French words, phrases, and sentences. Use the teacher's and students' grading detail area to compare earlier recordings to later ones to mark growth.

EXPANSION

Mini-dictée Use these sentences with open and closed vowel sounds for additional practice or dictation. **1. Elle a deux ordinateurs neufs. 2. Ma sœur est jeune et sérieuse. 3. J'aime mieux être coiffeur ou ingénieur. 4. Tu veux ce vieux tailleur?**

EXPANSION

Tongue Twisters Teach students these French tongue-twisters that contain the open and closed vowel sounds on this page. **Pépé paie peu, mémé m'émeut. Je veux un feutre bleu.**

243

Section Goals

In this section, students will learn functional phrases for talking about clothing and gifts through comprehensible input.

Key Standards
1.2, 2.1, 2.2, 4.1, 4.2

Video Recap: Leçon 6A
Before doing this **Roman-photo**, review the previous one with this activity.

1. Qu'est-ce que Sandrine a préparé pour l'anniversaire de Stéphane? (les desserts: une mousse au chocolat, des biscuits et un gâteau)

2. Qu'est-ce que Rachid et Astrid ont acheté comme cadeaux? (une calculatrice, des livres et une montre)

3. Qui a fait la décoration au café? (Astrid, Valérie et Amina)

4. Qu'est-ce qu'Amina a apporté à la fête? (un cadeau et de la glace au chocolat)

Video Synopsis Stéphane arrives at his surprise party. Sandrine explains that David is in Paris with his parents. Sandrine admires Amina's outfit, and Stéphane opens his presents. Valérie gives him a leather jacket and gloves. When he opens the books and calculator from Rachid and Astrid, he tries to act pleased. Then he realizes they were gag gifts when he sees the watch.

Suggestions

- Have students read the title, glance at the video stills, and predict what the episode will be about. Record their predictions.
- Have students read the **Roman-photo** conversation in groups of six.
- Have students scan the captions for vocabulary related to clothing and colors.
- Review students' predictions and ask them which ones were correct.

L'anniversaire vhlcentral

AP® Theme: Contemporary Life
Context: Holidays and Celebrations

PERSONNAGES

Amina

Astrid

Rachid

Sandrine

Stéphane

Valérie

Au café...

VALÉRIE, SANDRINE, AMINA, ASTRID ET RACHID Surprise! Joyeux anniversaire, Stéphane!
STÉPHANE Alors là, je suis agréablement surpris!
VALÉRIE Bon anniversaire, mon chéri!
SANDRINE On a organisé cette surprise ensemble...

VALÉRIE Pas du tout! C'est Sandrine qui a presque tout préparé.
SANDRINE Oh, je n'ai fait que les desserts et ton gâteau d'anniversaire.
STÉPHANE Tu es un ange.
RACHID Bon anniversaire, Stéphane. Tu sais, à ton âge, il ne faut pas perdre son temps. Alors cette année, tu travailles sérieusement, c'est promis?
STÉPHANE Oui, oui.

AMINA Rachid a raison. Dix-huit ans, c'est une étape importante dans la vie! Il faut fêter ça.
ASTRID Joyeux anniversaire, Stéphane.
STÉPHANE Oh, et en plus, vous m'avez apporté des cadeaux!

AMINA Oui. J'ai tout fait moi-même: ce tee-shirt, cette jupe et j'ai acheté ces chaussures.
SANDRINE Tu es une véritable artiste, Amina! Ta jupe est très originale! J'adore!
AMINA J'ai une idée. Tu me prêtes ta robe grise samedi et je te prête ma jupe. D'accord?
SANDRINE Bonne idée!

STÉPHANE Eh! C'est super cool, ce blouson en cuir noir. Avec des gants en plus! Merci, maman!
AMINA Ces gants vont très bien avec le blouson! Très à la mode!
STÉPHANE Tu trouves?

RACHID Tiens, Stéphane.
STÉPHANE Mais qu'est-ce que c'est? Des livres?
RACHID Oui, la littérature, c'est important pour la culture générale!
VALÉRIE Tu as raison, Rachid.
STÉPHANE Euh oui... euh... c'est gentil... euh... merci, Rachid.

A C T I V I T É S

1 Vrai ou faux? Indiquez si ces affirmations sont **vraies** ou **fausses**.

1. David ne veut pas (*doesn't want*) aller à la fête.
Faux.
2. Sandrine porte une jupe bleue.
Faux.
3. Amina a fait sa jupe elle-même (*herself*).
Vrai.
4. Le tee-shirt d'Amina est en soie.
Vrai.
5. Valérie donne un blouson en cuir et une ceinture à Stéphane.
Faux.

6. Sandrine n'aime pas partager ses vêtements.
Faux.
7. Pour Amina, 18 ans, c'est une étape importante.
Vrai.
8. Sandrine n'a rien fait (*didn't do anything*) pour la fête.
Faux.
9. Rachid donne des livres de littérature à Stéphane.
Vrai.
10. Stéphane pense que ses amis sont drôles.
Faux.

244 *deux cent quarante-quatre*

TEACHING OPTIONS

L'anniversaire Before viewing the video, have students work in pairs and make a list of words and expressions they might hear at a surprise birthday party.

TEACHING OPTIONS

Regarder la vidéo Show the video episode and tell students to check off the words or expressions they hear on their lists. Then show the episode again and have students give you a play-by-play description of the action. Write their descriptions on the board.

Les amis fêtent l'anniversaire de Stéphane.

SANDRINE Ah au fait, David est désolé de ne pas être là. Ce week-end, il visite Paris avec ses parents. Mais il pense à toi.
STÉPHANE Je comprends tout à fait. Les parents de David sont de Washington, n'est-ce pas?
SANDRINE Oui, c'est ça.

AMINA Merci, Sandrine. Je trouve que tu es très élégante dans cette robe grise! La couleur te va très bien.
SANDRINE Vraiment? Et toi, tu es très chic. C'est du coton?
AMINA Non, de la soie.
SANDRINE Cet ensemble, c'est une de tes créations, n'est-ce pas?

STÉPHANE Une calculatrice rose... pour moi?
ASTRID Oui, c'est pour t'aider à répondre à toutes les questions en maths, et avec le sourire.
STÉPHANE Euh, merci beaucoup! C'est très... utile.
ASTRID Attends! Il y a encore un cadeau pour toi...

STÉPHANE Ouah, cette montre est géniale, merci!
ASTRID Tu as aimé notre petite blague? Nous, on a bien ri.
RACHID Eh Stéphane! Tu as vraiment aimé tes livres et ta calculatrice?
STÉPHANE Ouais, vous deux, ce que vous êtes drôles.

Expressions utiles

Talking about your clothes

- **Et toi, tu es très chic. C'est du coton/de la soie?**
  And you, you are very chic. Is it cotton/silk?
- **J'ai tout fait moi-même.**
  I did/made everything myself.
- **La couleur te va très bien.**
  The color suits you well.
- **Tu es une véritable artiste! Ta jupe est très originale!**
  You are a true artist! Your skirt is very original!
- **Tu me prêtes ta robe grise samedi et je te prête ma jupe.**
  You lend me your gray dress Saturday and I'll lend you my skirt.
- **C'est super cool, ce blouson en cuir/laine/velours noir(e). Avec des gants en plus!**
  It's really cool, this black leather/wool/velvet jacket. With gloves as well!

Additional vocabulary

- **Vous m'avez apporté des cadeaux!**
  You brought me gifts!
- **Tu sais, à ton âge, il ne faut pas perdre son temps.**
  You know, at your age, one should not waste time.
- **C'est pour t'aider à répondre à toutes les questions en maths, et avec le sourire.**
  It's to help you answer all the questions in math, with a smile.
- **agréablement surpris(e)** — *pleasantly surprised*
- **véritable** — *true, genuine*
- **C'est promis?** — *Promise?*
- **Pour moi?** — *For me?*
- **Il pense à toi.** — *He's thinking of you.*
- **Attends!** — *Wait!*
- **tout à fait** — *absolutely*
- **On a bien ri.** — *We had a good laugh.*
- **Vraiment?** — *Really?*

---

2 Identifiez Indiquez qui a dit (*said*) ces phrases: Amina (**A**), Astrid (**As**), Rachid (**R**), Sandrine (**S**), Stéphane (**St**) ou Valérie (**V**).

- **S** 1. Tu es une véritable artiste.
- **As** 2. On a bien ri.
- **A** 3. Très à la mode.
- **St** 4. Je comprends tout à fait.
- **V** 5. C'est Sandrine qui a presque tout préparé.
- **R** 6. C'est promis?

3 À vous! Ce sont les soldes. Sandrine, David et Amina vont dans un magasin pour acheter des vêtements. Ils essaient différentes choses, donnent leur avis (*opinion*) et parlent de leurs préférences, des prix et des matières (*fabrics*). Avec un(e) partenaire, écrivez la conversation et jouez la scène devant la classe.

ACTIVITÉS

Expressions utiles

- Model the pronunciation of the **Expressions utiles** and have students repeat them.
- As you work through the list, point out expressions with indirect object pronouns, disjunctive pronouns, and **-re** verbs. Tell students that these grammar structures will be formally presented in **Structures**.
- Respond briefly to questions about indirect object pronouns and **-re** verbs. Reinforce correct forms, but do not expect students to produce them consistently at this time.
- Point out that the pronouns **tu**, **te**, and **toi** all mean *you*, but they cannot be used interchangeably because they are different parts of speech.
- To practice different fabrics and other materials, ask students yes/no and either/or questions about their clothing. Examples: ____, **votre chemisier, c'est du coton ou de la soie?** ____, **votre blouson, c'est du cuir ou de la laine? Avez-vous des gants en cuir noir?**

1 Expansion Have students write corrections for false statements on the board.

1 Expansion For additional practice, give students these items. **11. Stéphane n'est pas content de la fête. (Faux.) 12. David est à Paris avec ses parents. (Vrai.) 13. Sandrine aime bien la jupe d'Amina. (Vrai.) 14. Stéphane n'aime pas la montre. (Faux.)**

2 Expansion In addition to identifying the speaker, have students give the name of the person to whom each one is speaking. **1. Amina 2. Stéphane 3. Stéphane 4. Sandrine 5. Stéphane 6. Stéphane**

3 Suggestion Tell students to use an idea map or outline to plan their conversation before they begin to write it.

TEACHING OPTIONS

Using Games Divide the class into two teams. Give one team member a card with the name of an item of clothing or an accessory. This person has 30 seconds to draw the item and one player on his or her team has to guess what it is. Give a point for each correct answer. If a player cannot guess the item within the time limit, the next player on the opposing team may "steal" the point.

EXPANSION

Magazines Bring in photos from French fashion magazines or catalogues, such as **3 Suisses** or **La Redoute**, and have students give their opinions about the clothing and accessories.

Section Goals

In this section, students will:
- learn about fashion in France and where to buy clothes
- learn terms related to fashion
- read about traditional clothing and fabrics in some Francophone regions
- read about Coco Chanel

Key Standards

2.1, 2.2, 3.1, 3.2, 4.2

21st Century Skills

Global Awareness
Students will gain perspectives on the Francophone world to develop respect and openness toward others and to interact appropriately and effectively with citizens of Francophone cultures.

Culture à la loupe

Avant la lecture Have students read the title, look at the photo, and predict what this reading is about. Then ask them to share any information they know about fashion in France.

Lecture
- Point out the **Coup de main** and have students compare the clothing sizes. Example: **Si une femme porte la taille 8 aux États-Unis, quelle taille porte-t-elle en France? (38)**
- Explain that a **hypermarché** is similar to a Wal-Mart or Target in the United States.

Après la lecture Ask students: **Où les Français achètent-ils leurs vêtements? (dans les boutiques indépendantes, dans les chaînes françaises et américaines, dans les hypermarchés et dans les centres commerciaux)**

1 **Suggestion** Have students work in pairs to correct the false statements. Discuss them with the class.

AP® Theme: Beauty and Aesthetics
Context: Ideals of Beauty

vhlcentral | CULTURE À LA LOUPE

La mode° en France

Pour la majorité des Français, la mode est un moyen° d'expression. Les jeunes adorent les marques°, surtout les marques américaines. Avoir un *hoody* de style américain est considéré comme à la mode. C'est pareil° pour les chaussures. Bien sûr, les styles varient beaucoup. Il y a le style BCBG (bon chic bon genre), par exemple, plus classique avec la prédominance de la couleur bleu marine°. Il y a aussi le style «baba cool», c'est-à-dire° *hippie*.

Les marques coûtent cher, mais en France il y a encore beaucoup de boutiques indépendantes où les vêtements sont bon marché. Souvent les vendeurs et les vendeuses sont aussi propriétaires° du magasin. Ils encouragent plus les clients à acheter. Mais il y a aussi beaucoup de chaînes françaises comme Lacoste, Promod et Camaïeu. Et les chaînes américaines sont de plus en plus présentes dans les villes. Les Français achètent aussi des vêtements dans les hypermarchés°, comme Monoprix, Auchan ou Carrefour, et dans les centres commerciaux.

L'anthropologue américain Lawrence Wylie a écrit° sur les différences entre les vêtements français et américains. Les Américains portent des vêtements plus amples et plus confortables. Pour les Français, l'aspect esthétique est plus important que le confort. Les femmes mettent des baskets uniquement pour faire du sport. Les costumes français sont plus serrés et plus près du corps° et les épaules° sont en général plus étroites°.

Coup de main

Comparaison des tailles°

FEMMES						
France	32	34	36	38	40	42
USA	2	4	6	8	10	12

HOMMES (PANTALONS)						
France	36	38	40	42	44	46
USA	26	28	30	32	34	36

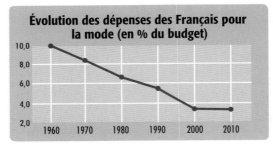

Évolution des dépenses des Français pour la mode (en % du budget)

(1960: 10,0; 1970: ~8,5; 1980: ~6,5; 1990: ~5,5; 2000: ~3,5; 2010: ~3,5)

La mode *Fashion* **moyen** *means* **marques** *brand names* **pareil** *the same* **marine** *navy* **c'est-à-dire** *in other words* **propriétaires** *owners* **hypermarchés** *large supermarkets* **a écrit** *wrote* **corps** *body* **épaules** *shoulders* **étroites** *narrow* **tailles** *sizes*

ACTIVITÉS

1 **Vrai ou faux?** Indiquez si les phrases sont **vraies** ou **fausses**.

1. Pour beaucoup de Français, la mode est un moyen d'expression. Vrai.
2. Un *hoody* de style américain est considéré comme du mauvais goût (*taste*) par les jeunes. Faux.
3. La couleur bleu marine prédomine dans le style BCBG. Vrai.
4. En France les boutiques indépendantes sont rares. Faux.

5. Les vendeurs et les vendeuses des boutiques indépendantes sont souvent aussi propriétaires. Vrai.
6. Lacoste, Promod et Camaïeu sont des chaînes françaises. Vrai.
7. Il est possible d'acheter des vêtements dans les hypermarchés. Vrai.
8. Lawrence Wylie a écrit sur la mode italienne. Faux.
9. Les Français portent des vêtements plus amples et plus confortables. Faux.
10. Les costumes français sont très larges. Faux.

EXPANSION

Cultural Comparison Have students work in groups of three and compare where French people and Americans shop for clothing. Tell them to list the similarities and differences in a two-column chart under the headings **Similitudes** and **Différences**. After they complete their charts, have two groups get together and compare their lists.

DIFFERENTIATION

For Visual Learners First, ask students what information the graph **Évolution des dépenses des Français pour la mode** shows. (The percentage of total budget that the French spent on fashion from 1960–2010.) Then ask: **Quel pourcentage de leur budget les Français ont-ils dépensé pour la mode en 1960? (10,0%) Et en 1980, ils ont dépensé plus ou moins? (moins).**

LE FRANÇAIS QUOTIDIEN

Les vêtements et la mode

fringues (f.)	clothes
look (m.)	style
vintage (m.)	vintage clothing
BCBG (bon chic bon genre)	chic and preppy
ringard(e)	out-of-style
être bien/ mal sapé(e)	to be well/ badly dressed
être sur son 31	to be well dressed

LE MONDE FRANCOPHONE

Vêtements et tissus

Voici quelques vêtements et tissus° traditionnels du monde francophone.

En Afrique centrale et de l'Ouest
Le boubou tunique plus ou moins° longue et souvent très colorée
Les batiks tissus traditionnels très colorés

En Afrique du Nord
La djellaba longue tunique à capuche°
Le kaftan sorte de djellaba portée à la maison

À la Martinique
Le madras tissu typique aux couleurs vives

À Tahiti
Le paréo morceau° de tissu attaché au-dessus de la poitrine° ou à la taille°

tissus fabrics **plus ou moins** more or less **à capuche** hooded **morceau** piece **poitrine** chest **taille** waist

---

PORTRAIT

AP® Theme: Beauty and Aesthetics   **Context:** Ideals of Beauty

Coco Chanel, styliste° parisienne

«La mode se démode°, le style jamais.»
—Coco Chanel

Coco Chanel (1883–1971) est considérée comme l'icône du parfum et de la mode du vingtième siècle°. Dans les années 1910, elle a l'idée audacieuse° d'intégrer la mode «à la garçonne» dans ses créations: les lignes féminines empruntent aux° éléments de la mode masculine. C'est la naissance du fameux tailleur Chanel. Pour «Mademoiselle Chanel», l'important dans la mode, c'est que les vêtements permettent de bouger°; ils doivent° être simples et confortables. Son invention de «la petite robe noire» illustre l'esprit° classique et élégant de ses collections. De nombreuses célébrités ont immortalisé le nom de Chanel: Jacqueline Kennedy avec le tailleur et Marilyn Monroe avec le parfum No. 5, par exemple.

styliste designer **vingtième siècle** twentieth century **idée audacieuse** daring idea **empruntent aux** borrow from **bouger** move **doivent** have to **esprit** spirit

AP® Theme: Beauty and Aesthetics   **Context:** Ideals of Beauty

Sur Internet

Combien de couturiers présentent leurs collections dans les défilés de mode, à Paris, chaque hiver?

Go to **vhlcentral.com** to find more information related to this **Culture** section.

---

2 **Coco Chanel** Complétez les phrases.

1. Coco Chanel était (*was*) _styliste de mode_.
2. Le style Chanel est inspiré de _la mode masculine_.
3. Les vêtements Chanel sont _simples et confortables_.
4. Jacqueline Kennedy portait souvent des _tailleurs_ Chanel.
5. D'après «Mademoiselle Chanel», il est très important de pouvoir (*to be able to*) _bouger_ dans ses vêtements.
6. C'est Coco Chanel qui a inventé _la petite robe noire_.

3 **Le «relookage»** Vous êtes conseiller/conseillère en image (*image counselors*), spécialisé(e) dans le «relookage». Votre nouveau (nouvelle) client(e), une célébrité, vous demande de l'aider à sélectionner un nouveau style. Discutez de ce nouveau look avec un(e) partenaire.

A C T I V I T É S

Le français quotidien
- Model the pronunciation of each term and have students repeat it.
- Ask students to give some examples of vintage clothing.
- Have volunteers create sentences using these words.

Portrait
- Have students look at the photo of Coco Chanel and describe her appearance and clothing.
- Tell students that **la petite robe noire** is a simple black evening dress that many consider to be an essential item in a woman's wardrobe.

Le monde francophone
- Bring in photos from magazines or the Internet of people wearing these types of clothing and fabrics to show the class.
- Ask a few content questions based on the reading. Examples: **1. Comment s'appelle la tunique que les gens portent en Afrique centrale? (le boubou) 2. On porte le kaftan en ville ou à la masion? (à la maison) 3. À la Martinique, on porte des vêtements faits de batik ou de madras? (des vêtements faits de madras) 4. Où porte-t-on le kaftan? (en Afrique du Nord)**

2 **Expansion** For additional practice, give students these items. **7. Les collections de Chanel sont classiques et ____. (élégantes) 8. Marilyn Monroe a immortalisé ____ de Chanel. (le parfum No. 5)**

3 **Suggestions** Have students write their descriptions and read them aloud for the class.

21st Century Skills

Information and Media Literacy: Sur Internet
Students access and critically evaluate information from the Internet.

EXPANSION

Vêtements et tissus Have students create five true/false statements based on the content in **Le monde francophone**. Then have students get together with a classmate and take turns reading their statements and responding **vrai** or **faux**.

EXPANSION

Les couturiers Have students research one of the **couturiers** from the **Sur Internet** activity and write a short paragraph about the person. Tell them to include information about the person's accomplishments, type(s) of clothing he or she designs, where it is sold, and any other important details.

6B.1

Indirect object pronouns **vhl**central

Point de départ An indirect object expresses *to whom* or *for whom* an action is done. It is always a person or animal and preceded by the preposition **à** in French. In the example below, the indirect object answers this question: **À qui parle Gisèle?** (*To whom does Gisèle speak?*)

SUBJECT	VERB	INDIRECT OBJECT NOUN
Gisèle	**parle**	**à sa mère.**
Gisèle	*speaks*	*to her mother.*

- Indirect object pronouns replace indirect object nouns and the prepositions that precede them.

Indirect object pronouns			
me	*to/for me*	nous	*to/for us*
te	*to/for you*	vous	*to/for you*
lui	*to/for him/her*	leur	*to/for them*

Gisèle parle **à sa mère**.
Gisèle speaks to her mother.

J'envoie des cadeaux **à mes nièces**.
I send gifts to my nieces.

Gisèle **lui** parle.
Gisèle speaks to her.

Je **leur** envoie des cadeaux.
I send them gifts.

Vous m'avez apporté des cadeaux!

Je te prête ma jupe. D'accord?

- The indirect object pronoun usually precedes the conjugated verb.

Antoine, je **te** parle.
Antoine, I'm talking to you.

Notre père **nous** a envoyé un e-mail.
Our father sent us an e-mail.

- In a negative statement, place the indirect object pronoun between **ne** and the conjugated verb.

Antoine, je ne **te** parle pas de ça.
Antoine, I'm not talking to you about that.

Notre père ne **nous** a pas envoyé d'e-mail.
Our father didn't send us an e-mail.

- When an infinitive follows a conjugated verb, the indirect object pronoun precedes the infinitive.

Nous allons **lui** donner une cravate.
We're going to give him a tie.

Il ne va pas **vous** prêter le costume.
He's not going to lend you the suit.

- In the **passé composé**, the indirect object pronoun comes before the auxiliary verb **avoir**.

Tu **lui** as parlé?
Did you speak to her?

Non, je ne **lui** ai pas parlé.
No, I didn't speak to her.

> **Boîte à outils**
>
> When asking a question using inversion, follow the same rules outlined on this page for the placement of the indirect object pronoun.
>
> **Lui parles-tu?**
>
> **Lui as-tu parlé?**
>
> **Vas-tu lui parler?**

Section Goals

In this section, students will learn:
- indirect object pronouns
- some additional uses of disjunctive pronouns

Key Standards

4.1, 5.1

Note Direct object pronouns are presented after indirect object pronouns in **Leçon 7A** so that students will already be familiar with the forms the two types of object pronouns share in common (**me**, **te**, **nous**, **vous**). They therefore will be able to focus on the new third-person forms (**le**, **la**, **l'**, **les**). Moreover, past participle agreement with preceding direct object pronouns is a difficult concept for many students and could pose a distraction while they are still learning about the **passé composé**.

Suggestions: Scaffolding
- Present **Point de départ**. Then write on the board: **Valérie achète un blouson à Stéphane.** Ask students to indicate the indirect object of the verb. (**Stéphane**) Point out that **un blouson** is the direct object of the verb.
- Present the indirect object pronouns and their placement rules, using the bullet points on p. 248. Point out in the presentation examples how the indirect object pronoun in French precedes the verb while in English it follows the verb. Then do the Expansion: Extra Practice activities.
- Practice asking questions by having students convert the examples on p. 248 into questions using **est-ce que** and inversion.

EXPANSION

Extra Practice Write the indirect object pronouns on the board. Show students some photos and say: **Je vous montre mes photos.** Give a student an object, such as a book, and say: **Je vous prête mon livre.** Continue the same procedure with the remaining indirect object pronouns.

EXPANSION

Extra Practice Write sentences with indirect objects on the board. Examples: **Anne-Laure ne te donne pas de biscuits. Pierre ne me parle pas. Loïc prête de l'argent à Louise. Marie nous pose une question. Je téléphone à mes amis.** Have students come to the board and circle the indirect objects.

- The indirect object pronouns **me** and **te** become **m'** and **t'** before a verb beginning with a vowel sound.

Ton petit ami **t'**envoie des e-mails.
Your boyfriend sends you e-mails.

Isabelle **m'**a prêté son sac à main.
Isabelle lent me her handbag.

M'a-t-il acheté ce pull?
Did he buy me this sweater?

Elles ne **t'**ont pas téléphoné hier?
Didn't they call you yesterday?

Verbs used with indirect object pronouns

demander à	*to ask, to request*	**parler à**	*to speak/talk to*
donner à	*to give to*	**poser une question à**	*to pose/ask a question (to)*
envoyer à	*to send to*	**prêter à**	*to lend to*
montrer à	*to show to*	**téléphoner à**	*to phone, to call*

Disjunctive pronouns

- Disjunctive pronouns can be used alone or in phrases without a verb.

Qui prend du café?
Who's having coffee?

Moi!
Me!

Eux aussi?
Them, too?

- Disjunctive pronouns emphasize the person to whom they refer.

Moi, je porte souvent une casquette.
Me, I often wear a cap.

Mon frère, **lui**, il déteste les casquettes.
My brother, he hates caps.

- To say *myself, ourselves,* etc., add **-même(s)** after the disjunctive pronoun.

Tu fais ça **toi-même**?
Are you doing that yourself?

Ils organisent la fête **eux-mêmes**.
They're planning the party themselves.

- Some French verbs and expressions use a stressed pronoun instead of an indirect object pronoun to replace people or animals that follow the preposition **à**. One such expression is **penser à**.

Il **pense** souvent **à** ses grands-parents, n'est-ce pas?
He often thinks about his grandparents, doesn't he?

Oui, il **pense** souvent **à** eux.
DISJUNCTIVE PRONOUN
Yes, he often thinks about them.

Vérifiez

Boîte à outils

The following are disjunctive pronouns, which can be used alone or after a preposition:

moi *me*		**nous** *us*	
toi *you*		**vous** *you*	
lui *him*		**eux** *them*	
elle *her*		**elles** *them*	

Vérifiez

Essayez!   Complétez les phrases avec le pronom d'objet indirect approprié.

1. Tu ___*nous*___ montres tes photos? (*us*)
2. Luc, je ___*te*___ donne ma nouvelle adresse. (*you, fam.*)
3. Vous ___*me*___ posez de bonnes questions. (*me*)
4. Nous ___*leur*___ avons demandé. (*them*)
5. On ___*vous*___ achète une nouvelle robe. (*you, form.*)
6. Ses parents ___*lui*___ ont acheté un tailleur. (*her*)
7. Je vais ___*lui*___ téléphoner à dix heures. (*him*)
8. Elle va ___*me*___ prêter sa jupe. (*me*)
9. Je ___*vous*___ envoie des vêtements. (*you, plural*)
10. Est-ce que tu ___*leur*___ as apporté ces chaussures? (*them*)
11. Il ne ___*te*___ donne pas son anorak? (*you, fam.*)
12. Nous ne ___*leur*___ parlons pas! (*them*)

Suggestions: Scaffolding
- Present elision rules with **me** and **te**, and verbs that use indirect objects. Have students complete **Vérifiez**.
- Go over the disjunctive pronouns. Explain the use of **-même(s)** and provide a few examples. Then have students create some sentences with the disjunctive pronouns.
- Tell students that there are relatively few expressions followed by **à** plus a person or animal that use the disjunctive pronoun instead of the indirect object pronoun. Encourage students to keep a running list as they come across them.
- Have students complete the **Vérifiez** activity.
- Have students complete **Essayez!**, then follow the suggestion below. For students who still struggle to grasp the concepts, have them watch the Grammar Tutorial and repeat the **Vérifiez** and **Essayez!** activities.

Essayez! Have students restate items 1, 2, 4, 5, 6, 9, 10, 11 and 12 using the **futur proche**. Example:
1. Tu vas nous montrer tes photos?

TEACHING OPTIONS

Extra Practice Have students write six sentences containing indirect objects on a sheet of paper. Ask them to exchange sheets with another student, who should rewrite the sentences replacing the indirect objects with pronouns. Ask volunteers to go to the board and write the two versions (with/without pronouns) of some of their sentences.

EXPANSION

Small Groups Working in groups of three, the first student lends an object to the second and says: **Je te prête mon/ma…**. The second student responds: **Tu me prêtes ton/ta…**. The third student says: **Marc lui prête son/sa…**. Groups repeat the process until everyone has begun the chain twice. To practice plural pronouns, have two groups get together. Then two students lend something to two other students.

249

Mise en pratique

1 **Complétez** Corinne fait du shopping avec sa copine Célia. Trouvez le bon pronom d'objet indirect ou disjonctif pour compléter ses phrases.

1. Je __leur__ achète des baskets. (à mes cousins)
2. Je __te__ prends une ceinture. (à toi, Célia)
3. Nous __lui__ achetons une jupe. (à notre copine Christelle)
4. Célia __nous__ prend des lunettes de soleil. (à ma mère et à moi)
5. Je __vous__ achète des gants. (à ta mère et à toi, Célia)
6. Célia __m'__ achète un pantalon. (à moi)
7. Et, c'est l'annversaire de Magalie demain. Tu penses à __elle__, j'espère! (à Magalie)

2 **Dialogues** Complétez les dialogues.

1. **M. SAUNIER** Tu m'as posé une question, chérie?
   MME SAUNIER Oui. Je __t'__ ai demandé l'heure.
2. **CLIENT** Je cherche un beau pull.
   VENDEUSE Je vais __vous__ montrer ce pull noir.
3. **VALÉRIE** Tu as l'air triste. Tu penses à ton petit ami?
   MÉGHANE Oui, je pense à __lui__.
4. **PROF 1** Mes étudiants ont passé l'examen.
   PROF 2 Tu __leur__ envoies les résultats?
5. **MÈRE** Qu'est-ce que vous allez faire?
   ENFANTS On va aller au cinéma. Tu __nous__ donnes de l'argent?
6. **PIERRE** Tu __me__ téléphones ce soir?
   CHARLOTTE D'accord. Je te téléphone.
7. **GÉRARD** Christophe a oublié son pull. Il a froid!
   VALENTIN Je __lui__ prête mon blouson.
8. **MÈRE** Tu ne penses pas à Théo et Sophie?
   PÈRE Mais si, je pense souvent à __eux__.

3 **Assemblez** Avec un(e) partenaire, assemblez les éléments pour comparer vos familles et vos amis. Answers will vary.

MODÈLE

Élève 1: *Mon père me prête souvent ses pulls.*
Élève 2: *Mon père, lui, il nous prête de l'argent.*

A	B	C
je	acheter	argent
tu	apporter	biscuits
mon père	envoyer	cadeaux
ma mère	expliquer	devoirs
mon frère	faire	e-mails
ma sœur	montrer	problèmes
mon/ma meilleur(e) ami(e)	parler	vêtements
mes copains	payer	vélo
?	prêter	?
	?	

Communication

4 Qu'allez-vous faire? Avec un(e) partenaire, dites ce que vous allez faire dans ces situations. Employez les verbes de la liste et présentez vos réponses à la classe. Answers will vary.

MODÈLE

Un ami a soif.
On va lui donner de l'eau.

acheter	montrer
apporter	parler
demander	poser des questions
donner	préparer
envoyer	prêter
faire	téléphoner

1. Une personne âgée a froid.
2. Des touristes sont perdus (*lost*).
3. Un homme est sans abri (*homeless*).
4. Votre tante est à l'hôpital.
5. Vos cousins vous invitent à manger chez eux.
6. Votre chien a faim.
7. Un(e) ami(e) fête son anniversaire.
8. Votre meilleur(e) (*best*) ami(e) a des problèmes.
9. Vous ne comprenez pas le prof.
10. Vos parents voyagent en France pendant (*for*) un mois.

5 Les cadeaux de l'année dernière Par groupes de trois, parlez des cadeaux que vous avez achetés à votre famille et à vos amis l'année dernière. Que vous ont-ils acheté? Présentez vos réponses à la classe. Answers will vary.

MODÈLE

Élève 1: *Qu'est-ce que tu as acheté à ta mère?*
Élève 2: *Je lui ai acheté un ordinateur.*
Élève 3: *Ma copine Dominique m'a donné une montre.*

6 Au grand magasin Par groupes de trois, jouez les rôles de deux client(e)s et d'un(e) vendeur/vendeuse. Les client(e)s cherchent des vêtements pour faire des cadeaux. Ils parlent de ce qu'ils (*what they*) cherchent et le/la vendeur/vendeuse leur fait des suggestions.

Answers will vary.

4 Suggestion Have pairs write their suggestions. Encourage them to come up with multiple responses for each item.

4 Virtual Chat You can also assign Activity 4 on vhlcentral.com. Students record individual responses that appear in your gradebook.

5 Suggestion Before students begin the activity, have them make a list of gifts they gave to family members and friends, and vice versa. Then have three volunteers read the **modèle** aloud.

6 Suggestions
• Before beginning the activity, have students describe what is happening in the photo.
• Videotape the scenes in class or have students videotape themselves outside of class. Show the videos so students can critique their role-plays.

Activity Pack For additional activities, go to the Activity Pack in the Resources section of vhlcentral.com.

EXPANSION

Video Have students read along as you show the video episode again. Tell them to note each time an indirect object pronoun or a disjunctive pronoun is used. After the video, ask them to read the sentences they identified and to say to whom each pronoun refers.

EXPANSION

Pairs Have students work in pairs. Tell them to write five questions they would like to ask their partner that require an indirect object pronoun in the answer. They should then take turns asking and answering each other's questions.

Section Goals

In this section, students will learn:
- regular **-re** verbs
- irregular **-re** verbs

Key Standards

4.1, 5.1

Suggestions: Scaffolding
- Present **Point de départ** and the first three bullets. Have students find the pattern for forming **-re** verbs.
- Model the pronunciation of the **-re** verbs and have students repeat. Go through all forms for each verb. Do the Extra Practice on TE p. 252.
- Talk about yourself and ask students follow-up questions. Examples: **Je réponds à tous mes e-mails. Et vous, répondez-vous à tous vos e-mails? Je rends visite à ma grand-mère le week-end. Rendez-vous visite à vos grands-parents le week-end?**
- Explain that the past participles of regular **-re** verbs add **-u** to the stem. Example: **attendre: attendu.** Then say the verbs listed and have students respond with the corresponding past participles.
- Repeat questions used earlier in the **passé composé.** Examples: **J'ai répondu à tous mes e-mails hier. Et vous, avez-vous répondu à tous vos e-mails hier? J'ai rendu visite à ma grand-mère le week-end dernier. Avez-vous rendu visite à vos grands-parents le week-end dernier?**
- Have students complete the **Vérifiez** activity.

6B.2

Regular and irregular *-re* verbs **vhl**central

Point de départ You've already learned the present tense and **passé composé** forms for infinitives that end in **-er** and **-ir**. Now you will learn the forms for a family of verbs that end in **-re**.

- Many **-re** verbs, such as **attendre** (*to wait*), follow a regular pattern of conjugation, as shown below.

attendre	
j'attends	nous attendons
tu attends	vous attendez
il/elle/on attend	ils/elles attendent

Tu **attends** devant le café?
Are you waiting in front of the café?

Nous **attendons** dans le magasin.
We're waiting in the store.

Où **attendez**-vous?
Where are you waiting?

Il faut **attendre** dans la bibliothèque.
You have to wait in the library.

- The verb **attendre** means *to wait* or *to wait for*. Unlike English, it does not require a preposition.

Marc **attend le bus.**
Marc is waiting for the bus.

Ils **attendent Robert.**
They're waiting for Robert.

Il **attend** ses parents à l'école.
He's waiting for his parents at school.

J'**attends** les soldes.
I'm waiting for a sale.

Other regular *-re* verbs			
descendre	to go down; to take down	rendre (à)	to give back, to return (to)
entendre	to hear	rendre visite (à)	to visit someone
perdre (son temps)	to lose; to waste (one's time)	répondre (à)	to answer, to respond (to)
		vendre	to sell

- **Rendre visite à** means *to visit a person*, while **visiter** means *to visit a place*.

Tu **rends visite à ta grand-mère** le lundi.
You visit your grandmother on Mondays.

Cécile va **visiter le musée** aujourd'hui.
Cécile is going to visit the museum today.

Vous **rendez visite à vos cousins**?
Are you visiting your cousins?

Nous **visitons Rome** ce week-end.
We are visiting Rome this weekend.

- To form the past participle of regular **-re** verbs, drop the **-re** from the infinitive and add **-u.**

Les étudiants ont **vendu** leurs livres.
The students sold their books.

Il a **entendu** arriver la voiture de sa femme.
He heard his wife's car arrive.

J'ai **répondu** à ton e-mail.
I answered your e-mail.

Nous avons **perdu** patience.
We lost patience.

Vérifiez

DIFFERENTIATION

For Kinesthetic Learners Make statements with regular and irregular **-re** verbs, and have students act them out.
Ex: **J'attends le bus.** (Students imitate waiting for the bus.)
Je conduis une voiture. (They imitate driving a car.)
Extra Practice Divide the class into teams of three. Each team has a piece of paper. Call out an infinitive and a person.
Ex: **traduire / première personne du pluriel.** Each team has

TEACHING OPTIONS

to compose a sentence, with each member writing one part. The first team member thinks of an appropriate subject or proper name and writes it down (Ex: **Ellene et moi**). The second writes the correct form of the verb (Ex: **traduisons**). The third completes the sentence in a logical way (Ex: **un livre**). The first team to write a logical and correct sentence wins. Team members should rotate positions each time a new verb is given.

● Some verbs whose infinitives end in **-re** are irregular.

Irregular -re verbs

	conduire *(to drive)*	mettre *(to put (on))*	rire *(to laugh)*
je	conduis	mets	ris
tu	conduis	mets	ris
il/elle/on	conduit	met	rit
nous	conduisons	mettons	rions
vous	conduisez	mettez	riez
ils/elles	conduisent	mettent	rient

Je **conduis** la voiture.
I'm driving the car.

Thérèse **met** ses gants.
Thérèse puts on her gloves.

Elles **rient** pendant le spectacle.
They laugh during the show.

Other irregular -re verbs

like *conduire*		like *mettre*	
construire	to build, to construct	permettre	to allow
détruire	to destroy	promettre	to promise
produire	to produce	**like *rire***	
réduire	to reduce		
traduire	to translate	sourire	to smile

● The past participle of the verb **mettre** is **mis**. Verbs derived from **mettre** (**permettre**, **promettre**) follow the same pattern: **permis, promis**.

Où est-ce que tu **as mis** mes livres?
Where did you put my books?

Je lui **ai promis** de faire la cuisine.
I promised her that I'd cook.

● The past participle of **conduire** is **conduit**. Verbs like **conduire** follow the same pattern: **construire → construit**; **détruire → détruit**; **produire → produit**; **traduire → traduit**.

● The past participle of **rire** is **ri**. The past participle of **sourire** is **souri**.

● Like for the other verb groups, use present tense verb forms to give commands.

Conduis moins vite!
Drive more slowly!

Souriez!
Smile!

Mets ta jupe noire!
Wear your black skirt!

 Boîte à outils

The French verbs **permettre** and **promettre** are followed by the preposition **à** and an indirect object to mean *to allow someone* or *to promise someone*: **permettre à quelqu'un** and **promettre à quelqu'un**.

***Leur* avez-vous permis de commencer à dix heures?**
Did you allow them to start at 10 o'clock?

Je *te* promets de ne pas partir.
I promise you I won't leave.

Vérifiez

Essayez!   Complétez les phrases avec la forme correcte du présent du verbe.

1. Ils __attendent__ (attendre) l'arrivée du train.
2. Nous __répondons__ (répondre) aux questions du professeur.
3. Je __souris__ (sourire) quand je suis heureuse.
4. Si on __construit__ (construire) trop, on __détruit__ (détruire) la nature.
5. Quand il fait froid, vous __mettez__ (mettre) un pull.
6. Est-ce que les élèves __entendent__ (entendre) le professeur?
7. Keiko __conduit__ (conduire) sa voiture ce week-end.
8. Si le sandwich n'est pas bon, je __mets__ (mettre) du sel (salt).

deux cent cinquante-trois **253**

Suggestions: Scaffolding
● Introduce the irregular **-re** verbs using TPR. Have students repeat the infinitives after you. Then, have students find the verb stems and patterns in each verb in the chart on p. 253. Point out the two different stems for **conduire (condui-, conduis-)** and **mettre (met, mett-)**. Explain that affirmative command forms are the same as the present tense.
● Do the Extra Practice on TE p. 253 for the present tense.
● Present the past participles of irregular **-re** verbs. Say the verbs listed and have students respond with the corresponding past participles.
● Explain that the verbs **permettre** and **promettre** are often followed by **de** + *an infinitive*. Write these examples on the board: **Je te promets d'arriver à 10 heures. Mes parents ne me permettent pas de sortir lundi soir.**
● Talk about yourself and ask students questions using the irregular verbs in the present tense and **passé composé**. Example: **D'habitude, je mets un pantalon. Aujourd'hui, j'ai mis une jupe/un costume. Et vous, que mettez-vous, en général?** Have students complete the **Vérifiez** activity.
● Have students review the Grammar Tutorial, and then complete **Essayez!**

Essayez! For additional practice, change the subjects of the sentences and have students restate them.

EXPANSION

Extra Practice Do a rapid-response drill. Write an infinitive from the list of **-re** verbs on the board. Call out subject pronouns and/or names, and have students respond with the correct verb form. Then repeat the drill, having students respond with the correct forms of the **passé composé**.

EXPANSION

Pairs Have students make a list of five things their parents allow them to do and five things their parents don't allow them to do. Then have them get together in pairs and compare their lists. Have volunteers report to the class the items they have in common. Example: **Mes parents ne me permettent pas de mettre des vêtements trop serrés. Ils me permettent parfois de sortir avec des amis.**

Mise en pratique

1 Qui fait quoi? Quelles phrases vont avec les illustrations?

1.   2.   3.   4.

___3___ **a.** Martin attend ses copains.

___4___ **b.** Nous rendons visite à notre grand-mère.

___1___ **c.** Vous vendez de jolis vêtements.

___2___ **d.** Je ris en regardant un film.

2 Les clients difficiles Henri et Gilbert travaillent pour un grand magasin. Complétez leur conversation.

GILBERT Tu n'as pas encore mangé?

HENRI Non, j' (1) ___attends___ (attendre) Jean-Michel.

GILBERT Il ne (2) ___descend___ (descendre) pas tout de suite. Il (3) ___perd___ (perdre) son temps avec un client difficile. Il (4) ___met___ (mettre) des cravates, des costumes, des chaussures...

HENRI Nous ne (5) ___vendons___ (vendre) pas souvent à des clients comme ça.

GILBERT C'est vrai. Ils (6) ___promettent___ (promettre) d'acheter quelque chose, puis ils partent les mains vides (*empty*).

3 Au centre commercial Daniel et ses copains ont passé (*spent*) la journée au centre commercial hier. Utilisez le passé composé et les éléments donnés pour faire des phrases complètes. Ajoutez d'autres éléments nécessaires. Answers will vary.

1. Mon frère et moi / conduire / centre commercial Mon frère et moi, nous avons conduit au centre commercial.

2. Guillaume / attendre / dix minutes / devant / cinéma Guillaume a atttendu dix minutes devant le cinéma.

3. Hervé et Thérèse / vendre / pulls Hervé et Thérèse ont vendu des pulls.

4. Lise / perdre / sac à main Lise a perdu son sac à main.

5. tu / mettre / robe / bleu Tu as mis une robe bleue.

6. Sandrine et toi / ne pas répondre / vendeur Sandrine et toi, vous n'avez pas répondu au vendeur.

4 La journée de Béatrice Hier, Béatrice a fait une liste des choses à faire. Avec un(e) partenaire, utilisez les verbes de la liste au passé composé pour dire (*to say*) tout ce qu'elle a fait. Answers will vary.

attendre	mettre
conduire	rendre visite
entendre	traduire

1. devoir d'espagnol	4. tante Albertine
2. parler d'un CD super	5. gants dans mon sac
3. e-mail de Sébastien	6. vieille voiture

Communication

5 **Fréquence** Employez les verbes de la liste et d'autres verbes pour dire (*to tell*) à un(e) partenaire ce que (*what*) vous faites tous les jours, une fois par mois et une fois par an. Alternez les rôles. Answers will vary.

> **MODÈLE**
>
> **Élève 1:** *J'attends mes copains à la cantine tous les jours.*
> **Élève 2:** *Moi, je rends visite à mes grands-parents une fois par mois.*

attendre	perdre
conduire	rendre
entendre	répondre
mettre	sourire

6 **Les charades** Par groupes de quatre, jouez aux charades. Chaque élève pense à une phrase différente avec un des verbes en **-re**. La première personne qui devine (*guesses*) propose la prochaine charade. Answers will vary.

7 **Questions personnelles** Avec un(e) partenaire, posez-vous ces questions à tour de rôle. Answers will vary.

1. Réponds-tu tout de suite (*immediately*) à tes e-mails?
2. As-tu promis à tes parents de faire quelque chose? Quoi?
3. Que mets-tu quand tu vas à un mariage? Pour aller à l'école? Pour sortir avec des copains?
4. Tes parents te permettent-ils de sortir tard pendant la semaine?
5. Tes parents conduisent une voiture? Comment conduisent-ils?
6. À qui rends-tu visite pendant les vacances?
7. Quelle est la dernière fois que tu as beaucoup ri? Avec qui?
8. As-tu déjà vendu quelque chose sur Internet? Quoi?

8 **La journée des vendeuses** Votre professeur va vous donner, à vous et à votre partenaire, une série d'illustrations qui montrent la journée d'Aude et d'Aurélie. Attention! Ne regardez pas la feuille de votre partenaire. Answers will vary.

> **MODÈLE**
>
> **Élève 1:** *Le matin, elles ont conduit pour aller au magasin.*
> **Élève 2:** *Après,...*

---

5 **Suggestion** Have two volunteers read the **modèle** aloud. Tell students that they may also make a negative statement, such as **Je ne conduis jamais**.

5 **Expansion** To practice the **passé composé**, have students specify when they did these things. Example: **J'ai rendu visite à mes grands-parents en avril.**

5 **Partner Chat** You can also assign Activity 5 on vhlcentral.com. Students work in pairs to record the activity online. The pair's recorded conversation will appear in your gradebook.

6 **Suggestion** This activity can also be used as a game by dividing the class into two teams with players from each team acting out the charades.

7 **Expansion** When pairs are done with the activity, have them share with the class some areas where they differ from their partner. Example: **Mes parents ne me permettent pas de sortir tard mais les parents de Gina lui permettent de sortir très tard le week-end.**

8 **Suggestion** Divide the class into pairs and distribute the Info Gap Handouts found in the Activity Pack on vhlcentral.com.

EXPANSION

Questions Ask students personalized questions using **-re** verbs. Examples: **1. Comment les élèves perdent-ils leur temps? 2. Est-ce que l'argent rend les gens heureux? 3. Que vend-on dans une boutique? 4. Vos parents vous permettent-ils de sortir le soir? 5. Rendez-vous souvent visite à votre famille? 6. Où mettez-vous vos livres en classe?**

EXPANSION

Writing Practice Have students work in pairs. Tell them to write a conversation between a clerk in a clothing store and a customer who has lost some item like sunglasses, a scarf, or gloves. The customer should explain the situation, and the clerk should ask for details, such as when the item was lost and a description. Alternatively, pairs can role-play this situation.

255

Révision

1 Je leur téléphone Par groupes de quatre, interviewez vos camarades. Préparez dix questions avec un verbe et une personne de la liste. Écrivez les réponses. *Answers will vary.*

MODÈLE

Élève 1: *Est-ce que tu parles souvent à tes cousines?*
Élève 2: *Oui, je leur parle toutes les semaines.*

verbes	personnes
donner un cadeau	copain ou copine
envoyer une carte/un e-mail	cousin ou cousine
parler	grands-parents
rendre visite	petit(e) ami(e)
téléphoner	sœur ou frère

2 Mes e-mails Ces personnes vous envoient des e-mails. Que faites-vous? Vous ne répondez pas, vous attendez quelques jours, vous leur téléphonez? Par groupes de trois, comparez vos réactions. *Answers will vary.*

MODÈLE

Élève 1: *Ma sœur m'envoie un e-mail tous les jours.*
Élève 2: *Tu lui réponds tout de suite?*
Élève 3: *Tu préfères ne pas lui répondre?*

1. un e-mail anonyme
2. un e-mail d'un(e) camarade de classe
3. un e-mail d'un professeur
4. un e-mail d'un(e) ami(e) d'enfance
5. un e-mail d'un(e) copain (copine)
6. un e-mail de vos grands-parents

3 Une liste Des membres de votre famille ou des amis vous ont donné ou acheté des vêtements que vous n'aimez pas du tout. Faites une liste de quatre ou cinq de ces vêtements. Comparez votre liste à la liste d'un(e) camarade. *Answers will vary.*

MODÈLE

Élève 1: *Ma sœur m'a donné une écharpe verte et laide et mon père m'a acheté des chaussettes marron trop petites!*
Élève 2: *L'année dernière, un ami m'a donné...*

4 Quoi mettre? Vous et votre partenaire allez faire des choses différentes. Un(e) partenaire va fêter la retraite de ses grands-parents à Tahiti. L'autre va skier dans les Alpes. Qu'allez-vous porter? Demandez des vêtements à votre partenaire si vous n'aimez pas tous les vêtements de votre ensemble. *Answers will vary.*

MODÈLE

Élève 1: *Est-ce que tu me prêtes ton tee-shirt violet?*
Élève 2: *Ah non, j'ai besoin de ce tee-shirt. Tu me prêtes ton pantalon?*

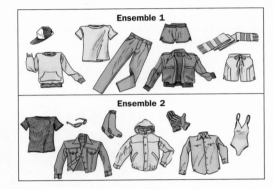

Ensemble 1

Ensemble 2

5 S'il te plaît Votre ami(e) a acheté un nouveau vêtement que vous aimez beaucoup. Vous essayez de convaincre (*to convince*) cet(te) ami(e) de vous prêter ce vêtement. Préparez un dialogue avec un(e) partenaire où vous employez tous les verbes. Jouez la scène pour la classe. *Answers will vary.*

aller avec	montrer
aller bien	prêter
donner	promettre
mettre	rendre

6 Bon anniversaire, Nicolas! Votre professeur va vous donner, à vous et à votre partenaire, deux feuilles d'activités différentes. Attention! Ne regardez pas la feuille de votre partenaire. *Answers will vary.*

MODÈLE

Élève 1: *Les amis de Nicolas lui téléphonent.*
Élève 2: *Ensuite, ...*

À l'écoute vhlcentral

STRATÉGIE

Listening for linguistic cues

You can improve your listening comprehension by listening for specific linguistic cues. For example, if you listen for the endings of conjugated verbs, or for familiar constructions, such as the **passé composé** with **avoir**, **avoir envie de** + [*infinitive*] or **aller** + [*infinitive*], you can find out whether a person did something in the past, wants to do something, or will do something in the future.

🔊 To practice listening for linguistic cues, you will listen to four sentences. As you listen, note whether each sentence refers to a past, present, or future action.

Préparation

Regardez la photo. Où sont Pauline et Sarah? Que font-elles? Décrivez les vêtements qu'elles regardent. À votre avis, pour quelle occasion cherchent-elles des vêtements?

🔊 À vous d'écouter

Écoutez la conversation entre Pauline et Sarah. Après une deuxième écoute, indiquez si les actions suivantes sont du **passé (p)**, du **présent (pr)** ou du **futur (f)**.

_p_ 1. la fête de la cousine de Pauline

_p_ 2. beaucoup danser

_p_ 3. rencontrer un musicien

_f_ 4. déjeuner avec un garçon intéressant

_pr_ 5. chercher de nouveaux vêtements

_f_ 6. mettre des chaussures en cuir noir

_pr_ 7. aimer une robe bleue

_f_ 8. acheter la robe bleue

Compréhension

Complétez Complétez les phrases.

1. Pauline cherche des vêtements pour ___c___.
   a. un dîner b. une fête c. un rendez-vous

2. Pauline va acheter un pantalon noir et ___b___.
   a. un tee-shirt b. une chemise rose c. un maillot de bain

3. Sarah pense que ___b___ ne vont pas avec les nouveaux vêtements.
   a. l'écharpe verte b. les baskets roses c. les lunettes de soleil

4. D'après Sarah, les chaussures ___a___ sont élégantes.
   a. en cuir noir b. roses c. en soie

5. La couleur préférée de Sarah n'est pas le ___c___.
   a. rose b. jaune c. vert

6. Sarah cherche un vêtement pour ___b___.
   a. un déjeuner b. la fête de retraite de son père c. un mariage

7. Sarah va acheter une robe en soie ___a___.
   a. à manches courtes b. à manches longues c. rouge

8. La robe existe en vert, en bleu et en ___c___.
   a. noir b. marron c. blanc

Une occasion spéciale Décrivez la dernière fois que vous avez fêté une occasion spéciale. Qu'est-ce que vous avez fêté? Où? Comment? Avec qui? Qu'est-ce que vous avez mis comme vêtements? Et les autres?

MODÈLE

Samedi, nous avons fêté l'anniversaire de mon frère. Mes parents ont invité nos amis Paul, Marc, Julia et Naomi dans un restaurant élégant. Moi, j'ai mis une belle robe verte en coton. Mon frère a mis un costume gris. Paul a mis...

S: Oui, mais elle a l'air un peu serrée. Je préfère les robes larges.
P: Et cette belle robe en soie à manches courtes?
S: Je déteste le vert. Ils l'ont en bleu?

P: Oui, et en blanc aussi.
S: Super. Je vais prendre la bleue.
Teacher Resources DVD

le marché de Douz, en Tunisie

L'Algérie

Le pays en chiffres

▶ **Superficie:** *2.381.741 km²*

▶ **Population:** *40.263.711*

▶ **Industries principales:** *agriculture, gaz naturel, pétrole°*

▶ **Ville capitale:** *Alger*　▶ **Monnaie:** *dinar algérien*

▶ **Langues:** *arabe, français, tamazight*

Le Maroc

Le pays en chiffres

▶ **Superficie:** *446.550 km²*

▶ **Population:** *33.655.786*

▶ **Industries principales:** *agriculture, exploitation minière°*

▶ **Ville capitale:** *Rabat*　▶ **Monnaie:** *dirham*

▶ **Langues:** *arabe, tamazight, français*

La Tunisie

Le pays en chiffres

▶ **Superficie:** *163.610 km²*

▶ **Population:** *11.134.588*

▶ **Industries principales:** *agriculture, exploitation minière*

▶ **Ville capitale:** *Tunis*　▶ **Monnaie:** *dinar tunisien*

▶ **Langues:** *arabe, français, tamazight*

Personnes célèbres

▶ Albert Memmi, *Tunisie, écrivain (1920–)*

▶ Nezha Chekrouni, *Maroc, politicienne (1955–)*

▶ Khaled, *Algérie, chanteur (1960–)*

pétrole *oil* exploitation minière *mining* ne... que *only*
Grâce aux *Thanks to* sources *springs* sable *sand*
faire pousser *grow* En plein milieu *Right in the middle*

L'OCÉAN ATLANTIQUE
LE PORTUGAL
L'ESPAGNE
LA MER MÉDITERRANÉE
Bizerte
Sétif
Tunis
Tanger
Oran
Alger
Rabat
Constantine
Fès
Sfax
Casablanca
LA TUNISIE
Marrakech
LES CHAÎNES DE L'ATLAS
LE MAROC
L'ALGÉRIE
LA LIBYE
LE SAHARA OCCIDENTAL
LA MAURITANIE
LE SAHARA
LE NIGER
LE MALI

0　500 miles
0　500 kilomètres

la mosquée Hassan II à Casablanca, au Maroc

un café à Tlemcen, en Algérie

Incroyable mais vrai!

Des oranges du Sahara? Dans ce désert, il ne tombe que° 12 cm de pluie par an. Grâce aux° sources° et aux rivières sous le sable°, les Sahariens ont développé un système d'irrigation pour faire pousser° des fruits et des légumes dans les oasis. En plein milieu° du désert, on peut trouver des tomates, des abricots ou des oranges!

AP® Theme: Global Challenges
Context: Diversity Issues

Les régions

Le Maghreb

La région du Maghreb, en Afrique du Nord, se compose° du Maroc, de l'Algérie et de la Tunisie. Envahis° aux 7e et 8e siècles par les Arabes, les trois pays deviennent plus tard des colonies françaises avant de retrouver leur indépendance dans les années 1950–1960. La population du Maghreb est composée d'Arabes, d'Européens et de Berbères, les premiers résidents de l'Afrique du Nord. Le Grand Maghreb inclut ces trois pays, plus la Libye et la Mauritanie. En 1989, les cinq pays ont formé l'Union du Maghreb Arabe dans l'espoir° de créer une union politique et économique, mais des tensions entre l'Algérie et le Maroc ont ralenti° le projet.

AP® Theme: Contemporary Life
Context: Travel

Les destinations

Marrakech

La ville de Marrakech, fondée en 1062, est un grand symbole du Maroc médiéval. Sa médina, ou vieille ville, est entourée° de fortifications et fermée aux automobiles. On y trouve la mosquée de Kutubiyya et la place Djem'a el-Fna. La mosquée est le joyau° architectural de la ville, et la place Djem'a el-Fna est la plus active de toute l'Afrique à tout moment de la journée, avec ses nombreux artistes et vendeurs. La médina a aussi le plus grand souk (grand marché couvert°) du Maroc, où toutes sortes d'objets sont proposés, au milieu de délicieuses odeurs de thé à la menthe°, d'épices et de pâtisseries au miel°.

AP® Theme: Beauty and Aesthetics
Context: Literature and Visual Arts

Les arts

Assia Djebar (1936–2015)

Lauréate de nombreux prix littéraires et cinématographiques, Assia Djebar était° une écrivaine et cinéaste algérienne très talenteuse. Dans ses œuvres°, Djebar présente le point de vue° féminin avec

l'intention de donner une voix° aux femmes algériennes. *La Soif*, son premier roman°, sort en 1957. C'est plus tard, pendant qu'elle enseigne l'histoire à l'Université d'Alger, qu'elle devient cinéaste et sort son premier film, *La Nouba des femmes du Mont Chenoua*, en 1979. Le film reçoit le prix de la critique internationale au festival du film de Venise. En 2005, Assia Djebar devient le premier écrivain du Maghreb, homme ou femme, à être élue° à l'Académie française.

AP® Theme: Families and Communities
Context: Customs and Ceremonies

Les traditions

Les hammams

Inventés par les Romains et adoptés par les Arabes, les hammams, ou «bains turcs», sont très nombreux et populaires en Afrique du Nord. Ce sont des bains de vapeur° composés de plusieurs pièces—souvent trois—où la chaleur est plus ou moins forte. L'architecture des hammams varie d'un endroit à un autre, mais ces bains de vapeur servent tous de lieux où se laver° et de centres sociaux très importants dans la culture régionale. Les gens s'y réunissent aux grandes occasions de la vie, comme les mariages et les naissances, et y vont aussi de manière habituelle pour se détendre et parler entre amis.

 Qu'est-ce que vous avez appris? Répondez aux questions par des phrases complètes.

1. Qui est un chanteur algérien célèbre?
   Khaled est un chanteur algérien célèbre.
2. Où fait-on pousser des fruits et des légumes dans le Sahara?
   On en fait pousser dans les oasis.
3. Pourquoi le français est-il parlé au Maghreb?
   Parce que ces trois pays ont été des colonies françaises.
4. Combien de pays composent le Grand Maghreb? Lesquels?
   Cinq pays le composent: l'Algérie, la Libye, le Maroc, la Mauritanie et la Tunisie.
5. Qui est Assia Djebar?
   C'est une écrivaine et une cinéaste algérienne.
6. Qu'essaie-t-elle de faire dans ses œuvres?
   Elle essaie de présenter le point de vue féminin et de donner une voix aux femmes algériennes.
7. Qu'est-ce qu'un souk?
   C'est un grand marché couvert.
8. Quel est l'autre nom pour la vieille ville de Marrakech?
   Elle s'appelle aussi la médina.
9. Où peut-on aller au Maghreb pour se détendre et parler entre amis?
   On peut aller au hammam.
10. Qui a inventé les hammams?
    Les Romains les ont inventés.

 Sur Internet

1. Cherchez plus d'information sur les Berbères. Où se trouvent les grandes populations de Berbères? Ont-ils encore une identité commune?

2. Le henné est une tradition dans le monde maghrébin. Comment et pourquoi est-il employé?

3. Cherchez des informations sur les oasis du Sahara. Comment est la vie là-bas? Que peut-on y faire?

se compose *is made up* **Envahis** *Invaded* **espoir** *hope*
ont ralenti *slowed down* **était** *was* **œuvres** *works*
point de vue *point of view* **voix** *voice* **roman** *novel* **élue** *elected*
entourée *surrounded* **joyau** *jewel* **couvert** *covered* **menthe** *mint*
miel *honey* **bains de vapeur** *steam baths* **se laver** *to wash oneself*

Le Maghreb In Arabic, *Maghreb* means *west*. Prior to the Arab conquest, the Maghreb region was part of the Roman Empire.

Assia Djebar (1936–2015)
Assia Djebar (whose given name was Fatima-Zohra Imalayen) was a well-known and prolific Algerian woman writer. She chronicled the complexities and evolution of life for North-African women in the Muslim world. Her works have been translated into over 20 languages.

Marrakech
- The **mosquée de Kutubiyya**, or **mosquée des Libraires**, was built in the twelfth century. It is a symbol of the Berber city and a principal landmark.
- The souk district is an intricate maze of covered streets where vendors sell their wares, such as carpets, iron work, leather products, clothes, and basketwork. Have students describe what they see in the photo.

Les hammams
- The **hammams** usually offer separate quarters or special days for men and women. The experience begins with a warm steam room where people relax and socialize, then a massage and an exfoliating scrub and soak, ending with a period of relaxation.

 21st Century Skills

Information and Media Literacy: Sur Internet
Go to vhlcentral.com to complete the **Sur Internet** activity associated with **Panorama** for additional practice accessing and using culturally authentic sources.

 TELL Connection

Environment 4 *Why:* Support your cultural goals. *What:* Using the **Sur internet** and other resources, have student groups prepare visuals of foods, traditions, and specialized products to connect the classroom environment to cultural content.

PRE-AP®

Presentational Speaking with Cultural Comparison Have students work in groups of three. Tell them to compare a **hammam** to a spa in the United States. Have them list the similarities and differences in a two-column chart under the headings **Similitudes** and **Différences**. Then have groups present and explain their lists to the class.

EXPANSION

Cultural Activity Have students discuss the various elements these three countries have in common. Tell them to give specific examples. Ask: **Quels sont les éléments que ces trois pays ont en commun?** Examples: **les langues, la religion, l'histoire et la culture.**

Lecture vhlcentral

Avant la lecture

STRATÉGIE

Recognizing word families

Recognizing related words can help you guess the meaning of words in context, ensuring better comprehension of a reading selection. Using this strategy will enrich your French vocabulary.

Examinez le texte

Voici quelques mots que vous avez déjà appris. Pour chaque mot, trouvez un terme de la même famille dans le texte et utilisez un dictionnaire pour donner son équivalent en anglais.

MODÈLE

ami	*amitié*	*friendship*
1. diplôme	diplômés	graduates
2. commencer	le commencement	beginning
3. sortir	la sortie	exit
4. timide	la timidité	shyness
5. difficile	les difficultés	difficulties
6. préférer	les préférences	preferences

Familles de mots

Avec un(e) partenaire, trouvez le bon mot pour compléter chaque famille de mots. (Note: vous avez appris tous les mots qui manquent (*all the missing words*) dans cette unité et il y a un mot de chaque famille dans le texte.)

MODÈLE

attendre	*l'attente*	*attendu(e)*
VERBE	**NOM**	**ADJECTIF**
1. boire	la boisson	bu(e)
2. fêter	la fête	festif/festive
3. vivre	la vie	vif/vive
4. rajeunir	la jeunesse	jeune
5. surprendre	la surprise	surpris(e)
6. répondre	la réponse	répondu(e)

Ça y est, c'est officiel!

Bravo, jeunes diplômés°! C'est le commencement d'une nouvelle vie. Il est maintenant temps de fêter ça!

Pour faire retomber la pression°, Mathilde, Christophe, Alexandre et Laurence vous invitent à fêter entre amis votre diplôme bien mérité°!

À laisser chez vous:
La timidité, la fatigue, les soucis° et les difficultés des études et de la vie quotidienne° pour une ambiance festive

Quoi d'autre?
Un groupe de musique (le frère de Mathilde et sa bande) va venir° jouer pour nous!

À apporter:
Nourriture° et boissons: Chaque invité apporte quelque chose pour le buffet: salades, plats° froids/chauds, fruits, desserts, boissons
Activités: Jeux de cartes, ballons°, autres jeux selon° vos préférences, chaises pliantes°, maillot de bain (pour la piscine), crème solaire
Surprenez-nous!

Quand:
Le samedi 16 juillet (de 16h00 à minuit)

Où:
Chez les parents de Laurence, 14 route des Mines, Allouagne, Nord-Pas-de-Calais

Comment y aller°:
À la sortie d'Allouagne, prenez la route de Lozinghem. Tournez à gauche sur la route des Mines. Le numéro 14 est la grande maison sur la droite. (Nous allons mettre des ballons° de couleurs sur la route pour indiquer l'endroit.)

Au programme:
Faire la fête, bien sûr! Manger (buffet et barbecue), rire, danser et fêter la fin des cours! Attendez-vous à passer un bon moment!

Autres activités:
Activités en plein air° (football, badminton, volley, piscine... et surtout détente°!)

Pour répondre à cette invitation:
Téléphonez à Laurence (avant le 6 juillet, SVP°) au 06.14.55.85.80 ou par e-mail:
laurence@courriel.fr

Ça y est! *That's it!* **diplômés** *graduates* **faire retomber la pression** *to unwind* **bien mérité** *well deserved* **soucis** *worries* **vie quotidienne** *daily life* **va venir** *is going to come* **Nourriture** *Food* **plats** *dishes* **ballons** *balls* **selon** *depending on* **pliantes** *folding* **y aller** *get there* **ballons** *balloons* **en plein air** *outdoor* **détente** *relaxation* **svp** *please*

Après la lecture

Vrai ou faux? Indiquez si les phrases sont **vraies** ou **fausses**. Corrigez les phrases fausses. *Answers may vary slightly.*

1. C'est une invitation à une fête d'anniversaire.
   Faux. C'est une invitation pour fêter le diplôme.
2. Les invités vont passer un mauvais moment.
   Faux. Les invités vont passer un bon moment.
3. On va manger des salades et des desserts.
   Vrai.
4. Les invités vont faire toutes les activités dans la maison.
   Faux. Les invités vont faire des activités en plein air.
5. Un groupe de musique va jouer à la fête.
   Vrai.
6. La fête commence à 16h00.
   Vrai.

Conseillez Vous êtes Laurence, l'organisatrice de la fête. Les invités veulent (*want*) assister à la fête, mais ils vous contactent pour parler de leurs soucis respectifs. Donnez-leur des conseils (*advice*) pour les mettre à l'aise (*at ease*). *Answers may vary. Suggested answers:*

MODÈLE

Isabelle: J'ai beaucoup de soucis cette semaine.
Vous: *Tu vas laisser tes soucis à la maison et venir* (*come*) *à la fête.*

1. Thomas: Je ne sais (*know*) pas quoi apporter.
   Vous: Tu vas apporter des boissons gazeuses.
2. Sarah: Je me perds (*get lost*) facilement quand je conduis.
   Vous: Tu vas chercher les ballons de couleurs sur la route.
3. Sylvie: Je ne fais pas de sport.
   Vous: Tu vas jouer aux cartes et discuter.
4. Salim: Je veux (*want*) répondre à l'invitation, mais je n'ai pas d'ordinateur.
   Vous: Tu vas me téléphoner.
5. Sandra: Je n'aime pas le barbecue.
   Vous: Tu vas manger des salades.
6. Véronique: J'aime faire du sport en plein air, mais je n'aime pas le football.
   Vous: Tu vas faire du badmington et du volley.

On va à la fête? Vous êtes invité(e) à cette fête et vous allez amener un(e) ami(e). Téléphonez à cet(te) ami(e) (votre partenaire) pour l'inviter. Donnez des détails et répondez aux questions de votre ami(e) sur les hôtes, les invités, les activités de l'après-midi et de la soirée, les choses à apporter, etc.

Vrai ou faux? Go over the answers with the class. For the false items, have students point out where they found the correct answer in the text.

Conseillez
- This activity can be done in pairs. Remind students to switch roles after items 1–3.
- Have pairs write two more situations for the activity. Then have them exchange papers with another pair and complete the situations.

On va à la fête? After students have completed the activity, take a quick class poll. Ask: **Qui va assister à la fête? Qui ne va pas assister à la fête? Pourquoi?**

21st Century Skills

Creativity and Innovation
Ask students to prepare a presentation on the ideal graduation party, inspired by the information on these two pages.

Écriture

STRATÉGIE

How to report an interview

There are several ways to prepare a written report about an interview. For example, you can transcribe the interview, or you can summarize it. In any event, the report should begin with an interesting title and a short introduction that answers the five *W*'s (*who, what, when, where, why*) and the *H* (*how*) of the interview. The report should end with an interesting conclusion. Note that when you transcribe a conversation in French, you should pay careful attention to format and punctuation.

Écrire une interview en français

- Pour indiquer qui parle dans une interview, on peut mettre le nom de la personne qui parle devant sa phrase.

  MONIQUE Lucie, qu'est-ce que tu vas mettre pour l'anniversaire de Julien?

  LUCIE Je vais mettre ma robe en soie bleue à manches courtes. Et toi, tu vas mettre quoi?

  MONIQUE Eh bien, une jupe en coton et un chemisier, je pense. Ou peut-être mon pantalon en cuir avec... Tiens, tu me prêtes ta chemise jaune et blanche?

  LUCIE Oui, si tu me la rends (*return it to me*) dimanche. Elle va avec le pantalon que je vais porter la semaine prochaine.

- On peut aussi commencer les phrases avec des tirets (*dashes*) pour indiquer quand une nouvelle personne parle.

  — Qu'est-ce que tu as acheté comme cadeau pour Julien?

  — Une cravate noire et violette. Elle est très jolie. Et toi?

  — Je ne lui ai pas encore acheté de cadeau. Des lunettes de soleil peut-être?

  — Oui, c'est une bonne idée! Et il y a des soldes à Saint-Louis Lunettes.

Thème

Écrire une interview

Avant l'écriture

1. Clarisse Deschamps est une styliste suisse. Elle dessine des vêtements pour les jeunes et va présenter sa nouvelle collection sur votre campus. Vous allez interviewer Clarisse pour le journal de votre lycée.

   Préparez une liste de questions à poser à Clarisse Deschamps sur elle ou sur sa nouvelle collection. Vous pouvez (*can*) poser des questions sur:

   ■ les types de vêtements

   ■ les couleurs

   ■ le style

   ■ les prix

Quoi?	
Comment?	
Pour qui?	
Combien?	
Pourquoi?	
Où?	
Quand?	

2. Vérifiez que vous avez au moins (*at least*) une question pour chaque mot interrogatif du tableau (*chart*).

3. Ensuite (*Then*), choisissez 5-6 questions à poser pendant (*during*) l'interview.

Écriture

Écrivez un compte rendu (*report*) de l'interview.

- Commencez par une courte introduction.

> **MODÈLE** *Voici une interview de Clarisse Deschamps, styliste suisse. Elle va présenter sa nouvelle collection sur notre campus vendredi, le 10 novembre.*

- Inventez une conversation de 10 à 12 lignes entre vous et Clarisse. Indiquez qui parle, avec des tirets (*dashes*) ou avec les noms des personnes.

> **MODÈLE** *—Quel genre de vêtements préférez-vous porter pour sortir?*
> *—Moi, je préfère porter une robe noire. C'est très élégant.*

- Terminez par une brève (*brief*) conclusion.

> **MODÈLE** *On vend la collection de Clarisse Deschamps à Vêtements & Co à côté du lycée. Cette semaine, il y a des soldes!*

Tête-à-tête avec Clarisse Deschamps

Voici une interview de Clarisse Deschamps, styliste suisse. Elle va présenter sa nouvelle collection sur notre campus vendredi, le 10 novembre.

- Quel genre de vêtements préférez-vous porter pour sortir?
- Moi, je préfère porter une robe noire. C'est très élégant...

On vend la collection de Clarisse Deschamps à Vêtements & Co dans le magasin qui est à côté de notre lycée. Cette semaine, il y a des soldes!

Après l'écriture

1. Échangez votre compte rendu avec celui (*the one*) d'un(e) partenaire. Répondez à ces questions pour commenter son travail.

- Votre partenaire a-t-il/elle organisé les questions de manière logique?

- A-t-il/elle inclu une introduction, une interview de 10 à 12 lignes et une conclusion?

- A-t-il/elle utilisé le bon style pour écrire l'interview?

- A-t-il/elle utilisé les bonnes formes verbales?

2. Corrigez votre compte rendu d'après (*according to*) les commentaires de votre partenaire. Relisez votre travail pour éliminer ces problèmes:

- des fautes (*errors*) d'orthographe

- des fautes de ponctuation

- des fautes de conjugaison

- des fautes d'accord (*agreement*) des adjectifs

- un mauvais emploi (*use*) de la grammaire

Key Standards

4.1

Suggestion Tell students that an easy way to study from **Vocabulaire** is to cover up the French half of each section, leaving only the English equivalents exposed. They can then quiz themselves on the French items. To focus on the English equivalents of the French entries, they simply reverse this process.

Creativity and Innovation

Ask students to prepare a list of three products or perspectives they learned about in this unit to share with the class. Consider asking them to focus on the **Culture** and **Panorama** sections.

Leadership and Responsibility: Extension Project

If you have access to students in a Francophone country, have students decide on three questions they want to ask the partner class related to this unit's topic. Based on the responses they receive, work as a class to explain to the partner class one aspect of their responses that surprised the class and why.

Leçon 6A

Les fêtes

faire une surprise (à quelqu'un)	to surprise (someone)
fêter	to celebrate
organiser une fête	to plan a party
un biscuit	cookie
un bonbon	candy
un dessert	dessert
un gâteau	cake
la glace	ice cream
un glaçon	ice cube
un cadeau	present, gift
une fête	party; celebration
un hôte/une hôtesse	host(ess)
un(e) invité(e)	guest
un jour férié	holiday
une surprise	surprise

Les relations

l'amitié (f.)	friendship
l'amour (m.)	love
le bonheur	happiness
un couple	couple
un(e) fiancé(e)	fiancé; fiancée
des jeunes mariés (m.)	newlyweds
un rendez-vous	date; appointment
ensemble	together

Périodes de la vie

l'adolescence (f.)	adolescence
l'âge adulte (m.)	adulthood
un divorce	divorce
l'enfance (f.)	childhood
une étape	stage
la jeunesse	youth
un mariage	marriage; wedding
la mort	death
la naissance	birth
la vie	life
la vieillesse	old age
prendre sa retraite	to retire
tomber amoureux/amoureuse	to fall in love
avant-hier	the day before yesterday
hier	yesterday

Expressions utiles

See p. 227.

Demonstrative adjectives

ce(t)(te)/ces	this/these; that/those
...-ci	...here
...-là	...there

Leçon 6B

Les vêtements

aller avec	to go with
porter	to wear
un anorak	ski jacket, parka
des baskets (f.)	des baskets (f.)
un blouson	jacket
une casquette	(baseball) cap
une ceinture	belt
un chapeau	hat
une chaussette	sock
une chaussure	shoe
une chemise (à manches courtes/longues)	shirt (short-/long-sleeved)
un chemisier	blouse
un costume	(man's) suit
une cravate	tie
une écharpe	scarf
un gant	glove
un jean	jeans
une jupe	skirt
des lunettes (de soleil) (f.)	(sun)glasses
un maillot de bain	swimsuit, bathing suit
un manteau	coat
un pantalon	pants
un pull	sweater
une robe	dress
un sac à main	purse, handbag
un short	shorts
un sous-vêtement	underwear
une taille	clothing size
un tailleur	(woman's) suit; tailor
un tee-shirt	tee shirt
des vêtements (m.)	clothing
des soldes (m.)	sales
un vendeur/une vendeuse	salesman/saleswoman
bon marché	inexpensive
chaque	each
cher/chère	expensive
large	loose; big
serré(e)	tight

Les couleurs

De quelle couleur...?	In what color...?
blanc(he)	white
bleu(e)	blue
gris(e)	gray
jaune	yellow
marron	brown
noir(e)	black
orange	orange
rose	pink
rouge	red
vert(e)	green
violet(te)	purple; violet

Expressions utiles

See p. 245.

Indirect object pronouns

me	to/for me
te	to/for you
lui	to/for him/her
nous	to/for us
vous	to/for you
leur	to/for them

Disjunctive pronouns

moi	me
toi	you
lui/elle	him/her
nous	us
vous	you
eux/elles	them
moi-même	myself
toi-même	yourself
lui-/elle-même	him-/herself
nous-mêmes	ourselves
vous-même(s)	yourself (yourselves)
eux-/elles-mêmes	themselves

Verbes en -re

attendre	to wait
conduire	to drive
construire	to build; to construct
descendre	to go down; to take down
détruire	to destroy
entendre	to hear
mettre	to put (on); to place
perdre (son temps)	to lose; to waste (one's time)
permettre	to allow
produire	to produce
promettre	to promise
réduire	to reduce
rendre (à)	to give back; to return (to)
rendre visite (à)	to visit someone
répondre (à)	to respond, to answer (to)
rire	to laugh
sourire	to smile
traduire	to translate
vendre	to sell

264 *deux cent soixante-quatre*

En vacances

Pour commencer

- Indiquez les couleurs qu'on voit (*sees*) sur la photo.
- Quel temps fait-il? C'est quelle saison, à votre avis?
- Où a été prise cette photo? Dans un hôtel à la plage? Dans une maison de campagne? À la montagne?
- Avez-vous envie de passer vos vacances dans cet endroit? Pourquoi ou pourquoi pas?

Unit Goals
Leçon 7A

In this lesson, students will learn:
- terms for travel and vacation
- names of countries and nationalities
- the role of diacriticals
- about Tahiti and **le musée d'Orsay**
- more about transportation and lodging through specially shot video footage
- the **passé composé** with **être**
- direct object pronouns
- about modern youth hostels

Leçon 7B

In this lesson, students will learn:
- terms related to hotels and accommodations
- ordinal numbers
- expressions for sequencing events
- the pronunciation of **ti, sti,** and **ssi**
- how and where the French vacation
- the formation and usage of adverbs; the irregular verbs **dire, écrire** and **lire**
- the **imparfait**
- to recognize the genre of spoken discourse

Savoir-faire

In this section, students will learn:
- cultural and historical information about French Polynesia and Southeast Asia
- to predict the content of a text from its title
- to make an outline
- to write a brochure

Pour commencer

- **On voit du bleu, du violet, du vert, de l'orange.**
- **Il fait beau et chaud. Le ciel est bleu et il y a du soleil. C'est l'été.**
- **Dans un hôtel à la plage.**
- Answers will vary.

Section Goals

In this section, students will learn and practice vocabulary related to:
- travel and vacations
- names of countries and nationalities

Key Standards

1.1, 1.2, 4.1

Suggestions

- Use the digital image for this page and describe what the people are doing. Examples: **Cette femme achète un billet. Cet homme utilise un plan.**
- Ask students questions about travel and transportation using the vocabulary. **Aimez-vous voyager? Comment préférez-vous voyager? Aimez-vous prendre l'avion/le train? Préférez-vous rouler en voiture ou prendre l'autobus? Quels pays avez-vous visités?** At this time, introduce additional countries, states, provinces, and their prepositions as needed. Explain that although there are exceptions, students should use **en** with feminine singular countries or masculine countries beginning with a vowel sound, **au** with masculine, singular countries, and **aux** with plural countries.
- Point out that **un (auto)bus** is a local bus; a bus that goes from town to town is **un (auto)car**.
- Point out that **les vacances** is always plural.
- Tell students that **un plan** is a city or town map; **une carte** is a map of a region or country.
- Explain that the word **un ticket** is used for a bus, subway, or other small ticket. A plane or train ticket or a ticket to an event, such as a concert, is called **un billet.**

You will learn how to...

- describe trips you have taken
- tell where you went

◁) **vhl**central

Bon voyage!

Vocabulaire

faire du shopping	to go shopping
faire les valises	to pack one's bags
faire un séjour	to spend time (somewhere)
partir en vacances	to go on vacation
prendre un train (un taxi, un (auto)bus, un bateau)	to take a train (taxi, bus, boat)
rouler en voiture	to ride in a car
un aéroport	airport
un arrêt d'autobus (de bus)	bus stop
un billet aller-retour	round-trip ticket
un billet (d'avion, de train)	(plane, train) ticket
un congé	time off, leave
une douane	customs
une gare (routière)	train station (bus terminal)
un passager/une passagère	passenger
une station (de métro)	(subway) station
une station de ski	ski resort
un ticket (de bus, de métro)	(bus, subway) ticket
des vacances (f.)	vacation
un vol	flight
à l'étranger	abroad, overseas
la campagne	country(side)
une capitale	capital
le monde	world
un pays	country
(en/l') Allemagne (f.)	(to/in) Germany
(en/l') Angleterre (f.)	(to/in) England
(en/la) Belgique (belge)	(to/in) Belgium (Belgian)
(au/le) Brésil (brésilien(ne))	(to/in) Brazil (Brazilian)
(en/la) Chine (chinois(e))	(to/in) China (Chinese)
(en/l') Irlande (irlandais(e)) (f.)	(to/in) Ireland (Irish)
(en/l') Italie (f.)	(to/in) Italy
(au/le) Japon	(to/in) Japan
(en/la) Suisse	(to/in) Switzerland

une sortie

Il utilise un plan. (utiliser)

la plage

le soleil!

Elle bronze. (bronzer)

la mer

les gens (m.)

Le Figaro

le journal

EXPANSION

Oral Drill Call out names of countries and nationalities at random, including adjectives of nationality from previous lessons. Have students classify them as either **un pays** or **une nationalité.** You might want to list the words on the board in two columns or have students write them on the board.

TEACHING OPTIONS

Using Games Write vocabulary for means of transportation on index cards. On another set of cards, draw or paste pictures to match each term. Tape them face down on the board in random order. Divide the class into two teams. Play a game of Concentration in which students match words with pictures. When a match is made, that player's team collects those cards. When all pairs have been matched, the team with the most cards wins.

Mise en pratique

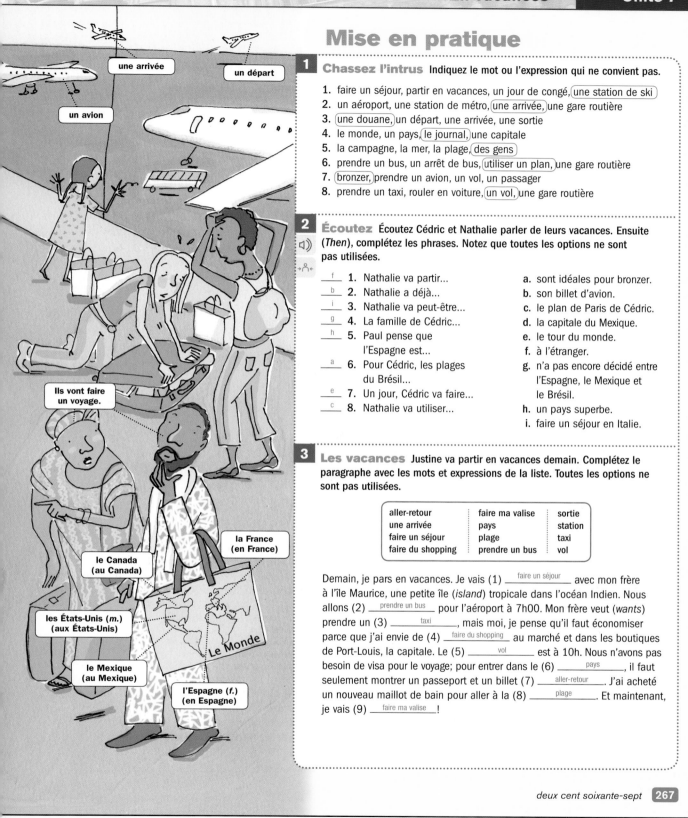

une arrivée
un départ
un avion
Ils vont faire un voyage.
le Canada (au Canada)
les États-Unis (*m.*) (aux États-Unis)
le Mexique (au Mexique)
l'Espagne (*f.*) (en Espagne)
la France (en France)
Le Monde

1 **Chassez l'intrus** Indiquez le mot ou l'expression qui ne convient pas.

1. faire un séjour, partir en vacances, un jour de congé, (une station de ski)
2. un aéroport, une station de métro, (une arrivée,) une gare routière
3. (une douane,) un départ, une arrivée, une sortie
4. le monde, un pays, (le journal,) une capitale
5. la campagne, la mer, la plage, (des gens)
6. prendre un bus, un arrêt de bus, (utiliser un plan,) une gare routière
7. (bronzer,) prendre un avion, un vol, un passager
8. prendre un taxi, rouler en voiture, (un vol,) une gare routière

2 **Écoutez** Écoutez Cédric et Nathalie parler de leurs vacances. Ensuite (*Then*), complétez les phrases. Notez que toutes les options ne sont pas utilisées.

_f_ 1. Nathalie va partir...
_b_ 2. Nathalie a déjà...
_i_ 3. Nathalie va peut-être...
_g_ 4. La famille de Cédric...
_h_ 5. Paul pense que l'Espagne est...
_a_ 6. Pour Cédric, les plages du Brésil...
_e_ 7. Un jour, Cédric va faire...
_c_ 8. Nathalie va utiliser...

a. sont idéales pour bronzer.
b. son billet d'avion.
c. le plan de Paris de Cédric.
d. la capitale du Mexique.
e. le tour du monde.
f. à l'étranger.
g. n'a pas encore décidé entre l'Espagne, le Mexique et le Brésil.
h. un pays superbe.
i. faire un séjour en Italie.

3 **Les vacances** Justine va partir en vacances demain. Complétez le paragraphe avec les mots et expressions de la liste. Toutes les options ne sont pas utilisées.

aller-retour	faire ma valise	sortie
une arrivée	pays	station
faire un séjour	plage	taxi
faire du shopping	prendre un bus	vol

Demain, je pars en vacances. Je vais (1) ___faire un séjour___ avec mon frère à l'île Maurice, une petite île (*island*) tropicale dans l'océan Indien. Nous allons (2) ___prendre un bus___ pour l'aéroport à 7h00. Mon frère veut (*wants*) prendre un (3) ___taxi___, mais moi, je pense qu'il faut économiser parce que j'ai envie de (4) ___faire du shopping___ au marché et dans les boutiques de Port-Louis, la capitale. Le (5) ___vol___ est à 10h. Nous n'avons pas besoin de visa pour le voyage; pour entrer dans le (6) ___pays___, il faut seulement montrer un passeport et un billet (7) ___aller-retour___. J'ai acheté un nouveau maillot de bain pour aller à la (8) ___plage___. Et maintenant, je vais (9) ___faire ma valise___!

Communication

4 Répondez Avec un(e) partenaire, posez-vous ces questions et répondez-y (*them*) à tour de rôle. Answers will vary.

1. Où pars-tu en vacances cette année? Quand?
2. Quand fais-tu tes valises? Avec combien de valises voyages-tu?
3. Préfères-tu la mer, la campagne ou les stations de ski?
4. Comment vas-tu à l'aéroport? Prends-tu l'autobus? Le métro?
5. Quelles sont tes vacances préférées?
6. Quand utilises-tu un plan?
7. Quel est ton pays favori? Pourquoi?
8. Dans quel(s) pays as-tu envie de voyager?

5 Décrivez Avec un(e) partenaire, écrivez (*write*) une description des images. Donnez beaucoup de détails. Ensuite (*Then*), rejoignez un autre groupe et lisez vos descriptions. L'autre groupe doit deviner (*must guess*) quelle image vous décrivez (*describe*). Answers will vary.

1.   2.   3.

4.   5.   6.

6 Conversez Votre professeur va vous donner, à vous et à votre partenaire, une feuille d'activités. L'un de vous est client(e), et l'autre est agent(e) de voyages. Travaillez ensemble pour finaliser la réservation et compléter vos feuilles respectives. Attention! Ne regardez pas la feuille de votre partenaire. Answers will vary.

7 Un voyage Vous allez faire un voyage en Europe et rendre visite à votre cousin, Jean-Marc, qui étudie en Belgique. Écrivez-lui (*Write him*) un e-mail et utilisez les mots de la liste. Answers will vary.

un aéroport	la France
la Belgique	prendre un taxi
un billet	la Suisse
faire un séjour	un vol
faire les valises	un voyage

- Parlez des détails de votre départ.
- Expliquez votre tour d'Europe.
- Organisez votre arrivée en Belgique.
- Parlez de ce que (*what*) vous allez faire ensemble.

Les sons et les lettres 🔊 vhlcentral

Diacriticals for meaning

Some French words with different meanings have nearly identical spellings except for a diacritical mark (*accent*). Sometimes a diacritical does not affect pronunciation at all.

ou	**où**	**a**	**à**
or	*where*	*has*	*to, at*

Sometimes, you can clearly hear the difference between the words.

côte	**côté**	**sale**	**salé**
coast	*side*	*dirty*	*salty*

Very often, two similar-looking words are different parts of speech. Many similar-looking word pairs are those with and without an **-é** at the end.

âge	**âgé**	**entre**	**entré (entrer)**
age (n.)	*elderly* (adj.)	*between* (prep.)	*entered* (p.p.)

In such instances, context should make their meaning clear.

Tu as quel âge?
How old are you? / What is your age?

C'est un homme âgé.
He's an elderly man.

Prononcez Répétez les mots suivants à voix haute.

1. la (*the*)   là (*there*)
2. êtes (*are*)   étés (*summers*)
3. jeune (*young*)   jeûne (*fasting*)
4. pêche (*peach*)   pêché (*fished*)

Articulez Répétez les phrases suivantes à voix haute.

1. J'habite dans une ferme (*farm*). Le magasin est fermé (*closed*).
2. Les animaux mangent du maïs (*corn*). Je suis suisse, mais il est belge.
3. Est-ce que tu es prête? J'ai prêté ma voiture (*car*) à Marcel.
4. La lampe est à côté de la chaise. J'adore la côte ouest de la France.

Dictons Répétez les dictons à voix haute.

À vos marques, prêts, partez! [1]

C'est un prêté pour un rendu.[2]

[1] On your mark, get set, go!
[2] One good turn deserves another. (lit. It is one loaned for one returned.)

Section Goals

In this section, students will learn functional phrases for talking about vacations.

Key Standards

1.2, 2.1, 2.2, 4.1, 4.21

Video Recap: Leçon 6B
Before doing this **Roman-photo**, review the previous one with this activity.

1. _____ a fêté ses dix-huit ans. (Stéphane)
2. _____ a fait un gâteau d'anniversaire. (Sandrine)
3. _____ a visité Paris avec ses parents. (David)
4. _____ a fait une jupe originale. (Amina)
5. _____ ont donné une montre à Stéphane. (Rachid et Astrid)
6. _____ lui a donné un blouson en cuir noir. (Valérie)

Video Synopsis At the train station, David tells Rachid about his trip to Paris. At the café, he tells Stéphane about his trip and that he loved the museums. Stéphane wants to go to Tahiti. David gives Stéphane sunglasses for his birthday. When Sandrine hears about David's trip, she remembers she needs to make reservations for her ski trip to Albertville.

Suggestions

• Ask students to read the title, glance at the video stills, and predict what the episode will be about. Record their predictions.
• Have students read the **Roman-photo** aloud in groups of four.
• Point out the expressions **bon voyage** and **bon séjour**. Explain that **un voyage** refers to travel to and from a destination; **un séjour** is extended time spent at the place itself.
• Review predictions and ask which ones were correct.

De retour au P'tit Bistrot   vhlcentral

AP® Theme: Contemporary Life
Context: Travel

PERSONNAGES

David

Rachid

Sandrine

Stéphane

À la gare...
RACHID Tu as fait bon voyage?
DAVID Salut! Excellent, merci.
RACHID Tu es parti pour Paris avec une valise et te voici avec ces énormes sacs en plus!
DAVID Mes parents et moi sommes allés aux Galeries Lafayette. On a acheté des vêtements et des trucs pour l'appartement aussi.

RACHID Ah ouais?
DAVID Mes parents sont arrivés des États-Unis jeudi soir. Ils ont pris une chambre dans un bel hôtel, tout près de la tour Eiffel.
RACHID Génial!
DAVID Moi, je suis arrivé à la gare vendredi soir. Et nous sommes allés dîner dans une excellente brasserie. Mmm!

DAVID Samedi, on a pris un bateau-mouche sur la Seine. J'ai visité un musée différent chaque jour: le musée du Louvre, le musée d'Orsay...
RACHID En résumé, tu as passé de bonnes vacances dans la capitale... Bon, on y va?
DAVID Ah, euh, oui, allons-y!

STÉPHANE Pour moi, les vacances idéales, c'est un voyage à Tahiti. Ahhh... la plage, et moi en maillot de bain avec des lunettes de soleil... et les filles en bikini!
DAVID Au fait, je n'ai pas oublié ton anniversaire.
STÉPHANE Ouah! Super, ces lunettes de soleil! Merci, David, c'est gentil.

DAVID Désolé de ne pas avoir été là pour ton anniversaire, Stéphane. Alors, ils t'ont fait la surprise?
STÉPHANE Oui, et quelle belle surprise! J'ai reçu des cadeaux trop cool. Et le gâteau de Sandrine, je l'ai adoré.
DAVID Ah, Sandrine... elle est adorable... Euh, Stéphane, tu m'excuses une minute?

DAVID Coucou! Je suis de retour!
SANDRINE Oh! Salut, David. Alors, tu as aimé Paris?
DAVID Oui! J'ai fait plein de choses... de vraies petites vacances! On a fait...

A C T I V I T É S

1   **Les événements** Mettez ces événements dans l'ordre chronologique.

  __1__ a. Rachid va chercher David.
  __6__ b. Stéphane parle de son anniversaire.
 __10__ c. Sandrine va faire une réservation.
  __5__ d. David donne un cadeau à Stéphane.
  __2__ e. Rachid mentionne que David a beaucoup de sacs.

  __7__ f. Stéphane met les lunettes de soleil.
  __4__ g. Stéphane décrit (*describes*) ses vacances idéales.
  __8__ h. David parle avec Sandrine.
  __9__ i. Sandrine pense à ses vacances.
  __3__ j. Rachid et David repartent en voiture.

TEACHING OPTIONS

De retour au P'tit Bistrot Before viewing the video episode **De retour au P'tit Bistrot**, have pairs of students make a list of things someone might say when describing a trip and talking about means of transportation.

TEACHING OPTIONS

Regarder la vidéo Download and print the videoscript on vhlcentral.com, and white out words related to travel and transportation. Distribute the scripts to pairs or groups to complete as cloze paragraphs as they watch the video.

David parle de ses vacances.

STÉPHANE Alors, ces vacances? Tu as fait un bon séjour?
DAVID Oui, formidable!
STÉPHANE Alors, vous êtes restés combien de temps à Paris?
DAVID Quatre jours. Ce n'est pas très long, mais on a visité pas mal d'endroits.
STÉPHANE Comment est-ce que vous avez visité la ville? En voiture?

DAVID En voiture!? Tu es fou! On a pris le métro, comme tout le monde.
STÉPHANE Tes parents n'aiment pas conduire?
DAVID Si, à la campagne, mais pas en ville, surtout une ville comme Paris. On a visité les monuments, les musées...
STÉPHANE Et Monsieur l'artiste a aimé les musées de Paris?
DAVID Je les ai adorés!

SANDRINE Oh! Des vacances!
DAVID Oui... Des vacances? Qu'est-ce qu'il y a?
SANDRINE Je vais à Albertville pour les vacances d'hiver. On va faire du ski!

SANDRINE Est-ce que tu skies?
DAVID Un peu, oui...
SANDRINE Désolée, je dois partir. J'ai une réservation à faire! Rendez-vous ici demain, David. D'accord? Ciao!

Expressions utiles

Talking about vacations

- **Tu es parti pour Paris avec une valise et te voici avec ces énormes sacs en plus!**
  You left for Paris with one suitcase and here you are with these huge extra bags!
- **Nous sommes allés aux Galeries Lafayette.**
  We went to Galeries Lafayette.
- **On a acheté des trucs pour l'appartement aussi.**
  We also bought some things for the apartment.
- **Moi, je suis arrivé à la gare vendredi soir et nous sommes allés dîner.**
  I got to/arrived at the station Friday night and we went to dinner.
- **On a pris un bateau-mouche sur la Seine.**
  We took a sightseeing boat on the Seine.
- **Vous êtes restés combien de temps à Paris?**
  How long did you stay in Paris?
- **On a pris le métro, comme tout le monde.**
  We took the subway, like everyone else.
- **J'ai fait plein de choses.**
  I did a lot of things.
- **Les musées de Paris, je les ai adorés!**
  The museums in Paris, I loved them!

Additional vocabulary

- **Alors, ils t'ont fait la surprise?**
  So, they surprised you?
- **J'ai reçu des cadeaux trop cool.**
  I got the coolest gifts.
- **Le gâteau, je l'ai adoré.**
  I loved the cake.
- **Tu m'excuses une minute?**
  Would you excuse me a minute?
- **Oui, formidable!**
  Yes, wonderful!
- **Qu'est-ce qu'il y a?**
  What is the matter?
- **Désolé(e), je dois partir.**
  Sorry, I have to leave.

---

2 **Questions** Répondez aux questions. *Answers may vary slightly.*

1. David est parti pour Paris avec combien de valises? À son retour (*Upon his return*), est-ce qu'il a le même nombre de valises?
   Il est parti avec une valise. Non, à son retour, il a des sacs en plus.
2. Qu'est-ce que David a fait pour ses vacances?
   Il a visité Paris avec ses parents.
3. Qu'est-ce que David donne à Stéphane comme cadeau d'anniversaire? Stéphane aime-t-il le cadeau?
   Il donne des lunettes de soleil à Stéphane. Oui, Stéphane aime beaucoup le cadeau.
4. Quelles sont les vacances idéales de Stéphane? C'est un voyage à Tahiti. Stéphane est à la plage en maillot de bain avec des lunettes de soleil.
5. Qu'est-ce que Sandrine va faire pour ses vacances d'hiver?
   Elle va faire du ski à Albertville.

3 **Écrivez** Imaginez: vous êtes David, Stéphane ou Sandrine et vous allez en vacances à Paris, Tahiti ou Albertville. Écrivez un e-mail à Valérie. Quel temps fait-il? Où est-ce que vous séjournez? Quels vêtements est-ce que vous avez apportés? Qu'est-ce que vous faites chaque jour?

A C T I V I T É S

EXPANSION

Les bateaux-mouches Touring by **bateau-mouche** is an excellent way to see the famous sights along the River Seine. Tourists can listen to narrations in various languages as they pass by **la cathédrale de Notre-Dame**, **la Conciergerie**, under the ornate **pont Alexandre III**, under the oldest bridge in Paris **le Pont Neuf**, **la tour Eiffel**, and even a miniature version of the **statue de la Liberté**.

PRE-AP®

Interpersonal Speaking Have students work in groups of four to prepare a skit to present to the class. In the skit, the group of friends is on vacation and decides what they feel like doing. Tell them to describe what city they are visiting and explain what activities they want to do while they are visiting the city.

Expressions utiles

- Model the pronunciation of the **Expressions utiles** and have students repeat them after you.
- Draw attention to expressions with direct object pronouns and the **passé composé** with **être** in the video still captions, in the **Expressions utiles** box, and as they occur in your conversation with students. Point out that this material will be formally presented in **Structures**.
- Respond briefly to questions about direct object pronouns and the **passé composé** with **être**. Reinforce correct forms, but do not expect students to produce them consistently at this time.
- Point out that **cool** is invariable since it is an adopted word.
- Point out to students that the word **formidable** is a **faux ami**, meaning *wonderful*, not *formidable*.
- Remind students that **désolée** in the last sentence is feminine because Sandrine is talking about herself. A man would say, **(je suis) désolé**.

1 Suggestion Form several groups of five students. Write each of these sentences on individual strips of paper and distribute them among the students in each group (two per student). Copy a set of sentences for each group. Have students read their sentences aloud in the proper order.

1 Expansion Have students write sentences to fill in parts of the story not mentioned in this activity.

2 Expansion Give students time to write out their answers to these questions. Then ask volunteers to write them on the board.

3 Suggestion Before starting this activity, review vocabulary for weather, clothing, and activities by asking questions. Examples: **Quel temps fait-il à Paris en été? à Albertville en hiver? Qu'est-ce que vous aimez faire à la plage? à la montagne? Qu'est-ce que vous mettez quand il fait chaud? quand il fait froid?**

271

AP® Theme: Contemporary Life
Context: Travel

vhlcentral | *Flash culture*   CULTURE À LA LOUPE

Tahiti

Tahiti, dans le sud° de l'océan Pacifique, est la plus grande île° de la Polynésie française. Elle devient° un protectorat français en 1842, puis° une colonie française en 1880. Depuis 1959, elle fait partie° de la collectivité d'outre-mer° de Polynésie française. Les langues officielles de Tahiti sont le français et le tahitien.

Le tourisme est une source d'activité très importante pour l'île. Ses hôtels de luxe et leurs fameux bungalows sur l'eau accueillent° près de 170.000 visiteurs par an. Les touristes apprécient Tahiti pour son climat chaud, ses plages superbes et sa culture riche en traditions. À Tahiti, il y a la possibilité de faire toutes sortes d'activités aquatiques comme du bateau, de la pêche, de

la planche à voile ou de la plongée°. On peut aussi faire des randonnées en montagne ou explorer les nombreux lagons bleus de l'île. Si on n'a pas envie de faire de sport, on peut se détendre° dans un spa, bronzer à la plage ou se promener° sur l'île. Papeete, capitale de la Polynésie française et ville principale de Tahiti, offre de bons restaurants, des boutiques variées et un marché.

> ### Coup de main
>
> Si introduces a hypothesis. It may come at the beginning or at the middle of a sentence.
>
> *si + subject + verb + subject + verb*
>
> **Si on n'a pas envie de faire de sport, on peut se détendre dans un spa.**
>
> *subject + verb + si + subject + verb*
>
> **On peut se détendre dans un spa si on n'a pas envie de faire de sport.**

sud *south* **la plus grande île** *the largest island* **devient** *becomes*
puis *then* **fait partie** *is part of* **collectivité d'outre-mer** *overseas territory*
accueillent *welcome* **plongée** *scuba diving* **se détendre** *relax* **se promener** *go for a walk*

A C T I V I T É S

1 Répondez Répondez aux questions par des phrases complètes.

1. Où est Tahiti?
   Tahiti est dans le sud de l'océan Pacifique.
2. Quand est-ce que Tahiti devient une colonie française?
   Tahiti devient une colonie en 1880.
3. De quoi fait partie Tahiti?
   Tahiti fait partie de la collectivité d'outre-mer de Polynésie française.
4. Quelles langues parle-t-on à Tahiti?
   On parle français et tahitien.
5. Quelle particularité ont les hôtels de luxe à Tahiti?
   Les hôtels de luxe ont des bungalows sur l'eau.
6. Combien de personnes par an visitent Tahiti?
   Près de 170.000 touristes par an visitent Tahiti.
7. Pourquoi est-ce que les touristes aiment visiter Tahiti? *Les touristes aiment visiter Tahiti parce qu'il fait chaud et parce que les plages sont superbes.*
8. Quelles sont deux activités sportives que les touristes aiment faire à Tahiti?
   Answers may vary. Possible answer: Ils aiment faire du bateau et de la plongée.
9. Comment s'appelle la ville principale de Tahiti?
   La ville principale de Tahiti s'appelle Papeete.
10. Où va-t-on à Papeete pour acheter un cadeau pour un ami?
    On va au marché ou dans les boutiques.

EXPANSION

Oral Practice Have students imagine arriving in Tahiti to meet a friend who lives there. The "visitor" should ask about possible ways to spend time during the visit and the "resident" should propose activities (basing information on the reading and the vocabulary from **Contextes**).

Then combine two pairs for a reflection on each pair's experiences while together in Tahiti. One pair should ask the other pair what they did, using **les pronoms disjoints** for emphasis and contrast. Encourage students to use an array of verbs conjugated in the **passé composé** with **avoir**.

LE FRANÇAIS QUOTIDIEN

À la gare

contrôleur	*ticket inspector*
couchette	*berth*
guichet	*ticket window*
horaire	*schedule*
quai	*train/metro platform*
voie	*track*
wagon-lit	*sleeper car*
composter	*to punch one's (train) ticket*

LE MONDE FRANCOPHONE

AP® Theme: Contemporary Life
Context: Travel

Les transports

Voici quelques faits insolites° dans les transports.
Au Canada Inauguré en 1966, le métro de Montréal est le premier du monde à rouler sur des pneus° et non sur des roues° en métal. Chaque station a été conçue° par un architecte différent.
En France Le tunnel sous la Manche° permet aux trains Eurostar de transporter des voyageurs et des marchandises entre la France et l'Angleterre.
En Mauritanie Le train du désert, en Mauritanie, en Afrique, est peut-être le train de marchandises le plus long° du monde. Long de 2 km en général, le train fait six voyages chaque jour du Sahara à la côte ouest°. C'est un voyage de plus de 700 km qui dure jusqu'à° 18 heures. Un des seuls moyens° de transport dans la région, ce train est aussi un train de voyageurs.

faits insolites *unusual facts* **pneus** *tires* **roues** *wheels* **conçue** *designed* **Manche** *English Channel* **le plus long** *the longest* **côte ouest** *west coast* **dure jusqu'à** *lasts up to* **seuls moyens** *only means*

PORTRAIT

AP® Theme: Beauty and Aesthetics
Context: Architecture

Le musée d'Orsay

Le musée d'Orsay est un des musées parisiens les plus° visités. Le lieu n'a pourtant° pas toujours été un musée. À l'origine, ce bâtiment° est une gare, construite par l'architecte Victor Laloux et inaugurée en 1900 à l'occasion de l'Exposition universelle°. Les voies de la gare d'Orsay deviennent° trop courtes et en 1939, on décide de limiter le service aux trains de banlieue. Plus tard, la gare sert de décor à des films, comme *Le Procès* de Kafka adapté par Orson Welles, puis° elle devient théâtre, puis salle de ventes aux enchères°. En 1986, le bâtiment est transformé en musée. Il est principalement dédié° à l'art du dix-neuvième siècle°, avec une magnifique collection d'art impressionniste.

Danseuses en bleu, **Edgar Degas**

les plus *the most* **pourtant** *however* **bâtiment** *building* **Exposition universelle** *World's Fair* **deviennent** *become* **puis** *then* **ventes aux enchères** *auction* **principalement dédié** *mainly dedicated* **siècle** *century*

Sur Internet

AP® Theme: Contemporary Life
Context: Travel

Qu'est-ce que le funiculaire de Montmartre?

Go to **vhlcentral.com** to find more information related to this **Culture** section and to watch the corresponding **Flash culture** video.

---

2 Vrai ou faux? Indiquez si les phrases sont **vraies** ou **fausses**. Corrigez les phrases fausses.

1. Le musée d'Orsay a été un théâtre.
   Vrai.
2. Le musée d'Orsay a été une station de métro.
   Faux. Il a été une gare.
3. Le musée d'Orsay est dédié à la sculpture moderne.
   Faux. Le musée d'Orsay est dédié à l'art du dix-neuvième siècle.
4. Il y a un tunnel entre la France et la Guyane française.
   Faux. Il y a un tunnel entre la France et l'Angleterre.
5. Le métro de Montréal roule sur des roues en métal.
   Faux. Le métro de Montréal roule sur des pneus.
6. Le train du désert transporte aussi des voyageurs.
   Vrai.

3 Comment voyager? Vous allez passer deux semaines en France. Vous avez envie de visiter Paris et deux autres régions. Par petits groupes, parlez des moyens (*means*) de transport que vous allez utiliser pendant votre voyage. Expliquez vos choix (*choices*).

ACTIVITÉS

EXPANSION

Cultural Comparison Have students explore Paris's public transportation website (ratp.fr) and plot itineraries in the city using the website. Then have them do the same for an American city, such as New York City. Ask students: **Quel moyen de transport préférez-vous à Paris? à New York?** Tell them to list similarities (**Similitudes**) and differences (**Différences**) between the two systems.

EXPANSION

Les transports You may want to supplement this section by telling students about travel between **Tanger (Maroc)** and **Algésiras (Espagne)** via hydrofoil; between **la Corse**, **l'Italie**, and **la Tunisie** by ferry; **le funiculaire de Montmartre**; **les canaux** in France; and **le bus amphibie** in **Montréal**.

273

Section Goals

In this section, students will learn the **passé composé** with **être**.

Key Standards

4.1, 5.1

Suggestions: Scaffolding
- Quickly review the **passé composé** with **avoir**. Go over **Point de départ** and past participles for the verbs listed.
- Introduce the **passé composé** with **être** by describing where you went yesterday. Example: **Hier, je suis allé(e) à la bibliothèque. Ensuite, je suis allé(e) chez moi.** Then ask students: **Et vous, où êtes-vous allé(e) hier?**
- Explain the agreement of past participles in the **passé composé** with **être** using the chart and examples in bullet two.
- Go over all the verbs that take **être** by drawing a house with doors, windows, and a staircase. Write captions that include verbs that take **être** in the **passé composé** to describe what various people are doing. Stress the irregular past participles **né** and **mort**. Also, consider giving students the mnemonic device **DR & MRS P. VANDERTRAMP**, which includes many of these verbs and their derivatives.
- Follow the Teaching Options suggestion for practicing agreement. Then assign the **Vérifiez** activity.

7A.1

The *passé composé* with *être*   **vhl**central

Point de départ In **Leçon 6A**, you learned to form the **passé composé** with **avoir**. Some verbs, however, form the **passé composé** with **être**. Many such verbs involve motion. You already know a few: **aller, arriver, descendre, partir, sortir, passer, rentrer,** and **tomber**.

- To form the **passé composé** of these verbs, use a present-tense form of the auxiliary verb **être** and the past participle of the verb that expresses the action.

PRESENT TENSE	PAST PARTICIPLE		PRESENT TENSE	PAST PARTICIPLE
Je **suis**	**allé.**		Il **est**	**sorti.**

Tu es parti pour Paris.

Mes parents sont arrivés des États-Unis.

Boîte à outils

Remember, the **passé composé** has three English equivalents. Example: **Nous sommes sortis**. = *We went out. We have gone out. We did go out.*

- The past participles of verbs conjugated with **être** agree with their subjects in number and gender.

aller au passé composé	
je suis allé(e)	nous sommes allé(e)s
tu es allé(e)	vous êtes allé(e)(s)
il/on est allé	ils sont allés
elle est allée	elles sont allées

Charles, tu **es allé** à Montréal?
Charles, did you go to Montreal?

Mes frères **sont rentrés**.
My brothers came back.

Florence **est partie** en vacances.
Florence went on vacation.

Elles **sont arrivées** hier soir.
They arrived last night.

- Here is a list of verbs that take **être** in the **passé composé**.

Verbs that take *être* in the *passé composé*			
aller	*to go*	passer	*to pass by; to spend time*
arriver	*to arrive*	rentrer	*to return (home)*
partir	*to leave*	sortir	*to go out*
descendre	*to go down*	tomber	*to fall*
entrer	*to enter*	rester	*to stay*
monter	*to go up; to get in/on*	retourner	*to return*
mourir	*to die*	naître	*to be born*

TEACHING OPTIONS

Agreement To practice gender and number agreement of past participles in the **passé composé** with **être**, write a pattern sentence on the board. Ex: **Je suis allé à la plage**. Give students a different subject (e.g. Sylvie et Marie) and ask volunteers to go to the board and re-write the sentence making the necessary changes. Ex: **Sylvie et Marie sont allées à la plage**.

EXPANSION

Small Groups Have students work in small groups and talk about where they have already gone/haven't gone yet. Encourage them to find similarities and differences among them. Once they have spoken for a few minutes, ask them to stop and share their responses with the whole class. Ex: **Je suis déjà allé(e) à Orlando. Nous ne sommes jamais allé(e)s en France.**

- These verbs have irregular past participles in the **passé composé**.

naître ▶ **né**

Mes parents **sont nés** en 1958 à Paris.
My parents were born in Paris in 1958.

mourir ▶ **mort**

Ma grand-mère **est morte** l'année dernière.
My grandmother died last year.

〜 **Vérifiez**

Asking questions and negation

- To form a question using inversion in the **passé composé**, invert the subject pronoun and the conjugated form of **être**.

Est-elle restée à l'hôtel Aquabella?
Did she stay at the Aquabella Hotel?

Êtes-vous arrivée ce matin, Madame Roch?
Did you arrive this morning, Mrs. Roch?

- To make a verb negative in the **passé composé**, place **ne/n'** and **pas** around the auxiliary verb, in this case, **être**.

Marie-Thérèse **n'est pas sortie**?
Marie-Thérèse didn't go out?

Je **ne suis pas passé** chez mon amie.
I didn't drop by my friend's house.

Nous **ne sommes pas allées** à la plage.
We didn't go to the beach.

Tu **n'es pas rentré** à la maison hier.
You didn't come home yesterday.

Verbs that can take *avoir* or *être*

- Note that the verb **passer** takes **être** when it means *to pass by,* but it takes **avoir** when it means *to spend time.*

Maryse **est passée** à la douane.
Maryse passed through customs.

Je **suis passé** par là hier.
I went by there yesterday.

Maryse **a passé** trois jours à la campagne.
Maryse spent three days in the country.

J'**ai passé** l'après-midi avec lui.
I spent the afternoon with him.

- The verb **sortir** takes **être** in the **passé composé** when it means *to go out* or *to leave,* but it takes **avoir** when it means *to take someone or something out.*

Elle **est sortie** de chez elle.
She left her house.

Elle **a sorti** la voiture du garage.
She took the car out of the garage.

Essayez! Choisissez le participe passé approprié.

1. Vous êtes (nés/**né**) en 1959, Monsieur?
2. Les élèves sont (**partis**/parti) le 2 juin.
3. Les filles sont (**rentrées**/rentrés) de vacances.
4. Simone de Beauvoir est-elle (mort/**morte**) en 1986?
5. Mes frères sont (**sortis**/sortie).
6. Paul n'est pas (**resté**/restée) chez sa grand-mère.
7. Tu es (arrivés/**arrivée**) avant dix heures, Sophie.
8. Jacqueline a (passée/**passé**) une semaine en Suisse.
9. Nous sommes (descendu/**descendus**) à l'arrêt d'autobus.
10. Maman est (monté/**montée**) dans la voiture.

Mise en pratique

1 **Un week-end sympa** Carole raconte son week-end à Paris. Complétez l'histoire avec les formes correctes des verbes au passé composé.

Thomas et moi, nous (1) ___sommes partis___ (partir) de Lyon samedi et nous (2) ___sommes arrivés___ (arriver) à Paris à onze heures. Nous (3) ___sommes passés___ (passer) à l'hôtel et puis je (4) ___suis allée___ (aller) au Louvre. En route, je (5) ___suis tombée___ (tomber) sur un vieil ami, et nous (6) ___sommes allés___ (aller) prendre un café. Ensuite, je (7) ___suis entrée___ (entrer) dans le musée. Samedi soir, Thomas et moi (8) ___sommes montés___ (monter) au sommet de la tour Eiffel et après nous (9) ___sommes sortis___ (sortir) danser. Dimanche, nous (10) ___sommes retournés___ (retourner) au Louvre. Alors aujourd'hui, je suis fatiguée.

2 **La routine** Voici ce que Nadia et Éric font aujourd'hui. Dites qu'ils ont fait les mêmes activités samedi dernier.

1. Ils vont au parc.   Ils sont allés au parc.
2. Nadia fait du cheval.   Nadia a fait du cheval.
3. Éric passe une heure à la bibliothèque.   Éric a passé une heure à la bibliothèque.
4. Nadia sort avec ses amis.   Nadia est sortie avec ses amis.
5. Ils rentrent tard le soir.   Ils sont rentrés tard le soir.
6. Ils jouent au golf.   Ils ont joué au golf.

3 **Dimanche dernier** Dites ce que (*what*) ces personnes ont fait dimanche dernier. Utilisez les verbes de la liste.   Suggested answers

▶ **MODÈLE**

Laure est allée à la piscine.

aller	rentrer
arriver	rester
monter	sortir

Laure

1. je
Je suis rentré tard.

2. tu
Tu es restée à l'hôtel.

3. nous
Nous sommes allés à l'église.

4. Pamela et Caroline
Pamela et Caroline sont sorties.

4 **L'accident** Le mois dernier, Djénaba et Safiatou sont allées au Sénégal. Complétez les phrases au passé composé. Ensuite, mettez-les dans l'ordre chronologique.

___1___ **a.** les filles / partir pour Dakar en avion   Les filles sont parties pour Dakar en avion.

___5___ **b.** Djénaba / tomber de vélo   Djénaba est tombée de vélo.

___4___ **c.** elles / aller faire du vélo dimanche matin   Elles sont allées faire du vélo dimanche matin.

___2___ **d.** elles / arriver à Dakar tard le soir   Elles sont arrivées à Dakar tard le soir.

___3___ **e.** elles / rester à l'hôtel Sofitel   Elles sont restées à l'hôtel Sofitel.

___6___ **f.** elle / aller à l'hôpital   Elle est allée à l'hôpital.

Communication

5 **Les vacances de printemps** Avec un(e) partenaire, parlez de vos dernières vacances. Répondez à toutes ses questions. Answers will vary.

MODÈLE

quand / partir
Élève 1: *Quand es-tu parti(e)?*
Élève 2: *Je suis parti(e) vendredi soir.*

1. où / aller
2. avec qui / partir
3. comment / voyager
4. à quelle heure / arriver
5. où / dormir

6. combien de temps / rester
7. que / visiter
8. sortir / souvent le soir
9. que / acheter
10. quand / rentrer

6 **Enquête** Votre professeur va vous donner une feuille d'activités. Circulez dans la classe et demandez à différents camarades s'ils ont fait ces choses récemment (*recently*). Présentez les résultats de votre enquête à la classe. Answers will vary.

MODÈLE

Élève 1: *Es-tu allé(e) au musée récemment?*
Élève 2: *Oui, je suis allé(e) au musée jeudi dernier.*

Questions	Nom
1. aller au musée	François
2. passer chez ses amis	
3. sortir au cinéma	
4. rester à la maison pour écouter de la musique	
5. partir en week-end avec sa famille	
6. monter en avion	

7 **À l'aéroport** Imaginez une mauvaise expérience dans un aéroport et parlez-en (*talk about it*) en petits groupes. À tour de rôle, racontez (*tell*) vos aventures et posez le plus (*most*) de questions possible. Utilisez les expressions de la liste et d'autres aussi. Answers will vary.

MODÈLE

Élève 1: *Quand je suis rentré(e) de la Martinique, j'ai attendu trois heures à la douane.*
Élève 2: *Quelle horreur! Pourquoi?*

aller	passer
arriver	perdre
attendre	plan
avion	prendre un avion
billet (aller-retour)	sortir
douane	tomber
partir	valise
passagers	vol

5 Suggestion Have two volunteers read the **modèle** aloud.

5 Partner Chat You can also assign Activity 5 on vhlcentral.com. Students work in pairs to record the activity online. The pair's recorded conversation will appear in your gradebook.

6 Suggestion Distribute the **Feuilles d'activités** found in the Activity Pack on vhlcentral.com.

7 Suggestion Before beginning the activity, ask the students about their travel experiences. Example: **Êtes-vous déjà allé(e)s dans un autre pays?**

Activity Pack For additional activities, go to the **Activity Pack** in the **Resources** section of vhlcentral.com.

EXPANSION

Video Show the video episode again to give students more input regarding the **passé composé** with **être** and **avoir**. Pause the video where appropriate to discuss how certain verbs were used and to ask comprehension questions.

EXPANSION

Extra Practice Using the information in the **Roman-photo**, have students write a summary of David's trip to Paris. Then have students get together with a partner and exchange papers. Tell them to peer edit each other's work. Remind them to check for the correct usage of **avoir** and **être** in the **passé composé,** subject-verb agreement, and the correct forms of past participles.

277

7A.2 Direct object pronouns **vhl**central

Point de départ In **Leçon 6B**, you learned about indirect objects. You are now going to learn about direct objects.

- A direct object is a noun that receives the action of a verb. An indirect object is usually the person or thing that receives the direct object.

DIRECT   INDIRECT
OBJECT   OBJECT

J'ai fait **un cadeau à ma sœur.**
I gave a present to my sister.

- While indirect objects are frequently preceded by the preposition **à**, no preposition is needed before a direct object.

DIRECT OBJECT   *but*   INDIRECT OBJECT
J'emmène **mes parents.**   Je parle **à mes parents.**
I'm taking my parents.   *I'm talking to my parents.*

Boîte à outils

Some French verbs do not take a preposition although their English equivalents do: **écouter** (*to listen to*), **chercher** (*to look for*) and **attendre** (*to wait for*). In deciding whether an object is direct or indirect, always check if the French verb takes the preposition **à**.

Direct object pronouns			
singular		**plural**	
me/m'	*me*	nous	*us*
te/t'	*you*	vous	*you*
le/la/l'	*him/her/it*	les	*them*

Boîte à outils

Like indirect objects, the direct object pronouns **me, te, nous,** and **vous** replace people. However, the direct objects **le, la,** and **les** can replace a person, a place, or a thing.

- You can use a direct object pronoun in the place of a direct object noun.

Tu fais **les valises**? ▶ Tu **les** fais?
Are you packing the suitcases?   *Are you packing them?*

Ils retrouvent **Luc** à la gare. ▶ Ils **le** retrouvent à la gare.
They're meeting Luc at the train station.   *They're meeting him at the train station.*

Tu visites souvent **la Belgique**? ▶ Tu **la** visites souvent?
Do you visit Belgium often?   *Do you visit there often?*

Vérifiez

Direct object pronouns with the present tense

- In the present tense, the direct object pronoun precedes the conjugated verb unless that verb is followed by an infinitive.

Les langues? Laurent et Xavier **les** étudient.   Les élèves ne **vous** entendent pas.
Languages? Laurent and Xavier study them.   *The students don't hear you.*

M'attendez-vous à l'aéroport?   Et Daniel? Tu ne **le** retrouves pas au cinéma?
Are you waiting for me at the airport?   *And Daniel? Aren't you meeting him at the movies?*

- When an infinitive follows a conjugated verb, the direct object pronoun precedes the infinitive.

Marcel va **nous écouter.**   Tu ne préfères pas **la porter** demain?
Marcel will listen to us.   *Wouldn't you rather wear it tomorrow?*

Direct object pronouns with the *passé composé*

- In the **passé composé**, place the direct object pronoun before the conjugated form of the auxilary verb **avoir**.

  Le billet? Je **l'**ai acheté.
  The ticket? I bought it.

  Comment est-ce que tu **m'**as trouvé?
  How did you find me?

  Elle ne **l'a** pas pris à 14 heures?
  She didn't take it at 2 o'clock?

  Le plan? Non, nous ne **l'**avons pas utilisé.
  The map? No, we didn't use it.

- When a direct object pronoun is used with the **passé composé**, the past participle must agree with it in both gender and number.

  J'ai mis **la valise** dans la voiture ce matin.
  I put the suitcase in the car this morning.

  ▶ Je **l'ai mise** dans la voiture ce matin.
  I put it in the car this morning.

  J'ai attendu **les filles** à la gare.
  I waited for the girls at the train station.

  ▶ Je **les** ai **attendues** à la gare.
  I waited for them at the train station.

- When the gender of the direct object pronoun is ambiguous, the past participle agreement will indicate the gender of the direct object to which it refers.

  Ses copains ne **l'**ont pas **trouvée**.
  Her friends didn't find her.

  Mon père **nous** a **entendus**.
  My father heard us.

Et le gâteau, je l'ai adoré!

Les musées, je les ai adorés!

À noter

Verbs that take **être** in the **passé composé** are intransitive verbs. This means that they do not take objects.

Vérifiez

Boîte à outils

When a direct object precedes a form of the **passé composé**, the past participle must agree in number and gender with the direct object.

Quelle plage as-tu préférée?

Which beach did you prefer?

Voilà les pays que j'ai visités.

Here are the countries I visited.

Vérifiez

Essayez! Répondez aux questions en remplaçant l'objet direct par un pronom d'objet direct.

1. Thierry prend le train? Oui, il ___le___ prend.
2. Tu attends ta mère? Oui, je ___l'___ attends.
3. Vous entendez Olivier et Vincent? Oui, on ___les___ entend.
4. Le professeur te cherche? Oui, il ___me___ cherche.
5. Barbara et Caroline retrouvent Linda? Oui, elles ___la___ retrouvent.
6. Vous m'invitez? Oui, nous ___t'/vous___ invitons.
7. Tu nous as compris? Oui, je ___vous___ ai compris.
8. Elles ont regardé les gens? Oui, elles ___les___ ont regardés.
9. Chloé a aimé le concert? Oui, elle ___l'___ a aimé.
10. Vous avez regardé le film *Chacun cherche son chat*? Oui, nous ___l'___ avons regardé.

Suggestions: Scaffolding

- Go over placement rules with the **passé composé**. Point out the information in **À noter**. Then play the Game on p. 279. Assign the **Vérifiez** activity.
- Explain the agreement of past participles with direct object pronouns in the **passé composé**.
- Point out that in the second-to-last bullet, **trouvée** indicates that **l'** refers to a female, while **entendus** indicates that **nous** refers to at least two males or a mixed group of males and females. Tell students that this strategy works well for written French. In the spoken language, however, only a handful of past participles ending in a consonant, such as **fait** and **mis**, predictably reveal the gender of the direct object: **faite(s)**, **mise(s)**. Assign the **Vérifiez** activity. Then have students watch the Grammar Tutorial before completing **Essayez!**

Essayez! For additional practice, have students restate or rewrite the answers in the negative.

EXPANSION

Game Send a student out of the room. Give his or her belongings to other students to hide. Then have the person return. To get the belongings back, the person must ask students yes/no questions. They should respond using direct object pronouns. Example: **Tu as mon livre? (Oui, je l'ai./Non, je ne l'ai pas.)**

EXPANSION

Pairs Have students work in pairs. Write the following list on the board. Tell them to take turns asking each other who does these activities: **acheter le billet, prendre le bus, aimer les sports, passer la douane,** and **étudier les mathématiques.** Example: **Qui prend le bus? (Mon ami Patrick le prend.)**

2 Suggestion Have students ask questions with a direct object pronoun for each item. Example: **Qui l'écoute?**

3 Suggestion Before beginning the activity, have students identify the direct objects.

4 Suggestion Tell students to add two of their own questions with direct objects to the list.

Mise en pratique

1 **À l'aéroport** Jules est à l'aéroport et il parle à sa mère. Choisissez le pronom d'objet direct approprié pour compléter ses phrases.

1. Ton CD préféré? Marie (le, la, **l'**) écoute.
2. Le plan? Les Cartier (la, les, **le**) regardent.
3. Notre amie? Roger et Emma (l', le, **la**) cherchent.
4. Le journal français? Papa (la, **l'**, le) achète.
5. Nos billets? Coralie (le, l', **les**) a pris.

2 **Des activités** Dites ce que (*what*) ces gens font le week-end. Employez des pronoms d'objet direct.

▶ **MODÈLE**

Il l'écoute.

Dominique / ce CD

1. Benoît / ses films
Il les regarde.

2. ma mère / cette robe
Elle l'admire.

3. Philippe / son gâteau
Il le mange.

4. Stéphanie et Marc / ces lunettes
Ils les achètent.

3 **À la plage** La famille de Dalila a passé une semaine à la mer. Dalila parle de ce que (*what*) chaque membre de sa famille a fait. Employez des pronoms d'objet direct.

MODÈLE

J'ai conduit Ahmed à la plage. *Je l'ai conduit à la plage.*

1. Mon père a acheté le journal tous les matins.   Il l'a acheté tous les matins.
2. Ma sœur a retrouvé son petit ami au café.   Elle l'a retrouvé au café.
3. Mes parents ont emmené les enfants au cinéma.   Ils les ont emmenés au cinéma.
4. Mon frère a invité sa fiancée au restaurant.   Il l'a invitée au restaurant.
5. Anissa a porté ses lunettes de soleil.   Elle les a portées.
6. Noah a pris les cartes.   Il les a prises.

4 **Des doutes** Julie est au parc avec son amie Caroline et répond à ses questions sur leurs vacances avec les parents de Julie. Formez les questions que pose Caroline. Avec un(e) partenaire, jouez les deux rôles. Ensuite, présentez la scène à la classe.   Suggested answers

1. Oui, mes parents t'invitent au bord de la mer.   Tes parents m'invitent au bord de la mer?
2. Oui, je vais t'attendre à l'aéroport.   Quelqu'un va m'attendre à l'aéroport?
3. Oui, mon frère va nous emmener sur son bateau.   Ton frère va-t-il nous emmener sur son bateau?
4. Oui, je pense que ma famille va bien t'aimer.   Penses-tu que ta famille va bien m'aimer?
5. J'ai choisi d'emporter (*take*) les chaussures vertes.   Quelle chaussures as-tu choisies d'emporter?
6. J'ai pris le maillot de bain bleu.   Quel maillot de bain as-tu pris?

TEACHING OPTIONS

Small Groups Split the class into small groups. Have students take turns asking the group who does these activities: **prendre le train, pratiquer le cyclisme, gagner tous les matchs, rendre visite à ses grands-parents pendant les vacances, écrire des e-mails, écouter les professeurs, aller à la piscine.** Ex: **Qui prend le train? Je le prends.**

EXPANSION

Extra Practice Have students work in pairs to write 5-6 sentences describing what they did on a recent trip, using direct object pronouns. The sentences should not be in chronological order. Have them exchange papers and order each other's sentences, then read them aloud to each other.

Communication

5 **Le départ** Clémentine va partir au Cameroun chez sa correspondante (*pen pal*) Léa. Sa mère veut (*wants*) être sûre qu'elle est prête, mais Clémentine n'a encore rien (*nothing*) fait. Avec un(e) partenaire, jouez leur conversation en utilisant les phrases de la liste. *Answers will vary.*

MODÈLE

Élève 1: *Tu as acheté le cadeau pour ton amie?*
Élève 2: *Non, je ne l'ai pas encore acheté.*
Élève 1: *Quand vas-tu l'acheter?*
Élève 2: *Je vais l'acheter cet après-midi.*

Coup de main

Place short adverbs, such as **déjà** and **encore**, between the auxiliary verb and the past participle when using the **passé composé**.

acheter ton billet d'avion	faire tes valises
avoir l'adresse de Léa	finir ton shopping
chercher un maillot de bain	prendre tes lunettes
choisir le cadeau de Léa	préparer tes vêtements
confirmer l'heure de l'arrivée	trouver ton passeport

6 **À Tahiti** Imaginez que vous alliez partir à Tahiti. Avec un(e) partenaire, posez-vous ces questions. Il/Elle vous répond en utilisant le pronom d'objet direct approprié. Ensuite, changez de rôles. *Answers will vary.*

MODÈLE

Est-ce que tu prends le bus pour aller à la plage?
Non, je ne le prends pas.

1. Aimes-tu la mer?

2. Est-ce que tu prends l'avion?

3. Qui va t'attendre à l'aéroport?

4. Quand as-tu fait tes valises?

5. Est-ce que tu as acheté ton maillot de bain?

6. Est-ce que tu prends ton appareil photo?

7. Où as-tu acheté tes vêtements?

8. As-tu déjà choisi ton hôtel à Tahiti?

9. Est-ce que tu as réservé ta chambre d'hôtel?

10. Tu vas regarder la télévision tahitienne?

11. Vas-tu essayer les plats typiques de Tahiti?

12. As-tu regardé le plan de Tahiti?

---

5 Suggestions
• Before beginning the activity, have students underline the direct objects in the phrases.
• Have two volunteers read the **modèle** aloud.

5 Partner Chat You can also assign Activity 5 on vhlcentral.com. Students work in pairs to record the activity online. The pair's recorded conversation will appear in your gradebook.

6 Suggestions
• Before beginning the activity, have students describe the photo.
• Tell students to add three of their own questions with direct objects to the list.

Activity Pack For additional activities, go to the **Activity Pack** in the **Resources** section of vhlcentral.com.

EXPANSION

Extra Practice Make a list of twenty questions requiring direct object pronouns in the answer. Arrange students in two concentric circles. Students in the inner circle ask questions from the list to those in the outer circle until you say stop (**Arrêtez-vous**). The outer circle then moves one person to the right and the questions begin again. Continue for five minutes, and then have the students in the outer circle ask the questions.

EXPANSION

Pairs Have students work in pairs. Tell them to invent a romantic dialogue between Simone and Jean-Claude, two protagonists of a soap opera. They should include direct object pronouns in their dialogues and these verbs: **adorer, aimer, détester,** and **attendre**. Example: **Jean-Claude: Simone, je t'adore.**

Révision

Key Standards

1.1

1 Suggestion Tell students to write their sentences. Remind them that verbs that indicate motion often require the **passé composé** with **être**.

1 Partner Chat You can also assign Activity 1 on vhlcentral.com. Students work in pairs to record the activity online. The pair's recorded conversation will appear in your gradebook.

2 Suggestions
• Distribute the **Feuilles d'activités** from the Activity Pack.
• Have two volunteers read the **modèle** aloud. Remind students to use direct object pronouns in their responses.

3 Suggestions
• Some students may not have traveled to another country. Tell them they can "make up" countries they have visited.
• Tell students to jot down notes during their interviews.

4 Expansion To practice **vous** forms, bring in a small suitcase with various items and tell the class you just returned from a trip. Students must ask you questions about your vacation based on the items and figure out where you went. Example: a suitcase with gloves, a hat, a parka, and ski goggles.

5 Expansion Have groups decide who had the best or most interesting weekend, then ask them to tell the class about it.

6 Suggestion Divide the class into pairs and distribute the Info Gap Handouts from the Activity Pack. Give students ten minutes to complete the activity.

1 Il y a dix minutes Avec un(e) partenaire, décrivez (*describe*) dans cette scène les actions qui se sont passées (*happened*) il y a dix minutes. Utilisez les verbes de la liste pour écrire (*write*) des phrases. Ensuite, comparez vos phrases avec les phrases d'un autre groupe. Answers will vary.

MODÈLE

Élève 1: *Il y a dix minutes, M. Hamid est parti.*
Élève 2: *Il y a dix minutes, …*

aller	partir
arriver	rentrer
descendre	sortir
monter	tomber

2 Qui aime quoi? Votre professeur va vous donner une feuille d'activités. Circulez dans la classe pour trouver un(e) camarade différent(e) qui aime ou qui n'aime pas chaque lieu de la liste. Answers will vary.

MODÈLE

Élève 1: *Est-ce que tu aimes les aéroports?*
Élève 2: *Je ne les aime pas du tout; je les déteste.*

3 À l'étranger Par groupes de quatre, interviewez vos camarades. Dans quels pays sont-ils déjà allés? Dans quelles villes? Comparez vos destinations, puis présentez toutes les réponses à la classe. N'oubliez pas de demander: Answers will vary.

• quand vos camarades sont parti(e)s
• où ils/elles sont allé(e)s
• où ils/elles sont resté(e)s
• combien de temps ils/elles ont passé là-bas

4 La valise Sandra et John sont partis en vacances. Voici leur valise. Avec un(e) partenaire, faites une description écrite (*written*) de leurs vacances. Où sont-ils allés? Comment sont-ils partis? Answers will vary.

5 Un long week-end Avec un(e) partenaire, préparez huit questions sur le dernier long week-end. Utilisez les verbes de la liste. Ensuite, par groupes de quatre, répondez à toutes les questions. Answers will vary.

MODÈLE

Élève 1: *Où es-tu allé(e) vendredi soir?*
Élève 2: *Vendredi soir, je suis resté(e) chez moi. Mais samedi, je suis sorti(e)!*

aller	rentrer
arriver	rester
partir	retourner
passer	sortir

6 Mireille et les Girard Votre professeur va vous donner, à vous et à votre partenaire, une feuille sur le week-end de Mireille et de la famille Girard. Posez des questions à votre partenaire pour compléter votre feuille. Attention! Ne regardez pas la feuille de votre partenaire. Answers will vary.

MODÈLE

Élève 1: *Qu'est-ce que Mireille a fait vendredi soir?*
Élève 2: *Elle est allée au cinéma.*

EXPANSION

Dehydrated Sentences Write these phrases on the board. Tell students to write complete sentences, using the **passé composé**. 1. Janine et moi / faire du shopping 2. Nous / partir / une heure 3. Nous / prendre / métro / Galeries Lafayette / et / nous / passer / après-midi / là 4. Nous / arriver / chez Janine / fatigué 5. Elle / ne pas / avoir besoin / sortir / pour manger / et / nous / rester / la maison

PRE-AP®

Presentational Writing Have students write a composition about a memorable vacation they took with friends or family. Remind them to use the **passé composé**. They should also use object pronouns to avoid unnecessary repetition.

Reportage de CETELEM

Oubliez les dortoirs° de 10 à 15 lits°...

vhlcentral

AP® Theme: Contemporary Life
Context: Travel

Préparation Répondez aux questions suivantes. Answers will vary.

1. Qu'est-ce que vous aimez faire pendant les vacances?
2. Préférez-vous faire du camping, descendre (*stay*) dans un hôtel ou rester chez des amis pendant les vacances? Pourquoi?

Des auberges de jeunesse° nouvelle génération

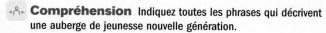

Après avoir terminé° leurs études à l'université et avant de commencer leur vie professionnelle, beaucoup de jeunes partent en voyage à l'étranger. Avec très peu d'argent, ils arrivent à° passer plusieurs semaines, quelques mois, ou même une année entière à visiter les pays du monde. Ils voyagent seuls ou avec des amis et souvent, ils passent la nuit dans une auberge de jeunesse pour économiser de l'argent. Autrefois°, ces auberges offraient° peu de confort. Il fallait° dormir dans de grands dortoirs et partager la salle de bains au bout du couloir°. Mais aujourd'hui, les auberges s'adaptent aux jeunes qui sont de plus en plus exigeants°. Elles sont beaucoup plus confortables, mais restent bon marché°.

dortoirs *dormitories* **lits** *beds* **auberges de jeunesse** *youth hostels* **Après avoir terminé** *After having finished* **arrivent à** *manage to* **Autrefois** *In the past* **offraient** *offered* **Il fallait** *It was necessary* **au bout du couloir** *at the end of the hall* **exigeants** *demanding* **bon marché** *inexpensive*

Vocabulaire utile

la douche	*shower*
la couverture	*blanket, cover*
la chambre	*room*
l'armoire (*f.*)	*wardrobe*
sécurisé(e)	*locked*
gratuit(e)	*free*
privé(e)	*private*

 Compréhension Indiquez toutes les phrases qui décrivent une auberge de jeunesse nouvelle génération.

_____ 1. Il y a des dortoirs de 10 à 15 lits.

_____ 2. Les douches sont dans le couloir.

✓ 3. Il y a des armoires sécurisées et du Wi-Fi gratuit.

_____ 4. Le petit-déjeuner (*breakfast*) est gratuit.

✓ 5. Les chambres coûtent entre 60–100 euros la nuit.

Conversation Avec un partenaire, décidez si vous êtes d'accord avec ces déclarations et expliquez pourquoi. Answers will vary.

1. Voyager forme (*shapes*) la jeunesse.
2. C'est important d'aider financièrement les jeunes à voyager.

 Application Trouvez sur Internet deux auberges de jeunesse dans une région ou un pays francophone. Notez les services qu'elles offrent. Ensuite, utilisez ces informations pour préparer une présentation qui propose la construction d'une auberge de jeunesse dans votre région. Dans votre présentation, expliquez les services que l'auberge de jeunesse va offrir et les différents avantages qu'elle peut apporter aux jeunes et la communauté.

Section Goals

In this section, students will:
- read about youth hostels
- watch a video about modern youth hostels
- answer questions about youth travel

Key Standards

1.1, 1.2, 1.3, 2.1, 4.2

Préparation Tell students to base their answers on what they would like to do if they have not traveled widely.

Des auberges de jeunesse nouvelle génération

To check comprehension, have students complete these statements: 1. **Les jeunes partent en voyage après…** (avoir terminé leurs études à l'université) 2. **…offraient peu de confort.** (Les auberges de jeunesse d'autrefois) 3. **…s'adaptent aux jeunes qui sont de plus en plus exigeants.** (Les auberges de nouvelle génération)

PRE-AP®

Interpretive Communication
- Have students look at the image and read the caption to predict what the video is about.
- Explain that students will not understand every word they hear. Tell them to listen for cognates and pay attention to images that support the vocabulary they hear.

Compréhension After students complete the activity, show the video again so they can check their answers. Have them revise the unchecked statements so they describe the youth hostel in the video.

Section Goals

In this section, students will learn and practice vocabulary related to:
• hotels
• ordinal numbers
• sequencing events

Key Standards

1.1, 1.2, 4.1

Suggestions

• Use the digital image for this page. Point out people and things in the illustration and describe what the people are doing. Example: **Ils sont à la réception d'un hôtel. Ils ont une réservation. Voici la clé de leur chambre.**

• Have students look over the new vocabulary. They should notice that many terms related to hotels and travel are cognates (**réservation, réception, passeport**).

• Point out that the word **libre** means *free*, as in *available*, not *free of charge*.

• Emphasize that, in this context, **complet/complète** means *full*, not *complete*.

• Go through ordinal numbers and have students repeat after you. Emphasize the difference in pronunciation between **deuxième** and **douzième**.

• Tell students that the word **second(e)** is used instead of **deuxième** when there are only two items to list. Example: **La Seconde Guerre mondiale.**

You will learn how to...

• make hotel reservations
• give instructions

◁)) **vhl**central

À l'hôtel

Vocabulaire

annuler une réservation	to cancel a reservation
réserver	to reserve, to book
premier/première	first
cinquième	fifth
neuvième	ninth
vingt et unième	twenty-first
vingt-deuxième	twenty-second
trente et unième	thirty-first
centième	hundredth
une agence de voyages	travel agency
un agent de voyages	travel agent
une auberge de jeunesse	youth hostel
une chambre individuelle	single room
un hôtel	hotel
complet/complète	full (no vacancies)
libre	available
alors	so, then; at that moment
après (que)	after
avant (de)	before
d'abord	first
donc	therefore
enfin	finally, at last
ensuite	then, next
finalement	finally
pendant (que)	during, while
puis	then
tout à coup	suddenly
tout de suite	right away

la réception

Bienvenue!

le lit

l'hôtelier (m.)

l'hôtelière (f.)

le passeport

la clé

les client(e)s

DIFFERENTIATION

For Kinesthetic Learners Ask ten volunteers to line up facing the class. Make sure students know what number they are in line. Call out ordinal numbers at random. The student whose cardinal number corresponds to the called ordinal number has three seconds to step forward. If that student is too slow, he or she sits down. The order changes for the rest of the students standing further down the line. The last students standing win.

EXPANSION

Les étages Point out to students that a second floor in the U.S. would be called **le premier étage** in the Francophone world. Tell them that an **étage** is a floor above another floor. Elevators usually indicate the ground floor by the letter **R** (the abbreviation of **rez-de-chaussée**) or the number **0**. Add that, in buildings with only two floors, people say **à l'étage** for *on the second floor*.

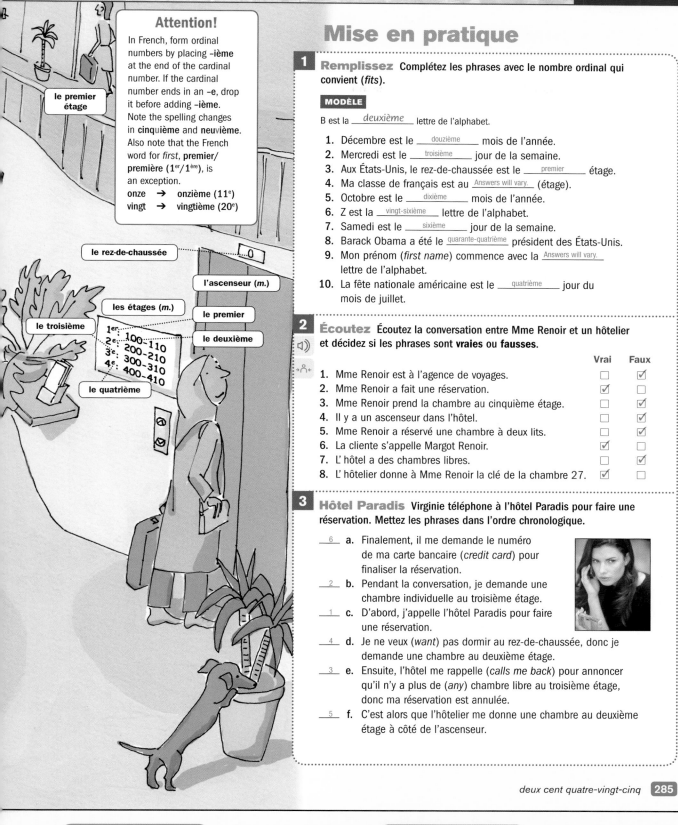

Attention!

In French, form ordinal numbers by placing –ième at the end of the cardinal number. If the cardinal number ends in an –e, drop it before adding –ième. Note the spelling changes in **cinquième** and **neuvième**. Also note that the French word for *first*, premier/première (1ᵉʳ/1ᵉʳᵉ), is an exception.

onze → onzième (11ᵉ)

vingt → vingtième (20ᵉ)

le premier étage

le rez-de-chaussée

l'ascenseur (m.)

les étages (m.)

le troisième

le premier

le deuxième

le quatrième

1ᵉʳ 100–110
2ᵉ 200–210
3ᵉ 300–310
4ᵉ 400–410

Mise en pratique

1 Remplissez Complétez les phrases avec le nombre ordinal qui convient (*fits*).

MODÈLE

B est la ___deuxième___ lettre de l'alphabet.

1. Décembre est le ___douzième___ mois de l'année.
2. Mercredi est le ___troisième___ jour de la semaine.
3. Aux États-Unis, le rez-de-chaussée est le ___premier___ étage.
4. Ma classe de français est au ___Answers will vary.___ (étage).
5. Octobre est le ___dixième___ mois de l'année.
6. Z est la ___vingt-sixième___ lettre de l'alphabet.
7. Samedi est le ___sixième___ jour de la semaine.
8. Barack Obama a été le ___quarante-quatrième___ président des États-Unis.
9. Mon prénom (*first name*) commence avec la ___Answers will vary.___ lettre de l'alphabet.
10. La fête nationale américaine est le ___quatrième___ jour du mois de juillet.

2 Écoutez Écoutez la conversation entre Mme Renoir et un hôtelier et décidez si les phrases sont **vraies** ou **fausses**.

	Vrai	Faux
1. Mme Renoir est à l'agence de voyages.	☐	☑
2. Mme Renoir a fait une réservation.	☑	☐
3. Mme Renoir prend la chambre au cinquième étage.	☐	☑
4. Il y a un ascenseur dans l'hôtel.	☐	☑
5. Mme Renoir a réservé une chambre à deux lits.	☐	☑
6. La cliente s'appelle Margot Renoir.	☑	☐
7. L'hôtel a des chambres libres.	☐	☑
8. L'hôtelier donne à Mme Renoir la clé de la chambre 27.	☑	☐

3 Hôtel Paradis Virginie téléphone à l'hôtel Paradis pour faire une réservation. Mettez les phrases dans l'ordre chronologique.

___6___ a. Finalement, il me demande le numéro de ma carte bancaire (*credit card*) pour finaliser la réservation.

___2___ b. Pendant la conversation, je demande une chambre individuelle au troisième étage.

___1___ c. D'abord, j'appelle l'hôtel Paradis pour faire une réservation.

___4___ d. Je ne veux (*want*) pas dormir au rez-de-chaussée, donc je demande une chambre au deuxième étage.

___3___ e. Ensuite, l'hôtel me rappelle (*calls me back*) pour annoncer qu'il n'y a plus de (*any*) chambre libre au troisième étage, donc ma réservation est annulée.

___5___ f. C'est alors que l'hôtelier me donne une chambre au deuxième étage à côté de l'ascenseur.

deux cent quatre-vingt-cinq **285**

285

Communication

4 Suggestions
- Tell students that the verb **descendre** means *to stay* when used with **hôtel** and that in some countries hotel guests must leave their passports at the reception desk.
- Have students explore different hotel websites to find a hotel to describe.

4 Expansion Ask volunteers to describe their **vacances idéales** to the class.

4 Virtual Chat You can also assign Activity 4 on vhlcentral.com. Students record individual responses that appear in your gradebook.

5 Suggestion Have students consider other details that might come up while making a hotel reservation and include them in their conversation. Examples: **Est-ce qu'il y a un ascenseur? Il y a une télévision dans la chambre?**

6 Expansion Assign each group a different Francophone location. Tell students to include any nearby attractions (**la plage, la campagne, le centre-ville**) and hotel amenities (**la piscine, le restaurant**) in their poster. For inspiration, have students explore French-language hotel booking websites.

21st Century Skills

6 Flexibility and Adaptability Remind students to include input from all team members, adapting their presentation so it represents the whole group.

7 Suggestion Before starting this activity, have students brainstorm a list of steps involved in making a hotel reservation as well as a list of possible complications.

Successful Language Learning Remind students to accept some corrections without explanation, especially when they are attempting to use language and structures above their current level. Tell them not to overanalyze and to trust that it will make more sense as their language skills develop.

---

4 **Conversez** Interviewez votre camarade à propos de (*about*) ses vacances idéales dans un hôtel. Answers will vary.

1. Quelles sont les dates de ton séjour?
2. Où vas-tu? Dans quel pays, quelle région ou quelle ville? Vas-tu à la mer, à la campagne, ...?
3. À quel hôtel descends-tu (*do you stay*)?
4. Qui fait la réservation?
5. Comment est l'hôtel? Est-ce que l'hôtel a un ascenseur, une piscine, ...?
6. À quel étage est ta chambre?
7. Combien de lits a ta chambre?
8. Laisses-tu ton passeport à la réception?

5 **Notre réservation** Par groupes de trois, travaillez pour préparer une présentation où deux touristes font une réservation dans un hôtel ou une auberge de jeunesse francophone. N'oubliez pas d'ajouter (*add*) les informations de la liste. Answers will vary.

- le nom de l'hôtel
- le type de chambre(s)
- l'étage
- le nombre de lits
- les dates
- le prix

6 **Mon hôtel** Vous allez ouvrir (*open*) votre propre hôtel. Par groupes de quatre, créez une affiche (*poster*) pour le promouvoir (*promote*) avec l'information de la liste et présentez votre hôtel au reste de la classe. Votre professeur va ensuite donner à chaque groupe un budget. Avec ce budget, vous allez faire la réservation à l'hôtel qui convient le mieux (*best suits*) à votre groupe. Answers will vary.

- le nom de votre hôtel
- le nombre d'étoiles (*stars*)
- les services offerts
- le prix pour une nuit

★ une étoile	★★ deux étoiles	★★★ trois étoiles	★★★★ quatre étoiles	★★★★★ cinq étoiles

7 **Pour faire une réservation** Écrivez un paragraphe où vous décrivez (*describe*) ce qu'un touriste doit (*must*) faire pour réserver une chambre. Utilisez au moins cinq mots de la liste. Échangez et comparez votre paragraphe avec celui (*the one*) d'un camarade de classe. Answers will vary.

alors	d'abord	puis
après (que)	donc	tout à coup
avant (de)	enfin	tout de suite

TEACHING OPTIONS

Logical Associations Give each student a card with either (1) a noun from the **Vocabulaire**, such as **chambre, clé,** or **passeport** or (2) a related verb, such as **réserver, prendre, oublier,** or **perdre**. Tell students to find someone whose word can be combined logically with their own. Then have them write an original sentence in the **passé composé**. Compile the sentences on the board. Then use sequencing expressions to combine them into a story.

EXPANSION

Combien d'étoiles préférez-vous? Tell students that the French government regulates hotel ratings and requires that they be posted. Hotels must meet standards to qualify for a certain number of stars. A two-star hotel is a comfortable budget hotel. A five-star hotel is luxurious. While the level of comfort is standardized, prices are not.

Les sons et les lettres 🔊 vhlcentral

ti, sti, and ssi

The letters **ti** followed by a consonant are pronounced like the English word *tea*, but without the puff released in the English pronunciation.

ac**ti**f	pe**ti**t	**ti**gre	u**ti**les

When the letter combination **ti** is followed by a vowel sound, it is often pronounced like the sound linking the English words *miss you*.

dic**ti**onnaire	pa**ti**ent	ini**ti**al	addi**ti**on

Regardless of whether it is followed by a consonant or a vowel, the letter combination **sti** is pronounced *stee*, as in the English word *steep*.

ge**sti**on	que**sti**on	Séba**sti**en	arti**sti**que

The letter combination **ssi** followed by another vowel or a consonant is usually pronounced like the sound linking the English words *miss you*.

pa**ssi**on	expre**ssi**on	mi**ssi**on	profe**ssi**on

Words that end in **-sion** or **-tion** are often cognates with English words, but they are pronounced quite differently. In French, these words are never pronounced with a *sh* sound.

compre**ssi**on	na**ti**on	atten**ti**on	addi**ti**on

Prononcez Répétez les mots suivants à voix haute.

1. artiste
2. mission
3. réservation
4. impatient
5. position
6. initiative
7. possession
8. nationalité
9. compassion
10. possible

Articulez Répétez les phrases suivantes à voix haute.

1. L'addition, s'il vous plaît.
2. Christine est optimiste et active.
3. Elle a fait une bonne première impression.
4. Laëtitia est impatiente parce qu'elle est fatiguée.
5. Tu cherches des expressions idiomatiques dans le dictionnaire.

Dictons Répétez les dictons à voix haute.

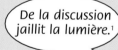
De la discussion jaillit la lumière.[1]

Il n'est de règle sans exception.[2]

[1] Discussion brings light.
[2] The exception proves the rule.

Section Goals
In this section, students will learn about the letter combinations **ti**, **sti**, and **ssi**.

Key Standards
4.1

Suggestions
- Pronounce each of the example words and have students repeat them after you.
- To practice **ti**, have students put the palm of their hand in front of their lips and say the English word *tea*. Ask them if they felt the puff of air when they pronounced the letter **t**. Then have them pronounce the French word **petit** holding their hand in front of their mouth. Explain that they should not feel a puff of air when they pronounce the letters **ti** in French.
- Point out that **-sion** as in the word **télévision** has a [z] sound. Additionally, **-cia** as in the name **Patricia** has an unvoiced [s] sound.
- Many words that end in **-sion**, **-ssion**, **-stion**, and **-tion** are cognates. Contrast the French and English pronunciation of words such as **attention** and **mission**.
- Mention words from the **Vocabulaire** that contain **ti**, **sti**, or **ssi**. Then have students repeat after you. Alternatively, ask students to recall such vocabulary. Examples: **réception, réservation, vingtième**. See if a volunteer is able to recall any words from previous lessons. Examples: **pessimiste, dessiner, l'addition,** and **attention**.

Dictons Tell students that the word **lumière** is used figuratively in the proverb «**De la discussion jaillit la lumière.**» Ask students what they think it means in this context (*clarity, ideas*).

EXPANSION

Pronunciation Here are some sentences to use for additional practice with these letter combinations. **1. C'est utile d'étudier la gestion et l'informatique. 2. La profession de Sébastien? Il est dentiste. 3. Patricia utilise un plan de la station de ski. 4. Martine est-elle pessimiste ou optimiste?**

EXPANSION

Tongue Twisters Teach your students the following French tongue-twisters that contain **ti** and **ssi**: **1. Pauvre petit pêcheur, prend patience pour pouvoir prendre plusieurs petits poissons. 2. Un pâtissier qui pâtissait chez un tapissier qui tapissait, dit un jour au tapissier qui tapissait: vaut-il mieux pâtisser chez un tapissier qui tapisse ou tapisser chez un pâtissier qui pâtisse?**

287

Section Goals

In this section, students will learn functional phrases for getting help and making reservations.

Key Standards

1.2, 2.1, 2.2, 4.1, 4.2

Video Recap: Leçon 7A

Before doing this **Roman-photo**, review the previous one with this activity.

1. **Où est allé David? (à Paris)**
2. **Avec qui a-t-il visité Paris? (avec ses parents)**
3. **Qu'a-t-il fait à Paris? (Il a visité les musées et les monuments. Il a pris un bateau-mouche.)**
4. **Qu'est-ce qu'il a rapporté à Stéphane? (des lunettes de soleil)**
5. **Où Sandrine va-t-elle passer ses vacances d'hiver? (à Albertville)**

Video Synopsis Sandrine goes to a travel agency to find a hotel in Albertville. They are all too expensive, so she leaves without making a reservation. She asks Amina to help find a cheaper hotel. Then Pascal says he can't go to Albertville after all. Disappointed, Sandrine tells Amina to cancel the reservation because she and Pascal are finished. Amina then tells Sandrine about Cyberhomme, her electronic pen pal.

Suggestions

- Ask students to read the title, glance at the video stills, and predict what the episode will be about.
- Have students read the **Roman-photo** aloud in groups of four.
- Have students scan the captions to find at least three sentences that contain words and expressions related to travel and accommodations. Examples: **Ou alors, à l'hôtel Le Mont Blanc, deux chambres individuelles pour 171 euros par personne. Les hôtels les moins chers sont déjà complets.**
- Review students' predictions and ask which ones were correct.

La réservation d'hôtel vhlcentral

AP® Theme: Contemporary Life
Context: Travel

PERSONNAGES

Agent de voyages

Amina

Pascal

Sandrine

À l'agence de voyages...

SANDRINE J'ai besoin d'une réservation d'hôtel, s'il vous plaît. C'est pour les vacances de Noël.

AGENT Où allez-vous? En Italie?

SANDRINE Nous allons à Albertville.

AGENT Et c'est pour combien de personnes?

SANDRINE Nous sommes deux, mais il nous faut deux chambres individuelles.

AGENT Très bien. Quelles sont les dates du séjour, Mademoiselle?

SANDRINE Alors, le 25, c'est Noël, donc je fête en famille. Disons du 26 décembre au 2 janvier.

AGENT Ce n'est pas possible à Albertville, mais à Megève, j'ai deux chambres à l'hôtel Le Vieux Moulin pour 143 euros par personne. Ou alors, à l'hôtel Le Mont Blanc pour 171 euros par personne.

SANDRINE Oh non, mais Megève, ce n'est pas Albertville... et ces prix! C'est vraiment trop cher.

AGENT C'est la saison, Mademoiselle. Les hôtels les moins chers sont déjà complets.

SANDRINE Oh là là. Je ne sais pas quoi faire... J'ai besoin de réfléchir. Merci, Monsieur. Au revoir!

AGENT Au revoir, Mademoiselle.

Chez Sandrine...

SANDRINE Oui, Pascal. Amina nous a trouvé une auberge à Albertville. C'est génial, non? En plus, c'est pas cher!

PASCAL Euh, en fait... Albertville, maintenant, c'est impossible.

SANDRINE Qu'est-ce que tu dis?

PASCAL C'est que... j'ai du travail.

SANDRINE Du travail! Mais c'est Noël! On ne travaille pas à Noël! Et Amina a déjà tout réservé... Oh! C'est pas vrai!

PASCAL *(à lui-même)* Elle n'est pas très heureuse maintenant, mais quelle surprise en perspective!

Un peu plus tard...

AMINA On a réussi, Sandrine! La réservation est faite. Tu as de la chance! Mais, qu'est-ce qu'il y a?

SANDRINE Tu es super gentille, Amina, mais Pascal a annulé pour Noël. Il dit qu'il a du travail... Lui et moi, c'est fini. Tu as fait beaucoup d'efforts pour faire la réservation, je suis désolée.

A C T I V I T É S

1 Vrai ou faux? Indiquez si ces affirmations sont **vraies** ou **fausses**.

1. Sandrine fait une réservation à l'agence de voyages. Faux.
2. Sandrine a envie de voyager le 25 décembre. Faux.
3. Amina fait une réservation à l'hôtel Le Mont Blanc. Faux.
4. Cent soixante et onze euros, c'est beaucoup d'argent pour Sandrine. Vrai.
5. Amina ne peut pas (*can't*) aider Sandrine. Faux.
6. Il y a beaucoup de touristes à Albertville en décembre. Vrai.
7. Pascal dit qu'il travaille à Noël. Vrai.
8. Pascal est fâché contre Sandrine. Faux.
9. Sandrine est fâchée contre Pascal. Vrai.
10. Il faut annuler la réservation à l'auberge de la Costaroche. Vrai.

TEACHING OPTIONS

La réservation d'hôtel Before viewing the video episode **La réservation d'hôtel**, have students brainstorm a list of things people might say when arranging a hotel reservation. For example, what questions might a travel agent ask? How might the traveler respond?

TEACHING OPTIONS

Regarder la vidéo Play the video episode once without sound and have the class create a plot summary based on the visual cues. Afterward, show the video with sound and have the class correct any mistaken guesses and fill in any gaps in the plot summary they created.

Sandrine essaie d'organiser son voyage.

Au P'tit Bistrot...

SANDRINE Amina, je n'ai pas réussi à faire une réservation pour Albertville. Tu peux m'aider?

AMINA C'est que... je suis connectée avec Cyberhomme.

SANDRINE Avec qui?

AMINA J'écris un e-mail à... Bon, je t'explique plus tard. Dis-moi, comment est-ce que je peux t'aider?

Un peu plus tard...

AMINA Bon, alors... Sandrine m'a demandé de trouver un hôtel pas cher à Albertville. Pas facile à Noël... Je vais essayer... Voilà! L'auberge de la Costaroche... 39 euros la nuit pour une chambre individuelle. L'hôtel n'est pas complet et il y a deux chambres libres. Quelle chance, cette Sandrine! Bon, nom... Sandrine Aubry...

AMINA Bon, la réservation, ce n'est pas un problème. C'était facile de réserver. Mais toi, Sandrine, c'est évident, ça ne va pas.

SANDRINE C'est vrai. Mais, alors, c'est qui, ce «Cyberhomme»?

AMINA Oh, c'est juste un ami virtuel. On correspond sur Internet, c'est tout. Ce soir, c'est son dixième message!

SANDRINE Lis-le-moi!

AMINA Euh non, c'est personnel...

SANDRINE Alors, dis-moi comment il est!

AMINA D'accord... Il est étudiant, sportif mais sérieux. Très intellectuel.

SANDRINE S'il te plaît, écris-lui: «Sandrine cherche aussi un cyberhomme»!

Expressions utiles

Getting help

- **Je ne sais pas quoi faire... J'ai besoin de réfléchir.**
  I don't know what to do... I have to think.
- **Je n'ai pas réussi à faire une réservation pour Albertville.**
  I didn't manage to make a reservation for Albertville.
- **Tu peux m'aider?**
  Can you help me?
- **Dis-moi, comment est-ce que je peux t'aider?**
  Tell me, how can I help you?
- **Qu'est-ce que tu dis?**
  What are you saying/did you say?
- **On a réussi.**
  We succeeded./We got it.
- **S'il te plaît, écris-lui.**
  Please, write to him.

Additional vocabulary

- **C'est trop tard?**
  Is it too late?
- **Disons...**
  Let's say...
- **La réservation est faite.**
  The reservation has been made.
- **C'est fini.**
  It's over.
- **Je suis connectée avec...**
  I am online with...
- **Lis-le-moi.**
  Read it to me.
- **Il dit que...**
  He says that...
- **les moins chers**
  the least expensive
- **en fait**
  in fact

2 **Questions** Répondez aux questions.

1. Pourquoi est-il difficile de faire une réservation pour Albertville?
   C'est difficile parce que c'est Noël.
2. Pourquoi est-ce que Sandrine ne veut pas (*doesn't want*) descendre à l'hôtel Le Vieux Moulin?
   L'hôtel Le Vieux Moulin est très cher.
3. Pourquoi Pascal dit-il qu'il ne peut pas (*can't*) aller à Albertville?
   Il dit qu'il a du travail.
4. Qui est Cyberhomme?
   C'est l'ami virtuel d'Amina.
5. À votre avis (*In your opinion*), Sandrine va-t-elle rester (*stay*) avec Pascal? Answers will vary.

3 **Devinez** Inventez-vous une identité virtuelle. Écrivez un paragraphe dans lequel (*in which*) vous vous décrivez, vous et vos loisirs préférés. Donnez votre nom d'internaute (*cybername*). Votre professeur va afficher (*post*) vos messages. Devinez (*Guess*) à qui correspondent les descriptions.

A C T I V I T É S

Expressions utiles
- Model the pronunciation of the **Expressions utiles** and have students repeat them. Contrast the pronunciation of the following expressions: **en fait, on fait**.
- As you work through the list, point out expressions that use a form of **dire** or **écrire**. Tell students that these irregular verbs will be formally presented in **Structures**.
- Respond briefly to questions regarding **dire** and **écrire**. Reinforce correct forms, but do not expect students to produce them consistently at this time.
- Point out the differences between direct and indirect discourse by writing these two sentences on the board: **Il dit qu'il a du travail. Il dit: «J'ai du travail.»** Ask students to respond to questions about who says what. Example: **Qui dit que c'est facile de réserver une chambre d'hôtel? (Amina)**

1 **Suggestion** Have students correct the items that are false.

1 **Expansion** Give these statements to the class.
11. Sandrine a besoin de deux chambres individuelles. (Vrai.) 12. Amina ne fait pas de réservation. (Faux.) 13. Cyberhomme est l'ami virtuel de Sandrine. (Faux.)

2 **Suggestion** Have students discuss these questions in small groups.

2 **Expansion** Discuss question #5 as a class. Have students make other predictions about what will happen. Ask what kind of surprise they think Pascal has in mind.

3 **Suggestion** Without revealing students' identities, match students with common interests and have them write back to one another.

PRE-AP®

Interpersonal Speaking Ask volunteers to act out the **Roman-photo** episode for the class. Assure them that it is not necessary to memorize the episode or to stick strictly to its content. Give them time to prepare. You may want to assign this as homework and do it the next class period as a review activity.

PRE-AP®

Presentational Writing Have students write a brief paragraph recapping the major events in this episode and using sequencing expressions, such as **d'abord, donc, ensuite, avant de, alors,** etc. Ask volunteers to read their synopses aloud.

289

AP® Theme: Contemporary Life
Context: Travel

vhlcentral

CULTURE À LA LOUPE

Les vacances des Français

Cassis

Les Français, aujourd'hui, ont beaucoup de vacances.
En 1936, les Français obtiennent° leurs premiers congés payés: deux semaines par an. En 1956, les congés payés passent à trois semaines, puis à quatre en 1969, et enfin à cinq semaines en 1982. Aujourd'hui, les Français sont parmi ceux qui° ont le plus de vacances en Europe. Pendant longtemps, les Français prenaient° un mois de congés l'été, en août, et beaucoup d'entreprises°, de bureaux et de magasins fermaient° tout le mois (la fermeture annuelle). Aujourd'hui, les Français ont tendance à prendre des vacances plus courtes (sept jours en moyenne°), mais plus souvent. Quant aux° destinations de vacances, 70,2% (pour cent) des Français restent en France métropolitaine°. S'ils partent à l'étranger, leurs destinations préférées sont l'Espagne, l'Italie et l'Afrique. Environ° 23% des Français vont à la campagne, 31% vont en ville, 22% vont à la mer, et 20% vont à la montagne.

Ce sont les personnes âgées et les agriculteurs° qui partent le moins souvent en vacances et les étudiants qui voyagent le plus, parce qu'ils ont beaucoup de vacances. Pour eux, les cours commencent en septembre ou octobre avec la rentrée des classes. Puis, il y a deux semaines de vacances plusieurs fois dans l'année: les vacances de Noël en décembre-janvier, les vacances d'hiver en février-mars et les vacances de printemps en avril-mai. Les élèves (de la maternelle° au lycée) ont une semaine en plus pour les vacances de la Toussaint en octobre-novembre. L'été, les étudiants et les élèves ont les grandes vacances de juin jusqu'à° la rentrée.

Les destinations de vacances des Français aujourd'hui

PAYS / CONTINENT	SÉJOURS
France	70,2%
Espagne	4,1%
Italie	3,0%
Afrique	2,2%
Royaume-Uni	1,8%
Belgique et Luxembourg	1,8%
Allemagne	1,5%
Amérique	1,8%
Asie et Océanie	1,4%
Les DOM°	0,7%

SOURCE: Direction Générale des Entreprises (DGE)

obtiennent *obtain* parmi ceux qui *among the ones who* prenaient *took* entreprises *companies* fermaient *closed* en moyenne *on average* Quant aux *As for* métropolitaine *mainland* Environ *Around* agriculteurs *farmers* maternelle *pre-school* jusqu'à *until* DOM *Overseas Departments*

Coup de main

To form the superlative of nouns, use **le plus (de)** + (*noun*) to say *the most* and **le moins (de)** + (*noun*) to say *the least*.

Les étudiants ont le plus de vacances.

Les personnes âgées prennent le moins de congés.

A C T I V I T É S

1 Complétez Complétez les phrases.

1. C'est en 1936 que les Français obtiennent leurs premiers __congés payés__.

2. Depuis (*Since*) 1982, les Français ont __cinq semaines__ de congés payés.

3. Pendant longtemps, les Français ont pris leurs vacances au mois __d'août__.

4. Pendant __la fermeture annuelle__, beaucoup de magasins sont fermés.

5. __La France__ est la destination de vacances préférée de 70,2% des Français.

6. Les destinations étrangères préférées des Français sont __l'Espagne, l'Italie et l'Afrique__.

7. Le lieu de séjour favori des Français est __la ville__.

8. __Les personnes âgées et les agriculteurs__ ne partent pas souvent en vacances.

9. Ce sont __les étudiants__ qui ont beaucoup de vacances.

10. Les étudiants ont __deux semaines de vacances__ plusieurs fois par an.

Section Goals

In this section, students will:
• learn about how and where the French vacation
• learn some terms used in youth hostels
• find out about vacation spots in the Francophone world
• read about the Alps, a popular destination for skiers

Key Standards

2.1, 2.2, 3.1, 3.2, 4.2

 21ˢᵗ Century Skills

Global Awareness
Students will gain perspectives on the Francophone world to develop respect and openness to other cultures.

Culture à la loupe

Avant la lecture Ask students how much vacation their parents can take annually, how much is typical in this country, and how much they think working people need to be happy in their work. You might also ask what vacation activities Americans enjoy and what the students imagine is popular in France.

Lecture
• Mention to students that when experts anticipate the **grands départs** on the **autoroutes**, these days are labeled **rouges** throughout France.
• Explain the **Coup de main** box on superlatives to help students understand the text.

Après la lecture Ask students to compare American and French vacation habits. Example: **Les élèves au lycée ici commencent leurs vacances en mai, mais les élèves en France terminent l'année scolaire en juillet.**

1 Expansion Continue the activity with these fill-in-the-blank statements.
11. Les Français d'aujourd'hui prennent des vacances qui durent _____ en moyenne. (sept jours) 12. Les vacances les moins populaires à l'étranger sont _____. (dans les DOM)

DIFFERENTIATION

For Visual Learners Ask students what they can learn in the chart **Les destinations de vacances des Français aujourd'hui**. (percentages showing where the French spend their vacations today) Have students quiz each other on the chart, so they can practice geography and percentages.

PRE-AP®

Presentational Speaking with Cultural Comparison Ask students to work with a partner to tell in their own words three main points described in **Les vacances des Français**. You might brainstorm a list on the board: the history of employee vacations, the change in how the French take their vacations, and the time periods of student vacations. Ask students to make comparisons with the way Americans spend their vacation.

LE FRANÇAIS QUOTIDIEN

À l'auberge de jeunesse

bagagerie (*f.*)	*baggage check room*
cadenas (*m.*)	*padlock*
casier (*m.*)	*locker*
couvre-feu (*m.*)	*curfew*
dortoir (*m.*)	*dormitory*
espace détente	*relaxation area*
laverie	*laundry*
sac (*m.*) **de couchage**	*sleeping bag*

AP® **Theme:** Contemporary Life   **Context:** Travel

LE MONDE FRANCOPHONE

Des vacances francophones

Si votre famille veut° partir en vacances dans un pays francophone, vous pouvez° aller en France, bien sûr, mais il y a aussi beaucoup d'autres destinations.

Près des États-Unis

En hiver, dans les Antilles, il y a la Guadeloupe et la Martinique. Ces deux îles° tropicales sont des départements français. Leurs habitants ont donc des passeports français.

Dans l'océan Pacifique

De la Côte Ouest des États-Unis, au sud° de Hawaï, vous pouvez aller dans les îles de la Polynésie française: les îles Marquises; les îles du Vent, avec Tahiti; les îles Tuamotu. Au total il y a 118 îles, dont° 67 sont habitées°.

veut *wants* **pouvez** *can* **îles** *islands* **sud** *south* **dont** *of which* **habitées** *inhabited*

PORTRAIT   AP® **Theme:** Contemporary Life   **Context:** Travel

Les Alpes et le ski

Les Français qui partent à la montagne pendant les vacances d'hiver privilégient° les stations de ski des Alpes françaises. La chaîne° des Alpes est la plus grande chaîne de montagnes d'Europe. Elle fait plus de 1.000 km de long et va de la Méditerranée à l'Autriche°. Plusieurs pays la partagent: entre autres° la France, la Suisse, l'Allemagne et l'Italie. Le Mont-Blanc, le sommet° le plus haut° d'Europe occidentale°, est à plus de 4.800 mètres d'altitude.

On trouve d'excellentes pistes° de ski dans les Alpes, comme à Chamonix, Tignes, Val d'Isère et aux Trois Vallées.

privilégient *favor* **chaîne** *range* **l'Autriche** *Austria* **entre autres** *among others* **sommet** *peak* **le plus haut** *the highest* **occidentale** *Western* **pistes** *trails*

AP® **Theme:** Contemporary Life   **Context:** Travel

Sur Internet

Chaque année, depuis (*since*) 1982, plus de 4 millions de Français utilisent des Chèques-Vacances pour payer leurs vacances. Qu'est-ce que c'est, un Chèque-Vacances?

Go to **vhlcentral.com** to find more information related to this **Culture** section.

---

2 **Répondez** Répondez aux questions par des phrases complètes.

1. Que peut-on (*can one*) utiliser à la place des draps?
   On peut utiliser un sac de couchage.
2. Quand on passe la nuit dans le dortoir d'une auberge de jeunesse, où met-on ses affaires (*belongings*)?
   On les met dans un casier.
3. Qu'est-ce que c'est, les Alpes?
   C'est la plus grande chaîne de montagnes d'Europe.
4. Quel est le sommet le plus haut d'Europe occidentale?
   Le Mont-Blanc est le sommet le plus haut d'Europe occidentale.
5. Quelles îles des Antilles sont françaises?
   La Guadeloupe et la Martinique sont françaises.

3 **À l'agence de voyages** Vous travaillez dans une agence de voyages en France. Votre partenaire, un(e) client(e), va vous parler des activités et du climat qu'il/elle aime. Faites quelques suggestions de destinations. Votre client(e) va vous poser des questions sur les différents voyages que vous suggérez.

A C T I V I T É S

EXPANSION

Les vacances Have students imagine that, while studying in France, they are planning a trip for an upcoming vacation. They can speak **au présent** and **au futur proche**. Examples: **Où est-ce qu'on va aller? Qui va réserver l'hôtel/l'auberge de jeunesse? Qu'est-ce qu'on a envie de faire?** Encourage them to consult **Les vacances des Français** to plan a trip when French schools are actually on break. Then have them refer to **Le monde**

francophone to discuss which place they would most like to visit. You might want to come up with some questions as a class before students continue in pairs. Examples: **Que préférez-vous, les Antilles ou la Polynésie française? Entre la Guadeloupe et la Martinique, que préférez-vous? Moi, j'ai envie de visiter Tahiti, et vous?**

7B.1

Adverbs and the verbs vhlcentral
dire, écrire, and *lire*

Point de départ Adverbs modify verbs, adjectives, and other adverbs. Adverbs you have already learned include **bien, déjà, encore, surtout,** and **très.**

- To form an adverb from an adjective that ends in a consonant, take the feminine form and add **-ment.** This ending is equivalent to the English *-ly.*

masc. adjective	fem. adjective	adverb	
actif	**active**	**activement**	*actively*
franc	**franche**	**franchement**	*frankly, honestly*
heureux	**heureuse**	**heureusement**	*fortunately*

Malheureusement, il ne va pas être là.
Unfortunately, he is not going to be there.

Il n'est pas passé **dernièrement.**
He hasn't passed by lately.

- If an adjective's masculine form ends in a vowel, just add **-ment.**

masc. adjective	adverb	
absolu	**absolument**	*absolutely*
vrai	**vraiment**	*really*

J'ai **vraiment** sommeil aujourd'hui.
I'm really sleepy today.

Le musée est **absolument** magnifique.
The museum is absolutely magnificent.

- If an adjective's masculine form ends in **-ant** or **-ent,** replace the ending with **-amment** or **-emment,** respectively.

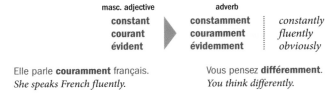

masc. adjective	adverb	
constant	**constamment**	*constantly*
courant	**couramment**	*fluently*
évident	**évidemment**	*obviously*

Elle parle **couramment** français.
She speaks French fluently.

Vous pensez **différemment.**
You think differently.

- Some adverbs are irregular.

masc. adjective	adverb	
bon	**bien**	*well*
gentil	**gentiment**	*nicely*
mauvais	**mal**	*badly*
petit	**peu**	*little*

Son français est bon; il le parle **bien.**
His French is good; he speaks it well.

Leurs devoirs sont mauvais; ils écrivent **mal.**
Their homework is bad; they write badly.

- Although the adverb **rapidement** can be formed from the adjective **rapide,** you can also use the adverb **vite** to say *fast.*

M. Bellay parle trop **rapidement.**
Mr. Bellay speaks too quickly.

Bérénice court **vite.**
Bérénice runs fast.

Boîte à outils

The exception to this rule is the adjective **lent.** Its adverb is **lentement** (*slowly*).

Il marche lentement.
He walks slowly.

Vérifiez

Section Goals

In this section, students will learn:
- the formation of adverbs using [*adjective*] + **-ment**
- irregular adverbs
- adverb placement
- the irregular verbs **dire, écrire,** and **lire**

Key Standards

4.1, 5.1

Suggestions: Scaffolding
- To start the lesson, ask volunteers to give examples of adverbs already learned and use them in a sentence. Examples: **Je vais très bien/mal. Ils ont déjà fait leurs devoirs. Elle travaille souvent le samedi.**
- Use magazine pictures of people doing various things to further review known adverbs and introduce a few new ones. Examples: **Ce chien mange beaucoup. Cette fille-ci nettoie rarement sa chambre. Cet homme-là se sent mal.**
- Brainstorm a list of masculine adjectives with the whole class. Have students write the feminine forms, reminding them that some do not change. Examples: **heureux (heureuse), facile (facile).**
- Go over points 1-3. Then ask questions with adverbs that correspond to the adjectives mentioned earlier. Example: **Faites-vous facilement vos devoirs?** Assign the **Vérifiez** activity.
- Present the irregular adverbs and **vite.**

EXPANSION

Extra Practice Have pairs of students write sentences using adverbs such as **bien, rapidement, facilement,** and so forth. When they have finished, ask volunteers to dictate their sentences to you to write on the board. After you have written a sentence and checked it for accuracy, ask a volunteer to create a sentence that uses the antonym of the adverb.

EXPANSION

Extra Practice Have students write a short paragraph about their daily lives using at least eight of the common adverbs taught in this lesson. Ask them to share their paragraphs with a classmate. Once the pairs have compared their two paragraphs, ask them to report to the class any differences they find. Ex: **Je mange rapidement mais Paul mange lentement.**

- You've learned **jamais, parfois, rarement,** and **souvent.** Three more adverbs of frequency are: **de temps en temps** (*from time to time*), **en général** (*in general*), and **quelquefois** (*sometimes*).

  Elle visite la capitale **de temps en temps**.
  She visits the capital from time to time.

  En général, nous prenons le bus.
  In general, we take the bus.

- Place an adverb that modifies an adjective or adverb before the word it modifies.

  La chambre est **assez** grande.
  The room is pretty big.

  Ils courent **très** vite.
  They run very fast.

- Place an adverb that modifies a verb immediately after the verb.

  Elle parle **bien** le français?
  Does she speak French well?

  Ils parlent **constamment**.
  They talk constantly.

- In the **passé composé**, short adverbs are typically placed before the past participle.

  Ils sont **vite** partis.
  They left quickly.

  but

  Ils ont gagné **facilement**.
  They won easily.

The verbs *dire, lire,* and *écrire*

dire, lire, écrire			
	dire (*to say*)	**lire** (*to read*)	**écrire** (*to write*)
je/j'	dis	lis	écris
tu	dis	lis	écris
il/elle/on	dit	lit	écrit
nous	disons	lisons	écrivons
vous	dites	lisez	écrivez
ils/elles	disent	lisent	écrivent

Elle m'**écrit**.
She writes to me.

Ne **dis** pas ton secret.
Don't tell your secret.

Lisez cet e-mail.
Read that e-mail.

- The past participles of **dire, écrire,** and **décrire**, respectively, are **dit, écrit,** and **décrit**. The past participle of **lire** is **lu**.

  Ils l'**ont dit**.
  They said it.

  Tu l'**as écrit**.
  You wrote it.

  Nous l'**avons lu**.
  We read it.

Essayez! Donnez les adverbes qui correspondent à ces adjectifs. Ensuite, donnez la forme correcte des verbes.

1. complet __complètement__
2. sérieux __sérieusement__
3. séparé __séparément__
4. constant __constamment__
5. mauvais __mal__
6. actif __activement__
7. gentil __gentiment__

8. Je __lis__ (lire) le journal.
9. Nous __disons__ (dire) la vérité (*truth*).
10. Viviane __écrit__ (écrire) bien.
11. Les filles __décrivent__ (décrire) l'accident.
12. Vous __dites__ (dire) ce que (*what*) vous pensez.
13. As-tu déjà __lu__ (lire) ce livre?
14. Je l'ai __décrit__ (décrire) comme je l'ai vu.

Mise en pratique

1 **Assemblez** Trouvez l'adverbe opposé.

_e_ 1. gentiment		a. rarement
_d_ 2. bien		b. faiblement
_f_ 3. lentement		c. impatiemment
_c_ 4. patiemment		d. mal
_a_ 5. fréquemment		e. méchamment
_b_ 6. fortement		f. vite

2 **Invitation aux vacances** Béatrice parle de ses vacances chez sa cousine. Complétez les phrases avec les adverbes qui correspondent aux adjectifs entre parenthèses.

Ma cousine Caroline m'a invitée à passer les vacances chez elle, à Nice. (1) __Évidemment__ (Évident), j'ai été très contente et j'ai (2) __rapidement__ (rapide) accepté son invitation. J'ai lu (3) __attentivement__ (attentif) les brochures touristiques et j'ai parlé (4) __constamment__ (constant) de mon voyage. (5) __Finalement__ (Final), le jour de mon départ est arrivé. J'ai fait (6) __prudemment__ (prudent) ma valise. À Paris, j'ai attendu le train très (7) __impatiemment__ (impatient). (8) __Franchement__ (Franc), j'avais hâte (was eager) d'arriver!

3 **On le fait comment?** Décrivez comment Gilles et ses amis font ces actions. Employez l'adverbe logique correspondant à un des adjectifs.

1. Marc et Marie écrivent. (bon, gentil) Ils écrivent bien.
2. J'attends mon ami. (rapide, impatient) J'attends impatiemment mon ami.
3. Ousmane dit des secrets. (fréquent, intelligent) Il dit fréquemment des secrets.
4. Tu conduis ta voiture. (fort, prudent) Tu conduis prudemment ta voiture.
5. Salima lit le texte. (courant, attentif) Elle lit attentivement le texte.

4 **Les activités** Avec un(e) partenaire, assemblez les éléments des colonnes pour décrire à tour de rôle comment on fait ces activités pendant les vacances. Answers will vary.

MODÈLE

Élève 1: *Je ne travaille pas sérieusement.*
Élève 2: *Mon frère joue constamment.*

A	B	C
je	aider	constamment
mon frère	dire	facilement
ma sœur	écrire	franchement
mon ami(e)	jouer	gentiment
mes profs	lire	patiemment
ma mère	travailler	rapidement
mon père	voyager	sérieusement
?	?	?

Communication

5 **Au lycée** Vous désirez mieux connaître (*know better*) vos camarades de classe. Répondez aux questions de votre partenaire avec les adverbes de la liste ou d'autres. Answers will vary.

attentivement	lentement	rapidement
bien	mal	rarement
difficilement	parfois	sérieusement
élégamment	patiemment	souvent
facilement	prudemment	quelquefois

1. Quand vas-tu à la cantine?
2. Comment étudies-tu en général?
3. Quand tes amis et toi étudiez-vous ensemble?
4. Comment les élèves écoutent-ils leur prof?
5. Comment ton prof de français parle-t-il?
6. Quand les élèves ne disent-ils pas la vérité (*truth*) au prof?
7. Quand lisez-vous pour le plaisir (*pleasure*)?
8. Quand allez-vous au cinéma, tes amis et toi?
9. Tes amis et toi, mangez-vous toujours (*always*) à la cantine?
10. Quand écrivez-vous des messages à vos amis?

6 **Fréquences** Votre professeur va vous donner une feuille d'activités. Circulez dans la classe et demandez à vos camarades à quelle fréquence ils/elles font ces choses. Trouvez une personne différente pour chaque réponse, puis présentez-les à la classe. Answers will vary.

MODÈLE

Élève 1: À quelle fréquence pars-tu en vacances?
Élève 2: Je pars fréquemment en vacances.

7 **Notre classe** Par groupes de quatre, choisissez les camarades de votre classe qui correspondent à ces descriptions. Trouvez le plus (*most*) de personnes possible. Answers will vary.

Qui dans la classe...

1. ... bavarde constamment avec ses voisins?
2. ... parle bien français?
3. ... chante bien?
4. ... apprend facilement les langues?
5. ... lit attentivement les instructions?
6. ... travaille sérieusement après les cours?
7. ... aime beaucoup les maths?
8. ... travaille trop?
9. ... écrit souvent des messages pendant le cours?
10. ... dort parfois pendant le cours?
11. ... oublie fréquemment ses devoirs?
12. ... mange rarement à la cantine?

5 **Expansion** Have students work in pairs to write three more questions like those in the activity. Students then switch questions with another pair and answer them orally.

5 **Virtual Chat** You can also assign Activity 5 on vhlcentral.com. Students record individual responses that appear in your gradebook.

6 **Suggestions**
• Have two volunteers read the **modèle** aloud, and then distribute the **Feuilles d'activités** found on vhlcentral.com.
• If some students finish early, have them form pairs or a small group to begin comparing their findings. Teach them to ask questions, such as: **Quels camarades de classe font les choses différemment? Et semblablement** (*similarly*)**?**

7 **Suggestion** Remind the class that the adverbs in these sentences modify the verb, so they immediately follow the verb.

Activity Pack For additional activities, go to the **Activity Pack** in the **Resources** section of vhlcentral.com.

EXPANSION

Extra Practice Tell students to research travel to a French-speaking location. For maximum cultural variety, assign a different location to each student or simply have students select their preferred destination. Have them find information online or in the library about what there is to see and do there. After they have completed their research, have them create a brochure with images of the place and write short descriptive captions.

EXPANSION

After that, tell students to plan an imaginary itinerary, telling what they will and won't do when they go and how often they will do each activity. Remind them to use frequency adverbs like **jamais**, **parfois**, **rarement**, **souvent**, **de temps en temps**, etc. Finally, have students present their brochures to the class and talk about their plans.

Section Goals

In this section, students will learn:
• the imperfect tense
• être in the imperfect tense

Key Standards
4.1, 5.1

Suggestions: Scaffolding
• Remind students that they can already express actions that are over and done with in the past using the **passé composé**. Tell them that now they will learn another tense needed to express themselves in the past. Mention that the **imparfait** expresses the past in a different way.
• Introduce the **imparfait** by describing something you used to do when you were little. Example: **Quand j'étais petit(e), je passais souvent les vacances chez mes grands-parents. Quand il faisait froid, nous jouions aux cartes à la maison. En été, ma famille louait une maison au bord de la mer**. Ask students what these actions have in common (you don't know exactly when they begin or end). Then ask what they noticed about the verb forms.
• Review the present tense **nous** forms of various verbs and explain that the stem without **-ons** is also the **imparfait** stem. Go through the conjugation of the different families of verbs. Go over the spelling changes with verbs ending in **-ger** and **-cer**. Then play the Game on p. 297.

7B.2

The *imparfait* vhlcentral

Point de départ You've learned how the **passé composé** can express past actions. Now you'll learn another past tense, the **imparfait** (*imperfect*).

• The **imparfait** can be translated into English in several ways.

Hakim **buvait** beaucoup de thé.
Hakim drank a lot of tea.
Hakim used to drink a lot of tea.
Hakim would drink a lot of tea.
Hakim was drinking a lot of tea.

Nina **chantait** sous la douche tous les matins.
Nina sang in the shower every morning.
Nina used to sing in the shower every morning.
Nina would sing in the shower every morning.
Nina was singing in the shower every morning.

• To form the **imparfait**, drop the **-ons** ending from the **nous** form of the present tense and replace it with these endings.

Boîte à outils

Note that the forms ending in **-ais**, **-ait**, and **-aient** are all pronounced identically. To avoid confusion when writing these forms, remember that the **je** and **tu** forms never end in a **-t**.

The *imparfait*				
	parler (parl**ons**)	finir (finiss**ons**)	vendre (vend**ons**)	boire (buv**ons**)
je	parlais	finissais	vendais	buvais
tu	parlais	finissais	vendais	buvais
il/elle/on	parlait	finissait	vendait	buvait
nous	parlions	finissions	vendions	buvions
vous	parliez	finissiez	vendiez	buviez
ils/elles	parlaient	finissaient	vendaient	buvaient

• Verbs whose infinitives end in **-ger** add an **e** before all endings of the **imparfait** except in the **nous** and **vous** forms. Verbs whose infinitives end in **-cer** change **c** to **ç** before all endings except in the **nous** and **vous** forms.

tu **déménageais**   *but*   nous **déménagions**

les invités **commençaient**   *but*   vous **commenciez**

Mes parents **voyageaient** en Afrique.
My parents used to travel to Africa.

Vous **mangiez** toujours des pâtes le soir?
Did you always have pasta for dinner?

À quelle heure **commençait** l'école?
What time did school start?

Nous **commencions** notre journée à huit heures.
We used to start our day at 8 o'clock.

• The **nous** and **vous** forms of infinitives ending in **-ier** have a double **i** in the **imparfait**.

Vous **skiiez** dans les Alpes en janvier.
You used to ski in the Alps in January.

Nous **étudiions** parfois jusqu'à minuit.
We studied until midnight sometimes.

À noter

You'll learn more about the uses of the **imparfait** and the **passé composé** in **Unité 8**.

• The **imparfait** is used to talk about actions that took place repeatedly or habitually in the past.

Je **passais** l'hiver à Lausanne.
I spent the winters in Lausanne.

Vous m'**écriviez** tous les jours.
You would write to me every day.

Nous **achetions** des fleurs au marché.
We used to buy flowers at the market.

Il **vendait** des meubles.
He used to sell furniture.

EXPANSION

Rapid Drill Write a few sentences in present tense on the board. Ask volunteers to come to the board and change the sentences to the imperfect tense. Then change the subjects of the sentences and ask other students to change the verbs accordingly.
Large Group Write a list of activities on the board. Ex: **1. jouer au foot, 2. boire du lait le matin, 3. parler avec un ami imaginaire.** Have students copy the list on a sheet of paper and check off

TEACHING OPTIONS

the items that they used to do when they were little kids. Then have them circulate around the room and find other students who used to do the same activities. Ex: **Tu buvais du lait le matin?** When they find a student who used to do the same activity, have them write that student's name next to the item. Then have students report back to the class. Ex: **Mark et moi parlions avec un ami imaginaire.**

Suggestions: Scaffolding
- Go over the different uses of the imperfect. Repeat your earlier story, pausing after each sentence for students to identify the usage.
- Present the points on **être** and third-person expressions.
- Ask volunteers to answer questions about their childhoods. Example: **Quand vous étiez petit(e), où alliez-vous en vacances avec votre famille? Aimiez-vous aller au cinéma? À la piscine?**
- Follow the Extra Practice suggestion on p. 297.

Essayez! Have students identify the infinitive of each verb in the activity. Examples: **1. louer 2. partager**

- The **imparfait** is also used to talk about ongoing actions over an unspecified period of time in the past.

Nous **parlions** à l'hôtelier.
We were talking to the hotel clerk.

Il **bronzait** sur la plage.
He was tanning on the beach.

Vous **écriviez** dans votre journal de voyage.
You were writing in your travel journal.

Je **faisais** du shopping en Chine.
I was shopping in China.

- The **imparfait** is used for description as well, often with the verb **être**, which is irregular in this tense.

The *imparfait* of *être*	
j'étais	nous étions
tu étais	vous étiez
il/elle/on était	ils/elles étaient

La cuisine **était** à côté du salon.
The kitchen was next to the living room.

Les toilettes **étaient** au rez-de-chaussée.
The restrooms were on the ground floor.

Étiez-vous heureux avec Francine?
Were you happy with Francine?

Nous **étions** dans le jardin.
We were in the garden.

- Note the imperfect forms of these expressions.

Il **pleuvait** chaque matin.
It rained every morning.

Il **neigeait** parfois au printemps.
It snowed sometimes in the spring.

Il **y avait** deux lits et une lampe.
There were two beds and a lamp.

Il **fallait** payer le loyer.
We had to pay rent.

Essayez!   **Choisissez la réponse correcte pour compléter les phrases.**

1. Muriel (louait/louais) un appartement en ville.
2. Rodrigue (partageait/partagiez) une chambre avec un autre étudiant.
3. Nous (écrivait/écrivions) beaucoup à nos amis.
4. Il y (avait/était) des balcons au premier étage.
5. Vous (mangeait/mangiez) chez Arnaud le samedi.
6. Je n'(avais/étais) pas peur du chien.
7. Il (neigeait/fallait) mettre le chauffage (*heat*) quand il (faisaient/faisait) froid.
8. Qu'est-ce que tu (faisait/faisais) dans le couloir?
9. Vous (aimiez/aimaient) beaucoup le quartier?
10. Nous (étaient/étions) trois dans le petit studio.
11. Rémy et Nathalie (voyagiez/voyageaient).
12. Il (avais/pleuvait) constamment en juillet.
13. Il (pleuvait/neigeait) beaucoup dans les Alpes en décembre.
14. Jean-Luc (finissait/finissais) toujours les devoirs en premier.
15. Tous les étés, nous (vendaient/vendions) des bonbons pour notre équipe de futbol.

EXPANSION

Game Divide the class into two teams. Choose one team member at a time to go to the board, alternating between teams. Say a subject pronoun and an infinitive. The student at the board must write and say the correct **imparfait** form. Example: **je: parler (je parlais)**. Give a point for each correct answer. Play to five or ten points, depending on how much time you have.

EXPANSION

Extra Practice Have students write five true/false sentences with the **imparfait** describing things they did while on vacation when they were younger. Have pairs read their descriptions aloud, one sentence at a time, listening for the **imparfait** and guessing what is true or false. Encourage follow-up discussion. Example: **L'hôtel où je suis resté avait 99 étages.** The other students might say: **Ce n'est pas vrai! Combien d'étages avait-il vraiment?**

Mise en pratique

1 **Nos voyages** La famille d'Emmanuel voyageait souvent quand il était petit. Complétez son histoire en mettant les verbes à l'imparfait.

Quand j' (1) ___étais___ (être) jeune, mon père (2) ___travaillait___ (travailler) pour une société canadienne et nous (3) ___voyagions___ (voyager) souvent. Quand nous (4) ___partions___ (partir), je (5) ___faisais___ (faire) ma valise et je (6) ___préparais___ (préparer) toutes mes affaires. Ma petite sœur (7) ___détestait___ (détester) voyager. Elle (8) ___disait___ (dire) qu'elle (9) ___aimait___ (aimer) rester chez nous près de ses amis et que ce n' (10) ___était___ (être) pas juste!

2 **Rien n'a changé** Laurent parle de l'école à son grand-père, qui lui explique que les choses n'ont pas changé. Employez l'imparfait pour transformer les phrases de Laurent et donner les phrases de son grand-père.

Laurent: Les cours commencent à 7h30. Je prends le bus pour aller à l'école. J'ai beaucoup d'amis. Mes copains et moi, nous mangeons à midi. Mon dernier cours finit à 16h00. Mon école est très sympa et je l'adore!

Grand-père: Les cours... _commençaient à 7h30. Je prenais le bus pour aller à l'école. J'avais_ _beaucoup d'amis. Mes copains et moi, nous mangions à midi. Mon dernier cours_ _finissait à 16h00. Mon école était très sympa et je l'adorais!_

3 **Le samedi** Dites ce que (*what*) ces personnes faisaient habituellement le samedi. Suggested answers

▶ **MODÈLE**

Paul dormait.

Paul

1. je
Je faisais du jogging.

2. ils
Ils finissaient leurs devoirs.

3. vous
Vous mangiez des glaces.

4. tu
Tu prenais du café.

4 **Maintenant et avant** Qu'est-ce qu'Emmanuel et sa famille font différemment aujourd'hui? Écrivez des phrases à l'imparfait et trouvez les adverbes opposés. Suggested answers

MODÈLE

beaucoup travailler (je)
Maintenant je travaille beaucoup, mais avant je travaillais peu.

1. rarement voyager (je)
... je voyage rarement, ... je voyageais constamment.
2. facilement prendre le train (nous)
... nous prenons facilement le train..., ... nous prenions difficilement le train.
3. souvent aller à la piscine (on)
... on va souvent à la piscine, ... on allait rarement à la piscine.
4. parfois acheter des cartes postales (mes parents)
... ils achètent parfois des cartes postales, ... ils achetaient souvent des cartes postales.
5. bien bricoler (vous)
... vous bricolez bien, ... vous bricoliez mal.
6. patiemment attendre son anniversaire (ma sœur)
... elle attend patiemment ..., ... elle attendait impatiemment...

298 Unit 7 • Lesson 7B

---

1 Suggestion Before assigning this activity, review the forms of the imperfect by calling out an infinitive and a series of subject pronouns. Ask volunteers to give the corresponding forms. Example: **détester, nous** (**nous détestions**).

3 Expansion After completing the activity, have students complete the sentences using the **passé composé** instead.

4 Suggestion Divide the class into two groups, **l'imparfait** and **le présent**. Have the first group give one phrase about what Emmanuel and his family used to do. The second group should describe what he and his family do differently now, using an opposite verb in the present tense.

EXPANSION

Extra Practice To provide oral practice with the imperfect tense, change the subjects in **Essayez!** on page 297. Have students give the appropriate forms for each infinitive listed.

DIFFERENTIATION

For Kinesthetic Learners Have the class stand and form a circle. Call out a name or subject pronoun and an infinitive (Ex: **elles/boire**). Toss a ball to a student, who will say the correct imperfect form (Ex: **buvaient**). He or she should then name a new subject and infinitive and throw the ball to another student.

Communication

5 **Quand tu avais dix ans** À tour de rôle, posez ces questions à votre partenaire pour savoir (*to know*) les détails de sa vie quand il/elle avait dix ans. Answers will vary.

1. Où habitais-tu?
2. Est-ce que tu faisais beaucoup de vélo?
3. Où est-ce que ta famille et toi alliez en vacances?
4. Pendant combien de temps partiez-vous en vacances?
5. Est-ce que tes amis et toi, vous sortiez tard le soir?
6. Que faisaient tes parents le week-end?
7. Quels sports pratiquais-tu?
8. Quel genre de musique écoutais-tu?
9. Comment était ton école?
10. Aimais-tu l'école? Pourquoi?

6 **Discutez** Regardez l'image. Votre partenaire et vous avez passé vos vacances à Saint-Barthélemy. À deux, écrivez un paragraphe d'au moins six phrases pour décrire le temps qu'il faisait et ce que (*what*) vous faisiez le plus souvent quand vous étiez là-bas. Utilisez l'imparfait dans votre description. Answers will vary.

7 **Chez les grands-parents** Quand vous étiez petit(e), vous passiez toujours les vacances à la campagne chez vos grands-parents. À tour de rôle, décrivez à votre partenaire une journée typique de vacances. Answers will vary.

> **MODÈLE**
>
> *Notre journée commençait très tôt le matin. Mémé préparait du pain...*

8 **Une énigme** La nuit dernière, quelqu'un est entré dans le bureau de votre professeur et a emporté (*took away*) l'examen de français. Vous devez (*must*) trouver qui. Qu'est-ce que vos camarades de classe faisaient hier soir? Interviewez-les. Ensuite, relisez vos notes et dites qui est le voleur (*thief*). Présentez vos conclusions à la classe. Answers will vary.

---

5 Expansion Have students share their partner's answers with the class using the third person pronouns **il/elle**.

5 Virtual Chat You can also assign Activity 5 on vhlcentral.com. Students record individual responses that appear in your gradebook.

7 Suggestion Consider giving students the option of describing a vacation by the sea, in the mountains, or in their favorite city if they prefer.

7 Expansion Have pairs of students present their imaginary vacations to another pair or to the whole class. Using the imperfect, compile a list of activities on the board.

8 Suggestion Before doing this activity, remind students that the imperfect form of **être** is irregular.

Activity Pack For additional activities, go to the **Activity Pack** in the **Resources** section of vhlcentral.com.

EXPANSION

Game Label the four corners of the room with different historical periods. Examples: la Préhistoire, le Moyen Âge, la Renaissance, and le **vingtième** siècle. Tell students to go to the corner that best represents the historical period they would visit if they could. Each group then discusses their reasons for picking that period using the imparfait. A spokesperson will summarize his or her group's responses to the class.

DIFFERENTIATION

For Visual Learners Bring in, or choose a few students to bring in, video clips from popular movies. Show clips to the class. Brainstorm important vocabulary. After viewing each clip, have students use the imparfait to describe what was happening and what people in the clip were doing.

299

Révision

Key Standards
1.1

1 **Suggestion** Have students write out the questions and answers. Check use of subject pronouns and the **imparfait** forms of **être**.

2 **Suggestion** Have two volunteers model a question and answer for the class.

2 **Expansion** After group members finish questioning each other, have a student from each group read the answers from another student. The class will then guess which student's childhood birthday celebration was described.

3 **Suggestions**
- Ask two students to read the **modèle** aloud. Then distribute the **Feuilles d'activités** from the Activity Pack.
- Encourage students to add sports and leisure activities not already found in their survey.

4 **Suggestion** Before beginning the activity, have students describe what the people in the drawing are doing in the present tense.

5 **Expansion** Tell students to imagine they are the **ancien prof de français** and have decided to give the student a second chance. Have them write an email to the student discussing his or her past versus present behavior at school.

5 **Partner Chat** You can also assign Activity 5 on vhlcentral.com. Students work in pairs to record the activity online. The pair's recorded conversation will appear in your gradebook.

6 **Suggestion** Divide the class into pairs and distribute the Info Gap Handouts from the Activity Pack.

---

1 **Mes affaires** Vous cherchez vos affaires (*belongings*). À tour de rôle, demandez de l'aide à votre partenaire. Où étaient-elles la dernière fois? Answers will vary.

MODÈLE

Élève 1: *Je cherche mes clés. Où sont-elles?*
Élève 2: *Tu n'as pas cherché à la réception? Elles étaient à la réception.*

baskets	passeport
journal	pull
livre	sac à dos
parapluie	valise

à la réception	sur la chaise
au rez-de-chaussée	sous le lit
dans la chambre	dans ton sac
au deuxième étage	à l'auberge de jeunesse

2 **Les anniversaires** Avec un(e) partenaire, préparez huit questions pour savoir (*know*) comment vos camarades de classe célébraient leur anniversaire quand ils étaient enfants. Employez l'imparfait et des adverbes dans vos questions, puis posez-les à un autre groupe. Answers will vary.

MODÈLE

Élève 1: *Que faisais-tu souvent pour ton anniversaire?*
Élève 2: *Quand j'étais petit, mes parents organisaient souvent une fête.*

3 **Sports et loisirs** Votre professeur va vous donner une feuille d'activités. Circulez dans la classe et demandez à vos camarades s'ils pratiquaient ces activités avant d'entrer au lycée. Trouvez une personne différente qui dise (*says*) oui pour chaque activité. Présentez les réponses à la classe. Answers will vary.

MODÈLE

Élève 1: *Est-ce que tu faisais souvent du jogging avant d'entrer au lycée?*
Élève 2: *Oui, je courais souvent le matin.*

4 **Pendant les vacances** Par groupes de trois, créez le texte d'un article qui décrit ce que (*what*) faisaient ces gens. Utilisez des verbes à l'imparfait et des adverbes dans vos descriptions. Ensuite, présentez vos articles à la classe. Answers will vary.

5 **Mes mauvaises habitudes** Vous aviez de mauvaises habitudes, mais vous les avez changées. Maintenant, vous parlez avec votre ancien prof de français que vous rencontrez dans la rue. Avec un(e) partenaire, préparez la conversation. Answers will vary.

MODÈLE

Élève 1: *Vous dormiez tout le temps en cours!*
Élève 2: *Je dormais souvent, mais je travaillais aussi. Maintenant, je travaille sérieusement.*

6 **Un week-end en vacances** Votre professeur va vous donner, à vous et à votre partenaire, une feuille de dessins sur le week-end de M. et Mme Bardot et de leur fille Alexandra. Attention! Ne regardez pas la feuille de votre partenaire. Answers will vary.

MODÈLE

Élève 1: *En général, ils logeaient dans un hôtel.*
Élève 2: *Tous les jours, …*

TEACHING OPTIONS

Mini-dictée Use these sentences containing adverbs and verbs in the **imparfait** as a dictation. Read each sentence twice, pausing after the second time for students to write.
1. Heureusement, il y avait beaucoup d'élèves dans la classe.
2. Conduisait-il vite la voiture? 3. J'étais vraiment très heureuse de te voir. 4. Il fallait constamment travailler le samedi.

TEACHING OPTIONS

Skits Have small groups organize a skit about a birthday or other party that took place recently. Guide them to first make general comments about the party, such as **C'était vraiment amusant!** Then describe a few specific things that were going on, what people were talking about, what they were wearing, and any other appropriate details. After the skits are performed, have students vote for their favorite one.

À l'écoute vhlcentral

Recognizing the genre of spoken discourse

You will encounter many different types of spoken discourse in French. For example, you may hear a political speech, a radio interview, a commercial, a message on an answering machine, or a news broadcast. Try to identify the context of what you hear so that you can activate your background knowledge about that type of discourse and identify the speaker's motives and intentions.

 To practice this strategy, you will listen to two short selections. Identify the genre of each one.

Préparation

Quand vous partez en vacances, qui décide où aller? Qui fait les réservations? Est-ce que vous utilisez les services d'une agence de voyages? Internet?

À vous d'écouter

Écoutez la publicité. Puis écoutez une deuxième fois et notez les informations qui manquent (*that are missing*). Notez aussi un détail supplémentaire pour chaque voyage.

Pays (ville/région)	Nombre de jours/semaines	Prix par personne	Détail supplémentaire
1. Italie (Venise)	3 jours	395 euros	Answers will vary.
2. Brésil	1 semaine	1.500 euros	Answers will vary.
3. Irlande (Dublin)	5 jours	575 euros	Answers will vary.
4. Amérique du Nord (États-Unis, Canada, Mexique)	2 semaines	2.000 euros	Answers will vary.
5. France (Avignon)	7 jours	487 euros	Answers will vary.

Compréhension

Où vont-ils? Vous travaillez pour l'agence Vacances Pour Tous cet été. Indiquez où chaque personne va aller.

1. Madame Dupuis n'a pas envie d'aller à l'étranger.
   Madame Dupuis va aller à Avignon.

2. Le fils de Monsieur Girard a besoin de pratiquer son espagnol et son anglais.
   Il va aller en Amérique du Nord.

3. Madame Leroy a envie de visiter une capitale européenne.
   Elle va aller en Irlande.

4. Yves Marignaud a seulement trois jours de congé.
   Il va aller en Italie (Venise).

5. Justine adore la plage et le soleil.
   Elle va aller au Brésil.

6. La famille Abou a envie de passer ses vacances à la campagne.
   Ils vont aller à Avignon.

Votre voyage Vous avez fait un des voyages proposés par l'agence Vacances Pour Tous. C'est le dernier jour et vous écrivez une carte postale (*postcard*) à un(e) ami(e) francophone. Parlez-lui de votre séjour. Quel voyage avez-vous fait? Pourquoi? Comment avez-vous voyagé? Qu'est-ce que vous avez fait pendant votre séjour? Est-ce que vous avez aimé vos vacances? Expliquez pourquoi.

trois cent un **301**

Section Goals

In this section, students will:
- learn to recognize the genre of spoken discourse
- listen to a radio ad for a travel agency

Key Standards
1.2, 2.1

Stratégie
Scripts 1. Bonjour et bienvenue à l'hôtel Belle Plage de Monaco. Nous sommes à quelques minutes de la plage, au 14 avenue des Anges, et nous avons des bus directs pour l'aéroport et la gare routière. Ce week-end, notre hôtel a encore six chambres libres. Si vous désirez des informations sur nos chambres, nos prix et notre hôtel en général, faites le 1. Pour faire ou confirmer une réservation, faites le 2. Pour contacter des clients de l'hôtel, faites le 3. Merci de nous avoir appelés et bonne journée. (message enregistré)
2. Mesdames, Messieurs, nous allons bientôt arriver à notre destination. À l'arrivée à l'aéroport de Montréal, sortez vos passeports pour passer la douane. Ensuite, allez au troisième étage pour prendre vos valises. Nous espérons que vous allez passer un agréable séjour au Canada. Merci d'avoir voyagé avec Air Vacances et à bientôt. (annonce d'avion)
Teacher Resources DVD

Préparation Have students discuss the questions in pairs or groups. Then have them describe the photo.

À vous d'écouter
Script Envie de partir en vacances? Pour un petit week-end en amoureux ou pour des vacances au soleil, l'agence Vacances Pour Tous a la formule idéale! Nos promotions de la semaine: Week-end à Venise, en Italie. Avion au départ de Paris vendredi matin, retour dimanche soir. Logement à l'hôtel; 395 euros par personne. Envie de mer et de plage? Séjour d'une semaine au Brésil; 1.500 euros par personne. Découvrez la capitale irlandaise avec un séjour de 5 jours à Dublin; 575 euros par personne. En train et bateau. Autre super promotion pour étudiants: un voyage de deux

semaines en Amérique. Une semaine aux États-Unis, quatre jours au Canada et trois jours au Mexique; 2.000 euros par personne. En avion et autobus. Logement en auberge de jeunesse. Vous n'avez pas envie de partir à l'étranger, mais vous avez une semaine de congé? Nous avons une promotion incroyable sur la

France. Sept jours à la campagne. Voyage en train. Logement dans un petit hôtel près d'Avignon; 487 euros par personne. Appelez tout de suite le 01.42.46.46.46 pour faire vos réservations!
Teacher Resources DVD

301

Section Goals

In this section, students will learn historical and cultural information about French Polynesia and Southeast Asia.

Key Standards

2.2, 3.1, 3.2, 5.1

21st Century Skills

Global Awareness
Students will gain perspectives on the Francophone world to develop respect and openness toward others and to interact appropriately and effectively with citizens of Francophone cultures.

Carte de la Polynésie française et de l'Asie du Sud-Est
- Have students look at the map or use the digital image for this page. Ask volunteers to read the names of countries and islands aloud.
- Point out that Southest Asia is the region between India and China.
- Mention that **la Polynésie française** is made up of 118 islands scattered over 1,200 miles of ocean. They are grouped into several archipelagos.

Les archipels et les pays en chiffres
- Have volunteers read the sections aloud. After each section, ask students questions about the content.
- Explain that an archipelago is a large group of islands. Point out that the **îles Gambier** and **îles de la Société** are composed of atolls (ring-shaped coral reefs).

Incroyable mais vrai! Ankor Wat is part of a 400 km² archaeological park that protects ruins of capital cities built under the Khmer Empire (9th–15th centuries). A Hindu temple at first, it became Buddhist in the 16th century.

Savoir-faire

vhlcentral

Panorama

La Polynésie française

Les archipels en chiffres

▶ Îles Australes: *(7.112), Tubuai*
▶ Îles de la Société: *(239.852), Papeete*
▶ Îles Marquises: *(9.835), Nuku Hiva*
▶ Îles Tuamotu-Gambier: *(16.664), Fakarava, Rankiroa*
SOURCE: INSEE

Personnages célèbres

▶ Henri Hiro, *Tahiti, îles de la Société, poète (1944–1991)*
▶ Rodolphe Vinh Tung, *Raiatea, îles de la Société, professionnel du wakeboard (1974–)*
▶ Célestine Hitiura Vaite, *Tahiti, îles de la Société, écrivaine° (1966–)*

L'Asie du Sud-Est

Les pays en chiffres

▶ Le Viêt-Nam: *(85.789.573), Hanoï, Hô Chi Minh, Haïphong*
▶ Le Cambodge: *(13.400.000), Phnom Penh, Battambang, Siem Reap*
▶ Le Laos: *(6.700.000), Luang Prabang, Savannakhet, Paksé*

Personnages célèbres

▶ Hô Chi Minh, *Viêt-Nam, révolutionnaire et homme d'État° (1890–1969)*
▶ Soma Serei Norodom, *Cambodge, chroniqueuse et philanthrope (1969–)*
▶ Bryan Thao Worra, *Laos, écrivain (1973–)*

écrivaine *writer* **homme d'État** *statesman* **redécouvre** *rediscovers* **caché** *hidden* **ouvriers** *workers* **d'après certains** *according to some* **courses de pirogues** *dugout canoe races*

---

le fleuve° Mékong au Laos

LA CHINE

Hanoï

Luang Prabang

LE LAOS
Vientiane

Savannakhet

THAÏLANDE

Hué
Da Nang

LA MER DE CHINE DU SUD

Pakxé

LE VIÊT-NAM

Siem Reap
Battambang
LE CAMBODGE
le Tonle Sap

Phnom Penh

LE GOLFE DE THAÏLANDE

Sihanoukville

Hô-Chi-Minh-Ville

Can Tho

le delta du Mékong

les courses de pirogues° en Polynésie française

La Polynésie française

Taiohae LES ÎLES MARQUISES
LES ÎLES DE LA SOCIÉTÉ
LES ÎLES TUAMOTU
Papeete
Tahiti
LES ÎLES GAMBIER
LES ÎLES AUSTRALES

0 — 1000 miles
0 — 1000 kilomètres

0 — 200 miles
0 — 200 kilomètres

Incroyable mais vrai!

En 1860 l'explorateur français Henri Mouhot redécouvre° un temple gigantesque caché° par la forêt dans le nord du Cambodge: Angkor Vat. Construit au XIIe siècle par 300.000 ouvriers° et 6.000 éléphants d'après certains°, ce «Temple Cité Royale» est le plus grand temple religieux du monde. Aujourd'hui il est aussi le symbole emblématique du pays et son attraction touristique principale.

Personnages célèbres **Henri Hiro** was responsible for a cultural resurgence of the traditional Polynesian customs in Tahitian theater, dance, music, and film. **Célestine Hitiura Vaite** writes novels that describe life in Tahiti from a contemporary perspective. Although a native French speaker, she writes primarily in English. **Ho Chi Minh**, a pseudonym for Nguyễn Sinh Cung, was a nationalist revolutionary leader who was president of Vietnam from 1954 to 1969. **Somo Serei Norodom** is a member of the royal family of Norodom, and considers herself a rebel. She writes columns for newspapers, has worked for several NGO's, and founded the non-profit Soma Norodom Foundation. **Bryan Thao Worra**, a poet and freelance journalist, writes about transience, identity, and home. He represented Laos as a Cultural Olympian at the London Summer Games in 2012.

AP® **Theme:** Beauty and Aesthetics
Context: Visual Arts

Les arts

Les peintures° de Gauguin

En 1891, le peintre Paul Gauguin (1848–1903) vend ses œuvres° à Paris et déménage° à Tahiti, dans les îles de la Société, pour échapper à° la vie moderne. Il y reste° deux ans avant de rentrer en France et, en 1895, il retourne en Polynésie française pour y habiter jusqu'à sa mort° en 1903. Inspirée par le nouvel environnement du peintre et la nature qui l'entoure°, l'œuvre «tahitienne» de Gauguin est célèbre° pour sa représentation du peuple indigène et l'emploi° de couleurs vives°. Ses peintures de femmes font partie de ses meilleurs tableaux°.

AP® **Theme:** Global Challenges
Context: Peace and War

L'histoire

L'Indochine française

Le Viêt-Nam, le Laos et le Cambodge faisaient autrefois partie° de l'Indochine, ancienne colonie de la France. Bien que° la présence française sur la péninsule date du 17e siécle, les Français ne s'y installent définitivement qu'à partir de° 1858, moment où ils sont intervenus° pour protéger les missionnaires catholiques contre l'harcèlement gouvernementale. Ils y resteront°, développant leurs intérêts économiques en exploitant les ressources du territoire, jusqu'à leur défaite° dans la guerre° d'Indochine en 1954. Aujourd'hui, on voit toujours des traces de la langue et de la culture françaises dans l'architecture, l'urbanisation des villes et la gastronomie de la région.

L'économie

AP® **Theme:** Global Challenges
Context: Economic Issues

La perle° noire

La Polynésie française est le principal producteur de perles noires. Dans la nature, les perles sont très rares; on en trouve dans une huître° sur 15.000. Par contre°, aujourd'hui, la Polynésie française produit plusieurs tonnes de perles noires chaque année. Des milliers de Tahitiens vivent de° l'industrie perlière. Parce qu'elle se trouve dans les lagons, la perliculture° aide à repeupler° certaines îles et certains endroits ruraux, abandonnés par les gens partis° en ville. Les perles sont très variées et présentent différentes formes et nuances de noir.

La gastronomie

La fusion des cuisines

Avant l'arrivée des colons° français au Viêt-Nam au 19e siècle, la viande de bœuf et les produits laitiers° ne figuraient pas dans sa gastronomie. Les Français, habitués°

à ces produits, les y ont introduit ainsi que° le café, la baguette et certains légumes, fruits et herbes tels que les fraises, le chou° et le basilic. Aujourd'hui, ces ingrédients maintenant font partie° des plats traditionnels comme *le pho*, une soupe de bouillon et nouilles°, et *le banh-mi*, un sandwich de baguette au porc rôti°.

Qu'est-ce que vous avez appris? Répondez aux questions.

1. Où se trouve Angkor Vat et qui le redécouvre?
   Dans le nord du Cambodge, Henri Mouhot
2. Quelle est la principale particularité d'Angkor Vat?
   C'est le plus grand temple réligieux du monde.
3. Pour quelle raison Gauguin déménage-t-il à Tahiti?
   Pour échapper à la vie moderne.
4. Pour quelles raisons l'œuvre «tahitienne» de Gauguin est-elle célèbre?
   Pour sa représentation du peuple indigène et pour l'emploi de couleurs vives.
5. Pendant combien de temps dure (*last*) la colonie de l'Indochine française?
   96 ans
6. Où trouve-t-on des traces de la culture française dans l'Asie du Sud-Est?
   Dans l'architecture, l'urbanisation des villes, la gastronomie et la langue.
7. D'où viennent la majorité des perles noires?
   De Polynésie française.
8. Comment la perliculture influence la population de la Polynésie?
   Elle aide à repeupler certaines îles et certains endroits ruraux.
9. Quels aliments (*foods*) les Français ont-ils introduit au Viêt-Nam?
   La viande de bœuf, les produits laitiers, le café, la baguette, certains légumes, fruits et herbes
10. Quels sont deux plats qui représentent la fusion des gastronomies françaises et vietnamiennes?
    Le pho et le banh-mi

Sur Internet

1. Cherchez des informations sur la gastronomie vietnamienne. Quels sont les ingrédients principaux des plats traditionnels?
2. Trouvez des informations sur Angkor Vat. Dans quel état (*state*) se trouve les ruines aujourd'hui?
3. Cherchez des informations sur les courses de pirogues en Polynésie française. Quelle est leur signification?

peinture *painting* **vend ses oeuvres** *sells his artwork* **déménage** *moves* **échapper à** *escape* **y reste** *stays there* **jusqu'à sa mort** *until his death* **entoure** *surrounds* **célèbre** *famous* **emploi** *use* **vives** *bright* **peintures** *paintings* **tableaux** *paintings* **anciennement faisaient partie** *was formerly part of* **Bien que** *Although* **qu'à partir de** *beginning only* **intervenus** *intervened* **resteront** *will stay* **défaite** *defeat* **perle** *pearl* **huître** *oyster* **Par contre** *On the other hand* **vivent de** *make a living from* **perliculture** *pearl farming* **repeupler** *repopulate* **gens partis** *people who left* **colons** *colonists* **laitiers** *dairy* **habitués** *used to* **ainsi que** *as well as* **chou** *cabbage* **font partie** *are part of* **nouilles** *noodles* **porc rôti** *roasted pork*

trois cent trois **303**

Les peintures de Gauguin

- Gauguin tried to capture authentic aspects of traditional Tahitian culture, emulated Oceanic traditions in his woodcuts, and often used the Tahitian language for titles of his works.
- Have students describe the painting. Tell them the title, **Femmes de Tahiti [sur la plage]**, and that the original is in the **Musée d'Orsay** in Paris.

L'Indochine française

- **La guerre d'Indochine** (1946–1954), called the First or French Indochina War, led to the independence of Vietnam, Cambodia, and Laos. Have students research the causes and consequences of the war for the French and the peoples of Southeast Asia.
- Tell students that around 654,000 people speak French in Vietnam, 423,000 in Cambodia, and 190,000 in Laos. Mention that French is also widely spoken in Thailand.

La perle noire Baby oysters are collected from the ocean and raised in pearl farms for three years. A small round piece of mother-of-pearl is inserted into the oyster, and the oyster begins the natural process of secreting nacre in layers onto the foreign substance which becomes a pearl after several years.

La fusion des cuisines Tell students that Vietnamese food is considered one of the healthiest and most refined cuisines in the world. Influenced by both Chinese and French traditions, Vietnamese cuisine also has many regional variations. Researchers have recorded over 500 national dishes.

21st Century Skills

Information and Media Literacy
Go to vhlcentral.com to complete the Sur Internet activity associated with **Panorama** for additional practice accessing and using culturally authentic sources.

EXPANSION

Une tradition tahitienne The **Hawaiki Nui Va'a** is one of the world's premier outrigger canoe competitions, and it is an important celebration of Tahiti's traditional sports. Each year in late October or early November, canoeists compete on an 80-mile, four-island course over the span of three days.
Cultural Comparisons **La guerre d'Indochine** (1946–1954) and the Vietnam War (1955–1975), known by many as the First and

EXPANSION

Second Indochina Wars, were unpopular wars. Have students research the reactions of the French to the First Indochina War and the reactions of Americans to the Vietnam War. Then lead a discussion in which you guide students to compare responses in both countries. In what ways did the two societies express their displeasure? How were these reactions the same and/or different?

Lecture vhlcentral

Avant la lecture

STRATÉGIE

Predicting content from the title

Prediction is an invaluable strategy in reading for comprehension. We can usually predict the content of a newspaper article from its headline, for example. More often than not, we decide whether or not to read the article based on its headline. Predicting content from the title will help you increase your reading comprehension in French.

Examinez le texte

Regardez le titre (*title*) et les sous-titres (*subtitles*) du texte. À votre avis, quel type de document est-ce? Avec un(e) camarade, faites une liste des informations que vous allez probablement trouver dans chaque section du document.

Des titres

Regardez ces titres et indiquez en quelques mots le sujet possible du texte qui suit (*follows*) chaque titre. Où pensez-vous qu'on trouve ces titres (dans un journal, un magazine, une brochure, un guide, etc.)?

Cette semaine à Paris:
un journal

Encore un nouveau restaurant pour chiens
un journal, un magazine

L'Égypte des pyramides en 8 jours
une brochure, un guide

À L'AÉROPORT CHARLES-DE-GAULLE, 155 BAGAGES D'UN VOL ALLEMAND PERDUS
un journal

Plan du centre-ville
un guide

France-Angleterre: Résultats du 7ᵉ match de foot
un journal

Hôtel confortable près de la gare routière
une brochure

TOUR DE CORSE

Voyage organisé de 12 jours

3.000 euros tout compris°
Promotion spéciale de Vacances–Voyages, agence de voyages certifiée

[Map: LA FRANCE, L'ITALIE, La Corse, LA MER MÉDITERRANÉE, 200 miles, 200 kilomètres]

ITINÉRAIRE

JOUR 1 Paris–Ajaccio

Rendez-vous à l'aéroport CDG et embarquement° sur votre vol à destination d'Ajaccio. Transfert en bus à votre hôtel. Votre séjour commence avec une visite de la ville à pied°. Dîner à l'hôtel.

JOUR 2 Ajaccio–Bonifacio

Le matin, départ en autobus pour Bonifacio, la belle ville côtière° où vous déjeunez dans un petit restaurant italien avant de visiter la ville. L'après-midi, promenade en mer à bord° d'un bateau, occasion idéale d'observer les falaises rocailleuses° et les plages blanches de l'île°. Le soir, installation à l'hôtel à Bonifacio et dîner sur place.

JOUR 3 Bonifacio–Corte

Départ pour la forêt de l'Ospédale, l'endroit idéal pour une randonnée à pied. Pique-nique à Zonza, petite ville montagneuse, avant de continuer vers Corte, l'ancienne° capitale de la Corse. Vous passez la soirée et la nuit à Corte.

JOUR 4 Corte–Bastia

Arrivée à Bastia. Journée libre pour visiter la ville. Spectacle de danse à 20h et nuit à l'hôtel.

JOUR 5 Bastia–Calvi

Visite du Cap Corse, la péninsule au nord° de la Corse. Puis, vous continuez vers le désert des Agriates, zone de montagnes désertiques où la chaleur est très forte. Ensuite, c'est l'Île-Rousse et une promenade à vélo dans la ville de Calvi. Vous dînez à votre hôtel.

Après la lecture

Les questions du professeur Vous avez envie de faire ce voyage en Corse et vous parlez du voyage organisé avec votre professeur de français. Répondez à ses questions par des phrases complètes, d'après la brochure.

1. Comment allez-vous aller en Corse?
   Je vais prendre l'avion à Paris.

2. Où le vol arrive-t-il en Corse?
   Le vol arrive à Ajaccio.

3. Combien de temps est-ce que vous allez passer en Corse?
   Je vais passer douze jours en Corse.

4. Est-ce que vous allez dormir dans des auberges de jeunesse?
   Non. Je vais dormir à l'hôtel./dans des hôtels.

5. Qu'est-ce que vous allez faire à Bastia?
   Je vais visiter la ville, aller à un spectacle de danse, puis passer la nuit à l'hôtel.

6. Est-ce que vous retournez à Ajaccio le neuvième jour?
   Non. Je retourne à Ajaccio le septième jour.

7. Qu'est-ce que vous allez prendre comme transports en Corse?
   Je vais prendre l'autobus et des bateaux.

8. Avez-vous besoin de faire toutes les réservations?
   Non. Le voyage est organisé par une agence de voyages.

Partons en Corse! Vous allez en France avec votre famille pour trois semaines et vous aimeriez *(would like)* faire le voyage organisé en Corse au départ de Paris. Vous téléphonez à l'agence de voyages pour avoir plus de détails. Posez des questions sur le voyage et demandez des précisions sur les villes visitées, les visites et les activités au programme, les hôtels, les transports, etc. Votre conversation doit aussi aborder *(should also touch on)* ces points:

- Vous aimez faire des randonnées, mais votre frère/sœur préfère voir *(to see)* des spectacles et faire du shopping.

- L'agent va expliquer pourquoi vous allez aimer ce voyage en Corse.

- Demandez à l'agent de vous trouver des billets d'avion aller-retour pour aller de votre ville à Paris.

- Demandez aussi un hôtel à Paris pour la troisième semaine de votre séjour en France.

- Vous expliquez à l'agent que votre famille veut *(wants)* avoir du temps libre pendant le voyage.

JOUR 6 Calvi–Porto

Départ en bus le matin pour la vallée du Fango et le golfe de Galéria à l'ouest° de l'île. Puis, visite du parc naturel régional et du golfe de Porto. Ensuite, promenade en bateau avant de passer la soirée dans la ville de Porto.

JOUR 7 Porto–Ajaccio

Visite en bateau des calanques°, particularité géographique de la région méditerranéenne, avant de retourner à Ajaccio.

JOURS 8 à 11 Ajaccio

À Ajaccio, vous avez trois jours pour explorer la ville. Vous avez la possibilité de visiter la cathédrale, la maison natale° de Napoléon ou des musées, et aussi de faire du shopping ou d'aller à la plage.

JOUR 12 Ajaccio–Paris

Retour à Paris en avion.

tout compris *all-inclusive* **embarquement** *boarding* **à pied** *on foot* **côtière** *coastal*
à bord *aboard* **falaises rocailleuses** *rocky cliffs* **île** *island* **ancienne** *former*
nord *north* **ouest** *west* **calanques** *rocky coves or creeks* **natale** *birth*

Les questions du professeur Have students quickly review the brochure before answering the questions. Suggest that pairs take turns answering them.

Partons en Corse! Have groups act out their conversations for the rest of the class.

Expansion Tell students that the travel agency is planning to create additional brochures to help them promote their **Tour de Corse** excursion. Their goal is to have several slightly different brochures about the same trip that may appeal to different types of people. Ask students to come up with 3 or 4 short, interesting titles for these new brochures.

 21ˢᵗ Century Skills

Creativity and Innovation
Ask students to prepare a presentation on the ideal 12-day tour to a different European destination, departing from Paris, inspired by the information on these two pages.

 TELL Connection

Learning Tools 2 *Why:* Use available technology to develop real-world language and cultural competencies. *What:* Increase students' reading and listening comprehension skills with vhlcentral.com auto-sync reading as well as their interpersonal and presentational communication skills with activities in the text, on vhlcentral.com, and in the teacher's wrap.

EXPANSION

Interviews Ask students if they have ever been on an organized tour. If students have not been on a tour similar to the one to Corsica described in **Lecture**, have them interview someone they know who has. Have students answer questions like these: **Où êtes-vous allé(e)? Avec quelle agence? Avez-vous aimé toutes les activités organisées? Expliquez pourquoi.**

EXPANSION

Narrative Have students work together in pairs. Tell them to divide the twelve-day **Tour de Corse** itinerary between them. Each student will then write at least five questions asking about their chosen parts of the trip. They will then answer each other's questions.

Écriture

STRATÉGIE

Making an outline

When we write to share information, an outline can serve to separate topics and subtopics, providing a framework for presenting the data. Consider the following excerpt from an outline of the tourist brochure on pages 304–305.

I. Itinéraire et description du voyage

    A. Jour 1
      1. ville: Ajaccio
      2. visites: visite de la ville à pied
      3. activités: dîner

    B. Jour 2
      1. ville: Bonifacio
      2. visites: la ville de Bonifacio
      3. activités: promenade en bateau, dîner

II. Description des hôtels et des transports

    A. Hôtels
    B. Transports

Schéma d'idées

Idea maps can be used to create outlines. The major sections of an idea map correspond to the Roman numerals in an outline. The minor sections correspond to the outline's capital letters, and so on. Consider the idea map that led to the outline above.

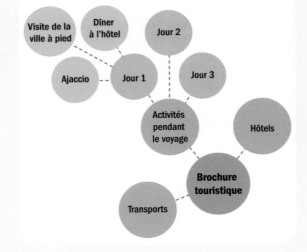

Thème

Écrivez une brochure

Avant l'écriture

1. Vous allez préparer une brochure pour un voyage organisé que vous avez envie de faire dans un pays francophone. Utilisez un schéma d'idées pour vous aider. Voici des exemples d'informations que votre brochure peut (*can*) donner.

- le pays et la ville/les villes

- le nombre de jours

- la date et l'heure du départ et du retour

- les transports utilisés (train, avion, …) et le lieu de départ (aéroport JFK, gare de Lyon, …)

- le temps qu'il va faire et quelques suggestions de vêtements à porter

- où on va dormir (hôtel, auberge de jeunesse, camping, …)

- où on va manger (restaurant, café, pique-nique dans un parc, …)

- les visites culturelles (monuments, musées, …)

- les autres activités au programme (explorer la ville, aller au marché, faire du sport, …)

- le prix du voyage par personne

2. Complétez le schéma d'idées pour vous aider à visualiser ce que (*what*) vous allez présenter dans votre brochure.

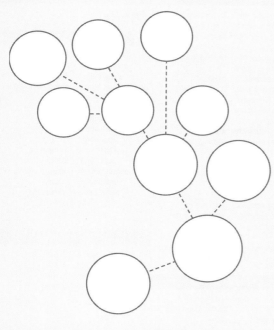

3. Une fois (*Once*) votre schéma d'idées créé, pensez à d'autres informations importantes pour la création de votre brochure.

Écriture

Utilisez votre schéma d'idées pour créer la brochure de votre voyage. Donnez un titre (*title*) à la présentation et aux différentes catégories. Chaque section et sous-section (*minor section*) doit (*must*) avoir son titre et être présentée séparément. Incorporez au moins (*at least*) quatre sous-sections. Vous pouvez inclure (*can include*) des visuels. Faites attention à bien les placer dans les sections correspondantes. Utilisez les constructions grammaticales et le vocabulaire que vous avez appris dans cette unité.

Après l'écriture

1. Échangez votre brochure avec celle (*the one*) d'un(e) partenaire. Répondez à ces questions pour commenter son travail.

- La brochure de votre partenaire correspond-elle au schéma d'idées qu'il/elle a créé?

- Votre partenaire a-t-il/elle inclu au moins quatre sections?

- Toutes les sections et sous-sections ont-elles un titre?

- Votre partenaire a-t-il/elle décrit en détail chaque catégorie?

- Chaque sous-section présente-t-elle des informations supplémentaires sur le sujet?

- Si votre partenaire a ajouté (*added*) des visuels, illustrent-ils vraiment le texte qu'ils accompagnent?

- Votre partenaire a-t-il/elle correctement utilisé les constructions grammaticales et le vocabulaire de l'unité?

2. Corrigez votre brochure d'après (*according to*) les commentaires de votre partenaire. Relisez votre travail pour éliminer ces problèmes:

- des fautes (*errors*) d'orthographe

- des fautes de ponctuation

- des fautes de conjugaison

- des fautes d'accord (*agreement*) des adjectifs

- un mauvais emploi (*use*) de la grammaire

trois cent sept   **307**

EVALUATION

Criteria

Content Contains both an idea map and an outline that provide all the information requested in bulleted list of tasks.
Scale: 1 2 3 4 5

Organization An outline or idea map that is then converted into a brochure with a title and minor sections that correspond to the outline or idea map.
Scale: 1 2 3 4 5

Accuracy Uses forms of **aller** and direct object pronouns correctly. Spells words, conjugates verbs, and modifies adjectives correctly throughout.
Scale: 1 2 3 4 5

Creativity Includes additional information that is not included in the task and/or designs a brochure with photos, drawings, or extra embellishments.
Scale: 1 2 3 4 5

Scoring

Excellent	18–20 points
Good	14–17 points
Satisfactory	10–13 points
Unsatisfactory	< 10 points

21st Century Skills

Productivity and Accountability
Provide the rubric to students before they hand their work in for grading. Ask students to make sure they have met the highest standard possible on the rubric before submitting their work.

Suggestion Tell students that an easy way to study from **Vocabulaire** is to cover up the French half of each section, leaving only the English equivalents exposed. They can then quiz themselves on the French items. To focus on the English equivalents of the French entries, they simply reverse this process.

21st Century Skills

Creativity and Innovation
Ask students to prepare a list of three products or perspectives they learned about in this unit to share with the class. Consider asking them to focus on the **Culture** and **Panorama** sections.

21st Century Skills

Leadership and Responsibility
Extension Project
If you have access to students in a Francophone country, have students decide on three questions they want to ask the partner class related to this unit's topic. Based on the responses they receive, work as a class to explain to the partner class one aspect of their responses that surprised the class and why.

Leçon 7A

Partir en voyage

partir en vacances	to go on vacation
prendre un train (un avion, un taxi, un (auto)bus, un bateau)	to take a train (plane, taxi, bus, boat)
un aéroport	airport
un arrêt d'autobus (de bus)	bus stop
une arrivée	arrival
un avion	plane
un billet aller-retour	round-trip ticket
un billet (d'avion, de train)	(plane, train) ticket
un départ	departure
une douane	customs
une gare (routière)	train station (bus station)
un passager/une passagère	passenger
une sortie	exit
une station (de métro)	(subway) station
un vol	flight
un voyage	trip
à l'étranger	abroad, overseas
le monde	world
un pays	country

Les pays

(en/l') Allemagne (f.)	(to, in) Germany
(en/l') Angleterre (f.)	(to, in) England
(en/la) Belgique (belge)	(to, in) Belgium (Belgian)
(au/le) Brésil (brésilien(ne))	(to, in) Brazil (Brazilian)
(au/le) Canada	(to, in) Canada
(en/la) Chine (chinois(e))	(to, in) China (Chinese)
(en/l') Espagne (f.)	(to, in) Spain
(aux/les) États-Unis (m.)	(to, in) the United States
(en/la) France	(to, in) France
(en/l') Irlande (f.) (irlandais(e))	(to, in) Ireland (Irish)
(en/l') Italie (f.)	(to, in) Italy
(au/le) Japon	(to, in) Japan
(au/le) Mexique	(to, in) Mexico
(en/la) Suisse	(to, in) Switzerland

Les vacances

bronzer	to tan
faire du shopping	to go shopping
faire les valises	to pack one's bags
faire un séjour	to spend time (somewhere)
rouler en voiture	to ride in a car
utiliser un plan	to use/read a map
la campagne	country(side)
une capitale	capital
un congé	time off, leave
des gens (m.)	people
le journal	newspaper
la mer	sea
une plage	beach
une station de ski	ski resort
un ticket de bus, de métro	bus, subway ticket
des vacances (f.)	vacation

Expressions utiles

See p. 271.

Verbes

aller	to go
arriver	to arrive
descendre	to go/take down
entrer	to enter
monter	to go/come up; to get in/on
mourir	to die
naître	to be born
partir	to leave
passer	to pass by; to spend time
rentrer	to return
rester	to stay
retourner	to return
sortir	to go out; to take someone or something out
tomber (sur quelqu'un)	to fall (to run into somebody)

Direct object pronouns

me/m'	me
te/t'	you
le/la/l'	him/her/it
nous	us
vous	you
les	them

Leçon 7B

Faire une réservation

annuler une réservation	to cancel a reservation
réserver	to reserve
une agence/un agent de voyages	travel agency/agent
un ascenseur	elevator
une auberge de jeunesse	youth hostel
une chambre individuelle	single room
une clé	key
un(e) client(e)	client; guest
un étage	floor
un hôtel	hotel
un hôtelier/une hotelière	hotel keeper
un lit	bed
un passeport	passport
la réception	reception desk
le rez-de-chaussée	ground floor
complet/complète	full (no vacancies)
libre	available

Adverbes et locutions de temps

alors	so, then; at that moment
après (que)	after
avant (de)	before
d'abord	first
donc	therefore
enfin	finally, at last
ensuite	then, next
finalement	finally
pendant (que)	during, while
puis	then
tout à coup	suddenly
tout de suite	right away

Ordinal numbers

premier/première	first
deuxième	second
troisième	third
quatrième	fourth
cinquième	fifth
neuvième	ninth
onzième	eleventh
vingtième	twentieth
vingt et unième	twenty-first
vingt-deuxième	twenty-second
trente et unième	thirty-first
centième	hundredth

Expressions utiles

See p. 289.

Adverbes

absolument	absolutely
constamment	constantly
couramment	fluently
de temps en temps	from time to time
dernièrement	lately
en général	in general
évidemment	obviously
franchement	frankly
gentiment	nicely
heureusement	fortunately
lentement	slowly
malheureusement	unfortunately
rapidement	quickly
quelquefois	sometimes
vite	fast
vraiment	really

Verbes irréguliers

décrire	to describe
dire	to say
écrire	to write
lire	to read

Chez nous

Pour commencer
- Où sont ces personnes?
  a. dans la cuisine b. dans la salle de bains
  c. dans la chambre
- Qu'est-ce qu'il y a sur la photo?
  a. une lampe b. une table c. une télévision
- Que font ces personnes?
  a. Elles étudient. b. Elles cuisinent.
  c. Elles regardent la télé.

Unit Goals
Leçon 8A

In this lesson, students will learn:
- terms for parts of the house
- terms for furniture
- the pronunciation of **s** and **ss**
- about housing in France and **le château Frontenac**
- more about housing in France through specially shot video footage
- the uses of the **passé composé** and the **imparfait**, and the verb **vivre**
- about an entrepreneur who makes cardboard furniture

Leçon 8B

In this lesson, students will learn:
- terms for household chores
- terms for appliances
- the pronunciation of semi-vowels
- about the interiors of French homes and the French Quarter in New Orleans
- more about the uses of the **passé composé** and the **imparfait**
- the uses of **savoir** and **connaître**
- to use visual cues to understand spoken French

Savoir-faire

In this section, students will learn:
- cultural and historical information about **Paris** and the French region **l'Île-de-France**
- to guess the meaning of unknown words from context
- to write a narrative using the **passé composé** and the **imparfait**

 21st Century Skills

Initiative and Self-Direction
Students can monitor their progress online using the activities and assessments on vhlcentral.com.

Pour commencer
- **a. dans la cuisine**
- **b. une table**
- **b. Elles cuisinent.**

SUPPORT FOR BACKWARD DESIGN

Unité 8 **Essential Questions**
1. How do people describe their homes?
2. How do people talk about specific past actions contrasted with how things used to be?
3. How do people talk about household chores?

Unité 8 **Integrated Performance Assessment**
Before teaching the chapter, review the Integrated Performance Assessment (IPA) and its accompanying scoring rubric provided in the Testing Program. Use the IPA to assess students' progress toward proficiency targets at the end of the chapter.
IPA Context: It is four years from now. You and a friend are planning to spend a semester in Paris and you are looking for an apartment to rent.

 FORUMS

Forums on vhlcentral.com allow you and your students to record and share audio messages.
Use Forums for presentations, oral assessments, discussions, directions, etc.

You will learn how to...
▪ describe your home
▪ talk about habitual past actions

◁)) **vhl**central

La maison

AP® Theme: Contemporary Life
Context: Housing and Shelter

Vocabulaire

déménager	*to move out*
emménager	*to move in*
louer	*to rent*
un appartement	*apartment*
une cave	*cellar; basement*
un couloir	*hallway*
une cuisine	*kitchen*
un escalier	*staircase*
un immeuble	*building*
un jardin	*garden; yard*
un logement	*housing*
un loyer	*rent*
une pièce	*room*
un quartier	*area, neighborhood*
une salle à manger	*dining room*
un salon	*formal living/sitting room*
un studio	*studio (apartment)*
une armoire	*armoire, wardrobe*
une douche	*shower*
un lavabo	*bathroom sink*
un meuble	*piece of furniture*
un placard	*closet, cupboard*
un tiroir	*drawer*
un(e) propriétaire	*owner*

le balcon
la salle de bains
les toilettes (f.)/ les W.C. (m.)
le miroir
la lampe
la baignoire
le canapé
le tapis
le fauteuil
une fleur
le sous-sol
la salle de séjour

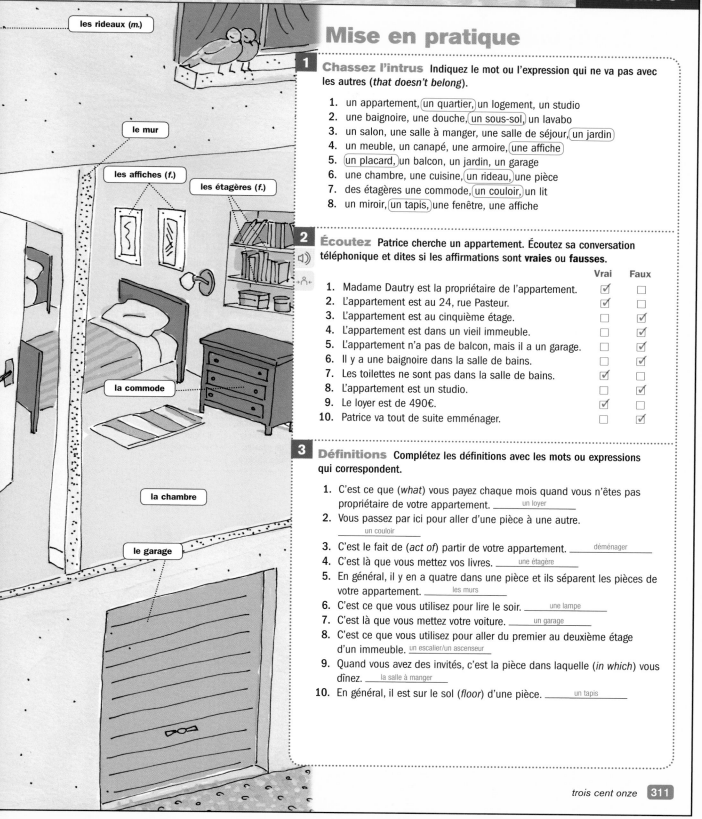

les rideaux (*m.*)

le mur

les affiches (*f.*)

les étagères (*f.*)

la commode

la chambre

le garage

Mise en pratique

1 **Chassez l'intrus** Indiquez le mot ou l'expression qui ne va pas avec les autres (*that doesn't belong*).

1. un appartement, un quartier, un logement, un studio
2. une baignoire, une douche, un sous-sol, un lavabo
3. un salon, une salle à manger, une salle de séjour, un jardin
4. un meuble, un canapé, une armoire, une affiche
5. un placard, un balcon, un jardin, un garage
6. une chambre, une cuisine, un rideau, une pièce
7. des étagères une commode, un couloir, un lit
8. un miroir, un tapis, une fenêtre, une affiche

2 **Écoutez** Patrice cherche un appartement. Écoutez sa conversation téléphonique et dites si les affirmations sont **vraies** ou **fausses**.

	Vrai	Faux
1. Madame Dautry est la propriétaire de l'appartement.	☑	☐
2. L'appartement est au 24, rue Pasteur.	☑	☐
3. L'appartement est au cinquième étage.	☐	☑
4. L'appartement est dans un vieil immeuble.	☐	☑
5. L'appartement n'a pas de balcon, mais il a un garage.	☐	☑
6. Il y a une baignoire dans la salle de bains.	☐	☑
7. Les toilettes ne sont pas dans la salle de bains.	☑	☐
8. L'appartement est un studio.	☐	☑
9. Le loyer est de 490€.	☑	☐
10. Patrice va tout de suite emménager.	☐	☑

3 **Définitions** Complétez les définitions avec les mots ou expressions qui correspondent.

1. C'est ce que (*what*) vous payez chaque mois quand vous n'êtes pas propriétaire de votre appartement. _____un loyer_____
2. Vous passez par ici pour aller d'une pièce à une autre. _____un couloir_____
3. C'est le fait de (*act of*) partir de votre appartement. _____déménager_____
4. C'est là que vous mettez vos livres. _____une étagère_____
5. En général, il y en a quatre dans une pièce et ils séparent les pièces de votre appartement. _____les murs_____
6. C'est ce que vous utilisez pour lire le soir. _____une lampe_____
7. C'est là que vous mettez votre voiture. _____un garage_____
8. C'est ce que vous utilisez pour aller du premier au deuxième étage d'un immeuble. _____un escalier/un ascenseur_____
9. Quand vous avez des invités, c'est la pièce dans laquelle (*in which*) vous dînez. _____la salle à manger_____
10. En général, il est sur le sol (*floor*) d'une pièce. _____un tapis_____

trois cent onze 311

---

1 **Expansion** Have students create one or two additional sets using at least three of the new vocabulary words in each one. Collect their papers and write some of the items on the board.

2 **Script** PATRICE: Allô, Madame Dautry, s'il vous plaît. MADAME: Oui, c'est moi. J'écoute.
P: Mon nom est Patrice Leconte. Je vous appelle au sujet de votre appartement du 24, rue Pasteur. Est-ce qu'il est toujours libre?
M: Oui, jeune homme. Il est toujours libre.
P: Parfait. Comment est-il?
M: Il est au quatrième étage d'un immeuble moderne. Il y a un balcon, mais pas de garage. La chambre est plutôt petite, mais il y a beaucoup de placards.
P: Et la salle de bains?
M: Elle est petite aussi, avec une douche, un lavabo et un grand miroir. Les toilettes sont séparées.
P: Et le salon?
M: C'est la pièce principale. Elle est plutôt grande. La cuisine est juste à côté.
P: C'est combien, le loyer?
M: Le loyer est de 490€.
P: Oh, c'est cher!
M: Mais vous êtes à côté de l'université et l'appartement est libre le premier septembre.
P: Bon, je vais y penser. Merci beaucoup. Au revoir, Madame.
M: Au revoir, Monsieur.
Teacher Resources DVD

2 **Expansion** Play the recording again, stopping at the end of each sentence that contains an answer. Have students verify true statements and correct the false ones.

3 **Expansion** Have students work in pairs to create definitions for five other words or expressions. Before beginning this activity, teach them expressions for circumlocution. Examples: **C'est un objet qu'on utilise pour… C'est une pièce où…**

TEACHING OPTIONS

Using Games Write vocabulary words related to home furnishings on index cards. On another set of cards, draw or paste pictures to match each term. Tape them face down on the board in random order. Divide the class into two teams. Play a game of Concentration in which students match words with pictures. When a player has a match, his or her team collects those cards. When all cards are matched, the team with the most cards wins.

EXPANSION

Classifying Words Write **Logements** and **Meubles** at the top of two columns on the board or on a transparency. Say vocabulary words and have students classify them in the correct category. Examples: **un appartement (logement), une résidence (logement), un studio (logement), un canapé (meuble), un lit (meuble),** and **une armoire (meuble).**

Communication

4 Répondez À tour de rôle avec un(e) partenaire, posez-vous ces questions et répondez-y (*them*). Answers will vary.

1. Où est-ce que tu habites?
2. Combien de pièces y a-t-il chez toi?
3. Quand est-ce que ta famille a emménagé?
4. Est-ce qu'il y a un jardin? Un garage?
5. Combien de placards est-ce qu'il y a? Où sont-ils?
6. Quels meubles avez-vous? Comment sont-ils?
7. Quels meubles est-ce que tu voudrais (*would like*) avoir dans ta chambre?
   (Répondez: **Je voudrais...**)
8. Qu'est-ce que tu n'aimes pas au sujet de ta chambre?

5 Votre chambre Écrivez une description de votre chambre. À tour de rôle, lisez votre description à votre partenaire. Il/Elle va vous demander d'autres détails et dessiner un plan. Ensuite, regardez le dessin (*drawing*) de votre partenaire et dites s'il correspond à votre chambre ou non. N'oubliez pas d'utiliser des prépositions pour indiquer où sont certains meubles et objets. Answers will vary.

6 Sept différences Votre professeur va vous donner, à vous et à votre partenaire, deux feuilles d'activités différentes. Il y a sept différences entre les deux images. Comparez vos dessins et faites une liste de ces différences. Attention! Ne regardez pas la feuille de votre partenaire. Answers will vary.

MODÈLE
Élève 1: *Dans mon appartement, il y a un lit. Il y a une lampe à côté du lit.*
Élève 2: *Dans mon appartement aussi, il y a un lit, mais il n'y a pas de lampe.*

7 La décoration Formez un groupe de trois. L'un de vous est un décorateur d'intérieur qui a rendez-vous avec deux clients qui veulent (*want*) redécorer leur maison. Les clients sont très difficiles. Imaginez votre conversation et jouez la scène devant la classe. Utilisez les mots de la liste. Answers will vary.

un canapé	un fauteuil
une chambre	un meuble
une cuisine	un mur
un escalier	un placard
une étagère	un tapis

EXPANSION

Finding the Correct Room Call out words for furnishings and other objects, and have students write or say the room(s) where they might be found. Examples: **la télévision (la salle de séjour), le lit (la chambre),** and **la table (la salle à manger).**

PRE-AP®

Interpersonal Speaking Have the class label various parts of the classroom with the names of rooms one would typically find in a house. Then have groups of three perform a skit in which the owner is showing the house to two exchange students who are going to spend the semester there.

Les sons et les lettres  **vhl**central

s and ss

You've already learned that an **s** at the end of a word is usually silent.

lavabos   **copains**   **vas**   **placards**

An **s** at the beginning of a word, before a consonant, or after a pronounced consonant is pronounced like the s in the English word *set*.

soir   **salon**   **studio**   **ab**solument

A double **s** is pronounced like the ss in the English word *kiss*.

grosse   **a**ssez   **inté**ressant   **rou**sse

An **s** at the end of a word is often pronounced when the following word begins with a vowel sound. An **s** in a liaison sounds like a z, like the s in the English word *rose*.

très élégant   **trois hommes**

The other instance where the French **s** has a z sound is when there is a single **s** between two vowels within the same word. The **s** is pronounced like the s in the English word *music*.

musée   **amu**sant   **oi**seau   **be**soin

These words look alike, but have different meanings. Compare the pronunciations of each word pair.

poison   **poi**sson   **dé**sert   **de**ssert

Prononcez Répétez les mots suivants à voix haute.

1. sac
2. triste
3. suisse
4. chose
5. bourse
6. passer
7. surprise
8. assister
9. magasin
10. expressions
11. sénégalaise
12. sérieusement

Articulez Répétez les phrases suivantes à voix haute.

1. Le spectacle est très amusant et la chanteuse est superbe.
2. Est-ce que vous habitez dans une maison?
3. De temps en temps, Suzanne assiste à l'inauguration d'expositions au musée.
4. Heureusement, mes professeurs sont sympathiques, sociables et très sincères.

Dictons Répétez les dictons à voix haute.

Si jeunesse savait, si vieillesse pouvait. [1]

Les oiseaux de même plumage s'assemblent sur le même rivage. [2]

[2] Birds of a feather flock together.
[1] (lit. If youth but knew, if old age but could.)
Youth is wasted on the young.

trois cent treize 313

313

Section Goals
In this section, students will learn about the sounds of **s** and **ss**.

Key Standards
4.1

Suggestions
• Model the pronunciation of the example words and have students repeat them after you.
• Ask students to provide more examples of words from this lesson or previous lessons with these sounds. Examples: **cuisine, salon,** and **expression.**
• Dictate five familiar words containing **s** and **ss**, repeating each one at least two times. Then write them on the board or on a transparency and have students check their spelling.

TELL Connection

Environment 5 *Why:* Create a word-rich environment to support performance objectives. *What:* Have students create their own labeled illustrations of the proverbs from each lesson and of the tongue-twisters in the Teacher's Edition so that they can see the language patterns they have learned on a daily basis.

EXPANSION
Mini-dictée Use these sentences for additional practice or dictation. **1. Serge est professeur de sociologie. 2. Solange est paresseuse et pessimiste. 3. Ces étudiants sénégalais sont très intelligents. 4. Sylvain essaie les chaussures sans chaussettes.**

EXPANSION
Tongue-twisters Teach students these French tongue-twisters that contain the **s** and **ss** sounds. **1. Ces six saucissons-ci sont si secs qu'on ne sait si c'en sont. 2. Zazie causait avec sa cousine en cousant.**

La visite surprise vhlcentral

AP® Theme: Contemporary Life
Context: Housing and Shelter

Section Goals

In this section, students will learn functional phrases for talking about their home.

Key Standards
1.2, 2.1, 2.2, 4.1, 4.2

Video Recap: Leçon 7B
Before doing this **Roman-photo**, review the previous one with this activity.
1. Pourquoi Sandrine est-elle allée à l'agence de voyages? (pour faire une réservation d'hôtel à Albertville)
2. Pourquoi n'a-t-elle pas fait la réservation? (Les hôtels moins chers sont complets.)
3. Comment Amina a-t-elle réussi à trouver un hôtel? (Elle a cherché sur Internet.)
4. Pourquoi Sandrine n'est-elle pas contente? (parce que Pascal ne va pas aller à Albertville)

Video Synopsis Pascal arrives in Aix-en-Provence. He runs into Rachid, who helps him pick up his flowers. He has never met Rachid before. Rachid and David then take a tour of Sandrine's apartment, which is very nice and big. Pascal shows up unexpectedly. Sandrine is not pleased by his surprise visit and breaks up with him.

Suggestions
- Have students scan the **Roman-photo** and find words related to the home.
- Have students read the **Roman-photo** conversation in groups of four.

PERSONNAGES

David

Pascal

Rachid

Sandrine

En ville, Pascal fait tomber (drops) ses fleurs.
PASCAL Aïe!
RACHID Tenez. *(Il aide Pascal.)*
PASCAL Oh, merci.
RACHID Aïe!
PASCAL Oh pardon, je suis vraiment désolé!
RACHID Ce n'est rien.
PASCAL Bonne journée!

Chez Sandrine...
RACHID Eh, salut, David! Dis donc, ce n'est pas un logement d'étudiants ici! C'est grand chez toi! Tu ne déménages pas, finalement?
DAVID Heureusement, Sandrine a décidé de rester.
SANDRINE Oui, je suis bien dans cet appartement. Seulement, les loyers sont très chers au centre-ville.

RACHID Oui, malheureusement! Tu as combien de pièces?
SANDRINE Il y a trois pièces: le salon, la salle à manger, ma chambre. Bien sûr, il y a une cuisine et j'ai aussi une grande salle de bains. Je te fais visiter?

SANDRINE Et voici ma chambre.
RACHID Elle est belle!
SANDRINE Oui... j'aime le vert.

RACHID Dis, c'est vrai, Sandrine, ta salle de bains est vraiment grande.
DAVID Oui! Et elle a un beau miroir au-dessus du lavabo et une baignoire!
RACHID Chez nous, on a seulement une douche.
SANDRINE Moi, je préfère les douches, en fait.

Le téléphone sonne (rings).
RACHID Comparé à cet appartement, le nôtre, c'est une cave! Pas de décorations, juste des affiches, un canapé, des étagères et mon bureau.
DAVID C'est vrai. On n'a même pas de rideaux.

A C T I V I T É S

1 **Vrai ou faux?** Indiquez si ces affirmations sont **vraies** ou **fausses**. Corrigez les phrases fausses. Answers may vary.

1. C'est la première fois que Rachid visite l'appartement. Vrai.
2. Sandrine ne déménage pas. Vrai.
3. Les loyers au centre-ville ne sont pas chers. Faux. Les loyers au centre-ville sont très chers.
4. Sandrine invite ses amis chez elle. Vrai.

5. Rachid préfère son appartement à l'appartement de Sandrine. Faux. Rachid préfère l'appartement de Sandrine.
6. Chez les garçons, il y a une baignoire et des rideaux. Faux. Les garçons ont une douche et n'ont pas de rideaux.
7. Quand Pascal arrive, Sandrine est contente (*pleased*). Faux. Sandrine n'est pas contente.
8. Pascal doit (*must*) travailler ce week-end. Faux. Pascal ne travaille pas ce week-end.

TEACHING OPTIONS

La visite surprise Before viewing the video, have students read the title and predict what might happen in this episode. Write their predictions on the board. After students have watched the video, review their predictions and ask them which ones were correct.

TEACHING OPTIONS

Regarder la vidéo Show the video episode without sound and have the class create a plot summary based on the visual cues. Then show the video again with sound and have the class correct any mistakes and fill in any gaps in the plot summary they created.

Pascal arrive à Aix-en-Provence.

SANDRINE Voici la salle à manger.
RACHID Ça, c'est une pièce très importante pour nous, les invités.

SANDRINE Et puis, la cuisine.
RACHID Une pièce très importante pour Sandrine...
DAVID Évidemment!

SANDRINE Mais Pascal... je pensais que tu avais du travail... Quoi? Tu es ici, maintenant? C'est une blague!
PASCAL Mais ma chérie, j'ai pris le train pour te faire une surprise...

SANDRINE Une surprise! Nous deux, c'est fini! D'abord, tu me dis que les vacances avec moi, c'est impossible et ensuite tu arrives à Aix sans me téléphoner!
PASCAL Bon, si c'est comme ça, reste où tu es. Ne descends pas. Moi, je m'en vais. Voilà tes fleurs. Tu parles d'une surprise!

Expressions utiles

Talking about your home

- **Tu ne déménages pas, finalement?**
  You are not moving, after all?
- **Heureusement, Sandrine a décidé de rester.**
  Thankfully/Happily, Sandrine has decided to stay.
- **Seulement, les loyers sont très chers au centre-ville.**
  However, rents are very expensive downtown.
- **Je te fais visiter?**
  Shall I give you a tour?
- **Ta salle de bains est vraiment grande.**
  Your bathroom is really big.
- **Elle a un beau miroir au-dessus du lavabo.**
  It has a nice mirror above the sink.
- **Chez nous, on a seulement une douche.**
  At our place, we only have a shower.

Additional vocabulary

- **Aïe!**
  Ouch!
- **Tenez.**
  Here.
- **Je pensais que tu avais du travail.**
  I thought you had work to do.
- **Mais ma chérie, j'ai pris le train pour te faire une surprise.**
  But sweetie, I took the train to surprise you.
- **sans**
  without
- **Moi, je m'en vais.**
  I am leaving/getting out of here.

2 **Quel appartement?** Indiquez si ces objets sont dans l'appartement de Sandrine (S) ou dans l'appartement de David et Rachid (D & R).

1. baignoire S
2. douche D & R
3. rideaux S
4. canapé D & R, S
5. trois pièces S
6. étagères D & R
7. miroir S
8. affiches D & R

3 **Conversez** Sandrine décide que son loyer est vraiment trop cher. Elle cherche un appartement à partager avec Amina. Avec deux partenaires, écrivez leur conversation avec un agent immobilier (*real estate agent*). Elles décrivent l'endroit idéal, le prix et les meubles qu'elles préfèrent. L'agent décrit plusieurs possibilités.

A C T I V I T É S

Expressions utiles
- Model the pronunciation of the **Expressions utiles** and have students repeat them.
- As you work through the list, point out verbs in the **passé composé** and verbs in the **imparfait**. Then tell them that the uses of these two past tenses will be formally presented in the **Structures** section.

1 **Suggestion** Have students write their corrections for false statements on the board.

1 **Expansion** For additional practice, give students these items. **9. Rachid et Pascal sont de bons amis. (Faux.) 10. La chambre de Sandrine est rose. (Faux.) 11. L'appartement de Sandrine est une cave. (Faux.)**

2 **Expansion** For additional practice, give students these items. **9. bureau (D & R) 10. grande salle de bains (S) 11. douche (D & R)**

3 **Suggestions**
- Before writing the conversation, tell students that the person playing the real estate agent should make a list of questions to ask prospective clients, and the two people playing Sandrine and Amina should decide on the features they are looking for in an apartment.
- You might want to bring in some real estate ads in French from newspapers or the Internet for the agents to use.
- Have students role-play their conversations.

 TELL Connection

Planning 8 *Why:* Media engages students in a broad range of thinking processes. *What:* Bring to students' attention the role and importance of each type of thinking process they use when engaged with media and associated activities: e.g. observation, remembering, understanding, analyzing, evaluating, applying, and creating.

PRE-AP®

Interpersonal Speaking Have groups of three interview each other about their dream house, with one student conducting the interview, one answering, and one taking notes. At three-minute intervals, have students switch roles until each has been interviewer, interviewee, and note-taker. Then have two groups get together and take turns describing their dream houses to one another using their notes.

EXPANSION

Writing Practice Have students work in pairs. Tell them to write an alternate ending to this episode, in which Sandrine is pleased to see Pascal and invites him upstairs to meet Rachid and David. Encourage students to use some of the **Expressions utiles**. Then have volunteers perform their role-plays for the class.

AP® **Theme:** Contemporary Life
Context: Housing and Shelter

vhlcentral | *Flash culture*

CULTURE À LA LOUPE

Le logement en France

Il y a différents types de logements. En ville, on habite dans une maison ou un appartement. À la campagne, on peut° habiter dans une villa, un château, un chalet ou un mas° provençal.

Vous avez peut-être remarqué° dans un film français qu'il y a une grande diversité de style d'habitation°. En effet°, le style et l'architecture varient d'une région à l'autre, souvent en raison° du climat et des matériaux disponibles°. Dans le Nord°, les maisons sont traditionnellement en briques° avec des toits en ardoise°. Dans l'Est°, en Alsace-Lorraine, il y

a de vieilles maisons à colombages° avec des parties de mur en bois°. Dans le Sud°, il y a des villas de style méditerranéen avec des toits en tuiles° rouges et des mas provençaux (de vieilles maisons en pierre°). Dans les Alpes, en Savoie, les chalets sont en bois avec de grands balcons très fleuris°, comme en Suisse. Les maisons traditionnelles de l'Ouest° ont des toits en chaume°. Presque toutes les maisons françaises ont des volets° et les fenêtres sont assez différentes aussi des fenêtres aux États-Unis. Très souvent il n'y a pas de moustiquaire°, même° dans le sud de la France où il fait très chaud en été.

En France les trois quarts des gens habitent en ville. Beaucoup habitent dans la banlieue, où il y a beaucoup de grands immeubles mais aussi de petits pavillons individuels (maisons avec de petits jardins). Dans les centres-villes et dans les banlieues, il y a des HLM. Ce sont des habitations à loyer modéré°. Les HLM sont construits par l'État°. Ce sont souvent des logements réservés aux familles qui ont moins d'argent.

peut *can* **mas** *farmhouse* **remarqué** *noticed* **habitation** *housing* **En effet** *Indeed* **en raison du** *due to the* **disponibles** *available* **Nord** *North* **en briques** *made of bricks* **toits en ardoise** *slate roofs* **Est** *East* **à colombages** *half-timbered* **en bois** *made of wood* **Sud** *South* **en tuiles** *made of tiles* **en pierre** *made of stone* **fleuris** *full of flowers* **Ouest** *West* **en chaume** *thatched* **volets** *shutters* **moustiquaire** *window screen* **même** *even* **habitations à loyer modéré** *low-cost housing* **construits par l'État** *built by the State (government)*

Coup de main

Here are some terms commonly used in statistics.

un quart = *one quarter*

un tiers = *one third*

la moitié = *half*

la plupart de = *most of*

un sur cinq = *one in five*

ACTIVITÉS

1   **Vrai ou faux?** Indiquez si les phrases sont **vraies** ou **fausses**.

1. Les maisons sont similaires dans les différentes régions françaises. Faux.
2. Dans le Nord les maisons sont traditionnellement en briques. Vrai.
3. En Alsace-Lorraine il y a des chalets. Faux.
4. Dans les Alpes il y a des mas provençaux. Faux.
5. Les mas provençaux sont des maisons en bois. Faux.
6. Presque toutes les maisons françaises ont des volets. Vrai.

7. Les maisons françaises n'ont pas toujours des moustiquaires. Vrai.
8. La plupart (*majority*) des Français habite à la campagne. Faux.
9. Le pavillon individuel est une sorte de grand immeuble. Faux.
10. Les millionnaires habitent dans des HLM. Faux.

LE FRANÇAIS QUOTIDIEN

Location d'un logement

agence (f.) de location	rental agency
bail (m.)	lease
caution (f.)	security deposit
charges (f.)	basic utilities
chauffage (m.)	heating
électricité (f.)	electricity
locataire (m./f.)	tenant
petites annonces (f.)	(rental) ads

AP® Theme: Beauty and Aesthetics Context: Architecture

LE MONDE FRANCOPHONE

L'architecture

Voici quelques exemples d'habitations traditionnelles.

En Afrique centrale et de l'Ouest des maisons construites sur pilotis°, avec un grenier à riz°

En Afrique du Nord des maisons en pisé (de la terre° rouge mélangée° à de la paille°) construites autour d'un patio central et avec, souvent, une terrasse sur le toit°

Aux Antilles des maisons en bois de toutes les couleurs avec des toits en métal

En Polynésie française des bungalows, construits sur pilotis ou sur le sol, souvent en bambou avec des toits en paille ou en feuilles de cocotier°

Au Viêt-nam des maisons sur pilotis construites sur des lacs, des rivières ou simplement au-dessus du sol°

pilotis *stilts* **grenier à riz** *rice loft* **terre** *clay* **mélangée** *mixed* **paille** *straw* **toit** *roof* **feuilles de cocotier** *coconut palm leaves* **au-dessus du sol** *off the ground*

PORTRAIT   AP® Theme: Contemporary Life Context: Travel

Le château Frontenac

Le château Frontenac est un hôtel de luxe et un des plus beaux° sites touristiques de la ville de Québec. Construit entre la fin° du

XIXᵉ siècle et le début° du XXᵉ siècle sur le Cap Diamant, dans le quartier du Vieux-Québec, le château offre une vue° spectaculaire sur la ville. Aujourd'hui, avec ses 618 chambres sur 18 étages, ses restaurants gastronomiques, sa piscine et son centre sportif, le château Frontenac est classé parmi° les 500 meilleurs° hôtels du monde.

un des plus beaux *one of the most beautiful* **fin** *end* **début** *beginning* **vue** *view* **classé parmi** *ranked among* **meilleurs** *best*

AP® Theme: Contemporary Life Context: Holidays and Celebrations

Sur Internet

Qu'est-ce qu'une pendaison de crémaillère? D'où vient cette expression?

Go to **vhlcentral.com** to find more information related to this **Culture** section and to watch the corresponding **Flash culture** video.

---

2 **Répondez** Répondez aux questions, d'après les informations données dans les textes.

1. Qu'est-ce que le château Frontenac?
Un hôtel de luxe.
2. De quel siècle date le château Frontenac?
De la fin du XIXᵉ et du début du XXᵉ siècles.
3. Dans quel quartier de la ville de Québec le trouve-t-on?
Le quartier du Vieux-Québec.
4. Où trouve-t-on des maisons sur pilotis?
En Afrique centrale et de l'Ouest, au Viêt-nam et en Polynésie française.
5. Quelles sont les caractéristiques des maisons d'Afrique du Nord?
Le pisé, le patio central et la terrasse sur le toit.

3 **Une année en France** Vous allez habiter en France. Téléphonez à un agent immobilier (*real estate*) (votre partenaire) et expliquez-lui le type de logement que vous recherchez. Il/Elle va vous donner des renseignements sur les logements disponibles (*available*). Posez des questions pour avoir plus de détails.

ACTIVITÉS

317

8A.1

The *passé composé* vs. the *imparfait* (Part 1)

vhlcentral

Point de départ Although the **passé composé** and the **imparfait** are both past tenses, they have very distinct uses and are not interchangeable. The choice between these two tenses depends on the context and on the point of view of the speaker.

À noter

The two basic uses of the **passé composé** are:
· to express completed actions in the past
· to describe changes in state of being

The explanations on this page point out further details regarding these two basic uses.

Boîte à outils

You have learned that **pendant** can mean *while* or *during*. When used with a time expression, however, it means *for*.

Pendant combien de temps as-tu habité à Paris?

For how long did you live in Paris?

J'ai habité à Paris pendant un an.

I lived in Paris for a year.

Uses of the *passé composé*	
To express specific actions that started and ended in the past	J'**ai nettoyé** la salle de bains deux fois. *I cleaned the bathroom twice.*
	Nous **avons acheté** un tapis. *We bought a rug.*
	L'enfant **est né** à la maison. *The child was born at home.*
	Il **a plu** hier. *It rained yesterday.*
To tell about events that happened at a specific point in time or within a specific length of time in the past	Je **suis allé** à la pêche avec papa **l'année dernière.** *I went fishing with dad last year.*
	Il **est allé** au concert **vendredi.** *He went to the concert on Friday.*
	Nous **avons passé** une journée fantastique à la plage. *We spent a fantastic day at the beach.*
	Elle **a étudié** à Paris **pendant six mois.** *She studied in Paris for six months.*
To express the beginning or end of a past action	Le film **a commencé** à huit heures. *The movie began at 8 o'clock.*
	Ils **ont fini** leurs devoirs samedi matin. *They finished their homework Saturday morning.*
To narrate a series of past actions or events	Ce matin, j'**ai fait** du jogging, j'**ai nettoyé** ma chambre et j'**ai fait** la cuisine. *This morning, I jogged, I cleaned my bedroom, and I cooked.*
	Pour la fête d'anniversaire de papa, maman **a envoyé** les invitations, elle **a acheté** un cadeau et elle **a fait** les décorations. *For dad's birthday party, mom sent out the invitations, bought a gift, and did the decorations.*
To signal a change in someone's mental, physical, or emotional state	Il **est mort** dans un accident. *He died in an accident.*
	J'**ai eu** peur quand j'ai vu le serpent. *I got scared when I saw the snake.*
	Elle **a eu** soif. *She got thirsty.*

Uses of the *imparfait*

To describe an ongoing past action with no reference to its beginning or end	Vous **dormiez** sur le canapé. *You were sleeping on the couch.* Tu **attendais** dans le café? *You were waiting in the café?* Nous **regardions** la télé chez Fanny. *We were watching TV at Fanny's house.* Les enfants **lisaient** tranquillement. *The children were reading peacefully.*
To express habitual or repeated past actions and events	Nous **faisions** un tour en voiture le dimanche matin. *We used to go for a drive on Sunday mornings.* Elle **mettait** toujours la voiture dans le garage. *She always put the car in the garage.* Maman **travaillait** souvent dans le jardin. *Mom would often work in the garden.*
To describe an ongoing mental, physical, or emotional state or condition	Karine **était** très inquiète. *Karine was very worried.* Simon et Marion **étaient** fatigués et ils **avaient** sommeil. *Simon and Marion were tired and sleepy.* Mon ami **avait** faim et il **avait** envie de manger quelque chose. *My friend was hungry and felt like eating something.* Quand j'**étais** jeune, j'**aimais** faire du camping. *When I was young, I used to like to go camping.*

Boîte à outils

Note that the verb **avoir** has a different meaning when used in the **imparfait** versus the **passé composé**:

J'avais sommeil.
I was sleepy.

J'ai eu sommeil.
I got sleepy.

Essayez! **Complétez chaque phrase avec le verbe correct.**

1. Avant de partir, ils (donnaient / ont donné) leurs clés aux voisins. ___ont donné___
2. Vous (étiez / avez été) souvent fatigué. ___étiez___
3. Je (naissait / suis né) en 2003. ___suis né___
4. On (rendait / a rendu) visite à oncle Marc deux fois le mois dernier. ___a rendu___
5. Tu es rentré à la maison, et ensuite tu (regardais / as regardé) la télé. ___as regardé___
6. Quand j'étais petite, j' (habitais / ai habité) une grande maison. ___habitais___
7. À minuit, la température (tombait / est tombée) et nous avons eu froid. ___est tombée___
8. Papa (lisait / a lu) le journal tranquillement et Maman écrivait un email. ___lisait___

Suggestions: Scaffolding

• Go through all the uses of the **imparfait** on this page and discuss **Boîte à outils**.

• Contrast again the uses of the **passé composé** and **imparfait** by giving personalized examples of things you and/ or your family did yesterday versus things you and your family used to do when you were young. Examples: **Hier soir, je suis allée au centre commercial. Quand j'étais petite, je jouais au foot.** Then make two columns on the board, one labeled **Hier, je/j'…** and the other labeled **Quand j'étais petit(e)…** Have volunteers take turns writing complete sentences about themselves under each column.

• As you compare the **passé composé** and the **imparfait**, have students focus on the pronunciation of these tenses. You might have them practice the following sentences: **J'ai travaillé. / Je travaillais. Il parlait. / Il a parlé. Tu allais. / Tu es allé(e). Elle chantait. / Elle a chanté.**

• Follow the Extra Practice suggestion on p. 319.

Essayez! Have students explain why they chose the **passé composé** or the **imparfait** for each of their responses.

EXPANSION

Extra Practice Make cards that contain a verb or noun and an expression that signals a past tense. Example: **hier / parc** or **Quand j'étais jeune / voyager**. Mix them up in a hat and have each student pick a card at random. Have each student state the cues on his or her card and use them in a sentence with the **passé composé** or the **imparfait**. Have the student say which tense he or she will use before formulating the sentence.

EXPANSION

Small Groups Have students work in groups to pick a popular holiday and write a few sentences in the past tense to describe it. Students might talk about typical activities they did that day, the weather, or how they felt on that day. Then, have them share their description with the class without revealing the holiday and have their classmates guess what holiday it is.

1 Expansion Have volunteers explain why they chose the **passé composé** or the **imparfait** in each case. Ask them to point out any words or expressions that triggered one tense or the other.

2 Suggestion Before assigning the activity, remind students that actions viewed as completed by the speaker take the **passé composé**. Have students give personal examples of actions in the past using this verb tense.

3 Expansion ↔�🯀↔ Have students use this activity as a model to write a short journal entry about a vacation of their own using the **passé composé** and the **imparfait**.

Mise en pratique

1 Une surprise désagréable Récemment, Benoît a fait un séjour à Strasbourg avec sa grande sœur. Complétez ses phrases avec l'imparfait ou le passé composé.

Ce matin, il (1) ____faisait____ (faire) chaud. J' (2) ____étais____ (être) content de partir pour Strasbourg. Je (3) ____suis parti____ (partir) pour la gare, où j' (4) ____ai retrouvé____ (retrouver) Émile. Le train (5) ____est arrivé____ (arriver) à Strasbourg à midi. Nous (6) ____avons commencé____ (commencer) notre promenade en ville. Nous (7) ____avions____ (avoir) besoin d'un plan. J' (8) ____ai cherché____ (chercher) mon portefeuille (*wallet*), mais il (9) ____était____ (être) toujours dans le train! Émile et moi, nous (10) ____avons couru____ (courir) à la gare!

2 Le week-end dernier Qu'est-ce que la famille Tran a fait le week-end dernier? Utilisez les éléments donnés et le passé composé ou l'imparfait pour écrire des phrases.

> **MODÈLE** nous / passer le week-end / chez des amis
> *Nous avons passé le week-end chez des amis.*

1. faire / beau / quand / nous / arriver   Il faisait beau quand nous sommes arrivés.
2. nous / être / fatigué / mais content   Nous étions fatigués mais contents.
3. Audrey et son amie / aller / à la piscine   Audrey et son amie sont allées à la piscine.
4. moi, je / décider de / dormir un peu   Moi, j'ai décidé de dormir un peu.
5. samedi soir / pleuvoir / quand / nous / sortir / cinéma   Samedi soir, il pleuvait quand nous sommes sortis du cinéma.
6. nous / rire / beaucoup / parce que / film / être / amusant   Nous avons beaucoup ri parce que le film était amusant.
7. minuit / nous / rentrer / chez nous   À minuit, nous sommes rentrés chez nous.
8. Lanh / regarder / télé / quand / nous / arriver   Lanh regardait la télé quand nous sommes arrivés.
9. dimanche matin / nous / passer / chez des amis   Dimanche matin, nous sommes passés chez des amis.
10. nous / passer / cinq heures / chez eux   Nous avons passé cinq heures chez eux.
11. ce / être / très / sympa   C'était très sympa.

3 Vacances à la montagne Hugo raconte ses vacances. Complétez ses phrases avec un des verbes de la liste au passé composé ou à l'imparfait.

aller	neiger	retourner
avoir	passer	skier
faire	rester	venir

1. L'hiver dernier, nous _avons passé_ les vacances à la montagne.
2. Quand nous sommes arrivés sur les pistes de ski, il _neigeait_ beaucoup et il _faisait_ un temps épouvantable.
3. Ce jour-là, nous _sommes restés_ à l'hôtel tout l'après-midi.
4. Le jour suivant, nous _sommes retournés_ sur les pistes.
5. Nous _avons skié_ et papa _est allé_ faire une randonnée.
6. Quand ils _avaient_ mon âge, papa et oncle Hervé _venaient_ tous les hivers à la montagne.

DIFFERENTIATION

For Auditory Learners Have your students make a list of 10 true and false sentences about what happened yesterday (or last week) in school using both the **passé composé** and the **imparfait**. For example: **Nous sommes allés à la gym; Marie était malade.** Encourage them to write sentences that contain both tenses, if they can. Ask them to read their sentences out loud. When someone in the class hears something that is not true, he or she should correct the sentence. Ex: **Non, Marie n'était pas malade. Elle allait bien et elle est venue en classe.**

Communication

4 Situations Avec un(e) partenaire, parlez de ces situations en utilisant le passé composé ou l'imparfait. Comparez vos réponses, puis présentez-les à la classe. Answers will vary.

MODÈLE

Le premier jour de cours...
Élève 1: *Le premier jour de cours, j'étais tellement nerveux/nerveuse que j'ai oublié mes livres.*
Élève 2: *Moi, j'étais nerveux/nerveuse aussi, alors j'ai quitté la maison très tôt.*

1. Quand j'étais petit(e),...
2. L'été dernier,...
3. Hier soir, mon/ma meilleur(e) ami(e)...
4. Hier, le professeur...
5. La semaine dernière, mon/ma camarade de classe...
6. Ce matin, au lycée,...
7. Quand j'avais dix ans,...
8. La dernière fois que j'étais en vacances,...

5 Votre premier/première ami(e) Posez ces questions à un(e) partenaire. Ajoutez (*Add*) d'autres questions si vous le voulez (*want*). Answers will vary.

1. Qui a été ton/ta premier/première ami(e)?
2. Quel âge avais-tu quand tu as fait sa connaissance?
3. Comment était-il/elle?
4. Est-ce que tu as fait la connaissance de sa famille?
5. Pendant combien de temps avez-vous resté(e)s ami(e)s?
6. À quoi jouiez-vous ensemble?
7. Aviez-vous les mêmes (*same*) centres d'intérêt?
8. Avez-vous perdu contact?

6 Conversation Sébastien est sorti avec des amis hier. Quand il est rentré plus tard que prévu (*later than planned*), sa mère était furieuse. Préparez leur conversation et présentez-la à la classe. Answers will vary.

MODÈLE

Élève 1: *Que faisais-tu cet après-midi?*
Élève 2: *Mes copains et moi, nous sommes allés manger une pizza...*

7 Un crime Vous avez été témoin (*witness*) d'un crime dans votre quartier et la police vous pose beaucoup de questions. Avec un(e) partenaire et à tour de rôle, jouez le détective et le témoin. Answers will vary.

MODÈLE

Élève 1: *Où étiez-vous vers huit heures hier soir?*
Élève 2: *Chez moi.*
Élève 1: *Avez-vous vu quelque chose?*

---

4 Expansion Have students choose one of these sentences to begin telling a short story in the past. Encourage students to use both the **passé composé** and the **imparfait**.

5 Expansion After completing the pair work, assign this activity as a short written composition.

5 Virtual Chat You can also assign Activity 5 on vhlcentral.com. Students record individual responses that appear in your gradebook.

6 Suggestion Act out the **modèle** with a volunteer before assigning this activity to pairs. Have pairs of students role-play their dialogues in front of the class.

6 Partner Chat You can also assign Activity 6 on vhlcentral.com. Students work in pairs to record the activity online. The pair's recorded conversation will appear in your gradebook.

Activity Pack For additional activities, go to the **Activity Pack** in the **Resources** section of vhlcentral.com.

EXPANSION

Fashion Show Have students work in pairs to write a critical review about a fashion show they attended last week. Have them give details about what the models were wearing and how they looked. They might also want to include comparisons between clothing styles they saw last week and how they were different from those in the past.

TEACHING OPTIONS

Small Groups Have students work in groups of four to write a brief account of a surprise party they organized last weekend. Have them tell how they prepared for the party, which rooms they decorated, what the weather was like, and how everyone felt after the party. Then, have them share their summary with the rest of the class.

Section Goals

In this section, students will learn:
- the use of the **passé composé** vs. the **imparfait** in narration, to describe interrupted actions, and to express cause and effect
- common expressions indicating the past tense
- the verb **vivre**

Key Standards

4.1, 5.1

Suggestions: Scaffolding
- Work with students to write the uses of the **passé composé** and the **imparfait** from pp. 318–319 on the board. Have students work in pairs to write example sentences for each use. When going over the sentences, emphasize that the **passé composé** is used to express completed actions in the past or a change in state or condition, and that the **imparfait** expresses actions with an undefined beginning or end. Then, have them explain the difference between these two sentences: **J'ai téléphoné quand ma mère est arrivée. Je téléphonais quand ma mère est arrivée.** (In the first case, I called after my mother arrived. In the second case, I was in the process of calling when my mother arrived.) Have students come up with other examples of sentences where the message changes based on which past tense form is used.
- Move through the bullet points on this page. Have students explain how the examples in each point relate to the uses listed earlier.
- Use timelines to illustrate an interrupted action and a cause and effect statement. The verb in the imperfect is a continuous line while the **passé composé** is a point on or at the end of that line.

8A.2

The *passé composé* vs. the *imparfait* (Part 2) and the verb *vivre* **vhl**central

Point de départ You have already seen some uses of the **passé composé** versus the **imparfait** for talking about actions and events in the past. Here are some other contexts in which the choice of tense is important.

- The **passé composé** and the **imparfait** are often used together to narrate a story or describe an incident. The **imparfait** provides the background description, such as time, weather, and location. The **passé composé** highlights specific events in the story.

Uses of the *passé composé* and the *imparfait*	
Le passé composé *is used to talk about:*	**L' imparfait** *is used to describe:*
• main facts	• the framework of the story: *weather, date, time, background scenery*
• specific, completed events	• descriptions of people: *age, physical and personality traits, clothing, feelings, state of mind*
• actions that advance the plot	• background setting: *what was going on, what others were doing*

Il **était** minuit et le temps **était** orageux. J'**avais** peur parce que j'**étais** seule dans la maison. Soudain, quelqu'un **a frappé** à la porte. J'**ai regardé** par la fenêtre et j'**ai vu** un vieil homme habillé en noir...
It was midnight and the weather was stormy. I was afraid because I was home alone. Suddenly, someone knocked at the door. I looked through the window and I saw an old man dressed in black...

- When the **passé composé** and the **imparfait** occur in the same sentence, the action in the **passé composé** often interrupts the ongoing action in the **imparfait**.

ACTION IN PROGRESS	INTERRUPTING ACTION
Je **chantais**	quand mon ami **est arrivé**.
I was singing	*when my friend arrived.*
Céline et Maxime **dormaient**	quand le téléphone **a sonné**.
Céline and Maxime were sleeping	*when the phone rang.*

- Sometimes the use of the **passé composé** and the **imparfait** in the same sentence expresses a cause and effect.

CAUSE	EFFECT
J'avais faim,	alors j'ai mangé un sandwich.
I was hungry,	*so I ate a sandwich.*
Elle est partie	parce qu'elle était fatiguée.
She left	*because she was tired.*

Vérifiez

EXPANSION

Pairs Ask students to narrate an embarrassing moment. Tell them to describe what happened and how they felt, using the **passé composé** and the **imparfait.** Then have volunteers retell their partner's embarrassing moment using the third person. You may want to let students make up a fake embarrassing moment.

TEACHING OPTIONS

Small Groups Have students work in groups of four to write a short article about an imaginary road trip they took last summer. Students should use the **imparfait** to set the scene and the **passé composé** to narrate events. Each student should contribute three sentences to the article. When finished, have students read their articles to the class.

Expressions that signal a past tense

- Use **pendant que** to indicate that one action was completed while another was still happening.

> Mes parents **sont arrivés** pendant que nous **répétions** dans le sous-sol.
> *My parents arrived while we were rehearsing in the basement.*

- Certain adverbs often indicate a particular past tense.

Expressions that signal a past tense

passé composé		imparfait	
soudain	*suddenly*	d'habitude	*usually*
tout d'un coup/ tout à coup	*all of a sudden*	parfois	*sometimes*
		souvent	*often*
une (deux, etc.) fois	*once (twice, etc.)*	toujours	*always*
un jour	*one day*	tous les jours	*every day*

The verb *vivre*

- While talking about the past or narrating a story, you might use the verb **vivre** (*to live*) which is irregular.

vivre

je vis	nous vivons
tu vis	vous vivez
il/elle/on vit	ils/elles vivent

Les enfants **vivent** avec leurs grands-parents.
The children live with their grandparents.

Je **vis** à Paris.
I live in Paris.

- The past participle of **vivre** is **vécu**. The **imparfait** is formed like that of other –re verbs, by dropping –**ons** from the **nous** form, and adding the imperfect endings.

Rémi **a vécu** à Nice pendant deux ans.
Rémi lived in Nice for two years.

Nous **vivions** avec mon oncle.
We used to live with my uncle.

∞ **Vérifiez**

Essayez!   Choisissez la forme correcte du verbe au passé.

1. Lise (a étudié /(étudiait)) toujours avec ses amis.
2. Anne ((lisait)/a lu) quand le téléphone à sonné.
3. Les garçons avaient soif, alors ils (buvaient /(ont bu)).
4. D'habitude, ils ((arrivaient)/sont arrivés) toujours en retard.
5. Tout à coup, le professeur (entrait /(est entré)) dans la classe.
6. Autrefois, plusieurs générations ((vivaient)/ont vécu) dans la même maison.

Suggestions: Scaffolding

- Present Expressions that signal a past tense. Give students these other expressions that signal the **imparfait: de temps en temps** (*from time to time*), **en général** (*in general, usually*), **quelquefois** (*sometimes*), **autrefois** (*in the past*).
- Write the following sentences on the board: **1. Je vais au cinéma avec un ami. 2. Nous prenons le bus. 3. Après le film, nous mangeons au restaurant. 4. Ensuite, nous allons danser dans une boîte de nuit. 5. Nous rentrons tard à la maison.** Have students change the sentences above first to the **passé composé** and then to the **imparfait.** Have them add adverbs or expressions they've learned that signal a past tense wherever possible. Assign the **Vérifiez** activity.
- Go over the forms for all tenses of **vivre.** Call on volunteers to use **vivre** in a sentence. Assign the **Vérifiez** activity.

Essayez! Give the following items as additional practice: **7. Autrefois, Nathan (a amené / amenait) sa sœur au cours de danse. (amenait) 8. Je/J' (ai parlé / parlais) deux fois à ma cousine la semaine dernière. (ai parlé) 9. Parfois, nous (faisions / avons fait) une randonnée en montagne. (faisions) 10. Elle (voyait / a vu) mes parents une fois à la mairie. (a vu)**

EXPANSION

Extra Practice Have students recall a memorable day from their childhood. Ask them to describe this day, giving as many details as possible: the weather, who was there, what happened, how they felt, etc. Alternatively, you could do this as a written activity and have students create a journal entry about their memorable day.

EXPANSION

Pairs Distribute illustrations or photos from magazines of everyday activities and vacation activities. Have students arrange the pictures in pairs and create sentences to say that one activity was going on when the other one interrupted it. Call on pairs of students to hold up their pictures and present their sentences to the rest of the class.

1 Expansion Have students redo this activity, this time coming up with their own explanations for why Sabine did or did not do the activities.

2 Suggestion Have students come up with different sentences using the same illustrations.

2 Expansion Have students come up with a short story for each illustration.

3 Suggestion Have students compare their answers with a partner's. For sentences where their answers differ, they should explain why they chose the **passé composé** or the **imparfait** and decide which tense is appropriate.

3 Expansion Have volunteers explain why they chose the **passé composé** or **imparfait** in each sentence. Ask them to point out any words or expressions that triggered one tense or the other.

Mise en pratique

1 Pourquoi? Expliquez pourquoi Sabine a fait ou n'a pas fait ces choses.

> **MODÈLE** ne pas faire de tennis / être fatigué
> *Sabine n'a pas fait de tennis parce qu'elle était fatiguée.*

1. aller au centre commercial / aimer faire les soldes — Sabine est allée au centre commercial parce qu'elle aimait faire les soldes.
2. ne pas travailler / avoir sommeil — Sabine n'a pas travaillé parce qu'elle avait sommeil.
3. ne pas sortir / pleuvoir — Sabine n'est pas sortie parce qu'il pleuvait.
4. mettre un pull / faire froid — Sabine a mis un pull parce qu'il faisait froid.
5. manger une pizza / avoir faim — Sabine a mangé une pizza parce qu'elle avait faim.
6. acheter une nouvelle robe / sortir avec des amis — Sabine a acheté une nouvelle robe parce qu'elle sortait avec des amis.
7. vendre son fauteuil / déménager — Sabine a vendu son fauteuil parce qu'elle déménageait.
8. ne pas bien dormir / être inquiet — Sabine n'a pas bien dormi parce qu'elle était inquiète.

2 Qu'est-ce qu'ils faisaient quand...? Dites ce qui (*what*) est arrivé quand ces personnes faisaient ces activités. Utilisez les mots donnés et d'autres mots. Suggested answers.

▶ **MODÈLE**

Tu nageais quand ton oncle est arrivé.

tu / oncle / arriver

1. Tristan / entendre / chien
Tristan nettoyait sa chambre quand il a entendu le chien.

2. nous / petite fille / tomber
Nous patinions quand la petite fille est tombée.

3. vous / perdre / billet
Vous partiez pour la France quand vous avez perdu votre billet.

4. Paul et Éric / téléphone / sonner
Paul et Éric déjeunaient dans la salle à manger quand le téléphone a sonné.

3 Rien d'extraordinaire Matthieu a passé une journée assez banale (*ordinary*). Réécrivez ce paragraphe au passé.

Il est 6h30. Il pleut. Je prends mon petit-déjeuner, je mets mon imperméable et je quitte la maison. J'attends une demi-heure à l'arrêt de bus et finalement, je cours au restaurant où je travaille. J'arrive en retard. Le patron (*boss*) n'est pas content. Le soir, après mon travail, je rentre à la maison et je vais directement au lit.

Il était 6h30. Il pleuvait. J'ai pris mon petit-déjeuner, j'ai mis mon imperméable et j'ai quitté la maison. J'ai attendu une demi-heure à l'arrêt de bus et finalement, j'ai couru au restaurant où je travaillais. Je suis arrivé en retard. Le patron n'était pas content. Le soir, après mon travail, je suis rentré à la maison et je suis allé directement au lit.

EXPANSION

Extra Practice Divide the class into teams. Make a list of all the adverbs or expressions that signal a past tense. As you read out each expression, a member from each team should come to the board and write a sentence in the past using that expression. The team that completes a correct sentence first gets a point.

EXPANSION

Small Groups Have students work in small groups to discuss their favorite movie or book. Students should use appropriate past tense forms to describe the main characters and give a brief summary of the plot. Encourage students to ask their classmates questions about the film or text.

Communication

4   La curiosité Votre tante Louise veut tout savoir. Elle vous pose beaucoup de questions. Avec un(e) partenaire, répondez aux questions d'une manière logique et échangez les rôles. *Answers will vary.*

MODÈLE retourner au lycée

Élève 1: *Pourquoi est-ce que tu es retourné(e) au lycée?*
Élève 2: *Je suis retourné(e) au lycée parce que j'avais beaucoup de devoirs.*

1. aller à la bibliothèque
2. aller au magasin
3. sortir avec des amis
4. téléphoner à ton cousin
5. rentrer tard
6. aller au café
7. inviter des gens
8. être triste

5   Une entrevue Avec un(e) partenaire, posez-vous ces questions à tour de rôle. *Answers will vary.*

1. Où allais-tu souvent quand tu étais petit(e)?
2. Qu'est-ce que tu aimais lire?
3. Est-ce que tu as vécu dans un autre pays?
4. Comment étais-tu quand tu avais dix ans?
5. Qu'est-ce que ta sœur/ton frère faisait quand tu es rentré(e) hier?
6. Qu'est-ce que tu as fait hier soir?
7. Qu'est-ce que tu as pris au petit-déjeuner ce matin?
8. Qu'est-ce que tu as porté hier?

6   Je me souviens! Racontez à votre partenaire un événement spécial de votre vie qui s'est déjà passé. Votre partenaire vous pose des questions pour avoir plus de détails sur cet événement. Vous pouvez (*can*) parler d'un anniversaire, d'une fête familiale, d'un mariage ou d'un concert. *Answers will vary.*

MODÈLE

Élève 1: *Nous avons fait une grande fête d'anniversaire pour ma grand-mère l'année dernière.*
Élève 2: *Quel âge a-t-elle eu?*

7   Scénario Par groupes de trois, créez une histoire au passé. La première personne commence par une phrase. La deuxième personne doit (*must*) continuer l'histoire. La troisième personne reprend la suite d'une manière logique. Continuez l'histoire une personne à la fois jusqu'à ce que vous ayez (*until you have*) un petit scénario. Soyez créatif! Ensuite, présentez votre scénario à la classe. *Answers will vary.*

trois cent vingt-cinq **325**

4 Expansion Have students redo the activity, reframing the questions in the negative and asking why their partner did not do those activities. Example: **Pourquoi est-ce que tu n'es pas allé(e) à la cantine?**

5 Suggestion Ask students some warm-up questions as a model, before they begin the activity in pairs. Examples: **Comment étaient tes profs l'année dernière? Qu'est-ce que tu as fait le week-end dernier?**

5 Expansion Have students do questions 1, 2, 3, 6, 7, and 8 as a survey by circulating around the classroom and interviewing at least five classmates. Have them tabulate the responses of each classmate in a chart and see how similar or different the responses were.

5 Virtual Chat You can also assign Activity 5 on vhlcentral.com. Students record individual responses that appear in your gradebook.

6 Suggestions
• Act out the **modèle** with a volunteer before assigning this activity to pairs.
• Encourage students to use key adverbs to indicate the appropriate verb tenses in the dialogue. Examples: **soudain, tout à coup, autrefois**, etc.

7 Suggestion This activity can be done either orally or in writing.

Activity Pack For additional activities, go to the **Activity Pack** in the **Resources** section of vhlcentral.com.

Révision

Key Standards

1.1

1 Suggestion Before beginning the activity, review prepositions of location.

2 Expansion You can expand this activity by having students do this in groups of three or four where one student plays the role of the detective and the others are possible witnesses who all claim to have seen the suspects. When questioned, the witnesses give the detective conflicting information about the suspects.

3 Suggestion As the students take turns being the interviewer and interviewee, have one of them answer the questions as if he or she had a wonderful vacation, the house was lovely, the weather was great, and everything went well while the other person had a negative experience where nothing was satisfactory.

4 Expansion Expand this activity by showing the class an **avant** and **après** picture of a person or place in a magazine. Divide the students into two groups. Have one group describe the person or place in the before picture. Have the other group describe the after picture using the present tense.

5 Suggestion Remind students that the floors are counted differently in France than in the U.S. The first floor in the U.S. would be the **rez-de-chaussée** in France while the second floor would be the **premier étage**. Ask students if they know other countries which refer to floors in the same way as the French do.

1 **Mes affaires** Vous cherchez vos affaires (*belongings*). À tour de rôle, demandez de l'aide à votre partenaire. Où étaient-elles? Utilisez l'illustration pour les trouver.
Answers will vary.

MODÈLE

Élève 1: *Je cherche mes baskets. Où sont-elles?*
Élève 2: *Tu n'as pas cherché sur l'étagère? Elles étaient sur l'étagère.*

baskets	ordinateur
casquette	parapluie
journal	pull
livre	sac à dos

2 **Un bon témoin** Il y a eu un cambriolage (*burglary*) chez votre voisin M. Cachetout. Le détective vous interroge parce que vous avez vu deux personnes suspectes sortir de la maison du voisin. Avec un(e) partenaire, créez cette conversation et jouez cette scène devant la classe. Utilisez ces éléments dans votre scène. Answers will vary.

- une description physique des suspects
- leurs attitudes
- leurs vêtements
- ce que (*what*) vous faisiez quand vous avez vu les suspects

MODÈLE

Élève 1: *À quelle heure est-ce que vous avez vu les deux personnes sortir?*
Élève 2: *À dix heures. Elles sont sorties du garage.*

3 **Quel séjour!** Vous venez de passer une semaine de vacances dans une maison à la campagne et votre partenaire veut tout savoir (*wants to know everything*). Répondez à ses questions sur la maison, le temps, les activités dans la région et votre opinion en général. Utilisez l'imparfait et le passé composé. Ensuite, changez de rôle. Answers will vary.

MODÈLE

Élève 1: *Combien de pièces y avait-il dans cette maison?*
Élève 2: *Il y avait six pièces dans la maison.*

4 **Avant et après** Voici la chambre d'Annette avant et après une visite de sa mère. Comment était sa chambre à l'origine? Avec un(e) partenaire, décrivez la pièce et cherchez les différences entre les deux illustrations. Answers will vary.

MODÈLE

Avant, la lampe était à côté de l'ordinateur. Maintenant, elle est à côté du canapé.

5 **La maison de mon enfance** Décrivez l'appartement ou la maison de votre enfance à un(e) partenaire. Où se trouvait-il/elle? Comment les pièces étaient-elles orientées? Y avait-il une piscine, un sous-sol? Qui vivait avec vous dans cet appartement ou cette maison? Racontez (*Tell*) des anecdotes.
Answers will vary.

MODÈLE

Ma maison se trouvait au bord de la mer.
C'était une maison à deux étages (floors).
Au rez-de-chaussée, il y avait...

EXPANSION

Floor Plan Have students work in pairs to draw the floor plan of their childhood home on a sheet of paper or cardboard. Have them cut out the floor plan into pieces by individual rooms. Then have them give these pieces to their partner who will reassemble the floor plan based on their memories of the house.

EXPANSION

Skits Have small groups organize a skit about a birthday or other party that took place recently. Guide them to first make general comments about the party, such as **C'était vraiment amusant!** Then describe a few specific things that were going on, what people were talking about, what they were wearing, and what happened.

AP® **Theme:** Beauty and Aesthetics
Context: Visual Arts

Préparation Répondez aux questions. Answers will vary.

1. Aimez-vous bricoler? Créez-vous des objets ou des meubles? Ou préférez-vous acheter les meubles et la décoration? Expliquez.

2. De quelle manière votre chambre reflète-t-elle votre personnalité?

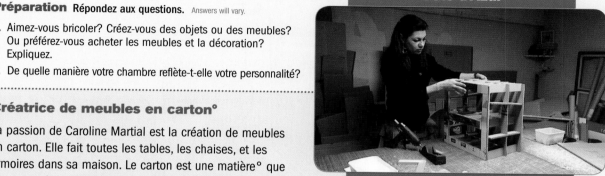

Reportage de France 3
Côte d'Azur

Ça va être un petit meuble...
une petite table de chevet.°

Créatrice de meubles en carton°

La passion de Caroline Martial est la création de meubles en carton. Elle fait toutes les tables, les chaises, et les armoires dans sa maison. Le carton est une matière° que d'autres voient comme laide et inutile, mais elle y voit plein de possibilités. Il suffit d'°un peu d'imagination pour le transformer en objet utile et beau. De quelques bouts° de carton ondulé°, elle peut construire un fauteuil et utiliser des plumes°, des boutons° ou des paillettes° pour le décorer. Des meubles en carton pour toute la maison? Pourquoi pas! Grâce à° Caroline Martial, les possibilités sont illimitées.

table de chevet *bedside table* **carton** *cardboard* **matière** *material* **Il suffit de** *All that's necessary is* **bouts** *bits* **ondulé** *corrugated* **plumes** *feathers* **boutons** *buttons* **paillettes** *glitter* **Grâce à** *Thanks to*

Vocabulaire utile

l'emballage (*m.*)	*packaging*
une niche	*small space*
ultraléger	*very lightweight*
laisser libre cours	*to give free reign*
une réalisation	*creation*

Compréhension Indiquez si les phrases sont vraies ou fausses.

1. Au début de la vidéo, Caroline Martial crée une commode.
   Faux.
2. Les meubles peuvent (*can*) résister à un poids (*weight*) important.
   Vrai.
3. Les meubles sont faciles à décorer.
   Vrai.
4. On voit une commode, une table de chevet et une mini-bibliothèque en carton dans les chambres des enfants de Caroline Martial.
   Vrai.
5. Le carton impose certaines limites à ce qu'on peut (*what one can*) créer.
   Faux.

Application

Choisissez un(e) artiste qui vous intéresse et préparez un reportage sur son œuvre (*work*). Montrez une de ses créations et expliquez leur impact sur la société.

Conversation En petits groupes, discutez des questions.
Answers will vary.

1. Aimez-vous les créations de Caroline Martial? Pourquoi ou pourquoi pas?

2. Quels sont des exemples de l'art fonctionnel dans votre vie?

3. Quels artistes admirez-vous? Pourquoi les admirez-vous? Quelle influence ont-ils sur la société?

trois cent vingt-sept **327**

Section Goals
In this section, students will:
• read about an entrepreneur who makes cardboard furniture
• watch a news report about her
• answer questions about the report and creativity in general

Key Standards
1.1, 1.2, 1.3, 2.1, 4.2

Préparation Have students discuss the questions in small groups. You may also ask students who are creative to bring in some examples of their work to share with the class.

PRE-AP®

Interpretive Communication
• Have students look at the image and read the caption to predict what the video is about.
• Explain that students will not understand every word they hear. Tell them to listen for cognates and words they already know. Point out that the images they see will also help them understand the words they hear.

Créatrice de meubles en carton
To check comprehension, ask:
1. Que fait Caroline Martial?
(des meubles en carton)
2. Qu'est-ce qu'il suffit d'avoir pour transformer du carton en meuble? (de l'imagination)
3. Qu'est-ce qu'elle utilise pour décorer ses créations?
(des plumes, des boutons ou des paillettes)

Compréhension After students complete the activity, show the video again so they can check their answers. Guide them in revising false statements so they are true.

Conversation Once they finish their discussions, have groups share their thoughts with the class. Encourage students to express their opinions regarding the purpose of art.

EXPANSION

Craft Vocabulary Share the following craft terms used in the video with students: **le papier peint** (*wallpaper*), **les papiers artisanaux** (*hand-made papers*), **le poudre d'or** (*gold dust*), **la strasse** (*silk scraps*). Ask them what materials they use when they do crafts, and have them look up the French words for them to share with the class.

EXPANSION

Cultures Have students work in pairs or small groups to research crafts popular in other Francophone cultures. Assign each group a different Francophone area and have them research a craft that's popular there. Then discuss with the class how these crafts vary from the one seen in the video and those popular in their own region. Also discuss the purpose crafts serve in a community. What do they say about the community's culture and people?

🔊 **vhl**central

Les tâches ménagères

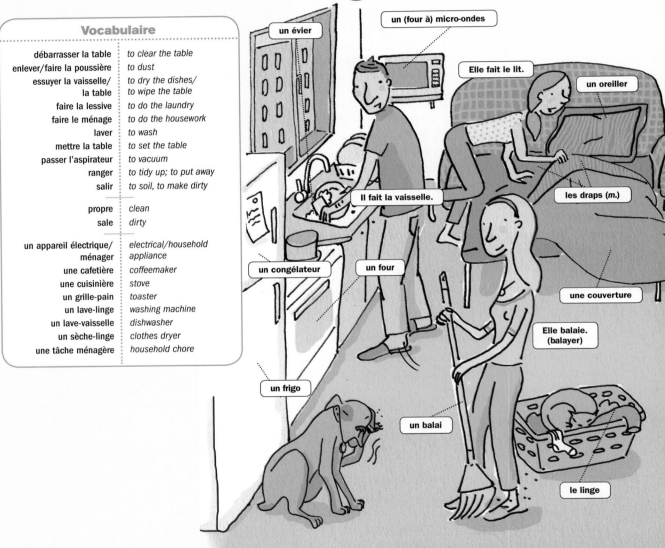

Vocabulaire

débarrasser la table	*to clear the table*
enlever/faire la poussière	*to dust*
essuyer la vaisselle/ la table	*to dry the dishes/ to wipe the table*
faire la lessive	*to do the laundry*
faire le ménage	*to do the housework*
laver	*to wash*
mettre la table	*to set the table*
passer l'aspirateur	*to vacuum*
ranger	*to tidy up; to put away*
salir	*to soil, to make dirty*
propre	*clean*
sale	*dirty*
un appareil électrique/ ménager	*electrical/household appliance*
une cafetière	*coffeemaker*
une cuisinière	*stove*
un grille-pain	*toaster*
un lave-linge	*washing machine*
un lave-vaisselle	*dishwasher*
un sèche-linge	*clothes dryer*
une tâche ménagère	*household chore*

Labels in illustration: un (four à) micro-ondes · un évier · Elle fait le lit. · un oreiller · Il fait la vaisselle. · les draps (m.) · un congélateur · un four · une couverture · Elle balaie. (balayer) · un frigo · un balai · le linge

Mise en pratique

1　On fait le ménage　Complétez les phrases avec le bon mot.

1. On balaie avec _____un balai_____.
2. On repasse le linge avec _____un fer à repasser_____.
3. On fait la lessive avec _____un lave-linge_____.
4. On lave la vaisselle avec _____un lave-vaisselle_____.
5. On prépare le café avec _____une cafetière_____.
6. On sèche les vêtements avec _____un sèche-linge_____.
7. On met la glace dans _____un congélateur_____.
8. Pour faire le lit, on doit arranger _____les draps_____, _____la couverture_____ et _____l'oreiller/les oreillers_____.

2　Écoutez　Écoutez la conversation téléphonique (*phone call*) entre Laurent et un conseiller à la radio (*radio psychologist*). Ensuite, indiquez les tâches ménagères que faisaient Laurent et Paul l'année dernière.

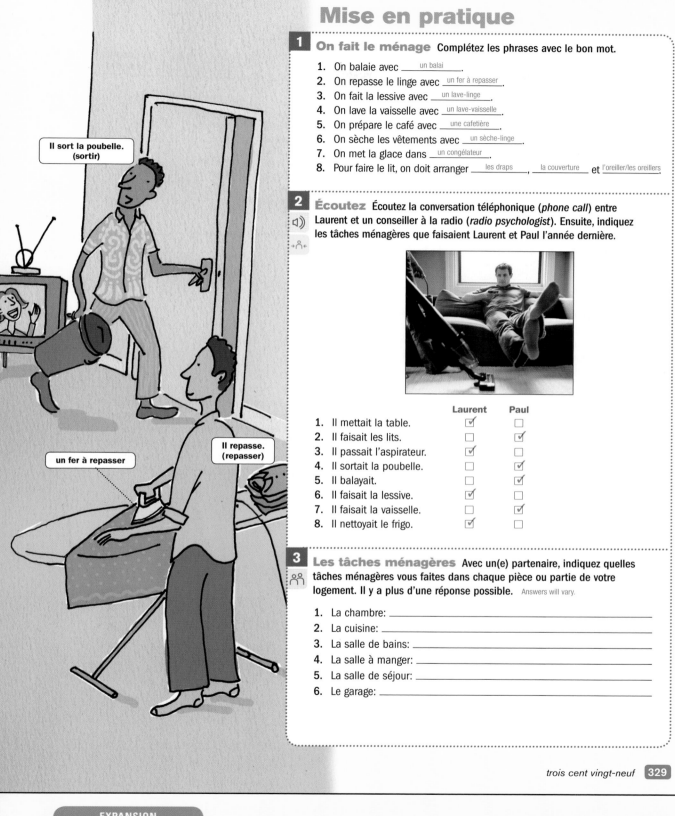

	Laurent	Paul
1. Il mettait la table.	☑	☐
2. Il faisait les lits.	☐	☑
3. Il passait l'aspirateur.	☑	☐
4. Il sortait la poubelle.	☐	☑
5. Il balayait.	☐	☑
6. Il faisait la lessive.	☑	☐
7. Il faisait la vaisselle.	☐	☑
8. Il nettoyait le frigo.	☑	☐

Labels in illustration: Il sort la poubelle. (sortir) · un fer à repasser · Il repasse. (repasser)

3　Les tâches ménagères　Avec un(e) partenaire, indiquez quelles tâches ménagères vous faites dans chaque pièce ou partie de votre logement. Il y a plus d'une réponse possible.　Answers will vary.

1. La chambre: _____
2. La cuisine: _____
3. La salle de bains: _____
4. La salle à manger: _____
5. La salle de séjour: _____
6. Le garage: _____

trois cent vingt-neuf **329**

1 Expansion Reverse this activity and ask students what each appliance is used for. Example: **Que fait-on avec une cuisinière? (On fait la cuisine.)**

2 Script J'ai un problème avec Paul, mon frère, parce qu'il ne m'aide pas à faire le ménage. L'année dernière, il faisait la vaisselle, il sortait la poubelle et il balayait. Parfois, il faisait même mon lit. Paul ne mettait jamais la table parce qu'il détestait ça. C'est moi qui la mettais. Je faisais aussi la lessive, je passais l'aspirateur et je nettoyais le frigo. Maintenant, Paul ne fait jamais son lit et il ne m'aide pas. C'est moi qui fais tout. Qu'est-ce que vous me suggérez de faire? *Teacher Resources DVD*

2 Suggestion After listening to the recording, have students identify Paul and Laurent in the photo and describe what they are doing.

2 Expansion Have students describe how they share household chores with their siblings or others at home.

3 Suggestion Have students get together with another pair and compare their answers.

🌐 **TELL Connection**

Learning Tools 6 *Why:* Integrated technology provides tools for students to meet performance objectives. *What:* Use tools on vhlcentral.com to encourage students to speak and write about their daily lives and environments. Tools include: audio and visual vocabulary practice, My Vocabulary, scaffolded listening activities, Partner and Virtual Chats for synchronous and asynchronous interpersonal speaking, Instructor Note function for guiding performance expectations, and Instructor-created activities for open-ended communication.

EXPANSION

Analogies Have students complete these analogies.
1. passer l'aspirateur : tapis / lave-vaisselle : _____ (verre/tasse)
2. chaud : froid / cuisinière : _____ (frigo/congélateur)
3. ordinateur : bureau / armoire : _____ (chambre)
4. tasse : cuisine / voiture : _____ (garage)

5. café : cafetière / pain : _____ (grille-pain)
6. mauvais : bon / sale : _____ (propre)
7. chaud : four à micro-ondes / froid : _____ (frigo/congélateur)
8. arriver : partir / nettoyer : _____ (salir)
9. table : verre / lit : _____ (draps/couverture/oreiller(s))

Communication

4 Qui fait quoi? Votre professeur va vous donner une feuille d'activités. Dites si vous faites les tâches indiquées en écrivant (*by writing*) **Oui** ou **Non** dans la première colonne. Ensuite, posez des questions à vos camarades de classe, et écrivez leur nom dans la deuxième colonne quand ils répondent **Oui**. Présentez vos réponses à la classe. Answers will vary.

MODÈLE

mettre la table pour prendre le petit-déjeuner
Élève 1: Est-ce que tu mets la table pour prendre le petit-déjeuner?
Élève 2: Oui, je mets la table chaque matin./ Non, je ne prends pas de petit-déjeuner, donc je ne mets pas la table.

Activités	Moi	Mes camarades de classe
1. mettre la table pour prendre le petit-déjeuner		
2. passer l'aspirateur tous les jours		
3. salir ses vêtements quand on mange		
4. nettoyer les toilettes		
5. balayer la cuisine		
6. débarrasser la table après le dîner		
7. souvent enlever la poussière sur son ordinateur		
8. laver les vitres (*windows*)		

5 Conversez Interviewez un(e) camarade de classe. Answers will vary.

1. Qui fait la vaisselle chez toi?
2. Qui fait la lessive chez toi?
3. Fais-tu ton lit tous les jours?
4. Quelles tâches ménagères as-tu faites le week-end dernier?
5. Repasses-tu tous tes vêtements?
6. Quelles tâches ménagères détestes-tu faire?
7. Quels appareils électriques as-tu chez toi?
8. Ranges-tu souvent ta chambre?

6 Au pair Vous partez dans un pays francophone pour vivre dans une famille pendant (*for*) un an. Travaillez avec deux camarades de classe et préparez un dialogue dans lequel (*in which*) vous: Answers will vary.

- parlez des tâches ménagères que vous détestez/aimez faire.
- posez des questions sur vos nouvelles responsabilités.
- parlez de vos passions et de vos habitudes.
- décidez si cette famille vous convient.

7 Écrivez L'appartement de Martine est un désastre: la cuisine est sale et le reste de l'appartement est encore pire (*worse*). Préparez un paragraphe où vous décrivez les problèmes que vous voyez (*see*) et que vous imaginez. Ensuite, écrivez la liste des tâches que Martine va faire pour tout nettoyer. Answers will vary.

Les sons et les lettres 🔊 vhlcentral
Semi-vowels

French has three semi-vowels. Semi-vowels are sounds that are produced in much the same way as vowels, but also have many properties in common with consonants. Semi-vowels are also sometimes referred to as *glides* because they glide from or into the vowel they accompany.

Lucien   **ch**ien   s**oif**   **nuit**

The semi-vowel that occurs in the word **bien** is very much like the *y* in the English word *yes*. It is usually spelled with an **i** or a **y** (pronounced *ee*), then glides into the following sound. This semi-vowel sound is also produced when **ll** follows an **i**.

nation   **bala**yer   **bien**   **brill**ant

The semi-vowel that occurs in the word **soif** is like the *w* in the English words *was* and *we*. It usually begins with **o** or **ou**, then glides into the following vowel.

trois   **fro**id   **oui**   **oui**stiti

The third semi-vowel sound occurs in the word **nuit**. It is spelled with the vowel **u**, as in the French word **tu**, then glides into the following sound.

lui   **suis**   **cru**el   **intellect**uel

Prononcez Répétez les mots suivants à voix haute.

1. oui
2. taille
3. suisse
4. fille
5. mois
6. cruel
7. minuit
8. jouer
9. cuisine
10. juillet
11. échouer
12. croissant

Articulez Répétez les phrases suivantes à voix haute.

1. Voici trois poissons noirs.
2. Louis et sa famille sont suisses.
3. Parfois, Grégoire fait de la cuisine chinoise.
4. Aujourd'hui, Matthieu et Damien vont travailler.
5. Françoise a besoin de faire ses devoirs d'histoire.
6. La fille de Monsieur Poirot va conduire pour la première fois.

Dictons Répétez les dictons à voix haute.

La nuit, tous les chats sont gris.[1]

Vouloir, c'est pouvoir.[2]

[1] All cats are gray in the dark.
[2] Where there's a will, there's a way.

Section Goals
In this section, students will learn about semi-vowels.

Key Standards
4.1

Suggestions
• Model the pronunciation of the example words and have students repeat them after you.
• Ask students to provide more examples of words from this or previous lessons with these sounds. Examples: **essuyer, évier, moi, minuit, juillet.**
• Dictate five familiar words containing semi-vowels, repeating each one at least two times. Then write them on the board or on a transparency and have students check their spelling.
• Remind students that many vowels combine to make a single sound with no glide. Examples: **ai** and **ou**
• Explain that **un ouistiti** is a marmoset.

EXPANSION

Mini-dictée Use these sentences with semi-vowels for additional practice or dictation. **1. Nous balayons bien la cuisine. 2. J'ai soif, mais tu as froid. 3. Une fois, ma fille a oublié son parapluie. 4. Parfois, mon chien aime jouer entre minuit et trois heures du matin.**

EXPANSION

Tongue-twisters Teach students these French tongue-twisters that contain semi-vowels. **1. Trois petites truites non cuites, trois petites truites crues. 2. Une bête noire se baigne dans une baignoire noire.**

La vie sans Pascal vhlcentral

PERSONNAGES

Amina

Michèle

Sandrine

Stéphane

Valérie

Au P'tit Bistrot...

MICHÈLE Tout va bien, Amina?
AMINA Oui, ça va, merci. *(Au téléphone)* Allô?... Qu'est-ce qu'il y a, Sandrine?... Non, je ne le savais pas, mais franchement, ça ne me surprend pas... Écoute, j'arrive chez toi dans quinze minutes, d'accord? ... À tout à l'heure!

MICHÈLE Je débarrasse la table?
AMINA Oui, merci, et apporte-moi l'addition, s'il te plaît.
MICHÈLE Tout de suite.

VALÉRIE Tu as fait ton lit, ce matin?
STÉPHANE Oui, maman.
VALÉRIE Est-ce que tu as rangé ta chambre?
STÉPHANE Euh... oui, ce matin, pendant que tu faisais la lessive.

Chez Sandrine...

SANDRINE Salut, Amina! Merci d'être venue.
AMINA Mmmm. Qu'est-ce qui sent si bon?
SANDRINE Il y a des biscuits au chocolat dans le four.
AMINA Oh, est-ce que tu les préparais quand tu m'as téléphoné?

SANDRINE Tu as soif?
AMINA Un peu, oui.
SANDRINE Sers-toi, j'ai des jus de fruits au frigo.

Sandrine casse (breaks) une assiette.

SANDRINE Et zut!
AMINA Ça va, Sandrine?
SANDRINE Oui, oui... passe-moi le balai, s'il te plaît.
AMINA N'oublie pas de balayer sous la cuisinière.
SANDRINE Je sais! Excuse-moi, Amina. Comme je t'ai dit au téléphone, Pascal et moi, c'est fini.

A C T I V I T É S

1 **Questions** Répondez aux questions par des phrases complètes. Answers may vary slightly.

1. Avec qui Amina parle-t-elle au téléphone?
   Elle parle avec Sandrine.
2. Comment va Sandrine aujourd'hui? Pourquoi?
   Elle est de mauvaise humeur parce que c'est fini avec Pascal.
3. Est-ce que Stéphane a fait toutes ses tâches ménagères?
   Non, il n'a pas fait toutes ses tâches ménagères.
4. Qu'est-ce que Sandrine préparait quand elle a téléphoné à Amina? Elle préparait des biscuits au chocolat.

5. Amina a faim et a soif. À votre avis (*opinion*), que va-t-elle prendre? Elle va prendre un jus de fruits et elle va manger des biscuits.
6. Pourquoi Amina n'est-elle pas fâchée (*angry*) contre Sandrine? Elle comprend pourquoi Sandrine est un peu triste/de mauvaise humeur.
7. Pourquoi Amina pense-t-elle que Sandrine aimerait (*would like*) un cyberhomme américain? Amina pense que Sandrine aime David.
8. Sandrine pense qu'Amina devrait (*should*) rencontrer Cyberhomme, mais Amina pense que ce n'est pas une bonne idée. À votre avis, qui a raison? Answers will vary.

Amina console Sandrine.

VALÉRIE Hmm... et la vaisselle? Tu as fait la vaisselle?
STÉPHANE Non, pas encore, mais...
MICHÈLE Il me faut l'addition pour Amina.
VALÉRIE Stéphane, tu dois faire la vaisselle avant de sortir.
STÉPHANE Bon, ça va, j'y vais!

VALÉRIE Ah, Michèle, il faut sortir les poubelles pour ce soir!
MICHÈLE Oui, comptez sur moi, Madame Forestier.
VALÉRIE Très bien! Moi, je rentre, il est l'heure de préparer le dîner.

SANDRINE Il était tellement pénible. Bref, je suis de mauvaise humeur aujourd'hui.
AMINA Ne t'en fais pas, je comprends.
SANDRINE Toi, tu as de la chance.
AMINA Pourquoi tu dis ça?
SANDRINE Tu as ton Cyberhomme. Tu vas le rencontrer un de ces jours?
AMINA Oh... Je ne sais pas si c'est une bonne idée.

SANDRINE Pourquoi pas?
AMINA Sandrine, il faut être prudent dans la vie, je ne le connais pas vraiment, tu sais.
SANDRINE Comme d'habitude, tu as raison. Mais finalement, un cyberhomme, c'est peut-être mieux qu'un petit ami. Ou alors, un petit ami artistique, charmant et beau garçon.
AMINA Et américain?

Expressions utiles

Talking about what you know

- **Je ne le savais pas, mais franchement, ça ne me surprend pas.**
  I didn't know that, but frankly, I'm not surprised.
- **Je sais!**
  I know!
- **Je ne sais pas si c'est une bonne idée.**
  I don't know if that's a good idea.
- **Je ne le connais pas vraiment, tu sais.**
  I don't really know him, you know.

Additional vocabulary

- **Comptez sur moi.**
  Count on me.
- **Ne t'en fais pas.**
  Don't worry about it.
- **J'y vais!**
  I'm going there!/I'm on my way!
- **pas encore**
  not yet
- **tu dois**
  you must
- **être de bonne/mauvaise humeur**
  to be in a good/bad mood

2 **Le ménage** Indiquez qui a fait ou va faire ces tâches ménagères: Amina (A), Michèle (M), Sandrine (S), Stéphane (St), Valérie (V) ou personne (no one) (P).

1. sortir la poubelle   M
2. balayer   S & A
3. passer l'aspirateur   P
4. faire la vaisselle   St
5. faire le lit   St
6. débarrasser la table   M
7. faire la lessive   V
8. ranger sa chambre   St

3 **Écrivez** Vous avez gagné un pari (*bet*) avec votre grande sœur et elle doit faire (*must do*) en conséquence toutes les tâches ménagères que vous lui indiquez pendant un mois. Écrivez une liste de dix tâches minimum. Pour chaque tâche, précisez la pièce du logement et combien de fois par semaine elle doit l'exécuter.

A C T I V I T É S

Expressions utiles
- Model the pronunciation of the **Expressions utiles** and have students repeat them.
- As you work through the list, point out the forms of **savoir** and **connaître**. See if students can discern the difference in meaning between the two verbs from the example sentences. Respond briefly to their questions, but tell them that these verbs will be formally presented in **Structures 8B.2**.

1 **Suggestion** Have volunteers write their answers on the board. Go over them as a class.

2 **Expansion** Ask students who works the hardest of all these people. Have them support their opinion with details from this episode and previous ones.

3 **Suggestion** To review past tenses, have students write a one-paragraph summary at the end of the month telling what their "sister" actually did or did not do, and why.

Presentational Writing Practice Ask students to reflect on what they think might happen in the next episode of **Roman-photo**, and have them create a story-board like the one shown here that represents their predictions.

TEACHING OPTIONS

Debate Divide the class into two groups based on their answers to question 8 on page 332 (whether or not Amina should meet Cyberhomme) and have a debate about who is right. Tell groups to brainstorm a list of arguments to support their point of view and anticipate rebuttals for what the other team might say.

EXPANSION

Predicting Future Episodes Have students work in pairs. Tell them to reread the last lines of the **Roman-photo** and write a short paragraph predicting what will happen in future episodes. Do they think Amina will meet Cyberhomme in person? What do they think will happen in Sandrine's love life? Have volunteers read their paragraphs aloud to the class.

333

AP® **Theme:** Contemporary Life
Context: Housing and Shelter

CULTURE À LA LOUPE

L'intérieur des logements français

L'intérieur des maisons et des appartements français est assez° différent de celui chez les Américains. Quand on entre dans un immeuble ancien en France, on est dans un hall° où il y a des boîtes aux lettres°. Ensuite, il y a souvent une deuxième porte. Celle-ci conduit à° l'escalier. Il n'y a pas souvent d'ascenseur, mais s'il y en a un°, en général, il est très petit et il est au milieu de° l'escalier. Le hall de l'immeuble peut aussi avoir une porte qui donne sur une cour° ou un jardin, souvent derrière le bâtiment°.

À l'intérieur des logements, les pièces sont en général plus petites que° les pièces américaines, surtout les cuisines et les salles de bains. Dans la cuisine, on trouve tous les appareils ménagers nécessaires (cuisinière, four, four à micro-ondes, frigo), mais ils sont plus petits qu'aux États-Unis. Les lave-vaisselle sont assez rares dans les appartements et plus communs dans les maisons. On a souvent une seule° salle de bains et les toilettes sont en général dans une autre petite pièce séparée°. Les lave-linge sont aussi assez petits et on les trouve, en général, dans la cuisine ou dans la salle de bains. Dans les chambres, en France, il n'y a pas de grands placards et les vêtements sont rangés la plupart° du temps dans une armoire ou une commode. Les fenêtres s'ouvrent° sur l'intérieur, un peu comme des portes, et il est très rare d'avoir des moustiquaires°. Par contre°, il y a presque toujours des volets°.

assez *rather* **hall** *entryway* **boîtes aux lettres** *mailboxes* **conduit à** *leads to* **s'il y en a un** *if there is one* **au milieu de** *in the middle of* **cour** *courtyard* **bâtiment** *building* **plus petites que** *smaller than* **une seule** *only one* **séparée** *separate* **la plupart** *most* **s'ouvrent** *open* **moustiquaires** *screens* **Par contre** *On the other hand* **volets** *shutters*

Combien de logements ont ces appareils ménagers?	
Réfrigérateur	99,8%
Cuisinière / Four	96,4%
Lave-linge	95,6%
Congélateur	91,2%
Four à micro-ondes	88,3%
Lave-vaisselle	57,1%
Sèche-linge	28,7%

SOURCE: INSEE

Coup de main

Demonstrative pronouns help to avoid repetition.

	S.	P.
M.	**celui**	**ceux**
F.	**celle**	**celles**

Ce lit est grand, mais le lit de Monique est petit.

Ce lit est grand, mais **celui** de Monique est petit.

A C T I V I T É S

1 Complétez Complétez chaque phrase logiquement.
Answers will vary. Possible answers provided.
1. Dans le hall d'un immeuble français, on trouve... des boîtes aux lettres et des portes.
2. Au milieu de l'escalier, dans les vieux immeubles français, ... il y a parfois un ascenseur.
3. Derrière les vieux immeubles, on trouve souvent... une cour ou un jardin.
4. Les cuisines et les salles de bains françaises sont... assez petites.
5. Dans les appartements français, il est assez rare d'avoir... un lave-vaisselle.
6. Les logements français ont souvent une seule... salle de bains.
7. En France, les toilettes sont souvent... dans une pièce séparée.
8. Les Français rangent souvent leurs vêtements dans une armoire parce qu'ils... n'ont pas souvent de placards.
9. On trouve souvent le lave-linge... dans la cuisine ou dans la salle de bains.
10. En général, les fenêtres dans les logements français... ont des volets.

EXPANSION

Cultural Comparison Take a quick class survey to find out how many students have the appliances listed in the chart in their homes. Tally the results on the board and have students calculate the percentages. Example: **Combien de personnes ont un réfrigérateur à la maison?**

Then have students compare the results of this survey with those in the chart. Examples: **Plus d'Américains ont un sèche-linge dans leur maison./Moins de Français ont un sèche-linge dans leur maison.**

LE FRANÇAIS QUOTIDIEN

Quelles conditions!

boxon (*m.*)	shambles
piaule (*f.*)	pad, room
souk (*m.*)	mess
impeccable	spic-and-span
nickel	spotless
ringard	cheesy, old-fashioned
crécher	to live
semer la pagaille	to make a mess

AP® Theme: Beauty and Aesthetics **Context:** Architecture

LE MONDE FRANCOPHONE

Architecture moderne et ancienne

Architecte suisse

Le Corbusier Originaire du canton de Neuchâtel, il est l'un des principaux représentants du mouvement moderne au début° du 20ᵉ siècle. Il est connu° pour être l'inventeur de l'unité d'habitation°, concept sur les logements collectifs qui rassemblent dans un même lieu garderie° d'enfants, piscine, écoles, commerces et lieux de rencontre. Il est naturalisé français en 1930.

Architecture du Maroc

Les riads, mot° qui à l'origine signifie «jardins» en arabe, sont de superbes habitations anciennes° construites pour préserver la fraîcheur°. On les trouve au cœur° des ruelles° de la médina (quartier historique).
Les kasbahs, bâtisses° de terre° dans le Sud marocain, sont des exemples d'un art typiquement berbère et rural.

début *beginning* **connu** *known* **unité d'habitation** *housing unit*
garderie *daycare center* **mot** *word* **anciennes** *old* **fraîcheur** *coolness*
cœur *heart* **ruelles** *alleyways* **bâtisses** *dwellings* **terre** *earth*

PORTRAIT

AP® Theme: Beauty and Aesthetics
Context: Architecture

Le Vieux Carré

Le Vieux Carré, aussi appelé le Quartier Français, est le centre historique de La Nouvelle-Orléans. Il a conservé le souvenir° des époques° coloniales du 18ᵉ siècle°. La culture française est toujours présente avec des noms de rues° français comme *Toulouse* ou *Chartres*, qui sont de grandes villes françaises. Cependant° le style architectural n'est pas français; il est espagnol. Les maisons avec les beaux balcons sont l'héritage de l'occupation espagnole de la deuxième moitié° du 18ᵉ siècle. Mardi gras, en février, est la fête la plus populaire de La Nouvelle-Orléans, qui est aussi très connue° pour son festival de jazz, en avril.

souvenir *memory* **époques** *times* **siècle** *century* **noms de rues** *street names*
Cependant *However* **moitié** *half* **connue** *known*

Sur Internet

Qu'est-ce qu'on peut voir (*see*) au musée des Arts décoratifs de Paris?

Go to **vhlcentral.com** to find more information related to this **Culture** section.

2 Complétez Complétez les phrases.

1. Le Vieux Carré est aussi appelé le Quartier Français .
2. Toulouse et Chartres sont deux noms de rues français à La Nouvelle-Orléans.
3. Le style architectural du Vieux Carré n'est pas français mais espagnol .
4. La Nouvelle-Orléans est connue pour son festival de jazz .
5. Le Corbusier est l'inventeur de l'unité d'habitation .
6. On trouve les riads parmi (*among*) les ruelles de la médina .

3 C'est le souk!
Votre oncle favori vient vous rendre visite et votre petit frère a semé la pagaille dans votre chambre. C'est le souk! Avec un(e) partenaire, inventez une conversation où vous lui donnez des ordres pour nettoyer avant l'arrivée de votre oncle. Jouez la scène devant la classe.

A C T I V I T É S

Le français quotidien
- Model the pronunciation of each term and have students repeat it.
- Have volunteers create sentences using these words.

Portrait Ask students: **Que désirez-vous faire ou visiter dans le Vieux Carré de La Nouvelle-Orléans?**

Le monde francophone
- Bring in photos from magazines, books, or the Internet of buildings designed by Le Corbusier, as well as images showing **riads** and **kasbahs** in Morocco. Ask students to compare and contrast the buildings and dwellings in the photos and to say which they prefer, and why.
- Ask a few content questions based on the text. Examples: **1. Quel mouvement architectural est-ce que Le Corbusier représente? (moderne) 2. Qu'est-ce qu'on trouve dans une unité d'habitation? (des garderies d'enfants, des piscines, des écoles, des commerces, des lieux de rencontre) 3. Quel style d'art représentent les kasbahs marocaines? (un art berbère et rural)**

2 Expansion For additional practice, give students these items. 7. _____ est la fête la plus populaire de La Nouvelle-Orléans. (Mardi gras) 8. On trouve des kasbahs dans le _____. (Sud marocain) 9. Au Maroc, _____ est appelé un riad. (un jardin)

3 Suggestion Encourage students to use terms in **Le français quotidien** in their role-plays.

21ˢᵗ Century Skills

Information and Media Literacy: Sur Internet
Students access and critically evaluate information from the Internet.

EXPANSION

Le Vieux Carré Share the following information about two important historical sites in New Orleans with students. **Le Cabildo** was completed in 1799. The ceremonies finalizing the Louisiana Purchase were held there in 1803. Since 1903, it has been the Louisiana State Museum. The museum contains a number of objects from Napoleonic history.

The present-day **cathédrale Saint-Louis** was completed in 1851. Made of bricks, the cathedral is dedicated to King Louis IX of France (1214–1270), who was canonized in 1297. His life is depicted in ten of the stained glass windows.

8B.1　The *passé composé* vs. the *imparfait* (Summary)

vhlcentral

Point de départ　You have learned the uses of the **passé composé** versus the **imparfait** to talk about things and events in the past. These tenses are distinct and are not used in the same way. Remember always to keep the context and the message you wish to convey in mind while deciding which tense to use.

Uses of the *passé composé*

To talk about events that happened at a specific moment or for a precise duration in the past	Je **suis allé** au concert vendredi. *I went to the concert on Friday.*
To express an action or a sequence of actions that started and ended in the past	Tu **as fait** le lit, tu **as sorti** la poubelle et tu **as mis** la table. *You made the bed, took out the trash, and set the table.*
To indicate a change in the mental, emotional or physical state of a person	Tout à coup, elle **a eu** soif. *Suddenly, she got thirsty.*
To narrate the facts in a story	Nous **avons passé** une journée fantastique à la plage. *We spent a fantastic day at the beach.*
To describe actions that move the plot forward in a narration	Soudain, Thomas **a trouvé** la réponse à leur question. *Suddenly, Thomas found the answer to their question.*

Uses of the *imparfait*

To talk about actions that lasted for an unspecified duration of time	Elle **dormait** tranquillement. *She was sleeping peacefully.*
To relate habitual or repeated past actions and events	Nous **faisions** une promenade au parc tous les dimanches matins. *We used to walk in the park every Sunday morning.*
To describe mental, emotional or physical states or conditions	Elle **avait** toujours soif. *She was always thirsty.*
To describe the background scene and setting of a story	Il **faisait** beau et le ciel **était** bleu. *The weather was nice and the sky was blue.*
To describe people and things	C'**était** une photo d'une jolie fille. *It was a photograph of a pretty girl.*

Section Goals

In this section, students will review:
• the uses and meanings of the **passé composé** and the **imparfait**
• common expressions indicating past tenses

Key Standards

4.1, 5.1

Note　If you feel that your students have sufficiently mastered the uses of the **passé composé** and the **imparfait**, you may wish to skip **Structures 8B.1** and move on to **Structures 8B.2**; or, you may wish to assign this section as remediation.

Suggestions: Scaffolding
• To practice contrasting the **passé composé** vs. the **imparfait,** first do a review of each tense and its uses. Then write the following sentences on the board: **1. Je vais au cinéma avec un ami. 2. Nous prenons le bus. 3. Après le film, nous mangeons au restaurant. 4. Ensuite, nous faisons une promenade. 5. Nous rentrons tard à la maison.** Have students change the sentences above first to the **passé composé** and then to the **imparfait.** Have them add adverbs or expressions they've learned that signal a past tense.
• Follow the Oral Practice suggestion on p. 336. Then have students work in pairs to complete the interview in the suggestion on p. 337.

EXPANSION

Oral Practice　Have students recall a misunderstanding or a dispute they've had with a friend or family member in the past. Ask them to describe what happened using the **passé composé** and the **imparfait.** Example: **Mon ami et moi avions rendez-vous au cinéma pour voir un film. Il faisait mauvais et il pleuvait. J'ai attendu mon ami pendant une heure devant le cinéma, mais il n'est pas venu!**

TEACHING OPTIONS

Video　Divide the class into small groups. Show the video of the **Roman-photo** again and have the groups write a summary of the episode, using the **passé composé** and the **imparfait.** Have the groups present their summaries and have the class vote for the best one.

Suggestion Before students complete **Essayez!**, have them reread all the points on pp. 336–337.

Essayez! Give the following items as additional practice.
**9. La semaine dernière, mon ami et moi _____ (faire) de la planche à voile. (avons fait)
10. Avant, ils _____ (répondre) toujours aux questions du prof. (répondaient) 11. Papa _____ (acheter) un nouveau frigo hier. (a acheté) 12. D'habitude, nous _____ (mettre) nos vêtements dans le placard. (mettions)**

- The **imparfait** and the **passé composé** are sometimes used in the same sentence to say what was going on when something else happened. Use the **imparfait** to say what was going on and the **passé composé** to say what happened to interrupt that action.

Je **travaillais** dans le jardin quand mon amie **a téléphoné**.
I was working in the garden when my friend called.

Ils **faisaient** de la planche à voile quand j'**ai pris** cette photo.
They were wind-surfing when I took this photo.

- A cause and effect relationship is sometimes expressed by using the **passé composé** and the **imparfait** in the same sentence.

Marie **avait** envie de faire du shopping, alors elle **est allée** au centre commercial.
Marie felt like shopping so she went to the mall.

Mon ami **a balayé** la maison parce qu'elle **était** sale.
My friend swept the house because it was dirty.

- The verb **avoir** has a different meaning when used in the **imparfait** versus the **passé composé**.

J'**avais** sommeil.
I was sleepy.

J'**ai eu** sommeil.
I got sleepy.

Expressions that signal a past tense

- Certain expressions like **soudain, tout à coup, autrefois, une fois, d'habitude, souvent, toujours,** etc. serve as clues to signal a particular past tense.

Autrefois, mes parents et moi **vivions** en Belgique.
In the past, my parents and I used to live in Belgium.

Un jour, j'**ai rencontré** Nathalie au cinéma.
One day, I met Nathalie at the movies.

D'habitude, j'**allais** au centre-ville avec mes amis.
Usually, I used to go downtown with my friends.

J'**ai fait** du cheval deux fois dans ma vie.
I have gone horseback riding two times in my life.

Essayez! Écrivez la forme correcte du verbe au passé.

1. D'habitude, vous _mangiez_ (manger) dans la salle à manger.
2. Quand mes copines étaient petites, elles _jouaient_ (jouer) de la guitare.
3. Tout à coup, ma sœur _est arrivée_ (arriver) à l'école.
4. Ce matin, Matthieu _a repassé_ (repasser) le linge.
5. Ils _ont vécu_ (vivre) en France pendant un mois.
6. Les chats _dormaient_ (dormir) toujours sur le tapis.
7. Je/J' _ai loué_ (louer) un studio en ville pendant trois semaines.
8. Vous _laviez_ (laver) toujours les rideaux?
9. Lise _avait_ (avoir) quinze ans quand elle a déménagé.
10. Soudain, nous _avons eu_ (avoir) peur.

TEACHING OPTIONS

Interview Have students interview each other about the first time they met their best friends, using the **passé composé** and the **imparfait**. Encourage them to include time expressions such as those presented on this page.

EXPANSION

Extra Practice Distribute the handout for the activity **Les souvenirs** from the online Resources (Unité 8/Activity Pack/ Vocabulary and Grammar Activities). Have students read the instructions and give them 10 minutes to complete the activity. Ask volunteers to share their answers once everyone has finished.

1 & **2 Expansions** Have volunteers explain why they chose the **passé composé** or the **imparfait** in each case. Ask them to point out any words or expressions that triggered one tense or the other.

3 Expansion ←👥→ Have students come up with a short story for each illustration.

TELL Connection

Learning Experience 4 *Why:* It is important to maintain 90% or more target language usage in the classroom, even when presenting grammar. *What:* Have students use the grammar explanations in English on the previous pages outside of class. In class, use the scaffolded activities as jumping-off points for more personalized activities that practice the structures in context. Use kinesthetic and visual approaches to clarify meaning without resorting to English, and to tap into the different learning styles in your classroom.

Mise en pratique

1 **À l'étranger!** Choisissez l'imparfait ou le passé composé pour compléter cette histoire.

Lise (1) ___avait___ (avoir) vraiment envie de travailler en France après le lycée. Alors, un jour, elle (2) ___a quitté___ (quitter) son petit village près de Bruxelles et elle (3) ___a pris___ (prendre) le train pour Paris. Elle (4) ___est arrivée___ (arriver) à Paris. Elle (5) ___a trouvé___ (trouver) une chambre dans un petit hôtel. Pendant six mois, elle (6) ___a balayé___ (balayer) le couloir et (7) ___a nettoyé___ (nettoyer) les chambres. Au bout de (*After*) six mois, elle (8) ___a pris___ (prendre) des cours au Cordon Bleu et maintenant, elle est chef dans un petit restaurant!

2 **Explique-moi!** Dites pourquoi vous et vos amis n'avez pas fait les choses qu'il fallait faire. Utilisez le passé composé pour dire ce que (*what*) vous n'avez pas fait et l'imparfait pour expliquer la raison. Faites des phrases complètes.

MODÈLE

Élise / étudier / avoir sommeil
Élise n'a pas étudié parce qu'elle avait sommeil.

1. Carla / faire une promenade / pleuvoir   Carla n'a pas fait de promenade parce qu'il pleuvait.
2. Alexandre et Mia / ranger la chambre / regarder la télé   Alexandre et Mia n'ont pas rangé la chambre parce qu'ils regardaient la télé.
3. nous / répondre au prof / ne pas faire attention   Nous n'avons pas répondu au prof parce que nous ne faisions pas attention.
4. Jade et Noémie / venir au café / nettoyer la maison   Jade et Noémie ne sont pas venues au café parce qu'elles nettoyaient la maison.
5. Léo / mettre un short / aller à un entretien (*interview*)   Léo n'a pas mis son short parce qu'il allait à un entretien.
6. je / manger au restaurant / ne pas avoir d'argent   Je n'ai pas mangé au restaurant parce que je n'avais pas d'argent.
7. Amadou / promener son chien / neiger   Amadou n'a pas promené son chien parce qu'il neigeait.
8. Marc et toi, vous / aller à la piscine / laver la voiture   Marc et toi, vous n'êtes pas allés à la piscine parce que vous laviez la voiture.
9. on / téléphoner à nos amis / ne pas avoir de portable   On n'a pas téléphoné à nos amis parce qu'on n'avait pas de portable.
10. toi, tu / faire du surf / avoir peur   Toi, tu n'as pas fait de surf parce que tu avais peur.

3 **Qu'est-ce qu'ils faisaient quand...?** Que faisaient ces personnes au moment de l'interruption?

► **MODÈLE**

Papa débarrassait la table quand mon frère est arrivé.

débarrasser / arriver

1. sortir / dire
Ils sortaient la poubelle quand le voisin a dit bonjour.

2. passer / tomber
Michel passait l'aspirateur quand l'enfant est tombé.

3. faire / partir
Sa mère faisait la lessive quand Anne est partie.

4. laver / commencer
Ils lavaient la voiture quand il a commencé à pleuvoir.

TEACHING OPTIONS

Extra Practice ←👥→ Have students work in small groups to write a story about a Francophone student who came to your school as part of a year-long exchange program. Tell them to use Activity 1 as a model and to include as much detail as possible in their stories.

TEACHING OPTIONS

Extra Practice 👥↔👥 Have students prepare questions to interview a classmate about something they did last weekend. Tell them to find out what their partner did, the circumstances surrounding the event, how they felt, etc. After students conduct their interviews, have them write a summary of what they learned.

Communication

4 Situations Avec un(e) partenaire, complétez ces phrases avec le passé composé ou l'imparfait. Comparez vos réponses, puis présentez-les à la classe. *Answers will vary.*

1. Autrefois, ma famille...
2. Je faisais une promenade quand...
3. Mon/Ma meilleur(e) ami(e)... tous les jours.
4. D'habitude, au petit-déjeuner, je...
5. Une fois, mon copain et moi...
6. Hier, je rentrais des cours quand...
7. Parfois, ma mère...
8. Hier, il faisait mauvais. Soudain, ...
9. Souvent, quand j'étais petit(e)...
10. La semaine dernière, en cours de français, nous...

5 À votre tour Demandez à un(e) partenaire de compléter ces phrases avec le passé composé ou l'imparfait. Ensuite, présentez ses phrases à la classe. *Answers will vary.*

1. Mes profs l'année dernière...
2. Quand je suis rentré(e) chez moi hier, ...
3. Le week-end dernier, ...
4. Quand j'ai fait la connaissance de mon/ma meilleur(e) ami(e), ...
5. La première fois que mon/ma meilleur(e) ami(e) et moi sommes sorti(e)s, ...
6. Quand j'avais dix ans, ...
7. Le jour de mon dernier anniversaire, ...
8. Pendant les vacances d'été, ...
9. Quand Leonardo DiCaprio a gagné son premier Oscar, ...
10. Hier soir, je regardais la télé quand...
11. Quand mes parents étaient plus jeunes, ...
12. La dernière fois que j'ai fait un voyage, ...

6 Je me souviens! Racontez à votre partenaire un événement spécial de votre vie qui s'est déjà passé. Votre partenaire vous pose des questions pour avoir plus de détails sur cet événement. Vous pouvez (*can*) parler d'un anniversaire, d'une fête familiale, d'un mariage ou d'un concert. Utilisez le passé composé et l'imparfait. *Answers will vary.*

MODÈLE

Élève 1: *Nous avons fait une grande fête d'anniversaire pour ma grand-mère l'année dernière.*
Élève 2: *Quel âge a-t-elle eu?*
Élève 1: *Elle a eu soixante ans.*
Élève 2: *Vous avez fait la fête chez toi?*
Élève 1: *Nous avons fait la fête dans le jardin parce qu'il faisait très beau.*

4 Expansion Have students choose one of these sentences to begin telling a short story in the past. Encourage students to use both the **passé composé** and the **imparfait**.

4 Partner Chat You can also assign Activity 4 on vhlcentral.com. Students work in pairs to record the activity online. The pair's recorded conversation will appear in your gradebook.

5 Expansion You could also have students do this activity as a survey by turning the phrases into questions and adding additional questions in the past. Examples: **Comment étaient tes profs l'année dernière? Que faisait ta mère quand tu es rentré(e) chez toi hier? Qu'est-ce que tu as fait le week-end dernier?**

Activity Pack For additional activities, go to the **Activity Pack** in the **Resources** section of vhlcentral.com.

Section Goals

In this section, students will learn the uses of **savoir** and **connaître**.

Key Standards

4.1, 5.1

Suggestions: Scaffolding

- Go over **Point de départ**. Model **savoir** by asking several questions with it. Examples: _____, **savez-vous faire du ski? Et vous, _____, savez-vous où est la bibliothèque?** Next, write **connaître** on the board and ask questions, such as: _____, **connaissez-vous mon frère? Connaissez-vous La Nouvelle-Orléans?** Ask students further questions using both verbs to help them infer the difference in use between the two.
- Discuss the images and captions from **Roman-photo**. Ask: **Que sait Amina? Est-ce qu'elle connaît Cyberhomme? (qu'il faut balayer sous la cuisinière, non)**
- Point out that the context of the phrase will indicate which verb to use. Using examples in English, have students say which verb would be used for the French translation. Examples: I know how to swim. (**savoir**) He doesn't know the president. (**connaître**)
- Go over the conjugations of both **savoir** and **connaître** in the present tense.

8B.2

The verbs *savoir* and *connaître* vhlcentral

Point de départ Savoir and connaître both mean *to know*. The choice of verb in French depends on the context in which it is being used.

> N'oublie pas de balayer sous la cuisinière.

> Je sais!

> Je ne le connais pas vraiment, tu sais.

savoir	
je	sais
tu	sais
il/elle/on	sait
nous	savons
vous	savez
ils/elles	savent

🏃 Boîte à outils

Always use the construction **savoir** + [*infinitive*] to mean *to know how to do something*.

- **Savoir** means *to know a fact* or *to know how to do something*.

  Je **sais** tout sur lui.
  I know everything about him.

  Ils ne **savent** pas qu'il est parti.
  They don't know that he left.

  Elle **sait** jouer du piano
  She knows how to play piano.

  Savez-vous faire la cuisine?
  Do you know how to cook?

- The verb **savoir** is often followed by **que, qui, où, quand, comment,** or **pourquoi**.

  Nous **savons que** tu arrives mardi.
  We know that you're arriving on Tuesday.

  Ils **savent comment** aller à la gare.
  They know how to get to the train station.

  Je **sais où** je vais.
  I know where I am going.

  Tu **sais qui** a fait la lessive?
  Do you know who did the laundry?

  Vous **savez quand** on part?
  Do you know when we're leaving?

  Elle **comprend pourquoi** tu es en colère.
  She understands why you're angry.

- The past participle of **savoir** is **su**. When used in the **passé composé**, **savoir** means *found out*.

  J'**ai su** qu'il y avait une fête.
  I found out there was a party.

  Je **savais** qu'il y avait une fête.
  I knew there was a party.

TEACHING OPTIONS

Large Groups Divide the class into two teams (**savoir** and **connaître**), and have them line up. Indicate the first member of each team and call out a sentence in English that uses *to know* (Ex: *We know the answer.*). The team member whose verb corresponds to the English sentence has to step forward and provide the French translation.

EXPANSION

Extra Practice Prepare dehydrated sentences such as these: **tu / savoir / que tu / ne pas connaître / mon meilleur ami; nous / connaître / les nouveaux élèves**. Write them on the board one at a time and have students create complete sentences using the fragments.

Suggestions: Scaffolding
- Present the conjugations of **savoir** and **connaître** in the **passé composé** and **imparfait**.
- Review the changes in meaning when **savoir** and **connaître** are used in the **imparfait** and **passé composé**.
- Point out that **connaître** can also be used with feelings or emotions, as in the advertisement on this page.

Essayez! Have students change the sentences to the past tense. Examples: **1. Je connaissais de bons restaurants. 2. Ils ne savaient pas parler allemand.**

connaître	
je	connais
tu	connais
il/elle/on	connaît
nous	connaissons
vous	connaissez
ils/elles	connaissent

- **Connaître** means *to know* or *be familiar with a person, place, or thing.*

Avec les sofas par **Côte-Nord**, vous connaissez le confort et la joie d'être chez vous.

Vous **connaissez** le prof.
You know the teacher.

Nous **connaissons** bien Paris.
We know Paris well.

Tu **connais** ce quartier?
Do you know that neighborhood?

Je ne **connais** pas ce magasin.
I don't know this store.

Boîte à outils

The verb **connaître** is never followed by an infinitive. It is always followed by a noun.

- The past participle of **connaître** is **connu**. **Connaître** in the **passé composé** means *met (for the first time)*.

Nous **avons connu** son père.
We met his father.

Nous **connaissions** son père.
We knew his father.

- **Reconnaître** means *to recognize*. It follows the same conjugation patterns as **connaître**.

Mes anciens profs me **reconnaissent** encore.
My former teachers still recognize me.

Nous **avons reconnu** vos enfants à la soirée.
We recognized your children at the party.

Essayez! Complétez les phrases avec les formes correctes des verbes **savoir** et **connaître**.

1. Je _connais_ de bons restaurants.
2. Ils ne _savent_ pas parler allemand.
3. Vous _savez_ faire du cheval?
4. Tu _connais_ une bonne coiffeuse?
5. Nous ne _connaissons_ pas Jacques.
6. Claudette _sait_ jouer aux échecs.
7. Laure et Béatrice _connaissent_ -elles tes cousins?
8. Nous _savons_ que vous n'aimez pas faire le ménage.

EXPANSION

Video Replay the video episode, having students focus on forms of **savoir** and **connaître**, as well as the use of the **imparfait** and the **passé composé**. Tell them to note when each one is used. Afterward, ask the class to describe the conversations that took place and what tenses were used. Have students identify the reason for the tense choice (a series of past actions, ongoing actions in the past, etc.).

EXPANSION

Extra Practice Ask individual students questions using **savoir** and **connaître** that are most likely not true for them. When students give a negative answer, they should indicate someone else who would answer in the affirmative. Example: ____, **connaissez-vous le président des États-Unis? (Non, je ne le connais pas, mais le président de la France le connaît.)**

341

Mise en pratique

1 Les passe-temps Qu'est-ce que ces personnes savent faire?

Patrick

▶ **MODÈLE**

Patrick sait skier.

1. Halima
Halima sait patiner.

2. vous
Vous savez nager.

3. tu
Tu sais jouer au tennis.

4. nous
Nous savons jouer au foot.

2 Dialogues Complétez les conversations avec le présent du verbe **savoir** ou **connaître**.

1. Marie _____sait_____ faire la cuisine?
   Oui, mais elle ne _____connaît_____ pas beaucoup de recettes (*recipes*).
2. Vous _____connaissez_____ les parents de François?
   Non, je _____connais_____ seulement sa cousine.
3. Tes enfants _____savent_____ nager dans la mer.
   Et mon fils aîné _____connaît_____ toutes les espèces de poissons.
4. Je _____sais_____ que le train arrive à trois heures.
   Est-ce que tu _____sais_____ à quelle heure il part?
5. Vous _____connaissez_____ le numéro de téléphone de Dorian?
   Oui, je le _____connais_____.
6. Nous _____connaissons_____ bien la musique arabe.
   Ah, bon? Tu _____sais_____ qu'il y a un concert de raï en ville demain?

3 Assemblez Assemblez les éléments des colonnes pour construire des phrases. Answers will vary.

MODÈLE   *Je sais parler une langue étrangère.*

A	B	C
Marion Cotillard	(ne pas) connaître	des célébrités
Oprah Winfrey	(ne pas) savoir	faire la cuisine
je		jouer dans un film
ton/ta camarade de classe		Julia Roberts
		parler une langue étrangère

Communication

4 **Enquête** Votre professeur va vous donner une feuille d'activités. Circulez dans la classe pour trouver au moins une personne différente qui répond oui à chaque question. Answers will vary.

Sujet	Nom
1. Sais-tu faire une mousse au chocolat?	Jacqueline
2. Connais-tu New York?	
3. Connais-tu le nom des sénateurs de cet état (state)?	
4. Connais-tu quelqu'un qui habite en Californie?	

5 **Je sais faire** Michelle et Maryse étudient avec un(e) nouvel/nouvelle ami(e). Par groupes de trois, jouez les rôles. Chacun(e) (*Each one*) essaie de montrer toutes les choses qu'il/elle sait faire. Answers will vary.

MODÈLE

Élève 1: *Alors, tu sais faire la vaisselle?*
Élève 2: *Je sais faire la vaisselle, et je sais faire la cuisine aussi.*
Élève 3: *Moi, je sais faire la cuisine, mais je ne sais pas passer l'aspirateur.*

6 **Questions** À tour de rôle, posez ces questions à un(e) partenaire. Ensuite, présentez vos réponses à la classe. Answers will vary.

1. Quel bon restaurant connais-tu près d'ici? Est-ce que tu y (*there*) manges souvent?
2. Dans ta famille, qui sait chanter le mieux (*best*)?
3. Connais-tu l'Europe? Quelles villes connais-tu?
4. Reconnais-tu toutes les chansons (*songs*) que tu entends à la radio?
5. Tes grands-parents savent-ils utiliser Internet? Le font-ils bien?
6. Connais-tu un(e) acteur/actrice célèbre? Une autre personne célèbre?
7. Ton/Ta meilleur(e) (*best*) ami(e) sait-il/elle écouter quand tu lui racontes (*tell*) tes problèmes?
8. Connais-tu la date d'anniversaire de tous les membres de ta famille et de tous tes amis? Donne des exemples.
9. Connais-tu des films français? Lesquels (*Which ones*)? Les aimes-tu? Pourquoi?
10. Sais-tu parler une langue étrangère? Laquelle? (*Which one*)?

4 Suggestions
• Distribute the **Feuilles d'activités** found in the Activity Pack on vhlcentral.com.
• Have students read through the list of questions using **savoir** and **connaître** for comprehension before completing the activity.

5 Suggestion Ask for three volunteers to act out the **modèle** for the class.

6 Expansion Ask these questions of the whole class. Ask students who answer in the affirmative for additional information. Examples: **Qui sait chanter? Chantez-vous bien? Chantiez-vous à l'école quand vous étiez petit(e)?**

6 Virtual Chat You can also assign Activity 6 on vhlcentral.com. Students record individual responses that appear in your gradebook.

Activity Pack For additional activities, go to the **Activity Pack** in the **Resources** section of vhlcentral.com.

EXPANSION

Extra Practice Have students write down three things they know how to do well (using **savoir bien** + [*infinitive*]). Collect the papers, and then read the sentences. Tell students that they must not identify themselves when they hear their sentence. The rest of the class takes turns trying to guess who wrote each sentence. Repeat this activity with **connaître**.

EXPANSION

Pairs Ask students to write brief, but creative, paragraphs in which they use **savoir** and **connaître**. Then have them exchange their papers with a partner. Tell students to help each other, through peer editing, to make the paragraphs as error-free as possible. Collect the papers for grading.

Révision

1 Un grand dîner Émilie et son mari Vincent ont invité des amis à dîner ce soir. Qu'ont-ils fait cet après-midi pour préparer la soirée? Que vont-ils faire ce soir après le départ des invités? Conversez avec un(e) partenaire. Answers will vary.

MODÈLE

Élève 1: Cet après-midi, Émilie et Vincent ont mis la table.

Élève 2: Ce soir, ils vont faire la vaisselle.

2 Mes connaissances Votre professeur va vous donner une feuille d'activités. Interviewez vos camarades. Pour chaque activité, trouvez un(e) camarade différent(e) qui réponde affirmativement. Answers will vary.

Élève 1: Connais-tu une personne qui aime faire le ménage?

Élève 2: Oui, autrefois, mon père aimait bien faire le ménage.

Activités	Noms
1. ne pas faire souvent la vaisselle	
2. aimer faire le ménage	Farid
3. dormir avec une couverture en été	
4. faire son lit tous les jours	
5. repasser rarement ses vêtements	

3 Qui faisait le ménage? Par groupes de trois, interviewez vos camarades. Qui faisait le ménage à la maison quand ils étaient petits? Préparez des questions avec ces expressions et comparez vos réponses. Answers will vary.

balayer	mettre et débarrasser la table
faire la lessive	passer l'aspirateur
faire le lit	ranger
faire la vaisselle	repasser le linge

4 Soudain! Tout était calme quand soudain... Avec un(e) partenaire, choisissez l'une des deux photos et écrivez un texte de dix phrases. Faites cinq phrases pour décrire la photo, et cinq autres pour raconter (*to tell*) un événement qui s'est passé soudainement (*that suddenly happened*). Employez des adverbes et soyez imaginatifs. Answers will vary.

5 J'ai appris... Avec un(e) partenaire, faites une liste de cinq choses que vous ne saviez pas avant ce cours de français, et cinq choses ou personnes que vous ne connaissiez pas. Utilisez l'imparfait et le présent dans vos explications. Answers will vary.

MODÈLE

Élève 1: Avant, je ne savais pas comment dire bonjour en français, et puis j'ai commencé ce cours, et maintenant, je sais le dire.

Élève 2: Avant, je ne connaissais pas tous les pays francophones, et maintenant, je les connais.

6 Élise fait sa lessive Votre professeur va vous donner, à vous et à votre partenaire, une feuille sur la journée d'Élise. Décrivez sa journée d'après (*according to*) les dessins. Attention! Ne regardez pas la feuille de votre partenaire. Answers will vary.

MODÈLE

Élève 1: Hier matin, Élise avait besoin de faire sa lessive.

Élève 2: Mais, elle...

TEACHING OPTIONS

Assigning Verbs Divide the class into three groups. One group is **savoir** (present tense with infinitive, **imparfait**), the second group is **connaître** (present tense, **imparfait**), and the third group is **savoir** and **connaître** (**passé composé**). Have each group brainstorm a list of phrases using their assigned verbs and tenses. A volunteer from each group should present their results to the class.

Example: Group 1 – **Je sais chanter. (présent) Ma mère savait parler français. (imparfait)** Group 2 – **Nous connaissons les nouveaux élèves. (présent) Il connaissait le président des États-Unis. (imparfait)** Group 3 – **J'ai su que l'examen de français était très difficile. (passé composé) Mon père a connu mon meilleur ami. (passé composé)**

À l'écoute vhlcentral

AP® **Theme:** Contemporary Life
Context: Housing and Shelter

STRATÉGIE

Using visual cues

Visual cues like illustrations and headings provide useful clues about what you will hear.

 To practice this strategy, you will listen to a passage related to the image. Jot down the clues the image gives you as you listen. Answers will vary.

Préparation

Qu'est-ce qu'il y a sur les trois photos à droite? À votre avis, quel va être le sujet de la conversation entre M. Duchemin et Mme Lopez?

À vous d'écouter

Écoutez la conversation. M. Duchemin va proposer trois logements à Mme Lopez. Regardez les annonces et écrivez le numéro de référence de chaque possibilité qu'il propose.

1. Possibilité 1: __Réf. 521__
2. Possibilité 2: __Réf. 522__
3. Possibilité 3: __Réf. 520__

À LOUER

 Appartement en ville, moderne, avec balcon
1.200 €
(Réf. 520)

 5 pièces, jardin, proche parc Victor Hugo
950 €
(Réf. 521)

 Maison meublée en banlieue, grande, tt confort, cuisine équipée
1.200 €
(Réf. 522)

Compréhension

Les détails Après une deuxième écoute, complétez le tableau (*chart*) avec les informations données dans la conversation.

	Où?	Maison ou appartement?	Meublé ou non?	Nombre de chambres?	Garage?	Jardin?
Logement 1	ville	maison	non	trois	non	oui
Logement 2	banlieue	maison	oui	quatre	oui	oui
Logement 3	centre-ville	appartement	non	deux	oui	non

Quel logement pour les Lopez? Lisez cette description de la famille Lopez. Décidez quel logement cette famille va probablement choisir et expliquez votre réponse.

M. Lopez travaille au centre-ville. Le soir, il rentre tard à la maison et il est souvent fatigué parce qu'il travaille beaucoup. Il n'a pas envie de passer son temps à travailler dans le jardin. Mme Lopez adore le cinéma et le théâtre. Elle n'aime pas beaucoup faire le ménage. Les Lopez ont une fille qui a seize ans. Elle adore retrouver ses copines pour faire du shopping en ville. Les Lopez ont beaucoup de beaux meubles modernes. Ils ont aussi une nouvelle voiture: une grosse BMW qui a coûté très cher!

Section Goals

In this section, students will:
- use visual cues to understand an oral description
- listen to a conversation and complete several activities

Key Standards
1.2, 2.1

Stratégie
Script Nous avons trouvé un appartement super dans le quartier du Marais. Il est au premier étage, dans un immeuble très calme. Il y a une salle de séjour assez grande, une cuisine avec frigo, cuisinière et lave-linge, une petite salle de bains et deux chambres très jolies. Il y a aussi des placards dans toutes les pièces et un garage en sous-sol pour notre voiture. On peut emménager la semaine prochaine et le loyer n'est pas très cher. Nous sommes vraiment heureux, tu sais!
Teacher Resources DVD

À vous d'écouter
Script AGENT: Allô, bonjour. Madame Lopez, s'il vous plaît.
CLIENTE: C'est elle-même.
A: Ah, bonjour, Madame. Ici Monsieur Duchemin de l'agence immobilière. Vous cherchez un logement à louer à Avignon ou dans la banlieue, c'est bien ça?
C: Oui, Monsieur, c'est exact. Vous avez une maison à me proposer?
A: Oui, j'ai trois possibilités. La première est une maison en ville, dans un quartier calme près du parc Victor Hugo. Elle n'est pas très grande, mais elle est très jolie et elle a un petit jardin. Il y a un salon, une salle à manger, une grande cuisine avec beaucoup de placards, une salle de bains, les W.-C. et trois chambres.
C: Il y a un garage?
A: Non, Madame, mais il y a toujours des places dans le quartier.
C: Bon. Et qu'est-ce que vous avez d'autre?
A: J'ai aussi une très grande maison meublée avec jardin et garage en banlieue, à une demi-heure de la ville.
C: C'est un peu loin, mais bon... Il y a combien de chambres?
A: Quatre chambres.

C: Et qu'est-ce qu'il y a comme meubles?
A: Un canapé, des fauteuils et des étagères dans le salon, un grand lit et une commode dans la grande chambre... et voyons, quoi d'autre? Ah, oui! La cuisine est équipée avec tout le nécessaire: frigo, congélateur, cuisinière, four à micro-ondes, lave-linge et sèche-linge.
C: Très bien. Et la troisième possibilité?
A: C'est un grand appartement dans le centre-ville, sur la place des Halles. Il n'y a pas de jardin.

C: Et combien de chambres y a-t-il?
A: Deux chambres avec des balcons. Si vous aimez le moderne, cet appartement est parfait pour vous. Et il a un garage.
C: Bon, je vais en parler avec mon mari.
A: Très bien, Madame. Au revoir.
C: Au revoir, Monsieur Duchemin.
Teacher Resources DVD

Savoir-faire

vhlcentral

Panorama

Paris

La ville en chiffres

▶ **Superficie:** *105 km²*

▶ **Population:** *2.229.621 (deux millions deux cents vingt-neuf mille six cents vingt et un)*
SOURCE: INSEE

Paris est la capitale de la France. On a l'impression que Paris est une grande ville—et c'est vrai si on compte° ses environs°. Mais Paris mesure moins de° 10 kilomètres de l'est à l'ouest°. On peut très facilement visiter la ville à pied°. Paris est divisée en 20 arrondissements°. Chaque° arrondissement a son propre maire° et son propre caractère.

▶ **Industries principales:** *haute couture, finances, transports, technologie, tourisme*

▶ **Musées:** *plus de° 150 (cent cinquante): le musée du Louvre, le musée d'Orsay, le centre Georges Pompidou et le musée Rodin*

Parisiens célèbres

▶ **Victor Hugo,** *écrivain° et activiste (1802–1885)*

▶ **Charles Baudelaire,** *poète (1821–1867)*...

▶ **Auguste Rodin,** *sculpteur (1840–1917)*

▶ **Jean-Paul Sartre,** *philosophe (1905–1980)*

▶ **Simone de Beauvoir,** *écrivain (1908–1986)*

▶ **Édith Piaf,** *chanteuse (1915–1963)*...

▶ ...**Emmanuelle Béart,** *actrice (1965–)*

si on compte *if one counts* environs *surrounding areas* moins de *less than* de l'est à l'ouest *from east to west* à pied *on foot* arrondissements *districts* Chaque *Each* son propre maire *its own mayor* plus de *more than* écrivain *writer* rues *streets* reposent *lie; rest* provenant *from* repos *rest*

l'Arc de Triomphe

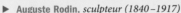

Basilique du Sacré-Cœur

Place du Tertre

Le Moulin Rouge

Parc Monceau

BOULEVARD HAUSSMANN

Arc de Triomphe

Opéra Garnier BLVD. DES ITALIENS

AVENUE DES CHAMPS-ÉLYSÉES

La Madeleine BLVD. DES CAPUCINES AVE. DE L'OPÉRA

Bois de Boulogne

Jeu de Paume

Grand Palais

Place de la Concorde

RUE DE RIVOLI

Les Halles

BOULEVARD DE SÉBASTOPOL

Beaubourg/Centre Georges Pompidou-Centre National d'Art et de Culture

Jardins du Trocadéro

Jardin des Tuileries Orangerie

Seine

QUAI D'ORSAY

Assemblée Nationale

BLVD ST. GERMAIN

Musée d'Orsay

Musée du Louvre

RUE DE RIVOLI

Tour Eiffel

Concergerie

Hôtel de Ville

Place des Vosges

Île de la Cité

Opéra de Paris Bastille

Parc du Champ de Mars

Hôtel des Invalides

BOULEVARD RASPAIL

BOULEVARD ST. GERMAIN

Cathédrale Notre-Dame

Île St-Louis

École Militaire

Jardin du Luxembourg

Tour Montparnasse

BOULEVARD SAINT-MICHEL

Sorbonne

Panthéon

Seine

l'opéra Garnier

0 ——— 0.5 mile
0 ——— 0.5 kilomètre

une terrasse de café

Incroyable mais vrai!

Sous les rues° de Paris, il y a une autre ville: les catacombes. Ici reposent° les squelettes d'environ 6.000.000 (six millions) de personnes provenant° d'anciens cimetières de Paris et de ses environs. Plus de 500.000 (cinq cent mille) touristes par an visitent cette ville de repos° éternel.

AP® **Theme:** Beauty and Aesthetics
Context: Architecture

Les monuments

La tour Eiffel

La tour Eiffel a été construite° en 1889 (mille huit cent quatre-vingt-neuf) pour l'Exposition universelle, à l'occasion du centenaire° de la Révolution française. Elle mesure 324 (trois cent vingt-quatre) mètres de haut et pèse° 10.100 (dix mille cent) tonnes. La tour attire près de° 7.000.000 (sept millions) de visiteurs par an°.

AP® **Theme:** Contemporary Life
Context: Leisure and Sports

Les gens

Paris-Plages

Pour les Parisiens qui ne voyagent pas pendant l'été, la ville de Paris a créé° Paris-Plages pour apporter la plage° aux Parisiens! Inauguré en 2001 pour la première fois sur les berges° de la Seine, puis prolongé sur le bassin de la Villette en 2007, Paris-Plages consiste en plusieurs kilomètres de sable et de pelouse°, plein° d'activités comme la natation° et le volley. Ouvert en° juillet et en août, près de 4.000.000 (quatre millions) de personnes visitent Paris-Plages chaque° année.

Les musées

AP® **Theme:** Beauty and Aesthetics
Context: Visual Arts

Le musée du Louvre

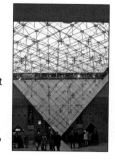

Ancien° palais royal, le musée du Louvre est aujourd'hui un des plus grands musées du monde avec sa vaste collection de peintures°, de sculptures et d'antiquités orientales, égyptiennes, grecques et romaines. L'œuvre° la plus célèbre de la collection est *La Joconde*° de Léonard de Vinci. La pyramide de verre°, créée par l'architecte américain I.M. Pei, marque l'entrée° principale du musée.

AP® **Theme:** Beauty and Aesthetics
Context: Architecture

Les transports

Le métro

L'architecte Hector Guimard a commencé à réaliser° des entrées du métro de Paris en 1898 (mille huit cent quatre-vingt-dix-huit). Ces entrées sont construites dans le style Art Nouveau: en forme de plantes et de fleurs°. Le métro est aujourd'hui un système très efficace° qui permet aux passagers de traverser° Paris rapidement.

 Qu'est-ce que vous avez appris? Complétez les phrases.

1. La ville de Paris est divisée en vingt _arrondissements_.

2. Chaque arrondissement a ses propres _maire_ et _caractère_.

3. Charles Baudelaire est le nom d'un _poète_ français.

4. Édith Piaf est une _chanteuse_ française.

5. Plus de 500.000 personnes par an visitent _les catacombes_ sous les rues de Paris.

6. La tour Eiffel mesure _324_ mètres de haut.

7. En 2001, la ville de Paris a créé _Paris-Plages_ au bord (*banks*) de la Seine.

8. Le musée du Louvre est un ancien _palais_.

9. _La pyramide de verre_ est une création de I.M. Pei.

10. Certaines entrées du métro sont de style _Art Nouveau_.

 Sur Internet

1. Quels sont les monuments les plus importants à Paris? Qu'est-ce qu'on peut faire (*can do*) dans la ville?

2. Trouvez des informations sur un des musées de Paris.

3. Recherchez la vie (*Research the life*) d'un(e) Parisien(ne) célèbre.

4. Cherchez un plan du métro de Paris et trouvez comment aller du Louvre à la tour Eiffel.

construite *built* **centenaire** *100-year anniversary* **pèse** *weighs* **attire près de** *attracts nearly* **par an** *per year* **a créé** *created* **apporter la plage** *bring the beach* **berges** *banks* **de sable et de pelouse** *of sand and grass* **plein** *full* **natation** *swimming* **Ouvert en** *Open in* **chaque** *each* **Ancien** *Former* **peintures** *paintings* **L'œuvre** *The work (of art)* **La Joconde** *The Mona Lisa* **verre** *glass* **entrée** *entrance* **réaliser** *create* **fleurs** *flowers* **efficace** *efficient* **traverser** *to cross*

Side column

La tour Eiffel Constructed of wrought iron, the architectural design of the Eiffel Tower was an engineering masterpiece for its time. Critics of Gustave Eiffel's design said it couldn't be built, but he proved them wrong. Later, some of the engineering techniques employed would be used to build the first steel skyscrapers. The Eiffel Tower remained the world's tallest building until 1930.

Paris-Plages Paris-Plages, with its numerous organized sports activities, dances, and concerts, is one of the most popular events in Paris during the summer months. All activities, beaches, and playgrounds are open and free to the public; however, the cost to the city of Paris can reach up to 4 million euros each year. Ask students if they think that **Paris-Plages** is worth the money.

Le musée du Louvre Bring in photos or slides of the **Louvre** and some of the most famous artwork in its collection, such as the *Mona Lisa*, the *Venus de Milo*, Vermeer's *The Lacemaker*, and Delacroix's *Liberty Leading the People* (**La Liberté guidant le peuple**). Ask students to describe the woman in the *Mona Lisa*. Point out that only a fraction of the 300,000 works owned by the museum are on display.

Le métro The Paris public transportation system, **le métro** (short for **le Métropolitain**), has 14 lines. It is the most convenient and popular means of transportation in the city since every building in Paris is within 500 meters of a **métro** station. Ask students what cities in the United States have metro or subway systems.

21ˢᵗ Century Skills

Information and Media Literacy Go to vhlcentral.com to complete the **Sur Internet** activity associated with **Panorama** for additional practice accessing and using culturally authentic sources.

PRE-AP®

Presentational Writing Assign each student a famous site in Paris. Examples: l'Île de la Cité, la Sainte-Chapelle, le quartier latin, etc. Tell students to research the site and write a brief description. Encourage them to include photos from the Internet or magazines. Ask a few volunteers to share their descriptions with the class.

EXPANSION

Mon itinéraire Have students work in pairs. Tell them that they have three days in Paris, and they have to make a list of places they want to see or visit each day so that they can make the most of their time there. Remind students that many famous sights, other than those mentioned in the text, appear on the map. Example: **Jour 1: visiter le musée du Louvre.** Ask volunteers to share their lists with the class.

Savoir-faire

vhlcentral

Panorama

L'Île-de-France

La région en chiffres

▶ **Superficie:** *12.012 km²*

▶ **Population:** *12.027.565*
SOURCE: INSEE

▶ **Industries principales:** *aéronautique, automobile, énergie nucléaire, santé°, services*

▶ **Villes principales:** *Paris, Meaux, Provins, Saint-Denis, Fontainebleau, Montreuil, Nanterre, Versailles, Argenteuil*

Franciliens célèbres

▶ **Jean Cocteau,** *poète, dramaturge° et cinéaste° (1889–1963)*

▶ **Dominique Voynet,** *femme politique° (1958–)*

▶ **Thierry Henry,** *footballeur (1977–)*

▶ **Jaques Prévert,** *poète, scénariste et artiste (1900–1977)*

▶ **Omar Sy,** *acteur (1978–)*

▶ **Vanessa Paradis,** *chanteuse et actrice (1972–)*

▶ **Les impressionnistes** *Plusieurs peintres impressionnistes du XIXᵉ siècle se sont inspirés des grands espaces° de l'Île-de-France. Quand Claude Monet a habité à Argenteuil pendant sept ans, il a réalisé° près de 250 peintures, comme «La Liseuse» (1872) et «Le pont d'Argenteuil» (1874). Auvers-sur-Oise aussi a été le sujet de plusieurs œuvres° impressionnistes, y compris° soixante-dix par Vincent Van Gogh. Aujourd'hui, on peut suivre° les quatre chemins de randonnée pédestre° aux Yveliennes qui sont dédiés aux impressionnistes pour voir° les sites où les artistes ont planté leur chevalet°.*

santé health **dramaturge** playwright **femme politique** politician **grands espaces** natural spaces **réalisé** created **œuvres** works of art **y compris** including **suivre** follow **chemins de randonnée pédestre** walking paths **voir** see **chevalet** easel **closerie** enclosed property **comprend** includes **abrite** houses **pont** bridge **jardin** garden

le pont° d'Argenteuil

LA FRANCE

40 miles
40 kilomètres

la Seine
l'Oise
la Marne

Saint-Denis
Meaux
Nanterre
Marne-la-Vallée
Versailles
Paris
ÎLE-DE-FRANCE
Provins
la Seine
Melun
Fontainebleau
Nemours
la Loire

un tombeau royal de la basilique Saint-Denis

le jardin° de Versailles

Incroyable mais vrai!

La closerie° Falbala a été construite entre 1971 et 1973 par l'artiste Jean Dubuffet, qui voulait créer un «espace mental» pour son énorme œuvre d'art, *Cabinet logologique*. Située sur l'île Saint-Germain, la closerie comprend° une sorte de jardin avec, au centre, la villa Falbala qui abrite° sa création. C'est l'un des monuments historiques les plus jeunes de France.

AP® Theme: Families and Communities
Context: Customs and Ceremonies

L'histoire

Provins

La ville de Provins a joué un rôle commercial très important en Europe au Moyen Âge. C'est ici que neuf chemins° commerciaux se croisaient. Donc, Provins est devenu la ville avec les plus grandes foires° de Champagne. Ces foires attiraient les marchands les plus important de l'Europe. Ces rassemblements, qui avaient lieu périodiquement et duraient° plusieurs semaines, permettaient les échanges internationaux. Aujourd'hui, la ville, classée au Patrimoine mondial par l'UNESCO, est toujours entourée° par des remparts° du Moyen Âge et la tradition des foires se perpétue avec des spectacles sur la thématique médiévale.

AP® Theme: Beauty and Aesthetics
Context: Architecture

Les gens

André Le Nôtre

Né le 12 mars 1613, André Le Nôtre passe sa jeunesse à travailler avec son père, jardinier aux Tuileries. Ensuite, il suit des cours d'archicture. Il devient jardinier du roi Louis XIV en 1637. Il amasse° une fortune énorme et gagne° une réputation internationale. Considéré «architecte paysagiste°,» Le Nôtre est connu pour ses «jardins de la française.» Ses œuvres les plus connus sont les jardins de Versailles, des Tuileries, et de Vaux-le-Vicomte. Ses créations précises et méticuleuses sont souvent caractérisées par des plantes en formes géométriques, ainsi que des éléments formelles et théâtrales.

AP® Theme: Contemporary Life
Context: Leisure and Sport

Les sports

En forêt de Fontainebleau

Chaque année, des millions de visiteurs vont en forêt de Fontainebleau attirés par les plus de 1.600 kilomètres de routes et de chemins de randonnée forestiers, par le site naturel d'escalade° et par les parcours acrobatiques en hauteur, ou PAH. Souvent appelée accrobranche, l'activité consiste à explorer la forêt en hauteur sur des structures fixées entre les arbres ou entre des supports artificiels. L'escalade naturelle est une autre activité populaire. Les rochers° de faible hauteur permettent aux grimpeurs° de pratiquer un type d'escalade sans corde, appelé «le bloc.» Réserve de bioshpère, la forêt de Fontainebleau offre un paysage varié et des vues exceptionnelles à ceux qui y pratiquent une activité physique.

AP® Theme: Contemporary Life
Context: Travel

Les destinations

Disneyland Paris

Ouvert° en 1992 sous le nom *Euro Disney Resort*, le parc d'attractions aujourd'hui appelé Disneyland Paris se trouve° à trente-deux kilomètres à l'est de° Paris. Le complexe compte° deux parcs à thèmes (un royaume° enchanté et un parc sur les thèmes du cinéma et de l'animation) et une soixantaine d'attractions. Le symbôle le plus connu du complexe, le Château de la Belle au bois dormant°, possède une particularité remarquable: son architecture est dans le style des contes de fée°, tandis que° les châteaux des autres parcs Disney représentent un style historique. Disneyland Paris est le parc d'attractions le plus visité de l'Europe, avec plus de 320 millions de visites depuis son ouverture°.

Qu'est-ce que vous avez appris? Complétez les phrases.

1. __Jean Dubuffet__ était le créateur de la closerie Falbala.

2. L'artiste a construit la villa Falbala parce qu'il voulait créer un __espace mental__ pour son œuvre.

3. __Euro Disney Resort__ était le nom original de Disneyland Paris.

4. À Disneyland Paris, l'architecture du château est dans le style des __contes de fée__.

5. Au Moyen Âge, neuf chemins principaux ont croisé à __Provins__.

6. Les plus grandes __foires de Champagne__ ont eu lieu à Provins.

7. Le jardinier principal du roi Louis XIV s'appelait __André Le Nôtre__.

8. Les plantes dans les jardins de Le Nôtre sont souvent en formes __géométriques__.

9. L'acronyme PAH signifie __parcours acrobatique en hauteur__

10. Le site d'escalade de la forêt de Fontainebleau est connu pour ses __rochers de faible hauteur__

Sur Internet

1. Trouvez quelques images des jardins de Le Nôtre. De quelle manière sont-ils similaires? Lequel est le plus visité?

2. Quelles autres particularités trouve-t-on à Disneyland Paris?

3. Trouvez un parc dans l'île-de-France où vous pouvez faire de l'accrobranche. Quels autres activités sont offertes?

---

chemins *routes* **foires** *fairs* **duraient** *lasted* **entourée** *surrounded* **remparts** *walls* **jardinier** *gardener* **suivi** *took* **illustre** *famed* **gagné** *earned* **architecte paysagiste** *landscape architect* **d'escalade** *rock climbing* **rochers** *boulders* **grimpeurs** *climbers* **Ouvert** *Opened* **se trouve** *is located* **à l'est de** *east of* **compte** *includes* **royaume** *kingdom* **Belle au bois dormant** *Sleeping Beauty* **contes de fée** *fairytales* **tandis que** *while* **ouverture** *opening*

Provins The city is also known for its famous **roses de Provins**, which have been cultivated there for centuries. During the Middle Ages the roses were said to have medicinal benefits. Today they are cultivated in **roseraies** and are used in both cuisine and cosmetics.

André Le Nôtre Le Nôtre's gardens require meticulous upkeep to maintain their manicured perfection. The gardens at Versailles cover almost 2,000 acres and have undergone five major replantations.

En forêt de Fontainebleau It wasn't until the early 2000s that adventure parks featuring ropes courses became popular recreation destinations in France. There are now about 500 locations in France dedicated to the activity, including an indoor facility in downtown Lyon.

Disneyland Paris In the 1990s, Disney considered hundreds of locations for its new park, including London and Barcelona, before choosing Paris, in part because of its flat terrain and moderate climate. Disneyland Paris celebrated its twenty-fifth anniversary in 2017 by renovating and adding several attractions and shows, including a new HyperSpace Mountain ride with a *Star Wars* theme, and a Disney Stars on Parade show.

 21st Century Skills

Information and Media Literacy: Sur Internet Students access and critically evaluate information from the Internet.

EXPANSION

Cultural Comparison Have students work in pairs to find out about another Disney theme park, such as the one in California or the one in Florida, and compare it with the one in Paris. They should visit the websites and compare prices, maps, cuisine, and lodging. Have them make a chart or diagram showing the results of their research and share it with the class. If any students have been to a Disney theme park, ask them to describe the experience to the class.

PRE-AP®

Presentational Speaking Have students prepare a one-minute presentation on Fontainebleau, Versailles, or Provins, in which they try to persuade their classmates to visit the location. They should include information not mentioned in the textbook, such as popular restaurants, monuments, and activities to do there. After they give their presentations, have the class vote on which location they will visit.

Savoir-faire

Lecture vhlcentral

Avant la lecture

AP® Theme: Beauty and Aesthetics
Context: Architecture, Contributions to World Artistic Heritage

STRATÉGIE

Guessing meaning from context

As you read in French, you will often see words you have not learned. You can guess what they mean by looking at surrounding words. Read this note and guess what **un deux-pièces** means.

> Johanne,
>
> Je cherchais un studio, mais j'ai trouvé un appartement plus grand: un deux-pièces près de mon travail! Le salon est grand et la chambre a deux placards. La cuisine a un frigo et une cuisinière, et la salle de bains a une baignoire. Et le loyer? Seulement 450 euros par mois!

If you guessed *a two-room apartment,* you are correct. You can conclude that someone is describing an apartment he or she will rent.

Examinez le texte

Regardez le texte et décrivez les photos. Quel va être le sujet de la lecture? Puis, trouvez ces mots et expressions dans le texte. Essayez de deviner leur sens (*to guess their meaning*).

ont été rajoutées were added	**autour du** around	**de haut** in height
de nombreux bassins numerous pools/fountains	**légumes** vegetables	**roi** King

Expérience personnelle

Avez-vous visité une résidence célèbre ou historique? Où? Quand? Comment était-ce? Un personnage historique a-t-il habité là? Qui? Parlez de cette visite à un(e) camarade.

À visiter près de Paris:
Le château de Versailles

La construction du célèbre° château de Versailles a commencé en 1623 sous le roi Louis XIII. Au départ, c'était un petit château où le roi logeait° quand il allait à la chasse°. Plus tard, en 1678, Louis XIV, aussi appelé le Roi-Soleil, a décidé de faire de Versailles sa résidence principale. Il a demandé à son architecte, Louis Le Vau, d'agrandir° le château, et à son premier peintre°, Charles Le Brun, de le décorer. Le Vau a fait construire, entre autres°, le Grand Appartement du Roi. La décoration de cet appartement de sept pièces était à la gloire du Roi-Soleil. La pièce la plus célèbre du château de Versailles est la galerie des Glaces°. C'est une immense pièce de 73 mètres de long, 10,50 mètres de large et 12,30 mètres de haut°. D'un côté, 17 fenêtres donnent° sur les jardins, et

de l'autre côté, il y a 17 arcades embellies de miroirs immenses. Au nord° de la galerie des Glaces, on trouve le salon de la Guerre°, et, au sud°, le salon de la Paix°. Quand on visite le château de Versailles, on peut également° voir de nombreuses autres pièces, ajoutées à différentes périodes, comme la chambre de la Reine°,

À l'intérieur du palais

plusieurs cuisines et salles à manger d'hiver et d'été, des bibliothèques, divers salons et cabinets, et plus de 18.000 m²° de galeries qui racontent°

Le château de Versailles et une fontaine

l'histoire de France en images. L'opéra, une grande salle où plus de° 700 personnes assistaient souvent à divers spectacles et bals, a aussi été ajouté plus tard. C'est dans cette salle que le futur roi Louis XVI et Marie-Antoinette ont été mariés. Partout° dans le château, on peut admirer une collection unique de meubles (lits, tables, fauteuils et chaises, bureaux, etc.) et de magnifiques tissus° (tapis, rideaux et tapisseries°). Le château de Versailles a aussi une chapelle et d'autres bâtiments, comme le Grand et le Petit Trianon. Autour du château, il y a des serres° et de magnifiques jardins avec de nombreux bassins°, fontaines et statues. Dans l'Orangerie, on trouve plus de 1.000 arbres°, et de nombreux fruits et légumes sont toujours cultivés dans le Potager° du Roi. L'Arboretum de Chèvreloup était le terrain de chasse des rois et on y° trouve aujourd'hui des arbres du monde entier°.

célèbre *famous* logeait *stayed* chasse *hunting* agrandir *enlarge* peintre *painter* entre autres *among other things* Glaces *Mirrors* haut *high* donnent *open* nord *north* Guerre *War* sud *south* Paix *Peace* également *also* Reine *Queen* m² (mètres carrés) *square meters* racontent *tell* plus de *more than* Partout *Everywhere* tissus *fabrics* tapisseries *tapestries* serres *greenhouses* bassins *ponds* arbres *trees* Potager *vegetable garden* y *there* entier *entire*

Après la lecture

Vrai ou faux? Indiquez si les phrases sont **vraies** ou **fausses**. Corrigez les phrases fausses.

1. Louis XIII habitait à Versailles toute l'année.
   Faux. Louis XIII logeait à Versailles quand il allait à la chasse.

2. Louis Le Vau est appelé le Roi-Soleil.
   Faux. Louis XIV est appelé le Roi-Soleil.

3. La galerie des Glaces est une grande pièce avec beaucoup de miroirs et de fenêtres.
   Vrai.

4. Il y a deux salons près de la galerie des Glaces.
   Vrai.

5. Aujourd'hui, au château de Versailles, il n'y a pas de meubles.
   Faux. Il y a une collection unique de meubles (lits, tables, fauteuils et chaises, bureaux, etc.).

6. Le château de Versailles n'a pas de jardins parce qu'il a été construit en ville.
   Faux. Il a des jardins: l'Orangerie, le Potager et l'Arboretum de Chèvreloup.

Répondez Répondez aux questions par des phrases complètes.

1. Comment était Versailles sous Louis XIII? Quand logeait-il là?
   C'était un petit château où le roi logeait quand il allait à la chasse.

2. Qu'est-ce que Louis XIV a fait du château?
   Il a fait de Versailles sa résidence principale. Il l'a agrandi et l'a décoré.

3. Qu'est-ce que Louis Le Vau a fait à Versailles?
   Il a construit, entre autres, le Grand Appartement du Roi.

4. Dans quelle salle Louis XVI et Marie-Antoinette ont-ils été mariés? Comment est cette salle?
   Ils ont été mariés dans l'Opéra. C'est une grande salle où plus de 700 personnes assistaient souvent à divers spectacles et bals.

5. Louis XVI est-il devenu roi avant ou après son mariage?
   Il est devenu roi après son mariage.

6. Le château de Versailles est-il composé d'un seul bâtiment? Expliquez.
   Non, le château a aussi une chapelle et d'autres bâtiments comme le Grand et le Petit Trianon.

Les personnages célèbres de Versailles

Par groupes de trois ou quatre, choisissez une des personnes mentionnées dans la lecture et faites des recherches (*research*) à son sujet. Préparez un rapport écrit (*written report*) à présenter à la classe. Vous pouvez (*may*) utiliser les ressources de votre bibliothèque ou Internet.

Vrai ou faux? Go over the answers with the class. For false items, have students point out where they found the correct information in the text. Expect and allow for some errors in vocabulary and grammar in students' answers.

Répondez Have students work with a partner and compare their answers. If they don't agree, tell them to locate the answer in the text. Expect and allow for some errors in vocabulary and grammar in students' answers.

Les personnages célèbres de Versailles Before assigning this activity, have students identify the people mentioned in the article and write their names on the board. To avoid duplication of efforts, you may want to assign each group a specific person. Encourage students to provide visuals with their presentations.

21ˢᵗ Century Skills

Creativity and Innovation Ask students to prepare a presentation on another French castle, inspired by the information on these two pages.

EXPANSION

Discussion Working in groups of three or four, have students discuss the features that they find most interesting or appealing about **le château de Versailles** and make a list of them.

TEACHING OPTIONS

Skimming Tell students to skim the text and underline all of the verbs in the **passé composé** and the **imparfait**. Then go through the text and ask volunteers to explain why each verb is in the **passé composé** or the **imparfait**.

Section Goals

In this section, students will:
- learn to write a narrative using the **passé composé** and the **imparfait**
- write a story about the past

Key Standards

1.3, 3.1, 5.1

Stratégie Write these sentences on the board. **1. Le film a fini à minuit. 2. J'ai fait mon lit, j'ai rangé ma chambre et j'ai passé l'aspirateur. 3. Le bébé a dormi parce qu'il avait sommeil. 4. Quand nous étions au restaurant, nous avons parlé avec nos copains.** Ask volunteers to explain why the **passé composé** or the **imparfait** was used in each case. Then have the class write sentences for their compositions.

Presentational Writing: Thème Explain that the story students are going to write will be about events that occurred in the past. Encourage them to brainstorm as many details as possible before they begin writing.

Écriture

STRATÉGIE

Mastering the past tenses

In French, when you write about events that occurred in the past, you need to know when to use the **passé composé** and when to use the **imparfait**. A good understanding of the uses of each tense will make it much easier to determine which one to use as you write.

Look at the following summary of the uses of the **passé composé** and the **imparfait**. Write your own example sentence for each of the rules described.

Passé composé vs. imparfait

Passé composé

1. Actions viewed as completed

   _____

2. Beginning or end of past actions

   _____

3. Change in mental, emotional or physical state

   _____

Imparfait

1. Ongoing past actions

   _____

2. Habitual past actions

   _____

3. Mental, physical, and emotional states and characteristics of the past

   _____

With a partner, compare your example sentences. Use the sentences as a guide to help you decide which tense to use as you are writing a story about something that happened in the past.

Thème

Écrire une histoire

Avant l'écriture

1. Quand vous étiez petit(e), vous habitiez dans la maison ou l'appartement de vos rêves (*of your dreams*).

   ■ Vous allez décrire cette maison ou cet appartement.

   ■ Vous allez décrire les différentes pièces, les meubles et les objets décoratifs.

   ■ Vous allez parler de votre pièce préférée et de ce que (*what*) vous aimiez faire dans cette pièce.

Ensuite, imaginez qu'il y ait eu (*was*) un cambriolage (*burglary*) dans cette maison ou dans cet appartement. Vous allez alors décrire ce qui est arrivé (*what happened*).

> ### Coup de main
>
> Here are some terms that you may find useful in your narration.
>
> | | |
> |---|---|
> | **le voleur** | *thief* |
> | **casser** | *to break* |
> | **j'ai vu** | *I saw* |
> | **manquer** | *to be missing* |

TEACHING OPTIONS

Avant l'écriture Say or read aloud some French past-tense sentences and have students identify the **passé composé** and **imparfait** forms. For each sentence, have students say why one form or the other was used. Review with them the situations and contexts that trigger the use of each tense.

Preview the use of the arrow diagram. Copy it on the board, making sure it is large enough to write inside. Start out with a description of the setting using the **imparfait** and write those sentences inside the arrow. Then have students volunteer possible completed actions using the **passé composé** and write them on the lines that intersect the arrow.

2. Utilisez le diagramme pour noter les éléments de votre histoire. Écrivez les éléments où il faut employer l'imparfait dans la partie IMPARFAIT et les éléments où il faut employer le passé composé dans les parties PASSÉ COMPOSÉ.

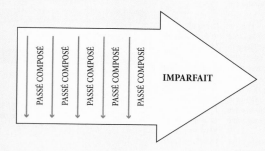

3. Échangez votre diagramme avec le diagramme d'un(e) partenaire. Est-ce qu'il faut changer quelque chose sur son diagramme? Si oui, expliquez pourquoi.

Écriture

Utilisez le diagramme pour écrire votre histoire. Écrivez trois paragraphes:

- le premier sur la présentation générale de la maison ou de l'appartement

- le deuxième sur votre pièce préférée et pourquoi vous l'avez choisie

- le troisième sur le cambriolage: les faits (*facts*) et vos réactions.

Quand j'étais petit(e), j'habitais dans un château, en France. Le château était dans une petite ville près de Paris. Il y avait un grand jardin, avec beaucoup d'animaux. Il y avait douze pièces...

Ma pièce préférée était la cuisine parce que j'aimais faire la cuisine et...

Un jour, mes parents et moi, nous sommes rentrés de vacances...

Après l'écriture

1. Échangez votre histoire avec celle (*the one*) d'un(e) partenaire. Répondez à ces questions pour commenter son travail.

- Votre partenaire a-t-il/elle correctement utilisé l'imparfait et le passé composé?

- A-t-il/elle écrit trois paragraphes qui correspondent aux descriptions de sa maison ou de son appartement, de sa pièce préférée et du cambriolage?

- Quel(s) détail(s) ajouteriez-vous (*would you add*)? Quel(s) détail(s) enlèveriez-vous (*would you delete*)? Quel(s) autre(s) commentaire(s) avez-vous pour votre partenaire?

2. Corrigez votre histoire d'après (*according to*) les commentaires de votre partenaire. Relisez votre travail pour éliminer ces problèmes:

- des fautes (*errors*) d'orthographe

- des fautes de ponctuation

- des fautes de conjugaison

- des fautes d'accord (*agreement*) des adjectifs

- un mauvais emploi (*use*) de la grammaire

TEACHING OPTIONS

Écriture Supply students with some useful expressions to use for their compositions. 1. Ongoing past-tense description: **toujours, tous les jours, d'habitude, normalement, en général/ généralement, chaque fois, de temps en temps** 2. Completed past actions: **tout à coup, à un moment, à ce moment-là, puis, ensuite, après, plus tard, enfin, finalement**

TEACHING OPTIONS

Après l'écriture When students have completed their stories, have them work in pairs or small groups to create a dramatic reenactment of the story. They can use voiceover narration for the descriptive part, then act out the completed actions that are part of the robbery and its aftermath. Encourage students to be creative and to use props and posters to set the stage and tell the story.

Key Standards

4.1

Suggestion Tell students that an easy way to study from **Vocabulaire** is to cover up the French half of each section, leaving only the English equivalents exposed. They can then quiz themselves on the French items. To focus on the English equivalents of the French entries, they simply reverse this process.

21ˢᵗ Century Skills

Creativity and Innovation
Ask students to prepare a list of three products or perspectives they learned about in this unit to share with the class. Consider asking them to focus on the **Culture** and **Panorama** sections.

21ˢᵗ Century Skills

Leadership and Responsibility: Extension Project
If you have access to students in a Francophone country, have students decide on three questions they want to ask the partner class related to this unit's topic. Based on the responses they receive, work as a class to explain to the partner class one aspect of their responses that surprised the class and why.

Leçon 8A

Les parties d'une maison

un balcon	balcony
une cave	basement, cellar
une chambre	bedroom
un couloir	hallway
une cuisine	kitchen
un escalier	staircase
un garage	garage
un jardin	garden; yard
un mur	wall
une pièce	room
une salle à manger	dining room
une salle de bains	bathroom
une salle de séjour	living/family room
un salon	formal living/sitting room
un sous-sol	basement
les toilettes/W.-C.	restrooms/toilet

Chez soi

un(e) propriétaire	owner
un appartement	apartment
un immeuble	building
un logement	housing
un loyer	rent
un quartier	area, neighborhood
un studio	studio (apartment)
une affiche	poster
une armoire	armoire, wardrobe
une baignoire	bathtub
un canapé	couch
une commode	dresser, chest of drawers
une douche	shower
une étagère	shelf
un fauteuil	armchair
une fleur	flower
une lampe	lamp
un lavabo	bathroom sink
un meuble	piece of furniture
un miroir	mirror
un placard	closet, cupboard
un rideau	drape, curtain
un tapis	rug
un tiroir	drawer
déménager	to move out
emménager	to move in
louer	to rent

Expressions utiles

See p. 315.

Expressions that signal a past tense

d'habitude	usually
une (deux, etc.) fois	once (twice, etc.)
un jour	one day
parfois	sometimes
soudain	suddenly
souvent	often
toujours	always
tous les jours	everyday
tout à coup/tout d'un coup	all of a sudden

Verbes

vivre	to live

Leçon 8B

Les tâches ménagères

une tâche ménagère	household chore
balayer	to sweep
débarrasser la table	to clear the table
enlever/faire la poussière	to dust
essuyer la vaisselle/la table	to dry the dishes/to wipe the table
faire la lessive	to do the laundry
faire le lit	to make the bed
faire le ménage	to do the housework
faire la vaisselle	to do the dishes
laver	to wash
mettre la table	to set the table
passer l'aspirateur	to vacuum
ranger	to tidy up; to put away
repasser (le linge)	to iron (the laundry)
salir	to soil, to make dirty
sortir la/les poubelle(s)	to take out the trash
propre	clean
sale	dirty

Chez soi

un balai	broom
une couverture	blanket
les draps (m.)	sheets
un évier	kitchen sink
un oreiller	pillow

Les appareils ménagers

un appareil électrique/ménager	electrical/household appliance
une cafetière	coffeemaker
un congélateur	freezer
une cuisinière	stove
un fer à repasser	iron
un four (à micro-ondes)	(microwave) oven
un frigo	refrigerator
un grille-pain	toaster
un lave-linge	washing machine
un lave-vaisselle	dishwasher
un sèche-linge	clothes dryer

Expressions utiles

See p. 333.

Locutions de temps

autrefois	in the past

Verbes

connaître	to know, to be familiar with
reconnaître	to recognize
savoir	to know (facts), to know how to do something

Appendices

The *impératif*

Point de départ The **impératif** is the form of a verb that is used to give commands or to offer directions, hints, and suggestions. With command forms, you do not use subject pronouns.

- Form the **tu** command of **-er** verbs by dropping the **-s** from the present tense form. Note that **aller** also follows this pattern.

Réserve deux chambres.
Reserve two rooms.

Ne travaille pas.
Don't work.

Va au marché.
Go to the market.

- The **nous** and **vous** command forms of **-er** verbs are the same as the present tense forms.

Nettoyez votre chambre.
Clean your room.

Mangeons au restaurant ce soir.
Let's eat at the restaurant tonight.

- For **-ir** verbs, **-re** verbs, and most irregular verbs, the command forms are identical to the present tense forms.

Finis la salade.
Finish the salad.

Attendez dix minutes.
Wait ten minutes.

Faisons du yoga.
Let's do some yoga.

The *impératif* of *avoir* and *être*

	avoir	être
(tu)	aie	sois
(nous)	ayons	soyons
(vous)	ayez	soyez

- The forms of **avoir** and **être** in the **impératif** are irregular.

Aie confiance.
Have confidence.

Ne **soyons** pas en retard.
Let's not be late.

- An object pronoun can be added to the end of an affirmative command. Use a hyphen to separate them. Use **moi** and **toi** for the first- and second-person object pronouns.

Permettez-moi de vous aider.
Allow me to help you.

Achète le dictionnaire et **utilise-le**.
Buy the dictionary and use it.

- In negative commands, place object pronouns between **ne** and the verb. Use **me** and **te** for the first- and second-person object pronouns.

Ne **me montre** pas les réponses, **s'il te plaît.**
Please don't show me the answers.

Cette photo est fragile. Ne **la touchez** pas.
That picture is fragile. Don't touch it.

Glossary of Grammatical Terms

ADJECTIVE A word that modifies, or describes, a noun or pronoun.

des livres **amusants**
*some **funny** books*

une **jolie** fleur
*a **pretty** flower*

Demonstrative adjective An adjective that specifies which noun a speaker is referring to.

cette chemise
***this** shirt*

ce placard
***this** closet*

cet hôtel
***this** hotel*

ces boîtes
***these** boxes.*

Possessive adjective An adjective that indicates ownership or possession.

ma belle montre
***my** beautiful watch*

C'est **son** cousin.
*This is **his/her** cousin.*

tes crayons
***your** pencils*

Ce sont **leurs** tantes.
*Those are **their** aunts.*

ADVERB A word that modifies, or describes, a verb, adjective, or other adverb.

Michael parle **couramment** français.
*Michael speaks French **fluently**.*

Elle lui parle **très** franchement.
*She speaks to him **very** honestly.*

ARTICLE A word that points out a noun in either a specific or a non-specific way.

Definite article An article that points out a noun in a specific way.

le marché
***the** market*

la valise
***the** suitcase*

les dictionnaires
***the** dictionaries*

les mots
***the** words*

Indefinite article An article that points out a noun in a general, non-specific way.

un vélo
a bike

une fille
a girl

des oiseaux
***some** birds*

des affiches
***some** posters*

CLAUSE A group of words that contains both a conjugated verb and a subject, either expressed or implied.

Main (or Independent) clause A clause that can stand alone as a complete sentence.

J'ai un manteau vert.
I have a green coat.

Subordinate (or Dependent) clause A clause that does not express a complete thought and therefore cannot stand alone as a sentence.

Je travaille dans un restaurant **parce que j'ai besoin d'argent**.
*I work in a restaurant **because I need money**.*

COMPARATIVE A construction used with an adjective or adverb to express a comparison between two people, places, or things.

Thomas est **plus petit** qu'Adrien.
*Thomas is **shorter than** Adrien.*

En Corse, il pleut **moins souvent qu'**en Alsace.
*In Corsica, it rains **less often than** in Alsace.*

Cette maison n'a pas **autant de fenêtres** que l'autre.
*This house does not have **as many windows as** the other one.*

CONJUGATION A set of the forms of a verb for a specific tense or mood, or the process by which these verb forms are presented.

Imparfait conjugation of **chanter**:

je chant**ais**	nous chant**ions**
tu chant**ais**	vous chant**iez**
il/elle chant**ait**	ils/elles chant**aient**

CONJUNCTION A word used to connect words, clauses, or phrases.

Suzanne **et** Pierre habitent en Suisse.
*Suzanne **and** Pierre live in Switzerland.*

Je ne dessine pas très bien, **mais** j'aime les cours de dessin.
*I don't draw very well, **but** I like art classes.*

CONTRACTION The joining of two words into one. In French, the contractions are **au**, **aux**, **du**, and **des**.

Ma sœur est allée **au** concert hier soir.
*My sister went **to a** concert last night.*

Il a parlé **aux** voisins cet après-midi.
*He talked **to the** neighbors this afternoon.*

Je retire de l'argent **du** distributeur automatique.
*I withdraw money **from the** ATM machine.*

Nous avons campé près **du** village.
*We camped **near the** village.*

DIRECT OBJECT A noun or pronoun that directly receives the action of the verb.

Thomas lit **un livre**.   Je **l'**ai vu hier.
*Thomas reads **a book**.*   *I saw **him** yesterday.*

GENDER The grammatical categorizing of certain kinds of words, such as nouns and pronouns, as masculine, feminine, or neuter.

Masculine
articles **le, un**
pronouns **il, lui, le, celui-ci, celui-là, lequel**
adjective **élégant**

Feminine
articles **la, une**
pronouns **elle, la, celle-ci, celle-là, laquelle**
adjective **élégante**

IMPERSONAL EXPRESSION A third-person expression with no expressed or specific subject.

Il pleut.   **C'est** très important.
It's raining.   *It's very important.*

INDIRECT OBJECT A noun or pronoun that receives the action of the verb indirectly; the object, often a living being, to or for whom an action is performed.

Éric donne un livre **à Linda**.
*Éric gave a book **to Linda**.*

Le professeur **m'**a donné une bonne note.
*The teacher gave **me** a good mark.*

INFINITIVE The basic form of a verb. Infinitives in French end in **-er**, **-ir**, **-oir**, or **-re**.

parler	**finir**	**savoir**	**prendre**
to speak	*to finish*	*to know*	*to take*

INTERROGATIVE An adjective or pronoun used to ask a question.

Qui parle?
***Who** is speaking?*

Combien de biscuits as-tu achetés?
***How many** cookies did you buy?*

Que penses-tu faire aujourd'hui?
***What** do you plan to do today?*

INVERSION Changing the word order of a sentence, often to form a question.

Statement: Elle a vendu sa voiture.

Inversion: A-t-elle vendu sa voiture?

MOOD A grammatical distinction of verbs that indicates whether the verb is intended to make a statement or command or to express a doubt, emotion, or condition contrary to fact.

Conditional mood Verb forms used to express what would be done or what would happen under certain circumstances, or to make a polite request, soften a demand, express what someone could or should do, or to state a contrary-to-fact situation.

Il irait se promener s'il avait le temps.
He would go for a walk if he had the time.

Pourrais-tu éteindre la lumière, s'il te plaît?
Would you turn off the light, please?

Je devrais lui parler gentiment.
I should talk to her nicely.

Imperative mood Verb forms used to make commands or suggestions.

Parle lentement.	**Venez** avec moi.
***Speak** slowly.*	***Come** with me.*

Indicative mood Verb forms used to state facts, actions, and states considered to be real.

Je sais qu'**il a** un chat.
*I know that **he has** a cat.*

Subjunctive mood Verb forms used principally in subordinate (dependent) clauses to express wishes, desires, emotions, doubts, and certain conditions, such as contrary-to-fact situations.

Il est important que **tu finisses** tes devoirs.
*It's important that **you finish** your homework.*

Je doute que **Louis ait** assez d'argent.
*I doubt that **Louis has** enough money.*

NOUN A word that identifies people, animals, places, things, and ideas.

homme	**chat**	**Belgique**
man	*cat*	*Belgium*
maison	**livre**	**amitié**
house	*book*	*friendship*

NUMBER A grammatical term that refers to singular or plural. Nouns in French and English have number. Other parts of a sentence, such as adjectives, articles, and verbs, can also have number.

Singular	**Plural**
une chose	**des** choses
a thing	*some things*
le professeur	**les** professeurs
the professor	*the professors*

NUMBERS Words that represent amounts.

Cardinal numbers Words that show specific amounts.

cinq minutes	l'année **deux mille six**
***five** minutes*	*the year **2006***

Ordinal numbers Words that indicate the order of a noun in a series.

le **quatrième** joueur	la **dixième** fois
*the **fourth** player*	*the **tenth** time*

PAST PARTICIPLE A past form of the verb used in compound tenses. The past participle may also be used as an adjective, but it must then agree in number and gender with the word it modifies.

Ils ont beaucoup **marché**.
*They have **walked** a lot.*

Je n'ai pas **préparé** mon examen.
*I haven't **prepared** for my exam.*

Il y a une fenêtre **ouverte** dans le salon.
*There is an **open** window in the living room.*

PERSON The form of the verb or pronoun that indicates the speaker, the one spoken to, or the one spoken about. In French, as in English, there are three persons: first, second, and third.

Person	Singular		Plural	
1st	**je**	*I*	**nous**	*we*
2nd	**tu**	*you*	**vous**	*you*
3rd	**il/elle**	*he/she/it*	**ils/elles**	*they*
	on	*one*		

PREPOSITION A word or words that describe(s) the relationship, most often in time or space, between two other words.

Annie habite **loin de** Paris.
*Annie lives **far from** Paris.*

Le blouson est **dans** la voiture.
*The jacket is **in** the car.*

Martine s'est coiffée **avant de** sortir.
*Martine combed her hair **before** going out.*

PRONOUN A word that takes the place of a noun or nouns.

Demonstrative pronoun A pronoun that takes the place of a specific noun.

Je veux **celui-ci**.
*I want **this one**.*

*Marc préférait **ceux-là**.*
*Marc preferred **those**.*

Object pronoun A pronoun that functions as a direct or indirect object of the verb.

Elle **lui** donne un cadeau.
*She gives **him** a present.*

Frédéric **me l'**a apporté.
*Frédéric brought **it** to **me**.*

Reflexive pronoun A pronoun that indicates that the action of a verb is performed by the subject on itself. These pronouns are often expressed in English with -*self*: *myself, yourself,* etc.

Je **me lave** avant de sortir.
*I **wash (myself)** before going out.*

Marie **s'est couchée** à onze heures et demie.
*Marie **went to bed** at eleven-thirty.*

Relative pronoun A pronoun that connects a subordinate clause to a main clause.

Le garçon **qui** nous a écrit vient nous voir demain.
*The boy **who** wrote us is coming to visit tomorrow.*

Je sais **que** nous avons beaucoup de choses à faire.
*I know **that** we have a lot of things to do.*

Subject pronoun A pronoun that replaces the name or title of a person or thing, and acts as the subject of a verb.

Tu vas partir.
***You** are going to leave.*

Il arrive demain.
***He** arrives tomorrow.*

SUBJECT A noun or pronoun that performs the action of a verb and is often implied by the verb.

Marine va au supermarché.
***Marine** goes to the supermarket.*

Ils travaillent beaucoup.
***They** work a lot.*

Ces livres sont très chers.
***Those books** are very expensive.*

SUPERLATIVE A word or construction used with an adjective, adverb or a noun to express the highest or lowest degree of a specific quality among three or more people, places, or things.

Le cours de français est **le plus intéressant**.
*The French class is **the most interesting**.*

Romain court **le moins rapidement**.
*Romain runs **the least fast**.*

C'est son jardin qui a **le plus d'arbres**.
*It is her garden that has **the most trees**.*

TENSE A set of verb forms that indicates the time of an action or state: past, present, or future

Compound tense A two-word tense made up of an auxiliary verb and a present or past participle. In French, there are two auxiliary verbs: **être** and **avoir**.

Le colis n'**est** pas encore **arrivé**.
*The package **has** not **arrived** yet.*

Elle **a réussi** son examen.
*She **has passed** her exam.*

Simple tense A tense expressed by a single verb form.

Timothée **jouait** au volley-ball pendant les vacances.
*Timothée **played** volleyball during his vacation.*

Joëlle **parlera** à sa mère demain.
*Joëlle **will speak** with her mom tomorrow.*

VERB A word that expresses actions or states-of-being.

Auxiliary verb A verb used with a present or past participle to form a compound tense. **Avoir** is the most commonly used auxiliary verb in French.

Ils **ont** vu les éléphants.
*They **have** seen the elephants.*

J'espère que tu **as** mangé.
*I hope you **have** eaten.*

Reflexive verb A verb that describes an action performed by the subject on itself and is always used with a reflexive pronoun.

Je **me suis acheté** une voiture neuve.
*I **bought myself** a new car.*

Pierre et Adeline **se lèvent** très tôt.
*Pierre and Adeline **get (themselves) up** very early.*

Spelling-change verb A verb that undergoes a predictable change in spelling in the various conjugations.

acheter	e → è	nous achetons	j'ach**è**te
espérer	é → è	nous espérons	j'esp**è**re
appeler	l → ll	nous appelons	j'appe**ll**e
envoyer	y → i	nous envoyons	j'envo**i**e
essayer	y → i	nous essayons	j'essa**i**e/ j'essaye

Verb Conjugation Tables

Each verb in this list is followed by a model verb conjugated according to the same pattern. The number in parentheses indicates where in the verb tables you can find the conjugated forms of the model verb. Reminder: All reflexive (pronominal) verbs use **être** as their auxiliary verb in the **passé composé**. The infinitives of reflexive verbs begin with **se (s')**.

* = This verb, unlike its model, takes **être** in the **passé composé**.
† = This verb, unlike its model, takes **avoir** in the **passé composé**.
In the tables you will find the infinitive, past participles, and all the forms of each model verb you have learned.

abolir like finir (2)
aborder like parler (1)
abriter like parler (1)
accepter like parler (1)
accompagner like parler (1)
accueillir like ouvrir (31)
acheter (7)
adorer like parler (1)
afficher like parler (1)
aider like parler (1)
aimer like parler (1)
aller (13) **p.c.** with **être**
allumer like parler (1)
améliorer like parler (1)
amener like acheter (7)
animer like parler (1)
apercevoir like recevoir (36)
appeler (8)
applaudir like finir (2)
apporter like parler (1)
apprendre like prendre (35)
arrêter like parler (1)
arriver* like parler (1)
assister like parler (1)
attacher like parler (1)
attendre like vendre (3)
attirer like parler (1)
avoir (4)
balayer like essayer (10)
bavarder like parler (1)
boire (15)
bricoler like parler (1)
bronzer like parler (1)
célébrer like préférer (12)
chanter like parler (1)
chasser like parler (1)

chercher like parler (1)
choisir like finir (2)
classer like parler (1)
commander like parler (1)
commencer (9)
composer like parler (1)
comprendre like prendre (35)
compter like parler (1)
conduire (16)
connaître (17)
consacrer like parler (1)
considérer like préférer (12)
construire like conduire (16)
continuer like parler (1)
courir (18)
coûter like parler (1)
couvrir like ouvrir (31)
croire (19)
cuisiner like parler (1)
danser like parler (1)
débarrasser like parler (1)
décider like parler (1)
découvrir like ouvrir (31)
décrire like écrire (22)
décrocher like parler (1)
déjeuner like parler (1)
demander like parler (1)
démarrer like parler (1)
déménager like manger (11)
démissionner like parler (1)
dépasser like parler (1)
dépendre like vendre (3)
dépenser like parler (1)
déposer like parler (1)
descendre* like vendre (3)
désirer like parler (1)

dessiner like parler (1)
détester like parler (1)
détruire like conduire (16)
développer like parler (1)
devenir like venir (41)
devoir (20)
dîner like parler (1)
dire (21)
diriger like parler (1)
discuter like parler (1)
divorcer like commencer (9)
donner like parler (1)
douter (20)
dormir† like partir (32)
douter like parler (1)
durer like parler (1)
échapper like parler (1)
échouer like parler (1)
écouter like parler (1)
écrire (22)
effacer like commencer (9)
embaucher like parler (1)
emménager like manger (11)
emmener like acheter (7)
employer like essayer (10)
emprunter like parler (1)
enfermer like parler (1)
enlever like acheter (7)
enregistrer like parler (1)
enseigner like parler (1)
entendre like vendre (3)
entourer like parler (1)
entrer* like parler (1)
entretenir like tenir (40)
envahir like finir (2)
envoyer like essayer (10)
épouser like parler (1)

dessiner like parler (1)

espérer like préférer (12)
essayer (10)
essuyer like essayer (10)
éteindre (24)
éternuer like parler (1)
étrangler like parler (1)
être (5)
étudier like parler (1)
éviter like parler (1)
exiger like manger (11)
expliquer like parler (1)
explorer like parler (1)
faire (25)
falloir (26)
fermer like parler (1)
fêter like parler (1)
finir (2)
fonctionner like parler (1)
fonder like parler (1)
freiner like parler (1)
fréquenter like parler (1)
fumer like parler (1)
gagner like parler (1)
garder like parler (1)
garer like parler (1)
gaspiller like parler (1)
enfler like parler (1)
goûter like parler (1)
graver like parler (1)
grossir like finir (2)
guérir like finir (2)
habiter like parler (1)
imprimer like parler (1)
indiquer like parler (1)
interdire like dire (21)
inviter like parler (1)

jeter like appeler (8)
jouer like parler (1)
laisser like parler (1)
laver like parler (1)
lire (27)
loger like manger (11)
louer like parler (1)
lutter like parler (1)
maigrir like finir (2)
maintenir like tenir (40)
manger (11)
marcher like parler (1)
mêler like préférer (12)
mener like parler (1)
mettre (28)
monter* like parler (1)
montrer like parler (1)
mourir (29); **p.c.** with **être**
nager like manger (11)
naître (30); **p.c.** with **être**
nettoyer like essayer (10)
noter like parler (1)
obtenir like tenir (40)
offrir like ouvrir (31)
organiser like parler (1)
oublier like parler (1)
ouvrir (31)
parler (1)
partager like manger (11)
partir (32); **p.c.** with **être**
passer like parler (1)
patienter like parler (1)
patiner like parler (1)
payer like essayer (10)
penser like parler (1)
perdre like vendre (3)
permettre like mettre (28)
pleuvoir (33)
plonger like manger (11)
polluer like parler (1)
porter like parler (1)
poser like parler (1)
posséder like préférer (12)
poster like parler (1)
pouvoir (34)
pratiquer like parler (1)
préférer (12)

prélever like parler (1)
prendre (35)
préparer like parler (1)
présenter like parler (1)
préserver like parler (1)
prêter like parler (1)
prévenir like tenir (40)
produire like conduire (16)
profiter like parler (1)
promettre like mettre (28)
proposer like parler (1)
protéger like préférer (12)
provenir like venir (41)
publier like parler (1)
quitter like parler (1)
raccrocher like parler (1)
ranger like manger (11)
réaliser like parler (1)
recevoir (36)
recommander like parler (1)
reconnaître like connaître (17)
recycler like parler (1)
réduire like conduire (16)
réfléchir like finir (2)
regarder like parler (1)
régner like préférer (12)
remplacer like parler (1)
remplir like finir (2)
rencontrer like parler (1)
rendre like vendre (3)
rentrer* like parler (1)
renvoyer like essayer (10)
réparer like parler (1)
repasser like parler (1)
répéter like préférer (12)
repeupler like parler (1)
répondre like vendre (3)
réserver like parler (1)
rester* like parler (1)
retenir like tenir (40)
retirer like parler (1)
retourner* like parler (1)
retrouver like parler (1)
réussir like finir (2)
revenir like venir (41)

revoir like voir (42)
rire (37)
rouler like parler (1)
salir like finir (2)
s'amuser like se laver (6)
s'asseoir (14)
sauvegarder like parler (1)
sauver like parler (1)
savoir (38)
se brosser like se laver (6)
se coiffer like se laver (6)
se composer like se laver (6)
se connecter like se laver (6)
se coucher like se laver (6)
se croiser like se laver (6)
se dépêcher like se laver (6)
se déplacer* like commencer (9)
se déshabiller like se laver (6)
se détendre* like vendre (3)
se disputer like se laver (6)
s'embrasser like se laver (6)
s'endormir like partir (32)
s'énerver like se laver (6)
s'ennuyer* like essayer (10)
s'excuser like se laver (6)
se fouler like se laver (6)
s'installer like se laver (6)
se laver (6)
se lever* like acheter (7)
se maquiller like se laver (6)
se marier like se laver (6)
se promener* like acheter (7)
se rappeler* like appeler (8)
se raser like se laver (6)
se rebeller like se laver (6)
se réconcilier like se laver (6)
se relever* like acheter (7)
se reposer like se laver (6)
se réveiller like se laver (6)

servir† like partir (32)
se sécher* like préférer (12)
se souvenir like venir (41)
se tromper like se laver (6)
s'habiller like se laver (6)
sentir† like partir (32)
signer like parler (1)
s'inquiéter* like préférer (12)
s'intéresser like se laver (6)
skier like parler (1)
s'occuper like se laver (6)
sonner like parler (1)
s'orienter like se laver (6)
sortir like partir (32)
sourire like rire (37)
souffrir like ouvrir (31)
souhaiter like parler (1)
subvenir† like venir (41)
suffire like lire (27)
suggérer like préférer (12)
suivre (39)
surfer like parler (1)
surprendre like prendre (35)
télécharger like parler (1)
téléphoner like parler (1)
tenir (40)
tomber* like parler (1)
tourner like parler (1)
tousser like parler (1)
traduire like conduire (16)
travailler like parler (1)
traverser like parler (1)
trouver like parler (1)
tuer like parler (1)
utiliser like parler (1)
valoir like falloir (26)
vendre (3)
venir (41); **p.c.** with **être**
vérifier like parler (1)
visiter like parler (1)
vivre like suivre (39)
voir (42)
vouloir (43)
voyager like manger (11)

Regular verbs

Infinitive	INDICATIVE					CONDITIONAL	SUBJUNCTIVE	IMPERATIVE
Past participle	Subject Pronouns	Present	Passé composé	Imperfect	Future	Present	Present	
1 parler *(to speak)* parlé	je (j')	parle	ai parlé	parlais	parlerai	parlerais	parle	
	tu	parles	as parlé	parlais	parleras	parlerais	parles	parle
	il/elle/on	parle	a parlé	parlait	parlera	parlerait	parle	
	nous	parlons	avons parlé	parlions	parlerons	parlerions	parlions	parlons
	vous	parlez	avez parlé	parliez	parlerez	parleriez	parliez	parlez
	ils/elles	parlent	ont parlé	parlaient	parleront	parleraient	parlent	
2 finir *(to finish)* fini	je (j')	finis	ai fini	finissais	finirai	finirais	finisse	
	tu	finis	as fini	finissais	finiras	finirais	finisses	finis
	il/elle/on	finit	a fini	finissait	finira	finirait	finisse	
	nous	finissons	avons fini	finissions	finirons	finirions	finissions	finissons
	vous	finissez	avez fini	finissiez	finirez	finiriez	finissiez	finissez
	ils/elles	finissent	ont fini	finissaient	finiront	finiraient	finissent	
3 vendre *(to sell)* vendu	je (j')	vends	ai vendu	vendais	vendrai	vendrais	vende	
	tu	vends	as vendu	vendais	vendras	vendrais	vendes	vends
	il/elle/on	vend	a vendu	vendait	vendra	vendrait	vende	
	nous	vendons	avons vendu	vendions	vendrons	vendrions	vendions	vendons
	vous	vendez	avez vendu	vendiez	vendrez	vendriez	vendiez	vendez
	ils/elles	vendent	ont vendu	vendaient	vendront	vendraient	vendent	

Auxiliary verbs: *avoir* and *être*

Infinitive / Past participle	Subject Pronouns	INDICATIVE Present	INDICATIVE Passé composé	INDICATIVE Imperfect	INDICATIVE Future	CONDITIONAL Present	SUBJUNCTIVE Present	IMPERATIVE
4 avoir *(to have)*	j'	ai	ai eu	avais	aurai	aurais	aie	
	tu	as	as eu	avais	auras	aurais	aies	aie
	il/elle/on	a	a eu	avait	aura	aurait	ait	
eu	nous	avons	avons eu	avions	aurons	aurions	ayons	ayons
	vous	avez	avez eu	aviez	aurez	auriez	ayez	ayez
	ils/elles	ont	ont eu	avaient	auront	auraient	aient	
5 être *(to be)*	je (j')	suis	ai été	étais	serai	serais	sois	
	tu	es	as été	étais	seras	serais	sois	sois
	il/elle/on	est	a été	était	sera	serait	soit	
été	nous	sommes	avons été	étions	serons	serions	soyons	soyons
	vous	êtes	avez été	étiez	serez	seriez	soyez	soyez
	ils/elles	sont	ont été	étaient	seront	seraient	soient	

Reflexive (Pronominal)

Infinitive / Past participle	Subject Pronouns	INDICATIVE Present	INDICATIVE Passé composé	INDICATIVE Imperfect	INDICATIVE Future	CONDITIONAL Present	SUBJUNCTIVE Present	IMPERATIVE
6 se laver *(to wash oneself)*	je	me lave	me suis lavé(e)	me lavais	me laverai	me laverais	me lave	
	tu	te laves	t'es lavé(e)	te lavais	te laveras	te laverais	te laves	lave-toi
	il/elle/on	se lave	s'est lavé(e)	se lavait	se lavera	se laverait	se lave	
lavé	nous	nous lavons	nous sommes lavé(e)s	nous lavions	nous laverons	nous laverions	nous lavions	lavons-nous
	vous	vous lavez	vous êtes lavé(e)s	vous laviez	vous laverez	vous laveriez	vous laviez	lavez-vous
	ils/elles	se lavent	se sont lavé(e)s	se lavaient	se laveront	se laveraient	se lavent	

Verb Conjugation Tables

Verbs with spelling changes

Infinitive / Past participle	Subject Pronouns	INDICATIVE Present	Passé composé	Imperfect	Future	CONDITIONAL Present	SUBJUNCTIVE Present	IMPERATIVE
7 acheter *(to buy)*	j'	achète	ai acheté	achetais	achèterai	achèterais	achète	
	tu	achètes	as acheté	achetais	achèteras	achèterais	achètes	achète
	il/elle/on	achète	a acheté	achetait	achètera	achèterait	achète	
acheté	nous	achetons	avons acheté	achetions	achèterons	achèterions	achetions	achetons
	vous	achetez	avez acheté	achetiez	achèterez	achèteriez	achetiez	achetez
	ils/elles	achètent	ont acheté	achetaient	achèteront	achèteraient	achètent	
8 appeler *(to call)*	j'	appelle	ai appelé	appelais	appellerai	appellerais	appelle	
	tu	appelles	as appelé	appelais	appelleras	appellerais	appelles	appelle
	il/elle/on	appelle	a appelé	appelait	appellera	appellerait	appelle	
appelé	nous	appelons	avons appelé	appelions	appellerons	appellerions	appelions	appelons
	vous	appelez	avez appelé	appeliez	appellerez	appelleriez	appeliez	appelez
	ils/elles	appellent	ont appelé	appelaient	appelleront	appelleraient	appellent	
9 commencer *(to begin)*	je (j')	commence	ai commencé	commençais	commencerai	commencerais	commence	
	tu	commences	as commencé	commençais	commenceras	commencerais	commences	commence
	il/elle/on	commence	a commencé	commençait	commencera	commencerait	commence	
commencé	nous	commençons	avons commencé	commencions	commencerons	commencerions	commencions	commençons
	vous	commencez	avez commencé	commenciez	commencerez	commenceriez	commenciez	commencez
	ils/elles	commencent	ont commencé	commençaient	commenceront	commenceraient	commencent	
10 essayer *(to try)*	j'	essaie	ai essayé	essayais	essaierai	essaierais	essaie	
	tu	essaies	as essayé	essayais	essaieras	essaierais	essaies	essaie
	il/elle/on	essaie	a essayé	essayait	essaiera	essaierait	essaie	
essayé	nous	essayons	avons essayé	essayions	essaierons	essaierions	essayions	essayons
	vous	essayez	avez essayé	essayiez	essaierez	essaieriez	essayiez	essayez
	ils/elles	essayent	ont essayé	essayaient	essaieront	essaieraient	essaient	
11 manger *(to eat)*	je (j')	mange	ai mangé	mangeais	mangerai	mangerais	mange	
	tu	manges	as mangé	mangeais	mangeras	mangerais	manges	mange
	il/elle/on	mange	a mangé	mangeait	mangera	mangerait	mange	
mangé	nous	mangeons	avons mangé	mangions	mangerons	mangerions	mangions	mangeons
	vous	mangez	avez mangé	mangiez	mangerez	mangeriez	mangiez	mangez
	ils/elles	mangent	ont mangé	mangeaient	mangeront	mangeraient	mangent	
12 préférer *(to prefer)*	je (j')	préfère	ai préféré	préférais	préférerai	préférerais	préfère	
	tu	préfères	as préféré	préférais	préféreras	préférerais	préfères	préfère
	il/elle/on	préfère	a préféré	préférait	préférera	préférerait	préfère	
préféré	nous	préférons	avons préféré	préférions	préférerons	préférerions	préférions	préférons
	vous	préférez	avez préféré	préfériez	préférerez	préféreriez	préfériez	préférez
	ils/elles	préfèrent	ont préféré	préféraient	préféreront	préféreraient	préfèrent	

Irregular verbs

Infinitive / Past participle	Subject Pronouns	INDICATIVE Present	Passé composé	Imperfect	Future	CONDITIONAL Present	SUBJUNCTIVE Present	IMPERATIVE
13 aller (to go) / allé	je (j')	vais	suis allé(e)	allais	irai	irais	aille	
	tu	vas	es allé(e)	allais	iras	irais	ailles	va
	il/elle/on	va	est allé(e)	allait	ira	irait	aille	
	nous	allons	sommes allé(e)s	allions	irons	irions	allions	allons
	vous	allez	êtes allé(e)s	alliez	irez	iriez	alliez	allez
	ils/elles	vont	sont allé(e)s	allaient	iront	iraient	aillent	
14 s'asseoir (to sit down, to be seated) / assis	je	m'assieds	me suis assis(e)	m'asseyais	m'assiérai	m'assiérais	m'asseye	
	tu	t'assieds	t'es assis(e)	t'asseyais	t'assiéras	t'assiérais	t'asseyes	assieds-toi
	il/elle/on	s'assied	s'est assis(e)	s'asseyait	s'assiéra	s'assiérait	s'asseye	
	nous	nous asseyons	nous sommes assis(es)	nous asseyions	nous assiérons	nous assiérions	nous asseyions	asseyons-nous
	vous	vous asseyez	vous êtes assis(es)	vous asseyiez	vous assiérez	vous assiériez	vous asseyiez	asseyez-vous
	ils/elles	s'asseyent	se sont assis(es)	s'asseyaient	s'assiéront	s'assiéraient	s'asseyent	
15 boire (to drink) / bu	je (j')	bois	ai bu	buvais	boirai	boirais	boive	
	tu	bois	as bu	buvais	boiras	boirais	boives	bois
	il/elle/on	boit	a bu	buvait	boira	boirait	boive	
	nous	buvons	avons bu	buvions	boirons	boirions	buvions	buvons
	vous	buvez	avez bu	buviez	boirez	boiriez	buviez	buvez
	ils/elles	boivent	ont bu	buvaient	boiront	boiraient	boivent	
16 conduire (to drive; to lead) / conduit	je (j')	conduis	ai conduit	conduisais	conduirai	conduirais	conduise	
	tu	conduis	as conduit	conduisais	conduiras	conduirais	conduises	conduis
	il/elle/on	conduit	a conduit	conduisait	conduira	conduirait	conduise	
	nous	conduisons	avons conduit	conduisions	conduirons	conduirions	conduisions	conduisons
	vous	conduisez	avez conduit	conduisiez	conduirez	conduiriez	conduisiez	conduisez
	ils/elles	conduisent	ont conduit	conduisaient	conduiront	conduiraient	conduisent	
17 connaître (to know, to be acquainted with) / connu	je (j')	connais	ai connu	connaissais	connaîtrai	connaîtrais	connaisse	
	tu	connais	as connu	connaissais	connaîtras	connaîtrais	connaisses	connais
	il/elle/on	connaît	a connu	connaissait	connaîtra	connaîtrait	connaisse	
	nous	connaissons	avons connu	connaissions	connaîtrons	connaîtrions	connaissions	connaissons
	vous	connaissez	avez connu	connaissiez	connaîtrez	connaîtriez	connaissiez	connaissez
	ils/elles	connaissent	ont connu	connaissaient	connaîtront	connaîtraient	connaissent	
18 courir (to run) / couru	je (j')	cours	ai couru	courais	courrai	courrais	coure	
	tu	cours	as couru	courais	courras	courrais	coures	cours
	il/elle/on	court	a couru	courait	courra	courrait	coure	
	nous	courons	avons couru	courions	courrons	courrions	courions	courons
	vous	courez	avez couru	couriez	courrez	courriez	couriez	courez
	ils/elles	courent	ont couru	couraient	courront	courraient	courent	
19 croire (to believe) / cru	je (j')	crois	ai cru	croyais	croirai	croirais	croie	
	tu	crois	as cru	croyais	croiras	croirais	croies	crois
	il/elle/on	croit	a cru	croyait	croira	croirait	croie	
	nous	croyons	avons cru	croyions	croirons	croirions	croyions	croyons
	vous	croyez	avez cru	croyiez	croirez	croiriez	croyiez	croyez
	ils/elles	croient	ont cru	croyaient	croiront	croiraient	croient	

Irregular verbs (continued)

Infinitive / Past participle	Subject Pronouns	Present	Passé composé	Imperfect	Future	Present (Conditional)	Present (Subjunctive)	Imperative
			INDICATIVE			CONDITIONAL	SUBJUNCTIVE	IMPERATIVE
20 devoir *(to have to; to owe)* dû	je (j')	dois	ai dû	devais	devrai	devrais	doive	
	tu	dois	as dû	devais	devras	devrais	doives	dois
	il/elle/on	doit	a dû	devait	devra	devrait	doive	
	nous	devons	avons dû	devions	devrons	devrions	devions	devons
	vous	devez	avez dû	deviez	devrez	devriez	deviez	devez
	ils/elles	doivent	ont dû	devaient	devront	devraient	doivent	
21 dire *(to say, to tell)* dit	je (j')	dis	ai dit	disais	dirai	dirais	dise	
	tu	dis	as dit	disais	diras	dirais	dises	dis
	il/elle/on	dit	a dit	disait	dira	dirait	dise	
	nous	disons	avons dit	disions	dirons	dirions	disions	disons
	vous	dites	avez dit	disiez	direz	diriez	disiez	dites
	ils/elles	disent	ont dit	disaient	diront	diraient	disent	
22 écrire *(to write)* écrit	j'	écris	ai écrit	écrivais	écrirai	écrirais	écrive	
	tu	écris	as écrit	écrivais	écriras	écrirais	écrives	écris
	il/elle/on	écrit	a écrit	écrivait	écrira	écrirait	écrive	
	nous	écrivons	avons écrit	écrivions	écrirons	écririons	écrivions	écrivons
	vous	écrivez	avez écrit	écriviez	écrirez	écririez	écriviez	écrivez
	ils/elles	écrivent	ont écrit	écrivaient	écriront	écriraient	écrivent	
23 envoyer *(to send)* envoyé	j'	envoie	ai envoyé	envoyais	enverrai	enverrais	envoie	
	tu	envoies	as envoyé	envoyais	enverras	enverrais	envoies	envoie
	il/elle/on	envoie	a envoyé	envoyait	enverra	enverrait	envoie	
	nous	envoyons	avons envoyé	envoyions	enverrons	enverrions	envoyions	envoyons
	vous	envoyez	avez envoyé	envoyiez	enverrez	enverriez	envoyiez	envoyez
	ils/elles	envoient	ont envoyé	envoyaient	enverront	enverraient	envoient	
24 éteindre *(to turn off)* éteint	j'	éteins	ai éteint	éteignais	éteindrai	éteindrais	éteigne	
	tu	éteins	as éteint	éteignais	éteindras	éteindrais	éteignes	éteins
	il/elle/on	éteint	a éteint	éteignait	éteindra	éteindrait	éteigne	
	nous	éteignons	avons éteint	éteignions	éteindrons	éteindrions	éteignions	éteignons
	vous	éteignez	avez éteint	éteigniez	éteindrez	éteindriez	éteigniez	éteignez
	ils/elles	éteignent	ont éteint	éteignaient	éteindront	éteindraient	éteignent	
25 faire *(to do; to make)* fait	je (j')	fais	ai fait	faisais	ferai	ferais	fasse	
	tu	fais	as fait	faisais	feras	ferais	fasses	fais
	il/elle/on	fait	a fait	faisait	fera	ferait	fasse	
	nous	faisons	avons fait	faisions	ferons	ferions	fassions	faisons
	vous	faites	avez fait	faisiez	ferez	feriez	fassiez	faites
	ils/elles	font	ont fait	faisaient	feront	feraient	fassent	
26 falloir *(to be necessary)* fallu	il	faut	a fallu	fallait	faudra	faudrait	faille	

Infinitive		INDICATIVE				CONDITIONAL	SUBJUNCTIVE	IMPERATIVE
Past participle	Subject Pronouns	Present	Passé composé	Imperfect	Future	Present	Present	
27 lire (to read)	je (j')	lis	ai lu	lisais	lirai	lirais	lise	
	tu	lis	as lu	lisais	liras	lirais	lises	lis
	il/elle/on	lit	a lu	lisait	lira	lirait	lise	
lu	nous	lisons	avons lu	lisions	lirons	lirions	lisions	lisons
	vous	lisez	avez lu	lisiez	lirez	liriez	lisiez	lisez
	ils/elles	lisent	ont lu	lisaient	liront	liraient	lisent	
28 mettre (to put)	je (j')	mets	ai mis	mettais	mettrai	mettrais	mette	
	tu	mets	as mis	mettais	mettras	mettrais	mettes	mets
	il/elle/on	met	a mis	mettait	mettra	mettrait	mette	
mis	nous	mettons	avons mis	mettions	mettrons	mettrions	mettions	mettons
	vous	mettez	avez mis	mettiez	mettrez	mettriez	mettiez	mettez
	ils/elles	mettent	ont mis	mettaient	mettront	mettraient	mettent	
29 mourir (to die)	je	meurs	suis mort(e)	mourais	mourrai	mourrais	meure	
	tu	meurs	es mort(e)	mourais	mourras	mourrais	meures	meurs
	il/elle/on	meurt	est mort(e)	mourait	mourra	mourrait	meure	
mort	nous	mourons	sommes mort(e)s	mourions	mourrons	mourrions	mourions	mourons
	vous	mourez	êtes mort(e)s	mouriez	mourrez	mourriez	mouriez	mourez
	ils/elles	meurent	sont mort(e)s	mouraient	mourront	mourraient	meurent	
30 naître (to be born)	je	nais	suis né(e)	naissais	naîtrai	naîtrais	naisse	
	tu	nais	es né(e)	naissais	naîtras	naîtrais	naisses	nais
	il/elle/on	naît	est né(e)	naissait	naîtra	naîtrait	naisse	
né	nous	naissons	sommes né(e)s	naissions	naîtrons	naîtrions	naissions	naissons
	vous	naissez	êtes né(e)s	naissiez	naîtrez	naîtriez	naissiez	naissez
	ils/elles	naissent	sont né(e)s	naissaient	naîtront	naîtraient	naissent	
31 ouvrir (to open)	j'	ouvre	ai ouvert	ouvrais	ouvrirai	ouvrirais	ouvre	
	tu	ouvres	as ouvert	ouvrais	ouvriras	ouvrirais	ouvres	ouvre
	il/elle/on	ouvre	a ouvert	ouvrait	ouvrira	ouvrirait	ouvre	
ouvert	nous	ouvrons	avons ouvert	ouvrions	ouvrirons	ouvririons	ouvrions	ouvrons
	vous	ouvrez	avez ouvert	ouvriez	ouvrirez	ouvririez	ouvriez	ouvrez
	ils/elles	ouvrent	ont ouvert	ouvraient	ouvriront	ouvriraient	ouvrent	
32 partir (to leave)	je	pars	suis parti(e)	partais	partirai	partirais	parte	
	tu	pars	es parti(e)	partais	partiras	partirais	partes	pars
	il/elle/on	part	est parti(e)	partait	partira	partirait	parte	
parti	nous	partons	sommes parti(e)s	partions	partirons	partirions	partions	partons
	vous	partez	êtes parti(e)(s)	partiez	partirez	partiriez	partiez	partez
	ils/elles	partent	sont parti(e)s	partaient	partiront	partiraient	partent	
33 pleuvoir (to rain)	il	pleut	a plu	pleuvait	pleuvra	pleuvrait	pleuve	
plu								

Irregular verbs (continued)

Infinitive / Past participle	Subject Pronouns	Present	Passé composé	Imperfect	Future	Present (Conditional)	Present (Subjunctive)	Imperative
			INDICATIVE			CONDITIONAL	SUBJUNCTIVE	IMPERATIVE
34 pouvoir (to be able) / pu	je (j')	peux	ai pu	pouvais	pourrai	pourrais	puisse	
	tu	peux	as pu	pouvais	pourras	pourrais	puisses	
	il/elle/on	peut	a pu	pouvait	pourra	pourrait	puisse	
	nous	pouvons	avons pu	pouvions	pourrons	pourrions	puissions	
	vous	pouvez	avez pu	pouviez	pourrez	pourriez	puissiez	
	ils/elles	peuvent	ont pu	pouvaient	pourront	pourraient	puissent	
35 prendre (to take) / pris	je (j')	prends	ai pris	prenais	prendrai	prendrais	prenne	
	tu	prends	as pris	prenais	prendras	prendrais	prennes	prends
	il/elle/on	prend	a pris	prenait	prendra	prendrait	prenne	
	nous	prenons	avons pris	prenions	prendrons	prendrions	prenions	prenons
	vous	prenez	avez pris	preniez	prendrez	prendriez	preniez	prenez
	ils/elles	prennent	ont pris	prenaient	prendront	prendraient	prennent	
36 recevoir (to receive) / reçu	je (j')	reçois	ai reçu	recevais	recevrai	recevrais	reçoive	
	tu	reçois	as reçu	recevais	recevras	recevrais	reçoives	reçois
	il/elle/on	reçoit	a reçu	recevait	recevra	recevrait	reçoive	
	nous	recevons	avons reçu	recevions	recevrons	recevrions	recevions	recevons
	vous	recevez	avez reçu	receviez	recevrez	recevriez	receviez	recevez
	ils/elles	reçoivent	ont reçu	recevaient	recevront	recevraient	reçoivent	
37 rire (to laugh) / ri	je (j')	ris	ai ri	riais	rirai	rirais	rie	
	tu	ris	as ri	riais	riras	rirais	ries	ris
	il/elle/on	rit	a ri	riait	rira	rirait	rie	
	nous	rions	avons ri	riions	rirons	ririons	riions	rions
	vous	riez	avez ri	riiez	rirez	ririez	riiez	riez
	ils/elles	rient	ont ri	riaient	riront	riraient	rient	
38 savoir (to know) / su	je (j')	sais	ai su	savais	saurai	saurais	sache	
	tu	sais	as su	savais	sauras	saurais	saches	sache
	il/elle/on	sait	a su	savait	saura	saurait	sache	
	nous	savons	avons su	savions	saurons	saurions	sachions	sachons
	vous	savez	avez su	saviez	saurez	sauriez	sachiez	sachez
	ils/elles	savent	ont su	savaient	sauront	sauraient	sachent	
39 suivre (to follow) / suivi	je (j')	suis	ai suivi	suivais	suivrai	suivrais	suive	
	tu	suis	as suivi	suivais	suivras	suivrais	suives	suis
	il/elle/on	suit	a suivi	suivait	suivra	suivrait	suive	
	nous	suivons	avons suivi	suivions	suivrons	suivrions	suivions	suivons
	vous	suivez	avez suivi	suiviez	suivrez	suivriez	suiviez	suivez
	ils/elles	suivent	ont suivi	suivaient	suivront	suivraient	suivent	
40 tenir (to hold) / tenu	je (j')	tiens	ai tenu	tenais	tiendrai	tiendrais	tienne	
	tu	tiens	as tenu	tenais	tiendras	tiendrais	tiennes	tiens
	il/elle/on	tient	a tenu	tenait	tiendra	tiendrait	tienne	
	nous	tenons	avons tenu	tenions	tiendrons	tiendrions	tenions	tenons
	vous	tenez	avez tenu	teniez	tiendrez	tiendriez	teniez	tenez
	ils/elles	tiennent	ont tenu	tenaient	tiendront	tiendraient	tiennent	

Infinitive / Past participle	Subject Pronouns	INDICATIVE Present	INDICATIVE Passé composé	INDICATIVE Imperfect	INDICATIVE Future	CONDITIONAL Present	SUBJUNCTIVE Present	IMPERATIVE
41 venir *(to come)*	je	viens	suis venu(e)	venais	viendrai	viendrais	vienne	
	tu	viens	es venu(e)	venais	viendras	viendrais	viennes	viens
	il/elle/on	vient	est venu(e)	venait	viendra	viendrait	vienne	
venu	nous	venons	sommes venu(e)s	venions	viendrons	viendrions	venions	venons
	vous	venez	êtes venu(e)(s)	veniez	viendrez	viendriez	veniez	venez
	ils/elles	viennent	sont venu(e)s	venaient	viendront	viendraient	viennent	
42 voir *(to see)*	je (j')	vois	ai vu	voyais	verrai	verrais	voie	
	tu	vois	as vu	voyais	verras	verrais	voies	vois
	il/elle/on	voit	a vu	voyait	verra	verrait	voie	
vu	nous	voyons	avons vu	voyions	verrons	verrions	voyions	voyons
	vous	voyez	avez vu	voyiez	verrez	verriez	voyiez	voyez
	ils/elles	voient	ont vu	voyaient	verront	verraient	voient	
43 vouloir *(to want, to wish)*	je (j')	veux	ai voulu	voulais	voudrai	voudrais	veuille	
	tu	veux	as voulu	voulais	voudras	voudrais	veuilles	veuille
	il/elle/on	veut	a voulu	voulait	voudra	voudrait	veuille	
voulu	nous	voulons	avons voulu	voulions	voudrons	voudrions	voulions	veuillons
	vous	voulez	avez voulu	vouliez	voudrez	voudriez	vouliez	veuillez
	ils/elles	veulent	ont voulu	voulaient	voudront	voudraient	veuillent	

Guide to Vocabulary

This glossary contains the words and expressions listed on the **Vocabulaire** page found at the end of each unit in **D'accord!** Levels 1 & 2. The numbers following an entry indicate the **D'accord!** level and unit where the term was introduced. For example, the first entry in the glossary, **à**, was introduced in **D'accord!** Level 1, Unit 4. Note that **II–P** refers to the **Unité Préliminaire** in **D'accord!** Level 2.

Abbreviations used in this glossary

adj.	adjective	*f.*	feminine	*i.o.*	indirect object	*prep.*	preposition
adv.	adverb	*fam.*	familiar	*m.*	masculine	*pron.*	pronoun
art.	article	*form.*	formal	*n.*	noun	*refl.*	reflexive
comp.	comparative	*imp.*	imperative	*obj.*	object	*rel.*	relative
conj.	conjunction	*indef.*	indefinite	*part.*	partitive	*sing.*	singular
def.	definite	*interj.*	interjection	*p.p.*	past participle	*sub.*	subject
dem.	demonstrative	*interr.*	interrogative	*pl.*	plural	*super.*	superlative
disj.	disjunctive	*inv.*	invariable	*poss.*	possessive	*v.*	verb
d.o.	direct object						

French-English

A

à *prep.* at; in; to I-4
À bientôt. See you soon. I-1
à condition que on the condition that, provided that II-7
à côté de *prep.* next to I-3
À demain. See you tomorrow. I-1
à droite (de) *prep.* to the right (of) I-3
à gauche (de) *prep.* to the left (of) I-3
à ... heure(s) at ... (o'clock) I-4
à la radio on the radio II-7
à la télé(vision) on television II-7
à l'étranger abroad, overseas I-7
à mi-temps half-time (*job*) II-5
à moins que unless II-7
à plein temps full-time (*job*) II-5
À plus tard. See you later. I-1
À quelle heure? What time?; When? I-2
À qui? To whom? I-4
À table! Let's eat! Food is on! II-1
à temps partiel part-time (*job*) II-5
À tout à l'heure. See you later. I-1
au bout (de) *prep.* at the end (of) II-4

au contraire on the contrary II-7
au fait by the way I-3
au printemps in the spring I-5
Au revoir. Good-bye. I-1
au secours help II-3
au sujet de on the subject of, about II-6
abolir *v.* to abolish II-6
absolument *adv.* absolutely I-7
accident *m.* accident II-3
avoir un accident to have/to be in an accident II-3
accompagner *v.* to accompany II-4
acheter *v.* to buy I-5
acteur *m.* actor I-1
actif/active *adj.* active I-3
activement *adv.* actively I-8, II-P
actrice *f.* actress I-1
addition *f.* check, bill I-4
adieu farewell II-6
adolescence *f.* adolescence I-6
adorer *v.* to love I-2
J'adore... I love... I-2
adresse *f.* address II-4
aérobic *m.* aerobics I-5
faire de l'aérobic *v.* to do aerobics I-5
aéroport *m.* airport I-7
affaires *f., pl.* business I-3
affiche *f.* poster I-8, II-P
afficher *v.* to post II-5
âge *m.* age I-6
âge adulte *m.* adulthood I-6
agence de voyages *f.* travel agency I-7
agent *m.* officer; agent II-3
agent de police *m.* police officer II-3

agent de voyages *m.* travel agent I-7
agent immobilier *m.* real estate agent II-5
agréable *adj.* pleasant I-1
agriculteur/agricultrice *m., f.* farmer II-5
aider (à) *v.* to help (*to do something*) I-5
aie (avoir) *imp. v.* have I-7
ail *m.* garlic II-1
aimer *v.* to like I-2
aimer mieux to prefer I-2
aimer que... to like that... II-6
J'aime bien... I really like... I-2
Je n'aime pas tellement... I don't like ... very much. I-2
aîné(e) *adj.* elder I-3
algérien(ne) *adj.* Algerian I-1
aliment *m.* food item; a food II-1
Allemagne *f.* Germany I-7
allemand(e) *adj.* German I-1
aller *v.* to go I-4
aller à la pêche to go fishing I-5
aller aux urgences to go to the emergency room II-2
aller avec to go with I-6
aller-retour *adj.* round-trip I-7
billet aller-retour *m.* round-trip ticket I-7
Allons-y! Let's go! I-2
Ça va? What's up?; How are things? I-1
Comment allez-vous? *form.* How are you? I-1
Comment vas-tu? *fam.* How are you? I-1

Je m'en vais. I'm leaving. I-8, II-P

Je vais bien/mal. I am doing well/badly. I-1

J'y vais. I'm going/coming. I-8, II-P

Nous y allons. We're going/coming. II-1

allergie *f.* allergy II-2

Allez. Come on. I-5

allô *(on the phone)* hello I-1

allumer *v.* to turn on II-3

alors *adv.* so, then; at that moment I-2

améliorer *v.* to improve II-5

amende *f.* fine II-3

amener *v.* to bring (*someone*) I-5

américain(e) *adj.* American I-1

  football américain *m.* football I-5

ami(e) *m., f.* friend I-1

  petit(e) ami(e) *m., f.* boyfriend/girlfriend I-1

amitié *f.* friendship I-6

amour *m.* love I-6

amoureux/amoureuse *adj.* in love I-6

  tomber amoureux/amoureuse *v.* to fall in love I-6

amusant(e) *adj.* fun I-1

an *m.* year I-2

ancien(ne) *adj.* ancient, old; former II-7

ange *m.* angel I-1

anglais(e) *adj.* English I-1

angle *m.* corner II-4

Angleterre *f.* England I-7

animal *m.* animal II-6

année *f.* year I-2

  cette année this year I-2

anniversaire *m.* birthday I-5

  C'est quand l'anniversaire de ... ? When is ...'s birthday? I-5

  C'est quand ton/votre anniversaire? When is your birthday? I-5

annuler (une réservation) *v.* to cancel (a reservation) I-7

anorak *m.* ski jacket, parka I-6

antipathique *adj.* unpleasant I-3

août *m.* August I-5

apercevoir *v.* to see, to catch sight of II-4

aperçu (apercevoir) *p.p.* seen, caught sight of II-4

appareil *m.* (on the phone) telephone II-5

  appareil (électrique/ménager) *m.* (electrical/household) appliance I-8, II-P

appareil photo (numérique) *m.* (digital) camera II-3

  C'est M./Mme/Mlle ... à l'appareil. It's Mr./Mrs./Miss ... on the phone. II-5

  Qui est à l'appareil? Who's calling, please? II-5

appartement *m.* apartment II-7

appeler *v.* to call I-7

applaudir *v.* to applaud II-7

applaudissement *m.* applause II-7

apporter *v.* to bring, to carry (*something*) I-4

apprendre (à) *v.* to teach; to learn (*to do something*) I-4

appris (apprendre) *p.p., adj.* learned I-6

après (que) *adv.* after I-2

après-demain *adv.* day after tomorrow I-2

après-midi *m.* afternoon I-2

  cet après-midi this afternoon I-2

  de l'après-midi in the afternoon I-2

  demain après-midi *adv.* tomorrow afternoon I-2

  hier après-midi *adv.* yesterday afternoon I-7

arbre *m.* tree II-6

architecte *m., f.* architect I-3

argent *m.* money II-4

  dépenser de l'argent *v.* to spend money I-4

  déposer de l'argent *v.* to deposit money II-4

  retirer de l'argent *v.* to withdraw money II-4

armoire *f.* armoire, wardrobe I-8, II-P

arrêt d'autobus (de bus) *m.* bus stop I-7

arrêter (de faire quelque chose) *v.* to stop (doing something) II-3

arrivée *f.* arrival I-7

arriver (à) *v.* to arrive; to manage (*to do something*) I-2

art *m.* art I-2

  beaux-arts *m., pl.* fine arts II-7

artiste *m., f.* artist I-3

ascenseur *m.* elevator I-7

aspirateur *m.* vacuum cleaner I-8, II-P

  passer l'aspirateur to vacuum I-8, II-P

aspirine *f.* aspirin II-2

Asseyez-vous! (s'asseoir) *imp. v.* Have a seat! II-2

assez *adv.* (*before adjective or adverb*) pretty; quite I-8, II-P

assez (de) (*before noun*) enough (of) I-4

  pas assez (de) not enough (of) I-4

assiette *f.* plate II-1

assis (s'asseoir) *p.p., adj.* (*used as past participle*) sat down; (*used as adjective*) sitting, seated II-2

assister *v.* to attend I-2

assurance (maladie/vie) *f.* (health/life) insurance II-5

athlète *m., f.* athlete I-3

attacher *v.* to attach II-3

  attacher sa ceinture de sécurité to buckle one's seatbelt II-3

attendre *v.* to wait I-6

attention *f.* attention I-5

  faire attention (à) *v.* to pay attention (to) I-5

au (à + le) *prep.* to/at the I-4

auberge de jeunesse *f.* youth hostel I-7

aucun(e) *adj.* no; *pron.* none II-2

  ne... aucun(e) none, not any II-4

augmentation (de salaire) *f.* raise (in salary) II-5

aujourd'hui *adv.* today I-2

auquel (à + lequel) *pron., m., sing.* which one II-5

aussi *adv.* too, as well; as I-1

  Moi aussi. Me too. I-1

  aussi ... que (*used with an adjective*) as ... as II-1

autant de ... que *adv.* (*used with noun to express quantity*) as much/as many ... as II-6

auteur/femme auteur *m., f.* author II-7

autobus *m.* bus I-7

  arrêt d'autobus (de bus) *m.* bus stop I-7

  prendre un autobus to take a bus I-7

automne *m.* fall I-5

  à l'automne in the fall I-5

autoroute *f.* highway II-3

autour (de) *prep.* around II-4

autrefois *adv.* in the past I-8, II-P

aux (à + les) *prep.* to/at the I-4

auxquelles (à + lesquelles) *pron., f., pl.* which ones II-5

auxquels (à + lesquels) *pron., m., pl.* which ones II-5

avance *f.* advance I-2

  en avance *adv.* early I-2

avant (de/que) *adv.* before I-7

avant-hier *adv.* day before yesterday I-7

avec *prep.* with I-1
  Avec qui? With whom? I-4
aventure *f.* adventure II-7
  film d'aventures *m.*
  adventure film II-7
avenue *f.* avenue II-4
avion *m.* airplane I-7
  prendre un avion *v.* to take
  a plane I-7
avocat(e) *m., f.* lawyer I-3
avoir *v.* to have I-2
  aie *imp. v.* have I-2
  avoir besoin (de) to need
  (*something*) I-2
  avoir chaud to be hot I-2
  avoir de la chance to be
  lucky I-2
  avoir envie (de) to feel like
  (*doing something*) I-2
  avoir faim to be hungry I-4
  avoir froid to be cold I-2
  avoir honte (de) to be
  ashamed (of) I-2
  avoir mal to have an ache II-2
  avoir mal au cœur to feel
  nauseated II-2
  avoir peur (de/que) to be
  afraid (of/that) I-2
  avoir raison to be right I-2
  avoir soif to be thirsty I-4
  avoir sommeil to be sleepy I-2
  avoir tort to be wrong I-2
  avoir un accident to have/to
  be in an accident II-3
  avoir un compte bancaire to
  have a bank account II-4
  en avoir marre to be fed up I-3
avril *m.* April I-5
ayez (avoir) *imp. v.* have I-7
ayons (avoir) *imp. v.* let's have I-7

B

bac(calauréat) *m.* an important
  exam taken by high-school
  students in France I-2
baguette *f.* baguette I-4
baignoire *f.* bathtub I-8, II-P
bain *m.* bath I-6
  salle de bains *f.* bathroom
  I-8, II-P
balai *m.* broom I-8, II-P
balayer *v.* to sweep I-8, II-P
balcon *m.* balcony I-8, II-P
banane *f.* banana II-1
banc *m.* bench II-4
bancaire *adj.* banking II-4
  avoir un compte bancaire *v.*
  to have a bank account II-4
bande dessinée (B.D.) *f.*
  comic strip I-5
banlieue *f.* suburbs I-4

banque *f.* bank II-4
banquier/banquière *m., f.*
  banker II-5
barbant *adj.,* **barbe** *f.* drag I-3
baseball *m.* baseball I-5
basket(-ball) *m.* basketball I-5
baskets *f., pl.* tennis shoes I-6
bateau *m.* boat I-7
  prendre un bateau *v.* to take
  a boat I-7
bateau-mouche *m.* riverboat I-7
bâtiment *m.* building II-4
batterie *f.* drums II-7
bavarder *v.* to chat I-4
beau (belle) *adj.* handsome;
  beautiful I-3
  **faire quelque chose de
  beau** *v.* to be up to something
  interesting II-4
  Il fait beau. The weather is
  nice. I-5
beaucoup (de) *adv.* a lot (of) 4
  Merci (beaucoup). Thank
  you (very much). I-1
beau-frère *m.* brother-in-law I-3
beau-père *m.* father-in-law;
  stepfather I-3
beaux-arts *m., pl.* fine arts II-7
belge *adj.* Belgian I-7
Belgique *f.* Belgium I-7
belle *adj., f. (feminine form of*
  beau) beautiful I-3
belle-mère *f.* mother-in-law;
  stepmother I-3
belle-sœur *f.* sister-in-law I-3
besoin *m.* need I-2
  avoir besoin (de) to need
  (*something*) I-2
beurre *m.* butter 4
bibliothèque *f.* library I-1
bien *adv.* well I-7
  bien sûr *adv.* of course I-2
  Je vais bien. I am doing
  well. I-1
  Très bien. Very well. I-1
bientôt *adv.* soon I-1
  À bientôt. See you soon. I-1
bienvenu(e) *adj.* welcome I-1
bijouterie *f.* jewelry store II-4
billet *m. (travel)* ticket I-7;
  (*money*) bills, notes II-4
  billet aller-retour *m.* round-
  trip ticket I-7
biologie *f.* biology I-2
biscuit *m.* cookie I-6
blague *f.* joke I-2
blanc(he) *adj.* white I-6
blessure *f.* injury, wound II-2
bleu(e) *adj.* blue I-3
blond(e) *adj.* blonde I-3
blouson *m.* jacket I-6
bœuf *m.* beef II-1

boire *v.* to drink I-4
bois *m.* wood II-6
boisson (gazeuse) *f.* (carbonated)
  drink/beverage I-4
boîte *f.* box; can II-1
  boîte aux lettres *f.* mailbox II-4
  boîte de conserve *f.* can
  (of food) II-1
bol *m.* bowl II-1
bon(ne) *adj.* kind; good I-3
  bon marché *adj.* inexpensive I-6
  Il fait bon. The weather is
  good/warm. I-5
bonbon *m.* candy I-6
bonheur *m.* happiness I-6
Bonjour. Good morning.;
  Hello. I-1
Bonsoir. Good evening.;
  Hello. I-1
bouche *f.* mouth II-2
boucherie *f.* butcher's shop II-1
boulangerie *f.* bread shop,
  bakery II-1
boulevard *m.* boulevard II-4
  suivre un boulevard *v.* to
  follow a boulevard II-4
bourse *f.* scholarship, grant I-2
bout *m.* end II-4
  au bout (de) *prep.* at the end
  (of) II-4
bouteille (de) *f.* bottle (of) I-4
boutique *f.* boutique, store II-4
brancher *v.* to plug in, to
  connect II-3
bras *m.* arm II-2
brasserie *f.* restaurant II-4
Brésil *m.* Brazil II-2
brésilien(ne) *adj.* Brazilian I-7
bricoler *v.* to tinker; to do odd
  jobs I-5
brillant(e) *adj.* bright I-1
bronzer *v.* to tan I-6
brosse (à cheveux/à dents) *f.*
  (hair/tooth)brush II-2
brun(e) *adj. (hair)* dark I-3
bu (boire) *p.p.* drunk I-6
bureau *m.* desk; office I-1
  bureau de poste *m.* post
  office II-4
bus *m.* bus I-7
  arrêt d'autobus (de bus)
  m. bus stop I-7
  prendre un bus *v.* to take a
  bus I-7

C

ça *pron.* that; this; it I-1
 Ça dépend. It depends. I-4
 Ça ne nous regarde pas. That has nothing to do with us.; That is none of our business. II-6
 Ça suffit. That's enough. I-5
 Ça te dit? Does that appeal to you? II-6
 Ça va? What's up?; How are things? I-1
 ça veut dire that is to say II-2
 Comme ci, comme ça. So-so. I-1
cadeau *m.* gift I-6
 paquet cadeau wrapped gift I-6
cadet(te) *adj.* younger I-3
cadre/femme cadre *m., f.* executive II-5
café *m.* café; coffee I-1
 terrasse de café *f.* café terrace I-4
 cuillére à café *f.* teaspoon II-1
cafetière *f.* coffeemaker I-8, II-P
cahier *m.* notebook I-1
calculatrice *f.* calculator I-1
calme *adj.* calm I-1; *m.* calm I-1
camarade de classe *m., f.* classmate I-1
caméra vidéo *f.* camcorder II-3
caméscope *m.* camcorder II-3
campagne *f.* country(side) I-7
 pain de campagne *m.* country-style bread I-4
 pâté (de campagne) *m.* pâté, meat spread II-1
camping *m.* camping I-5
 faire du camping *v.* to go camping I-5
Canada *m.* Canada I-7
canadien(ne) *adj.* Canadian I-1
canapé *m.* couch I-8, II-P
candidat(e) *m., f.* candidate; applicant II-5
cantine *f.* (school) cafeteria I-2
capitale *f.* capital I-7
capot *m.* hood II-3
carafe (d'eau) *f.* pitcher (of water) II-1
carotte *f.* carrot II-1
carrefour *m.* intersection II-4
carrière *f.* career II-5
carte *f.* map I-1; menu II-1; card II-4
 payer par carte (bancaire/ de crédit) to pay with a (debit/credit) card II-4

carte postale *f.* postcard II-4
cartes *f. pl.* (*playing*) cards I-5
casque *f.* **à écouteurs** *m., pl.* headphones II-3
casquette *f.* (baseball) cap I-6
cassette vidéo *f.* videotape II-3
catastrophe *f.* catastrophe II-6
cave *f.* basement, cellar I-8, II-P
ce *dem. adj., m., sing.* this; that I-6
 ce matin this morning I-2
 ce mois-ci this month I-2
 Ce n'est pas grave. It's no big deal. I-6
 ce soir this evening I-2
 ce sont... those are... I-1
 ce week-end this weekend I-2
ceinture *f.* belt I-6
 attacher sa ceinture de sécurité *v.* to buckle one's seatbelt II-3
célèbre *adj.* famous II-7
célébrer *v.* to celebrate I-5
célibataire *adj.* single I-3
celle *pron., f., sing.* this one; that one; the one II-6
celles *pron., f., pl.* these; those; the ones II-6
celui *pron., m., sing.* this one; that one; the one II-6
cent *m.* one hundred I-3
 cent mille *m.* one hundred thousand I-5
 cent un *m.* one hundred one I-5
 cinq cents *m.* five hundred I-5
centième *adj.* hundredth I-7
centrale nucléaire *f.* nuclear plant II-6
centre commercial *m.* shopping center, mall I-4
centre-ville *m.* city/town center, downtown I-4
certain(e) *adj.* certain II-1
 Il est certain que... It is certain that... II-7
 Il n'est pas certain que... It is uncertain that... II-7
ces *dem. adj., m., f., pl.* these; those I-6
c'est... it/that is... I-1
 C'est de la part de qui? On behalf of whom? II-5
 C'est le 1ᵉʳ (premier) octobre. It is October first. I-5
 C'est M./Mme/Mlle ... (à l'appareil). It's Mr./Mrs./Miss ... (on the phone). II-5
 C'est quand l'anniversaire de... ? When is ...'s birthday? I-5

 C'est quand ton/votre anniversaire? When is your birthday? I-5
 Qu'est-ce que c'est? What is it? I-1
cet *dem. adj., m., sing.* this; that I-6
 cet après-midi this afternoon I-2
cette *dem. adj., f., sing.* this; that I-6
 cette année this year I-2
 cette semaine this week I-2
ceux *pron., m., pl.* these; those; the ones II-6
chaîne (de télévision) *f.* (television) channel II-3
chaise *f.* chair I-1
chambre *f.* bedroom I-8, II-P
 chambre (individuelle) *f.* (single) room I-7
champ *m.* field II-6
champignon *m.* mushroom II-1
chance *f.* luck I-2
 avoir de la chance *v.* to be lucky I-2
chanson *f.* song II-7
chanter *v.* to sing I-5
chanteur/chanteuse *m., f.* singer I-1
chapeau *m.* hat I-6
chaque *adj.* each I-6
charcuterie *f.* delicatessen II-1
charmant(e) *adj.* charming I-1
chasse *f.* hunt II-6
chasser *v.* to hunt II-6
chat *m.* cat I-3
châtain *adj.* (*hair*) brown I-3
chaud *m.* heat I-2
 avoir chaud *v.* to be hot I-2
 Il fait chaud. (*weather*) It is hot. I-5
chauffeur de taxi/de camion *m.* taxi/truck driver II-5
chaussette *f.* sock I-6
chaussure *f.* shoe I-6
chef d'entreprise *m.* head of a company II-5
chef-d'œuvre *m.* masterpiece II-7
chemin *m.* path; way II-4
 suivre un chemin *v.* to follow a path II-4
chemise (à manches courtes/ longues) *f.* (short-/long-sleeved) shirt I-6
chemisier *m.* blouse I-6
chèque *m.* check II-4
 compte-chèques *m.* checking account II-4
 payer par chèque *v.* to pay by check II-4

cher/chère *adj.* expensive I-6
chercher *v.* to look for I-2
  chercher un/du travail to look for a job/work II-4
chercheur/chercheuse *m., f.* researcher II-5
chéri(e) *adj.* dear, beloved, darling I-2
cheval *m.* horse I-5
  faire du cheval *v.* to go horseback riding I-5
cheveux *m., pl.* hair II-1
  brosse à cheveux *f.* hairbrush II-2
  cheveux blonds blond hair I-3
  cheveux châtains brown hair I-3
  se brosser les cheveux *v.* to brush one's hair II-1
cheville *f.* ankle II-2
  se fouler la cheville *v.* to twist/sprain one's ankle II-2
chez *prep.* at (*someone's*) house I-3, at (*a place*) I-3
  passer chez quelqu'un *v.* to stop by someone's house I-4
chic *adj.* chic I-4
chien *m.* dog I-3
chimie *f.* chemistry I-2
Chine *f.* China I-7
chinois(e) *adj.* Chinese 7
chocolat (chaud) *m.* (hot) chocolate I-4
chœur *m.* choir, chorus II-7
choisir *v.* to choose I-4
chômage *m.* unemployment II-5
  être au chômage *v.* to be unemployed II-5
chômeur/chômeuse *m., f.* unemployed person II-5
chose *f.* thing I-1
  quelque chose *m.* something; anything I-4
chrysanthèmes *m., pl.* chrysanthemums II-1
chut shh II-7
-ci (*used with demonstrative adjective* **ce** *and noun or with demonstrative pronoun* **celui**) here I-6
  ce mois-ci this month I-2
ciel *m.* sky II-6
cinéma (ciné) *m.* movie theater, movies I-4
cinq *m.* five I-1
cinquante *m.* fifty I-1
cinquième *adj.* fifth 7
circulation *f.* traffic II-3
clair(e) *adj.* clear II-7
  Il est clair que... It is clear that... II-7
classe *f.* (*group of students*) class I-1

camarade de classe *m., f.* classmate I-1
  salle de classe *f.* classroom I-1
clavier *m.* keyboard II-3
clé *f.* key I-7
  clé USB *f.* USB drive II-3
client(e) *m., f.* client; guest I-7
cœur *m.* heart II-2
  avoir mal au cœur to feel nauseated II-2
coffre *m.* trunk II-3
coiffeur/coiffeuse *m., f.* hairdresser I-3
coin *m.* corner II-4
colis *m.* package II-4
colocataire *m., f.* roommate (*in an apartment*) I-1
Combien (de)... ? *adv.* How much/many... ? I-1
  Combien coûte... ? How much is... ? I-4
combiné *m.* receiver II-5
comédie (musicale) *f.* comedy (musical) II-7
commander *v.* to order II-1
comme *adv.* how; like, as I-2
  Comme ci, comme ça. So-so. I-1
commencer (à) *v.* to begin (*to do something*) I-2
comment *adv.* how I-4
  Comment? *adv.* What? I-4
  Comment allez-vous?, *form.* How are you? I-1
  Comment t'appelles-tu? *fam.* What is your name? I-1
  Comment vas-tu? *fam.* How are you? I-1
  Comment vous appelez-vous? *form.* What is your name? I-1
commerçant(e) *m., f.* shopkeeper II-1
commissariat de police *m.* police station II-4
commode *f.* dresser, chest of drawers I-8, II-P
complet (complète) *adj.* full (no vacancies) I-7
composer (un numéro) *v.* to dial (a number) II-3
compositeur *m.* composer II-7
comprendre *v.* to understand I-4
compris (comprendre) *p.p., adj.* understood; included I-6
comptable *m., f.* accountant II-5
compte *m.* account (*at a bank*) II-4
  avoir un compte bancaire *v.* to have a bank account II-4
  compte de chèques *m.* checking account II-4

compte d'épargne *m.* savings account II-4
  se rendre compte *v.* to realize II-2
compter sur quelqu'un *v.* to count on someone I-8, II-P
concert *m.* concert II-7
condition *f.* condition II-7
  à condition que on the condition that..., provided that... II-7
conduire *v.* to drive I-6
conduit (conduire) *p.p., adj.* driven I-6
confiture *f.* jam II-1
congé *m.* time off, leave I-7
  jour de congé *m.* day off I-7
  prendre un congé *v.* to take time off II-5
congélateur *m.* freezer I-8, II-P
connaissance *f.* acquaintance I-5
  faire la connaissance de *v.* to meet (*someone*) I-5
connaître *v.* to know, to be familiar with I-8, II-P
connecté(e) *adj.* connected II-3
  être connecté(e) avec quelqu'un *v.* to be online with someone I-7, II-3
connu (connaître) *p.p., adj.* known; famous I-8, II-P
conseil *m.* advice II-5
conseiller/conseillère *m., f.* consultant; advisor II-5
considérer *v.* to consider I-5
constamment *adv.* constantly I-7
construire *v.* to build, to construct I-6
conte *m.* tale II-7
content(e) *adj.* happy II-5
  être content(e) que... *v.* to be happy that... II-6
continuer (à) *v.* to continue (*doing something*) II-4
contraire *adj.* contrary II-7
  au contraire on the contrary II-7
copain/copine *m., f.* friend I-1
corbeille (à papier) *f.* wastebasket I-1
corps *m.* body II-2
costume *m.* (*man's*) suit I-6
côte *f.* coast II-6
coton *m.* cotton II-4
cou *m.* neck II-2
couche d'ozone *f.* ozone layer II-6
  trou dans la couche d'ozone *m.* hole in the ozone layer II-6
couleur *f.* color 6
  De quelle couleur... ? What color... ? I-6

couloir *m.* hallway I-8, II-P
couple *m.* couple I-6
courage *m.* courage II-5
courageux/courageuse *adj.* courageous, brave I-3
couramment *adv.* fluently I-7
courir *v.* to run I-5
courrier *m.* mail II-4
cours *m.* class, course I-2
course *f.* errand II-1
  faire les courses *v.* to go (grocery) shopping II-1
court(e) *adj.* short I-3
  chemise à manches courtes *f.* short-sleeved shirt I-6
couru (courir) *p.p.* run I-6
cousin(e) *m., f.* cousin I-3
couteau *m.* knife II-1
coûter *v.* to cost I-4
  Combien coûte... ? How much is... ? I-4
couvert (couvrir) *p.p.* covered II-3
couverture *f.* blanket I-8, II-P
couvrir *v.* to cover II-3
covoiturage *m.* carpooling II-6
cravate *f.* tie I-6
crayon *m.* pencil I-1
crème *f.* cream II-1
  crème à raser *f.* shaving cream II-2
crêpe *f.* crêpe I-5
crevé(e) *adj.* deflated; blown up II-3
  pneu crevé *m.* flat tire II-3
critique *f.* review; criticism II-7
croire (que) *v.* to believe (that) II-7
  ne pas croire que... to not believe that… II-7
croissant *m.* croissant I-4
croissant(e) *adj.* growing II-6
  population croissante *f.* growing population II-6
cru (croire) *p.p.* believed II-7
cruel/cruelle *adj.* cruel I-3
cuillère (à soupe/à café) *f.* (soup/tea)spoon II-1
cuir *m.* leather II-4
cuisine *f.* cooking; kitchen 5
  faire la cuisine *v.* to cook 5
cuisiner *v.* to cook II-1
cuisinier/cuisinière *m., f.* cook II-5
cuisinière *f.* stove I-8, II-P
curieux/curieuse *adj.* curious I-3
curriculum vitæ (C.V.) *m.* résumé II-5

D

d'abord *adv.* first I-7
d'accord *(tag question)* all right? I-2; *(in statement)* okay I-2
  être d'accord to be in agreement I-2
d'autres *m., f.* others I-4
d'habitude *adv.* usually I-8, II-P
danger *m.* danger, threat II-6
dangereux/dangereuse *adj.* dangerous II-3
dans *prep.* in I-3
danse *f.* dance II-7
danser *v.* to dance I-4
danseur/danseuse *m., f.* dancer II-7
date *f.* date I-5
  Quelle est la date? What is the date? I-5
de/d' *prep.* of I-3; from I-1
  de l'après-midi in the afternoon I-2
  de laquelle *pron., f., sing.* which one I-5
  De quelle couleur... ? What color... ? I-6
  De rien. You're welcome. I-1
  de taille moyenne of medium height I-3
  de temps en temps *adv.* from time to time I-7
débarrasser la table *v.* to clear the table I-8, II-P
déboisement *m.* deforestation II-6
début *m.* beginning; debut II-7
décembre *m.* December I-5
déchets toxiques *m., pl.* toxic waste II-6
décider (de) *v.* to decide (*to do something*) II-3
découvert (découvrir) *p.p.* discovered II-3
découvrir *v.* to discover II-3
décrire *v.* to describe I-7
décrocher *v.* to pick up II-5
décrit (décrire) *p.p., adj.* described I-7
degrés *m., pl.* (*temperature*) degrees I-5
  Il fait ... degrés. (*to describe weather*) It is ... degrees. I-5
déjà *adv.* already I-5
déjeuner *m.* lunch II-1; *v.* to eat lunch I-4
de l' *part. art., m., f., sing.* some I-4
de la *part. art., f., sing.* some I-4
délicieux/délicieuse delicious I-8, II-P
demain *adv.* tomorrow I-2

À demain. See you tomorrow. I-1
  après-demain *adv.* day after tomorrow I-2
  demain matin/après-midi/ soir *adv.* tomorrow morning/ afternoon/evening I-2
demander (à) *v.* to ask (*someone*), to make a request (*of someone*) I-6
  demander que... *v.* to ask that… II-6
démarrer *v.* to start up II-3
déménager *v.* to move out I-8, II-P
demie half I-2
  et demie half past … (o'clock) I-2
demi-frère *m.* half-brother, stepbrother I-3
demi-sœur *f.* half-sister, stepsister I-3
démissionner *v.* to resign II-5
dent *f.* tooth II-1
  brosse à dents *f.* tooth brush II-2
  se brosser les dents *v.* to brush one's teeth II-1
dentifrice *m.* toothpaste II-2
dentiste *m., f.* dentist I-3
départ *m.* departure I-7
dépasser *v.* to go over; to pass II-3
dépense *f.* expenditure, expense II-4
dépenser *v.* to spend I-4
  dépenser de l'argent *v.* to spend money I-4
déposer de l'argent *v.* to deposit money II-4
déprimé(e) *adj.* depressed II-2
depuis *adv.* since; for II-1
dernier/dernière *adj.* last I-2
dernièrement *adv.* lastly, finally I-7
derrière *prep.* behind I-3
des *part. art., m., f., pl.* some I-4
des (de + les) *m., f., pl.* of the I-3
dès que *adv.* as soon as II-5
désagréable *adj.* unpleasant I-1
descendre (de) *v.* to go downstairs; to get off; to take down I-6
désert *m.* desert II-6
désirer (que) *v.* to want (that) I-5
désolé(e) *adj.* sorry I-6
  être désolé(e) que... to be sorry that… II-6
desquelles (de + lesquelles) *pron., f., pl.* which ones II-5
desquels (de + lesquels) *pron., m., pl.* which ones II-5

dessert *m.* dessert I-6
dessin animé *m.* cartoon II-7
dessiner *v.* to draw I-2
détester *v.* to hate I-2
  Je déteste... I hate... I-2
détruire *v.* to destroy I-6
détruit (détruire) *p.p., adj.*
  destroyed I-6
deux *m.* two I-1
deuxième *adj.* second I-7
devant *prep.* in front of I-3
développer *v.* to develop II-6
devenir *v.* to become II-1
devoir *m.* homework I-2; *v.* to
  have to, must II-1
dictionnaire *m.* dictionary I-1
différemment *adv.* differently
  I-8, II-P
différence *f.* difference I-1
différent(e) *adj.* different I-1
difficile *adj.* difficult I-1
dimanche *m.* Sunday I-2
dîner *m.* dinner II-1; *v.* to have
  dinner I-2
diplôme *m.* diploma, degree I-2
dire *v.* to say I-7
  Ça te dit? Does that appeal
  to you? II-6
  ça veut dire that is to say II-2
  veut dire *v.* means, signifies
  II-1
diriger *v.* to manage II-5
discret/discrète *adj.* discreet;
  unassuming I-3
discuter *v.* discuss I-6
disque dur *m.* hard drive II-3
dissertation *f.* essay II-3
distributeur automatique/de
  billets *m.* ATM II-4
dit (dire) *p.p., adj.* said I-7
divorce *m.* divorce I-6
divorcé(e) *adj.* divorced I-3
divorcer *v.* to divorce I-3
dix *m.* ten I-1
dix-huit *m.* eighteen I-1
dixième *adj.* tenth I-7
dix-neuf *m.* nineteen I-1
dix-sept *m.* seventeen I-1
documentaire *m.*
  documentary II-7
doigt *m.* finger II-2
doigt de pied *m.* toe II-2
domaine *m.* field II-5
dommage *m.* harm II-6
  Il est dommage que... It's a
  shame that... II-6
donc *conj.* therefore I-7
donner (à) *v.* to give (*to*
  someone) I-2
dont *rel. pron.* of which; of
  whom; that II-3
dormir *v.* to sleep I-5

dos *m.* back II-2
  sac à dos *m.* backpack I-1
douane *f.* customs I-7
douche *f.* shower I-8, II-P
  prendre une douche *v.* to
  take a shower II-2
doué(e) *adj.* talented, gifted II-7
douleur *f.* pain II-2
douter (que) *v.* to doubt
  (that) II-7
douteux/douteuse *adj.*
  doubtful II-7
  Il est douteux que... It is
  doubtful that... II-7
doux/douce *adj.* sweet; soft I-3
douze *m.* twelve I-1
dramaturge *m.* playwright II-7
drame (psychologique) *m.*
  (psychological) drama II-7
draps *m., pl.* sheets I-8, II-P
droite *f.* the right (side) I-3
  à droite de *prep.* to the right
  of I-3
drôle *adj.* funny I-3
du *part. art., m., sing.* some I-4
du (de + le) *m., sing.* of the I-3
dû (devoir) *p.p., adj. (used with*
  infinitive) had to; (*used with*
  noun) due, owed II-1
duquel (de + lequel) *pron., m.,*
  sing. which one II-5

E

eau (minérale) *f.* (mineral)
  water I-4
  carafe d'eau *f.* pitcher of
  water II-1
écharpe *f.* scarf I-6
échecs *m., pl.* chess I-5
échouer *v.* to fail I-2
éclair *m.* éclair I-4
école *f.* school I-2
écologie *f.* ecology II-6
écologique *adj.* ecological II-6
économie *f.* economics I-2
écotourisme *m.* ecotourism II-6
écouter *v.* to listen (to) I-2
écran *m.* screen 11
écrire *v.* to write I-7
écrivain(e) *m., f.* writer II-7
écrit (écrire) *p.p., adj.* written I-7
écureuil *m.* squirrel II-6
éducation physique *f.* physical
  education I-2
effacer *v.* to erase II-3
effet de serre *m.* greenhouse
  effect II-6
égaler *v.* to equal I-3
église *f.* church I-4

égoïste *adj.* selfish I-1
Eh! *interj.* Hey! I-2
électrique *adj.* electric I-8, II-P
  appareil électrique/ménager
  m. electrical/household
  appliance I-8, II-P
électricien/électricienne *m., f.*
  electrician II-5
élégant(e) *adj.* elegant 1
élevé *adj.* high II-5
élève *m., f.* pupil, student I-1
elle *pron., f.* she; it I-1; her I-3
  elle est... she/it is... I-1
elles *pron., f.* they I-1; them I-3
  elles sont... they are... I-1
e-mail *m.* e-mail II-3
emballage (en plastique) *m.*
  (plastic) wrapping/
  packaging II-6
embaucher *v.* to hire II-5
embrayage *m.* (*automobile*)
  clutch II-3
émission (de télévision) *f.*
  (television) program II-7
emménager *v.* to move in
  I-8, II-P
emmener *v.* to take (*someone*) I-5
emploi *m.* job II-5
  emploi à mi-temps/à temps
  partiel *m.* part-time job II-5
  emploi à plein temps *m.*
  full-time job II-5
employé(e) *m., f.* employee II-5
employer *v.* to use, to employ I-5
emprunter *v.* to borrow II-4
en *prep.* in I-3
  en automne in the fall I-5
  en avance early I-2
  en avoir marre to be fed up I-6
  en effet indeed; in fact II-6
  en été in the summer I-5
  en face (de) *prep.* facing,
  across (from) I-3
  en fait in fact I-7
  en général *adv.* in general I-7
  en hiver in the winter I-5
  en plein air in fresh air II-6
  en retard late I-2
  en tout cas in any case 6
  en vacances on vacation 7
  être en ligne to be online II-3
en *pron.* some of it/them; about
  it/them; of it/them; from it/
  them II-2
  Je vous en prie. *form.*
  Please.; You're welcome. I-1
  Qu'en penses-tu? What do
  you think about that? II-6
enceinte *adj.* pregnant II-2
Enchanté(e). Delighted. I-1
encore *adv.* again; still I-3
endroit *m.* place I-4

énergie (nucléaire/solaire) *f.* (nuclear/solar) energy II-6
enfance *f.* childhood I-6
enfant *m., f.* child I-3
enfin *adv.* finally, at last I-7
enlever la poussière *v.* to dust I-8, II-P
ennuyeux/ennuyeuse *adj.* boring I-3
énorme *adj.* enormous, huge I-2
enregistrer *v.* to record II-3
enregistreur DVR *m.* DVR II-3
enseigner *v.* to teach I-2
ensemble *adv.* together I-6
ensuite *adv.* then, next I-7
entendre *v.* to hear I-6
entracte *m.* intermission II-7
entre *prep.* between I-3
entrée *f.* appetizer, starter II-1
entreprise *f.* firm, business II-5
entrer *v.* to enter I-7
entretien: passer un entretien *to have an interview* II-5
enveloppe *f.* envelope II-4
envie *f.* desire, envy I-2
  avoir envie (de) to feel like (*doing something*) I-2
environnement *m.* environment II-6
envoyer (à) *v.* to send (*to someone*) I-5
épargne *f.* savings II-4
  compte d'épargne *m.* savings account II-4
épicerie *f.* grocery store I-4
épouser *v.* to marry I-3
épouvantable *adj.* dreadful 5
  Il fait un temps épouvantable. The weather is dreadful. I-5
époux/épouse *m., f.* husband/wife I-3
équipe *f.* team I-5
escalier *m.* staircase I-8, II-P
escargot *m.* escargot, snail II-1
espace *m.* space II-6
Espagne *f.* Spain 7
espagnol(e) *adj.* Spanish I-1
espèce (menacée) *f.* (endangered) species II-6
espèces *m.* cash II-4
espérer *v.* to hope I-5
essayer *v.* to try I-5
essence *f.* gas II-3
  réservoir d'essence *m.* gas tank II-3
  voyant d'essence *m.* gas warning light II-3
essentiel(le) *adj.* essential II-6
  Il est essentiel que... It is essential that... II-6

essuie-glace *m.* (**essuie-glaces** *pl.*) windshield wiper(s) II-3
essuyer (la vaisselle/la table) *v.* to wipe (the dishes/the table) I-8, II-P
est *m.* east II-4
Est-ce que... ? (*used in forming questions*) I-2
et *conj.* and I-1
  Et toi? *fam.* And you? I-1
  Et vous? *form.* And you? I-1
étage *m.* floor I-7
étagère *f.* shelf I-8, II-P
étape *f.* stage I-6
États-Unis *m., pl.* United States I-7
été *m.* summer I-5
  en été in the summer I-5
été (être) *p.p.* been I-6
éteindre *v.* to turn off II-3
éternuer *v.* to sneeze II-2
étoile *f.* star II-6
étranger/étrangère *adj.* foreign I-2
  langues étrangères *f., pl.* foreign languages I-2
étranger *m.* (*places that are*) abroad, overseas I-7
  à l'étranger abroad, overseas I-7
étrangler *v.* to strangle II-5
être *v.* to be I-1
  être bien/mal payé(e) to be well/badly paid II-5
  être connecté(e) avec quelqu'un to be online with someone I-7, II-3
  être en ligne avec to be online with II-3
  être en pleine forme to be in good shape II-2
études (supérieures) *f., pl.* studies; (higher) education I-2
étudiant(e) *m., f.* student I-1
étudier *v.* to study I-2
eu (avoir) *p.p.* had I-6
eux *disj. pron., m., pl.* they, them I-3
évidemment *adv.* obviously, evidently; of course I-7
évident(e) *adj.* evident, obvious II-7
  Il est évident que... It is evident that... II-7
évier *m.* sink I-8, II-P

éviter (de) *v.* to avoid (*doing something*) II-2
exactement *adv.* exactly II-1
examen *m.* exam; test I-1
  être reçu(e) à un examen *v.* to pass an exam I-2

passer un examen *v.* to take an exam I-2
Excuse-moi. *fam.* Excuse me. I-1
Excusez-moi. *form.* Excuse me. I-1
exercice *m.* exercise II-2
  faire de l'exercice *v.* to exercise II-2
exigeant(e) *adj.* demanding II-5
  profession (exigeante) *f.* a (demanding) profession II-5
exiger (que) *v.* to demand (that) II-6
expérience (professionnelle) *f.* (professional) experience II-5
expliquer *v.* to explain I-2
explorer *v.* to explore I-4
exposition *f.* exhibit II-7
extinction *f.* extinction II-6

F

facile *adj.* easy I-2
facilement *adv.* easily I-8, II-P
facteur *m.* mailman II-4
faible *adj.* weak I-3
faim *f.* hunger I-4
  avoir faim *v.* to be hungry I-4
faire *v.* to do; to make I-5
  faire attention (à) *v.* to pay attention (to) I-5
  faire quelque chose de beau *v.* to be up to something interesting II-4
  faire de l'aérobic *v.* to do aerobics I-5
  faire de la gym *v.* to work out I-5
  faire de la musique *v.* to play music II-5
  faire de la peinture *v.* to paint II-7
  faire de la planche à voile *v.* to go windsurfing I-5
  faire de l'exercice *v.* to exercise II-2
  faire des projets *v.* to make plans II-5
  faire du camping *v.* to go camping I-5
  faire du cheval *v.* to go horseback riding I-5
  faire du jogging *v.* to go jogging I-5
  faire du shopping *v.* to go shopping I-7
  faire du ski *v.* to go skiing I-5
  faire du sport *v.* to do sports I-5
  faire du vélo *v.* to go bike riding I-5

faire la connaissance de v. to meet (*someone*) I-5
faire la cuisine v. to cook I-5
faire la fête v. to celebrate I-6
faire la lessive v. to do the laundry I-8, II-P
faire la poussière v. to dust I-8, II-P
faire la queue v. to wait in line II-4
faire la vaisselle v. to do the dishes I-8, II-P
faire le lit v. to make the bed I-8, II-P
faire le ménage v. to do the housework I-8, II-P
faire le plein v. to fill the tank II-3
faire les courses v. to run errands II-1
faire les musées v. to go to museums II-7
faire les valises v. to pack one's bags I-7
faire mal v. to hurt II-2
faire plaisir à quelqu'un v. to please someone II-5
faire sa toilette v. to wash up II-2
faire une piqûre v. to give a shot 10
faire une promenade v. to go for a walk I-5
faire une randonnée v. to go for a hike I-5
faire un séjour v. to spend time (*somewhere*) I-7
faire un tour (en voiture) v. to go for a walk (drive) I-5
faire visiter v. to give a tour I-8, II-P
fait (faire) p.p., adj. done; made I-6
falaise f. cliff II-6
faut (falloir) v. (*used with infinitive*) is necessary to... I-5
  Il a fallu... It was necessary to... I-6
  Il fallait... One had to... I-8, II-P
  Il faut que... One must.../It is necessary that... II-6
fallu (falloir) p.p. (*used with infinitive*) had to... I-6
  Il a fallu... It was necessary to... I-6
famille f. family I-3
fatigué(e) adj. tired I-3
fauteuil m. armchair I-8, II-P
favori/favorite adj. favorite I-3
fax m. fax (machine) II-3

félicitations congratulations II-7
femme f. woman; wife I-1
  femme d'affaires businesswoman I-3
  femme au foyer housewife II-5
  femme auteur author II-7
  femme cadre executive II-5
  femme peintre painter II-7
  femme politique politician II-5
  femme pompier firefighter II-5
fenêtre f. window I-1
fer à repasser m. iron I-8, II-P
férié(e) adj. holiday I-6
  jour férié m. holiday I-6
fermé(e) adj. closed II-4
fermer v. to close; to shut off II-3
festival (festivals pl.**)** m. festival II-7
fête f. party; celebration I-6
  faire la fête v. to celebrate I-6
fêter v. to celebrate I-6
feu de signalisation m. traffic light II-4
feuille de papier f. sheet of paper I-1
feuilleton m. soap opera II-7
février m. February I-5
fiancé(e) adj. engaged I-3
fiancé(e) m., f. fiancé I-6
fichier m. file II-3
fier/fière adj. proud I-3
fièvre f. fever II-2
  avoir de la fièvre v. to have a fever II-2
fille f. girl; daughter I-1
film (d'aventures, d'horreur, de science-fiction, policier) m. (adventure, horror, science-fiction, crime) film II-7
fils m. son I-3
fin f. end II-7
finalement adv. finally I-7
fini (finir) p.p., adj. finished, done, over I-4
finir (de) v. to finish (*doing something*) I-4
fleur f. flower I-8, II-P
fleuve m. river II-6
fois f. time I-8, II-P
  une fois adv. once I-8, II-P
  deux fois adv. twice I-8, II-P
fonctionner v. to work, to function II-3
fontaine f. fountain II-4
foot(ball) m. soccer I-5
  football américain m. football I-5
forêt (tropicale) f. (tropical) forest II-6

formation f. education; training II-5
forme f. shape; form II-2
  être en pleine forme v. to be in good shape II-2
formidable adj. great I-7
formulaire m. form II-4
  remplir un formulaire to fill out a form II-4
fort(e) adj. strong I-3
fou/folle adj. crazy I-3
four (à micro-ondes) m. (microwave) oven I-8, II-P
fourchette f. fork II-1
frais/fraîche adj. fresh; cool I-5
  Il fait frais. (*weather*) It is cool. I-5
fraise f. strawberry II-1
français(e) adj. French I-1
France f. France I-7
franchement adv. frankly, honestly I-7
freiner v. to brake II-3
freins m., pl. brakes II-3
fréquenter v. to frequent; to visit I-4
frère m. brother I-3
  beau-frère m. brother-in-law I-3
  demi-frère m. half-brother, stepbrother I-3
frigo m. refrigerator I-8, II-P
frisé(e) adj. curly I-3
frites f., pl. French fries I-4
froid m. cold I-2
  avoir froid to be cold I-2
  Il fait froid. (*weather*) It is cold. I-5
fromage m. cheese I-4
fruit m. fruit II-1
fruits de mer m., pl. seafood II-1
funérailles f., pl. funeral II-1
furieux/furieuse adj. furious II-6
  être furieux/furieuse que... v. to be furious that... II-6

G

gagner v. to win I-5; to earn II-5
gant m. glove I-6
garage m. garage I-8, II-P
garanti(e) adj. guaranteed 5
garçon m. boy I-1
garder la ligne v. to stay slim II-2
gare (routière) f. train station (bus station) I-7
gaspillage m. waste II-6
gaspiller v. to waste II-6
gâteau m. cake I-6
gauche f. the left (side) I-3
  à gauche (de) prep. to the left (of) I-3

gazeux/gazeuse *adj.* carbonated, fizzy **4**
boisson gazeuse *f.* carbonated drink/beverage **I-4**
généreux/généreuse *adj.* generous **I-3**
génial(e) *adj.* great **I-3**
genou *m.* knee **II-2**
genre *m.* genre **II-7**
gens *m., pl.* people **I-7**
gentil/gentille *adj.* nice **I-3**
gentiment *adv.* nicely **I-8, II-P**
géographie *f.* geography **I-2**
gérant(e) *m., f.* manager **II-5**
gestion *f.* business administration **I-2**
glace *f.* ice cream **I-6**
glaçon *m.* ice cube **I-6**
glissement de terrain *m.* landslide **II-6**
golf *m.* golf **I-5**
enfler *v.* to swell **II-2**
gorge *f.* throat **II-2**
goûter *m.* afternoon snack **II-1**; *v.* to taste **II-1**
gouvernement *m.* government **II-6**
grand(e) *adj.* big **I-3**
grand magasin *m.* department store **I-4**
grand-mère *f.* grandmother **I-3**
grand-père *m.* grandfather **I-3**
grands-parents *m., pl.* grandparents **I-3**
gratin *m.* gratin **II-1**
gratuit(e) *adj.* free **II-7**
grave *adj.* serious **II-2**
Ce n'est pas grave. It's okay.; No problem. **I-6**
grille-pain *m.* toaster **I-8, II-P**
grippe *f.* flu **II-2**
gris(e) *adj.* gray **I-6**
gros(se) *adj.* fat **I-3**
grossir *v.* to gain weight **I-4**
guérir *v.* to get better **II-2**
guitare *f.* guitar **II-7**
gym *f.* exercise **I-5**
faire de la gym *v.* to work out **I-5**
gymnase *m.* gym **I-4**

H

habitat *m.* habitat **II-6**
sauvetage des habitats *m.* habitat preservation **II-6**
habiter (à) *v.* to live (in/at) **I-2**
haricots verts *m., pl.* green beans **II-1**
Hein? *interj.* Huh?; Right? **I-3**
herbe *f.* grass **II-6**
hésiter (à) *v.* to hesitate (*to do something*) **II-3**

heure(s) *f.* hour, o'clock; time **I-2**
à ... heure(s) at ... (o'clock) **I-4**
À quelle heure? What time?; When? **I-2**
À tout à l'heure. See you later. **I-1**
Quelle heure avez-vous? *form.* What time do you have? **I-2**
Quelle heure est-il? What time is it? **I-2**
heureusement *adv.* fortunately **I-8, II-P**
heureux/heureuse *adj.* happy **I-3**
être heureux/heureuse que... to be happy that... **II-6**
hier (matin/après-midi/soir) *adv.* yesterday (morning/afternoon/evening) **I-7**
avant-hier *adv.* day before yesterday **I-7**
histoire *f.* history; story **I-2**
hiver *m.* winter **I-5**
en hiver in the winter **I-5**
homme *m.* man **I-1**
homme d'affaires *m.* businessman **I-3**
homme politique *m.* politician **II-5**
honnête *adj.* honest **II-7**
honte *f.* shame **I-2**
avoir honte (de) *v.* to be ashamed (of) **I-2**
hôpital *m.* hospital **I-4**
horloge *f.* clock **I-1**
hors-d'œuvre *m.* hors d'œuvre, appetizer **II-1**
hôte/hôtesse *m., f.* host **I-6**
hôtel *m.* hotel **I-7**
hôtelier/hôtelière *m., f.* hotel keeper **I-7**
huile *f.* oil **II-1**
huile *f.* (automobile) oil **II-3**
huile d'olive *f.* olive oil **II-1**
vérifier l'huile to check the oil **II-3**
voyant d'huile *m.* oil warning light **II-3**
huit *m.* eight **I-1**
huitième *adj.* eighth **I-7**
humeur *f.* mood **I-8, II-P**
être de bonne/mauvaise humeur *v.* to be in a good/bad mood **I-8, II-P**

I

ici *adv.* here **I-1**
idée *f.* idea **I-3**
il *sub. pron.* he; it **I-1**
il est... he/it is... **I-1**

Il n'y a pas de quoi. It's nothing.; You're welcome. **I-1**
Il vaut mieux que... It is better that... **II-6**
Il faut (falloir) *v.* (*used with infinitive*) It is necessary to... **I-6**
Il a fallu... It was necessary to... **I-6**
Il fallait... One had to... **I-8, II-P**
Il faut (que)... One must.../ It is necessary that... **II-6**
il y a there is/are **I-1**
il y a eu there was/were **6**
il y avait there was/were **I-8, II-P**
Qu'est-ce qu'il y a? What is it?; What's wrong? **I-1**
Y a-t-il... ? Is/Are there... ? **I-2**
il y a... (*used with an expression of time*) ... ago **II-1**
île *f.* island **II-6**
ils *sub. pron., m., pl.* they **I-1**
ils sont... they are... **I-1**
immeuble *m.* building **I-8, II-P**
impatient(e) *adj.* impatient **I-1**
imperméable *m.* rain jacket **I-5**
important(e) *adj.* important **I-1**
Il est important que... It is important that... **II-6**
impossible *adj.* impossible **II-7**
Il est impossible que... It is impossible that... **II-7**
imprimante *f.* printer **II-3**
imprimer *v.* to print **II-3**
incendie *m.* fire **II-6**
prévenir l'incendie to prevent a fire **II-6**
incroyable *adj.* incredible **II-3**
indépendamment *adv.* independently **I-8, II-P**
indépendant(e) *adj.* independent **I-1**
indications *f.* directions **II-4**
indiquer *v.* to indicate **I-5**
indispensable *adj.* essential, indispensable **II-6**
Il est indispensable que... It is essential that... **II-6**
individuel(le) *adj.* single, individual **I-7**
chambre individuelle *f.* single (hotel) room **I-7**
infirmier/infirmière *m., f.* nurse **II-2**
informations (infos) *f., pl.* news **II-7**
informatique *f.* computer science **I-2**
ingénieur *m.* engineer **I-3**
inquiet/inquiète *adj.* worried **I-3**

instrument *m.* instrument I-1
intellectuel(le) *adj.* intellectual I-3
intelligent(e) *adj.* intelligent I-1
interdire *v.* to forbid, to prohibit II-6
intéressant(e) *adj.* interesting I-1
inutile *adj.* useless I-2
invité(e) *m., f.* guest I-6
inviter *v.* to invite I-4
irlandais(e) *adj.* Irish I-7
Irlande *f.* Ireland I-7
Italie *f.* Italy I-7
italien(ne) *adj.* Italian I-1

J

jaloux/jalouse *adj.* jealous I-3
jamais *adv.* never I-5
  ne... jamais never, not ever II-4
jambe *f.* leg II-2
jambon *m.* ham I-4
janvier *m.* January I-5
Japon *m.* Japan I-7
japonais(e) *adj.* Japanese I-1
jardin *m.* garden; yard I-8, II-P
jaune *adj.* yellow I-6
je/j' *sub. pron.* I I-1
  Je vous en prie. *form.* Please.; You're welcome. I-1
jean *m., sing.* jeans I-6
jeter *v.* to throw away II-6
jeu *m.* game I-5
  jeu télévisé *m.* game show II-7
  jeu vidéo (des jeux vidéo) *m.* video game(s) II-3
jeudi *m.* Thursday I-2
jeune *adj.* young I-3
  jeunes mariés *m., pl.* newlyweds I-6
jeunesse *f.* youth I-6
  auberge de jeunesse *f.* youth hostel I-7
jogging *m.* jogging I-5
  faire du jogging *v.* to go jogging I-5
joli(e) *adj.* handsome; beautiful I-3
joue *f.* cheek II-2
jouer (à/de) *v.* to play (*a sport/a musical instrument*) I-5
  jouer un rôle *v.* to play a role II-7
joueur/joueuse *m., f.* player I-5
jour *m.* day I-2
  jour de congé *m.* day off I-7
  jour férié *m.* holiday I-6
  Quel jour sommes-nous? *What day is it?* I-2
journal *m.* newspaper; journal I-7

journaliste *m., f.* journalist I-3
journée *f.* day I-2
juillet *m.* July I-5
juin *m.* June I-5
jungle *f.* jungle II-6
jupe *f.* skirt I-6
jus (d'orange/de pomme) *m.* (orange/apple) juice I-4
jusqu'à (ce que) *prep.* until II-4
juste *adv.* just; right I-3
  juste à côté right next door I-3

K

kilo(gramme) *m.* kilo(gram) II-1
kiosque *m.* kiosk I-4

L

l' *def. art., m., f. sing.* the I-1; *d.o. pron., m., f.* him; her; it I-7
la *def. art., f. sing.* the I-1; *d.o. pron., f.* her; it I-7
là(-bas) (over) there I-1
-là (*used with demonstrative adjective* **ce** *and noun or with demonstrative pronoun* **celui**) there I-6
lac *m.* lake II-6
laid(e) *adj.* ugly I-3
laine *f.* wool II-4
laisser *v.* to let, to allow II-3
  laisser tranquille *v.* to leave alone II-2
  laisser un message *v.* to leave a message II-5
  laisser un pourboire *v.* to leave a tip I-4
lait *m.* milk I-4
laitue *f.* lettuce II-1
lampe *f.* lamp I-8, II-P
langues (étrangères) *f., pl.* (foreign) languages I-2
lapin *m.* rabbit II-6
laquelle *pron., f., sing.* which one II-5
  à laquelle *pron., f., sing.* which one II-5
  de laquelle *pron., f., sing.* which one II-5
large *adj.* loose; big I-6
lavabo *m.* bathroom sink I-8, II-P
lave-linge *m.* washing machine I-8, II-P
laver *v.* to wash I-8, II-P
laverie *f.* laundromat II-4
lave-vaisselle *m.* dishwasher I-8, II-P
le *def. art., m. sing.* the I-1; *d.o. pron.* him; it I-7
légume *m.* vegetable II-1
lent(e) *adj.* slow I-3

lentement *adv.* slowly I-7
lequel *pron., m., sing.* which one II-5
  auquel (à + lequel) *pron., m., sing.* which one II-5
  duquel (de + lequel) *pron., m., sing.* which one II-5
les *def. art., m., f., pl.* the I-1; *d.o. pron., m., f., pl.* them I-7
lesquelles *pron., f., pl.* which ones II-5
  auxquelles (à + lesquelles) *pron., f., pl.* which ones II-5
  desquelles (de + lesquelles) *pron., f., pl.* which ones II-5
lesquels *pron., m., pl.* which ones II-5
  auxquels (à + lesquels) *pron., m., pl.* which ones II-5
  desquels (de + lesquels) *pron., m., pl.* which ones II-5
lessive *f.* laundry I-8, II-P
  faire la lessive *v.* to do the laundry I-8, II-P
lettre *f.* letter II-4
  boîte aux lettres *f.* mailbox II-4
  lettre de motivation *f.* letter of application II-5
  lettre de recommandation *f.* letter of recommendation, reference letter II-5
lettres *f., pl.* humanities I-2
leur *i.o. pron., m., f., pl.* them I-6
leur(s) *poss. adj., m., f.* their I-3
librairie *f.* bookstore I-1
libre *adj.* available I-7
lien *m.* link II-3
lieu *m.* place I-4
ligne *f.* figure, shape II-2
  garder la ligne *v.* to stay slim II-2
limitation de vitesse *f.* speed limit II-3
limonade *f.* lemon soda I-4
linge *m.* laundry I-8, II-P
  lave-linge *m.* washing machine I-8, II-P
  sèche-linge *m.* clothes dryer I-8, II-P
lire *v.* to read I-7
lit *m.* bed I-7
  faire le lit *v.* to make the bed I-8, II-P
littéraire *adj.* literary II-7
littérature *f.* literature I-1
livre *m.* book I-1
logement *m.* housing I-8, II-P
logiciel *m.* software, program II-3
loi *f.* law II-6
loin de *prep.* far from I-3
loisir *m.* leisure activity I-5
long(ue) *adj.* long I-3

chemise à manches longues *f.* long-sleeved shirt I-6
longtemps *adv.* a long time I-5
louer *v.* to rent I-8, II-P
loyer *m.* rent I-8, II-P
lu (lire) *p.p.* read I-7
lui *pron., sing.* he I-1; him I-3; *i.o. pron.* (*attached to imperative*) to him/her II-1
l'un(e) à l'autre to one another II-3
l'un(e) l'autre one another II-3
lundi *m.* Monday I-2
Lune *f.* moon II-6
lunettes (de soleil) *f., pl.* (sun)glasses I-6
lycée *m.* high school I-1
lycéen(ne) *m., f.* high school student I-2

M

ma *poss. adj., f., sing.* my I-3
Madame *f.* Ma'am; Mrs. I-1
Mademoiselle *f.* Miss I-1
magasin *m.* store I-4
grand magasin *m.* department store I-4
magazine *m.* magazine II-7
magnétophone *m.* tape recorder II-3
magnétoscope *m.* videocassette recorder (VCR) II-3
mai *m.* May I-5
maigrir *v.* to lose weight I-4
maillot de bain *m.* swimsuit, bathing suit I-6
main *f.* hand I-5
sac à main *m.* purse, handbag I-6
maintenant *adv.* now I-5
maintenir *v.* to maintain II-1
mairie *f.* town/city hall; mayor's office II-4
mais *conj.* but I-1
mais non (but) of course not; no I-2
maison *f.* house I-4
rentrer à la maison *v.* to return home I-2
mal *adv.* badly I-7
Je vais mal. I am doing badly. I-1
le plus mal *super. adv.* the worst II-1
se porter mal *v.* to be doing badly II-2
mal *m.* illness; ache, pain II-2
avoir mal *v.* to have an ache II-2
avoir mal au cœur *v.* to feel nauseated II-2
faire mal *v.* to hurt II-2
malade *adj.* sick, ill II-2

tomber malade *v.* to get sick II-2
maladie *f.* illness II-5
assurance maladie *f.* health insurance II-5
malheureusement *adv.* unfortunately I-7
malheureux/malheureuse *adj.* unhappy I-3
manche *f.* sleeve I-6
chemise à manches courtes/ longues *f.* short-/long-sleeved shirt I-6
manger *v.* to eat I-2
salle à manger *f.* dining room I-8, II-P
manteau *m.* coat I-6
maquillage *m.* makeup II-2
marchand de journaux *m.* newsstand II-4
marché *m.* market I-4
bon marché *adj.* inexpensive I-6
marcher *v.* to walk (*person*) I-5; to work (*thing*) II-3
mardi *m.* Tuesday I-2
mari *m.* husband I-3
mariage *m.* marriage; wedding (*ceremony*) I-6
marié(e) *adj.* married I-3
mariés *m., pl.* married couple I-6
jeunes mariés *m., pl.* newlyweds I-6
marocain(e) *adj.* Moroccan I-1
marron *adj., inv.* (not for hair) brown I-3
mars *m.* March I-5
martiniquais(e) *adj.* from Martinique I-1
match *m.* game I-5
mathématiques (maths) *f., pl.* mathematics I-2
matin *m.* morning I-2
ce matin *adv.* this morning I-2
demain matin *adv.* tomorrow morning I-2
hier matin *adv.* yesterday morning I-7
matinée *f.* morning I-2
mauvais(e) *adj.* bad I-3
Il fait mauvais. The weather is bad. I-5
le/la plus mauvais(e) *super. adj.* the worst II-1
mayonnaise *f.* mayonnaise II-1
me/m' *pron., sing.* me; myself I-6
mec *m.* guy II-2
mécanicien *m.* mechanic II-3
mécanicienne *f.* mechanic II-3
méchant(e) *adj.* mean I-3
médecin *m.* doctor I-3
médicament (contre/pour) *m.* medication (against/for) II-2
meilleur(e) *comp. adj.* better II-1

le/la meilleur(e) *super. adj.* the best II-1
membre *m.* member II-7
même *adj.* even II-5; same
-même(s) *pron.* -self/-selves I-6
menacé(e) *adj.* endangered II-6
espèce menacée *f.* endangered species II-6
ménage *m.* housework I-8, II-P
faire le ménage *v.* to do housework I-8, II-P
ménager/ménagère *adj.* household I-8, II-P
appareil ménager *m.* household appliance I-8, II-P
tâche ménagère *f.* household chore I-8, II-P
mention *f.* distinction II-5
menu *m.* menu II-1
mer *f.* sea I-7
Merci (beaucoup). Thank you (very much). I-1
mercredi *m.* Wednesday I-2
mère *f.* mother I-3
belle-mère *f.* mother-in-law; stepmother I-3
mes *poss. adj., m., f., pl.* my I-3
message *m.* message II-5
laisser un message *v.* to leave a message II-5
messagerie *f.* voicemail II-5
météo *f.* weather II-7
métier *m.* profession II-5
métro *m.* subway I-7
station de métro *f.* subway station I-7
metteur en scène *m.* director (*of a play*) II-7
mettre *v.* to put, to place 6
mettre la table to set the table I-8, II-P
meuble *m.* piece of furniture I-8, II-P
mexicain(e) *adj.* Mexican I-1
Mexique *m.* Mexico I-7
Miam! *interj.* Yum! I-5
micro-onde *m.* microwave oven I-8, II-P
four à micro-ondes *m.* microwave oven I-8, II-P
midi *m.* noon I-2
après-midi *m.* afternoon I-2
mieux *comp. adv.* better II-1
aimer mieux *v.* to prefer I-2
le mieux *super. adv.* the best II-1
se porter mieux *v.* to be doing better II-2
mille *m.* one thousand I-5
cent mille *m.* one hundred thousand I-5
million, un *m.* one million I-5
deux millions *m.* two million I-5

minuit *m.* midnight I-2
miroir *m.* mirror I-8, II-P
mis (mettre) *p.p.* put, placed I-6
mode *f.* fashion I-2
modeste *adj.* modest II-5
moi *disj. pron., sing.* I, me I-3; *pron. (attached to an imperative)* to me, to myself II-1
  Moi aussi. Me too. I-1
  Moi non plus. Me neither. I-2
moins *adv.* before … (o'clock) I-2
moins (de) *adv.* less (of); fewer I-4
  le/la moins *super. adv. (used with verb or adverb)* the least II-1
  le moins de… *(used with noun to express quantity)* the least… II-6
  moins de… que… *(used with noun to express quantity)* less… than… II-6
mois *m.* month I-2
  ce mois-ci this month I-2
moment *m.* moment I-1
mon *poss. adj., m., sing.* my I-3
monde *m.* world I-7
monnaie *f.* change, coins; money II-4
Monsieur *m.* Sir; Mr. I-1
montagne *f.* mountain I-4
monter *v.* to go up, to come up; to get in/on I-7
montre *f.* watch I-1
montrer (à) *v.* to show *(to someone)* I-6
morceau (de) *m.* piece, bit (of) I-4
mort *f.* death I-6
mort (mourir) *p.p., adj. (as past participle)* died; *(as adjective)* dead I-7
mot de passe *m.* password II-3
moteur *m.* engine II-3
mourir *v.* to die I-7
moutarde *f.* mustard II-1
moyen(ne) *adj.* medium I-3
  de taille moyenne of medium height I-3
MP3 *m.* MP3 II-3
mur *m.* wall I-8, II-P
musée *m.* museum I-4
  faire les musées *v.* to go to museums II-7
musical(e) *adj.* musical II-7
  comédie musicale *f.* musical II-7
musicien(ne) *m., f.* musician I-3
musique: faire de la musique *v.* to play music II-7

N

nager *v.* to swim I-4
naïf/naïve *adj.* naïve I-3
naissance *f.* birth I-6
naître *v.* to be born I-7
nappe *f.* tablecloth II-1
nationalité *f.* nationality I-1
  Je suis de nationalité… I am of … nationality. I-1
  Quelle est ta nationalité? *fam.* What is your nationality? I-1
  Quelle est votre nationalité? *fam., pl., form.* What is your nationality? I-1
nature *f.* nature II-6
naturel(le) *adj.* natural II-6
  ressource naturelle *f.* natural resource II-6
né (naître) *p.p., adj.* born I-7
ne/n' no, not I-1
  ne… aucun(e) none, not any II-4
  ne… jamais never, not ever II-4
  ne… ni… ni… neither… nor… II-4
  ne… pas no, not I-2
  ne… personne nobody, no one II-4
  ne… plus no more, not anymore II-4
  ne… que only II-4
  ne… rien nothing, not anything II-4
  N'est-ce pas? *(tag question)* Isn't it? I-2
nécessaire *adj.* necessary II-6
  Il est nécessaire que… It is necessary that… II-6
neiger *v.* to snow I-5
  Il neige. It is snowing. I-5
nerveusement *adv.* nervously I-8, II-P
nerveux/nerveuse *adj.* nervous I-3
nettoyer *v.* to clean I-5
neuf *m.* nine I-1
neuvième *adj.* ninth I-7
neveu *m.* nephew I-3
nez *m.* nose II-2
ni nor II-4
  ne… ni… ni… neither… nor II-4
nièce *f.* niece I-3
niveau *m.* level II-5
noir(e) *adj.* black I-3
non no I-2
  mais non (but) of course not; no I-2
nord *m.* north II-4

nos *poss. adj., m., f., pl.* our I-3
note *f. (academics)* grade I-2
notre *poss. adj., m., f., sing.* our I-3
nourriture *f.* food, sustenance II-1
nous *pron.* we I-1; us I-3; ourselves II-2
nouveau/nouvelle *adj.* new I-3
nouvelles *f., pl.* news II-7
novembre *m.* November I-5
nuage de pollution *m.* pollution cloud II-6
nuageux/nuageuse *adj.* cloudy I-5
  Le temps est nuageux. It is cloudy. I-5
nucléaire *adj.* nuclear II-6
  centrale nucléaire *f.* nuclear plant II-6
  énergie nucléaire *f.* nuclear energy II-6
nuit *f.* night I-2
  boîte de nuit *f.* nightclub I-4
nul(le) *adj.* useless I-2
numéro *m. (telephone)* number II-3
  composer un numéro *v.* to dial a number II-3
  recomposer un numéro *v.* to redial a number II-3

O

objet *m.* object I-1
obtenir *v.* to get, to obtain II-5
occupé(e) *adj.* busy I-1
octobre *m.* October I-5
œil (les yeux) *m.* eye (eyes) II-2
œuf *m.* egg II-1
œuvre *f.* artwork, piece of art II-7
  chef-d'œuvre *m.* masterpiece II-7
  hors-d'œuvre *m.* hors d'œuvre, starter II-1
offert (offrir) *p.p.* offered II-3
office du tourisme *m.* tourist office II-4
offrir *v.* to offer II-3
oignon *m.* onion II-1
oiseau *m.* bird I-3
olive *f.* olive II-1
  huile d'olive *f.* olive oil II-1
omelette *f.* omelette I-5
on *sub. pron., sing.* one (we) I-1
  on y va let's go II-2
oncle *m.* uncle I-3
onze *m.* eleven I-1
onzième *adj.* eleventh I-7
opéra *m.* opera II-7
optimiste *adj.* optimistic I-1
orageux/orageuse *adj.* stormy I-5
  Le temps est orageux. It is stormy. I-5

Vocabulary

orange *adj. inv.* orange I-6;
  f. orange II-1
orchestre *m.* orchestra II-7
ordinateur *m.* computer I-1
ordonnance *f.* prescription II-2
ordures *f., pl.* trash II-6
  ramassage des ordures *m.*
  garbage collection II-6
oreille *f.* ear II-2
oreiller *m.* pillow I-8, II-P
organiser (une fête) *v.* to
  organize/to plan (a party) I-6
origine *f.* heritage I-1
  Je suis d'origine... I am of...
  heritage. I-1
orteil *m.* toe II-2
ou *or* I-3
où *adv., rel. pron.* where 4
ouais *adv.* yeah I-2
oublier (de) *v.* to forget (*to do
  something*) I-2
ouest *m.* west II-4
oui *adv.* yes I-2
ouvert (ouvrir) *p.p., adj. (as past
  participle)* opened; (*as adjective*)
  open II-3
ouvrier/ouvrière *m., f.* worker,
  laborer II-5
ouvrir *v.* to open II-3
ozone *m.* ozone II-6
  **trou dans la couche
  d'ozone** *m.* hole in the ozone
  layer II-6

P

page d'accueil *f.* home page II-3
pain (de campagne) *m.*
  (country-style) bread I-4
panne *f.* breakdown,
  malfunction II-3
  tomber en panne *v.* to break
  down II-3
pantalon *m., sing.* pants I-6
pantoufle *f.* slipper II-2
papeterie *f.* stationery store II-4
papier *m.* paper I-1
  corbeille à papier
  f. wastebasket I-1
  feuille de papier *f.* sheet of
  paper I-1
paquet cadeau *m.* wrapped
  gift I-6
par *prep.* by I-3
  par jour/semaine/mois/an
  per day/week/month/year I-5
parapluie *m.* umbrella I-5
parc *m.* park I-4
parce que *conj.* because I-2
Pardon. Pardon (me). I-1
Pardon? What? I-4
pare-brise *m.* windshield II-3
pare-chocs *m.* bumper II-3

parents *m., pl.* parents I-3
paresseux/paresseuse *adj.*
  lazy I-3
parfait(e) *adj.* perfect I-4
parfois *adv.* sometimes I-5
parking *m.* parking lot II-3
parler (à) *v.* to speak (to) I-6
  parler (au téléphone) *v.* to
  speak (on the phone) I-2
partager *v.* to share I-2
partir *v.* to leave I-5
  partir en vacances *v.* to go
  on vacation I-7
pas (de) *adv.* no, none II-4
  ne... pas no, not I-2
  pas de problème no
  problem II-4
  pas du tout not at all I-2
  pas encore not yet I-8, II-P
  Pas mal. Not badly. I-1
passager/passagère *m., f.*
  passenger I-7
passeport *m.* passport I-7
passer *v.* to pass by; to spend
  time I-7
  passer chez quelqu'un *v.* to
  stop by someone's house I-4
  passer l'aspirateur *v.* to
  vacuum I-8, II-P
  passer un examen *v.* to take
  an exam I-2
passe-temps *m.* pastime,
  hobby I-5
pâté (de campagne) *m.* pâté,
  meat spread II-1
pâtes *f., pl.* pasta II-1
patiemment *adv.* patiently
  I-8, II-P
patient(e) *m., f.* patient II-2;
  adj. patient I-1
patienter *v.* to wait (on the
  phone), to be on hold II-5
patiner *v.* to skate I-4
pâtisserie *f.* pastry shop, bakery,
  pastry II-1
patron(ne) *m., f.* boss II-5
pauvre *adj.* poor I-3
payé (payer) *p.p., adj.* paid II-5
  être bien/mal payé(e) *v.* to
  be well/badly paid II-5
payer *v.* to pay I-5
  **payer par carte (bancaire/
  de crédit)** *v.* to pay with a
  (debit/credit) card II-4
  payer en espèces *v.* to pay
  in cash II-4
  payer par chèque *v.* to pay
  by check II-4
pays *m.* country I-7
peau *f.* skin II-2
pêche *f.* fishing I-5; peach II-1
  aller à la pêche *v.* to go
  fishing I-5

peigne *m.* comb II-2
peintre/femme peintre *m., f.*
  painter II-7
peinture *f.* painting II-7
pendant (que) *prep.* during,
  while I-7
  pendant (*with time expression*)
  prep. for II-1
pénible *adj.* tiresome I-3
penser (que) *v.* to think (that) I-2
  ne pas penser que... to not
  think that... II-7
  Qu'en penses-tu? What do
  you think about that? II-6
perdre *v.* to lose I-6
  perdre son temps *v.* to waste
  time I-6
perdu *p.p., adj.* lost II-4
  être perdu(e) to be lost II-4
père *m.* father I-3
  beau-père *m.* father-in-law;
  stepfather I-3
permettre (de) *v.* to allow (*to
  do something*) I-6
permis *m.* permit; license II-3
  permis de conduire *m.* driver's
  license II-3
permis (permettre) *p.p., adj.*
  permitted, allowed I-6
personnage (principal) *m.*
  (main) character II-7
personne *f.* person I-1; *pron.* no
  one II-4
  ne... personne nobody, no
  one II-4
pessimiste *adj.* pessimistic I-1
petit(e) *adj.* small I-3; short
  (*stature*) I-3
  petit(e) ami(e) *m., f.* boy-
  friend/girlfriend I-1
petit-déjeuner *m.* breakfast II-1
petite-fille *f.* granddaughter I-3
petit-fils *m.* grandson I-3
petits-enfants *m., pl.* grandchildren I-3
petits pois *m., pl.* peas II-1
peu (de) *adv.* little; not much
  (of) I-2
peur *f.* fear I-2
  avoir peur (de/que) *v.* to be
  afraid (of/that) I-2
peut-être *adv.* maybe, perhaps I-2
phares *m., pl.* headlights II-3
pharmacie *f.* pharmacy II-2
pharmacien(ne) *m., f.*
  pharmacist II-2
philosophie *f.* philosophy I-2
photo(graphie) *f.* photo
  (graph) I-3
physique *f.* physics I-2
piano *m.* piano II-7
pièce *f.* room I-8, II-P
pièce de théâtre *f.* play II-7

pièces de monnaie *f., pl.* change II-4
pied *m.* foot II-2
pierre *f.* stone II-6
pilule *f.* pill II-2
pique-nique *m.* picnic II-6
piqûre *f.* shot, injection II-2
  faire une piqûre *v.* to give a shot II-2
pire *comp. adj.* worse II-1
  le/la pire *super. adj.* the worst II-1
piscine *f.* pool I-4
placard *m.* closet; cupboard I-8, II-P
place *f.* square; place I-4; *f.* seat II-7
plage *f.* beach I-7
plaisir *m.* pleasure, enjoyment II-5
  faire plaisir à quelqu'un *v.* to please someone II-5
plan *m.* map I-7
  utiliser un plan *v.* to use a map I-7
planche à voile *f.* windsurfing I-5
  faire de la planche à voile *v.* to go windsurfing I-5
planète *f.* planet II-6
  sauver la planète *v.* to save the planet II-6
plante *f.* plant II-6
plastique *m.* plastic II-6
  emballage en plastique *m.* plastic wrapping/packaging II-6
plat (principal) *m.* (main) dish II-1
plein air *m.* outdoor, open-air II-6
pleine forme *f.* good shape, good state of health II-2
  être en pleine forme *v.* to be in good shape II-2
pleurer *v.* to cry
pleuvoir *v.* to rain I-5
  Il pleut. It is raining. I-5
plombier *m.* plumber II-5
plu (pleuvoir) *p.p.* rained I-6
pluie acide *f.* acid rain II-6
plus *adv. (used in comparatives, superlatives, and expressions of quantity)* more I-4
  le/la plus ... *super. adv. (used with adjective)* the most II-1
  le/la plus mauvais(e) *super. adj.* the worst II-1
  le plus *super. adv. (used with verb or adverb)* the most II-1
  le plus de... *(used with noun to express quantity)* the most... II-6
  le plus mal *super. adv.* the worst II-1
  plus... que *(used with adjective)* more... than II-1

plus de more of I-4
plus de... que *(used with noun to express quantity)* more... than II-6
plus mal *comp. adv.* worse II-1
plus mauvais(e) *comp. adj.* worse II-1
plus *adv.* no more, not any-more II-4
  ne... plus no more, not any-more II-4
plusieurs *adj.* several I-4
plutôt *adv.* rather I-2
pneu (crevé) *m.* (flat) tire II-3
  vérifier la pression des pneus *v.* to check the tire pressure II-3
poème *m.* poem II-7
poète/poétesse *m., f.* poet II-7
point *m. (punctuation mark)* period II-3
poire *f.* pear II-1
poisson *m.* fish I-3
poissonnerie *f.* fish shop II-1
poitrine *f.* chest II-2
poivre *m. (spice)* pepper II-1
poivron *m. (vegetable)* pepper II-1
poli(e) *adj.* polite I-1
police *f.* police II-3
  agent de police *m.* police officer II-3
  commissariat de police *m.* police station II-4
policier *m.* police officer II-3
  film policier *m.* detective film II-7
policière *f.* police officer II-3
poliment *adv.* politely I-8, II-P
politique *adj.* political I-2
  femme politique *f.* politician II-5
  homme politique *m.* politician II-5
  sciences politiques (sciences po) *f., pl.* political science I-2
polluer *v.* to pollute II-6
pollution *f.* pollution II-6
  nuage de pollution *m.* pollution cloud II-6
pomme *f.* apple II-1
pomme de terre *f.* potato II-1
pompier/femme pompier *m., f.* firefighter II-5
pont *m.* bridge II-4
population croissante *f.* growing population II-6
porc *m.* pork II-1
portable *m.* cell phone II-3
porte *f.* door I-1
porter *v.* to wear I-6
portière *f.* car door II-3
portrait *m.* portrait I-5
poser une question (à) *v.* to ask (*someone*) a question I-6

posséder *v.* to possess, to own I-5
possible *adj.* possible II-7
  Il est possible que... It is possible that... II-6
poste *f.* postal service; post office II-4
  bureau de poste *m.* post office II-4
poste *m.* position II-5
poster une lettre *v.* to mail a letter II-4
postuler *v.* to apply II-5
poulet *m.* chicken II-1
pour *prep.* for I-5
  pour qui? for whom? I-4
  pour rien for no reason I-4
  pour que so that II-7
pourboire *m.* tip I-4
  laisser un pourboire *v.* to leave a tip I-4
pourquoi? *adv.* why? I-2
poussière *f.* dust I-8, II-P
  enlever/faire la poussière *v.* to dust I-8, II-P
pouvoir *v.* to be able to; can II-1
pratiquer *v.* to play regularly, to practice I-5
préféré(e) *adj.* favorite, preferred I-2
préférer (que) *v.* to prefer (that) I-5
premier *m.* the first (*day of the month*) I-5
  C'est le 1ᵉʳ (premier) octobre. It is October first. I-5
premier/première *adj.* first I-2
prendre *v.* to take I-4; to have I-4
  prendre sa retraite *v.* to retire I-6
  prendre un train/avion/ taxi/autobus/bateau *v.* to take a train/plane/taxi/bus/ boat I-7
  prendre un congé *v.* to take time off II-5
  prendre une douche *v.* to take a shower II-2
  prendre (un) rendez-vous *v.* to make an appointment II-5
  prendre une photo(graphe) *v.* to take a photo(graph) II-3
préparer *v.* to prepare (for) I-2
près (de) *prep.* close (to), near I-3
  tout près (de) very close (to) II-4
présenter *v.* to present, to introduce II-7
  Je te présente... *fam.* I would like to introduce... to you. I-1
  Je vous présente... *fam., form.* I would like to introduce... to you. I-1

préservation *f.* protection II-6
préserver *v.* to preserve II-6
presque *adv.* almost I-2
pressé(e) *adj.* hurried II-1
pression *f.* pressure II-3
   vérifier la pression des pneus
   to check the tire pressure II-3
prêt(e) *adj.* ready I-3
prêter (à) *v.* to lend
   (*to someone*) I-6
prévenir l'incendie *v.* to prevent
   a fire II-6
principal(e) *adj.* main,
   principal II-1
   personnage principal *m.*
   main character II-7
   plat principal *m.* main dish II-1
printemps *m.* spring I-5
   au printemps in the spring I-5
pris (prendre) *p.p., adj.* taken I-6
prix *m.* price I-4
problème *m.* problem I-1
prochain(e) *adj.* next I-2
produire *v.* to produce I-6
produit *m.* product II-6
produit (produire) *p.p., adj.*
   produced I-6
professeur *m.* teacher, professor I-1
profession (exigeante) *f.*
   (demanding) profession II-5
professionnel(le) *adj.*
   professional II-5
   expérience professionnelle *f.*
   professional experience II-5
profiter (de) *v.* to take advantage
   (of); to enjoy II-7
programme *m.* program II-7
projet *m.* project II-5
   faire des projets *v.* to make
   plans II-5
promenade *f.* walk, stroll I-5
   faire une promenade *v.* to go
   for a walk I-5
promettre *v.* to promise I-6
promis (promettre) *p.p., adj.*
   promised I-6
promotion *f.* promotion II-5
proposer (que) *v.* to propose
   (that) II-6
   proposer une solution *v.* to
   propose a solution II-6
propre *adj.* clean I-8, II-P
propriétaire *m., f.* owner I-8, II-P
protection *f.* protection II-6
protéger *v.* to protect 5
psychologie *f.* psychology I-2
psychologique *adj.*
   psychological II-7
psychologue *m., f.* psychologist II-5
pu (pouvoir) *p.p. (used with
   infinitive)* was able to 9

publicité (pub) *f.* advertisement II-7
publier *v.* to publish II-7
puis *adv.* then I-7
pull *m.* sweater I-6
pur(e) *adj.* pure II-6

Q

quand *adv.* when I-4
   **C'est quand l'anniversaire
   de … ?** When is …'s
   birthday? I-5
   **C'est quand ton/votre
   anniversaire?** When is your
   birthday? I-5
quarante *m.* forty I-1
quart *m.* quarter I-2
   et quart a quarter after…
   (o'clock) I-2
quartier *m.* area,
   neighborhood I-8, II-P
quatorze *m.* fourteen I-1
quatre *m.* four I-1
quatre-vingts *m.* eighty I-3
quatre-vingt-dix *m.* ninety I-3
quatrième *adj.* fourth I-7
que/qu' *rel. pron.* that; which II-3;
   conj. than II-1, II-6
   plus/moins … que *(used with
   adjective)* more/less … than II-1
   plus/moins de … que *(used
   with noun to express quantity)*
   more/less … than II-6
que/qu'…? *interr. pron.* what? I-4
   Qu'en penses-tu? What do
   you think about that? II-6
   Qu'est-ce que c'est? What is
   it? I-1
   Qu'est-ce qu'il y a? What is
   it?; What's wrong? I-1
que *adv.* only II-4
   ne… que only II-4
québécois(e) *adj.* from Quebec I-1
quel(le)(s)? *interr. adj.* which? I-4;
   what? I-4
   À quelle heure? What time?;
   When? I-2
   Quel jour sommes-nous?
   What day is it? I-2
   Quelle est la date? What is
   the date? I-5
   Quelle est ta nationalité?
   fam. What is your nationality? I-1
   Quelle est votre nationalité?
   form. What is your nationality? I-1
   Quelle heure avez-vous?
   form. What time do you have? I-2
   Quelle heure est-il? What
   time is it? I-2
   Quelle température fait-il?
   (weather) What is the
   temperature? I-5

   Quel temps fait-il? What is
   the weather like? I-5
quelqu'un *pron.* someone II-4
quelque chose *m.* something;
   anything I-4
   Quelque chose ne va pas.
   Something's not right. I-5
quelquefois *adv.* sometimes I-7
quelques *adj.* some I-4
question *f.* question I-6
   poser une question (à) to ask
   (*someone*) a question I-6
queue *f.* line II-4
   faire la queue *v.* to wait in
   line II-4
qui? *interr. pron.* who? I-4;
   whom? I-4; *rel. pron.* who,
   that II-3
   à qui? to whom? I-4
   avec qui? with whom? I-4
   C'est de la part de qui? On
   behalf of whom? II-5
   Qui est à l'appareil? Who's
   calling, please? II-5
   Qui est-ce? Who is it? I-1
quinze *m.* fifteen I-1
quitter (la maison) *v.* to leave
   (the house) I-4
   Ne quittez pas. Please
   hold. II-5
quoi? *interr. pron.* what? I-1
   Il n'y a pas de quoi. It's
   nothing.; You're welcome. I-1
   quoi que ce soit whatever it
   may be II-5

R

raccrocher *v.* to hang up II-5
radio *f.* radio II-7
   à la radio on the radio II-7
raide *adj.* straight I-3
raison *f.* reason; right I-2
   avoir raison *v.* to be right I-2
ramassage des ordures *m.*
   garbage collection II-6
randonnée *f.* hike I-5
   faire une randonnée *v.* to go
   for a hike I-5
ranger *v.* to tidy up, to put away
   I-8, II-P
rapide *adj.* fast I-3
rapidement *adv.* quickly I-7
rarement *adv.* rarely I-5
rasoir *m.* razor II-2
ravissant(e) *adj.* beautiful;
   delightful II-5
réalisateur/réalisatrice *m., f.*
   director (*of a movie*) II-7
récent(e) *adj.* recent II-7
réception *f.* reception desk I-7
recevoir *v.* to receive II-4

réchauffement de la Terre *m.* global warming II-6

recharger *v.* to charge (battery) II-3

rechercher *v.* to search for, to look for II-5

recommandation *f.* recommendation II-5

recommander (que) *v.* to recommend (that) II-6

recomposer (un numéro) *v.* to redial (a number) II-3

reconnaître *v.* to recognize I-8, II-P

reconnu (reconnaître) *p.p., adj.* recognized I-8, II-P

reçu *m.* receipt II-4

reçu (recevoir) *p.p., adj.* received I-7

être reçu(e) à un examen to pass an exam I-2

recyclage *m.* recycling II-6

recycler *v.* to recycle II-6

redémarrer *v.* to restart, to start again II-3

réduire *v.* to reduce I-6

réduit (réduire) *p.p., adj.* reduced I-6

référence *f.* reference II-5

réfléchir (à) *v.* to think (about), to reflect (on) I-4

refuser (de) *v.* to refuse (*to do something*) II-3

regarder *v.* to watch I-2

Ça ne nous regarde pas. That has nothing to do with us.; That is none of our business. II-6

régime *m.* diet II-2

être au régime *v.* to be on a diet II-1

région *f.* region II-6

regretter (que) *v.* to regret (that) II-6

remplir (un formulaire) *v.* to fill out (a form) II-4

rencontrer *v.* to meet I-2

rendez-vous *m.* date; appointment I-6

prendre (un) rendez-vous *v.* to make an appointment II-5

rendre (à) *v.* to give back, to return (to) I-6

rendre visite (à) *v.* to visit I-6

rentrer (à la maison) *v.* to return (home) I-2

rentrer (dans) *v.* to hit II-3

renvoyer *v.* to dismiss, to let go II-5

réparer *v.* to repair II-3

repartir *v.* to go back II-7

repas *m.* meal II-1

repasser *v.* to take again II-7

repasser (le linge) *v.* to iron (the laundry) I-8, II-P

fer à repasser *m.* iron I-8, II-P

répéter *v.* to repeat; to rehearse I-5

répondeur (téléphonique) *m.* answering machine II-3

répondre (à) *v.* to respond, to answer (to) I-6

réseau (social) *m.* (social) network II-3

réservation *f.* reservation I-7

annuler une réservation *v.* to cancel a reservation I-7

réservé(e) *adj.* reserved I-1

réserver *v.* to reserve I-7

réservoir d'essence *m.* gas tank II-3

responsable *m., f.* manager, supervisor II-5

ressource naturelle *f.* natural resource II-6

restaurant *m.* restaurant I-4

rester *v.* to stay I-7

résultat *m.* result I-2

retenir *v.* to keep, to retain II-1

retirer (de l'argent) *v.* to withdraw (money) II-4

retourner *v.* to return I-7

retraite *f.* retirement I-6

prendre sa retraite *v.* to retire I-6

retraité(e) *m., f.* retired person II-5

retrouver *v.* to find (again); to meet up with I-2

rétroviseur *m.* rear-view mirror II-3

réunion *f.* meeting II-5

réussir (à) *v.* to succeed (*in doing something*) I-4

réussite *f.* success II-5

réveil *m.* alarm clock II-2

revenir *v.* to come back II-1

rêver (de) *v.* to dream about II-3

revoir *v.* to see again II-7

Au revoir. Good-bye. I-1

revu (revoir) *p.p.* seen again II-7

rez-de-chaussée *m.* ground floor I-7

rhume *m.* cold II-2

ri (rire) *p.p.* laughed I-6

rideau *m.* curtain I-8, II-P

rien *m.* nothing II-4

De rien. You're welcome. I-1

ne... rien nothing, not anything II-4

ne servir à rien *v.* to be good for nothing II-1

rire *v.* to laugh I-6

rivière *f.* river II-6

riz *m.* rice II-1

robe *f.* dress I-6

rôle *m.* role II-6

jouer un rôle *v.* to play a role II-7

roman *m.* novel II-7

rose *adj.* pink I-6

roue (de secours) *f.* (emergency) tire II-3

rouge *adj.* red I-6

rouler en voiture *v.* to ride in a car I-7

rue *f.* street II-3

suivre une rue *v.* to follow a street II-4

S

s'adorer *v.* to adore one another II-3

s'aider *v.* to help one another II-3

s'aimer (bien) *v.* to love (like) one another II-3

s'allumer *v.* to light up II-3

s'amuser *v.* to play; to have fun II-2

s'amuser à *v.* to pass time by II-3

s'apercevoir *v.* to notice; to realize II-4

s'appeler *v.* to be named, to be called II-2

Comment t'appelles-tu? *fam.* What is your name? I-1

Comment vous appelez-vous? *form.* What is your name? I-1

Je m'appelle... My name is... I-1

s'arrêter *v.* to stop II-2

s'asseoir *v.* to sit down II-2

sa *poss. adj., f., sing.* his; her; its I-3

sac *m.* bag I-1

sac à dos *m.* backpack I-1

sac à main *m.* purse, handbag I-6

sain(e) *adj.* healthy II-2

saison *f.* season I-5

salade *f.* salad II-1

salaire (élevé/modeste) *m.* (high/low) salary II-5

augmentation de salaire *f.* raise in salary II-5

sale *adj.* dirty I-8, II-P

salir *v.* to soil, to make dirty I-8, II-P

salle *f.* room I-8, II-P

salle à manger *f.* dining room I-8, II-P

salle de bains *f.* bathroom I-8, II-P

salle de classe *f.* classroom I-1

salle de séjour *f.* living/family room I-8, II-P

salon *m.* formal living room, sitting room I-8, II-P
  salon de beauté *m.* beauty salon II-4

Salut! Hi!; Bye! I-1

samedi *m.* Saturday I-2

sandwich *m.* sandwich I-4

sans *prep.* without I-8, II-P
  sans que *conj.* without II-7

santé *f.* health II-2
  être en bonne/mauvaise santé *v.* to be in good/bad health II-2

saucisse *f.* sausage II-1

sauvegarder *v.* to save II-3

sauver (la planète) *v.* to save (the planet) II-6

sauvetage des habitats *m.* habitat preservation II-6

savoir *v.* to know (*facts*), to know how to do something I-8, II-P
  savoir (que) *v.* to know (that) II-7
  Je n'en sais rien. I don't know anything about it. II-6

savon *m.* soap II-2

sciences *f., pl.* science I-2
  sciences politiques (sciences po) *f., pl.* political science I-2

sculpture *f.* sculpture II-7

sculpteur/sculptrice *m., f.* sculptor II-7

se/s' *pron., sing., pl. (used with reflexive verb)* himself; herself; itself; 10 *(used with reciprocal verb)* each other II-3

séance *f.* show; screening II-7

se blesser *v.* to hurt oneself II-2

se brosser (les cheveux/les dents) *v.* to brush one's (hair/ teeth) II-1

se casser *v.* to break II-2

sèche-linge *m.* clothes dryer I-8, II-P

se coiffer *v.* to do one's hair II-2

se connaître *v.* to know one another II-3

se coucher *v.* to go to bed II-2

secours *m.* help II-3
  Au secours! Help! II-3

s'écrire *v.* to write one another II-3

sécurité *f.* security; safety
  attacher sa ceinture de sécurité *v.* to buckle one's seatbelt II-3

se dépêcher *v.* to hurry II-2

se déplacer *v.* to move, to change location II-4

se déshabiller *v.* to undress II-2

se détendre *v.* to relax II-2

se dire *v.* to tell one another II-3

se disputer (avec) *v.* to argue (with) II-2

se donner *v.* to give one another II-3

se fouler (la cheville) *v.* to twist/to sprain one's (ankle) II-2

se garer *v.* to park II-3

seize *m.* sixteen I-1

séjour *m.* stay I-7
  faire un séjour *v.* to spend time (*somewhere*) I-7
  salle de séjour *f.* living room I-8, II-P

sel *m.* salt II-1

se laver (les mains) *v.* to wash oneself (one's hands) II-2

se lever *v.* to get up, to get out of bed II-2

semaine *f.* week I-2
  cette semaine this week I-2

s'embrasser *v.* to kiss one another II-3

se maquiller *v.* to put on makeup II-2

se mettre *v.* to put (*something*) on (yourself) II-2
  se mettre à *v.* to begin to II-2
  se mettre en colère *v.* to become angry II-2

s'endormir *v.* to fall asleep, to go to sleep II-2

s'énerver *v.* to get worked up, to become upset II-2

sénégalais(e) *adj.* Senegalese I-1

s'ennuyer *v.* to get bored II-2

s'entendre bien (avec) *v.* to get along well (with one another) II-2

sentier *m.* path II-6

sentir *v.* to feel; to smell; to sense I-5

séparé(e) *adj.* separated I-3

se parler *v.* to speak to one another II-3

se porter mal/mieux *v.* to be ill/better II-2

se préparer (à) *v.* to get ready; to prepare (*to do something*) II-2

se promener *v.* to take a walk II-2

sept *m.* seven I-1

septembre *m.* September I-5

septième *adj.* seventh I-7

se quitter *v.* to leave one another II-3

se raser *v.* to shave oneself II-2

se réconcilier *v.* to make up II-7

se regarder *v.* to look at oneself; to look at each other II-2

se relever *v.* to get up again II-2

se rencontrer *v.* to meet one another, to make each other's acquaintance II-3

se rendre compte *v.* to realize II-2

se reposer *v.* to rest II-2

se retrouver *v.* to meet one another (*as planned*) II-3

se réveiller *v.* to wake up II-2

se sécher *v.* to dry oneself II-2

se sentir *v.* to feel II-2

sérieux/sérieuse *adj.* serious I-3

serpent *m.* snake II-6

serre *f.* greenhouse II-6
  effet de serre *m.* greenhouse effect II-6

serré(e) *adj.* tight I-6

serveur/serveuse *m., f.* server I-4

serviette *f.* napkin II-1
  serviette (de bain) *f.* (bath) towel II-2

servir *v.* to serve I-5

ses *poss. adj., m., f., pl.* his; her; its I-3

se souvenir (de) *v.* to remember II-2

se téléphoner *v.* to phone one another II-3

se tourner *v.* to turn (oneself) around II-2

se tromper (de) *v.* to be mistaken (about) II-2

se trouver *v.* to be located II-2

seulement *adv.* only I-8, II-P

s'habiller *v.* to dress II-2

shampooing *m.* shampoo II-2

shopping *m.* shopping I-7
  faire du shopping *v.* to go shopping I-7

short *m., sing.* shorts I-6

si *conj.* if II-5

si *adv. (when contradicting a negative statement or question)* yes I-2

signer *v.* to sign II-4

S'il te plaît. *fam.* Please. I-1

S'il vous plaît. *form.* Please. I-1

sincère *adj.* sincere I-1

s'inquiéter *v.* to worry II-2

s'intéresser (à) *v.* to be interested (in) II-2

site Internet/web *m.* web site II-3

six *m.* six I-1

sixième *adj.* sixth I-7

ski *m.* skiing I-5
  faire du ski *v.* to go skiing I-5
  station de ski *f.* ski resort I-7

skier *v.* to ski I-5

smartphone *m.* smartphone II-3

SMS *m.* text message II-3

s'occuper (de) *v.* to take care (*of something*), to see to II-2

sociable *adj.* sociable I-1

sociologie *f.* sociology I-1

sœur *f.* sister I-3
  belle-sœur *f.* sister-in-law I-3

demi-sœur *f.* half-sister, stepsister I-3
soie *f.* silk I-4
soif *f.* thirst I-4
  avoir soif *v.* to be thirsty I-4
soir *m.* evening I-2
  ce soir *adv.* this evening I-2
  demain soir *adv.* tomorrow evening I-2
  du soir *adv.* in the evening I-2
  hier soir *adv.* yesterday evening I-7
soirée *f.* evening I-2
sois (être) *imp. v.* be I-2
soixante *m.* sixty I-1
soixante-dix *m.* seventy I-3
solaire *adj.* solar II-6
  énergie solaire *f.* solar energy II-6
soldes *f., pl.* sales I-6
soleil *m.* sun I-5
  Il fait (du) soleil. It is sunny. I-5
solution *f.* solution II-6
  proposer une solution *v.* to propose a solution II-6
sommeil *m.* sleep I-2
  avoir sommeil *v.* to be sleepy I-2
son *poss. adj., m., sing.* his; her; its I-3
sonner *v.* to ring II-3
s'orienter *v.* to get one's bearings II-4
sorte *f.* sort, kind II-7
sortie *f.* exit I-7
sortir *v.* to go out, to leave I-5; to take out I-8, II-P
  sortir la/les poubelle(s) *v.* to take out the trash I-8, II-P
soudain *adv.* suddenly I-8, II-P
souffrir *v.* to suffer II-3
souffert (souffrir) *p.p.* suffered II-3
souhaiter (que) *v.* to wish (that) II-6
soupe *f.* soup I-4
  cuillère à soupe *f.* soupspoon II-1
sourire *v.* to smile I-6; *m.* smile II-4
souris *f.* mouse II-3
sous *prep.* under I-3
sous-sol *m.* basement I-8, II-P
sous-vêtement *m.* underwear I-6
souvent *adv.* often I-5
soyez (être) *imp. v.* be I-7
soyons (être) *imp. v.* let's be I-7
spécialiste *m., f.* specialist II-5
spectacle *m.* show I-5
spectateur/spectatrice *m., f.* spectator II-7
sport *m.* sport(s) I-5

faire du sport *v.* to do sports I-5
sportif/sportive *adj.* athletic I-3
stade *m.* stadium I-5
stage *m.* internship; professional training II-5
station (de métro) *f.* (subway) station I-7
station de ski *f.* ski resort I-7
station-service *f.* service station II-3
statue *f.* statue II-4
steak *m.* steak II-1
studio *m.* studio (*apartment*) I-8, II-P
stylo *m.* pen I-1
su (savoir) *p.p.* known I-8, II-P
sucre *m.* sugar I-4
sud *m.* south II-4
suggérer (que) *v.* to suggest (that) II-6
sujet *m.* subject II-6
  au sujet de on the subject of; about II-6
suisse *adj.* Swiss I-1
Suisse *f.* Switzerland I-7
suivre (un chemin/une rue/ un boulevard) *v.* to follow (a path/a street/a boulevard) II-4
supermarché *m.* supermarket II-1
sur *prep.* on I-3
sûr(e) *adj.* sure, certain II-1
  bien sûr of course I-2
  Il est sûr que... It is sure that... II-7
  Il n'est pas sûr que... It is not sure that... II-7
surpopulation *f.* overpopulation II-6
surpris (surprendre) *p.p., adj.* surprised I-6
  être surpris(e) que... *v.* to be surprised that... II-6
  faire une surprise à quelqu'un *v.* to surprise someone I-6
surtout *adv.* especially; above all I-2
sympa(thique) *adj.* nice I-1
symptôme *m.* symptom II-2
syndicat *m.* (*trade*) union II-5

T

ta *poss. adj., f., sing.* your I-3
table *f.* table I-1
  À table! Let's eat! Food is ready! II-1
  débarrasser la table *v.* to clear the table I-8, II-P
  mettre la table *v.* to set the table I-8, II-P

tableau *m.* blackboard; picture I-1; *m.* painting II-7
tablette (tactile) *f.* tablet II-3
tâche ménagère *f.* household chore I-8, II-P
taille *f.* size; waist I-6
  de taille moyenne of medium height I-3
tailleur *m.* (*woman's*) suit; tailor I-6
tante *f.* aunt I-3
tapis *m.* rug I-8, II-P
tard *adv.* late I-2
  À plus tard. See you later. I-1
tarte *f.* pie; tart I-8, II-P
tasse (de) *f.* cup (of) I-4
taxi *m.* taxi I-7
  prendre un taxi *v.* to take a taxi I-7
te/t' *pron., sing., fam.* you I-7; yourself II-2
tee-shirt *m.* tee shirt I-6
télécharger *v.* to download II-3
télécommande *f.* remote control II-3
téléphone *m.* telephone I-2
  parler au téléphone *v.* to speak on the phone I-2
téléphoner (à) *v.* to telephone (*someone*) I-2
télévision *f.* television I-1
  à la télé(vision) on television II-7
  chaîne (de télévision) *f.* television channel II-3
tellement *adv.* so much I-2
  Je n'aime pas tellement... I don't like... very much. I-2
température *f.* temperature I-5
  Quelle température fait-il? What is the temperature? I-5
temps *m., sing.* weather I-5
  Il fait un temps épouvantable. The weather is dreadful. I-5
  Le temps est nuageux. It is cloudy. I-5
  Le temps est orageux. It is stormy. I-5
  Quel temps fait-il? What is the weather like? I-5
temps *m., sing.* time I-5
  de temps en temps *adv.* from time to time I-7
  emploi à mi-temps/à temps partiel *m.* part-time job II-5
  emploi à plein temps *m.* full-time job II-5
  temps libre *m.* free time I-5
Tenez! (tenir) *imp. v.* Here! II-1
tenir *v.* to hold II-1
tennis *m.* tennis I-5
terrasse (de café) *f.* (café) terrace I-4

Terre *f.* Earth II-6
  réchauffement de la Terre *m.* global warming II-6
tes *poss. adj., m., f., pl.* your I-3
tête *f.* head II-2
texto *m.* text message II-3
thé *m.* tea I-4
théâtre *m.* theater II-7
thon *m.* tuna II-1
ticket de bus/métro *m.* bus/subway ticket I-7
Tiens! (tenir) *imp. v.* Here! II-1
timbre *m.* stamp II-4
timide *adj.* shy I-1
tiret *m. (punctuation mark)* dash; hyphen II-3
tiroir *m.* drawer I-8, II-P
toi *disj. pron., sing., fam.* you I-3; *refl. pron., sing., fam. (attached to imperative)* yourself II-2
  toi non plus you neither I-2
toilette *f.* washing up, grooming II-2
  faire sa toilette to wash up II-2
toilettes *f., pl.* restroom(s) I-8, II-P
tomate *f.* tomato II-1
tomber *v.* to fall I-7
  tomber amoureux/amoureuse *v.* to fall in love I-6
  tomber en panne *v.* to break down II-3
  tomber/être malade *v.* to get/be sick II-2
  tomber sur quelqu'un *v.* to run into someone I-7
ton *poss. adj., m., sing.* your I-3
tort *m.* wrong; harm I-2
  avoir tort *v.* to be wrong I-2
tôt *adv.* early I-2
toujours *adv.* always I-8, II-P
tour *m.* tour I-5
  faire un tour (en voiture) *v.* to go for a walk (drive) I-5
tourisme *m.* tourism II-4
  office du tourisme *m.* tourist office II-4
tourner *v.* to turn II-4
tousser *v.* to cough II-2
tout *m., sing.* all I-4
  tous les *(used before noun)* all the... I-4
  tous les jours *adv.* every day I-8, II-P
  toute la *f., sing. (used before noun)* all the... I-4
  toutes les *f., pl. (used before noun)* all the... I-4
  tout le *m., sing. (used before noun)* all the... I-4
  tout le monde everyone II-1

tout(e) *adv. (before adjective or adverb)* very, really I-3
  À tout à l'heure. See you later. I-1
  tout à coup suddenly I-7
  tout à fait absolutely; completely II-4
  tout de suite right away I-7
  tout droit straight ahead II-4
  tout d'un coup *adv.* all of a sudden I-8, II-P
  tout près (de) really close by, really close (to) I-3
toxique *adj.* toxic II-6
  déchets toxiques *m., pl.* toxic waste II-6
trac *m.* stage fright II-5
traduire *v.* to translate I-6
traduit (traduire) *p.p., adj.* translated I-6
tragédie *f.* tragedy II-7
train *m.* train I-7
tranche *f.* slice II-1
tranquille *adj.* calm, serene II-2
  laisser tranquille *v.* to leave alone II-2
travail *m.* work II-4
  chercher un/du travail *v.* to look for a job/work II-4
  trouver un/du travail *v.* to find a job/work II-5
travailler *v.* to work I-2
travailleur/travailleuse *adj.* hard-working I-3
traverser *v.* to cross II-4
treize *m.* thirteen I-1
trente *m.* thirty I-1
très *adv. (before adjective or adverb)* very, really I-8, II-P
  Très bien. Very well. I-1
triste *adj.* sad I-3
  être triste que... *v.* to be sad that... II-6
trois *m.* three I-1
troisième *adj.* third 7
trop (de) *adv.* too many/much (of) I-4
tropical(e) *adj.* tropical II-6
  forêt tropicale *f.* tropical forest II-6
trou (dans la couche d'ozone) *m.* hole (in the ozone layer) II-6
troupe *f.* company, troupe II-7
trouver *v.* to find; to think I-2
  trouver un/du travail *v.* to find a job/work II-5
truc *m.* thing I-7
tu *sub. pron., sing., fam.* you I-1

U

un *m. (number)* one I-1
un(e) *indef. art.* a; an I-1
urgences *f., pl.* emergency room II-2
  aller aux urgences *v.* to go to the emergency room II-2
usine *f.* factory II-6
utile *adj.* useful I-2
utiliser (un plan) *v.* to use (a map) I-7

V

vacances *f., pl.* vacation I-7
  partir en vacances *v.* to go on vacation I-7
vache *f.* cow II-6
vaisselle *f.* dishes I-8, II-P
  faire la vaisselle *v.* to do the dishes I-8, II-P
  lave-vaisselle *m.* dishwasher I-8, II-P
valise *f.* suitcase I-7
  faire les valises *v.* to pack one's bags I-7
vallée *f.* valley II-6
variétés *f., pl.* popular music II-7
vaut (valloir) *v.*
  Il vaut mieux que It is better that II-6
vélo *m.* bicycle I-5
  faire du vélo *v.* to go bike riding I-5
velours *m.* velvet II-4
vendeur/vendeuse *m., f.* seller I-6
vendre *v.* to sell I-6
vendredi *m.* Friday I-2
venir *v.* to come II-1
  venir de *v. (used with an infinitive)* to have just II-1
vent *m.* wind I-5
  Il fait du vent. It is windy. I-5
ventre *m.* stomach II-2

vérifier (l'huile/la pression des pneus) *v.* to check (the oil/the tire pressure) II-3
véritable *adj.* true, real II-4
verre (de) *m.* glass (of) I-4
vers *adv.* about I-2
vert(e) *adj.* green I-3
  haricots verts *m., pl.* green beans II-1
vêtements *m., pl.* clothing I-6
  sous-vêtement *m.* underwear I-6
vétérinaire *m., f.* veterinarian II-5
veuf/veuve *adj.* widowed I-3

veut dire (vouloir dire) *v.* means, signifies II-1
viande *f.* meat II-1
vie *f.* life I-6
    assurance vie *f.* life insurance II-5
vieille *adj., f. (feminine form of vieux)* old I-3
vieillesse *f.* old age I-6
vietnamien(ne) *adj.* Vietnamese I-1
vieux/vieille *adj.* old I-3
ville *f.* city; town I-4
vingt *m.* twenty I-1
vingtième *adj.* twentieth I-7
violet(te) *adj.* purple; violet I-6
violon *m.* violin II-7
visage *m.* face II-2
visite *f.* visit I-6
    rendre visite (à) *v.* to visit (*a person or people*) I-6
visiter *v.* to visit (*a place*) I-2
    faire visiter *v.* to give a tour I-8, II-P
vite *adv.* fast I-7
vitesse *f.* speed II-3
vivre *v.* to live I-8, II-P
voici here is/are I-1
voilà there is/are I-1
voir *v.* to see II-7
voisin(e) *m., f.* neighbor I-3
voiture *f.* car II-3
    faire un tour en voiture *v.* to go for a drive I-5
    rouler en voiture *v.* to ride in a car I-7
vol *m.* flight I-7
volant *m.* steering wheel II-3
volcan *m.* volcano II-6
volley(-ball) *m.* volleyball I-5
volontiers *adv.* willingly II-2
vos *poss. adj., m., f., pl.* your I-3
votre *poss. adj., m., f., sing.* your I-3
vouloir *v.* to want; to mean (*with* **dire**) II-1
    ça veut dire that is to say II-2
    veut dire *v.* means, signifies II-1
    vouloir (que) *v.* to want (that) II-6
voulu (vouloir) *p.p., adj. (used with infinitive)* wanted to… ; (*used with noun*) planned to/for II-1
vous *pron., sing., pl., fam., form.* you I-1; *d.o. pron.* you I-7; yourself, yourselves II-2
voyage *m.* trip I-7
    agence de voyages *f.* travel agency I-7
    agent de voyages *m.* travel agent I-7
voyager *v.* to travel I-2

voyant (d'essence/d'huile) *m.* (gas/oil) warning light 11
vrai(e) *adj.* true; real I-3
    Il est vrai que… It is true that… II-7
    Il n'est pas vrai que… It is untrue that… II-7
vraiment *adv.* really I-7
vu (voir) *p.p.* seen II-7

W

W.-C. *m., pl.* restroom(s) I-8, II-P
week-end *m.* weekend I-2
    ce week-end this weekend I-2

Y

y *pron.* there; at (*a place*) II-2
    j'y vais I'm going/coming I-8, II-P
    nous y allons we're going/coming II-1
    on y va let's go II-2
    Y a-t-il… ? Is/Are there… ? I-2
yaourt *m.* yogurt II-1
yeux (œil) *m., pl.* eyes I-3

Z

zéro *m.* zero I-1
zut *interj.* darn I-6

English-French

A

a **un(e)** *indef. art.* I-1
able: to be able to **pouvoir** *v.* II-1
abolish **abolir** *v.* II-6
about **vers** *adv.* I-2
abroad **à l'étranger** I-7
absolutely **absolument**
   adv. I-7;
   tout à fait *adv.* I-6
accident **accident** *m.* II-2
   to have/to be in an accident
   avoir un accident *v.* II-3
accompany **accompagner** *v.* II-4
account *(at a bank)* **compte**
   m. I-4
   checking account **compte** *m.*
   de chèques II-4
   to have a bank account **avoir**
   un compte bancaire *v.* II-4
accountant **comptable** *m., f.* II-5
acid rain **pluie acide** *f.* II-6
across from **en face de** *prep.* I-3
acquaintance **connaissance** *f.* I-5
active **actif/active** *adj.* I-3
actively **activement** *adv.* I-8, II-P
actor **acteur/actrice** *m., f.* I-1
address **adresse** *f.* II-4
administration: business
   administration **gestion** *f.* I-2
adolescence **adolescence** *f.* I-6
adore **adorer** I-2
   I love... **J'adore...** I-2
   to adore one another
   s'adorer *v.* II-3
adulthood **âge adulte** *m.* I-6
adventure **aventure** *f.* II-7
   adventure film **film** *m.*
   d'aventures II-7
advertisement **publicité (pub)**
   f. II-7
advice **conseil** *m.* II-5
advisor **conseiller/conseillère**
   m., f. II-5
aerobics **aérobic** *m.* I-5
   to do aerobics **faire de**
   l'aérobic *v.* I-5
afraid: to be afraid of/that **avoir**
   peur de/que *v.* II-6
after **après (que)** *adv.* I-7
afternoon **après-midi** *m.* I-2
   ... (o'clock) in the afternoon
   ... heure(s) de l'après-midi I-2
afternoon snack **goûter** *m.* II-1
again **encore** *adv.* I-3
age **âge** *m.* I-6

agent: travel agent **agent de**
   voyages *m.* I-7
   real estate agent **agent**
   immobilier *m.* II-5
ago *(with an expression of time)*
   il y a... II-1
agree: to agree (with) **être**
   d'accord (avec) *v.* I-2
airport **aéroport** *m.* I-7
alarm clock **réveil** *m.* II-2
Algerian **algérien(ne)** *adj.* I-1
all **tout** *m., sing.* I-4
   all of a sudden **soudain** *adv.*
   I-8, II-P; **tout à coup** *adv.*; **tout**
   d'un coup *adv.* I-7
all right? *(tag question)*
   d'accord? I-2
allergy **allergie** *f.* II-2
allow *(to do something)* **laisser** *v.*
   II-3; **permettre (de)** *v.* I-6
allowed **permis (permettre)**
   p.p., adj. I-6
all the... *(agrees with noun that*
   follows) **tout le...** *m., sing;*
   toute la... *f., sing;* **tous les...**
   m., pl.; **toutes les...** *f., pl.* I-4
almost **presque** *adv.* I-5
a lot (of) **beaucoup (de)** *adv.* I-4
alone: to leave alone **laisser**
   tranquille *v.* II-2
already **déjà** *adv.* I-3
always **toujours** *adv.* I-8, II-P
American **américain(e)** *adj.* I-1
an **un(e)** *indef. art.* I-1
ancient *(placed after noun)*
   ancien(ne) *adj.* II-7
and **et** *conj.* I-1
   And you? **Et toi?,** *fam.;* **Et**
   vous? *form.* I-1
angel **ange** *m.* I-1
angry: to become angry
   s'énerver *v.* II-2; **se mettre**
   en colère *v.* II-2
animal **animal** *m.* II-6
ankle **cheville** *f.* II-2
answering machine **répondeur**
   téléphonique *m.* II-3
apartment **appartement** *m.* I-7
appetizer **entrée** *f.* II-1;
   hors-d'œuvre *m.* II-1
apple **pomme** *f.* II-1
appliance **appareil** *m.* I-8, II-P
   electrical/household appliance
   appareil *m.* **électrique/**
   ménager I-8, II-P
applicant **candidat(e)** *m., f.* II-5
apply **postuler** *v.* II-5

appointment **rendez-vous** *m.* II-5
   to make an appointment
   prendre (un) rendez-vous
   v. II-5
April **avril** *m.* I-5
architect **architecte** *m., f.* I-3
Are there... ? **Y a-t-il... ?** I-2
area **quartier** *m.* I-8, II-P
argue (with) **se disputer**
   (avec) *v.* II-2
arm **bras** *m.* II-2
armchair **fauteuil** *m.* I-8, II-P
armoire **armoire** *f.* I-8, II-P
around **autour (de)** *prep.* II-4
arrival **arrivée** *f.* I-7
arrive **arriver (à)** *v.* I-2
art **art** *m.* I-2
   artwork, piece of art **œuvre**
   f. II-7
   fine arts **beaux-arts** *m., pl.* II-7
artist **artiste** *m., f.* I-3
as *(like)* **comme** *adv.* I-6
   as ... as *(used with adjective to*
   compare) **aussi ... que** II-1
   as much ... as *(used with*
   noun to express comparative
   quatity) **autant de ... que** II-6
   as soon as **dès que** *adv.* II-5
ashamed: to be ashamed of
   avoir honte de *v.* I-2
ask **demander** *v.* I-2
   to ask *(someone)* **demander**
   (à) *v.* I-6
   to ask *(someone)* a question
   poser une question (à) *v.* I-6
   to ask that... **demander**
   que... II-6
aspirin **aspirine** *f.* II-2
at **à** *prep.* I-4
   at ... (o'clock) **à ... heure(s)** I-4
   at the doctor's office **chez le**
   médecin *prep.* I-2
   at (someone's) house **chez...**
   prep. I-2
   at the end (of) **au bout (de)**
   prep. II-4
   at last **enfin** *adv.* II-3
athlete **athlète** *m., f.* I-3
ATM **distributeur** *m.* **automa-**
   tique/de billets *m.* II-4
attend **assister** *v.* I-2
August **août** *m.* I-5
aunt **tante** *f.* I-3
author **auteur/femme auteur**
   m., f. II-7
autumn **automne** *m.* I-5
   in autumn **en automne** I-5
available *(free)* **libre** *adj.* I-7
avenue **avenue** *f.* II-4
avoid **éviter de** *v.* II-2

B

back **dos** *m.* II-2
backpack **sac à dos** *m.* I-1
bad **mauvais(e)** *adj.* I-3
  to be in a bad mood **être de mauvaise humeur** I-8, II-P
  to be in bad health **être en mauvaise santé** II-2
badly **mal** *adv.* I-7
  I am doing badly. **Je vais mal.** I-1
  to be doing badly **se porter mal** *v.* II-2
baguette **baguette** *f.* I-4
bakery **boulangerie** *f.* II-1
balcony **balcon** *m.* I-8, II-P
banana **banane** *f.* II-1
bank **banque** *f.* II-4
  to have a bank account **avoir un compte bancaire** *v.* II-4
banker **banquier/banquière** *m., f.* II-5
banking **bancaire** *adj.* II-4
baseball **baseball** *m.* I-5
baseball cap **casquette** *f.* I-6
basement **sous-sol** *m.;* **cave** *f.* I-8, II-P
basketball **basket(-ball)** *m.* I-5
bath **bain** *m.* I-6
bathing suit **maillot de bain** *m.* I-6
bathroom **salle de bains** *f.* I-8, II-P
bathtub **baignoire** *f.* I-8, II-P
be **être** *v.* I-1
  sois (être) *imp. v.* I-7;
  soyez (être) *imp. v.* I-7
beach **plage** *f.* I-7
beans **haricots** *m., pl.* II-1
  green beans **haricots verts** *m., pl.* II-1
bearings: to get one's bearings **s'orienter** *v.* II-4
beautiful **beau (belle)** *adj.* I-3
beauty salon **salon** *m.* **de beauté** II-4
because **parce que** *conj.* I-2
become **devenir** *v.* II-1
bed **lit** *m.* I-7
  to go to bed **se coucher** *v.* II-2
bedroom **chambre** *f.* I-8, II-P
beef **bœuf** *m.* II-1
been **été (être)** *p.p.* I-6
before **avant (de/que)** *adv.* I-7
  before (*o'clock*) **moins** *adv.* I-2
begin (*to do something*) **commencer (à)** *v.* I-2; **se mettre à** *v.* II-2
beginning **début** *m.* II-7
behind **derrière** *prep.* I-3
Belgian **belge** *adj.* I-7

Belgium **Belgique** *f.* I-7
believe (that) **croire (que)** *v.* II-7
believed **cru (croire)** *p.p.* II-7
belt **ceinture** *f.* I-6
  to buckle one's seatbelt **attacher sa ceinture de sécurité** *v.* II-3
bench **banc** *m.* II-4
best: the best **le mieux** *super. adv.* II-1; **le/la meilleur(e)** *super. adj.* II-1
better **meilleur(e)** *comp. adj.;* **mieux** *comp. adv.* II-1
  It is better that… **Il vaut mieux que/qu'…** II-6
  to be doing better **se porter mieux** *v.* II-2
  to get better (*from illness*) **guérir** *v.* II-2
between **entre** *prep.* I-3
beverage (carbonated) **boisson** *f.* **(gazeuse)** I-4
bicycle **vélo** *m.* I-5
  to go bike riding **faire du vélo** *v.* I-5
big **grand(e)** *adj.* I-3; (*clothing*) **large** *adj.* I-6
bill (*in a restaurant*) **addition** *f.* I-4
bills (*money*) **billets** *m., pl.* II-4
biology **biologie** *f.* I-2
bird **oiseau** *m.* I-3
birth **naissance** *f.* I-6
birthday **anniversaire** *m.* I-5
bit (of) **morceau (de)** *m.* I-4
black **noir(e)** *adj.* I-3
blackboard **tableau** *m.* I-1
blanket **couverture** *f.* I-8, II-P
blonde **blond(e)** *adj.* I-3
blouse **chemisier** *m.* I-6
blue **bleu(e)** *adj.* I-3
boat **bateau** *m.* I-7
body **corps** *m.* II-2
book **livre** *m.* I-1
bookstore **librairie** *f.* I-1
bored: to get bored **s'ennuyer** *v.* II-2
boring **ennuyeux/ennuyeuse** *adj.* I-3
born: to be born **naître** *v.* I-7; **né (naître)** *p.p., adj.* I-7
borrow **emprunter** *v.* II-4
bottle (of) **bouteille (de)** *f.* I-4
boulevard **boulevard** *m.* II-4
boutique **boutique** *f.* II-4
bowl **bol** *m.* II-1
box **boîte** *f.* II-1
boy **garçon** *m.* I-1
boyfriend **petit ami** *m.* I-1
brake **freiner** *v.* II-3
brakes **freins** *m., pl.* II-3
brave **courageux/courageuse** *adj.* I-3

Brazil **Brésil** *m.* I-7
Brazilian **brésilien(ne)** *adj.* I-7
bread **pain** *m.* I-4
  country-style bread **pain** *m.* **de campagne** I-4
bread shop **boulangerie** *f.* II-1
break **se casser** *v.* II-2
breakdown **panne** *f.* II-3
break down **tomber en panne** *v.* II-3
break up (*to leave one another*) **se quitter** *v.* II-3
breakfast **petit-déjeuner** *m.* II-1
bridge **pont** *m.* II-4
bright **brillant(e)** *adj.* I-1
bring (*a person*) **amener** *v.* I-5; (*a thing*) **apporter** *v.* I-4
broom **balai** *m.* I-8, II-P
brother **frère** *m.* I-3
brother-in-law **beau-frère** *m.* I-3
brown **marron** *adj., inv.* I-3
  brown (*hair*) **châtain** *adj.* I-3
brush (hair/tooth) **brosse** *f.* **(à cheveux/à dents)** II-2
  to brush one's hair/teeth **se brosser les cheveux/les dents** *v.* II-1
buckle: to buckle one's seatbelt **attacher sa ceinture de sécurité** *v.* II-3
build **construire** *v.* I-6
building **bâtiment** *m.* II-4; **immeuble** *m.* I-8, II-P
bumper **pare-chocs** *m.* II-3
bus **autobus** *m.* I-7
bus stop **arrêt d'autobus (de bus)** *m.* I-7
bus terminal **gare** *f.* **routière** I-7
business (*profession*) **affaires** *f., pl.* I-3; (*company*) **entreprise** *f.* II-5
business administration **gestion** *f.* I-2
businessman **homme d'affaires** *m.* I-3
businesswoman **femme d'affaires** *f.* I-3
busy **occupé(e)** *adj.* I-1
but **mais** *conj.* I-1
butcher's shop **boucherie** *f.* II-1
butter **beurre** *m.* I-4
buy **acheter** *v.* I-5
by **par** *prep.* I-3
Bye! **Salut!** *fam.* I-1

C

cabinet **placard** *m.* I-8, II-P
café **café** *m.* I-1
  café terrace **terrasse** *f.* **de café** I-4
cafeteria (school) **cantine** *f.* I-2

cake **gâteau** *m.* I-6
calculator **calculatrice** *f.* I-1
call **appeler** *v.* II-5
calm **calme** *adj.* I-1; **calme** *m.* I-1
camcorder **caméra vidéo** *f.* II-3; **caméscope** *m.* II-3
camera **appareil photo** *m.* II-3
   digital camera **appareil photo** *m.* **numérique** II-3
camping **camping** *m.* I-5
   to go camping **faire du camping** *v.* I-5
can (of food) **boîte (de conserve)** *f.* II-1
Canada **Canada** *m.* I-7
Canadian **canadien(ne)** *adj.* I-1
cancel (a reservation) **annuler (une réservation)** *v.* I-7
candidate **candidat(e)** *m., f.* II-5
candy **bonbon** *m.* I-6
cap: baseball cap **casquette** *f.* I-6
capital **capitale** *f.* I-7
car **voiture** *f.* II-3
   to ride in a car **rouler en voiture** *v.* I-7
card (letter) **carte postale** *f.* II-4; credit card **carte** *f.* **de crédit** II-4
   to pay with a (debit/credit) card **payer par carte (bancaire/de crédit)** *v.* II-4
   cards (playing) **cartes** *f.* I-5
carbonated drink/beverage **boisson** *f.* **gazeuse** I-4
career **carrière** *f.* II-5
carpooling **covoiturage** *m.* II-6
carrot **carotte** *f.* II-1
carry **apporter** *v.* I-4
cartoon **dessin animé** *m.* II-7
case: in any case **en tout cas** I-6
cash **espèces** *m.* II-4
   to pay in cash **payer en espèces** *v.* II-4
cat **chat** *m.* I-3
catastrophe **catastrophe** *f.* II-6
catch sight of **apercevoir** *v.* II-4
celebrate **célébrer** *v.* I-5; **fêter** *v.* I-6; **faire la fête** *v.* I-6
celebration **fête** *f.* I-6
cellar **cave** *f.* I-8, II-P
cell(ular) phone **portable** *m.* II-3
center: city/town center **centre-ville** *m.* I-4
certain **certain(e)** *adj.* II-1; **sûr(e)** *adj.* II-7
   It is certain that… **Il est certain que…** II-7
   It is uncertain that… **Il n'est pas certain que…** II-7
chair **chaise** *f.* I-1
change (coins) **(pièces** *f. pl.* **de) monnaie** II-4

channel (television) **chaîne** *f.* **(de télévision)** II-3
character **personnage** *m.* II-7
   main character **personnage principal** *m.* II-7
charge (battery) **recharger** *v.* II-3
charming **charmant(e)** *adj.* I-1
chat **bavarder** *v.* I-4
check **chèque** *m.* II-4; (bill) **addition** *f.* I-4
   to pay by check **payer par chèque** *v.* II-4;
   to check (the oil/the air pressure) **vérifier (l'huile/la pression des pneus)** *v.* II-3
checking account **compte** *m.* **de chèques** II-4
cheek **joue** *f.* II-2
cheese **fromage** *m.* I-4
chemistry **chimie** *f.* I-2
chess **échecs** *m., pl.* I-5
chest **poitrine** *f.* II-2
   chest of drawers **commode** *f.* I-8, II-P
chic **chic** *adj.* I-4
chicken **poulet** *m.* II-1
child **enfant** *m., f.* I-3
childhood **enfance** *f.* I-6
China **Chine** *f.* I-7
Chinese **chinois(e)** *adj.* I-7
choir **chœur** *m.* II-7
choose **choisir** *v.* I-4
chorus **chœur** *m.* II-7
chrysanthemums **chrysanthèmes** *m., pl.* II-1
church **église** *f.* I-4
city **ville** *f.* I-4
city hall **mairie** *f.* II-4
city/town center **centre-ville** *m.* I-4
class (group of students) **classe** *f.* I-1; (course) **cours** *m.* I-2
classmate **camarade de classe** *m., f.* I-1
classroom **salle** *f.* **de classe** I-1
clean **nettoyer** *v.* I-5; **propre** *adj.* I-8, II-P
clear **clair(e)** *adj.* II-7
   It is clear that… **Il est clair que…** II-7
   to clear the table **débarrasser la table** I-8, II-P
client **client(e)** *m., f.* I-7
cliff **falaise** *f.* II-6
clock **horloge** *f.* I-1
   alarm clock **réveil** *m.* II-2
close (to) **près (de)** *prep.* I-3
   very close (to) **tout près (de)** II-4
close **fermer** *v.* II-3
closed **fermé(e)** *adj.* II-4
closet **placard** *m.* I-8, II-P

clothes dryer **sèche-linge** *m.* I-8, II-P
clothing **vêtements** *m., pl.* I-6
cloudy **nuageux/nuageuse** *adj.* I-5
   It is cloudy. **Le temps est nuageux.** I-5
clutch **embrayage** *m.* II-3
coast **côte** *f.* II-6
coat **manteau** *m.* I-6
coffee **café** *m.* I-1
coffeemaker **cafetière** *f.* I-8, II-P
coins **pièces** *f. pl.* **de monnaie** II-4
cold **froid** *m.* I-2
   to be cold **avoir froid** *v.* I-2
   (weather) It is cold. **Il fait froid.** I-5
cold **rhume** *m.* II-2
color **couleur** *f.* I-6
   What color is… ? **De quelle couleur est… ?** I-6
comb **peigne** *m.* II-2
come **venir** *v.* I-7
come back **revenir** *v.* II-1
Come on. **Allez.** I-2
comedy **comédie** *f.* II-7
comic strip **bande dessinée (B.D.)** *f.* I-5
company (troop) **troupe** *f.* II-7
completely **tout à fait** *adv.* I-6
composer **compositeur** *m.* II-7
computer **ordinateur** *m.* I-1
computer science **informatique** *f.* I-2
concert **concert** *m.* II-7
congratulations **félicitations** II-7
connect **brancher** *v.* II-3
consider **considérer** *v.* I-5
constantly **constamment** *adv.* I-7
construct **construire** *v.* I-6
consultant **conseiller/ conseillère** *m., f.* II-5
continue (doing something) **continuer (à)** *v.* II-4
cook **cuisiner** *v.* II-1; **faire la cuisine** *v.* I-5; **cuisinier/ cuisinière** *m., f.* II-5
cookie **biscuit** *m.* I-6
cooking **cuisine** *f.* I-5
cool: (weather) It is cool. **Il fait frais.** I-5
corner **angle** *m.* II-4; **coin** *m.* II-4
cost **coûter** *v.* I-4
cotton **coton** *m.* I-6
couch **canapé** *m.* I-8, II-P
cough **tousser** *v.* II-2
count (on someone) **compter (sur quelqu'un)** *v.* I-8, II-P
country **pays** *m.* I-7
   country(side) **campagne** *f.* I-7

country-style **de campagne**
   adj. I-4
couple **couple** *m.* I-6
courage **courage** *m.* II-5
courageous **courageux/
   courageuse** *adj.* I-3
course **cours** *m.* I-2
cousin **cousin(e)** *m., f.* I-3
cover **couvrir** *v.* II-3
covered **couvert
   (couvrir)** *p.p.* II-3
cow **vache** *f.* II-6
crazy **fou/folle** *adj.* I-3
cream **crème** *f.* II-1
credit card **carte** *f.* **de crédit**
   II-4
   to pay with a debit/credit
   card **payer par carte
   bancaire/de crédit** *v.* II-4
crêpe **crêpe** *f.* I-5
crime film **film policier** *m.* II-7
croissant **croissant** *m.* I-4
cross **traverser** *v.* II-4
cruel **cruel/cruelle** *adj.* I-3
cry **pleurer** *v.*
cup (of) **tasse (de)** *f.* I-4
cupboard **placard** *m.* I-8, II-P
curious **curieux/
   curieuse** *adj.* I-3
curly **frisé(e)** *adj.* I-3
currency **monnaie** *f.* II-4
curtain **rideau** *m.* I-8, II-P
customs **douane** *f.* I-7

D

dance **danse** *f.* II-7
   to dance **danser** *v.* I-4
danger **danger** *m.* II-6
dangerous **dangereux/
   dangereuse** *adj.* II-3
dark (*hair*) **brun(e)** *adj.* I-3
darling **chéri(e)** *adj.* I-2
darn **zut** II-3
dash (*punctuation mark*) **tiret**
   m. II-3
date (*day, month, year*) **date** *f.* I-5;
   (*meeting*) **rendez-vous** *m.* I-6
   to make a date **prendre (un)
   rendez-vous** *v.* II-5
daughter **fille** *f.* I-1
day **jour** *m.* I-2; **journée** *f.* I-2
   day after tomorrow **après-
   demain** *adv.* I-2
   day before yesterday **avant-
   hier** *adv.* I-7
   day off **congé** *m.,* **jour de
   congé** I-7
dear **cher/chère** *adj.* I-2
death **mort** *f.* I-6
December **décembre** *m.* I-5
decide (*to do something*)
   décider (de) *v.* II-3

deforestation **déboisement**
   m. II-6
degree **diplôme** *m.* I-2
degrees (*temperature*) **degrés**
   m., pl. I-5
   It is... degrees. **Il fait...
   degrés.** I-5
delicatessen **charcuterie** *f.* II-1
delicious **délicieux/délicieuse**
   adj. I-4
Delighted. **Enchanté(e).** *p.p.,
   adj.* I-1
demand (that) **exiger (que)**
   v. II-6
demanding **exigeant(e)** *adj.*
   demanding profession
   profession *f.* **exigeante** II-5
dentist **dentiste** *m., f.* I-3
department store **grand magasin**
   m. I-4
departure **départ** *m.* I-7
deposit: to deposit money
   déposer de l'argent *v.* II-4
depressed **déprimé(e)** *adj.* II-2
describe **décrire** *v.* I-7
described **décrit (décrire)** *p.p.,
   adj.* I-7
desert **désert** *m.* II-6
desire **envie** *f.* I-2
desk **bureau** *m.* I-1
dessert **dessert** *m.* I-6
destroy **détruire** *v.* I-6
destroyed **détruit (détruire)**
   p.p., adj. I-6
detective film **film policier** *m.* II-7
detest **détester** *v.* I-2
   I hate... **Je déteste...** I-2
develop **développer** *v.* II-6
dial (a number) **composer
   (un numéro)** *v.* II-3
dictionary **dictionnaire** *m.* I-1
die **mourir** *v.* I-7
died **mort (mourir)** *p.p., adj.* I-7
diet **régime** *m.* II-2
   to be on a diet **être au
   régime** II-1
difference **différence** *f.* I-1
different **différent(e)** *adj.* I-1
differently **différemment**
   adv. I-8, II-P
difficult **difficile** *adj.* I-1
digital camera **appareil photo**
   m. **numérique** II-3
dining room **salle à manger**
   f. I-8, II-P
dinner **dîner** *m.* II-1
   to have dinner **dîner** *v.* I-2
diploma **diplôme** *m.* I-2
directions **indications** *f.* II-4
director (*movie*) **réalisateur/
   réalisatrice** *m., f.;* (*play/show*)
   metteur en scène *m.* II-7
dirty **sale** *adj.* I-8, II-P

discover **découvrir** *v.* II-3
discovered **découvert
   (découvrir)** *p.p.* II-3
discreet **discret/discrète** *adj.* I-3
discuss **discuter** *v.* II-3
dish (*food*) **plat** *m.* II-1
   to do the dishes **faire la
   vaisselle** *v.* I-8, II-P
dishwasher **lave-vaisselle**
   m. I-8, II-P
dismiss **renvoyer** *v.* II-5
distinction **mention** *f.* II-5
divorce **divorce** *m.* I-6
   to divorce **divorcer** *v.* I-3
divorced **divorcé(e)** *p.p., adj.* I-3
do (*make*) **faire** *v.* I-5
   to do odd jobs **bricoler** *v.* I-5
doctor **médecin** *m.* I-3
documentary **documentaire**
   m. II-7
dog **chien** *m.* I-3
done **fait (faire)** *p.p., adj.* I-6
door (*building*) **porte** *f.* I-1;
   (*automobile*) **portière** *f.* II-3
doubt (that)... **douter (que)...**
   v. II-7
doubtful **douteux/douteuse**
   adj. II-7
   It is doubtful that... **Il est
   douteux que...** II-7
download **télécharger** *v.* II-3
downtown **centre-ville** *m.* I-4
drag **barbant** *adj.* I-3; **barbe** *f.* I-3
drape **rideau** *m.* I-8, II-P
draw **dessiner** *v.* I-2
drawer **tiroir** *m.* I-8, II-P
dreadful **épouvantable** *adj.* I-5
dream (about) **rêver (de)** *v.* II-3
dress **robe** *f.* I-6
   to dress **s'habiller** *v.* II-2
dresser **commode** *f.* I-8, II-P
drink (carbonated)
   boisson *f.* **(gazeuse)** I-4
   to drink **boire** *v.* I-4
drive **conduire** *v.* I-6
   to go for a drive **faire un tour
   en voiture** I-5
driven **conduit (conduire)**
   p.p. I-6
driver (taxi/truck) **chauffeur
   (de taxi/de camion)** *m.* II-5
driver's license **permis** *m.* **de
   conduire** II-3
drums **batterie** *f.* II-7
drunk **bu (boire)** *p.p.* I-6
dryer (*clothes*) **sèche-linge**
   m. I-8, II-P
dry oneself **se sécher** *v.* II-2
due **dû(e) (devoir)** *adj.* II-1
during **pendant** *prep.* I-7
dust **enlever/faire la poussière**
   v. I-8, II-P
DVR **enregistreur DVR** *m.* II-3

E

each **chaque** *adj.* I-6
ear **oreille** *f.* II-2
early **en avance** *adv.* I-2; **tôt** *adv.* I-2
earn **gagner** *v.* II-5
Earth **Terre** *f.* II-6
easily **facilement** *adv.* I-8, II-P
east **est** *m.* II-4
easy **facile** *adj.* I-2
eat **manger** *v.* I-2
   to eat lunch **déjeuner** *v.* I-4
éclair **éclair** *m.* I-4
ecological **écologique** *adj.* II-6
ecology **écologie** *f.* II-6
economics **économie** *f.* I-2
ecotourism **écotourisme** *m.* II-6
education **formation** *f.* II-5
effect: in effect **en effet** II-6
egg **œuf** *m.* II-1
eight **huit** *m.* I-1
eighteen **dix-huit** *m.* I-1
eighth **huitième** *adj.* I-7
eighty **quatre-vingts** *m.* I-3
eighty-one **quatre-vingt-un** *m.* I-3
elder **aîné(e)** *adj.* I-3
electric **électrique** *adj.* I-8, II-P
   electrical appliance **appareil** *m.* **électrique** I-8, II-P
electrician **électricien/électricienne** *m., f.* II-5
elegant **élégant(e)** *adj.* I-1
elevator **ascenseur** *m.* I-7
eleven **onze** *m.* I-1
eleventh **onzième** *adj.* I-7
e-mail **e-mail** *m.* II-3
emergency room **urgences** *f., pl.* II-2
   to go to the emergency room **aller aux urgences** *v.* II-2
employ **employer** *v.* I-5
end **fin** *f.* II-7
endangered **menacé(e)** *adj.* II-6
   endangered species **espèce** *f.* **menacée** II-6
engaged **fiancé(e)** *adj.* I-3
engine **moteur** *m.* II-3
engineer **ingénieur** *m.* I-3
England **Angleterre** *f.* I-7
English **anglais(e)** *adj.* I-1
enormous **énorme** *adj.* I-2
enough (of) **assez (de)** *adv.* I-4
   not enough (of) **pas assez (de)** I-4
enter **entrer** *v.* I-7
envelope **enveloppe** *f.* II-4
environment **environnement** *m.* II-6
equal **égaler** *v.* I-3
erase **effacer** *v.* II-3
errand **course** *f.* II-1

escargot **escargot** *m.* II-1
especially **surtout** *adv.* I-2
essay **dissertation** *f.* II-3
essential **essentiel(le)** *adj.* II-6
   It is essential that… **Il est essentiel/indispensable que…** II-6
even **même** *adv.* I-5
evening **soir** *m.*; **soirée** *f.* I-2
   … (o'clock) in the evening … **heures du soir** I-2
every day **tous les jours** *adv.* I-8, II-P
everyone **tout le monde** *m.* II-1
evident **évident(e)** *adj.* II-7
   It is evident that… **Il est évident que…** II-7
evidently **évidemment** *adv.* I-7
exactly **exactement** *adv.* II-1
exam **examen** *m.* I-1
Excuse me. **Excuse-moi.** *fam.* I-1; **Excusez-moi.** *form.* I-1
executive **cadre/femme cadre** *m., f.* II-5
exercise **exercice** *m.* II-2
   to exercise **faire de l'exercice** *v.* II-2
exhibit **exposition** *f.* II-7
exit **sortie** *f.* I-7
expenditure **dépense** *f.* I-4
expensive **cher/chère** *adj.* I-6
explain **expliquer** *v.* I-2
explore **explorer** *v.* I-4
extinction **extinction** *f.* II-6
eye (eyes) **œil (yeux)** *m.* II-2

F

face **visage** *m.* II-2
facing **en face (de)** *prep.* I-3
fact: in fact **en fait** I-7
factory **usine** *f.* II-6
fail **échouer** *v.* I-2
fall **automne** *m.* I-5
   in the fall **en automne** I-5
   to fall **tomber** *v.* I-7
   to fall in love **tomber amoureux/amoureuse** *v.* I-6
   to fall asleep **s'endormir** *v.* II-2
family **famille** *f.* I-3
famous **célèbre** *adj.* II-7; **connu (connaître)** *p.p., adj.* I-8, II-P
far (from) **loin (de)** *prep.* I-3
farewell **adieu** *m.* II-6
farmer **agriculteur/agricultrice** *m., f.* II-5
fashion **mode** *f.* I-2
   fashion design **stylisme de mode** *m.* I-2
fast **rapide** *adj.* I-3; **vite** *adv.* I-7

fat **gros(se)** *adj.* I-3
father **père** *m.* I-3
father-in-law **beau-père** *m.* I-3
favorite **favori/favorite** *adj.* I-3; **préféré(e)** *adj.* I-2
fax machine **fax** *m.* II-3
fear **peur** *f.* I-2
   to fear that **avoir peur que** *v.* II-6
February **février** *m.* I-5
fed up: to be fed up **en avoir marre** *v.* I-3
feel *(to sense)* **sentir** *v.* I-5; *(state of being)* **se sentir** *v.* II-2
   to feel like *(doing something)* **avoir envie (de)** *v.*
   to feel nauseated **avoir mal au cœur** II-2
festival (festivals) **festival (festivals)** *m.* II-7
fever **fièvre** *f.* II-2
   to have fever **avoir de la fièvre** *v.* II-2
fiancé **fiancé(e)** *m., f.* I-6
field *(terrain)* **champ** *m.* II-6; *(of study)* **domaine** *m.* II-5
fifteen **quinze** *m.* I-1
fifth **cinquième** *adj.* I-7
fifty **cinquante** *m.* I-1
figure *(physique)* **ligne** *f.* II-2
file **fichier** *m.* II-3
fill: to fill out a form **remplir un formulaire** *v.* II-4
   to fill the tank **faire le plein** *v.* II-3
film **film** *m.* II-7
   adventure/crime film **film** *m.* **d'aventures/policier** II-7
finally **enfin** *adv.* I-7; **finalement** *adv.* I-7; **dernièrement** *adv.* I-7
find (a job/work) **trouver (un/du travail)** *v.* II-5
   to find again **retrouver** *v.* I-2
fine **amende** *f.* II-3
fine arts **beaux-arts** *m., pl.* II-7
finger **doigt** *m.* II-2
finish *(doing something)* **finir (de)** *v.* I-4, II-3
fire **incendie** *m.* II-6
firefighter **pompier/femme pompier** *m., f.* II-5
firm *(business)* **entreprise** *f.* II-5;
first **d'abord** *adv.* I-7; **premier/première** *adj.* I-2; **premier** *m.* I-5
   It is October first. **C'est le 1ᵉʳ (premier) octobre.** I-5
fish **poisson** *m.* I-3
fishing **pêche** *f.* I-5
   to go fishing **aller à la pêche** *v.* I-5

fish shop **poissonnerie** *f.* II-1
five **cinq** *m.* I-1
flat tire **pneu** *m.* **crevé** II-3
flight *(air travel)* **vol** *m.* I-7
floor **étage** *m.* I-7
flower **fleur** *f.* I-8, II-P
flu **grippe** *f.* II-2
fluently **couramment** *adv.* I-7
follow *(a path/a street/a boulevard)*
   **suivre (un chemin/une rue/
   un boulevard)** *v.* II-4
food item **aliment** *m.* II-1;
   nourriture *f.* II-1
foot **pied** *m.* II-2
football **football américain** *m.* I-5
for **pour** *prep.* I-5; **pendant**
   prep. II-1
   For whom? **Pour qui?** I-4
forbid **interdire** *v.* II-6
foreign **étranger/étrangère**
   adj. I-2
   foreign languages **langues**
   f., pl. **étrangères** I-2
forest **forêt** *f.* II-6
   tropical forest **forêt tropicale**
   f. II-6
forget *(to do something)* **oublier
   (de)** *v.* I-2
fork **fourchette** *f.* II-1
form **formulaire** *m.* II-4
former *(placed before noun)*
   ancien(ne) *adj.* II-7
fortunately **heureusement**
   adv. I-7
forty **quarante** *m.* I-1
fountain **fontaine** *f.* II-4
four **quatre** *m.* I-1
fourteen **quatorze** *m.* I-1
fourth **quatrième** *adj.* I-7
France **France** *f.* I-7
frankly **franchement** *adv.* I-7
free *(at no cost)* **gratuit(e)** *adj.* II-7
   free time **temps libre** *m.* I-5
freezer **congélateur** *m.* I-8, II-P
French **français(e)** *adj.* I-1
French fries **frites** *f., pl.* I-4
frequent *(to visit regularly)*
   fréquenter *v.* I-4
fresh **frais/fraîche** *adj.* I-5
Friday **vendredi** *m.* I-2
friend **ami(e)** *m., f.* I-1; **copain/
   copine** *m., f.* I-1
friendship **amitié** *f.* I-6
from **de/d'** *prep.* I-1
   from time to time **de temps en
   temps** *adv.* I-7
front: in front of **devant** *prep.* I-3
fruit **fruit** *m.* II-1
full *(no vacancies)* **complet
   (complète)** *adj.* I-7
full-time job **emploi** *m.*
   à plein temps II-5
fun **amusant(e)** *adj.* I-1

to have fun *(doing something)*
   s'amuser (à) *v.* II-3
funeral **funérailles** *f., pl.* II-1
funny **drôle** *adj.* I-3
furious **furieux/furieuse** *adj.* II-6
   to be furious that… **être
   furieux/furieuse que…** *v.* II-6

G

gain: gain weight **grossir** *v.* I-4
game *(amusement)* **jeu** *m.* I-5;
   (sports) **match** *m.* I-5
game show **jeu télévisé** *m.* II-7
garage **garage** *m.* I-8, II-P
garbage **ordures** *f., pl.* II-6
garbage collection **ramassage**
   m. **des ordures** II-6
garden **jardin** *m.* I-8, II-P
garlic **ail** *m.* II-1
gas **essence** *f.* II-3
gas tank **réservoir d'essence**
   m. II-3
gas warning light **voyant** *m.*
   d'essence II-3
generally **en général** *adv.* I-7
generous **généreux/généreuse**
   adj. I-3
genre **genre** *m.* II-7
gentle **doux/douce** *adj.* I-3
geography **géographie** *f.* I-2
German **allemand(e)** *adj.* I-1
Germany **Allemagne** *f.* I-7
get *(to obtain)* **obtenir** *v.* II-5
get along well (with) **s'entendre
   bien (avec)** *v.* II-2
get off **descendre (de)** *v.* I-6
get up **se lever** *v.* II-2
   get up again **se relever** *v.* II-2
gift **cadeau** *m.* I-6
   wrapped gift **paquet cadeau**
   m. I-6
gifted **doué(e)** *adj.* II-7
girl **fille** *f.* I-1
girlfriend **petite amie** *f.* I-1
give *(to someone)* **donner (à)** *v.* I-2
   to give a shot **faire une
   piqûre** *v.* II-2
   to give a tour **faire visiter**
   v. I-8, II-P
   to give back **rendre (à)** *v.* I-6
   to give one another **se donner**
   v. II-3
glass (of) **verre (de)** *m.* I-4
glasses **lunettes** *f., pl.* I-6
   sunglasses **lunettes de soleil**
   f., pl. I-6
global warming **réchauffement**
   m. **de la Terre** II-6
glove **gant** *m.* I-6
go **aller** *v.* I-4
   Let's go! **Allons-y!** I-4; **On y
   va!** II-2

I'm going. **J'y vais.** I-8, II-P
to go back **repartir** *v.* II-7
to go downstairs **descendre
   (de)** *v.* I-6
to go out **sortir** *v.* I-7
to go over **dépasser** *v.* II-3
to go up **monter** *v.* I-7
to go with **aller avec** *v.* I-6
golf **golf** *m.* I-5
good **bon(ne)** *adj.* I-3
   Good evening. **Bonsoir.** I-1
   Good morning. **Bonjour.** I-1
   to be good for nothing **ne
   servir à rien** *v.* II-1
   to be in a good mood **être de
   bonne humeur** *v.* I-8, II-P
   to be in good health **être en
   bonne santé** *v.* II-2
   to be in good shape **être en
   pleine forme** *v.* II-2
   to be up to something
   interesting **faire quelque
   chose de beau** *v.* II-4
Good-bye. **Au revoir.** I-1
government **gouvernement** *m.* II-6
grade *(academics)* **note** *f.* I-2
grandchildren **petits-enfants**
   m., pl. I-3
granddaughter **petite-fille** *f.* I-3
grandfather **grand-père** *m.* I-3
grandmother **grand-mère** *f.* I-3
grandparents **grands-parents**
   m., pl. I-3
grandson **petit-fils** *m.* I-3
grant **bourse** *f.* I-2
grass **herbe** *f.* II-6
gratin **gratin** *m.* II-1
gray **gris(e)** *adj.* I-6
great **formidable** *adj.* I-7;
   génial(e) *adj.* I-3
green **vert(e)** *adj.* I-3
green beans **haricots verts**
   m., pl. II-1
greenhouse **serre** *f.* II-6
   greenhouse effect **effet de serre**
   m. II-6
grocery store **épicerie** *f.* I-4
groom: to groom oneself *(in the
   morning)* **faire sa toilette** *v.* II-2
ground floor **rez-de-chaussée**
   m. I-7
growing population **population**
   f. **croissante** II-6
guaranteed **garanti(e)** *p.p.,*
   adj. I-5
guest **invité(e)** *m., f.* I-6;
   client(e)
   m., f. I-7
guitar **guitare** *f.* II-7
guy **mec** *m.* II-2
gym **gymnase** *m.* I-4

H

habitat **habitat** *m.* II-6
  habitat preservation **sauvetage des habitats** *m.* II-6
had **eu (avoir)** *p.p.* I-6
  had to **dû (devoir)** *p.p.* II-1
hair **cheveux** *m., pl.* II-1
  to brush one's hair **se brosser les cheveux** *v.* II-1
  to do one's hair **se coiffer** *v.* II-2
hairbrush **brosse** *f.* **à cheveux** II-2
hairdresser **coiffeur/coiffeuse** *m., f.* I-3
half **demie** *f.* I-2
  half past … (o'clock) **… et demie** I-2
half-brother **demi-frère** *m.* I-3
half-sister **demi-sœur** *f.* I-3
half-time job **emploi** *m.* **à mi-temps** II-5
hallway **couloir** *m.* I-8, II-P
ham **jambon** *m.* I-4
hand **main** *f.* I-5
handbag **sac à main** *m.* I-6
handsome **beau** *adj.* I-3
hang up **raccrocher** *v.* II-5
happiness **bonheur** *m.* I-6
happy **heureux/heureuse** *adj.;* **content(e)** II-5
  to be happy that… **être content(e) que…** *v.* II-6; **être heureux/heureuse que…** *v.* II-6
hard drive **disque (dur)** *m.* II-3
hard-working **travailleur/travailleuse** *adj.* I-3
hat **chapeau** *m.* I-6
hate **détester** *v.* I-2
  I hate… **Je déteste…** I-2
have **avoir** *v.* I-2; **aie (avoir)** *imp., v.* I-7; **ayez (avoir)** *imp. v.* I-7; **prendre** *v.* I-4
  to have an ache **avoir mal** *v.* II-2
to have to (*must*) **devoir** *v.* II-1
he **il** *sub. pron.* I-1
head (*body part*) **tête** *f.* II-2; (*of a company*) **chef** *m.* **d'entreprise** II-5
headache: to have a headache **avoir mal à la tête** *v.* II-2
headlights **phares** *m., pl.* II-3
headphones **casque** *f.* **à écouteurs** *m., pl.* II-3
health **santé** *f.* II-2
  to be in good health **être en bonne santé** *v.* II-2
health insurance **assurance** *f.* **maladie** II-5
healthy **sain(e)** *adj.* II-2

hear **entendre** *v.* I-6
heart **cœur** *m.* II-2
heat **chaud** *m.* 2
hello (*on the phone*) **allô** I-1; (*in the evening*) **Bonsoir.** I-1; (*in the morning or afternoon*) **Bonjour.** I-1
help **au secours** II-3
  to help (*to do something*) **aider (à)** *v.* I-5
  to help one another **s'aider** *v.* II-3
her **la/l'** *d.o. pron.* I-7; **lui** *i.o. pron.* I-6; (*attached to an imperative*) **-lui** *i.o. pron.* II-1
her **sa** *poss. adj., f., sing.* I-3; **ses** *poss. adj., m., f., pl.* I-3; **son** *poss. adj., m., sing.* I-3
Here! **Tenez!** *form., imp. v.* II-1; **Tiens!** *fam., imp., v.* II-1
here **ici** *adv.* I-1; (*used with demonstrative adjective* **ce** *and noun or with demonstrative pronoun* **celui**); **-ci** I-6; Here is…. **Voici…** I-1
heritage: I am of… heritage. **Je suis d'origine…** I-1
herself (*used with reflexive verb*) **se/s'** *pron.* II-2
hesitate (*to do something*) **hésiter (à)** *v.* II-3
Hey! **Eh!** *interj.* 2
Hi! **Salut!** *fam.* I-1
high **élevé(e)** *adj.* II-5
high school **lycée** *m.* I-1
  high school student **lycéen(ne)** *m., f.* 2
higher education **études supérieures** *f., pl.* 2
highway **autoroute** *f.* II-3
hike **randonnée** *f.* I-5
  to go for a hike **faire une randonnée** *v.* I-5
him **lui** *i.o. pron.* I-6; **le/l'** *d.o. pron.* I-7; (*attached to imperative*) **-lui** *i.o. pron.* II-1
himself (*used with reflexive verb*) **se/s'** *pron.* II-2
hire **embaucher** *v.* II-5
his **sa** *poss. adj., f., sing.* I-3; **ses** *poss. adj., m., f., pl.* I-3; **son** *poss. adj., m., sing.* I-3
history **histoire** *f.* I-2
hit **rentrer (dans)** *v.* II-3
hold **tenir** *v.* II-1
  to be on hold **patienter** *v.* II-5
hole in the ozone layer **trou dans la couche d'ozone** *m.* II-6
holiday **jour férié** *m.* I-6; **férié(e)** *adj.* I-6
home (*house*) **maison** *f.* I-4
  at (someone's) home **chez…** *prep.* 4

home page **page d'accueil** *f.* II-3
homework **devoir** *m.* I-2
honest **honnête** *adj.* II-7
honestly **franchement** *adv.* I-7
hood **capot** *m.* II-3
hope **espérer** *v.* I-5
hors d'œuvre **hors-d'œuvre** *m.* II-1
horse **cheval** *m.* I-5
  to go horseback riding **faire du cheval** *v.* I-5
hospital **hôpital** *m.* I-4
host **hôte/hôtesse** *m., f.* I-6
hot **chaud** *m.* I-2
  It is hot (weather). **Il fait chaud.** I-5
  to be hot **avoir chaud** *v.* I-2
hot chocolate **chocolat chaud** *m.* I-4
hotel **hôtel** *m.* I-7
  (single) hotel room **chambre** *f.* **(individuelle)** I-7
hotel keeper **hôtelier/hôtelière** *m., f.* I-7
hour **heure** *f.* I-2
house **maison** *f.* I-4
  at (someone's) house **chez…** *prep.* I-2
  to leave the house **quitter la maison** *v.* I-4
  to stop by someone's house **passer chez quelqu'un** *v.* I-4
household **ménager/ménagère** *adj.* I-8, II-P
household appliance **appareil** *m.* **ménager** I-8, II-P
household chore **tâche ménagère** *f.* I-8, II-P
housewife **femme au foyer** *f.* II-5
housework: to do the housework **faire le ménage** *v.* I-8, II-P
housing **logement** *m.* I-8, II-P
how **comme** *adv.* I-2; **comment?** *interr. adv.* I-4
  How are you? **Comment allez-vous?** *form.* I-1; **Comment vas-tu?** *fam.* I-1
  How many/How much (of)? **Combien (de)?** I-1
How much is… ? **Combien coûte… ?** I-4
huge **énorme** *adj.* I-2
Huh? **Hein?** *interj.* I-3
humanities **lettres** *f., pl.* I-2
hundred: one hundred **cent** *m.* I-5
  five hundred **cinq cents** *m.* I-5
  one hundred one **cent un** *m.* I-5
  one hundred thousand **cent mille** *m.* I-5
hundredth **centième** *adj.* I-7
hunger **faim** *f.* I-4

hungry: to be hungry **avoir faim** *v.* I-4

hunt **chasse** *f.* II-6
  to hunt **chasser** *v.* II-6

hurried **pressé(e)** *adj.* II-1

hurry **se dépêcher** *v.* II-2

hurt **faire mal** *v.* II-2
  to hurt oneself **se blesser** *v.* II-2

husband **mari** *m.;* **époux** *m.* I-3

hyphen *(punctuation mark)* **tiret** *m.* II-3

I

I **je** *sub. pron.* I-1; **moi** *disj. pron., sing.* I-3

ice cream **glace** *f.* I-6

ice cube **glaçon** *m.* I-6

idea **idée** *f.* I-3

if **si** *conj.* II-5

ill: to become ill **tomber malade** *v.* II-2

illness **maladie** *f.* II-5

immediately **tout de suite** *adv.* I-4

impatient **impatient(e)** *adj.* I-1

important **important(e)** *adj.* I-1
  It is important that... **Il est important que...** II-6

impossible **impossible** *adj.* II-7
  It is impossible that... **Il est impossible que...** II-7

improve **améliorer** *v.* II-5

in **dans** *prep.* I-3; **en** *prep.* I-3; **à** *prep.* I-4

included **compris (comprendre)** *p.p., adj.* I-6

incredible **incroyable** *adj.* II-3

independent **indépendant(e)** *adj.* I-1

independently **indépendamment** *adv.* I-8, II-P

indicate **indiquer** *v.* 5

indispensable **indispensable** *adj.* II-6

inexpensive **bon marché** *adj.* I-6

injection **piqûre** *f.* II-2
  to give an injection **faire une piqûre** *v.* II-2

injury **blessure** *f.* II-2

instrument **instrument** *m.* I-1

insurance (health/life) **assurance** *f.* **(maladie/vie)** II-5

intellectual **intellectuel(le)** *adj.* I-3

intelligent **intelligent(e)** *adj.* I-1

interested: to be interested (in) **s'intéresser (à)** *v.* II-2

interesting **intéressant(e)** *adj.* I-1

intermission **entracte** *m.* II-7

internship **stage** *m.* II-5

intersection **carrefour** *m.* II-4

interview: to have an interview **passer un entretien** II-5

introduce **présenter** *v.* I-1
  I would like to introduce *(name)* to you. **Je te présente...** , *fam.* I-1
  I would like to introduce *(name)* to you. **Je vous présente...** , *form.* I-1

invite **inviter** *v.* I-4

Ireland **Irlande** *f.* I-7

Irish **irlandais(e)** *adj.* I-7

iron **fer à repasser** *m.* I-8, II-P
  to iron (the laundry) **repasser (le linge)** *v.* I-8, II-P

isn't it? *(tag question)* **n'est-ce pas?** I-2

island **île** *f.* II-6

Italian **italien(ne)** *adj.* I-1

Italy **Italie** *f.* I-7

it: It depends. **Ça dépend.** I-4
  It is... **C'est...** I-1

itself *(used with reflexive verb)* **se/s'** *pron.* II-2

J

jacket **blouson** *m.* I-6

jam **confiture** *f.* II-1

January **janvier** *m.* I-5

Japan **Japon** *m.* I-7

Japanese **japonais(e)** *adj.* I-1

jealous **jaloux/jalouse** *adj.* I-3

jeans **jean** *m. sing.* I-6

jewelry store **bijouterie** *f.* II-4

jogging **jogging** *m.* I-5
  to go jogging **faire du jogging** *v.* I-5

joke **blague** *f.* I-2

journalist **journaliste** *m., f.* I-3

juice (orange/apple) **jus** *m.* **(d'orange/de pomme)** I-4

July **juillet** *m.* I-5

June **juin** *m.* I-5

jungle **jungle** *f.* II-6

just *(barely)* **juste** *adv.* I-3

K

keep **retenir** *v.* II-1

key **clé** *f.* I-7

keyboard **clavier** *m.* II-3

kilo(gram) **kilo(gramme)** *m.* II-1

kind **bon(ne)** *adj.* I-3

kiosk **kiosque** *m.* I-4

kiss one another **s'embrasser** *v.* II-3

kitchen **cuisine** *f.* I-8, II-P

knee **genou** *m.* II-2

knife **couteau** *m.* II-1

know *(as a fact)* **savoir** *v.* I-8, II-P; *(to be familiar with)* **connaître** *v.* I-8, II-P
  to know one another **se connaître** *v.* II-3
  I don't know anything about it. **Je n'en sais rien.** II-6
  to know that... **savoir que...** II-7

known *(as a fact)* **su (savoir)** *p.p.* I-8, II-P; *(famous)* **connu (connaître)** *p.p., adj.* I-8, II-P

L

laborer **ouvrier/ouvrière** *m., f.* II-5

lake **lac** *m.* II-6

lamp **lampe** *f.* I-8, II-P

landslide **glissement de terrain** *m.* II-6

language **langue** *f.* I-2
  foreign languages **langues** *f., pl.* **étrangères** I-2

last **dernier/dernière** *adj.* I-2

lastly **dernièrement** *adv.* I-7

late *(when something happens late)* **en retard** *adv.* I-2; *(in the evening, etc.)* **tard** *adv.* I-2

laugh **rire** *v.* I-6

laughed **ri (rire)** *p.p.* I-6

laundromat **laverie** *f.* II-4

laundry: to do the laundry **faire la lessive** *v.* I-8, II-P

law **loi** *f.* II-6

lawyer **avocat(e)** *m., f.* I-3

lay off *(let go)* **renvoyer** *v.* II-5

lazy **paresseux/paresseuse** *adj.* I-3

learned **appris (apprendre)** *p.p.* I-6

least **moins** II-1
  the least... *(used with adjective)* **le/la moins...** *super. adv.* II-1
  the least... , *(used with noun to express quantity)* **le moins de...** II-6
  the least... *(used with verb or adverb)* **le moins...** *super. adv.* II-1

leather **cuir** *m.* I-6

leave **partir** *v.* I-5; **quitter** *v.* I-4
  to leave alone **laisser tranquille** *v.* II-2
  to leave one another **se quitter** *v.* II-3
  I'm leaving. **Je m'en vais.** I-8, II-P

left: to the left (of) **à gauche (de)** *prep.* I-3

leg **jambe** *f.* II-2

leisure activity **loisir** *m.* I-5

lemon soda **limonade** *f.* I-4

lend *(to someone)* **prêter (à)** *v.* I-6
less **moins** *adv.* I-4
  less of... *(used with noun to express quantity)* **moins de...** I-4
  less … than *(used with noun to compare quantities)* **moins de... que** II-6
  less… than *(used with adjective to compare qualities)* **moins... que** II-1
let **laisser** *v.* II-3
  to let go *(to fire or lay off)* **renvoyer** *v.* II-5
  Let's go! **Allons-y!** I-4; **On y va!** II-2
letter **lettre** *f.* II-4
  letter of application **lettre** *f.* **de motivation** II-5
  letter of recommendation/reference **lettre** *f.* **de recommandation** II-5
lettuce **laitue** *f.* II-1
level **niveau** *m.* II-5
library **bibliothèque** *f.* I-1
license: driver's license **permis** *m.* **de conduire** II-3
life **vie** *f.* I-6
life insurance **assurance** *f.* **vie** II-5
light: warning light *(automobile)* **voyant** *m.* II-3
  oil/gas warning light **voyant** *m.* **d'huile/d'essence** II-3
  to light up **s'allumer** *v.* II-3
like *(as)* **comme** *adv.* I-6; to like **aimer** *v.* I-2
  I don't like … very much. **Je n'aime pas tellement...** I-2
  I really like… **J'aime bien...** I-2
  to like one another **s'aimer bien** *v.* II-3
  to like that... **aimer que...** *v.* II-6
line **queue** *f.* II-4
  to wait in line **faire la queue** *v.* II-4
link **lien** *m.* II-3
listen (to) **écouter** *v.* I-2
literary **littéraire** *adj.* II-7
literature **littérature** *f.* I-1
little *(not much)* (of) **peu (de)** *adv.* I-4
live **vivre** *v.* I-8, II-P
  live (in) **habiter (à)** *v.* I-2
living room *(informal room)* **salle de séjour** *f.* I-8, II-P; *(formal room)* **salon** *m.* I-8, II-P
located: to be located **se trouver** *v.* II-2
long **long(ue)** *adj.* I-3
  a long time **longtemps** *adv.* I-5

look *(at one another)* **se regarder** *v.* II-3; *(at oneself)* **se regarder** *v.* II-2
look for **chercher** *v.* I-2
  to look for work/a job **chercher du/un travail** II-4
loose *(clothing)* **large** *adj.* I-6
lose: to lose **perdre** *v.* I-6
  to lose weight **maigrir** *v.* I-4
lost: to be lost **être perdu(e)** *v.* II-4
lot: a lot of **beaucoup de** *adv.* I-4
love **amour** *m.* I-6
  to love **adorer** *v.* I-2
  I love… **J'adore...** I-2
  to love one another **s'aimer** *v.* II-3
  to be in love **être amoureux/amoureuse** *v.* I-6
luck **chance** *f.* I-2
  to be lucky **avoir de la chance** *v.* I-2
lunch **déjeuner** *m.* II-1
  to eat lunch **déjeuner** *v.* I-4

M

ma'am **Madame.** *f.* I-1
machine: answering machine **répondeur** *m.* II-3
mad: to get mad **s'énerver** *v.* II-2
made **fait (faire)** *p.p., adj.* I-6
magazine **magazine** *m.* II-7
mail **courrier** *m.* II-4
mailbox **boîte** *f.* **aux lettres** II-4
mailman **facteur** *m.* II-4
main character **personnage principal** *m.* II-7
main dish **plat (principal)** *m.* II-1
maintain **maintenir** *v.* II-1
make **faire** *v.* I-5
makeup **maquillage** *m.* II-2
  to put on makeup **se maquiller** *v.* II-2
make up **se réconcilier** *v.* II-7
malfunction **panne** *f.* II-3
man **homme** *m.* I-1
manage *(in business)* **diriger** *v.* II-5; *(to do something)* **arriver à** *v.* I-2
manager **gérant(e)** *m., f.* II-5, **responsable** *m., f.* II-5
many (of) **beaucoup (de)** *adv.* I-4
  How many (of)? **Combien (de)?** I-1
map *(of a city)* **plan** *m.* I-7; *(of the world)* **carte** *f.* I-1
March **mars** *m.* I-5
market **marché** *m.* I-4
marriage **mariage** *m.* I-6
married **marié(e)** *adj.* I-3
  married couple **mariés** *m., pl.* I-6
marry **épouser** *v.* I-3

Martinique: from Martinique **martiniquais(e)** *adj.* I-1
masterpiece **chef-d'œuvre** *m.* II-7
mathematics **mathématiques (maths)** *f., pl.* I-2
May **mai** *m.* I-5
maybe **peut-être** *adv.* I-2
mayonnaise **mayonnaise** *f.* II-1
mayor's office **mairie** *f.* II-4
me **moi** *disj. pron., sing.* I-3; *(attached to imperative)* **-moi** *pron.* II-1; **me/m'** *i.o. pron.* I-6; **me/m'** *d.o. pron.* I-7
  Me too. **Moi aussi.** I-1
  Me neither. **Moi non plus.** I-2
meal **repas** *m.* II-1
mean **méchant(e)** *adj.* I-3
  to mean *(with* **dire***)* **vouloir** *v.* II-1
means: that means **ça veut dire** *v.* II-1
meat **viande** *f.* II-1
mechanic **mécanicien/mécanicienne** *m., f.* II-3
medication (against/for) **médicament (contre/pour)** *m., f.* II-2
meet *(to encounter, to run into)* **rencontrer** *v.* I-2; *(to make the acquaintance of)* **faire la connaissance de** *v.* I-5, **se rencontrer** *v.* II-3; *(planned encounter)* **se retrouver** *v.* II-3
meeting **réunion** *f.* II-5; **rendez-vous** *m.* I-6
member **membre** *m.* II-7
menu **menu** *m.* II-1; **carte** *f.* II-1
message **message** *m.* II-5
  to leave a message **laisser un message** *v.* II-5
Mexican **mexicain(e)** *adj.* I-1
Mexico **Mexique** *m.* I-7
microwave oven **four à micro-ondes** *m.* I-8, II-P
midnight **minuit** *m.* I-2
milk **lait** *m.* I-4
mineral water **eau** *f.* **minérale** I-4
mirror **miroir** *m.* I-8, II-P
Miss **Mademoiselle** *f.* I-1
mistaken: to be mistaken *(about something)* **se tromper (de)** *v.* II-2
modest **modeste** *adj.* II-5
moment **moment** *m.* I-1
Monday **lundi** *m.* I-2
money **argent** *m.* II-4; *(currency)* **monnaie** *f.* II-4
  to deposit money **déposer de l'argent** *v.* II-4
month **mois** *m.* I-2
  this month **ce mois-ci** I-2
moon **Lune** *f.* II-6
more **plus** *adv.* I-4

more of **plus de** I-4
more … than *(used with noun to compare quantities)* **plus de… que** II-6
more … than *(used with adjective to compare qualities)* **plus… que** II-1
morning **matin** *m.* I-2; **matinée** *f.* I-2
this morning **ce matin** I-2
Moroccan **marocain(e)** *adj.* I-1
most **plus** II-1
the most… *(used with adjective)* **le/la plus…** *super. adv.* II-1
the most… *(used with noun to express quantity)* **le plus de…** II-6
the most… *(used with verb or adverb)* **le plus…** *super. adv.* II-1
mother **mère** *f.* I-3
mother-in-law **belle-mère** *f.* I-3
mountain **montagne** *f.* I-4
mouse **souris** *f.* II-3
mouth **bouche** *f.* II-2
move *(to get around)* **se déplacer** *v.* II-4
to move in **emménager** *v.* I-8, II-P
to move out **déménager** *v.* I-8, II-P
movie **film** *m.* II-7
adventure/horror/science-fiction/crime movie **film** *m.* **d'aventures/d'horreur/de science-fiction/policier** II-7
movie theater **cinéma (ciné)** *m.* I-4
MP3 **MP3** *m.* II-3
much (as much … as) *(used with noun to express quantity)* **autant de … que** *adv.* II-6
How much *(of something)*? **Combien (de)?** I-1
How much is… ? **Combien coûte… ?** I-4
museum **musée** *m.* I-4
to go to museums **faire les musées** *v.* II-7
mushroom **champignon** *m.* II-1
music: to play music **faire de la musique** II-7
musical **comédie** *f.* **musicale** II-7; **musical(e)** *adj.* II-7
musician **musicien(ne)** *m., f.* I-3
must *(to have to)* **devoir** *v.* II-1
One must **Il faut…** I-5
mustard **moutarde** *f.* II-1
my **ma** *poss. adj., f., sing.* I-3; **mes** *poss. adj., m., f., pl.* I-3; **mon** *poss. adj., m., sing.* I-3
myself **me/m'** *pron., sing.* II-2; *(attached to an imperative)* **-moi** *pron.* II-1

naïve **naïf (naïve)** *adj.* I-3
name: My name is… **Je m'appelle…** I-1
named: to be named **s'appeler** *v.* II-2
napkin **serviette** *f.* II-1
nationality **nationalité** *f.*
I am of … nationality. **Je suis de nationalité…** I-1
natural **naturel(le)** *adj.* II-6
natural resource **ressource naturelle** *f.* II-6
nature **nature** *f.* II-6
nauseated: to feel nauseated **avoir mal au cœur** *v.* II-2
near (to) **près (de)** *prep.* I-3
very near (to) **tout près (de)** II-4
necessary **nécessaire** *adj.* II-6
It was necessary… *(followed by infinitive or subjunctive)* **Il a fallu…** I-6
It is necessary…. *(followed by infinitive or subjunctive)* **Il faut que…** I-5
It is necessary that… *(followed by subjunctive)* **Il est nécessaire que/qu'…** II-6
neck **cou** *m.* II-2
need **besoin** *m.* I-2
to need **avoir besoin (de)** *v.* I-2
neighbor **voisin(e)** *m., f.* I-3
neighborhood **quartier** *m.* I-8, II-P
neither… nor **ne… ni… ni…** *conj.* II-4
nephew **neveu** *m.* I-3
nervous **nerveux/nerveuse** *adj.* I-3
nervously **nerveusement** *adv.* I-8, II-P
network (social) **réseau (social)** *m.* II-3
never **jamais** *adv.* I-5; **ne… jamais** *adv.* II-4
new **nouveau/nouvelle** *adj.* I-3
newlyweds **jeunes mariés** *m., pl.* I-6
news **informations (infos)** *f., pl.* II-7; **nouvelles** *f., pl.* II-7
newspaper **journal** *m.* I-7
newsstand **marchand de journaux** *m.* II-4
next **ensuite** *adv.* I-7; **prochain(e)** *adj.* I-2
next to **à côté de** *prep.* I-3
nice **gentil/gentille** *adj.* I-3; **sympa(thique)** *adj.* I-1
nicely **gentiment** *adv.* I-7
niece **nièce** *f.* I-3
night **nuit** *f.* I-2

nine **neuf** *m.* I-1
nine hundred **neuf cents** *m.* I-5
nineteen **dix-neuf** *m.* I-1
ninety **quatre-vingt-dix** *m.* I-3
ninth **neuvième** *adj.* I-7
no *(at beginning of statement to indicate disagreement)* **(mais) non** I-2; **aucun(e)** *adj.* II-2
no more **ne… plus** II-4
no problem **pas de problème** II-4
no reason **pour rien** I-4
no, none **pas (de)** II-4
nobody **ne… personne** II-4
none (not any) **ne… aucun(e)** II-4
noon **midi** *m.* I-2
no one **personne** *pron.* II-4
north **nord** *m.* II-4
nose **nez** *m.* II-2
not **ne… pas** I-2
not at all **pas du tout** *adv.* I-2
Not badly. **Pas mal.** I-1
to not believe that **ne pas croire que** *v.* II-7
to not think that **ne pas penser que** *v.* II-7
not yet **pas encore** *adv.* I-8, II-P
notebook **cahier** *m.* I-1
notes **billets** *m., pl.* II-3
nothing **rien** *indef. pron.* II-4
It's nothing. **Il n'y a pas de quoi.** I-1
notice **s'apercevoir** *v.* II-4
novel **roman** *m.* II-7
November **novembre** *m.* I-5
now **maintenant** *adv.* I-5
nuclear **nucléaire** *adj.* II-6
nuclear energy **énergie nucléaire** *f.* II-6
nuclear plant **centrale nucléaire** *f.* II-6
nurse **infirmier/infirmière** *m., f.* II-2

object **objet** *m.* I-1
obtain **obtenir** *v.* II-5
obvious **évident(e)** *adj.* II-7
It is obvious that… **Il est évident que…** II-7
obviously **évidemment** *adv.* I-7
o'clock: It's… (o'clock). **Il est… heure(s).** I-2
at … (o'clock) **à … heure(s)** I-4
October **octobre** *m.* I-5
of **de/d'** *prep.* I-3
of medium height **de taille moyenne** *adj.* I-3

of the **des (de + les)** I-3
of the **du (de + le)** I-3
of which, of whom **dont**
rel. pron. II-3
of course **bien sûr** *adv.* I-2;
évidemment *adv.* I-7
of course not *(at beginning
of statement to indicate
disagreement)* **(mais) non** I-2
offer **offrir** *v.* II-3
offered **offert (offrir)** *p.p.* II-3
office **bureau** *m.* I-4
at the doctor's office **chez le
médecin** *prep.* I-2
often **souvent** *adv.* I-5
oil **huile** *f.* II-1
automobile oil **huile** *f.* II-3
oil warning light **voyant** *m.*
d'huile II-3
olive oil **huile** *f.* **d'olive** II-1
to check the oil **vérifier
l'huile** *v.* II-3
okay **d'accord** I-2
old **vieux/vieille** *adj.; (placed
after noun)* **ancien(ne)** *adj.* I-3
old age **vieillesse** *f.* I-6
olive **olive** *f.* II-1
olive oil **huile** *f.* **d'olive** II-1
omelette **omelette** *f.* I-5
on **sur** *prep.* I-3
On behalf of whom? **C'est de
la part de qui?** II-5
on the condition that… **à
condition que** II-7
on television **à la
télé(vision)** II-7
on the contrary
au contraire II-7
on the radio **à la radio** II-7
on the subject of **au sujet
de** II-6
on vacation **en vacances** I-7
once **une fois** *adv.* I-8, II-P
one **un** *m.* I-1
one **on** *sub. pron., sing.* I-1
one another **l'un(e) à
l'autre** II-3
one another **l'un(e) l'autre** II-3
one had to… **il fallait…**
I-8, II-P
One must… **Il faut que/
qu'…** II-6
One must… **Il faut…** *(followed
by infinitive or subjunctive)* I-5
one million **un million** *m.* I-5
one million *(things)* **un
million de…** I-5
onion **oignon** *m.* II-1
online **en ligne** II-3
to be online **être en ligne** *v.* II-3
to be online *(with someone)*
**être connecté(e) (avec
quelqu'un)** *v.* I-7, II-3

only **ne… que** II-4; **seulement**
adv. I-8, II-P
open **ouvrir** *v.* II-3; **ouvert(e)**
adj. II-3
opened **ouvert (ouvrir)** *p.p.* II-3
opera **opéra** *m.* II-7
optimistic **optimiste** *adj.* I-1
or **ou** I-3
orange **orange** *f.* II-1; **orange**
inv.adj. I-6
orchestra **orchestre** *m.* II-7
order **commander** *v.* II-1
organize (a party) **organiser (une
fête)** *v.* I-6
orient oneself **s'orienter** *v.* II-4
others **d'autres** I-4
our **nos** *poss. adj., m., f., pl.* I-3;
notre *poss. adj., m., f., sing.* I-3
outdoor *(open-air)* **plein
air** II-6
over **fini** *adj., p.p.* I-7
overpopulation **surpopulation**
f. II-6
overseas **à l'étranger** *adv.* I-7
over there **là-bas** *adv.* I-1
owed **dû (devoir)** *p.p., adj.* II-1
own **posséder** *v.* I-5
owner **propriétaire** *m., f.* I-8, II-P
ozone **ozone** *m.* II-6
hole in the ozone layer
**trou dans la couche
d'ozone** *m.* II-6

P

pack: to pack one's bags **faire les
valises** I-7
package **colis** *m.* II-4
paid **payé (payer)** *p.p., adj.* II-5
to be well/badly paid **être bien/
mal payé(e)** II-5
pain **douleur** *f.* II-2
paint **faire de la peinture** *v.* II-7
painter **peintre/femme peintre**
m., f. II-7
painting **peinture** *f.* II-7;
tableau *m.* II-7
pants **pantalon** *m., sing.* I-6
paper **papier** *m.* I-1
Pardon (me). **Pardon.** I-1
parents **parents** *m., pl.* I-3
park **parc** *m.* I-4
to park **se garer** *v.* II-3
parka **anorak** *m.* I-6
parking lot **parking** *m.* II-3
part-time job **emploi** *m.* **à
mi-temps/à temps partiel**
m. II-5
party **fête** *f.* I-6
pass **dépasser** *v.* II-3; **passer**
v. I-7
to pass an exam **être reçu(e)
à un examen** *v.* I-2

passenger **passager/passagère**
m., f. I-7
passport **passeport** *m.* I-7
password **mot de passe** *m.* II-3
past: in the past **autrefois**
adv. I-8, II-P
pasta **pâtes** *f., pl.* II-1
pastime **passe-temps** *m.* I-5
pastry **pâtisserie** *f.* II-1
pastry shop **pâtisserie** *f.* II-1
pâté **pâté (de campagne)** *m.* II-1
path **sentier** *m.* II-6; **chemin**
m. II-4
patient **patient(e)** *adj.* I-1
patiently **patiemment**
adv. I-8, II-P
pay **payer** *v.* I-5
to pay by check **payer par
chèque** *v.* II-4
to pay in cash **payer en
espèces** *v.* II-4
to pay with a debit/credit
card **payer par carte
bancaire/de crédit** *v.* II-4
to pay attention (to) **faire
attention (à)** *v.* I-5
peach **pêche** *f.* II-1
pear **poire** *f.* II-1
peas **petits pois** *m., pl.* II-1
pen **stylo** *m.* I-1
pencil **crayon** *m.* I-1
people **gens** *m., pl.* I-7
pepper *(spice)* **poivre** *m.* II-1;
(vegetable) **poivron** *m.* II-1
per day/week/month/year
**par jour/semaine/mois/
an** I-5
perfect **parfait(e)** *adj.* I-2
perhaps **peut-être** *adv.* I-2
period *(punctuation mark)* **point**
m. II-3
permit **permis** *m.* II-3
permitted **permis (permettre)**
p.p., adj. I-6
person **personne** *f.* I-1
pessimistic **pessimiste** *adj.* I-1
pharmacist **pharmacien(ne)**
m., f. II-2
pharmacy **pharmacie** *f.* II-2
philosophy **philosophie** *f.* I-2
phone one another **se téléphoner**
v. II-3
photo(graph) **photo(graphie)**
f. I-3
physical education **éducation
physique** *f.* I-2
physics **physique** *f.* I-2
piano **piano** *m.* II-7
pick up **décrocher** *v.* II-5
picnic **pique-nique** *m.* II-6
picture **tableau** *m.* I-1
pie **tarte** *f.* II-1
piece (of) **morceau (de)** *m.* I-4

piece of furniture **meuble** *m.* I-8, II-P
pill **pilule** *f.* II-2
pillow **oreiller** *m.* I-8, II-P
pink **rose** *adj.* I-6
pitcher (of water) **carafe (d'eau)** *f.* II-1
place **endroit** *m.* I-4; **lieu** *m.* I-4
planet **planète** *f.* II-6
plans: to make plans **faire des projets** *v.* II-5
plant **plante** *f.* II-6
plastic **plastique** *m.* II-6
plastic wrapping **emballage en plastique** *m.* II-6
plate **assiette** *f.* II-1
play **pièce de théâtre** *f.* II-7
play **s'amuser** *v.* II-2; (*a sport/a musical instrument*) **jouer (à/de)** *v.* I-5
to play regularly **pratiquer** *v.* I-5
to play sports **faire du sport** *v.* I-5
to play a role **jouer un rôle** *v.* II-7
player **joueur/joueuse** *m., f.* I-5
playwright **dramaturge** *m.* II-7
pleasant **agréable** *adj.* I-1
please: to please someone **faire plaisir à quelqu'un** *v.* II-5
Please. **S'il te plaît.** *fam.* I-1
Please. **S'il vous plaît.** *form.* I-1
Please. **Je vous en prie.** *form.* I-1
Please hold. **Ne quittez pas.** II-5
plug in **brancher** *v.* II-3
plumber **plombier** *m.* II-5
poem **poème** *m.* II-7
poet **poète/poétesse** *m., f.* II-7
police **police** *f.* II-3; **policier** *adj.* II-7
police officer **agent de police** *m.* II-3; **policier** *m.* II-3; **policière** *f.* II-3
police station **commissariat de police** *m.* II-4
polite **poli(e)** *adj.* I-1
politely **poliment** *adv.* I-8, II-P
political science **sciences politiques (sciences po)** *f., pl.* I-2
politician **homme/femme politique** *m., f.* II-5
pollute **polluer** *v.* II-6
pollution **pollution** *f.* II-6
pollution cloud **nuage de pollution** *m.* II-6
pool **piscine** *f.* I-4
poor **pauvre** *adj.* I-3
popular music **variétés** *f., pl.* II-7
population **population** *f.* II-6
growing population **population** *f.* **croissante** II-6

pork **porc** *m.* II-1
portrait **portrait** *m.* I-5
position (*job*) **poste** *m.* II-5
possess (*to own*) **posséder** *v.* I-5
possible **possible** *adj.* II-7
It is possible that... **Il est possible que...** II-6
post **afficher** *v.* II-5
post office **bureau de poste** *m.* II-4
postal service **poste** *f.* II-4
postcard **carte postale** *f.* II-4
poster **affiche** *f.* I-8, II-P
potato **pomme de terre** *f.* II-1
practice **pratiquer** *v.* I-5
prefer **aimer mieux** *v.* I-2; **préférer (que)** *v.* I-5
pregnant **enceinte** *adj.* II-2
prepare (for) **préparer** *v.* I-2
to prepare (*to do something*) **se préparer (à)** *v.* II-2
prescription **ordonnance** *f.* II-2
present **présenter** *v.* II-7
preservation: habitat preservation **sauvetage des habitats** *m.* II-6
preserve **préserver** *v.* II-6
pressure **pression** *f.* II-3
to check the tire pressure **vérifier la pression des pneus** *v.* II-3
pretty **joli(e)** *adj.* I-3; (*before an adjective or adverb*) **assez** *adv.* I-8, II-P
prevent: to prevent a fire **prévenir l'incendie** *v.* II-6
price **prix** *m.* I-4
principal **principal(e)** *adj.* II-4
print **imprimer** *v.* II-3
printer **imprimante** *f.* II-3
problem **problème** *m.* I-1
produce **produire** *v.* I-6
produced **produit (produire)** *p.p., adj.* I-6
product **produit** *m.* II-6
profession **métier** *m.* II-5; **profession** *f.* II-5
demanding profession **profession** *f.* **exigeante** II-5
professional **professionnel(le)** *adj.* II-5
professional experience **expérience professionnelle** *f.* II-5
program **programme** *m.* II-7; (*software*) **logiciel** *m.* II-3; (*television*) **émission** *f.* **de télévision** II-7
prohibit **interdire** *v.* II-6
project **projet** *m.* II-5
promise **promettre** *v.* I-6
promised **promis (promettre)** *p.p., adj.* I-6

promotion **promotion** *f.* II-5
propose that... **proposer que...** *v.* II-6
to propose a solution **proposer une solution** *v.* II-6
protect **protéger** *v.* I-5
protection **préservation** *f.* II-6; **protection** *f.* II-6
proud **fier/fière** *adj.* I-3
psychological **psychologique** *adj.* II-7
psychological drama **drame psychologique** *m.* II-7
psychology **psychologie** *f.* I-2
psychologist **psychologue** *m., f.* II-5
publish **publier** *v.* II-7
pure **pur(e)** *adj.* II-6
purple **violet(te)** *adj.* I-6
purse **sac à main** *m.* I-6
put **mettre** *v.* I-6
to put (on) (yourself) **se mettre** *v.* II-2
to put away **ranger** *v.* I-8, II-P
to put on makeup **se maquiller** *v.* II-2
put **mis (mettre)** *p.p.* I-6

Q

quarter **quart** *m.* I-2
a quarter after ... (o'clock) **... et quart** I-2
Quebec: from Quebec **québécois(e)** *adj.* I-1
question **question** *f.* I-6
to ask (*someone*) a question **poser une question (à)** *v.* I-6
quickly **vite** *adv.* I-7; **rapidement** *adv.* I-7
quite (*before an adjective or adverb*) **assez** *adv.* I-8, II-P

R

rabbit **lapin** *m.* II-6
rain **pleuvoir** *v.* I-5
acid rain **pluie** *f.* **acide** II-6
It is raining. **Il pleut.** I-5
It was raining. **Il pleuvait.** I-8, II-P
rain forest **forêt tropicale** *f.* II-6
rain jacket **imperméable** *m.* I-5
rained **plu (pleuvoir)** *p.p.* I-6
raise (in salary) **augmentation (de salaire)** *f.* II-5
rarely **rarement** *adv.* I-5
rather **plutôt** *adv.* I-1
ravishing **ravissant(e)** *adj.* II-5
razor **rasoir** *m.* II-2
read **lire** *v.* I-7
read **lu (lire)** *p.p., adj.* I-7
ready **prêt(e)** *adj.* I-3

real (true) **vrai(e)** adj.; **véritable** adj. I-3

real estate agent **agent immobilier** m., f. II-5

realize **se rendre compte** v. II-2

really **vraiment** adv. I-7; (before adjective or adverb) **tout(e)** adv. I-3; really close by **tout près** I-3

rear-view mirror **rétroviseur** m. II-3

reason **raison** f. I-2

receive **recevoir** v. II-4

received **reçu (recevoir)** p.p., adj. II-4

receiver **combiné** m. II-5

recent **récent(e)** adj. II-7

reception desk **réception** f. I-7

recognize **reconnaître** v. I-8, II-P

recognized **reconnu (reconnaître)** p.p., adj. I-8, II-P

recommend that... **recommander que...** v. II-6

recommendation **recommandation** f. II-5

record **enregistrer** v. II-3

recycle **recycler** v. II-6

recycling **recyclage** m. II-6

red **rouge** adj. I-6

redial **recomposer (un numéro)** v. II-3

reduce **réduire** v. I-6

reduced **réduit (réduire)** p.p., adj. I-6

reference **référence** f. II-5

reflect (on) **réfléchir (à)** v. I-4

refrigerator **frigo** m. I-8, II-P

refuse (to do something) **refuser (de)** v. II-3

region **région** f. II-6

regret that... **regretter que...** II-6

relax **se détendre** v. II-2

remember **se souvenir (de)** v. II-2

remote control **télécommande** f. II-3

rent **loyer** m. I-8, II-P

to rent **louer** v. I-8, II-P

repair **réparer** v. II-3

repeat **répéter** v. I-5

research **rechercher** v. II-5

researcher **chercheur/ chercheuse** m., f. II-5

reservation **réservation** f. I-7

to cancel a reservation **annuler une réservation** I-7

reserve **réserver** v. I-7

reserved **réservé(e)** adj. I-1

resign **démissionner** v. II-5

resort (ski) **station** f. **(de ski)** I-7

respond **répondre (à)** v. I-6

rest **se reposer** v. II-2

restart **redémarrer** v. II-3

restaurant **restaurant** m. I-4

restroom(s) **toilettes** f., pl. I-8, II-P; **W.-C.** m., pl.

result **résultat** m. I-2

résumé **curriculum vitæ (C.V.)** m. II-5

retake **repasser** v. II-7

retire **prendre sa retraite** v. I-6

retired person **retraité(e)** m., f. II-5

retirement **retraite** f. I-6

return **retourner** v. I-7

to return (home) **rentrer (à la maison)** v. I-2

review (criticism) **critique** f. II-7

rice **riz** m. II-1

ride: to go horseback riding **faire du cheval** v. I-5

to ride in a car **rouler en voiture** v. I-7

right **juste** adv. I-3

to the right (of) **à droite (de)** prep. I-3

to be right **avoir raison** I-2

right away **tout de suite** I-7

right next door **juste à côté** I-3

ring **sonner** v. II-3

river **fleuve** m. II-6; **rivière** f. II-6

riverboat **bateau-mouche** m. I-7

role **rôle** m. II-6

room **pièce** f. I-8, II-P; **salle** f. I-8, II-P

bedroom **chambre** f. I-7

classroom **salle** f. **de classe** I-1

dining room **salle** f. **à manger** I-8, II-P

single hotel room **chambre** f. **individuelle** I-7

round-trip **aller-retour** adj. I-7

round-trip ticket **billet** m. **aller-retour** I-7

rug **tapis** m. I-8, II-P

run **courir** v. I-5; **couru (courir)** p.p., adj. I-6

to run into someone **tomber sur quelqu'un** v. I-7

S

sad **triste** adj. I-3

to be sad that... **être triste que...** v. II-6

safety **sécurité** f. II-3

said **dit (dire)** p.p., adj. I-7

salad **salade** f. II-1

salary (a high, low) **salaire (élevé, modeste)** m. II-5

sales **soldes** f., pl. I-6

salon: beauty salon **salon** m. **de beauté** II-4

salt **sel** m. II-1

sandwich **sandwich** m. I-4

sat (down) **assis (s'asseoir)** p.p. II-2

Saturday **samedi** m. I-2

sausage **saucisse** f. II-1

save **sauvegarder** v. II-3

save the planet **sauver la planète** v. II-6

savings **épargne** f. II-4

savings account **compte d'épargne** m. II-4

say **dire** v. I-7

scarf **écharpe** f. I-6

scholarship **bourse** f. I-2

school **école** f. I-2

science **sciences** f., pl. I-2

political science **sciences politiques (sciences po)** f., pl. I-2

screen **écran** m. II-3

screening **séance** f. II-7

sculpture **sculpture** f. II-7

sculptor **sculpteur/sculptrice** m., f. II-7

sea **mer** f. I-7

seafood **fruits de mer** m., pl. II-1

search for **chercher** v. I-2

to search for work/a job **chercher du/un travail** v. II-4

season **saison** f. I-5

seat **place** f. II-7

seatbelt **ceinture de sécurité** f. II-3

to buckle one's seatbelt **attacher sa ceinture de sécurité** v. II-3

seated **assis(e)** p.p., adj. II-2

second **deuxième** adj. I-7

security **sécurité** f. II-3

see **voir** v. II-7; (catch sight of) **apercevoir** v. II-4

to see again **revoir** v. II-7

See you later. **À plus tard.** I-1

See you later. **À tout à l'heure.** I-1

See you soon. **À bientôt.** I-1

See you tomorrow. **À demain.** I-1

seen **aperçu (apercevoir)** p.p. II-4; **vu (voir)** p.p. II-7

seen again **revu (revoir)** p.p. II-7

self/-selves **même(s)** pron. I-6

selfish **égoïste** adj. I-1

sell **vendre** v. I-6

seller **vendeur/vendeuse** m., f. I-6

send **envoyer** v. I-5

to send (to someone) **envoyer (à)** v. I-6

to send a letter **poster une lettre** II-4

Senegalese **sénégalais(e)** adj. I-1

sense **sentir** v. I-5
separated **séparé(e)** adj. I-3
September **septembre** m. I-5
serious **grave** adj. II-2;
  sérieux/sérieuse adj. I-3
serve **servir** v. I-5
server **serveur/serveuse**
  m., f. I-4
service station **station-service**
  f. II-3
set the table **mettre la table**
  v. I-8, II-P
seven **sept** m. I-1
seven hundred **sept cents** m. I-5
seventeen **dix-sept** m. I-1
seventh **septième** adj. I-7
seventy **soixante-dix** m. I-3
several **plusieurs** adj. I-4
shame **honte** f. I-2
  It's a shame that… **Il est**
  dommage que… II-6
shampoo **shampooing** m. II-2
shape (state of health) **forme** f. II-2
share **partager** v. I-2
shave (oneself) **se raser** v. II-2
shaving cream **crème à raser**
  f. II-2
she **elle** pron. I-1
sheet of paper **feuille de papier**
  f. I-1
sheets **draps** m., pl. I-8, II-P
shelf **étagère** f. I-8, II-P
shh **chut** II-7
shirt (short-/long-sleeved)
  chemise (à manches
  courtes/longues) f. I-6
shoe **chaussure** f. I-6
shopkeeper **commerçant(e)**
  m., f. II-1
shopping **shopping** m. I-7
  to go shopping **faire du**
  shopping v. I-7
  to go (grocery) shopping **faire**
  les courses v. II-1
shopping center **centre**
  commercial m. I-4
short **court(e)** adj. I-3;
  (stature) **petit(e)** I-3
shorts **short** m. I-6
shot (injection) **piqûre** f. II-2
  to give a shot **faire une piqûre**
  v. II-2
show **spectacle** m. I-5; (movie
  or theater) **séance** f. II-7
  to show (to someone) **montrer**
  (à) v. I-6
shower **douche** f. I-8, II-P
shut off **fermer** v. II-3
shy **timide** adj. I-1
sick: to get/be sick **tomber/être**
  malade v. II-2
sign **signer** v. II-4
silk **soie** f. I-6

since **depuis** adv. II-1
sincere **sincère** adj. I-1
sing **chanter** v. I-5
singer **chanteur/chanteuse**
  m., f. I-1
single (marital status) **célibataire**
  adj. I-3
  single hotel room **chambre** f.
  individuelle I-7
sink **évier** m. I-8, II-P;
  (bathroom) **lavabo** m. I-8, II-P
sir **Monsieur** m. I-1
sister **sœur** f. I-3
sister-in-law **belle-sœur** f. I-3
sit down **s'asseoir** v. II-2
sitting **assis(e)** adj. II-2
six **six** m. I-1
six hundred **six cents** m. I-5
sixteen **seize** m. I-1
sixth **sixième** adj. I-7
sixty **soixante** m. I-1
size **taille** f. I-6
skate **patiner** v. I-4
ski **skier** v. I-5; **faire du ski** I-5
skiing **ski** m. I-5
ski jacket **anorak** m. I-6
ski resort **station** f. **de ski** I-7
skin **peau** f. II-2
skirt **jupe** f. I-6
sky **ciel** m. II-6
sleep **sommeil** m. I-2
  to sleep **dormir** v. I-5
  to be sleepy **avoir sommeil**
  v. I-2
sleeve **manche** f. I-6
slice **tranche** f. II-1
slipper **pantoufle** f. II-2
slow **lent(e)** adj. I-3
slowly **lentement** adv. I-7
small **petit(e)** adj. I-3
smartphone **smartphone** m. II-3
smell **sentir** v. I-5
smile **sourire** m. I-6
  to smile **sourire** v. I-6
snack (afternoon) **goûter** m. II-1
snake **serpent** m. II-6
sneeze **éternuer** v. II-2
snow **neiger** v. I-5
  It is snowing. **Il neige.** I-5
  It was snowing… **Il**
  neigeait… I-8, II-P
so **si** II-3; **alors** adv. I-1
  so that **pour que** II-7
soap **savon** m. II-2
soap opera **feuilleton** m. II-7
soccer **foot(ball)** m. I-5
sociable **sociable** adj. I-1
sociology **sociologie** f. I-1
sock **chaussette** f. I-6
software **logiciel** m. II-3
soil (to make dirty) **salir** v. I-8, II-P
solar **solaire** adj. II-6

solar energy **énergie solaire** f. II-6
solution **solution** f. II-6
some **de l'** part. art., m., f., sing. I-4
  some **de la** part. art., f., sing. I-4
  some **des** part. art., m., f., pl. I-4
  some **du** part. art., m., sing. I-4
  some **quelques** adj. I-4
  some (of it/them) **en** pron. II-2
someone **quelqu'un** pron. II-4
something **quelque chose** m. I-4
  Something's not right.
  Quelque chose ne va pas. I-5
sometimes **parfois** adv. I-5;
  quelquefois adv. I-7
son **fils** m. I-3
song **chanson** f. II-7
sorry **désolé(e)** II-3
  to be sorry that… **être**
  désolé(e) que… v. II-6
sort **sorte** f. II-7
So-so. **Comme ci, comme**
  ça. I-1
soup **soupe** f. I-4
soupspoon **cuillère à soupe**
  f. II-1
south **sud** m. II-4
space **espace** m. II-6
Spain **Espagne** f. I-7
Spanish **espagnol(e)** adj. I-1
speak (on the phone) **parler**
  (au téléphone) v. I-2
  to speak (to) **parler (à)** v. I-6
  to speak to one another **se**
  parler v. II-3
specialist **spécialiste** m., f. II-5
species **espèce** f. II-6
  endangered species **espèce** f.
  menacée II-6
spectator **spectateur/**
  spectatrice m., f. II-7
speed **vitesse** f. II-3
speed limit **limitation de vitesse**
  f. II-3
spend **dépenser** v. I-4
  to spend money **dépenser de**
  l'argent I-4
  to spend time **passer** v. I-7
  to spend time (somewhere)
  faire un séjour I-7
spoon **cuillère** f. II-1
sport(s) **sport** m. I-5
  to play sports **faire du sport**
  v. I-5
sporty **sportif/sportive** adj. I-3
sprain one's ankle **se fouler la**
  cheville II-2
spring **printemps** m. I-5
  in the spring **au printemps** I-5
square (place) **place** f. I-4
squirrel **écureuil** m. II-6
stadium **stade** m. I-5
stage (phase) **étape** f. I-6
stage fright **trac** II-5

staircase **escalier** *m.* I-8, II-P
stamp **timbre** *m.* II-4
star **étoile** *f.* II-6
starter **entrée** *f.* II-1
start up **démarrer** *v.* II-3
station **station** *f.* I-7
   subway station **station** *f.* **de métro** I-7
   train station **gare** *f.* I-7
stationery store **papeterie** *f.* II-4
statue **statue** *f.* II-4
stay **séjour** *m.* I-7; **rester** *v.* I-7
   to stay slim **garder la ligne** *v.* II-2
steak **steak** *m.* II-1
steering wheel **volant** *m.* II-3
stepbrother **demi-frère** *m.* I-3
stepfather **beau-père** *m.* I-3
stepmother **belle-mère** *f.* I-3
stepsister **demi-sœur** *f.* I-3
still **encore** *adv.* I-3
stomach **ventre** *m.* II-2
   to have a stomach ache **avoir mal au ventre** *v.* II-2
stone **pierre** *f.* II-6
stop (doing something) **arrêter (de faire quelque chose)** *v.; (to stop oneself)* **s'arrêter** *v.* II-2
   to stop by someone's house **passer chez quelqu'un** *v.* I-4
   bus stop **arrêt d'autobus (de bus)** *m.* I-7
store **magasin** *m.;* **boutique** *f.* II-4
   grocery store **épicerie** *f.* I-4
stormy **orageux/orageuse** *adj.* I-5
   It is stormy. **Le temps est orageux.** I-5
story **histoire** *f.* I-2
stove **cuisinière** *f.* I-8, II-P
straight **raide** *adj.* I-3
   straight ahead **tout droit** *adv.* II-4
strangle **étrangler** *v.* II-5
strawberry **fraise** *f.* II-1
street **rue** *f.* II-3
   to follow a street **suivre une rue** *v.* II-4
strong **fort(e)** *adj.* I-3
student **étudiant(e)** *m., f.* 1; **élève** *m., f.* I-1
   high school student **lycéen(ne)** *m., f.* I-2
studies **études** *f.* I-2
studio (*apartment*) **studio** *m.* I-8, II-P
study **étudier** *v.* I-2
suburbs **banlieue** *f.* I-4
subway **métro** *m.* I-7
subway station **station** *f.* **de métro** I-7
succeed (*in doing something*) **réussir (à)** *v.* I-4

success **réussite** *f.* II-5
suddenly **soudain** *adv.* I-8, II-P; **tout à coup** *adv.* I-7.*; tout d'un coup* **adv.** I-8, II-P
suffer **souffrir** *v.* II-3
suffered **souffert (souffrir)** *p.p.* II-3
sugar **sucre** *m.* I-4
suggest (that) **suggérer (que)** *v.* II-6
suit (*man's*) **costume** *m.* I-6; (*woman's*) **tailleur** *m.* I-6
suitcase **valise** *f.* I-7
summer **été** *m.* I-5
   in the summer **en été** I-5
sun **soleil** *m.* I-5
   It is sunny. **Il fait (du) soleil.** I-5
Sunday **dimanche** *m.* I-2
sunglasses **lunettes de soleil** *f., pl.* I-6
supermarket **supermarché** *m.* II-1
supervisor **responsable** *m., f.* II-5
sure **sûr(e)** II-1
   It is sure that… **Il est sûr que…** II-7
   It is unsure that… **Il n'est pas sûr que…** II-7
surprise (someone) **faire une surprise (à quelqu'un)** *v.* I-6
surprised **surpris (surprendre)** *p.p., adj.* I-6
   to be surprised that… **être surpris(e) que…** *v.* II-6
sweater **pull** *m.* I-6
sweep **balayer** *v.* I-8, II-P
swell **enfler** *v.* II-2
swim **nager** *v.* I-4
swimsuit **maillot de bain** *m.* I-6
Swiss **suisse** *adj.* I-1
Switzerland **Suisse** *f.* I-7
symptom **symptôme** *m.* II-2

T

table **table** *f.* I-1
   to clear the table **débarrasser la table** *v.* I-8, II-P
tablecloth **nappe** *f.* II-1
tablet **tablette (tactile)** *f.* II-3
take **prendre** *v.* I-4
   to take a photo(graph) **prendre une photo(graphe)** *v.* II-3
   to take a shower **prendre une douche** II-2
   to take a train (plane, taxi, bus, boat) **prendre un train (un avion, un taxi, un autobus, un bateau)** *v.* I-7
   to take a walk **se promener** *v.* II-2
   to take advantage of **profiter de** *v.* II-7

   to take an exam **passer un examen** *v.* I-2
   to take care (of something) **s'occuper (de)** *v.* II-2
   to take out the trash **sortir la/les poubelle(s)** *v.* I-8, II-P
   to take time off **prendre un congé** *v.* II-5
   to take (*someone*) **emmener** *v.* I-5
taken **pris (prendre)** *p.p., adj.* I-6
tale **conte** *m.* II-7
talented (*gifted*) **doué(e)** *adj.* II-7
tan **bronzer** *v.* I-6
tape recorder **magnétophone** *m.* II-3
tart **tarte** *f.* II-1
taste **goûter** *v.* II-1
taxi **taxi** *m.* I-7
tea **thé** *m.* I-4
teach **enseigner** *v.* I-2
   to teach (*to do something*) **apprendre (à)** *v.* I-4
teacher **professeur** *m.* I-1
team **équipe** *f.* I-5
teaspoon **cuillére à café** *f.* II-1
tee shirt **tee-shirt** *m.* I-6
teeth **dents** *f., pl.* II-1
   to brush one's teeth **se brosser les dents** *v.* II-1
telephone (*receiver*) **appareil** *m.* II-5
   to telephone (*someone*) **téléphoner (à)** *v.* I-2
   It's Mr./Mrs./Miss … (on the phone.) **C'est M./Mme/Mlle … (à l'appareil.)** II-5
television **télévision** *f.* I-1
   television channel **chaîne** *f.* **(de télévision)** II-3
   television program **émission** *f.* **de télévision** II-7
tell one another **se dire** *v.* II-3
temperature **température** *f.* I-5
ten **dix** *m.* I-1
tennis **tennis** *m.* I-5
tennis shoes **baskets** *f., pl.* I-6
tenth **dixième** *adj.* I-7
terminal (bus) **gare** *f.* **routière** I-7
terrace (café) **terrasse** *f.* **de café** I-4
test **examen** *m.* I-1
text message **texto, SMS** *m.* II-3
than **que/qu'** *conj.* II-1, II-6
thank: Thank you (very much). **Merci (beaucoup).** I-1
that **ce/c', ça** I-1; **que** *rel. pron.* II-3
   Is that… ? **Est-ce… ?** I-2
   That's enough. **Ça suffit.** I-5

That has nothing to do with us.
That is none of our business. **Ça
ne nous regarde pas.** II-6
that is… **c'est…** I-1
that is to say **ça veut dire** II-2
theater **théâtre** *m.* II-7
their **leur(s)** *poss. adj., m., f.* I-3
them **les** *d.o. pron.* I-7, **leur**
i.o. pron., m., f., pl. I-6
then **ensuite** *adv.* I-7, **puis** *adv.*
I-7, **puis** I-4; **alors** *adv.* I-7
there **là** I-1; **y** *pron.* II-2
Is there… ? **Y a-t-il… ?** I-2
over there **là-bas** *adv.* I-1
(over) there (*used with
demonstrative adjective ce and
noun or with demonstrative
pronoun celui*) **-là** I-6
There is/There are… **Il y a…** I-1
There is/There are…. **Voilà…** I-1
There was… **Il y a eu…** I-6;
Il y avait… I-8, II-P
therefore **donc** *conj.* I-7
these/those **ces** *dem. adj., m., f.,
pl.* I-6
these/those **celles** *pron., f.,
pl.* II-6
these/those **ceux** *pron., m.,
pl.* II-6
they **ils** *sub. pron., m.* I-1;
elles *sub. and disj. pron., f.* I-1;
eux *disj. pron., pl.* I-3
thing **chose** *f.* I-1, **truc** *m.* I-7
think (about) **réfléchir (à)** *v.* I-4
to think (that) **penser
(que)** *v.* I-2
third **troisième** *adj.* I-7
thirst **soif** *f.* I-4
to be thirsty **avoir soif** *v.* I-4
thirteen **treize** *m.* I-1
thirty **trente** *m.* I-1
thirty-first **trente et unième**
adj. I-7
this/that **ce** *dem. adj., m.,
sing.* I-6; **cet** *dem. adj., m.,
sing.* I-6; **cette** *dem. adj., f.,
sing.* I-6
this afternoon **cet après-midi**
I-2
this evening **ce soir** I-2
this one/that one
celle *pron., f., sing.* II-6;
celui *pron., m., sing.* II-6
this week **cette semaine** I-2
this weekend **ce week-end** I-2
this year **cette année** I-2
those are… **ce sont…** I-1
thousand: one thousand **mille**
m. I-5
one hundred thousand
cent mille *m.* I-5
threat **danger** *m.* II-6
three **trois** *m.* I-1

three hundred **trois cents** *m.* I-5
throat **gorge** *f.* II-2
throw away **jeter** *v.* II-6
Thursday **jeudi** *m.* I-2
ticket **billet** *m.* I-7
round-trip ticket **billet** *m.*
aller-retour I-7 bus/subway
ticket **ticket de bus/de
métro** *m.* I-7
tie **cravate** *f.* I-6
tight **serré(e)** *adj.* I-6
time (*occurence*) **fois** *f.* I-8, II-P;
(*general sense*) **temps** *m.,
sing.* I-5
a long time **longtemps** *adv.* I-5
free time **temps libre** *m.* I-5
from time to time **de temps
en temps** *adv.* I-7
to waste time **perdre son
temps** *v.* I-6
tinker **bricoler** *v.* I-5
tip **pourboire** *m.* I-4
to leave a tip **laisser un
pourboire** *v.* I-4
tire **pneu** *m.* II-3
flat tire **pneu** *m.* **crevé** II-3
(emergency) tire **roue (de
secours)** *f.* II-3
to check the tire pressure
**vérifier la pression des
pneus** *v.* II-3
tired **fatigué(e)** *adj.* I-3
tiresome **pénible** *adj.* I-3
to **à** *prep.* I-4; **au (à + le)** I-4;
aux (à + les) I-4
toaster **grille-pain** *m.* I-8, II-P
today **aujourd'hui** *adv.* I-2
toe **orteil** *m.* II-2; **doigt de
pied** *m.* II-2
together **ensemble** *adv.* I-6
tomato **tomate** *f.* II-1
tomorrow (morning, afternoon,
evening) **demain (matin,
après-midi, soir)** *adv.* I-2
day after tomorrow
après-demain *adv.* I-2
too **aussi** *adv.* I-1
too many/much (of) **trop
(de)** I-4
tooth **dent** *f.* II-1
to brush one's teeth **se brosser
les dents** *v.* II-1
toothbrush **brosse** *f.* **à dents** II-2
toothpaste **dentifrice** *m.* II-2
tour **tour** *m.* I-5
tourism **tourisme** *m.* II-4
tourist office **office du tourisme**
m. II-4
towel (bath) **serviette (de
bain)** *f.* II-2
town **ville** *f.* I-4
town hall **mairie** *f.* II-4
toxic **toxique** *adj.* II-6

toxic waste **déchets toxiques**
m., pl. II-6
traffic **circulation** *f.* II-3
traffic light **feu de signalisation**
m. II-4
tragedy **tragédie** *f.* II-7
train **train** *m.* I-7
train station **gare** *f.* I-7; **station**
f. **de train** I-7
training **formation** *f.* II-5
translate **traduire** *v.* I-6
translated **traduit (traduire)**
p.p., adj. I-6
trash **ordures** *f., pl.* II-6
travel **voyager** *v.* I-2
travel agency **agence de voyages**
f. I-7
travel agent **agent de voyages**
m. I-7
tree **arbre** *m.* II-6
trip **voyage** *m.* I-7
troop (*company*) **troupe** *f.* II-7
tropical **tropical(e)** *adj.* II-6
tropical forest **forêt tropicale**
f. II-6
true **vrai(e)** *adj.* I-3; **véritable**
adj. I-6
It is true that… **Il est vrai
que…** II-7
It is untrue that… **Il n'est pas
vrai que…** II-7
trunk **coffre** *m.* II-3
try **essayer** *v.* I-5
Tuesday **mardi** *m.* I-2
tuna **thon** *m.* II-1
turn **tourner** *v.* II-4
to turn off **éteindre** *v.* II-3
to turn on **allumer** *v.* II-3
to turn (oneself) around **se
tourner** *v.* II-2
twelve **douze** *m.* I-1
twentieth **vingtième** *adj.* I-7
twenty **vingt** *m.* I-1
twenty-first **vingt et unième**
adj. I-7
twenty-second **vingt-deuxième**
adj. I-7
twice **deux fois** *adv.* I-8, II-P
twist one's ankle **se fouler la
cheville** *v.* II-2
two **deux** *m.* I-1
two hundred **deux cents**
m. I-5
two million **deux millions**
m. I-5
type **genre** *m.* II-7

U

ugly **laid(e)** *adj.* I-3
umbrella **parapluie** *m.* I-5
uncle **oncle** *m.* I-3
under **sous** *prep.* I-3

understand **comprendre** *v.* I-4
understood **compris
(comprendre)** *p.p., adj.* I-6
underwear **sous-vêtement**
m. I-6
undress **se déshabiller** *v.* II-2
unemployed person **chômeur/
chômeuse** *m., f.* II-5
to be unemployed **être au
chômage** *v.* II-5
unemployment **chômage** *m.* II-5
unfortunately **malheureusement**
adv. I-7
unhappy **malheureux/
malheureuse** *adj.* I-3
union **syndicat** *m.* II-5
United States **États-Unis** *m.,
pl.* I-7
unless **à moins que** *conj.* II-7
unpleasant **antipathique** *adj.*
I-3; **désagréable** *adj.* I-1
until **jusqu'à** *prep.* II-4; **jusqu'à
ce que** *conj.* II-7
upset: to become upset **s'énerver**
v. II-2
us **nous** *i.o. pron.* I-6; **nous** *d.o.
pron.* I-7
USB drive **clé USB** *f.* II-3
use **employer** *v.* I-5
to use a map **utiliser un plan**
v. I-7
useful **utile** *adj.* I-2
useless **inutile** *adj.* I-2; **nul(le)**
adj. I-2
usually **d'habitude** *adv.* I-8, II-P

V

vacation **vacances** *f., pl.* I-7
vacation day **jour de
congé** *m.* I-7
vacuum **aspirateur** *m.* I-8, II-P
to vacuum **passer
l'aspirateur** *v.* I-8, II-P
valley **vallée** *f.* II-6
vegetable **légume** *m.* II-1
velvet **velours** *m.* I-6
very *(before adjective)* **tout(e)**
adv. I-3
Very well. **Très bien.** I-1
veterinarian **vétérinaire** *m.,
f.* II-5
videocassette recorder (VCR)
magnétoscope *m.* II-3
video game(s) **jeu vidéo (des
jeux vidéo)** *m.* II-3
videotape **cassette vidéo**
f. II-3
Vietnamese **vietnamien(ne)**
adj. I-1
violet **violet(te)** *adj.* I-6
violin **violon** *m.* II-7
visit **visite** *f.* I-6

to visit *(a place)* **visiter** *v.* I-2;
(a person or people) **rendre visite (à)** *v.* I-6; *(to visit regularly)*
fréquenter *v.* I-4
voicemail **messagerie** *f.* II-5
volcano **volcan** *m.* II-6
volleyball **volley(-ball)** *m.* I-5

W

waist **taille** *f.* I-6
wait **attendre** *v.* I-6
to wait *(on the phone)* **patienter**
v. II-5
to wait in line **faire la
queue** *v.* II-4
wake up **se réveiller** *v.* II-2
walk **promenade** *f.* I-5;
marcher *v.* I-5
to go for a walk **faire une
promenade** I-5; **faire un
tour** I-5
wall **mur** *m.* I-8, II-P
want **désirer** *v.* I-5; **vouloir** *v.* II-1
wardrobe **armoire** *f.* I-8, II-P
warming: global warming
réchauffement de la Terre
m. II-6
warning light (gas/oil) **voyant**
m. **(d'essence/d'huile)** II-3
wash **laver** *v.* I-8, II-P
to wash oneself (one's hands)
se laver (les mains) *v.* II-2
to wash up (in the morning)
faire sa toilette *v.* II-2
washing machine **lave-linge**
m. I-8, II-P
waste **gaspillage** *m.* II-6;
gaspiller *v.* II-6
wastebasket **corbeille (à papier)**
f. I-1
waste time **perdre son temps**
v. I-6
watch **montre** *f.* I-1; **regarder**
v. I-2
water **eau** *f.* I-4
mineral water **eau
f. minérale** I-4
way *(by the way)* **au fait** I-3;
(path) **chemin** *m.* II-4
we **nous** *pron.* I-1
weak **faible** *adj.* I-3
wear **porter** *v.* I-6
weather **temps** *m., sing.*
I-5; **météo** *f.* II-7
The weather is bad. **Il fait
mauvais.** I-5
The weather is dreadful. **Il fait
un temps épouvantable.** I-5
The weather is good/warm. **Il
fait bon.** I-5
The weather is nice. **Il fait
beau.** I-5

web site **site Internet/web**
m. II-3
wedding **mariage** *m.* I-6
Wednesday **mercredi** *m.* I-2
weekend **week-end** *m.* I-2
this weekend **ce week-end**
m. I-2
welcome **bienvenu(e)** *adj.* I-1
You're welcome. **Il n'y a pas
de quoi.** I-1
well **bien** *adv.* I-7
I am doing well/badly. **Je vais
bien/mal.** I-1
west **ouest** *m.* II-4
What? **Comment?** *adv.* I-4;
Pardon? I-4; **Quoi?** I-1 *interr.
pron.* I-4
What day is it? **Quel jour
sommes-nous?** I-2
What is it? **Qu'est-ce que
c'est?** *prep.* I-1
What is the date? **Quelle est
la date?** I-5
What is the temperature?
**Quelle température
fait-il?** I-5
What is the weather like? **Quel
temps fait-il?** I-5
What is your name? **Comment
t'appelles-tu?** *fam.* I-1
What is your name? **Comment
vous appelez-vous?** *form.* I-1
What is your nationality?
Quelle est ta nationalité?
sing., fam. I-1
What is your nationality?
Quelle est votre nationalité?
sing., pl., fam., form. I-1
What time do you have?
Quelle heure avez-vous?
form. I-2
What time is it? **Quelle heure
est-il?** I-2
What time? **À quelle
heure?** I-2
What do you think about that?
Qu'en penses-tu? II-6
What's up? **Ça va?** I-1
whatever it may be **quoi que
ce soit** II-5
What's wrong? **Qu'est-ce qu'il
y a?** I-1
when **quand** *adv.* I-4
When is …'s birthday? **C'est
quand l'anniversaire de …?**
I-5
When is your birthday?
**C'est quand ton/votre
anniversaire?** I-5
where **où** *adv., rel. pron.* I-4
which? **quel(le)(s)?** *adj.* I-4
which one **à laquelle** *pron., f.,
sing.* II-5

which one **auquel (à + lequel)** *pron., m., sing.* II-5
which one **de laquelle** *pron., f., sing.* II-5
which one **duquel (de + lequel)** *pron., m., sing.* II-5
which one **laquelle** *pron., f., sing.* II-5
which one **lequel** *pron., m., sing.* II-5
which ones **auxquelles (à + lesquelles)** *pron., f., pl.* II-5
which ones **auxquels (à + lesquels)** *pron., m., pl.* II-5
which ones **desquelles (de + lesquelles)** *pron., f., pl.* II-5
which ones **desquels (de + lesquels)** *pron., m., pl.* II-5
which ones **lesquelles** *pron., f., pl.* II-5
which ones **lesquels** *pron., m., pl.* II-5
while **pendant que** *prep.* I-7
white **blanc(he)** *adj.* I-6
who? **qui?** *interr. pron.* I-4; **qui** *rel. pron.* II-3
   Who is it? **Qui est-ce?** I-1
   Who's calling, please? **Qui est à l'appareil?** II-5
whom? **qui?** *interr.* I-4
   For whom? **Pour qui?** I-4
   To whom? **À qui?** I-4
why? **pourquoi?** *adv.* I-2, I-4
widowed **veuf/veuve** *adj.* I-3
wife **femme** *f.* I-1; **épouse** *f.* I-3
willingly **volontiers** *adv.* II-2
win **gagner** *v.* I-5
wind **vent** *m.* I-5
   It is windy. **Il fait du vent.** I-5
window **fenêtre** *f.* I-1
windshield **pare-brise** *m.* II-3
windshield wiper(s) **essuie-glace (essuie-glaces** *pl.***)** *m.* II-3
windsurfing **planche à voile** *v.* I-5
   to go windsurfing **faire de la planche à voile** *v.* I-5
winter **hiver** *m.* I-5
   in the winter **en hiver** I-5
wipe (the dishes/the table) **essuyer (la vaisselle/la table)** *v.* I-8, II-P
wish that… **souhaiter que…** *v.* II-6
with **avec** *prep.* I-1
   with whom? **avec qui?** I-4
withdraw money **retirer de l'argent** *v.* II-4
without **sans** *prep.* I-8, II-P; **sans que** *conj.* I-5
woman **femme** *f.* I-1

wood **bois** *m.* II-6
wool **laine** *f.* I-6
work **travail** *m.* II-4
   to work **travailler** *v.* I-2; **marcher** *v.* II-3; **fonctionner** *v.* II-3
work out **faire de la gym** *v.* I-5
worker **ouvrier/ouvrière** *m., f.* II-5
world **monde** *m.* I-7
worried **inquiet/inquiète** *adj.* I-3
worry **s'inquiéter** *v.* II-2
worse **pire** *comp. adj.* II-1; **plus mal** *comp. adv.* II-1; **plus mauvais(e)** *comp. adj.* II-1
worst: the worst **le plus mal** *super. adv.* II-1; **le/la pire** *super. adj.* II-1; **le/la plus mauvais(e)** *super. adj.* II-1
wound **blessure** *f.* II-2
wounded: to get wounded **se blesser** *v.* II-2
write **écrire** *v.* I-7
   to write one another **s'écrire** *v.* II-3
writer **écrivain(e)** *m., f.* II-7
written **écrit (écrire)** *p.p., adj.* I-7
wrong **tort** *m.* I-2
   to be wrong **avoir tort** *v.* I-2

Y

yeah **ouais** I-2
year **an** *m.* I-2; **année** *f.* I-2
yellow **jaune** *adj.* I-6
yes **oui** I-2; *(when making a contradiction)* **si** I-2
yesterday (morning/afternoon evening) **hier (matin/après-midi/soir)** *adv.* I-7
   day before yesterday **avant-hier** *adv.* I-7
yogurt **yaourt** *m.* II-1
you **toi** *disj. pron., sing., fam.* I-3; **tu** *sub. pron., sing., fam.* I-1; **vous** *pron., sing., pl., fam., form.* I-1
   you neither **toi non plus** I-2
   You're welcome. **De rien.** I-1
young **jeune** *adj.* I-3
younger **cadet(te)** *adj.* I-3
your **ta** *poss. adj., f., sing.* I-3; **tes** *poss. adj., m., f., pl.* I-3; **ton** *poss. adj., m., sing.* I-3; **vos** *poss. adj., m., f., pl.* I-3; **votre** *poss. adj., m., f., sing.* I-3;
yourself **te/t'** *refl. pron., sing., fam.* II-2; **toi** *refl. pron., sing., fam.* II-2; **vous** *refl. pron., form.* II-2

youth **jeunesse** *f.* I-6
youth hostel **auberge de jeunesse** *f.* I-7
Yum! **Miam!** *interj.* I-5

Z

zero **zéro** *m.* I-1

Mots utiles

absent(e) *absent*
un département *department*
une dictée *dictation*
une phrase *sentence*
une feuille d'activités
  activity sheet
l'horaire des cours (m.)
  class schedule
un paragraphe *paragraph*
une épreuve *quiz*
un examen *exam; test*
suivant(e) *following*

Expressions utiles

Asseyez-vous, s'il vous plaît.
  Sit down, please.
Avez-vous des questions?
  Do you have any questions?
**Comment dit-on _____ en
français?** *How do you say
_____ in French?*
**Comment écrit-on _____ en
français?** *How do you write
_____ in French?*
Écrivez votre nom. *Write
your name.*
Étudiez la leçon trois. *Study
lesson 3.*
Fermez votre livre. *Close your
book(s).*
Je ne comprends pas. *I don't
understand.*
Je ne sais pas. *I don't know.*
Levez la main. *Raise your hand(s).*
**Lisez la phrase à voix
haute.** *Read the sentence aloud.*
**Ouvrez votre livre à la page
deux.** *Open your book to
page two.*
**Plus lentement, s'il vous
plaît.** *Slower, please.*
Que signifie _____? *What
does _____ mean?*
**Répétez, s'il vous
plaît.** *Repeat, please.*
**Répondez à la/aux
question(s).** *Answer the
question(s).*
Vous comprenez? *Do you
understand?*

Titres des sections
du livre

À l'écoute *Listening*
Après la lecture *After Reading*
Avant la lecture *Before Reading*
Coup de main *Helping Hand*
Culture à la loupe *Culture
  through a magnifying glass*
Écriture *Writing*
Essayez! *Try it!*
Incroyable mais vrai! *Incredible
  But True!*
Le français quotidien *Everyday
  French*
Le français vivant *French Live*
Lecture *Reading*
Les sons et les lettres *Sounds
  and Letters*
Mise en pratique *Putting it
  into Practice*
Le monde francophone *The
  Francophone World*
Pour commencer *To Begin*
Projet *Project*
Roman-photo *Story based
  on photographs*
Savoir-faire *Know-how*
Structures *Structures; Grammar*
Le zapping *Channel-surfing*

D'autres adjectifs de
nationalité en Europe

autrichien(ne) *Austrian*
belge *Belgian*
bulgare *Bulgarian*
danois(e) *Danish*
écossais(e) *Scottish*
finlandais(e) *Finnish*
grec/grecque *Greek*
hongrois(e) *Hungarian*
norvégien(ne) *Norwegian*
polonais(e) *Polish*
portugais(e) *Portuguese*
roumain(e) *Romanian*
russe *Russian*
slovaque *Slovakian*
slovène *Slovene; Slovenian*
suédois(e) *Swedish*
tchèque *Czech*

D'autres adjectifs de
nationalité en Afrique

africain(e) *African*
angolais(e) *Angolan*
béninois(e) *Beninese*
camerounais(e) *Cameroonian*
congolais(e) *Congolese*
égyptien(ne) *Egyptian*
éthiopien(ne) *Ethiopian*
kenyan(e) *Kenyan*
ivoirien(ne) *of the Ivory Coast*
nigérien(ne) *Nigerian*
somalien(ne) *Somali*
soudanais(e) *Sudanese*
sud-africain(e) *South African*
tchadien(ne) *Chadian*
togolais(e) *Togolese*
tunisien(ne) *Tunisian*

D'autres adjectifs
de nationalité dans
le monde

antillais(e) *Caribbean, West Indian*
argentin(e) *Argentinian*
asiatique *Asian*
australien(ne) *Australian*
bolivien(ne) *Bolivian*
chilien(ne) *Chilean*
colombien(ne) *Colombian*
cubain(e) *Cuban*
haïtien(ne) *Haitian*
indien(ne) *Indian*
irakien(ne) *Iraqi*
iranien(ne) *Iranian*
israélien(ne) *Israeli*
libanais(e) *Lebanese*
néo-zélandais(e) *New Zealander*
pakistanais(e) *Pakistani*
péruvien(ne) *Peruvian*
portoricain(e) *Puerto Rican*
syrien(ne) *Syrian*
turc/turque *Turkish*
vénézuélien(ne) *Venezuelan*

D'autres cours

l'agronomie (*f.*) *agriculture*
l'algèbre (*m.*) *algebra*
l'anatomie (*f.*) *anatomy*
l'anthropologie (*f.*) *anthropology*
l'archéologie (*f.*) *archaeology*
l'architecture (*f.*) *architecture*
l'astronomie (*f.*) *astronomy*
la biochimie *biochemistry*
la botanique *botany*
le commerce *business*
une filière *course of study*
le latin *Latin*
les langues romanes
    romance languages
la linguistique *linguistics*
le marketing *marketing*
les mathématiques
    supérieures,
    spéciales *calculus*
la médecine *medicine*
la musique *music*
la trigonométrie *trigonometry*
la zoologie *zoology*

D'autres mots utiles

un classeur *binder*
une gomme *eraser*
l'infirmerie (*f.*) *infirmary*
une règle *ruler*

D'autres animaux familiers

un cochon d'Inde *guinea pig*
un furet *ferret*
une gerbille *gerbil*
un hamster *hamster*
un rongeur *rodent*
une souris *mouse*
une tortue *turtle*

D'autres adjectifs pour décrire les gens

ambitieux/ambitieuse *ambitious*
arrogant(e) *arrogant*
calme *calm*
compétent(e) *competent*
excellent(e) *excellent*
franc/franche *frank, honest*
(mal)honnête *(dis)honest*
idéaliste *idealistic*
immature *immature*
mûr(e) *mature*
(ir)responsable *(ir)responsible*
romantique *romantic*
séduisant(e) *attractive*
sentimental(e) *sentimental*
souple *flexible*
studieux/ieuse *studious*
tranquille *quiet*

D'autres professions

un boucher/une
    bouchère *butcher*
un boulanger/une
    boulangère *baker*
un caissier/une
    caissière *cashier*
un cordonnier *cobbler*
un dessinateur/une
    dessinatrice *illustrator*
un fermier/une fermière *farmer*
un(e) informaticien(ne)
    computer scientist
un instituteur/une institutrice
    nursery/elementary school teacher
un(e) photographe *photographer*
un(e) pilote *pilot*
un(e) styliste *fashion designer*
un tailleur (pour dames)
    (ladies') tailor
un teinturier *dry cleaner*

Au café

une brioche *brioche, bun*
un café crème *espresso with milk*
un croque-monsieur *toasted
    ham and cheese sandwich*
de l'eau gazeuse (*f.*) *sparkling
    mineral water*
de l'eau plate (*f.*) *plain water*
un garçon de café *waiter*
une omelette au jambon/au
    fromage *omelet with ham/
    with cheese*
des œufs au/sur le plat
    (*m.*) *fried eggs*
une part de tarte *slice of a pie*
une tartine de beurre *slice of
    bread and butter*

Quelques fromages

du bleu des Causses *blue
    cheese made with cow's milk*
du camembert *soft cheese made
    with cow's milk*
du fromage de chèvre
    goat cheese
du gruyère *Swiss cheese*
du munster *semisoft cheese that
    can be sharp in flavor, made
    with cow's milk*
du reblochon *soft cheese made
    with cow's milk*
du roquefort *blue cheese made
    with sheep's milk*
de la tomme de Savoie
    *cheese from the Alps made of
    scalded curds*

Supplementary Vocabulary

D'autres loisirs

une bicyclette *bicycle*
bricolage (faire du)
  fixing things
collectionner les timbres *to*
  collect stamps
faire des mots croisés *to do a*
  crossword puzzle
une fête foraine/une foire *fair*
jouer à la pétanque/aux
  boules (f.) *to play the game*
  of petanque
jouer aux dames (f.)
  to play checkers
louer une vidéo/un DVD
  to rent a video/DVD
la natation (faire de) *swimming*
un parc d'attractions
  amusement park
tapisserie (faire de la)
  needlework
tricoter *knitting*

Des mots liés à la météo

une averse *shower*
la bise *North wind*
la brise *breeze*
un ciel couvert *overcast sky*
un ciel dégagé *clear sky*
une éclaircie *break in the*
  weather; sunny spell
la grêle *hale*
la grisaille *grayness*
de la neige fondue *sleet*
un nuage *cloud*
un orage *thunder storm*
une vague de chaleur *heat wave*
le verglas *black ice*

Des fêtes de famille

une bague de
  fiançailles *engagement ring*
un baptême *christening*
les fiançailles *engagement*
les noces d'argent *silver*
  wedding anniversary
les noces d'or *golden*
  wedding anniversary
un enterrement *funeral*

Des jours fériés

l'Action de grâce *Thanksgiving*
la fête de l'Indépendance
  Independence Day
une fête nationale
  National holiday
le Jour de l'an/la Saint-
  Sylvestre *New Year's Day*
le 14 juillet *Bastille Day*
la Saint-Valentin *Valentine's Day*

D'autres mots pour faire la fête

des accessoires de cotillon
  (m.) *party accessories*
des amuse-gueule (m.)
  appetizers; nibbles
un bal *ball*
des confettis *confetti*
des feux d'artifice *fireworks*
un serpentin *streamer*

Quelques vêtements

une doudoune *down coat*
un foulard *headscarf*
un gilet *cardigan; vest*
un moufle *mitten*
un pantacourt *capri pants*
un pull à col roulé *turtleneck*
un sweat-shirt *sweatshirt*
une veste *jacket*

Quelques pays d'Europe

l'/en Autriche (f.) *Austria*
la/en Bulgarie *Bulgaria*
le/au Danemark *Denmark*
l'/en Écosse (f.) *Scotland*
la/en Finlande *Finland*
la/en Grèce *Greece*
la/en Hongrie *Hungary*
la/en Norvège *Norway*
la/en Pologne *Poland*
le/au Portugal *Portugal*
la/en République tchèque
  Czech Republic
la/en Roumanie *Romania*
le/au Royaume-Uni
  United Kingdom
la/en Russie *Russia*
la/en Slovaquie *Slovakia*
la/en Slovénie *Slovenia*
la/en Suède *Sweden*

Quelques pays d'Afrique

l'/en Afrique du Sud (f.)
  South Africa
l'/en Algérie (f.) *Algeria*
l'/en Angola (f.) *Angola*
le/au Bénin *Benin*
le/au Cameroun *Cameroon*
le/au Congo *Congo*
la/en Côte d'Ivoire *Ivory Coast*
l'/en Égypte (f.) *Egypt*
l'/en Éthiopie (f.) *Ethiopia*
le/au Kenya *Kenya*
le/au Maroc *Morocco*
le/au Niger *Niger*
le/au Sénégal *Senegal*
la/en Somalie *Somalia*
le/au Soudan *Sudan*
le/au Soudan du Sud
  South Sudan
le/au Tchad *Chad*
le/au Togo *Togo*
la/en Tunisie *Tunisia*

D'autres pays

l'/en Argentine (f.) *Argentina*
l'/en Australie (f.) *Australia*
la/en Bolivie *Bolivia*
le/au Chili *Chile*
la/en Colombie *Colombia*
(à) Cuba (f.) *Cuba*
(à) Haïti *Haiti*
l'/en Inde (f.) *India*
l'/en Irak (m.) *Iraq*
l'/en Iran (m.) *Iran*
(en) Israël (m.) *Israel*
le/au Liban *Lebanon*
la/en Nouvelle-Zélande
  New Zealand
le/au Pakistan *Pakistan*
le/au Pérou *Peru*
(à) Porto Rico (f.) *Puerto Rico*
la/en Syrie *Syria*
la/en Turquie *Turkey*
le/au Venezuela *Venezuela*

Partir en vacances

atterrir *to land*
l'atterrissage (m.) *landing*
une compagnie aérienne *airline*
une crème solaire *sunscreen*
une croisière *cruise*
le décollage *take-off*
décoller *to take off*
défaire ses valises *to unpack*
un douanier *customs officer*
une frontière *border*
un groom *bellhop*
un numéro de vol *flight number*
dormir à la belle étoile *to*
  sleep out in the open
une station balnéaire
  seaside resort

Dans la maison

allumer la lumière *to turn on*
  the light
du bois *wood*
le chauffage central
  central heating
la cheminé *chimney; fireplace*
la climatisation *air-conditioning*
la décoration intérieure
  interior design
en bas *downstairs*
en haut *upstairs*
éteindre la lumière *to turn off*
  the light
le fioul *heating oil*
le gaz *natural gas*
le grenier *attic*
la lumière *light*
une penderie *walk-in closet*
un plafond *ceiling*
le sol *floor*
le toit *roof*

Des tâches ménagères

aérer une pièce *to air a room*
arroser les plantes *to water*
  the plants
étendre le linge *to hang out/*
  hang up washing
laver les vitres *to clean*
  the windows
une vitre *windowpane*

Des meubles et des objets de la maison

une ampoule *light bulb*
une bougie *candle*
un buffet *sideboard*
une corde à linge *clothesline*
une couette *comforter*
le linge de maison *linen*
une persienne *shutter*
une pince à linge *clothes pin*
un portemanteau *coat rack*
un radiateur *radiator*
un robot ménager *food*
  processor
un store *blind*
un volet *shutter*

AP® French Themes & Contexts

This index aligns the cultural content in **D'accord! 1** with the AP® French Language and Culture themes and recommended contexts to help you build the broad cultural understanding you need to succeed in class, on the AP® Exam, and beyond.

The numbers following each entry can be understood as follows:

(1) 9 = **(Unit)** page
As shown, the entry above would be found in Unit 1, page 9.

*Entries marked with an asterisk offer cultural information that supports the AP® theme and context but may not fully align with it.

Index of AP® Themes & Contexts

Families & Communities

Customs and Ceremonies
Les bonnes manières **(1)** 9
Les cafés nord-africains **(4)** 159
*Des spécialités à grignoter **(4)** 159
Les hammams **(6)** 259
Provins **(8)** 349

Family Structures
La famille de Marie Laval **(3)** 90
La famille en France **(3)** 96
*Fido en famille **(3)** 128
Les Noah **(3)** 97

Friendship and Love
L'amitié **(3)** 114
*Les copains **(1)** 24–25
La poignée de main ou la bise? **(1)** 8
*La vie sans Pascal **(8)** 332–333

Global Challenges

Diversity Issues
Le Maghreb **(6)** 259

Economic Issues
Des montres et des banques **(3)** 127
*L'industrie **(2)** 83
Jean-Jacques Rousseau **(3)** 127
La perle noire **(7)** 303

Environmental Issues
Les Cousteau **(3)** 115
Les parcs nationaux du Cameroun **(5)** 235
La perle noire **(7)** 303

Health Issues
Attention au sucre! **(1)** 19

Human Rights
Bineta Diop, la «vice-présidente» des
femmes **(5)** 215

Nutrition and Food Safety
*La fusion des cuisines **(7)** 303

Peace and War
L'Indochine française **(7)** 303

Personal & Public Identities

Beliefs and Values
Marianne **(1)** 27

Language and Identity
Haïti, première République noire **(1)** 39
*Incroyable mais vrai! **(1)** 38
Le français au Québec **(1)** 39
La Journée internationale de la
Francophonie **(1)** 39
Les langues **(1)** 27
La Louisiane **(1)** 39
Le verlan **(4)** 141

Multiculturalism
Qu'est-ce qu'un Français typique? **(1)** 26

Nationalism and Patriotism
Un Québec indépendant **(4)** 171

Science and Technology

Social Impact of Technology
Pages d'Or **(3)** 107

You can find a comprehensive index of AP® Themes & Contexts for all levels of **D'accord!** on the Supersite.

Grammar Index

Grammar Index

Photography and Art Credits

Cover: Yadid Levy/Offset.

Front Matter (TE): T36: SimmiSimons/iStockphoto; **T38:** Monkeybusinessimages/Bigstock.

Front Matter (SE): xix: (all) North Wind Picture Archives/Alamy; **xx:** (l) Courtesy of the Library of Congress; (r) Design Pics Inc/Alamy; **xxi:** Masterpics/Alamy; **xxii:** (tl) Moodboard/Fotolia; (bl) Moshimochi/Shutterstock; (br) Wavebreakmedia Ltd/Shutterstock; **xxiii:** JTB Photo Communications, Inc/Alamy; **xxiv:** (l) Gawrav/iStockphoto; (r) Yuri/iStockphoto; **xxv:** FMB/Isabel Schiffler/Future Image/WENN/Newscom; **xxvi:** (t) Monkey Business Images/Fotolia; (b) Yuri Arcurs/Fotolia; **xxvii:** (t) Monkeybusinessimages/iStockphoto; (b) Masterfile Royalty-Free; **xxviii:** David Schaffer/Media Bakery.

Unit 1: 1: Patrick Sheandell O'Carroll/Media Bakery; **4:** (t) VHL; A(b) Rossy Llano; **8:** (t) Anne Loubet; (b) Paula Diez; **9:** Ian G. Dagnall/Alamy; **13:** (tl) LdF/iStockphoto; (tm) Martín Bernetti; (tr) Jim Erickson/Media Bakery; (bl) Rawpixel/Fotolia; (bml) Sami Sert/iStockphoto; (bmr) WavebreakmediaMicro/Fotolia; (br) Laura Stevens; **15:** (bl) Anne Loubet; (br) Terex/Fotolia; **17:** Pascal Pernix; **22:** Martín Bernetti; **26:** (l) Andrew Bayda/Fotolia; (r) Huang Zheng/Shutterstock; **27:** Charles Platiau/Reuters/Newscom; **28:** (all) Anne Loubet; **29:** (tl) Annie Pickert Fuller; (tr) VHL; (bl) VHL; (br) Masson/Shutterstock; **30:** (tl) Martín Bernetti; (tm) BillionPhotos/Fotolia; (tr) Hongqi Zhang/Alamy; (bl) Niko Guido/iStockphoto; (bm) Michal Kowalski/Shutterstock; (br) Demidoff/Fotolia; **31:** (tl) Jstone/Shutterstock; (tm) Featureflash Photo Agency/Shutterstock; (tr) Jose Luis Pelaez/Media Bakery; (bl) Anne Loubet; (bml) Odilon Dimier/Media Bakery; (bmr) Martín Bernetti; (br) Colleen Cahill/Media Bakery; **35:** Masterfile Royalty-Free; **36:** (tl) Anne Loubet; (tr) Anne Loubet; (mtl) Robert Lerich/Fotolia; (mtr) Anne Loubet; (mbl) Rossy Llano; (mbr) Anne Loubet; (bl) Anne Loubet; (br) Anne Loubet; **37:** Pascal Pernix; **38:** (left col: t) Hulton Deutsch/Getty Images; (left col. mt) Sarah Lee/Eyevine/Redux Pictures; (left col: mb) Allstar Picture Library/Alamy; (left col: b) Eddy Lemaistre/Getty Images; (br) Eddy Lemaistre/Corbis; **39:** (tl) Rossy Llano; (tr) Frederic/Fotolia; (bl) Brent Hofacker/Shutterstock; (br) Courtesy of the International Organisation of La Francophonie; **42:** Inspirestock Royalty-Free/Inmagine.

Unit 2: 45: Auremar/Fotolia; **52:** Anne Loubet; **53:** Jose Luis Pelaez, Inc/Blend Images/MaXx Images; **60:** Anne Loubet; **66:** (l) Martín Bernetti; (r) Pascal Pernix; **70:** Pascal Pernix; **71:** Pascal Pernix; **72:** (all) VHL; **73:** (tl) OneClearVision/iStockphoto; (tr) Mihailomilovanovic/iStockphoto; (bl) Aleksander Mijatovic/Fotolia; (br) Sebra/Fotolia; **81:** Anne Loubet; **82:** (left col: t) Universal Images Group/Superstock; (left col: m) Bettmann/Getty Images; (left col: b) Antoine Gyori/Sygma/Getty Images; (t) Anne Loubet; (ml) Claude Coquilleau/Fotolia; (mr) Daniel Haller/iStockphoto; (b) Anne Loubet; **83:** (tl) David Gregs/Alamy; (tr) Anne Loubet; (bl) Anne Loubet; (br) Caroline Beecham/iStockphoto; **84:** (inset) Martín Bernetti; **84-85:** (background) Art Kowalsky/Alamy; **85:** (inset) Jon Feingersh/Blend Images/MaXx Images; **86:** Pascal Pernix; **87:** (l) Martín Bernetti; (r) Darío Eusse Tobón.

Unit 3: 89: Michael Simons/123RF; **92:** Hero/Media Bakery; **96:** Anne Loubet; **97:** (l) Alix William/SIPA/Newscom; (r) Nuccio DiNuzzo/TNS/Newscom; **98:** (l) Martín Bernetti; (r) FogStock LLC/Photolibrary; **100:** Hemera Technologies/AbleStock/Jupiterimages; **101:** (t) Tomasz Trojanowski/Shutterstock; (ml) Brian McEntire/iStockphoto; (mm) Anna Lurye/Shutterstock; (mr) RJGrant/Bigstock; (bl) Linda Kloosterhof/iStockphoto; (bm) Dmitry Pistrov/Shutterstock; (br) Oliveromg/Shutterstock; **104:** (tl) Martín Bernetti; (tm) Dmitry Kutlayev/iStockphoto; (tr) Zentilia/Fotolia; (bl) AHBE/Fotolia; (bml) VHL; (bmr) Anne Loubet; (br) Martín Bernetti; **105:** (t) Gladiolus/iStockphoto; (bl) Dynamic Graphics/Jupiterimages; (br) Rossy Llano; **109:** (l) Martín Bernetti; (m) Anne Loubet; (r) Anne Loubet; **110:** (t) Anne Loubet; (ml) Hemera Technologies/Photos.com; (mml) Anne Loubet; (mmr) Paula Diez; (mr) Vstock, LLC/Photolibrary; (bl) Martín Bernetti; (bml) Shock/Fotolia; (bmr) Keith Levit Photography/Photolibrary; (br) Anne Loubet; **114:** Anne Loubet; **115:** (tl) Album/Oronoz/Newscom; (tr) Xavier Collin/Celebrity Monitor/Newscom; (b) Panoramic/Zuma Press/Newscom; **117:** (top inset) Ray Levesque; Nigel Riches/Media Bakery; (bottom inset) Anne Loubet; **119:** (t) Martín Bernetti; (ml) David Lee/Alamy; (mml) Martín Bernetti; (mmr) TpaBMa/AGE Fotostock; (mr) Igor Tarasov/Fotolia; (bl) Creative Jen Designs/Shutterstock; (bml) Photofriday/Shutterstock; (bmr) F9photos/Shutterstock; (br) Martín Bernetti; **122:** (tl) Valua Vitaly/Shutterstock; (tm) Roy Hsu/Media Bakery; (tr) Don Mason/Getty Images; (bl) Simon Kolton/Alamy; (bml) Blend Images/Ariel Skelley/Getty Images; (bmr) Jacek Chabraszewski/iStockphoto; (br) Sergei Telegin/Shutterstock; **124:** Anne Loubet; **125:** Anne Loubet; **126:** (t) Sergey Dzyuba/Shutterstock; (m) Simona Dumitru/Alamy; (bl) Marta Perez/EFE/Newscom; (br) Nicole Paton/Shutterstock; **127:** (tl) Franky DeMeyer/iStockphoto; (tr) Dave Bartruff/Danita Delimont/Alamy; (bl) Erik Tham/Alamy; (br) Portrait of Jean Jacques Rousseau by Edouard Lacretelle. Gianni Dagli Orti/The Art Archive at Art Resource, NY; **128:** (t) Juniors Bildarchiv/Alamy; (b) Martín Bernetti; **129:** Anne Loubet; **130:** Anne Loubet; **131:** Anne Loubet.

Unit 4: 133: Pascal Pernix; **136:** (t) Buzzshotz/Alamy; (b) Martín Bernetti; **140:** Vincent Besnault/Getty Images; **141:** (t) Foc Kan/WireImage/Getty Images; (b) Romuald Meigheux/Sipa/Newscom; **145:** David Hughes/Photolibrary; **153:** Tetra Images/SuperStock; **154:** Anne Loubet; **158:** Carlos S. Pereyra/AGE Fotostock; **159:** (t) Kevin Foy/Alamy; (b) Yadid Levy/Alamy; **161:** VHL; **165:** Ana Cabezas Martín; **169:** Anne Loubet; **170:** (left col: t) Art Babych/Shutterstock; (left col: m) Yoan Valat/EPA/Newscom; (left col: b) Byron Purvis/AdMedia/Newscom; (t) Csp/123RF; (mt) Stephen Saks Photography/Alamy; (mb) Peter Spiro/iStockphoto; (b) Richard T. Nowitz/Getty Images; **171:** (tl) Mike Blake/Reuters; (tr) Grafxcom/iStockphoto; (bl) Rubens Abboud/Alamy; (br) Perry Mastrovito/Getty Images; **172-173:** Anne Loubet; **173:** (all) Anne Loubet; **174:** Martín Bernetti; **175:** Patrick Sheandell O'Carroll/Getty Images.

Unit 5: 177: Lagos Nigeria/Alamy; **180:** Martín Bernetti; **184:** Orban Thierry/ABACA/Newscom; **185:** (t) Marco Iacobucci EPP/Shutterstock; (b) Arko Datta/Reuters: **198:** Ron Koeberer/Getty Images; **200:** Anne Loubet; **203:** (l) Anne Loubet; (r) Benoit Tessier/Reuters/Newscom; **205:** Vanessa Bertozzi; **214:** (left col: t) ATB/ATP/WENN/Newscom; (left col: b) Shaun Best/Reuters; (t) Brianafrica/Alamy; (ml) Author's Image Ltd/Alamy; (mr) MJ Photography/Alamy; (b) Gerard Lacz Images/SuperStock; **215:** (tl) Seyllou/AFP/Getty Images; (tr) Sadaka Edmond/SIPA/Newscom; (bl) Kevin Schafer/Alamy; (br) Werner Forman Archive/Heritage Image Partnership Ltd/Alamy; **216:** (t) Perry Mastrovito/Corbis; (b) Rossy Llano; **217:** Anne Loubet; **218:** Pascal Pernix; **219:** (l) Martine Coquilleau/Fotolia; (r) Peter Adams Photography Ltd/Alamy.

Unit 6: 221: Jupiterimages/Getty Images; **228:** Fadi Al-barghouthy/123RF; **229:** (t) Mal Langsdon/Reuters; (b) Trevor Pearson/Alamy; **230:** Rachel Distler; **231:** (all) Martín Bernetti; **241:** (t) Ben Blankenburg/Corbis; (ml) Hemera Technologies/Getty Images; (mr) Purestock/Jupiterimages; (b) Ablestock.com/Getty Images; **246:** Poree-Wyters/ABACA/Newscom; **247:** (t) Evening Standard/Hulton Archive/Getty Images; (b) Graylock/MCT/Newscom; **251:** Anne Loubet; **255:** Anne Loubet; **257:** Anne Loubet; **258:** (t) Idealink Photography/Alamy; (ml) A.Anwar Sacca/Fotolia; (mr) Nik Wheeler/Getty Images; (bl) Abdelhak Senna/Getty Images; (br) Frans Lemmens/Getty Images; **259:** (tl) Stephen Lloyd Morocco/Alamy; (tr) Ulf Andersen/Getty Images; (bl) Paul Springett B/Alamy; (br) Romilly Lockyer/Getty Images; **260:** Trois-Rivieres Le Nouvelliste/The Canadian Press (Sylvain Mayer); **260-261:** (background) Corbis RF; **262:** Jeff Greenberg/Alamy; **263:** Brian McEntire/iStockphoto.

Unit 7: 265: Janet Dracksdorf; **268:** PeopleImages/iStockphoto; **272:** Courtesy of www.Tahiti-Tourisme.com; **273:** (l) Zonesix/Shutterstock; (r) Edgar Degas (1834–1917). Danseuses bleues, Blue dancers, c. 1890. Location: Musée d'Orsay, Paris, France. Photo credit: Alfredo Dagli Orti/The Art Archive/Art Resource; **281:** Courtesy of www.Tahiti-Tourisme.com; **285:** Photolibrary; **286:** Martín Bernetti; **290:** (l) Janet Dracksdorf; (r) Anne Loubet; **291:** Johner Images/Alamy; **299:** Alantide Phototravel/Getty Images; **301:** Anne Loubet; **302:** (left col: t) The AGE/Getty Images; (left col: b) Charles Bonnay/Gamma-Rapho/Getty Images; (t) Saiko3p/Shutterstock; (m) Melba Photo Agency/Alamy; (b) Ashit Desai/Getty Images; **303:** (tl) Photo Josse/Leemage/Getty Images; (tr) Neftali77/Deposit Photos; (bl) Courtesy of www.Tahiti-Tourisme.com; (br) AS Food Studio/Shutterstock; **304-305:** Andreas Prott/Shutterstock; **306:** Pascal Pernix; **307:** Jessica Beets.

Unit 8: 309: Helen & Bodil Sturesson/Johner Images; **316:** Anne Loubet; **317:** Maridav/Shutterstock; **329:** Giantstep Inc/Getty Images; **330:** Thinkstock/Corbis; **334:** Anne Loubet; **335:** David Redfern/Getty Images; **341:** 290712/Fotolia; **342:** (t) Stockshot/Alamy; (bl) Ben Blankenburg/Corbis; (bml) Martín Bernetti; (bmr) Martín Bernetti; (br) Martín Bernetti; **343:** Sigrid Olsson/AGE Fotostock; **344:** (all) Anne Loubet; **345:** (all) Anne Loubet; **346:** (left col: t) Historical Picture Archive/Getty Images; (left col: m) Keystone Pictures/AGE Fotostock; (left col: b) Kurt Krieger/Getty Images; (t) Jeremy Reddington/Shutterstock; (ml) Abadesign/Shutterstock; (mr) Anne Loubet; (b) Benjamin Herzog/Fotolia; **347:** (tl) Tom Delano; (tr) Anne Loubet; (bl) Janet Dracksdorf; (br) Anne Loubet; **348:** (left col, t) Aksaran/Gamma-Rapho/Getty Images; (left col, m) Stills Press/Alamy; (left col, b) AF Archive/Alamy; (t) Structurae/Nicolas Janberg; (ml) Paanna/Deposit Photos; (mr) Sigurcamp/Shutterstock; (b) Jean Dubuffet. Closerie Falbala (1971-1973). Painted epoxy resin and sprayed concrete. Surface area: 1.610 m2. Fondation Dubuffet, Perigny-sur-Marne (France). Copyright Fondation Dubuffet / ARS 2017. **349:** (tl) Kalpana Kartik/Alamy; (tr) Josse Christophel/Alamy; (bl) Tony C. French/Getty Images; (br) Bukki88/Depositphotos; **350-351:** Jessica Beets; **350:** (b) Jessica Beets; **351:** (inset) Jessica Beets; **352:** Anne Loubet; **353:** Terry J Alcorn/iStockphoto.

Back Cover: Demaerre/iStockphoto.

Credits

Television Credits

19 Courtesy of INPES.

63 Courtesy of Production: Via Storia - viastoria.com

107 Courtesy of Truvo Belgium.

151 Courtesy of Sid Lee Paris and PagesJaunes.

195 Courtesy of Canal 32.

239 Courtesy of ResoNews.

283 Courtesy of Tous Les Budgets, un site d'information propose por CETELEM.

327 Courtesy of France TV.

Chart Credits

140 Ipsos in France for the Centre National du Livre. The survey was conducted in France, by telephone on 1,012 people (aged 15 yo and more), from February 3rd to 11th, 2015.